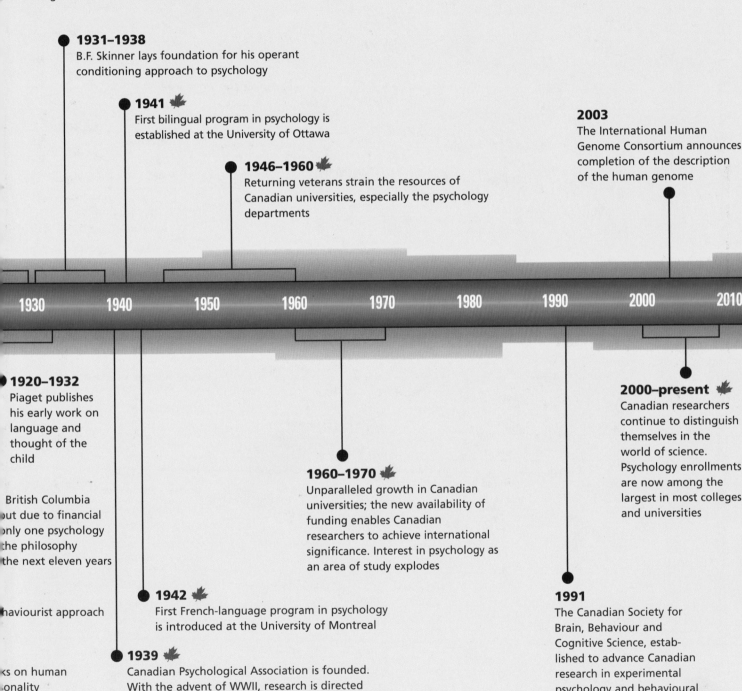

**1920–1930**
In Central Canada, psychology departments begin to separate from philosophy departments and emerge as distinct academic entities

**1931–1938**
B.F. Skinner lays foundation for his operant conditioning approach to psychology

**1941**
First bilingual program in psychology is established at the University of Ottawa

**1946–1960**
Returning veterans strain the resources of Canadian universities, especially the psychology departments

**2003**
The International Human Genome Consortium announces completion of the description of the human genome

1930 1940 1950 1960 1970 1980 1990 2000 2010

**1920–1932**
Piaget publishes his early work on language and thought of the child

British Columbia
out due to financial
only one psychology
the philosophy
the next eleven years

haviourist approach

ks on human
onality

**1939**
Canadian Psychological Association is founded. With the advent of WWII, research is directed at war-related issues, particularly personnel selection and training

**1942**
First French-language program in psychology is introduced at the University of Montreal

**1960–1970**
Unparalleled growth in Canadian universities; the new availability of funding enables Canadian researchers to achieve international significance. Interest in psychology as an area of study explodes

**1991**
The Canadian Society for Brain, Behaviour and Cognitive Science, established to advance Canadian research in experimental psychology and behavioural neuroscience, holds its first general meeting

**2000–present**
Canadian researchers continue to distinguish themselves in the world of science. Psychology enrollments are now among the largest in most colleges and universities

# Personalized Learning!

In MyPsychLab you are treated as an individual with specific learning needs.

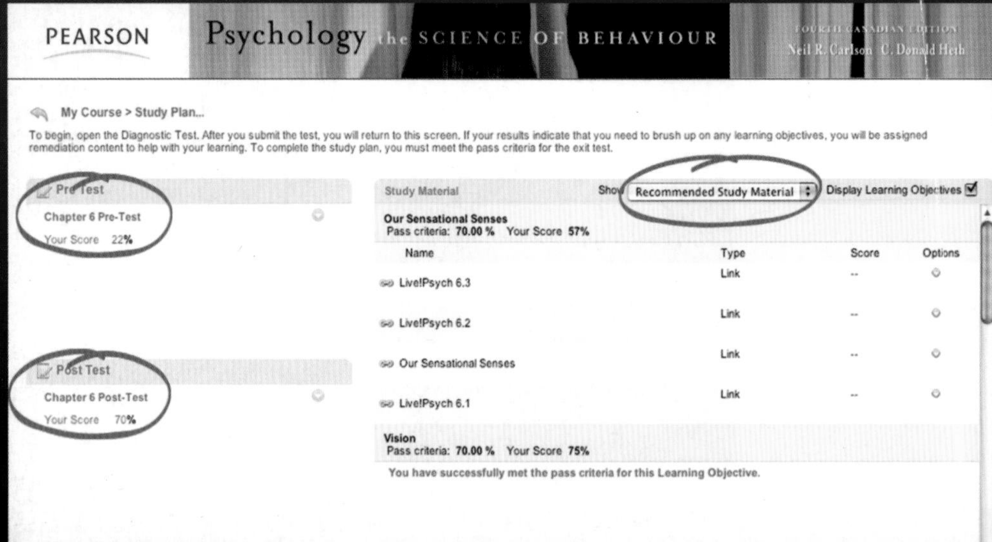


The study and assessment resources that complement your textbook allow you to review content and develop your skills and knowledge online, on your own time, and at your own pace.

## MyPsychLab provides

- learning and assessment activities with immediate scoring and feedback
- a custom study plan, based on those results, that directs you where to study. Improve your understanding of key content areas.
- a gradebook where you can store your grades and view reports showing your progress as the term unfolds
- instructor access to the gradebook. Some instructors assign homework, monitor class results, and adapt their lectures based on students' progress
- more than 100 video clips with closed captioning and post-viewing activities

Save Time. Improve Results. www.mypsychlab.com

FOURTH CANADIAN EDITION

# Psychology the SCIENCE OF BEHAVIOUR

**Neil R. Carlson** University of Massachusetts

**C. Donald Heth** University of Alberta

**Harold Miller** Brigham Young University

**John W. Donahoe** University of Massachusetts

**William Buskist** Auburn University

**G. Neil Martin** Middlesex University, UK

**Rodney M. Schmaltz** Grant MacEwan College

**Pearson Canada**
Toronto

**Library and Archives Canada Cataloguing in Publication**

Psychology : the science of behaviour / Neil R. Carlson . . . [et al.].—4th Canadian ed.

Includes index.
ISBN 978-0-205-64524-4

1. Psychology—Textbooks. I. Carlson, Neil R., 1942–

BF121.P835 2010 150 C2008-905789-9



ISBN-13: 978-0-205-64524-4
ISBN-10: 0-205-64524-0

Vice President, Editorial Director: Gary Bennett
Editor-in-Chief: Ky Pruesse
Executive Marketing Manager: Judith Allen
Developmental Editors: Joanne Sutherland, Suzanne Schaan
Production Editors: Susan Broadhurst, Kevin Leung
Copy Editor: Susan Broadhurst
Proofreader: Lenore Latta
Production Coordinator: Avinash Chandra
Permissions and Photo Research: Natalie Barrington
Composition: Macmillan Publishing Solutions
Art Director: Julia Hall
Cover Design: Michelle Bellemare
Cover Image: Lisa Johansson/Millennium Images, UK

For permission to reproduce copyrighted material, the publisher gratefully acknowledges the copyright holders listed on page 667, which are considered an extension of this copyright page.



1 2 3 4 5 13 12 11 10 09

Printed and bound in the United States of America.

# Foreword

I began writing textbooks in 1975, during my first sabbatical leave, which was spent at the University of Victoria in British Columbia. The roots of my writing, then, are Canadian. I received a warm welcome at UVic. The combination of a quiet, comfortable office, a good library, and interesting colleagues to talk with helped me do the best job I could. My first book, *Physiology of Behavior*, was published the next year, and its reception led my editor to suggest that I consider writing an introductory psychology textbook. I told him that I knew little about so many topics that would have to be covered in such a book, but his persuasive efforts—and the fact that I had enjoyed writing my first book—led me to agree to give the book a try.

*Psychology: The Science of Behavior* (sorry, I mean *Behaviour*) was received well enough that I revised it four times. Bill Buskist joined me on the fifth edition. Bill, a behavioural psychologist with a special interest in the role of evolution, helped strengthen the behavioural approach to psychological research, an approach for which I already had great respect.

From the beginning, I did all I could to give my books an international scope. I never assumed that they would be read only in the United States—and, indeed, I was gratified to learn that they were adopted in Canada, England, Australia, New Zealand, and even many countries where English is a second language. When an editor I knew at Pearson Allyn and Bacon in Canada proposed a Canadian edition of *Psychology*, I was delighted. As predicted, the book was well received. (If it had not been, there would not be a fourth Canadian edition for me to write about.) Don Heth and Mike Enzle, of the University of Alberta, did a splendid job of transforming the book into one appropriate for Canadian students, specifically designed to highlight the contribution of Canadian scientists to the study of behaviour. Now, Don and Rodney Schmaltz, of Grant McEwan College, have prepared this fourth Canadian edition.

Although Don and Rodney took primary responsibility for updating *Psychology: The Science of Behaviour,* we collaborated on this project, especially with respect to the advances that have been made in biological psychology. My own research includes studies of the role of the limbic system of the brain in species-typical behaviours (such as the care that a mother mouse gives to her offspring) and learned behaviours. During a sabbatical year spent at a medical centre, I also studied the behaviour of patients with brain damage, which led me to develop a course in human neuropsychology that I began teaching in the early 1980s. However, I found writing to be my most rewarding scholarly endeavour. I very much enjoy the challenge of finding and reading scientific literature, understanding it, and explaining it to students.

I have long believed that one of the most important approaches to the study of behaviour is biological psychology. After all, the brain is the organ responsible for all of the phenomena that psychologists study—for example, perception, learning and memory, thinking and cognition, language, and emotion. And psychological disorders are more than ever being understood as malfunctions of systems in the brain, caused by interactions between hereditary and environmental factors. Our knowledge of human brain functions has been expanding enormously as a result of studies using functional imaging, which permit us to see moment-to-moment activation of brain structures as volunteers perform various tasks. Advances in molecular genetics make it possible to investigate the role that genes play in the normal and abnormal development of brain mechanisms.

I am delighted to contribute this foreword to *Psychology: The Science of Behaviour* and to have collaborated with Don and Rodney on the fourth Canadian edition. Together, we hope that this textbook will spark further interest in the discipline of psychology and pave the way to further study of the understanding of human behaviour.

Neil R. Carlson
nrc@psych.umass.edu

# Dedications

*From Neil Carlson*

For Alexander, Gilbert, and Cedric.

*From Donald Heth*

For Sue.

*From Harold Miller*

Dedicated to Bill Buskist, prized student, prize-winning teacher, and beneficent co-author and friend.

*From John W. Donahoe*

Dedicated to my wife, Millie, and to our children, Kirk, Lisa, and Grant.

*From William Buskist*

Dedicated to the memory of my grandmother, Marion E. Short, and my uncle, Dr. Kenneth Trout.

*From Rodney M. Schmaltz*

Dedicated to my parents, Harold and Jeannie, for their support and inspiration.

# Brief Contents

# Contents

## Evolution, Heredity, and Behaviour 56

## Biology of Behaviour 86

# Preface

It was 10 years ago that the editors of Pearson Education began discussing with us the possibility of a Canadian adaptation of *Psychology: The Science of Behavior* by Neil Carlson and William Buskist. We, as authors, began our association with the text with one principal goal: to achieve for Canadian students what Carlson and Buskist had for their American audience—to present psychological research as an exciting and dynamic enterprise that is occurring around them at their own universities.

From the beginning, we felt that our students, as Canadians, should feel a sense of ownership of the scientific discoveries that form what we know of psychology. In part, this was pragmatic. Canadian research has always been at the forefront of psychology, both in the past and in the present; those who will shape research policy in the future need to be aware of this. However, as instructors, there is also a reason closer to our hearts. We want our students to feel that the discoveries they read about in the press, or the issues about human nature that crop up in popular culture, can be connected to the scholarly activity around them. We believe that many readers of this edition will find their own professors named in the text. Many others will see their universities mentioned at the end of each chapter, where we identify research that originates primarily in Canada. We hope that our readers will feel invited into the scientific narrative because of this connection.

The 10 years that have passed between the first Canadian adaptation and this edition have certainly reinforced our view of the dynamism of psychological research. As just one example, as the First Canadian Edition went to press, we noted the completion of the first draft of the human genome; in this Fourth Canadian Edition, we discuss the practical consequences of that knowledge in just about every chapter. It's not surprising that advances such as this are reflected in the way the media now portray psychological issues. The challenge to us, as instructors, will be to show the continuity of psychology's development in the face of so much change. We feel that Carlson and Buskist's emphasis on the process of research discovery will continue to serve us well in that challenge.

## Major Content Changes

This Fourth Canadian Edition has given us an opportunity to reorganize our presentation. In earlier editions, each chapter contained sections called *Biology and Culture* and *Evaluating Scientific Issues*. In this edition, the material featured in these sections has been integrated, where appropriate, within the main text. In their place, we have introduced a new feature—called *Then and Now*—which we use to illustrate the progressive nature of psychology. In these sections, we describe a model or viewpoint that has undergone significant transformation in theory or evidence. For example, in Chapter 2, we describe the evolution in psychology's approach to research ethics. In this instance, as in the sections in other chapters, our intention is not to critique well-intentioned efforts of the past, but to show how and why psychology has been enriched by newer perspectives.

In earlier editions, each chapter was introduced by a vignette that set the stage for the chapter's discussion. We've been pleased with this approach. In many cases, it has provided an opportunity to describe incidents of contemporary culture that personalize the chapter material. In this edition, we've developed these sections as prologues to each chapter, with an epilogue of commentary at the end.

The text has been reorganized in several places. The chapter on learning has been moved so that it now precedes the discussion of memory. In discussing psychology's history, we include collateral fields that have had an influence on the discipline's development: the pedagogical and psychiatric traditions that have shaped, among others, learning theory, developmental psychology, and clinical psychology. A major section on cultural psychology has been added to Chapter 15. And, of course, we have updated and expanded coverage in all 18 chapters.

Sadly, though, there is one change that was not welcome. Michael E. Enzle, our colleague on the First Canadian Edition and those that followed, passed away as this edition was in the planning stage. Mike's vision guided our work in fundamental ways. He exemplified the best of scholarship, recognizing as he did that it must be professed through integrity. As well, he was eloquent in his view that Canadian psychology could and should stand on its own, without rhetorical and editorial flourish. Mike believed that scholarly excellence spoke with its own voice. We hope this edition is a fitting continuation of that belief.

## Pedagogical Aids

After three successful Canadian editions, we believe that we have evolved a practical and efficient set of pedagogical features for an upper-level text. In this edition, we have concentrated on increasing the effectiveness of the features rather than on creating newer ones that could distract the reader from the central material. Each chapter begins with an ***outline*** that gives students a survey of what the chapter discusses. These outlines are designed both to engage students' interest and to present the scope of the chapter. The chapter outline is followed by a ***prologue***, a lively narrative that illustrates examples of phenomena covered in the chapter. An ***epilogue*** at the end of the chapter revisits the topic introduced in the prologue with insights based on the chapter content.

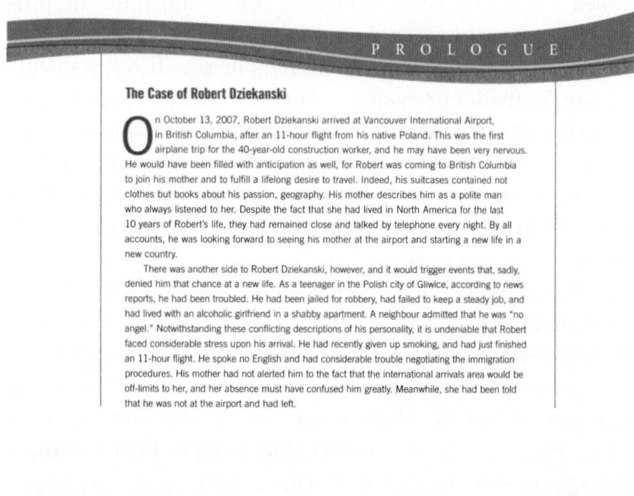

PROLOGUE

**The Case of Robert Dziekanski**

On October 13, 2007, Robert Dziekanski arrived at Vancouver International Airport, in British Columbia, after an 11-hour flight from his native Poland. This was the first airplane trip for the 40-year-old construction worker, and he may have been very nervous. He would have been filled with anticipation as well, for Robert was coming to British Columbia to join his mother and to fulfill a lifelong desire to travel. Indeed, his suitcases contained not clothes but books about his passion, geography. His mother describes him as a polite man who always listened to her. Despite the fact that she had lived in North America for the last 10 years of Robert's life, they had remained close and talked by telephone every night. By all accounts, he was looking forward to seeing his mother at the airport and starting a new life in a new country.

There was another side to Robert Dziekanski, however, and it would trigger events that, sadly, denied him that chance at a new life. As a teenager in the Polish city of Gliwice, according to news reports, he had been troubled. He had been jailed for robbery, had failed to keep a steady job, and had lived with an alcoholic girlfriend in a shabby apartment. A neighbour admitted that he was "no angel." Notwithstanding these conflicting descriptions of his personality, it is undeniable that Robert faced considerable stress upon his arrival. He had recently given up smoking, and had just finished an 11-hour flight. He spoke no English and had considerable trouble negotiating the immigration procedures. His mother had not alerted him to the fact that the international arrivals area would be off-limits to her, and her absence must have confused him greatly. Meanwhile, she had been told that he was not at the airport and had left.

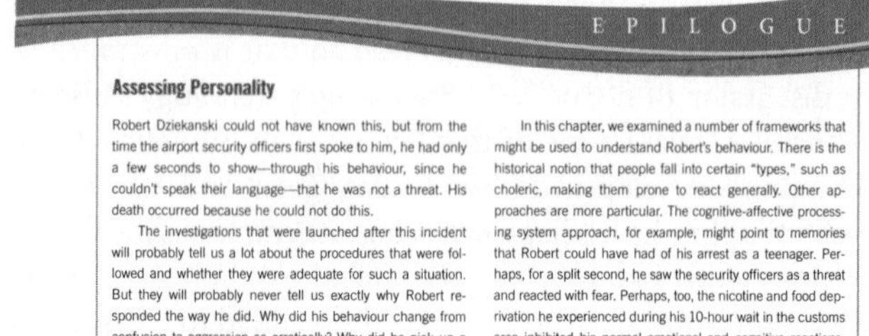

EPILOGUE

**Assessing Personality**

Robert Dziekanski could not have known this, but from the time the airport security officers first spoke to him, he had only a few seconds to show—through his behaviour, since he couldn't speak their language—that he was not a threat. His death occurred because he could not do this.

The investigations that were launched after this incident will probably tell us a lot about the procedures that were followed and whether they were adequate for such a situation. But they will probably never tell us exactly why Robert responded the way he did. Why did his behaviour change from confusion to aggression so erratically? Why did he pick up a table, of all things, and carry it around?

In this chapter, we examined a number of frameworks that might be used to understand Robert's behaviour. There is the historical notion that people fall into certain "types," such as choleric, making them prone to react generally. Other approaches are more particular. The cognitive-affective processing system approach, for example, might point to memories that Robert could have had of his arrest as a teenager. Perhaps, for a split second, he saw the security officers as a threat and reacted with fear. Perhaps, too, the nicotine and food deprivation he experienced during his 10-hour wait in the customs area inhibited his normal emotional and cognitive reactions.

As in previous editions, we have provided summaries where they will do the most good: immediately after a sizable chunk of material. Each chapter contains several of these ***interim summaries***, found after each major heading. They provide students with a place to relax a bit and review what they have just read. Taken together, they provide a much longer summary than students would tolerate at the end of a chapter and will, we believe, serve them better. ***Questions to consider***, designed to entice students to apply what they have learned to everyday issues, follow each interim summary. ***Terms and their definitions*** are printed at the bottom of each page, so that a student can see at a glance what new vocabulary is being introduced and can quickly scan the terms and definitions to review for an exam. ***Figure references*** are in boldface coloured type so that the student can easily find his or her place in the text after examining the figure.

Each chapter of this edition contains a special feature: a critical thinking section called ***Then and Now***. These features illustrate the progressive nature of psychology and show how and why psychology has been enriched by newer perspectives. Each feature describes a model or viewpoint that has undergone significant transformation in theory or evidence. Examples include the evolution in psychology's approach to research ethics, extrasensory perception, the James–Lange theory, autistic disorder, and the impact of media violence.

**Then and Now**

**The Impact of Media Violence**

As you will recall from Chapter 13, psychologists are strongly motivated to understand how media violence affects real-world behaviour. Tragedies such as the Columbine High School killings, the Montreal Massacre, the school shooting in Taber, Alberta, and the more recent mass murder at Virginia Tech have led to conclusions in the news media that violent media may be partially responsible for these horrific events. The killers in Columbine played *Doom*, a violent but popular video game, and there has been speculation in the news media that violent video games also may have played a role in the Virgina Tech murders. Does violence in television, music, or video games really lead to tragedy? Social psychologists have spent decades trying to answer this important question.

showed increased play with aggressive toys, such as guns, even though this had not been modelled by the adults.

Bandura's groundbreaking research demonstrated that, at least in some situations, children model violent behaviour. Hundreds of studies have been conducted following Bandura's work to better understand the role of violent media on aggressive behaviour. In the early 1970s, government-funded inquiries into the link between media violence and violent behaviour led some researchers to conclude that there is a relationship between violence on film and real-world acts of aggression (Gunter, 2008). These findings spurred more empirical research, some of which indicated that exposure to violence in television in the lab increases aggressive behaviour in children. For example, Liebert and Baron (1972) exposed children to a violent police drama. When these children were allowed free play with other children who had not seen the violent program, they behaved far more aggressively than a separate group of children who had watched only a non-

We noted in the First Canadian Edition the growing role of the World Wide Web in expanding educational material. As we did in that edition, we've used this tool to situate Canadian research contributions in their international context. You'll find these contributions noted at the end of each chapter in the section entitled ***Canadian Connections to Research in This Chapter***, where we have provided bibliographic references for Canadian research cited there. We've also provided URLs for the universities where these works were produced. In making these associations, we used the formal affiliation, when given, of the first author of the work. In some cases, of course, the authors of these works will no longer be associated with that university. However, in most cases, the research environment still reflects the same or similar research interests, and our links will provide a useful starting point for further investigation.

# Ancillary Materials

## For Instructors

Experience with the previous editions has guided the revision of the supplements package that accompanies the Fourth Canadian Edition. We have developed a high-quality package that will be a valuable resource for teaching creatively and effectively.

**MyPsychLab with peerScholar:** Pearson Education Canada's online resource, MyPsychLab, offers instructors and students all of their resources in one place, organized to accompany this text. With MyPsychLab, you will be able to enliven your lectures with a variety of material. As well, your students will be able to "study smarter" with an e-book and a diagnostic test that creates a customized study plan to help them prepare for, and perform better on, exams. MyPsychLab is available to instructors by going to www.mypsychlab.com and following the instructions on that page. Students get MyPsychLab with an access code that is made available with the purchase of a new textbook.

peerScholar

Bring critical thinking and writing assessment back into your psychology course!

- Are you looking for new ways to challenge your students to think critically?
- Would you like to free up your time to do other, more meaningful things like interacting with students or leading study groups?

If you answered "yes" to one or both of these questions, peerScholar is the solution you have been looking for.

peerScholar allows you to test your students' writing and critical thinking skills online. Thought-provoking new articles, with suggested writing assignments and grading rubrics, are included in the program. You can use these pre-loaded assignments or add your own. It's economical, reliable, easy to use, student-friendly, customizable, backed by solid and documented research and results, connected to a gradebook, and now it's available to every student in MyPsychLab! Access to MyPsychLab and peerScholar is available with every new copy of *Psychology: The Science of Behaviour.*

**MyTest** (www.pearsonmytest.com): MyTest from Pearson Education Canada is a powerful assessment generation program that helps instructors easily create and print quizzes, tests, exams, as well as homework or practice handouts. Questions and tests can all be authored online, allowing instructors ultimate flexibility and the ability to efficiently manage assessments at any time, from anywhere. MyTest for *Psychology: The Science of Behaviour*, Fourth Canadian Edition, includes approximately 4000 questions in multiple-choice, true/false, and essay format. These questions are also available in Microsoft Word format on the Instructor's Resource CD-ROM (see below).

**Instructor's Resource CD-ROM** (978-0-205-68252-2): This resource CD includes the following instructor supplements:

- **Instructor's Resource Manual**: This manual includes chapter-by-chapter outlines, lecture suggestions, and critical thinking problems.
- **Test Item File**: This test bank, in Microsoft Word format, includes approximately 4000 questions in multiple-choice, true/false, and essay format. The questions are also available in MyTest format (see above).
- **PowerPoints**: These presentations review the core concepts of each chapter, incorporating key figures from the text.
- **Image Gallery**: Key figures and tables from the text are provided in electronic format.

Most of these instructor supplements are also available for download from a password-protected section of Pearson Education Canada's online catalogue (www.pearsoned.ca/highered). Navigate to your book's catalogue page to view a list of those supplements that are available. See your local sales representative for details and access.

**Teaching Films Boxed Set:** This supplement offers qualified adopters an easy-to-use multi-DVD set of videos, organized by topic for easy lecture integration. It includes 100 short video clips of 5 to 15 minutes in length from many of the most popular video sources for psychology content, such as ABCNews, the Films for the Humanities series, PBS, Pennsylvania State Media Sales Video Classics, and more! Contact your local sales representative for more information.

**Classic Experiments in Psychology** (from Pennsylvania State Media, edited by Dennis Thompson, Georgia State University): This five-DVD set includes the best-known classic film footage for key concepts and researchers in the field of psychology. Most clips are 5 to 15 minutes in length. The set is available to qualified adopters. Contact your local sales representative for more information.

**Technology Specialists:** Pearson's Technology Specialists work with faculty and campus course designers to ensure that Pearson technology products, assessment tools, and online course materials are tailored to meet your specific needs. This highly qualified team is dedicated to helping schools take full advantage of a wide range of educational resources, by assisting in the integration of a variety of instructional materials and media formats. Your local sales representative can provide you with more details on this service program.

**CourseSmart:** CourseSmart is a new way for instructors and students to access textbooks online anytime from anywhere. With thousands of titles across hundreds of courses, CourseSmart helps instructors choose the best textbook for their class and give their students a new option for buying the assigned textbook as a lower-cost eTextbook. For more information, visit www.coursesmart.com.

## For Students

**MyPsychLab with peerScholar:** Supplied with every new copy of this textbook, MyPsychLab provides students with access to a wealth of resources, including

- Diagnostic tests that assess your understanding of the text
- A custom study program that creates a personalized study plan using the e-book and based on your diagnostic test results
- A media-enriched e-book loaded with animations, videos, and additional resources
- Live!Psych Experiments and Simulations
- Access to peerScholar, with written exercises assigned by your instructor

MyPsychLab includes access to Research Navigator, Pearson's fully searchable online collection of academic and popular journals.

Get started with the Student Access Code packaged with your new copy of the text. Student Access Codes for MyPsychLab can also be purchased separately at www.mypsychlab.com.

**Grade Aid Study Guide:** A comprehensive Study Guide has been developed for the Canadian edition of *Psychology: The Science of Behaviour*, based on a combination of the results of psychological research and the authors' own experience. Each chapter features two lessons (tied to learning objectives), a series of self-tests, and a set of concept cards, with key terms on one side and definitions on the other.

The Grade Aid Study Guide is available in two convenient formats. You can access the electronic version through MyPsychLab for *Psychology: The Science of Behaviour.* A printed version is also available. Please contact your instructor or local sales representative to get a copy.

# Acknowledgments

As in our previous editions, we have had the immense good fortune to work with the team at Pearson Education Canada. The first Canadian adaptation of the Carlson and Buskist text was the result of their vision and, in the intervening years, they have given us the encouragement and support to develop it in the directions that meet the needs of our audience. Ky Preusse, Acquisitions Editor, has been a part of our work for several years, and we thank him for his advice and guidance. Joanne Sutherland, Developmental Editor, has earned our appreciation for her ability to provide us with encouragement, helpful feedback, and, when needed, some gentle prodding regarding schedules. Susan Broadhurst is our Production Editor; we thank her for the special talent she possesses to bring all of the pieces together.

Our thanks also go to Brittany Weikum for her extensive research for Chapters 16, 17, and 18.

Professors who write do so with an invisible audience listening to their words—the audience of previous classes and former students. We've had the good fortune to teach many fine students who, through their questions and observations, have shaped our teaching. We've also had generous colleagues who reviewed our chapters and offered their advice. Some, such as David Pierce and Edward Cornell at the University of Alberta, are those we work with every day. Others have assisted us through formal reviews of our manuscript. They are listed below.

We end these comments by expressing our deepest appreciation to our spouses and our families. To our loved ones, who have tolerated the disruptions produced by our work and who have supported us during this project, goes our fondest acknowledgment.

## Reviewers of the Fourth Canadian Edition

George Alder
*Simon Fraser University*

Nicole Anderson
*Grant MacEwan College*

Melissa Boyce
*University of Calgary*

Jason Daniels
*University of Alberta*

Margaret L. Forgie
*The University of Lethbridge*

Donald R. Gorassini
*King's University College*

Linda L. Hatt, Ph.D.
*University of British Columbia, Okanagan*

Steve Joordens
*University of Toronto–Scarborough*

Rupert Klein
*Lakehead University*

Ara Norenzayan
*University of British Columbia*

Kristine A. Peace
*Grant MacEwan College*

Catharine Rankin
*University of British Columbia*

Heather Schellinck
*Dalhousie University*

Michael R. Woloszyn
*Thompson Rivers University*

# To the Reader

This is a book about something that belongs to you. That's true in an obvious sense, since this is a textbook that describes the mechanisms of behaviour that we, as humans, all share. You have inherited, through the intricate machinery of your ancestors' genes, a brain that once contemplated the African savannah and that now can comprehend the information age. You have also acquired, through your life's experiences, a tremendous store of knowledge and memories that affects your thoughts and emotions in ways distinctive to you. Your psychology, in that sense, belongs to you.

But there is something else about this book that also belongs to you. Psychology is an international discipline, built by scholars around the world. Canadian scientists have played central roles in much of what we know about the brain and about behaviour. Key distinctions regarding the way your memory stores information, to cite just one area, were developed by Canadian scholars. In creating this textbook, we've deliberately attempted to ensure that past Canadian contributions were noted and that research currently under way at Canadian universities is discussed in its broader context.

That Canadian research has figured so prominently in the development of psychology has been the result of years of dedicated support from private, provincial, and federal agencies. Canadian science, notably, has been guided by three federal institutions that review research proposals and recommend funding for the most meritorious. The discoveries that developed from these projects have advanced our understanding of psychological phenomena. So, you see, much of the knowledge in this book belongs to you as a Canadian. A significant goal in our adaptation of this text was to show how this investment has paid off.

There are some things you should know about the book before you start reading. Each chapter begins with a chapter outline and a brief overview of the material to be discussed. These overviews tell you what to expect when you read the chapter and help you keep track of your progress.

Because every discipline has its own vocabulary—and psychology is no exception—important terms are specially marked in the text. Each one appears in boldface where the definition or description is given. Succinct definitions of these terms are provided at the bottom of each page.

The book contains tables, graphs, diagrams, drawings, and photographs. They are there to illustrate important points and, in some cases, to say something that cannot be said with words alone. To help you quickly find your place again once you've looked at them, figure references are in boldface coloured type, like this: (See **Figure 5•10**.).

Rather than provide a long summary at the end of each chapter we have provided interim summaries—reviews of the information that has just been presented. These summaries divide chapters into more easily managed chunks. When you reach an interim summary in your reading, take the opportunity to relax and think about what you have read. You might even want to take a five-minute break after reading the interim summary, then read it again to remind yourself of what you just read before going on to the next section. If you read the material this way, you will learn it with much less effort than you would otherwise have to expend.

The study guide that accompanies this text (consult your instructor regarding availability) is an excellent aid to actively learning the material in the book. By thinking about and answering the study questions, you will be sure not to have missed some important points. In addition, each chapter in the study guide includes two short self-tests so you can assess your comprehension of the material.

Although this book has many authors—four American, one English, and three Canadian—and although it is a collaborative effort, each of us is ultimately responsible for what he wrote. You will see that the book is sometimes written in the first person; we wrote "I" and "me" rather than "we" and "us." Each of us has illustrated points with examples from our own lives or those of people we know, and these narratives demand personal pronouns. If you want to know which of us wrote a particular narrative, write to us and we will be happy to tell you.

We have not met you, but we feel as if we have been talking to you while working on this book. Writing is an "unsocial" activity in the sense that it is done alone. It is even an anti-social activity when the writer must say, "No, I'm too busy writing to talk with you now." So, as we wrote this book, we consoled ourselves by imagining that you were listening to us. You will get to meet us, or at least do so vicariously, through our words, as you read this book.

# 1

# THE SCIENCE OF PSYCHOLOGY

# CHAPTER OUTLINE

## What Is Psychology?

Why Behaviour Is Studied • Fields of Psychology

Psychology is the science of behaviour, and psychologists try to explain behaviour by discovering its causes. In addition, some psychologists try to apply the discoveries of psychological research to practical problems. Scientific psychology consists of many subfields, each investigating different types of behaviours or searching for different types of causes.

## The Growth of Psychology as a Science

Philosophical Roots of Psychology • Biological Roots of Psychology • Applications in Education and Therapy

The science of psychology is rooted in philosophy, biology, education, and medicine. Philosophers developed the principles of materialism and empiricism, which made it possible to conceive of studying the human mind and, eventually, behaviour. Biologists developed experimental methods that enabled us to study the brain and discover its role in the control of behaviour. Improvements in education and medicine became public policy goals of governments during the 1800s. Educators devised methods of instruction based on principles of human development, while many medical doctors stressed the role of environmental factors in the treatment of psychological disorders.

## Major Trends in the Development of Psychology

Structuralism • Functionalism • Freud's Psychodynamic Theory • Psychology in Transition • Behaviourism • Humanistic Psychology • Reaction against Behaviourism: The Emphasis on Cognition • Reaction against Behaviourism: The Emphasis on Neurobiology • *Then and Now: Psychology Compared to the Other Sciences*

The first laboratory of experimental psychology was established by Wilhelm Wundt in Germany in 1879. Wundt's structuralism was soon abandoned, but other laboratories developed new methods to study the causes of behaviour. Charles Darwin's principle of natural selection led to the development of functionalism, which in turn inspired the development of behaviourism, a movement in psychology that insisted that only observable behaviour could be studied scientifically. Sigmund Freud's psychodynamic theory and humanistic psychologists have had wide appeal with the general public. More recently, cognitive psychologists have restored an emphasis on the study of mental processes. New developments in the research methods of neurobiology have strengthened the biological emphasis in psychological research.

# PROLOGUE

## An Assignment

The moment she entered the classroom, I knew Laura had something she wanted to say. She sat down, looked at me, and said, "This book is freaking us out!"

I had to stifle a smile. It isn't often you can make a senior psychology student outraged about a single book. "Oh?" I responded, with as much innocence as I could muster.

"It isn't so much the part in the book that talks about replacing some of our nervous system with electronics . . . we realize that might be possible. But this guy says that we'll soon be able to replace all of it. And get this: he talks about actually having sex with a computer! Is this guy for real?"

"Well, that's for you to decide," was my rather unhelpful response. You see, Laura and three of her classmates had been assigned to read a book by one of America's foremost authorities on technology, Raymond Kurzweil, called *The Age of Spiritual Machines: When Computers Exceed Human Intelligence.* In it, he engaged in some heady speculation about the future of technology. We're all familiar with devices that amplify our senses, such as hearing aids and night-vision goggles. As these devices become more sophisticated, Kurzweil argues, they'll be able to perform all of the functions of our natural nervous system, and humans will be able to "enhance" their brains with sophisticated implants. As our knowledge of the brain increases, we will, says Kurzweil in his most shocking prediction, be able to download our consciousness to a computer. Laura's four years of study in psychology had given her a pretty good grounding in the biology of the brain. Now, she had to consider what it would mean to simulate this biology inside a computer program.

Laura and her team had to review Kurzweil's book in a special way: As part of their class assignment, they had to work with our campus radio station to produce a 30-minute radio documentary that would examine the plausibility of Kurzweil's predictions. The radio station would give them full access to its recording and interviewing facilities, but they had to come up with their own take on the problem. And it would be broadcast.

In the weeks after our classroom exchange, I noticed that Laura's team was becoming more and more involved in the project. I learned later that they had been spending long nights at each other's homes, working out a script and considering the interviews they had done with philosophers, psychologists, and computer scientists. One professor even complained to me that the students were spending more time on *my* assignment and not enough on *hers.* Then, halfway through the term, the team asked me if they could produce a 60-minute program. "This assignment has forced us to think about the meaning of everything we've learned about psychology," they said. "We can do something really special if we have the additional time." Thinking that I had created some kind of monster, I said yes.

On the day the assignment was due, I stopped by the radio station and picked up the CD of the team's program. The station manager had reviewed it and written a note on the CD. *Yikes!* was all it said.

Here are two facts about the world you live in:

- There is a man whose otherwise normal life is disturbed at night, when he will suddenly leap from his bed and prowl around his bedroom growling like a lion, his fingers curled into claws. In the morning, he remembers nothing of these episodes.
- When atoms are placed in a strong magnetic field, the axes around which their electrons spin become aligned with that magnetic field. If a radio pulse is directed at them, they will wobble like spinning tops and then return to their alignment. It takes different amounts of time for atoms of different elements to realign.

When you entered university, you undoubtedly expected to learn about such facts and to understand how they relate to other similar facts. For example, if you take a first-year course in physics, you expect to learn about wave patterns on the surface of a liquid and about wave patterns of light. You probably have a good understanding of what to expect from a course in chemistry, biology, history, or geography. But, entering a course in psychology, you may not have expected to encounter in the same textbook facts as different as the two just mentioned. Nevertheless, both of these facts are of interest to psychologists.

What does it mean to be a psychologist? If you asked your fellow students this question, you would receive several different answers. In fact, if you asked this question of several psychologists, you would still receive more than one answer. Psychologists are probably the most diverse group of people in our society to share the same title. At the time of the 2001 Census, there were 5275 men and 10 780 women in Canada employed as psychologists. They engage in research, teaching, counselling, and psychotherapy; they advise industry and governmental agencies about personnel matters, the design of products, advertising and marketing, and legislation; they devise and administer tests of personality, achievement, and ability. Psychologists study a wide variety of phenomena, including physiological processes within the nervous system, genetics, environmental events, personality characteristics, mental abilities, and social interactions. And yet psychology is a new discipline; the first person to call himself a psychologist was still alive in 1920, and the Canadian professors he trained lived into the 1960s and 1970s.

For me, and for my colleagues who wrote this textbook, psychology is exciting because is it so diverse and changing so rapidly. But it may sometimes be confusing to you, a student faced with understanding this large and complex field. So this first chapter will give you an overview of what it means to be a psychologist. It describes the nature of psychology, its goals, and its history.

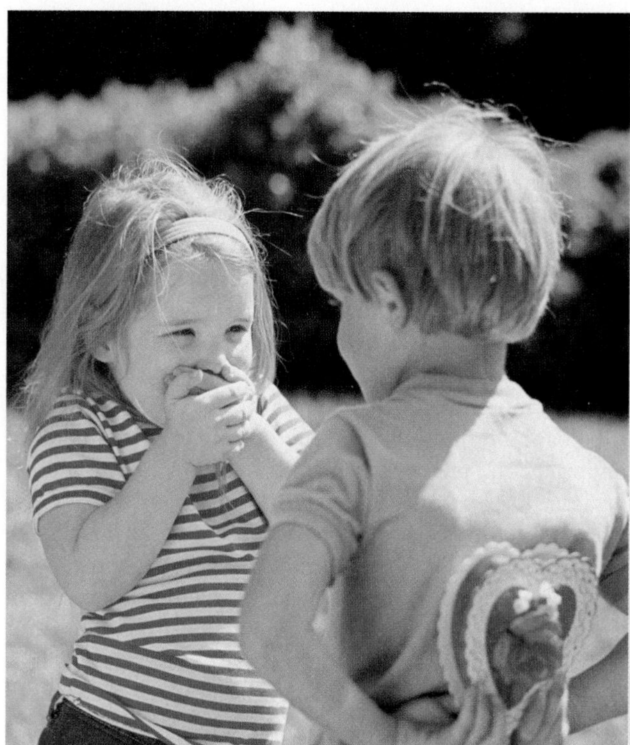

▲ *The research interests of psychologists vary widely. One might be interested in the nature of romantic attraction, while another might be interested in childhood memory. These different research questions are answered by the study of behaviour.*

# What Is Psychology?

In this book, my co-authors and I consider **psychology** as a science—a science with a special focus on behaviour. The primary emphasis is on discovering and explaining the causes of behaviour. Of course, we shall describe the applications of these discoveries to the treatment of psychological disorders and the improvement of society, but the focus will be on the way in which psychologists discover the facts that make these applications possible. This is an important guide to understanding psychology as a science. As you read this book, you should concentrate on how this process of discovery works. To help you, I should make a key distinction.

The word *psychology* comes from two Greek words: *psukhe*, meaning "breath" or "soul," and *logos*, meaning "word" or "reason." The modern meaning of *psycho-* is "mind" and the modern meaning of *-logy* is "science"; thus, the word *psychology* literally means "the science of the mind." However, this is a bit misleading. As the title of this book states, and as I just implied, psychology is the science of *behaviour*. The difference can be traced to the way that psychologists have thought about the mind. Early in the development of psychology, people conceived of the mind as an independent, free-floating spirit. Later, they described it as a characteristic of a functioning brain whose ultimate function was to control behaviour. Thus, the focus turned from the mind, which cannot be observed directly, to behaviour, which can. And because the brain is the organ that both contains the mind and controls behaviour, psychology very soon incorporated the study of the brain. (It is this recognition, by the way, that relates the two facts I cited at the start of this chapter. You will see how this is so in a later chapter.)

## Why Behaviour Is Studied

The ultimate goal of research in psychology is to understand human behaviour: to explain why people do what they do. But how do we, as psychologists, provide an "explanation" of behaviour? First, we must describe it. We must become familiar with the things that people (or other animals) do. We must learn how to categorize and measure behaviour so that we can be sure that different psychologists in different places are observing the same phenomena. Next, we must discover the causes of the behaviour we observe—the events responsible for a behaviour's occurrence. If we can discover the events that caused the behaviour, we have "explained" it. Events that cause other events (including behaviour) to occur are called **causal events.**

As you will see throughout this book, different kinds of psychologists are interested in different kinds of behaviour and in different levels of explanation. For example, one psychologist might be interested in how vision is coordinated with movement; another might be interested in courtship. But even when they are interested in the same behaviour, psychologists may study different categories of causal events—what I referred to as different "levels of explanation." Some look inside the organism in a literal sense, seeking physiological causes such as the activity of nerve cells or the secretions of glands. Others look inside the organism in a metaphorical sense, explaining behaviour in terms of hypothetical mental states such as anger, fear, curiosity, or love. Still others look

**psychology** The scientific study of the causes of behaviour; also, the application of the findings of psychological research to the solution of problems.
**causal event** An event that causes another event to occur.

only for events in the environment (including things that other people do) that cause behaviour to occur. The word *levels* does not mean that one approach is superior or is more fundamental than another. Instead, it refers to a common choice of causes to study and methods of research to use. The use of different levels of explanation is one reason why psychology is such a diverse discipline.

What is the purpose of this quest for explanations? Intellectual curiosity is one answer. An essential part of human nature seems to be a need to understand what makes things work, and what could be more interesting than trying to understand our fellow human beings? But psychological research is more than the idle endeavour of curious scientists; it holds the promise of showing us how to solve our most important and pressing problems.

One reason for studying behaviour, in contrast to studying a non-observable mind, is that human behaviour is the root of many of the world's problems: poverty, crime, overpopulation, drug addiction, bigotry, pollution, oppression, terrorism, and war. If global warming adversely affects our planet, or if forests and lakes die because of acid rain, it will be because of our behaviour. Many health-related problems—such as cardiovascular disease, some forms of cancer, and a large number of stress-related illnesses—are caused (or at least aggravated) by individuals' behaviour. Heavy smoking, obesity, lack of exercise, poor diet, unsanitary personal habits, and stressful lifestyles are responsible for illnesses found around the world. Inappropriate agricultural practices, inefficient distribution of food, and wars and tribal conflicts—which you will note are the products of human behaviour—are responsible for much of the hunger and starvation that exists in the world today.

Scientific research and technology have not yet provided us with complete solutions to these problems. We hope that while reading this book and learning what psychologists have discovered about human behaviour, you will think about the contribution that psychology could make to providing solutions to the problems mentioned. Sometimes, discoveries that originate from different sciences still need knowledge of psychology to facilitate their implementation. For example, when the celebrated British explorer James Cook experimented with the use of sauerkraut to prevent scurvy, he realized that his sailors would probably resist having something new in their diet. Cook did what any parent would think of doing: He increased the status of sauerkraut by ordering his officers to eat it (Berwick, 2003). After observing their officers eating this new meal, ordinary seamen were also demanding this "privilege." Cook had few problems with scurvy afterwards.

**physiological psychology** The branch of psychology that studies the physiological basis of behaviour.

**comparative psychology** The branch of psychology that studies the behaviours of a variety of organisms in an attempt to understand the adaptive and functional significance of the behaviours and their relation to evolution.

## Fields of Psychology

Psychologists sometimes identify themselves in terms of their activities. Some of us are scientists, trying to discover the causes of behaviour. Some of us are practitioners of *applied psychology*, applying what our scientific colleagues have learned to the solution of problems in the world outside the laboratory. And, of course, some psychologists perform both roles. This section describes the various fields of psychological research and the areas of applied psychology.

**Areas of Psychological Research** Most research psychologists work in colleges or universities or are employed by private or governmental research laboratories. Research psychologists differ from one another in two principal ways: in the types of *behaviour* they investigate, and in the *causal events* they analyze. That is, they explain different types of behaviours, and they explain them in terms of different types of causes. For example, two psychologists might both be interested in memory, but they might attempt to explain memory in terms of different causal events—one may focus on physiological events whereas the other may focus on environmental events.

To explore the areas of psychology, let's look at an important behavioural problem: drug abuse. As you know, drug abuse is one of the most serious problems that society presently faces. It cuts across both culture and geography—from the urban districts of East Hastings Street in Vancouver to the most remote reserves in Labrador. Alcohol abuse can lead to divorce, loss of employment, automobile accidents, birth defects, and cirrhosis of the liver. Heroin addiction can lead to fatal overdoses. Addicts who take drugs intravenously run a serious risk of contracting and spreading AIDS. Why do people use these drugs and subject themselves to these dangers? What can psychological research tell us about the causes of—and possible solutions to—the problem of drug abuse?

**Physiological psychology** examines the physiology of behaviour. The organism's physiology, especially its nervous system, is considered to be the appropriate level of explanation. Physiological psychologists study almost all behavioural phenomena that can be observed in non-human animals, including learning, memory, sensory processes, emotional behaviour, motivation, sexual behaviour, and sleep. Each phenomenon in non-human animals is considered a model that can help us understand the causal events in human behaviour.

Much about drug abuse can certainly be explained by referring to human physiology. Physiological psychologists have discovered that all drugs having the potential for addiction act on a particular system in the brain that is involved in our reactions to pleasurable events such as encountering food, warmth, and sexual contact. Some drugs artificially activate this system, providing effects on behaviour similar to those that pleasurable events naturally produce. Understanding how these drugs affect the brain may help us develop medications to help addicts break their habits.

**Comparative psychology** is the study of the behaviour of members of a variety of species in an attempt to explain behaviour in terms of evolutionary adaptation to the environment. Comparative psychologists study behavioural phenomena similar to those studied by physiological psychologists. They are likely to study inherited behavioural patterns, such as courting and mating, predation and aggression, defensive behaviours, and parental behaviours.

Comparative studies of the effects of drugs have shown that all species of mammals tested so far react like humans to addictive drugs. If laboratory animals are allowed to control the amount of drug injected into a vein, they will become addicted to this drug.

**Behaviour analysis** is the branch of psychology that studies the effect of the environmental events on behaviour. Behaviour analysts are primarily interested in learning and motivation. They believe that an important cause of a specific behaviour is the relationship between the behaviour and some consequent event. Behaviours that produce pleasant outcomes tend to be repeated, whereas those that produce unpleasant consequences (or no consequences at all) are less likely to be repeated. Behaviour analysts do their research in the laboratory or in applied settings, such as schools, homes, and businesses. Their findings have been applied to teaching, business management, and psychotherapy.

Behaviour analysts have contributed much to the study of drug addiction. They have developed methods for studying the way that pleasurable events (including the effects of drugs) lead people to repeat certain behaviours. They have discovered that some of the negative effects of addictive drugs, including withdrawal symptoms, are learned. They have developed methods that can indicate the abuse potential of newly developed drugs before they are tried on people. Psychotherapists have applied the discoveries of behaviour analysts to the treatment of people with drug addictions.

**Behaviour genetics** is the branch of psychology that studies the role of genetics in behaviour. The genes we inherit from our parents include a blueprint for the construction of a human brain. Each blueprint is a little different, which means that no two brains are exactly alike. Therefore, no two people will act exactly alike, even in identical situations. Behaviour geneticists study the role of genetics in behaviour by examining similarities in physical and behavioural characteristics of blood relatives, whose genes are more similar than those of unrelated individuals. They also perform breeding experiments with laboratory animals to see what aspects of behaviour can be transmitted to an animal's offspring. Using new techniques of molecular genetics, they can even alter parts of the gene during these experiments to determine how differences in the genetic code relate to behavioural differences among animals.

One of the major contributions of behaviour genetics to the study of drug abuse has been the development of strains of laboratory animals that are especially susceptible to the effects of drugs. Comparisons of these animals with others who tend not to become addicted may help us understand the physiological mechanisms involved in drug dependence.

**Cognitive psychology** is the study of mental processes and complex behaviours such as perception, attention, learning and memory, verbal behaviour, concept formation, and problem solving. To cognitive psychologists, the events that cause behaviour consist of functions of the human brain that occur in response to environmental events. Their explanations involve characteristics of inferred mental processes, such as imagery, attention, and mechanisms of language. Most of them do not study physiological mechanisms, but recently some have begun collaborating with neurologists and other professionals involved in brain scanning. The study of the biology of cognition has been greatly aided by the development of harmless brain-scanning methods that permit us to measure the activity of various parts of the human brain.

The primary contribution of cognitive psychology to the study of drug addiction has been the development of therapeutic methods that have proven themselves useful in the treatment of addictive behaviours. Cognitive behaviour therapists have discovered the importance of teaching people coping strategies that enable them to resist the temptations of addictive drugs better. perception, attention, etc.

**Cognitive neuroscience** is closely allied with both cognitive psychology and physiological psychology. This branch of psychology is generally interested in the same phenomena studied by cognitive psychologists, but it attempts to discover the particular brain mechanisms responsible for cognitive processes. One of the principal research techniques is to study the behaviour of people whose brains have been damaged by natural causes, such as diseases, strokes, or tumours.

Cognitive neuroscientists have developed many tests that are useful in assessing behavioural and cognitive deficits caused by abnormal brain functions. For example, they have developed tests that show the effects that the intake of alcohol, nicotine, and other drugs by pregnant women have on the development of their babies.

**Developmental psychology** is the study of physical, cognitive, emotional, and social development, especially of children. Some developmental psychologists study phenomena of adolescence or adulthood—in particular, the effects of aging. The causal events they study are as comprehensive as all of psychology: physiological processes, cognitive processes, and social influences.

**behaviour analysis** The branch of psychology that studies the effect of the environment on behaviour—primarily, the effects of the consequences of behaviours on the behaviours themselves.

**behaviour genetics** The branch of psychology that studies the role of genetics in behaviour.

**cognitive psychology** The branch of psychology that studies complex behaviours and mental processes such as perception, attention, learning and memory, verbal behaviour, concept formation, and problem solving.

**cognitive neuroscience** The branch of psychology that attempts to understand cognitive psychological functions by studying the brain mechanisms that are responsible for them.

**developmental psychology** The branch of psychology that studies the changes in behavioural, perceptual, and cognitive capacities of organisms as a function of age and experience.

Developmental psychologists have helped us understand how drug-taking behaviour can change over the course of an individual's life. In addition, their research on infant development has made it possible to describe the time at which specific cognitive abilities (such as memory) are normally present. This knowledge provides a baseline that can be used to develop tests to assess behavioural and cognitive deficits caused by the brain damage associated with addictive drugs.

**Social psychology** is the study of the effects of people on people. Social psychologists explore phenomena such as perception (of oneself as well as of others), cause-and-effect relations in human interactions, attitudes and opinions, interpersonal relationships, group dynamics, and emotional behaviours, including aggression and sexual behaviour.

Drug addiction is not affected by physiological factors alone: It also has causes in the phenomena that social psychologists study. For example, children who begin smoking do not do so because their first cigarette gives them pleasure—this experience is usually *unpleasant*. Instead, they smoke because their peers do, and because smoking is portrayed so attractively in advertisements. Social influences are also involved in addictions to alcohol and illegal drugs. If we want to try to do something about these influences, we must first understand them.

**Personality psychology** is the study of individual differences in temperament and patterns of behaviour. Personality psychologists look for causal events in a person's history, both genetic and environmental. Some personality psychologists are closely allied with social psychologists; others work on problems related to adjustment to society and hence study problems of interest to clinical psychologists.

Personality differences certainly play a role in a person's susceptibility to drug addiction. One of the major contributions of personality psychologists to our understanding of drug addiction has been the development of tests of personality that can be used to study the factors involved in susceptibility to drug abuse.

**Evolutionary psychology** seeks to explain cognitive, social, and personality aspects of psychology by looking at their adaptive significance during the evolution of modern species. Clearly, the discoveries of comparative psychologists and behavioural geneticists are of interest to evolutionary psychologists. However, evolutionary psychologists use the theory of evolution by means of natural selection as a guiding principle. Our species presumably evolved because certain traits (such as the ability to walk upright) gave us a competitive advantage over species without those traits. The task of the evolutionary psychologist is to trace the development of such differences and to explore how their adaptive advantages might explain the behaviours of modern humans.

On the surface, drug addiction might be a real conundrum for evolutionary psychology. Why would an advanced species like ours fall prey to substances that are so harmful? Evolutionary psychologists attempt to unravel such puzzles by looking at possible side effects of drug use. Perhaps addictions are caused by processes that normally work to our benefit but interact harmfully with respect to certain substances that were not originally part of the environment of early humans.

**Cross-cultural psychology** is the study of the impact of culture on behaviour. Because the ancestors of people of different racial and ethnic groups lived in different environments that presented different problems and opportunities, different cultures have developed different strategies for adapting to their environments. These strategies show themselves in laws, customs, myths, religious beliefs, and ethical principles.

Undoubtedly, cross-cultural research can teach us much about drug addiction. Some cultures have traditions of drug use that generally do not lead to drug abuse; others have more problems when their members encounter these drugs. While some differences may be genetic (for example, differences in the ability to metabolize alcohol or in the sensitivity of nerve cells to particular drugs), many of the differences can best be understood by studying the customs and habits surrounding drug use. In some societies, for example, drugs are associated with sacred rituals. Perhaps, by restricting drug use to these rituals, a society regulates the frequency and amount of drugs used by its members.

**Clinical psychology** is the study of psychological disorders and problems of adjustment. Most clinical psychologists are practitioners who try to help people solve their problems, whatever the causes. The rest are scientists who look for a wide variety of causal events, including genetic and physiological factors, and environmental factors such as parental upbringing, interactions with siblings, and other social stimuli. They also do research to evaluate and improve methods of psychotherapy.

Clinical psychologists (and other mental health professionals, such as psychiatrists) are the people we call on to apply to individuals what we have learned about the causes of a disorder. Their contribution to addressing the problem of drug addiction has been an important one: the development of therapeutic methods used to prevent and treat drug abuse.

You will have undoubtedly noted that some of the fields I have described take contrasting views of the way behaviours are to be explained. Behavioural analysts, for example, focus on the environment as a source of differences among individuals, while behavioural geneticists look at genetic variation.

**social psychology** The branch of psychology devoted to the study of the effects people have on each other's behaviour.

**personality psychology** The branch of psychology that attempts to categorize and understand the causes of individual differences in patterns of behaviour.

**evolutionary psychology** The branch of psychology that explains behaviour in terms of adaptive advantages that specific behaviours provided during the evolution of a species. Evolutionary psychologists use natural selection as a guiding principle.

**cross-cultural psychology** The branch of psychology that studies the effects of culture on behaviour.

**clinical psychology** The branch of psychology devoted to the investigation and treatment of abnormal behaviour and psychological disorders.

**TABLE 1•1 Some Applied Areas of Psychology**

| Type of Psychologist | Area of Application | Typical Employment Setting |
|---|---|---|
| **Clinical neuropsychologists** | Identification and treatment of the behavioural consequences of nervous system disorders and injuries | Hospitals, in association with specialists who treat diseases of the nervous system |
| **Clinical psychologists** | Identification, assessment, and treatment of psychological disorders | Private practice and hospitals |
| **Community psychologists** | Welfare of individuals in the social system, especially those who are disadvantaged | Community organizations |
| **Consumer psychologists** | Motivation, perception, learning, and purchasing behaviour of individuals in the marketplace | Corporations and advertising agencies |
| **Engineering psychologists and ergonomists** | Perceptual and cognitive factors in the use of machinery | Corporations and engineering agencies |
| **Forensic psychologists** | Behaviour as it relates to the legal and justice system | Private law firms and public agencies in the justice system |
| **Health psychologists** | Behaviour that affects health and lifestyle | Hospitals, government agencies, and corporations |
| **Organizational psychologists** | Behaviour in industrial work processes | Corporations and government agencies |
| **School psychologists** | Behavioural issues of students in the school setting | Educational agencies and institutions |

Similarly, cultural psychologists and evolutionary psychologists might point to different explanations for cultural practices. These contrasting views provide the field of psychology with a large part of its vitality. You will undoubtedly develop your own opinion of the worth of specific approaches as my co-authors and I discuss them throughout this book. Be alert, however, to the possible value of viewpoints opposed to your own. And remember, too, that psychologists may be working with different levels of explanation.

**Areas of Psychological Application** Although discovering the causes of behaviour is important, not all psychologists are involved in research. In fact, *most* psychologists work outside the laboratory, applying the findings of research psychologists to problems related to people's behaviour. Their fields of application are still closely related to the research specialties I've just described, but their employment situations may be quite different. **Table 1•1** lists some of these applied areas.

## Interim Summary

### What Is Psychology?

Psychology is the science of behaviour, and psychologists study a large variety of behaviours in humans and other animals. They attempt to explain these behaviours by studying the events that cause them. Different psychologists are interested in different behaviours and in different categories of causes.

In this section, we considered 12 different approaches to understanding the causes of behaviour. Physiological psychologists study the role of the brain in behaviour. Comparative psychologists study the evolution of behaviour by comparing the behavioural capacities of various species of animals. Behaviour analysts study the relation of the environment to behaviour—in particular, the effects of the consequences of behaviour. Behaviour geneticists study the genetics of behaviour. Cognitive psychologists study complex human behaviours such as cognition, memory, and attention. Cognitive neuroscientists study the brain mechanisms responsible for cognitive processes. Developmental psychologists study the development of behaviour throughout the lifespan. Social psychologists study the effects of people on the behaviour of other people. Personality psychologists study individual differences in temperament and patterns of behaviour. Evolutionary psychologists study the influence of natural selection on behaviour. Cross-cultural psychologists study the impact of culture on behaviour. Clinical psychologists study the causes and treatment of psychological disorders and problems of adjustment.

In addition to thinking of psychology as a scientific discipline, we can also consider it as a profession, in which psychologists apply their knowledge of behaviour to the solution of certain kinds of problems.

**QUESTIONS TO CONSIDER**

1. Before you read the previous section, how would you have answered the question, "What is psychology?" Would your answer be different now?
2. What problems would you like psychologists to work on? If you want to be a psychologist, which field do you think you would be most interested in? What questions might you want to answer?

# The Growth of Psychology as a Science

Psychology is a young science that started in the late nineteenth century in Germany. However, humans have certainly been curious about psychological issues for much longer than that. To understand how psychology as a science came into being, we must first trace its roots back through philosophy and the natural sciences, because these disciplines provided the methods we use to study human behaviour. These roots took many centuries to develop. Let's examine them and see how they set the stage for the emergence of the science of psychology in the late nineteenth century.

▲ *Animism attempts to explain natural phenomena by supernatural means. This painting, from the tomb of Ramses VI, depicts the Egyptian belief that the sun was a god, borne across the heavens on a special boat, to be swallowed each evening by Nut, the goddess of the sky.*

## Philosophical Roots of Psychology

Perhaps the most notable part of our mental experience is that each of us is conscious of our own existence. Furthermore, we are aware of this consciousness and tend to relate it to our own behaviours. That is, although we might sometimes find ourselves engaged in things we had not planned to do, we generally have the impression that our conscious mind controls our behaviour. We consider alternatives, make plans, and then act. We get our bodies moving; we engage in behaviour.

It is ironic that, although consciousness is a private experience, we give it such importance in our public lives. Even though we can experience only our own consciousness directly, we assume that our fellow human beings are also conscious, and, to at least some extent, we attribute consciousness to other animals as well. To the degree that our behaviours are similar, we tend to assume that our mental states, too, resemble one another. Much earlier in the history of our species, it was common to attribute a life-giving spirit to anything that seemed to move or grow independently. Because early people believed that the movements of their own bodies were controlled by their minds or spirits, they inferred that the sun, moon, wind, and tides were similarly animated. This primitive philosophy is called **animism** (from the Latin *animare*, "to quicken, enliven, endow with breath or soul"). Even gravity was explained in animistic terms: Rocks fell to the ground because the spirits within them wanted to be reunited with the earth.

Obviously, our interest in animism is historical. Scientific understanding of our natural world requires that we reject such notions as rocks falling because they "want to." Rather, we refer to the existence of natural forces inherent in physical matter, even if these forces are not completely understood. However, note that different interpretations can be placed on the same events. Surely, we are just as prone to subjective interpretations of natural phenomena, albeit more sophisticated ones, as our ancestors were. In fact, when we try to explain why people do what they do, we tend to attribute at least some of their behaviour to the action of a motivating spirit—namely, a will. In our daily lives, this explanation of behaviour may often suit our needs. However, on a scientific level, we need to base our explanations on phenomena that can be observed and measured. We cannot objectively and directly observe "will."

Psychology as a science must be based on the assumption that behaviour is strictly subject to physical laws, just as any other natural phenomenon is. This assumption allows us to discover these laws objectively, using the scientific method (to be described in Chapter 2). The rules of scientific research impose discipline on humans, whose natural inclinations might lead them to incorrect conclusions. It seemed natural for our ancestors to believe that rocks had spirits, just as it seems natural for people nowadays to believe that behaviour

**animism** The belief that all animals and all moving objects possess spirits providing their motive force.

▲ *René Descartes (1596–1650)*

**FIGURE 1•1** Descartes's diagram of a withdrawal reflex. The energy from the fire would be transmitted physically to the brain, where it would release a type of fluid that would inflate the muscles and cause movement.

can be affected by a person's will. In contrast, the idea that feelings, emotions, imagination, and other private experiences are the products of physical laws of nature did not come easily; it evolved through many centuries.

Although the history of Western philosophy properly begins with the ancient Greeks, we will begin here with René Descartes (1596–1650), a seventeenth-century French philosopher and mathematician. Descartes has been called the father of modern philosophy and of a biological tradition that led to modern physiological psychology. He advocated a sober, impersonal investigation of natural phenomena using sensory experience and human reasoning. He assumed that the world was a purely mechanical entity that, having once been set in motion by God, ran its course without divine interference. To understand the world, one had only to understand how it was constructed. This stance challenged the established authority of the Church, which believed that the purpose of philosophy was to reconcile human experiences with the truth of God's revelations.

To Descartes, animals were creatures of the natural world only; accordingly, their behaviours were controlled by natural causes and could be understood by the methods of science. His view of the human body was much the same: It was a machine affected by natural causes and producing natural effects. For example, the application of a hot object to a finger would cause an almost immediate withdrawal of the arm from the source of stimulation. Reactions like this did not require participation of the mind; they occurred automatically. Descartes called these actions **reflexes** (from the Latin *reflectere*, "to bend back upon itself"). Energy coming from the outside source would be reflected back through the nervous system to the muscles, which would contract. The term is still in use today, but, of course, we explain the operation of a reflex differently. (See **Figure 1•1**.)

What set humans apart from the rest of the world, according to Descartes, was their possession of a mind. The mind was not part of the natural world, and therefore it obeyed different laws. Thus, Descartes was a proponent of **dualism**, the belief that all reality can be divided into two distinct entities: mind and matter. He distinguished between "extended things," or physical bodies, and "thinking things," or minds. Physical bodies, he believed, do not think, and minds are not made of ordinary matter. Although Descartes was not the first to propose dualism, his thinking differed from that of his predecessors in one important way: He suggested that a causal link existed between the mind and its physical housing.

Although later philosophers pointed out that this theoretical link actually contradicted the belief in dualism, the proposal of a causal interaction between mind and matter was absolutely vital to the development of a psychological science. Descartes reasoned that the mind controlled the

**reflex** An automatic response to a stimulus, such as the blink reflex to the sudden unexpected approach of an object toward the eyes.
**dualism** The philosophical belief that reality consists of mind and matter.

Locke+Berkley → origin of knowledge+concept of learning

movements of the body, while the body, through its sense organs, supplied the mind with information about what was happening in the environment. Descartes hypothesized that this interaction between mind and body took place in the pineal body, a small organ situated on top of the brain stem, buried beneath the large cerebral hemispheres of the brain. When the mind decided to perform an action, it tilted the pineal body in a particular direction, causing fluid to flow from the brain into the proper set of nerves. This flow of fluid caused the appropriate muscles to inflate and move.

How did Descartes come up with this mechanical concept of the body's movements? Western Europe in the seventeenth century was the scene of great advances in the sciences. It was not just the practical application of science that impressed Europeans, but also the beauty, imagination, and fun of it. Craftsmen constructed many elaborate mechanical toys and devices during this period. The young René Descartes was greatly impressed by the moving statues in the Royal Gardens (Jaynes, 1970). These devices served as models for Descartes as he theorized about how the body worked. He conceived of the muscles as balloons. They became inflated when a fluid passed through the nerves that connected them to the brain and spinal cord, just as water flowed through pipes to activate the statues. This inflation was the basis of the muscular contraction that causes us to move.

Descartes's explanation was one of the first to use a technological device as a model of the nervous system. In science, a **model** is a relatively simple system that works on known principles and is able to do at least some of the things that a more complex system can do. For example, when scientists discovered that elements of the nervous system communicate by means of electrical impulses, researchers developed models of the brain based on telephone switchboards and, more recently, computers. Abstract models, which are completely mathematical in their properties, have also been developed.

Although Descartes's model of the human body was mechanical, it was controlled, as we have seen, by a nonmechanical (in fact, non-physical) mind. Thus, humans were born with a special capability that made them greater than simply the sum of their physical parts. Their knowledge was more than merely a physical phenomenon. Perhaps it was due to the Catholic culture in which he lived, but Descartes refused to deny a spiritual basis to human actions.

It was an English philosopher, John Locke (1632–1704), who took this analysis one step further. Locke did not exempt the mind from the laws of the material universe. Descartes's *rationalism* (pursuit of truth through reason) was replaced by **empiricism**—pursuit of truth through observation and experience. Locke rejected the belief, prevalent in the seventeenth century, that ideas were innately present in an infant's mind. Instead, he proposed that all knowledge must come through experience; it is empirically derived. (In Greek, *empeiria* means "experience.") His model of the mind was the *tabula rasa* or "cleaned slate"—the ancient method of writing on waxed tablets that were scraped clean before use. Locke meant to imply that our minds were empty at birth, and ready to accept the writings of experience.

Some of our knowledge is undoubtedly more than simple snippets of experiences. Locke believed that knowledge developed through linkages of simple, primary sensations: simple ideas combined to form complex ones. Amending this notion somewhat, the Irish bishop, philosopher, and mathematician George Berkeley (1685–1753) suggested that our knowledge of events in the world also requires inferences based on the accumulation of past experiences. In other words, we must learn how to perceive. For example, our visual perception of depth involves several elementary sensations, such as observing the relative movements of objects as we move our heads and the convergence of our eyes (turning inward toward each other or away) as we focus on near or distant objects. Although our knowledge of visual depth seems to be immediate and direct, it is actually a secondary, complex response constructed from a number of simple elements. Our perceptions of the world can also involve integrating the activity of different sense organs, such as when we see, hear, feel, and smell the same object.

As philosophers, Locke and Berkeley speculated on the origins of knowledge and dealt with the concept of learning. (In fact, modern psychologists are still concerned with the issues that Berkeley raised.) However, although they rejected Descartes's version of the mind, they were trying to fit a nonquantifiable variable—reason—into the equation.

With the work of the Scottish philosopher James Mill (1773–1836), speculation about the mind completed an intellectual swing from *animism* (physical matter animated by spirits) to *materialism* (mind composed entirely of matter). **Materialism** is the belief that reality can be known only through an understanding of the physical world, of which the mind is a part. Mill did not invent materialism, but he developed it into a complete system for looking at human nature. He worked on the assumption that humans and animals were fundamentally the same. Both were thoroughly physical in their makeups and were completely subject to the physical laws of the universe. Essentially, he agreed with Descartes's approach to understanding the human body but rejected the concept of an immaterial mind. Mind, to Mill, was as passive as the body. It responded to the environment in precisely the same way. The mind, no less than the body, was a machine.

## Biological Roots of Psychology

René Descartes and his model of muscular physiology provide a good beginning for a discussion of the biological roots of psychology. You may have noted from the dates that

**model** A relatively simple system that works on known principles and is able to do at least some of the things that a more complex system can do.
**empiricism** The philosophical view that all knowledge is obtained through the senses.
**materialism** A philosophical belief that reality can be known only through an understanding of the physical world, of which the mind is a part.

▲ *Johannes Müller (1801–1858)*

Descartes lived at the same time as Galileo, when the latter was exploring the use of simple models of inclined planks to investigate the physical laws of motion. Like Galileo's models of gravitational motion, Descartes's concept was based on an actual working model (the moving statue) whose movements seemed similar to those of human beings. Unlike Galileo, however, Descartes relied on simple similarity as "proof" of his theory; he did not have the means to offer a scientific proof. But technological development soon made experimentation and manipulation possible in the biological realm as well. For example, Descartes's hydraulic model of muscular movement was shown to be incorrect by Luigi Galvani (1737–1798), an Italian physiologist who discovered that muscles could be made to contract by applying an electrical current directly to them or to the nerves attached to them. The muscles themselves contained the energy needed to contract. They did not have to be inflated by pressurized fluid. Indeed, a British physician made the same assertion even more pointedly when he demonstrated, by flexing his arm in a barrel of water, that his muscles did not increase in volume as Descartes's theory would predict.

The work of the German physiologist Johannes Müller (1801–1858) clearly shows the way in which emerging biological knowledge shaped the evolution of psychology. Müller was a forceful advocate of applying experimental procedures to the study of physiology. He recommended that biologists should do more than observe and classify; they should remove or isolate animals' organs, test their responses to chemicals, and manipulate other conditions to see how the organism worked. His most important contribution to what would become the science of psychology was his **doctrine of specific nerve energies.** He noted that the basic message sent along all nerves was the same—an electrical impulse. And the impulse itself was the same, regardless of whether the message concerned, for example, a visual perception or an auditory one. What, then, accounts for the brain's ability to distinguish different kinds of sensory information? That is, why do we see what our eyes detect, hear what our ears detect, and so on? After all, the optic nerves and the auditory nerves both send the same kind of message to the brain.

Müller's answer was that the messages are sent over different channels. Because the optic nerves are attached to the eyes, the brain interprets impulses received from these nerves as visual sensations. You have probably already noticed that rubbing your eyes causes sensations of flashes of light. When you rub your eyes, the pressure against them stimulates visual receptors located inside. As a result of this stimulation, messages are sent through the optic nerves to the brain. The brain interprets these messages as sensations of light.

Müller's doctrine had important implications. If the brain recognizes the nature of a particular sensory input by means of the particular nerve that brings the message, then perhaps the brain is similarly specialized, with different parts having different functions. In other words, if different nerves convey messages about different kinds of information, then the regions of the brain that receive these messages must have different functions.

Pierre Flourens (1774–1867), a French physiologist, provided experimental evidence for the implications of Müller's doctrine of specific nerve energies. He operated on animals, removing various parts of the nervous system, and found that the resulting effects depended on which parts were removed. He observed what the animal could no longer do and concluded that the missing capacity must have been the function of the part that had been removed. For example, if an animal could not move its leg after part of its brain was removed, then that region must normally control leg movements. This method of removal of part of the brain, called **experimental ablation** (from the Latin *ablatus*, "carried away"), was soon adopted by neurologists, and it is still used by scientists today. Through experimental ablation, Flourens claimed to have discovered the regions of the brain that control heart rate and breathing, purposeful movements, and visual and auditory reflexes.

Paul Broca (1824–1880) applied Müller's logic, although not his method, to humans. In 1861, Broca, a French surgeon, performed an autopsy on the brain of a man who had had a stroke several years previously. The stroke (damage to the brain caused in this case by a blood clot) had caused the man to lose the ability to speak. Broca discovered that the stroke had damaged part of the cerebral cortex on the left side of the man's brain. He suggested that this region of the brain is a centre for speech.

Although subsequent research has found that speech is not controlled by a single "centre" in the brain, the area that Broca identified is indeed necessary for speech production.

**doctrine of specific nerve energies** Johannes Müller's observation that different nerve fibres convey specific information from one part of the body to the brain or from the brain to one part of the body.

**experimental ablation** The removal or destruction of a portion of the brain of an experimental animal for the purpose of studying the functions of that region.

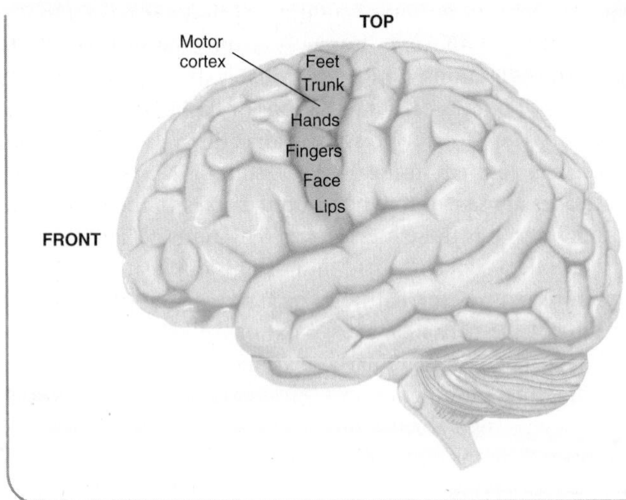


**FIGURE 1•2** Cortical motor map. Stimulation of various parts of the motor cortex causes contraction of muscles in various parts of the body.

▲ *Hermann von Helmholtz (1821–1894)*

The comparison of post-mortem anatomical findings with a patient's behavioural and intellectual deficits has become an important means of studying the functions of the brain. Psychologists can operate on the brains of laboratory animals, but they obviously cannot operate on the brains of humans. Instead, they must study the effects of brain damage that occurs from natural causes.

In 1870, the German physiologists Gustav Fritsch and Eduard Hitzig introduced the use of electrical stimulation as a tool for mapping the functions of the brain. The results of this method complemented those produced by the experimental destruction of nervous tissue and provided some answers that the method of experimental ablation could not. For example, Fritsch and Hitzig discovered that applying a small electrical shock to different parts of the cerebral cortex caused movements of different parts of the body. In fact, the body appeared to be "mapped" on the surface of the brain. (See **Figure 1•2**.) Decades later, when techniques of human brain surgery had advanced to the point where painless surgery could be performed on conscious patients, the Canadian neurosurgeon Wilder Penfield would be able to show that highly specific sensory experiences and even memories could be mapped in a similar way.

The work of the German physicist and physiologist Hermann von Helmholtz (1821–1894) did much to demonstrate that mental phenomena could be explained by physiological means. This extremely productive scientist made contributions to both physics and physiology. He actively dissociated himself from natural philosophy, from which many assumptions about the nature of the mind had been derived. Müller, under whom Helmholtz had conducted his first research, believed that human organs were endowed with a vital immaterial force that coordinated physiological behaviour, a force that was not subject to experimental investigation. Helmholtz would allow no such assumptions about unproved (and unprovable) phenomena. He advocated a purely scientific approach, with conclusions based on objective investigation and precise measurement.

Before Helmholtz's work, the transmission of impulses through nerves was thought to be as fast as the speed of electricity in wires; under this assumption, transmission would be virtually instantaneous, considering the small distances that impulses need to travel within the human body. Helmholtz successfully measured the speed of the nerve impulse and found that it was only about 27 metres per second, which is considerably slower than the speed of electricity in wires. This finding suggested to later researchers that the nerve impulse is more complex than a simple electrical current passing through a wire, which is indeed true.

Having shown that neural conduction was not instantaneous, Helmholtz next sought to measure the speed of a person's reaction to a physical stimulus. Here, however, he encountered a difficulty that no amount of careful measurement could solve: He discovered that there was too much variability from person to person to make the kind of scientific laws that were common in physics. This variability interested scientists who followed him and who tried to explain individual differences in behaviour. Because both the velocity of nerve impulses and a person's reactions to stimuli could be measured, researchers theorized that mental events themselves could be the subject of scientific investigation. Possibly, if the proper techniques could be developed, one could investigate what went on within the human brain. Thus, Helmholtz's research was very important in setting the stage for the science of psychology.

In Germany, a contemporary of Helmholtz's, Ernst Weber (1795–1878), began work that led to the development of a method for measuring the magnitude of human sensations. Weber, an anatomist and physiologist, found that people's ability to distinguish between two similar stimuli—such as the brightness of two lights, the heaviness of two objects, or the loudness of two tones—followed orderly laws. This regularity suggested to Weber and his followers that perceptual phenomena could be studied as scientifically as physics or biology. In Chapter 5, we will consider the study of the relation between the physical characteristics of a stimulus and the perceptions produced, a field called **psychophysics**.

## Applications in Education and Therapy

Descartes believed that the mind had *free will*—the ability to make decisions for which it was morally responsible. This viewpoint fit very well with Descartes's Catholic faith, which taught that an individual's soul had to choose between good and evil. However, it stood in opposition to a very different, even older, conception—that individual decisions were determined by outside forces, such as the Greek concept of *fate*, the Buddhist concept of *karma,* and the human desires mentioned in the poetic musings of the Persian mathematician Omar Khayyám.

As scientific knowledge expanded, scientists studying the physical world became increasingly precise in predicting phenomena from their antecedent causes. Philosophers began to recognize that a commitment to empiricism and materialism might also imply a commitment to **determinism**—the doctrine that behaviour is the result of prior events.

Psychologists differ concerning their views on determinism. Some, like Sigmund Freud, believed in a strong version of determinism based on internal psychological events (we will discuss Freud in the next section and in Chapter 14). Others, particularly those who practise humanistic psychology, emphasize autonomous choice as a factor (humanistic psychology is also discussed in the next section). Most psychologists assume some form of determinism, in part because of the philosophical and biological developments we've discussed. A third source of this assumption can be found in the political efforts of the nineteenth century to reform society and improve individual well-being.

The period from Descartes's life to Helmholtz's saw immense changes in Western politics and culture. The American and French revolutions (partly inspired by Locke's writings) ushered in a new conception of government as an institution to improve the lives of its citizens. Education was recognized as an important means of improvement, suggesting a role for the public in an area that had previously been provided by individuals, churches, or charities. At the same time, medical advances arising from the knowledge of biology promised cures for many diseases, including diseases of the mind.

Cures, of course, change or transform a person. Education likewise changes a person by introducing new knowledge. The notion of change, or of betterment, was to become an important topic of study in the 1800s. Educators and physicians began to consider the factors that cause change—whether it be either in a young pupil or in a patient. Much of this speculation began with an incident that, had it occurred in our own times, would have made the headlines of many a supermarket tabloid.

In January 1800, a boy about 12 years old was found living alone in the forests around Aveyron, France. Once captured by the authorities, he seemed completely divorced from human contact and unable to speak or understand language. His description seemed to match reports from a neighbouring district of a boy living alone in the fields; he had been living without human support for two or three years, getting what food he could by raiding village vegetable patches. He was wearing only a tattered shirt when found, but refused all attempts to clothe him. He seemed mainly to be interested in food and a place to sleep, and seemed not to care about human company or any kind of social interaction. When one of his caretakers showed him a mirror, the boy tried several times to reach through it to grab the object he saw reflected there (Shattuck, 1980).

The village commissioner, who had been active in the French Revolution, must have found something unique in the boy, for he arranged to house him in an orphanage and recommended that the authorities in Paris be contacted. Eventually, the boy was sent to Paris, where he quickly became the object of observation and debate among French scholars. Some assumed that he had grown up in the wild and saw him as an untainted example of the "noble savage"; others claimed that he suffered from a psychological disorder. When the argument died down, the poor boy was confined to a Parisian institute for the deaf. He lived there, or in the company of one of its caretakers, until his death in 1828.

The "Wild Boy of Aveyron" is one of the most famous case studies in the history of psychology. Although it was clear that the boy was not deaf, the Parisian institute seemed to be the only place where he could be housed. There, his case was taken up by a young physician, Jean-Marc Gaspard Itard (1774–1838), who had been hired by the institute only a few months before the boy's arrival. Itard worked with the boy (whom he named Victor) for about five years. Those who had studied Victor before Itard merely observed the boy's reactions and recorded his deficiencies of language and habits. In contrast, Itard sought to discover what Victor could learn. He devised a number of procedures to teach the boy words and then recorded his progress. His reports charted the successes and failures of different methods. Itard proceeded, in other words, on the assumption "that what the boy *was* hinged on what he could *become*." (Benzaquén, 2006, p. 167). His descriptions were couched in terms of Victor's development in response to this intervention.

Unfortunately, Victor's deficits in language improved only slightly under Itard's teaching. However, Itard's efforts have profound consequences beyond this single pupil. He had approached the problem of educating Victor much as a

**psychophysics** The branch of psychology that measures the quantitative relation between physical stimuli and perceptual experience.

**determinism** The doctrine that behaviour is the result of prior events.

doctor would approach a patient: by identifying the problem and devising a procedure to cure it. Itard stressed the identification of factors that could bring about change and inspired a new approach in Europe to the education of individuals with cognitive disabilities. More broadly, educators began to discuss whether *all* children should be educated by methods suited to an individual.

Child education had become an important issue in the United States at about this time. Most states had adopted a system known as the "American Common School" by the late 1800s. Reformers centralized school administration, organized classes according to age, and sought the best curriculum for a given age. Educators such as Booker T. Washington (1856–1915) and philosophers such as John Dewey (1859–1952) advocated reforms based on the needs and faculties of children. Dewey, in particular, argued that education must match the way in which children's abilities develop. He argued that children learn activities that are organized around goals, and that instruction should match this natural way of learning. A staunch empiricist and a passionate defender of the idea of democracy, Dewey believed that one aim of education should be to establish habits that integrate the child into the community. His views helped shape the movement in the United States known as Progressive Education.

It fell to one of Dewey's professional colleagues to suggest how such integrative habits might be learned. Edward Thorndike (1874–1949) originally studied the behaviour of animals, looking at responses that might indicate intelligence. He noticed that some events, usually those that one would expect to be pleasant, seemed to "stamp in" a response that had just occurred, thereby making it more likely to occur again. Noxious events seemed to "stamp out" the response, or make it less likely to occur. (Today, we call these processes *reinforcement* and *punishment;* they are described in more detail in Chapter 7.) Thorndike called this relationship the **law of effect** and defined it as follows:

> Any act which in a given situation produces satisfaction becomes associated with that situation, so that when the situation recurs the act is more likely than before to recur also. Conversely, any act which in a given situation produces discomfort becomes disassociated from that situation, so that when the situation recurs the act is less likely than before to recur. (Thorndike, 1905, p. 203)

The law of effect seemed to provide a universal principle by which habits could be learned: Goals were satisfiers that caused the action to recur more frequently. Larger activities could be built up from these activities; therefore, an ideal curriculum would be based on identifying the discrete units that make up the task to be learned. Extensive tests—some of which Thorndike himself developed and sold to school boards—would measure how well these units had been acquired.

If this sounds like a step backward from Itard's progressive ideas, you're probably correct. Thorndike's emphasis on "stamping in" responses implied that learning was automatic and inevitable. (To be sure, Thorndike did acknowledge the role of instinct and individual differences in behaviour. However, he was so fond of his law of effect that he had the words *stimulus* and *response* carved above the door to his laboratory, so that students would be reminded of how he had connected them.)

Meanwhile, an alternative view of children's learning was being developed in Italy by Maria Montessori (1870–1952). At a time when teaching was virtually the only profession open to women, Montessori decided to enter medical school and become a doctor. This must have taken extraordinary perseverance on her part. It was considered improper for a female student to see a naked body in the presence of men, so Montessori was banished from the classroom during dissections; she had to do them herself, alone, at night, surrounded by cadavers. Despite such hardships, Montessori became the first woman in Italy to earn a medical degree. (See Kramer, 1976, for additional details of her life.)

Ironically, she is best known as a teacher today. Appointed to administer an institution for children with developmental disabilities, Montessori discovered Itard's work with Victor. She applied Itard's approach to individualized instruction with considerable success. Reflecting upon the results, Montessori wondered whether children without disabilities would also benefit from this approach. She was given a chance to test these theories when she was asked to organize a school near Rome for poor preschool children. Montessori added some innovations of her own and developed a system now known as the Montessori method. This method was based on her belief that children matured through stages and were sensitive to different kinds

**law of effect** Thorndike's observation that stimuli that occur as a consequence of a response can increase or decrease the likelihood of making that response again.

▲ *Maria Montessori (1870–1952)*

of instruction at specific age ranges. Education was most effective when it provided exercises that matched the competency of the child at his or her stage. In contrast to Thorndike's emphasis on rewards as the basis for learning, Montessori felt that extrinsic rewards actually interfered with a child's natural incentive to learn. She also believed that movement was closely related to thought, and encouraged her pupils to move around in the classroom.

Montessori attracted considerable attention in Europe (Freud wrote to her once, contrasting the notoriety of his own name with "the brilliance that radiates from yours"), but her work had little effect on North American educational practices. Montessori herself may have been part of the problem: She was a bit of an autocrat and insisted that only she could train teachers in her methods. However, Thorndike's philosophy of learning did fit better with developing trends in psychology (we'll examine these in the next section). As a consequence, it's likely that the school system you experienced from kindergarten through high school was shaped more by Thorndike than by Montessori (Lillard, 2005).

Before Itard took responsibility for Victor, the boy was examined by Philippe Pinel (1745–1826). A physician like Itard, Pinel would influence how psychology thought about change, but in a different direction: He is widely regarded now as the father of psychiatry, the medical specialty that treats psychological disorders.

Prior to Pinel's time, people with mental illness were largely considered to be the responsibility of their family. Their treatment, typically provided by family members who feared or loathed their illness, could be abominable. Visitors to such households often told of how relatives would lock "the insane" in filthy cages, or chain them in pigsties. These reports eventually prompted activist governments to look for solutions, and to build asylums where persons with mental illness could be centrally cared for. Pinel was hired by the Revolutionary government of France to administer one such facility, the Salpêtrière hospital in Paris.

Pinel introduced some limited humanitarian reforms to the hospital, but his main influence was to propose that an asylum could, with proper practices, become a therapeutic institution. He and his followers tried new approaches to restore the cognitive abilities of an inmate. Mostly, these approaches took the form of social interventions, such as long conversations with a therapist or poetry readings. They were based on the belief that mental illness had a social cause and could be cured by similar factors.

For many reasons, the number of asylums grew rapidly during the 1800s, along with the number of people committed to them (Shorter, 1997). It could be argued that many of these people did not truly have mental illnesses, but were placed in these institutions for other reasons. Among this suspect category were the women of one ward of the Salpêtrière who were admitted with a collection of symptoms such as memory loss, intermittent paralysis, and insensitivity to painful stimuli. They were thought to be suffering from a nervous disorder that had been labelled *hysteria*. Beginning in 1862, a neurologist by the name of Jean-Martin Charcot (1825–1893) developed a clinical practice based on observations from the Salpêtrière ward. Neurology as a medical specialty deals with the treatment of diseases of the nervous system and is closely allied with psychiatry. Charcot proposed that hysteria was closely related to the condition produced by hypnosis and treated his patients by hypnotizing them. Although "hysteria" is no longer recognized as a disorder (its symptoms are now ascribed to other mental illnesses), Charcot's linking of hypnosis to the treatment of a mental illness would have important consequences. We'll explore hypnosis in Chapter 9 and its place in psychotherapy in Chapter 18.

## Interim Summary

### The Growth of Psychology as a Science

We can see that by the mid-nineteenth century, philosophy had embraced two concepts that would lead to the objective investigation of the human mind: the principles of materialism and empiricism. Materialism maintained that the mind was made of matter. Thus, all natural phenomena, including human behaviour, could be explained in terms of physical entities: the interaction of matter and energy. Empiricism emphasized that all knowledge was acquired by means of sensory experience; no knowledge was innate. By directing attention to the tangible, sensory components of human activity, these concepts laid the foundation for a scientific approach within psychology. At that time, the divisions between science and philosophy were still blurred. Subsequent developments in the natural sciences, especially in biology and physiology, provided the necessary ingredients that, united with the critical, analytical components of philosophy, formed the scientific discipline of psychology. These ingredients were experimentation and verification.

Materialism implies the doctrine of determinism, which is opposed to the concept of free will. Determinism makes possible the prediction that an outcome will follow some cause.

Education and psychiatry became matters of public concern during the early 1800s. Both fields emphasized the causal factors that can produce change. Progressive education stressed the natural development of the child and sought methods of teaching that would match the way children normally learned. Thorndike proposed the law of effect as a principle of this learning, while Montessori argued that different methods were appropriate at different ages of a child. Psychiatry saw mental illness as possibly having social causes and explored therapies that relied either on normal human discourse or on specialized techniques such as hypnosis.

**QUESTIONS TO CONSIDER**

1. Explaining things, whether scientifically or through myths and legends, seems to be a human need. It seems that people would rather invent a myth to explain a phenomenon than simply say, "I don't know." Can you think of a possible explanation for this need?
2. Which of the philosophers, scientists, educators, or therapists described in this section appeal to you the most? Would you like to know more about any of them and their times? What questions would you like to ask these people if it were possible to meet them?
3. Thorndike exerted immense influence on the development of schools in North America during the early 1900s. Do you see any vestiges of his beliefs about habits and the law of effect in your own school experience in Canada?

▲ *Wilhelm Wundt (1832–1920)*

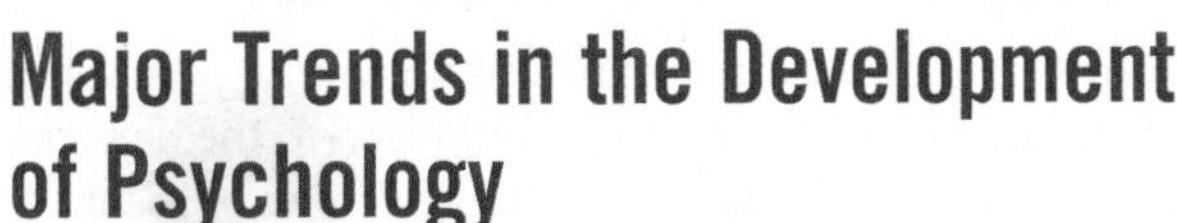

# Major Trends in the Development of Psychology

Psychology as a science, separate from philosophy and biology, began in Germany in the late nineteenth century with Wilhelm Wundt (1832–1920). Wundt was the first person to call himself a psychologist. He shared the conviction of other German scientists that all aspects of nature, including the human mind, could be studied scientifically. His book *Principles of Physiological Psychology* was the first textbook of psychology.

You may have already noted the high preponderance of German scholars in our survey of early influences on psychology. The fact that Germany was the birthplace of psychology had as much to do with social, political, and economic influences as with the abilities of its scientists and scholars. The German university system was well established, and professors were highly respected members of society. The academic tradition in Germany emphasized a scientific approach to a large number of subject areas, such as history, phonetics, archaeology, aesthetics, and literature. Thus, in contrast to French and British scholars, who adopted the more traditional, philosophical approach to the study of the human mind, German scholars were open to the possibility that it could be studied scientifically. German science also emphasized the importance of classification. We will see the significance of this to psychology shortly. Experimental physiology, one of the most important roots of experimental psychology, was well established in Germany. A more mundane and practical factor that favoured Germany as the birthplace of psychology was that its universities were well financed; there was money to support researchers who wanted to expand scientific investigation into new fields. It was in this climate that Müller, Helmholtz, and Wundt conducted their research.

## Structuralism

Wundt defined psychology as the "science of immediate experience." This approach was called **structuralism** by one of his students. Its subject matter was the *structure* of the mind, built from the elements of consciousness, such as ideas and sensations. Its raw material was supplied by trained observers who described their own experiences. The observers were taught to engage in **introspection** (literally, "looking within"); they observed stimuli and described their experiences. Wundt and his associates made inferences about the nature of mental processes by seeing how changes in the stimuli caused changes in trained observers' verbal reports.

Like George Berkeley, Wundt was particularly interested in the way that basic sensory information gave rise to complex perceptions. His trained observers attempted to ignore complex perceptions and report only the elementary ones. For example, the sensation of seeing a patch of red is immediate and elementary, whereas the perception of an apple is complex.

Wundt was an ambitious and prolific scientist who wrote many books and trained many other scientists in his laboratory. Many of them brought the new conception of psychology to North America, where it created quite a sensation. For example, in 1889, one of Wundt's proteges, James

**structuralism** The system of experimental psychology that began with Wundt; it emphasized introspective analysis of sensation and perception.
**introspection** Literally, "looking within," in an attempt to describe one's own memories, perceptions, cognitive processes, or motivations.

Mark Baldwin (1861–1934), was appointed professor of psychology at the University of Toronto. His appointment, which was the first of the "modern" psychologists in a Canadian university, was quite controversial. Students and prominent faculty members petitioned against him, a newspaper denounced his psychological training in an editorial, and the matter was eventually discussed in the Ontario Cabinet (Hoff, 1992). Professors trained by Wundt were also hired at Queen's University and the University of Alberta, although these appointments were much less controversial. Wright and Myers (1982) describe these early years at Canadian universities.

Wundt's method did not survive the test of time, however; structuralism died out in the early twentieth century. The major problem with his approach was the difficulty of reporting the raw data of sensation, unmodified by experience. Also, the emphasis of psychological investigation shifted from the study of the mind to the study of behaviour. More recently, psychologists have resumed the study of the human mind, but better methods are now available for studying it. Although structuralism has been supplanted, Wundt's contribution must be acknowledged. He established psychology as an experimental science independent of philosophy. He trained many psychologists, a number of whom established their own laboratories and continued to advance the new discipline.

## Functionalism

The next major trend in psychology was known as **functionalism**. This approach was in large part a reaction against Wundt's structuralism. Structuralists were interested in what they called the components of consciousness (ideas and sensations); in contrast, functionalists focused on the process of conscious activity (perceiving and learning). Functionalism grew from the new perspective on nature supplied by Charles Darwin and his followers. Proponents stressed the biological significance (the purpose, or *function*) of natural processes, including behaviours. The emphasis was on overt, observable behaviours, not on private mental events.

Charles Darwin (1809–1882) proposed the theory of evolution in his book *On the Origin of Species by Means of Natural Selection*, published in 1859. As you know, his work, more than that of any other person, revolutionized biology. The concept of *natural selection* showed how the consequences of an animal's characteristics affect its ability to survive. Instead of simply identifying, describing, and naming species, biologists now began to look at the adaptive significance of the ways in which species differed.

Darwin's theory was important to psychology because it suggested that behaviours, like other biological characteristics, could best be explained by understanding their role in the adaptation of an organism to its environment. Thus, behaviour has a biological context. Darwin assembled evidence that behaviours, like body parts, could be inherited. In *The Expression of the Emotions in Man and Animals*, published in 1872, he proposed that the facial gestures animals make in expressing emotions were descended from movements that previously had other functions. New areas of exploration were opened for psychologists by the ideas that an evolutionary continuity existed among various animal species and that behaviours, like parts of the body, had evolutionary histories.

▲ *James Mark Baldwin (1861–1934)*

The most important psychologist to embrace functionalism was the American scholar William James (1842–1910). As James said, "My thinking is first, last, and always for the sake of my doing." That is, thinking was not an end in itself; its function was to produce useful behaviours. Although James was a champion of experimental psychology, he did not appear to enjoy research, instead spending most of his time reading, thinking, teaching, and writing during his tenure as professor of philosophy (later, professor of psychology) at Harvard University. Although he did not produce any important experimental research, his teaching and writing influenced those who followed him. His theory of emotion is one of the most famous and durable psychological theories, and it is still quoted in modern textbooks. (Yes, you will read about it later in this book.) Psychologists still find it worthwhile to read James's writings, as he supplied ideas for experiments that still sound fresh and new today.

Unlike structuralism, functionalism was not supplanted. Functionalist textbooks were widely used in Canadian departments of psychology during their early years, and the tenets of functionalism strongly influenced the development of psychological explanations. One of the last functionalists, James Angell (1869–1949), described its basic principles:

1. Functional psychology is the study of mental operations and not mental *structures*. (For example, the mind

**functionalism** The strategy of understanding a species' structural or behavioural features by attempting to establish their usefulness with respect to survival and reproductive success.

remembers; it does not contain a memory.) It is not enough to compile a catalogue of what the mind does; one must try to understand what the mind accomplishes by this doing.

2. Mental processes are not studied as isolated and independent events but as part of the biological activity of the organism. These processes are aspects of the organism's adaptation to the environment and are a product of its evolutionary history. For example, the fact that we are conscious implies that consciousness has adaptive value for our species.
3. Functional psychology studies the relation between the environment and the response of the organism to the environment. There is no meaningful distinction between mind and body; they are part of the same entity.

Consider these points when you read the section on behaviourism.

## Freud's Psychodynamic Theory

When psychology was developing as a fledgling science, an important figure, Sigmund Freud (1856–1939), was formulating a theory of human behaviour that would greatly affect psychology and psychiatry and radically influence intellectuals of all kinds. Freud began his career as a neurologist, so his work was firmly rooted in biology. He soon became interested in behavioural and emotional problems and even attended one of Charcot's demonstrations on hypnosis at the Salpêtrière hospital. Freud was impressed with Charcot's demonstration of how a psychological event like hypnosis could cause a presumably neurological disorder like hysteria.

Freud's theory will be discussed in Chapter 14; we discuss him here only to mark his place in the history of psychology. His theory of the mind included structures, but his structuralism was quite different from Wundt's. He devised his concepts of ego, superego, id, and other mental structures through talking with his patients, not through laboratory experiments. His hypothetical mental operations included many that were unconscious and hence not available to introspection. And, unlike Wundt, Freud emphasized function; his mental structures served biological drives and instincts and reflected our animal nature.

## Psychology in Transition

Psychology as a science took a radical turn in the early decades of the twentieth century. Before we consider this change, it might help you to understand how the different intellectual contributions of the structuralists and the functionalists had shaped the way that psychology was practised at universities in Canada and the United States.

The controversy over James Mark Baldwin's appointment at the University of Toronto quickly died down, helped in part by the creation by the Ontario Minister of Education of a second position for Baldwin's rival. Baldwin was given a rather handsome budget of $1550 for equipment, which he promptly used to create the first psychological laboratory in the British Dominion (Baldwin, 1892). Like the laboratories of Wundt in Germany and of William James in the United States, it was designed for the experimental investigation of the mind, with attention to the control of noise and light. Baldwin went immediately to work in his new environment, even publishing a paper on handedness based on observations of his infant daughter.

The new emphasis on experiment and observation was becoming prominent in the classroom as well. Calkins (1892), for example, wrote a lengthy description of the senior class she taught in psychology at Wellesley College. Her students were taught the anatomy of the brain and received laboratory exercises in the dissection of lamb brains, the measurement of sensation, and the comparison of associations to simple words. She reported that the experiments on taste "were so unpopular that I should never repeat them in a general class of students who are not specializing in the subject." This leads the modern reader to wonder just what Calkins asked her students to taste.

Through the efforts of both researchers and instructors, psychology became part of university curricula throughout Canada. Professors of psychology joined academic societies and became recognized as members of an emerging scientific discipline. This trend would culminate in Canada in the summer of 1938 when, during a meeting of the American Association for the Advancement of Science in Ottawa, a group of psychologists began steps that led to the establishment of the Canadian Psychological Association (Dzinas, 2000).

Meanwhile, psychology textbooks began to reflect the prominence of physiological observation and the measurement of human reactivity. Shortly after setting up his laboratory in Toronto, Baldwin finished a major handbook of current psychological knowledge. In it, he incorporated not only the work of Mill and Wundt, but also that of Darwin and other natural historians. He formulated a special principle (now called the Baldwin effect) that he thought could explain the evolution of mental phenomena. As well, he speculated on the relationship between consciousness and muscular movement (Richards, 1987). Wundt had founded the science of psychology on the assumption that it should describe the contents of the mind. By the beginning of the twentieth century, however, psychologists like James and Baldwin had returned to the problem that vexed Descartes: How do we understand the actions that the mind supposedly determines?

## Behaviourism

The next major trend that we will discuss, behaviourism, likewise reflected this concern with action. It went further than James or Baldwin, however, by rejecting the special nature of mental events, denying that unobservable and unverifiable mental events were properly the subject matter of psychology. Behaviourists believe that because psychology is the study of observable behaviours, mental events, which cannot be observed, are outside the realm of psychology. **Behaviourism** is thus the study of the relation between people's environments and their behaviour, without appeal to hypothetical events occurring within their heads.

We have already examined one of the first behaviourists—Edward Thorndike, who formulated the law of effect. The law of effect is certainly in the functionalist tradition. It asserts that the consequences of a behaviour act back upon the organism, affecting the likelihood that the behaviour will occur again. This process is very similar to the principle of natural selection. Just as organisms that successfully adapt to their environments are more likely to survive and breed, so do behaviours that cause useful outcomes become more likely to recur.

Thorndike insisted that the subject matter of psychology was behaviour. However, his explanations contained mentalistic terms. For example, in his law of effect he spoke of "satisfaction," which is certainly not a phenomenon that can be observed directly. Later behaviourists recognized this contradiction and replaced terms such as *satisfaction* and *discomfort* with more objective concepts that reflected only the behaviour.

Another major figure in the development of the behaviouristic trend was not a psychologist at all but a physiologist: Ivan Pavlov (1849–1936), a Russian who studied the physiology of digestion (for which he later received a Nobel Prize). In the course of studying the stimuli that produce salivation, he discovered that hungry dogs would salivate at the sight of the attendant who brought in their dishes of food. Although first labelling this phenomenon a "psychic reflex," Pavlov soon traced it to the experience the dog had received. Pavlov found that a dog would salivate at completely arbitrary stimuli, such as the sound of a bell, if the stimuli were quickly followed by the delivery of a bit of food into the animal's mouth.

Pavlov's discovery had profound significance for psychology. He showed that through experience an animal could learn to make a response to a stimulus that had never caused this response before. This ability might explain how organisms learn cause-and-effect relations in the environment. In contrast, Thorndike's law of effect suggested an explanation for the adaptability of an individual's behaviour to its particular environment. So, from Thorndike's and Pavlov's studies, two important behavioural principles had been discovered.

▲ *Ivan Pavlov (1849–1936) in his laboratory with some of his collaborators. His research revealed valuable information about the principles of learning.*

▲ *John B. Watson (1878–1958)*

Behaviourism as a formal school of psychology began with the publication of a book by John B. Watson (1878–1958), *Psychology from the Standpoint of a Behaviourist.* Watson, a professor of psychology at Johns Hopkins University, was a popular teacher and writer and a very convincing advocate of behaviourism. Even after leaving Johns Hopkins for a highly successful career in advertising, he continued to lecture and write magazine articles about psychology.

According to Watson, psychology was a natural science whose domain was restricted to observable events: the behaviour of organisms. He believed that the elements of consciousness studied by the structuralists were too subjective to lend themselves to scientific investigation. He defined psychology as the objective study of stimuli and the behaviours they produced. Even thinking was reduced to a form of behaviour—talking to oneself:

> Now what can we observe? We can observe behaviour—*what the organism does or says*. And let us point out at once: that saying is doing—that is, behaving. Speaking overtly or to ourselves (thinking) is just as objective a type of behaviour as baseball. (Watson, 1930, p. 6)

Behaviourism is still very much in evidence today in psychology. Its advocates included B. F. Skinner (1904–1990), one of the most influential psychologists of the twentieth century. But psychologists, including modern behaviourists, have

**behaviourism** A movement in psychology that asserts that the only proper subject matter for scientific study in psychology is observable behaviour.

▲ *Margaret Floy Washburn (1871–1939)*

moved away from the strict behaviourism of Watson; mental processes such as imagery and attention are again considered to be proper subject matter for scientific investigation.

In this sense, modern psychologists have moved more toward a view advocated by Margaret Floy Washburn (1871–1939) early in the debate over behaviourism. Washburn (1922), although advocating her own version of structuralism, suggested to behaviourists that they regard introspection as a form of behaviour itself—one that could help us understand the inaccessible processes of mental life. As Washburn would have wished, Watson's emphasis on objectivity in psychological research remains. Even those modern psychologists who most vehemently protest against what they consider to be the narrowness of behaviourism use the same principles of objectivity to guide their research. As research scientists, they must uphold the principles of objectivity that evolved from empiricism to functionalism to behaviourism. A psychologist who studies private mental events realizes that these events can be studied only indirectly, by means of behaviour—verbal reports of inner experiences. Unlike Wundt, present-day psychologists realize that these reports are not pure reflections of these mental events; like other behaviours, these responses can be affected by many factors. Consequently, they strive to maintain an objective stance to ensure that their research findings will be valid and capable of being verified.

**humanistic psychology** An approach to the study of human behaviour that emphasizes human experience, choice and creativity, self-realization, and positive growth.

**Gestalt psychology** A movement in psychology that emphasized that cognitive processes could be understood by studying their organization, not their elements.

## Humanistic Psychology

For many years, philosophers and other intellectuals have been concerned with what they consider to be the special nature of humanity—with free will and spontaneity, with creativity and consciousness. As the science of psychology developed, these concerns received less attention because researchers could not agree on objective ways to study them. Humanistic psychology developed during the 1950s and 1960s as a reaction to both behaviourism and psychoanalysis. Although psychoanalysis certainly dealt with mental phenomena that could not be measured objectively, it viewed people as products of their environment and of innate, unconscious forces. Humanistic psychologists insist that human nature goes beyond environmental influences, and that psychologists should study conscious processes, not unconscious ones. In addition, they note that psychoanalysis seems preoccupied with disturbed people, ignoring positive phenomena such as happiness, satisfaction, love, and kindness.

**Humanistic psychology** is an approach to the study of human behaviour that emphasizes human experience, choice and creativity, self-realization, and positive growth. Humanistic psychologists emphasize the positive sides of human nature and the potential we all share for personal growth. In general, humanistic psychologists do not believe that we will understand human consciousness and behaviour through scientific research. Thus, the humanistic approach has not had a significant influence on psychology as a science. Its greatest impact has been on the development of methods of psychotherapy based on a positive and optimistic view of human potential.

## Reaction against Behaviourism: The Emphasis on Cognition

Proponents of behaviourism restricted the subject matter of psychology to observable behaviours. And, despite their differences from the structuralists, they also tended to analyze behaviour by dividing it into smaller elements. Even as behaviourism became the dominant trend in psychology, a contrasting school of thought began to emphasize how unobservable factors influence larger patterns of human consciousness.

This movement began when a German psychologist, Max Wertheimer (1880–1943), bought a toy that presented a series of pictures in rapid succession. Each picture was slightly different from the preceding one, resulting in the impression of continuous motion—like a movie. Wertheimer and his colleagues suggested that psychological processes provided the continuity. They therefore attempted to discover the *organization* of cognitive processes, not their elements. They called their approach **Gestalt psychology**. *Gestalt* is a German word that roughly translates as "unified form." Gestalt psychologists insisted that perceptions resulted from patterns of interactions among many elements, in the same way that we recognize a song by the relations between the notes, rather than by the individual notes themselves.

Although the Gestalt school of psychology no longer exists, its insistence that the elements of an experience are organized into larger units was very influential. These organizational processes are not directly observable, yet they still determine behaviour. During the past three decades, many psychologists likewise began to reject the restrictions of behaviourism and have turned to the study of consciousness, feelings, imagery, and other private events.

Much of *cognitive psychology* uses an approach called **information processing**—information received through the senses is "processed" by various systems of neurons in the brain. Some systems store the information in the form of memory; other systems control behaviour. Some systems operate automatically and unconsciously, while others are conscious and require effort. Because the information processing approach was first devised to describe the operations of complex physical systems such as computers, the modern model of the human brain is, for most cognitive psychologists, the computer. However, partly as a result of developments discussed in the next section, another model (the artificial neural network) is beginning to replace the computer.

Although cognitive psychologists now study mental structures and operations, they have not gone back to the introspective methods that structuralists such as Wundt employed. They use objective research methods, just as behaviourists do. For example, several modern psychologists have studied the phenomenon of imagery. If you close your eyes and imagine what the open pages of this book look like, you are viewing a mental image of what you have previously seen. This image exists only within your brain, and it can be experienced by you and no one else. I have no way of knowing whether your images are like mine any more than I can know whether the colour red looks the same to you as it does to me. The experience of imagery cannot be shared in a scientific sense.

However, behaviours that are based on images can indeed be measured. For example, Kosslyn (1973, 1975) asked a group of people to memorize several drawings. Then, he asked them to imagine one of them, focusing their attention on a particular feature of the image. Next, he asked a question about a detail of the image that was either "near" the point they were focusing on or "far" from it. For example, if they were picturing a boat, he might ask them to imagine that they were looking at its stern (back). Then he might ask whether the boat had a rudder at the stern, or whether a rope was fastened to its bow (front).

Kosslyn found that people could very quickly answer a question about a feature of the boat that was near the place they were focusing on, but they took longer to answer a question about a part that was farther away. It was as if they had to scan their mental image to get from one place to the other. (See **Figure 1•3**.)

**FIGURE 1•3** A drawing used in the imagery study by Kosslyn.

*(From Kosslyn, S. M. (1973).* Perception and Psychophysics, *14, 90–94. Reprinted with permission.)*

Because we cannot observe what is happening within a person's head, the concept of imagery remains hypothetical. However, this hypothetical concept very nicely explains and organizes some concrete results—namely, the time it takes for a person to give an answer. Although the explanation for the results of this experiment is phrased in terms of private events (mental images), the behavioural data (how long it takes to answer the questions) are empirical and objective.

## Reaction against Behaviourism: The Emphasis on Neurobiology

Although the first scientific roots of psychology were in biology and physiology, the biological approach to behaviour has become so strong in the past few years that it can properly be called a revolution. During the early and mid-twentieth century, the dominance of behaviourism led to a de-emphasis of biological factors in the study of behaviour. At the time, scientists had no way of studying what went on in the brain, but that did not prevent people from spinning elaborate theories of how the brain controlled behaviour. Behaviourists rejected such speculation. They acknowledged that the brain controlled behaviour, but argued that because we could not see what was happening inside the brain, we should refrain from inventing physiological explanations that could not be verified. One of the few dissenters from the prevailing behaviourist view of the time was a Canadian psychologist, Donald Hebb (1904–1985).

Hebb had graduated from Dalhousie University with aspirations of being a novelist. After a brief stint teaching in Quebec, he was admitted as a part-time student at McGill University. Although his initial academic record at McGill has been described by Ferguson (1982) as "dismal," Hebb was inspired by the physiological approach to psychology then taught at McGill by a professor who had worked with Pavlov. After completing his graduate work in the United States and teaching briefly at Queen's University, Hebb returned to McGill in 1947.

**information processing** An approach used by cognitive psychologists to explain the workings of the brain; information received through the senses is processed by systems of neurons in the brain.

▲ *Donald Hebb (1904–1985)*

Challenging the behaviourists, Hebb argued that behavioural and mental phenomena could be related directly to brain activity. In his most influential work, published soon after his return to McGill, he suggested several simple principles by which the nervous system organized itself into special "circuits" that could represent mental activity (Hebb, 1949).

Cognitive psychologists had inherited from early behaviourists a suspicion of the value of biology in explaining behaviour. Thus, the cognitive revolution did not lead to a renewed interest in biology. But the extraordinary advances in neurobiology in the late twentieth century revolutionized psychology and vindicated Hebb's viewpoint (Klein, 1999). Many of his students and associates were at the forefront of subsequent developments in psychology (Adair, Paivio, & Ritchie, 1996).

Neurobiologists (biologists who study the nervous system) and scientists and engineers in allied fields have developed ways to study the brain that were unthinkable just a few decades ago. We can study fine details of nerve cells, discover their interconnections, analyze the chemicals they use to communicate with each other, produce drugs that block the action of these chemicals or mimic their effects, see the internal structure of a living human brain, and measure the activity of different parts of the brain—regions as small as a few cubic millimetres—while people are watching visual displays, listening to words, or performing various kinds of cognitive tasks. In addition, it seems as though every day a new gene is discovered that plays a role in a particular behaviour, and drugs are being designed to duplicate or block the effects of these genes.

As one small indication of the strong influence that the biological revolution has had on psychology, the premier award of the Canadian Psychological Association was named in honour of Donald Hebb. Each year, this award honours the researcher who has made the greatest contribution to the discipline of psychology.

## Then and Now

### Psychology Compared to the Other Sciences

A discussion of a subject's history is a pretty conventional way to begin a textbook. Like most textbook authors, we feel that knowing the history of psychology will help you, as a student, to understand why psychologists choose certain topics to study and why they use certain methods. In the chapters to follow, we'll continue that approach with a series of sections like this, in which we examine the way our knowledge about behaviour has changed as a result of discovery. Sometimes progress is not always predictable, and we hope that following the twists and turns of psychological research will give you a better appreciation of what we know today . . . and, perhaps, of how much we still have to learn.

This chapter has looked at the historical development of the whole field of psychology. That development began with Descartes in the 1600s—about 50 years before Isaac Newton published his famous work *Philosophiæ Naturalis Principia Mathematica,* which can be fairly viewed as the foundation of modern physics. Thanks to Newton's pioneering work, physics, as a science, has advanced to a highly precise body of knowledge in the twenty-first century. Historically, psychology had a bit of a head start. How does it compare with physics or with the other sciences?

Simonton (2004) compared the scientific status of psychology with that of physics, chemistry, sociology, and biology. He identified a number of characteristics that typified a general science:

- the number of theories and laws mentioned in introductory textbooks (the higher the ratio of theory to law, the "softer"—that is, less scientific—the discipline)
- publication rate (the more frequent, the more scientific the discipline)
- the appearance of graphs in journal papers (the "harder" the discipline, the greater the number of graphs)
- the impact made by young researchers (the more scientific the discipline, the greater the agreement that a researcher's contribution is significant)
- how peers evaluated 60 of their colleagues in their own disciplines, and how often single papers are cited (referred to in research papers).

Simonton also looked at secondary measures of scientific standing: "lecture disfluency" (the number of pause words such as *uh, er,* and *um*: these are more common in less formal, structured, and factual disciplines), the extent

**FIGURE 1•4** According to Simonton's study, psychology's scientific status was more similar to that of biology than to another discipline traditionally associated with it: sociology.

*(From Simonton, D. K. (2004). Psychology's status as a scientific discipline: Its empirical placement within an implicit hierarchy of the sciences.* Review of General Psychology, 8, *65 (Figure 2). Published by APA. Reprinted with permission.)*

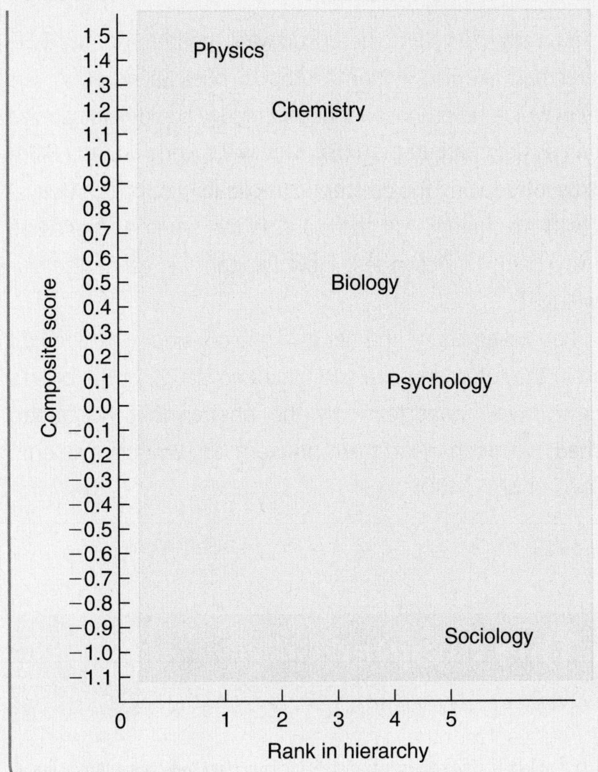


to which references in journal articles were recent, age at receipt of the Nobel Prize, and perceived difficulty of the discipline. Simonton combined these measures to provide a composite measure of scientific status.

Based on the first set of indicators, Simonton found that the natural sciences were judged to be more "scientific" than were the social sciences. Psychology fell right on the mean—at the junction between natural and social sciences (see **Figure 1•4**). However, psychology's score was much closer to biology's than to sociology's. In fact, the biggest gap in scores was found between psychology and sociology, suggesting that the discipline is closer to its natural science cousins than to its social science acquaintances. A gap also separated chemistry and biology, suggesting that the sciences might be grouped according to three clusters: the physical sciences (chemistry and physics), life sciences (biology and psychology), and social science (sociology).

Psychology's position in this clustering makes sense if we consider the history we've just discussed. Much of psychology's early history concerned issues of definition—what it would study and how that topic differed from the subject matter of philosophy. However, despite its commitment to materialism, it was pretty clear that psychology could not achieve the mathematical precision of Newtonian physics. The biological discoveries of the 1800s provided a more compatible scientific foundation, and psychology's growth as a science accelerated with new knowledge about the brain and the nervous system.

## Interim Summary

### Major Trends in the Development of Psychology

We can see that psychology has come a long way in a relatively short time. The first laboratory of experimental psychology was established in 1879, a little over a century ago. Wilhelm Wundt established psychology as a discipline that was independent of philosophy. It was based on the premise that, through introspection, the mind's contents could be described. Even though Wundt's structuralism did not last, interest in psychology continued to grow. It took on added breadth and scope with the emergence of functionalism, which grew out of Darwin's theory of evolution, and its stress on the adaptive value of biological phenomena. Functionalism gave rise to the objectivity of behaviourism, which still dominates the way we do research.

The cognitive revolution began because some psychologists believed that a strict emphasis on observable behaviour missed the complexity of human cognition and behaviour, an opinion that modern behaviourists contest. The biological revolution in psychology is manifested in the increased interest of psychologists in all fields—not just physiological psychology—in the role of biological factors in behaviour.

#### QUESTIONS TO CONSIDER

1. Although psychology began in Germany, it soon migrated to North America, where it flourished. Can you think of any characteristics of North American society that might explain why psychology developed faster there than elsewhere in the world?
2. As you have learned, psychologists study a wide variety of behaviours. Do you think that there are any behaviours that psychologists cannot explain (or should not try to explain)?

EPILOGUE

## The Bottom Line

I wasn't the only one who thought that reading Kurzweil's book would be a good exercise in shaking up one's assumptions about psychology. The director of the movie *I, Robot* reportedly required his entire cast to read this book before filming began. Whether it had any special inspiration for Will Smith is something you can decide on your own. But, for Laura and her group, the book accomplished what I had hoped.

Kurzweil attempted to construct a utopian vision of the future based on the scientific assumptions that have shaped contemporary psychology: historical themes such as materialism, empiricism, and determinism. It's a challenging notion to push the working assumptions of a science into a prescription for the future. Laura and her partners in this project had to consider whether our current knowledge from the science of behaviour is up to the task.

Ironically, 50 years before Kurzweil, the behaviourist B. F. Skinner had likewise written a utopian book (a novel, in this case) in which he proposed that psychology could revolutionize human society (Skinner, 1948). Kurzweil's work extends Skinner's by introducing the concept of replicating our nervous system with machinery, but the issue is the same and goes all the way back to Descartes: How far can we generalize our knowledge?

I had asked Laura and her group to consider what it might mean in the future to have complete knowledge of the brain's biology. If you want to know the answer that her group reached, you can hear their program at www.cjsr.ualberta.ca/news.php?s=p400.

## Canadian Connections to Research in This Chapter

Adair, J. G., Paivio, A., & Ritchie, P. (1996). Psychology in Canada. *Annual Review of Psychology, 47*, 341–370. (University of Manitoba: www.umanitoba.ca)

Baldwin, J. M. (1892). The psychological laboratory in the University of Toronto. *Science, 19*, 143–144. (University of Toronto: www.library.utoronto.ca)

Dzinas, K. (2000). Founding the Canadian Psychological Association: The perils of historiography. *Canadian Psychology, 41*, 205–212. (York University: www.yorku.ca)

Ferguson, G. A. (1982). Psychology at McGill. In Wright, M. J., & Myers, C. R. (Eds.), *History of academic psychology in Canada* (pp. 33–67). Toronto: Hogrefe. (McGill University: www.mcgill.ca)

Hebb, D. O. (1949). *The organization of behaviour.* New York: Wiley-Interscience. (McGill University: www.mcgill.ca)

Hoff, T. L. (1992). Psychology in Canada one hundred years ago: James Mark Baldwin at the University of Toronto. *Canadian Psychology, 33*, 683–694. (University of Saskatchewan: www.usask.ca)

Klein, R. M. (1999). The Hebb legacy. *Canadian Journal of Psychology, 53*, 1–3. (Dalhousie University: www.dal.ca)

Wright, M. J., & Myers, C. R. (Eds.). (1982). *History of academic psychology in Canada.* Toronto: Hogrefe. (University of Western Ontario: www.uwo.ca)

## Suggestions for Further Reading

Kurzweil, R. (1999). *The age of spiritual machines: When computers exceed human intelligence.* New York: Viking Penguin.

Skinner, B. F. (1948). *Walden two.* New York: Macmillan.

What would it be like if society followed psychological or neuroscientific principles? These two utopian books try to answer this question. Skinner's book is a classic that applies behaviouristic principles to life. Kurzweil's is the book referred to in my opening vignette. As I mentioned, my fourth-year university students found Kurzweil's scenarios plausible but disturbing. Is this our future? You be the judge.

Lawson, R. B., Graham, J. E., & Baker, K. M. (2007). *A history of psychology: Globalization, ideas, and applications.* Upper Saddle River: NJ: Pearson Prentice Hall.

Reese, R. J. (2005). *America's public schools: From the common school to "No Child Left Behind."* Baltimore, MD: Johns Hopkins University Press.

Shorter, E. (1997). *A history of psychiatry.* New York: John Wiley & Sons.

The book by Lawson, Graham, and Baker is an excellent history of psychology. Particularly notable is its inclusiveness: There are special chapters on the role of women in the history of psychology, the contribution of black Americans, and the development of psychology outside Europe and America. Reese's book is not centrally concerned with psychology, but you may find it of interest to know why your elementary, junior high, and high schools were organized the way they were. Shorter's work is a history of the medical profession of psychiatry. It skips around, but provides some interesting anecdotes on major figures.

# 2

# THE WAYS AND MEANS OF PSYCHOLOGY

C H A P T E R   O U T L I N E

## The Scientific Method in Psychology

Identifying the Problem: Getting an Idea for Research • Designing an Experiment • Performing an Experiment • Correlational Studies • Reporting and Generalizing a Study

The scientific method is the most effective procedure for understanding natural phenomena and cause-and-effect relations. Starting with hypotheses—guesses about the way variables are related—researchers use experiments and observational studies to investigate phenomena. Researchers must use valid and reliable operational definitions of independent and dependent variables. They must avoid confounding variables if their results are to be clear and understandable. Finally, they hope to generalize the results of their research beyond the particular participants they have studied.

## Ethics

Research with Human Participants • *Then and Now: Research and Ethics* • Research with Animal Participants

Psychologists must abide by the ethical principles established by governmental agencies and professional societies. Human participants have a right to informed consent prior to participating in a study. Their dignity must be respected and their well-being protected. Animals used in research must be housed properly and treated humanely.

## Understanding Research Results

Descriptive Statistics: What Are the Results? • Inferential Statistics: Are the Results Significant?

After researchers have collected data from a study, they analyze the results. They first describe the data using descriptive statistics, such as measures of central tendency, variability, and correlation. Then, they use inferential statistics to determine whether the results are statistically significant. They estimate the likelihood that the results could have occurred by chance.

P R O L O G U E

## Justine's Experiment

Justine's parents operate a small company that employs five people. The employees assemble custom testing devices used in the oil exploration industry. One summer, after her first year of university, Justine decided to put her skills to work by trying to increase the company's productivity. She reasoned that if the employees could complete more of the testing devices per day, the company would be more profitable for her parents and the workers themselves would benefit through their profit-sharing plan.

One evening, Justine stayed at the assembly laboratory to work on one of the devices herself. After a couple of hours, her neck was strained and her arms and hands tingled from maintaining a bent position over the bench at which she was working. Justine convinced her parents to invest in height-adjustable chairs to replace the existing stationary ones. When the chairs arrived, she adjusted them so that each employee seemed to be at a comfortable position. Justine held an informal meeting with the employees, and told them that she thought the new chairs would reduce discomfort and therefore permit them to be more productive. She said that she would keep track of how many units they finished over the next several days, and would let them know if the chairs had helped. At the end of the week, the employees eagerly asked Justine how they had done. She proudly announced that they had completed 20 percent more of the testing units than they had during the same period of time before the chairs arrived. The workers congratulated her for her insight and help.

Justine continued to check in with the employees and to collect data during the following week. She then got together with her friend Lawrence, who had recently taken a statistics course. Lawrence helped her conduct a formal statistical test to compare the production figures for the seven workdays before Justine introduced the new chairs, and for the seven workdays afterwards. They found that productivity had increased significantly more than would be expected by chance. Her intervention had worked, or so it appeared, and Justine stopped her daily visits with the employees.

A few weeks later, Justine happened to look at the employees' production figures and was disappointed to find that productivity had fallen to the same level as before the new chairs arrived. She decided to start over with the old chairs, monitor the employees' output, and then reintroduce the adjustable chairs to see what would happen. After a week with the old chairs, productivity inexplicably increased by 20 percent again. Justine was understandably perplexed. Increased productivity with the old chairs? She gave up on her project. What had happened? Justine was sure that she had diligently applied the scientific method and that her intervention should have had clear-cut results.

The goal of psychology as a science is the explanation of behaviour. As scientists, the vast majority of psychologists believe that behaviour, like other natural phenomena, can be studied objectively. The scientific method permits us to discover the nature and causes of behaviour. This chapter will show you how the scientific method is used in psychological research. What you learn here will help you understand the research described in the rest of the book. But even more than that, what you learn here can be applied to everyday life. Knowing how a psychologist can be misled by the results of improperly conducted research can help us all avoid being misled by more casual observations. Understanding the scientific method can also help us, as consumers of information, distinguish worthwhile research from flawed research reported in the mass media.

## The Scientific Method in Psychology

To explain behaviour, we must use a method that is both precise enough to be understood by others and general enough to apply to a wide variety of situations. We hope to find general statements about the events that cause phenomena to occur.

**scientific method** A set of rules that governs the collection and analysis of data gained through observational studies or experiments.
**naturalistic observation** The observation of the behaviour of people or other animals in their natural environments.
**clinical observation** The observation of the behaviour of people who are undergoing diagnosis or treatment.

Scientists use an agreed-upon approach to discovery and explanation—the scientific method. The **scientific method** consists of a set of rules that dictate the general procedure a scientist must follow in his or her research. These rules are not arbitrary; as we will see, they are based on logic and common sense. The rules were originally devised by philosophers who were attempting to determine how we could understand reality. By nature, we are all intuitive psychologists, trying to understand why others do what they do—so it is important to realize how easily we can be fooled about the actual causes of behaviour. Thus, everyone, not just professional psychologists, should know the basic steps of the scientific method.

Psychologists conduct three major types of scientific research. These classes of research are common across many of the sciences. The first type includes **naturalistic observation** and **clinical observation**—observation of people or animals in their natural environment or while they are undergoing treatment or diagnosis for a psychological condition. These methods are the least formal and are constrained by the fewest rules. Naturalistic observations provide the foundations of the biological and social sciences. For example, Charles Darwin's observation and classification of animals, plants, and fossils during his voyage around the world provided him with the raw material for his theory of evolution. Maria Montessori formed many of her ideas about child development by watching children in a classrooom. And Paul Broca suggested that language was located in a specific region of the brain after treating a man who had lost his ability to speak. As these examples illustrate, a researcher might perceive new facts following careful observation.

The second type, **correlational studies**, is observational in nature but involves more formal measurement—of environmental events, of individuals' physical and social characteristics, and of their behaviour. Researchers examine the relations of these measurements in an attempt to explain the observed behaviours.

Finally, **experiments** go beyond mere measurement. A psychologist performing an experiment makes things happen and observes the results. As you will see, only experiments can positively identify the causal relations among events.

Let us consider how we might use the scientific method to gain an understanding of a psychological experience you may have encountered. Every mall in Canada seems to have at least one shop that stocks those multicoloured posters that reveal a three-dimensional image of an object when you cross your eyes just the right amount. (See **Figure 2•1**.) When we lecture on the visual perception material discussed in Chapter 6 of this textbook, we show students samples of these images, which go by the long-winded label of *single image random dot stereograms*, or *SIRD stereograms*. Invariably, some students can identify the hidden object quickly while others fail to see it after long minutes of straining. Given that our individual visual systems are generally alike, why is there this difference? Would giving the students a picture of the hidden image help them find it in the stereogram?

The three classes of research often occur in progressive sequence, and provide increasingly more compelling evidence. Naturalistic observations of yourself or your friends at a shopping mall in front of a SIRD sterogram could provide the context of the problem. You likely would observe that some people take much longer than others to identify the hidden objects in these images. Observational evidence identifies the phenomenon and might indicate something about its magnitude. Correlational evidence arises when you start to observe relations between observations. For example, you might note that you and your friends seem to bring the three-dimensional object into focus much faster when a small two-dimensional picture of the object appears alongside the stereogram. Finally, systematic investigation of the phenomenon through experimentation can produce concrete evidence about the causal role that you believe visual hints play in seeing the three-dimensional objects.

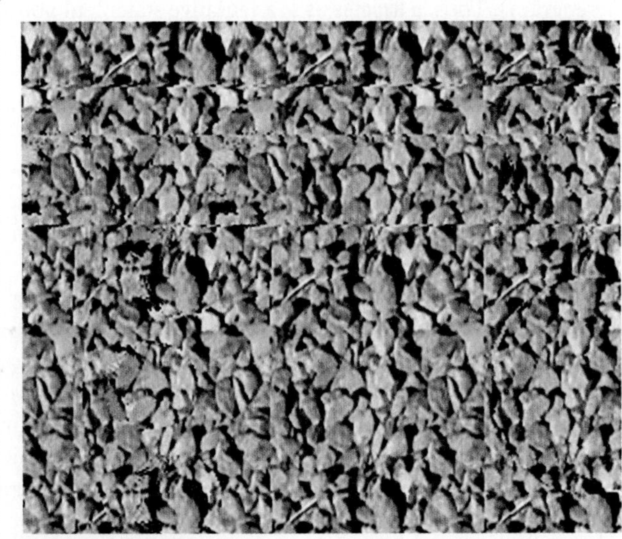

FIGURE 2•1 A SIRD stereogram. Hold the image 10 to 20 cm in front of you. As you look at the image, imagine that it is really much farther away. Do not focus on the image itself, but rather on a spot a metre or so behind the image. Seeing the three-dimensional image may take some time. If you cannot see it after a reasonable period, ask someone who can see it to give you a verbal clue and then try again.

Experiments provide evidence about the psychological processes that affect behaviour, and in this sense provide general accounts of phenomena. For example, suppose we give some of the students, but not others, a visual hint—an expectation of what the image looks like. If we found that those who received the hint were faster at finding the three-dimensional image, we would now have systematic evidence about the causal role of visual hints. Demonstrating the role of visual expectations in this situation might help us generalize the concept of expectation to other types of perception. To understand the confidence that psychologists place in experiments, we must understand how experiments are conducted.

The following five steps summarize the rules of the scientific method that apply to experiments—the form of scientific research that identifies cause-and-effect relations. As we will see later, many of these rules also apply to observational and correlational studies. Some new terms introduced here without definition will be described in detail later in this chapter.

1. *Identify the problem and formulate hypothetical cause-and-effect relations among variables.* This step involves identifying variables (particular behaviours and particular environmental and physiological events) and describing the relations among them in general terms. Consider the following hypothesis: Expectation of an image facilitates its detection in a SIRD stereogram. This statement describes a relation between two variables—expectation of an image and detection of that same image—and states that the first will increase the second.

2. *Design the experiment.* Experiments involve the manipulation of independent variables and the observation of dependent variables. For example, if we wanted to test the hypothesis about the relation between expectation and detection of an image, we would have to do something to produce an expectation (the independent variable) and see whether that experience altered a person's ability to detect a hidden image (the dependent variable). Each

**correlational study** The examination of relations between two or more measurements of behaviour or other characteristics of people or other animals.

**experiment** A study in which the researcher changes the value of an independent variable and observes whether this manipulation affects the value of a dependent variable. Only experiments can confirm the existence of cause-and-effect relations among variables.

variable must be *operationally defined*, and the independent variable must be controlled so that only it, and no other variable, is responsible for any changes in the dependent variable.

3. *Perform the experiment*. The researcher must organize the material needed to perform the experiment, train the people who will perform the research, recruit volunteers whose behaviour will be observed, and randomly assign each of these volunteers to an experimental group or a control group. The experiment is performed and the observations are recorded.
4. *Evaluate the hypothesis by examining the data from the study.* Do the results support the hypothesis, or do they suggest that it is wrong? This step often involves special mathematical procedures used to determine whether an observed effect is *statistically significant*.
5. *Communicate the results.* Once psychologists have learned something about the causes of a behaviour from an experiment, they must tell others about their findings. In most cases, scientists write an article that includes a description of the procedure and results and a discussion of their significance. They send the article to one of the many journals that publish results of psychological research. Journal editors and expert reviewers determine which research is methodologically sound and important enough to publish. In addition, researchers often present their findings at conferences or professional conventions. As a result, other psychologists will be able to incorporate these findings into their own thinking and hypothesizing.

Following these steps decreases the chances that we will be misled by our observations and come to incorrect conclusions in our research. As we shall see in Chapter 11, people have a tendency to accept some types of evidence even though the rules of logic indicate that they should not. This tendency sometimes serves us well in our daily lives, but it can lead us to make the wrong conclusions when we try to understand the true causes of natural phenomena, including our own behaviour.

Now that you have a general idea of what the scientific method is, let us consider its components and the rules that govern it.

## Identifying the Problem: Getting an Idea for Research

Like most professions, science is a very competitive enterprise. Most scientists want to be recognized for their work. They want to discover and explain interesting phenomena and have other scientists acknowledge their importance. They may hope that the fruits of their research will affect the public at large. They certainly need to be hard-working and dedicated, perhaps even obstinate and relentless.

More often, though, great science results from the cumulative work of many individual researchers who are part of a larger collective (international) endeavour. Most research occurs in institutional settings such as universities, where scientists, students, and technicians are all involved in the effort. Long-term projects require financial support. Psychological research in Canada has historically been supported by the three major research-funding agencies of the Canadian government: the Natural Sciences and Engineering Research Council, the Social Sciences and Humanities Research Council, and the Canadian Institutes of Health Research (previously called the Medical Research Council). Before providing funding, these agencies rigorously review the merits of a proposed research program and its potential for long-term scientific value. They provide an independent evaluation of the worth of a scientific idea.

In this environment of competition and rigorous evaluation, a successful scientist needs to have *good ideas*. Where do they come from?

**Hypotheses** A hypothesis is the starting point of any study. It is an idea, phrased as a general statement, that a scientist wishes to test through scientific research. In the original Greek, *hypothesis* means "suggestion," and the word still conveys the same meaning. When scientists form a hypothesis, they are suggesting that a relation exists among various phenomena (such as the one that might exist between expectation of an image and a person's ability to detect it in a SIRD stereogram). Thus, a **hypothesis** is a tentative statement about a cause-and-effect relation between two or more events.

**Theories** A **theory** is a set of statements that describes and explains known facts, proposes relations among variables, and makes new predictions. In a sense, then, a theory is an elaborate form of hypothesis. A scientific theory operates within the scientific method to organize a system of facts and related hypotheses to explain some larger aspect of nature.

A good theory is also one that generates *testable hypotheses*—hypotheses that can potentially be supported or proved wrong by scientific research. Some theories are so general or so abstract that they do not produce testable hypotheses and hence cannot be subjected to scientific rigour. For example, Sigmund Freud theorized that conflicts between mental structures such as the id and the superego were significant determinants of personality and behaviour. Because there is no way to observe or measure these structures, there is no way to test the idea of conflict among them (although we will see that testable hypotheses can be generated from other aspects of Freud's theorizing).

Many, but not all, research endeavours in psychology are directed at making a particular theory stronger. They try to show that the evidence is consistent with the hypothesis, or

**hypothesis** A statement, usually designed to be tested by an experiment, that tentatively expresses a cause-and-effect relationship between two or more events.

**theory** A set of statements designed to explain a set of phenomena; more encompassing than a hypothesis.

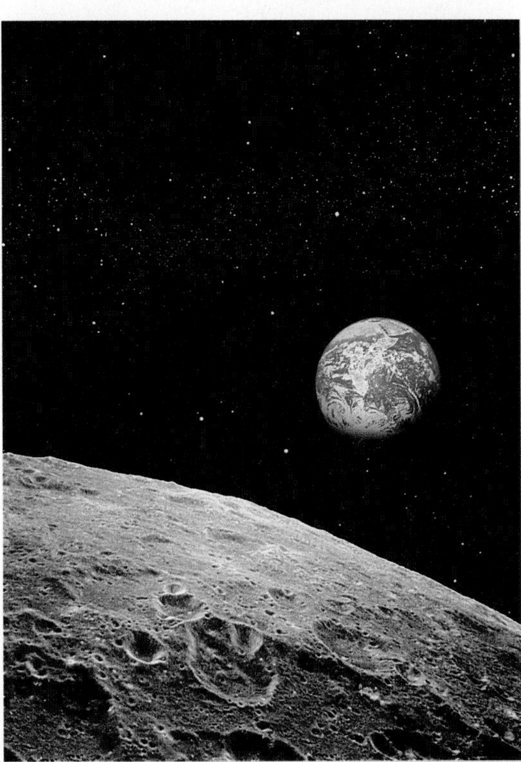

▲ *Some of the earliest scientific theories involved the movements of celestial bodies.*

they explore the relationship between concepts within the theory. Sometimes research stimulates researchers to think about old problems in new ways by showing how findings that did not appear to be related can be explained by a single concept. There is even a scientific journal, *Psychological Review*, devoted to articles of this type.

**Naturalistic and Clinical Observations as Sources of Hypotheses and Theories** Psychology is about behaviour. To understand human behaviour, or the behaviour of other animals, we first have to know something about that behaviour. Much of what we know about behaviour comes from ordinary experience: observing other people, listening to their stories, watching films, and reading novels. In effect, we perform naturalistic observations throughout our lives. However, careful, systematic observations permit trained observers, who are already well informed about a particular topic, to discover subtly different categories of behaviour and to develop hypotheses about their causes.

Naturalists are people who carefully observe animals in their natural environment, disturbing them as little as possible. Naturalistic observations, then, are what naturalists see and record. All sciences—physical, biological, and social—begin with simple observation. For example, people described mountains, volcanoes, canyons, plains, and the multitude of rocks and minerals found in these locations long before they attempted to understand their formation. Thus, observation

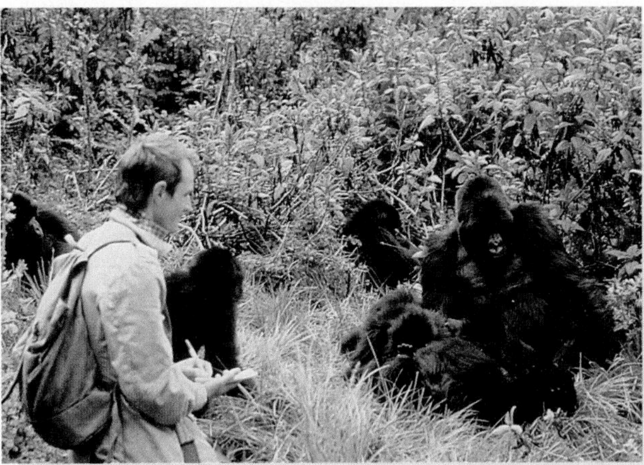

▲ *Much can be learned through careful observation of animals in their natural environment. The results of such observations often suggest hypotheses to be tested by subsequent studies.*

and classification of the landscape and its contents began long before the development of the science of geology.

Psychologists who are also naturalists apply observational procedures to questions of behaviour. The important feature of naturalistic observations is that the observer remains in the background, trying not to interfere with the people (or animals) being observed. For example, suppose we were interested in studying the social behaviour of preschoolers. We want to know under what conditions children share their toys or fight over them, how they react to newcomers to the group, and so on. The best way to begin to get some ideas is to watch groups of children. We would start by taking notes, classifying behaviours into categories, and seeing what events provoked them—and what the effects of these behaviours might be. These naturalistic observations would teach us how to categorize and measure the children's behaviour and would help us develop hypotheses that could be tested in experiments or in correlational studies.

Clinical observations are different. In the course of diagnosis or treatment, clinical psychologists can often observe important patterns of behaviour. They often report the results of their observations in detailed descriptions known as **case studies**. As with naturalistic observations, these could form the basis of hypotheses about the causes of behaviour. Unlike a naturalist, however, a clinical psychologist most likely does *not* remain in the background, because the object of therapy is to change the patient's behaviour and to solve problems. Indeed, the psychologist is ethically constrained to engage in activities designed to benefit the patient; he or she cannot arbitrarily withhold some treatment or apply another just for the sake of new observations. So, like the naturalist, a clinician is bound by certain rules that limit the kinds of observations that can be made: The clinician cannot interfere with the treatment regime prescribed for the patient.

**case study** A detailed description of an individual's behaviour during the course of clinical treatment or diagnosis.

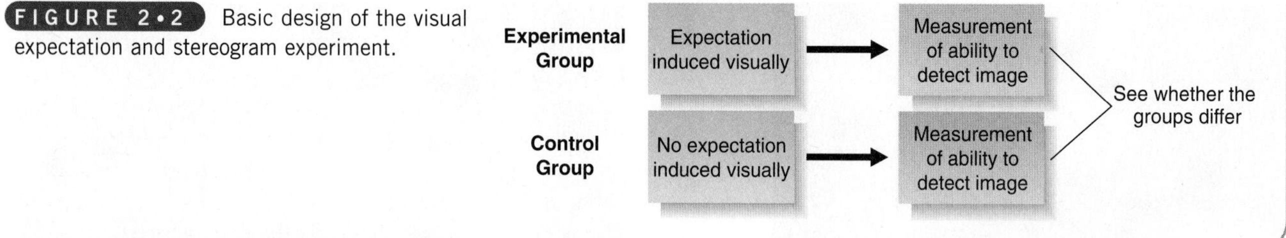


FIGURE 2•2 Basic design of the visual expectation and stereogram experiment.

In some cases, psychologists *do* interfere with a situation in a natural or clinical setting. They may, for example, ask questions at job sites or on the street—places that we might regard as naturalistic settings. In one common procedure, a **survey study**, researchers may ask people specially designed and controlled questions, perhaps about their beliefs, opinions, or attitudes. Survey studies are designed to elicit a special kind of behaviour: answers to the questions. The observations, then, are usually descriptions of the classes of responses to these questions. Many people may participate in a survey study, but they all are given the same, *standardized,* questions. As these questions become more specific and precise, they allow the same formal measurement of relations that underlies correlational studies.

A clinical psychologist, too, may manipulate the treatment given to a patient, with the desire of producing a more beneficial response. The psychologist may report the result in the manner of a case study, but such manipulation would make the process an experiment, not an observational study.

## Designing an Experiment

Although naturalistic or clinical observations enable a psychologist to classify behaviours into categories and provide hypothetical explanations for them, only an experiment can determine whether these explanations are correct. Let us see how to design an experiment. We will learn about the operational definition and control of experimental variables.

**Variables** The hypothesis proposed earlier—"Expectation of an image increases a person's ability to detect it in a SIRD stereogram"—describes a relation between expectation and the detection of an image. Scientists refer to these two components as **variables:** things that can vary in value. Thus, temperature is a variable, and so is happiness. Virtually anything that can differ in amount, degree, or presence versus absence is a variable.

Scientists either *manipulate* or *measure* the values of variables. **Manipulate** literally means "to handle" (from *manus,* "hand"). Because of abuses in the history of human research (which we will discuss later), the term *manipulation* is sometimes incorrectly understood to mean something that researchers do to participants. Psychologists use the word, however, to describe setting the values of a variable in order to examine that variable's effect on another variable. In the SIRD experiment, one value of the expectation variable would be set at "visual expectation present" and the other at "visual expectation absent." Measuring variables is what it sounds like. Just as we measure the variable of temperature with a thermometer, so psychologists devise instruments to measure psychological variables. The results of experimental manipulations and measurements of variables help us evaluate hypotheses.

To test the visual expectation hypothesis with an experiment, we would assemble two groups of volunteers to serve as participants. We would present participants in the **experimental group** with an experience that would give them an expectation about the nature of the image hidden in the SIRD stereogram. For example, we might show these participants an image somewhat similar to that in the SIRD. We would not give participants in the **control group** such an experience, and therefore they would have no expectation. We would then measure the ability of participants in both groups to detect the hidden image and determine whether the outcomes in the two groups differed. Provided that our two groups of volunteers were alike at the start of the experiment, which is usually accomplished by randomly assigning volunteers to the two groups, we could attribute any differences in detection ability to the experimental manipulation of expectation. (See **Figure 2•2.**)

Our imaginary experiment examines the effect of one variable on another. The variable that we manipulate (expectation of the image) is called the **independent variable.** The variable that we measure (recognition of the image) is the **dependent variable.** An easy way to keep the names of these variables straight is to remember that a hypothesis describes how the value of a dependent variable *depends* on the value of an independent variable. Our hypothesis proposes that recognition of the hidden image depends on prior expectation of what it looks like. (See **Figure 2•3.**)

**survey study** A study of people's responses to standardized questions.
**variable** Anything capable of assuming any of several values.
**manipulation** Setting the values of an independent variable in an experiment to see whether the value of another variable is affected.
**experimental group** A group of participants in an experiment, the members of which are exposed to a particular value of the independent variable, which has been manipulated by the researcher.
**control group** A comparison group used in an experiment, the members of which are exposed to the naturally occurring or zero value of the independent variable.
**independent variable** The variable that is manipulated in an experiment as a means of determining cause-and-effect relations.
**dependent variable** The variable that is measured in an experiment.

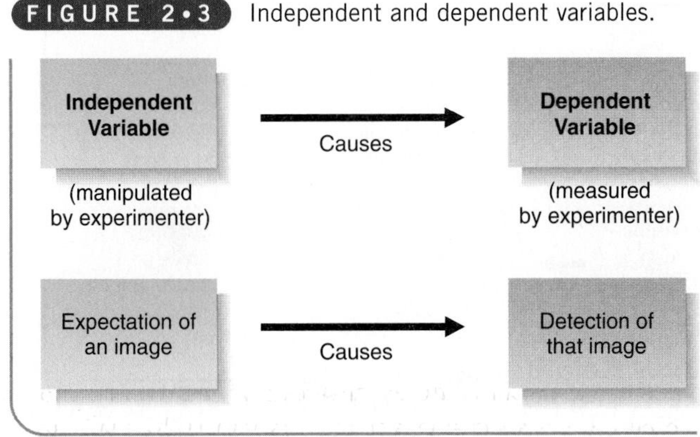


**FIGURE 2•3** Independent and dependent variables.

Scientists want to understand the causes of behaviour in more than one specific situation. Thus, the variables that hypotheses deal with are expressed in general terms. Independent and dependent variables are *categories* into which various behaviours are classified. For example, we would probably label all of the following behaviours as included within the category of "interpersonal aggression": hitting, kicking, and throwing something at someone. Presumably, these behaviours would have very similar causes. A psychologist must know enough about a particular type of behaviour to be able to classify it correctly.

Even though one of the first steps in psychological research involves naming and classifying behaviours, we must be careful to avoid committing the nominal fallacy. The **nominal fallacy** is the erroneous belief that one has explained an event merely by naming it. (*Nomen* means "name.") Classifying a behaviour does not explain it; classifying only prepares us to examine and discover events that cause a behaviour. For example, suppose that we see a man frown and shout at other people without provocation, criticize their work when it is really acceptable, and generally act unpleasantly toward everyone around him. Someone says, "Wow, he's really angry today!" Does this statement explain his behaviour?

No; it only *describes* the behaviour. Instead of saying he is angry, we might better say that his behaviour is hostile and aggressive. This statement does not claim to explain why he is acting the way he is. To say that he is angry suggests that an internal state is responsible for his behaviour—that anger is causing his behaviour. But all we have observed is his behaviour, not his internal state. Even if he is experiencing feelings of anger, these feelings are not a full account of his behaviour. What we really need to know is *what events made him act the way he did*. Perhaps he has a painful toothache. Perhaps he just learned that he failed to get a job he wanted. Perhaps he just read a book that promoted assertiveness. Events like these are causes of both the behaviour and the feelings. Unless these events are discovered and examined, we have not explained his behaviour in a scientifically meaningful way.

Yet, identifying causes is not as simple as just identifying preceding events. Many internal and external events may precede any behaviour. Some of these events are causal and some almost certainly will be completely unrelated to the observed behaviour. For example, you get off your commuter train because your stop is announced, not because someone coughs or someone else turns the page of a newspaper, even though all of these events could have happened just before you stood up and left the train. The task of a psychologist is to determine which of the many events that occurred before a particular behaviour caused that behaviour to happen.

**Operational Definitions** Hypotheses are phrased in general terms, but when we design an experiment (step 2 of the scientific method) we need to decide what *particular* variables we will manipulate and measure. For example, to produce an expectation of what the hidden image looks like, we must arrange a particular situation that has this effect. Similarly, we must measure the participants' detection of the image. Both expectation and ability to detect must be translated into specific operations.

This translation of generalities into specific operations is called an **operational definition:** Independent variables and dependent variables are defined in terms of the operations a researcher performs to set their values or to measure them. In our proposed experiment, the operational definition of the independent and dependent variables and the setting in which they are studied might be the following:

*Setting.* Participants of both groups were comfortably seated in front of a projection screen. Participants received 20 presentations of different SIRD stereograms and were asked to press a button when they had identified the object on the screen. Prior to each presentation, participants heard a verbal "priming stimulus" naming the hidden object.

*Independent variable.* A visual expectation was created for each participant in the experimental group by displaying for one second, during the verbal priming stimulus, a silhouette image of the target, of the same orientation and size as hidden in the stereogram. Participants in the control group received only the verbal priming stimulus and a random geometric shape not related to the hidden object.

*Dependent variable.* Detection of the image was measured by the time between the first appearance of the stereogram and the participant's pressing the response button. All participants were asked to be reasonably confident that they had detected the object before pressing the button. (See **Figure 2•4**.)

If research is to be understood, evaluated, and possibly replicated by other people (step 5 of the scientific method), the investigator must provide others with a thorough and adequate description of the procedures used to manipulate the independent variable and to measure the dependent variable.

**nominal fallacy** The false belief that one has explained the causes of a phenomenon by identifying and naming it; for example, believing that one has explained lazy behaviour by attributing it to "laziness."

**operational definition** The definition of a variable in terms of the operations the researcher performs to measure or manipulate it.

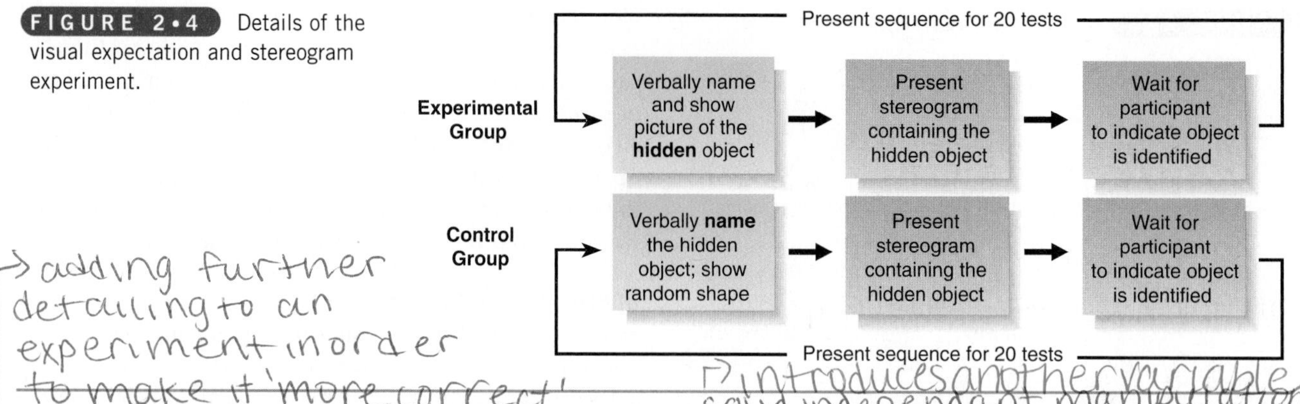


**FIGURE 2•4** Details of the visual expectation and stereogram experiment.

For example, a complete definition of the dependent variable (detection of the SIRD stereogram image) would need to include a detailed description of each stereogram used.

Any general concept can be operationalized in many different ways. By selecting one particular operational definition, the researcher may or may not succeed in manipulating the independent variable or in measuring the dependent variable. For example, there is certainly no single definition of visual expectation. Another investigator, using a different set of operations to produce an expectation, might obtain results that are different from ours. Which operational definition is correct? Which set of results should we believe? To answer these questions, we need to address the issue of *validity*.

The **validity** of operational definitions refers to how appropriate they are for testing the researcher's hypothesis—how accurately they represent the variables whose values have been manipulated or measured. Obviously, only experiments that use valid operational definitions of their variables can yield meaningful results. Let us consider this operational definition of detection: the time it takes from initial presentation of the stereogram to the pressing of the response button. How can we know that the participant has actually seen the hidden image? Even with the best of intentions, a person in an experiment like this might be reacting to imagination rather than actual visual perception. As one possible check, we could construct our stereograms so that the image appears in one of the four quadrants of the display screen. We could then ask participants to point to the quadrant in which they had seen the image. Using only those times that were associated with correct points would increase the validity of our measure.

### Control of Independent Variables

We have seen that a scientist performs an experiment by manipulating the value of the independent variable and then observing whether this change affects the dependent variable. If an effect is seen, the scientist can conclude that there is a cause-and-effect relation between the variables. That is, changes in the value of the independent variable cause changes in the value of the dependent variable.

When conducting an experiment, the researcher must manipulate the value of the independent variable—and *only* the independent variable. For example, if we want to determine whether general ambient (background) environmental noise has an effect on people's reading speed, we must choose our source of noise carefully. If we were to use the soundtrack from a television program to supply the noise and find that it slows people's reading speed, we could not conclude that the effect was caused purely by "noise." We might have selected an interesting program, thus distracting the participants' attention from the material they were reading because of the program rather than because of "noise." If we want to do this experiment properly, we should use noise that is neutral and not a source of interest by itself—for instance, noise like the *sssh* sound that is heard when an FM radio is tuned between stations.

If we used a TV program soundtrack as our manipulation of noise, we would inadvertently cause **confounding of variables**—we would introduce the effects of another variable besides noise on reading speed. One of the meanings of the word *confound* is "to fail to distinguish." If a researcher inadvertently introduces one or more extra, unwanted, independent variables that vary synchronously with the intended independent variable, he or she will not be able to distinguish the effects of any one of them on the dependent variable. That is, the effects of the variables will be confounded. In our example, the noise of the TV program would be mixed with the content of the program in the experimental condition, whereas in the control condition there would be neither noise nor content. You can see that any effect of the manipulation on reading could be due to either noise or content, or even to their combination. It would be impossible to reach any conclusion about the experimental hypothesis.

When I was a graduate student, I accompanied several fellow students to hear a talk that was presented by a visitor to the zoology department. He described research he had conducted in a remote area of South America. He was interested in determining whether a particular species of bird could recognize a large bird that normally preys upon it. He had constructed a set of cardboard models that bore varying

**validity** The degree to which the operational definition of a variable accurately reflects the variable it is designed to measure or manipulate.

**confounding of variables** Inadvertent simultaneous manipulation of more than one variable. The results of an experiment involving confounded variables permit no valid conclusions about cause and effect.

**FIGURE 2•5** A schematic representation of the flawed predator experiment.

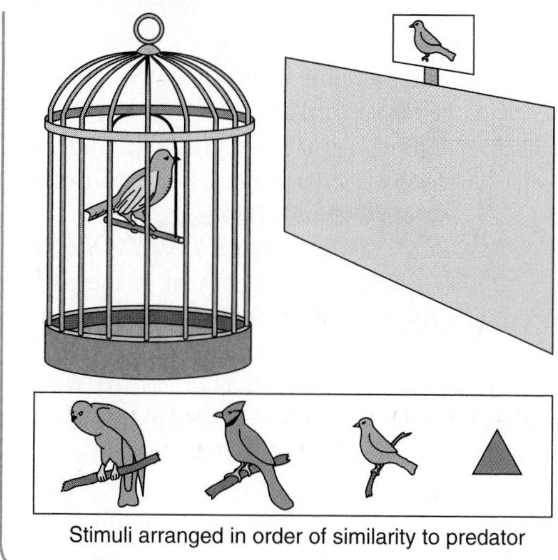

Stimuli arranged in order of similarity to predator


**FIGURE 2•6** Counterbalancing in the predator experiment. The predator experiment could be improved by changing the order of presentation of the models.

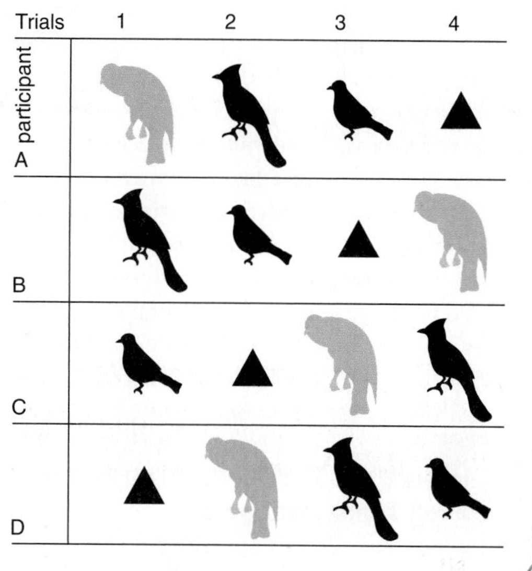


degrees of resemblance to the predator: from a perfect representation, to two models of non-carnivorous birds, to a neutral stimulus (a triangle, I think). The researcher restrained each bird he was testing and suddenly presented it with each of the test stimuli, in decreasing order of similarity to the predator—that is, from predator to harmless birds to triangle. He observed a relation between the amount of alarm that the birds showed and the similarity that the model bore to the predator. The most predator-like model produced the greatest response. (See **Figure 2•5.**)

One of us pointed out—to the embarrassment of the speaker—that the study contained a fatal flaw that made it impossible to conclude whether a relation existed between the independent variable (similarity of the model to the predator) and the dependent variable (amount of alarm). It's a fairly subtle, but important problem. Can you figure it out? Reread the previous paragraph, consult Figure 2.5, and think about the problem before you read on.

Now, the answer: When testing the birds' responses to the models, the investigator presented each model at a different time *but always in the same order*. Very likely, even if the birds had been shown the *same* model again and again, they would have exhibited less and less of a response. We very commonly observe this phenomenon, called *habituation*, when a stimulus is presented repeatedly. The last presentation produces a much smaller response than the first. Consequently, we do not know whether the decrease in signs of alarm occurred because the stimuli looked less and less like the predator or simply because the birds became habituated to the stimuli.

Could the zoologist have carried out his experiment in a way that would have permitted a causal relation to be inferred? Yes, he could have; perhaps the solution has occurred to you already. Here is the answer: The researcher should have presented the stimuli in different orders to different birds. Some birds would see the predator first, others would see the triangle first, and so on. Then he could have calculated the average amount of alarm that the birds showed to each of the stimuli, without the results being contaminated by habituation. This procedure is called **counterbalancing.** To *counterbalance* means to "weigh evenly," and counterbalancing would have been accomplished if the investigator had made sure that each of the models was presented equally often (to different participant birds, of course) as the first, second, third, or fourth stimulus. The effects of habituation would thus be spread equally among all of the stimuli. (See **Figure 2•6.**)

## Performing an Experiment

After designing a study with due regard for the dangers of confounds, we must decide how best to conduct it. We are now at step 3 of the scientific method: perform the experiment. We must decide what participants to use, what instructions to give, and what equipment and materials to use. We must ensure that the data collected will be accurate; otherwise, all effort will be in vain.

**Reliability of Measurements** A procedure described by an operational definition that produces consistent results under consistent conditions is said to have high **reliability.** For example, measurements of people's height and weight are extremely reliable. Measurements of their academic aptitude (by means of standard, commercial tests) are also reliable, but somewhat less so.

**counterbalancing** A systematic variation of conditions in an experiment, such as the order of presentation of stimuli, so that different participants encounter them in different orders; prevents confounding of independent variables with time-dependent processes such as habituation or fatigue.

**reliability** The repeatability of a measurement; the likelihood that if the measurement was made again it would yield the same value.

Suppose that we operationally define detection of a hidden image as the time it takes before the participant blinks. Eye blink measurements can be made reliably and accurately, but it is problematic to consider this a valid or true measure of image detection, because there are many reasons for a participant to blink other than having detected the hidden image. Achieving reliability is usually much easier than achieving validity. Reliability is mostly a result of care and diligence on the part of researchers in the planning and execution of their studies.

Let us look at an example of a factor that can decrease the reliability of an operationally defined variable. Suppose that in our study on the effects of visual expectation on detection of a hidden image, we present the stereograms by randomly drawing, from a large collection of digital stereogram images, 20 images to be presented to each participant. Unfortunately, some of our images were poorly scanned, so that they are out of focus when projected. You can easily appreciate how this extraneous factor would affect our measurement of detection, and would add to the differences we observe among the images and among participants.

Careful researchers can identify and control most of the extraneous factors that might affect the reliability of their measurements. Conditions throughout the experiment should always be as consistent as possible. For example, the same instructions should be given to each person who participates in the experiment, all equipment should be in good working order, and all assistants hired by the researcher should be well trained in performing their tasks. Noise and other sources of distraction should be kept to a minimum.

The degree of subjectivity in taking a measurement is another factor that affects reliability. Our definition of inducing an expectation is *objective*; that is, even a non-expert could follow our procedure and obtain the same results. But researchers often attempt to study variables whose measurement is *subjective*—that is, it requires judgment and expertise. For example, suppose that a psychologist wants to count the number of friendly interactions that a child has with other children in a group. This measurement requires someone to watch the child and note each time a friendly interaction occurs. However, it is difficult to be absolutely specific about what constitutes a friendly interaction and what does not. What if the child looks at another child and their gazes meet? One observer may say that the look conveyed interest in what the other child was doing and so should be scored as a friendly interaction. Another observer may disagree.

The solution in this case is, first, to try to specify as precisely as possible the criteria to be used for defining an interaction as friendly in order to make the measurement as objective as possible. Then, two or more people should watch the child's behaviour and score it independently; that is, neither person should be aware of the other person's ratings. If their ratings agree, we can say that the scoring system has high **interrater reliability**. If they disagree, interrater reliability is low, and there is no point in continuing the study. Instead, the rating system should be refined, and the raters should be trained to apply it consistently. Any investigator who performs a study that requires some degree of skill and judgment in measuring the dependent variables must do what is necessary to produce high interrater reliability.

**Selecting the Participants** Now let's turn to the participants in our experiment. How do we choose them? How do we assign them to the experimental or control group? These decisions must be considered carefully because just as independent variables can be confounded, so can variables that are inherent in participants whose behaviour is being observed.

Suppose a professor wants to determine which of two teaching methods works best. She teaches two courses in introductory psychology, one that meets at 8 a.m. and another that meets at 4 p.m. She considers using one teaching method for the morning class and another for the afternoon class. She then imagines that at the end of the term the final examination scores are higher for her morning class. If this proves correct, will she be able to conclude that the morning teaching method is superior to the method used in the afternoon? No; a good researcher would understand that the method considered here would produce a significant interpretation problem. There likely would be differences between the two groups of participants other than the teaching method they experienced. People who sign up for a class that meets at 8 a.m. are likely to differ, for many reasons, in some ways from those who sign up for a 4 p.m. class. Some people prefer to get up early while others prefer to sleep late. Perhaps the school schedules athletic practices late in the afternoon, which means that athletes will not be able to enroll in the 4 p.m. class. Therefore, the professor would not be able to conclude that any observed differences in final examination scores were caused solely by the differences in the teaching methods. Personal characteristics of the participant groups would be confounded with the two teaching methods.

The most common way to avoid confounding participant characteristics with the manipulated values of an independent variable is **random assignment**. Random assignment means that each participant has an equal chance of being assigned to any of the conditions or groups of the experiment. One way to accomplish random assignment is to list the names of the available participants and then toss a coin for each one to determine the participant's assignment to one of two groups. (More typically, the assignment is made by computer or by consulting a list of random numbers.) We can expect people to have different abilities, personality traits, and other characteristics that may affect the outcome of the experiment. However, if people are randomly assigned to the experimental conditions, these differences should be equally distributed across the groups. Randomly assigning students to two sections of a course meeting at the same time of day

**interrater reliability** The degree to which two or more independent observers agree in their ratings of another organism's behaviour.

**random assignment** Procedure in which each participant has an equally likely chance of being assigned to any of the conditions or groups of an experiment.

would help solve the problem faced by the professor who wants to study different teaching methods.

Even after researchers have designed an experiment and randomly assigned participants to the groups, they must remain alert to the problem of confounding participant characteristics with their independent variable manipulations. Some problems will not emerge until the investigation is actually performed. Suppose that we wish to learn whether anger decreases a person's ability to concentrate. We begin by acting very rudely toward the participants in the experimental group, which presumably makes them angry, but we treat the participants in the control group politely. After the rude or polite treatment, the participants watch a video that shows a constantly changing display of patterns of letters. Participants are instructed to press a button whenever a particular letter appears. This vigilance test is designed to reveal how carefully participants are paying attention to the letters.

The design of this experiment is sound. Assuming that the participants in the experimental group are really angry and that our letter identification test is a good dependent measure of concentration, we should be able to draw conclusions about the effects of anger on concentration. However, the experiment, as performed under real conditions, may not work out the way it was designed. Suppose that some of our "angry" participants simply walk away. All researchers must assure participants that their participation is voluntary and that they are free to leave at any time; some angry participants might well exercise this right and withdraw from the experiment. If they do, we will now be comparing the behaviour of two groups of participants that have a different mix of personal characteristics—one group composed of people who are willing to submit to the researcher's rude behaviour (because the objectors have withdrawn) and another group of randomly selected people, some of whom would have left had they been subjected to the rude treatment. Now the experimental group and the control group are no longer equivalent. (See **Figure 2•7**.)

The moral of this example is that a researcher must continue to attend to the possibility of confounded variables even after the experiment is under way. The solution in this case? There probably is none, given the particular method of producing anger. Because we cannot force participants to continue in the experiment, there is a strong possibility that some of them will leave. Some psychological variables are, by their very nature, difficult to investigate. But difficult does not mean impossible. The researcher in our example must go back to the drawing board and devise a better experiment with which to test the hypothesis.

**Expectancy Effects** Research participants are not passive beings whose behaviour is controlled solely by the independent variables manipulated by the researcher. In the opening vignette, we saw that Justine learned this fact when she tried to improve production at her parents' company. Participants in experiments know that they are being observed, and this knowledge is certain to affect their behaviour. This is a basic concept in the sciences: Observation can change that which you observe. The facts in Justine's case represent what is known as the *Hawthorne effect.* More than 70 years ago, the managers of the Hawthorne Plant of Western Electric wondered whether increasing the level of lighting in the plant would increase productivity. It did, but they found that the increase in productivity was short-lived. The managers went on to do some more investigating, and found that productivity actually went up when they lowered the level of lighting. The commonly accepted explanation of these findings is based on the fact that the workers knew that an experiment was being conducted and that they were being monitored. That knowledge may have made them work harder regardless of whether lighting levels were increased or decreased. The workers may even have been pleased, and motivated, by the fact that management was obviously trying to improve their work environment, and may have tried to return the favour. Of course, the effect would not last indefinitely, and eventually production returned to normal. Adair (1984) provides a detailed analysis of these original studies and the methods that have evolved in field experiments to counter the Hawthorne effect.

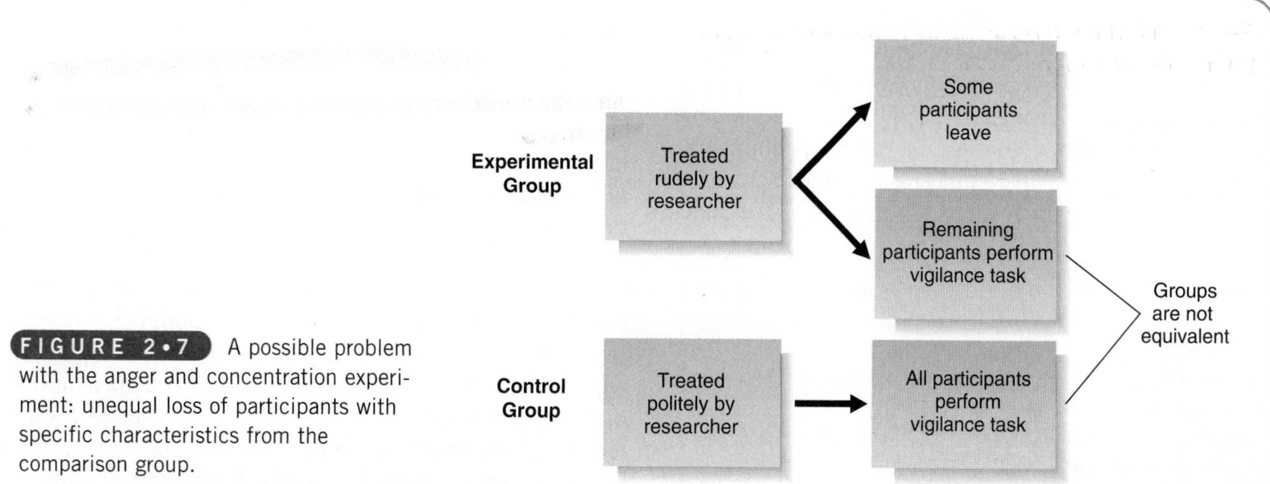


FIGURE 2•7 A possible problem with the anger and concentration experiment: unequal loss of participants with specific characteristics from the comparison group.

One way to think about the Hawthorne effect is that the participants were trying to help the researchers confirm their hypothesis that changes in lighting would improve productivity. There is compelling evidence that this type of co-operation with researchers can occur even in very sophisticated laboratory research. If research participants figure out the researcher's hypothesis, they will sometimes behave as if the hypothesis is true, even if it is not. This is a dangerous state of affairs for good science. For this reason, researchers routinely keep the details of their hypotheses to themselves when dealing with participants, at least until after the independent variable is manipulated and the dependent variable is measured. The situation is more troublesome, however, when participants can figure out the researcher's hypothesis and independent variable manipulations on their own. You may have heard that deception is sometimes used in psychological research. Overall, deception is relatively rare. When it *is* used, however, the sole reason is to disguise the nature of an independent variable manipulation (and perhaps the dependent measure). By providing the participant with an alternative explanation for the experimental events—an untrue one—the intention is to prevent the participant from acting as if the hypothesis is true when it might in fact not be. When deception is used, researchers take great pains to disclose the truth to participants at the earliest possible moment and to re-establish a trusting relationship. Interestingly, people who actually have participated in deception experiments are generally quite accepting of the rationale for the use of this technique (Sharpe, Adair, & Roese, 1992). Let's turn now to other techniques that have been developed to cope with problems of hypothesis awareness among research participants.

**Single-Blind Experiments** Suppose that we want to study the effects of a stimulant drug on a person's ability to perform a task that requires fine manual dexterity. We will administer the drug to one group of participants and leave another group untreated. (Of course, the experiment will have to be supervised by a physician, who will prescribe the drug.) We will count how many times each participant can thread a needle in a 10-minute period (our operational definition of fine manual dexterity). We will then see whether taking the drug had any effect on the number of needle threadings.

However, there is a problem in our design. For us to conclude that a cause-and-effect relation exists, the treatment of the two groups must be identical except for the single variable that is being manipulated. In this case, the mere administration of a drug may have effects on behaviour, independent of its pharmacological effects. The behaviour of participants who know that they have just taken a stimulant drug is very likely to be affected by this knowledge as well as by the drug circulating in their bloodstream.

To solve this problem, we would give pills to the members of both groups. People in one group would receive the stimulant, while those in the other group would receive an identical-looking pill that contained no active drug—a **placebo** pill. Participants would not be told which type of pill they are taking, but would know that they have a 50–50 chance of receiving either the stimulant or the inactive substance. By using this improved experimental procedure, called a **single-blind study**, we could infer that any observed differences in needle-threading ability of the two groups were produced solely by the pharmacological effects of the stimulant drug.

**Double-Blind Experiments** In a single-blind experiment, only the participants are kept unaware of their assignment to a particular experimental group; the researcher knows which treatment each participant receives. Now let us look at an example in which it is important to keep both the researcher and the participants in the dark. Suppose we believe that if patients with psychological disorders take a particular drug, they will be more willing to engage in conversation. This would be an important study because enhanced communicability could facilitate their therapy. So, we give the real drug to some patients and administer a placebo to others. We talk with all of the patients afterwards and rate the quality of the conversation. However, "quality of conversation" is a difficult dependent variable to measure, and the rating is therefore likely to be subjective. The fact that we, the researchers, know who received the drug and who received the placebo leaves open the possibility that we may tend to give higher conversation quality ratings to those who took the drug. Of course, we would not intentionally cheat, but even honest people tend to perceive results in a way that favours their own preconceptions.

The solution to this problem is simple. Just as the participants should not know whether they are receiving a drug or a placebo, neither should the researcher. That is, the researcher should use a **double-blind study**. Either another person should administer the pills, or the researcher should be given a set of identical-looking pills in coded containers so that both researcher and participants are unaware of the nature of the contents. Now the researcher's ratings of conversation quality cannot be affected by any preconceived ideas he or she may have. Keep in mind that someone who has no direct contact with the participants is keeping track of who gets which pills so that the effect of the independent variable manipulation can be tested.

The double-blind procedure does not apply only to experiments that use drugs as the independent variable. Suppose that the experiment just described attempted to evaluate the effects of a new form of psychotherapy, not a drug, on the willingness of a participant to talk. If the same person does both the psychotherapy and the rating, that person might tend to see the results in a light that is most favourable to his or her own expectations. In this case, then, one person should

**placebo** An inert substance that cannot be distinguished in appearance from a real medication; used as the control substance in a single-blind or double-blind experiment.

**single-blind study** An experiment in which the researcher but not the participant knows the value of the independent variable.

**double-blind study** An experiment in which neither the participant nor the researcher knows the value of the independent variable.

**FIGURE 2•8** An example of a correlation. Correlations do not necessarily indicate cause-and-effect relations: Daydreaming could cause shyness (upper), or shyness could cause daydreaming (lower).

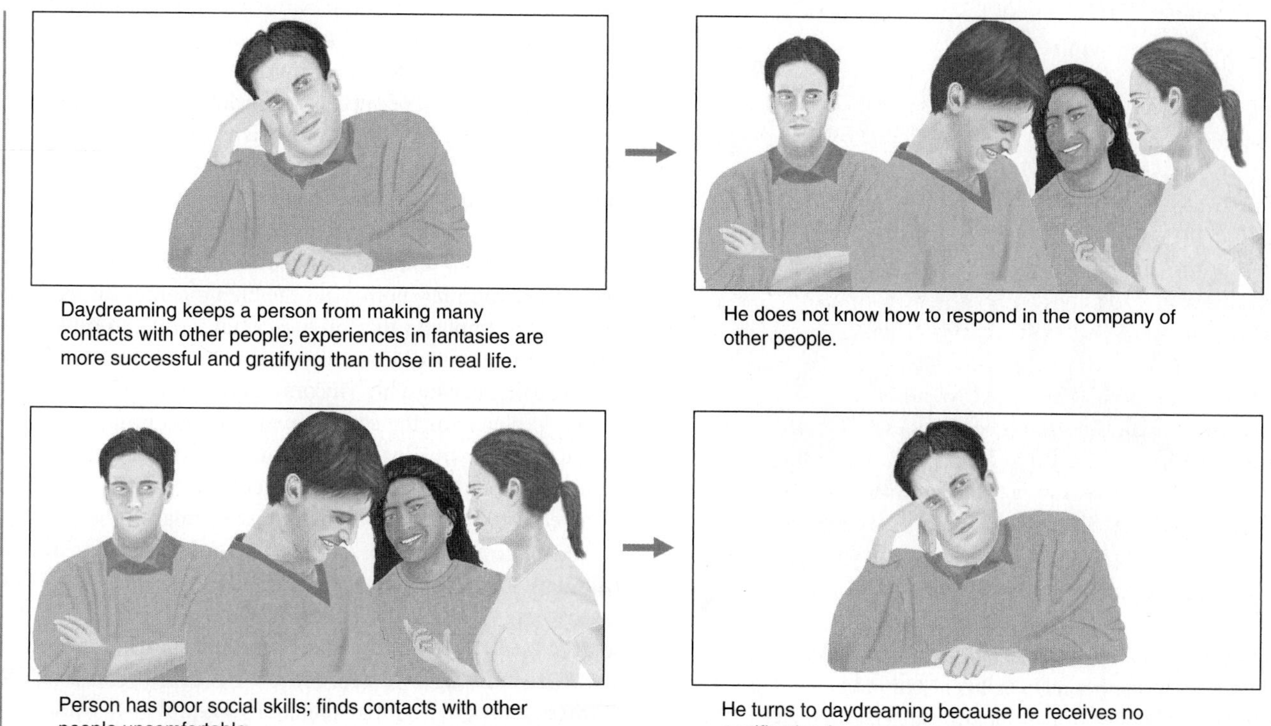


perform the psychotherapy and another person should evaluate the quality of conversation with the participants. The evaluator will not know whether a particular participant has just received the new psychotherapy or is a member of the control group that received the old standard therapy.

Daydreaming keeps a person from making many contacts with other people; experiences in fantasies are more successful and gratifying than those in real life.
He does not know how to respond in the company of other people.
Person has poor social skills; finds contacts with other people uncomfortable.
He turns to daydreaming because he receives no gratification from social contacts.

## Correlational Studies

To be sure that a cause-and-effect relation exists between variables, we must perform an experiment in which we manipulate an independent variable and measure its effects on a dependent variable. But there are some variables—especially participant variables—that a psychologist cannot manipulate. For example, a person's sex, genetic history, income, social class, family environment, and personality are obviously not under the researcher's control. Nevertheless, these variables are important and interesting because they often affect people's behaviour. Because they cannot be manipulated, they cannot be investigated in an experiment. A different method must therefore be used to study them: a **correlational study.**

The design and conduct of a correlational study is relatively simple: For each member of a group of people we measure two or more variables as they are found to exist, and we determine whether the variables are related by using a statistical procedure called *correlation*. Correlational studies are often conducted to investigate the effects of personality variables on behaviour. For example, we may ask whether shyness is related to daydreaming. Our hypothesis is that shy people tend to daydream more than do less shy people. We decide how to assess a person's shyness and the amount of daydreaming he or she engages in each day, and we then measure these two variables for a group of people. Some people will be very shy and some not shy at all. Some people will daydream a lot and others hardly at all. If we found that relatively shy people tend to daydream more (or less) than do relatively less shy people, we could conclude that the variables are related.

Suppose that we do, in fact, find that shy people spend more time daydreaming. Such a finding tells us that the variables are related—we say they are *correlated*—but it does not permit us to make any conclusions about cause and effect. Shyness may have caused the daydreaming, or daydreaming may have caused the shyness, or perhaps some other variable that we did not measure caused both shyness and an increase in daydreaming. In other words, *correlations do not necessarily indicate cause-and-effect relations.* (See **Figure 2•8.**)

This principle is illustrated by a study on a topic that may be of great interest to you: the employability of social science graduates. Using data from the 1991 Canadian census, Allen (1998) tracked the income growth of graduates with a bachelor's degree in the social sciences from their early twenties to the peak income period of their fifties. He then compared this growth to graduates from other educational programs. Allen found that males with a post-secondary diploma or certificate had an increase of 47 percent in

**correlational study** The examination of relations between two or more measurements of behaviour or other characteristics of people or other animals.

▲ *Correlation is not causation. Does being a Scout increase people's tendency to join community organizations later, or do young people who like to join groups continue to do so when they are adults? Without performing an experiment, we cannot tell.*

income over their careers; the increase was 69 percent for those with a degree in the agricultural or biological sciences and 78 percent for those with a degree in commerce. Male graduates with a degree in the social sciences, however, had income growth of 106 percent. These data indicate a correlation between graduating from a program in the social sciences, such as psychology, and long-term career growth.

As promising as these results look for psychology, however, they do not necessarily argue for changing one's major. The important question is whether choosing to pursue a degree in the social sciences improves career opportunities. That is, does the correlation imply a cause-and-effect relationship? It could be that people who already have good job prospects choose an arts degree in university because they already feel secure on a career path. Or it could be that a third factor, such as good people skills, leads both to choosing a major in the arts and to success in managerial positions.

(Allen's study was directed toward a different point: He was evaluating the popular belief that a degree in the social sciences or humanities was a poor economic choice. The data discussed here were part of a larger analysis, which indicates that the social sciences and humanities are valuable segments of the Canadian economy.)

Allen's data do indicate a relation. To determine whether that relation is a causal one, we would have to do an experiment. We would have to randomly assign some students entering university to a social sciences program and others to a different program. Later, we would evaluate each group's career success. Clearly, because we cannot interfere with people's lives this way, we cannot answer this important question definitively. Instead, we must accept the correlation as suggestive, but remain aware that other explanations might be possible.

The news media often report the results of correlational studies as if they implied causal relations. For example, one newspaper routinely points out the high incomes earned by its subscribers, implying that by subscribing, you can cause your own income to rise. But correlation does not prove causation. It could be that having a high income causes you to buy the newspaper (perhaps for the specific news of your profession). You might consider this logic when you receive that seductive recruiting brochure from a business faculty showing how its graduates earn 40 percent more than those from any other faculty.

Can anything be done to reduce some of the uncertainty inherent in correlational studies? The answer is yes. When attempting to study the effects of a variable that cannot be altered (such as sex, age, socio-economic status, or personality characteristics), we can use a procedure called **matching**. Rather than selecting participants randomly, we *match* the participants in each of the groups on all of the relevant variables except the one being studied. For instance, if we want to study the effects of shyness on daydreaming, we might select two groups of participants, one composed of people who score very high on the shyness test and another group composed of people who score very low on it. We could then place further restrictions so that the effects of other variables are minimized. We could make sure that average age, intelligence, income, and personality characteristics (other than shyness) of people in the two groups are the same. If we find that, say, the shy group is, on average, younger than the non-shy group, we will replace some of the people in the shy group with older shy people until the average age is the same.

If, after following this matching procedure, we find that shyness is still related to daydreaming, we can be more confident that the relation is one of cause and effect and that the differences between the two variables are not caused by a third variable. The limitation of the matching procedure is that we may not know all of the variables that should be held constant. If, unbeknownst to us, the two groups are not matched on an important variable, the results will be misleading. In any case, even the matching procedure does not permit us to decide which variable is the cause and which is the effect; we still do not know whether shyness causes daydreaming or daydreaming causes shyness.

The strengths and limitations of correlational studies will become evident in subsequent chapters in this book. For example, almost all studies that attempt to discover the environmental factors that influence personality characteristics or the relation between these characteristics and people's behaviour are correlational.

**matching** A systematic selection of participants in groups in an experiment or (more often) a correlational study to ensure that the mean values of important participant variables of the groups are similar.

## Reporting and Generalizing a Study

Scientists in all disciplines report the details of their research methods in sufficient detail that other investigators can repeat, or *replicate*, the research. **Replication** is one of the great strengths of science; it ensures that erroneous results and incorrect conclusions are weeded out. When scientists publish a study, they know that if the findings are important enough, others will try to replicate their work to be sure that the results were not just a statistical fluke—or the result of errors in the design or execution of the original study. Statistical anomalies and incompetently conducted research usually will be uncovered through unsuccessful attempts to replicate. The insistence on replicability of research results also helps inhibit fraud in science, because the unreliability of falsified findings is likely to be discovered.

When we carry out an experiment or a correlational study, we probably assume that our participants are representative of the larger population. In fact, a representative group of participants is usually referred to as a **sample** of the larger population. If we study the behaviour of a group of five-year-old children, we want to make conclusions about five-year-olds in general. We want to be able to **generalize** our specific results to the population as a whole—to conclude that the results tell us something about human nature in general, not simply about our particular participants.

Many researchers recruit their participants from introductory courses in psychology. The results of studies that use these students as participants can best be generalized to other groups of students who are similarly recruited. In the strictest sense, the results cannot be generalized to students in other courses, to adults in general, or even to all students enrolled in introductory psychology—after all, students who volunteer to serve as participants may be different from those who do not. Even if we used truly random samples of all age groups of adults in our area, we could not generalize the results to people who live in other geographical regions. If our ability to generalize is really so limited, is it worthwhile to do psychological research?

We are not so strictly limited, of course. Most psychologists assume that a relation among variables that is observed in one group of humans will also be seen in other groups as long as the sample of participants is not especially unusual. For example, we may expect data obtained from prisoners to have less generality than data obtained from university students. One feature of the scientific method we have discussed before helps achieve generalizability: replication. When results are replicated with different samples of people, we gain confidence in the generalizability of the results.

The problems associated with generalizing occur in observational and correlational studies as often as in experiments. During the 1993 Canadian federal election, the Conservative party ran several television advertisements that provoked a storm of controversy because they were perceived as mocking a speech mannerism of their opponent, Jean Chrétien. The ads are widely believed to have exacerbated the Conservatives' political loss. Yet the individuals who developed these advertisements had conducted opinion polls showing that even some of Chrétien's own supporters found him embarrassing, and they had also tested the ads by showing them to focus groups selected to represent the target audience. Somehow, this testing failed to generalize to the public's reaction. A more sophisticated before–after test, however, did reveal the effect of the ads. Haddock and Zanna (1997) polled opinions about Chrétien and about his opponent Kim Campbell both before and after the negative advertisements appeared. Attitudes toward Chrétien improved and those toward Campbell deteriorated.

There could have been two reasons that the advertisements failed. First, the focus groups might not have included a sufficient balance of individuals whose backgrounds and opinions represented the general public. Second, opinions given to a pollster may depend on context. For one thing, the advertisements had not yet actually appeared when presented to the focus group, and public reaction to them was not available to the focus group members (but was available to the participants in Haddock and Zanna's study). Perhaps as public criticism of the negative advertisements mounted, people who had expressed embarrassment regarding Chrétien might have felt compelled to defend him.

The lesson from this incident is that generalization occurs in two ways. We attempt to generalize from the observations of our sample to a different group. And we generalize from one context, usually under our control, to a different context. The better our research design, control, and sampling, the better our chances of successful generalization.

## Interim Summary

### The Scientific Method in Psychology

The scientific method allows us to determine the causes of phenomena. There are three basic forms of scientific research: naturalistic or clinical observations, experiments, and correlational studies. Only experiments permit us to be certain that a cause-and-effect relation exists. An experiment tests the truth of a hypothesis: a tentative statement about a relation between an independent variable and a dependent variable. Hypotheses come from information gathered through naturalistic observations, from previous experiments, or from formal theories.

To perform an experiment, a scientist manipulates the values of the independent variable and measures changes in the dependent variable. Because a hypothesis is stated in general terms, the scientist must specify the particular operations that

**replication** Repetition of an experiment or observational study to see whether previous results will be obtained.

**sample** A selection of elements from a larger population—for example, a group of participants selected to participate in an experiment.

**generalization** The conclusion that the results obtained from a sample apply also to the population from which the sample was taken.

he or she will perform to manipulate the independent variable and to measure the dependent variable. That is, the researcher must provide operational definitions, which may require some ingenuity and hard work. Operational definitions are a necessary part of the procedure of testing a hypothesis; they also can eliminate confusion by giving concrete form to the hypothesis, making its meaning absolutely clear to other scientists.

Validity is the degree to which an operational definition succeeds in producing a particular value of an independent variable or in measuring the value of a dependent variable. Reliability refers to the consistency and precision of an operational definition. Researchers achieve high reliability by carefully controlling the conditions of their studies and by ensuring that procedures are followed correctly. Measurement involving subjectivity requires researchers to seek high interrater reliability.

When designing an experiment, researchers must be sure to control extraneous variables that may confound their results. If an extra variable is inadvertently manipulated and if this extra variable has an effect on the dependent variable, then the results of the experiment will be invalid. Confounding of participant variables can be caused by improperly assigning participants to groups or by treatments that cause some participants to leave the experiment. Another problem involves participants' expectations. Most participants in psychological research try to figure out what the researcher is trying to accomplish, and their conclusions can affect their behaviour. If knowledge of the experimental condition could alter the participants' behaviour, one solution is to conduct the experiment with a single-blind procedure. Concealment or deception is sometimes a solution as well. If knowledge about the participants' condition might also alter the researcher's assessment of the participants' behaviour, a double-blind procedure can be used.

Correlational studies involve assessing relations among variables that the researcher cannot readily manipulate, such as personality characteristics, age, and sex. The investigator attempts to hold these variables constant by matching members in each of the groups on all relevant variables except for the one being studied. The problem is that investigators may miss a variable that affects the outcome. And, of course, even a well-designed correlational study cannot determine which variable is the cause and which is the effect.

Researchers are almost never interested only in the particular participants they study; they want to be able to generalize their results to a larger population. The confidence that researchers can have in their generalizations depends on the nature of the variables being studied and on the composition of the sample group of participants.

**QUESTIONS TO CONSIDER**

1. How might you apply the five steps of the scientific method to a question of your own—for example, does occasionally taking time out from studying for stretching and a little exercise affect a student's grades?
2. What is the relation between theories and hypotheses?
3. Suppose that you were interested in studying the effects of sleep deprivation on learning ability. Which of these two variables would be the independent variable and which would be the dependent variable? How might you operationally define these variables?
4. What is the difference between description and explanation in psychology?
5. In what ways might an operational definition be reliable yet not valid? Valid yet not reliable?

# Ethics

Because psychologists must study living participants, they must respect ethical rules as well as scientific rules. Great care is needed in the treatment of human participants because we can hurt people in very subtle ways.

## Research with Human Participants

Our federal research funding agencies require that all institutions that receive research support funds have one or more Research Ethics Boards (REBs) that review the ethics of human research (Canadian Institutes of Health Research, Natural Sciences and Engineering Council of Canada, & Social Sciences and Humanities Council of Canada, 1998). This Interagency Policy requires that all research be reviewed by an REB before it is conducted and that researchers comply with ethical principles and guidelines. Researchers in Canada also subscribe to the ethical principles described in the Canadian Code of Ethics for Psychologists (Canadian Psychological Association, 2000) and the Ethical Principles of Psychologists and Code of Conduct (American Psychological Association, 2002). These three guiding documents focus the attention of researchers on the same fundamental values and issues, because the codes have developed from common social and cultural roots (see Adair, 2001; Hadjistavropoulos et al., 2002).

You likely know that terrible medical experiments were conducted under the Nazi regime in Germany during the Second World War. Perhaps you did not know that starting in the 1930s, hundreds of poor African-American men, without their knowledge or valid consent, were allowed by medical researchers to progress through the devastating final stage of syphilis without treatment. And perhaps you did not know that during the 1950s and 1960s, CIA-sponsored brainwashing experiments were conducted at the Allan Memorial Institute in Montreal on unsuspecting psychiatric patients. Although you would be correct in suspecting that research ethics have been influenced by reactions to such violations of human rights, a major source of ethical principles in psychology has been the values and concerns of researchers themselves. In coping with the difficult business of conducting important and useful research, most psychological researchers over the decades have been concerned about respect for the dignity of their participants. Codes of research ethics have made these shared values explicit.

Codes of human research ethics can be understood as widely accepted values about everyday interpersonal relations translated to the context of human research. In their everyday lives, most people believe that (1) it is wrong to hurt others needlessly; (2) it is good to help others; (3) it is usually wrong to make others do things contrary to their wishes and best interests; (4) it is usually wrong to lie to others; (5) we should respect others' privacy; (6) under most circumstances we should not break our promises to keep others' secrets; and (7) we should afford special protection to those who are relatively powerless or especially vulnerable to harm.

How are these interpersonal values translated to research relationships between researchers and participants? Codes of research ethics tell us that (1) we should minimize harm to participants, whether physical or mental; (2) we should maximize the benefits of research to participants in particular and society in general; (3) participants should be fully informed about the nature of the research in which they are invited to participate, including risks and benefits, and their **informed consent** to participate must be voluntary; (4) deception in research is generally unacceptable, although it may be tolerated under limited circumstances; (5) we should not intrude into the private lives of participants without their permission; (6) with certain exceptions, we should guarantee participants that the information they provide will be kept anonymous or **confidential** unless they agree to make it public; and (7) vulnerable populations (e.g., children, prisoners, seriously ill patients, those with compromised cognitive abilities) should be treated with special care.

Difficulties sometimes arise when researchers try to translate everyday values to research. Research procedures that represent good science are sometimes in conflict with respect for participants' dignity. The interesting problem that researchers set for themselves is to resolve conflicts so that the best possible research is accomplished while simultaneously ensuring that participants are treated properly. We have chosen these words carefully here. Sometimes researchers speak as though the values of research themselves are contrary to the value of respecting people. This is not the case. Good research procedures, not the values of scientific inquiry, are sometimes in conflict with good treatment of participants. The goal is to identify and use research procedures that are both as ethical and as scientifically valid as possible.

You may have noticed that the list of research ethics values derived from interpersonal values includes exceptions to the general rules (as is the case for the interpersonal values themselves). For example, sometimes telling participants the full truth about the nature of the research will invalidate the research results. If I, as a researcher, tell you that I believe your enjoyment of your favourite activity will decline if I start to pay you for doing it, you may feel pressure to act as if I am correct, even if I am wrong. In this type of situation, the researcher may decide that concealing the hypothesis from you, or actively deceiving you about the nature of the hypothesis, would be good science. Yet there is a conflict with the interpersonal value of not telling lies. The result of ethical decision making and ethics review by REBs is sometimes to identify an acceptable balance. The researcher may be permitted to use concealment or minor deception, but only if there is no foreseeable harm to participants and if the researcher can re-establish trust with participants by immediately disclosing the truth to them in a **debriefing** upon completion of their participation. I think that it is interesting that this is also the nature of the corresponding values in interpersonal relations. Most of us believe that it is wrong to conceal important information from each other and to lie to one another. Yet many people at times do not strictly observe these interpersonal values, and still believe that they have acted properly. Good business practice, for example, sometimes involves concealing proprietary information from competitors to protect intellectual property rights. Neither opposing hockey teams nor chess players reveal their strategies. We may say to someone, "That's a lovely sweater you're wearing" even though our personal taste does not run to chartreuse. Sometimes telling the truth (e.g., revealing our dislike of the sweater) conflicts with our values of not harming others (e.g., not criticizing a friend's taste). Even so, we are likely to lie only if doing so does not undermine trust in the relationship—just as in the laboratory. The details of ethical conflicts in the laboratory and the living room differ, but the underlying problems and solutions are similar.

Another way to look at value conflicts is the old saying that "The exception proves the rule." In our daily lives most of us take seriously the confidences afforded us by others. Likewise, in our research we respect our promises of confidentiality. But the person in private life who promises to keep an as-yet-unstated secret and the researcher who makes the same promise can face a similar conflict of values if the secret turns out to pose a risk of harm to someone or to reveal ongoing harmful acts. A private citizen who learns that a neighbour is sexually abusing a child, or a researcher who learns that a participant is doing so, is compelled to intervene on the child's behalf. The conflicting value of protecting children from harm justifies breaking the promise of confidentiality by reporting the abuse to authorities. The shared basis for interpersonal and research values, as these examples illustrate, virtually guarantees that conflicts among values will arise in both contexts. The task then is to solve those problems in a sensitive and ethical manner.

**informed consent** Agreement to participate in an experiment after being informed about the nature of the research and any possible risks and benefits.

**confidentiality** Privacy of participants and non-disclosure of their participation in a research project.

**debriefing** Full disclosure to research participants of the nature and purpose of a research project after its completion.

## Then and Now

### Research and Ethics

In the late 1930s, a young psychologist at the University of Iowa, Wendell Johnson, was beginning to develop a new explanation for the speech problem known as stuttering. In contrast to the prevailing theory, which held it to be a result of brain physiology, Johnson felt that stuttering originated when children were overcorrected for minor lapses in correct speech.

To test this theory, Johnson and his graduate student devised a study in which children residing at a nearby orphanage were divided into different groups and given different types of feedback regarding their speech. Six children, judged not to be stutterers, were assigned to a group in which each hesitation in speaking was pointed out to them by the experimenter over a four- to five-month period. The objective was to see whether speech fluency could be adversely affected by this type of feedback (Reynolds, 2003).

Decades later, this study contrasts sharply with the research ethics we use today. The children and their caretakers (the teachers at the orphanage) were given false information to conceal the purpose of the study, and it's unclear how much the administrators knew about the intent of the project. Notice that the hypothesis envisioned that the treatment would produce speech impairments. Yet Johnson and his student apparently did not develop a preplanned debriefing or a prearranged means to ameliorate the possible harm that might ensue (Schwartz, 2006).

When contacted 60 years after the study and informed of its details, the people who had been subjected to this treatment reacted with dismay and outrage (Dyer, 2001). Some reported an adult life of shyness, speech deficits, and social difficulties and, when they heard the news, attributed these problems to the study. They sued. In August 2007, the state of Iowa agreed to pay $925 000 to three surviving participants and the estates of three others for the distress the study had caused them.

It's clearly difficult to compare an ethical decision made 70 years ago to one we would make today. However, it's informative to consider why the participants of this study felt so betrayed. Basically, their complaints were related to many of the principles we've just discussed: They were subjected to procedures that they felt were harmful (Principle 1); they had not given informed consent (Principle 3); they were deceived (Principle 4); and they felt that their status as wards of the state had made them vulnerable (Principle 7) (Luna, 2007). Their distress underlines the need for a code of ethics that addresses these possible results of research.

Johnson's colleagues considered him a kindly, altruistic man who would not knowingly subject children to a harmful procedure (Yairi, 2006). Furthermore, his project was based on a respectable scientific theory that, if supported, could have suggested important innovations in the treatment of speech problems. Yet, 70 years later, his university felt compelled to pay a significant amount of money to redress the effects of the project. The lesson we can take from this episode is that good intentions are not enough.

▲ *Hazel Dornbush was one of the children who participated in Wendell Johnson's study.*

## Research with Animal Participants

Although most psychologists study the behaviour of their fellow humans, some study the behaviour of other animals. Any time we use another species of animal for our own purposes, we should be sure that what we are doing is both humane and worthwhile. A good case can be made that such psychological research qualifies on both counts. Humane treatment is a matter of procedure. We know how to maintain laboratory animals in good health and in comfortable, sanitary conditions. For experiments that involve surgery, we know how to administer anaesthetics and analgesics so that animals do not suffer. Most industrially developed societies have very strict regulations about the care of animals and require approval of the procedures that will be used in the experiments in which they participate. Canadian researchers who use animals adhere to ethical guidelines developed by the Canadian Council on Animal Care (CCAC). Under these guidelines, all projects involving animals, including teaching and research projects, are reviewed by a committee composed of scientists, veterinarians, and members of the public community who meet regularly at the institution where the research is to be carried out. These committee members rigorously review the experimental procedures according to principles developed by the CCAC (Olfert, Cross, & McWilliam, 1993) and have the authority to prevent or halt a project that does not adhere to these principles. Nationally, members of humane societies and of professional scientific bodies like the Canadian

Psychological Association sit on the board of directors of the CCAC. They are responsible for developing the policies that the individual committees at each university and research institute will use.

Because we, as humans, have the power to decide whether a research project is carried out, and other animals do not, it is important to ask whether research involving animals is a form of exploitation. We use animals for many purposes. We eat their meat and their eggs and drink their milk; we turn their hides into leather; we extract insulin and other hormones from their organs to treat people with diseases; we train them to do useful work on farms or to entertain us. These are all forms of exploitation. Even having a pet is a form of exploitation: It is we—not they—who decide that they will live in our homes. The fact is, we have been using other animals throughout the history of our species.

Whether the use of animals in research is justified is more difficult to say. One factor to consider is the nature of the controls placed on research activity as compared to some other uses of animals. For example, we know that pet ownership causes much more suffering among animals than scientific research does. As Miller (1983) notes, pet owners are not required to receive permission to keep their pets from boards of experts that include veterinarians, nor are they subject to periodic inspections to ensure that their homes are clean and sanitary, that their pets have enough space to exercise properly, and that their diets are appropriate. In contrast, all research facilities in Canada are inspected by a special team of veterinarians and scientists every three years.

The core reality is that our species is beset by medical, mental, and behavioural problems, many of which can be solved only through research involving non-human animals. Research with laboratory animals has produced important discoveries about the possible causes or potential treatments of neurological and psychological disorders, including Parkinson's disease, schizophrenia, bipolar disorder, anxiety disorders, obsessive-compulsive disorders, anorexia nervosa, obesity, and drug addictions. Although much progress has been made, these problems are still with us and cause much human suffering.

▲ *Should animals be used in psychological research? Most psychologists and other researchers strongly believe that animal research, conducted humanely, is necessary and ethically justified. This rat is receiving a drink of a sweet liquid during its participation in a learning task.*

However, as a result of discoveries described in Chapter 4, we now have the ability to describe the inner workings of the human brain in healthy and alert people and even to produce motion pictures of the brain at work. This research has the promise of providing answers to the problems I mentioned, but only if we can understand the basic principles of neurology and behaviour. Often, this understanding can be gained only by research that involves animals. Some people have suggested that instead of using laboratory animals in our research, we could use tissue cultures or computer simulations. Unfortunately, tissue cultures or computer simulations are seldom interchangeable substitutes for living organisms. We have no way to study behavioural problems such as addictions in tissue cultures, nor can we program a computer to simulate the workings of an animal's nervous system. If we could, we would already have all of the answers.

## Interim Summary

### Ethics

Because psychologists study living organisms, they must follow ethical principles in the treatment of their participants. The three major federal research funding agencies in Canada have a joint policy incorporating ethical guidelines and requiring review by a Research Ethics Board prior to any human research being undertaken in institutions receiving funding from the agencies. Ethical principles for research are similar to those that guide people in their everyday lives and include minimizing harm to participants, ensuring informed consent, respecting confidentiality, and avoiding deception in most circumstances.

Research that involves the use of laboratory animals is also guided by ethical principles. It is incumbent on all scientists using these animals to see that they are housed comfortably and treated humanely, and laws have been enacted to ensure that they are. Such research has already produced many benefits to humankind and promises to continue to do so.

#### QUESTIONS TO CONSIDER

1. In your opinion, should principles of ethical research be absolute or should they be flexible? Suppose that a researcher proposed to perform an experiment, the results of which could have important and beneficial consequences for society, perhaps a real reduction in violent crime. However, the proposed study would violate ethical guidelines because it would involve deception and a significant degree of psychological pain for the participants.

Should the researcher be given permission to perform the experiment? Should an exception be made because of the potential benefits to society?

2. Why do you think some people apparently are more upset about using animals for research and teaching than for other purposes?

# Understanding Research Results

Our study is finished. We have a collection of data—numbers representing the measurements of behaviour we have made. Now what do we do? How do we know what we found? Was our hypothesis supported? To answer these questions, we must analyze the data we have collected. We will use some statistical methods to do so.

## Descriptive Statistics: What Are the Results?

In the examples we have considered so far, the behaviour of participants assigned to groups (conditions) was observed and measured. Once a study is finished, we need some way to compare these measurements. To do so, we will first use **descriptive statistics**, mathematical procedures that permit us to summarize sets of numbers. Using these procedures, we will calculate measures that summarize the performance of the participants in each group. Then we can compare these measures to see whether the groups of participants behaved differently (step 4 of the scientific method). We can also use these measures to describe the results of the experiment to others (step 5 of the scientific method). You are already familiar with some descriptive statistics. For example, you know how to calculate the average of a set of numbers; an average is a common measure of *central tendency*. You might be less familiar with measures of *variability*, which tell us how groups of numbers differ from one another, and with measures of *relations*, which tell us how closely related two sets of numbers are.

**Measures of Central Tendency** When we say that the average weight of an adult male in North America is 79 kilograms or that the average salary of a female university graduate was $32 669 in 1995, we are using a **measure of central tendency**, a statistic that represents many observations. There are several different measures of central tendency, but the most common is the average, also called the **mean**. The mean of a set of observations is calculated by adding the individual values and dividing by the number of observations. The mean is the most frequently used measure of central tendency in reports of psychological experiments.

Although the mean is usually selected to measure central tendency, it is not the most precise measure, especially if a set of numbers contains a few especially high or low values. Under these conditions, the most representative measure of central tendency is the **median**, the midpoint of a group of values arranged numerically. For this reason, we usually read "median family income" rather than "mean family income" in newspaper or magazine articles.

**Measures of Variability** Many experiments produce two sets of numbers, one consisting of the experimental group's scores and one of the control group's scores. If the mean scores of these two groups differ, the researcher can conclude that the independent variable had an effect. However, the researcher must decide whether the difference between the two groups is larger than what would probably occur by chance. To make this decision, the researcher calculates a **measure of variability**—a statistic that describes the degree to which scores in a set of numbers differ from each other. The psychologist then uses this measure as a basis for comparing the means of the two groups.

Two sets of numbers can have the same mean or median and still be very different in their overall character. For example, the mean and median of both sets of numbers listed in **Table 2•1** are the same, but the sets of numbers are clearly different. The variability of the scores in Sample B is greater.

One way of stating the difference between the two sets of numbers is to say that the numbers in Sample A range from 8 to 12 and the numbers in Sample B range from 0 to 20. The **range** of a set of numbers is simply the largest number minus the smallest. Thus, the range of Sample A is 4 and the range of Sample B is 20.

**descriptive statistics** Mathematical procedures for organizing collections of data, such as determining the mean, the median, the range, the variance, and the correlation coefficient.

**measure of central tendency** A statistical measure used to characterize the value of items in a sample of numbers.

**mean** A measure of central tendency; the sum of a group of values divided by their number; the arithmetical average.

**median** A measure of central tendency; the midpoint of a group of values arranged numerically.

**measure of variability** A statistical measure used to characterize the dispersion in values of items in a sample of numbers.

**range** The difference between the highest score and the lowest score of a sample.

**TABLE 2•1 Two Sets of Numbers Having the Same Mean and Median but Different Ranges**

| Sample A | Sample B |
|---|---|
| 8 | 0 |
| 9 | 5 |
| 10 Median | 10 Median |
| 11 | 15 |
| 12 | 20 |
| Total: 50 | Total: 50 |
| Mean: 50/5 = 10 | Mean: 50/5 = 10 |
| Range: 12 − 8 = 4 | Range: 20 − 0 = 20 |

**TABLE 2•2 Calculation of the Variance and Standard Deviation of Two Sets of Numbers Having the Same Mean**

**Sample A**

| Score | Difference between Score and Mean | Difference Squared |
|---|---|---|
| 8 | 10 − 8 = 2 | 4 |
| 9 | 10 − 9 = 1 | 1 |
| 10 | 10 − 10 = 0 | 0 |
| 11 | 11 − 10 = 1 | 1 |
| 12 | 12 − 10 = 2 | 4 |
| Total: 50 | Total: | 10 |
| Mean: 50/5 = 10 | Mean (variance): | 10/5 = 2 |
| | Square root (standard deviation): | $\sqrt{2} = 1.41$ |

**Sample B**

| Score | Difference between Score and Mean | Difference Squared |
|---|---|---|
| 0 | 10 − 0 = 10 | 100 |
| 5 | 10 − 5 = 5 | 25 |
| 10 | 10 − 10 = 0 | 0 |
| 15 | 15 − 10 = 5 | 25 |
| 20 | 20 − 10 = 10 | 100 |
| Total: 50 | Total: | 250 |
| Mean: 50/5 = 10 | Mean (variance): | 250/5 = 50 |
| | Square root (standard deviation): | $\sqrt{50} = 7.07$ |

The range is not used very often to describe the results of psychological experiments because another measure of variability—the standard deviation—has more useful mathematical properties. To calculate the standard deviation of a set of numbers, you first calculate the mean and then find the difference between each number and the mean. These different scores are squared (that is, multiplied by themselves). The mean of these squared numbers is called the *variance*; the **standard deviation** is the square root of the variance. The more different the numbers are from each other, the larger the standard deviation will be. (See **Table 2•2**.)

**Measurement of Relations** In correlational studies, the investigator measures the degree to which two variables are related. For example, suppose that a psychologist has developed a new aptitude test and is trying to persuade a university to adopt the test to evaluate applicants to its combined law and business administration program. We need to show a relation between scores on the test and measures of success (such as grades) in the program. Although universities in Canada use a number of different grading systems, suppose this one uses a letter grading system, in which A designates the top grade and F designates a failure. (There is no grade E.) To analyze the test quantitatively, we need to convert these labels into numerical scores; we use the convention that an A is 4, an F is 0, and the letters in between have corresponding values.

**TABLE 2•3 Test Score and Average Grades of 10 Students**

| Student | Test Score | Average Grade[a] |
|---|---|---|
| A. C. | 15 | 2.8 |
| B. F. | 12 | 3.2 |
| C. G. | 19 | 3.5 |
| L. H. | 8 | 2.2 |
| R. J. | 14 | 3.0 |
| S. K. | 11 | 2.6 |
| P. R. | 13 | 2.8 |
| A. S. | 7 | 1.5 |
| J. S. | 9 | 1.9 |
| P. V. | 18 | 3.8 |

[a]0 = F; 4 = A

We give the test to 10 students entering the program and later obtain their average grades. We will have two scores for each person, as shown in **Table 2•3**. We can examine the relation between these variables by plotting the scores on a graph. For example, student R. J. received a test score of 14 and earned an average grade of 3.0. We can represent this student's score as a point on the graph shown in **Figure 2•9**. The horizontal axis represents the test score, and the vertical axis represents the average grade. We put a point on the graph that corresponds to R. J.'s score on both of these measures.

We do this for each of the remaining students and then look at the graph, called a **scatterplot**, to determine whether the two variables are related. When we examine the scatterplot, we see that the points tend to be located along a diagonal line that runs from the lower left to the upper right, indicating that a rather strong relation exists between a student's test score and average grade. (See Figure 2.9.) High scores are associated with good grades, low scores with poor grades.

Although scatterplots are useful, we need a more convenient way to communicate the results to others, so we calculate the **correlation coefficient**, a number that expresses the strength of a relation. Calculating this statistic for the two sets of scores gives a correlation of +0.9 between the two variables.

The size of a correlation coefficient can vary from 0 (no relation) to plus or minus 1.0 (a perfect relation). A perfect

**standard deviation** A statistic that expresses the variability of a measurement; square root of the average of the squared deviations from the mean.

**scatterplot** A graph of items that have two values; one value is plotted against the horizontal axis and the other against the vertical axis.

**correlation coefficient** A measurement of the degree to which two variables are related.

**FIGURE 2•9** A scatterplot of the test scores and average grades of 10 students. An example of graphing one data point (student R. J.) is shown by the arrows.

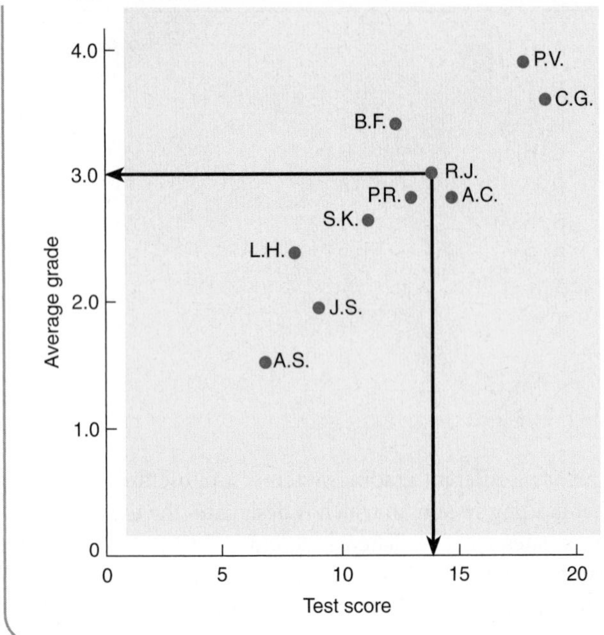


relation means that if we know the value of a person's score on one measure, then we can predict exactly what his or her score will be on the other. Thus, a correlation of +0.9 is very close to perfect; our hypothetical aptitude test is an excellent predictor of how well a student will do in the program. A *positive correlation* indicates that high values on one measure are associated with high values on the other, and that low values on one are associated with low values on the other.

Correlations can be negative as well as positive. A *negative correlation* indicates that high values on one measure are associated with low values on the other and vice versa. An example of a negative correlation is the relation between people's mathematical ability and the amount of time it takes them to solve a series of math problems. People with the highest level of ability will take the least time to solve the problems. For purposes of prediction, a negative correlation is just as good as a positive one. Examples of scatterplots illustrating high and low correlations, both positive and negative, are shown in **Figure 2•10**.

If the points in a scatterplot fall along a line, the relation is said to be *linear*. But many relations are non-linear. For example, consider the relation between level of illumination and reading speed. Obviously, it is impossible to read in the dark. As the light level increases, people's reading speed will increase, but once an adequate amount of light falls on a page, further increases in light will have no effect. Finally, the light becomes so bright and dazzling that people's reading speed will decline. (See **Figure 2•11**.) A correlation coefficient cannot accurately represent a non-linear relation such as this because the mathematics involved in calculating this measure assume that the relation is linear. Scientists who discover non-linear relations in their research usually present them in graphs or express them as non-linear mathematical formulas.

## Inferential Statistics: Are the Results Significant?

When we perform an experiment, we select a sample of participants from a larger population. In doing so, we hope that the results will be similar to those we might have obtained had we included all members of the population in the experiment. We randomly assign the participants to groups in an unbiased manner, manipulate only the relevant independent variables, and measure the dependent variable using a valid and reliable method. After the experiment is completed, we must examine the results and decide whether a relation really exists between independent and dependent variables.

But what does it mean to conclude that a relation "really" exists? As a matter of common sense, we'd like to say that our results are not due to some rare fluke or chance accident. Therefore, we must measure how likely it is that our results might be due to chance. If we find it improbable that our results are accidental, then we can describe them as possessing **statistical significance**—as being probably not due to chance. As we saw, descriptive statistics enable us to summarize our

**statistical significance** The likelihood that an observed relation or difference between two variables really exists rather than is due to chance factors.

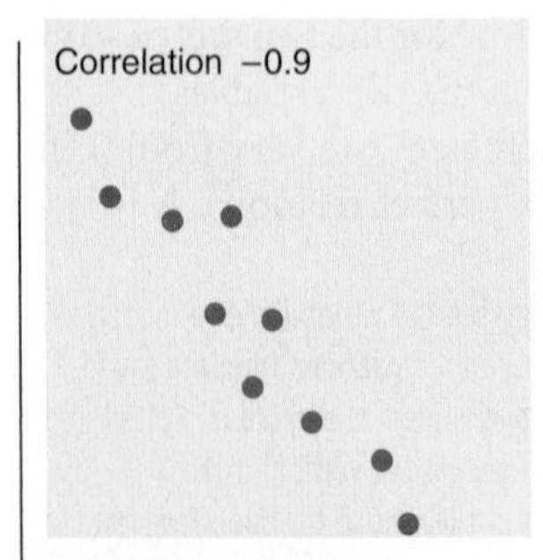

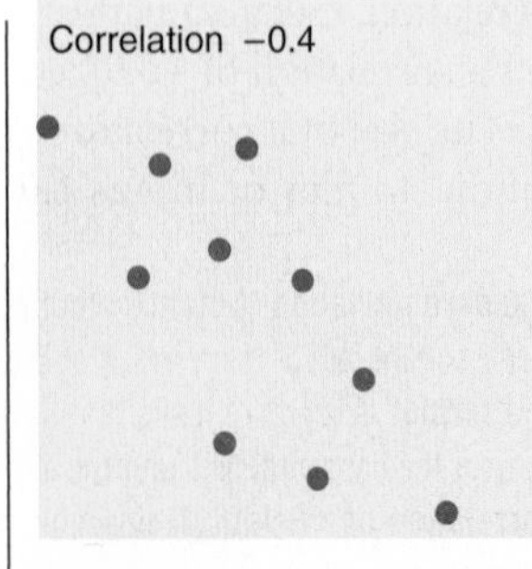

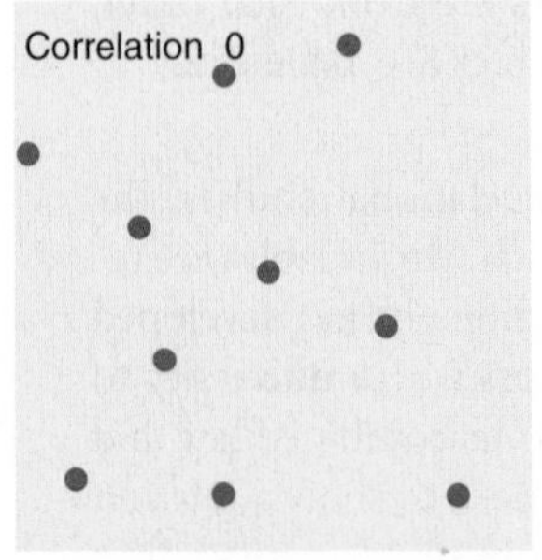

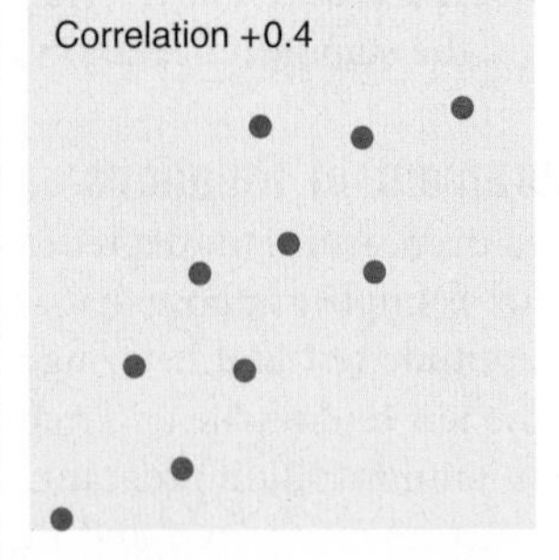


**FIGURE 2•10** Scatterplots of variables having several different levels of correlation.

**FIGURE 2•11** A non-linear relation. Results of a hypothetical experiment investigating the relation between level of illumination and reading speed. A correlation coefficient cannot adequately represent this kind of relation.

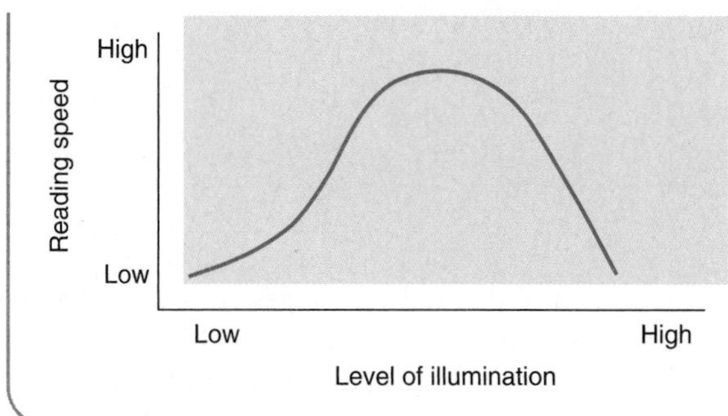


data. **Inferential statistics** enable us to calculate the probability that our results are due to chance and thereby tell us whether the results are statistically significant.

The concept of statistical significance is not an easy one to grasp, so we want to make sure you understand the purpose of this discussion. Recall our hypothesis that a visual expectation of an image increases detection of the image in a SIRD stereogram. We show some participants but not others a silhouette of the image. Next, we show stereograms to participants in both groups and record how long it takes them to detect the image. To see whether viewing the silhouette improved detection of an image, we calculate the mean response time for both groups. If the means are different, we can conclude that visual expectation *does* affect people's ability to recognize an image.

But how different is different? Suppose that we tested two groups of people, both treated exactly the same way. Would the mean scores of the two groups be precisely the same? Of course not. *By chance*, they would be at least slightly different. Suppose that we find that the mean score for the group that was shown the image is lower than the mean score for the control group. How much lower would it have to be before we could rightfully conclude that the difference between the groups was significant?

**TABLE 2•4 Height (in cm) of Selected Samples of Students**

| Name Ends in Consonant | | Name Ends in Vowel |
|---|---|---|
| 165 | 155 | 170 |
| 170 | 173 | 173 |
| 180 | 178 | 158 |
| 183 | 165 | 160 |
| 185 | 185 | 158 |
| 165 | 152 | 163 |
| 188 | 178 | 152 |
| 188 | 183 | 160 |
| 170 | 160 | 155 |
| 175 | 170 | 175 |
| 172 | 185 | 160 |
| 190 | 168 | 165 |
| 183 | 180 | 175 |
| 180 | 183 | 180 |
| 165 | 163 | 175 |
| 168 | 175 | 165 |
| 178 | 185 | 178 |
| 183 | 191 | 160 |
| 183 | 183 | 160 |
| 180 | 168 | 163 |
| 158 | 180 | 165 |
| 158 | 173 | 160 |
| 203 | 178 | 168 |
| 191 | | 158 |
| Total: 8272 | | 183 |
| Mean: 8272/47 = 176 | | 165 |
| | | 168 |
| | | 165 |
| | | 165 |
| | | Total: 4802 |
| | | Mean: 4802/29 = 165.6 |
| Difference between means: 176 − 165.6 = 10.4 | | |

**Assessment of Differences between Samples** The obvious way to determine whether two group means differ significantly is to look at the size of the difference. If it is large, then we can be fairly confident that the independent variable had a significant effect. If it is small, then the difference is probably due to chance. What we need are guidelines to help us determine when a difference is large enough to be statistically significant.

The following example, based on a real classroom demonstration and results, will explain how these guidelines are constructed. A few years ago, I performed a simple correlational study to test the following hypothesis: People whose first names end in vowels will, on average, be shorter than people whose first names end in consonants. (You will understand the rationale for this hypothesis later.)

The first step was to distribute a blank card to each student in a psychology class, and ask each student to print his or her first name on the card together with his or her height. Suppose that there are 76 students in the class, and that the mean height for all students is 172 cm (as was the case in the real demonstration). Next, I divided the participants into two groups: those whose first names ended in vowels and those whose first names ended in consonants. **Table 2•4** contains a listing of these two groups. In the real demonstration you can see that the means for the two groups differed by 10.4 cm.

**inferential statistics** Mathematical procedures for determining whether relations or differences between samples are statistically significant.

**TABLE 2•5 Height (in cm) of a Random Division of a Class into Two Groups**

| Group A | | Group B | |
|---|---|---|---|
| 165 | 180 | 160 | 158 |
| 183 | 160 | 158 | 160 |
| 183 | 188 | 178 | 165 |
| 175 | 183 | 178 | 191 |
| 155 | 180 | 165 | 180 |
| 175 | 165 | 163 | 203 |
| 168 | 180 | 191 | 180 |
| 178 | 170 | 160 | 173 |
| 168 | 183 | 178 | 180 |
| 165 | 168 | 191 | 185 |
| 168 | 183 | 170 | 158 |
| 165 | 185 | 165 | 183 |
| 163 | 160 | 173 | 165 |
| 183 | 175 | 160 | 183 |
| 160 | 158 | 175 | 168 |
| 165 | 152 | 170 | 185 |
| 158 | 178 | 173 | 165 |
| 170 | 173 | 152 | 185 |
| | 175 | | 155 |
| | 163 | | 188 |
| Total: 6506 | | Total: 6570 | |
| Mean: 171.2 | | Mean: 172.9 | |
| | Difference: –1.7 | | |

**TABLE 2•6 Mean Heights (in cm) of Five Random Divisions of the Class into Two Groups**

| Group A | Group B | Difference |
|---|---|---|
| 171.7 | 172.5 | –0.8 |
| 173.0 | 171.2 | 1.8 |
| 172.2 | 171.7 | 0.5 |
| 172.5 | 171.5 | 1.0 |
| 172.7 | 171.2 | 1.5 |

A difference of 10.4 cm seems large, but how can we be sure that it is not due to chance? What we really need to know is how large a difference there would be if the means had been calculated from two groups that were randomly selected. For comparison, I divided the class into two random groups by shuffling the cards with the students' names on them and dealing them out into two piles. Then I calculated the mean height of the people whose names were in each of the piles. This time, the difference between the means was 1.7 cm. (See **Table 2•5**.)

I divided the cards into two random piles five more times, calculating the means and the difference between the means each time. The differences ranged from 0.5 to 1.8 cm. (See **Table 2•6**.) It begins to look as though a mean difference of 10.4 cm was bigger than would be expected by chance.

Next, I divided the cards into two random piles 1000 times. (I used my computer to do the chore.) *Not once* in 1000 times was the difference between the means greater than 7.6 cm. Therefore, I can conclude that if the class is divided randomly into two groups, the chance that the means of their heights will differ by 10.4 cm is less than one time in a thousand, or 0.1 percent. Thus, I can safely say that when I divided the students into two groups according to the last letters of their first names, I was dividing them in a way that was somehow related to their height. The division was *not* equivalent to random selection; a person's height *really is* related to the last letter of his or her first name.

**Figure 2.12** presents a frequency distribution of the differences between the means of the two groups for 1000 random divisions of the class. The height of a point on the graph represents the number of times (the frequency) that the difference

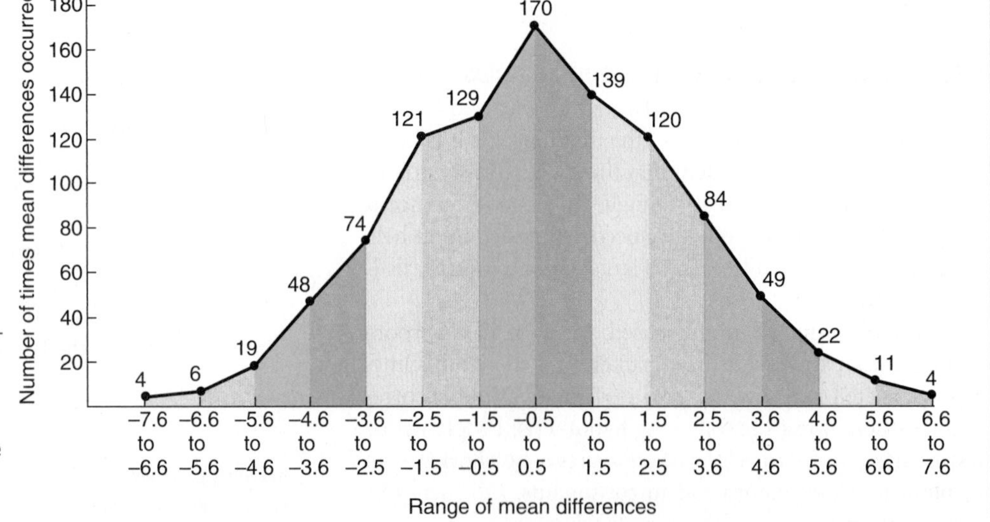


**FIGURE 2•12** A frequency distribution. This distribution illustrates the number of occurrences of various ranges of mean differences in height. The group of 76 people was divided randomly into 2 sets of numbers 1000 times.

Assessment between samples—
chance + experimentation



between the means fell into that particular range. For example, the difference between the means fell between –0.5 and +0.5 cm 170 times.

Suppose that the difference between the means in our observational study had been smaller than 10.4 cm—say, 5.8 cm. Would we conclude that the difference represented a real relation, or would we decide that the difference was due to chance? A look at Figure 2.12 will help us decide.

We can see that only 15 out of 1000 times (1.5 percent) is the difference between the means of the two groups as large as or larger than 5.8 cm: 11 + 4 = 15. (See Figure 2.12.) Therefore, if we had obtained a difference of 5.8 cm between the means of the groups and concluded that people whose first names end in vowels tend to be shorter than people whose first names end in consonants, *the likelihood of our being wrong would have been only 1.5 percent.* The calculations show that we will obtain a difference of at least 5.8 cm between the means purely by chance only 1.5 percent of the time. Because 1.5 percent is a small number, we are fairly safe in concluding that the relation is statistically significant.

The method used to determine the statistical significance of my findings employs the same principles that researchers use to determine whether the results observed in an experiment represent a real difference or are just due to chance. In this example we considered two possibilities: (1) that the difference between the means was due to chance, and (2) that the difference between the means occurred because the last letter of a person's first name is related to his or her height. Because a difference of 10.4 cm would be expected less than one time in a thousand, we rejected alternative 1 and concluded that alternative 2 was correct. The results supported my original hypothesis.

Ordinarily, psychologists who conduct experiments or correlational studies like this one do not use their computers to divide their participants' scores randomly 1000 times. Instead, they calculate the mean and standard deviation for each group and consult a table that statisticians have already prepared for them. The table (which is based on special mathematical properties of the mean and standard deviation) will tell them how likely it is that their results could have been obtained by chance. In other words, the table tells them how likely it is that the last letter of a person's first name is not related to his or her height. If the likelihood is low enough, they will conclude that the results they obtained are statistically significant. Most psychologists consider a 5 percent probability to be statistically significant but are much more comfortable with 1 percent or less.

Please note that statistical tests help us decide whether results are representative of the larger population but not whether they are *important*. In general usage, the word *significant* does mean "important," but *statistical* significance simply means that the results appear not to be caused by chance. For example, suppose a school board experiments with a new teaching method and finds that the test scores of students taught by the new method are higher than those of students taught by the old one. The difference is statistically significant, but is very small. (A small difference can be statistically significant if the variability within the groups is low enough or if the groups are very large.) Because changing over to the new method is very expensive, the school system would probably decide to continue with the present method.

▲ *Although individuals vary widely in height, men are taller, on average, than women—and this explains the finding in my classroom observational study.*

Oh yes, why would I ever guess (hypothesize) that the last letter of a person's first name is related to his or her height? The answer is that in English, feminine names are more likely than masculine names to end in a vowel (Paula, Anna, Marie, etc.). Because women tend to be shorter than men, I could expect that a group of students whose first names ended in vowels would be shorter, on average, than those whose first names ended in consonants.

## Interim Summary

### Understanding Research Results

Psychologists need ways to communicate their results to others accurately and concisely. They typically employ three kinds of descriptive statistics: measures of central tendency, variability, and relations. The most common examples of these measures are the mean, the median, the standard deviation, and the correlation coefficient.

If psychologists test a hypothesis by comparing the scores of two groups of participants, they must have some way of determining whether the observed difference in the mean scores is larger than what would be expected by chance. The first name–height example was a correlational study. However, the procedure I followed is based on the same logic that a psychologist would use in assessing the significance of the results of an experiment.

Psychologists perform experiments by observing the performance of two or more groups of participants who have been exposed to different conditions, each representing different values of the independent variable. Next, they calculate the group means and standard deviations of the values of the dependent variable that was measured. Finally, they determine the statistical significance of the results. To do so, they plug means and standard deviations into a formula and consult a special table that statisticians have devised. (This almost always happens via software!) The table indicates the likelihood of getting such results when the independent variable actually has no effect on the dependent variable. If the probability of obtaining these results by chance is sufficiently low, the psychologists will reject the possibility that the independent variable had *no effect* and decide in favour of the alternative—that it really did have an effect on the dependent variable.

The scientific method consists of a logical system of inquiry with sensible rules that must be followed if a person wants to draw accurate conclusions about the causes of natural phenomena. These rules were originally devised by philosophers who attempted to determine how we could understand reality. By nature, we are all intuitive psychologists, trying to understand why others do what they do, so it is important to realize how easily we can be fooled about the actual causes of behaviour. Thus, everyone, not just professional psychologists, should know the basic steps of the scientific method.

**QUESTIONS TO CONSIDER**

1. Can you think of some real-life variables that you would expect to be positively and negatively correlated?
2. What does it mean to say that a study produced statistically significant results?
3. Why might the results of a study be statistically significant but nevertheless unimportant?

EPILOGUE

## Bias and Sensitivity in Justine's Experiment

Our discussion of the ways and means of psychology gives us some insight into Justine's project described in the opening vignette. Though it cost her a sore neck and back, Justine's naturalistic observation generated her hypothesis about a possible cause. With Lawrence's help, her introduction of new chairs was a test of that hypothesis.

Justine was facing two issues common to any test of a hypothesis: Was her procedure sensitive and was it free of bias? Now that you understand the concepts of psychological research, we can explore these two issues further.

A procedure that tests a hypothesis is sensitive to the extent that it can detect whether the hypothesis is true. The fact that a hypothesis is correct could be obscured by the many chance factors that operate during an experiment. As we've seen, single-subject methods of research try to increase sensitivity by strict controls that eliminate random factors. Statistical approaches accomplish this by increasing the number of participants in a study so that random factors cancel each other out. Justine's experiment was clearly sensitive, since she was able to obtain a significant result.

Bias is a more subtle matter. Bias is the combination of factors that tend to produce positive research findings when they are not, in fact, true (Ioannidis, 2005). Irrespective of the sensitivity of a test, bias can make a non-effect look real or, in the case of reverse bias, make a real effect look false.

We have discussed several possible sources of bias. Assignment of participants to an experimental condition could be a source of bias: If Justine had given new employees the new chairs and compared their productivity to older employees, her experiment clearly would be susceptible to bias. As it was, Justine would have to be careful that the week in which she introduced the chairs didn't overlap with some other factor that could increase productivity (such as a week with a payday in it).

Bias can occur in each of the five steps of a research program. For example, Justine's eagerness to report a solution to her parents (akin to "publishing" an article) could also be a source of bias. The competitive nature of science similarly tends to induce a bias to publish research findings prematurely.

The lesson from Justine's story, of course, is that her very attempt to test her hypothesis was a source of bias—her own expectations and the desire of her parents' employees to match that expectation. By now, you understand this as the Hawthorne effect—a special case of expectancy effects. However, there's a general point to be made here as well. Aside from naturalistic studies and some kinds of correlational research, psychological investigation is itself a form of intervention. When we, as psychologists, study behaviour, we conceivably alter it. I devoted a large part of this chapter to the topic of research ethics to emphasize that point: that our procedures have consequences that we must always consider. Doing so makes us better psychologists and better neighbours to our fellow humans.

## Canadian Connections to Research in This Chapter

Adair, J. G. (1984). The Hawthorne effect: A reconsideration of the methodological artifact. *Journal of Applied Psychology, 69,* 334–345. (University of Manitoba: www.umanitoba.ca)

Adair, J. G. (2001). Ethics of psychological research: New policies; continuing issues; new concerns. *Canadian Psychology, 42,* 25–37. (University of Manitoba: www.umanitoba.ca)

Professor Adair received the Canadian Psychological Association's Gold Medal for Distinguished Lifetime Contributions to Canadian Psychology in 2000.

Allen, R. C. (1998). *The employability of university graduates in the humanities, social sciences, and education: Recent statistical evidence.* Ottawa: Social Sciences and Humanities Research Council. (University of British Columbia: www.ubc.ca)

Canadian Institutes of Health Research, Natural Sciences and Engineering Council of Canada, & Social Sciences and Humanities Research Council of Canada. (1998). *Tri-council policy statement: Ethical conduct for research involving humans.* Ottawa: Authors. (www.pre.ethics.gc.ca/english/index.cfm)

Canadian Psychological Association. (2000). *Canadian code of ethics for psychologists* (3rd ed.). Ottawa: Canadian Psychological Association. (www.cpa.ca)

Haddock, G., & Zanna, M. P. (1997). Impact of negative advertising on evaluations of political candidates: The 1993 Canadian federal election. *Basic and Applied Social Psychology, 19,* 205–223. (University of Waterloo: www.uwaterloo.ca)

Professor Zanna was elected Fellow of the Royal Society of Canada in 1999.

Hadjistavropoulos, T., Malloy, D. C., Sharpe, D., Green, S. M., & Fuchs-Lacelle, S. (2002). The relative importance of the ethical principles adopted by the American Psychological Association. *Canadian Psychology, 43,* 254–259. (University of Regina: www.uregina.ca)

Olfert, E. D., Cross, B. M., & McWilliam, A. A. (Eds.). (1993). *Guide to the care and use of experimental animals,* Vol. 1 (2nd ed.). Ottawa: Canadian Council on Animal Care. (www.ccac.ca)

Sharpe, D., Adair, J. G., & Roese, N. J. (1992). Twenty years of deception research: A decline in subjects' trust? *Personality and Social Psychology Bulletin, 18,* 585–590. (University of Manitoba: www.umanitoba.ca)

## Suggestions for Further Reading

Christensen, L. B. (2003). *Experimental methodology* (9th ed.). Boston: Allyn and Bacon.

Sternberg, R. J. (2005). *Reviewing scientific works in psychology.* Washington, DC: American Psychological Association.

Trochim, W. M. K. (2005). *Research methods: The concise knowledge base.* Cincinnati, OH: Atomic Dog.

Several standard textbooks discuss the scientific method in psychological research. The Christensen book covers ethical and practical issues as well as theoretical ones, while Trochim's is a general work on a variety of research methods. Sternberg's book is actually a manual written for researchers who review other researchers' work. It offers a good look at how research reports are evaluated for publication.

Bell, J. (1999). *Evaluating psychological information: Sharpening your critical thinking skills* (3rd ed.). Boston: Allyn and Bacon.

Bell's book provides what the title claims: an excellent way to sharpen your critical thinking skills. It is full of exercises to help you accomplish that goal.

Collins, A. (1988). *The sleep room.* Toronto: Lester & Orpen Dennys Limited.

Collins tells a stark story of the brainwashing experiments conducted in the 1950s and 1960s in Montreal at the Allan Memorial Institute. She received the Governor General's Literary Award (non-fiction) for this book in 1988.

PEARSON mypsychlab To access more tests and your own personalized study plan that will help you focus on the areas you need to master before your next class test, be sure to go to **www.MyPsychLab.com**, Pearson Education Canada's online Psychology website available with the access code packaged with your book.

# 3

# Evolution, Heredity, and Behaviour

C H A P T E R   O U T L I N E

## The Development of Evolutionary Theory

The Voyage of the *Beagle* • *The Origin of Species* • Natural Selection

Heredity and environment interact to influence our behaviour. To understand these influences, many psychologists study evolution, genetics, and events in the immediate environment that affect behaviour. Our understanding of biological evolution stems from Darwin's work on natural selection. Natural selection occurs because individual organisms vary physically, behaviourally, and genetically. Some physical and behavioural characteristics provide a competitive advantage for survival and reproduction. If these characteristics have a genetic basis, they are likely to increase in frequency in successive generations.

## Heredity and Genetics

Basic Principles of Genetics • The Importance of Genetic Diversity • Influences of Gender on Heredity • Mutations and Chromosomal Aberrations • Genetic Disorders • Heredity and Behaviour Genetics • Studying Genetic Influences • *Then and Now: The Central Dogma and Epigenetics*

Genes contain instructions for the synthesis of protein molecules. These molecules control bodily development and regulate physiological processes. Sexual reproduction provides for genetic diversity through the recombination of genes. Genetic diversity increases the chance that some members of a species may survive environmental changes. The expression of a gene depends on its interaction with other genes, the sex of the individual possessing that gene, and the environmental conditions under which that individual lives. Changes in genetic material caused by mutations or chromosomal aberrations produce changes in gene expression and play a primary role in the cause of genetic disorders. Artificial selection, segregation analysis, and allelic association studies are the primary ways that psychologists and other scientists study the relation between genes and behaviour. Epigenetics examines mechanisms of inheritance that do not involve changes in the genetic code.

## Humans and Evolution

Natural Selection in Human Evolution • Sociobiology

In human evolution, natural selection has favoured an upright posture and increases in brain size. These two factors contributed to the exploration and settling of new environments, and eventually to culture. Sociobiology, the study of the biological basis of social behaviour, represents an extension of Darwin's work to the explanation of complex human behaviour. Sex differences in the resources that parents invest in procreation and caring for their offspring have led to the evolution of four different patterns of selecting mates and rearing offspring. Altruism increases the reproductive success of other individuals with whom one may have many genes in common. We are likely to engage in altruistic acts toward others who may later be in a position to return the favour to us or to our relatives. Sociobiologists have been criticized for neglecting the role of the environment in determining human behaviour.

P R O L O G U E

## Sacrifice

The Beechcraft had taken off from Cambridge Bay on a mission of mercy. Inside it were four people, whose combination of culture and background one could perhaps find only in the northern communities of Canada. The person whose life had taken the most unpredictable route to this flight was the pilot, Martin Hartwell. Hartwell had been a member of the Luftwaffe, the German air force. Now, Hartwell had turned from warrior to healer: He was transporting two seriously ill passengers to a hospital in Yellowknife. Aboard, as nurse, was Judy Hill, who had come to the Northwest Territories from Great Britain. The passengers were Eunice Nimiqakruq Nuliayuk, who was having complications in her pregnancy, and David Pisurayak Kootook, who was suffering from appendicitis.

Four hundred kilometres from their destination, the plane hit a tree and crashed into a wooded slope. Judy Hill was killed on impact; Eunice Nimiqakruq Nuliayuk died a few hours later. Martin Hartwell survived the crash, but both of his ankles and one of his knees were fractured. The only person in any condition to walk was 14-year-old David Pisurayak Kootook.

Appendicitis is an agonizing condition. Even slight pressure on the swollen site can cause intense pain. The risk—and it is a lethal one—is that the appendix will rupture. Yet David nursed the injured Hartwell as best he could over the next desperate days. He built a shelter for him and collected what food and water he could. Each trip through the waist-deep snow must have caused him great pain. Together, he and Hartwell watched their small stock of food diminish until they had consumed it all.

Twenty days after the crash, David died. Twelve days after David's death, Hartwell was spotted by rescue aircraft. David's selfless struggle had kept Hartwell alive.

## The Development of Evolutionary Theory

You do not have to read much from popular culture to find some metaphor based on the idea of competition. "Survival," we are told, belongs to "the fittest," whether that is in business, sports, or even art. So, when we come across stories like that of David Pisurayak Kootook, we are struck by the contrast. That we see such tension in modern life between these two norms of behaviour is arguably due to one man: Charles Darwin.

> From my early youth I have had the strongest desire to understand and explain whatever I observed—that is, to group all facts under some general laws. . . . With such moderate abilities as I possess, it is truly surprising that I should have influenced to a considerable extent the belief of scientific men on some important points. (Darwin, 1888/1950, pp. 67–71)

These words seem surprisingly tentative coming as they do from a man who has influenced the course of scientific thought more than any other individual since Isaac Newton. Darwin argued that, over time, organisms originate and become adapted to their environments by biological means. Today, his concept of **biological evolution**—changes that take place in the genetic and physical characteristics of a population or group of organisms over time—stands as the primary explanation of the origin of life.

**biological evolution** Changes that take place in the genetic and physical characteristics of a population or group of organisms over time.
**adaptive significance** The effectiveness of behaviour in aiding organisms to adapt to changing environmental conditions.

Darwin's work transcends biology and has influenced other natural sciences, especially psychology. Psychologists have become increasingly aware of the way in which the modern synthesis of Darwin's theory and new discoveries in genetics can help us to understand behaviour. As you will see in this chapter, many behavioural differences among organisms, both within and across species, correspond to genetic and other biological differences. Understanding these differences and their evolution allows psychologists to understand behaviour in terms of its possible origins and **adaptive significance**—its effectiveness in aiding the organism to adapt to changing environmental conditions.

Consider novelty seeking, the tendency to engage in behaviours that lead to new experiences. Individuals who exhibit high scores on psychological tests for novelty seeking are described as "impulsive," "exploratory," or "excitable," while those who show low scores are considered "reflective," "stoic," and "slow-tempered." Is it beneficial to be one of the former . . . or one of the latter? To answer this question in terms of adaptive significance, we must ask ourselves two questions. First, what events and conditions in a person's lifetime might contribute to a tendency to seek or to avoid novelty; what function does novelty seeking (or its converse) serve in helping people adapt to the changing circumstances of life? Second, what events and conditions in the evolution of our species favoured or punished novelty seekers; what functions has novelty seeking served in the history of humankind? A complete understanding of novelty seeking, or any behaviour, requires that we understand both the past and the present conditions that influence it.

In other words, psychologists might research how *past environmental conditions* favoured novelty seeking over more conservative reactions and how the *immediate environment* influences day-to-day choices. They are interested in understanding both **ultimate causes** (from the Latin *ultimatus*, "to come to an end") of behaviour—events and conditions that, over successive generations, have slowly shaped the behaviour of our species—and **proximate causes** (from the Latin *proximus*, "near"), namely immediate environmental variables that affect behaviour.

Consider this puzzle, involving sexual behaviours of gerbils—the sand-coloured rodents with the tufted tails. As mammals, fetal gerbils gestate in their mother's uterus next to siblings of their litter. This intrauterine environment has profound effects on their subsequent sexual behaviours. For example, a male fetus that develops next to other males is exposed to high levels of the male sex hormone testosterone secreted by his brothers. As an adult, he reacts to a receptive female with a variety of sexual behaviours that help to propagate his kind. However, if a male gestates next to a female fetus, he grows up with a different repertoire of sexual behaviours. He will often act uninterested in females, or, if he does mate, the matings are less successful than those of his counterparts who developed next to other males. Clark and Galef (1998) have traced this difference between males to the presence or absence of testosterone during the gestation period. Testosterone from nearby brothers in the womb acts as a proximal cause for the development of sexual behaviours of these males; its absence, when a male develops next to sisters, causes a deficit in sexual proficiency.

Why should this happen? Specifically, why wouldn't natural selection have weeded out such differences, for example, by reducing the sensitivity of the fetus to intrauterine testosterone? A sexually competent male competes much more effectively for female attention and produces more offspring; this competition should have eliminated the genetic mechanisms that produce the poorer performance. A possible solution to this puzzle was discovered by Clark, DeSousa, Vonk, and Galef (1997) when they examined the subsequent behaviours of the males who gestated next to females. When they did mate successfully, these gerbils were good fathers. They spent more time in contact with pups, and their mates became sexually active more quickly. An ultimate cause of the difference in male gerbils might therefore be that in gerbils there are *two* breeding strategies: males who are better sexual performers and males who are better parents. The selective value of both strategies over the long history of gerbil evolution maintains this difference.

By understanding how adaptive behaviour developed through the long-term process of evolution, psychologists are able to gain a more thorough understanding of our ability to adjust to changes in our immediate environment. To understand the present, we must understand the past—the history of the individual and the history of our species. We behave as we do because we are members of the human species—an ultimate cause—and because we have learned to act in special ways—a proximate cause. Both biology and environment contribute to our personal development.

Considering the role of evolutionary factors in behaviour is becoming so widespread that a new subfield within psychology, evolutionary psychology, is beginning to emerge (Daly & Wilson, 1999; Tooby & Cosmides, 1989). This area of psychology investigates how an organism's evolutionary history contributes to the development of behaviour patterns and cognitive strategies related to reproduction and survival during its lifetime (Leger, 1991). As we will see throughout this book, evolutionary psychology has made significant contributions to our understanding of behaviour.

If evolutionary psychology succeeds in its quest to understand the relation between evolution and development, we might also arrive at a clearer understanding of the psychological adaptations of our species that have given rise to, and continue to augment, the ongoing evolution of culture. **Culture** is the sum of socially transmitted knowledge, customs, and behaviour patterns common to a particular group of people. Psychology's contribution to this understanding will be an explanation of how thinking and behaving shape cultural adaptations to changing environmental conditions. Arriving at such knowledge requires that the contribution of the evolutionary process be understood. No theory of behaviour can be complete without considering the role of evolution.

In this chapter, we will look at the development of Darwin's theory of evolution and explain how evolution operates. Then we'll discuss the general principles of heredity and genetics, the basic means by which biological and many behavioural characteristics are passed from one generation to the next. Finally, we'll examine sociobiology, a branch of biology that seeks to identify and understand evolutionary influences on social behaviour.

It is one of the ironies of the history of science that another British naturalist, Alfred Russell Wallace, devised the theory of natural selection at about the same time that Darwin did. Yet it is Darwin's work that we remember. The story of his theory illustrates the mix of hard work, intellect, and good fortune that often makes scientific discovery possible.

## The Voyage of the *Beagle*

After receiving a degree in theology from Christ's College, Cambridge (England), in 1831, Darwin met Captain Robert Fitz Roy. The captain was looking for someone to serve as an unpaid naturalist and travelling companion during a five-year voyage on board the HMS *Beagle*, a ten-gun brig converted to an ocean-going research vessel. The *Beagle*'s mission

**ultimate causes** Evolutionary conditions that have slowly shaped the behaviour of a species over generations.

**proximate causes** Immediate environmental events and conditions that affect behaviour.

**culture** The sum of socially transmitted knowledge, customs, and behaviour patterns common to a particular group of people.

▲ *Charles Darwin (1809–1882)*

was to explore and survey the coast of South America and to make hydrographic measurements worldwide. Darwin was eager to volunteer, although he needed to overcome his father's objections before he received his family's support for the voyage.

During the voyage, Darwin observed the flora and fauna of South America, Australia, South Africa, and the islands of the Pacific, South Atlantic, and Indian oceans, including, most notably, the Galapagos Islands off the west coast of South America. He spent most of his time doing what he enjoyed most: collecting. He collected creatures and objects of every sort. These specimens, which were sent to England at various stages of the trip, were later examined by naturalists from all over Europe.

Darwin did not form his theory of evolution while at sea. Although he was impressed by the tremendous amount of diversity among seemingly related animals, his original training was in theology, which ascribed to the doctrine of essentialism, a view dating back to Plato that all living things belong to a fixed class or "kind," defined by an essence that characterizes it alone (Mayr, 2001).

## The Origin of Species

Darwin's voyage ended in 1836. He returned to England still marvelling at the many ways that animals and plants adapt to their environments. He sifted through his collections, comparing the similarities and differences between the creatures he had found. He carefully reviewed the work of earlier naturalists (including his own grandfather), who had speculated about the concept of evolution but were unable to propose a believable process by which it occurred. He became interested in **artificial selection**, a procedure in which particular animals are deliberately mated to produce offspring that possess especially desirable characteristics. Using artificial selection, people select which animals will and will not breed based on specific, desirable characteristics of those animals. For example, if a pigeon fancier wanted to produce a pigeon with colourful plumage, he or she would examine the available stock and permit only the most colourful to reproduce. If this process is repeated over many generations of birds, the breeder's colony should become more colourful. Darwin was intrigued with artificial selection and, in fact, bred pigeons for a while. (See **Figure 3•1**.) He speculated: If artificial selection can produce such different varieties of pigeons, could a similar process result in different species?

It would be another year and a half before Darwin's intensive study of artificial selection would bear fruit. Darwin recalls the event in his autobiography:

> I happened to read for amusement Malthus on *Population*, and being well prepared to appreciate the struggle for existence which everywhere goes on from long continued observation of plants and animals, it at once struck me that under these circumstances favourable variations would tend to be preserved, and unfavourable ones to be destroyed. The result would be the formation of a new species. (Darwin, 1888/1950, p. 54)

What struck Darwin was the idea of **natural selection**, or the consequence of the fact that organisms reproduce differentially: Within any given population, some members of a given species will produce more offspring than will others. Any animal that possesses a characteristic that helps it to survive or adapt to changes in its environment is likely to live longer and to produce more offspring than are animals that do not have this characteristic.

Darwin came to this realization in September 1838, but did not publish his theory until 20 years later. Why did he wait so long? Among other things, he devoted considerable time to gathering supportive evidence. He took great pains to develop a clear, coherent, and accurate case for his theory. He examined and re-examined his specimens, carefully studied current research and theory in the natural sciences, conducted his own research on artificial selection, and, perhaps most importantly, tested his ideas on his closest colleagues, whom he often met at a pub in London.

Darwin might have been even slower in publishing his theory had Alfred Wallace not come to the same discovery of the principle of natural selection. Wallace had been reading the same book by Malthus that had inspired Darwin. Early in 1858, while suffering from a bout of fever in the Spice Islands, Wallace recognized that natural selection could be a force for the origin of new species. Quickly writing his ideas

**artificial selection** A procedure in which particular animals are deliberately mated to produce offspring that possess especially desirable characteristics.

**natural selection** The consequence of the fact that, because there are physical and behavioural differences among organisms, they reproduce differentially. Within a given population, some animals—the survivors—will produce more offspring than will other animals.

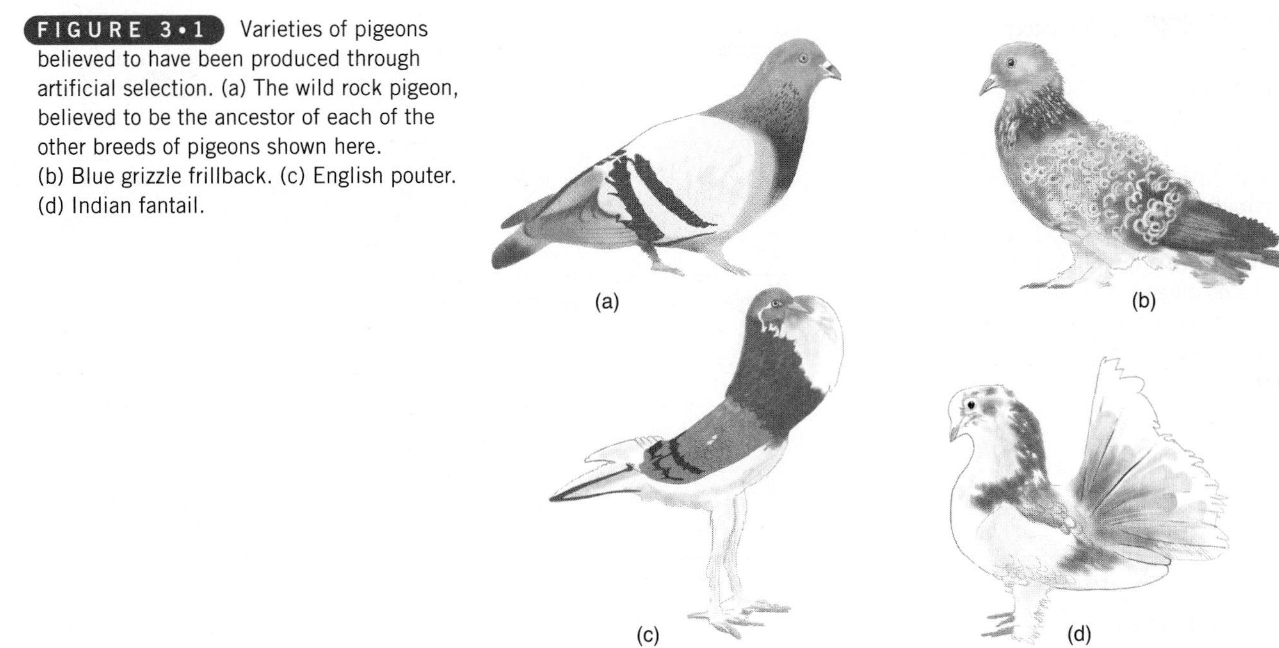


**FIGURE 3•1** Varieties of pigeons believed to have been produced through artificial selection. (a) The wild rock pigeon, believed to be the ancestor of each of the other breeds of pigeons shown here. (b) Blue grizzle frillback. (c) English pouter. (d) Indian fantail.

down, he sent a short description of them to, of all people, Charles Darwin.

What was Darwin to do? If he published his theory now, it would look like he had stolen the idea from Wallace; if he did not publish it, his 20 years of painstaking toil would be wasted. He presented the dilemma to his colleagues, who suggested that he and Wallace make a joint presentation of their separate works before a learned society—the Linnean Society—so that each might lay equal claim to the theory of natural selection. This was done, and a year later Darwin published his "abstract," which we know today as *The Origin of Species.*

## Natural Selection

Mayr (2000) has suggested that Darwin's immense contribution to modern thinking about evolution can be traced to four insights: that species are not fixed, but rather change over time; that evolution is a branching process, implying that all species descend from a single common ancestor; that evolution is continuous, with gradual changes; and that evolution is based on natural selection.

Natural selection is the key to the success of Darwin's version of evolution. It is based on two premises (Eldredge, 1998): First, individuals within a population show variability in heritable behavioural and physical characteristics. Second, the capacity of the environment to sustain a population of any species is limited, producing competition. Darwin and Wallace realized that these two factors meant that those individuals within the population with characteristics that compete better are more likely to survive and reproduce. To the extent that these characteristics are heritable, they would be likely to appear in the next generation. Darwin's careful study of natural history also convinced him that behavioural adaptations were especially important to survival and therefore an important part of evolution.

For example, wolves that are fleet of foot are better able to capture prey than are slower pack mates. Fast wolves will therefore tend to outlive and out-reproduce slower wolves. (See **Figure 3•2**.) If a wolf's tendency to run fast is a genetically controlled trait, it will be passed on to its offspring. These offspring will be more likely to catch prey and will therefore live longer and have more opportunities to reproduce.

The ability of an individual to produce offspring defines that individual's **reproductive success**—the number of viable offspring it produces relative to the number of viable offspring produced by other members of the same species. Contrary to popular interpretation, "survival of the fittest" does not always mean survival of the most physically fit or of the strongest. The evolutionary "bottom line" is not physical strength but reproductive success. Physical strength is only one factor that might contribute to such success. In humans, for example, good looks, charm, and intelligence play an important role in an individual's ability to provide for a family. These characteristics would therefore be possible factors for natural selection.

The two aspects of natural selection, variation and competition, are the critical factors that determine whether any particular animal and its offspring will enjoy reproductive success. Let's take a look at each of these aspects, beginning with variation.

**reproductive success** The number of viable offspring an individual produces relative to the number of viable offspring produced by other members of the same species.

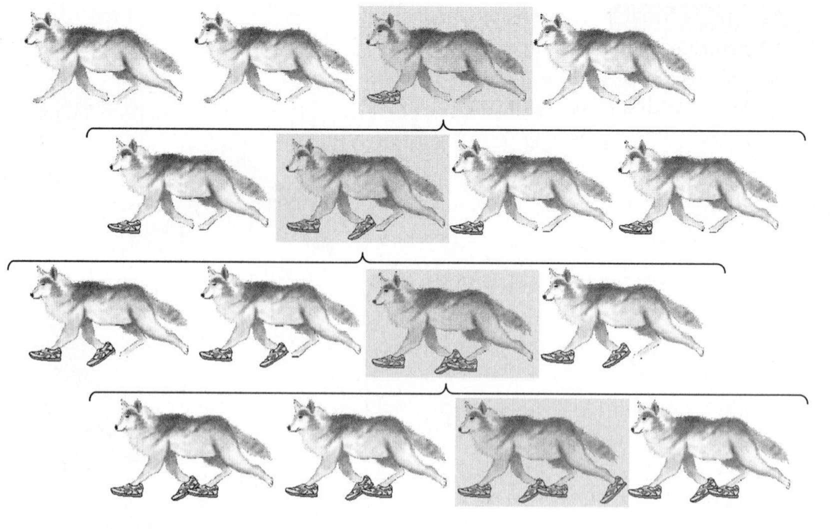

**FIGURE 3•2** Natural selection at work. Wolves that are fast (speed represented by the number of running shoes) will be better at escaping predators, capturing game, and reproducing than their slower pack mates. Because of the adaptive advantage that running fast confers upon a wolf's survival and reproductive success, the genotype for running speed will be passed on and increase in frequency across future generations. Shading shows the fastest wolf in each generation.

**Variation** **Variation** refers to the differences among members of a species, including physical characteristics such as size, strength, or physiology, and behavioural characteristics such as intelligence or sociability. What factors are responsible for these sorts of variations? First, an individual organism's genetic makeup, or its **genotype**, differs from that of all other individuals (except in the case of identical twins). As a result of these genetic differences, an individual organism's physical characteristics and behaviour, or its **phenotype**, also vary from every other individual.

It is important to recognize that every individual's phenotype is produced by the interaction of its genotype with the environment. In essence, the genotype determines how much the environment can influence an organism's development and behaviour. For instance, identical twins have exactly the same genotype. If they are separated at birth and one twin has a better diet than the other, their phenotypes will be different: The better-fed twin is likely to be taller and stronger. However, despite the difference in diet between the two, neither twin is likely to be exceptionally tall or muscular if the genotype shared by the twins does not promote these characteristics. Likewise, neither twin will realize his or her full potential for tallness and muscularity if he or she does not eat a nutritional diet. In this example, both the genotype (the genes related to tallness and muscularity) and a favourable environment (a well-balanced, nutritional diet) must be present for either twin to become tall and muscular.

Phenotypes and the genotypes responsible for them may or may not be selected, depending on the particular advantage they confer. Consider, for example, Darwin's finches, 13 species of finch that Darwin discovered in the Galapagos Islands. A striking physical difference among these birds is beak size. Some finches have a small, thin beak phenotype and others have a large, thick beak phenotype. Birds having small, thin beaks feed on small seeds covered by weak shells, and birds having large, thick beaks feed on large seeds covered by tough shells.

By studying the relationship between rainfall, food supply, and finch population on one island, Peter and Rosemary Grant (2002) discovered that the amount of rainfall and the size of the food supply directly affected the mortality of finches having certain kinds of beaks. During droughts, small seeds became scarce. As a result, the finches having small, thin beaks died at a higher rate than finches having bigger, thicker beaks. During the next few years, the number of finches having bigger, thicker beaks increased—just as the principle of natural selection would predict. During times of plentiful rain, small seeds became abundant, and the number of finches having small, thin beaks became more plentiful in subsequent years.

The Grants' study makes two important points. First, although evolution occurs over the long run, natural selection can produce important changes in the short run—in the space of only a few years. Second, phenotypic variation (in this case, differences in beak size) can produce important selective advantages that affect survival. Imagine if all the finches had had small, thin beaks. During the drought, most, if not all, of these finches might have died. None would be left to reproduce; these finches would have become extinct on this island. Fortunately, there was phenotypic variation in beak size among the finches. And because phenotypic variation is caused by genetic variation (different genotypes give rise to different phenotypes), some finches—those having large, thick beaks—had an advantage. Their food supply (the larger seeds) was relatively unaffected by the drought, enabling them to out-survive and out-reproduce the finches having small, thin beaks.

**variation** The differences found across individuals of any given species in terms of their genetic, biological (size, strength, physiology), and psychological (intelligence, sociability, behaviour) characteristics.
**genotype** An organism's genetic makeup.
**phenotype** The outward expression of an organism's genotype; an organism's physical characteristics and behaviour.

You might think that all finches should have developed large, thick beaks. However, when rain is plentiful and small seeds are abundant, birds having small, thin beaks find it easier to feed. Under these environmental conditions, these birds have a phenotypic (and genotypic) advantage. From the standpoint of the species, diversity in genotype can itself convey an advantage.

**Competition** **Competition** is the second premise underlying the concept of natural selection. Because individuals of a given species share the same environment, competition within a species for food, mates, and territory is inevitable. Every salmon captured and eaten by one bald eagle is a fish that cannot be captured and eaten by another bald eagle. If one bald eagle finds a suitable mate, then there is one fewer potential mate for other bald eagles.

Competition also occurs between species when members of different species vie for similar ecological resources, such as food and territory. For example, yellow-headed blackbirds and red-winged blackbirds eat the same foods and occupy the same type of breeding territories; thus, they compete for these resources. Such competition does not involve competition for mates (yellow-headed blackbirds do not court red-winged blackbirds and vice versa). However, although these species do not compete for mates, their competition for other resources indirectly influences reproductive success because the ability to find and court a suitable mate depends on the ability to stake out and defend a territory that has an adequate food supply. The probability of a yellow-headed blackbird finding a mate and successfully rearing a family depends not only on its success in competing against other yellow-headed blackbirds, but also on its success in competing against red-winged blackbirds.

A good example of competition at work has recently been found in the breeding behaviours of red squirrels in the Yukon. The average spring temperature in the region of Kluane Lake has increased by nearly 2 degrees Celsius since 1975, presumably as a result of global climate warming. This has, in turn, increased the availability of seeds that red squirrel mothers can use to support their newly born young—provided that they use the seeds before other animals exhaust the supply. Réale, McAdam, Boutin, and Berteaux (2003) found that the average time at which female squirrels gave birth has advanced more than two weeks in just ten years. The number of pine cones stored in treetops by the squirrels of this region also increased over the same period, suggesting that the squirrels were exploiting the increased availability of food. The old adage about early birds and their breakfast apparently applies just as well to the parturition of Yukon red squirrels.

Natural selection works because the members of any species have different phenotypes. Because these phenotypes are caused by different genotypes, successful individuals will pass on their genes to the next generation. Over time, competition for food and other resources will allow only the best-adapted phenotypes (and their corresponding genotypes) to survive, thereby producing evolutionary change. Under the right conditions, these changes can be measured using techniques based on the correlational methods described in the previous chapter. In the case of the red squirrels just discussed, Réale and colleagues (2003) found that the genotype of each new generation produced a birthdate that was about one day earlier than that of the previous generation.

## Interim Summary

### The Development of Evolutionary Theory

Understanding behaviour completely requires that psychologists learn more about both proximate causes of behaviour (how animals adapt to environmental changes through learning) and ultimate causes of behaviour (historical events and conditions in the evolution of a species that have shaped its behaviour). Evolutionary psychology is a relatively new subfield of psychology that is devoted to the study of how evolution and genetic variables influence adaptive behaviour.

Darwin's voyage on the HMS *Beagle* and his subsequent thinking and research in artificial selection led him to develop the idea of biological evolution, which explains how genetic and physical changes occur in groups of animals over time. The primary element of biological evolution is natural selection: the tendency of some members of a species to produce more offspring than other members do. Members of a species vary genetically, such that some possess specific traits to a greater or lesser extent than other individuals do. If any of these traits gives an animal a competitive advantage over other members of the species—for example, a better ability to escape predators, find food, or attract mates—then that animal is also more likely to have greater reproductive success. Its offspring will then carry its genes into future generations.

#### QUESTIONS TO CONSIDER

1. In what ways are psychology and biology related disciplines? How does understanding biological aspects of behaviour contribute to our understanding of psychological aspects of behaviour?
2. How do ultimate and proximate causes of behaviour influence human behaviour—for example, eating?
3. What might be the effects of reducing genetic variability in a population of organisms?
4. What argument might be made to support the suggestion that the human species is no longer evolving via natural selection? Is this a valid argument? Explain.

**competition** A striving or vying with others who share the same ecological niche for food, mates, and territory.

## Heredity and Genetics

Darwin's work unveiled the process of natural selection and pointed out new frontiers for exploration and experimentation. One of the most important of these frontiers is **genetics**, the study of the structure and functions of genes, how they are transmitted from one generation to another, and how they operate in populations (Suzuki, Griffiths, Miller, & Lewontin, 1989). Genetics, then, also involves the study of how the genetic makeup of an organism influences its physical and behavioural characteristics. Closely related to genetics are the principles of **heredity**, the sum of the traits and tendencies inherited from a person's parents and other biological ancestors.

Although Darwin had built a strong case for natural selection, he could not explain a key tenet of his theory—inheritance. He knew that individual differences occurred within a given species and that those differences were subject to natural selection. But he did not know how adaptations were passed from parent to offspring or why differences among offspring occurred.

Six years after *The Origin of Species* was published, Gregor Mendel, an Austrian monk who conducted experimental crossbreeding studies with pea plants, uncovered the basic principles of heredity. Mendel demonstrated conclusively how height, flower colour, seed shape, and other traits of pea plants could be transmitted from one generation to the next. Furthermore, his inspired analysis explained the source of the variation of inherited traits. Although little noticed during his lifetime, Mendel's work has since been applied to studying heredity in thousands of plants and animals.

Genetics has revolutionized the study of biology, but its importance to psychology is almost as great. It helps provide us with both proximal and ultimate explanations for psychological processes. Throughout the later chapters of this book, you will see many cases where psychologists have turned to genetic explanations to understand how people develop into who they are and why they behave the way they do. In addition, the study of genetics tells us much about our society and the extent to which the differences among us are due either to the culture we grew up in or to the ancestors we have. Finally, there are many psychological disorders and diseases with psychological effects that have genetic causes. Clinical psychologists who treat individuals with these diseases need to understand their genetic origins.

**genetics** The study of the genetic makeup of organisms and how it influences their physical and behavioural characteristics.
**heredity** The sum of the traits and tendencies inherited from a person's parents and other biological ancestors.
**DNA (deoxyribonucleic acid)** The DNA structure resembles that of a twisted ladder. Strands of sugar and phosphates are connected by rungs made from nucleotide molecules of adenine, thymine, guanine, and cytosine.
**genes** Small units of DNA that direct the synthesis of proteins and enzymes.

### Basic Principles of Genetics

Heredity is determined by genetic material called **DNA (deoxyribonucleic acid)**—strands of sugar and phosphate that are connected by nucleotide molecules of adenine, thymine, guanine, and cytosine. As discovered by James Watson and Francis Crick in 1953, DNA is configured like a twisted ladder: the sugar and phosphate form the sides and the four nucleotides form the rungs. (See **Figure 3•3.**) The location of a particular sequence of nucleotides along the DNA molecule is known as a **gene**. Some genes contain a short sequence of

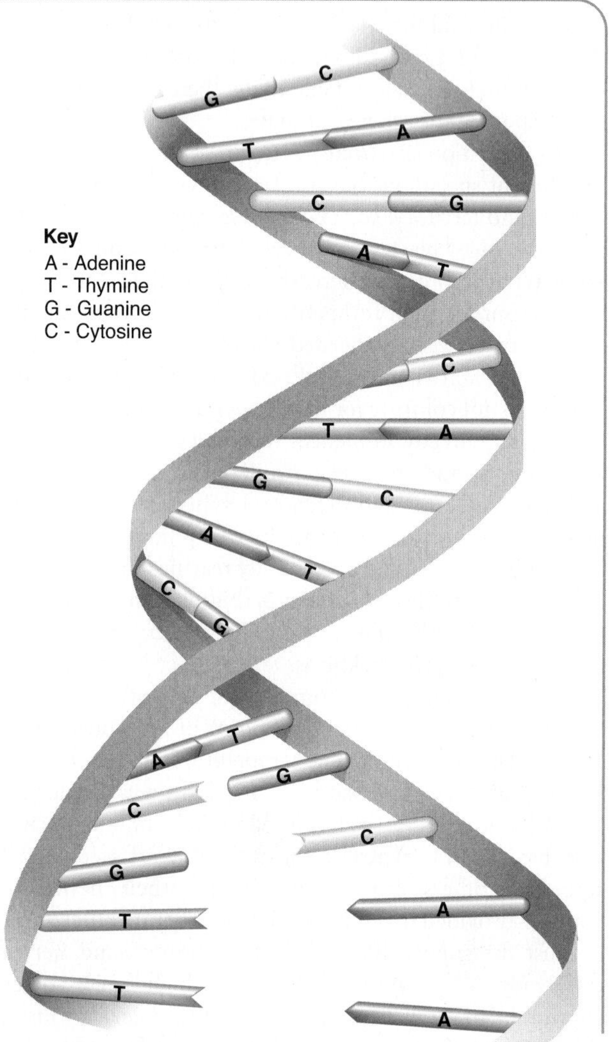


FIGURE 3•3 The structure and composition of DNA. The rungs of the "twisted ladder of DNA" are made up of combinations of four nucleotide bases: adenine, thymine, guanine, and cytosine. Genes are segments of DNA that direct the synthesis of proteins and enzymes according to the particular sequences of nucleotide bases they contain. In essence, genes serve as "recipes" for the synthesis of these proteins and enzymes, which regulate the cellular and other physiological processes of the body, including those responsible for behaviour. *(Based on Watson, J. D. (1976).* Molecular biology of the gene. *Menlo Park, CA: Benjamin.)*

nucleotides, whereas others may contain a sequence of millions. Regardless, the particular sequence of these nucleotide molecules directs the synthesis of protein molecules that regulate the biological and physical development of the body and all of its organs. The total set of genetic material is known as the **genome**. The human genome comprises 24 different DNA molecules in women and 25 different DNA molecules in men. There appear to be 30 000 to 40 000 genes within the human genome, which, surprisingly, is only about twice the number in a common housefly or worm (The Genome Sequencing Consortium, 2001).

**Genes as "Recipes" for Protein Synthesis** Genes influence our physical and behavioural development in only one way: through protein synthesis. Proteins are strings of amino acids, arranged in a chain whose order is specified by the way the nucleotides adenine, thymine, guanine, and cytosine are linked together on the DNA molecule. A sequence of three nucleotides corresponds to a particular amino acid. For example, a sequence of three adenine nucleotides might correspond to one amino acid, but a sequence of two adenines and a thymine would correspond to another. Thus, in a sense, genes are "recipes" consisting of different nucleotide sequences. In this case, the recipe is for combining the proteins necessary to create and develop physiological structures and for behaviour—how those structures might function in response to environmental stimulation.

Strictly speaking, though, there are no genes for behaviour, only for the physical structures and physiological processes that are related to behaviour. For example, if we were to look for a gene for the ability to learn, we would need to look for a gene that contains instructions for the synthesis of proteins that might affect this ability. Evidence from behavioural and pharmacological studies has indicated that a substance called dopamine (see Chapter 4) affects learning (Schultz, 2001). We might speak of the gene that affects dopamine as a "learning gene," but this would not be exact. The gene affects dopamine production, not learning. It is important to note that we are really speaking about its association with the chemical mechanisms that lead to dopamine production.

Genes also direct the synthesis of **enzymes**, which govern the processes that occur within every cell in the body, and thus control each cell's structure and function. As we will see later, a faulty gene may contain instructions for synthesis of faulty enzymes, which produces serious physiological and behavioural problems. There are also large segments of the DNA molecule consisting of so-called "junk" DNA. Junk DNA is not involved in the direct synthesis of proteins and for that reason is known as *non-coding DNA*. Nevertheless, non-coding sequences of DNA may play a critical role. They regulate the processes of other genes that synthesize proteins by genes. In this way, non-coding DNA can affect evolution, including human evolution (Greally, 2007).

**Chromosomes and Meiosis** Most genes are located on **chromosomes**, the threadlike structures made of DNA found in the nucleus of every cell, although a few are located in the cell's mitochondria. In essence, genes are particular regions of chromosomes that contain the recipes for particular proteins. Each set of chromosomes contains a different DNA molecule and, hence, a different sequence of genes. We inherit 23 individual chromosomes from each of our parents, giving us 23 pairs—46 individual chromosomes—in most cells of the body. In 22 of

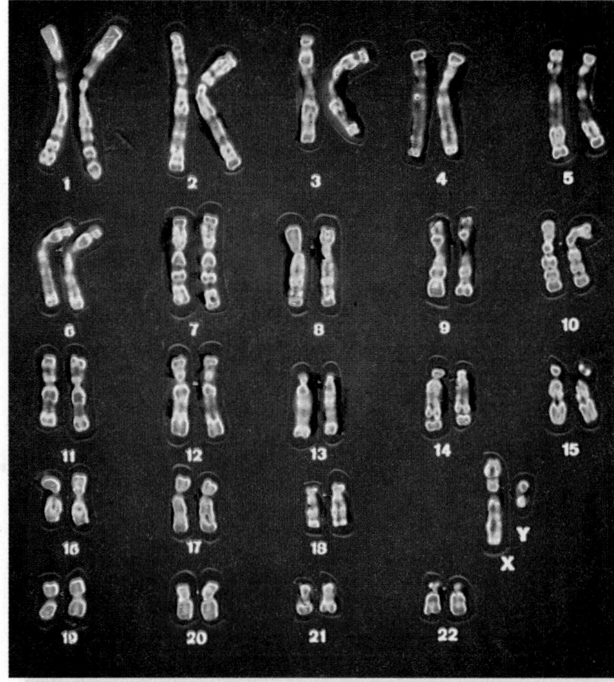

(a)

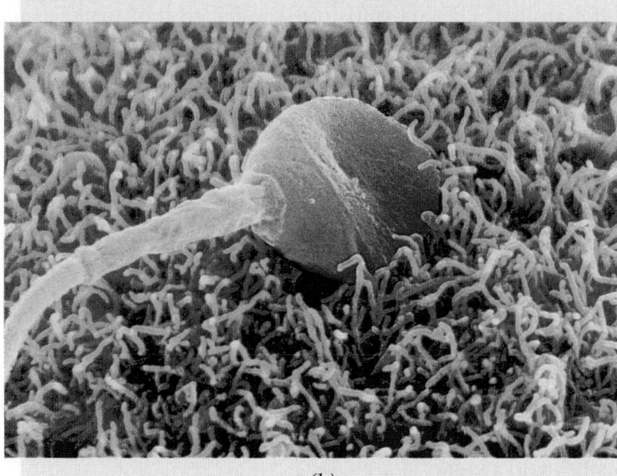
(b)

▲ *(a) Human chromosomes. The presence of a Y chromosome indicates that this sample came from a male. A sample from a female would include two X chromosomes. (b) Fertilization—a human sperm penetrating an egg.*

**genome** The total set of genetic material of an organism.
**enzymes** Proteins that regulate the structure of bodily cells and the processes occurring within those cells.
**chromosomes** Threadlike structures in the nuclei of living cells; contain genes.

these pairs of chromosomes, the two DNA molecules are of matching types. The remaining pair of chromosomes, the **sex chromosomes**, contains the instructions for the development of male or female sex characteristics—those characteristics that distinguish males from females. In females, the two sex chromosomes are matching DNA molecules, labelled as *X chromosomes*, but in males the two molecules are of different types, and labelled as *X* and *Y chromosomes*. (This is why the human male genome contains one more DNA molecule than the human female genome.) The chromosomes that are not sex chromosomes are known as **autosomes**.

Sexual reproduction involves the union of a sperm, which carries genetic instructions from the male, and an ovum (egg), which carries genetic instructions from the female. Sperm and ova differ from the other bodily cells in at least two very important ways. First, sperm and ova contain only one member of each chromosome pair. Second, some of the genetic information on one member of a pair has been exchanged with the information on the other member. The reason that sperm and ova differ from ordinary body cells is that they are produced by a special reproductive process known as **meiosis**. The 23 pairs of chromosomes break apart into two groups, with one member of each pair joining one of the groups. The cell splits into 2 cells, each of which contains 23 *individual* chromosomes. The assignment of the members of each pair of chromosomes to a particular group is a random process; thus, a single individual can produce $2^{23}$ (8 388 608) different ova or sperm.

Although brothers and sisters may resemble each other, they are not exact copies. Because the union of a particular sperm with an ovum is apparently random, a couple could produce 8 388 608 × 8 388 608, or 70 368 774 177 664 different possible children. Only identical twins are genetically identical. Identical twins occur when a fertilized ovum divides, giving rise to two identical individuals. Fraternal twins are no more similar than any other two siblings. They occur when a woman produces two ova, both of which are fertilized (by different sperm, of course).

Sex is determined by the twenty-third pair of chromosomes: the *sex chromosomes*. As noted, there are two different kinds of sex chromosomes, X chromosomes and Y chromosomes. Females have a pair of X chromosomes (XX); males have one of each type (XY). Because women's cells contain only X chromosomes, each of their ova contains a single X chromosome (along with 22 other single chromosomes). Because men's cells contain both an X chromosome and a Y chromosome, half of the sperm they produce contain an X chromosome and half contain a Y chromosome. Thus, the sex of a couple's offspring depends on which type of sperm fertilizes the ovum. A Y-bearing sperm produces a boy, and an X-bearing sperm produces a girl. (See **Figure 3•4**.)

**FIGURE 3•4** Determination of sex. The sex of human offspring depends on whether the sperm that fertilizes the ovum carries an X or a Y chromosome.

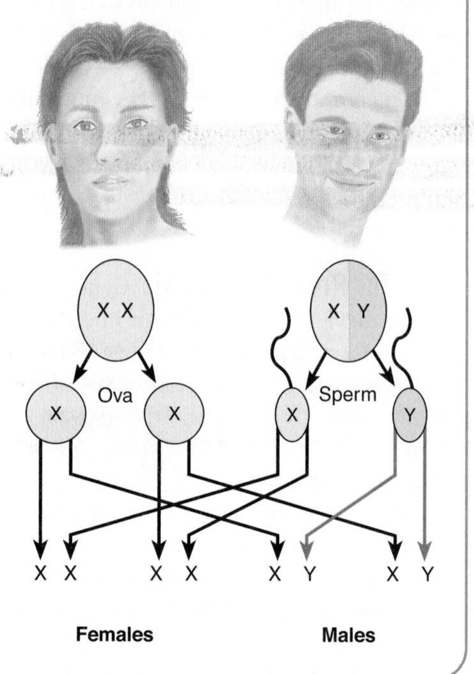


**sex chromosomes** The chromosomes that contain the instructional code for the development of male or female sex characteristics.
**autosomes** The chromosomes that are not sex chromosomes.
**meiosis** The form of cell division by which new sperm and ova are formed. The chromosomes within the cell are randomly rearranged so that new sperm and ova contain 23 individual chromosomes, or half of those found in other bodily cells.
**alleles** Alternative forms of the same gene.
**dominant trait** The trait that is exhibited when an individual possesses heterozygous alleles.
**recessive trait** A trait that occurs only when it is expressed by homozygous alleles.

**Dominant and Recessive Traits** Each pair of chromosomes contains pairs of genes: One gene in each pair is contributed by each parent. Genes, however, come in different forms. Alternative forms of genes are called **alleles**. (*Allele*, like *alias*, comes from the Greek *allos*, "other.") Consider eye colour. The pigment found in the iris of the eye is produced by a particular gene. If parents each contribute the same allele for eye colour to their child, the gene combination is called *homozygous* (from the Greek *homo*, "same," and *zygon*, "yolk"). However, if the parents contribute different alleles, the gene combination is said to be *heterozygous* (from the Greek *hetero*, "different"). The character or trait produced by heterozygous gene combinations is called the **dominant trait**. The character of brown eyes is dominant. When a child inherits the allele that codes for brown eye colour from one parent and the allele that codes for a different eye colour from the other parent, the child will have brown eyes. Blue eye colour, on the other hand, is a **recessive trait**—it is not present when an individual is heterozygous. Only if both of a child's alleles for eye colour are of the blue type will the child have blue eyes. Inheritance of two alleles for brown eyes will, of

FIGURE 3•5 Patterns of inheritance for eye colour. (a) If one parent is homozygous for the dominant eye colour (BB), and the other parent is homozygous for the recessive eye colour (bb), then all of their children will be heterozygous for eye colour (Bb) and will have brown eyes. (b) If one parent is heterozygous (Bb), and the other parent is homozygous recessive (bb), then their children will have a 50 percent chance of being heterozygous (brown eyes) and a 50 percent chance of being homozygous recessive (eye colours other than brown). (c) If one parent is homozygous dominant (BB), and the other parent is heterozygous (Bb), then their children will have a 50 percent chance of being homozygous for the dominant eye colour (BB) and will have brown eyes, and a 50 percent chance of being heterozygous (Bb) for the trait and will have brown eyes.

*(Adapted from Klug, W. S., & Cummings, M. R. (1986).* Concepts of genetics *(2nd ed.). Glenview, IL: Scott, Foresman.)*

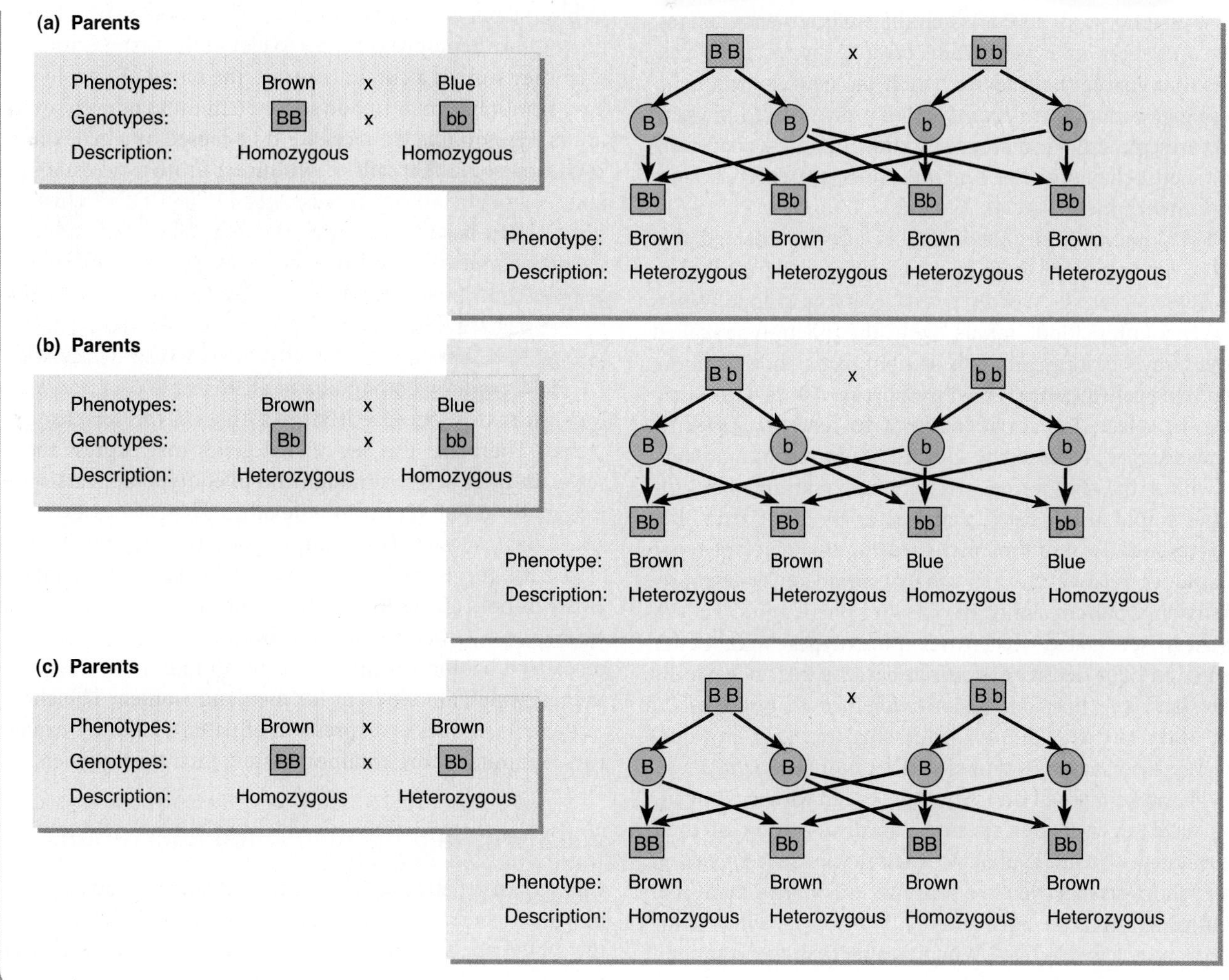


course, result in brown eyes. (See **Figure 3•5.**) Other eye colours, such as hazel or black, are produced by the effects of other genes, which influence the brown allele to code for more (black) or less (hazel) pigment in the iris.

It is important to remember that the genetic contributions to our personal development and behaviour are extremely complex. One reason for this complexity is that protein synthesis is often under *polygenic* control—that is, influenced by many pairs of genes, not just a single pair. The inheritance of behaviour is even more complicated, because different environments influence the expression of polygenic traits. Consider, for example, the ability to run. Running speed for any individual is the joint product of genetic factors that produce proteins for muscle, bone, blood, oxygen metabolism, and motor coordination (to name but a few) and environmental factors such as exercise patterns, age, nutrition, accidents, and so on.

## The Importance of Genetic Diversity

As discussed, no two individuals, except identical twins, are genetically identical. Such genetic diversity is a characteristic of all species that reproduce sexually.

Are there many organisms that reproduce asexually? Yeast and fungi may come to mind, and if you are familiar with horticultural practices you may know that nurseries often reproduce plants and trees through grafting, which is an asexual process. But when we examine the world around us, we find that the overwhelming majority of species reproduce sexually. Why?

One possible answer is that sexual reproduction increases a species' ability to adapt to environmental changes. Sexual reproduction leads to genetic diversity because there are two different copies of the DNA molecule in the child's genome—one from each parent. Genetically diverse species have a better chance of adapting to a changing environment (see West-Eberhard, 2005). When the environment changes, some members of a genetically diverse species may have genes that enable them to survive in the new environment. These genes manufacture proteins that give rise to physical structures, physiological processes, and, ultimately, adaptively significant behaviour that can withstand particular changes in the environment.

Sokolowski, Pereira, and Hughes (1997) observed this kind of adaptation at work in the behaviour of fruit fly larvae. These larvae show two types of reactions to food. When they encounter food, larvae with the phenotype called "rover" travel in long, generally straight paths; those with the phenotype called "sitter" crawl in short segments with many turns. In effect, the rovers respond to food by travelling longer distances to find new sources. Sitters respond by staying within the discovered patch. Sokolowski and her colleagues found that raising many generations of fruit flies under crowded conditions increased the frequency of rover phenotypes relative to sitter phenotypes. Conversely, low-density environments selected for sitter phenotypes. The researchers speculated that rover phenotypes were better adapted to high-density conditions because their behaviours were more likely to lead to a food patch that was not crowded with other larvae. When environments were not crowded, however, sitter larvae exploited patches more efficiently.

The advantages of diversity may explain why so many insects have survived our species' radical alteration of their environment. The lifespan of the moth species *Biston betularia* is very short, so that even in a short period of time, many different generations are born and die. The normal wing colour of these moths is very light. When we alter their environment, as we did when the Industrial Revolution coated many of the white trees where they rest, we may kill many of them by making them more visible to birds and hence more susceptible to predation. However, some survive because they have the right combination of genes that produce a darker wing colour. The survivors then reproduce. The latent capacity of the genome to produce a darker wing colour ensured that the species could survive this radical change to its environment (Dawkins, 1996). Natural selection, then, can favour species that reproduce sexually because of the adaptive value of genetic diversity.

**mutations** Accidental alterations in the DNA code within a single gene. Mutations can be either spontaneous, occurring naturally, or the result of environmental factors such as exposure to high-energy radiation.

## Influences of Gender on Heredity

The simple pattern of inheritance that I described for eye colour is appropriate for traits coded by single genes on the autosomes. When genes are located on the sex chromosomes, the situation will be more complicated. An individual's sex will play a crucial role in influencing the expression of such traits. A good example is hemophilia, an increased tendency to bleed from even minor injuries. The blood of people who do not have hemophilia begins to clot in the first few minutes after they sustain a cut. In contrast, the blood of people who have hemophilia may not do so for 30 minutes or even several hours. Hemophilia is a recessive trait caused by a gene on the X chromosome that fails to produce a protein necessary for normal blood clotting. Because females have two X chromosomes, they can carry an allele for hemophilia but still have normal blood clotting if the other allele is normal. Males, however, have only a single X chromosome, which they receive from their mothers. If the gene for blood clotting carried on this chromosome is faulty, they develop hemophilia.

The gene for hemophilia is an example of a *sex-linked gene*, so named because it resides only on the sex chromosomes. There are also sex-related genes that express themselves in both sexes, although the phenotype appears more frequently in one sex than in the other. These genes are called *sex-influenced genes*. For example, pattern baldness (thin hair across the top of the head) develops in men if they inherit either or both alleles for baldness, but this trait is not seen in women, even when they inherit both alleles. The expression of pattern baldness is influenced by an individual's sex hormones, which are different for men and women. The effects of these hormones on expression of pattern baldness explain why it is much more common among men than women.

## Mutations and Chromosomal Aberrations

Changes in genetic material are caused by mutations or chromosomal aberrations. **Mutations** are accidental alterations in the DNA code within a single gene. Mutations are the original source of genetic diversity. Although most mutations have harmful effects, some may produce characteristics that are beneficial in certain environments. Mutations can be either spontaneous, occurring naturally, or the result of environmental factors such as high-energy radiation.

Hemophilia provides one of the most famous examples of mutation. Although hemophilia has appeared many times in human history, no other case of hemophilia has had as far-reaching effects as the spontaneous mutation that was passed among the royal families of nineteenth-century Europe. Through genealogical analysis, researchers have discovered that this particular mutant gene arose with Queen Victoria (1819–1901). She was the first in her family line to bear affected children: two female carriers and an afflicted son. The tradition that dictates that nobility marry only other nobility caused the mutant gene to spread rapidly throughout the royal families.

The second type of genetic change, **chromosomal aberration**, involves either changes in parts of chromosomes or a change in the total number of chromosomes. An example of a disorder caused by a chromosomal aberration—in this case, a partial deletion of the genetic material in chromosome 5—is the *cri-du-chat syndrome*. Infants who have this syndrome have gastrointestinal and cardiac problems, have severe problems in mental functioning, and make crying sounds resembling a cat's mewing (hence the syndrome's name, "cry of the cat"). In general, the syndrome's severity appears to be related directly to the amount of genetic material that is missing. Psychologists and developmental disability specialists have discovered that early special education training permits many individuals having this syndrome to learn self-care and communication skills. This fact highlights an important point about genetics and behaviour: Even behaviour that has a genetic basis can often be modified to some extent through training or experience.

## Genetic Disorders

Many genes decrease an organism's viability—its ability to survive. These "killer genes" are actually quite common. On average, each of us has two to four of them. Fortunately, these lethal genes are usually expressed as recessive traits, and there are so many different types that most couples do not carry the same ones. (If these genes produced dominant traits and we had two to four of them, we would be dead!) When a child inherits a healthy gene from one parent and a lethal gene from the other, the destructive effects of the lethal gene are not expressed.

A few lethal genetic disorders are dominant, however. Different lethal genes express themselves at different times in the lifespan. A fetus may die and be spontaneously aborted before a woman even realizes that she is pregnant, a baby may be stillborn, or the lethal genes may not be expressed until adulthood.

There are many human genetic disorders. Here are several of the more common ones that impair mental functioning and behaviour and so are of special interest to psychologists.

**Down syndrome**, named after the British physician John Langdon Down who provided the first medical description of this condition, is caused by a chromosomal aberration consisting of an extra twenty-first chromosome. People having Down syndrome show impaired physical, psychomotor, and cognitive development. Many children born with this condition have heart and respiratory complications that require careful medical and surgical attention. The frequency of Down syndrome increases with the age of the mother (Rischer & Easton, 1992). About 40 percent of all Down syndrome children are born to women over 40. To a lesser extent, the age of the father also increases the chances of Down syndrome. Although Down syndrome is caused by a chromosomal aberration, it is not an inherited disorder.

**Huntington's disease** tends to emerge when the afflicted person is between 30 and 40 years old. It is a dominant trait caused by a lethal gene that results in degeneration in certain parts of the brain. Before the onset of this disease, an individual may be healthy in every respect. After onset, however, the individual experiences slow but progressive mental and physical deterioration, including loss of coordination and motor ability. (The word *chorea* comes from the Greek word for *dance* and is used to describe the uncoordinated movements that occur during this stage.) Death generally occurs 5 to 15 years after onset. Because age of onset for Huntington's chorea is long after sexual maturity, this lethal gene can be passed from parent to child before the parent even knows that he or she has the gene.

Individuals having the recessive trait **phenylketonuria (PKU)** are homozygous for a gene responsible for synthesis of a faulty enzyme, which renders them unable to break down phenylalanine, an amino acid found in many high-protein foods. As a result, blood levels of phenylalanine increase, causing severe brain damage and disruptions in mental functioning. PKU is one of many diseases for which infants are routinely tested before they leave the hospital. Infants diagnosed as having PKU are placed on a low-phenylalanine diet shortly after birth. If this diet is followed carefully, brain development will be normal.

## Heredity and Behaviour Genetics

It may surprise you to learn that humans differ from other primates in that we are genetically much less diverse. For example, we show less genetic diversity than our closest animal relatives, the chimpanzees (Strachan & Read, 1999). However, because each of us is born into a different environment and each of us does possess a unique combination of genetic instructions, we differ considerably from one another. Consider, for instance, your classmates. They come in different sizes and shapes, vary in personality and intelligence, and possess unequal artistic and athletic abilities. To what extent are these sorts of differences attributable to heredity or to the environment?

Before we explore this question, consider the way in which the answer is constrained by how genetics works. If all of your classmates had been reared in identical environments, any differences between them would necessarily be due to genetics. Conversely, if all of your classmates had come

**chromosomal aberration** The rearrangement of genes within chromosomes or a change in the total number of chromosomes.

**Down syndrome** A genetic disorder caused by a chromosomal aberration resulting in an extra twenty-first chromosome. People having Down syndrome show impairments in physical, psychomotor, and cognitive development.

**Huntington's disease** A genetic disorder caused by a dominant lethal gene in which a person experiences slow but progressive mental and physical deterioration.

**phenylketonuria (PKU)** A genetic disorder caused by a particular pair of homozygous recessive genes and characterized by the inability to break down phenylalanine, an amino acid found in many high-protein foods. The resulting high blood levels of phenylalanine cause mental retardation.

from the same fertilized egg but were subsequently raised in different environments, any differences in their personal characteristics would necessarily be due only to the environment. Our attribution of differences to either heredity or the environment will therefore depend on specifying the underlying variability.

**Heritability** is a statistical term that refers to the estimated amount of variability in a trait in a given population that is due to genetic differences among the individuals in that population. The more that a trait in a given population is influenced by genetic factors, the greater its heritability. Heritability is sometimes confused with *inheritance*, the tendency of a given trait to be passed from parent to individual offspring. But heritability does not apply to individuals; it pertains only to the variation of a trait in a *specific population*. At best, then, it is a partial answer to our question and its value depends on the specific environment within which it is measured.

A more inclusive scientific approach is to study the mechanisms of genetic influences on behaviour—a field called **behaviour genetics**. As noted by one of this field's most prolific researchers, Robert Plomin (1990), behaviour genetics is intimately involved with providing an explanation of why people differ. As we will see below, behaviour geneticists attempt to account for the roles that both heredity and the environment play in individual differences in a wide variety of physical and mental abilities.

## Studying Genetic Influences

Although farmers and animal breeders had experimented with artificial selection for thousands of years, only within the last 150 years has the relation between heredity and behaviour been formally studied in the laboratory. Of course, Mendel's careful analysis of genetic influences on specific characteristics gave us the first good clue that traits were actually heritable. His tracing of traits through biological pedigrees provided the foundation for the study of what are now called **mendelian traits**—traits that show standard patterns of inheritance like those depicted in Figure 3.5 (see page 67). Mendelian traits are determined by DNA coding at a single concentrated location on a chromosome.

Even before Mendel's work became well known, a cousin of Darwin's, Francis Galton (1869), had attempted to apply concepts of heredity to psychology. His studies showed that intelligence tends to run in families: If parents are intelligent, then, in general, so are their children. But intelligence, to the extent that it is a genetically determined characteristic, is a **non-mendelian trait**—a trait generally showing continuous variation and not the "either–or" pattern that was described by Mendel. Because non-mendelian traits are polygenic, they cannot be analyzed in the same way that Mendel analyzed his plant pedigrees. Nevertheless, they are quite important and, indeed, are probably the basis of the traits that underlie human evolution (Carroll, 2003). The search for genetic bases of behaviour has been active since Galton's time, with modern behaviour geneticists using techniques that rely on both Mendel's methods and statistical techniques developed by Galton. Three primary tools of modern behaviour genetics are artificial selection, segregation analysis, and allelic association.

**Artificial Selection in Animals** Any heritable trait, even a non-mendelian one, can be selected in a breeding program. The heritability of many traits in animals, such as aggression, docility, preference for alcohol, running speed, and mating behaviours, can be studied by means of artificial selection. A trait with a high measure of heritability should be modifiable by artificial selection.

For example, Robert Tryon (1940) conducted what is now considered a classic study concerning maze learning. Tryon wished to determine whether genetic variables influenced learning. He began his study with a large sample of genetically diverse rats. He trained them to learn a maze and recorded the number of errors that each rat made in the process. He then selected two groups of rats—those that learned the fastest (bright) and those that learned the slowest (dull). He mated "bright" rats with other "bright" rats and "dull" rats with other "dull" rats. To ensure that the rats were not somehow learning the maze from their mothers, he

▲ *Tryon's selective breeding study showed that a rat's ability to navigate successfully through a maze was affected by genetic factors.*

**heritability** The amount of variability in a given trait in a given population at a given time due to genetic factors.

**behaviour genetics** The study of genetic influences on behaviour.

**mendelian trait** A trait showing a classical dominant, recessive, or sex-linked pattern of inheritance. Mendelian traits are usually dichotomous and are controlled by a single locus.

**non-mendelian trait** A trait that does not show the inheritance pattern described by Mendel. Non-mendelian traits are usually polygenic and show continuous variation in the phenotype.

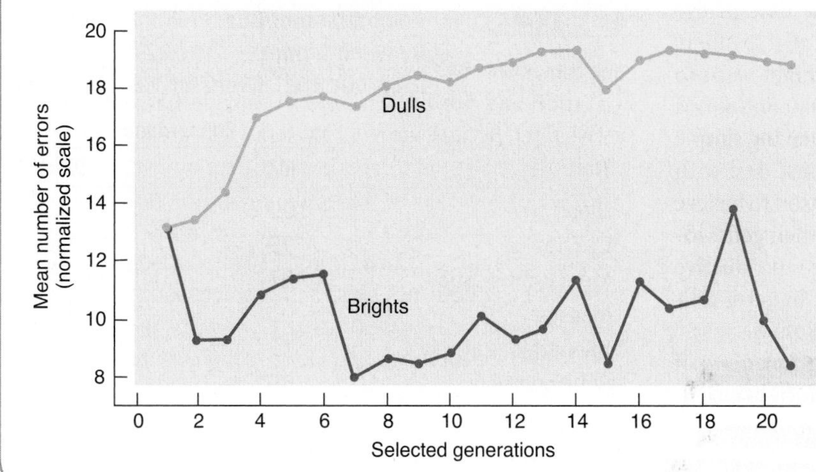


**FIGURE 3•6** Results from Tryon's 1940 artificial breeding research of rats' ability to learn a maze. Within a few generations, differences in the rats' ability to negotiate the maze became distinct.
*(Adapted from Tryon, R. C. (1940). Genetic differences in maze-learning ability in rats.* Yearbook of the National Society for the Study of Education, 39, *111–119.)*

"adopted out" some of the pups: Some of the bright pups were reared by dull mothers and some of the dull pups were reared by bright mothers. He found that parenting made little difference in his results, so this factor can be discounted.

Tryon continued this sequence of having rats learn the maze and selectively breeding the best with the best (bright) and the worst with the worst (dull) over many generations. Soon, the maze performance of each group virtually did not overlap. (See **Figure 3•6**.) He concluded that maze learning in rats could be manipulated through artificial selection.

However, remember that heritability applies only to a specific population living in a specific environment. Later studies showed that Tryon's results were limited by the standard laboratory cage environment in which rats lived when they were not running the maze. For example, Cooper and Zubek (1958) demonstrated that differences in maze ability were virtually eliminated when bright and dull strains of rats were reared in either enriched environments designed to stimulate learning (cages containing geometric objects such as tunnels, ramps, and blocks) or impoverished environments designed to inhibit learning (cages containing only food and water dishes). However, the rats in Cooper and Zubek's study who were reared in the standard laboratory cage performed similarly to Tryon's rats: The bright rats outperformed the dull rats. Thus, changing the environmental conditions in which the rats lived had an important result—reducing the effects of genetic differences between the bright and dull rats. This finding makes good sense when you consider the fact that genes are not expressed in the absence of an appropriate environmental factor.

Tryon's research shows that over successive generations a trait can be made to become more or less likely in a given population, but it does not tell us precisely why. We do not know whether genes related to learning or genes related to other traits were selected. Perhaps Tryon's rats were neither especially bright nor especially dull but differed in their motivation to obtain the food reward that awaited them at the end of the maze.

The rapidly growing field of molecular genetics has made impressive progress in mapping the sequence of nucleotide bases on human and animal chromosomes. On April 14, 2003, the International Human Genome Consortium announced that it had completed the description of the human genome. With this knowledge, behaviour geneticists not only can identify specific sequences within an individual, but also can synthesize sequences and insert them into an animal's genetic code using techniques that form the new discipline of **genetic engineering**. This type of direct manipulation of genetic material can sometimes be used to identify the function of a suspected gene and provide a more detailed description of its inheritance directly. For example, a type of manufactured mutation, called a **knockout mutation**, can be inserted into a gene to make it inactive, or the gene can be eliminated entirely. The phenotypic effect of this manipulation provides a clue to the function of the inactivated gene.

In contrast, it is also possible to insert an active mutation into a gene to see if the insertion changes the phenotype. Osborne and colleagues (1997) used such a procedure to show that the rover phenotype of fruit fly larvae discussed earlier is the result of a gene that controls the production of a special enzyme. Behaviour geneticists can also trace both natural and artificially induced mutations through breeding studies by means of **genetic markers**—known DNA sequences, usually neutral with respect to phenotype, that serve as landmarks along the chromosome. These and other techniques of molecular genetics will help scientists understand how specific DNA sequences in humans can influence physiological processes that affect behaviour, emotion, remembering, and thinking (Plomin & Rende, 1991).

**genetic engineering** The new scientific discipline of manipulating genetic sequences to alter an organism's genome.

**knockout mutation** An artificially constructed genetic sequence inserted into a gene to inactivate it.

**genetic marker** A known DNA sequence that occurs at a particular place in the chromosome.

**Segregation Analysis** Although we used the case of eye colour as an example of a human characteristic that is inherited, many of the psychological traits that we might want to study are non-mendelian. For example, they show continuous variation along some dimension. So, instead of having simple categories like "brown" or "blue," geneticists must deal with subtle gradations in a trait. Also, there is good reason to believe that many of these traits are polygenic, and have their genes located on many different chromosomes. Because reproductive cells are produced by meiosis, genes recombine in germ cells in new ways when they are on different chromosomes.

There are two other barriers to studying the effects of heredity on human behavioural traits. First, ethical considerations prevent psychologists and geneticists from manipulating people's genetic history or restricting the type of environment in which they are reared. For example, we cannot artificially breed people to learn the extent to which shyness or other personality characteristics are inherited or insert a knockout mutation to see if intelligence is affected by a change at a particular place on a chromosome. Second, in most cases, the non-mendelian character of the trait, and the enormous variability in human environments, effectively masks any correlation that might exist between genetics and trait expression.

Behaviour geneticists accommodate these constraints by several strategies. These strategies are generally based on the fact that, although we cannot manipulate a human's genotype, we can observe a person's phenotype and, with that person's informed consent, can analyze the sequences of nucleotides along the chromosome. Knowing that person's family history, a behaviour geneticist can infer the degree to which genetic influences are linked together as they are passed from generation to generation.

This method still leaves the problem of assessing the contribution of environmental influences on the expression of a trait. Nevertheless, psychologists have been able to circumvent the problem by taking advantage of an important quirk of nature: multiple births.

Recall that identical twins, also called *monozygotic (MZ) twins*, arise from a single fertilized ovum, called a zygote, that splits into two genetically identical cells. Fraternal twins, or *dizygotic (DZ) twins*, develop from the separate fertilization of two ova. DZ twins are no more alike genetically than any two siblings. Because MZ twins are genetically identical, they should be more similar to one another in terms of their psychological characteristics (such as personality or intelligence) than either DZ twins or non-twin siblings.

**Concordance research**, which examines the degree of similarity in traits expressed between twins, supports this rationale. Twins are *concordant* for a trait if both of them express it or if neither does, and they are *discordant* if only one expresses it. If concordance rates (which can range from 0 to 100 percent) of any given trait are substantially higher for MZ twins than for DZ twins, heredity is likely involved in the expression of that trait. **Table 3•1** compares concordance values between MZ and DZ twins for several traits. When we observe a trait exhibiting a high concordance for MZ twins but a low one for DZ twins, we can conclude that the trait is strongly affected by genetics. This is the case for a trait such as blood type, which has a heritability of 100 percent. If the concordance rates for the two types of twins are similar, the effect of heredity is low. For example, consider the characteristic of religious beliefs. In this case, a high concordance value (that is, both twins having similar beliefs) probably reflects the fact that they acquired their beliefs from their parents. In fact, the concordance rate for religious beliefs of DZ twins is generally just as high as that of MZ twins (Loehlin & Nichols, 1976). Thus, there is no evidence that religious beliefs are inherited.

**concordance research** Research that studies the degree of similarity between twins in traits expressed. Twins are said to be concordant for a trait if either both or neither twin expresses it and discordant if only one twin expresses it.

**TABLE 3•1 Comparison of Concordance Rates between Monozygotic (MZ) and Dizygotic (DZ) Twins for Various Traits**

| | Concordance | |
|---|---|---|
| **Trait** | **MZ** | **DZ** |
| Blood type | 100% | 66% |
| Eye colour | 99 | 28 |
| Mental retardation | 97 | 37 |
| Measles | 95 | 87 |
| Idiopathic epilepsy | 72 | 15 |
| Schizophrenia | 69 | 10 |
| Diabetes | 65 | 18 |
| Identical allergy | 59 | 5 |
| Tuberculosis | 57 | 23 |

*Source: Klug, W. S., & Cummings, M. R. (1986).* Concepts of genetics *(2nd ed.). Glenview, IL: Scott, Foresman.*

Twin studies, and a similar method using adopted individuals, have been used to study a wide range of psychological phenomena. This research has shown that genetic factors affect cognitive abilities such as language ability, mathematical ability, and vocabulary skills; personality traits such as extroversion (the tendency to be outgoing) and emotional stability; personality development; and the occurrence of psychological disorders such as schizophrenia and mental retardation (Bouchard & Propping, 1993). Further evidence for genetic influences on trait expression comes from extensive analyses of twin studies concerning heredity and intelligence (Bouchard & McGue, 1981).

However, we will have the clearest picture of the role of genetics in determining these traits only when we can identify the specific areas of the DNA code that underlie them. To gain this information, behaviour geneticists use the information on concordances to identify a trait that might show

▲ *Research with identical twins has provided psychologists with information about the role of heredity in behavioural traits.*

strong genetic influences. They then examine the segregation of various markers that they believe are close to a suspected gene on its chromosome. Essentially, these markers provide a means of treating a region of the chromosome in a mendelian fashion. Psychologists are especially interested in regions called "quantitative trait loci" that have large influences on a specific psychological characteristic.

Now that the human genome has been mapped, segregation analysis can be combined with detailed knowledge of the nucleotide sequences of a gene. A recent discovery has shown the power of this technique. Lai, Fisher, Hurst, Vargha-Khadem, and Monaco (2001) examined the genetic background of three generations of a family, given the pseudonym *KE*. Some members of the KE family show pronounced language deficits, involving both the processing of word sounds and the use of grammar. One gene on the seventh chromosome, designated with the letters FOXP2, showed a mutation unique to those members of the family with the language disorder. This mutation was not seen in a large sample of individuals unrelated to the KE family who did not possess the KE language disorder. However, another individual afflicted with a similar disorder and tested by Lai and colleagues showed an abnormality in the same gene.

The evidence strongly suggests, then, that a normally functioning FOXP2 gene may be important to language, particularly to the fine muscle movements of the face and mouth that make refined speech possible (Pinker, 2001). But, coupled with our new knowledge of the human genome, an even more startling conclusion is possible. Comparing the map of the human genome to the mouse genome, and to analogous genetic sequences in other primates, Enard and colleagues (2002) found that the FOXP2 gene has apparently changed quite rapidly in the time since humans diverged from the other great apes. Furthermore, using some standard assumptions of the rate at which mutations happen, Enard and colleagues could extrapolate a possible date at which the modern human form of FOXP2 first appeared. Although highly constrained by these assumptions, Enard and colleagues suggest that FOXP2, and its effects on language, developed within the last 200 000 years of human evolution. Later, you will see that this was during the time in which the modern line of *Homo sapiens* made its appearance on the evolutionary stage.

**Allelic Association Studies** The same advances that produced the mapping of the human genome now permit geneticists to identify the alleles present at a particular place along the chromosome. As a consequence, the genotype of an individual can be specified with precision if the location of the gene along the chromosome is known. If the gene also happens to be involved in synthesizing proteins that interact with brain neurochemicals, it is reasonable to look for associations between the different alleles present in the genotype and specific psychological traits. Let us consider a discovery that illustrates this approach.

Earlier, we discussed the variation across individuals in novelty seeking, a characteristic closely related to personality. Psychologists have debated for some time the nature of personality, but considerable data suggest that our personality is closely tied to five factors or dimensions. (Some of this evidence will be discussed in Chapter 14.) These dimensions can be measured with high reliability and show stability across an individual's life. Novelty seeking seems to be related to two of these dimensions: a high degree of *extroversion* and a low degree of *conscientiousness*. Twin studies have shown that these two dimensions have moderate heritability (about 40 to 60 percent). This would suggest a genetic mechanism contributing to novelty seeking.

Novelty seeking also seems to be related, pharmacologically, to the chemical dopamine. The gene D4DR not only contains instructions for the synthesis of proteins that react to dopamine but also is active in those areas of the brain that concern emotion and thinking. Consequently, D4DR seems like a gene that might possibly influence novelty seeking.

This hypothesis was supported by two studies that looked at the association between two alleles of D4DR and scores from psychological tests for novelty seeking. Both Ebstein and colleagues (1996) and Benjamin and colleagues (1996) found that the presence of one allele was associated with high novelty-seeking scores.

Yet, if D4DR is a "novelty-seeking gene," its effect is small and the trait itself is likely polygenetic. Wahlsten (1999) reviewed 10 allelic association studies involving D4DR and found that, collectively, they barely showed a significant effect. At best, the gene seems to influence about 3 to 4 percent of the total variability in novelty-seeking scores—about a tenth of the total genetic variation. If the balance of the variation were controlled by genes with similar effects, there would be about 10 genes that control this trait.

It is important to stress the relatively small amount of variance controlled by this gene. If the estimate of 10 genes is correct, then the contribution of any one gene to the trait we have labelled "novelty seeking" is small. The effects of these genes may be moderated by as yet unknown variables (Kluger, Siegfried, & Ebstein, 2002). And together, these genes determine only about half of the normal variation in this trait seen in individuals. Furthermore, this estimate applies only to the specific environment in which these individuals develop, and it is subject to the qualifications we mentioned in Chapter 2 when discussing the validity of concepts such as novelty seeking. We must recognize that genetic analysis is just one tool in a more complete understanding of behaviour. As investigation of such socially significant traits as intelligence becomes more refined (Plomin et al., 1994), we must avoid simplistic thinking about the role of heredity and human psychology and be mindful of the ethical implications (see Harper, 1995, for one laboratory's response to these issues).

Failure to do so can lead to disastrous results. In the late 1920s, for example, the Alberta government, in an attempt to control the genetic transmission of traits it deemed undesirable, authorized the sterilization of people with various psychological difficulties. The tragic consequences of this political venture into genetic engineering (described by Wahlsten, 1997a) hold an important lesson for us all.

## Then and Now

### The Central Dogma and Epigenetics

When Watson and Crick published their description of the DNA molecule in 1953, it seemed to provide a direct, although complicated, explanation for the way in which genes determined the biology of the individual. The genetic code was contained in the sequences of the four nucleotides. A particular sequence determined the amino acid that would be used to synthesize a given protein. The amount of particular proteins synthesized according to a cell's DNA might be regulated by other chemicals in the cell's environment (so that, for example, hair cells might produce a different colouring pigment than do skin cells), but the inherited information from one cell to another was determined by the sequence of nucleotides (see Figure 3.3 on page 64). This description of inheritance from one cell to its descendants was such a useful conceptual framework that it has been called the "central dogma of molecular biology" (Crick, 1970). However, like much of science, subsequent discoveries have suggested that it may need to be revised.

One possible exception is apparent from simply looking around you. Although men and women have obvious differences, the sexes are otherwise pretty similar. Yet, as we saw earlier (see Figure 3.4 on page 66), women have two copies of the X chromosome, while men have only one. Since the X chromosome is larger and has many more genes than the Y, it would be expected that women would produce more of the proteins controlled by X chromosome genes. Yet, this does not occur. Through a process known as *X chromosome inactivation*, one of the X chromosomes is "silenced" shortly after fertilization so that its genes do not produce the proteins it normally would. This means that, although a woman receives an X chromosome from her mother and another from her father, only one of these is active. (Which one is largely a matter of chance.) Furthermore, each cell passes along the inactivation to the next generation of cells, so that all cells in an adult woman reflect the silencing that occurred early in life. Interestingly, a woman's germ cells reactivate the silenced chromosome, so that a woman can pass along, say, her father's X chromosome—even if it was silenced in her.

Inactivation occurs because the proteins that surround the DNA molecule undergo complex chemical changes that condense the protein structure and make the DNA contained within it non-functional (Brockdorff & Turner, 2007). These changes persist through cell divisions, condensing the same part of the chromosome in the descendant cells and passing along the inactivation. In this way, a molecular change early in the life of a woman affects all the cells that develop thereafter, despite the fact that the DNA code itself has not changed.

X chromosome inactivation is one example of an **epigenetic modification**, a modification of cell inheritance that is not due to alterations of the DNA sequence itself. Biologists have identified a number of possible epigenetic mechanisms, some of which could revolutionize the central dogma of molecular biology. We'll look at two.

*Paramutations* are heritable changes in an organism due to the expression of an allele that is no longer present (Chandler, 2007). One example of a paramutation concerns a gene known as KIT that determines part of the coat colouring of mice. Homozygous mice with two copies of the normal allele show brown coats; those that are heterozygous, possessing one normal and one special mutant allele, show tails and feet that are white. However, the offspring of a heterozygous mouse will show white tails and feet, even if they are homozygous with the normal allele. (See **Figure 3•7**, and compare it with Figure 3.5 on page 67.) Somehow, even though the mutant allele for white colouring is no longer present in the DNA of the offspring, it still affects their coat colour (Rassoulzadegan et al., 2006).

*Prions* are proteins whose geometric structure is altered in such a way that they cause other proteins to adopt the altered shape. Through a process of chain reaction, the shape of a prion is self-perpetuating. A cell that contains prions will, when it replicates, pass those prions along to descendants. Prions are thought to be the root cause of a brain-wasting disease known as Creutzfeldt-Jakob disease. There has been some speculation that Creutzfeldt-Jakob disease can be acquired when one ingests food containing specific prions.

The study of epigenetics has the potential to change much of our thinking regarding the way that genetics and the environment interact to determine behaviour. One

**epigenetic modifications** Changes in cell inheritance that are not due to alterations in the sequence of DNA nucleotides.

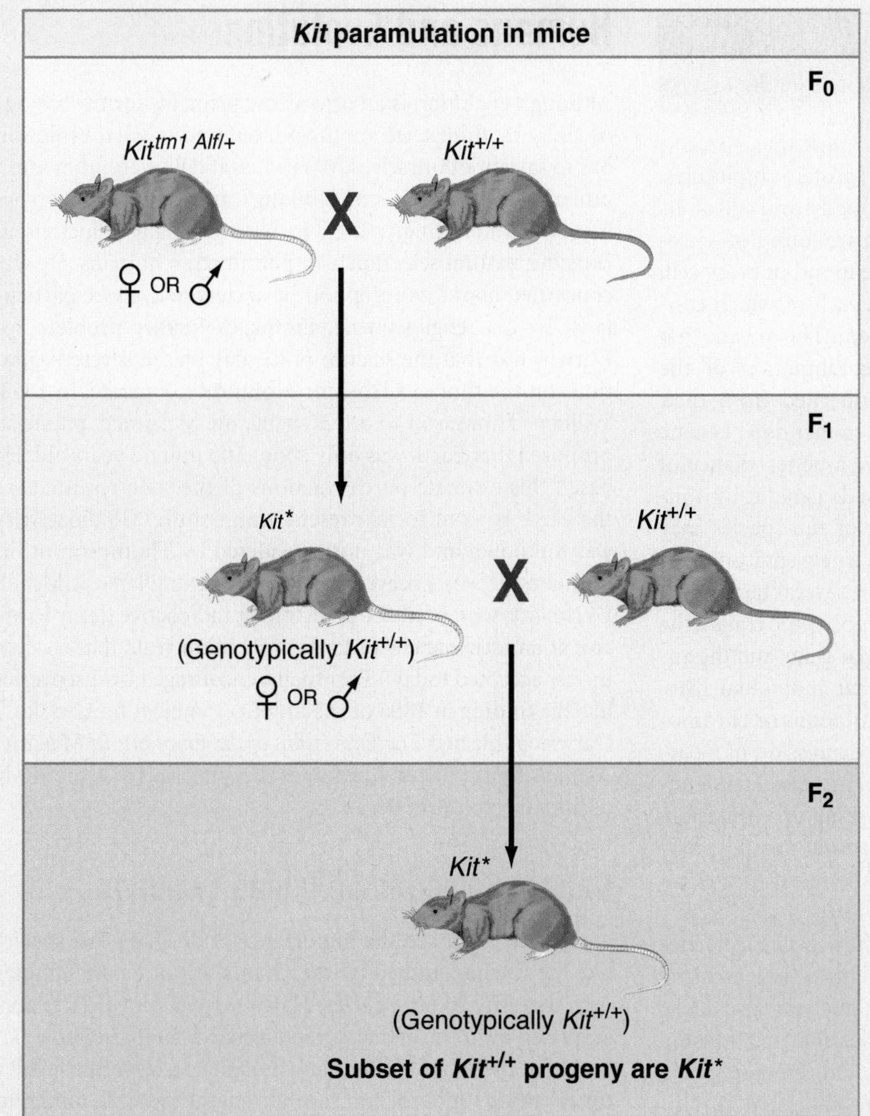


**FIGURE 3•7** Paramutation in mice. The top row shows a mouse on the right that is homozygous for the normal allele ("+"). The mouse on the left is heterozygous with a normal and a mutant allele ("tm1Alf"). Many offspring which are homozygous normal and genetically like the +/+ parent show the colouring of the other (designated here as Kit*). This colouring can also be transmitted to offspring, but the frequency of this phenotype decreases with each generation.
*(Reprinted from* Cell, *128(4), Chandler, V. L., Paramutation: From maize to mouse, 641–645, (2007) with permission from Elsevier. http://www.sciencedirect.com/science/journal/00928674)*

important influence of experience is on learning and memory, topics that we will discuss in Chapters 7 and 8. There has been considerable speculation that, at the molecular level, memories are maintained by different proteins (Hunter, 2008). Si, Lindquist, and Kandel (2004) have suggested that one protein involved in the maintenance of memories may be a prion, which would link an epigenetic effect to a very important psychological process. Later, in Chapter 12, we will discuss the effects of early parental care on the way an individual develops as an adult. Weaver and colleagues (2005) have shown that the reaction of adult rats to stress can be affected by the type of maternal care they received as pups, and that this relationship is due to epigenetic changes that can even be reversed.

An important, but controversial, question is whether epigenetic modifications caused by experience could be inherited from one individual to another. Paramutations suggest that such a possibility could exist, although they themselves are not triggered by environmental events. A tantalizing report of a possible *transgenerational* epigenetic modification was made by Pembrey and colleagues (2006), who examined the health records of several generations of people in an isolated region of Sweden. They found that the health of one's paternal grandparent could affect the health of a grandchild. Paternal grandfathers who ate plenty of food during their late childhood had grandsons with a higher rate of mortality; similarly, paternal grandmothers who ate well as children had granddaughters with higher rates of mortality. But there was no association with one's *maternal* grandparents, implying a sex-linked effect.

Modern evolutionary theory proposes that acquired characteristics cannot be inherited. If the new field of epigenetics were to show this claim to be false, then much of evolutionary biology would have to be reconsidered. Regardless, knowledge of epigenetics has helped shape our understanding of heredity.

## Interim Summary

### Heredity and Genetics

The instructions for the synthesis of protein molecules, which oversee the development of the body and all of its processes, are contained in genes. Genes are found on chromosomes, which consist of DNA and are found in every cell. We inherit 23 individual chromosomes, each of which contains thousands of genes, from each parent. This means that our genetic blueprint represents a recombination of the genetic instructions that our parents inherited from their parents. Such recombination makes for tremendous genetic diversity. Genetically diverse species have a better chance of adapting to a changing environment than do genetically non-diverse species because some members of the species may have genes that enable them to survive in a new environment.

The expression of a gene depends on several factors, including its interaction with other genes (polygenic traits), the sex of the individual carrying the particular gene, and the environmental conditions under which that individual lives. Changes in genetic material caused by mutations or chromosomal aberrations lead to changes in the expression of a particular gene. For example, hemophilia, an increased tendency to bleed from even minor injuries, is the result of a mutation; and Down syndrome, which involves impaired mental, physical, and psychomotor development, is the result of a chromosomal aberration.

Behaviour genetics is the study of how genes influence behaviour. Psychologists and other scientists use artificial selection studies of animals, segregation analysis, and allelic association studies to investigate the possible relationship between genes and behaviour in humans. One emerging field of research is epigenetics, which examines inherited modifications that do not involve changes in the genetic code. X chromosome inactivation, paramutations, and prion self-replication are examples of epigenetic changes.

#### QUESTIONS TO CONSIDER

1. How would you explain the fact that you might have blue eyes but your sister has brown eyes?
2. In scientific terms, what does it mean to say that there is a gene for shyness?
3. How might the gene related to the development of athletic ability interact with environmental variables to produce a specific phenotype (for example, a specific level of athletic ability in a specific individual)?
4. How would you design a study to assess the genetic basis of human aggression? Could you use more than one approach to gathering this information, and, if so, what would these other approaches entail?

# Humans and Evolution

Although evolution is an organizing principle for the biology of all living things, we are most interested in what evolution has to say about ourselves. What does it tell us about modern humans (*Homo sapiens*, or thinking human) and our own behaviour? Interestingly, Darwin was originally reluctant to consider natural selection as it pertained to humans. He was concerned about its reception by society and, more particularly, by his religious wife, Emma. A further problem for Darwin was that the science of his day placed severe limitations on the time available for evolution to operate. In 1858, William Thompson (Lord Kelvin), an acclaimed physicist, proposed that Earth was only about 100 million years old. He based this estimate on calculations of the time required for the earth to cool to its present temperature. (Radioactivity was unknown and was not considered by Thompson in his estimates. It was Ernest Rutherford, working later at McGill University, who used the principle of radioactive decay to arrive at an estimate closer to the 4.5 billion years that is commonly accepted today.) Eventually, encouraged by discoveries like the finding in 1856 of the first truly ancient human skull, Darwin published *The Expression of the Emotions in Man and Animals*. With the publication of this book in 1872, the study of human evolution began.

## Natural Selection in Human Evolution

Earlier, we discussed the importance of diversity to a species like the finches studied by the Grants. All of us are familiar with diversity in our species, *Homo sapiens*. However, it may surprise you to hear that some paleoarchaeologists now believe that there have been many human species in the history of evolution. Indeed, for several lengthy periods, different hominids have inhabited the same geographical areas (Tattersall, 2000). Not only did our species evolve over time, but as the only surviving descendant of the hominid line, we must have been competitively superior to other possible human species.

This fact raises the obvious question as to what made our particular evolutionary line so successful. There is not a single answer to this, since human evolution occurred across a large span of different times and conditions and may have included fortuitous events such as ice ages and volcanic catastrophes to our hominid competitors. However, a short overview of our own evolutionary history provides some interesting clues about the characteristics that defined us as a unique species.

Although it is unclear when our ancestral branch of evolution diverged from the other great apes, there are indications that an early hominid, named *Ardipithecus ramidus*, might have lived about 4.4 million years ago in Africa (Tattersall, 1997). It is unclear how human this creature really was, but two later species, *Australopithecus anamensis* and

*Australopithecus afarensis*, were clearly like us, in that they both exhibited **bipedalism**, the ability to walk upright on two feet. The fossilized remains of a female individual of the latter species, from about 3.8 to 3 million years ago, shows that our ancestors hedged their bets somewhat, since her body structure still shows signs of an ape-like ability to climb trees.

Evidence of early humans is rare and difficult to interpret. Accordingly, there are different viewpoints about what the fossil evidence tells us. However, one viewpoint supported by statistical evidence (Strait, Grine, & Moniz, 1997) is that over the period from 3 to 2 million years ago, the hominid line split in two. The African environment may have turned drier, altering sources of food. One line of hominids evolved into a genus with powerful jaws that could crush and chew plants and nuts. They comprise the genus *Paranthropus*. (See **Figure 3•8**.) The other line continued from *Australopithecus*. However, by about 2.5 to 1.8 million years ago, two very distinct new species, *Homo rudolfensis* and *Homo habilis*, had evolved from this line and were sufficiently different to be designated as members of a new genus, *Homo*.

The name of the latter species, *Homo habilis*, means "handy man" and was chosen because this species is thought to be the originator of the many stone tools found at *H. habilis* sites.

If these stone tools were indeed created by *Homo habilis*, then the species had a marked advantage. You will note in Figure 3.8 that, at about that time, there were at least four hominid species living in East Africa. The ability to make and use tools would have been a significant advantage in competing for food. Hominid skull fossils from this time show a marked **encephalization**, an increase in the size of the brain. Bigger brains require more metabolic energy (Aiello & Wheeler, 1995). Using tools to extract more calories from their environment would certainly have helped the first hominid species to discover Stone Age technology.

Archaeologists, however, still dispute the specific way that tool use altered hominid life (Mithen, 1996). It is possible that tool use was associated with a specific "home base" used by groups of early humans not only to share food but also to raise their children. Alternatively, it may be that early humans could only scavenge meals opportunistically and thus carried their tools with them.

Hominids apparently left their African home about 1.8 million years ago. One species, *Homo erectus*, has been discovered as far away from Africa as Java and China. Tool use was highly developed by these individuals, but it reflected a certain kind of technology. Tools were fashioned by chipping small flakes from a larger stone until the stone looked like a hand axe or other implement. However, 600 000 years ago in Africa, a new species, *Homo heidelbergensis*, apparently developed a different approach. These human ancestors built stone tools in a more planned way: the core of the stone was prepared so that a single well-directed blow would detach the finished tool.

**FIGURE 3•8** A reconstruction of the evolutionary history of hominid species. To construct a possible family tree, paleoarchaeologists examine fossil characteristics to determine similarities between species. Once the grouping of species is established, the age of the fossils can suggest a chronology. Reconstructions like this one, however, are speculative, because fossils are fragmentary and difficult to compare directly. *(From Tattersall, I. (2000, January). Once we were not alone.* Scientific American, *282, p. 60. Reprinted with permission.)*

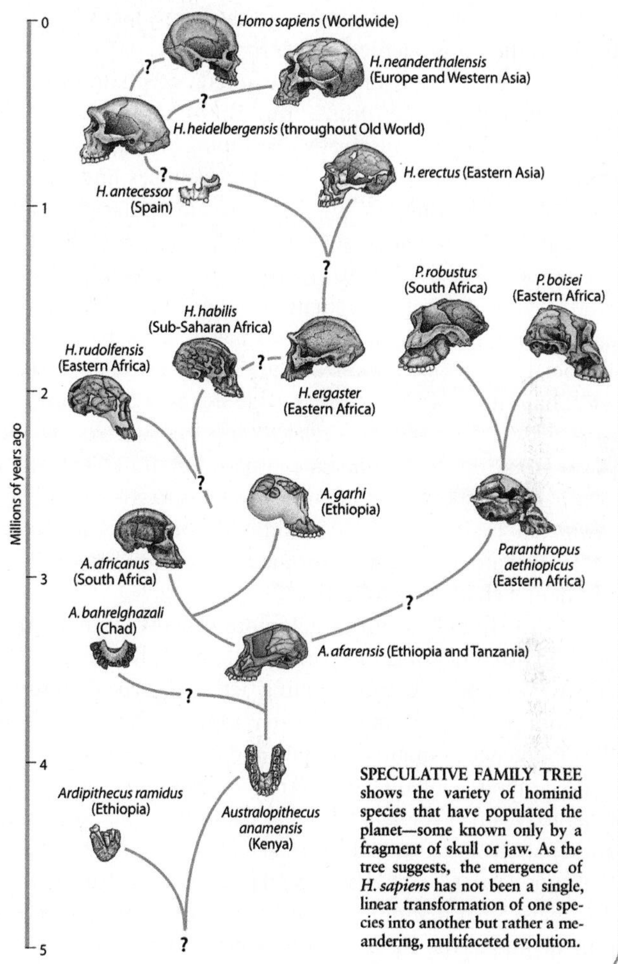


The last two major hominid groups apparently evolved from *heidelbergensis*. They were *Homo neanderthalensis*, the so-called Neanderthals, and us, *Homo sapiens*. The evidence currently suggests that our species originated in Africa about 150 000 to 200 000 years ago. If so, we shared our environment with Neanderthals for a considerable time. What is clear, though, is that the *Homo sapiens* line has survived to flourish in all parts of the world, despite the presence of hostile climates, terrains, and predators.

The remarkable success of our species in adapting to a variety of ecological niches stems from the fact that natural

**bipedalism** The ability to move about the environment upright on two feet.
**encephalization** An increase in brain size.

selection has favoured two important human characteristics we have already noted: bipedalism and encephalization. The ability to walk upright not only allowed greater mobility but also freed the hands for grabbing, holding, and throwing objects. The ability to grasp objects, in combination with an expanding capacity for learning and remembering new skills provided by a larger brain, led to advances in tool making, food gathering, hunting, and escaping predators. Humans who were able to fashion and use tools for hunting and self-defence lived longer and enjoyed greater reproductive success than did their less talented counterparts.

The selective pressures that favoured encephalization are less apparent. For example, the *Paranthropus* hominids adapted to drier conditions by developing stronger jaws and teeth so that they could add woody vegetables and nuts to their diet. Why did our ancestors develop a larger brain? Dunbar (1993) has suggested the intriguing possibility that *Homo* species evolved in an environment that favoured large groups. Large groups can remain together only if the individuals within them can remember the small nuances that underlie all social interactions. Dunbar found that, among primates, encephalization was correlated with the typical size of the species' social group. The relationship he observed would predict that modern humans can naturally function with a group size of about 148 individuals. Our ancestors may have competed better than other hominids because our larger brains initially helped us coordinate socially and meet environmental challenges collectively.

As the brain became larger, more of its volume became devoted to functions that organized social life more efficiently. Memorizing and recalling actions, such as hunting and tool production, may have developed early, followed by the emergence of linguistic ability and the capacity to manipulate symbols (Donald, 1993). Another important ability that emerged from encephalization was planning—the capacity to anticipate future events and to take into account the effects that those events might have on an individual or group of individuals. Such planning might have involved the organization of hunts, the institution of social customs and events (such as weddings and funerals), and the planting and harvesting of crops. Over time, the interaction of bipedalism and encephalization permitted humans to exploit new environments and establish well-organized communities.

Advances in tool making and hunting, combined with the use of fire for cooking, protection, and warmth, were adaptive; they helped humans live longer. The increased lifespan of humans may have aided the gradual accumulation of wisdom as the older members of early human communities began to share their knowledge with younger members through language. Although the fossil record cannot tell us when language first developed, we can be sure that those who were able to communicate with others through language had a distinct advantage over those who could not.

Language originated and subsequently evolved because of its immensely adaptive significance. As Skinner (1986) noted, language provided not only a simple means of warning others of danger, but also a means of communicating important information to others, such as the location of a good hunting spot or instructions on how to craft a tool. But perhaps the most important advantage conferred by language was its ability to reinforce the already strong social tendencies of early humans. Dunbar (1993) has made this point, suggesting that conversation ultimately replaced the typical grooming behaviour of primates as a more efficient way to reinforce social bonds. If so, this ability to converse may have ultimately led to the development and transmission of cultural traditions.

*Homo neanderthalensis* was a successful species that became extinct only 25 000 years ago, with evidence of its last settlements in southern Spain near Gibraltar (Finlayson et al., 2006). Our species, *Homo sapiens,* has thus far survived for about 200 000 years. For perhaps 10 000 of those years, we as a species overlapped with *Homo neanderthalensis* in southern Europe (Grine et al., 2007). It is a matter of debate whether interbreeding occurred between our species and *Homo neanderthalensis* (Noonan et al., 2006; Pennisi, 2007). Interestingly, there is little evidence that our last major rivals, the Neanderthals, developed much of a cultural tradition, especially one involving symbolic representations based on art (Tattersall, 2000). If this is the case, it may have been culture rather than physical endurance or strength that tipped our species' competition with the Neanderthals to our benefit.

As cultures continued evolving, humans gained an increasing ability to control and modify their environment. The same intellectual resourcefulness that permitted early humans to discover and use fire and to invent useful tools prompted the agricultural revolution of 10 000 years ago, the Industrial Revolution of 150 years ago, and the technological revolution that began only 50 years ago with the invention of the transistor, the integrated circuit, and the computer. **Cultural evolution**, or the adaptive changes of cultures in response to changes in the environment over time, is possible only because humans have been genetically endowed with a capacity for learning and language. As cultural anthropologist Marvin Harris (1991, p. 27) has noted, our capacity for learning has evolved because (1) it leads to "a more flexible and rapid method of achieving reproductive success" and (2) it allows entire groups of people to "adjust or take advantage of novel opportunities in a single generation without having to wait for the appearance and spread of genetic mutations." For example, advances in medicine have allowed us to control life-threatening diseases such as polio, smallpox, malaria, tetanus, typhoid fever, and diphtheria. It would take hundreds of thousands of years, maybe even millions, to evolve immunities to these diseases. Let's not forget, though, that cultural evolution is a mixed blessing. With it has come pollution, many social ills and injustices (for example, racism), and overpopulation.

**cultural evolution** The adaptive changes of cultures in response to environmental changes over time.

▲ *Cultural evolution includes the development of specific kinds of tools to accomplish specific tasks such as cutting, producing steel, and processing and storing complex information.*

## Sociobiology

**Sociobiology** is the study of the genetic basis of social behaviour. Sociobiology synthesizes research findings from many other fields of science, including those from evolutionary psychology and behaviour genetics. (Evolutionary psychology and behaviour genetics are broader fields than sociobiology in the sense that both are concerned with other phenomena, such as intelligence and cognition, in addition to social behaviour.) Sociobiologists are especially interested in understanding the evolutionary roots of our modern-day social actions. More often than not, sociobiologists study the evolutionary bases of social behaviour in non-human animals and then extrapolate from those species to humans. Sociobiology represents an interface between the biological sciences and psychology. However, not all psychologists are ardent supporters of sociobiology. As we will see, some think that sociobiology is too simplistic and that its emphasis on genetics inadequately explains the complexities of human behaviour.

**Reproductive Strategies and the Biological Basis of Parenting** Reproduction and parenting are among the most important social behaviours related to the survival of a species. Indeed, a focal point of sociobiological research and theory has been understanding more about the different kinds of social organization that result from particular **reproductive strategies**—systems of mating and rearing offspring.

| | | Male partner: One | Male partner: Multiple |
|---|---|---|---|
| Female partner | One | Monogamy | Polyandry |
| | Multiple | Polygyny | Polygynandry |

**FIGURE 3•9** Reproductive strategies. Different numbers of males mating with different numbers of females yields the four reproductive strategies of monogamy, polygyny, polyandry, and polygynandry.

You are likely quite accustomed to thinking about sex and family in terms of **monogamy**: the mating of one female and one male. If mating is successful, the individuals share in the raising of the child or children. However, monogamy is just one of several reproductive strategies that sexual creatures employ in mating and rearing offspring (Barash, 1982). Three other major classes of reproductive strategy are also possible. (See **Figure 3•9**.) **Polygyny** involves one male mating with more than one female; **polyandry** involves one female mating with more than one male; and **polygynandry** involves several females mating with several males.

According to Trivers (1972), these four reproductive strategies evolved because of important sex differences in the resources that parents invest in conceiving and rearing their offspring. **Parental investment** is the time, physical effort, and risks to life involved in procreation and in the feeding, nurturing, and protecting of offspring. Parental investment is a critical factor in mate selection. An individual who is willing and able to make a greater investment is generally more sought after as a mate and is often more selective or discriminating when selecting a mate (Trivers, 1972).

In some species, competition for mates leads to **sexual selection**—selection for traits specific to sex, such as body size or particular patterns of behaviour. For example, in some animals, such as buffalo, females select mates based on the male's ability to survive the skirmishes of the rutting (mating) season. In general, the larger and more aggressive males win these battles and gain access to more females and enjoy greater reproductive success.

**sociobiology** The study of the genetic bases of social behaviour.
**reproductive strategies** Different systems of mating and rearing offspring. These include monogamy, polygyny, polyandry, and polygynandry.
**monogamy** The mating of one female and one male.
**polygyny** The mating of one male with more than one female.
**polyandry** The mating of one female with more than one male.
**polygynandry** The mating of several females with several males.
**parental investment** The resources, including time, physical effort, and risks to life that a parent spends in procreation and in the feeding, nurturing, and protecting of offspring.
**sexual selection** Selection for traits specific to sex, such as body size or particular patterns of behaviour.

Among humans, polygyny is by far the most common reproductive strategy. In fact, 84 percent of human societies practise polygyny or allow men who are either wealthy or powerful to practise it (Badcock, 1991). Monogamy is the next most popular reproductive strategy, with about 15 percent of all human cultures practising it. Polyandry and polygynandry are both rare. Combined, these two reproductive strategies dominate in less than 1 percent of all human cultures.

Let us now consider each reproductive strategy individually, beginning with polygyny.

**Polygyny: High Female and Low Male Parental Investment** In many species, the female makes the greater parental investment. For example, in most mammals (including humans), there can be little doubt that the costs associated with reproduction are higher for females than for males. First, females have fewer opportunities than males to reproduce. Generally, females produce only one ovum or a few ova periodically, whereas males produce vast quantities of sperm over substantially shorter time intervals. Second, females carry the fertilized ovum in their bodies during a long gestation period, continuously diverting a major portion of their own metabolic resources to nourish the rapidly growing fetus. Females also assume all of the risks that accompany pregnancy and childbirth, including physical discomfort and possible death. The male's contributions to reproduction are, at a minimum, the sperm and the time needed for intercourse. Third, after the offspring is born, females may continue to devote some of their metabolic resources to the infant by nursing it. Just as important, they usually devote more time and physical energy than males to caring for the newborn.

In addition, a female can bear only a certain number of offspring in a lifetime, regardless of the number of males with whom she mates. In contrast, a male is limited in his reproductive success only by the number of females he can impregnate. For example, consider the differences between females and males in our species. If a woman became pregnant once a year for 10 years, she would have 10 children—only a fraction of the number of children a man is capable of fathering over the same interval. Suppose that a man impregnated a different woman every month for 10 years—he would have fathered 120 children. This example is hardly an exaggeration. According to the *Guinness Book of World Records* (Young, 1998), the largest number of live births to one woman is 69 (she had several multiple births). In contrast, King Ismail of Morocco is reported to have fathered 1056 children.

Because females in polygynous species invest so heavily in their offspring, they are usually highly selective of their mates, choosing to mate with only those males who possess specific attributes, such as physical size, strength, and aggressiveness. Such selectivity makes adaptive sense for both her and her progeny. After all, bearing the offspring of the victor means that her male offspring will tend to possess the same adaptively significant attributes as their father and thus be more likely to win their own quests for mating privileges. As a result, genes for large size, increased strength, and aggressiveness will continue to have greater representation in future generations than will genes for less adaptive attributes.

▲ *Large male elephant seals are more successful in competing for females than are smaller males. But is there a point at which larger size could become maladaptive?*

However, sexual selection may reach a point of diminishing returns. Consider the elephant seal. Male elephant seals have evolved to be several times larger than female elephant seals. The largest males almost always win mating privileges—with up to several dozen females. But growing to the point at which the male's mobility while foraging for food and fighting is impaired is maladaptive. An overly large male will be unable to find ample food to sustain his size and will be unlikely to win contests with leaner and more agile competitors. Thus, the male's adaptive attributes are kept in check by the costs of getting too large.

**Monogamy: Shared, but Not Always Equal, Parental Investment** Monogamy is common in species whose environments have favoured the contributions of both parents to the survival and reproductive success of their offspring. In these environments, two individuals sharing parental duties enjoy more reproductive success than does one individual who must do it all alone. For example, foxes must provide food, milk, and protection for their offspring. A single fox attempting to fulfill these responsibilities puts the pups at risk. Hunting for food would be difficult with the pups straggling along. However, leaving the pups in the den would put them at risk of predation and wandering off. The reproductive strategy exhibited by foxes is that both parents hunt and protect the cubs. By committing themselves to the joint care of their pups, both male and female foxes enhance the chance that their offspring will survive and reproduce.

Although both parents in monogamous species share offspring-rearing duties, each parent may not make an equal contribution toward that end. Like females in polygynous species, females in monogamous species generally have greater parental investment in the offspring, for many of the same reasons: the limited opportunity for mating relative to that for males, pregnancy and its accompanying risks, providing food to the newborns, and the time and energy spent in caring for them. As a result, very few monogamous species, including our own, are exclusively monogamous. In fact, there is a strong tendency in most monogamous species toward patterns of reproductive behaviour and parental investment that resemble those of polygynous species (Badcock, 1991; Shackelford & Weekes-Shackelford, 2004).

In our evolutionary past, those females who carefully selected their mates produced more offspring than did those who were less choosy. Males who successfully mated with a number of females produced more offspring than did males who mated with fewer females. From a sociobiological perspective, females tend to be more interested in the quality of their offspring, which, of course, leads females to be selective about the quality of the father and the kinds of resources he brings to the relationship. In contrast, males tend to be more interested in the sheer number of matings.

However, keep in mind that human sexual behaviour, although a product of natural selection, is subject to strong cultural influences, which explains why monogamy might be the dominant reproductive strategy in some cultures. Remember, too, that we tend to think of reproductive success today not in terms of the mere number of children we have, but in terms of raising healthy, happy, and well-adjusted children. Although most people have the biological capacity to produce a large number of children, many do not have the psychological or financial wherewithal to do so.

**Polyandry: High Male and Low Female Parental Investment** Polyandry is a rare reproductive strategy among humans and non-existent in other mammals. An example of polyandry in humans is found among some of the people who live in remote Himalayan villages. These people live in a harsh environment on land that is only marginally arable. Custom decrees that farmland is inherited through the paternal side of the family. To prevent the dissolution of family farms through marriage, families that have more than one son limit the number of marriages to only one per generation—several brothers may share the same wife. A female tends to marry more than one man (most often brothers) to guarantee that she will be adequately supported. The male's notable contribution to the success of reproduction—the farm, which is the source of food and some income for the family—is protected through polyandry.

**Polygynandry: Group Parental Investment** Many primates, such as chimpanzees, live in colonies in which few or no barriers are placed on which female mates with which male. In other words, the colonies are promiscuous—during periods of mating, intercourse is frequent and indiscriminate. What is the advantage of such a reproductive strategy?

The primary advantage seems to be the co-operation of males and females in the colony with respect to rearing offspring. Because the males in the colony are not sure which offspring belong to them, it is in their best interest to help rear and protect all offspring and defend their mothers. The unity in the colony and the lack of aggression among the males contribute directly to the general welfare of all colony members. Females and males have access to many mates, and the offspring are well cared for.

▲ *Although extremely rare, if not non-existent in Western cultures, polyandry is practised in some Eastern cultures. Shown here is a Nepalese wedding ceremony in which two men are being married to the same woman.*

This type of mating system is seen in other species, too, such as the Smith's longspur—a medium-sized bird found in the subarctic tundra. Female longspurs copulate with several males during the mating season, and males mate with several females. The clutch of eggs that results contains genetic material from several males. Briskie, Montgomerie, Põldmaa, and Boag (1998) looked at the parental care that males subsequently provided to the fledglings. In general, males tended to provide more care to nests where they had more offspring, but, regardless, did not discriminate among the young within a nest. Indeed, when a male was the sole supporter of a nest, his response was not related to the number of offspring that were his exclusively.

**The Biological Basis of Altruism** Sociobiologists attempt to explain social behaviours other than reproduction and parenting. A particularly interesting and important social behaviour central to sociobiological theory is **altruism**, the unselfish concern of one individual for the welfare of another. Examples of altruistic behaviour abound in our culture, and in their most extreme form are represented when one person risks his or her life to save the life of another. Remember David from the opening vignette? He nursed and cared for the injured Martin after their plane crashed, ultimately dying before help arrived to rescue Martin. Examples of altruism are not limited to our species. In fact, they are common throughout the animal kingdom. Consider, for example, the honeybee that sacrifices its life on behalf of its hive mates by stinging an intruder, or the prairie dog that gives an alarm call that warns other prairie dogs of the predator but increases its own chances of being captured. In each case, the altruist's chances of survival and reproductive success are lowered while those of the other individuals are raised. Examples of altruism are therefore problematic for models of social behaviour, such as sociobiology, that are based on the process of natural selection.

**altruism** The unselfish concern of one individual for the welfare of another.

**Kin Selection** The difficulty that altruism poses for sociobiology is that natural selection operates to select individuals. Recall that natural selection favours only those phenotypes that enhance one's reproductive success. How could altruistic behaviour have evolved given that, by definition, it is less adaptive than selfish or competitive behaviour?

Geneticist William D. Hamilton (1964, 1970) suggested an answer to this question in a series of mathematical papers. Hamilton's insights stemmed from examining natural selection from the perspective of the genotype instead of from the perspective of the whole, living organism. He argued that natural selection does not favour mere reproductive success but rather **inclusive fitness**, or the reproductive success of those individuals who share many of the same genes. Altruistic acts are generally aimed at close relatives such as parents, siblings, grandparents, and grandchildren. The closer the family relation is, the more likely the genetic similarity among the individuals involved. Such biologic favouritism toward relatives is called **kin selection** (Mayr, 2001).

The message here is clear: Under the proper circumstances, individuals behave altruistically toward others with whom they share a genetic history, with the willingness to do so decreasing as the relative becomes more distant. In this view, altruism is not necessarily a conscious act but rather an act driven by a biological prompt that has been favoured by natural selection. Natural selection would favour this kind of altruism simply because organisms who share genes also help each other survive.

Parenting is a special case of kin selection and an important contributor to one's survival and reproductive success. In the short run, parents' altruistic actions promote the continued survival of their offspring. In the long run, these actions increase the likelihood that the offspring, too, will become parents and that their genes will survive in successive generations. Such cycles continue according to biological schedule, generation after generation. In the words of sociobiologist David Barash (1982, pp. 69–70),

> It is obvious why genes for parenting have been selected: All living things are the offspring of parents who themselves were parents! It is a guaranteed, unbroken line stretching back into time. [Genes] that inclined their bearers to be less successful parents left fewer copies of themselves than did those [genes] that were more successful.

At stake, of course, is not the survival of individual organisms but the survival of the genes carried by those organisms. Hamilton's insightful contribution to sociobiological theory was to show that altruistic behaviour has a genetically selfish basis. In other words, genes allow organisms to maximize their inclusive fitness through altruistic behaviour directed at other organisms sharing the same genes (Dawkins, 1986). You carry copies of genes that have been in your family line for thousands of years. When the opportunity presents itself, you will most likely carry on the tradition—reproducing and thus projecting your biological endowment into yet another generation. But you did not reach sexual maturity on your own; the concern for your welfare by your parents, brothers, sisters, grandparents, and perhaps an aunt or uncle has contributed to your chances of being reproductively successful. Genes not projected into the next generation simply disappear.

**Reciprocal Altruism** Kin selection explains altruism toward relatives, but what about altruism directed toward nonrelatives? What about the kind of altruism that David Pisurayak Kootook showed to the injured pilot? Do sociobiologists have an explanation for a person's altruistic actions toward a non-relative? According to Trivers (1971), the answer is yes. This kind of altruism, called **reciprocal altruism**, is the expression of a crude biological version of the golden rule.

Reciprocal altruism can be adaptive, and hence promoted by natural selection, if it increases the chances that altruistic behaviour will be reciprocated. In other words, if you do something altruistic toward someone else, that person is likely to return the favour should he or she be in such a position to do so in the future.

Generally speaking, certain conditions must be satisfied before such reciprocity is likely. First, giving aid must carry with it a low risk to the altruist but a high benefit for the recipient. In other words, altruists behave as if they have calculated a cost–benefit ratio for their action: The lower the cost to themselves and the greater the benefit for others, the more likely the altruistic act. Second, there must be a good chance that the situation could be reversed. If the altruist is not likely ever to benefit from similar action on the part of the original recipient, the chances of altruism are lowered. Third, the recipient must be able to recognize the altruist. We are more likely to render assistance to people with whom we are most familiar.

## Evaluation of Sociobiology

Sociobiology has had its critics, both friendly and hostile. I have no way of knowing how you feel about sociobiology, but you may have been struck by two aspects in the evidence I've presented. First, you may have noticed that many of the explanations of sociobiology involve behaviours that are very broadly defined, such as "mating strategies." Second, you probably felt that the account I've presented switched pretty freely between examples of behaviour of humans and that of other animals.

Evolutionary psychologists, who are generally sympathetic to sociobiology, approach the first of these issues by trying to identify more particular aspects of psychological processes. For example, Daly and Wilson (2001) analyze some sex differences in behaviour in terms of the psychological mechanisms that allow us to evaluate decisions involving

**inclusive fitness** The reproductive success of those who share common genes.

**kin selection** A type of selection that favours altruistic acts aimed at individuals who share some of the altruist's genes, such as parents, siblings, grandparents, grandchildren, and, under certain conditions, distant relatives.

**reciprocal altruism** Altruism in which people behave altruistically toward one another because they are confident that such acts will be reciprocated toward either them or their kin.

risk. The intraspecific competition of males may relate to mechanisms that cause them to evaluate future gains and losses differently than do females. This approach has the advantage that behaviour may be more closely explained by the way the brain functions—the topic of the next chapter. Furthermore, these brain functions may be identified with the human genome (much as speech may be associated with the FOXP2 gene) and their evolutionary history might be traced. Evolutionary psychologists, in this way, attempt to "reverse engineer" behavioural mechanisms (Pinker, 1997).

Some less friendly critics focus on the second point and argue that sociobiology draws simplistic analogies between research done with non-human animals and human behaviour. This criticism maintains that we cannot learn anything important about human social behaviour from research that focuses on non-human animals. Sociobiologists reply that our understanding of human genetics and physiology is a direct result of research involving non-human animals and that advances in understanding human social behaviour are likely to follow a similar avenue.

Sociobiologists are also criticized for explaining human social behaviour only in terms of genetic determinants and for ignoring environmental factors such as experience and cultural influences. Sociobiologists point out that genes and environmental factors interact to produce any given phenotype. They stress that genes endow organisms only with a behavioural capacity; it is the environment that actually shapes specific behaviours.

The most intense criticism of sociobiology is political, not scientific. Opponents argue that sociobiology sanctions the superiority of one group over another, be it a race, a gender, or a political organization. Sociobiologists flatly deny such allegations and argue that it is the critics and not they who have confused the term *natural* with the terms *good* and *superior*. Sociobiologists contend that they study the biological bases of social behaviour only to understand it better, not to find justification for particular cultural practices and customs. Wilson has eloquently stated the sociobiological defence:

> The purpose of sociobiology is not to make crude comparisons between animal species or between animals and men. . . . Its purpose is to develop general laws of the evolution and biology of social behavior, which might then be extended in a disinterested manner to the study of human beings. . . . It is vital not to misconstrue the political implications of such generalizations. To devise a naturalistic description of human social behavior is to note a set of facts for further investigation, not to pass a value judgment or to deny that a great deal of the behavior can be deliberately changed if individual societies wish. . . . Human behavior is dominated by culture in the sense that the greater part, perhaps all, of the variation between societies is based on differences in cultural experiences. . . . To understand the evolutionary history . . . is to understand in a deeper manner the construction of human nature, to learn what we really are and not just what we hope we are, as viewed through the various prisms of our mythologies. (Wilson, cited in Barash, 1982, pp. xiv–xv)

## Interim Summary

### Humans and Evolution

Two important adaptations during the course of human evolution are *bipedalism*, the ability to walk upright on two feet, and *encephalization*, an increase in brain size. The combination of these two factors allowed early humans to explore and settle new environments and led to advances in tool making, hunting, food gathering, and self-defence. Encephalization appears to have been associated with language development and cultural evolution. The study of the evolution of our species suggests the nature of the circumstances under which adaptive behaviour first emerged and those circumstances that have been important for its continued expression to the present time.

The discovery of the genetic bases for social behaviour is the primary goal of sociobiology. Sociobiologists have been especially interested in studying social behaviour related to reproduction and the rearing of offspring. Different reproductive strategies are believed to have evolved because of sex differences in the resources that parents invest in procreative and child-rearing activities. These resources include the time, physical effort, and risks to life involved in procreation and in the feeding, nurturing, and protecting of offspring. Polygynous and monogamous strategies tend to require greater female investment, polyandrous strategies tend to require greater male investment, and polygynandrous strategies tend to require investment on the part of members of a large group, such as a colony of chimpanzees.

Altruism has also been an important topic of study among sociobiologists because it represents an intriguing scientific puzzle, which, on the surface, would seem difficult to explain by appealing to natural selection. After all, why would natural selection favour a trait that lowers one's own reproductive success while increasing the reproductive success of others? The answer to this question may be found in inclusive fitness, or the reproductive success of those who share many of the same genes. Altruistic behaviour generally involves one organism risking its life either for others with whom it shares some genes (kin selection) or for others who are likely to be in the position of later returning the favour (reciprocal altruism).

Sociobiology is augmented by evolutionary psychology, which attempts to explain behaviour by the adaptiveness of psychological mechanisms. Sociobiology has been criticized on the grounds that research on animal social behaviour is not relevant to understanding human social behaviour, that environmental factors play a greater role than genetic factors in shaping human behaviour, and that sociobiology is simply a way to justify the superiority of one group over another. Sociobiologists reply that natural selection has shaped and continues to shape the evolution of culture, that findings from animal research can be generalized to humans, that genes and environment interact to determine behaviour, and, finally, that sociobiology is an attempt to understand human social behaviour, not to justify it.

**QUESTIONS TO CONSIDER**

1. How might the course of human evolution have been different had natural selection not favoured encephalization?
2. Do you believe that human social behaviour has a genetic component? Explain your rationale.
3. How might a belief in the superiority of one's own culture have influenced human evolution? What factors contribute to its continued presence throughout the world?

EPILOGUE

## The Cost of Sacrifice

Two decades after the crash of the Beechcraft and, after a determined campaign by Edmonton city councillor and lawyer Kiviaq, David Pisurayak Kootook received the Governor General's Award for Bravery.

The kind of altruism shown by David does not seem to be completely explained by the models of altruism we have considered within a purely genetically based theory of human behaviour. The closest plausible model would be that of mutual altruism, but even that falls short of explaining his sacrifice. The risks to his own health were severe; while the situation could have been reversed, it did not seem especially likely; and while Martin Hartwell could recognize David Pisurayak Kootook, they were not a regular part of each other's lives.

David's story shows the way in which culture modifies the biological determinism of our genes. People in Canada's northern communities understand the risks they commonly face. Pulling together in times of adversity is a theme of much Canadian folklore. In addition to having the capacity to behave altruistically under certain circumstances, we also have the inherited capacity to learn to behave altruistically under different circumstances. It is not surprising to learn that all cultures have a version of the golden rule. Altruism and other forms of reciprocation appear to be highly valued and adaptive traits for individuals in any culture to possess. And cultures, in turn, have a vested interest in encouraging such traits. David's sacrifice, and Kiviaq's one-man crusade to have it recognized with the Governor General's Award for Bravery, are both examples of the way in which a stable and secure society maintains its cohesion.

## Canadian Connections to Research in This Chapter

Briskie, J. V., Montgomerie, R., Põldmaa, T., & Boag, P. T. (1998). Paternity and paternal care in the polygynandrous Smith's longspur. *Behavioral Ecology and Sociobiology, 43*, 181–190. (Queen's University: www.queensu.ca)

Clark, M. M., DeSousa, D., Vonk, J., & Galef, B. G. Jr. (1997). Parenting and potency: Alternative routes to reproductive success in male Mongolian gerbils. *Animal Behaviour, 54*, 635–642. (McMaster University: www.mcmaster.ca)

Clark, M. M., & Galef, B. G. Jr. (1998). Where the males are. *Natural History, 107*(9), 22–24. (McMaster University: www.mcmaster.ca)

Cooper, R. M., & Zubek, J. P. (1958). Effects of enriched and restricted early environments on the learning ability of bright and dull rats. *Canadian Journal of Psychology, 12*, 159–164. (University of Manitoba: www.umanitoba.ca)

Daly, M., & Wilson, M. I. (1999). Human evolutionary psychology and animal behaviour. *Animal Behaviour, 57*, 509–519. (McMaster University: www.mcmaster.ca)

Daly, M., & Wilson, M. I. (2001). Risk-taking, intrasexual competition, and homicide. *Nebraska Symposium on Motivation, 47*, 1–36. (McMaster University: www.mcmaster.ca)

Finlayson, C. et al. (2006). Late survival of Neanderthals at the southernmost extreme of Europe. *Nature, 443*, 850–853. (University of Toronto—Scarborough: www.scar.utoronto.ca)

Osborne, K. A., Robichon, A., Burgess, E., Butland, S., Shaw, R. A., Coulthard, A., Pereira, H. S., Greenspan, R. H., & Sokolowski, M. B. (1997). Natural behavior polymorphism due to a cGMP-dependent protein kinase of *Drosophila. Science, 277*, 834–836. (York University: www.yorku.ca)

Réale, D., McAdam, A. G., Boutin, S., & Berteaux, D. (2003). Genetic and plastic responses of a northern mammal to climate change. *Proceedings of the Royal Society of London, 270*, 591–596. (McGill University: www.mcgill.ca)

Sokolowski, M. B., Pereira, H. S., & Hughes, K. (1997). Evolution of foraging behavior in *Drosophila* by density-dependent selection. *Proceedings of the*

*National Academy of Sciences of the United States, 94*, 7373–7377. (York University: www.yorku.ca)

Marla Sokolowski was elected to the Royal Society of Canada in 1998.

Suzuki, D. T., Griffiths, A. J. F., Miller, J. H., & Lewontin, R. C. (1989). *An introduction to genetic analysis* (4th ed.). New York: Freeman. (University of British Columbia: www.ubc.ca)

Wahlsten, D. (1997a). Leilani Muir versus the philosopher king: Eugenics goes on trial in Alberta. *Genetica, 99*, 185–198. (University of Alberta: www.ualberta.ca)

Wahlsten, D. (1999). Single gene influences on brain and behavior. *Annual Review of Psychology, 50*, 599–624. (University of Alberta: www.ualberta.ca)

Weaver, I. C. G., Champagne, F. A., Brown, S. E., Dymov, S., Sharma, S., Meaney, M. J., & Szyf, M. (2005). Reversal of maternal programming of stress responses in adult offspring through methyl supplementation: Altering epigenetic marking later in life. *Journal of Neuroscience, 25*, 11045–11054. (McGill University: www.mcgill.ca)

## Suggestions for Further Reading

Darwin, C. (1859). *The origin of species by means of natural selection.* London: Murray.

This book contains the full argument that Darwin marshalled in defence of evolution by natural selection. It is a must for serious students of evolutionary psychology.

Dawkins, R. (1996). *Climb mount improbable.* New York: Norton.

This book provides an excellent discussion of the role of diversity in the natural world. Some beautiful graphics and illustrations supplement this readable text.

Dennett, D. (1995). *Darwin's dangerous idea.* New York: Simon and Schuster.

This is a literary and challenging look at the philosophical implications of natural selection, particularly with respect to human nature. Dennett takes issue with S. J. Gould, listed below, on the suitability of adaptation as an explanation in psychology and other biological sciences.

Gould, S. J. (1996). *Full house: The spread of excellence from Plato to Darwin.* New York: Harmony Books.

Until his death in 2002, Gould authored an extensive set of books on evolution, the history of biology, and genetic determinism. This book sets some of the principles of evolution in a wide context. Gould is a gifted and witty author; reading his work is a pleasure.

Plomin, R. (1990). *Nature and nurture: An introduction to behavioral genetics.* Pacific Grove, CA: Brooks/Cole.

This very brief book (144 pages), authored by one of the field's pre-eminent scholars, is an excellent, easy-to-read introduction to the field of behaviour genetics. The relevance of behaviour genetics to understanding the origins of common behaviours and problems comes across especially clearly.

Wilson, D. S. (2007). *Evolution for everyone: How Darwin's theory can change the way we think about our lives.* New York: Delacorte Press.

Another introduction to Darwin with particular reference to the implication of his ideas for our lives.

Wilson, E. O. (1975). *Sociobiology: The new synthesis.* Cambridge, MA: Harvard University Press.

This well-written and engaging graduate-level text represents the evolutionary argument for the biological basis of social behaviour. The last chapter contains applications of the theory to humans.

# 4

# Biology of Behaviour

# CHAPTER OUTLINE

## The Brain and Its Components

Structure of the Nervous System • Cells of the Nervous System • The Excitable Axon: The Action Potential • Synapses

The central nervous system consists of the brain and the spinal cord. The peripheral nervous system consists of nerves that connect the central nervous system to sense organs, muscles, and glands. The primary functions of the brain are to control behaviour, to process information about the environment, and to regulate the physiological processes of the body. Circuits of neurons (nerve cells) accomplish these functions, supported by glial cells. Neurons communicate with each other by releasing chemicals called transmitter substances. The message transmitted from place to place—the action potential—is a change in the electrochemical properties of the neuron. Synapses, the junctions between neurons, are either excitatory or inhibitory: Excitatory synapses increase a neuron's activity, and inhibitory synapses decrease it.

## Drugs and Behaviour

Effects of Drugs on Synaptic Transmission • Neurotransmitters, Their Actions, and Drugs That Affect Them

Drugs that affect behaviour do so by facilitating or interfering with synaptic transmission. The most important neurotransmitters are glutamate, which has excitatory effects, and GABA, which has inhibitory effects. Other important categories of neurotransmitters include acetylcholine, the monoamines (dopamine, norepinephrine, and serotonin), the peptides, and the cannabinoids.

## Study of the Brain

Experimental Ablation • Visualizing the Structure of the Brain • Measuring the Brain's Activity • Stimulating the Brain's Activity • Understanding the Limitations of Brain Methods • *Then and Now: Neurogenesis*

Physiological psychologists study the biological processes of the brain using experimental ablation, electrical and chemical recording or stimulation, and genetic manipulation. The development of scanning devices has revolutionized the study of the living human brain. Many techniques allow us to measure the activity of brain neurons as behaviour occurs. It is also possible to stimulate special areas of the brain in a way that mimics its normal function.

## Control of Behaviour

Organization of the Cerebral Cortex • Lateralization of Function • Vision: The Occipital and Temporal Lobes • Audition: The Temporal Lobe • Somatosensation and Spatial Perception: The Parietal Lobe • Planning and Moving: The Frontal Lobe

The cerebral cortex, the outer layer of the cerebral hemispheres, receives sensory information, controls perceptual and learning processes, and formulates plans and actions. Some brain functions are lateralized—controlled primarily by one side of the brain. Each of the four lobes of the brain is involved with specific activities: The occipital lobe and the temporal lobe control seeing; the temporal lobe controls hearing; the parietal lobe controls perception of the body and the space around it; and the frontal lobe controls motor activities, planning, attending to emotionally related stimuli, spontaneous behaviour, and speech.

## Control of Internal Functions and Automatic Behaviour

The Brain Stem • The Cerebellum • Structures within the Cerebral Hemispheres

The more primitive parts of the brain control homeostasis and species-typical behaviours, such as those involved in fighting, foraging, and reproduction. The cerebellum plays a crucial role in the execution of movement. The thalamus functions as a relay station for sensory information on its way to the cerebral cortex. The hypothalamus controls the autonomic nervous system and the endocrine system. Endocrine glands secrete hormones, which affect physiological functions and behaviour. The limbic system regulates the expression of emotion, defence, and aggression and is involved in learning and memory.

PROLOGUE

## The Left Is Gone

Miss S. was a 60-year-old woman who had a history of high blood pressure, which was not responding well to the medication she was taking. One evening, she was sitting in her reclining chair reading the newspaper when the phone rang. She got out of her chair and walked to the phone. As she did, she began to feel giddy and stopped to hold onto the kitchen table. She has no memory of what happened after that.

The next morning, a neighbour who usually stopped by to have coffee with Miss S. found her lying on the floor, mumbling incoherently. The neighbour called an ambulance, which took Miss S. to a hospital.

Two days after her admission, the neurological resident in charge of her case told a group of us that she had had a stroke in the back part of the right side of the brain. He attached a CT scan to an illuminated viewer mounted on the wall and showed us a white spot caused by the accumulation of blood in a particular region of her brain. (You can look at the scan yourself; it is shown in Figure 4.19.)

We then went to see Miss S. in her hospital room. She was awake but seemed a little confused. The resident greeted her and asked how she was feeling.

"Fine, I guess," she said. "I still don't know why I'm here."

"Can you see the other people in the room?"

"Why, sure."

"How many are there?"

She turned her head to the right and began counting. She stopped when she had counted the people at the foot of her bed. "Seven," she reported.

"What about us?" asked a voice from the left side of her bed.

"What?" she asked, looking at the people she had already counted.

"Here, to your left. No, toward your left!" the voice repeated.

Slowly, rather reluctantly, she began turning her head to the left. The voice kept insisting, and finally, she saw who was talking. "Oh," she said, "I guess there are more of you."

The resident approached the left side of her bed and touched her left arm. "What is this?" he asked.

"Where?" she asked.

"Here," he answered, holding up her arm and moving it gently in front of her face.

"Oh, that's an arm."

"An arm? Whose arm?"

"I don't know." She paused. "I guess it must be yours."

"No, it's yours. Look, it's a part of you." He traced with his fingers from her arm to her shoulder.

"Well, if you say so," she said, sounding unconvinced.

When we returned to the residents' lounge, the chief of neurology said that we had seen a classic example of unilateral (one-sided) neglect, caused by damage to a particular part of the brain. "I've seen many cases like this," he explained. "People can still perceive sensations from the left side of their bodies, but they just don't pay attention to them. A woman will put makeup on only the right side of her face, and a man will shave only half of his beard. When they put on a shirt or a coat, they will use their left hand to slip it over their right arm and shoulder, but then they'll just forget about their left arm and let the garment hang from one shoulder. They also don't look at things located toward the left—or even at the left halves of things. Once I saw a man who had just finished eating breakfast. He was sitting in his bed, with a tray in front of him. There was half a pancake on his plate. 'Are you all done?' I asked. 'Sure,' he said. I turned the plate around so that the uneaten part was on his right. He gave a startled look and said, 'Where the hell did that come from?'"

Of all the objects we know, the human brain is the most complex. As far as our species is concerned, it is the most important kilogram and a half of living tissue in the world. It is also the only object capable of studying itself. (If it could not do so, this chapter could not exist.) Our perceptions, our thoughts, our memories, our emotions, and our desires all reside in our brains. If a surgeon transplants a heart, a liver, or a kidney—or even all three organs—we do not ask ourselves whether the identity of the recipient has been changed. But if a brain transplant were feasible (it isn't), we would undoubtedly say that the owner of the brain was getting a new body rather than the reverse. If, in some futuristic scenario, your own brain was hopelessly injured and surgeons replaced it with the brain of a younger clone of yourself, your body would now contain the clone's memories, thoughts, and personality. Your experience, knowledge, and wisdom would be gone, even though your body still lived.

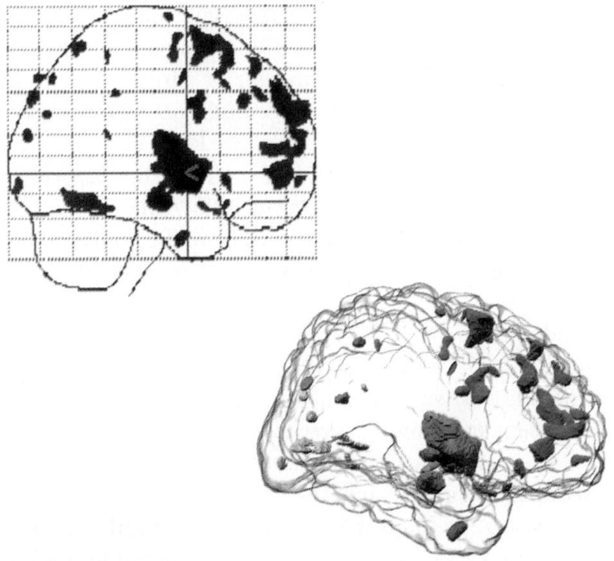

**FIGURE 4•1** Areas of the brain showing structural changes from adolescence to adulthood. Green clusters are locations in subcortical regions, purple are in the frontal lobe, red in the parietal lobe, yellow in the occipital lobe, and blue in the temporal lobe. These terms will be explained later in the chapter. *(From Sowell, E. R., Thompson, P. M., Holmes, C. J., Jernigan, T. L., & Toga, A. W. (1999).* In vivo *evidence for post-adolescent brain maturation in frontal and striatal regions.* Nature Neuroscience, 2, *859–861.)*

This is true because, even though the brain of a younger clone would be genetically identical to yours, it would be physically quite different. Maturation and experience create these differences and, as we will see, they have profound consequences for thought, memory, emotion, and other human characteristics.

As a short preview of the topics to come, consider the changes that have happened to you since you left high school. You're more mature, better able to plan, and more cognizant of your increased responsibility to yourself and your society. Now look at **Figure 4•1**, which is based on brain imaging techniques that can identify the change in a human brain that occurs from about the age of 14 to 26 (Sowell et al., 1999). The coloured areas represent regions of the brain that have changed structurally. Notice all of the areas on the right side of the figure, which corresponds to the front part of the brain. If you happen to be in the middle of this age range, your brain is likely changing in these areas now.

Are these regions the *physical* location of our increased maturity? What could cause these changes? What about the other areas that also show structural changes with maturation and experience? The answers to these questions are important statements about you and what makes your mind different from your friends' and relatives'. Finding these answers requires knowing about that kilogram and a half of tissue.

## The Brain and Its Components

The brain contains anywhere between 10 billion and 100 billion nerve cells—no one knows for sure—and about as many helper cells, which take care of important support and housekeeping functions. For many decades, neuroscientists have known that the brain contains many different types of nerve cells. These cells differ in shape, size, and the kinds of chemicals they produce. How they work together to control behaviour was not clear. Although early physiologists such as Pierre Flourens had emphasized that different parts of the nervous system were responsible for different functions, physiological psychologists had found conflicting evidence. Many memory functions, for example, seemed to be distributed over large areas of the brain.

Donald Hebb, whom we discussed in Chapter 1, provided the foundation for a better understanding 60 years ago (Hebb, 1949). He considered how individual nerve cells are organized into larger units. He proposed specific principles of organization by which these units were structurally organized and he suggested how they could generate the higher processes of the brain such as memory, thought, and decision making. By stressing the role of these larger units, Hebb showed how brain functioning could be understood in terms of both the individual cells and the larger networks they comprised.

Since Hebb's pioneering work, neuroscientists have learned that the nerve cells of the brain are indeed organized in *modules*—clusters of nerve cells that communicate with each other. Of course, individual modules do not stand alone; they are connected to other neural circuits, receiving information from some of them, processing this information, and sending the results to other modules. Particular modules have particular functions, just as the transistors, resistors, and capacitors in a computer chip do.

To understand how the brain works, we must follow much of the reasoning that Hebb used, although with more modern conceptions of neural mechanisms. (See Seung, 2000, for a recent retrospective on Hebb's work.) We need to understand how individual nerve cells work, how they connect with each other to form modules, and just what these modules do. Next, we have to understand the more complex neural circuits formed by connections among large numbers of modules. We will then know how these circuits control behaviour and how they are affected by outside agents such as drugs.

**central nervous system** The brain and the spinal cord.

**spinal cord** A long, thin collection of nerve cells attached to the base of the brain and running the length of the spinal column.

**nerve** A bundle of fibres that transmits information between the central nervous system and the body's sense organs, muscles, and glands.

**peripheral nervous system** The cranial and spinal nerves; that part of the nervous system peripheral to the brain and spinal cord.

**cranial nerve** A bundle of nerve fibres attached to the base of the brain; conveys sensory information from the face and head and carries messages to muscles and glands.

**spinal nerve** A bundle of nerve fibres attached to the spinal cord; conveys sensory information from the body and carries messages to muscles and glands.

**brain stem** The "stem" of the brain, including the medulla, pons, and midbrain.

**cerebral hemisphere** The largest part of the brain; covered by the cerebral cortex and containing parts of the brain that evolved most recently.

**cerebellum** A pair of hemispheres resembling the cerebral hemispheres but much smaller and lying beneath and in back of them; controls posture and movements, especially rapid ones.

**vertebra** One of the bones that encase the spinal cord and constitute the vertebral column.

## Structure of the Nervous System

The brain has three major functions: controlling behaviour, processing and retaining the information we receive from the environment, and regulating the body's physiological processes. How does it accomplish these tasks?

The brain cannot act alone. It needs to receive information from the body's sense receptors, and it must be connected with the muscles and glands of the body if it is to affect behaviour and physiological processes. The nervous system consists of two divisions. The brain and the spinal cord make up the **central nervous system.** The **spinal cord** is a long, thin collection of nerve cells attached to the base of the brain and running the length of the spinal column. The spinal cord contains circuits of nerve cells that control some simple reflexes, such as automatically pulling away from a painfully hot object. The central nervous system communicates with the rest of the body through **nerves**—bundles of fibres that transmit information in and out of the central nervous system. The nerves, which are attached to the spinal cord and to the base of the brain, make up the **peripheral nervous system.** (See **Figure 4•2.**) Sensory information (information about what is happening in the environment or within the body) is conveyed from sensory organs to the brain and spinal cord. Information from the head and neck region (for example, from the eyes, ears, nose, and tongue) reaches the brain through the **cranial nerves.** Sensory information from the rest of the body reaches the spinal cord (and ultimately the brain) through the **spinal nerves.** The cranial nerves and spinal nerves also carry information away from the central nervous system. The brain controls muscles, glands, and internal organs by sending messages to these structures through these nerves.

The human brain has three major parts: the *brain stem*, the *cerebellum*, and the *cerebral hemispheres.* **Figure 4•3** shows a view of the left side of the brain. The lower part of the cerebellum and brain stem projects beneath the left cerebral hemisphere; the upper part is normally hidden.

If the human brain is removed from the skull, it looks as if it has a handle or a stem. The **brain stem** is one of the most primitive regions of the brain, and its functions are correspondingly basic ones: primarily control of physiological functions and automatic behaviours. In fact, the brains of some animals, such as amphibians, consist primarily of a brain stem and a simple cerebellum.

The pair of **cerebral hemispheres** constitutes the largest part of the human brain. The cerebral hemispheres contain the parts of the brain that evolved most recently—and thus are involved in behaviours of particular interest to psychologists. The **cerebellum**, attached to the back of the brain stem, looks like a miniature version of the cerebral hemispheres. Its primary function is to control and coordinate movements. (See Figure 4.3.)

Because the central nervous system is vital to an organism's survival, it is exceptionally well protected. The brain is encased in the skull, and the spinal cord runs through the middle of a column of hollow bones known as **vertebrae.**

FIGURE 4•2 The central nervous system (brain and spinal cord) and the peripheral nervous system (cranial nerves and spinal nerves).

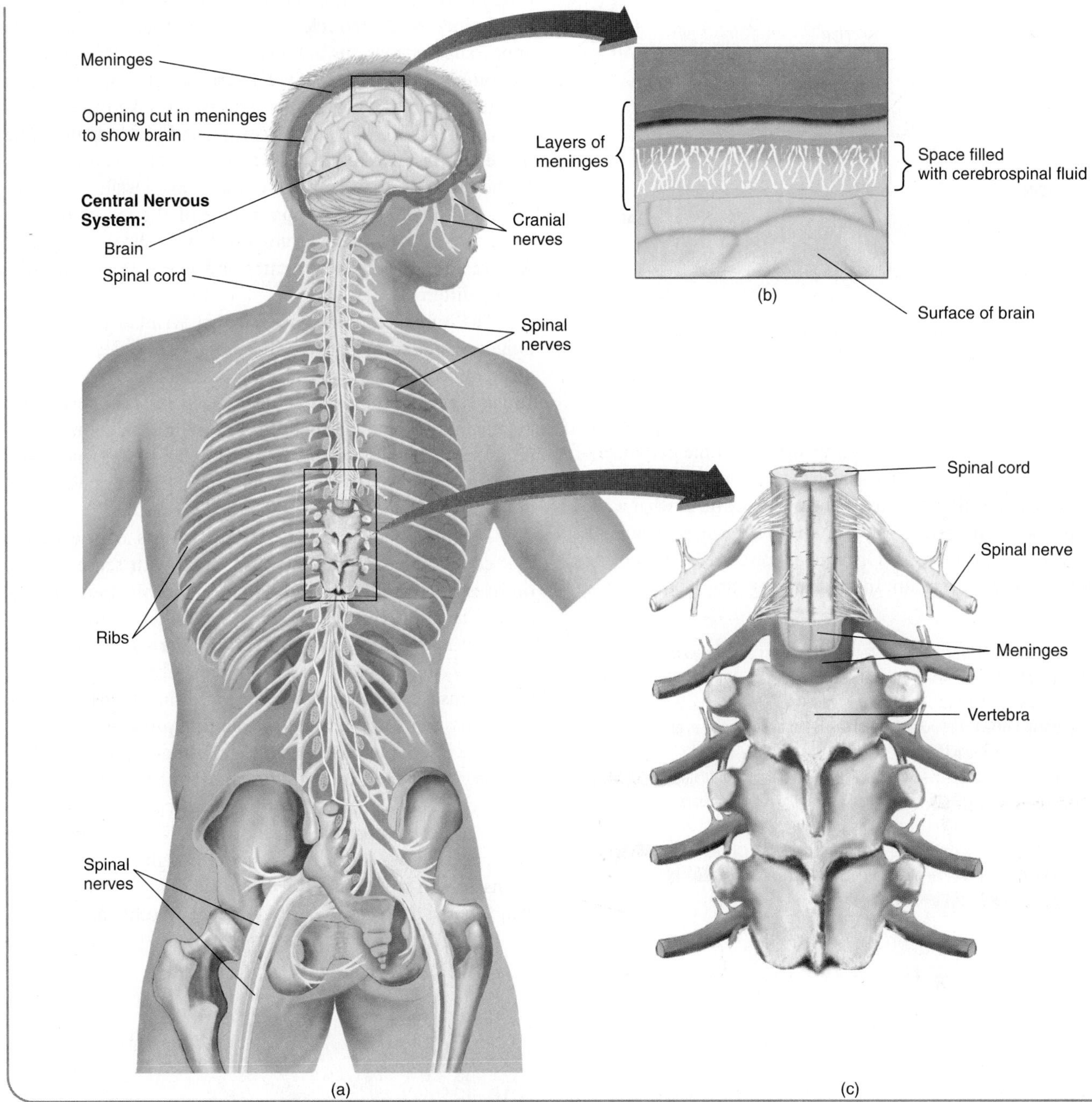


(Refer to Figure 4.2.) Both the brain and the spinal cord are enclosed by a three-layered set of membranes called the **meninges**. (*Meninges* is the plural of *meninx*, the Greek word for "membrane." You have probably heard of meningitis, which is an inflammation of the meninges.) The brain and spinal cord do not come into direct contact with the bones of the skull and vertebrae. Instead, they float in a clear liquid called **cerebrospinal fluid (CSF)**. This liquid fills the space between two of the meninges, thus providing a liquid cushion surrounding the brain and spinal cord and protecting them from being bruised by the bones that encase them.

The brain is protected from chemical assault as well as physical shock. The cells of the body receive water and nutrients from the capillaries, the smallest of the blood vessels. In most of the body, the walls of the capillaries have small openings that let chemicals pass freely from the blood into the surrounding tissue. The brain is an exception: Its capillaries do

**meninges** The three-layered set of membranes that enclose the brain and spinal cord.

**cerebrospinal fluid (CSF)** The liquid in which the brain and spinal cord float; provides a shock-absorbing cushion.

**FIGURE 4•3** The three major parts of the brain: brain stem, cerebellum, and cerebral hemisphere. Only the left side of the brain is shown.

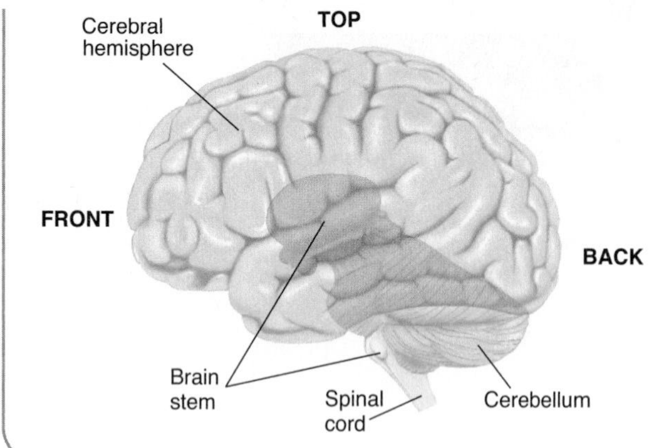


not have these openings, so fewer substances can pass from the blood to the brain. This impediment to the exchange of chemicals is called the **blood–brain barrier**. Its major function is to make it less likely that toxic chemicals found in what we eat or drink can find their way into the brain, where they might do damage to neurons. Of course, there are many poisons that can affect the brain, so this barrier is not foolproof.

**blood–brain barrier** A barrier between the blood and the brain produced by the cells in the walls of the brain's capillaries; prevents some substances from passing from the blood into the brain.
**cerebral cortex** The outer layer of the cerebral hemispheres of the brain, approximately 3 mm thick.
**grey matter** The portions of the central nervous system that are abundant in cell bodies of neurons rather than axons. The colour appears grey relative to white matter.
**white matter** The portions of the central nervous system that are abundant in axons rather than cell bodies of neurons. The colour derives from the presence of the axons' myelin sheaths.

The surface of the cerebral hemispheres is covered by the **cerebral cortex.** (The word *cortex* means "bark" or "rind.") The cerebral cortex consists of a thin layer of tissue approximately 3 mm thick. It is often referred to as **grey matter** because of its appearance. It contains billions of nerve cells. (The structure and functions of nerve cells are described in the next section.) It is in the cerebral cortex that perceptions take place, memories are stored, and plans are formulated and executed. The nerve cells in the cerebral cortex are connected to other parts of the brain by a layer of nerve fibres called **white matter** because of the shiny white appearance of the substance that coats and insulates them. **Figure 4•4** shows a slice of the brain. As you can see, the grey matter and white matter are distinctly different.

The human cerebral cortex is very wrinkled; it is full of bulges separated by grooves. The bulges are called *gyri* (singular, *gyrus*), and the large grooves are called *fissures*. Fissures and gyri expand the amount of surface area of the cortex and greatly increase the number of nerve cells it can contain. Animals with the largest and most complex brains, including humans and the higher primates, have the most wrinkled brains and, thus, the largest cerebral cortexes.

The peripheral nervous system consists of the nerves that connect the central nervous system with sense organs, muscles, and glands. Nerves carry both incoming and outgoing information. The sense organs detect changes in the environment and send signals through the nerves to the central nervous system. The brain sends signals through the nerves to the muscles (causing behaviour) and the glands (producing adjustments in internal physiological processes).

Nerves are bundles of many thousands of individual fibres, all wrapped in a tough, protective membrane. Under a microscope, nerves look something like telephone cables, with their bundles of wires. Like the individual wires in a telephone cable, nerve fibres transmit messages through the nerve, from a sense organ to the brain or from the brain to a muscle or gland. These make up the white matter and other axon tracts.

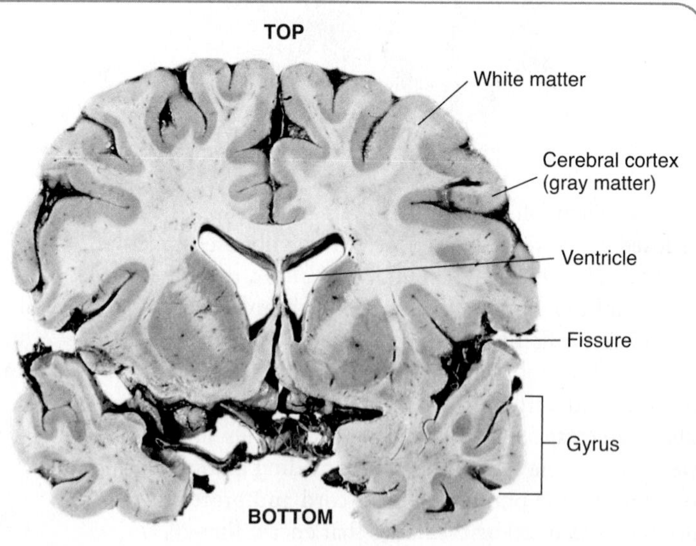


**FIGURE 4•4** A photograph of a slice of a human brain showing fissures and gyri and the layer of cerebral cortex that follows these convolutions.
*(Harvard Medical School/Betty G. Martindale.)*

**FIGURE 4•5** The basic parts of a neuron and its connections with other neurons (synapses). The inset depicts the structure of a synapse.

*(Adapted from Carlson, N. R. (2004).* Physiology of behaviour *(8th ed.). Needham Heights, MA: Allyn & Bacon, pp. 31, 52. Reprinted with permission.)*

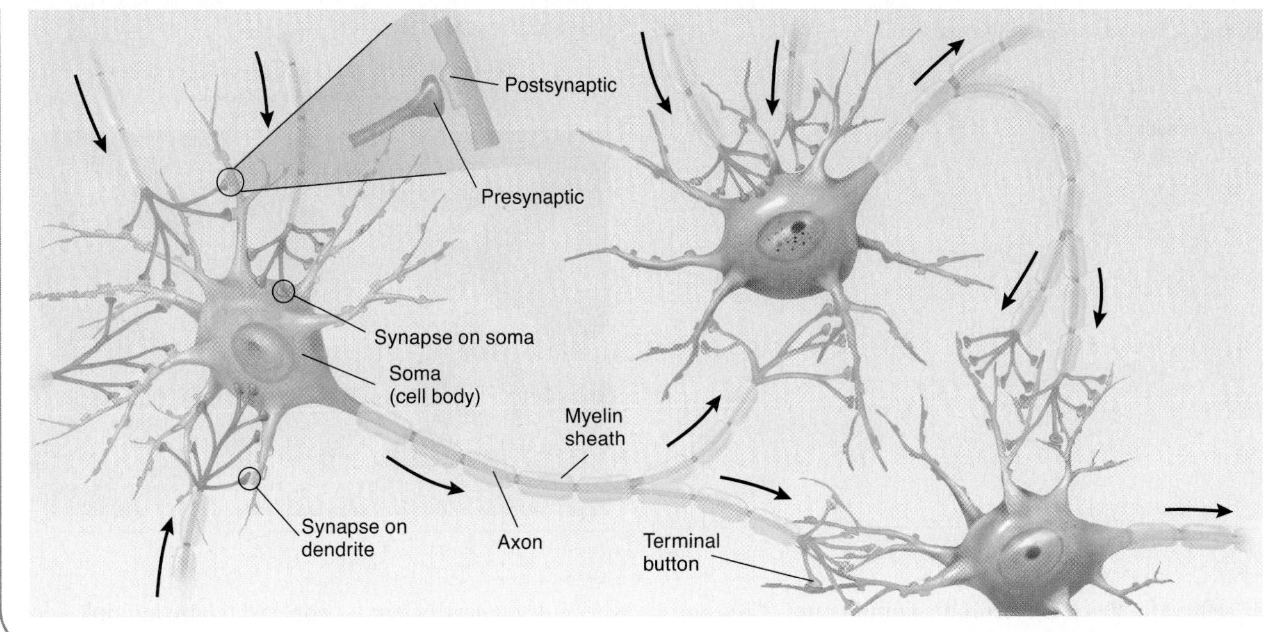


## Cells of the Nervous System

**Neurons**, or nerve cells, are the elements of the nervous system that bring sensory information to the brain, store memories, reach decisions, and control the activity of the muscles. Neurons can receive information from other neurons (or from cells in sense organs), process this information, and communicate the processed information to other neurons (or to cells in muscles, glands, or internal organs). Thus, neurons contain structures specialized for receiving, processing, and transmitting information. These structures are shown in **Figure 4•5**.

Neurons are assisted in their task by another kind of cell: the **glia**. Glia (or *glial cells*) get their name from the Greek word for "glue." At one time, scientists thought that glia simply held neurons—the important elements of the nervous system—in place. They do that, but they also do much more. During development of the brain, some types of glial cells form long fibres that guide developing neurons from their place of birth to their final resting place. Other types of glia manufacture chemicals that neurons need to perform their tasks and absorb chemicals that might impair neurons' functioning. Others form protective insulating sheaths around nerve fibres. Still others serve as the brain's immune system, protecting it from invading micro-organisms that might infect it.

**Dendrites**, tree-like growths attached to the body of a nerve cell, function principally to receive messages from other neurons. (*Dendron* means "tree.") They transmit the information they receive down their "trunks" to the cell body. **Dendritic spines** are small protuberances on the surface of dendrites. They appear on neurons in the brain. The **soma**, or cell body, is the largest part of the neuron and contains the mechanisms that control the metabolism and maintenance of the cell. In most neurons, the soma also receives messages from other neurons. The nerve fibre, or **axon**, carries messages away from the soma toward the cells with which the neuron communicates. These messages, called *action potentials*, consist of brief changes in the electrical charge of the axon.

Axons end in **terminal buttons**, which are located at the ends of the "twigs" that branch off from their ends. Terminal buttons rest against dendrites, dendritic spines, the soma, or the axon of another neuron. (See **Figure 4•6**.) Terminal buttons secrete a chemical called a **neurotransmitter** whenever an action potential is sent down the axon (that is, whenever the axon *fires*). The neurotransmitter affects the activity of the

**neuron** A nerve cell; consists of a cell body with dendrites and an axon whose branches end in terminal buttons that synapse with muscle fibres, gland cells, or other neurons.

**glial cell** A cell of the central nervous system that provides support for neurons and supplies them with some essential chemicals.

**dendrite** A tree-like part of a neuron on which other neurons form synapses.

**dendritic spine** A small bud-like protuberance on the surface of a neuron's dendrite.

**soma** A cell body; the largest part of a neuron.

**axon** A long, thin part of a neuron attached to the soma; divides into a few or many branches, ending in terminal buttons.

**terminal button** The rounded swelling at the end of the axon of a neuron; releases transmitter substance.

**neurotransmitter** A chemical released by the terminal buttons that causes the postsynaptic neuron to be excited or inhibited.

**FIGURE 4•6** Types of synapses. Axodendritic synapses can occur on the smooth surface of a dendrite (a) or on dendritic spines (b).

*(Carlson,* Physiology of Behavior, *pp. 52, "Figure: Types of synapses", © 2004. Reproduced by permission of Pearson Education, Inc.)*

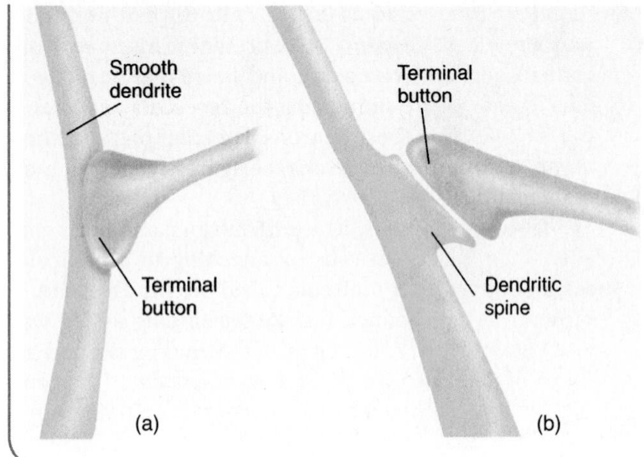


**FIGURE 4•7** A scanning electron micrograph of a neuron.

*(From* Tissues and organs: A text-atlas of scanning electron microscopy, *by Richard G. Kessel and Randy H. Kardon. San Francisco: W. H. Freeman, 1979. Reprinted by permission of the authors and Visuals Unlimited.)*

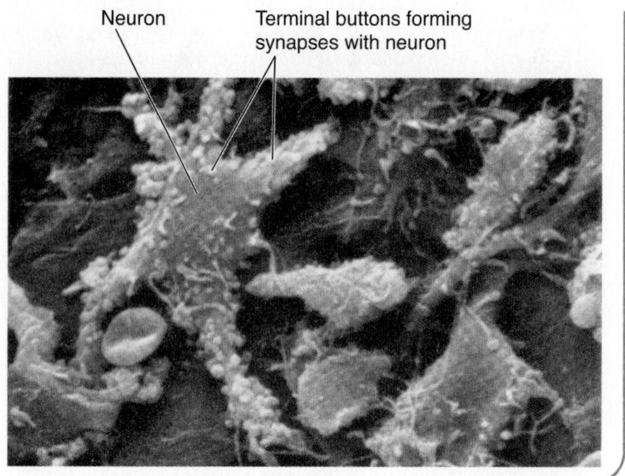


other cells with which the neuron communicates. Thus, the message is conveyed *chemically* from one neuron to another. Most drugs that affect the nervous system and hence alter a person's behaviour do so by affecting the chemical transmission of messages between cells.

Many axons, especially long ones, are insulated with a substance called *myelin*. The white matter located beneath the cerebral cortex gets its colour from the **myelin sheaths** around the axons that travel through these areas. Myelin, part protein and part fat, is produced by glial cells that wrap parts of themselves around segments of the axon, leaving small bare patches of the axon between them. (Refer to Figure 4.5.) The principal function of myelin is to insulate axons from one another and thus to prevent the scrambling of messages. Myelin also increases the speed of the action potential.

To appreciate how important the myelin sheath is, consider the symptoms of a neurological disease: *multiple sclerosis* (MS). In this disorder, a person's immune system begins to attack parts of his or her central nervous system. Multiple sclerosis is so named because an autopsy of the brain and spinal cord will show numerous patches of hardened, damaged tissue. (*Skleros* is Greek for "hard.") The immune system of a person with multiple sclerosis attacks a protein in the myelin sheath of axons in the central nervous system, stripping it away. Although most of the axons survive this assault, they can no longer function normally, and so—depending on where the damage occurs—people who have multiple sclerosis suffer from a variety of neurological symptoms.

**Figure 4•7** is a photograph made with a scanning electron microscope. It shows the actual appearance of a neuron and some terminal buttons that form synapses with it. The terminal buttons were broken off from their axons when the tissue was being prepared, but by comparing this photograph with Figure 4.5 you can begin to imagine some of the complexity of the nervous system.

**myelin sheath** The insulating material that encases most large axons.
**action potential** A brief electrochemical event that is carried by an axon from the soma of the neuron to its terminal buttons; causes the release of a transmitter substance.
**ion** A positively or negatively charged particle; produced when many substances dissolve in water.

## The Excitable Axon: The Action Potential

The message carried by the axon—the action potential—involves an electrical current, but it does not travel down the axon the way that electricity travels through a wire. Electricity travels through a wire at hundreds of millions of metres per second. However, as we saw in Chapter 1, Helmholtz discovered that the axon transmits information at a much slower rate: less than 30 metres per second.

The membrane of an axon is electrically charged. When the axon is resting (that is, when no action potential is occurring), the inside is charged at –70 millivolts (thousandths of a volt) with respect to the outside. An **action potential** is an abrupt, short-lived reversal in the electrical charge of an axon. This temporary reversal begins at the end of the axon that attaches to the soma and is transmitted to the end that divides into small branches capped with terminal buttons.

The electrical charge of the axon occurs because of an unequal distribution of positively and negatively charged particles inside the axon and in the fluid that surrounds it. These particles, called **ions**, are produced when various substances—including ordinary table salt—are dissolved in water. Normally, ions cannot penetrate the membrane that surrounds axons. However, the axonal membrane contains

**FIGURE 4•8** Ion channels and ion transporters. These structures regulate the number of ions found inside and outside the axon. An unequal distribution of positively and negatively charged ions is responsible for the axon's electrical charge.

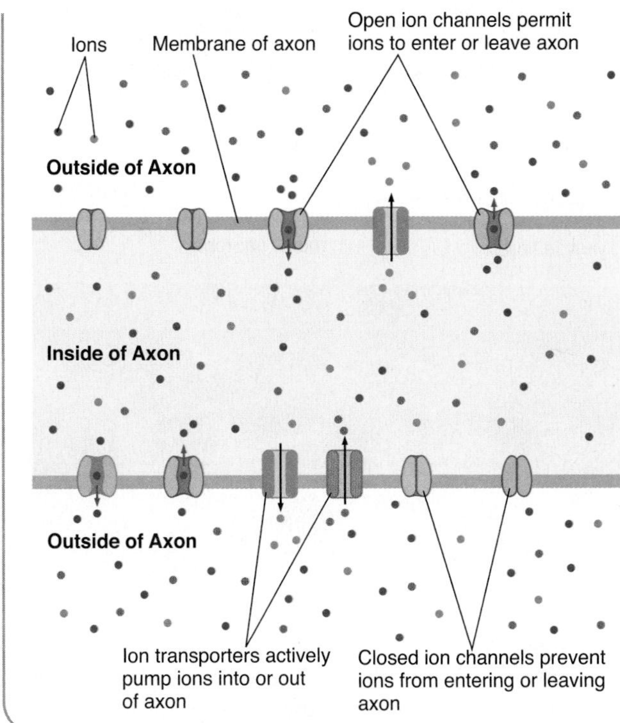


special submicroscopic proteins that serve as ion channels or ion transporters. **Ion channels** can open or close; when they are open, a particular ion can enter or leave the axon. As we will see, the membrane of the axon contains two types of ion channels: sodium channels and potassium channels. **Ion transporters** work like pumps. They use the energy resources of the cell to transport particular ions into or out of the axon. (See **Figure 4•8.**)

When the axon is in a resting state, the outside of the membrane is positively charged (and the inside is negatively charged) because the fluid inside the axon contains more negatively charged ions and fewer positively charged ions. In the resting state, the axon's ion channels are closed, so ions cannot move into or out of the axon. An action potential is caused by the opening of some ion channels in the membrane at the end of the axon nearest the soma. The opening of these ion channels permits positively charged sodium ions to enter, which reverses the membrane potential at that location. This reversal causes nearby ion channels to open, which produces another reversal at *that* point. The process continues all the way to the terminal buttons located at the other end of the axon.

Note that an action potential is a *brief* reversal of the membrane's electrical charge. As soon as the charge reverses, the ion channels close and another set of ion channels opens for a short time, letting positively charged potassium ions out of the axon. This outflow of positive ions restores the normal electrical charge. Thus, an action potential resembles the "wave" that sports fans often make in a stadium during a game. People in one part of the stadium stand up, raise their arms over their heads, and sit down again. People seated next to them see that a wave is starting, so they do the same—and the wave travels around the stadium. Everyone remains at the same place, but the effect is that of something circling in the stands around the playing field. Similarly, electricity does not really travel down the length of an axon. Instead, the entry of positive ions in one location reverses the charge at that point and causes ion channels in the adjacent region to open, and so on. (See **Figure 4•9.**)

You may be wondering what happens to the sodium ions that enter the axon and the potassium ions that leave it. This

**ion channel** A special protein molecule located in the membrane of a cell; controls the entry or exit of particular ions.

**ion transporter** A special protein molecule located in the membrane of a cell; actively transports ions into or out of the cell.

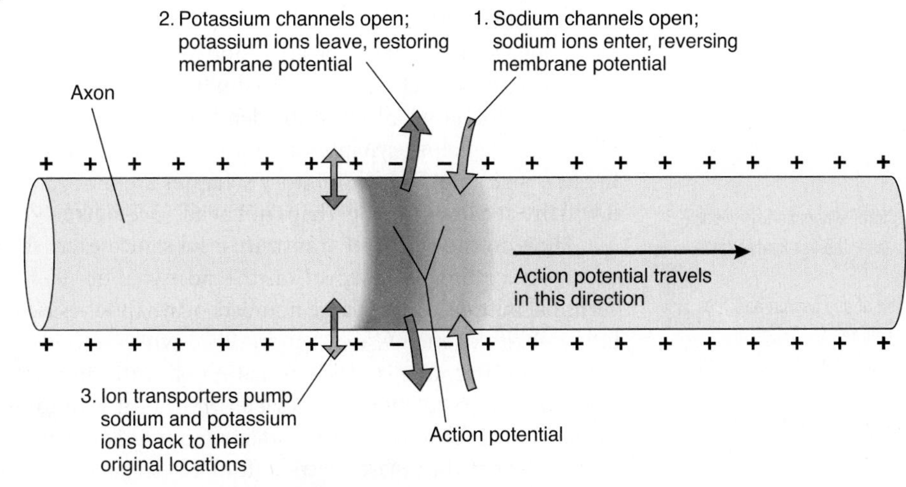


**FIGURE 4•9** Movement of sodium and potassium ions during the action potential. Sodium ions are represented by red arrows, potassium ions by green arrows.

is where the ion transporters come in. The ion transporters pump sodium ions out of the axon and pump potassium ions back in, restoring the normal balance. (See Figure 4.9.)

An action potential is an all-or-none event; either it happens or it does not. Action potentials in a given axon are all the same size; there are no large or small action potentials. This fact has been stated as the **all-or-none law**. However, if action potentials cannot vary in size, how can axons convey quantitative information? For example, how can **sensory neurons**—neurons that receive information from sensory organs such as the eyes—tell other neurons in the brain about the strength of a stimulus? And how can **motor neurons**—neurons whose axons form synapses with a muscle—tell the muscle how forcefully to contract? The answer is simple: A single action potential is not the basic element of information; rather, quantitative information is represented by an axon's rate of firing. Strong stimuli (such as bright lights) trigger a high rate of firing in axons of sensory neurons that receive visual information. Similarly, a high rate of firing in the axons of motor neurons causes strong muscular contractions.

## Synapses

Neurons communicate with other cells by means of synapses. A **synapse** is the conjunction of a terminal button of one neuron and the membrane of another cell—neuron, muscle cell, or gland cell. Let us first consider synapses between one neuron and another. The terminal button belongs to the **presynaptic neuron**—the neuron that sends the message. As discussed, when terminal buttons become active, they release a chemical called a transmitter substance. The neuron that receives the message (that is, detects the transmitter substance) is called the **postsynaptic neuron**. (Refer to inset, Figure 4.5, on page 93.) A neuron receives messages from many terminal buttons, and in turn its terminal buttons form synapses with many other neurons. The drawing in Figure 4.5 is greatly simplified; thousands of terminal buttons can form synapses with a single neuron.

**Figure 4.10** illustrates the relation between a motor neuron and a muscle. When the axon of a motor neuron fires, all of the muscle fibres with which it forms synapses will contract with a brief twitch. A muscle consists of thousands of individual muscle fibres. It is controlled by a large number of motor neurons, each of which forms synapses with different groups of muscle fibres. The strength of a muscular contraction, then, depends on the rate of firing of the axons that control it. If they fire at a high rate, the muscle contracts forcefully; if they fire at a low rate, the muscle contracts weakly.

**FIGURE 4•10** Synapses between terminal buttons of the axon of a motor neuron and a muscle.

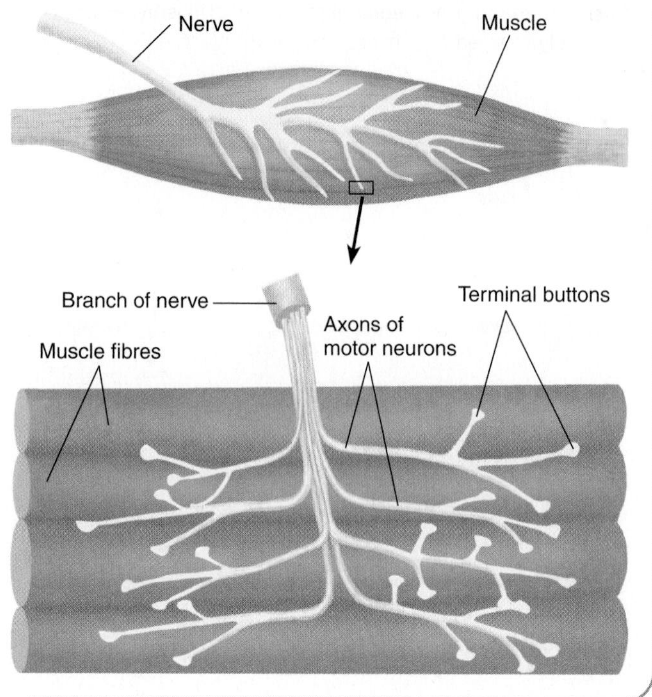


There are basically two types of synapses: *excitatory synapses* and *inhibitory synapses*. Excitatory synapses do just what their name implies: When the axon fires, the terminal buttons release a transmitter substance that excites the postsynaptic neurons with which they form synapses. The effect of this excitation is to make it more likely that the axons of the postsynaptic neurons will fire. Inhibitory synapses do just the opposite: When they are activated, they *lower* the likelihood that the axons of the postsynaptic neurons will fire.

The rate at which a particular axon fires is determined by the activity of all synapses on the dendrites and soma of the cell. If the excitatory synapses are more active, the axon will fire at a high rate. If the inhibitory synapses are more active, it will fire at a low rate or perhaps not at all. (See **Figure 4•11**.)

How do molecules of transmitter substance exert their excitatory or inhibitory effect on the postsynaptic neuron? Terminal buttons contain large numbers of synaptic vesicles—little bubbles of membrane that are filled with molecules of the neurotransmitter. (*Vesicle* is Latin for "little bladder.") When an action potential reaches a terminal button, it causes the terminal button to release a small amount of transmitter substance into the **synaptic cleft**, a fluid-filled space between

**all-or-none law** The principle that once an action potential is triggered in an axon, it is propagated, without getting smaller, to the end of the axon.
**sensory neuron** A neuron that detects changes in the external or internal environment and sends information about these changes to the central nervous system.
**motor neuron** A neuron whose terminal buttons form synapses with muscle fibres. When an action potential travels down its axon, the associated muscle fibres will twitch.
**synapse** The junction between the terminal button of one neuron and the membrane of a muscle fibre, a gland, or another neuron.
**presynaptic neuron** A neuron whose terminal buttons form synapses with and excite or inhibit another neuron.
**postsynaptic neuron** A neuron with which the terminal buttons of another neuron form synapses and that is excited or inhibited by that neuron.

**FIGURE 4•11** Interaction between the effects of excitatory and inhibitory synapses. Excitatory and inhibitory effects combine to determine the rate of firing of the neuron on the right.

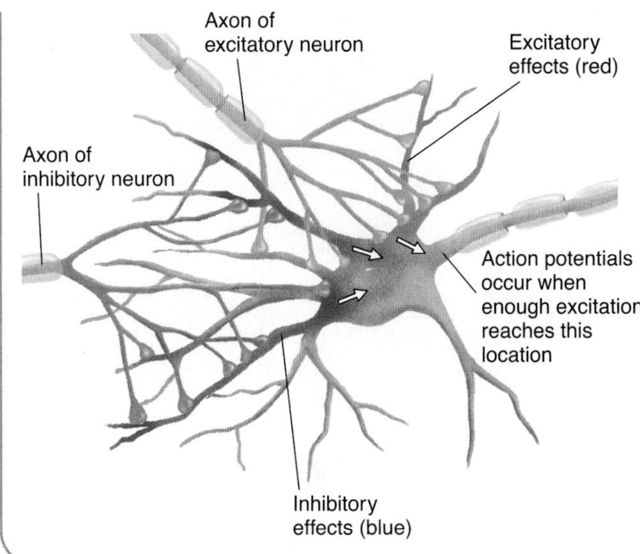


**FIGURE 4•12** The release of a transmitter substance from a terminal button. The drawing depicts the inset portion of Figure 4.5 (see page 93). **Top:** Before the arrival of an action potential. **Middle:** Just after the arrival of an action potential. Molecules of transmitter substance have been released. **Bottom:** Activation of receptor molecules. The molecules of transmitter substance diffuse across the synaptic cleft and some of them activate receptor molecules in the postsynaptic membrane.

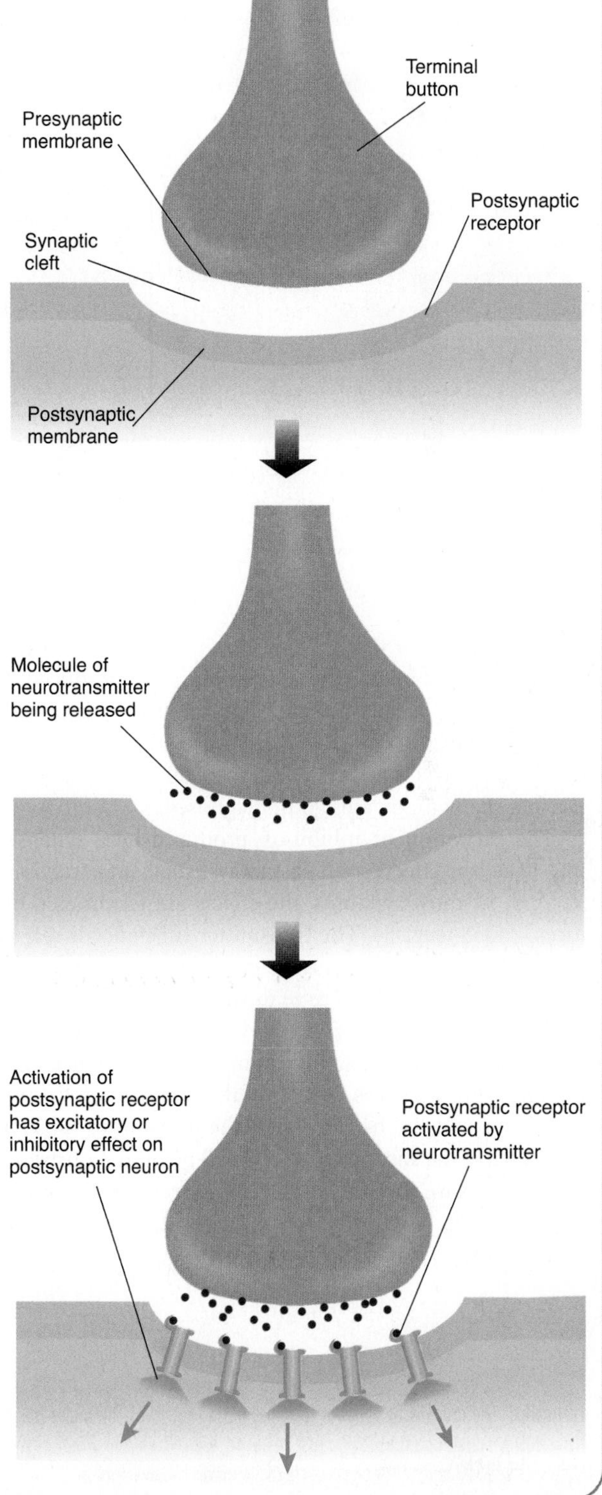


the terminal button and the membrane of the postsynaptic neuron. (Note that the terminal button and the postsynaptic membrane do not touch each other.) The transmitter substance causes reactions in the postsynaptic neuron that either excite or inhibit it. These reactions are triggered by special submicroscopic protein molecules embedded in the postsynaptic membrane called **neurotransmitter receptors.** (See **Figure 4•12.**)

A molecule of a transmitter substance attaches to a receptor molecule the way a key fits in a lock. After their release from a terminal button, molecules of transmitter substance find their way to the receptor molecules, attach to them, and activate them. Once they are activated, the receptor molecules produce excitatory or inhibitory effects on the postsynaptic neuron. They do so by opening ion channels. Most ion channels found at excitatory synapses permit sodium ions to enter the neuron; most of those found at inhibitory synapses permit potassium ions to leave it. (See **Figure 4•13.**)

As mentioned earlier, multiple sclerosis is caused by an autoimmune disorder that attacks a protein in the myelin sheaths of axons in the central nervous system. Another autoimmune disorder attacks a different protein: the neuro-

**synaptic cleft** A fluid-filled space between the presynaptic and postsynaptic membranes; the terminal button releases transmitter substance into this space.

**neurotransmitter receptor** A special protein molecule located in the membrane of the postsynaptic neuron that responds to molecules of the neurotransmitter.

FIGURE 4•13 Ion-channel receptors. The ion channel opens when a molecule of neurotransmitter attaches to the binding site. For purposes of clarity, the drawing is schematic; molecules of neurotransmitter are actually much larger than individual ions.

*(From Carlson, N. R. (2004).* Physiology of behaviour *(8th ed.). Needham Heights, MA: Allyn & Bacon, p. 56. Reprinted with permission.)*

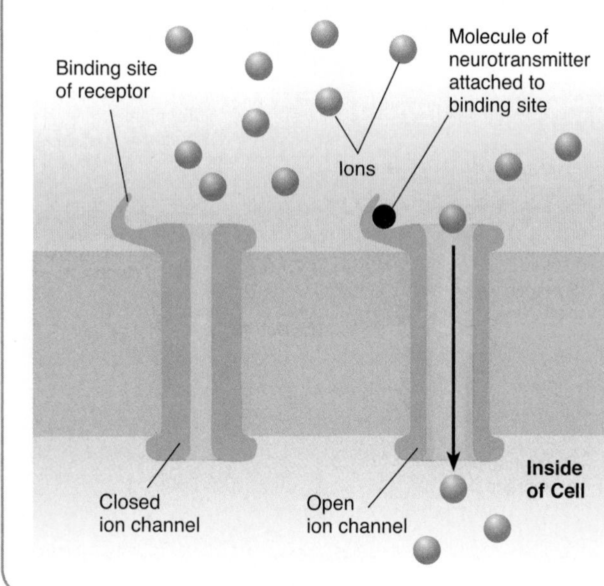


FIGURE 4•14 Reuptake of molecules of transmitter substance.

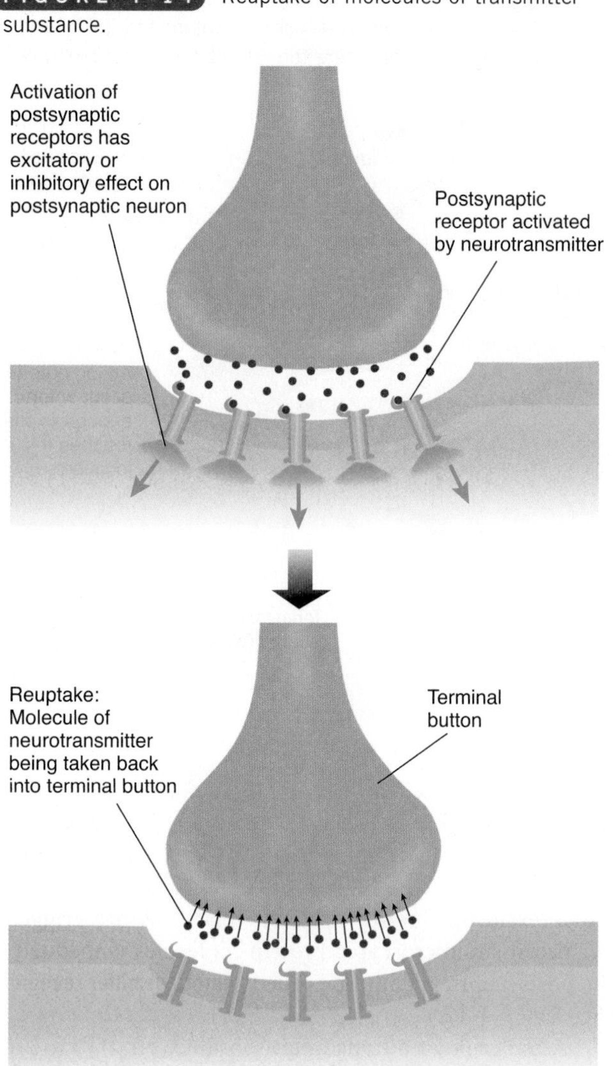


transmitter receptor that is found in the membrane of muscle fibres. Almost as fast as new receptors are produced, the immune system destroys them. The result of this attack is progressive *myasthenia gravis*, or "grave muscle weakness." Myasthenia gravis is not very common, but most experts believe that many mild cases go undiagnosed.

The excitation or inhibition produced by a synapse is short-lived; the effects soon pass away, usually in a fraction of a second. At most synapses, the effects are terminated by a process called **reuptake.** The transmitter substance is released and quickly taken up again by the terminal button, so it therefore has only a short time to stimulate the postsynaptic receptor molecules. (See **Figure 4•14.**) The rate at which the terminal button takes back the transmitter substance determines how prolonged the effects of the chemical on the postsynaptic neuron will be. The faster the transmitter substance is taken back, the shorter its effects will be on the postsynaptic neuron. As we will see, some drugs affect the nervous system by slowing down the rate of reuptake, thus prolonging the effects of the transmitter substance.

**reuptake** The process by which a terminal button retrieves the molecules of transmitter substance that it has just released; terminates the effect of the transmitter substance on the receptors of the postsynaptic neuron.

## Interim Summary

### The Brain and Its Components

The brain has three major functions: control of behaviour, processing and storing of information about the environment, and regulation of the body's physiological processes.

The central nervous system consists of the spinal cord and the three major divisions of the brain: the brain stem, the cerebellum, and the cerebral hemispheres. The cerebral cortex, which covers the cerebral hemispheres, is wrinkled by fissures and gyri. The brain communicates with the rest of the body through the peripheral nervous system, which includes the spinal nerves and cranial nerves.

The basic element of the nervous system is the neuron, with its soma, dendrites, and axon. Neurons are assisted in their tasks by glia, which provide physical support, aid in the development of the nervous system, provide neurons with chemicals they need, remove unwanted chemicals, provide myelin sheaths for axons, and protect neurons from infections.

One neuron communicates with another (or with muscle or gland cells) at synapses. A synapse is the junction of the terminal button of the presynaptic neuron with the membrane of the postsynaptic neuron. Synaptic communication is chemical; when an action potential travels down an axon (when the axon "fires"), it causes a transmitter substance to be released by the terminal buttons. An action potential consists of a brief change in the electrical charge of the axon, produced by a brief entry of positively charged sodium ions into the axon followed by a brief exit of positively charged potassium ions. Ions enter the axon through ion channels, and ion transporters eventually restore the proper concentrations of ions inside and outside the cell.

Molecules of the transmitter substance released by terminal buttons either excite or inhibit the firing of the postsynaptic neuron. The combined effects of excitatory and inhibitory synapses on a particular neuron determine the rate of firing of that neuron.

**QUESTIONS TO CONSIDER**

1. The brain is the seat of our perceptions, thoughts, memories, and feelings. Why, then, do we so often refer to our hearts as the location of our feelings and emotions? For example, why do you think we say, "He acted with his heart, not with his head"?
2. The blood–brain barrier keeps many chemicals in the blood out of the brain. There are a few places in the brain where this barrier does not exist, including the part of the brain stem that contains the neural circuits that trigger vomiting. Can you think of an explanation for the lack of a blood–brain barrier in this region?

# Drugs and Behaviour

Long ago, people discovered that the sap, fruit, leaves, bark, or roots of various plants could alter their perceptions and behaviour, could be used to relieve pain or treat diseases, or could be used as poisons to kill animals for food. They also discovered that some substances affected people's moods in ways that they wanted to experience again and again.

Why do plants produce chemicals that have specific effects on the cells of our nervous system? They do so because these chemicals are toxic to animals—primarily insects—that eat them. Of course, some chemicals produced by plants have beneficial effects in humans and have consequently been extracted or synthesized in the laboratory for use as therapeutic drugs. The therapeutic use of drugs is of obvious benefit to society, and the abuse of addictive drugs is responsible for much misery and unhappiness. But drugs are also important tools to help scientists discover how the brain works. For example, we know that certain drugs relieve anxiety and others reduce the symptoms of schizophrenia. Discovering how these drugs affect the brain can help our understanding of the causes of these disorders and can provide information we need to develop even better forms of treatments.

## Effects of Drugs on Synaptic Transmission

Drugs that affect our thoughts, perceptions, emotions, and behaviour do so by affecting the activity of neurons in the brain. As we saw, communication between neurons involves the release of neurotransmitters, which bind with receptors and either excite or inhibit the activity of the postsynaptic cell. Drugs can affect this process in many ways. They can stimulate or inhibit the release of neurotransmitters, mimic the effects of neurotransmitters on postsynaptic receptors, block these effects, or interfere with the reuptake of a neurotransmitter once it is released. Through these mechanisms (and others too complicated to describe here), a drug can alter the perceptions, thoughts, and behaviours controlled by particular neurotransmitters. Let's briefly examine some of these mechanisms.

**Stimulating or Inhibiting the Release of Neurotransmitters** Some drugs stimulate certain terminal buttons to release their neurotransmitter continuously, even when the axon is not firing. Other drugs prevent certain terminal buttons from releasing their neurotransmitter when the axon fires. The effects of a particular drug are usually specific to one neurotransmitter. (See step 1 in **Figure 4•15**.)

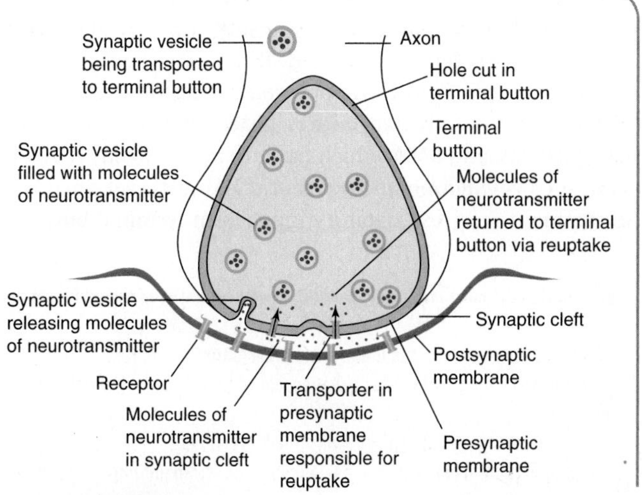


**FIGURE 4•15** A summary of the ways in which drugs can affect the synaptic transmission.

**Stimulating or Blocking Postsynaptic Receptors** Neurotransmitters produce their effects by stimulating postsynaptic receptors; this excites or inhibits postsynaptic neurons by opening ion channels and permitting ions to enter or leave the neurons. Some drugs mimic the effects of particular neurotransmitters by directly stimulating particular kinds of receptors. If we use the lock-and-key analogy to describe the effects of a neurotransmitter on a receptor, then a drug that stimulates receptors works like a master key, turning the receptors on even when the neurotransmitter is not present. (See step 2 in Figure 4.15.)

Some drugs bind with receptors and do not stimulate them. This action blocks receptors, making them inaccessible to the neurotransmitter and thus inhibiting synaptic transmission. To continue the lock-and-key analogy, a drug that blocks receptors plugs up the lock so that the key will no longer fit into it.

**Inhibiting Reuptake** As we saw, the effects of most neurotransmitters are kept brief by the process of reuptake. Molecules of the neurotransmitter are released by a terminal button, stimulate the receptors in the postsynaptic membrane for a fraction of a second, and are then taken back into the terminal button. Some drugs inhibit the process of reuptake so that molecules of the neurotransmitter continue to stimulate the postsynaptic receptors for a long time. Therefore, inhibition of reuptake increases the effect of the neurotransmitter. (See step 3 in Figure 4.15.)

## Neurotransmitters, Their Actions, and Drugs That Affect Them

Now that we've seen the most important ways that drugs can affect synaptic transmission, let's look at the most important neurotransmitters and consider some examples of drugs that interact with them. Because neurotransmitters have two general effects on postsynaptic membranes—excitatory or inhibitory—you might expect that there would be two kinds of neurotransmitters. However, in reality, there are many different kinds—several dozen, at least.

In the brain, most synaptic communication is accomplished by two neurotransmitters: **glutamate**, which has excitatory effects, and **GABA**, which has inhibitory effects. (GABA stands for *gamma-amino butyric acid.*) Almost every neuron in the brain receives excitatory input from terminal buttons that secrete glutamate and inhibitory input from terminal buttons that secrete GABA. (Another inhibitory neurotransmitter, *glycine*, is found in the lower brain stem and the spinal cord.)

What do all of the other neurotransmitters do? In general, they have modulating effects rather than information-transmitting effects. That is, the release of neurotransmitters other than glutamate and GABA tends to activate or inhibit entire circuits of neurons that are involved in particular brain functions. These effects include facilitation of learning, control of wakefulness and vigilance, suppression of impulsive behaviour, and suppression or enhancement of anxiety. Thus, because particular drugs can selectively affect neurons that secrete particular neurotransmitters, these drugs can have specific effects on behaviour.

Given the importance of glutamate and GABA, let's look at these two neurotransmitters first.

**Glutamate** As mentioned, glutamate is the most important excitatory neurotransmitter in the brain. It is also the major excitatory neurotransmitter in the spinal cord. With the exception of neurons that detect painful stimuli, all sensory organs transmit information to the brain through axons whose terminals release glutamate.

One type of glutamate receptor (the *NMDA receptor*) plays a critical role in the effects of environmental stimulation on the developing brain and is also responsible for many of the changes in synaptic connections that are responsible for learning. This receptor is partially deactivated by alcohol, which accounts for the fact that binge drinkers often have no memory of what happened while they were drunk.

**GABA** Some drugs depress behaviour, causing relaxation, sedation, or even loss of consciousness. Most of these drugs act on a particular type of GABA receptor (the $GABA_A$ receptor), increasing its sensitivity to the neurotransmitter. **Barbiturates** act this way. In low doses, barbiturates have a calming effect. In progressively higher doses, they produce difficulty in walking and talking, unconsciousness, coma, and death. A dose of a barbiturate sufficient to cause relaxation is not much lower than a fatal dose; thus, these drugs do not have much of a safety factor. Physicians rarely prescribe barbiturates.

By far the most commonly used depressant drug is ethyl alcohol, the active ingredient in alcoholic beverages. This drug also acts on the $GABA_A$ receptor. The effects of alcohol and barbiturates are additive: A moderate dose of alcohol plus a moderate dose of barbiturates can be fatal.

Many **antianxiety drugs** are members of a family known as the **benzodiazepines**, which include the well-known tranquilizer Valium (diazepam). These drugs, too, act on $GABA_A$ receptors on neurons in various parts of the brain, including a region that is involved in fear and anxiety. Benzodiazepines are much safer than barbiturates; a lethal dose is more than a hundred times higher than a therapeutic dose. They are sometimes used to treat people who are afflicted by periodic

**glutamate** The most important excitatory neurotransmitter in the brain and spinal cord.
**GABA** The most important inhibitory neurotransmitter in the brain.
**barbiturate** A drug that causes sedation; one of several derivatives of barbituric acid.
**antianxiety drug** A "tranquilizer," which reduces anxiety.
**benzodiazepine** A class of drug having anxiolytic ("tranquilizing") effects, such as diazepam (Valium).

attacks of severe anxiety. In addition, some benzodiazepines serve as sleep medications.

**Acetylcholine** **Acetylcholine (ACh)** is the primary neurotransmitter secreted by the axons of motor neurons; it is also released by several groups of neurons in the brain. Because all muscular movement is accomplished by the release of acetylcholine, you will not be surprised to learn that the immune systems of people with myasthenia gravis (described in the previous section) attack acetylcholine receptors.

The axons and terminal buttons of acetylcholinergic neurons are distributed widely throughout the brain. Three systems have received the most attention from neuroscientists. One system activates the brain mechanisms responsible for REM sleep—the phase of sleep during which most dreaming occurs. Another system is involved in activating neurons in the cerebral cortex and facilitating learning, especially perceptual learning. A third system controls the functions of another part of the brain involved in learning: the hippocampus. (You will see this structure later in this chapter.)

Two drugs, botulinum toxin and the venom of the black widow spider, affect the release of acetylcholine. **Botulinum toxin**, produced by a bacterium that can grow in improperly canned food, prevents the release of ACh. The drug is an extremely potent poison. Very dilute solutions (they had better be!) of this drug, usually referred to as botox, can be injected into people's facial muscles to stop muscular contractions that are causing wrinkles. **Black widow spider venom** has the opposite effect: It stimulates the release of ACh. Although the effects of black widow spider venom can also be fatal to infants or to frail, elderly people, the venom is much less toxic than botulinum toxin.

Although the effects of most neurotransmitters on the postsynaptic membrane are terminated by reuptake, acetylcholine is an exception. After being released by the terminal button, ACh is deactivated by an enzyme that is present in the postsynaptic membrane. This enzyme, acetylcholinesterase (AChE), can be inactivated by various drugs. One of them, **neostigmine**, can help people with myasthenia gravis. The drug allows the patients to regain some strength, because the acetylcholine that is released in their muscles has a more prolonged effect on the few acetylcholine receptors that remain. (Fortunately, neostigmine cannot cross the blood–brain barrier, so it does not affect the AChE found in the central nervous system.)

The best-known drug that affects acetylcholine receptors is **nicotine**, found in the leaves of the tobacco plant, *Nicotiana tabacum*. Nicotine is a highly addictive drug; as evidence, consider the fact that after undergoing surgery for lung cancer, approximately 50 percent of patients continue to smoke (Hyman & Malenka, 2001). The addictive nature of nicotine indicates that acetylcholine plays a role in the reinforcement (reward) mechanisms of the brain. You'll learn more about the nature of reinforcement later in this chapter and in Chapters 7 and 13.

▲ *The venom of the black widow spider causes the release of acetylcholine, which can cause numbness, muscle pain and cramps, sweating, salivation, and difficulty breathing. Fortunately, a single bite is very rarely fatal for a healthy adult.*

Another drug, **curare**, blocks acetylcholine receptors. Because these are the receptors on muscles, curare, like botulinum toxin, causes paralysis. However, the effects of curare are much faster. The drug is extracted from several species of plants found in South America, where it was discovered long ago by people who used it to coat the tips of arrows and darts. Within minutes of being struck by one of these points, an animal collapses, ceases breathing, and dies. Nowadays, curare (or any of various drugs with the same site of action) is used to paralyze patients who are to undergo surgery so that their muscles will relax completely and not contract when they are cut with a scalpel. An anaesthetic also must be used, because a person who receives only curare will remain perfectly conscious and sensitive to pain, even though paralyzed. Of course, a respirator must supply air to the lungs during the procedure.

**Monoamines** Dopamine, norepinephrine, and serotonin are three chemicals that belong to a family of compounds called **monoamines.** Because the molecular structures of these substances are similar, some drugs affect the activity of all

**acetylcholine (ACh)** A neurotransmitter found in the brain, spinal cord, and parts of the peripheral nervous system; responsible for muscular contraction.

**botulinum toxin** A drug that prevents the release of acetylcholine by terminal buttons.

**black widow spider venom** A drug that stimulates the release of acetylcholine by terminal buttons.

**neostigmine** A drug that enhances the effects of acetylcholine by blocking the enzyme that destroys it.

**nicotine** A drug that binds with and stimulates acetylcholine receptors, mimicking the effects of this neurotransmitter.

**curare** A drug that binds with and blocks acetylcholine receptors, preventing the neurotransmitter from exerting its effects.

**monoamine** A category of neurotransmitters that includes dopamine, norepinephrine, and serotonin.

▲ *This native of Peru is inserting a curare-tipped dart into his blowgun. Curare kills animals by blocking acetylcholine receptors, which paralyzes muscles and causes suffocation.*

of them to some degree. The monoamines are produced by several systems of neurons in the brain. Most of these systems consist of a relatively small number of cell bodies located in the brain stem, whose axons branch repeatedly and give rise to an enormous number of terminal buttons distributed throughout many regions of the brain. Monoaminergic neurons thus serve to modulate the function of widespread regions of the brain, increasing or decreasing the activities of particular brain functions.

**Dopamine (DA)** has been implicated in several important functions, including movement, attention, learning, and the reinforcing effects of drugs that people tend to abuse. A progressive degenerative disease that destroys one set of DA neurons causes **Parkinson's disease**, a movement disorder characterized by tremors, rigidity of the limbs, poor balance, and difficulty in initiating movements. People with Parkinson's disease are given a drug called L-DOPA. Once this chemical reaches the brain, it is taken up by the DA neurons that still survive and is converted to dopamine. As a result, these neurons release more dopamine, which alleviates the patients' symptoms.

**dopamine (DA)** A monoamine neurotransmitter involved in control of brain mechanisms of movement and reinforcement.
**Parkinson's disease** A neurological disorder characterized by tremors, rigidity of the limbs, poor balance, and difficulty in initiating movements; caused by degeneration of a system of dopamine-secreting neurons.
**norepinephrine (NE)** A monoamine neurotransmitter involved in alertness and vigilance and control of REM sleep.
**serotonin** A monoamine neurotransmitter involved in the regulation of mood; in the control of eating, sleep, and arousal; and in the regulation of pain.
**LSD** Lysergic acid diethylamide; a hallucinogenic drug that blocks a category of serotonin receptors.
**neuromodulator** A substance secreted in the brain that modulates the activity of neurons that contain the appropriate receptors.

Dopamine has also been implicated as a neurotransmitter that might be involved in schizophrenia, a serious psychological disorder whose symptoms include hallucinations, delusions, and disruption of normal, logical thought processes. Drugs such as Thorazine (chlorpromazine) and Clozaril (clozapine) relieve the symptoms of this disorder, apparently by blocking particular types of dopamine receptors. The physiology of schizophrenia is discussed in Chapter 17.

Several drugs inhibit the reuptake of dopamine, thus serving to prolong and strengthen its effects. The best known of these drugs are amphetamine and cocaine. The fact that people abuse these drugs indicates that dopamine plays an important role in reinforcement. (In fact, nicotine exerts its reinforcing effect by indirectly increasing the activity of terminal buttons that release dopamine.)

Almost every region of the brain receives input from neurons that secrete the second monoamine, **norepinephrine (NE)**. Release of NE (also known as *noradrenaline*) appears to cause an increase in vigilance—attentiveness to events in the environment.

The third monoamine neurotransmitter, **serotonin**, has complex behavioural effects. Serotonin plays a role in the regulation of mood; in the control of eating, sleep, and arousal; and in the regulation of pain. A deficiency in the release of serotonin in the cerebral cortex is associated with alcoholism and anti-social behaviour. Like NE neurons, serotonin-secreting neurons are involved in the control of REM sleep. Drugs such as Prozac (fluoxetine), which inhibit the reuptake of serotonin and thus strengthen and prolong its effects, are used to treat depression, anxiety disorder, and obsessive-compulsive disorder. A drug that causes the release of serotonin (fenfluramine) was used as an appetite suppressant in the 1990s, but adverse side effects took this drug off the market.

Several hallucinogenic drugs appear to produce their effects by interacting with serotonergic transmission. For example, **LSD** (lysergic acid diethylamide) produces distortions of visual perceptions that some people find awesome and fascinating but that simply frighten other people. This drug, which is effective in extremely small doses, stimulates one category of serotonin receptor.

**Peptides** As we saw earlier, terminal buttons excite or inhibit postsynaptic neurons by releasing neurotransmitters. These chemicals travel a very short distance and affect receptors located on a small patch of the postsynaptic membrane. But some neurons release chemicals that get into the general circulation of the brain and stimulate receptors on many thousands of neurons, some located a considerable distance away. These chemicals are called **neuromodulators**, because they modulate the activity of the neurons they affect. We can think of neuromodulators as the brain's own drugs. As these chemicals diffuse through the brain, they can activate or inhibit circuits of neurons that control a variety of functions; thus, they can modulate particular categories of behaviour.

Most neuromodulators are peptides. (The most important exception to this rule is described in the next subsection.)

**Peptides** are molecules that consist of two or more amino acids attached by special chemical links called peptide bonds. One of the best-known families of peptides is the **endogenous opioids.** *Endogenous* means "produced from within"; *opioid* means "like opium." Several years ago, it became clear that opiates—drugs such as opium, morphine, and heroin—reduce pain because they have direct effects on the brain. (Please note that the term *opioid* refers to endogenous chemicals, and *opiate* refers to drugs.) The endogenous opioids stimulate special opioid receptors located on neurons in several parts of the brain. Their behavioural effects include decreased sensitivity to pain and a tendency to persist in ongoing behaviour. Opioids are released while an animal is engaging in important species-typical behaviours, such as mating or fighting. The behavioural effects of opioids ensure that a mating animal or an animal fighting to defend itself is less likely to be deterred by pain; thus, conception is more likely to occur and a defence is more likely to be successful.

People abuse opiates not because opiates reduce pain, but because they cause the release of dopamine in the brain, which has a reinforcing effect on behaviour. This reinforcing effect normally encourages an animal performing a useful and important behaviour to continue in that behaviour. Unfortunately, the reinforcing effect is not specific to useful and important behaviours and can lead to addiction.

To help drug addicts, pharmacologists have developed drugs that block opioid receptors. One of them, **naloxone**, is used clinically to reverse opiate intoxication. This drug has saved the lives of many drug abusers brought to the emergency room in heroin-induced comas. An injection of naloxone blocks the effects of the heroin, and the person quickly revives.

Various peptide neuromodulators other than the opioids play roles in behaviours important to survival, such as control of eating and metabolism, drinking, mineral balance, mating, parental care, and social bonding. Some reduce anxiety; others increase it. Some promote eating; others curb appetite. Research on the effects of these chemicals is discussed in later chapters.

**Cannabinoids** You have undoubtedly heard of *Cannabis sativa*, the plant that produces hemp and marijuana. You probably also know that it produces a resin that has physiological effects on the brain. The principal active ingredient in this resin is tetrahydrocannabinol (THC), which affects perception and behaviour by activating receptors located on neurons in the brain. THC mimics the effects of **endogenous cannabinoids**—chemicals produced and released by neurons in the brain.

THC produces analgesia and sedation, stimulates appetite, reduces nausea caused by drugs used to treat cancer, relieves asthma attacks, decreases pressure within the eyes in patients with glaucoma, and reduces the symptoms of certain motor disorders. On the other hand, THC interferes with concentration and memory, alters visual and auditory perception, and distorts perception of the passage of time (Iversen, 2003). Devane and colleagues (1992) discovered the first—and most important—endogenous cannabinoid: a lipid-like (fat-like) substance they named **anandamide**, from the Sanskrit word *ananda*, or "bliss."

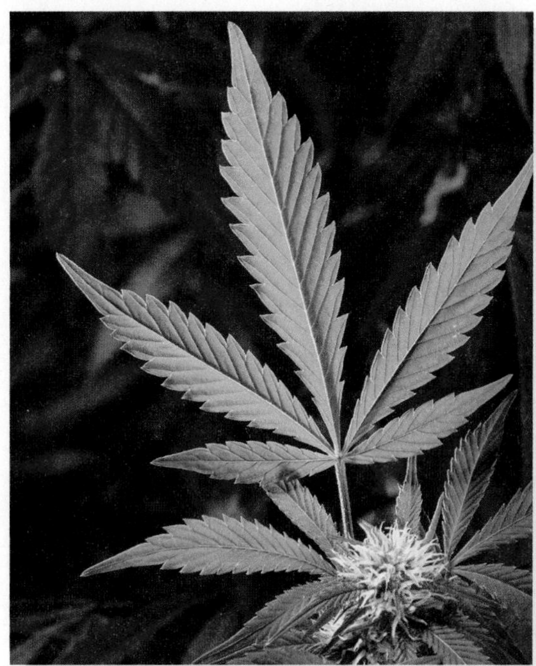

▲ *The effects of endogenous cannabinoids, produced and released in the brain, are mimicked by THC, the active ingredient of* Cannabis sativa, *the marijuana plant.*

Cannabinoid receptors are found on terminal buttons of neurons that secrete glutamate, GABA, acetylcholine, dopamine, norepinephrine, and serotonin. (That is, almost all of the neurotransmitters I've mentioned in this chapter.) Thus, the secretion of anandamide—or the smoking of marijuana—alters the release of these neurotransmitters, and this has widespread effects in the brain. Recent research indicates that the endogenous cannabinoids modulate the synaptic changes that appear to be responsible for learning, which accounts for the fact that THC disrupts short-term memory (Fegley et al., 2004).

**Table 4•1** lists the neurotransmitters discussed in this section, summarizes their effects, and lists some drugs that interact with them.

**peptide** A category of neurotransmitters and neuromodulators that consist of two or more amino acids, linked by peptide bonds.

**endogenous opioid** A neuromodulator whose action is mimicked by a natural or synthetic opiate, such as opium, morphine, or heroin.

**naloxone** A drug that binds with and blocks opioid receptors, preventing opiate drugs or endogenous opioids from exerting their effects.

**endogenous cannabinoid** A neuromodulator whose action is mimicked by THC and other drugs present in marijuana.

**anandamide** The most important endogenous cannabinoid.

TABLE 4•1 **The Major Neurotransmitters, Their Primary Effects, and Drugs That Interact with Them**

| Neurotransmitter | Primary Effects | Drugs That Interact with Neurotransmitter | Effects of Drugs |
|---|---|---|---|
| Glutamate | Primary excitatory neurotransmitter in brain | Alcohol | Desensitization of NMDA receptor |
| GABA | Primary excitatory neurotransmitter in brain | Barbiturates<br>Benzodiazepines ("tranquilizers")<br>Alcohol | Desensitization of $GABA_A$ receptor |
| Acetylcholine (ACh) | Excites muscular contraction, activates cerebral cortex, controls REM sleep, controls hippocampus | Botulinum toxin<br>Black widow spider venom<br>Neostigmine<br>Nicotine | Blocks release of ACh<br>Stimulates release of ACh<br>Blocks AChE, enhances effects of ACh<br>Stimulates ACh receptors |
| Monoamines | | | |
| Dopamine (DA) | Facilitates movement, attention, learning, reinforcement | L-DOPA<br>Amphetamine, cocaine<br>Antipsychotic drugs | Increases synthesis of dopamine<br>Inhibit reuptake of dopamine<br>Block dopamine receptors |
| Norepinephrine (NE) | Increases vigilance, controls REM sleep | | |
| Serotonin | Regulates mood; controls eating, sleep, arousal, regulation of pain; suppresses risky behaviours | Fluoxetine (Prozac)<br>LSD | Inhibits reuptake of serotonin<br>Stimulates certain serotonin receptors |
| Endogenous opioids | Reduce pain, reinforce ongoing behaviour | Opiates (heroin, morphine, etc.)<br>Naloxone | Stimulate opioid receptors<br>Blocks opioid receptors |
| Anandamide (endogenous cannabinoid) | Analgesia, nausea reduction, decreased pressure in eyes, interference with short-term memory, increased appetite | THC | Stimulates cannabinoid receptors |

## Interim Summary

### Drugs and Behaviour

Drugs can facilitate or interfere with synaptic activity. Facilitating drugs include those that cause the release of a neurotransmitter (such as the venom of the black widow spider); drugs that directly stimulate postsynaptic receptors, thus duplicating the effects of the neurotransmitter itself (such as nicotine); and drugs that inhibit the reuptake of a neurotransmitter (such as amphetamine and cocaine). Drugs that interfere with synaptic activity include those that inhibit the release of a neurotransmitter (such as botulinum toxin) and those that block receptors (such as curare).

In the brain, most synaptic communication is accomplished by two neurotransmitters: glutamate, which has excitatory effects, and GABA, which has inhibitory effects. Acetylcholine (ACh) controls muscular movements and is involved in control of REM sleep, activation of the cerebral cortex, and modulation of a brain structure involved in memory. Nicotine stimulates ACh receptors, and curare blocks them (and causes paralysis). Neostigmine, which is used to treat myasthenia gravis, suppresses the destruction of ACh by an enzyme. The monoamines also modulate important brain functions. Dopamine (DA) facilitates movements and plays a role in reinforcing behaviours. L-DOPA, which stimulates production of DA, is used to treat Parkinson's disease, and cocaine produces reinforcing effects on behaviour by blocking the reuptake of dopamine. Drugs that block dopamine receptors are used to treat the symptoms of schizophrenia. The release of norepinephrine (NE) increases vigilance. The release of serotonin helps suppress aggressive behaviour and risk-taking behaviour, and drugs that inhibit the reuptake of serotonin are used to treat anxiety disorders, depression, and obsessive-compulsive disorder.

Most peptides serve as neuromodulators, which resemble neurotransmitters but travel farther and are dispersed more widely within the brain, where they can modulate the activity of many neurons. The best-known neuromodulators are the endogenous opioids, which are released when an animal is engaged in important behaviour. Anandamide, the most important of the endogenous cannabinoids, helps regulate the release of many neurotransmitters. THC, the active ingredient in marijuana, acts on cannabinoid receptors and mimics the effects of anandamide. Cannabinoids have some beneficial effects but also impair short-term memory.

**QUESTIONS TO CONSIDER**

1. As we saw, opioids are useful neuromodulators because they encourage an animal to continue fighting or mating. Can you think of other behaviours that might be influenced by neuromodulators? Can you think of mental or behavioural problems that might be caused if too much or too little of these neuromodulators were secreted?
2. Suppose that a woman is taking a drug for anxiety. Suppose further that she is planning to go out for drinks with friends. Her husband advises her to enjoy an evening with her friends but not have any drinks. Why is this a good suggestion?
3. If you were in charge of the research department of a pharmaceutical company, what new behaviourally active drugs would you seek? Analgesics? Antianxiety drugs? Antiaggression drugs? Memory-improving drugs? Should behaviourally active drugs be taken only by people who clearly have afflictions such as schizophrenia, depression, or obsessive-compulsive disorder? Or should we try to find drugs that help people who want to improve their intellectual performance or social adjustment or who simply want to feel happier?

# Study of the Brain

Recent advances in science and technology have given us the means to study—and perhaps someday understand—the brain. We now have at our disposal a range of research methods that would have been impossible to imagine just a few decades ago. We have ways to identify neurons that contain particular chemicals. We have ways to use special microscopes to observe particular ions entering living neurons when the appropriate ion channels open. We have ways to inactivate individual genes or to insert new genes in laboratory animals to see what happens to the animals' physiology and behaviour. We have ways to view details of the structure of a living human brain and to study the activity of various brain regions while the person is performing various perceptual or behavioural tasks. In this section, we'll look at the most important research methods, which will introduce you to the research performed by physiological psychologists.

## Experimental Ablation

As we saw in Chapter 1, physiological knowledge has been important to psychology since the time of Johannes Müller. Naturally, much of this knowledge has concerned the physiology of the brain, which requires study of its biological processes. As a biological organ, the brain changes in response to disease or accident, it shows electrical and chemical responses, and it responds to the instructions encoded in its genes. Physiological psychologists have developed methods that permit detailed study of how these processes occur in the brain and what consequences they show for behaviour.

The earliest research method of physiological psychology involved the study of change. Using experimental ablation, Pierre Flourens and Paul Broca came to their insights about the brain by correlating a behavioural deficit with physical disruption of a specific part of the nervous system. Although disruption of the brain can occur through illness or accident, as in the case studied by Broca, it is much more informative if this disruption can be studied under laboratory conditions using the ethical safeguards I discussed earlier. To study the experimental effect of brain disruption in animal behaviour, the investigator produces a **brain lesion**, an injury to a particular part of the brain, and then studies the effects of the lesion on the animal's behaviour. If particular behaviours are disrupted, the damaged part of the brain must be involved in those behaviours.

To produce a brain lesion, the researcher first anaesthetizes an animal, prepares it for surgery, and drills a hole in its skull. In most cases, the region under investigation is located deep within the brain. To reach this region, the investigator uses a special device called a **stereotaxic apparatus** to insert a fine wire (called an electrode) or a thin tube (called a cannula) into a particular location in the brain. (The term *stereotaxic* refers to the ability to manipulate an object in three-dimensional space.)

Once the correct region is located, its function can be altered. *Electrolytic lesions* are produced by passing an electrical current through the electrode, which produces heat that destroys a small portion of the brain around the tip of the electrode. Alternatively, *excitotoxic lesions* are established by injecting a chemical through the cannula that causes lethal overstimulation of the neurons. It is also possible to produce *reversible lesions* through special anaesthetics that temporarily suppress action of the region. After a few days, the animal recovers from the operation and the researcher can assess its behaviour. (See **Figure 4•16**.)

Thanks to the advances in genetics we discussed in Chapter 3, physiological psychologists can now manipulate

**brain lesion** Damage to a particular region of the brain; a synonym for experimental ablation.

**stereotaxic apparatus** A device used to insert an electrode into a particular part of the brain for the purpose of recording electrical activity, stimulating the brain electrically, or producing localized damage.

**FIGURE 4•16** A stereotaxic apparatus, used to insert a wire into a specific portion of an animal's brain.

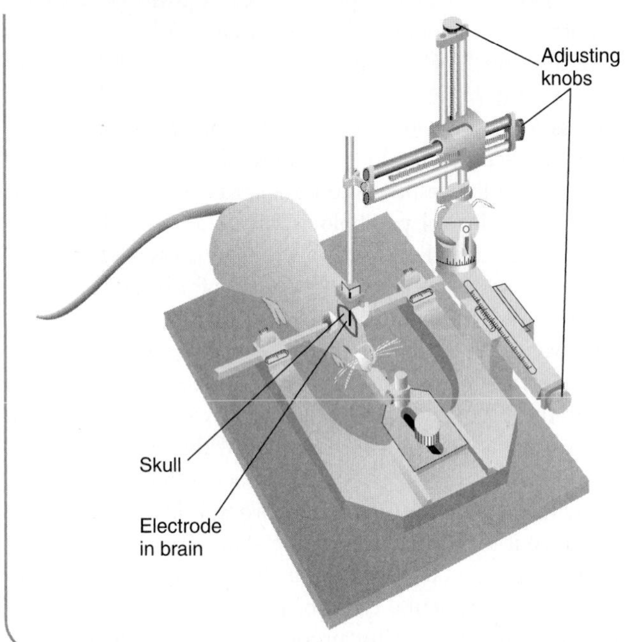


genetic mechanisms that control the nervous system. This control allows them to perform the neurochemical version of experimental ablation. For example, suppose that a specific neurotransmitter is hypothesized to perform some function. A **targeted mutation** (a "genetic knockout gene") can be synthesized to produce only a non-functional version of this neurotransmitter. If implanting this knockout gene then eliminates the function, the researcher has additional evidence of the neurotransmitter's role. For example, a targeted mutation that prevents production of a particular peptide causes a hereditary sleep disorder known as narcolepsy, which, we now know, is caused by degeneration of the neurons that secrete this peptide (Chemelli et al., 1999). Of course, knowledge of the nervous system can also advance our knowledge of genetic mechanisms. Sections of new genetic code for a different species can be implanted into an animal's genome to determine how that gene regulates neural development or function (Milner, Squire, & Kandell, 1998). In one demonstration of this, Tang and colleagues (1999) found that a genetic modification that increased the production of a particular type of receptor increased the animals' learning ability in a particular task.

**targeted mutation** A mutated gene (also called a "knockout gene") produced in the laboratory and inserted into the chromosomes of mice; abolishes the normal effects of the gene.

**neural plasticity** The production of changes in the structure and functions of the nervous system, induced by environmental events.

**CT scanner** A device that uses a special X-ray machine and a computer to produce images of the brain that appear as slices taken parallel to the top of the skull.

## Visualizing the Structure of the Brain

It is important to remember that the brain is a physical, three-dimensional object. Much of its ability to process information derives from the physical connections of neurons to each other or from the clustering of neurons into larger brain modules. Psychologists use several techniques that are designed to trace or map these connections.

Obviously, the brain grows in volume as an individual develops from an embryo to an adult. However, it is also modified by experience after its physical maturation is finished (Kolb & Whishaw, 1998). New synapses form, old ones disappear, dendrites grow or shrink, and the axons of some neurons become myelinated. The brain exhibits **neural plasticity**—structural changes resulting from experience.

Psychologists and neuroscientists can trace the effects of physical maturation and plasticity by using techniques that mark or "stain" neurons chemically. There are many such techniques, adapted for different purposes. Some chemical stains, for example, are particularly good at marking a certain percentage of neurons and making their dendrites especially prominent. These techniques would be helpful in estimating the growth of dendrites and inferring possible changes in the number of synapses. Other staining techniques could highlight axonal growth, showing the way axons grow to connect with specific areas of the brain. **Figure 4•17**, for example, shows how this technique was used to distinguish the effects of four artificial mutations in mice. Two of the mutations show a large collection of axons in the olfactory organ of a mouse converging on one small area; the other two mutations do not show this convergence. The staining technique used in this study can distinguish the effects on neuronal development of the different mutations.

Psychologists and neuroscientists also must examine larger areas of the brain. Chemical staining techniques are sometimes used, for example, when a human patient has died from a brain injury and an autopsy is performed to find the location of the injury. However, recent advances in radiography and nuclear medicine have given us additional methods that allow us to look at the brains of living individuals and construct a realistic image of them.

Until recently, the most useful technique to study the structure of the brain was the **CT scanner**. (See **Figure 4•18**.) (CT stands for *computerized tomography*. *Tomos*, meaning "cut," describes the CT scanner's ability to produce a picture that looks like a slice of the brain.) The scanner sends a narrow beam of X-rays through a person's head. The beam is moved around the patient's head, and a computer calculates the amount of radiation that passes through it at various points along each angle. The result is a two-dimensional image of a "slice" of the person's head, parallel to the top of the skull.

Although the use of X-rays obviously requires extensive safeguards, the CT scanner can provide valuable information regarding the large-scale structure of the brain. Using the CT scanner, for example, an investigator can determine

**FIGURE 4•17** Chemical staining of olfactory neural tissue in mice given artificial mutations. Two of the mutations, depicted in the upper panels of this figure (a, c), produce neurons whose axons project to a single area; two other mutations, depicted in the lower panels (d, e), do not produce this convergence.

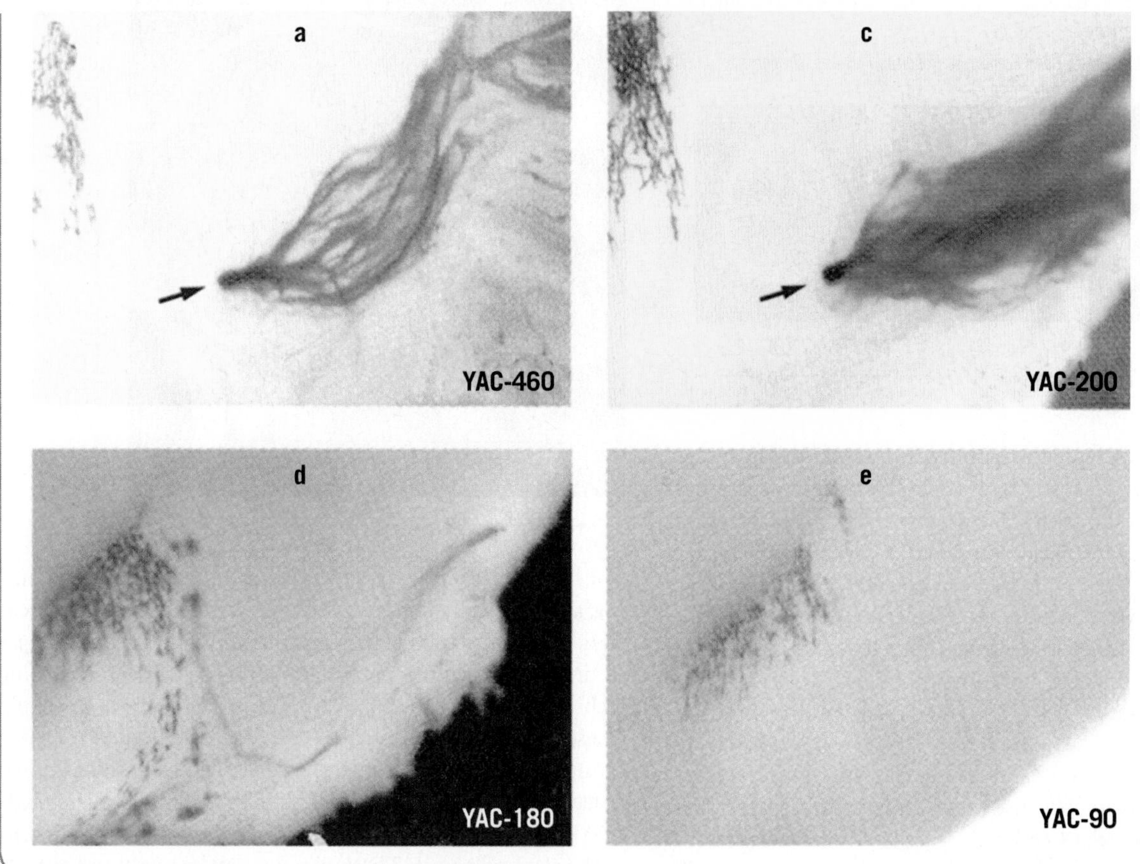


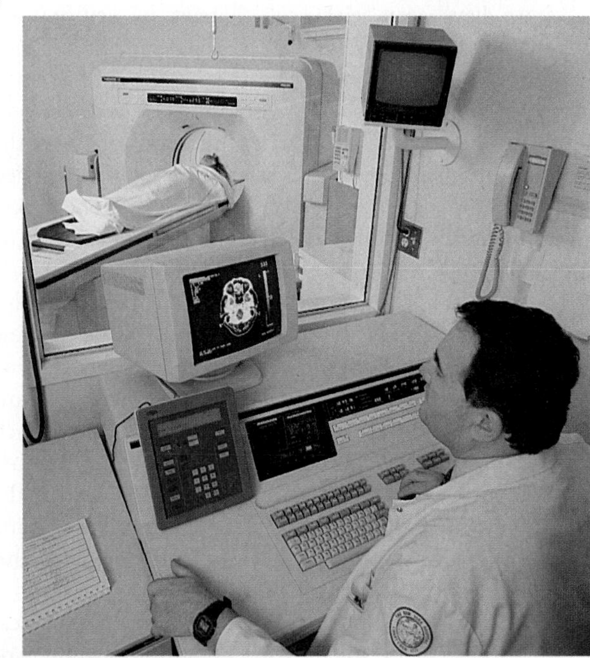

**FIGURE 4•18** A patient being placed in a computerized tomography (CT) scanner.

the approximate location of a brain injury in a living patient. **Figure 4•19** shows several CT scans of the brain of a patient with an injury—Miss S., whose case is described in the opening vignette. The scans are arranged from the bottom of the brain (scan 1) to the top (scan 3). You can easily see the damaged area, a white spot, in the lower left corner of scan 2.

Recent developments in technology have given us two other ways to produce images of the brain. One of these is called *positron emission tomography,* or PET. PET scans rely on radioactive processes to provide tomographical information. A person is given a harmless dose of a radioactive substance. The substance is incorporated into brain tissue metabolically, where it emits an antimatter particle (the positron). This particle travels about 2 cm through brain tissue before it collides with a matter particle. When it does, a photon is emitted, which can be measured and used to construct the brain image.

The other imaging technique is known as *magnetic resonance imaging,* or MRI. (See **Figure 4•20**.) MRI scans are produced by placing an individual within a strong magnetic field. This field causes the molecules within its influence to become aligned with the lines of magnetic force. A radio signal is then generated around the person, which has the

FIGURE 4•19 A set of CT scans from a patient with a brain lesion caused by a damaged area (the white spot in the lower left corner of scan 2). Because left and right are traditionally reversed on CT scans, the damaged area is actually in the right hemisphere.

*(Courtesy of Dr. J. McA. Jones, Good Samaritan Hospital, Portland, Oregon.)*

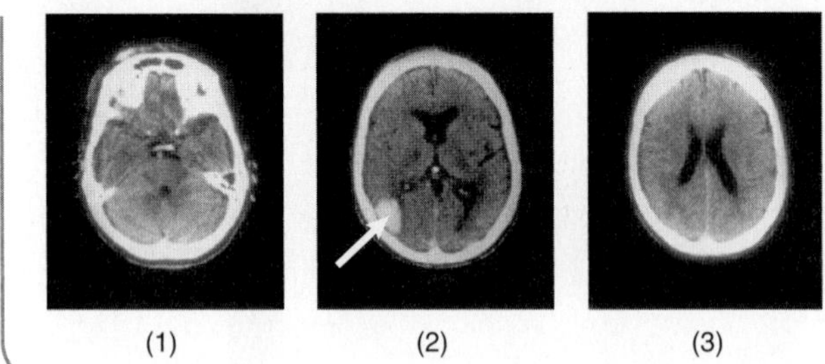


FIGURE 4•20 An MRI scan of a human brain.

*(ISM/Phototake, Inc)*

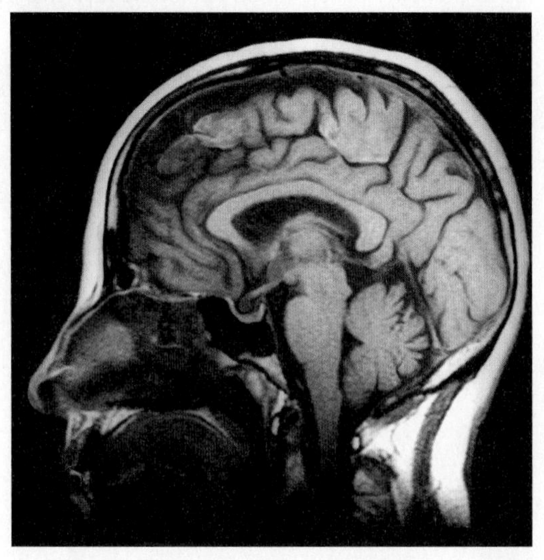

effect of tilting these aligned atoms, just as you might nudge a spinning top and cause it to wobble. The scanner measures the time it takes the molecules to stop wobbling and recover to their aligned state. Because different molecules take different times to recover, an image can be constructed based on the relative amounts of different materials within the scanner. For example, myelinated neurons recover at a different rate than unmyelinated neurons, producing a contrast between white matter and grey matter when the brain is scanned. The data in Figure 4.1 (see page 89) are based on this contrast. MRI scans can produce high-resolution images of brain regions and, because they do not involve radioactivity, are safe to use. Paus and colleagues (1999) have used MRI technology to trace the development of white matter as children matured into adolescents. And one study has even found evidence of significant brain plasticity resulting from learning to drive a taxicab in London (Maguire et al., 2000).

## Measuring the Brain's Activity

In addition to structural features, the brain also shows the effects of the action potentials and synaptic changes of its myriad neurons. These effects can be detected using *recording* techniques and deliberately triggered using *stimulation* methods.

Because the brain's physiology involves both electrical and chemical processes, recording techniques have been developed for each. **Microelectrodes** are extremely thin electrical sensors able to detect the electrical currents of individual neurons. They are either a fine metal wire or a thin glass tube containing an electrically conductive fluid. With suitable amplification, they can be used to measure the minute electrical changes of individual action potentials. Other electrical recording techniques involve larger electrodes placed outside the skull. These electrodes can measure the electrical activity of large groups of neurons. One recently developed technique, known as **magnetoencephalography**, detects the minute magnetic fields that accompany the ionic currents of action potentials in cells of the cerebral cortex. These currents can be measured outside the skull, and have provided substantial evidence of changes in the cerebral cortex (Buonomano & Merzenich, 1998).

As we have seen, electrical changes in neurons are brought about by chemical processes. These can also be studied in the brain. **Microdialysis** is a procedure that collects small amounts of the brain's chemical solutions. It uses a set of concentric tubes to circulate a carrier fluid into and out of the brain; neurotransmitters and similar secretions are carried off through this current, collected, and analyzed. The procedure is sufficiently sensitive to detect the amounts of specific neurotransmitters that escape from the synaptic cleft.

The chemical processes that occur in the brain can also be detected through *neurochemical* methods. Some of these methods mimic the body's own machinery for detecting chemicals. When a foreign protein enters the body, the immune system produces *antibodies* that chemically attach themselves to the protein. The antibodies serve as homing beacons for the white blood cells that can then destroy the invader. Synthetic antibodies that recognize proteins specific to neurons can be produced. If these antibodies are also attached to a special chemical dye, they will show up in a microscope. Using such labelled antibodies, physiological psychologists can detect the presence of neurotransmitters or the enzymes that create them.

**microelectrode** A thin electrode made of wire or glass that can measure the electrical activity of a single neuron.

**magnetoencephalography** A method of brain study that measures the changes in magnetic fields that accompany action potentials in the cerebral cortex.

**microdialysis** A procedure that collects solutions surrounding the brain's neurons for subsequent chemical analysis.

One of the fastest growing areas of psychology and neuroscience uses methods that permit researchers to measure neural activity as the brain performs some function. These methods combine knowledge of the brain's physiology and the visualization technology we discussed in the previous section. One example of these methods, a version of MRI called *functional MRI*, or fMRI, measures the different recovery times of blood hemoglobin. Hemoglobin reacts to the magnetic fields of the MRI scanner, but its recovery time after the radio signal is applied depends on whether it has released its complement of oxygen. The contrast between oxygenated and deoxygenated hemoglobin can be measured in an MRI scanner very quickly, allowing a sequence of scans to be taken in a short span of time. By synchronizing the scans with some psychological task, the fMRI scan shows what parts of the brain are metabolically active at the time the task is performed.

In principle, this method could show regions of the brain that are active as a person undertakes some mental task. However, to make this connection, we must assume that oxygen levels correlate with neural activity. Neuroscientists have found support for this assumption by comparing human fMRI scans to electrode recording data from monkeys (Rees, Friston, & Koch, 2000) in visual areas of the brain.

Even before this evidence was available, fMRI studies were having an explosive impact on the study of brain functioning. Psychologists can use the technique to see how the brain reacts to particular stimuli or to particular requirements of a psychological task. As several psychologists recently wrote, "There is something particularly captivating about coming into the lab each day to literally watch your own brain at work" (Heeger, Juk, Geisler, & Albrecht, 2000).

PET scans can also be used in this way, although the physics of the radioactive agents limits the spatial resolution of the method. Despite this limitation, however, PET scans are ideally suited to measuring biochemical processes in the brain, and can therefore trace neurotransmitter substances (Morgan, Brodie, & Dewey, 1998). **Figure 4•21** shows PET scans after the use of a chemical that becomes concentrated in regions of the brain that contain the most activity. As you can see, different regions become active when the person sees images, hears sounds, or talks.

**FIGURE 4•21** PET scans of the left side of the brain showing the regions having the highest amount of activity. The scans show that different regions of the brain are activated by different tasks.

(*Discover*. (1989). 10(3), p. 61. Reprinted by permission of the publisher.)

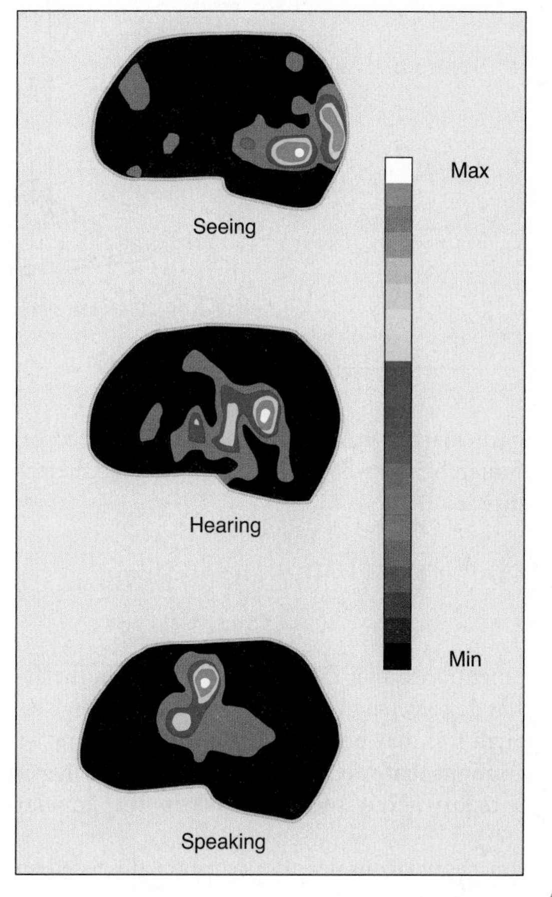


## Stimulating the Brain's Activity

Ideally, recording techniques study the physiology of the brain without greatly changing it. However, it is also useful to examine the effects of activating regions of the brain through stimulation. Moderate currents delivered through an electrode can mimic the effects of an action potential and activate neurons located near the tip of the electrode. The researcher can then see how this artificial stimulation affects the animal's behaviour. One example of an experiment that uses this technique is shown in **Figure 4•22**. A rat presses a lever attached to an electrical switch that turns on a stimulator. The stimulator sends a brief pulse of electricity through an electrode placed in the rat's brain. Olds and Milner (1954) discovered that if the tip of the electrode is located in certain parts of the brain, the animal will press the lever again and again. This finding suggests that these parts of the brain play a role in reward mechanisms. One functional MRI study of heterosexual male college students even found that the sight of a photograph of a beautiful woman activates this region (Aharon et al., 2001).

Some methods of direct stimulation of the brain do not require the invasive implanting of electrodes. The neurons of the outer regions of the brain can be stimulated through magnetic fields. **Transcranial magnetic stimulation** stimulates neurons of the cerebral cortex by inducing an electrical current in the neurons through large electric magnets placed on the scalp. Physiological psychologists find this

**transcranial magnetic stimulation** Direct stimulation of the cerebral cortex induced by magnetic fields generated outside the skull.

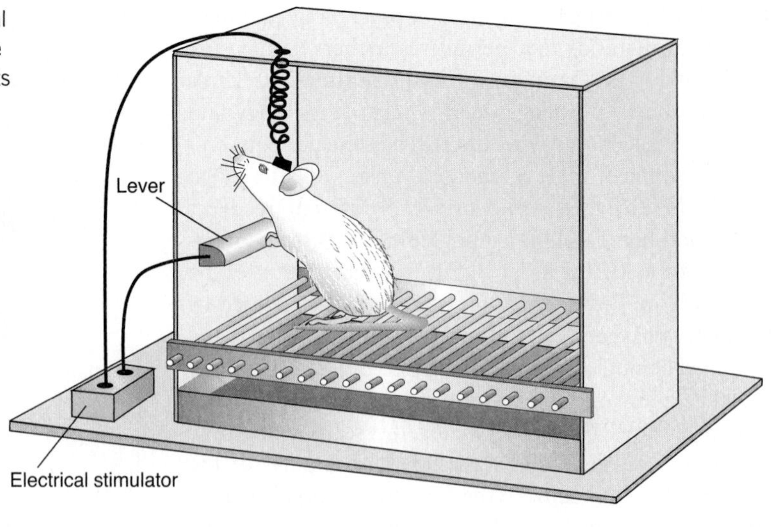


FIGURE 4•22 An example of an electrical stimulation experiment. When the rat presses the switch, it receives a brief pulse of electricity to its brain through electrodes.

technique particularly valuable because it can be used on conscious human beings who can then describe the subjective experience.

## Understanding the Limitations of Brain Methods

I've already mentioned that fMRI results depend on the assumption that deoxygenated hemoglobin reflects neural activity. Although this may be a sound assumption, there are other qualifications that you should bear in mind whenever you hear a report about such methods in the popular media.

First, you should consider the issues we discussed in Chapter 2. Studies using fMRI basically compare the scan of an individual performing one task to the scan when the individual is performing a control task. As in any experiment, the strength of the conclusion depends on the quality of the control. Are all factors controlled? The difference between the scan during the task and the scan during a control activity may be due to some confounding factor.

Similarly, we must be cautious when we interpret the functional role of a particular brain region, regardless of the technique being used. Vanderwolf and Cain (1994) point out many of the possible confounds that can occur in a system as complicated as the brain. Modules within the brain are highly interconnected, with many feedback loops between different regions.

Finally, you should be alert to problems of generalization. The research that we have examined is highly specialized, and the tasks that are used are developed for specific purposes. More study is needed before many of these findings can be applied to real-world problems. For example, the work on brain plasticity has led some politicians and social commentators to recommend early sensory stimulation for human infants. CD recordings of "Mozart for Babies" have been recommended, for example, without careful consideration of whether the studies warrant this intervention or whether the effects would be desirable (Editorial, *Nature Neuroscience*, 1999). Although the new methods of brain imaging and description have great potential, we must always maintain scientific rigour when drawing our conclusions.

## Then and Now

### Neurogenesis

If you've ever had a relative suffer damage to the brain through a stroke or accident, you know how persistent the behavioural effects can be. Unlike many of the body's cells, such as bone, muscle, or skin cells, neurons do not seem to regenerate in adult animals. Indeed, for decades, it was considered a truism that, in mammals, no new neurons were ever formed in the adult brain. Colucci-D'Amato and di Porzio (2008) provide examples of basic medical and biological textbooks from 1881 to 2002 that made this claim. No less an authority than Donald Hebb used to give a talk in which he would gloomily snap his fingers about once a second, while informing his audience that a brain cell died with each snap, never to be replaced. (Hebb went on to reassure his audience by pointing out the large number of neurons that our brains possess.)

Even as knowledge of cell biology improved, evidence seemed to back this textbook view. For example, Rakic (1985) examined adult monkey brain cells that had been stained with a chemical known to label cells specifically when DNA replicates. Although other somatic cells showed clear evidence of regeneration, no brain neurons showed convincing evidence of DNA division. Rakic concluded, like others, that brain cells did not regenerate in adult primates and speculated that this was an evolutionary development designed to preserve the brain's ability to retain information.

However, despite this prevailing opinion, evidence was accumulating that the neurons of many non-mammals could regenerate. Adult songbirds, reptiles, amphibians, and some fish exhibit instances of this **neurogenesis** (Chapouton, Jagasia, & Bally-Cuif, 2007). New neurons seem to appear throughout all stages of life in these species. So, are mammals unique? In fact, the adult mammalian brain *can* produce new neurons.

Before I describe this evidence, let's take a brief look at the basics of human brain development. Early in development, the brain consists of a hollow tube (the *neural tube*) that later develops into the ventricles. This tube is surrounded by the **ventricular zone**, which consists of a layer of *founder cells*—a special type of **stem cell**. During the first phase of development, founder cells divide, making new ones and increasing the size of the ventricular zone. This phase is referred to as *symmetrical division,* because the division of each founder cell produces two identical cells. Then, seven weeks after conception, founder cells receive a chemical signal to begin a period of *asymmetrical division.* During this phase, founder cells divide asymmetrically, producing another founder cell, which remains in place, and a neuron, which travels outward into the developing brain.

The period of asymmetrical division lasts about three months. The end of this stage of development occurs when the founder cells receive a chemical signal that causes them to die—a phenomenon known as **apoptosis** (literally, a "falling away"). All cells contain killer genes, but only certain cells—including the brain's founder cells—contain receptors that detect the chemical death signal and activate these genes.

But that is not the end of the matter. The adult brain contains some stem cells that can divide asymmetrically and produce neurons. Researchers detect the presence of newly produced cells in the brains of laboratory animals by administering a small amount of a radioactive form of one of the molecules that cells use to produce the DNA, which is needed for neurogenesis. The next day, the animals' brains are removed and examined with methods described earlier in this chapter.

Neurogenesis takes place in at least two regions of the ventricular zone in the mammalian brain (Doetsch & Hen, 2005). Stem cells in the *subventricular zone* produce neurons that migrate to the olfactory bulbs, stalk-like protrusions of the brain that receive information from the odour receptors in the nose. Stem cells in the *subgranular zone* produce neurons that migrate to the hippocampus, a brain region that plays a critical role in the formation of new memories. Some preliminary but inconclusive evidence suggests that neurogenesis may take place in other parts of the brain,

**FIGURE 4•23** Effects of learning on neurogenesis, seen in sections through a part of the hippocampus of rats that received training on a learning task or were exposed to a control condition that did not lead to learning. Arrows indicate newly formed cells.

*(From Leuner, B., Mendolia-Loffredo, S., Kozorovitskiy, Y., Samburg, D., Gould, E., and Shors, T. J. (2004). Learning enhances the survival of new neurons beyond the time when the hippocampus is required for memory.* Journal of Neuroscience, *24, 7477–7481. Copyright © 2004 by the Society of Neuroscience.)*

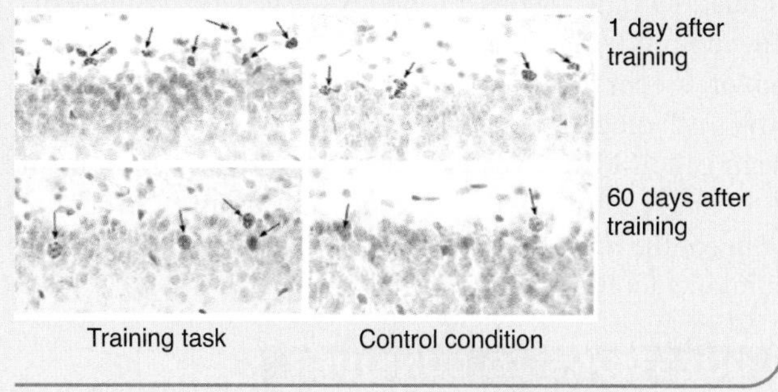


including the cerebral cortex (Gould, 2007). There is even evidence from functional imaging studies that neurogenesis takes place not only in the brains of laboratory animals but also in the human brain (Pereira et al., 2007).

New neurons quickly grow dendrites and axons, and establish functional synaptic connections with existing neurons that surround them (Ramirez-Amaya et al., 2006; Toni et al., 2007). Furthermore, environmental events can influence this process: Exposure to new odours increases the numbers of new neurons in the olfactory bulbs of rats, and training on a learning task enhances neurogenesis in the hippocampus. (See **Figure 4•23**.)

Some evidence suggests a link between stress, depression, and neurogenesis. Depression and exposure to stress suppress neurogenesis in the hippocampus, and drugs or other treatments (including exercise) that reduce stress and depression reinstate neurogenesis (Paizanis, Hamon, & Lanfumey, 2007). Unfortunately, there is no clear evidence that neurogenesis can repair the effects of brain damage, such as that caused by head injury or strokes (Zhao, Deng, & Gage, 2008).

**neurogenesis** The generation of new neurons.

**ventricular zone** The area that surrounds the neural tube; consists of a layer of founder cells.

**stem cell** Undifferentiated cells that can divide and produce any one of a variety of differentiated cells.

**apoptosis** The death of founder cells, caused by a chemical signal at the end of asymmetrical division.

## Interim Summary

### Study of the Brain

The brain's complexity requires a good description of how individual neurons are connected to each other. Several methods have been developed to study the brain. Some, using animals, alter brain function. These techniques selectively destroy parts of the brain, electrically or chemically record or stimulate specific regions, or modify the genetic components of neural processes. Other techniques provide a visual depiction of the brain's structure. Chemical staining methods allow psychologists to see neural structures. CT scans, PET imaging, and MRI scans provide large-scale descriptions of the brain. A third class of methods can measure the functioning of the brain by detecting chemical changes that reflect neural metabolism.

**QUESTIONS TO CONSIDER**

1. Remember that Donald Hebb proposed his view of the nervous system long before most of the techniques we've discussed were invented. Hebb felt that the brain worked by the activation of groups of neurons. He called these groups "cell assemblies" and theorized that cell assemblies corresponded to the brain processes underlying thinking and remembering. Which of the techniques we have discussed would be useful in testing some of Hebb's ideas?
2. Would you like to have an electrode placed in your brain so that you could see what reinforcing ("rewarding") brain stimulation feels like?
3. Suppose it were necessary to make an MRI scan of your brain. Would you want to see the scans afterwards?
4. Suppose you had a PET scanner and many volunteers. You could present various types of stimuli while PET scans were being taken, and you could have the volunteers perform various types of mental tasks and behaviours that did not involve their moving around. What kinds of experiments would you perform?
5. Although the basic program that controls brain development is contained in our chromosomes, environmental factors can also influence this process. Why do you think the process of development is not completely automatic and programmed? What is the point of letting the environment influence it? Would we be better off if development was simply automatic, or does such flexibility have some potential benefits?

**anterior** Toward the front.
**posterior** Toward the back.
**frontal lobe** The front portion of the cerebral cortex, including Broca's speech area and the motor cortex; damage impairs movement, planning, and flexibility in behavioural strategies.
**parietal lobe** The region of the cerebral cortex behind the frontal lobe and above the temporal lobe; contains the somatosensory cortex; is involved in spatial perception and memory.
**temporal lobe** The portion of the cerebral cortex below the frontal and parietal lobes; contains the auditory cortex.
**occipital lobe** The rearmost portion of the cerebral cortex; contains the primary visual cortex.

# Control of Behaviour

As mentioned, the brain has three roles: controlling the movements of the muscles, processing and retaining information about the environment, and regulating the physiological functions of the body. The first two roles look outward toward the environment and the third looks inward. The outward-looking roles include several functions: perceiving events in the environment, learning about them, making plans, and acting. The inward-looking role requires the brain to measure and regulate internal characteristics such as body temperature, blood pressure, and nutrient levels. The outward-looking roles are, of course, of particular interest to psychology. Therefore, in this section, we will examine the portions of the brain that control behaviour and process information. The following section describes the brain's regulatory functions.

## Organization of the Cerebral Cortex

If we want to understand the brain functions most important to the study of behaviour—perceiving, learning, planning, and moving—we should start with the cerebral cortex. Since we will be discussing the various regions of the cerebral cortex, it will be good to start with the names used for them. The cerebral cortex contains a large groove, or fissure, called the *central fissure.* The central fissure provides an important dividing line between the **anterior** (front) part of the cerebral cortex and the **posterior** (back) regions. (See **Figure 4•24.**)

The cerebral cortex is divided into four areas, or *lobes*, named for the bones of the skull that cover them: frontal lobe, parietal lobe, temporal lobe, and occipital lobe. (See Figure 4.24.) Of course, the brain contains two of each lobe, one in each hemisphere, on each side of the brain. The **frontal lobe** (the "front") includes everything in front of the central fissure. The **parietal lobe** (the "wall") is located on the side of the cerebral hemisphere, just behind the central fissure, in back of the frontal lobe. The **temporal lobe** (the "temple") juts forward from the base of the brain, beneath the frontal and parietal lobes. The **occipital lobe** (*ob*, "in back of"; *caput*, "head") lies at the very back of the brain, behind the parietal and temporal lobes.

**Regions of Primary Sensory and Motor Cortex** We become aware of events in our environment by means of the five major senses: vision, audition, olfaction, gustation (taste),

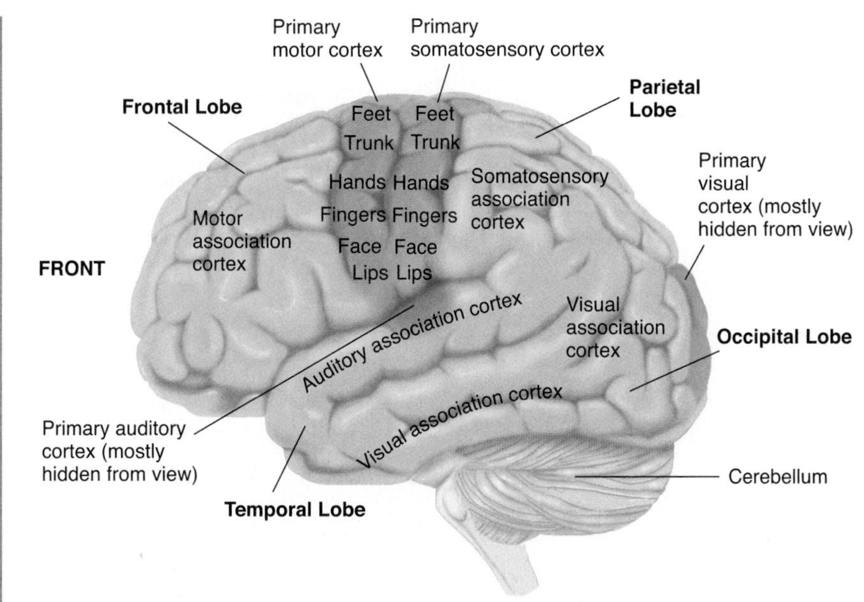


**FIGURE 4•24** A side view of the human brain, showing the location of the four lobes of the cerebral cortex, the primary sensory and motor areas, and the regions of association cortex. The central fissure is the dividing line between the primary motor cortex and the primary somatosensory cortex.

and the somatosenses ("body" senses: touch, pain, and temperature). Three areas of the cerebral cortex receive information from the sensory organs. The **primary visual cortex**, which receives visual information, is located at the back of the brain, on the inner surfaces of the occipital lobe. The **primary auditory cortex**, which receives auditory information, is located within the temporal lobe on the inner surface of a deep fissure in the side of the brain. The **primary somatosensory cortex**, a vertical strip near the middle of the cerebral hemispheres on the parietal lobe, receives information from the body senses. As Figure 4.24 shows, different regions of the primary somatosensory cortex receive information from different regions of the body. In addition, the base of the somatosensory cortex receives information concerning taste.

The three regions of primary sensory cortex in each hemisphere receive information from the opposite side of the body. Thus, the primary somatosensory cortex of the left hemisphere learns what the right hand is holding, the left primary visual cortex learns what is happening to the person's right, and so on. The connections between the sensory organs and the cerebral cortex are said to be **contralateral** (*contra*, "opposite"; *lateral*, "side").

The region of the cerebral cortex most directly involved in the control of movement is the **primary motor cortex** within the frontal lobe, located just in front of the primary somatosensory cortex. (Note that in this context *motor* is used in its original sense and refers to *movement*, not to mechanical engines.) Neurons in different parts of the primary motor cortex are connected to muscles in different parts of the body. The connections, like those of the sensory regions of the cerebral cortex, are contralateral; the left primary motor cortex controls the right side of the body and vice versa. Thus, for example, if a surgeon electrically stimulates the "hand" region of the left primary motor cortex, the patient's right hand will move. (See Figure 4.24.) Evidence from animal studies suggests that these movements may be organized by the cortex as patterns (Whishaw, 2000). I like to think of the strip of primary motor cortex as the keyboard of a piano, with each key controlling a different movement pattern. (We will see shortly who the "player" of this piano is.)

**Association Cortex** The regions of primary sensory and motor cortex occupy only a small part of the cerebral cortex. The rest of the cerebral cortex accomplishes what is done between sensation and action: perceiving, learning and remembering, planning, and acting. These processes take place in the *association areas* of the cerebral cortex. The anterior region is involved in movement-related activities, such as planning and executing behaviours. The posterior part is involved in perceiving and learning.

Each primary sensory area of the cerebral cortex sends information to adjacent regions, called the **sensory association cortex**. Circuits of neurons in the sensory association cortex

**primary visual cortex** The region of the cerebral cortex that receives information directly from the visual system; located in the occipital lobes.
**primary auditory cortex** The region of the cerebral cortex that receives information directly from the auditory system; located in the temporal lobes.
**primary somatosensory cortex** The region of the cerebral cortex that receives information directly from the somatosensory system (touch, pressure, vibration, pain, and temperature); located in the front part of the parietal lobes.
**contralateral** Residing in the side of the body opposite the reference point.
**primary motor cortex** The region of the cerebral cortex that directly controls the movements of the body; located posterior to the frontal lobes.
**sensory association cortex** Those regions of the cerebral cortex that receive information from the primary sensory areas.

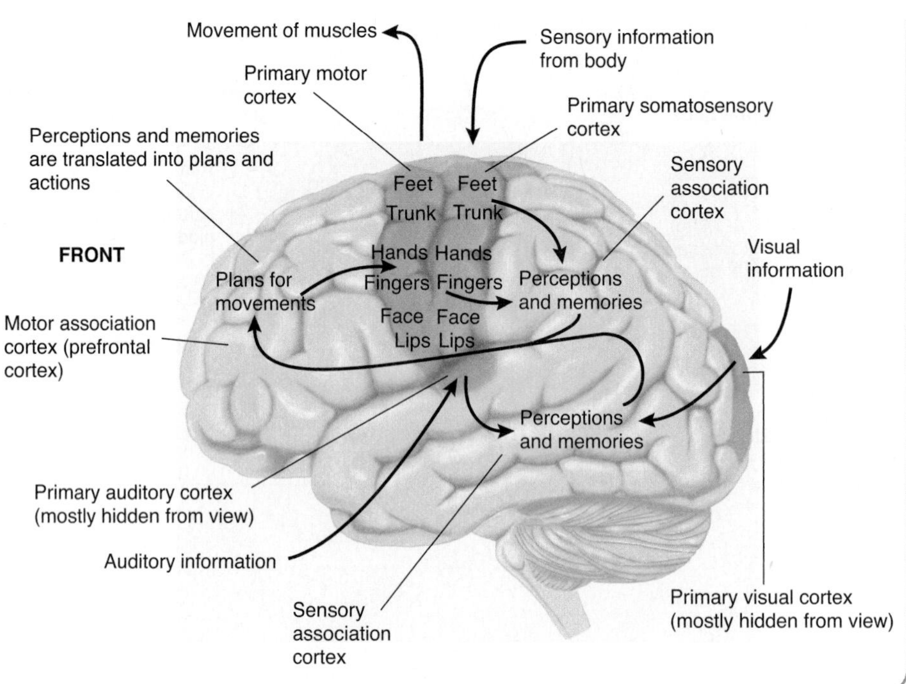


**FIGURE 4•25** The relation between the association cortex and the regions of primary sensory and motor cortex. Arrows refer to the flow of information.

analyze the information received from the primary sensory cortex; perception takes place there, and memories are stored there. The regions of the sensory association cortex located closest to the primary sensory areas receive information from only one sensory system. For example, the region closest to the primary visual cortex analyzes visual information and stores visual memories. Regions of the sensory association cortex located far from the primary sensory areas receive information from more than one sensory system; thus, they are involved in several kinds of perceptions and memories. These regions make it possible to integrate information from more than one sensory system. For example, we can learn the connection between the sight of a particular face and the sound of a particular voice. (See **Figure 4•25.**)

Just as regions of the sensory association cortex of the posterior part of the brain are involved in perceiving and remembering, so the frontal association cortex is involved in the planning and execution of movements. The anterior part of the frontal lobe—known as the **prefrontal cortex**—contains the **motor association cortex**. The motor association cortex controls the primary motor cortex; thus, it directly controls behaviour. If the primary motor cortex is the keyboard of the piano, then the motor association cortex is the piano player.

Obviously, we behave in response to events happening in the world around us. Therefore, the sensory association cortex of the posterior part of the brain sends information about the environment to the motor association cortex (prefrontal cortex), which translates the information into plans and actions. (See Figures 4•24 and 4•25.)

**prefrontal cortex** The anterior part of the frontal lobe; contains the motor association cortex.

**motor association cortex** Those regions of the cerebral cortex that control the primary motor cortex; involved in planning and executing behaviours.

## Lateralization of Function

Although the two cerebral hemispheres co-operate with each other, they do not perform identical functions. Some functions are *lateralized*—located primarily on one side of the brain. In general, the left hemisphere participates in the *analysis* of information—the extraction of the elements that make up the whole of an experience. This ability makes the left hemisphere particularly good at recognizing *serial events*—events whose elements occur one after the other. The left hemisphere is also involved in controlling serial behaviours. (In a few people, the functions of the left and right hemispheres are reversed.) The serial functions performed by the left hemisphere include verbal activities, such as talking, understanding the speech of other people, reading, and writing. These abilities are disrupted by damage to the various regions of the left hemisphere. (We'll look at language and the brain in more detail in Chapters 9 and 10.)

In contrast, the right hemisphere is specialized for *synthesis*; it is particularly good at putting isolated elements together to perceive things as a whole. For example, our ability to draw sketches (especially of three-dimensional objects), read maps, and construct complex objects out of smaller elements depends heavily on circuits of neurons located in the right hemisphere. Damage to the right hemisphere disrupts these abilities.

**FIGURE 4•26** A view of a brain that has been sliced through the midline. The corpus callosum unites the cerebral cortex of the two hemispheres.

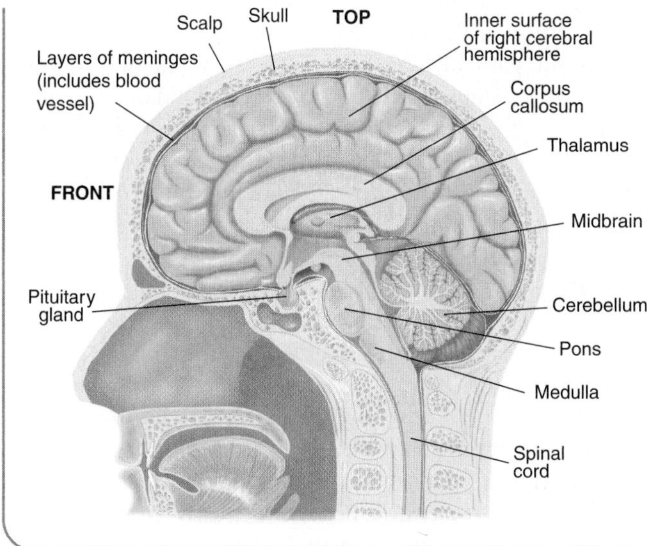


We are not aware of the fact that each hemisphere perceives the world differently. Although the two cerebral hemispheres perform somewhat different functions, our perceptions and our memories are unified. This unity is accomplished by the **corpus callosum**, a large band of axons that connects the two cerebral hemispheres. The corpus callosum connects corresponding parts of the left and right hemispheres: The left and right temporal lobes are connected, the left and right parietal lobes are connected, and so on. Because of the corpus callosum, each region of the association cortex knows what is happening in the corresponding region of the opposite side of the brain.

**Figure 4•26** shows a brain that has been sliced through the middle, from top to bottom. We see the inner surface of the right hemisphere. The corpus callosum has been cut; if we looked at it closely we would see the ends of millions of severed axons. We also see the names of several structures that have not yet been discussed. Do not worry; we'll get to those soon.

If the corpus callosum unites the two hemispheres and permits them to exchange information, what would happen if the corpus callosum were cut? In fact, neurosurgeons sometimes deliberately cut the corpus callosum to treat a certain type of epilepsy. I'll describe the interesting effects of this operation on perceptions and consciousness in Chapter 9.

## Vision: The Occipital and Temporal Lobes

The primary business of the occipital lobe—and the lower part of the temporal lobe—is seeing. (Refer to Figure 4.24.) Total damage to the primary visual cortex, located in the inner surface of the posterior occipital lobe, produces blindness. Because the visual field is "mapped" onto the surface of the primary visual cortex, a small lesion in the primary visual cortex produces a "hole" in a specific part of the field of vision.

The visual association cortex is located in the rest of the occipital lobe and in the lower portion of the temporal lobe. (Refer to Figure 4.24.) Damage to the visual association cortex will not cause blindness. In fact, visual acuity may be very good; the person may be able to see small objects and may even be able to read. However, the person will not be able to *recognize* objects by sight. For example, when looking at a drawing of a clock, the person may say that he or she sees a circle, two short lines forming an angle in the centre of a circle, and some dots spaced along the inside of the circle, but will not be able to recognize what the picture shows. On the other hand, if handed a real clock, he or she will immediately recognize it by touch. This fact tells us that the person has not simply forgotten what clocks are. Similarly, the person may fail to recognize his or her spouse by sight but will be able to do so from the sound of the spouse's voice. This deficit in visual perception is called **visual agnosia** (*a-*, "without"; *gnosis*, "knowledge"). We'll deal with this phenomenon further in Chapter 6.

## Audition: The Temporal Lobe

The temporal lobe contains both the primary auditory cortex and the auditory association cortex. The primary auditory cortex is hidden from view on the inner surface of the upper temporal lobe. The auditory association cortex is located on the lateral surface of the upper temporal lobe. (Refer to Figure 4.24.) Damage to the primary auditory cortex leads to hearing losses, while damage to the auditory association cortex produces more complex deficits. Damage to the left auditory association cortex causes severe language deficits. People with such damage are no longer able to comprehend speech, presumably because they have lost the circuits of neurons that decode speech sounds. However, the deficit is more severe than that. They also lose the ability to produce meaningful speech; their speech becomes a jumble of words. We'll look again at language deficits produced by brain damage in Chapter 10.

Damage to the right auditory association cortex does not seriously affect speech perception or production, but it does affect the ability to recognize non-speech sounds, including patterns of tones and rhythms. The damage can also impair the ability to perceive the location of sounds in the environment. As we will see later, the right hemisphere is very

**corpus callosum** A large bundle of axons ("white matter") that connects the cortex of the two cerebral hemispheres.

**visual agnosia** The inability of a person who is not blind to recognize the identity or use of an object by means of vision; usually caused by damage to the brain.

important in the perception of space. The contribution of the right temporal lobe to this function is to participate in perceiving the placement of sounds.

## Somatosensation and Spatial Perception: The Parietal Lobe

The primary sensory function of the parietal lobe is perception of the body. (Refer to Figure 4.24.) However, the association cortex of the parietal lobe is involved in much more than somatosensation. Damage to a particular region of the association cortex of the left parietal lobe can disrupt the ability to read or write without causing serious impairment in the ability to talk and understand the speech of other people. Damage to another part of the parietal lobe impairs a person's ability to draw. When the left parietal lobe is damaged, the primary deficit seems to be in the person's ability to make precise hand movements; his or her drawing looks shaky and sloppy. In contrast, the primary deficit produced by damage to the right parietal lobe is perceptual. The person can analyze a picture into its parts but has trouble integrating these parts into a consistent whole. Thus, he or she has difficulty drawing a coherent picture. (See **Figure 4•27**.)

The right parietal lobe also plays a role in people's ability to pay attention to stimuli located toward the opposite (left) side of the body. As we saw in the prologue, Miss S. displayed a symptom called unilateral neglect. A CT scan of her brain (shown in Figure 4.19) reveals that her stroke damaged part of the association cortex of the right parietal lobe.

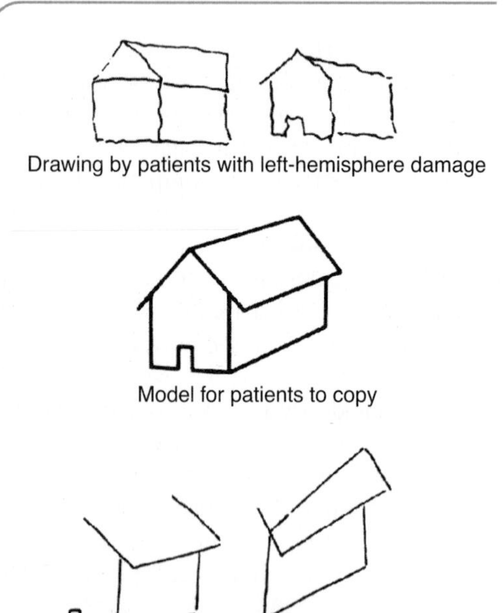


**FIGURE 4•27** Attempts to copy a drawing of a house by patients with damage to the left and right parietal lobes.

*(Reprinted from* Neuropsychologia, *8(3), Gainotti, G. & Tiacci, C., Patterns of drawing disability in right and left hemispheric patients Pages 379–384, (1970), with permission from Elsevier. http://www.sciencedirect.com/science/journal/00283932)*

Most neuropsychologists believe that the left parietal lobe plays an important role in our ability to keep track of the location of the moving parts of our own body, whereas the right parietal lobe helps us keep track of the space around us. People with right parietal lobe damage usually have difficulty with spatial tasks, such as reading a map. People with left parietal lobe damage usually have difficulty identifying parts of their own bodies by name. For example, when asked to point to their elbows, they may actually point to their shoulders.

People with damage to the left parietal lobe often have difficulty performing arithmetic calculations. This deficit is probably related to other spatial functions of the parietal lobe. For example, try to multiply 55 by 12 without using pencil and paper. Close your eyes and work on the problem for a while. Try to analyze how you did it.

Most people report that they try to imagine the numbers arranged one above the other as they would be if paper and pencil were being used. In other words, they "write" the problem out mentally. Apparently, damage to the parietal lobes makes it impossible for people to keep the imaginary numbers in place and remember what they are.

## Planning and Moving: The Frontal Lobe

Although the principal function of the frontal lobe is motor activity, it is also involved in planning, changing strategies, being aware of oneself, evaluating emotionally related stimuli, and performing a variety of spontaneous behaviours. It also contains a region involved in the control of speech. (Refer to Figure 4.24.)

Damage to the primary motor cortex produces a very specific effect: paralysis of the side of the body opposite to the brain damage. If a portion of the region is damaged, then only the corresponding parts of the body will be paralyzed. However, damage to the prefrontal cortex produces more complex behavioural deficits.

1. *Slowing of thoughts and behaviour and loss of spontaneity.* The person will react to events in the environment but show deficits in initiating behaviour. When a person with damage to the prefrontal cortex is asked to say or write as many words as possible, he or she will have great difficulty coming up with more than a few, even though he or she has no problem understanding words or identifying objects by name.
2. *Perseveration.* People with damage to the frontal lobes tend to have difficulty changing strategies. If given a task to solve, they may solve it readily; however, they will fail to abandon the strategy and learn a new one if the problem is changed.
3. *Loss of self-awareness and changes in emotional reactions.* People with damaged frontal lobes often have rather bland personalities. They seem indifferent to events that

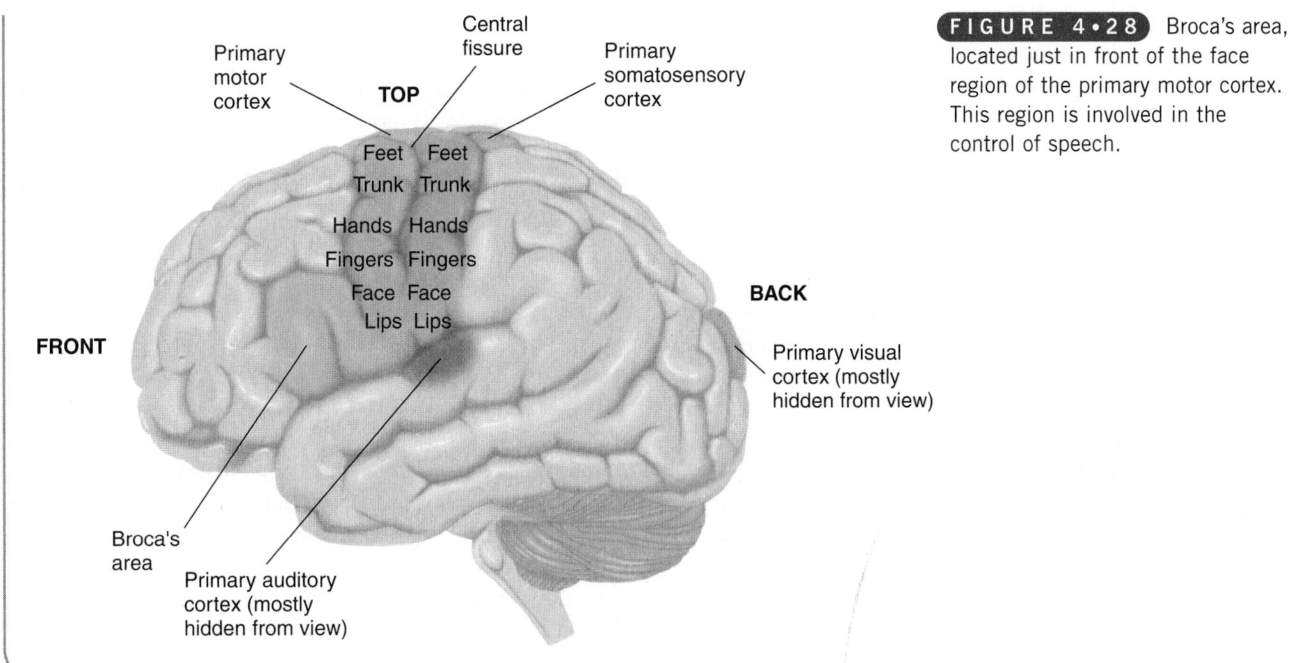


**FIGURE 4•28** Broca's area, located just in front of the face region of the primary motor cortex. This region is involved in the control of speech.

would normally be expected to affect them emotionally. For example, they may show no signs of distress at the death of a close relative. They have little insight into their own problems and are uncritical of their performance on various tasks. They do not even seem to be bothered by pain, although they may say that they still feel it.

4. *Deficiencies in foresight and planning.* In terms of daily living, the most important consequences of damage to the frontal lobes are probably lack of foresight and difficulty planning. A person with frontal lobe damage might perform fairly well on a test of intelligence but be unable to hold a job. Presumably, planning is related to the general motor functions of the frontal lobes. Just as we can use the posterior regions of the brain to imagine something we have perceived, so we can use the frontal region to imagine something we might do. Perhaps we test various possible actions by imagining ourselves doing them and guessing what the consequences of these actions might be. When people's frontal lobes are damaged, they often do or say things that have unfavourable consequences because they have lost the ability to plan their actions.

As we saw in Chapter 1, Paul Broca discovered that damage to a region of the left frontal lobe disrupts speech. This region, which we now call Broca's area, lies just in front of the "face" region of the primary motor cortex. (See **Figure 4•28**.) Thus, Broca's area controls the muscles used for talking. Circuits of neurons located in Broca's area appear to contain the memories of the sequences of muscle movements that are needed to pronounce words. We'll discuss more on the effects of lesions in Broca's area in Chapter 10.

## Interim Summary

### Control of Behaviour

Anatomically, the cerebral cortex is divided into four lobes: frontal, parietal, occipital, and temporal. Functionally, the cerebral cortex is organized into five major regions: the three regions of the primary sensory cortex (visual, auditory, and somatosensory), the primary motor cortex, and the association cortex. The association cortex consists of sensory regions that are responsible for perceiving and learning and the motor regions that are responsible for planning and acting.

Suppose that you see a rose and then pick it and smell it. The visual stimulation is transmitted from the eyes to the brain through the optic nerves, one of the pairs of cranial nerves. The information is sent to the primary visual cortex in the occipital lobe. Your perception of the rose causes you to remember how beautiful a rose on looks in a vase on your desk. This memory, located in the visual association cortex, causes messages to be sent forward to the motor association cortex (the "piano player") in your frontal lobes. There, plans are made to pick the rose so that you can display it on your desk. Impulses are sent to your primary motor cortex and from there to the muscles that control your legs. As you move toward the rose, new sensory information received by the posterior lobes informs the frontal lobes about the appropriate movements. You reach for the rose and pick it.

When you pick the rose, you feel the stem with your fingers. The somatosensory information is transmitted from your fingers to the spinal cord by means of a spinal nerve. It is then sent up through the spinal cord and is relayed to the primary somatosensory cortex. Next, your frontal lobes direct your hand to bring the rose under your nose and then command your muscles to make you sniff in some air to smell the rose. Information about the aromatic molecules is transmitted to your brain through the olfactory nerves, another pair of cranial nerves.

The right and left hemispheres are involved with somewhat different functions; that is, some brain functions are lateralized. The left hemisphere is mostly concerned with analysis—with the extraction of information about details of perception, such as the series of sounds that constitute speech or the symbols that constitute writing. The right hemisphere is mostly concerned with synthesis—with putting together a perception of the general form and shape of things from smaller elements that are present at the same time. The two hemispheres share information through the corpus callosum, a large bundle of axons.

The frontal lobes are concerned with motor functions, including the planning of strategies for action. A region of the left frontal cortex (Broca's area) is specialized for control of speech. The three lobes behind the central fissure are generally concerned with perceiving, learning, and remembering: somatosensory information in the parietal lobe, visual information in the occipital and lower temporal lobes, and auditory information in the upper temporal lobe. The other functions of these lobes are related to these perceptual processes; for example, the parietal lobes are concerned with perception of space as well as knowledge about the body.

**QUESTIONS TO CONSIDER**

1. If you were to have a stroke (and let's hope you don't), in which region of the cerebral cortex and in which hemisphere would you prefer the brain damage to be located? Why?
2. Damage to the anterior or posterior corpus callosum produces different behavioural deficits. Why do you think this is so?
3. Suppose you suspected that someone had a lesion in the left parietal lobe. What behavioural tests would you devise to try to determine whether the person did indeed have a lesion there?
4. Explain why a brain lesion that impairs a person's speech often also affects movements of the right side of the body.

**homeostasis** The process by which important physiological characteristics (such as body temperature and blood pressure) are regulated so that they remain at their optimum level.

**species-typical behaviour** A behaviour seen in all or most members of a species, such as nest building, special food-getting behaviours, or reproductive behaviours.

**medulla** The part of the brain stem closest to the spinal cord; controls vital functions such as heart rate and blood pressure.

**pons** The part of the brain stem just anterior to the medulla; involved in control of sleep.

**midbrain** The part of the brain stem just anterior to the pons; involved in control of fighting and sexual behaviour and in decreased sensitivity to pain during these behaviours.

# Control of Internal Functions and Automatic Behaviour

So far, we've looked at brain regions involved in perceiving, remembering, planning, and acting. We have primarily discussed the role of the cerebral cortex in these activities. However, there is much more to the brain than the cerebral cortex. After all, the cortex consists of only the outer 3 mm of the surface of the cerebral hemispheres. What roles do the brain stem, the cerebellum, and the interior of the cerebral hemispheres play?

As we shall see, the primary function of the cerebellum is to help the cerebral hemispheres control movements and to initiate some automatic movements—such as postural adjustment—on its own. The brain stem and much of the interior of the cerebral hemispheres are involved in homeostasis and control of species-typical behaviours. **Homeostasis** (from the root words *homoios*, "similar," and *stasis*, "standstill") refers to maintaining a proper balance of physiological variables such as temperature, concentration of fluids, and the amount of nutrients stored within the body. **Species-typical behaviours** are the more-or-less automatic behaviours exhibited by most members of a species that are important to survival, such as eating, drinking, fighting, courting, mating, and caring for offspring.

## The Brain Stem

The brain stem contains three structures: the *medulla*, the *pons*, and the *midbrain*. **Figure 4•29** shows a view of the left side of the brain. The brain has been rotated slightly so that we can see some of the front of the brain stem, and the cerebral hemispheres are shown lightly so that the details of the brain stem can be seen. We also see the *thalamus*, the *hypothalamus*, and the *pituitary gland*. (We will discuss these later.)

The brain stem contains circuits of neurons that control functions vital to the survival of the organism in particular and the species in general. For example, circuits of neurons in the **medulla**, the part of the brain stem closest to the spinal cord, control heart rate, blood pressure, rate of respiration, and—especially in simpler animals—crawling or swimming motions. Circuits of neurons in the **pons**, the part of the brain stem just above the medulla, control some of the stages of sleep. Circuits of neurons in the **midbrain**, the part of the brain

**FIGURE 4•29** The divisions of the brain stem: the medulla, the pons, and the midbrain. The thalamus, hypothalamus, and pituitary gland are attached to the end of the brain stem.

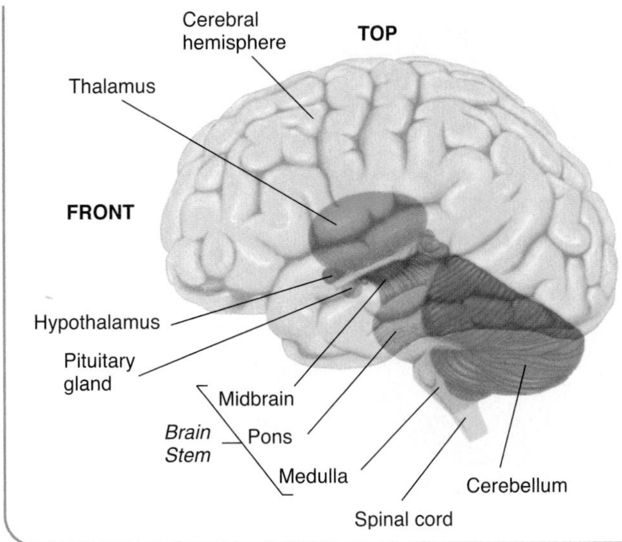


stem just above the pons, control movements used in fighting and sexual behaviour and decrease sensitivity to pain while engaged in these activities.

## The Cerebellum

The cerebellum plays an important role in the control of movement. It receives sensory information, especially about the position of body parts, so it knows what the parts of the body are doing. It also receives information from the cortex of the frontal lobes, so it knows what movements the frontal lobes intend to accomplish. The cerebellum is basically a computer that compares the location of the body parts with the intended movements and assists the frontal lobes in executing these movements. Without the cerebellum, the frontal lobes would produce jerky, uncoordinated, inaccurate movements—which is exactly what happens when a person's cerebellum is damaged. Besides helping the frontal lobes accomplish their tasks, the cerebellum monitors information regarding posture and balance, to keep us from falling down when we stand or walk, and produces eye movements that compensate for changes in the position of the head. It also exhibits the plasticity I spoke of earlier, in response to skilled motor movement (Kleim et al., 1998).

Recently, researchers have discovered that the cerebellum may also play a role in people's cognitive abilities. For a long time, neurologists have known that cerebellar damage can interfere with people's ability to speak, but the deficit seems to involve control of the speech muscles rather than the cognitive abilities involved in language. However, a few years ago, researchers making PET scans of the brains of people working on various types of cognitive tasks discovered that parts of their cerebellums became active—even when the people were not moving. Many neuroscientists now suspect that as we learn more about the cerebellum we will discover that its functions are not limited to motor tasks.

## Structures within the Cerebral Hemispheres

So far, we have been directing most of our attention to the surface of the brain. Now let's see what's inside it.

**The Thalamus** If you stripped away the cerebral cortex and the white matter that lies under it, you would find the **thalamus**, located in the heart of the cerebral hemispheres. (*Thalamos* is Greek for "inner chamber.") The thalamus is divided into two parts, one in each cerebral hemisphere. Each part looks rather like a football, with the long axis oriented from front to back. (See Figure 4.29.)

The thalamus performs two basic functions. The first—and most primitive—is similar to that of the cerebral cortex. Parts of the thalamus receive sensory information, other parts integrate the information, and still other parts assist in the control of movements through their influence on circuits of neurons in the brain stem. However, the second role of the thalamus—that of a relay station for the cortex—is even more important. As the cerebral hemispheres evolved, the cerebral cortex grew in size and its significance for behavioural functions increased. The thalamus took on the function of receiving sensory information from the sensory organs, performing some simple analyses, and passing the results on to the primary sensory cortex. Thus, all sensory information (except for olfaction, which is the most primitive of all sensory systems) is sent to the thalamus before it reaches the cerebral cortex.

**The Hypothalamus** *Hypo-* means "less than" or "beneath" and, as its name suggests, the **hypothalamus** is located below the thalamus, at the base of the brain. The hypothalamus is a small region, consisting of less than 1 cc of tissue (smaller than a grape). Its relative importance far exceeds its size. (See Figure 4.29.)

The hypothalamus, like the brain stem, participates in homeostasis and species-typical behaviours. It receives sensory information, including information from receptors inside the organs of the body; thus, it is informed about changes in the organism's physiological status. It also contains specialized sensors that monitor various characteristics of the blood that flows through the brain, such as temperature, nutrient

**thalamus** A region of the brain near the centre of the cerebral hemispheres. All sensory information except smell is sent to the thalamus and then relayed to the cerebral cortex.

**hypothalamus** A region of the brain located just above the pituitary gland; controls the autonomic nervous system and many behaviours related to regulation and survival, such as eating, drinking, fighting, shivering, and sweating.

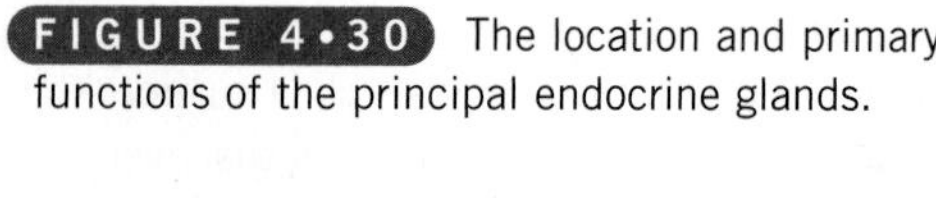

**FIGURE 4•30** The location and primary functions of the principal endocrine glands.

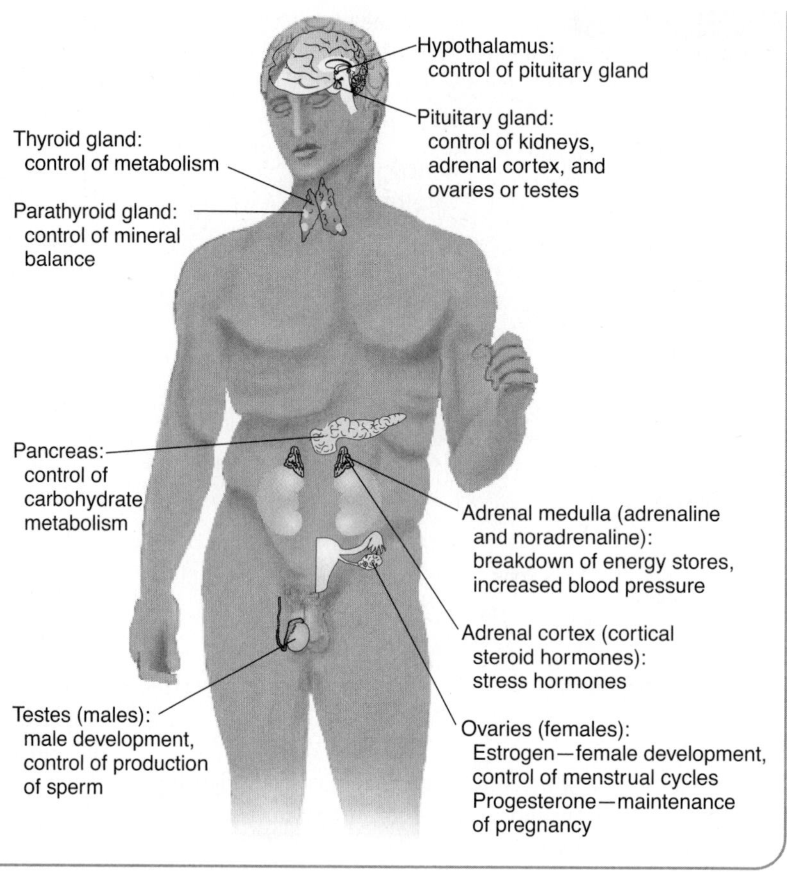


content, and amount of dissolved salts. In turn, the hypothalamus controls the **pituitary gland**, an *endocrine gland* attached by a stalk to the base of the hypothalamus.

Hormones are chemicals produced by *endocrine glands* (from the Greek *endo-*, "within," and *krinein*, "to secrete"). **Endocrine glands** secrete hormones into the blood supply, which carries them to all parts of the body. **Hormones** are similar to transmitter substances or neuromodulators, except that they act over much longer distances. Like transmitter substances and neuromodulators, they produce their effects by stimulating receptor molecules. These receptor molecules are located on (or in) particular cells. The presence of a hormone causes physiological reactions in these cells, which are known as **target cells**. Almost every cell of the body contains hormone receptors of one kind or another. This includes neurons; hormones that affect behaviour do so by altering the activity of particular groups of neurons in the brain. For example, the sex hormones have important effects on behaviour and will be discussed in later chapters.

The pituitary gland has been called the "master gland" because the hormones it secretes act on target cells in other endocrine glands; thus, the pituitary gland controls the activity of other endocrine glands. By controlling the pituitary gland, the hypothalamus controls the entire endocrine system. **Figure 4.30** shows some of the endocrine glands and the functions they regulate.

The hypothalamus also controls much of the activity of the **autonomic nervous system**, which consists of nerves that control the functions of the glands and internal organs. The nerves of the autonomic nervous system control activities such as sweating, shedding tears, salivating, secreting digestive juices, changing the size of blood vessels (which alters blood pressure), and secreting some hormones. The autonomic nervous system has two branches. The **sympathetic branch** directs activities that involve the expenditure of energy. For example, activity of the sympathetic branch can increase the flow of blood to the muscles when we are about to fight someone or run away from a dangerous situation.

**pituitary gland** An endocrine gland attached to the hypothalamus at the base of the brain.
**endocrine gland** A gland that secretes a hormone.
**hormone** A chemical substance secreted by an endocrine gland that has physiological effects on target cells in other organs.
**target cell** A cell whose physiological processes are affected by a particular hormone; contains special receptor molecules that respond to the presence of the hormone.
**autonomic nervous system** The portion of the peripheral nervous system that controls the functions of the glands and internal organs.
**sympathetic branch** The portion of the autonomic nervous system that activates functions that accompany arousal and expenditure of energy.

**FIGURE 4•31** The organs controlled by the autonomic nervous system. The reciprocal actions of the sympathetic and parasympathetic branches are noted next to each organ.

| | Sympathetic Nervous System | Parasympathetic Nervous System |
|---|---|---|
| Eye (Lachrymal gland) | Lachrymal glands: secretion of tears<br>Pupil: dilation | Pupil: constriction |
| Blood vessels | Abdomen: constriction<br>Muscles: dilation<br>Skin: constriction | Abdomen: dilation<br>Muscles: constriction<br>Skin: dilation |
| Stomach | Inhibition of contractions and secretion of stomach acid | Contractions, secretion of stomach acid |
| Intestines | Decreased activity | Increased activity |
| Bladder | Inhibition of contraction | Contraction |
| Salivary gland | Secretion of thick saliva | Secretion of thin saliva |
| Skin (Hair follicle, Sweat gland) | Sweating, piloerection ("goose bumps") | |
| Heart | Faster rate of contraction | Slower rate of contraction |
| Adrenal gland | Secretion of adrenaline | |
| External genitalia | Ejaculation/orgasm | Erection/vaginal lubrication |

The **parasympathetic branch** controls quiet activities, such as digestion of food. Activity of the parasympathetic branch stimulates the secretion of digestive enzymes and increases the flow of blood to the digestive system. (See **Figure 4•31**.)

Psychophysiologists can monitor the activity of the autonomic nervous system and its relation to psychological phenomena such as emotion. For example, when a person is angry, his or her heart rate and blood pressure rise. The lie detector (described in Chapter 13) works by recording emotional responses controlled by the autonomic nervous system.

The homeostatic functions of the hypothalamus can involve either internal physiological changes or behaviour. For example, the hypothalamus is involved in the control of body temperature. It can directly lower body temperature by causing sweating to occur, or it can raise it by causing shivering to occur. If these measures are inadequate, it can send messages to the cerebral cortex that will cause the person to engage in

**parasympathetic branch** The portion of the autonomic nervous system that activates functions that occur during a relaxed state.

a learned behaviour, such as turning on an air conditioner or putting another log on the fire. Damage to the hypothalamus can cause impaired regulation of body temperature, changes in food intake, sterility, and stunting of growth.

**The Limbic System** The **limbic system**, a set of structures located in the cerebral hemispheres, plays an important role in learning and in the expression of emotion. The limbic system consists of several regions of the **limbic cortex**—the cerebral cortex located around the edge of the cerebral hemispheres where they join with the brain stem. (*Limbus* means "border"; hence the term *limbic* system.) Besides the limbic cortex, the most important components of the limbic system are the *amygdala* and the *hippocampus.* The amygdala and the hippocampus get their names from their shapes; *amygdala* means "almond" and *hippocampus* means "sea horse."

**Figure 4•32** shows a view of the right hemisphere of the brain, rotated slightly and seen from the left. We can see the limbic cortex, located on the inner surface of the right cerebral hemisphere. The left hippocampus and amygdala, located in the middle of the temporal lobe, are shown projecting out into the place where the missing left hemisphere would be. We can also see the right hippocampus and amygdala, "ghosted in." We also see a structure that does not belong to the limbic system—the corpus callosum. As we saw earlier, the corpus callosum consists of a band of nerve fibres that enables the left and right cerebral hemispheres to communicate with each other.

Damage to the **amygdala**, a cluster of neurons located deep in the temporal lobe, affects emotional behaviour—especially negative emotions, such as those caused by painful, threatening, or stressful events. In addition, the amygdala controls physiological reactions that help provide energy for short-term activities such as fighting or fleeing. If an animal's amygdala is destroyed, it no longer reacts to prevent events that normally produce stress and anxiety (Treit & Menard, 1997). We might think that an animal would be better off if it did not become "stressed out" by unpleasant or threatening situations. However, research has shown that animals with damaged amygdalas cannot survive in the wild. These animals fail to compete successfully for food and other resources, and often act in ways that provoke attacks by other animals. We'll look at the role of the amygdala in emotion and stress in Chapters 13 and 16.

The **hippocampus**, a collection of structures located just behind the amygdala, plays an important role in memory. For example, rats with damage to the hippocampus lose their ability to use landmarks that locate hidden objects (Duva et al., 1997). People with lesions in the area of the hippocampus lose the ability to learn anything new. For them, "yesterday" is always the time before their brain damage occurred; everything after that slips away, just as the memory of dreams often slips away from a person soon after awakening. We'll look at this form of amnesia again in Chapter 8, which discusses human memory.

**FIGURE 4•32** The principal structures of the limbic system.

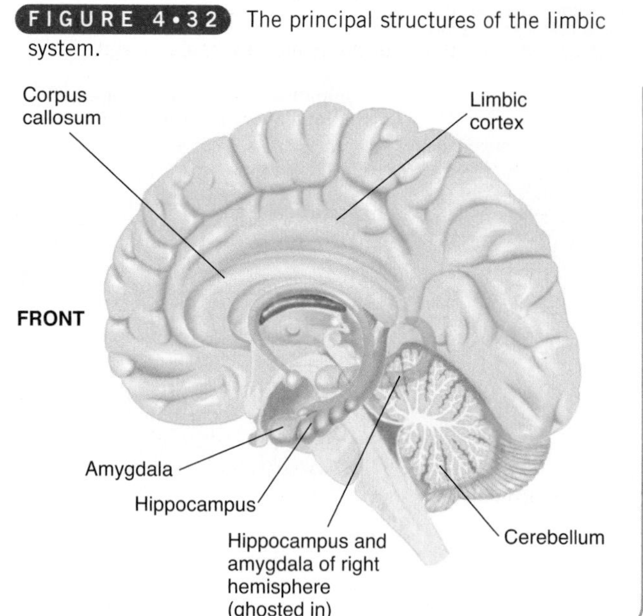


**limbic system** A set of interconnected structures of the brain important in emotional and species-typical behaviour; includes the amygdala, hippocampus, and limbic cortex.

**limbic cortex** The cerebral cortex located around the edge of the cerebral hemispheres where they join with the brain stem; part of the limbic system.

**amygdala** A part of the limbic system of the brain located deep in the temporal lobe; damage causes changes in emotional and aggressive behaviour.

**hippocampus** A part of the limbic system of the brain, located in the temporal lobe; plays important roles in learning.

## Interim Summary

### Control of Internal Functions and Automatic Behaviour

The more primitive parts of the brain control homeostasis and species-typical behaviours. The brain stem, which consists of the medulla, the pons, and the midbrain, contains neural circuits that control vital physiological functions and produce automatic movements such as those used in locomotion, fighting, and sexual behaviour. The cerebellum assists the cerebral cortex in carrying out movements; it coordinates the control of muscles, resulting in smooth movements. It also regulates postural adjustments and appears to play some role in cognitive abilities.

Within the cerebral hemispheres, the thalamus participates in the control of movements and relays sensory information to the cerebral cortex. The hypothalamus receives sensory information from sense receptors elsewhere in the body and also contains its own specialized receptors, such as those used to monitor body temperature. It controls the pituitary gland, which, in turn, controls most of the endocrine glands of the body, and it also controls the internal organs through the autonomic nervous system. Hormones, secreted by endocrine glands, are chemicals that act on hormone receptors in target cells and produce physiological reactions in these cells. The hypothalamus can control homeostatic processes directly and automatically through its control of the pituitary gland and the autonomic nervous system, or it can cause neural circuits in the cerebral cortex to execute more complex, learned behaviour.

The amygdala and the hippocampus, both located within the temporal lobe, are important parts of the limbic system. The amygdala is involved in emotions and emotional behaviours, such as defence and aggression, and it plays an important role in physiological reactions that have beneficial effects in the short run but can lead to stress-related illnesses if they become chronic. The hippocampus is involved in learning and memory; people with damage to this structure can recall old memories but are unable to learn anything new.

### QUESTIONS TO CONSIDER

1. The cerebellum is one of the largest parts of the brain and contains billions of neurons. What does this fact suggest about the complexity of the task of coordinating movements of the body?
2. Suppose that you wanted to build a lie detector. You would monitor reactions that might indicate emotional responses produced by the act of lying. What behavioural and physiological functions would you want to record?
3. Tranquilizers reduce negative emotional reactions. In what part (or parts) of the brain do you think these drugs might act? Why?

# EPILOGUE

## Unilateral Neglect

When we see people like Miss S., the woman with unilateral neglect described in the prologue of this chapter, we realize that perception and attention are somewhat independent. The perceptual mechanisms of our brain provide the information, and the mechanisms involved in attention determine whether we become conscious of this information.

Unilateral ("one-sided") neglect occurs when the right parietal lobe is damaged. As we saw, the parietal lobe is concerned with the body and its position. But that is not all; the association cortex of the parietal lobe also receives auditory and visual information from the association cortex of the occipital and temporal lobes. Its most important function seems to be to put together information about the movements and location of the parts of the body with the locations of objects in space around us.

If unilateral neglect consisted of simply blindness in the left side of the visual field and anaesthesia of the left side of the body, it would not be nearly as interesting. But individuals with unilateral neglect are neither half-blind nor half-numb. Under the proper circumstances, they *can* see things located to their left, and they *can* tell when someone touches the left side of their bodies. However, normally, they ignore such stimuli and act as if the left side of the world and of their bodies does not exist.

Volpe, LeDoux, and Gazzaniga (1979) presented pairs of visual stimuli to people with unilateral neglect—one stimulus in the left visual field and one stimulus in the right visual field. Invariably, the people reported seeing only the right-hand stimulus. However, when the investigators asked the people to say whether the two stimuli were identical, they answered correctly *even though they said that they were unaware of the left-hand stimulus.*

If you think about the story that the chief of neurology told about the man who ate only the right half of a pancake, you will realize that people with unilateral neglect *must* be able to perceive more than the right visual field. Remember that people with unilateral neglect fail to notice not only things to their left but also the *left halves* of things. But, to distinguish between the left and right halves of an object, you first have to perceive the entire object—otherwise, how would you know where the middle is?

## Canadian Connections to Research in This Chapter

Duva, C. A., Floresco, S. B., Wunderlich, G. R., Lao, T. L., Pinel, J. P. J., & Phillips, A. G. (1997). Disruption of spatial but not object-recognition memory by neurotoxic lesions of the dorsal hippocampus in rats. *Behavioral Neuroscience, 111,* 1184–1196. (University of British Columbia: www.ubc.ca)

Anthony Phillips was the 1995 winner of the Donald O. Hebb Award of the Canadian Psychological Association.

Hebb, D. O. (1949). *The organization of behavior.* New York: Wiley-Interscience. (McGill University: www.mcgill.ca)

Donald Hebb was the first winner (in 1980) of the Donald O. Hebb Award of the Canadian Psychological Association and the 1961 winner of the American Psychological Association's Award for Distinguished Scientific Contributions.

Kolb, B., & Whishaw, I. Q. (1998). Brain plasticity and behavior. *Annual Review of Psychology, 49,* 43–64. (University of Lethbridge: www.uleth.ca)

Bryan Kolb was the 2000 winner of the Donald O. Hebb Award of the Canadian Psychological Association and was elected to the Royal Society of Canada in 2000. Ian Whishaw was elected to the Royal Society of Canada in 1998.

Milner, B., Squire, L. R., & Kandel, E. R. (1998). Cognitive neuroscience and the study of memory. *Neuron, 20,* 445–468. (McGill University: www.mcgill.ca)

Brenda Milner was the 1981 winner of the Donald O. Hebb Award of the Canadian Psychological Association and the 1973 winner of the American Psychological Association's Award for Distinguished Scientific Contributions. Larry Squire was the 1993 winner of the American Psychological Association's Award for Distinguished Scientific Contributions. Eric Kandel was the 2000 winner of the Nobel Prize in Medicine.

Olds, J., & Milner, P. (1954). Positive reinforcement produced by electrical stimulation of the septal area and other regions of the rat brain. *Journal of Comparative and Physiological Psychology, 47,* 419–427. (McGill University: www.mcgill.ca)

James Olds was the 1967 winner of the American Psychological Association's Award for Distinguished Scientific Contributions.

Paus, T., Zijdenbos, A., Worsley, K., Collins, D. L., Blumenthal, J., Giedd, J. N., Rapoport, J. L., & Evans, A. C. (1999). Structural maturation of neural pathways in children and adolescents: In vivo study. *Science, 283,* 1908–1911. (McGill University: www.mcgill.ca)

Treit, D., & Menard, J. (1997). Dissociations among the anxiolytic effects of septal, hippocampal, and amygdaloid lesions. *Behavioral Neuroscience, 111,* 653–658. (University of Alberta: www.ualberta.ca)

Vanderwolf, C. H., & Cain, D. P. (1994). The behavioral neurobiology of learning and memory: A conceptual reorientation. *Brain Research Reviews, 19,* 264–297. (University of Western Ontario: www.uwo.ca)

Whishaw, I. Q. (2000). Loss of the innate cortical engram for action patterns used in skilled reaching and the development of behavioral compensation following motor cortex lesions in the rat. *Neuropharmacology, 39,* 788–805. (University of Lethbridge: www.uleth.ca)

Ian Whishaw was elected to the Royal Society of Canada in 1998.

## Suggestions for Further Reading

Grilly, D. M. (2002). *Drugs and human behavior* (4th ed.). Boston: Allyn and Bacon.

Meyer, J. S., & Quenzer, L. F. (2005) *Psychopharmacology: Drugs, the brain, and behavior.* Sunderland, MA: Sinauer Associates.

If you are interested in learning more about the effects of drugs that are often abused, you may want to read these books, both of which contain much helpful information about the effects of popular drugs and their use and abuse in society.

Carlson, N. R. (2008). *Foundations of physiological psychology* (7th ed.). Boston: Allyn and Bacon.

My introductory textbook of physiological psychology discusses the topics presented in this chapter in more detail.

# 5

# SENSATION

# CHAPTER OUTLINE

## Sensory Processing

Transduction • Sensory Coding • Psychophysics

The primary function of the sense organs is to provide information that can guide behaviour. The translation of information about environmental events into neural activity is called transduction. In the nervous system, sensory information must be translated into one of two types of neural code: anatomical or temporal. Psychophysics is the study of the relation between the physical characteristics of stimuli and the perceptions they produce.

## Vision

Light • The Eye and Its Functions • Transduction of Light by Photoreceptors • Adaptation to Light and Dark • Eye Movements • Colour Vision

Light is a form of electromagnetic radiation. Images of the visual scene are focused on the retina, the inner layer at the back of the eye. Photoreceptors, specialized neurons located in the retina, contain chemicals called photopigments that transduce light into neural activity. Chemical changes in the photopigments are responsible for our ability to see in dim or bright light. The eyes make small involuntary movements that prevent the image from fading and three types of purposive movements. Light can vary in wavelength, intensity, and purity. Three types of cones in the retina, each most sensitive to a particular wavelength of light, detect colours. Most genetic defects affecting colour vision cause the inability to produce one of the three photopigments found in cones.

## Audition

Sound • The Ear and Its Functions • Detecting and Localizing Sounds in the Environment • Age-Related Losses in Hearing

Sound waves can vary in frequency, intensity, and complexity, giving rise to differences in perceptions of pitch, loudness, and timbre. The bones of the middle ear transmit sound vibrations from the eardrum to the cochlea, which contains the auditory receptors—the hair cells. The auditory system detects individual frequencies by means of place coding and rate coding. Left–right localization is accomplished by two means: arrival time and differences in intensity. With age, people may lose the ability to hear sound against a noisy background and to hear certain frequencies.

## Gustation

Receptors and the Sensory Pathway • The Five Qualities of Taste

Taste receptors on the tongue respond to bitterness, sourness, sweetness, saltiness, and umami and, together with the olfactory system, provide us with information about complex flavours.

## Olfaction

Anatomy of the Olfactory System • The Dimensions of Odour

The olfactory system detects the presence of aromatic molecules. Several hundred different types of receptors may be involved in olfactory discrimination, giving humans the capacity, through pattern recognition, to discriminate among thousands of different odours.

## The Somatosenses

The Skin Senses • The Internal Senses • The Vestibular Senses • *Then and Now: Extrasensory Perception . . . A Case Study*

Sensory receptors in the skin provide information about touch, pressure, vibration, changes in temperature, and stimuli that cause tissue damage. Pain perception helps protect us from harmful stimuli. Sensory endings located in the internal organs, joints, and muscles convey information about our own movements and about events occurring in our organs. The vestibular system helps us maintain our balance and makes compensatory eye movements to help us maintain fixation when our heads move.

PROLOGUE

## Monsters from the Forest

He didn't mention it at the time he told me this story, but my friend Ken Hill must have started his shift with a fear that the day would end in heartbreak. Ken is a social psychologist, but on that day he was working in his other role: as a search and rescue manager for the Province of Nova Scotia.

Ken's job is to prevent the tragedy that can occur in Canada's open spaces: a child or adult loses her or his bearings in the wilderness and dies of exposure. There are many police and civilian agencies throughout Canada whose members assist in the search for lost persons. Shortly after moving to Nova Scotia to teach, Ken saw the tragedy that occurs when these efforts fail and a lost child is not found in time. Since then, he has devoted his free time to learning search and rescue techniques and much of his professional time to studying the behaviour of lost people. He is now one of the foremost experts in North America on search and rescue management.

But the search mission that day was not looking good. They were searching for a lost four-year-old boy who had been missing for three days after wandering away from his family. The weather had turned cold and rainy. Alone in such conditions, survival is problematic even for an adult. However, young children sometimes beat the odds because they often cuddle up in a warm place, whereas an older child might panic and wander far. That hope was keeping Ken's team going.

Search and rescue doctrine emphasizes that, because a lost person might be hard to spot in heavy undergrowth, the searchers themselves should be as easy to detect as possible. Having the lost person spot you is as useful as you spotting him or her. Searchers dress in bright clothing, use loud whistles, and, at night, wear bright headlights—all in an attempt to get a response from the person they are seeking. Canada is in the forefront of research on the best search and rescue procedures, with people like Martin Colwell of British Columbia doing systematic work regarding these techniques. Ken's responsibility as a manager is to apply this research to optimize the search. Searchers must be spaced far enough apart to cover ground quickly, for example, but not so far apart that they are out of earshot of each other. For whatever reason, though, the searchers had failed to locate the lost boy over the last three days.

Ken's anxiety vanished with a single radio report. A truck bringing food to the searchers' camp found the boy when he stepped onto the road and flagged it down. "I want my mommy," he said. All things considered, the boy was remarkably fit after his experience—even a little nonchalant about it.

Part of Ken's skill as a search manager arises from his attention to debriefing the lost person so he can learn what the person did. Ken got a chance to talk to the boy shortly after he was found.

"What was it like being lost in the woods?" Ken asked.

"Oh, it was okay," the boy said. "Except at night. When the monsters came out."

"Monsters?" Ken asked. This was a wilderness risk new to him.

"Yes. They were tall and scary. I could see them at night moving around, because they had one big glowing eye on the tops of their heads. And what was worse was that they knew I was there. They kept calling out my name. Over and over again. I'm glad I found you first."

Our senses are the means by which we experience the world; everything we learn is detected by sense organs and transmitted to our brains by sensory nerves. Without sensory input, a human brain would be utterly useless; it would learn nothing, think no thoughts, and have no experiences.

The sense organs and the sensory nerves have evolved to provide us with useful information about the external world. Using vision as their example, Milner and Goodale (1996, p. 11) make this point succinctly: "Vision [evolved] to provide distal sensory control of the movements that the animal makes in order to survive and reproduce in that world." How the sense systems do that depends not only on the specific modality of the information, but also on the characteristics of the information and the state of the brain at the time it receives it. Differences between sources of information in the environment have important consequences for the way in which sensory systems process that information.

For example, consider the difference between the world as we see it and as we hear it. The visual scene received by our eyes changes rapidly as we move our body, our head, and our eyes. Think of it as a visual picture frame, and consider how quickly it moves as we shift our eyes around a room. Yet we sense our visual world as stable. The visual system must provide that stability in the face of rapid shifts in its input. Sound, on the other hand, is not so variable. While its intensity changes as we move toward or away from its origin, on the whole these changes are more gradual than those faced by the visual system. Furthermore, sounds carry around obstacles in ways that light does not. Our auditory sense, then, has more time to process signals. As we will see, it uses this time to discriminate complex waveforms of the underlying sounds.

Because they are attuned to different aspects of our world, the senses contribute to the richness of experience. Given the role that speech plays in human culture, audition is extremely important for social behaviour. With vision, it provides information about distant events, as does the sense of smell, which can tell us about sources of aromatic molecules far upwind. The other senses deal with events occurring immediately nearby—for instance, the taste of our favourite foods or the touch of a loved one. The body senses are closely tied to our own movements. When we feel an object, the experience is active, not passive; we move our hands over it to determine its shape, texture, and temperature. And information from specialized organs in the inner ear and from receptors in the muscles and joints is actually produced by our own movements. This information helps us maintain our balance as we engage in our everyday activities.

▲ *Our senses are the means by which we experience the world.*

## Sensory Processing

Experience is traditionally studied by distinguishing between sensation and perception. Most psychologists define **sensation** as the detection of simple properties of stimuli, such as brightness, colour, warmth, and sweetness. **Perception** is the detection of objects (both animate and inanimate), their locations, their movements, and their backgrounds. According to these definitions, seeing the colour red is a *sensation*, but seeing a red apple is a *perception*. Similarly, seeing a movement is a sensation, but seeing a soccer ball coming toward us and realizing that we will have to move to the left to block it is a perception. As Ken Hill's story about the lost four-year-old demonstrates, detecting a sound is not the same as identifying what the source of the sound means. Psychologists used to believe that perceptions depended heavily on learning whereas pure sensations involved innate, "prewired" physiological mechanisms. However, neither behavioural nor physiological research has been able to establish a clear boundary between "simple" sensations and "complex" perceptions. Indeed, research has shown that experience is essential to the development of some of the most elementary features of sensory systems.

This chapter describes our sensory mechanisms: the visual, auditory, gustatory, olfactory, and somatosensory systems. According to tradition, we have five senses, but, in fact, we have several more. For example, the somatosensory system includes separate components that are able to detect touch, warmth, coolness, vibration, physical damage (pain), head tilt, head movement, limb movement, muscular contraction, and various events occurring within our bodies. Whether we choose to call each of these components "senses" is a matter of terminology.

### Transduction

Your brain, floating in cerebrospinal fluid, swaddled in its protective sheath of meninges, and sheltered in a thick skull, is isolated from the world around you. The only sense receptors that the brain possesses detect such things as temperature and salt concentration of the blood, and these receptors cannot inform it about what is going on outside.

**sensation** The detection of the elementary properties of a stimulus.
**perception** The detection of the more complex properties of a stimulus, including its location and nature; involves learning.

**TABLE 5•1 The Types of Transduction Accomplished by the Sense Organs**

| Location of Sense Organ | Environmental Stimuli | Energy Transduced |
|---|---|---|
| Eye | Light | Radiant energy |
| Ear | Sound | Mechanical energy |
| Vestibular system | Tilt and rotation of head | Mechanical energy |
| Tongue | Taste | Recognition of molecular shape |
| Nose | Odour | Recognition of molecular shape |
| Skin, Internal organs | Touch | Mechanical energy |
| | Temperature | Thermal energy |
| | Vibration | Mechanical energy |
| Muscle | Pain | Chemical reaction |
| | Stretch | Mechanical energy |

Useful actions require information about the external world, and such information is gathered by the sense organs located outside the brain.

Sense organs detect stimuli provided by light, sound, odour, taste, or mechanical contact with the environment. Information about these stimuli is transmitted to the brain through neural impulses—action potentials carried by the axons in sensory nerves. The task of the sense organs is to transmit signals to the brain that are coded in such a way as to represent faithfully the events that have occurred in the environment. The task of the brain is to analyze this information and reconstruct what has occurred.

**Transduction** (literally, "leading across") is the process by which the sense organs convert energy from environmental events into neural activity. Each sense organ responds to a particular form of energy given off by an environmental stimulus and translates that energy into neural firing to which the brain can respond. The means of transduction are as diverse as the kinds of stimuli we can perceive. In most senses, specialized neurons called **receptor cells** release chemical transmitter substances that stimulate other neurons, thus altering the rate of firing of their axons. In the somatosenses ("body senses"), dendrites of neurons respond directly to physical stimuli without the intervention of specialized receptor cells. However, some of these neurons do have specialized endings that enable them to respond to particular kinds of sensory information. **Table 5•1** summarizes the types of transduction accomplished by our sense organs.

**transduction** The conversion of physical stimuli into changes in the activity of receptor cells of sensory organs.
**receptor cell** A neuron that directly responds to a physical stimulus, such as light, vibrations, or aromatic molecules.
**anatomical coding** A means by which the nervous system represents information; different features are coded by the activity of different neurons.

## Sensory Coding

Sensory information must accurately represent the environment. But, as we saw in Chapter 4, nerves are bundles of axons, each of which can do no more than transmit action potentials. These action potentials are fixed in size and duration; they cannot be altered. Thus, different stimuli cannot be translated into different types of action potentials. Yet we can detect an enormous number of different stimuli with each of our sense organs. For example, we are capable of discriminating among approximately 7.5 million different colours. We can recognize up to 10 000 odours. We can also identify touches to different parts of the body, and we can further discriminate the degree of pressure involved and the sharpness or bluntness, softness or hardness, and temperature of the object touching us. How, then, if action potentials cannot be altered, do the sense organs tell the brain that, for instance, a red apple or a yellow lemon has been seen—or that the right hand is holding a small, cold object or a large, warm one? The information from the sense organs must somehow be coded in the activity of axons carrying information from the sense organs to the brain.

A *code* is a system of symbols or signals representing information. Spoken English, written French, traffic lights, tones produced by the number keys on a cellphone, and the electrical zeros and ones in the memory of a computer are all examples of codes. As long as we know the rules of a code, we can convert a message from one medium to another without losing any information. Although we do not know the precise rules by which the sensory systems transmit information to the brain, we do know that they take two general forms: *anatomical coding* and *temporal coding*.

**Anatomical Coding** Since the early 1800s, when Johannes Müller formulated his doctrine of specific nerve energies (discussed in Chapter 1), we have known that the brain learns what is happening through the activity of specific sets of neurons. Sensory organs located in different places in the body send their information to the brain through different nerves. Because the brain has no direct information about the physical energy impinging on a given sense organ, it uses **anatomical coding** to interpret the location and type of sensory stimulus according to which incoming nerve fibres are active. For example, if you rub your eyes, you will mechanically stimulate the light-sensitive receptors located there. This stimulation produces action potentials in the axons of the nerves that connect the eyes with the brain (the *optic nerves*). The visual system of the brain has no way of knowing that the light-sensitive receptors of the eyes have been activated by a non-visual stimulus. As a result, the brain acts as if the neural activity in the optic nerves was produced by light—so you see stars and flashes. Experiments performed during surgery have shown that artificial stimulation of the nerves that convey taste produces a sensation of taste, electrical stimulation of the auditory nerve produces a sensation of a buzzing noise, and so forth.

Sensory coding for the body surface is anatomical. The primary somatosensory cortex contains a neural "map" of the skin. Receptors in the skin in different parts of the body send information to different parts of the primary somatosensory cortex. Similarly, the primary visual cortex maintains a map of the visual field.

**Temporal Coding** **Temporal coding** is the coding of information in terms of time. The simplest form of temporal code is *rate.* By firing at a faster or slower rate according to the intensity of a stimulus, an axon can communicate quantitative information to the brain. For example, a light touch to the skin can be encoded by a low rate of firing and a more forceful touch by a high rate. Thus, the firing of a particular set of neurons (an anatomical code) tells *where* the body is being touched; the rate at which these neurons fire (a temporal code) tells *how intense* that touch is. As far as we know, all sensory systems use rate of firing to encode the intensity of stimulation.

## Psychophysics

As you learned in Chapter 1, nineteenth-century Europe was the birthplace of **psychophysics**, the systematic study of the relation between the physical characteristics of stimuli and the sensations they produce (the "physics of the mind"). To study perceptual phenomena, scientists had to find reliable ways to measure people's sensations. We will examine two of these methods—the just-noticeable difference and the procedures of signal detection theory—in the following subsections.

**The Principle of the Just-Noticeable Difference** In Germany, Ernst Weber (1795–1878), an anatomist and physiologist, investigated the ability of humans to discriminate between various stimuli. He measured the **just-noticeable difference (jnd)**—the smallest change in the magnitude of a stimulus that a person can detect. He discovered a principle that held true for many sensory systems: The jnd is directly related to the magnitude of that stimulus. For example, when he presented participants with two metal objects and asked them to say whether they differed in weight, the participants reported that the two weights felt the same unless they differed by a factor of 1 in 40. That is, a person could just barely distinguish a 40-gram weight from a 41-gram weight, an 80-gram weight from an 82-gram weight, or a 400-gram weight from a 410-gram weight. Psychologically, the difference between a 40-gram weight and a 41-gram weight is equivalent to the difference between an 80-gram weight and an 82-gram weight: one jnd. Different senses had different ratios. For example, the ratio for detecting differences in the brightness of white light is approximately 1 in 60. These ratios are called **Weber fractions.**

Gustav Fechner (1801–1887), another German physiologist, used Weber's concept of the just-noticeable difference to measure people's sensations. Assuming that the jnd was the basic unit of a sensory experience, he measured the absolute

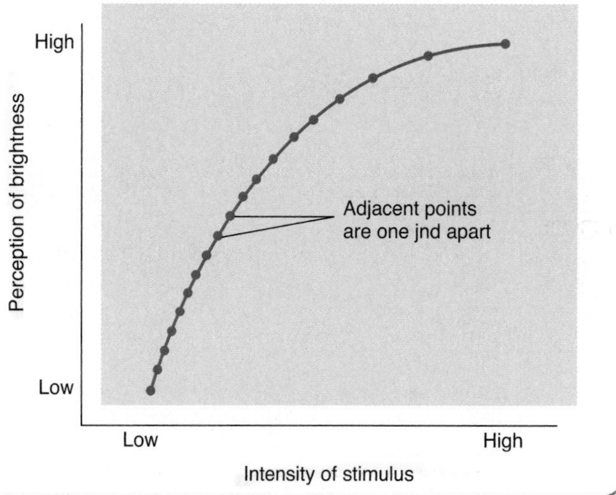


**FIGURE 5•1** A hypothetical range of perceived brightness (in jnds) as a function of intensity.

magnitude of a sensation in jnds. For example, suppose we want to measure the strength of a person's sensation of light of a particular intensity. We seat the participant in a darkened room facing two discs of frosted glass, each having a light bulb behind it; the brightness of the light bulb is adjustable. One of the discs serves as the sample stimulus, the other as the comparison stimulus. We start with the sample and comparison stimuli turned off completely and increase the brightness of the comparison stimulus until our participant can just detect a difference. That value is one jnd. Then we set the sample stimulus to that intensity (one jnd) and again increase the brightness of the comparison stimulus just until our participant can again tell them apart. The new value of the comparison stimulus is two jnds. We continue making these measurements until our stimuli are as bright as we can make them or until they become uncomfortably bright for our participant. Finally, we construct a graph indicating the strength of a sensation of brightness (in jnds) in relation to the intensity of a stimulus. The graph, which relates strength of a sensory experience to physical intensity, might look something like **Figure 5•1.**

How should you interpret a graph like the one in Figure 5.1? First, note the two scales. The values along the X axis are measures of physical intensity—something measured with

**temporal coding** A means by which the nervous system represents information; different features are coded by the pattern of activity of neurons.

**psychophysics** A branch of psychology that measures the quantitative relation between physical stimuli and perceptual experience.

**just-noticeable difference (jnd)** The smallest difference between two similar stimuli that can be distinguished; also called difference threshold.

**Weber fraction** The ratio between a just-noticeable difference and the magnitude of a stimulus; reasonably constant over the middle range of most stimulus intensities.

**FIGURE 5•2** The relationship between stimulus and perception when less energy is required to produce a jnd at higher intensities.

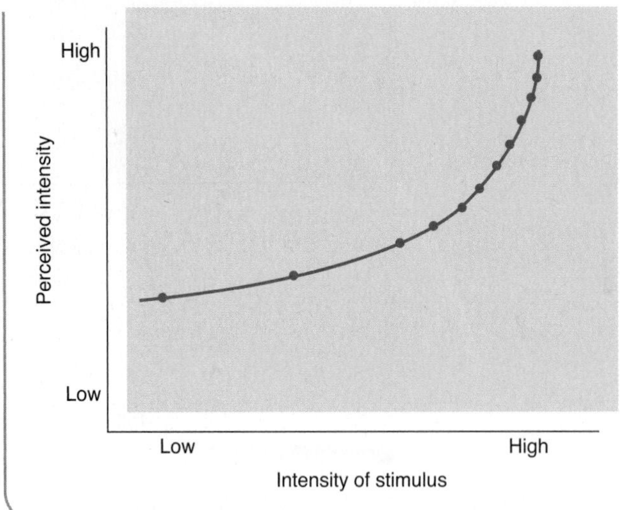


respect to the objective world. The values along the Y axis are very different. Each unit is a jnd—a measure of the extent that the subjective perception is increasing. So, in other words, Figure 5.1 provides a mapping between the physical and the psychological worlds.

Second, notice that if you trace the distance between dots on the X axis, the distances become larger as you move to the right on the graph. This is a consequence of Weber's principle. Each dot marks another jnd. The amount of physical energy necessary to produce a jnd increases with the magnitude of the stimulus.

Finally, note the shape of the curve. It rises steeply at first, but then begins to level off. This kind of curve is characteristic of the mathematical function of a logarithm. Fechner's great contribution to psychology was to show how a logarithmic function could be derived from Weber's principle. Norwich and Wong (1997) provide a technical overview of how these two perspectives relate to each other.

What would the function shown in Figure 5.1 look like if Weber's principle did not hold? The question is not an idle one, because there are some sensations (e.g., the pain from electric shock) for which it takes less energy to produce a jnd at higher intensities. The kind of function that describes this situation looks like the one in **Figure 5•2.** Notice that the points of physical energy that produce a more intense sensation are closer together at the higher levels of physical sensation. The shape of the curve is different as a result.

Is there a way to reconcile these two contrasting functions? Almost 100 years after Fechner's work, S. S. Stevens proposed another viewpoint, which has become very influential. Stevens suggested a power function to relate physical intensity to the magnitude of sensation. In mathematical notation, if $S$ is the psychological magnitude of the sensation, and $I$ is the intensity of the physical stimulus, then, according to the Stevens' power function,

$$S = kI^b$$

The symbol $k$ stands for a mathematical constant that adjusts for the way physical intensity is measured. The important change is that the intensity ($I$) is raised to the power $b$.

The mathematical properties of a power function are such that when $b$ is a number between zero and one (i.e., a fraction) the curve for sensation looks somewhat like Fechner's (see Figure 5.1). However, if the value of $b$ is greater than 1, the curve looks like the one in Figure 5.2. Stevens' power function, then, provides a single principle that can account for both types of results. The only substantive difference is the value of $b$.

For example, with our sense of taste, the value of $b$ for saccharin is 0.8 (see Schiffman, 1996). What the power function implies, for this value, is that if we were to taste two solutions, one containing twice as high a concentration of saccharin as the other, the first solution would taste only about 1.7 times as sweet. In contrast, the value of $b$ for salt is 1.3. A solution with twice the concentration of salt would therefore taste about two-and-one-half times as salty. The larger effect of doubling the concentration of salt compared to the effect of doubling the concentration of saccharin is reflected in the two exponents. The power law therefore provides a systematic way to compare different sensory systems.

**Signal Detection Theory** Psychophysical methods rely heavily on the concept of a **threshold**, the line between not perceiving and perceiving. The just-noticeable difference can also be called a **difference threshold**, the minimum detectable difference between two stimuli. An **absolute threshold** is the minimum value of a stimulus that can be detected—that is, discriminated from no stimulus at all. Thus, the first comparison in the experiment just described—using a dark disc as the sample stimulus—measured an absolute threshold. The subsequent comparisons measured difference thresholds.

Even early psychophysicists realized that a threshold was not an absolutely fixed value. When a researcher flashes a very dim light, a participant may report seeing it on some trials but not on others. By convention, the threshold is the point at which a participant detects the stimulus 50 percent of the time. This definition is necessary because of the inherent variability of activity in the nervous system. Even when they are not being stimulated, neurons are never absolutely still; they fire every now and then. If a very weak stimulus occurs when neurons in the visual system happen to be quiet, the brain is likely to detect it. But if the neurons happen to be firing, the effects of the stimulus are likely to be lost in the "noise."

**threshold** The point at which a stimulus, or a change in the value of a stimulus, can just be detected.
**difference threshold** An alternative name for just-noticeable difference (jnd).
**absolute threshold** The minimum value of a stimulus that can be detected.

▲ *According to signal detection theory, we must discriminate between the signal, conveying information, and noise, contributed by background stimuli and random activity of our own nervous systems.*

An alternative method of measuring a person's sensitivity to changes in physical stimuli takes account of random changes in the nervous system (Green & Swets, 1974). According to **signal detection theory**, every stimulus event requires discrimination between *signal* (stimulus) and *noise* (consisting of both background stimuli and random activity of the nervous system).

Suppose you are seated in a quiet room, facing a small warning light. The researcher tells you that when the light flashes, you *may* hear a faint tone one second later. Your task is to say "yes" or "no" after each flash of the warning light, according to whether you hear the tone. At first, the task is easy: Some flashes are followed by an easily heard tone; others are followed by silence. You are confident about your yes and no decisions. But as the experiment progresses, the tone gets fainter and fainter, until it is so soft that you have doubts about how you should respond. The light flashes. What should you say? Did you really hear a tone or were you just imagining it?

At this point, your *response bias*—your tendency to say "yes" or "no" when you are not sure whether you detected the stimulus—can have an effect. According to the terminology of signal detection theory, *hits* are saying "yes" when the stimulus is presented; *misses* are saying "no" when it is presented; *correct negatives* are saying "no" when the stimulus is not presented; and *false alarms* are saying "yes" when the stimulus is not presented. Hits and correct negatives are correct responses; misses and false alarms are incorrect responses. (See **Figure 5•3**.) Suppose you want to be very sure that you are

**FIGURE 5•3** Four possibilities in judging the presence or absence of a stimulus.

| Event | | Judgment: "Yes" | Judgment: "No" |
|---|---|---|---|
| | Light *did* flash | Hit | Miss |
| | Light *did not* flash | False alarm | Correct negative |

correct when you say "yes" because you would feel foolish saying you have heard something that is not there. Your response bias is to err in favour of avoiding false alarms, even at the risk of making misses. Someone else's response bias might be to err in favour of detecting all stimuli, even at the risk of making false alarms.

A person's response bias can seriously affect an investigator's estimate of the threshold of detection. A person with a response bias to avoid false alarms will appear to have a higher threshold than will someone who does not want to let a tone go by without saying "yes." To avoid this problem, signal detection theorists have developed a method of assessing people's sensitivity, regardless of their initial response bias. They deliberately manipulate the response biases and observe the results of these manipulations on the people's judgments.

Suppose you are a participant in the experiment just described, and the researcher promises you a dollar every time you make a hit, with no penalty for false alarms. You would undoubtedly tend to say "yes" on every trial, even if you were not sure you had heard the tone; after all, you have nothing to lose and everything to gain. In contrast, suppose the researcher announced that she would fine you a dollar every time you made a false alarm and give you nothing for making hits. You would undoubtedly say "no" every time, because you would have everything to lose and nothing to gain: You would be extremely conservative in your judgments.

Now consider your response bias under a number of intermediate conditions. If you receive a dollar for every hit but are also fined 50 cents for every miss, you will say "yes" whenever you are reasonably sure you heard the tone. If you receive 50 cents for every hit but are fined a dollar for each

**signal detection theory** A mathematical theory of the detection of stimuli, which involves discriminating a signal from the noise in which it is embedded and which takes into account participants' willingness to report detecting the signal.

**FIGURE 5•4** A receiver operating characteristic (ROC) curve. The percentage of hits and false alarms in judging the presence of a stimulus under several payoff conditions.

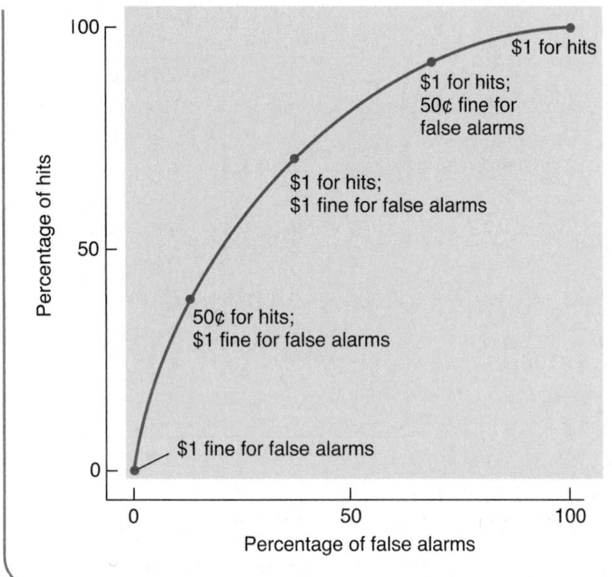


**FIGURE 5•5** Two ROC curves, obtained by presenting a more discriminable stimulus (magenta curve) and a less discriminable stimulus (yellow curve).

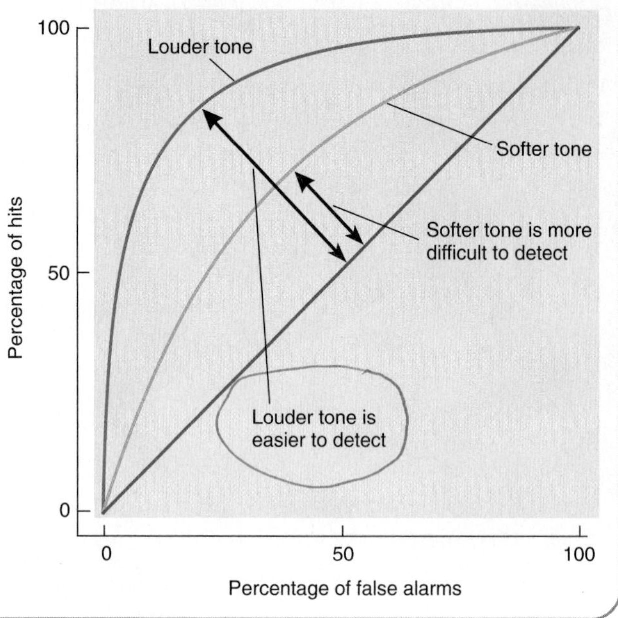


false alarm, you will be more conservative. But if you are sure you heard the tone, you will say "yes" to earn 50 cents. (Note, however, that there are other, less expensive ways to change people's response biases besides offering them payment, which is fortunate for researchers on limited budgets.) **Figure 5•4** graphs your performance over this range of payoff conditions.

The graph in Figure 5.4 is a **receiver operating characteristic curve (ROC curve)**, named for its original use in research at the Bell Laboratories to measure the intelligibility of speech transmitted through a telephone system. The curve shows performance when the sound is difficult to detect. If the sound were louder, so that you rarely doubted whether you heard it, you would make almost every possible hit and very few false alarms. The few misses you made would be under the low-payoff condition, when you wanted to be absolutely certain you heard the tone. The few false alarms would occur when guessing did not matter because the fine for being wrong was low or non-existent. The ROC curve (magenta) reflecting this new condition is shown with the original one (yellow) in **Figure 5•5**. The difference between the two curves demonstrates that the louder tone is easier to detect. Detectability is measured by the relative distances of the curves from a 45-degree line (blue).

The signal detection method is the best way to determine a person's sensitivity to the occurrence of a particular stimulus. Note that the concept of threshold is not used. Instead, a stimulus is more or less detectable. The person *decides* whether a stimulus occurred, and the consequences of making hits or false alarms can bias this decision. Signal detection theory emphasizes that sensory experience involves factors other than the activity of the sensory systems, such as motivation and prior experience.

**receiver operating characteristic curve (ROC curve)** A graph of hits and false alarms of participants under different motivational conditions; indicates people's ability to detect a particular stimulus.

## Interim Summary

### Sensory Processing

We experience the world through our senses. Our knowledge of the world stems from the accumulation of sensory experience and subsequent learning. All sensory experiences are the result of energy from events that is transduced into activity of receptors, which are specialized neurons. Transduction causes changes in the activity of axons of sensory nerves, and these changes in activity inform the sensory mechanisms of the brain about the environmental event. The information received from the receptors is transmitted to the brain by means of two coding schemes: anatomical coding and temporal coding.

To study the nature of experience scientifically, we must be able to measure it. In nineteenth-century Germany, Weber devised the concept of the just-noticeable difference, and Fechner used the jnd to measure the magnitude of sensations.

Stevens modified this formulation and suggested a power function to describe the relation between physical intensity and sensation. In the twentieth century, signal detection theory gave rise to methods that enabled psychologists to assess people's sensitivity to stimuli despite individual differences in response bias. The methods of psychophysics apply to all sensory modalities, including sight, smell, taste, hearing, and touch.

**QUESTIONS TO CONSIDER**

1. What sense modalities would you least want to lose? Why?
2. If you could design a new sense modality, what kind of information would it detect? What advantages would this new ability provide? Or do you think that our sensory organs already detect all of the useful information that is available? Why or why not?

# Vision

The visual system performs a remarkable job. We take for granted the fact that in a quick glance we can recognize what there is to see: people, objects, and landscapes in depth and full colour. Researchers who have tried to program computers to recognize scenes visually realize just how complex this task is. This section begins our tour of the visual system. We will consider the eye and its functions in this chapter and explore the nature of visual perception in Chapter 6. But first, let's start with the stimulus: light.

## Light

As we all know, the eye is sensitive to light. But what is light? Light consists of radiant energy similar to radio waves. Radiant energy oscillates as it is transmitted from its source. For example, the antenna that broadcasts the programs of my favourite FM station transmits radio waves that oscillate at 88.5 MHz (megahertz, or million times per second). Because electromagnetic energy travels at 298 000 km per second, the waves transmitted by this antenna are approximately 3.4 metres apart. (One 88.5 millionth of 298 000 km equals 3.367 m.) Thus, the **wavelength** of the signal from the station—the distance between the waves of radiant energy—is 3.4 m.

The wavelength of visible light is much shorter, ranging from 380 through 760 nanometres (a nanometre, nm, is one billionth of a metre). When viewed by a human eye, different wavelengths of visible light have different colours: for instance, 380 nm light looks violet and 760 nm light looks red.

All other radiant energy is invisible to our eyes. Ultraviolet radiation, X-rays, and gamma rays have shorter wavelengths than visible light has, whereas infrared radiation, radar, and (as we saw) radio waves have longer wavelengths. The entire range of wavelengths is known as the *electromagnetic spectrum*; the part our eyes can detect—the part we see as light—is referred to as the *visible spectrum*. (See **Figure 5•6**.)

The definition of the visible spectrum is based on the human visual system. Some other species of animals would undoubtedly define the visible spectrum differently. For example, bees can see ultraviolet radiation that is invisible to us. Some plants have taken advantage of this fact and produce flowers that contain dyes that reflect ultraviolet radiation, presenting patterns that attract bees to them. Some snakes (notably, pit vipers such as the rattlesnake) have special organs that detect infrared radiation. This ability enables them to find their prey in the dark by detecting the heat emitted by small mammals in the form of infrared radiation.

## The Eye and Its Functions

The eyes are important and delicate sense organs—and they are well protected. Each eye is housed in a bony socket and can be covered by the eyelid to keep dust and dirt out. The eyelids are edged by eyelashes, which help keep foreign matter from falling into the open eye. The eyebrows prevent sweat on the forehead from dripping into the eyes. Reflex mechanisms provide additional protection: The sudden approach of an object toward the face or a touch on the surface of the eye causes automatic eyelid closure and withdrawal of the head.

**Figure 5•7** shows a cross-section of a human eye. The transparent **cornea** forms a bulge at the front of the eye and admits light. A tough white membrane called the **sclera** (from the Greek *skleros*, "hard") coats the rest of the eye. The **iris** consists of two bands of muscles that control the amount of

**wavelength** The distance between adjacent waves of radiant energy; in vision, most closely associated with the perceptual dimension of hue.
**cornea** The transparent tissue covering the front of the eye.
**sclera** The tough outer layer of the eye; the "white" of the eye.
**iris** The pigmented muscle of the eye that controls the size of the pupil.

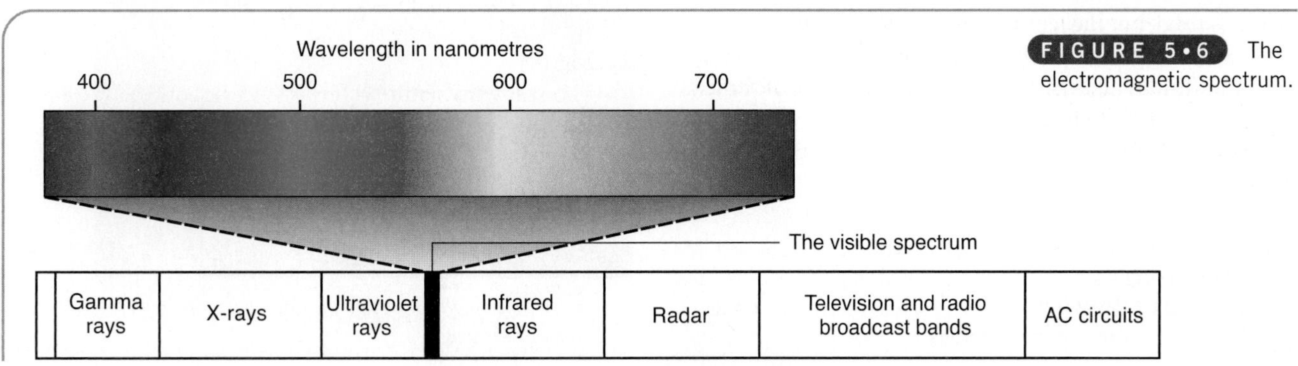


FIGURE 5•6 The electromagnetic spectrum.

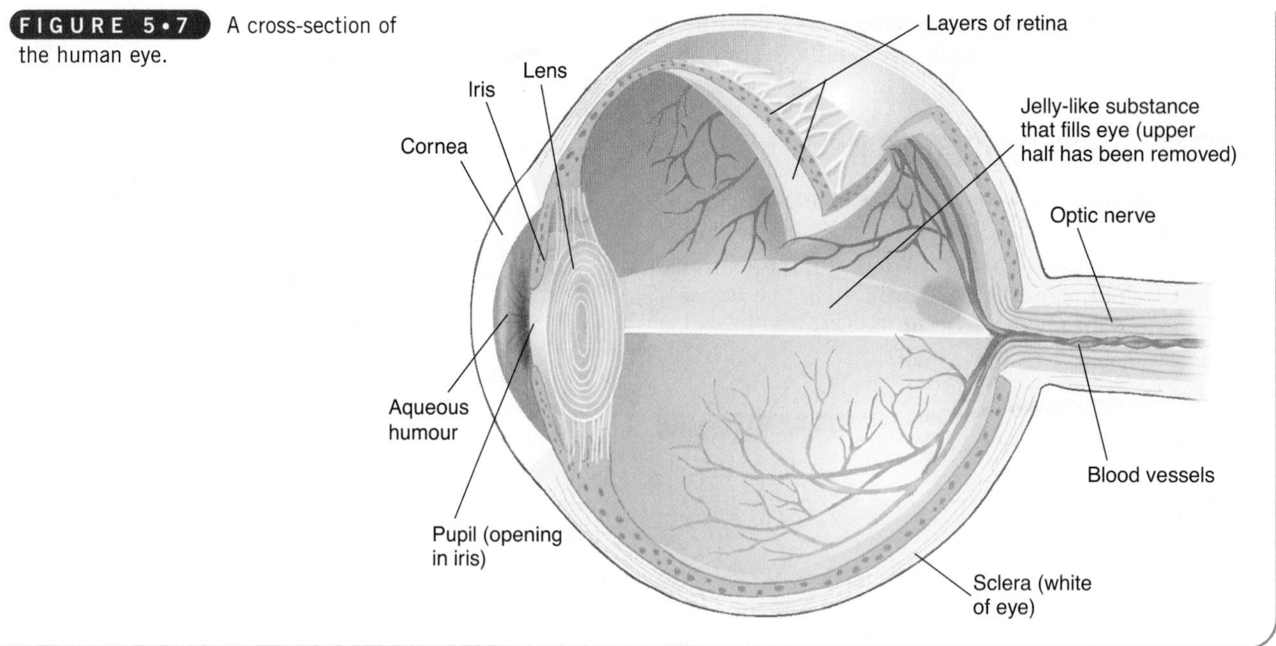


**FIGURE 5•7** A cross-section of the human eye.

light admitted into the eye. The brain controls these muscles and thus regulates the size of the pupil, constricting it in bright light and dilating it in dim light. The space immediately behind the cornea is filled with *aqueous humour*, which simply means "watery fluid." This fluid is constantly produced by tissue behind the cornea that filters the fluid from the blood. In place of blood vessels, the aqueous humour nourishes the cornea and other portions of the front of the eye; this fluid must circulate and be renewed. (If aqueous humour is produced too quickly or if the passage that returns it to the blood becomes blocked, the pressure within the eye can increase and cause damage to vision—a disorder known as *glaucoma*.) Because of its transparency, the cornea must be nourished in this unusual manner. Our vision would be less clear if we had a set of blood vessels across the front of our eyes.

The curvature of the cornea and of the **lens**, which lies immediately behind the iris, causes images to be focused on the inner surface of the back of the eye. Although this image is upside down and reversed from left to right, the brain compensates for this alteration and interprets the information appropriately. The lens has a special limitation: Because it must remain transparent, the lens contains no blood vessels and is therefore functionally dead tissue. The shape of the cornea is fixed, but the lens is flexible; a special set of muscles can alter its shape so that the eye can obtain images of either nearby or distant objects. This change in the shape of the lens to adjust for distance is called **accommodation.**

Normally, the length of the eye matches the bending of light rays produced by the cornea and the lens so that the

▲ *To a nearsighted person, distant objects are blurry and out of focus.*

**lens** The transparent organ situated behind the iris of the eye; helps focus an image on the retina.
**accommodation** Changes in the thickness of the lens of the eye that focus images of near or distant objects on the retina.

**FIGURE 5•8** Lenses used to correct nearsightedness and farsightedness.

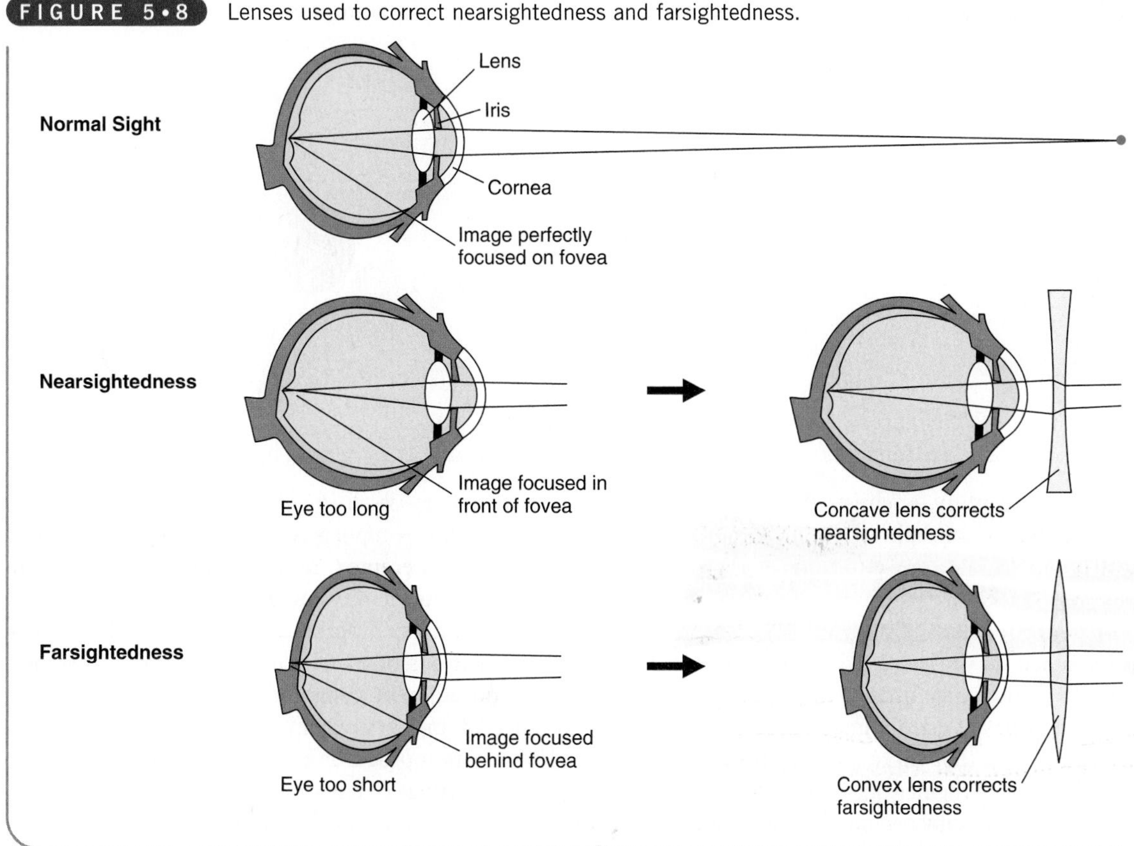


image of the visual scene is sharply focused on the retina. However, for some people these two factors are not matched, and the image on the retina is therefore out of focus. These people need an extra lens in front of their eyes (in the form of eyeglasses or contact lenses) to correct the discrepancy and bring the image into focus. People whose eyes are too long (front to back) are said to be *nearsighted*; they need a concave lens to correct the focus. People whose eyes are too short are said to be *farsighted*; they need a convex lens. As people get older, the lenses of their eyes become less flexible and it becomes difficult for them to focus on objects close to them. These people need reading glasses with convex lenses (or bifocals, if they already wear glasses). (See **Figure 5•8**.)

The **retina**, which lines the inner surface of the back of the eye, performs the sensory functions of the eye. Embedded in the retina are more than 130 million **photoreceptors**—specialized neurons that transduce light into neural activity. The information from the photoreceptors is transmitted to neurons that send axons toward one point at the back of the eye—the **optic disc**. All axons leave the eye at this point and join the optic nerve, which travels to the brain. (See Figures 5•7 and **5•9**.) Because there are no photoreceptors directly in front of the optic disc, this portion of the retina is blind. If you have not located your own blind spot, you might want to try the demonstration shown in **Figure 5•10**.

**FIGURE 5•9** A view of the back of the eye. The photograph shows the retina, the optic disc, and blood vessels. *(Courtesy of Douglas G. Mollerstuen, New England Medical Center.)*

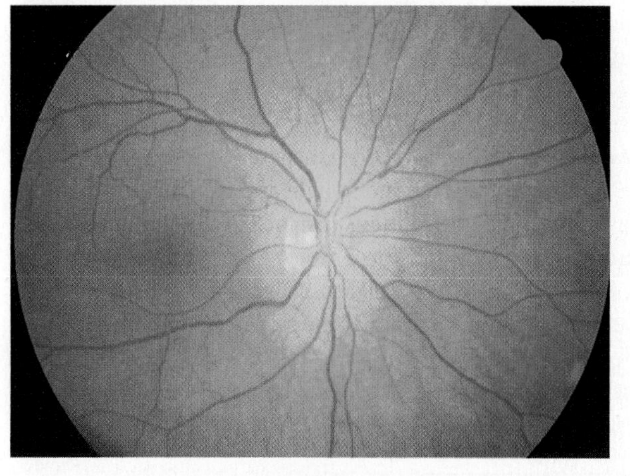

**retina** The tissue at the back inside surface of the eye that contains the photoreceptors and associated neurons.

**photoreceptor** A receptive cell for vision in the retina; a rod or a cone.

**optic disc** A circular structure located at the exit point from the retina of the axons of the ganglion cells that form the optic nerve.

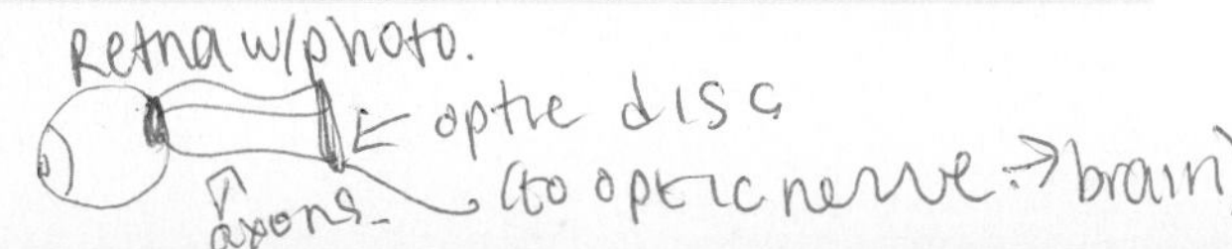

**FIGURE 5•10** A test for the blind spot. With your left eye closed, look at the + with your right eye and move the page back and forth, toward and away from yourself. At about 20 centimetres, the coloured circle disappears from your vision because its image falls on your blind spot.

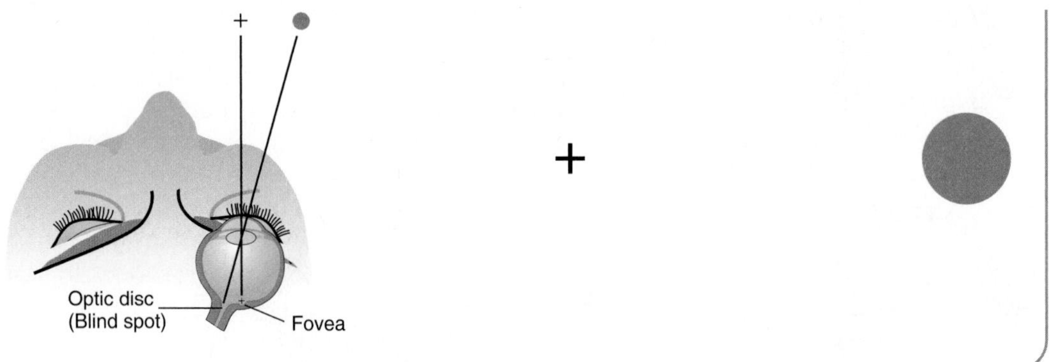


Before the seventeenth century, scientists thought that the lens sensed the presence of light. Johannes Kepler (1571–1630), the astronomer who discovered the true shape of the planets' orbits around the sun, is credited with the suggestion that the retina, not the lens, contained the receptive tissue of the eye. It remained for Christoph Scheiner (another German astronomer) to demonstrate in 1625 that the lens is simply a focusing device. (Perhaps astronomers had a special interest in vision and gave some thought to it during the long nights spent watching the sky.) Scheiner obtained an ox's eye from a slaughterhouse. After carefully peeling the sclera away from the back of the eye, he was able to see an upside-down image of the world through the thin, translucent membrane that remained. As an astronomer, he was familiar with the fact that convex glass lenses could cast images, so he recognized the function of the lens of the eye.

**Figure 5•11** shows a cross-section of the retina. The retina has three principal layers. Light passes successively through the *ganglion cell layer* (front), the *bipolar cell layer* (middle), and the *photoreceptor layer* (back). Early anatomists were surprised to find the photoreceptors in the deepest layer of the retina. As you might expect, the cells that are located above the photoreceptors are transparent.

Photoreceptors respond to light and pass the information on by means of a transmitter substance to the **bipolar cells**, the neurons with which they form synapses. Bipolar cells transmit this information to the **ganglion cells**, neurons whose axons travel across the retina and through the optic nerves. Thus, visual information passes through a three-cell chain to the brain: photoreceptor → bipolar cell → ganglion cell → brain.

A single photoreceptor responds only to light that reaches its immediate vicinity, but a ganglion cell can receive information from many different photoreceptors. The retina also contains neurons that interconnect both adjacent photoreceptors and adjacent ganglion cells. (See Figure 5.11.) The existence of this neural circuitry indicates that some kinds of information processing are performed in the retina.

The human retina contains two general types of photoreceptors: 125 million rods and 6 million cones, so called because of their shapes. **Rods** function mainly in dim light; they are very sensitive to light but are insensitive to differences between colours. **Cones** function when the level of illumination is bright enough to see things clearly. They are also responsible for colour vision. The **fovea**, a small pit in the back of the retina approximately 1 mm in diameter, contains only cones. (Refer to Figure 5.8.) Most cones are connected to only one ganglion cell apiece. As a consequence, the fovea is responsible for our finest, most detailed vision. When we look at a point in our visual field, we move our eyes so that the image of that point falls directly on the cone-packed fovea.

**bipolar cell** A neuron in the retina that receives information from photoreceptors and passes it on to the ganglion cells, from which axons proceed through the optic nerves to the brain.
**ganglion cell** A neuron in the retina that receives information from photoreceptors by means of bipolar cells and from which axons proceed through the optic nerves to the brain.
**rod** A photoreceptor that is very sensitive to light but cannot detect changes in hue.
**cone** A photoreceptor that is responsible for acute daytime vision and for colour perception.
**fovea** A small pit near the centre of the retina containing densely packed cones; responsible for the most acute and detailed vision.

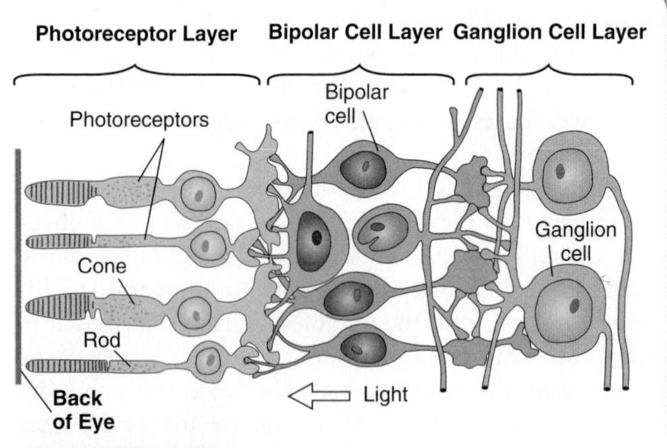


**FIGURE 5•11** The cells of the retina.

*(Redrawn by permission of the Royal Society and the authors from Dowling, J. E., & Boycott, B. B. (1966).* Proceedings of the Royal Society *(London), Series B, 166, 80–111.)*

Farther away from the fovea, the number of cones decreases and the number of rods increases. Up to 100 rods may converge on a single ganglion cell. A ganglion cell that receives information from so many rods is sensitive to very low levels of light. Rods are therefore responsible for our sensitivity to very dim light, but, because many of them from different areas connect to just one ganglion cell, visual information they provide lacks sharpness.

## Transduction of Light by Photoreceptors

Although light-sensitive sensory organs have evolved independently in a wide variety of animals—from insects to fish to mammals—the chemistry is essentially the same in all species: A molecule derived from vitamin A is the central ingredient in the transduction of the energy of light into neural activity. (Carrots are said to be good for vision because they contain a substance that the body easily converts to vitamin A.) In the absence of light, this molecule is attached to another molecule, a protein. The two molecules together form a **photopigment.** The photoreceptors of the human eye contain four kinds of photopigments (one for rods and three for cones), but their basic mechanism is the same. When a photon (a particle of light) strikes a photopigment, the photopigment splits into its two constituent molecules. This event starts the process of transduction. The splitting of the photopigment causes a series of chemical reactions that stimulate the photoreceptor and cause it to send a message to the bipolar cell with which it forms a synapse. The bipolar cell sends a message to the ganglion cell, which then sends one on to the brain. (See **Figure 5•12.**)

Intact photopigments have a characteristic colour. **Rhodopsin**, the photopigment of rods, is pink (*rhodon* means "rose" in Greek). However, once the photopigments are split by the action of light, they lose their colour—they become bleached. Franz Boll discovered this phenomenon in 1876 when he removed an eye from an animal and pointed it toward a window that opened onto a brightly lit scene. He then examined the retina under dim light and found that the image of the scene was still there. The retina was pink where little light had fallen and pale where the image had been bright. Boll's discovery led investigators to suspect that a chemical reaction was responsible for the transduction of light into neural activity.

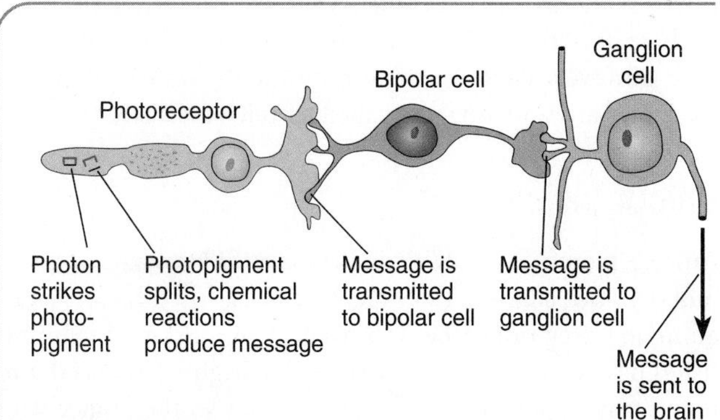
Photoreceptor
Bipolar cell
Ganglion cell
Photon strikes photo- pigment
Photopigment splits, chemical reactions produce message
Message is transmitted to bipolar cell
Message is transmitted to ganglion cell
Message is sent to the brain

**FIGURE 5•12** Transduction of light into neural activity. A photon strikes a photoreceptor and causes the photopigment to split. This event initiates the transmission of information to the brain.

After light has caused a molecule of photopigment to split and become bleached, energy from the photoreceptor's metabolism causes the two molecules to recombine. The photopigment is then ready to be bleached by light again. Each photoreceptor contains many thousands of molecules of photopigment. The number of intact, unbleached molecules of photopigment in a given cell depends on the relative rates at which they are being split by light and being put back together by the cell's energy. The brighter the light, the more bleached photopigment there is.

## Adaptation to Light and Dark

The detection of light requires that photons split molecules of rhodopsin or one of the other photopigments. When high levels of illumination strike the retina, the rate of regeneration of rhodopsin falls behind the rate of the bleaching process. With only a small percentage of the rhodopsin molecules intact, the rods are not very sensitive to light. If you enter a dark room after being in a brightly lit room or in sunlight, there are too few intact rhodopsin molecules for your eyes to respond immediately to dim light. The probability that a photon will strike an intact molecule of rhodopsin is very low. However, after a while the regeneration of rhodopsin overcomes the bleaching effects of the light energy. The rods become full of unbleached rhodopsin, and a photon passing through a rod is likely to find a target. The eye has undergone **dark adaptation.**

## Eye Movements

Our eyes are never completely at rest, even when our gaze is fixed on a particular place called the *fixation point.* Our eyes make fast, aimless, jittering movements, similar to the fine tremors our hands and fingers make when we try to keep them still. They also make occasional slow movements away from the target they are fixed on, which are terminated by quick movements that bring the image of the fixation point back to the fovea.

Although the small, jerky movements that the eyes make when at rest are random, they appear to serve a useful function. Riggs, Ratliff, Cornsweet, and Cornsweet (1953) devised a way to project *stabilized images* onto the retina—images

**photopigment** A complex molecule found in photoreceptors; when struck by light, it splits and stimulates the membrane of the photoreceptor in which it resides.
**rhodopsin** The photopigment contained by rods.
**dark adaptation** The process by which the eye becomes capable of distinguishing dimly illuminated objects after going from a bright area to a dark one.

that remain in the same location on the retina. They mounted a small mirror in a contact lens worn by the participant and bounced a beam of light off it. They then projected the image onto a white screen in front of the participant, bounced it off several more mirrors, and finally directed it toward the participant's eye. The path of the light was arranged so that the image on the screen moved in perfect synchrony with the eye movements. If the eye moved, so did the image; thus, the image that the researchers projected always fell on precisely the same part of the retina despite the participant's eye movements. Under these conditions, details of visual stimuli began to disappear. At first, the image was clear, but then a "fog" drifted over the participant's field of view, obscuring the image. After a while, some images could not be seen at all.

The disappearance of stabilized images suggests that elements of the visual system are not responsive to an unchanging stimulus. The photoreceptors or the ganglion cells, or perhaps both, apparently cease to respond to a constant stimulus. The small, involuntary movements of our eyes keep the image moving and thus keep the visual system responsive to the details of the scene before us. Without these involuntary movements, our vision would become blurry soon after we fixed our gaze on a single point and our eyes became still.

The eyes also make three types of "purposive" movements: vergence movements, saccadic movements, and pursuit movements. **Vergence movements** are co-operative movements that keep both eyes fixed on the same target—or, more precisely, that keep the image of the target object on corresponding parts of the two retinas. If you hold up a finger in front of your face, look at it, and then bring your finger closer to your face, your eyes will make vergence movements toward your nose. If you then look at an object on the other side of the room, your eyes will rotate outward, and you will see two separate blurry images of your finger. As you will learn in Chapter 6, vergence eye movements assist in depth perception—the perception of distance.

When you scan the scene in front of you, your gaze travels from point to point as you examine important or interesting features. As you do so, your eyes make jerky **saccadic movements**—you shift your gaze abruptly from one point to another. (See **Figure 5•13**.) For example, when you read a line in this book, your eyes stop several times, moving very quickly between each stop. You cannot consciously control the speed of movement between stops; during each *saccade* the eyes move as fast as they can. Scialfa and Joffe (1998) have found that these movements are important to the way we search visually for an object. Ross and Ma-Wyatt (2004) have suggested that they help us remember the spatial relationships of objects in our visual field. These researchers found that saccadic movements enhance something called the McCollough effect—a phenomenon we will discuss shortly that seems to involve learning about visual features.

**vergence movement** The co-operative movement of the eyes, which ensures that the image of an object falls on identical portions of both retinas.
**saccadic movement** The rapid movement of the eyes that is used in scanning a visual scene, as opposed to the smooth pursuit movements used to follow a moving object.
**pursuit movement** The movement that the eyes make to maintain an image of a moving image upon the fovea.

**FIGURE 5•13** Saccadic eye movements are the shifts in gaze made as we examine a scene. The white line traces a representative series of saccadic movements that might be made by an individual looking at this scene.

*(From Nature Publishing Group. (2004).* Nature Neuroscience, *7, cover image. Reprinted with permission.)*

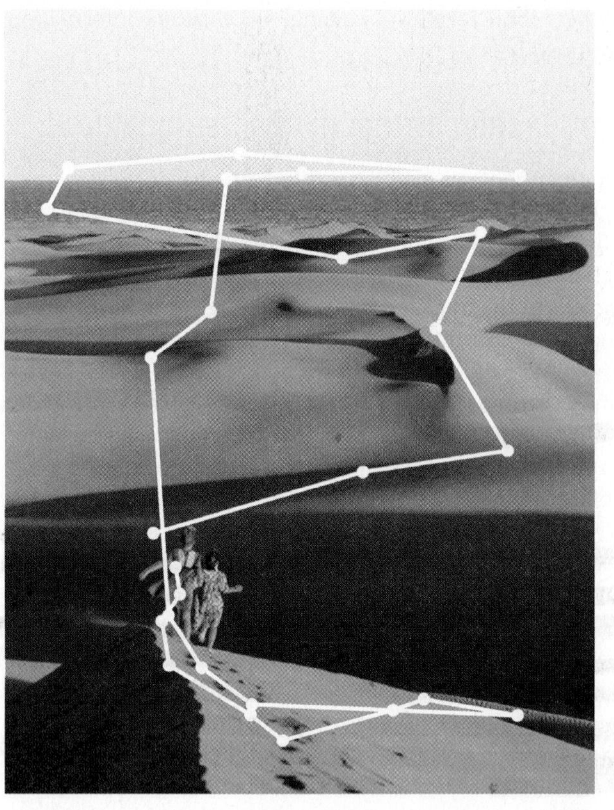

Much of the time, the scene in front of us contains moving objects: objects blown by the wind, automobiles, airplanes, animals, other people. When we concentrate on one of these objects, we fix our gaze on it and track its movements with our eyes. These tracking movements, which follow the object we are watching, are called **pursuit movements.**

## Colour Vision

Among mammals, only primates have full colour vision. A bull does not charge a red cape; he charges what he sees as an annoying grey object being waved at him. Many birds and fishes have excellent colour vision; the brightly coloured lure may really appeal to the fish as much as to the angler who buys it.

Light (as we humans define it) consists of radiant energy having wavelengths between 380 and 760 nm. Light of different wavelengths gives rise to sensations of different colours.

▲ *The spectral colours, contained in a rainbow, do not include all of the colours we can see. Thus, differences in wavelength do not account for all differences in the colours we can perceive.*

How can we tell the difference between different wavelengths of light? Experiments have shown that there are three types of cones in the human eye, each containing a different type of photopigment. Each type of photopigment is most sensitive to light of a particular wavelength. That is, light of a particular wavelength most readily causes a particular photopigment to split. Thus, different types of cones are stimulated by different wavelengths of light. Information from the cones enables us to perceive colours.

Wavelength is related to colour, but the terms are not synonymous. For example, the *spectral colours* (the colours we see in a rainbow, which contains the entire spectrum of visible radiant energy) do not include all of the colours we can see, such as brown, pink, and the metallic colours silver and gold. The fact that not all colours are found in the spectrum means that differences in wavelength alone do not account for the differences in the colours we can perceive.

**The Dimensions of Colour** Most colours can be described in terms of three physical dimensions: wavelength, intensity, and purity. Three perceptual dimensions—hue, brightness, and saturation—corresponding to these physical dimensions describe what we see. The **hue** of most colours is determined by wavelength; for example, light having a wavelength of 540 nm is perceived as green. A colour's **brightness** is determined by the intensity, or amount of energy, of the light that is being perceived, all other factors being equal. A colour of maximum brightness dazzles us with a lot of light. A colour of minimum brightness is simply black. The third perceptual dimension of colour, **saturation**, is roughly equivalent to purity. A fully saturated colour consists of light of only one wavelength—for example, pure red or pure blue. Desaturated colours look pastel or washed out. (See **Table 5•2**.)

Saturation is probably the most difficult dimension of colour to understand. White light consists of a mixture of all wavelengths of light. Although its components consist of light of all possible hues, we perceive it as being colourless.

**TABLE 5•2 Physical and Perceptual Dimensions of Colour**

| Perceptual Dimension | Physical Dimension | Physical Characteristics |
|---|---|---|
| Hue | Wavelength | Length of oscillation of light radiation |
| Brightness | Intensity | Amount of energy of light radiation |
| Saturation | Purity | Intensity of dominant wavelength relative to total radiant energy |

White light is completely desaturated; no single wavelength is dominant. If we begin with light of a single wavelength (a pure, completely saturated colour) and then mix in a little amount of white light, we will have reduced the saturation of that colour. For example, when white light is added to red light (700 nm), the result is pink light. The dominant wavelength of 700 nm gives the colour a reddish hue, but the addition of white light to the mixture decreases the colour's saturation. In other words, pink is a less saturated version of red. **Figure 5•14** illustrates how a colour having a particular dominant wavelength (hue) can vary in brightness and saturation.

**Colour Mixing** Vision is a *synthetic* sensory modality. It synthesizes (puts together) rather than analyzes (takes apart). When two wavelengths of light are present, we see an

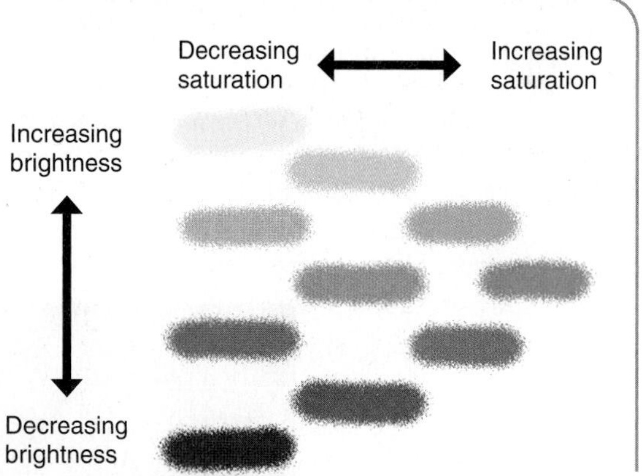


**FIGURE 5•14** Hue, brightness, and saturation. The colours shown have the same dominant wavelength (hue) but different saturation and brightness.

**hue** A perceptual dimension of colour, most closely related to the wavelength of a pure light.

**brightness** A perceptual dimension of colour, most closely related to the intensity or degree of radiant energy emitted by a visual stimulus.

**saturation** A perceptual dimension of colour, most closely associated with purity of a colour.

**FIGURE 5•15** Colour mixing. White light can be split into a spectrum of colours with a prism and recombined through another prism.

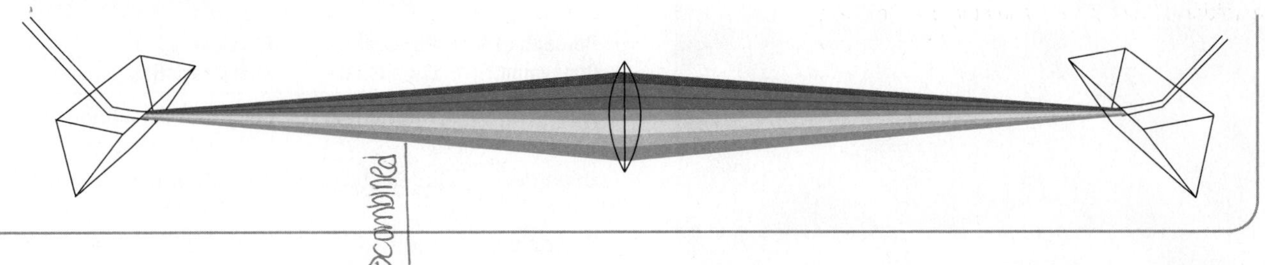

intermediate colour rather than the two components. (In contrast, the auditory system is *analytical*. If a high note and a low note are played together on a piano, we hear both notes instead of a single, intermediate tone.) The addition of two or more lights of different wavelengths is called **colour mixing**. Colour mixing is an additive process and is very different from paint mixing. So are its results. If we pass a beam of white light through a prism, we break it into the spectrum of the different wavelengths it contains. If we recombine these colours by passing them through another prism, we obtain white light again. (See **Figure 5•15**.)

Do not confuse colour mixing with pigment mixing—what we do when we mix paints. An object has a particular colour because it contains pigments that absorb some wavelengths of light (converting them into heat) and reflect other wavelengths. For example, the chlorophyll found in the leaves of plants absorbs less green light than light of other wavelengths. When a leaf is illuminated by white light, it reflects a high proportion of green light and appears green to us.

**colour mixing** The perception of two or more lights of different wavelengths seen together as light of an intermediate wavelength.
**trichromatic theory** The theory that colour vision is accomplished by three types of photoreceptors, each of which is maximally sensitive to a different wavelength of light.

When we mix paints, we are subtracting colours, not adding them. Mixing two paints yields a darker result. For example, adding blue paint to yellow paint yields green paint, which certainly looks darker than yellow. But mixing two beams of light of different wavelengths always yields a brighter colour. For example, when red and green light are shone together on a piece of white paper, we see yellow. In fact, we cannot tell a pure yellow light from a synthesized one made of the proper intensities of red and green light. To our eyes, both yellows appear identical.

To reconstitute white light, we do not even have to recombine all of the wavelengths in the spectrum. If we shine a blue light, a green light, and a red light together on a sheet of white paper and properly adjust their intensities, the place where all three beams overlap will look perfectly white. A colour television or a computer display screen uses this system. When white appears on the screen, it actually consists of tiny dots of red, blue, and green light. (See **Figure 5.16**.)

**Colour Coding in the Retina** In 1802, Thomas Young, a British physicist and physician, noted that the human visual system can synthesize any colour from various amounts of almost any set of three colours of different wavelengths. Young proposed a **trichromatic theory** ("three-colour" theory) of colour vision. He hypothesized that the eye contains three types of colour receptors, each sensitive to a different hue,

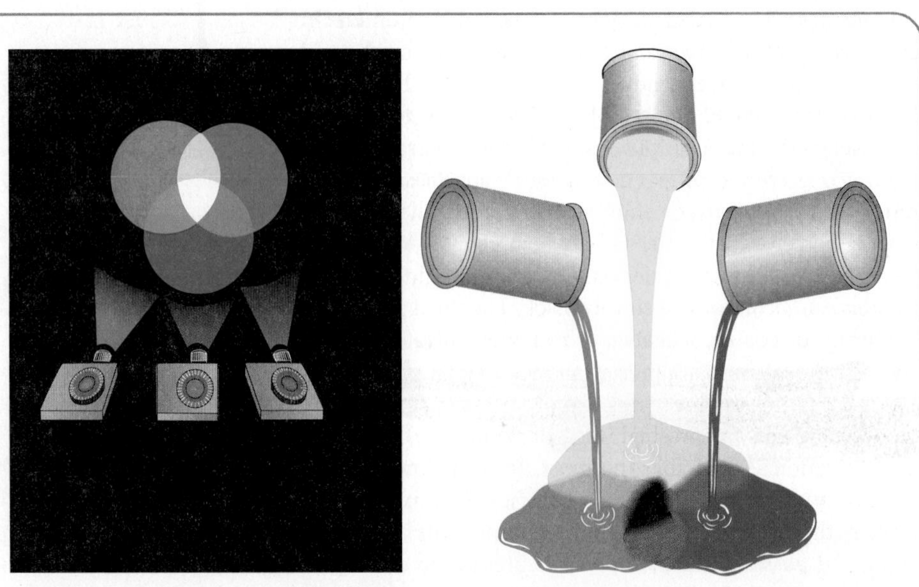

**FIGURE 5•16** Additive colour mixing and paint mixing. When blue, red, and green light of the proper intensity are all shone together, the result is white light. When red, blue, and yellow paints are mixed together, the result is a dark grey.

**FIGURE 5•17** Colour coding in the retina. (a) Red light stimulating a "red" cone, which causes excitation of a red/green ganglion cell. (b) Green light stimulating a "green" cone, which causes inhibition of a red/green ganglion cell. (c) Yellow light stimulating "red" and "green" cones equally. The stimulation of "red" and "green" cones causes excitation of a yellow/blue ganglion cell. The arrows labelled E and I represent neural circuitry within the retina that translates excitation (E) of a cone into excitation or inhibition (I) of a ganglion cell. For clarity, only some of the circuits are shown.

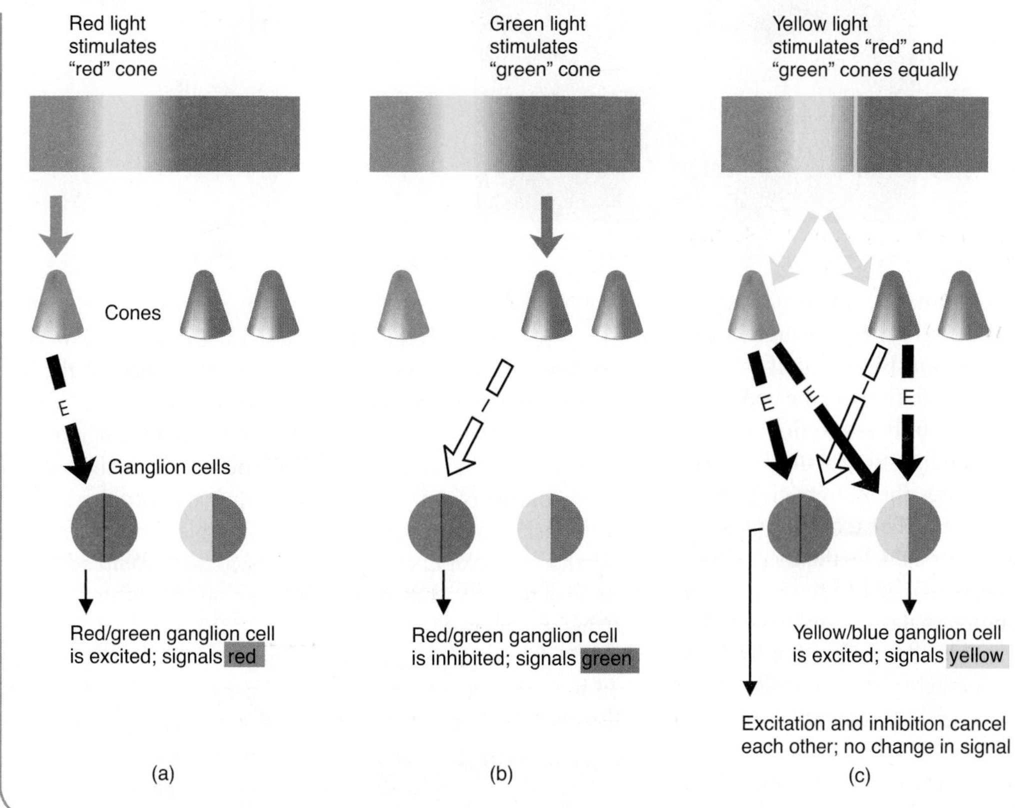


and that the brain synthesizes colours by combining the information received by each type of receptor. He suggested that these receptors were sensitive to three of the colours that people perceive as "pure": blue, green, and red. (His theory ignored the fact that people also perceive yellow as a pure colour; more about this fact later.) Young's suggestion was incorporated into a more elaborate theory of colour vision by Hermann von Helmholtz.

Experiments in recent years have shown that the cones in the human eye do contain three types of photopigments, each of which preferentially absorbs light of a particular wavelength: 420, 530, and 560 nm. Although these wavelengths actually correspond to blue-violet, green, and yellow-green, most investigators refer to these receptors as *blue*, *green*, and *red* cones. To simplify the discussion here, let's pretend that the three cones respond to these three pure hues. Red and green cones are present in about equal proportions. There are far fewer blue cones.

The eye uses the principle of the colour television screen, but in reverse: Instead of displaying colours, it senses them.

If a spot of white light shines on the retina, it stimulates all three types of cones equally, and we perceive white light. If a spot of pure blue, green, or red light shines on the retina, it stimulates mainly one of the three classes of cones, and a pure colour is perceived. If a spot of yellow light shines on the retina, it stimulates red and green cones equally well but has little effect on blue cones. (You can see in **Figure 5•17** that yellow is located between red and green.) Stimulation of red and green cones, then, is the signal that yellow light has been received.

Several scientists after Young and Helmholtz devised theories that took into account the fact that people also perceive yellow as a psychologically pure hue. Late in the nineteenth century, Ewald Hering, a German physiologist, noted that the four primary hues appeared to belong to pairs of opposing colours: red/green and yellow/blue. We can imagine a bluish green or a yellowish green, or a bluish red or a yellowish red. However, we cannot imagine a greenish red or a yellowish blue. Hering originally suggested that we cannot imagine these blends because there are two types of photoreceptors, one kind responding to green and red and the other kind responding to yellow and blue. (We'll look at the reasoning behind this statement shortly.)

Hering's hypothesis about the nature of photoreceptors was wrong, but his principle describes the characteristics of the information that the retinal ganglion cells send to the

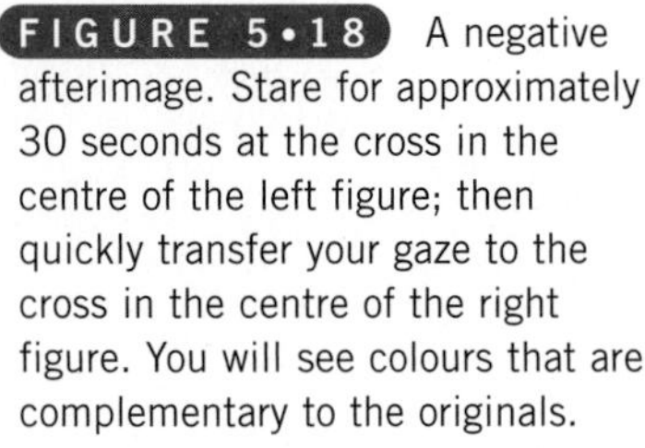

**FIGURE 5•18** A negative afterimage. Stare for approximately 30 seconds at the cross in the centre of the left figure; then quickly transfer your gaze to the cross in the centre of the right figure. You will see colours that are complementary to the originals.

brain. Two types of ganglion cells encode colour vision: *red/green cells* and *yellow/blue cells.* Both types of ganglion cells fire at a steady rate when they are not stimulated. If a spot of red light shines on the retina, excitation of the red cones causes the red/green ganglion cells to begin to fire at a high rate. Conversely, if a spot of green light shines on the retina, excitation of the green cones causes the red/green ganglion cells to begin to fire at a slow rate. Thus, the brain learns about the presence of red or green light by the increased or decreased rate of firing of axons attached to red/green ganglion cells. Similarly, yellow/blue ganglion cells are excited by yellow light and inhibited by blue light. Because red and green light, and yellow and blue light, have opposite effects on the rate of axon firing, this coding scheme is called an **opponent process**.

Figure 5.17 provides a schematic explanation of the opponent-process coding that takes place in the retina. Stimulation of a red cone by red light excites the red/green ganglion cell, whereas stimulation of a green cone by green light inhibits the red/green ganglion cell. If the photoreceptors are stimulated by yellow light, both the red and green cones are stimulated equally. Because of the neural circuitry between the photoreceptors and the ganglion cells, the result is that the yellow/blue ganglion cell is excited, signalling yellow.

The retina contains red/green and yellow/blue ganglion cells because of the nature of the connections between the cones, bipolar cells, and ganglion cells. The brain detects various colours by comparing the rates of firing of the axons in the optic nerve that signal red or green and yellow or blue. Now you can see why we cannot perceive a reddish green or a bluish yellow: An axon that signals red or green (or yellow or blue) can either increase or decrease its rate of firing. It cannot do both at the same time. A reddish green would have to be signalled by a ganglion cell firing slowly and rapidly at the same time, which is obviously impossible.

**opponent process** The representation of colours by the rate of firing of two types of neurons: red/green and yellow/blue.

**negative afterimage** The image seen after a portion of the retina is exposed to an intense visual stimulus; a negative afterimage consists of colours complementary to those of the physical stimulus.

**Negative Afterimages** **Figure 5•18** demonstrates an interesting property of the visual system: the formation of a **negative afterimage**. Stare at the cross in the centre of the image on the left for approximately 30 seconds. Then quickly look at the cross in the centre of the white rectangle to the right. You will have a fleeting experience of seeing the red and green colours of a radish—colours that are complementary, or opposite, to the ones on the left. Complementary items go together to make up a whole. In this context, *complementary colours* are those that make white (or shades of grey) when added together.

The most important cause of negative afterimages is adaptation to the rate of firing of retinal ganglion cells. When ganglion cells are excited or inhibited for a prolonged period of time, they later show a *rebound effect*, firing faster or slower than normal. For example, the reddish leaves in Figure 5.18 cause some red/green ganglion cells to fire faster. When this region of the retina is then stimulated with the neutral-coloured light reflected off the white rectangle, the red/green ganglion cells—no longer excited by the red light—fire more slowly than normal. Thus, we see a green afterimage of the leafy part of the image.

A related phenomenon, which is not completely understood, is that of contingent colour after-effects. In one type of contingent colour after-effect, discovered by Celeste McCollough in 1965, people are asked to look at two differently oriented and differently coloured fields of lines. For example, a person could be asked to look at a set of alternating black and red horizontal bars for three seconds, and then asked to look at a set of alternating black and green vertical bars for another three seconds. After several minutes of this, the person is then asked to look at black bars that alternate with white ones. The usual result is that the white areas between the horizontal bars now seem to be tinted with green, while the white areas between the vertical bars seem pinkish. This effect is long lasting compared to the simple after-effects we have just examined, sometimes lasting for days. **Figure 5•19** shows the stimuli used in the experiment by Ross and Ma-Wyatt (2004) that I mentioned earlier.

The explanation of contingent after-effects is still debated. Dodwell and Humphrey (1990) suggested that the contour information of the grating acts somewhat like the opponent

**FIGURE 5•19** A demonstration of the McCollough effect. Cover the red patch and gaze for a few seconds at the green patch. You should not fixate your gaze, as in the demonstration of negative afterimages; instead, move your eyes around the grey border now and then. Then cover the green patch and gaze at the red one. Alternate gazing at these two patches. After a few minutes, look at the patch on the right. Does one half look a different colour? How do the two sides differ in colour? Some people report seeing this effect long after they have stopped looking at the coloured patches on the left.

*(Adapted from Ross, J., & Ma-Wyatt, A. (2004). Saccades actively maintain perceptual continuity.* Nature Neuroscience, *7, 65–69. Reprinted with permission.)*

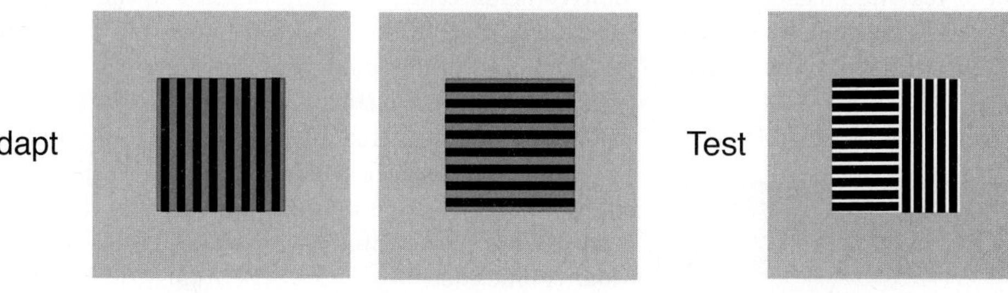


processes of colour; the visual system uses this information to adapt to the artificial correlation experienced between the bars and the colour. It has also been suggested that the different sensations are associated in a way similar to classical conditioning—a topic we will discuss in Chapter 7. This latter account is interesting, because it suggests that sensory experiences can be learned, but it is disputed. Allan and colleagues (1997) and Humphrey, Herbert, Hazlewood, and Stewart (1998) provide contrasting views on these explanations.

**Defects in Colour Vision** Approximately 1 in 20 males has some form of defective colour vision. These defects are sometimes called *colour blindness*, but this term should probably be reserved for the very few people who cannot see any colour at all. Males are affected more than females because many of the genes for producing photopigments are located on the X chromosome. Because males have only one X chromosome (females have two), a defective gene there will always be expressed.

There are many different types of defective colour vision. Two of the three described here involve the red/green system. People with these defects confuse red and green. Their primary colour sensations are yellow and blue; red and green both look yellowish. **Figure 5•20** shows one of the figures from a commonly used test for defective colour vision. A person who confuses red and green will not be able to see the 5 in this image. Another test for defective colour vision is a questionnaire developed by Coren and Hakstian (1988).

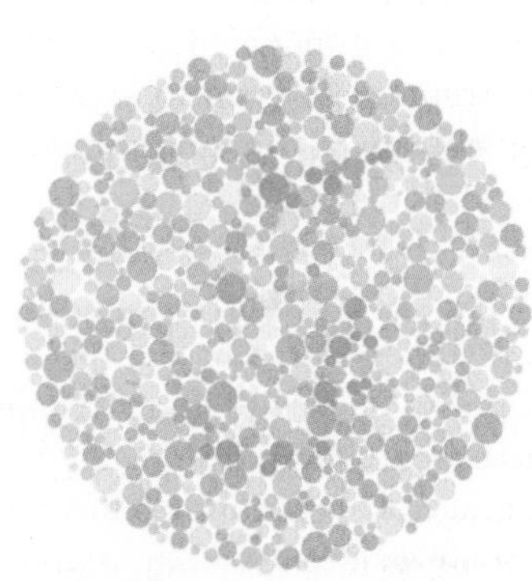

**FIGURE 5•20** A figure commonly used to test for defective colour vision. People with red/green colour blindness will fail to see the 5.

*(Courtesy of American Optical Corporation.)*

The most common defect, called **protanopia** (literally, "first-colour defect"), appears to result from a lack of the photopigment for red cones. The fact that people with protanopia have relatively normal sharpness of vision suggests that they have red cones but that these cones are filled with green photopigment (Boynton, 1979). If red cones were missing, almost half of the cones would be gone from the retina, and vision would be less acute. To a protanope, red looks much darker than green. The second form of red/green defect, called **deuteranopia** ("second-colour defect"), appears to result from the opposite kind of substitution: Green cones are filled with red photopigment.

As you can see, the nature of the problem for people with either protanopia or deuteranopia is that the red and green cones contain photopigments that respond similarly to light. Normally, genetic coding on the X chromosome will produce a different photopigment for red cones than for green cones. Provided there is even a slight difference in the way each cone's photopigment absorbs light, the person will be able to distinguish red from green (Neitz, He, & Shevell, 1999); when the two are the same, however, red/green defects will result. Among mammals, only primates exhibit the genetic mechanisms by which red and green cones contain different photopigments (Mollon, 1989). The recent evolutionary development of this characteristic may be the reason that the two red/green colour defects are more prevalent than the third form of colour defect.

**protanopia** A form of hereditary anomalous colour vision; caused by defective "red" cones in the retina.

**deuteranopia** A form of hereditary anomalous colour vision; caused by defective "green" cones in the retina.

This third form of colour defect, called **tritanopia** ("third-colour defect"), involves the yellow/blue system and is much rarer: It affects fewer than 1 in 10 000 people. Tritanopes see the world in greens and reds; to them, a clear blue sky is a bright green, and yellow looks pink. The faulty gene that causes tritanopia is not carried on a sex chromosome; therefore, it is equally common in males and females. This defect appears to involve the loss of blue cones. However, because there are far fewer of these than of red and green cones to begin with, investigators have not yet determined whether the cones are missing or are filled with one of the other photopigments.

## Interim Summary

### Vision

Imagine yourself watching an ice-skating competition on television with a friend. Right now, your eyes are directed toward the television screen. The cornea and lens of your eyes cast an image of the screen on your retinas, which contain photoreceptors: rods and cones. Because the room and the television screen are brightly illuminated, only your cones are gathering visual information; your rods work only when the light is very dim. The energy from the light that reaches the cones in your retinas is transduced into neural activity when photons strike molecules of photopigment, splitting them into their two constituents. This event causes the cones to send information through the bipolar cells to the ganglion cells. The axons of the ganglion cells travel through the optic nerves and form synapses with neurons in the brain.

Vision requires the behaviour of looking, which consists of moving our eyes and head. The eyes have a repertoire of movements that function for visual perception. Experiments using stabilized images show that small, involuntary movements keep an image moving across the photoreceptors, thus preventing them from adapting to a constant stimulus. (As you will see later in this chapter, other sensory systems also respond better to changing stimuli than to constant ones.) As the skaters glide across the ice, your eyes follow them with pursuit movements. Now your friend says something, so you turn your head toward him. Your eyes make rapid saccadic movements so that you can look directly at your friend's face. Vergence movements keep each eye fixed on the same point. Because your friend is closer to you than the television screen is, you must also accommodate the change in distance, adjusting the focus of the lenses of your eyes.

When an image of the visual scene—your friend's face or the television screen—is cast upon the retina, each part of the image has a different colour, which can be specified in terms of its hue (dominant wavelength), brightness (intensity), and saturation (purity). Information about colour is encoded trichromatically by your cones; the red, green, and blue cones respond in proportion to the amount of the appropriate wavelength contained in the light striking them. This information is transformed into an opponent-process coding, signalled by the firing rates of red/green and yellow/blue ganglion cells, and is transmitted to the brain. If you stare for a while at the television screen and then look at a blank wall, you will see a negative afterimage of the screen. If you are a male, the chances are about 1 in 20 that you will have some defect in red/green colour vision. If this is the case, your red or green cones contain the wrong photopigment. Male or female, chances are very slim that you will have a blue/yellow confusion, caused by the absence of functioning blue cones.

#### QUESTIONS TO CONSIDER

1. Why is colour vision useful? Birds, some fish, and some primates have full, three-cone colour vision. Considering our own species, what benefits derive from the evolution of colour vision?
2. Did you notice that an afterimage seems to be fuzzier than the original? Why do you think that might be? (Hint: Remember that negative afterimages are produced by fatigue in ganglion cells.)

# Audition

Vision involves the perception of objects in three dimensions, at a variety of distances, and with a multitude of colours and textures. These complex stimuli may occur at a single point in time or over an extended period. They may also involve an unchanging scene or a rapidly changing one. The other senses analyze much simpler stimuli (such as an odour or a taste) or depend on time and stimulus change for the development of a complex perception. For example, to perceive a solid object in three dimensions by means of touch, we must manipulate it—turn it over in our hands or move our hands over its surface. The stimulus must change over time for a full-fledged perception of form to emerge. The same is true for audition: We hear nothing meaningful in an instant.

## Sound

Sound consists of rhythmical pressure changes in air. As an object vibrates, it causes the air around it to move. When the object is in the phase of vibration in which it moves toward you, it compresses molecules of air; as it moves away, it pulls

**tritanopia** A form of hereditary anomalous colour vision; caused by a lack of "blue" cones in the retina.

▲ *Sound consists of rhythmical pressure changes in air, which can convey an incredible diversity of auditory sensations.*

**FIGURE 5•21** Sound waves. Changes in air pressure from sound waves move the eardrum in and out. Air molecules are closer together in regions of higher pressure and farther apart in regions of lower pressure.

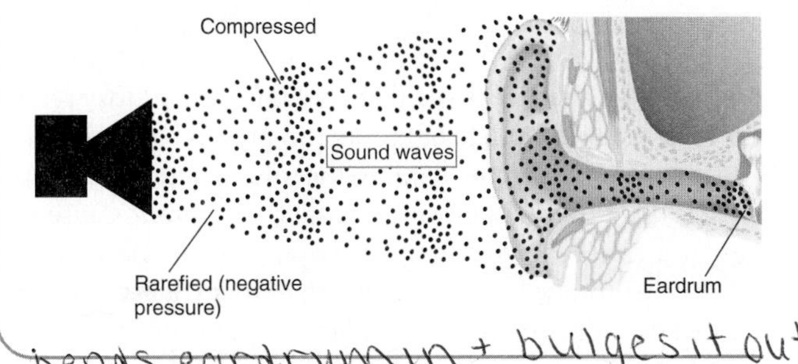


the molecules of air farther apart. As a pressure wave arrives at your ear, it bends your eardrum in. The following wave of negative pressure (when the molecules are pulled farther apart) causes your eardrum to bulge out. (See **Figure 5•21**.)

Sound waves are measured in frequency units of cycles per second called **hertz (Hz)**. The human ear perceives vibrations between approximately 30 and 20 000 Hz. Sound waves can vary in intensity and frequency. These variations produce corresponding changes in sensations of loudness and pitch. Consider a loudspeaker, a device that contains a paper cone moved back and forth by a coil of wire located in a magnetic field. Alternations in the electrical current transmitted from an amplifier to this coil cause the coil (and the paper cone) to move back and forth. If the cone begins vibrating more rapidly, the pitch of the sound increases. If the vibrations become more intense (that is, if the cone moves in and out over a greater distance), the loudness of the sound increases. (See **Figure 5•22**.) A third perceptual dimension, *timbre,* corresponds to the complexity of the sound vibration. We'll look at timbre in a later section of this chapter.

## The Ear and Its Functions

When people refer to the ear, they usually mean what anatomists call the *pinna*—the flesh-covered cartilage attached to the side of the head. (*Pinna* means "wing" in Latin.) However, the pinna performs only a small role in audition. It helps funnel sound through the *ear canal* toward the middle and inner ear, where the business of hearing gets done. (See **Figure 5•23**.)

The *eardrum* (tympanic membrane) is a thin, flexible membrane that vibrates back and forth in response to sound waves and passes these vibrations on to the receptor cells in the inner ear. The eardrum is attached to the first of a set of three middle ear bones called the **ossicles** (literally, "little bones"). The three ossicles are known as the *hammer* (malleus), the *anvil* (incus), and the *stirrup* (stapes), because of their shapes. These bones act together, in lever fashion, to transmit the vibrations of the eardrum to the fluid-filled structure of the inner ear that contains the receptive organ.

The bony structure that contains the receptive organ is called the **cochlea** (*kokhlos* means "snail," which accurately describes its shape; see Figure 5.23). The cochlea is filled with a liquid. A bony chamber attached to the cochlea (the *vestibule*) contains two openings, the oval window and the round window. The last of the three ossicles (the stirrup) presses against a membrane behind an opening in the bone surrounding the

**hertz (Hz)** The primary measure of the frequency of vibration of sound waves; cycles per second.
**ossicle** One of the three bones of the middle ear (the hammer, anvil, and stirrup) that transmit acoustical vibrations from the eardrum to the membrane behind the oval window of the cochlea.
**cochlea** A snail-shaped chamber set in bone in the inner ear, where auditory transduction takes place.

| Physical Dimension | Perceptual Dimension | | |
|---|---|---|---|
| Amplitude (intensity) | Loudness | loud | soft |
| Frequency | Pitch | low | high |
| Complexity | Timbre | simple | complex |

**FIGURE 5•22** The physical and perceptual dimensions of sound waves.

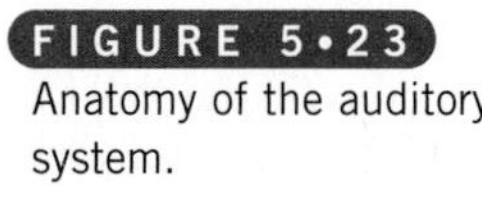

FIGURE 5•23 Anatomy of the auditory system.

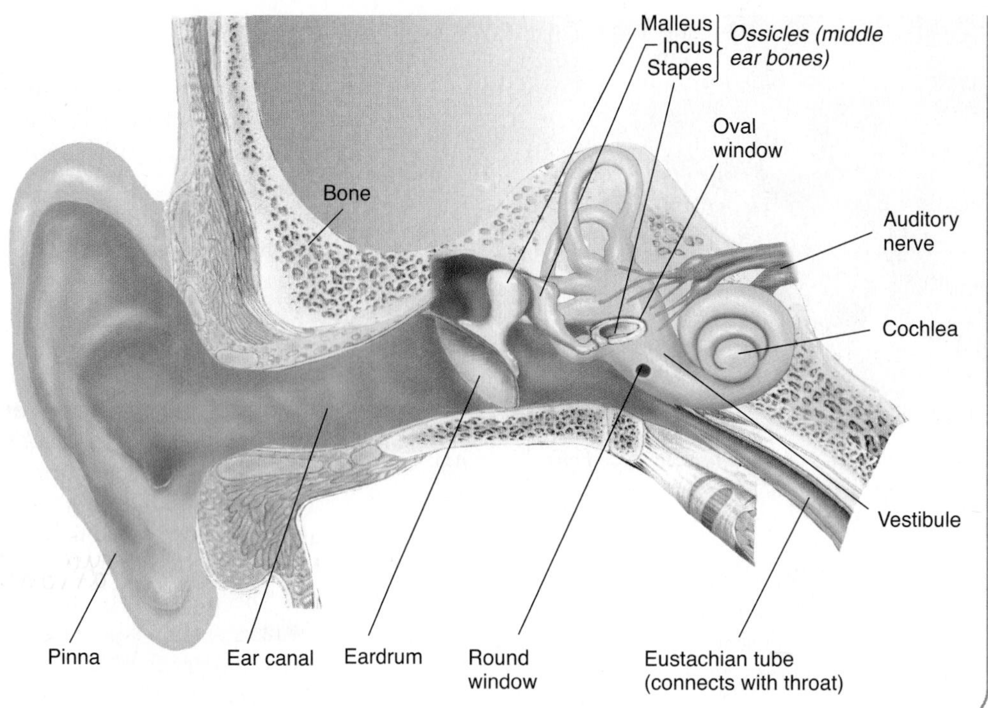


cochlea called the **oval window**, thus transmitting sound waves into the liquid inside the cochlea, where it can reach the receptive organ for hearing. The cochlea is divided into three chambers by two membranes, one of which is the **basilar membrane**—a sheet of tissue that contains the auditory receptor cells. As the footplate of the stirrup presses back and forth against the membrane behind the oval window, pressure changes in the fluid above the basilar membrane cause the basilar membrane to vibrate back and forth. Because the basilar membrane varies in its width and flexibility, different frequencies of sound cause different parts of the basilar membrane to vibrate. High-frequency sounds cause the end near the oval window to vibrate, medium-frequency sounds cause the middle to vibrate, and low-frequency sounds cause the tip to vibrate. (See **Figure 5•24**.)

**oval window** An opening in the bone surrounding the cochlea. The stirrup presses against a membrane behind the oval window and transmits sound vibrations into the fluid within the cochlea.
**basilar membrane** One of two membranes that divide the cochlea of the inner ear into three compartments; the receptive organ for audition resides here.

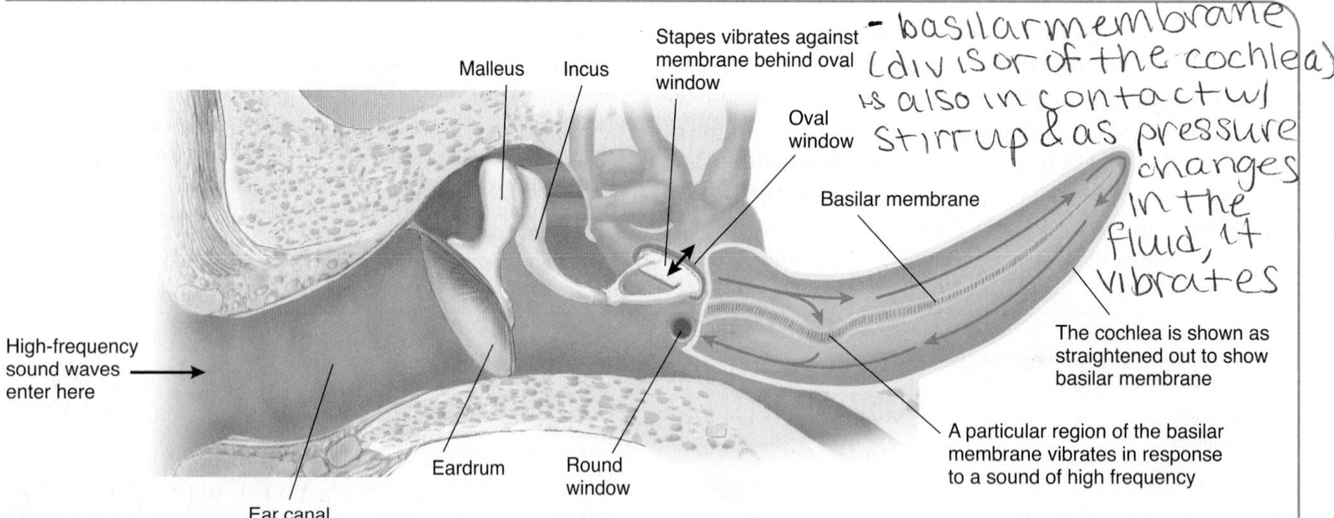


FIGURE 5•24 Responses to sound waves. When the stirrup pushes against the membrane behind the oval window, the membrane behind the round window bulges outward. Different high-frequency and medium-frequency sound vibrations cause flexing of different portions of the basilar membrane. In contrast, low-frequency sound vibrations cause the tip of the basilar membrane to flex in synchrony with the vibrations.

**FIGURE 5•25** The transduction of sound vibrations in the auditory system.

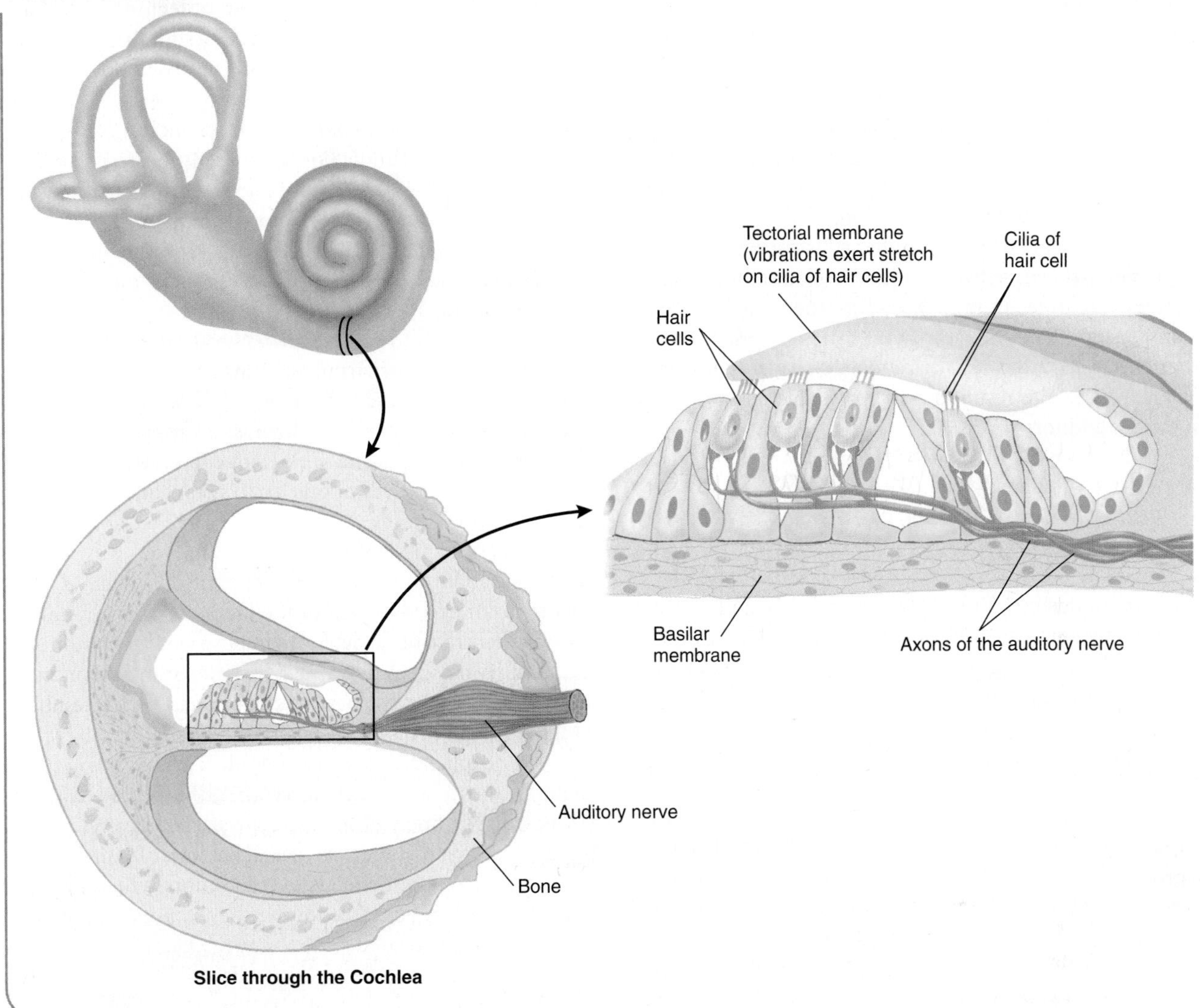


The basilar membrane can vibrate freely only if the fluid in the lower chamber of the cochlea has somewhere to go—unlike gases, liquids cannot be compressed. Free space is provided by the **round window**. When the basilar membrane flexes down, the displacement of the fluid causes the membrane behind the round window to bulge out. In turn, when the basilar membrane flexes up, the membrane behind the round window bulges in.

Sounds are detected by special neurons known as auditory hair cells, located on the basilar membrane. **Auditory hair cells** transduce mechanical energy caused by the flexing of the basilar membrane into neural activity. These cells possess hair-like protrusions called **cilia** ("eyelashes"). The ends of the cilia are embedded in a fairly rigid shelf (the **tectorial membrane**) that hangs over the basilar membrane like a balcony. When sound vibrations cause the basilar membrane to flex back and forth, the cilia are stretched. This pull on the cilia is translated into neural activity. (See **Figure 5•25**.)

When a mechanical force is exerted on the cilia of the auditory hair cells, the electrical charge across the membrane is altered. What causes the change in potential is not fully known, although pressure on the cilia is known to increase calcium flow into the hair cells (Kennedy, Evans, Crawford, & Fettiplace, 2003). These calcium currents are very fast, and may alter the temporal duration of the depolarization. The change in the electrical charge causes a transmitter substance to be released at a synapse between the auditory hair cell and the dendrite of a neuron of the auditory nerve, similar to the way that bipolar cells connect to a ganglion cell in the retina.

**round window** An opening in the bone surrounding the cochlea. Movements of the membrane behind this opening permit vibrations to be transmitted through the oval window into the cochlea.

**auditory hair cell** The sensory neuron of the auditory system; located on the basilar membrane.

**cilium** A hair-like appendage of a cell; involved in movement or in transducing sensory information. Cilia are found on the receptors in the auditory and vestibular systems.

**tectorial membrane** A membrane located above the basilar membrane; serves as a shelf against which the cilia of the auditory hair cells move.

- auditory haircells w/cilia on tectorial membrane vibrate + make basilar membrane flex, stretching cilia + turning it into neural activity

However, one hair cell will be connected to many auditory neurons (Trussell, 2002), so, unlike the case with visual cells, one hair cell has a large effect on subsequent nerve activity.

The synapses are likewise slightly different. Earlier, I described how stabilized visual stimuli can actually disappear; small movements of the eyes normally keep this from happening by changing the location of the stimuli on the retina. The auditory system does not have this capacity and must instead deal with sounds that persist for long intervals—intervals long enough to deplete the transmitter substance in a normal synapse. The synapses between the hair cells and the auditory nerve therefore differ in function from others in the central nervous system. They involve more synaptic vesicles with shorter effects. Also, the depolarization is stronger (Glowatzki & Fuchs, 2002). The result is a more reliable signal passed along to the auditory nerve.

## Detecting and Localizing Sounds in the Environment

As we saw, sounds can differ in loudness, pitch, and timbre. They also have sources; they come from particular locations. How does the ear distinguish these characteristics? As we will see, the ear's ability to distinguish sounds by their timbre depends on its ability to distinguish loudness and pitch. So let's examine these two characteristics first.

**Loudness and Pitch** Scientists originally thought that the neurons of the auditory system represented pitch by firing in synchrony with the vibrations of the basilar membrane. However, they subsequently learned that axons cannot fire rapidly enough to represent the high frequencies that we can hear. A good, young ear can hear frequencies of more than 20 000 Hz, but axons cannot fire more than 1000 times per second. Therefore, high-frequency sounds, at least, must be encoded in some other way.

As we saw, high-frequency and medium-frequency sounds cause different parts of the basilar membrane to vibrate. Thus, sounds of different frequencies stimulate different groups of auditory hair cells located along the basilar membrane. At least for high-frequency and medium-frequency sounds, therefore, the brain is informed of the pitch of a sound by the activity of different sets of axons from the auditory nerve. When medium-frequency sound waves reach the ear, the middle of the basilar membrane vibrates, and auditory hair cells located in this region are activated. In contrast, high-frequency sounds activate auditory hair cells located at the base of the basilar membrane, near the oval window. (Refer to Figure 5.24.)

Two kinds of evidence indicate that pitch is detected in this way. First, direct observation of the basilar membrane has shown that the region of maximum vibration depends on the frequency of the stimulating tone (von Békésy, 1960). Second, experiments have found that damage to specific regions of the basilar membrane causes loss of the ability to perceive specific frequencies.

Although high-frequency and medium-frequency sounds are detected because they cause different regions of the basilar membrane to vibrate, low-frequency sounds are detected by a different method. Kiang (1965) recorded the electrical activity of single axons in the auditory nerve and found many that responded to particular frequencies. Presumably, these axons were stimulated by hair cells located on different regions of the basilar membrane. However, Kiang did not find any axons that responded uniquely to particular frequencies lower than 200 Hz—and yet tones lower than 200 Hz are easily perceived. How, then, are the lower frequencies encoded?

The answer is this: Frequencies lower than 200 Hz cause the very tip of the basilar membrane to vibrate in synchrony with the sound waves. Neurons that are stimulated by hair cells located there are able to fire in synchrony with these vibrations, thus firing at the same frequency as the sound. The brain "counts" these vibrations (so to speak) and thus detects low-frequency sounds. As you may have recognized, this process is an example of temporal coding.

What about loudness? The axons of the cochlear nerve appear to inform the brain of the loudness of a stimulus by altering their rate of firing. More intense vibrations stimulate the auditory hair cells more intensely. This stimulation causes them to release more transmitter substance, which results in a higher rate of firing by the axons in the auditory nerve.

This explanation works for the axons involved in anatomical coding of pitch; in this case, pitch is signalled by which neurons fire, and loudness is signalled by their rate of firing. However, the neurons that signal lower frequencies do so with their rate of firing. If they fire more frequently, they signal a higher pitch. Obviously, they cannot signal both loudness and pitch by the same means. Therefore, most investigators believe that the loudness of low-frequency sounds is signalled by the number of auditory hair cells that are active at a given time. A louder sound excites a larger number of hair cells.

**Timbre** You can easily distinguish between the sounds of a violin and a clarinet, even if they are playing tones of the same pitch and loudness. So, clearly, pitch and loudness are not the only characteristics of a sound. Sounds can vary greatly in complexity. They can start suddenly or gradually increase in loudness, be short or long, and seem thin and reedy or full and vibrant. The enormous variety of sounds that we can distinguish is in large part due to an important characteristic of sound called timbre.

The combining, or synthesis, of two or more simple tones, each consisting of a single frequency, can produce a complex tone. For example, an electronic synthesizer produces a mixture of sounds of different frequencies, each of which can be varied in amplitude (intensity). Thus, it can synthesize the complex sounds of a clarinet or violin or can assemble completely new sounds not produced by any other source. Conversely, complex sounds that have a regular sequence of waves can be reduced by means of analysis into

**FIGURE 5•26** Analysis of timbre. The shape of a sound wave from a clarinet is shown at the top. The waveforms under it show the frequencies into which it can be analyzed.

*(Copyright © 1977 by CBS Magazines. Reprinted from* Stereo Review, *June 1977, with permission.)*

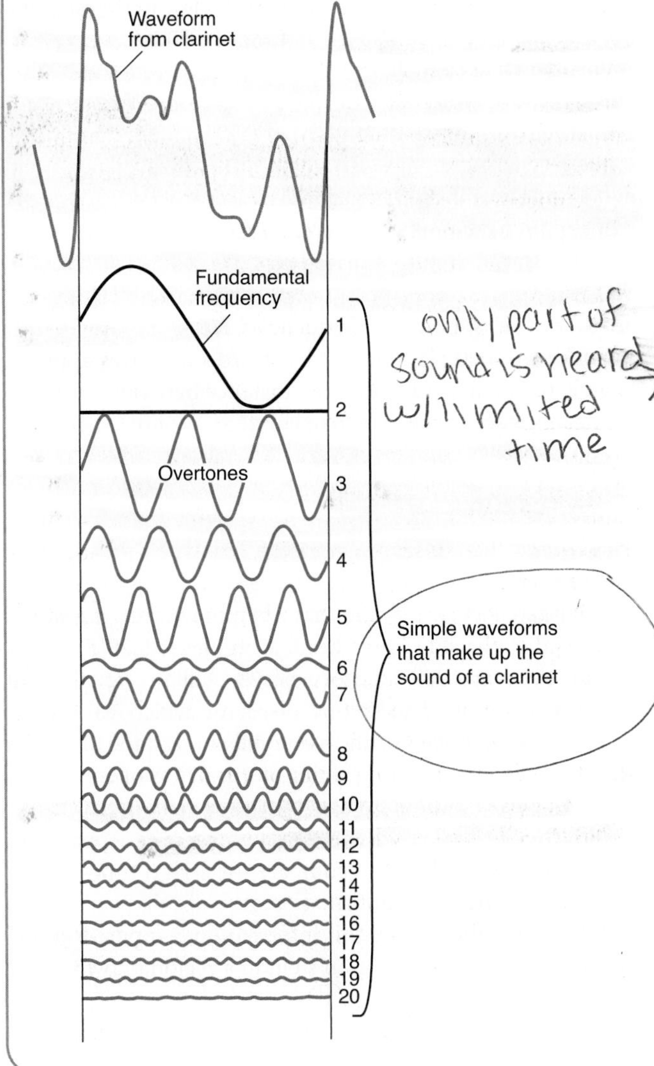


several simple tones. **Figure 5•26** shows a waveform produced by the sound of a clarinet (upper curve). The curves beneath it show the amplitude and frequency of the simple waves that can be shown, mathematically, to produce the waveform of the sound made by a clarinet.

An analysis like the one shown in Figure 5.26 specifies the timbre of a sound. We can tell a clarinet from another instrument because each instrument produces sounds consisting of a unique set of simple tones called **harmonics** (also called *overtones*). Their frequencies are multiples of the **fundamental frequency**, or the basic pitch of the sound. **Timbre** is the distinctive combination of harmonics with the fundamental frequency. The fundamental frequency causes one part of the basilar membrane to flex, while each of the harmonics causes another portion to flex. During a complex sound, many different portions of the basilar membrane are flexing simultaneously. Thus, the ear analyzes a complex sound, just as the person who devised Figure 5.26 did. Information about the fundamental frequency and each of the harmonics is sent to the brain through the auditory nerve, and the person hears a complex tone having a particular timbre. When you consider that we can listen to an orchestra and identify several instruments playing simultaneously, you can appreciate the complexity of the analysis performed by the auditory system.

This kind of analysis puts special demands on the auditory system. Look closely at Figure 5.26 and you will notice that it takes a relatively long interval to describe the sound wave fully. But some sounds are brief. What if only the left half of the top curve was heard? Would the sound still have the timbre of a clarinet? Not quite. There is, in other words, a trade-off between time and complexity when analyzing sound. Engineers speak of "filters" that can distinguish aspects of sound; a filter that is good at analyzing a brief sound may not be good at analyzing a complex one. Lewicki (2002) has examined the kinds of filters that can best discriminate different kinds of sounds: environmental sounds such as twigs snapping, animal vocalizations such as hyena calls, and sounds in between such as human speech. He found that the human auditory system is similar to a theoretical combination of filters attuned to a mixture of sounds in which environmental noises predominate. Significantly, this theoretical system also performs quite well within the range of human speech sounds.

Basically, the task of the auditory system in identifying particular sound sources is one of *pattern recognition.* The auditory system must recognize that particular patterns of constantly changing activity received from the hair cells on the basilar membrane belong to different sound sources. And few patterns are simple mixtures of fixed frequencies. Consider the complexity of sounds that occur in the environment: cars honking, birds chirping, people coughing, doors slamming, and so on. (An even more complicated task—speech recognition—is discussed in Chapter 10.)

A functional imaging study by Lewis and colleagues (2004) presented subjects with recordings of environmental sounds—sounds made by various tools, animals, dropped objects, and poured or dripping liquids. They also presented these sounds recorded backward, which preserved their complexity but made it impossible for them to be recognized. All

**harmonic** A component of a complex tone; one of a series of tones whose frequency is a multiple of the fundamental frequency. In music theory, also known as an overtone.

**fundamental frequency** The lowest, and usually most intense, frequency of a complex sound; most often perceived as the sound's basic pitch.

**timbre** A perceptual dimension of sound, determined by the complexity of the sound—for example, as shown by a mathematical analysis of the sound wave.

**FIGURE 5•27** Localizing the source of high-frequency sounds. The head casts a "sound shadow" for high-frequency sound vibrations. The brain uses the difference in loudness to detect the location of the source of the sound.

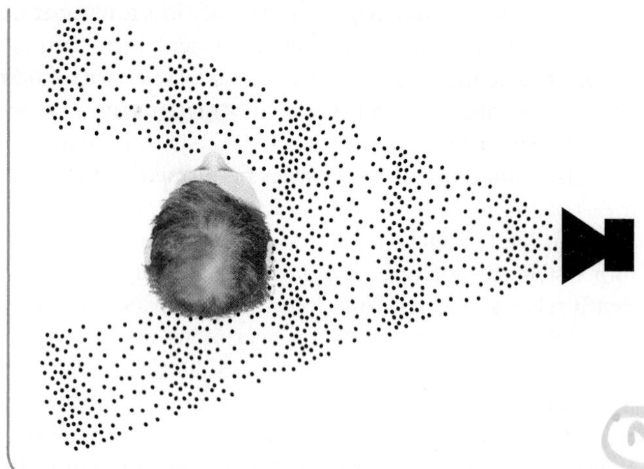

sounds activated the auditory cortex, but only recognized sounds activated a region of the left hemisphere centred on the posterior temporal lobe—a region also activated by the recognition of objects by seeing them or hearing verbal descriptions of them.

**Locating the Source of a Sound** When we hear an unexpected sound, we usually turn our heads quickly to face its source. Even newborn infants can make this response with reasonably good accuracy. Once our faces are oriented toward the source of the sound, we can detect changes in its location by as little as 1 degree. To do so, we make use of two qualities of sound: relative loudness and difference in arrival time.

Relative loudness is the most effective means of perceiving the location of high-frequency sounds. Acoustic energy, in the form of vibrations, does not actually pass through solid objects. Low-frequency sounds can easily make a large solid object, such as a wall, vibrate, setting the air on the other side in motion and producing a *new* sound across the barrier. But large, solid objects cannot vibrate rapidly, so they effectively damp out high-frequency sounds. Thus, they cast a "sound shadow," just as opaque objects cast a shadow in the sunlight. The head is one such large solid object, and it damps out high-frequency sounds so that they appear much louder to the ear nearer the source of the sound. Thus, if a source on your right produces a high-frequency sound, your right ear will receive more intense stimulation than your left ear will. The brain uses this difference to calculate the location of the source of the sound. (See **Figure 5•27**.)

The second method involves detecting differences in the arrival time of sound pressure waves at each eardrum. This method works best for frequencies below approximately 3000 Hz. A 1000 Hz tone produces pressure waves approximately 0.3 m apart. Because the distance between a person's eardrums is somewhat less than half that, a source of 1000 Hz sound located to one side of the head will cause one eardrum to be pushed in while the other eardrum is pulled out. In contrast, if the source of the sound is directly in front of the listener, both eardrums will move in synchrony. (See **Figure 5•28**.)

Researchers have found that when the source of a sound is located to the side of the head, as in Figure 5.28(a), axons in the right and left auditory nerves will fire at different times. The brain detects this disparity, which causes the sound to be perceived as off to one side. In fact, the brain can detect differences in firing times of a fraction of a millisecond. The easiest stimuli to locate are those that produce brief clicks, which cause brief bursts of neural activity. Apparently, it is easiest for the brain to compare the arrival times of single bursts of incoming information.

Where in the brain is this information computed? Initial processing occurs in the brain stem in a region known as the

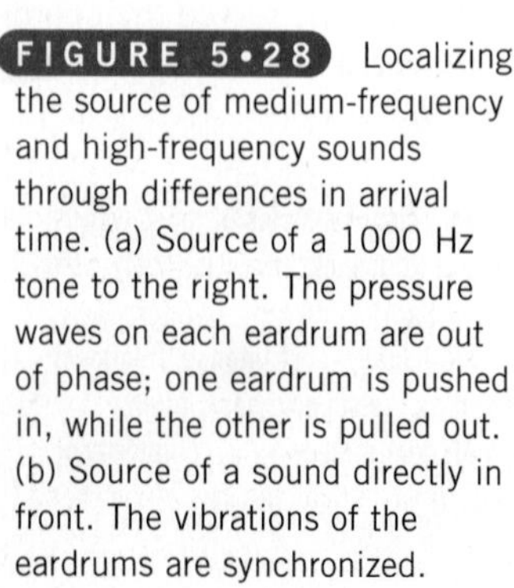

**FIGURE 5•28** Localizing the source of medium-frequency and high-frequency sounds through differences in arrival time. (a) Source of a 1000 Hz tone to the right. The pressure waves on each eardrum are out of phase; one eardrum is pushed in, while the other is pulled out. (b) Source of a sound directly in front. The vibrations of the eardrums are synchronized.

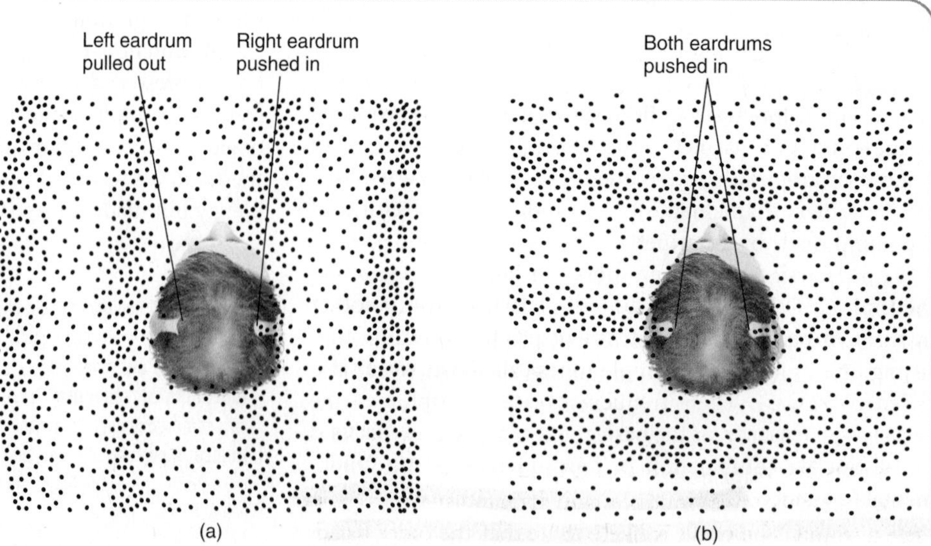

superior olive. Stimulation involving different temporal discrepancies activates different regions of the superior olive but, unlike the retina, these areas do not have a simple relationship of sectors within this region to locations of sounds in space (Oliver et al., 2003). Zatorre, Bouffard, Ahad, and Belin (2002) used a PET scan technique to examine cortical brain functioning as people listened to environmental sounds with both loudness and time difference cues to location. When all sounds were the same, but differed in location, no single part of the auditory cortex seemed to respond to differences in sound location. But when the sounds were different and came from different locations, the area at the top of the temporal cortex, close to the parietal lobe, showed a strong response. Apparently, spatial location in general is processed quite widely in the auditory cortex. But when the location concerns a particular object, it is processed in an area close to the parietal lobe. Recall from Chapter 4 that the parietal lobe is a region of the brain that helps us maintain a sense of spatial orientation.

Sound localization seems to show contingent aftereffects similar to those discussed earlier for colour vision. Dong, Swindale, and Cynader (1999) asked people to listen to tones produced by a loudspeaker that moved back and forth in front of them. As the loudspeaker moved to the left, the frequency of the tone increased; as it moved to the right, the frequency decreased. After 10 minutes of adaptation, several test tones were presented. Some of these tones were stationary in location, but changed in pitch. Dong and colleagues found that stationary tones that increased in pitch were judged as moving to the right. Stationary tones that decreased in frequency were judged as moving to the left. That is, the apparent motion of the tone was, like a negative afterimage, opposite to the initial experience.

## Age-Related Losses in Hearing

Earlier, we looked at how visual sharpness changes as the eye's lens becomes less flexible with age. The auditory system also changes with age, but the result is not merely a general loss of sensitivity. In absolute terms, significant hearing losses generally do not occur until the sixth or seventh decade of life (Cheesman, 1997). What is important, however, is the way these cumulative losses interact with normal hearing processes.

An important capacity in hearing, for example, is our ability to use background information to process a sound. Under laboratory conditions, if you are trying to hear a tone against some background noise, your threshold is better if the noise goes to both ears rather than to one. The difference is called the masking-level difference (MLD) and it can be measured in various ways. Pichora-Fuller and Schneider (1998), among others, have found that older listeners (about 69 years of age) show smaller MLDs than younger listeners (about 23 years of age) over a wide range of noise levels. These results imply age-related degradation in the auditory system's ability to use loudness and arrival disparities to isolate a sound. The result is likely to be that the older listener will find it difficult to follow a conversation in a noisy environment, or may confuse the sound of a telephone heard over the television with one heard from the kitchen.

Other age-related changes concern loss of sensitivity to different bands of frequencies. Sensitivity loss for higher frequencies occurs earlier and with more severity than for lower frequencies. Also, there is a loss in selectivity to certain frequencies, as if the tuner on your radio were somehow receptive to several stations at once. The result may be a loss in the ability to perceive the finer distinctions in sound that convey the informational content of speech (Schneider, 1997).

## Interim Summary

### Audition

Were you to sit at a synthesizer, you would have at your fingertips the means to produce a vast array of sounds. You would also have at your disposal (in your head) an auditory system sophisticated enough to differentiate among those sounds. The physical dimensions of the synthesizer's sound—amplitude, frequency, and complexity—would be translated into the perceptual dimensions of loudness, pitch, and timbre for sounds ranging from 30 to 20 000 Hz. Sound pressure waves put the process in motion by setting up vibrations in the eardrum, which are passed on to the ossicles. Vibrations of the stirrup against the membrane behind the oval window create pressure changes in the fluid within the cochlea that cause the basilar membrane to flex back and forth. This vibration causes the auditory hair cells on the basilar membrane to move relative to the tectorial membrane. The resulting pull on the cilia of the hair cells stimulates them to secrete a transmitter substance that excites neurons of the auditory nerve. This process informs the brain of the presence of a sound.

Two different methods of detection enable the brain to recognize the pitch of a sound. Different high-frequency and medium-frequency sounds are perceived when different parts of the basilar membrane vibrate in response to these frequencies. Low-frequency vibrations are detected when the tip of the basilar membrane vibrates in synchrony with the sound, which causes some axons in the auditory nerve to fire at the same frequency.

To locate the source of a sound (for example, if your synthesizer is hooked up to different speakers), you have available two means: Low-frequency sounds are located by differences in the arrival time of the sound waves in each ear. High-frequency sounds are located by differences in intensity caused by the "sound shadow" cast by your head.

As you produce sounds of more and more complex timbre, the auditory system will analyze them into their constituent frequencies, each of which causes a particular part of the basilar membrane to vibrate. All of these functions proceed automatically, so that when you press some keys on your synthesizer, your brain will then hear what you have played, whether it resembles the sound of a clarinet or some new combination of fundamental frequency and harmonics. With age, people may lose the ability to hear sound against a noisy background and to hear certain frequencies.

**QUESTIONS TO CONSIDER**

1. A naturalist once noted that when a male bird stakes out his territory, he sings with a very sharp, staccato song that says, in effect, "Here I am, and stay away!" In contrast, if a predator appears in the vicinity, many birds will emit alarm calls that consist of steady whistles that start and end slowly. Knowing what you do about the two means of localizing sounds, why do you think these two types of calls have different characteristics?
2. If you had a child who was born deaf, would you send him or her to a school that taught sign language or to one that emphasized speaking and lip reading? Why? Now imagine that you are deaf (or, if you are deaf, that you are hearing). Would your answer change?

**chemosense** One of the two sense modalities (gustation and olfaction) that detect the presence of particular molecules present in the environment.
**gustation** The sense of taste.
**papilla** A small bump on the tongue that contains a group of taste buds.
**taste bud** A small organ on the tongue that contains a group of gustatory receptor cells.

# Gustation

We have two senses specialized for detecting chemicals in our environment: taste and smell. Together, they are referred to as the **chemosenses.** Taste, or **gustation,** is the simplest of the sense modalities. Taste is not the same as flavour; the flavour of a food includes its odour, texture, and touch as well as its taste. You have probably noticed that the flavours of foods are diminished when you have a head cold. This loss of flavour occurs not because your taste buds are inoperative but because mucus congestion makes it difficult for odour-laden air to reach your receptors for the sense of smell. Without their characteristic odours to serve as cues, onions taste much like apples (although apples do not make your eyes water).

## Receptors and the Sensory Pathway

The tongue has a somewhat corrugated appearance, being marked by creases and bumps. The bumps are called **papillae** (from the Latin, meaning "nipple"). Each papilla contains a number of taste buds (in some cases as many as 200). A **taste bud** is a small organ that contains a number of receptor cells, each of which is shaped rather like a segment of an orange. The cells have hair-like projections called *microvilli* that protrude through the pore of the taste bud into the saliva that coats the tongue and fills the trenches of the papillae. (See **Figure 5•29.**) Molecules of chemicals dissolved in the saliva stimulate the receptor cells, probably by interacting with special receptors on the microvilli that are

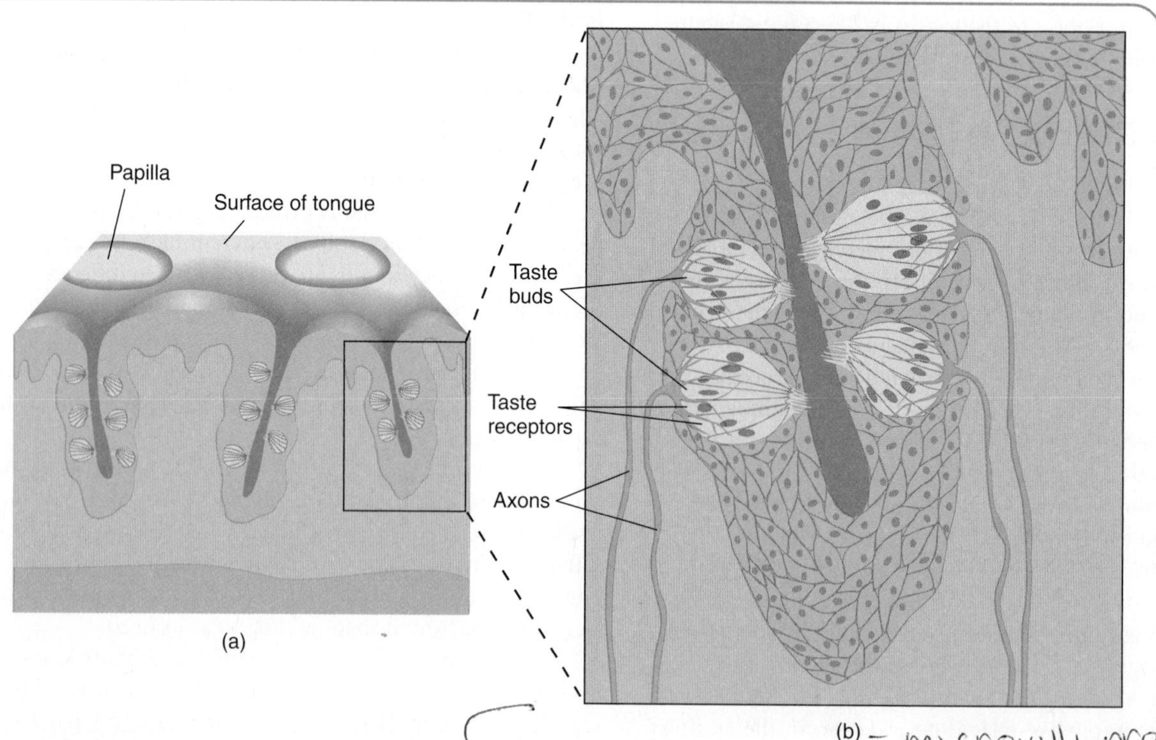


**FIGURE 5•29** The tongue. (a) Papillae on the surface of the tongue. (b) Taste buds.

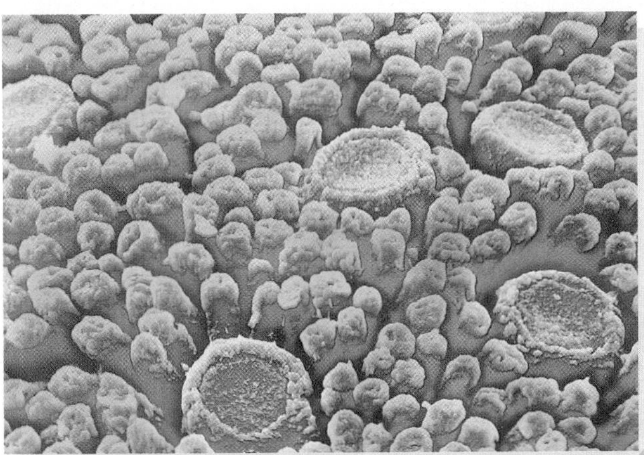

▲ *A photograph of taste buds taken with a scanning electron microscope.*

similar to the postsynaptic receptors found on other neurons. The receptor cells form synapses with dendrites of neurons that send axons to the brain through three different cranial nerves.

## The Five Qualities of Taste

The physical properties of the molecules that we taste determine the nature of the taste sensations (Lindemann, 2001). Traditionally, it has been thought that there were four taste qualities: sourness, sweetness, saltiness, and bitterness. Recently, however, investigators have found evidence for another taste: *umami* (a Japanese word that means "good taste"). Umami refers to the taste of monosodium glutamate; genes that code for its receptors have been identified (Chaudhari, Landin, & Roper, 2000). These five taste qualities arise when different molecules stimulate different types of receptors. For example, all substances that taste salty ionize (break into charged particles) when they dissolve. The most important salty substance is, of course, table salt—sodium chloride (NaCl). Other chlorides, such as lithium or potassium chloride, and some other salts, such as bromides or sulphates, are also salty in taste; however, none tastes quite as salty as sodium chloride. This finding suggests that the specific function of salt-tasting receptors is to identify sodium chloride. Most likely, salt-tasting receptors respond when sodium enters a taste cell through sodium channels in the membrane. The influx of sodium depolarizes the cell, causing it to release neurotransmitters. Sodium plays a unique role in the regulation of our body fluid. If the body's store of sodium falls, we cannot retain water, and our blood volume will fall. The result can be heart failure. Loss of sodium stimulates a strong craving for the salty taste of sodium chloride.

Both bitter and sweet substances seem to consist of large, non-ionizing molecules. Scientists cannot predict, merely on the basis of shape, whether a molecule will taste bitter or sweet (or neither). Some molecules (such as saccharin) stimulate both sweet and bitter receptors. Most likely, the function of the bitterness receptor is to avoid ingesting poisons. Many plants produce alkaloids that serve to protect them against being eaten by insects or browsing animals. Some of these alkaloids are poisonous to humans, and most of them taste bitter. In contrast, the sweetness receptor enables us to recognize the sugar content of fruits and other nutritive plant foods. When sweet-loving animals gather and eat fruit, they tend to disperse the seeds and help propagate the plant; thus, the presence of sugar in the fruit is to the plant's advantage as well.

Most sour tastes are produced by acids—in particular, by the hydrogen ion (H+) contained in acid solutions. The sourness receptor probably serves as a warning device against substances that have undergone bacterial decomposition, most of which become acidic. In earlier times, most wholesome, natural foods tasted sweet or salty, not bitter or sour. (Nowadays, we can mix sweet-tasting and sour-tasting substances to make tasty beverages such as lemonade.)

You probably recognized monosodium glutamate—the chemical that stimulates the umami receptor—as a taste-enhancing agent used in many, especially oriental, dishes. Why would we have a gene for such a taste sensation? Glutamate is an abundant amino acid, and is present in many proteins, which may explain why animals have evolved a taste for it (Lindemann, 2000). There also may be receptors for groups of amino acids (Nelson et al., 2002) to enhance our preference for fuel-rich foods.

# Olfaction

The sense of smell—**olfaction**—is one of the most interesting and puzzling of the sense modalities. It is unlike other sense modalities in two important ways. First, people have difficulty describing odours in words. Second, odours have a powerful ability to evoke old memories and feelings, even many years after an event (Chu & Downes, 2000). At some time in their lives, most people encounter an odour that they recognize as having some childhood association, even though they cannot identify it. The phenomenon may occur because the olfactory system sends information to the limbic system, a part of the brain that plays a role in both emotions and memories.

The sense shows other interesting patterns as well: Women, for example, seem to have a more acute sense of smell than do men. And it is possible that humans have not one, but two, olfactory systems. The second system would be the "accessory olfactory system," which is possessed by many mammals and detects special chemicals called **pheromones** that regulate sexual and social behaviour in many animals (Bartoshuk & Beauchamp, 1994). Humans possess some vestigial elements of an accessory olfactory system and there has

**olfaction** The sense of smell.
**pheromones** Chemical signals, usually detected by smell or taste, that regulate reproductive and social behaviours between animals.

been some evidence that women's menstrual cycles can be affected by chemical signals (Stern & McClintock, 1998). However, there is no evidence showing that the anatomical units of a human accessory olfactory system are fully functional. Therefore, we'll look only at the primary olfactory system.

Olfaction, like audition, seems to be an analytical sense modality. That is, when we sniff air that contains a mixture of familiar odours, we can usually identify the individual components. The molecules do not blend together and produce a single odour the way lights of different wavelengths produce a single colour.

Although other animals, such as dogs, have more sensitive olfactory systems than humans do, we should not underrate our own. The olfactory system is second only to the visual system in the number of sensory receptor cells, with an estimated 10 million receptor cells. We can smell some substances at lower concentrations than our most sensitive laboratory instruments can detect. One reason for the difference in sensitivity between our olfactory system and those of other mammals is that other mammals put their noses where odours are the strongest—just above ground level. For example, watch a dog following an odour trail. The dog sniffs along the ground, where the odours of the passing animal will have clung. Even a bloodhound's nose would not be very useful if it were located almost two metres above the ground, as ours is. When people sniff the ground like dogs do, their olfactory system works much better. Porter and colleagues (2007) prepared a scent trail—a string moistened with essential oil of chocolate—and laid it down in a grassy field. Research subjects were blindfolded and wore earmuffs, kneepads, and gloves, which prevented them from using anything other than their noses to follow the scent trail. They did quite well, and adopted the same zigzag strategy used by dogs. That being said, though, it is true that dogs have many more sensory receptors: Doty (2001) notes that in humans the area of olfactory reception is about 22 $cm^2$; in dogs it is 7 $m^2$!

**olfactory mucosa** The mucous membrane lining the top of the nasal sinuses; contains the cilia of the olfactory receptors.

**olfactory bulbs** Stalk-like structures located at the base of the brain that contain neural circuits that perform the first analysis of olfactory information.

## Anatomy of the Olfactory System

**Figure 5•30** shows the anatomy of the olfactory system. The receptor cells lie in the **olfactory mucosa**, patches of mucous membrane located on the roof of the nasal sinuses, just under the base of the brain. The receptor cells have cilia that are embedded in the olfactory mucosa. They also have axons that pass through small holes in the bone above the olfactory mucosa and form synapses with neurons in the olfactory bulbs. The **olfactory bulbs** are stalk-like structures located at the base of the brain that contain neural circuits that perform the first analysis of olfactory information.

The interaction between odour molecule and receptor appears to be similar to that of transmitter substance and postsynaptic receptor on a neuron. That is, when a molecule of an odorous substance fits a receptor molecule located on the cilia of a receptor cell, the cell becomes excited. This excitation is passed on to the brain by the axon of the receptor cell. Thus, similar mechanisms may detect the stimuli for taste and olfaction.

Unlike information from all other sensory modalities, olfactory information is not sent to the thalamus and then relayed to a specialized region of the cerebral cortex. Instead, olfactory information is sent directly to several regions of the limbic system—in particular, to the amygdala and to the limbic cortex of the frontal lobe. One intriguing clue about the

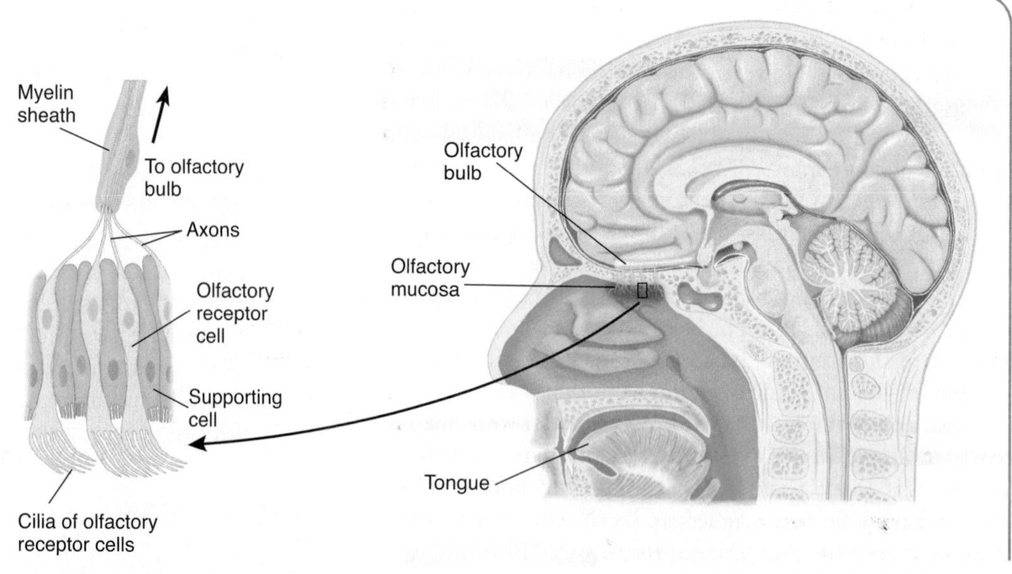


FIGURE 5•30 The olfactory system.

way olfactory stimuli are processed is that olfaction shows *cross-modal* integration with taste stimuli. Dalton, Doolittle, Nagata, and Breslin (2000) tested people's sensitivity to benzaldehyde, an odour that smells like cherry and almonds. They found that the threshold for detecting the odour was lower when the participants in their study held a sweet solution of saccharin in their mouths. Dalton and colleagues suggested that connections in the amygdala may be responsible for the increased sensitivity to the odour when it is paired with a relevant flavour.

## The Dimensions of Odour

We know that there are five qualities of taste and that a colour can be specified in terms of hue, brightness, and saturation. Research in molecular biology has found that the olfactory system contains several hundred different receptor molecules, located in the membrane of the cilia of the receptor cells (Buck & Axel, 1991). These receptor molecules detect different categories of odours. Humans have 339 different types of olfactory receptors, while mice have 913 (Godfrey, Malnic, & Buck, 2004; Malnic, Godfrey, & Buck, 2004).

Humans can recognize up to 10 000 different odorants, and other animals can probably recognize even more than that (Shepherd, 1994). Even with 339 different olfactory receptors, that leaves many odours unaccounted for. As well, every year, chemists synthesize new chemicals, many with odours unlike those that anyone has previously detected. How can we use a relatively small number of receptors to detect so many different odorants?

The answer is that a particular odorant binds to more than one receptor. Thus, the brain eventually receives signals from several receptors. Recognizing a particular odour, then, is a matter of recognizing a particular pattern of activity. The task of chemical recognition is thereby transformed into a task of pattern recognition.

**Figure 5•31** illustrates this process (Malnic, Hironi, Sato, & Buck, 1999). The left side of the figure shows the shapes of eight hypothetical odorants. The right side shows four hypothetical odorant receptor molecules. If a portion of the odorant molecule fits the binding site of the receptor molecule, it will activate it and stimulate the olfactory neuron. As you can see, each odorant molecule fits the binding site of at least one of the receptors, and in most cases fits more than one of them. Notice also that the *pattern* of receptors activated by each of the eight odorants is different, which means that if we know which pattern of receptors is activated, we know which odorant is present. Of course, even though a particular odorant might bind with several different types of receptor molecules, it might not bind equally well with each of them. For example, it might bind very well with one receptor molecule, moderately well with another, weakly with another, and so on. Presumably, the brain recognizes particular odours by recognizing different patterns of activation that it receives from the olfactory bulbs.

**FIGURE 5•31** A hypothetical explanation of coding of olfactory information. Different odorant molecules attach to different combinations of receptor molecules. (Activated receptor molecules are shown in blue.) Unique patterns of activation represent particular odorants.

*(Adapted from Malnic, B., Hirono, J., Sato, T., & Buck, L. B. (1999).* Cell, 96, *713–723.)*

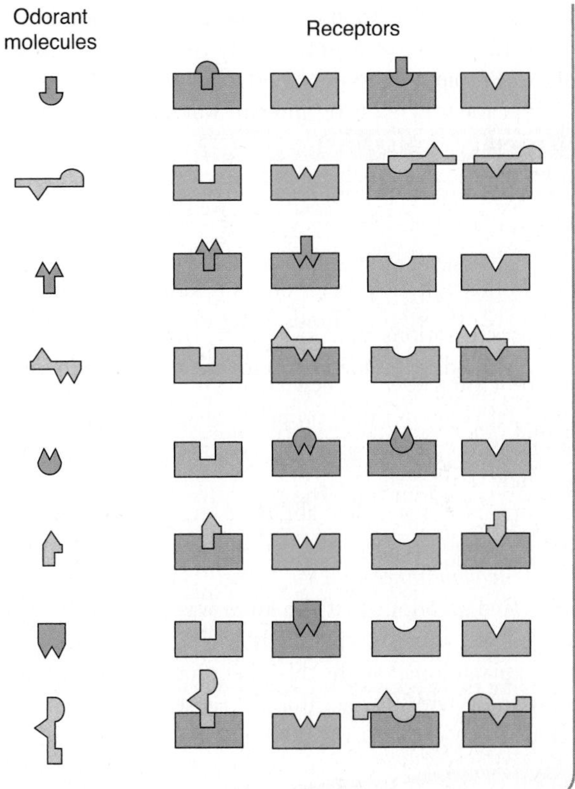


## Interim Summary

### Gustation and Olfaction

Both gustation and olfaction are served by cells having receptors that respond selectively to various kinds of molecules. Taste buds have at least five kinds of receptors, responding to molecules that we perceive as sweet, salty, sour, bitter, or umami. To most organisms, sweet, umami, and moderately salty substances taste pleasant, whereas sour or bitter substances taste unpleasant. Sweet, umami, and salty receptors permit us to detect nutritious foods and sodium chloride. Sour and bitter receptors help us avoid substances that might be poisonous.

Olfaction is a remarkable sense modality. Olfactory information combines with information about taste to provide us with the flavour of a food present in our mouths. We can distinguish thousands of different odours and can recognize smells from childhood, even when we cannot remember when or where we first encountered them. Although we recognize similarities between different odours, most seem unique. Unlike visual stimuli, odours do not blend easily. For example, when visiting a carnival, we can distinguish the odours of popcorn, cotton candy, crushed grass, and diesel oil in a single sniff. The detection of different odours appears to be accomplished by a little more than 300 different receptor molecules located in the membrane of the cilia of the olfactory receptor cells. The brain recognizes particular odours by analyzing the pattern of neural activity produced by activation of these receptors.

**QUESTIONS TO CONSIDER**

1. Bees and birds can taste sweet substances, but cats and alligators cannot. Obviously, the ability to taste particular substances is related to the range of foods a species eats. If, through the process of evolution, a species develops a greater range of foods, what do you think comes first, the food or the receptor? Would a species start to eat something having a new taste (say, something sweet) and later develop the appropriate taste receptors, or do the taste receptors evolve first and then lead the animal to a new taste?
2. Odours have a peculiar ability to evoke memories—a phenomenon vividly described by Marcel Proust in his novel *Remembrance of Things Past.* Have you ever encountered an odour that you knew was somehow familiar, but you couldn't say exactly why? Can you think of any explanations? Might this phenomenon have something to do with the fact that the sense of olfaction developed very early during the evolution of our brain?

## The Somatosenses

The body senses, or **somatosenses**, include our ability to respond to touch, vibration, pain, warmth, coolness, limb position, muscle length and stretch, tilt of the head, and changes in the speed of head rotation. The number of sense modalities represented in this list depends on one's definition of a sense modality. However, it does not really matter whether we say that we respond to warmth and coolness by means of one sense modality or two different ones; the important thing is to understand how our bodies are able to detect changes in temperature.

Many experiences require simultaneous stimulation of several different sense modalities. For example, taste and odour alone do not determine the flavour of spicy food; mild (or sometimes not-so-mild) stimulation of pain detectors in the mouth and throat gives Thai food its special characteristic. Sensations such as tickle and itch are apparently mixtures of varying amounts of touch and pain. Similarly, our perception of the texture and three-dimensional shape of an object that we touch involves co-operation among our senses of pressure, muscle and joint sensitivity, and motor control (to manipulate the object). If we handle an object and find that it moves smoothly in our hand, we conclude that it is slippery. If, after handling this object, our fingers subsequently slide across each other without much resistance, we perceive a feeling of oiliness. If we sense vibrations when we move our fingers over an object, it is rough. And so on. If you close your eyes as you manipulate some soft and hard, warm and cold, and smooth and rough objects, you can make yourself aware of the separate sensations that interact and give rise to a complex perception.

The following discussion of the somatosenses groups them into three major categories: the skin senses, the internal senses, and the vestibular senses.

**somatosense** Bodily sensations; sensitivity to such stimuli as touch, pain, and temperature.
**free nerve ending** A dendrite of somatosensory neurons.
**Pacinian corpuscle** A specialized somatosensory nerve ending that detects mechanical stimuli, especially vibrations.

### The Skin Senses

The entire surface of the human body is *innervated* (supplied with nerve fibres) by the dendrites of neurons that transmit somatosensory information to the brain. Cranial nerves convey information from the face and front portion of the head (including the teeth and the inside of the mouth and throat); spinal nerves convey information from the rest of the body's surface. All somatosensory information is detected by the dendrites of neurons; the system uses no separate receptor cells. However, some of these dendrites have specialized endings that modify the way they transduce energy into neural activity.

Figure 5.32 shows the sensory receptors found in hairy skin and in smooth, hairless skin (such as skin on the palms of the hands or the soles of the feet). The most common type of skin sensory receptor is the **free nerve ending**, which resembles the fine roots of a plant. Free nerve endings infiltrate the middle layers of both smooth and hairy skin and surround the hair follicles in hairy skin. If you bend a single hair on your forearm, you will see how sensitive the free nerve endings are. (Try it; then see **Figure 5•32**.)

The largest of the special receptive endings, called the **Pacinian corpuscle**, is actually visible to the naked eye. Pacinian corpuscles are very sensitive to touch. When they are moved, their axons fire a brief burst of impulses. Among the possible functions of Pacinian corpuscles is providing information about vibration.

Other specialized receptors detect other sensory qualities, including pressure, warmth, coolness, and pain.

**Touch and Pressure** Psychologists speak of touch and pressure as two separate sensations. They define touch as the sensation of very light contact of an object with the skin, and pressure as the sensation produced by more forceful contact.

**FIGURE 5•32** Sensory receptors in hairy skin (left) and in hairless skin (right).

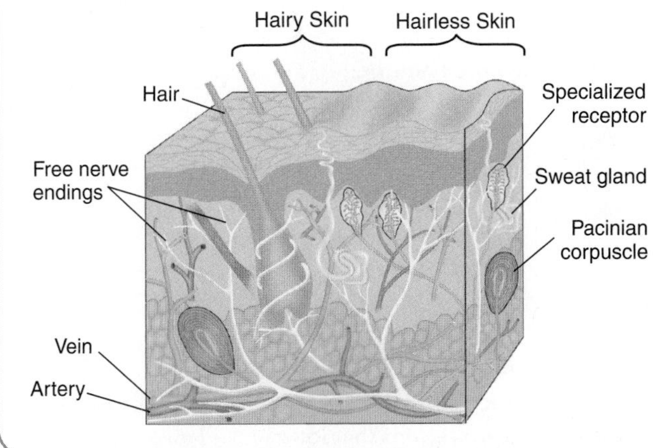


Sensations of pressure occur only when the skin is actually moving (being pushed in), which means that the pressure detectors respond only while they are being bent. If you rest your forearm on a table and place a small weight on your skin, you will feel the pressure at first, but eventually you will feel nothing at all, if you keep your arm still. You fail to feel the pressure not because your brain "ignores" incoming stimulation but because the sensory endings no longer send impulses to your brain. Studies that have measured very slow, very minute movements of a weight sinking down into the skin have shown that sensory transmission ceases when the movements stop. With the addition of another weight on top of the first one, movement and sensory transmission begin again (Nafe & Wagoner, 1941). Of course, a person will feel a very heavy weight indefinitely, but the sensation will be that of pain rather than pressure.

The ability to precisely localize the part of the body being touched varies widely across the surface of the body. The most sensitive regions are the lips and the fingertips. The most common measure of tactile discrimination (the ability to tell touches apart) is the **two-point discrimination threshold**. To determine this measure, a researcher touches a person with one or both legs of a caliper and asks the person to say whether the sensation is coming from one or two points. (See **Figure 5•33**.) The farther apart the legs of the caliper must be before the person reports feeling two separate sensations, the lower the sensitivity of that region of skin.

**Temperature** We can detect thermal stimuli over a very wide range of temperatures, from less than 8 degrees Celsius (noxious cold) to more than 52 degrees Celsius (noxious heat). Investigators have long believed that no single receptor could detect such a range of temperatures, and recent research indicates that this belief is correct. At present, we know of six mammalian thermoreceptors (Voets et al., 2004). One of these receptors, which is sensitive to ranges of temperatures close to body temperature, is found in the anterior hypothalamus (Güler et al., 2002), the region of the brain that is responsible for measuring and maintaining our body temperature.

**FIGURE 5•33** The method for determining the two-point discrimination threshold.

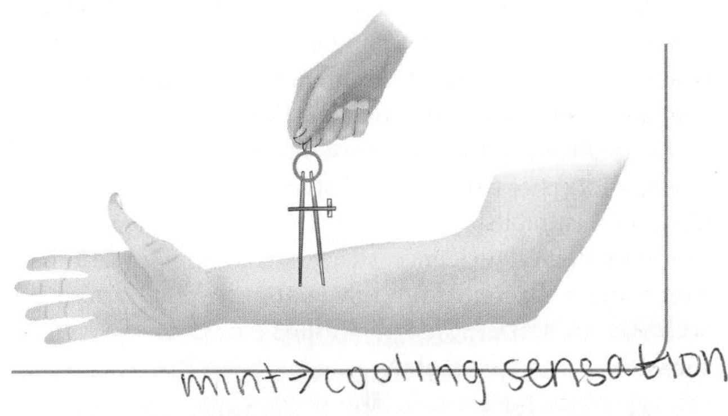

Some of the thermal receptors respond to particular chemicals as well as to changes in temperature. For example, one of them is stimulated by menthol, a compound found in the leaves of many members of the mint family. As you undoubtedly know, peppermint tastes cool in the mouth, and menthol is added to some cigarettes to make the smoke feel cooler (and perhaps to try to delude smokers into thinking that the smoke is less harsh and damaging to the lungs). Menthol provides a cooling sensation because it binds with and stimulates this thermal receptor and produces neural activity that the brain interprets as coolness. As we will see in the next subsection, chemicals can produce the sensation of heat also.

**Pain** Pain reception, like temperature reception, is accomplished by the networks of free nerve endings in the skin. There appear to be at least three types of pain receptors (usually referred to as *nociceptors,* or "detectors of noxious stimuli"). High-threshold mechanoreceptors are free nerve endings that respond to intense pressure, which might be caused by something striking, stretching, or pinching the skin. A second type of free nerve ending appears to respond to extremes of heat, to acids, and to the presence of *capsaicin,* the active ingredient in chile peppers (Kress & Zeilhofer, 1999). (Note that we say that chile peppers make food taste "hot.") Caterina and colleagues (2000) found that mice with a targeted mutation against this receptor showed less sensitivity to painful high-temperature stimuli and would drink water to which capsaicin had been added. Ghilardi and colleagues (2005) found that a drug that blocks this type of receptor reduced pain in patients with bone cancer—apparently the pain is caused by acid produced by the tumours.

Another type of nociceptor contains receptors that are sensitive to *ATP,* a chemical that serves as an energy source in all cells of the body (Burnstock & Wood, 1996). ATP is also released when the blood supply to a region of the body is disrupted or when a muscle is damaged. As well, it is released by rapidly growing tumours. Thus, these nociceptors may be at

**two-point discrimination threshold** The minimum distance between two small points that can be detected as separate stimuli when pressed against a particular region of the skin.

least partly responsible for the pain caused by angina, migraine, damage to muscles, and some kinds of cancer.

Pain is a complex sensation involving not only intense sensory stimulation but also an emotional component. That is, a given sensory input to the brain might be interpreted as pain in one situation and as pleasure in another. For example, when people are sexually aroused, they become less sensitive to many forms of pain and may even find such intense stimulation pleasurable.

Physiological evidence suggests that the sensation of pain is quite different from the emotional reaction to pain. Opiates such as morphine diminish the sensation of pain by stimulating opioid receptors on neurons in the brain; these neurons block the transmission of pain information to the brain. In contrast, some tranquilizers (such as Valium) depress neural systems that are responsible for the emotional reaction to pain but do not diminish the intensity of the sensation. Thus, people who have received a drug like Valium will report that they feel the pain just as much as they did before but that it does not bother them much.

Evidence from surgical procedures also supports the distinction between sensation and emotion. Prefrontal lobotomy (a form of brain surgery), like the use of tranquilizers such as Valium, blocks the emotional component of pain but does not affect the primary sensation. Therefore, operations similar to prefrontal lobotomy (but much less drastic) are sometimes performed to treat people who suffer from chronic pain that cannot be alleviated by other means.

Many noxious stimuli elicit two kinds of pain: an immediate sharp, or "bright," pain followed by a deep, dull, sometimes throbbing pain. Some stimuli elicit only one of these two kinds of pain. For example, a pinprick will produce only the superficial "bright" pain, whereas a hard blow from a blunt object to a large muscle will produce only the deep, dull pain. Different sets of axons mediate these two types of pain.

A particularly interesting form of pain sensation occurs after a limb has been amputated. After their limbs are gone, up to 70 percent of amputees report that they feel as though their missing limbs still exist, and that they often hurt. This phenomenon is referred to as the **phantom limb** (Melzack, 1992). People who have phantom limbs report that the limbs feel very real, and often say that if they try to reach out with their missing limbs, it feels as though the limbs are responding. Sometimes, they perceive the limbs as sticking out, and may feel compelled to avoid knocking them against the side of a door frame or sleeping in a position that would make the limbs come between them and the mattress. People have reported all sorts of sensations in phantom limbs, including pain, pressure, warmth, cold, wetness, itching, sweatiness, and prickliness.

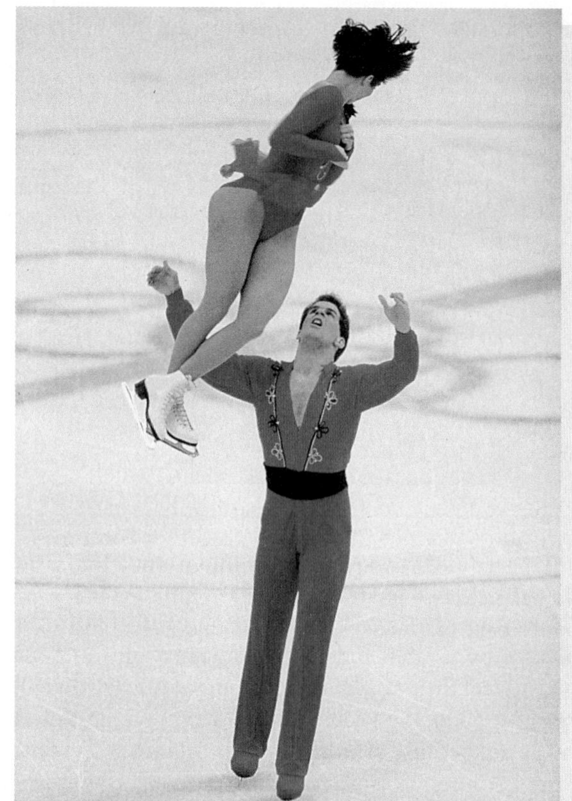

▲ *Information from the internal senses, along with visual information, tells these skaters about the location and movements of their bodies and helps them gauge the force they need to exert to perform their intricate manoeuvres.*

Melzack suggests that the phantom limb sensation is inherent in the organization of the parietal cortex. As we saw in Chapter 4, the parietal cortex is involved in our awareness of our own bodies. Indeed, people who have sensory neglect, caused by lesions of the right parietal lobe, have been known to push their own legs out of bed, believing that they actually belong to someone else. Melzack reports that some people who were born missing limbs nevertheless experience phantom limb sensations, which would suggest that our brains are genetically programmed to provide sensations for all four limbs—even if we do not have them.

## The Internal Senses

Sensory endings located in our internal organs, bones and joints, and muscles convey painful, neutral, and in some cases pleasurable sensory information. For example, the internal senses convey the pain of arthritis, the perception of the location of our limbs, and the pleasure of a warm drink descending to our stomachs.

Muscles contain special sensory endings. One class of receptors, located at the junction between muscles and the tendons that connect them to the bones, provides information about the amount of force the muscle is exerting. These receptors protect the body by inhibiting muscular contractions when they become too forceful. During competition, some weightlifters have received injections of a local anaesthetic

**phantom limb** Sensations that appear to originate in a limb that has been amputated.

near the tendons of some muscles to eliminate this protective mechanism. As a result, they are able to lift even heavier weights. Unfortunately, if they use this tactic, some tendons may snap or some bones may break.

Another set of stretch detectors consists of spindle-shaped receptors distributed throughout the muscle. These receptors, appropriately called **muscle spindles**, inform the brain about changes in muscle length. People are not conscious of the specific information provided by the muscle spindles, but the brain uses the information from these receptors and from joint receptors to keep track of the location of parts of the body and to control muscular contractions.

## The Vestibular Senses

What we call our "sense of balance" in fact involves several senses, not just one. If we stand on one foot and then close our eyes, we immediately realize how important a role vision plays in balance. The **vestibular apparatus** of the inner ear provides only part of the sensory input that helps us remain upright.

The three **semicircular canals**—located in the inner ear—oriented at right angles to one another, detect changes in rotation of the head in any direction. (See **Figure 5•34**.) These canals contain a liquid. Rotation of the head makes the liquid flow, stimulating the receptor cells located in the canals.

Another set of inner ear organs, the **vestibular sacs**, contain crystals of calcium carbonate that are embedded in a gelatin-like substance attached to receptive hair cells. In one sac, the receptive tissue is on the wall; in the other, it is on the floor. When the head tilts, the weight of the calcium carbonate crystals shifts, producing different forces on the cilia of the hair cells. These forces change the activity of the hair cells, and the information is transmitted to the brain. However, they must also be coordinated with information from the semicircular canals. Taking a rapid step forward shifts the calcium carbonate crystals in the same way that tilting your head back does. Yet you probably don't feel as if you've accelerated forward whenever you tilt your head. Evidence, reviewed by Snyder (1999), suggests that the semicircular canals help us disambiguate the information from the vestibular sacs.

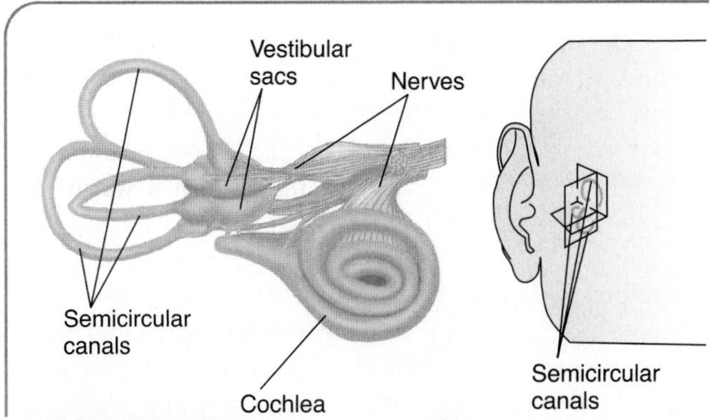


**FIGURE 5•34** The three semicircular canals and two vestibular sacs located in the inner ear.

The vestibular sacs are very useful in maintaining an upright head position. They also participate in a reflex that enables us to see clearly even when the head is being jarred. When we walk, our eyes are jostled back and forth. The jarring of the head stimulates the vestibular sacs to cause reflex movements of the eyes that partially compensate for the head movements. You can see the effect of this reflex with the following demonstration. Hold this textbook steady and move your head from side to side. Notice that it is relatively easy to keep the text in the centre of your vision. Now, try to keep your head still and move the textbook from side to side. The relative motion is the same, but it is very difficult to keep the text in view. The reflexive eye movements are linked to the specific vestibular information from the head. People who lack this reflex because of localized brain damage must stop walking in order to see things clearly—for example, to read a street sign.

## Interim Summary

### The Somatosenses

The somatosenses gather several different kinds of information from different parts of the body. The skin senses of temperature, touch and pressure, vibration, and pain inform us about the nature of objects that come in contact with our skin. Imagine a man attempting to climb a rock cliff. As he reaches for a firm handhold overhead, the Pacinian corpuscles in his fingers detect vibration caused by movement of his fingers over the rock, which helps him determine its texture and find cracks into which he can insert anchors for his rope. Perhaps temperature receptors in his fingers tell him whether the rock is exposed to the sun and has warmed up or whether it is in the cool shade. If he cuts his skin against some sharp rock, free nerve endings give rise to sensations of pain. Presumably he is too intent on his task to notice sensations from his internal organs, although he would certainly feel a painful stimulus like a kidney stone. If he thinks that he is slipping, he will feel a queasy sensation caused by his internal reaction to a sudden release of adrenaline. As he climbs, he relies heavily on sensory receptors in his muscles and joints, which inform his brain of the movement and location of his arms and legs. The vestibular senses help him keep his balance.

**muscle spindle** A muscle fibre that functions as a stretch receptor; arranged parallel to the muscle fibres responsible for contraction of the muscle, it detects muscle length.
**vestibular apparatus** The receptive organs of the inner ear that contribute to balance and perception of head movement.
**semicircular canal** One of a set of three organs in the inner ear that respond to rotational movements of the head.
**vestibular sac** One of a set of two receptor organs in each inner ear that detect changes in the tilt of the head.

QUESTION TO CONSIDER

1. Why can slow, repetitive vestibular stimulation (like that provided by a boat ride in stormy weather) cause nausea and vomiting? Can you think of any useful functions this response might serve?

## Then and Now

### Extrasensory Perception . . . A Case Study

Extrasensory perception, or ESP, is a staple of the tabloid press or bad science fiction writing. *That* version of ESP—the supposed sensing of another's thoughts, future events, or ghosts of the departed—is not possible. However, in general terms, the notion that we might experience sensations in addition to the ones discussed in this chapter (vision, audition, gustation, olfaction, and the somatosenses) is hypothetically possible under certain conditions. For example, we've looked at the internal senses as a group, but they really comprise a number of very different physiological systems with different kinds of receptors. As scientific knowledge of the nervous system improves, additional receptors undoubtedly will be identified. In this box, we'll look at some of the considerations that might be involved in discovering a sense "extra" to the ones we already know about. In this case, it involves an ability that, if humans do possess it, would be quite extraordinary. Indeed, it might even bring us back to the spooky type of ESP that I just dismissed.

Many animals inhabit an ecological niche that involves long migrations. Green sea turtles, for example, breed on Ascension Island in the South Atlantic; they migrate there from feeding grounds that are more than 2000 km away, off the coast of Brazil (Lohmann, Luschi, & Hays, 2008). These incredible feats of navigation are thought to be partly based on the ability of sea turtles to discriminate variations in the characteristics of the earth's magnetic field over large distances. For example, Lohmann and Lohmann (1996) found that newly hatched loggerhead turtles would swim in different directions when placed in magnetic fields of different intensities. Interestingly, the directions in which they swam were identical to their normal migratory orientation at regions of the earth with corresponding magnetic strengths.

Young turtles can discriminate different levels of magnetic energy. Do humans have this ability? If so, could it help us to find our way home as well? This provocative possibility was first raised by Baker (1980), who tested a number of British adolescents on their ability to point toward home after being blindfolded and taken to a site many kilometres away. **Figure 5.35** shows the result of one such test. Home was the town of Barnard Castle. The participants were blindfolded and taken by bus to a site to the southwest (the lower left white square in Figure 5.35) and then to the southeast (the lower right white square). At each of these locations, they were asked to name the direction back to Barnard Castle. The results are shown in the lower part of

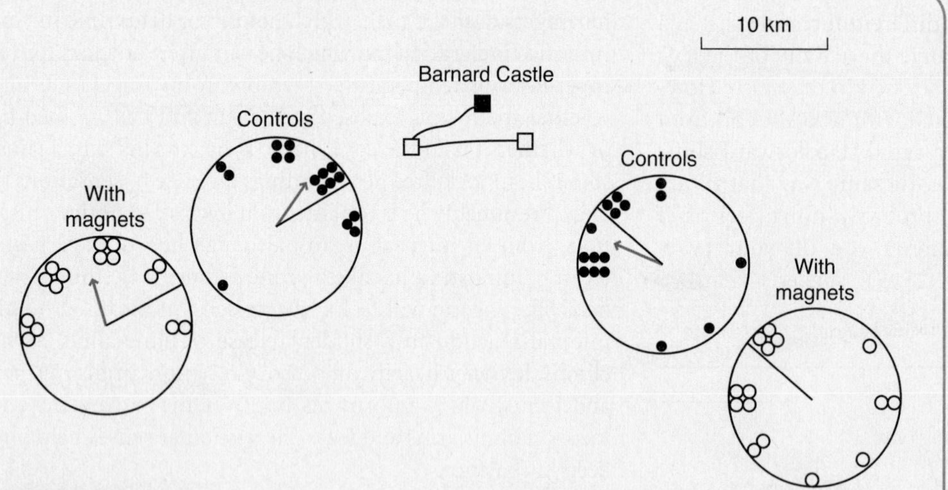


FIGURE 5•35 A test of whether humans can sense their location when transported. Participants were moved from Barnard Castle (black square) to two locations (white squares) and asked to describe the direction toward their starting point. Black dots on the two inner circles represent individual choices. Within each circle, the black line shows the true direction and the red line shows the average direction. White dots in the two outer circles show judgments made by people who wore magnets during the voyage. Their judgments were not as accurate and, in the case of the rightmost group, had no consistent mean direction.

*(Source: Adapted from Baker, R. R. (1980). Goal orientation by blindfolded humans after long-distance displacement: Possible involvement of a magnetic sense.* Science, 210, *555–557. Reprinted with permission from AAAS.)*

Figure 5.35. Each black dot represents a person's judgment about the correct direction home. As you can see, most of the black dots cluster around the correct direction. Despite wearing blindfolds and riding on a bus that took a circuitous route, people seemed capable of locating their home base.

Baker suggested that they might do this using a magnetic sensory ability. In Figure 5.35 is a group of white dots that also represent participant judgments. These people, however, rode by bus wearing magnets taped to their blindfolds—a method designed to disrupt any stimulation from the earth's magnetic field. As you can see in Figure 5.35, these people were much less accurate in identifying the correct direction home.

Baker's suggestion in 1980 was a remarkable claim, since few people, if any, seem aware of this "sense." To assess this claim, we should examine several issues: How is it possible to transduce magnetic force fields? Could such a sense be traced through our own evolutionary history? And finally, at an empirical level, can Baker's results be replicated?

Although it's an exotic source of information, there are at least three possible ways that biological cells could respond to variations in magnetic fields: magnetic induction, chemical magnetoreception, and magnetite torque (see Johnsen & Lohmann, 2005). Magnetic induction would activate a sensory receptor by producing an electrical current as the receptor crossed magnetic lines of force. The nervous systems of some species of fish possess cells that could function in this way. Chemical magnetoreception could occur if magnetic energy alters the characteristic of electrons in a biological chemical. We've already seen a similar mechanism in the way that light alters photopigments. Consequently, a chemical magnetoreceptor might also be a photoreceptor. However, no such receptors have so far been identified. Finally, magnetites are small crystals of magnetized material. If they were embedded in pressure-sensitive cells, they could produce a sensation in response to the magnetic forces acting on them. Magnetites have been detected in the beaks of some birds, suggesting this type of receptor may be a source of a magnetic sense in these species.

Are there mammals that show sensitivity to magnetic information? The answer seems to be yes. Muheim, Edgar, Sloan, and Phillips (2006) found that mice can sense directional information from magnetic fields, and use it to position their nests within a large enclosure. Compared to sea turtles or birds, mice are closer to our evolutionary ancestry, so it is at least possible that a similar sense could have appeared in the evolutionary history of humans.

This brings us back to the question of empirical evidence. Shortly after Baker's study was published, there were many attempts to replicate his findings (Gould & Able, 1981). They all failed.

It's worth pointing out, however, that these replications were tests of people's ability to orient and to point homeward. Orientation is a complex skill and requires the capacity to sense two separate directional dimensions, so it's not surprising that humans would not be able to show it based on a magnetic sensory system. The possibility remains that we might be able to discriminate less informative, but still detectable, magnetic field variations.

If this turns out to be the case, it might explain a rather strange finding reported by Wiseman and colleagues (2003). They asked people to tour sites in England and Scotland famous for reported sightings of ghosts. Indeed, when participants of this study visited locations that had a reputation for being "haunted," they reported unusual experiences. Generally, ghost sightings seemed to be correlated with variations in local magnetic fields.

# EPILOGUE

## Seeing the Forest and All That's within It

Ironically, the boy that Ken was looking for likely could hear better than Ken could. Although the hearing loss that we examined earlier in this chapter becomes a significant factor only in old age, it is still the case that hearing becomes progressively worse with age for anyone older than adolescence. This is particularly true with regards to high-frequency sounds (Kaewboonchoo, Saleekul, & Jaipukdee, 2007; Takeda et al., 1992). One possible reason is that the auditory hair cells near the oval window are more prone to nerve damage from exposure to noise. So it's quite possible that the auditory environment of the four-year-old was subtly different from that of his searchers: the snap of a broken twig, the rustling of leaves, perhaps even the sound of keys jingling on the belts of the searcher could have been especially salient, sudden, and, perhaps, menacing.

It's easy to see, then, why the boy thought the searchers were monsters lurking in the night. Their noises were strange; their clothing and helmets would have made them look especially big; and, of course, their headlamps would have looked just like an evil, glowing eye. If you think back to our discussion of signal detection theory, the imagined threat of alien abduction would have produced a strong response bias to stay quiet.

As this chapter has emphasized, "sensing" something involves more than the physiological transduction of information. We don't respond to everything that we sense and often, as in the case of McCollough effects or even one-eyed monsters in the woods, what we think we respond to is not what is actually there. Much of our world, psychologically, is a construction. Sensory reception is the first part of that construction, but ultimately those sensations produce our reaction to people and objects. How that construction occurs is the topic of our next chapter.

## Canadian Connections to Research in This Chapter


Allan, L. G., Siegel, S., Kulatunga-Moruzi, C., Eissenberg, T., & Chapman, A. (1997). Isoluminance and contingent color aftereffects. *Perception & Psychophysics, 59,* 1327–1334. (McMaster University: www.mcmaster.ca)

Cheesman, M. F. (1997). Speech perception by elderly listeners: Basic knowledge and implications for audiology. *Journal of Speech-Language Pathology and Audiology, 21,* 104–110. (University of Western Ontario: www.uwo.ca)

Coren, S., & Hakstian, A. R. (1988). Color vision screening without the use of technical equipment: Scale development and cross-validation. *Perception and Psychophysics, 43,* 115–120. (University of British Columbia: www.ubc.ca)

Stanley Coren was elected to the Royal Society of Canada in 1999.

Dodwell, P. C., & Humphrey, G. K. (1990). A function theory of the McCollough effect. *Psychological Review, 97,* 78–89. (Queen's University: www.queensu.ca)

Peter Dodwell was the 1992 winner of the Donald O. Hebb Award of the Canadian Psychological Association.

Dong, C.-J., Swindale, N. V., & Cynader, M. S. (1999). A contingent aftereffect in the auditory system. *Nature Neuroscience, 2,* 863–865. (University of British Columbia: www.ubc.ca)

Humphrey, G. K., Herbert, A. M., Hazlewood, S., & Stewart, J. A. D. (1998). The indirect McCollough effect: An examination of an associative account. *Perception & Psychophysics, 60,* 1188–1196. (University of Western Ontario: www.uwo.ca)

Melzack, R. (1992). Phantom limbs. *Scientific American, 266*(4), 120–126. (McGill University: www.mcgill.ca)

Ronald Melzack was the 1986 winner of the Donald O. Hebb Award of the Canadian Psychological Association.

Norwich, K. H., & Wong, W. (1997). Unification of psychophysical phenomena: The complete form of Fechner's Law. *Perception and Psychophysics, 59,* 929–940. (University of Toronto: www.utoronto.ca)

Pichora-Fuller, M. K., & Schneider, B. A. (1998). Masking-level differences in older adults: The effect of the level of the masking noise. *Perception & Psychophysics, 60,* 1197–1205. (University of British Columbia: www.ubc.ca)

Schneider, B. (1997). Psychoacoustics and aging: Implications for everyday listening. *Journal of Speech-Language Pathology and Audiology, 21,* 111–124. (University of Toronto: www.utoronto.ca)

Scialfa, C. T., & Joffe, K. M. (1998). Response times and eye movements in feature and conjunctive search as a function of target eccentricity. *Perception & Psychophysics, 60,* 1067–1082. (University of Calgary: www.ucalgary.ca)

Zatorre, R. J., Bouffard, M., Ahad, P., & Belin, P. (2002). Where is "where" in the human auditory cortex? *Nature Neuroscience, 5,* 905–909. (McGill University: www.mcgill.ca)


## Suggestions for Further Reading


Coren, S., Ward, L. M., & Enns, J. T. (2003). *Sensation and perception* (6th ed.). New York: Wiley.

Gregory, R. L. (1997). *Eye and brain: The psychology of seeing* (5th ed.). Princeton, NJ: Princeton University Press.

Many books have been written about vision and visual perception. Gregory's book is an excellent starting point, based on a thorough knowledge of the subject, written with wit and style, and well illustrated. After you have read Chapter 6, the book by Coren, Ward, and Enns will provide an excellent next step in enlarging your understanding of the sensory systems.

Gulick, W. L., Gescheider, G. A., & Frisina, R. D. (1989). *Hearing: Physiological acoustics, neural coding, and psychoacoustics.* New York: Oxford University Press.

Yost, W. A. (2000). *Fundamentals of hearing: An introduction* (4th ed.). San Diego: Academic Press.

There are many excellent books on hearing. I can especially recommend these two for their thoroughness and accuracy.

Matlin, M., & Foley, H. J. (1997). *Sensation and perception* (4th ed.). Boston: Allyn and Bacon.

Sekuler, R., & Blake, R. (2002). *Perception* (4th ed.). Boston: McGraw-Hill.

Both of these books provide good introductions to the functions of the sensory systems. The book by Matlin and Foley has an excellent chapter on taste, with many applications for food and beverage tasting.

# 6

# Perception

# CHAPTER OUTLINE

Visual perception is a rapid, automatic, unconscious process. We experience the results of this process, not its steps. The function of visual perception is to guide our action. This guidance can occur immediately, or it can provide us with memories that we can use much later.

## Brain Mechanisms of Visual Perception

The Primary Visual Cortex • The Visual Association Cortex

The visual system of the brain is arranged hierarchically. Information is analyzed at each level, and the results are passed on to the next level for further analysis. The primary visual cortex contains a "map" of the retina and, hence, of the visual field. Visual images are broken down into small pieces, each analyzed by clusters of neurons that provide information about such features as lines, edges, and colours. Particular regions of the first level of the visual association cortex are responsible for the analysis of details of shape, colour, location, and movement. The visual cortex consists of the primary visual cortex and the visual association cortex. The visual association cortex consists of two streams. The ventral stream is involved with the visual perception of objects and colours. The dorsal streram is involved in perception of space; in guiding our reaching, grasping, and manipulating; and in the perception of motion.

## Visual Perception of Objects

Figure and Ground • Gestalt Laws of Perceptual Organization • Models of Pattern Perception • Bottom-Up and Top-Down Processing: The Role of Context • Perceptual ("What") and Action ("Where") Systems: A Possible Synthesis • *Then and Now: Language and Perception*

The Gestalt organizational laws of proximity, similarity, good continuation, closure, and common fate describe how the grouping of elements of the visual scene help us distinguish between figure and ground—objects and their backgrounds. Psychologists have proposed several models—templates, prototypes, and distinctive features—to explain how we can recognize particular patterns of visual stimuli and thus identify particular objects. The fact that we can recognize complex objects such as faces as quickly as we can recognize simple geometric shapes suggests that the visual system performs many tasks at the same time. Bottom-up processing assembles a complex perception from simple elements provided by clusters of neurons in the primary visual cortex. Top-down processing refers to the powerful effect that context can have on the interpretation of the information about these simple elements. Top-down information may be provided by a system of object perception that is distinct from a system that guides controlled movement.

## Visual Perception of Space and Motion

Depth Perception • Constancies of Visual Perception • Perception of Motion

Although perceiving the shapes of objects is an important task, we must also perceive their locations in space and their movements for our own behaviour to be effective. Depth perception is accomplished by both binocular and monocular cues. When there are changes in the brightness of the light that illuminates an object or when an object rotates or its distance from us changes, our perception of the object remains relatively constant. The perception of motion enables us to predict the future locations of objects. We can perceive shapes of objects even when we have only scanty information about the movements of their parts. We can also perceive non-existent movement when two objects are alternately illuminated.

PROLOGUE

## Believing That You Don't See

Dr. L., a young neuropsychologist, was presenting the case of Mrs. R. to a group of medical students doing a rotation in the neurology department at the medical centre. The chief of the department had shown them Mrs. R.'s CT scans, and now Dr. L. was addressing the students. He told them that Mrs. R.'s stroke had not impaired her ability to talk or to move about, but it had affected her vision.

A nurse ushered Mrs. R. into the room and helped her find a seat at the end of the table.

"How are you, Mrs. R.?" asked Dr. L.

"I'm fine. I've been home for a month now, and I can do just about everything that I did before I had my stroke."

"Good. How is your vision?"

"Well, I'm afraid that's still a problem."

"What seems to give you the most trouble?"

"I just don't seem to be able to recognize things. When I'm working in my kitchen, I know what everything is as long as no one moves anything. A few times my husband tried to help me by putting things away, and I couldn't see them anymore." She laughed. "Well, I could see them, but I just couldn't say what they were."

Dr. L. took some objects out of a paper bag and placed them on the table in front of her.

"Can you tell me what these are?" he asked. "No," he said, "please don't touch them."

Mrs. R. stared intently at the objects. "No, I can't rightly say what they are."

Dr. L. pointed to one of them, a wristwatch. "Tell me what you see here," he said.

Mrs. R. looked thoughtful, turning her head one way and then the other. "Well, I see something round, and it has two things attached to it, one on the top and one on the bottom." She continued to stare at it. "There are some things inside the circle, I think, but I can't make out what they are."

"Pick it up."

She did so, made a wry face, and said, "Oh. It's a wristwatch." At Dr. L.'s request, she picked up the rest of the objects, one by one, and identified each of them correctly.

"Do you have trouble recognizing people, too?" asked Dr. L.

"Oh, yes!" she sighed. "While I was still in the hospital, my husband and my son both came in to see me, and I couldn't tell who was who until my husband said something—then I could tell which direction his voice was coming from. Now I've trained myself to recognize my husband. I can usually see his glasses and his bald head, but I have to work at it. And I've been fooled a few times." She laughed. "One of our neighbours is bald and wears glasses, too, and one day when he and his wife were visiting us, I thought he was my husband, so I called him 'honey.' It was a little embarrassing at first, but everyone understood."

"What does a face look like to you?" asked Dr. L.

"Well, I know that it's a face, because I can usually see the eyes, and it's on top of a body. I can see a body pretty well, by how it moves." She paused a moment. "Oh, yes, I forgot, sometimes I can recognize a person by how he moves. You know, you can often recognize friends by the way they walk, even when they're far away. I can still do that. That's funny, isn't it? I can't see people's faces very well, but I can recognize the way they walk."

Dr. L. made some movements with his hands. "Can you tell what I'm doing?" he asked.

"Yes, you're mixing something—like some cake batter."

He mimed the gestures of turning a key, writing, and dealing out playing cards, and Mrs. R. recognized them without any difficulty.

"Do you have any trouble reading?" he asked.

"Well, a little, but I don't do too badly."

Dr. L. handed her a magazine, and she began to read the article aloud—somewhat hesitantly, but accurately. "Why is it," she asked, "that I can see the words all right but have so much trouble with things and with people's faces?"

The primary function of the sense organs is to provide information to guide behaviour. But the sensory mechanisms cannot achieve this function by themselves. Consider, for example, our vision. The brain receives fragments of information from approximately 1 million axons in each of the optic nerves. It combines and organizes these fragments into the perception of a scene—objects having different forms, colours, and textures, residing at different locations in three-dimensional space. Even when our bodies or our eyes move, exposing the photoreceptors to entirely new patterns of visual information, our perception of the scene before us does not change. We see a stable world, not a moving one, because the brain keeps track of our own movements and those of our eyes and compensates for the constantly changing patterns of neural firing that these movements cause.

Because vision is so important to humans, it has received the most attention from psychologists and we know the most about it. However, similar considerations apply to the other senses. When we hear someone talking, we locate that person using the sensations discussed in Chapter 5. But moving our head, or changing our own position, doesn't alter our knowledge of the speaker's location, despite the change in sensation. **Perception** is the process by which we recognize what is represented by the information provided by our sense organs. This process gives unity and coherence to this input.

Perception is a rapid, automatic, unconscious process; it is not a deliberate, effortful activity in which we puzzle out the meaning of what we see. We do not first see an object and then perceive it; we simply perceive the object. Although occasionally what we see is ambiguous, requiring us to reflect on what it might be or gather further evidence to decide what it is, this situation is more problem solving than perception. If we look at a scene carefully, we can describe the elements of the objects that are present, but we do not necessarily become aware of the elements before we perceive the objects and the background of which they are a part. For example, if you look at a tall, cylindrical object on a countertop, you immediately perceive a glass and subsequently perceive the smudges near its top, the lettering on its side, and the few sips of beverage remaining at its bottom. Also note that our awareness of the process of visual perception comes only after it is complete; we are presented with a finished product, not the details of the process.

The distinction between sensation and perception is not easy to make. For some sensory systems, such as pain and our vestibular sense, the distinction is arbitrary, since they help us to react rather than to provide a representation of the world around us. Probably because of the importance we give to vision and because of the richness of the information provided by our visual system, psychologists make a more explicit distinction between visual sensation and perception than they do for any other sensory system. Hence, this chapter will focus primarily on visual perception. We will examine the most important task of auditory perception—recognizing spoken words—in Chapter 10.

## Brain Mechanisms of Visual Perception

Visual perception by the brain is often described as a hierarchy of information processing. According to this scheme, circuits of neurons analyze particular aspects of visual information and send the results of their analysis to another circuit, which performs further analysis. At each step in the process, successively more complex features are analyzed. Eventually, the process leads to perception of the scene and all objects in it. The higher levels of the perceptual process interact with memories: The viewer recognizes familiar objects and learns the appearance of new, unfamiliar ones.

**perception** A rapid, automatic, unconscious process by which we recognize what is represented by the information provided by our sense organs.

## The Primary Visual Cortex

Our knowledge of the earliest stages of visual analysis has come from investigations of the activity of individual neurons in the thalamus and the primary visual cortex. For example, in their pioneering studies, Nobel Prize laureates David Hubel and Torsten Wiesel inserted microelectrodes—extremely small wires with microscopically sharp points—into various regions of the visual systems of cats and monkeys to detect the action potentials produced by individual neurons (Hubel & Wiesel, 1977, 1979, 2004). The signals picked up by the microelectrodes are electronically amplified and sent to a recording device for later analysis.

After positioning a microelectrode close to a neuron, Hubel and Wiesel presented various stimuli on a large screen in front of the open-eyed but anaesthetized animal. The anaesthesia makes the animal unconscious but does not prevent neurons in the visual system from responding. The researchers moved a stimulus around on the screen until they located the point where it had the largest effect on the electrical activity of the neuron. Next, they presented stimuli of various shapes to learn which ones produced the greatest response from the neuron.

Hubel and Wiesel concluded that the geography of the visual field is retained in the primary visual cortex (refer to Figure 4.25 on page 114). That is, the surface of the retina is "mapped" on the surface of the primary visual cortex. However, this map on the brain is distorted, with the largest amount of area given to the centre of the visual field, where our vision is most precise. The map is actually like a mosaic—a picture made of individual tiles or pieces of glass. Each "tile" or, in neural terms, **module** consists of a block of tissue approximately 0.5 × 0.7 mm in size and containing approximately 150 000 neurons. All of the neurons within a module receive information from the same small region of the retina. The primary visual cortex contains approximately 2500 of these modules.

Because each module in the primary visual cortex receives information from a small region of one retina, this means it receives information from a small region of the visual field—the scene that is currently projected onto the retina. Hubel and Wiesel found that neural circuits within each module analyzed various characteristics of their own particular part of the visual field—that is, of their **receptive field**. For example, some circuits detected the presence of lines passing through the field and signalled the orientation of these lines (that is, the angle they made with respect to the horizon). Other circuits detected the width of these lines. Others detected the movement of the lines and the direction of these movements. Still others detected the lines' colours.

**Figure 6•1** shows a recording of the responses of an orientation-sensitive neuron in the primary visual cortex. This neuron is located in a cluster of neurons that receive information from a small portion of the visual field. (That is, the neuron has a small receptive field.) The neuron responds maximally when a line oriented at 50 degrees to the vertical is placed in this location, especially when the line is moving through the receptive field. This response is highly specific to orientation; the neuron responds very little when a line having a 70-degree or 30-degree orientation is passed through the receptive field. Other neurons in this cluster share the same receptive field but respond to lines of different orientations. Thus, the orientation of lines that pass through this receptive field is signalled by an increased rate of firing of particular neurons in the cluster.

## The Visual Association Cortex

Although the primary visual cortex is necessary for visual perception, the perception of objects and of the totality of the visual scene does not take place there. If you closed one eye and looked at the scene in front of you through a drinking straw, you would see about the same amount of information received by an individual module of the primary visual cortex. Thus, for us to perceive objects and entire visual scenes, the information from these individual modules must be combined. That combination takes place in the visual association cortex.

**Two Streams of Visual Analysis** Visual information analyzed by the primary visual cortex is further analyzed in the visual association cortex. So far, investigators have identified more than two dozen distinct regions and sub-regions of the visual cortex of the rhesus monkey. These regions are arranged hierarchically, beginning with the primary visual cortex (Grill-Spector & Malach, 2004). Circuits of neurons analyze particular aspects of visual information and send the results of their analysis to other circuits, which perform further analysis. At each step in the process, successively more complex features are analyzed. Remarkably, within a matter of milliseconds, the process leads to the perception of the scene and the objects in it. The higher levels of the perceptual process also interact with memories. The viewer recognizes familiar objects and learns to recognize new, unfamiliar ones.

Neurons in the primary visual cortex send axons to the region of the visual association cortex that surrounds the striate cortex. At this point, the visual association cortex divides into two pathways: the **ventral stream** and the **dorsal stream** (Ungerleider & Mishkin, 1982). The ventral stream continues forward and ends in the inferior temporal cortex. The dorsal

**module** A block of cortical tissue that receives information from the same group of receptor cells.

**receptive field** That portion of the visual field in which the presentation of visual stimuli will produce an alternation in the firing rate of a particular neuron.

**ventral stream** The flow of information from the primary visual cortex to the visual association area in the lower temporal lobe; used to form the perception of an object's shape, colour, and orientation (the "what" system).

**dorsal stream** The flow of information from the primary visual cortex to the visual association area in the parietal lobe; used to form the perception of an object's location in three-dimensional space (the "where" system).

**FIGURE 6•1** Responses of a single neuron to lines of particular orientations that are passed through its receptive field.

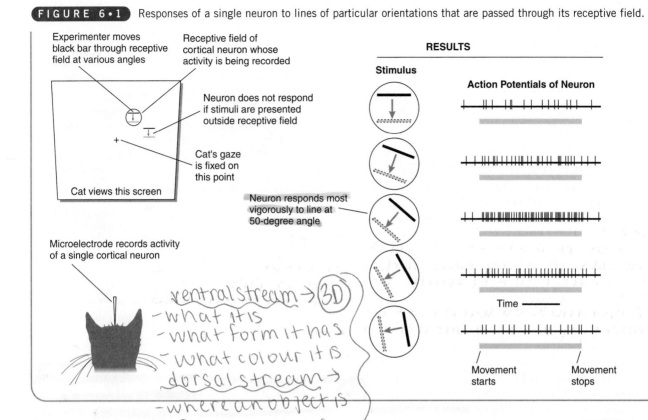

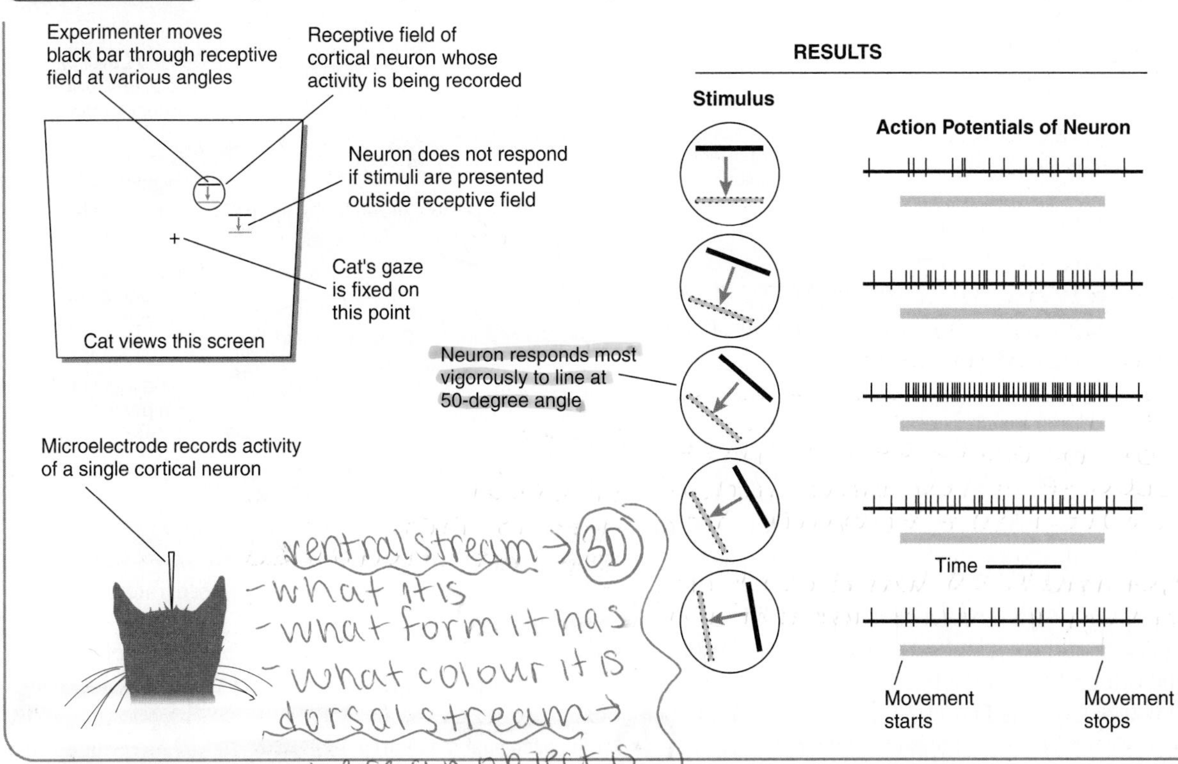
Experimenter moves black bar through receptive field at various angles
Receptive field of cortical neuron whose activity is being recorded
Neuron does not respond if stimuli are presented outside receptive field
Cat's gaze is fixed on this point
Cat views this screen
Neuron responds most vigorously to line at 50-degree angle
Microelectrode records activity of a single cortical neuron
RESULTS
Stimulus
Action Potentials of Neuron
Time
Movement starts
Movement stops

stream ascends into the posterior parietal cortex. The ventral stream functions in the recognition of *what* an object is—that is, what *form* it has, as well as what *colour* it is. The dorsal stream identifies *where* an object is located and whether it is *moving*. (See **Figure 6•2**.)

**The Ventral Stream: Perception of Form** Studies with laboratory animals have found that the recognition of visual patterns and identification of particular objects takes place in the inferior temporal cortex, located at the end of the ventral stream. It is there that analyses of form and colour are put together and perceptions of three-dimensional objects emerge.

Functional-imaging studies and the study of people with damage to the visual association cortex confirm the conclusions of animal studies. Brain damage can cause a category of deficits known as **visual agnosia**. *Agnosia* ("failure to know") refers to an inability to perceive or identify a stimulus that exists within a specific sensory modality. The inability occurs even though the person can perceive the details of the stimulus and otherwise retains relatively normal intellectual capacity. Mrs. R., whose case was described in this chapter's prologue, had visual agnosia. She could not identify common objects by sight, even though she had relatively normal visual acuity. When she was permitted to hold an object that she could not recognize visually, she could immediately recognize it by touch and say what it was. Clearly she had not lost her memory of the object or simply forgotten how to say its name.

A common symptom of visual agnosia is **prosopagnosis**, the inability to recognize particular faces (*prosopon* is Greek for "face"). That is, patients with this disorder can recognize that they are looking at a face, but they cannot say whose face it is—even if it belongs to a relative or close friend. They see eyes, ears, a nose, a mouth, but they cannot recognize the particular configuration of these features that identifies a specific individual's face. They still remember who these people are and will usually recognize them when they hear their voices.

Studies with brain-damaged people and functional imaging studies indicate that face-recognizing circuits are found in the **fusiform face area (FFA)**, a region of the ventral stream located at the base of the brain.

Several kinds of evidence suggest that face-recognition circuits develop as a result of experience with seeing people's faces. For example, brain lesions that produce prosopagnosia can also impair the ability of a farmer to recognize his cows or the ability of a driver to recognize her own car except by reading its licence plate (Bornstein, Sroka, & Munitz, 1969; Damasio, Damasio, & Van Hoesen, 1982). In other words, the failure of recognition is not confined to faces. Two functional

**visual agnosia** The inability of a person who is not blind to recognize the identity of an object visually; caused by damage to the visual association cortex.

**prosopagnosia** A form of visual agnosia characterized by difficulty in the recognition of people's faces; caused by damage to the visual association cortex.

**fusiform face area (FFA)** A region of the ventral stream of the visual system that contains face-recognizing circuits.

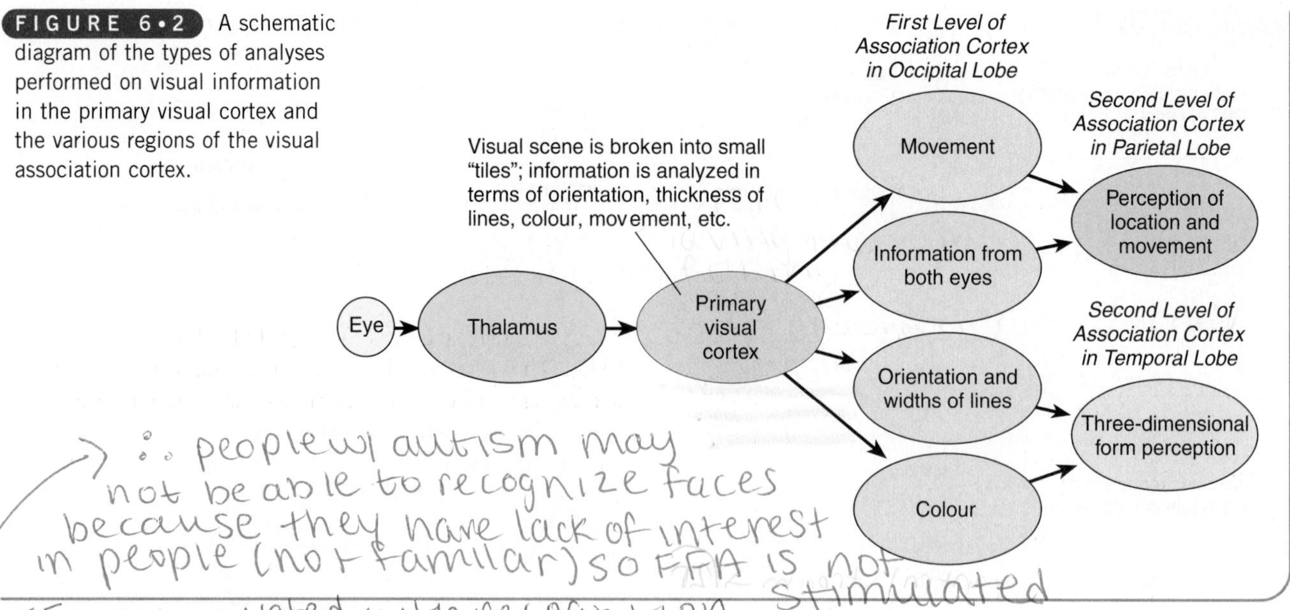


**FIGURE 6•2** A schematic diagram of the types of analyses performed on visual information in the primary visual cortex and the various regions of the visual association cortex.

imaging studies (Gauthier, Skudlarski, Gore, & Anderson, 2000; Xu, 2005) found that when bird or car experts viewed pictures of birds or cars, the FFA was activated. This did not occur when non-experts viewed the same pictures. Thus, Tarr and Gauthier (2000) suggested that the FFA be relabelled as the *flexible* fusiform area, given its participation in the visual recognition of diverse objects.

As we will see in Chapter 17, people with autistic disorder fail to develop normal social relations. In severe cases, they give no indication that other people exist. Grelotti, Gauthier, and Schultz (2002) found that people with autistic disorder showed a deficit in the ability to recognize faces and that looking at faces failed to activate the FFA. They speculated that other brain abnormalities associated with autistic disorder may result in a lack of interest in other people and consequently in the failure to acquire face recognition during childhood, as normally would occur.

Functional-imaging studies have revealed several additional regions of the ventral stream that respond differently to particular categories of visual stimuli. For example, a region next to the primary visual cortex, the **extrastriate body area (EBA)**, is specifically activated by photographs, silhouettes, or stick figures of human bodies or body parts and not by control stimuli such as photographs or drawings of tools, scrambled silhouettes, or scrambled stick drawings of bodies (Downing, Jiang, Shuman, & Kanwisher, 2001). Urgesi, Berlucchi, and Aglioti (2004) found that when the EBA was temporarily inactivated by transcranial magnetic stimulation, people lost the ability to recognize photographs of body parts but not parts of faces or motorcycles. A separate region of the ventral stream located below the hippocampus, the **parahippocampal place area (PPA)**, is activated by visual scenes (collections of several objects) and backgrounds. Steeves and colleagues (2004) reported the case of a woman with bilateral damage to the ventral stream that resulted in profound visual agnosia for objects. Functional imaging showed that her PPA was undamaged. She was still able to recognize both natural and human-made scenes such as beaches, forests, deserts, cities, markets, and rooms. However, she was unable to recognize the specific objects that belonged to these scenes.

**The Ventral Stream: Perception of Colour** Laboratory research has shown that individual neurons in a region of the ventral stream respond to particular colours, which suggests that this region is involved in combining the information from red/green and yellow/blue signals that originate in retinal ganglion cells (see Chapter 5). In fact, Heywood, Gaffan, and Cowey (1995) found that damage to this region disrupted the ability of monkeys to distinguish different colours. The animals could still distinguish between different shades of grey, so the deficit was not caused by a more general impairment of visual perception.

Lesions of a particular region of the human ventral stream can also cause loss of colour vision without disrupting visual acuity. The patients describe their vision as resembling a black-and-white film (Damasio et al., 1980; Heywood & Kentridge, 2003). The condition is known as **cerebral achromatopsia** (ey-krow-muh-TOP-see-uh, which means "vision without colour"). If the brain damage occurs on only one side of the brain, people will lose their colour vision in only half of the visual field (see **Figure 6•3**). If the damage is bilateral, they lose all colour vision and cannot even imagine colours or remember the colours of objects they saw before their brain damage occurred.

**extrastriate body area (EBA)** A region of the occipital cortex, next to the primary visual cortex, that responds to forms resembling the human body.
**parahippocampal place area (PPA)** A region of the ventral stream, below the hippocampus, that is activated by visual scenes.
**cerebral achromatopsia** The inability to discriminate among different hues; caused by damage to the visual association cortex.

**FIGURE 6•4** A drawing in which figure and ground can be reversed. You can see either two faces against a white background or a goblet against a dark background.

**FIGURE 6•6** Illusory contours. Even when boundaries are not present, we can be fooled into seeing them. The triangle with its point down looks brighter than the surrounding area.

front of them. Psychologists use the terms **figure** and **ground** to label an object and its background, respectively. The classification of an item as a figure or as a part of the background is not an intrinsic property of the item. Rather, it depends on the behaviour of the observer. If you are watching some birds fly overhead, they are figures, and the blue sky and the clouds behind them are part of the background. If, instead, you are watching the clouds move, then the birds become background. If you are looking at a picture hanging on a wall, it is an object. If you are looking at a person standing between you and the wall, the picture is part of the background. Sometimes, we receive ambiguous clues about what is object and what is background. For example, does **Figure 6•4** illustrate two faces or a wine goblet?

What are the characteristics of the complex patterns of light—varying in brightness, saturation, and hue—that give rise to perceptions of figures, of *things?* One of the most important aspects of form perception is the existence of a *boundary*. If the visual field contains a sharp and distinct change in brightness, colour, or texture, we perceive an edge. If this edge forms a continuous boundary, we will probably perceive the space enclosed by the boundary as a figure. (See **Figure 6•5**.)

## Gestalt Laws of Perceptual Organization

Although most figures are defined by a boundary, the presence of a boundary is not necessary for the perception of form. **Figure 6•6** demonstrates *illusory contours*—lines that do not exist. In this figure, the orientation of the pie-shaped objects and the three 45-degree segments make us perceive two triangles, one on top of the other. The one that looks like it is superimposed on the three green circles even appears to be brighter than the background.

Early in the twentieth century, a group of psychologists developed a theory of perception based on our tendency to organize elements and empty spaces into cohesive forms (see Hothersall, 2004). They called their movement **Gestalt psychology** (*Gestalt* is the German word for "form") and

**figure** A visual stimulus that is perceived as a self-contained object.
**ground** A visual stimulus that is perceived as a formless background against which objects are seen.
**Gestalt psychology** A branch of psychology that asserts that the perception of objects is produced by particular configurations of the elements of stimuli.

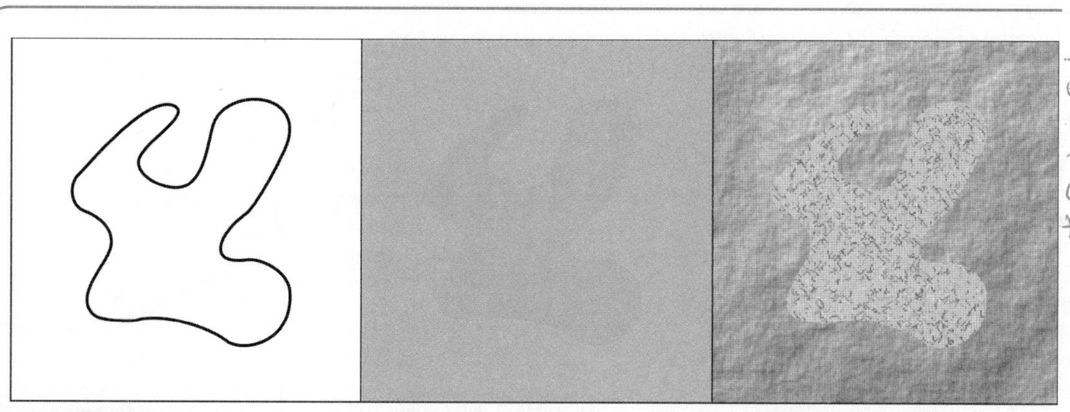

**FIGURE 6•5** Form perception and boundaries. We immediately perceive even an unfamiliar figure when its outline is closed.

**FIGURE 6•7** The Gestalt principle of proximity. Different spacing of the dots produces five vertical or five horizontal lines.

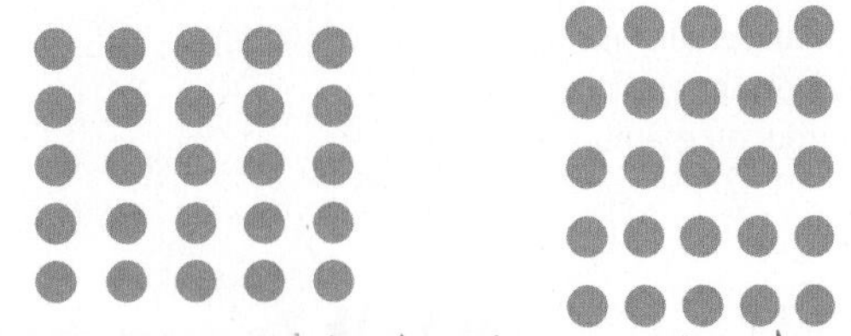

**FIGURE 6•8** The Gestalt principle of similarity. Similar elements are perceived as belonging to the same form.

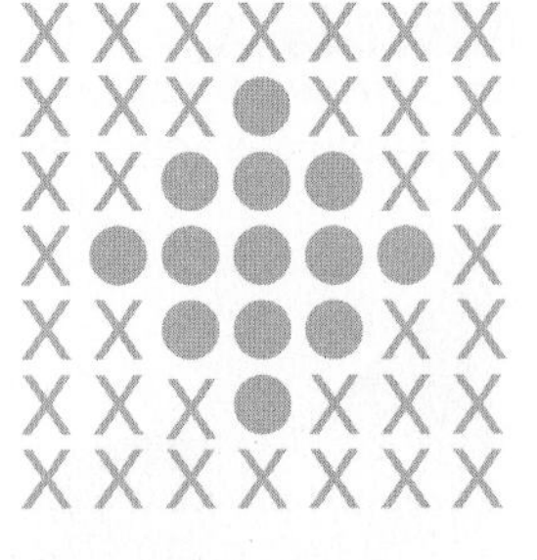

maintained that the task of perception was to recognize objects in the environment according to the organization of their elements. They argued that in perception the whole is more than the sum of its parts. Because of the characteristics of the visual system of the brain, visual perception cannot be understood simply by analyzing the scene into its elements. Instead, what we see depends on the *relationships* of these elements to one another.

The components of a visual scene can combine in various ways to produce different forms. Gestalt psychologists have observed that several principles of grouping can predict the combination of these elements. The fact that our visual system groups and combines elements is useful because we can then perceive forms even if they are fuzzy and incomplete. The real world presents us with objects partly obscured by other objects and with backgrounds that are the same colour as parts of the objects in front of them. The outlines of objects are very often not distinct. As I look out the window of my office, I see a large bush against a background of trees. It is summer, and I see countless shades of green in the scene before me. I cannot distinguish the bush from the trees behind it simply by differences in colour. However, I can clearly see the outline of the bush because of subtle differences in its texture (the leaves are smaller than those of the tree) and because the wind causes its branches to move in a pattern different from that of the tree branches. The laws of grouping discovered by Gestalt psychologists describe my ability to distinguish this figure from its background.

The **law of proximity** states that elements that are closest together will be perceived as belonging together. **Figure 6•7** demonstrates this principle. The pattern on the left looks like five vertical columns because the dots are closer to their neighbours above and below them than to those located to the right and to the left. The pattern on the right looks like five horizontal rows.

The **law of similarity** states that elements that look similar will be perceived as part of the same form. We can easily see the diamond inside the square in **Figure 6•8**.

**Good continuation** refers to predictability or simplicity. Which of the two sets of coloured dots best describes the continuation of the line of black dots in **Figure 6•9**? If you see the figure the way I do, you will choose the coloured dots that continue the curve down and to the right. It is simpler to perceive the line as following a smooth course than as suddenly making a sharp bend.

Often, one object partially hides another, but we nevertheless perceive the incomplete image. The **law of closure** states that our visual system often supplies missing information and "closes" the outline of an incomplete figure. For example, **Figure 6•10** looks a bit like a triangle, but if you place a pencil on the page so that it covers the gaps, the figure undeniably looks like a triangle. (Try it.)

The final Gestalt law of organization relies on movement. The **law of common fate** states that elements that move in the same direction will be perceived as belonging together and forming a figure. In the forest, an animal is camouflaged if its surface is covered with the same elements found in the background—spots of brown, tan, and green—because its boundary is obscured. There is no basis for grouping the

**law of proximity** A Gestalt law of organization; elements located closest to each other are perceived as belonging to the same figure.

**law of similarity** A Gestalt law of organization; similar elements are perceived as belonging to the same figure.

**good continuation** A Gestalt law of organization; given two or more interpretations of elements that form the outline of the figure, the simplest interpretation will be preferred.

**law of closure** A Gestalt law of organization; elements missing from the outline of a figure are "filled in" by the visual system.

**law of common fate** A Gestalt law of organization; elements that move together give rise to the perception of a particular figure.

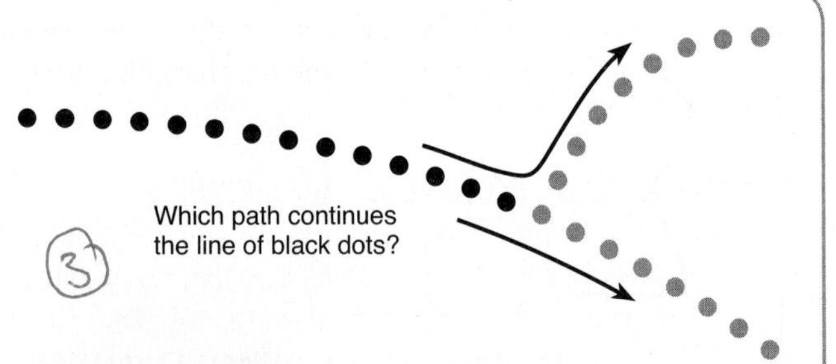
Which path continues
the line of black dots?

**FIGURE 6•9** The Gestalt principle of good continuation. It is easier to perceive a smooth continuation than an abrupt shift.

**FIGURE 6•10** The Gestalt principle of closure. We tend to supply missing information to close a figure and separate it from its background. Lay a pencil across the gaps and see how strong the perception of a complete triangle becomes.

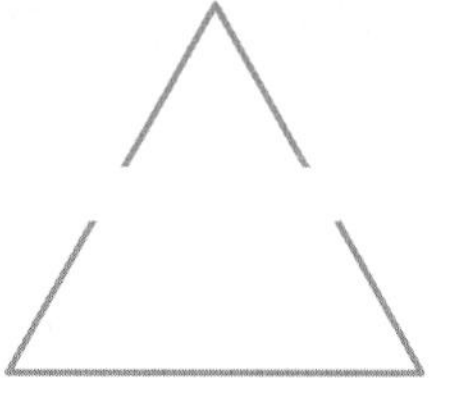

elements on the animal. As long as the animal is stationary, it remains well hidden. However, once it moves, the elements on its surface will move together, and the animal's form will quickly be perceived. The ability to distinguish figure from ground on the basis of motion seems to develop at a different rate from some of the other cues we have looked at, suggesting that motion-defined segregation may have different pathways in the human visual system (Giaschi & Regan, 1997).

Alais, Blake, and Lee (1998) have found that the principle of common fate applies to changes other than movement. Visual objects stand out from their background to the extent that they exhibit contrasts in colour or brightness. Alais and colleagues showed people several groups of lines and rapidly changed the contrast between the lines and their backgrounds. When this temporal variation in contrast was the same across different groups of lines, the different groups were perceived as being together. The researchers described this "common tempo" effect as a variation on the law of common fate.

And how did I distinguish the bush from the trees in my forest example? You will recall that the primary cues were differences in leaf size and in the movement induced by the wind, examples of similarity and common fate, respectively.

▲ *The template model for pattern recognition seems inadequate for explaining how we can recognize a human hand, in its many sizes, colours, and positions.*

## Models of Pattern Perception

Stimulus objects large and small can come together simultaneously or in a sequence and be perceived as a pattern. Cognitive psychologists interested in the cognitive processes responsible for perception attempt to identify and analyze the steps that take place between the time a person's eye is exposed to objects and the time when a pattern is perceived (Peterson, 2005). They collect behavioural data and try to make inferences about the nature of these intervening processes. Let's look at some of the models that cognitive psychologists have proposed.

**Templates and Prototypes** Our ability to recognize shapes of objects might be explained by our use of **templates**, which are special kinds of memories used by the visual system. A template is a type of pattern used to manufacture a series of objects. For example, a cookie cutter is a template used to cut out identical shapes from a flat piece of dough. Perhaps the visual system reverses the process; when a particular pattern of visual stimulation is encountered, our visual system searches through its set of templates and compares each of them with the pattern provided by the stimulus. If it finds a match, it knows that the pattern is a familiar one. Connections between the appropriate template and memories in other parts of the brain could provide the name of the object and other information about it, such as its function, when it was seen before, and so forth.

The template model of pattern recognition has the virtue of simplicity. However, most psychologists do not believe that it could actually work—the visual system would have to store an unreasonably large number of templates.

A more feasible model of pattern perception suggests that patterns of visual stimulation are compared with prototypes rather than templates. **Prototypes** (Greek for "original model") are idealized patterns of a particular shape; they resemble templates but are used in a much more flexible way. The visual system does not look for exact matches between the pattern being perceived and the memories of shapes of objects but accepts a degree of disparity; for instance, it accepts the various patterns produced when we look at a particular object from different viewpoints.

**template** A hypothetical pattern that resides in the nervous system and is used to perceive objects or shapes by a process of comparison.

**prototype** A hypothetical idealized pattern that resides in the nervous system and is used to perceive objects or shapes by a process of comparison; recognition can occur even when an exact match is not found.

▲ *We can recognize particular objects as well as general categories of objects.*

Most psychologists believe that pattern recognition by the visual system does involve prototypes, at least in some form. For example, you can undoubtedly identify maple trees, fir trees, and palm trees when you see them. In nature, each tree looks different from all others, but maples resemble other maples more than they resemble firs, and so on. A reasonable assumption is that your visual system has memories of the prototypical visual patterns that represent these objects. Recognizing particular types of trees, then, is a matter of finding the best fit between stimulus and prototype.

The visual system of the brain may indeed contain generic prototypes that help us recognize objects we have never seen before: coffee cups, maple trees, human faces. But we do more than recognize categories of objects; we can recognize *particular* coffee cups, maple trees, or human faces. In fact, we can learn to recognize enormous numbers of objects. Think of how many different people you can recognize by sight, how many buildings in your town you can recognize, how many pieces of furniture in your house and in your friends' houses you are familiar with—the list will be very long.

I strongly suspect that many objects have to be represented by more than one prototype, such as profile and frontal views of a face. Perhaps there are even various levels of prototypes: generic ones such as maples or human faces and more specific ones such as the tree in your backyard or the face of a friend. In fact, evidence from studies of nonhuman primates suggests that familiarity with categories of objects may lead to the development of specific types of prototypes (Humphrey, 1974).

**FIGURE 6•11** Distinctive features. We easily recognize all of these items as the letter *N*.

**Distinctive Features** How complete does the information in a prototype have to be? Does a prototype have to contain a detailed representation of an image of the object it represents, or can the information be represented in some shorthand way? Some psychologists suggest that the visual system encodes images of familiar patterns in terms of **distinctive features**—collections of important physical features that specify particular items. For example, **Figure 6•11** contains several examples of the letter *N*. Although the examples vary in size and style, you have no trouble recognizing them. How do you do so? Perhaps your visual system contains a specification of the distinctive features that fit the criterion for an *N*: two parallel vertical lines connected by a diagonal line sloping downward from the top of the left one to the bottom of the right one.

A classic experiment by Neisser (1964) supports the hypothesis that perception involves analysis of distinctive features. Figure 6.12 shows one of the tasks he asked people to do. The figure shows two columns of letters. Scan through them until you find the letter *Z*, which occurs once in each column. (See **Figure 6•12**.)

Chances are good that you found the letter in the left column much faster than you did the one in the right column, just as the individuals in Neisser's study did. Perhaps you guessed why: The letters in the left column have few features in common with those found in the letter *Z*, so the *Z* stands out from the others. In contrast, the letters in the right column have many features in common with the target letter, and thus the *Z* is camouflaged, so to speak.

Some phenomena cannot easily be explained by the distinctive-features model. The model suggests that the perception of an object consists of analysis and synthesis; the visual system first identifies the component features of an object and then adds up the features to determine what the object is. We might expect, then, that more complex objects, having more distinctive features, would take longer to perceive. But often, the addition of more features, in the form of

**distinctive feature** A physical characteristic of an object that helps distinguish it from other objects.

**FIGURE 6•12** A letter-search task. Look for the letter *Z* hidden in each column.
*(Adapted from Neisser, U. (1964).* Scientific American, 210, *94–102.)*

| GDOROC | IVEMXW |
|---|---|
| COQUCD | XVIWME |
| DUCOQG | VEMIXW |
| GRUDQO | WEXMVI |
| OCDURQ | XIMVWE |
| DUCGRO | IVMWEX |
| ODUCQG | VWEMXI |
| CQOGRD | IMEWXV |
| DUZORQ | EXMZWI |
| UCGROD | IEMWVX |
| QCUDOG | EIVXWM |
| RQGUDO | WXEMIV |
| DRGOQC | MIWVXE |
| OQGDRU | IMEVXW |
| UGCODQ | IEMWVX |
| ODRUCQ | IMWVEX |
| UDQRGC | XWMVEI |
| ORGCUD | IWEVXM |
| QOGRUC | VMIWEX |

contextual cues, *speeds up* the process of perception. The tendency for some stimuli to "pop out" during visual search of a larger display has proven to be very informative for identifying cases where perception does not seem to involve a strict search of features. Enns and Rensink (1991) found that orientation of wire-frame objects like those in **Figure 6•13** was quickly detected in a search. If the vertices of the drawing were not connected, however, the implicit orientation was much more difficult to detect. Pilon and Friedman (1998) similarly found that misaligned vertices were difficult to detect when wire-frame models were not connected. Presumably, closing the figures provided sufficient organization to make orientation more immediately perceptible, despite the additional features.

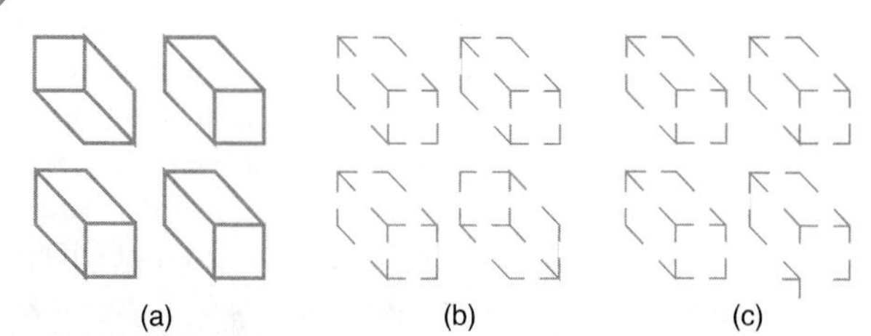


**FIGURE 6•13** Wire-frame figures similar to those used by Enns and Rensink (1991) and Pilon and Friedman (1998). Panel (a) depicts the wire-frame figures with connected vertices; panel (b) depicts figures with unconnected vertices. Pilon and Friedman used figures like those depicted in panel (c), in which the individual vertices of figures in panel (b) were individually rotated and misaligned with the rest of the figure.
*(Redrawn from Enns and Rensink (1991) and Pilon and Friedman (1998). Copyright 1998. Canadian Psychological Association. Reprinted with permission.)*

**FIGURE 6•14** Simple elements that are difficult to recognize without a context.

## Bottom-Up and Top-Down Processing: The Role of Context

We often must perceive objects under conditions that are less than optimal: the object is in a shadow, camouflaged against a similar background, or obscured by fog. Nevertheless, we usually manage to recognize the item correctly. We are often helped in our endeavour by the context in which we see the object. For example, look at the four items in **Figure 6•14**. Can you tell what they represent? Now, look at **Figure 6•16**. With the aid of a context, the items are easily recognized.

Palmer (1975) showed that even more general forms of context can aid in the perception of objects. He first showed his participants familiar scenes, such as a kitchen. (See **Figure 6•15**.) Next, he showed drawings of individual

Contextual scene

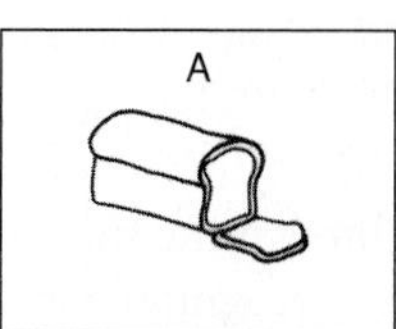


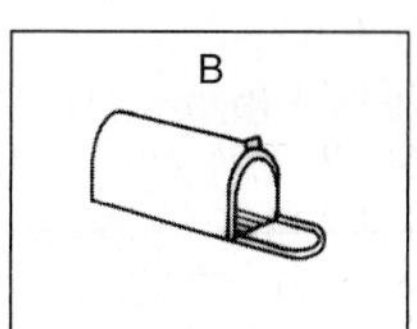


Target object (presented very briefly)

**FIGURE 6•15** Stimuli from the experiment by Palmer (1975). After looking at the contextual scene, the participants were shown one of the stimuli below it very briefly.
*(From Palmer, S. E. (1975).* Memory and cognition, 3, *519–526. Reprinted by permission of the Psychonomic Society, Inc.)*

**FIGURE 6•16** An example of top-down processing. The context facilitates our recognition of the items shown in Figure 6.14.

*(Adapted from Palmer, S. E. (1975). In D. A. Norman, D. E. Rumelhart, & the LNR Research Group (Eds.),* Explorations in cognition. *San Francisco: W. H. Freeman.)*

**FIGURE 6•17** Sample stimuli from the Wolfe, Butcher, Lee, & Hyle (2003) study that varied the relative influence of bottom-up and top-down information

*(Adapted from Wolfe, J. M., Butcher, S. J., Lee, C., & Hyle, M. (2003). Changing your mind: On the contributions of top-down and bottom-up guidance in visual search for feature singletons.* Journal of Experimental Psychology: Human Perception and Performance, 29, *483–502. Published by APA. Reprinted with permission.)*

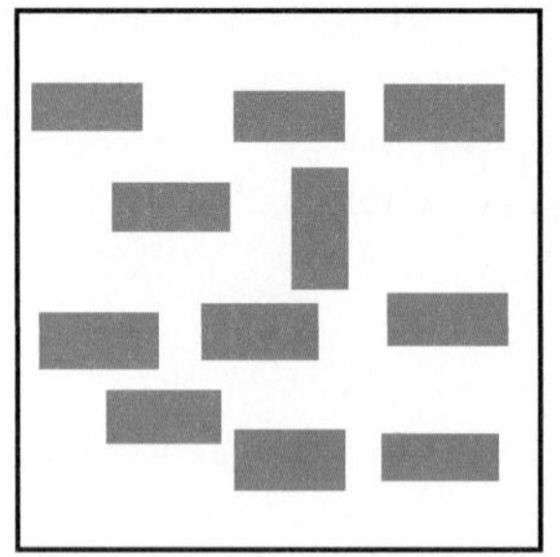

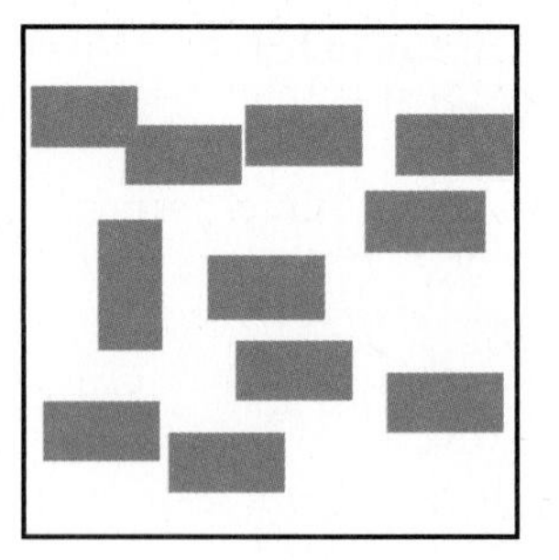

items and asked the participants to identify them. The drawings were shown very rapidly, making them difficult to identify. Sometimes, the participants saw an object that was appropriate to the scene, such as a loaf of bread. Other times, they saw an inappropriate but similarly shaped object, such as a mailbox. Palmer found that when the objects fit the context that had been set by the scene, the participants correctly identified about 84 percent of them. But when they did not, performance fell to about 50 percent. Performance was intermediate in the no-context control condition, under which participants did not first see a scene. Thus, compared with the no-context control condition, an appropriate context facilitated recognition and an inappropriate one interfered with it.

The Palmer study suggests the parallel operation of two processes: one that uses information directly available from the stimulus (the drawing of a loaf of bread) and another that uses information from memory (objects that a typical kitchen would contain). Cognitive psychologists often refer to the first process as bottom-up processing and to the second process as top-down processing. In **bottom-up processing** (also called data-driven or stimulus-driven processing), the process starts with the features—the bits and pieces—of the stimulus, beginning with the image that falls on the retina. This information is processed hierarchically by successively higher levels of the visual system until the highest levels (the "top" of the system) are reached, and the object is perceived. **Top-down processing** (also called knowledge-driven processing) involves the use of contextual information supplied from memory: the "big picture." The application of this model to Palmer's study, for example, suggests that information from memory about kitchen-specific features was sent from the "top" of the system down through lower levels. Then, when the participant saw a drawing of a loaf of bread, information about its features came up more readily through the successive levels of the bottom-up system, and recognition was faster and more accurate. In other words, information from the top (typical kitchen contents) primed the processing of information from the bottom (the loaf of bread).

The relative contribution of top-down and bottom-up processing to visual search was the focus of a series of experiments reported by Wolfe, Butcher, Lee, and Hyle (2003). In the design of their studies, the researchers sought to minimize top-down information in order to isolate the bottom-up process. In one study designed to vary the extent of top-down information available to participants, the researchers presented stimuli containing red or green lines that were arranged either vertically or horizontally. On each trial, the participant judged whether or not the stimulus met the description provided by the experimenter (the target). Feedback (right or wrong) followed each trial. In addition to recording the participant's answer, the researchers also recorded reaction time.

To separate top-down processing from bottom-up processing, Wolfe and colleagues varied the extent to which the dimensions of colour or orientation defined the target. For example, in one condition that maximized the influence of top-down information, any stimulus that contained the colour red was the target; the orientation of the lines was irrelevant. For example, in **Figure 6•17** the stimulus on the left would be correct, and the stimulus on the right incorrect. Thus, a participant could use the simple top-down rule of "always pick red when it appears" and be assured of success. On the other hand, to reduce the influence of top-down information, the experimenters introduced a condition in which the target was never consistently red, green, horizontal, or vertical. Instead it was any stimulus in which one of the lines that appeared was discrepant from all of the other lines in colour or orientation. Thus, in Figure 6.17, both of the stimuli would be correct. Now there was no simple top-down rule. The researchers argued that this allowed bottom-up influences a larger role in the participants' judgments. Consequently, average reaction time was slowest in that

**bottom-up processing** A perception based on successive analyses of the details of the stimuli that are present.

**top-down processing** A perception based on information provided by the context in which a particular stimulus is encountered.

condition. It was fastest in the condition with full top-down information.

## Perceptual ("What") and Action ("Where") Systems: A Possible Synthesis

Our discussion of form perception has brought us to a puzzle. It is clear that features play some role in our ability to identify objects, but it is less clear that theories of feature analysis can fully explain it. Top-down factors such as context exert powerful influences, but we can still ask how specific contextual states are activated.

In most cases, visual perception would seem to consist of a combination of top-down and bottom-up processing. **Figure 6•18** shows several examples of objects that can be recognized only by a combination of both forms of processing. Our knowledge of the configurations of letters in words (top-down processing) provides us with the contexts that permit us to organize (and expedite) the flow of feature information from the bottom up. However, concluding that the perception of objects requires the interaction of both types of processing still leaves unanswered the question of what that interaction is composed of. How do bottom-up and top-down processing come together to produce object recognition?

**FIGURE 6•18** Examples of combined top-down/bottom-up processing. The effect of context enables us to perceive the letters despite the missing or ambiguous features. Note that a given letter may be perceived in more than one way, depending on the letters surrounding it.
*(Adapted from McClelland, J. L., Rumelhart, D. E., & Hinton, G. E. (1986). In D. E. Rumelhart, J. L. McClelland, & the PDP Research Group (Eds.),* Parallel distributed processing. Vol. I: Foundations. *Cambridge, MA: The MIT Press. © 1986 The Massachusetts Institute of Technology.)*

Perhaps this puzzle will remain unsolved for some time. But findings from cognitive neuroscience are providing some provocative hints about where to look. For example, Goodale and Milner (2004) have described a large number of observations of a Scottish woman named "Dee" with a very unusual condition. Dee suffered an accident from carbon monoxide poisoning that left her unable to identify objects visually. Nonetheless, she is still able to reach for specific objects in a way that is behaviourally appropriate. For example, Dee would be unable to tell you whether the slot on a mailbox was oriented horizontally or vertically, but if you gave her an envelope and asked her to deposit it in the slot, her motor movements would be completely accurate. Goodale and Milner's work suggests that Dee's abilities show a strong dissociation between "vision for perception" and "vision for action." These two categories of vision are consistent with the ventral and dorsal streams in the visual association cortex that were introduced earlier in the chapter. The "what" system provides us with information about objects and their meanings and involves pathways that lead to the temporal lobe (the ventral stream). The "where" system provides us with information necessary for acting on objects with guided movement and involves pathways leading through the parietal lobe (the dorsal stream). (See Figure 6.2 on page 172.)

Dee's brain damage apparently affected her perception of objects—her "what" system—but left intact her ability to respond to the location and orientation of objects—her "where" system. The dorsal stream system provides information necessary for guiding our actions toward objects but does not provide us with the ability to recognize or name them. In fact, Dee's condition is reminiscent of that of Mrs. R. (from this chapter's prologue), who could not identify an object as a watch. However, when asked to pick it up, she did so readily, and having done so, could now say what it was. Goodale and Milner argue that visual perception involves the interplay between these two systems. The dorsal stream responds to the location and orientation of objects and coordinates the actions we take with respect to them. The ventral stream gives us information about what the objects are so that we know, for example, that it will take less effort to turn this page than it will to turn the cover of this book.

This differentiation produces some intricate differences between Dee's interaction with the world and yours. Suppose, for example, that you reach for either a screwdriver or a ruler on your workbench. Both are oblong and, as you reach for them, your wrist will orient your hand appropriately. Dee's wrist will do the same. But now, suppose that the handle of the screwdriver faces away from you. Your object identification system knows that what you reach for is a screwdriver and that a screwdriver has a "handle part." As you reach for it, you will adjust your hand so that you grab the handle—even if it means an awkward backhand grasp. This is the ability that Dee has lost. Her object perception system is no longer fully functional. As a result, her reaching does not adjust to the position of the "handle part" of the screwdriver.

## Then and Now

### Language and Perception

You've probably heard that snippet of urban myth claiming that Inuit people have many more words for "snow" than English speakers. This particular belief is linguistically silly (Martin, 1986) since it is like saying that we have many words for "car" because we can say "speeding car," "red car," and so on. Yet, this particular myth has a connection to a more legitimate idea, advanced by Benjamin Whorf, known as the **principle of linguistic relativity**. Briefly stated, this principle asserts that language used by the members of a particular culture is related to these people's thoughts and perceptions. According to Whorf (1956, p. 212), "the background linguistic system . . . of each language is not merely a reproducing instrument for voicing ideas but rather is itself a shaper of ideas, the program and guide for the individual's mental activity, for his analysis of impressions, for his synthesis of his mental stock-of-trade." In other words, perception is determined by language.

The principle of linguistic relativity has been most closely associated with the names that a language uses for colour. Proponents of linguistic relativity suggested that colour names are cultural conventions—that members of a given culture could divide the countless combinations of hue, saturation, and brightness that we call colours into any number of different categories. Each category was assigned a name, and when members of that culture looked at the world they perceived each of the colours they saw as belonging to one of these categories.

Two anthropologists tested this hypothesis (Berlin & Kay, 1969; Kay, 1975). Berlin and Kay studied a wide range of languages and found the following 11 primary colour terms: black, white, red, yellow, green, blue, brown, purple, pink, orange, and grey. (Of course, the words for these terms are different in different languages. For example, Japanese speakers say *aka*, Navahos say *lichi*, Inuit say *aupaluktak*, and English speakers say *red*.) Berlin and Kay referred to these as *focal colours*. Not all languages used all 11 terms (as English does). In fact, some languages used only two terms: black and white. If a language contained words for three primary colours, they were black, white, and red. If it contained words for six primary colours, they were black, white, red, yellow, green, and blue. (See **Figure 6•19**.) The fact that all cultures agree about what categories of colours deserve names suggests that the physiology of the visual system—and not arbitrary cultural conventions—is responsible for the selection of colour names.

**principle of linguistic relativity** The hypothesis that the language a person speaks determines his or her thoughts and perceptions.

Other evidence tends to suggest that this conclusion is correct. Heider (1971) found that both children and adults found it easier to remember a colour chip of a focal colour (such as red or blue) than one of a non-focal colour (such as turquoise or peach). Rosch (formerly Heider) studied members of the Dani culture of New Guinea. The language of the Dani people has only two basic colour terms: *mili* ("black") and *mola* ("white"). Rosch assembled two sets of colour chips, one containing focal colours and the other containing non-focal colours. She taught her participants arbitrary names that she made up for the colours. Even though the participants had no words in their language for any of the colours, the group learning names for focal colours learned the names faster and remembered them better (Heider, 1972; Rosch, 1973).

Rosch's experiments have been taken as showing little evidence that perception of colour is shaped by cultural codes. Roberson, Davies, and Davidoff (2000) have recently found more positive evidence. They compared British adults with adult speakers of Berinmo, a language spoken by a stone-age cultural group who lives in Papua New Guinea.

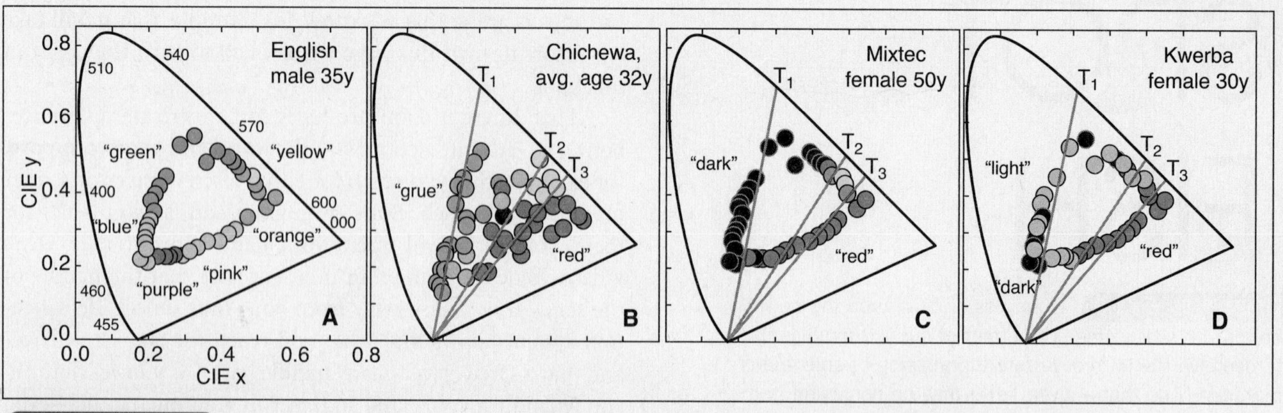


**FIGURE 6•19** Examples of colour naming in different languages: Chichewa is an African language, Mixtec is spoken in Mexico, and Kwerba is spoken in Indonesia. The term *grue* in B refers to either a green or a blue hue.

*(Lindsey, D. T., & Brown, A. M. Color naming and the phototoxic effects of sunlight on the eye.* Psychological Science, *13(6), 506–512. Copyright © 2002. Reproduced with permission of Blackwell Publishing Ltd.)*

Berinmo speakers have five basic colour terms, including *nol*, which describes shades of green, blue, and purple, and *wor*, which covers yellow, orange, brown, and khaki. Unlike British adults, then, Berinmo speakers do not distinguish green and blue as colours with separate names, nor do they discriminate between the different colours that comprise the word *wor*.

Roberson and colleagues showed participants from both linguistic groups three cards, each with a colour on it, and asked them to pick the colour that was different from the other two. For English speakers, when shown two shades of green and a shade of blue, the choice was obvious: the shade of blue was different. For the Berinmo speakers, however, the distinction between two greens and a blue was arbitrary; all three were *nol* colours. They chose the blue only about half of the time. However, when shown cards with yellow, khaki, and green shades, the tables were turned. For the Berinmo speakers, the choice was between two *wor* cards and a *nol*. For the English speakers, the distinction looked arbitrary. Roberson and her colleagues found that each group of speakers could distinguish colours across its own linguistic category boundaries, but was only at a chance level when making decisions relevant in the other group's language.

Kay and Regier (2006) have suggested a resolution of this controversy by suggesting that the Whorf hypothesis be qualified somewhat. They note that, with respect to colours, there do seem to be focal colours that most linguistic groups would distinguish. For example, Regier, Kay, and Cook (2005) asked speakers of languages from 110 non-industrialized societies to point to the "best example" of one of their colour names. Choices seemed to cluster around the same hues, showing that, regardless of the language, there is good agreement as to what hue actually represents a particular colour. So, some colours are universal, and the Whorf hypothesis does not apply to these colours. However, as the experiment by Roberson, Davies, and Davidoff (2000) showed, people speaking different languages can show differences in their ability to discriminate colours and, in this case, their colour perception is affected by their linguistic background. However, the source of these differences remains to be discovered (Lindsey & Brown, 2002; Regier & Kay, 2004).

## Interim Summary

### Visual Perception of Objects

Perception of form requires, first, recognition of figure and ground. The Gestalt organizational laws of proximity, similarity, good continuation, and common fate describe some of the ways we distinguish figure from ground even when the outlines of the figures are not explicitly bounded by lines.

Psychologists have advanced two major hypotheses about the mechanism of pattern perception, or visual recognition of particular shapes. The first hypothesis suggests that our brain contains templates of all of the shapes we can perceive. We compare a particular pattern of visual input with these templates until we find a fit. But how many different patterns can the brain hold? The second hypothesis suggests that our brain contains prototypes, which are more flexible than simple templates. Some psychologists believe that prototypes are collections of distinctive features (such as the two parallel lines and the connecting diagonal of the letter *N*).

Perception involves both bottom-up and top-down processing. Our perceptions are influenced not only by the details of the particular stimuli we see, but also by their relations to each other and our expectations. Evidence from cognitive neuroscience suggests that our perceptions arise from a system that is specialized for object identification. A second system, to guide actions in space, may be an independent source of visual information.

The Whorf hypothesis suggested that language could strongly affect the way we perceive the world. This hypothesis has been recently supported by cross-cultural analyses of the way people perceive colour.

#### QUESTIONS TO CONSIDER

1. Explore your environment a little and look for examples of figure and ground. Can you change your focus of attention and make items previously seen as figures become part of the background, and vice versa? Can you find some examples of when the Gestalt principles of grouping help you perceive particular objects?
2. How many unique objects do you think you can recognize? How many more do you think you will learn to recognize during the years ahead? Are you learning "new" objects, or relating them to older, familiar ones?
3. What principles do you use when you try to assemble the pieces of a complex picture puzzle? Can you relate these principles to the concepts of templates, prototypes, and distinctive features?
4. Suppose that Goodale and Milner are correct about a visual system that is specialized for movements such as reaching. Are you "aware" of orienting your hand when you reach for, say, a knife and a fork at odd angles on a tabletop? What might this say about consciousness?

# Visual Perception of Space and Motion

We not only are able to perceive the forms of objects in our environment but also can judge quite accurately their relative location in space and their movements. Perceiving where things are and what they are doing are obviously important functions of the visual system.

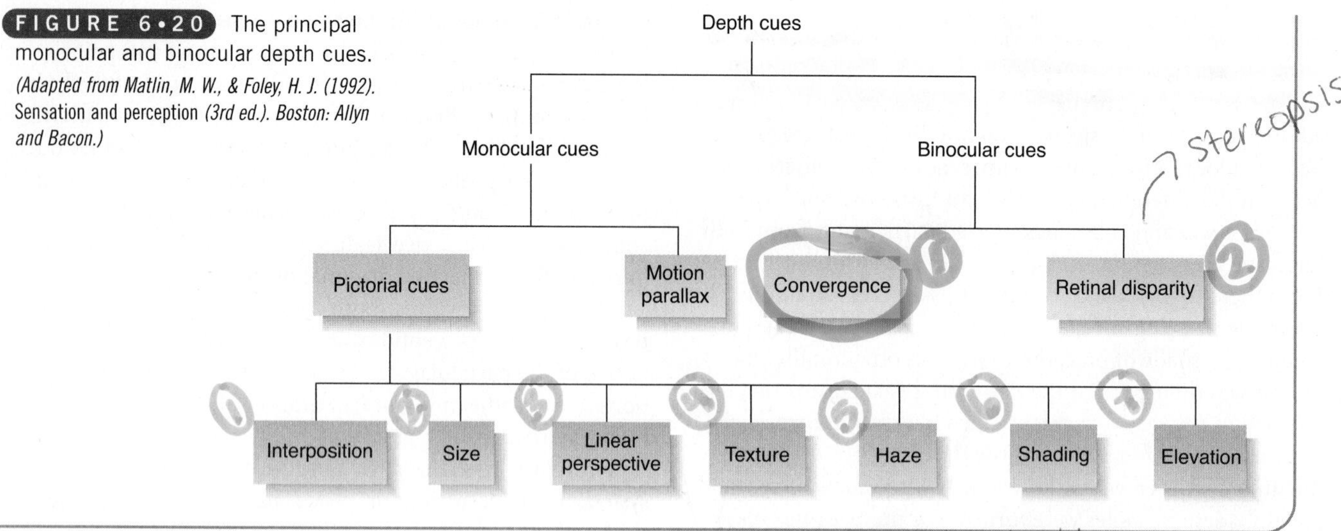


**FIGURE 6•20** The principal monocular and binocular depth cues. *(Adapted from Matlin, M. W., & Foley, H. J. (1992).* Sensation and perception *(3rd ed.). Boston: Allyn and Bacon.)*

## Depth Perception

Depth perception requires that we perceive the distance of objects in the environment from us and from each other. We do so by means of two kinds of cues: binocular ("two-eye") and monocular ("one-eye"). Binocular cues arise from the fact that the visual fields of both eyes overlap. Only animals that have eyes on the front of the head (such as primates, cats, and some avian species) have **binocular cues** as well as **monocular cues** available to them. Animals that have eyes on the sides of their heads (such as rabbits and fish) are strictly dependent on monocular cues.

One monocular cue involves movement and thus must be experienced in the natural environment or in a motion picture. The other monocular cues can be represented in a drawing or a photograph. In fact, most of these cues were originally discovered by artists and only later studied by psychologists. Artists wanted to represent the world realistically, and they studied their visual environments to identify the features that indicated the distance of objects from the viewer. Art historians can show us the evidence of their discoveries.

**Figure 6•20** shows the most important sources of distance cues (terms highlighted in colour).

**Binocular Cues** An important cue about distance is supplied by **convergence**. Recall from Chapter 5 that the eyes make vergence movements so that both look at (*converge* on) the same point of the visual scene. If an object is very close to your face, your eyes are turned inward. If it is farther away, they look more nearly straight ahead. Thus, the eyes can be used like rangefinders. The brain controls the extraocular muscles, so it knows the angle between them, which is related to the distance between the object and the eyes. Convergence is most important for perceiving the distance of objects located close to us, especially those we can reach with our hands. (See **Figure 6•21**.)

Another important factor in the perception of distance is the information provided by **retinal disparity**. (*Disparity* means "unlikeness" or "dissimilarity.") Hold up a finger of one hand at arm's length and then hold up a finger of the other hand midway between your nose and the distant finger. If you look at one of the fingers, you will see a double image of the other one. (Try it.) Whenever your eyes are pointed toward a particular point, the images of objects at different distances will fall on different portions of the retina in each eye. The disparity between the images of an object on the two retinas provides an important clue about its distance from us.

The perception of depth resulting from retinal disparity is called **stereopsis.** A *stereoscope* is a device that shows two slightly different pictures, one to each eye. The pictures are taken by a camera equipped with two lenses, located a few inches apart, just as our eyes are. When you look through a stereoscope, you see a three-dimensional image. An experiment by Julesz (1965, 2006) demonstrated that retinal disparity is what produces the effect of depth. Using a computer, he produced two displays of randomly positioned dots in which the location of some dots differed slightly. If some of the dots in one of the displays were displaced slightly to the right or the left, the two displays gave the impression of depth when viewed through a stereoscope.

**Figure 6•22** shows a pair of these random-dot stereograms. If you look at them very carefully, you will see that some of the dots near the centre have been moved slightly to the left. Some people can look at these figures without using a stereoscope and see depth. If you want to try this, hold the

**binocular cues** Cues to distance that depend on input from two eyes.
**monocular cues** Cues to distance that depend on input from only one eye.
**convergence** The result of vergence eye movements whereby the fixation point for each eye is identical; feedback from these movements provides information about the distance of objects from the viewer.
**retinal disparity** The fact that points on objects located at different distances from the observer will fall on slightly different locations on the two retinas; provides the basis for stereopsis, one of the forms of depth perception.
**stereopsis** A form of depth perception based on retinal disparity.

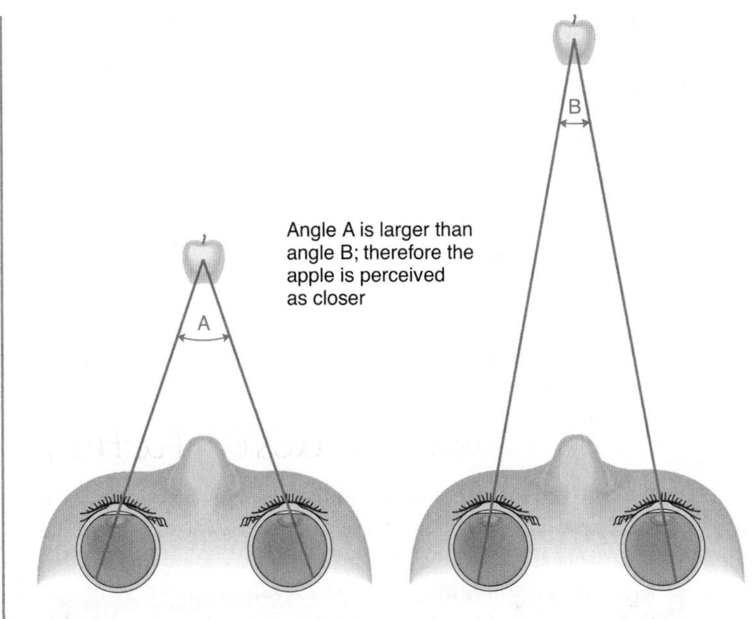


Angle A is larger than angle B; therefore the apple is perceived as closer

**FIGURE 6•21** Convergence. When the eyes converge on a nearby object, the angle between them is greater than when they converge on a distant object. The brain uses this information in perceiving the distance of an object.

book at arm's length and look at the space between the figures. Now pretend you are looking "through" the book, into the distance. Each image will become double, since your eyes are no longer converged properly. If you keep looking, you might make two of these images fuse into one, located right in the middle. Eventually, you might see a small square in the centre of the image, raised above the background.

The necessary condition for this perception is that the two images are fused together, so that the visual system can analyze the disparity. The single image random dot (SIRD) stereograms that I described in Chapter 2 induce stereopsis by tricking the visual system into fusing different parts of the image together. If you have seen one of these stereograms, you probably will have noticed how they show a kind of "wallpaper" structure, with repetitions of visual elements along the length of the image. The result is a little like staring at the tiles on your bathroom floor. Under the right conditions, the visual system may fuse an individual tile from one eye with the tile's neighbouring image on the other eye. The SIRD stereogram is constructed to exploit this fusion by additional disparity cues to provide the illusion of an object in depth (Schiffman, 1996).

Electrical recordings of individual neurons in the visual system of the brain have found a class of cells that receive information from both eyes and respond only when there is a slight disparity between the image of an object on both retinas. (This effect would occur if an object was slightly nearer or farther from you than the point at which you are gazing.) Thus, some neurons at this level apparently compare the activity of neurons with corresponding receptive fields for both eyes and respond when there is a disparity. These neurons participate in stereopsis.

**Monocular Cues** One of the most important sources of information about the relative distance of objects is **interposition** (*interposed* means "placed between"). If one object is placed between us and another object so that the closer object partially obscures our view of the more distant one, we can immediately perceive which object is closer to us.

Obviously, interposition works best when we are familiar with the objects and know what their shapes should look like. But it works even with unfamiliar objects. Just as the Gestalt law of good continuation plays a role in form perception, the *principle of good form* affects our perception of the relative location of objects: We perceive the object having the simpler border as being closer. **Figure 6•23(a)** can be seen either as two rectangles located one in front of the other (**Figure 6•23(b)**) or as a rectangle nestled against an L-shaped object (**Figure 6•23(c)**). Because we tend to perceive an ambiguous drawing according to the principle of good form, we are more likely to perceive Figure 6.23(a) as two simple shapes—rectangles—one partly hiding the other.

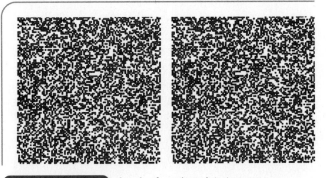

**FIGURE 6•22** A pair of random dot stereograms.
*(From Julesz, B. (1965). Texture and visual perception.* Scientific American, 12, *38–48. Copyright © 1965 by Scientific American, Inc. All rights reserved.)*

**interposition** A monocular cue of depth perception; an object that partially blocks another object is perceived as closer.

**FIGURE 6•23** Use of the principle of good form in the perception of depth. The two objects shown in (a) could be two identical rectangles, one in front of the other, as shown in (b), or a rectangle and an L-shaped object, as shown in (c). The principle of good form states that we will see the ambiguous object in its simplest (best) form—in this case, a rectangle. As a result, the shape to the right is perceived as being partly hidden and thus farther away from us.

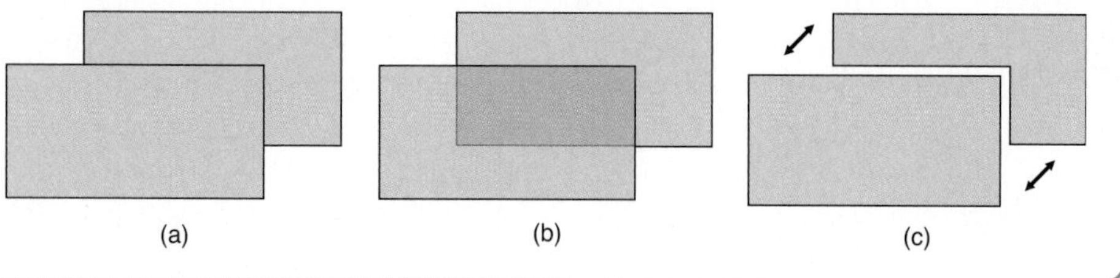


Another important monocular distance cue is provided by our familiarity with the sizes of objects. For example, if an automobile casts a very small image on our retinas, we will perceive it as being far away. Knowing how large cars are, our visual system can automatically compute the approximate distance based on the size of the retinal image.

**Figure 6•24** shows two columns located at different distances. The drawing shows **linear perspective:** the tendency for parallel lines that recede from us to converge at a single point. Because of perspective, we perceive the columns as being the same size even though they produce retinal images of different sizes. We also perceive the segments of the wall between the columns as rectangular, even though the image they cast on the retina does not contain any right angles.

In a natural environment that has not been altered by humans, we seldom see actual converging lines that denote perspective. For example, earlier in our evolutionary history, people did not see streets, large buildings, and railroad tracks. Did we acquire the ability to use perspective cues only after producing these features of the landscape, or is there a counterpart of perspective to be found in nature? This is one of the questions being studied by cross-cultural psychologists interested in the role of experience in visual perception.

**Texture**, especially the texture of the ground, provides another cue we use to perceive the distance of objects sitting on the ground. A coarser texture looks closer, and a finer texture looks more distant. (See **Figure 6•25**.) The earth's atmosphere, which always contains a certain amount of haze, can also supply cues about the relative distance of objects or parts of the landscape. Parts of the landscape that are farther away become less distinct because of haze in the air. Thus, **haze** provides a monocular distance cue. (See **Figure 6•26**.)

**linear perspective** A monocular cue of depth perception; the arrangement or drawing of objects on a flat surface such that parallel lines receding from the viewer are seen to converge at a point on the horizon.

**texture** A monocular cue of depth perception; the fineness of detail present in the surfaces of objects or in the ground or floor of a scene.

**haze** A monocular cue of depth perception; objects that are less distinct in their outline and texture are seen as farther from the viewer.

**shading** A monocular cue of depth perception; determines whether portions of the surface of an object are perceived as concave or convex.

The patterns of light and shadow in a scene—its **shading**—can provide us with cues about the three-dimensional shapes of objects. Although the cues that shading provides do not usually tell us much about the absolute distances of objects from us, they can tell us which *parts* of objects are closer and which are farther. **Figure 6•27** illustrates the power of this phenomenon. Some of the circles look as if they bulge out toward us; others look as if they are hollowed out (dimpled). You may notice a tendency to perceive this figure as a collection of dimples surrounded by bumps. Try turning the page upside down. The only difference is the direction of the shading, but your perception has changed. Our visual system appears to interpret such stimuli as if they were illuminated from above. Thus, the top of a convex (bulging) object will be light and the bottom will be in shadow. Actually, our visual system may be more specific than that. Using a

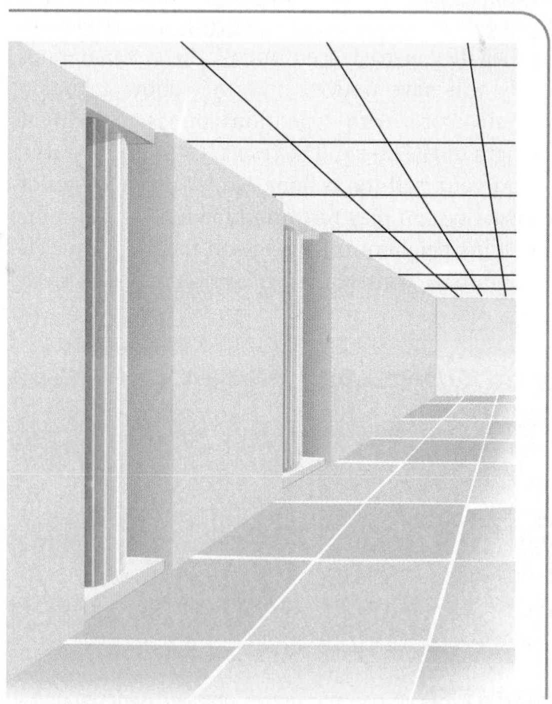

**FIGURE 6•24** Principle of perspective. Perspective gives the appearance of distance and makes the two columns look similar in size.

**FIGURE 6•25** Texture cues. Variations in texture can produce an appearance of distance. The stones diminish in size toward the top of the photo; we therefore perceive the top of the photo as being farther away from us.

**FIGURE 6•26** Cues from atmospheric haze. Variation in detail, owing to haze, produces an appearance of distance.

**FIGURE 6•27** Depth cues supplied by shading. A viewer tends to interpret this configuration as a group of bumps surrounding a group of dimples.
*(From Sun, J., & Perona, P. (1998).* Nature Neuroscience, 1.*)*

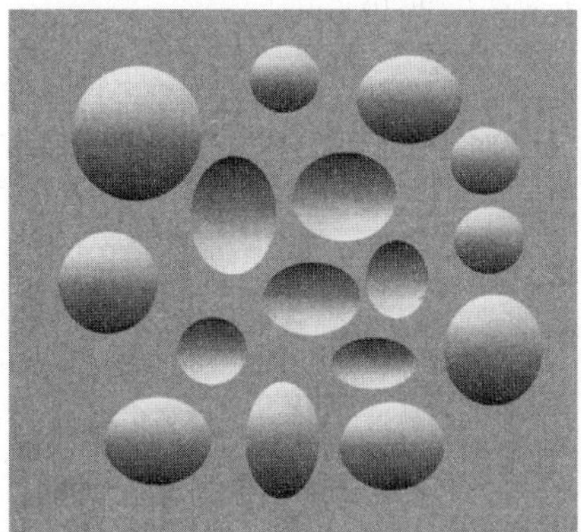

"pop-out" procedure similar to the one depicted in Figure 6.27, Sun and Perona (1998) found that dimples tended to pop out faster when the perceived direction of lighting was slightly from the top left. Next time you visit an art gallery, check the shadows on portraits and see if artists have followed this convention.

When we are able to see the horizon, we perceive objects near it as being distant and those above or below it as being nearer to us. Thus, **elevation** provides an important monocular depth cue. For example, cloud B and triangle B in **Figure 6•28** appear farther away from us than cloud A and triangle A.

So far, all of the monocular distance cues discussed have been those that can be rendered in a drawing or captured by a camera (pictorial cues). However, another important source of distance information depends on our own movement. Try the following demonstrations: If you focus your eyes on an object close to you and move your head from side to side, your image of the scene moves back and forth behind the nearer object. If you focus your eyes on the background while moving your head from side to side, the image of the nearer object passes back and forth across the background. Head and body movements cause the images from the scene before us to change; the closer the object, the more it changes relative to the background. The information contained in this relative movement helps us perceive distance.

**Figure 6•29** illustrates the kinds of cues supplied when we move with respect to features in the environment. The top part of the figure shows three objects at different distances from the observer: a man, a house, and a tree. The lower part shows the views that the observer will see from five different places ($P_1$–$P_5$). The changes in the relative locations of the objects provide cues concerning their distance from the observer. The phenomenon is known as **motion parallax** (*parallax* comes from a Greek word meaning "change").

**elevation** A monocular cue of depth perception; objects nearer the horizon are seen as farther from the viewer.
**motion parallax** A monocular cue of depth perception. As we pass by a scene, objects closer to us pass in front of objects farther away.

**FIGURE 6•28** Depth cues supplied by elevation. The objects nearest the horizontal line appear farthest away from us.

*(Adapted from Matlin, M. W., & Foley, H. J. (1992).* Sensation and perception *(3rd ed.). Boston: Allyn and Bacon.)*

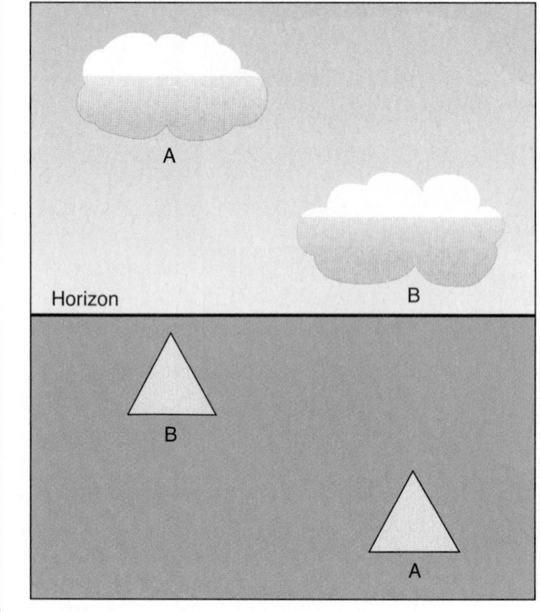


## Constancies of Visual Perception

Though Gestalt psychologists argued that similarities in human brains assure perceptual regularities—the Gestalt laws of perception—learning also plays a role in perception. Repeated exposure to a particular set of objects may allow us eventually to classify them accurately despite dramatic differences in the sensory information they produce. If you close the book you are reading and turn it around in front of you, the light reflected from the book will create quite different retinal images. Now imagine that another person is holding the same book while standing several feet from you and turns it around in much the same way. The retinal images will be much smaller. In both cases, however, you will recognize the book easily. As well, you will recognize that its size has not changed even though it is at a distance from you. A book remains a book regardless of large-scale shifts in the images it produces on our retinas. Such experience-based invariance in our recognition of objects is referred to as **perceptual constancy** and comes in several types: *form* (or shape) *constancy*, *size constancy*, *colour constancy*, and *brightness constancy*. Even though the viewing conditions may vary considerably, we learn that certain characteristics of objects remain the same.

**perceptual constancy** A mechanism that maintains a perceptual judgment as the external stimulus changes.

**FIGURE 6•29** Motion parallax. As we move from P1 to P5, the relative locations of the man, tree, and house change. These changes enable us to make inferences about the relative positions of these objects.

*(From Haber, R. N., & Hershenson, M. (1973).* The psychology of visual perception. *Holt, Rinehart & Winston, Inc. Reprinted by permission of Holt, Rinehart & Winston, Inc.)*

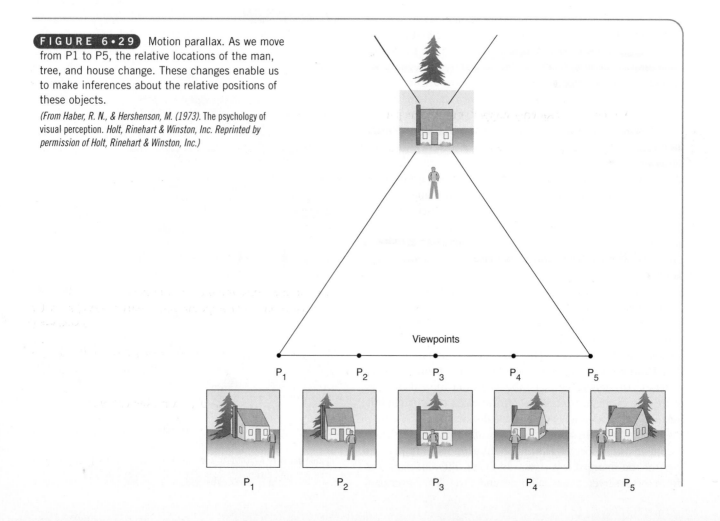

## Perception of Motion

Detection of movement is one of the most primitive aspects of visual perception. This ability is seen even in animals whose visual systems do not obtain detailed images of the environment. For animals that must avoid obstacles and elude predators, accurate estimation of motion is essential. Pigeons are a good example, since they are prey to fast-moving predators able to catch them in flight. Sun and Frost (1998) found that the pigeon's visual system contains three distinct classes of neurons that, separately, carry information about looming objects. The information provided by these neurons provides a sort of "early warning" system of an impending collision, as well as an accurate estimate of the time to collision. Of course, our visual system can detect more than the mere presence of movement. We can see what is moving in our environment and can detect the direction in which it is moving.

▲ *The combat soldier's survival depends on the ability to detect movement in the environment.*

**Adaptation and Long-Term Modification** One of the most important characteristics of all sensory systems is that they show adaptation and rebound effects. For example, when you stare at a spot of colour, the adaptation of neurons in your visual system will produce a negative afterimage if you shift your gaze to a neutral background; if you put your hand in some hot water, warm water will feel cool to that hand immediately afterwards.

Motion, like other kinds of stimuli, can give rise to adaptation and after-effects. This phenomenon was first reported in writing in 1834 by a Mr. Adams, who noticed it after watching the descent of a waterfall. Tootell, Reppas, Dale, and Look (1995) presented people with a display showing a series of concentric rings moving outward like the ripples in a pond. When the rings suddenly stopped moving, the participants had the impression of the opposite movement—that the rings were moving inward. As in the case of a negative afterimage, the illusion is the perceptual result of fatigue affecting one type of detector: those detecting the outward movement had become fatigued, so that they no longer balanced the other detectors. The researchers scanned the participants' brains to measure their metabolic activity while the illusion was present. The scans showed increased activity in the motion-sensitive region of the visual association cortex, which lasted as long as the illusion did. Thus, the neural circuits that give rise to this illusion appear to be located in the same region that responds to actual moving stimuli.

A study by Ball and Sekuler (1982) suggests that even the long-term characteristics of the system that detects movement can be modified by experience. The researchers trained people to detect extremely small movements. Each person sat in front of a display screen. A series of dots appeared, scattered across the face of the screen, and either all moved a very small distance or all remained stationary. The dots always moved in the same direction, but the direction was different for each person. After several sessions, the researchers assessed sensitivity to movements of the dots. They found that each person was especially good at detecting movement *only in the direction in which he or she had been trained*; the training did not increase their detection of movements in other directions. The effect was still present 10 weeks later.

The fact that these people learned to detect a small movement in a particular direction, and not small movements in general, shows that particular aspects of their visual systems were modified by experience. Did they acquire new sets of feature detectors, or were parallel networks of neurons modified in some way? As yet, we have no way of knowing.

**Interpretation of a Moving Retinal Image** As you read this book, your eyes are continuously moving. Naturally, the eye movements cause the image on your retina to move. You can also cause the retinal image to move by holding the book close to your face, looking straight ahead, and moving it back and forth. (Try it.) In the first case, when you were reading normally, you perceived the book as being still. In the second case, you perceived it as moving. Why does your brain interpret the movement differently in these two cases? Try another demonstration. Pick a letter on this page, stare at it, and then move the book around, following the letter with your eyes. This time you will perceive the book as moving, even though the image on your retina remains stable. Thus, perception of movement requires coordination between movements of the image on the retina and those of the eyes.

Haarmeier, Thier, Repnow, and Petersen (1997) reported the case of a patient with bilateral damage to the visual association cortex who could not compensate for image movement caused by head and eye movements. When the patient moved his eyes, it looked to him as if the world were moving in the opposite direction. Without the ability to compensate for head and eye movements, any movement of the image on the retina was perceived as movement of objects in the environment.

**Combining Information from Vision and Audition** So far in this chapter, I have discussed only the visual perceptual system. Space and movement, however, often involve sound. You're probably familiar with the *Doppler effect*, in which an approaching sound, like that of an oncoming train, increases in frequency. Changes in both pitch and loudness are therefore good clues to whether a sound is coming toward you. As you saw in Chapter 5, our two ears receive slightly different versions of the same sound, allowing us to localize its source. So, how does our *auditory* construction of space relate to our visual one?

The fact that we have two auditory sense organs (that is, our two ears) seems to be recapitulated in our auditory perceptual system. Using the human ability to detect a temporal gap in an ongoing sound, Boehnke and Phillips (1999) found that we have two spatial channels for sound localization: one to each side, with about 30 degrees of overlap on each side of the point directly in front of us. That doesn't mean that we can tell only if sounds come from the left and right. Remember that we have only three kinds of colour receptors, and yet can distinguish millions of different hues. Indeed, our discrimination of sound locations is quite good for sounds directly in front of us (Recanzone, Makhamra, & Guard, 1998).

The **ventriloquism effect** demonstrates that this auditory ability to locate a sound interacts with our vision. As stage performers have known for a long time, when an auditory cue and a visual cue signal conflicting sources of a sound, the visual cue tends to dominate. The source of the sound is judged to be closer to the apparent visual location (Vroomen, Bertelson, & de Gelder, 2001). Ventriloquists don't "throw" their voices; they throw off your perception of their voices' source by the movements of the puppets.

This interaction occurs in other phenomenon as well. Remember Mr. Adams' waterfall phenomenon? There is an auditory equivalent, in which rising or falling sounds are used to suggest movement. If that movement "stops," a person perceives an opposing movement. This auditory waterfall illusion is affected by visual cues: A visual cue to movement enhances the suggestion of opposing movement (Kitagawa & Ichihara, 2002).

Both of these observations suggest an important question: How do we connect the visual and auditory sources? What leads us, for example, to think that the squeaky voice is coming from the ventriloquist's dummy rather than from the human beside him? This issue is sometimes called "the binding problem" and it is a puzzle to psychologists and neuroscientists at present. Clearly, when combining auditory and visual perceptions of space, the brain must connect these two sources of sensory input. How it accomplishes this connection is still a mystery, although the functional imaging techniques discussed in Chapter 4 are providing new insights. For example, Bushara and colleagues (2003) used fMRI procedures to look at one type of binding, depicted in **Figure 6•30**. In their experiment, people watch a screen. Two vertical lines move from the edges toward the centre. When the two lines reach the centre, they then move toward the edges at the same rate. Observers either perceive the lines as passing through each other or as colliding and bouncing back. The tendency to report a collision is greatly enhanced if a "crash" noise is sounded at the moment the two lines meet. The noise binds with the visual event to produce a special perception. Bushara and colleagues found, not surprisingly, that this binding was associated with areas of the brain that respond to multimodal sensory input. However, binding was also associated with decreased activity in purely auditory or visual cortical areas. The connection, then, between auditory and visual localities may be established early in spatial processing.

**Perception of Movement in the Absence of Motion** If you sit in a darkened room and watch two small lights that are alternately turned on and off, your perception will be of a single light moving back and forth. You will not see the light turn off at one position and then turn on at the second position. If the distance and timing are just right, the light will appear to stay on at all times, quickly moving between the positions. This response is known as the **phi phenomenon.** Theatre marquees, "moving" neon signs, and some computer animations make use of it.

This characteristic of the visual system accounts for the fact that we perceive the images in motion pictures and on television as continuous rather than separate. The images actually jump from place to place, but we see smooth movement.

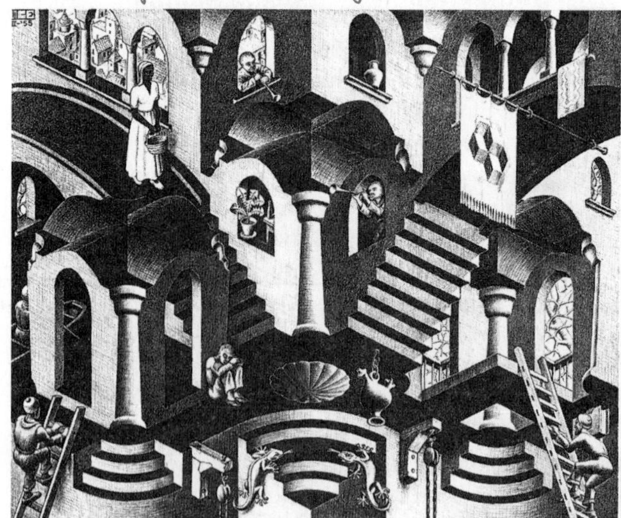

▲ *This lithograph,* Convex and Concave, *by M. C. Escher, shows how contradictory depth clues can be combined to provide an "impossible" scene.*

*M. C. Escher's "Convex and Concave"* 

**ventriloquism effect** The apparent shift in location of a sound from its auditory source to its perceived visual location.

**phi phenomenon** The perception of movement caused by the turning on of two or more lights, one at a time, in sequence; often used on theatre marquees; responsible for the apparent movement of images in movies and television.

FIGURE 6•30 A schematic of the procedure used in the Bushara and colleagues (2003) study. Study participants viewed a white rectangular window (a). At the beginning of a trial, two identical bars appeared at the left and right edges (b) and moved horizontally to the centre. After coinciding at the centre (c), the two bars moved away from each other to the edges and disappeared (d and e). Five seconds later, the screen went blank (f), and participants were asked to indicate whether the two bars bypassed each other or collided and bounced back. A collision sound (the waveform indicated in the diagram) was synchronized with the point of overlap (c).

*(From Bushara, K. O., Hanakawa, T., Immisch, I., Toma, K., Kansaku, K., & Hallett, M. (2003). Neural correlates of cross-modal binding.* Nature Neuroscience, 6, *190–195.)*

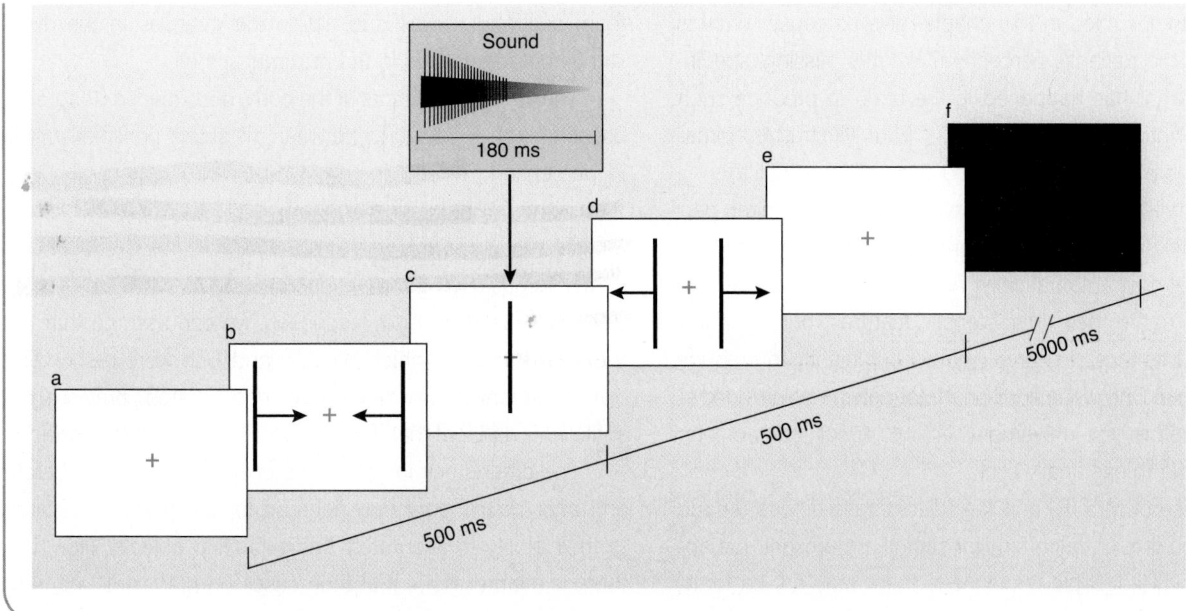


## Interim Summary

### Visual Perception of Space and Motion

Our visual system accomplishes a remarkable feat: It manages to perceive objects accurately even in the face of movement and changes in levels of illumination. Because the size and shape of a retinal image vary with the location of an object relative to the eye, accurate form perception requires depth perception—perception of the locations of objects in space. Depth perception comes from binocular cues (from convergence and retinal disparity) and monocular cues (from interposition, size, linear perspective, texture, haze, shading, elevation, and the effects of head and body movements).

We perceive the brightness of an object relative to that of objects around it; thus, objects retain a constant brightness under a variety of conditions of illumination. In addition, our perception of the relative distance of objects helps us maintain form constancy.

Because our bodies may well be moving while we are visually following some activity in the outside world, the visual system has to make further compensations. It keeps track of the commands to the eye muscles and compensates for the direction in which the eyes are pointing. Movement is perceived when objects move relative to one another. In particular, a smaller object is likely to be perceived as moving across a larger one. Movement is also perceived when our eyes follow a moving object, even though its image remains on the same part of the retina.

Vision is not our only perceptual system that can locate objects; we also rely on sound. Usually, the two systems provide similar information but when they conflict, as in the case of ventriloquism, the visual system seems to dominate.

The phi phenomenon describes our tendency to see an instantaneous disappearance of an object and its reappearance somewhere else as movement of that object. Because of the phi phenomenon, we perceive television shows and movies as representations of reality, not as a series of disconnected images.

#### QUESTIONS TO CONSIDER

1. Why do you suppose that artists often hold their thumbs in front of them while looking at the scenes they are painting?
2. When we ride in an automobile and can see the sun or moon through a side window, why does it look as if these objects are following us?

EPILOGUE

## The Outside World

The case studies cited in this chapter give us pause: What is going on in the patient's perception? What is missing, specifically? And what has happened to the brain to produce such unusual symptoms? The case of Mrs. R. is illustrative. Somehow, a cerebral stroke had altered her brain so that she—a perfectly intelligent woman otherwise—could no longer perform what children could easily perform and what she had long performed almost automatically: naming familiar objects. She often could name their characteristic features, but somehow she couldn't tie those features together sufficiently to produce the right name. Only when additional information was provided—through gesture or movement or by direct contact, for example—did things finally click.

The case of Mrs. R. and the related case of Dee remind us that, even though once-familiar stimuli are present, the appropriate knowledgeable response to them may not be forthcoming. Something about the disruption of cerebrovascular functioning in Mrs. R. and the too-long exposure to carbon monoxide in Dee had changed their brains sufficiently to render them visually agnostic.

In analyzing perception, psychologists sometimes make a distinction between distal and proximal stimuli. A distal stimulus is, as the term implies, at a distance—out there. A proximal stimulus is close by, immediate—in here. In the case of Mrs. R. and Dee, the distal stimuli used by the cognitive neuroscientists who examined them—the items used in formal or informal testing—were similar to those the two women had encountered many times prior to their brain injury. The new strangeness of their responses to those items—namely, their inability to name them accurately—was due not to the changes in the distal stimuli but to changes in the proximal stimuli.

The sensory receptors of the body, described in Chapter 5, constitute the dividing line between distal and proximal stimuli in perception. The images that fall on the retina are distal. What occurs thereafter in the optic nerve, the thalamus, the primary visual cortex, and the levels of the visual association cortex constitutes the proximal stimuli for perceptual responses. Based on their responses, we can assume that the proximal stimuli to which Mrs. R. and Dee were responding were different from those that had existed previously—sufficiently different that they could no longer respond correctly.

The differences in the brains of Mrs. R. and Dee before and after brain injury may account for the dramatic change in their ability to accurately name familiar objects. However, there is a larger issue that their cases bring to light—namely, that all of us are dependent on the proximal stimuli that are available to us. None of us has direct access to the distal stimuli. We are, as Plato famously put it, captives of our senses. We perceive only what is proximal.

What this implies is that the "world out there"—the world of other people and of non-human objects, the world that includes the parts of our own bodies that perceive—is a construction. It is a provisional reality. We could never perceive it directly; instead, we are able to perceive only the proximal stimuli it is presumed to induce. There is a fundamental conundrum here: namely, what it means to perceive reality. Our study of perception may make us more humble about offering such claims.

## Canadian Connections to Research in This Chapter


Bernstein, L. J., & Robertson, L. C. (1998). Illusory conjunctions of color and motion with shape following bilateral parietal lesions. *Psychological Science, 9*, 167–175. (University of Toronto: www.utoronto.ca)

Boehnke, S. E., & Phillips, D. P. (1999). Azimuthal tuning of human perceptual channels for sound location. *Journal of the Acoustical Society of America, 106*, 1948–1955. (Dalhouse University: www.dal.ca)

Enns, J. T., & Rensink, R. A. (1991). Preattentive recovery of three dimensional orientation from line drawings. *Psychological Review, 98*, 335–352. (University of British Columbia: www.ubc.ca)

Giaschi, D., & Regan, D. (1997). Development of motion-defined figure-ground segregation in preschool and older children, using a letter-identification task. *Optometry and Vision Science, 74*, 761–767. (University of British Columbia: www.ubc.ca)

David Regan was the 1997 winner of the Sir William Dawson medal of the Royal Society of Canada.

Goodale, M. A., & Humphrey, G. K. (1998). The objects of action and perception. *Cognition, 67*, 181–207. (University of Western Ontario: www.uwo.ca)

Goodale, M. A., Meenan, J. P., Bulthoff, H. H., Nicolle, D. A., Murphy, K. J., Racicot, C. I. (1994). Separate neural pathways for the visual analysis of object shape in perception and prehension. *Current Biology, 4*, 604–610. (University of Western Ontario: www.uwo.ca)

Goodale, M. A., & Milner, A. D. (1992). Separate visual pathways for perception and action. *Trends in Neurosciences, 15*, 20–25. (University of Western Ontario: www.uwo.ca)

Goodale, M., & Milner, D. (2005). *Sight unseen*. Oxford, UK: Oxford University Press. (University of Western Ontario: www.uwo.ca)

Goodale, M. A. & Westwood, D. A. (2004). An evolving view of duplex vision: Separate but interacting cortical pathways for perception and action. *Current Opinion in Neurobiology, 14*, 203–211. (University of Western Ontario: www.uwo.ca)

Hebb, D. O. (1949). *The organization of behavior.* New York: Wiley-Interscience. (McGill University: www.mcgill.ca)

Donald Hebb was the first winner (in 1980) of the Donald O. Hebb Award of the Canadian Psychological Association and the 1961 winner of the American Psychological Association's Award for Distinguished Scientific Contributions.

Jakobson, L. S., Archibald, Y. M., Carey, D. P., & Goodale, M. A. (1991). A kinematic analysis of reaching and grasping movements in a patient recovering from optic ataxia. *Neuropsychologia, 29*, 803–809. (University of Western Ontario: www.uwo.ca)

Pilon, D. J., & Friedman, A. (1998). Grouping and detecting vertices in 2-D, 3-D, and quasi-3-D objects. *Canadian Journal of Experimental Psychology, 52*, 114–126. (University of Alberta: www.ualberta.ca)

Steeves, J. K. E., Humphrey, G. K., Culham, J. C., Menon, R. S., Milner, A. D., & Goodale, M. A. (2004). Behavioral and neuroimaging evidence for a contribution of color and texture information to scene classification in a patient with visual form agnosia. *Journal of Cognitive Neuroscience, 16*, 955–965. (University of Western Ontario: www.uwo.ca)

Sun, H., & Frost, B. J. (1998). Computation of different optical variables of looming objects in pigeon nucleus rotundus neurons. *Nature Neuroscience, 1*, 296–303. (Queen's University: www.queensu.ca)

## Suggestions for Further Reading

Goodale, M., & Milner, D. (2005). *Sight unseen.* Oxford, UK: Oxford University Press.

Goodale and Milner's book presents the provocative suggestion that we have two visual systems: one for the perception of objects, and another for the control of movement. They base their hypothesis on intriguing observations of an individual with "blindsight." Their case is presented with compelling evidence and remarkable insight. I will also discuss the implications of Goodale and Milner's work in Chapter 9 on consciousness.

Hoffman, D. D. (1998). *Visual intelligence: How we create what we see.* New York: Norton.

Pinker, S. (1997). *How the mind works.* New York: Norton.

Hoffman's book is a thoughtful and engaging discussion of how the visual system constructs a model of the world. Pinker's book contains some intriguing ideas about the origin and the function of our perceptual systems.

# 7

# Learning and Behaviour

## CHAPTER OUTLINE

Learning is an adaptive process in which the tendency to perform a particular behaviour is changed by experience. As environmental conditions change, we learn new behaviours and eliminate old ones. However, changes in behaviour do not always reflect learning, and learning may occur without obvious changes in behaviour.

### Habituation

Habituation—the simplest form of learning—involves learning not to respond to insignificant events that occur repeatedly. Habituation helps an organism's behaviour become sensitive to more important stimuli, such as those involving survival and procreation.

### Classical Conditioning

Pavlov's Serendipitous Discovery • The Biological Significance of Classical Conditioning • Basic Principles of Classical Conditioning • Conditional Emotional Responses • What Is Learned in Classical Conditioning?

In classical conditioning, an organism's behaviour is elicited by one stimulus—the conditional stimulus—that predicts the occurrence of another stimulus—the unconditional stimulus. Different relations between the conditional and unconditional stimuli may lead to extinction, spontaneous recovery, generalization, and discrimination of the conditional response. Classical conditioning plays an important role in emotion.

### Operant Conditioning

The Law of Effect • Skinner and Operant Behaviour • The Three-Term Contingency • Reinforcement, Punishment, and Extinction • Other Operant Procedures and Phenomena • *Then and Now: Cellular Basis of Learning*

Operant conditioning enables an organism's behaviour to be modified by its consequences. Positive and negative reinforcement increase the frequency of a behaviour, and punishment and extinction decrease it. New, complex behaviours can be acquired through the process of shaping.

### Conditioning of Complex Behaviours

Aversive Control of Behaviour • Observation and Imitation • Spatial Learning and Navigation • Combining Behaviours: Insight • The Analysis of Human Behaviour

Punishment and negative reinforcement are effective means of controlling operant behaviour, but they may produce undesirable side effects. An aversion to a flavour can be conditioned by a single pairing of the flavour with illness—a finding that has had useful applications with cancer patients. Spatial behaviours are controlled by landmarks, which provide complex configurations of stimuli. Insight was once thought to involve a sudden—almost magical—solution to a problem. Research using animals has shown that insight may not be so sudden after all: Insight seems to require previous experience with the elements of the problem.

## PROLOGUE

### Which Way?

For some time, Dave had been expecting a call like the one he told me about. Dave is a park ranger at a large provincial park in southwestern Alberta. Part of his responsibility is to assist lost hikers and campers, which usually involves responding to calls for help from friends or relatives of the lost individual. However, in this age of cellphones, Dave knew it wouldn't be long before a lost hiker would call him directly. This call was the first, and it reached him as he sat at his desk.

"Hello? I think I'm lost . . ." the caller began.

Dave knows the backcountry pretty well, and as he listened to the man's story he got a pretty clear picture of what had happened. The man and his wife had left a popular trailhead, but had taken a wrong turn on the way back. Dave thought he could guide the pair back without activating a full-scale search.

"Okay," Dave said, when the man was finished. "I want you to look to the east and tell me what you see."

"I can't see anything. The sun's in my eyes," the caller replied. Dave sighed. It was late in the afternoon; his lost hiker apparently believed that the sun set in the east.

"Okay. Turn around. I'll bet you see three large mountains all in a row."

"Yeah . . . How did you know?" the voice asked. Dave ignored this but, having confirmed his hunch, gave the man directions back to the parking lot. Thirty minutes later, the phone rang again.

"Well, we came to a fork in the trail. My wife said we should go left, but I was sure that we should go right. We went right and now I think we're lost again . . ."

"No, you should have gone left. Backtrack to the junction and try again," Dave said.

The phone rang again half an hour later. It was the same story: The couple had come to another junction; the woman had felt they should go one way, but the man had chosen the other, wrong, way. They were lost as a result. And this time, the cellphone batteries were obviously getting low.

"Put your wife on," Dave directed. "Listen," he said to her, "your husband may be a fine person, but he's a poor navigator. Do you think you know how to get back?" The woman described the route she thought they should take. Dave approved. "Don't let him talk you out of it," were his last words before the phone connection died.

Dave heard from them again about an hour later: "We're at the parking lot, calling from a pay phone. Thanks for your help."

Our discussion of reflexive pathways in the nervous system (in Chapter 4) may have given you the impression that behaviour is controlled by neural circuits that are fixed and unchanging. Nothing could be further from the truth. Dave's brain was not built with inborn knowledge of the backcountry trail system. Dave acquired that knowledge from his experience hiking or reading maps. In contrast, the couple that lacked his experience showed very different knowledge: they got lost. Our behaviour, in other words, is changeable in response to certain experiences. The many times that Dave has hiked a trail and returned back has strengthened the behaviour of left and right turns—to the point that he could describe it over the phone as well as navigate it in person. Instructions can also change behaviour. The woman in this anecdote acquired enough knowledge from Dave's directions to guide her less-well-oriented husband. The conditions under which experiences change behaviour, and the nature of those changes, are the topics of this chapter.

**Learning** is an adaptive process in which the tendency to perform a particular behaviour is changed by experience. As conditions change, we learn new behaviours and eliminate old ones. Learning cannot be observed directly; it can only be inferred from changes in behaviour. However, not all changes in behaviour are caused by learning. For example, your performance on an examination or the skill with which you operate an automobile can be affected by your physical or mental condition—such as fatigue, fearfulness, or preoccupation. Moreover, learning may occur without noticeable changes in observable behaviour taking place. You may have received training in how to change a flat tire in a driver's education class, but your behaviour will not be noticeably different unless you need to change a flat tire.

Experience alters the structure and chemistry of the brain. These alterations affect how the nervous system responds to subsequent events. **Performance** is the behavioural change (or new behaviour) produced by the internal change. Performance, in other words, is the evidence that learning has occurred. But it is imperfect evidence, because other factors,

**learning** An adaptive process in which the tendency to perform a particular behaviour is changed by experience.

**performance** The behavioural change produced by the internal changes brought about by learning.

such as fatigue and motivation, also affect behaviour. Psychologists who study learning therefore look for special aspects of performance, such as its durability and specificity, to conclude that learning has taken place.

This chapter considers three kinds of learning: habituation, classical conditioning, and operant conditioning. All three involve cause-and-effect relations between the environment and behaviour. We learn which stimuli are trivial and which are important; we learn to make adaptive responses and to avoid maladaptive ones. We learn to recognize those conditions under which a particular response is useful and those under which a different response is more appropriate. The types of learning described in this chapter serve as the building blocks for more complex behaviours, such as problem solving and thinking, which we'll discuss in later chapters.

▲ *Unexpected events trigger an orienting response that rapidly habituates. We may be startled the first time we see a frightening scene in a movie, but repeated viewings will result in habituation. Really sudden and intense events elicit a strong startle response that may enter into more complex forms of learning.*

# Habituation

We react automatically to many events. For example, a sudden, unexpected noise causes an **orienting response**: We become alert and turn our heads toward the source of the sound. However, if the noise occurs repeatedly, we gradually cease to respond to it; we eventually ignore it. **Habituation**, learning *not* to respond to an unimportant event that occurs repeatedly, is one of the simplest forms of learning. Even animals with very primitive nervous systems are capable of habituation. George Humphrey (1933) made this point in an early textbook on psychology, in which he described a simple experiment he had conducted using land snails. (Humphrey was one of the scholars who studied with Wundt before coming to Canada to teach the new science of psychology; his interest in snails was certainly a change in pace from what he learned in Germany.) Humphrey placed several snails on a glass plate, and tapped sharply on the plate. All of the snails immediately and reflexively withdrew into their shells—showing a snail's version of how we might react to a sudden and scary scene in a movie. Humphrey waited until all of the snails re-emerged and then gave the plate another tap. This time, not all of the snails withdrew. With each further tap, fewer snails withdrew into their shells, until, after many taps, none would respond. For any individual snail, the probability of reacting to the tap decreased with each exposure to it.

Habituation makes sense from an evolutionary perspective. If a once-novel stimulus occurs again and again without any important result, the stimulus has no significance to the organism. Obviously, responding to a stimulus of no importance wastes time and energy. Consider what would happen to a land snail in a rainstorm if the withdrawal response never habituated: The snail would remain in its shell until the rain stopped falling. And consider how distracting it would be to have your attention diverted every time a common household noise occurred.

Now, you might object that there is nothing in this example to show that learning has occurred in the sense outlined earlier. For example, it could be that when a snail repeatedly withdraws into its shell it becomes fatigued and thereby less likely to respond the next time. In other words, the performance that Humphrey observed could have been affected by factors other than learning. Although this is indeed a possibility that must be considered, it is clear that even simple organisms show much greater specificity.

For example, consider a series of experiments done by Rankin and colleagues using a rather simple participant: a tiny worm from the class Nematoda (e.g., Giles, Rose, & Rankin, 2005). Like the snails, these worms respond to a tap on the substrate in which they move by withdrawing or retreating. It is known that this response occurs through neurons that respond to the mechanical stimulus of the tap. However, these worms also withdraw from sources of heat, using much the same neural pathway. Wicks and Rankin (1997) showed that they could produce habituation to a tap-elicited withdrawal without affecting withdrawal to a heat stimulus. In a way, you could say that these worms had learned something about the tap, and that they distinguished this learning from their reaction to a source of heat. What is surprising is that these worms do this with only 302 neurons in their entire nervous system.

The simplest form of habituation is temporary, and is known as *short-term habituation*. Suppose that we tap a snail's shell over and over until the withdrawal response ceases. If we tap it again after a few days, we will find that the

**orienting response** Any response by which an organism directs appropriate sensory organs (eyes, ears, nose) toward the source of a novel stimulus.
**habituation** The simplest form of learning; learning not to respond to an unimportant event that occurs repeatedly.

withdrawal response reoccurs and continues for several more taps. It takes just as long for habituation to occur as it did before. If we repeat our experiment every few days after that, the same thing will happen; the snail does not remember what happened previously.

Animals, particularly those that have more complex nervous systems, are capable of *long-term habituation.* For example, a hunting dog may be frightened the first few times it hears the sound of a shotgun, but it soon learns not to respond to the blast. This habituation carries across from day to day and even from one hunting season to the next. Likewise, your behaviour has habituated to stimuli that you have probably not thought about for a long time. When people move to new houses or apartments, they often complain about being kept awake by unfamiliar noises. But, after a while, they no longer notice them.

What distinguishes short-term habituation from long-term habituation? The pattern of experience plays a role. When stimuli are *massed* into quick repetitions, habituation is rapid but short term; when these stimuli are presented in small groups that are *spaced* in time, habituation is slower but long term (Stopfer et al., 1996). There is evidence that short-term and long-term habituation are produced by different neural mechanisms, even in so simple a nervous system as that of nematode worms (Rose & Rankin, 2001).

# Classical Conditioning

Habituation involves learning about single events. Unlike habituation, classical conditioning involves learning about the conditions that predict that a significant event will occur. We acquire much of our behaviour through classical conditioning. For example, if you are hungry and smell a favourite food cooking, your mouth is likely to water. You are reacting to the predictive relationship between the smell and your experience of the food. If you see someone with whom you have recently had a serious argument, you are likely to experience again some of the emotional reactions that occurred during the encounter. If you hear a song that you used to listen to with a loved one, you are likely to experience a feeling of nostalgia.

Here's a simple example of a conditioned behaviour. You are watching a B-grade horror movie. The heroine is walking through an abandoned warehouse when the background music switches to a creepy, dissonant theme. You know that some menace—perhaps a gooey one, at that—is about to pop out of the shadows. Yet, even though you expect a surprise, and relish the anticipation, you find your muscles tensing and your heart pounding. Your fear is the behaviour that shows you have learned the predictive relationship between the music and the upcoming fright. Or, as the young son of one of my colleagues once said, "Man, if I heard *that* music, I would never go in that building!"

Now consider how he might have learned this reaction. The first time he watched a horror movie, he might not have paid much attention to the music. After all, there's nothing in the sound of a horror film that is inherently frightening; if you heard the music outside a theatre, you probably would find it pretty boring. However, when something threatening bursts onto the screen—such as an alien creature exploding from a human body—it elicits a defensive startle reaction. (See **Figure 7•1**.) Sudden sights and sounds can cause an automatic, *unlearned* reaction. In the case of the B-grade horror movie, this reaction occurs in the presence of the threatening music.

It doesn't take many experiences with this pairing of music and fright to produce the kind of reaction we all associate with horror films. Our movie-theatre fear has been *classically conditioned* to certain musical motifs that were once neutral sounds. (See **Figure 7•2**.) Indeed, a clever director will use these sounds to elicit fright during other scenes, just to keep the fear going throughout the movie.

## Pavlov's Serendipitous Discovery

Louis Pasteur once said that chance favours the prepared mind. And indeed, in science, it pays to be observant. There is a story that, shortly before the German physicist Roentgen discovered X-rays, a British scientist had made the same discovery. His assistant reported to him that photographic film tended to get fogged if it was stored next to the laboratory uranium sample. The scientist only told his assistant to move the film, and thereby missed his chance at a Nobel Prize.

**FIGURE 7•1** The process of classical conditioning. The moviegoer watches the movie as the music changes tempo. Shortly after this tempo change, something frightening happens on the screen that causes a defensive startle response.

FIGURE 7•2 The conditional response. After the person's first experience with a horror movie, the change in music tempo elicits anxiety, tension, and fear.

The discovery of classical conditioning has a happier outcome. In December 1904, the Russian physiologist Ivan Pavlov was considered one of the foremost scientists of his time. Pavlov's chief ambition as a physiologist was to discover the neural mechanisms controlling glandular secretions during digestion. He measured the secretions during the course of a meal. For example, he inserted a small tube in a duct in an animal's mouth and collected drops of saliva as they were secreted by the salivary gland. It was while conducting routine studies of salivation in dogs that his interest in digestion became forever sidetracked by a serendipitous discovery.

Pavlov's strategy was to study salivary processes in individual dogs over many test sessions. During each session, he placed dry food powder inside the dog's mouth and then collected the saliva. All went well until the dogs became experienced participants. After several testing sessions, the dogs began salivating *before* being fed, usually as soon as they saw the laboratory assistant enter the room with the food powder. What Pavlov discovered was a form of learning in which one stimulus predicts the occurrence of another. In this case, the appearance of the laboratory assistant predicted the appearance of food.

Rather than ignoring this phenomenon or treating it as a confounding variable to be controlled, Pavlov designed experiments to discover exactly why the dogs were salivating before being given the opportunity to eat. He suspected that salivation might be triggered by stimuli that were initially unrelated to eating. Somehow, these neutral stimuli came to control what is normally a natural, reflexive behaviour. After all, dogs do not naturally salivate when they see laboratory assistants. Pavlov's new ambition was to understand the variables that controlled this unexpected behaviour.

To do so, he placed an inexperienced dog in a harness and occasionally gave it small amounts of food powder. (See **Figure 7•3**.) Just prior to placing the food powder in the dog's mouth, Pavlov sounded a bell, a buzzer, or some other auditory stimulus. At first, the dog showed only a startle response to the sound, perking its ears and turning its head toward the sound. The dog salivated only when the food powder was placed in its mouth. However, after only a dozen or so pairings of the bell and food powder, the dog began to salivate when the bell rang. Placing the food powder in the dog's mouth was no longer necessary to elicit salivation; the sound by itself was sufficient. Pavlov showed that a neutral stimulus can elicit a response similar to the original reflex when the stimulus predicts the occurrence of a significant stimulus (in this case, food powder). This type of learning is called **classical conditioning.** (Pavlov performed such an impressive and authoritative series of experiments that this form of learning is called "classical" out of respect for his work. It is also sometimes referred to as *Pavlovian conditioning.*)

FIGURE 7•3 Pavlov's original procedure for classical conditioning. The researcher rings a bell and then presents the food. Saliva is collected in a tube.

Pavlov demonstrated that conditioning occurred only when the food powder followed the bell within a short time. If there was a long delay between the sound and the food

**classical conditioning** The process by which a response normally elicited by one stimulus (the unconditional stimulus or UCS) comes to be controlled by another stimulus (the conditional stimulus or CS) as well.

FIGURE 7•4 Basic components of the classical conditioning procedure. Prior to conditioning, the UCS, but not the CS, elicits a response (the UCR). During conditioning, the CS is presented in conjunction with the UCS. Once the conditioning is completed, the CS alone elicits a response (the CR).

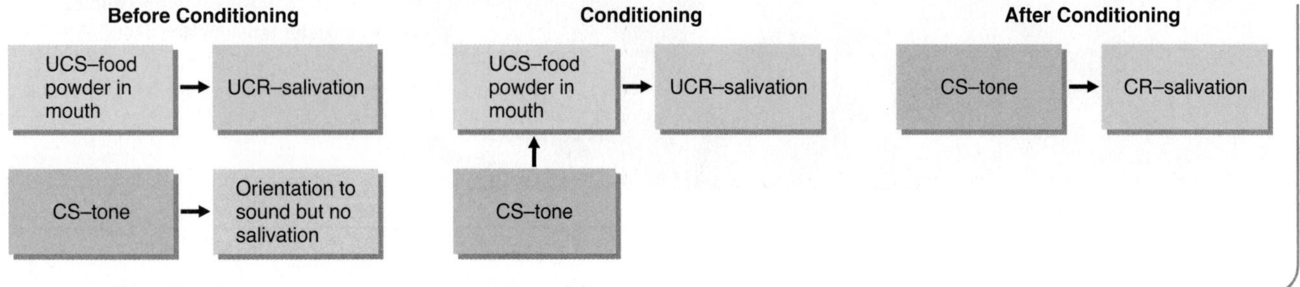


powder or if the sound followed the food powder (backward conditioning), the animal never learned to salivate when it heard the sound. Thus, the sequence and timing of events are important factors in classical conditioning. Classical conditioning provides us with a way to learn cause-and-effect relations between environmental events. We are able to learn about the stimuli that warn us that an important event is about to occur. Obviously, warning stimuli must occur prior to the event about which we are being warned.

**Figure 7•4** shows the basic classical conditioning procedure—the special conditions that must exist for an organism to respond to a previously neutral stimulus. A stimulus, such as food, that naturally elicits reflexive behaviour, such as salivation, is called an **unconditional stimulus (UCS)**. The reflexive behaviour itself is called the **unconditional response (UCR)**. If, for a certain dog, a bell signals food, then the bell may also come to elicit salivation through classical conditioning. Another dog may hear the sound of an electric can opener just before it is fed, in which case that sound will come to elicit salivation. A neutral stimulus paired with the unconditional stimulus that eventually elicits a response is called a **conditional stimulus (CS)**. The behaviour elicited by a conditional stimulus is called a **conditional response (CR)**. In the case of Pavlov's dogs, food powder was the UCS. It elicited the UCR, salivation. At first, when Pavlov presented the sound of the bell or buzzer, the dogs did not salivate; the sound was merely a neutral stimulus, not a CS. However, with repeated pairings of the sound and the food powder, the sound became a CS, reliably eliciting the CR (salivation).

**unconditional stimulus (UCS)** In classical conditioning, a stimulus, such as food, that naturally elicits a reflexive response, such as salivation.
**unconditional response (UCR)** In classical conditioning, a response, such as salivation, that is naturally elicited by the UCS.
**conditional stimulus (CS)** In classical conditioning, a stimulus that, because of its repeated association with the UCS, eventually elicits a conditional response (CR).
**conditional response (CR)** In classical conditioning, the response elicited by the CS.

## The Biological Significance of Classical Conditioning

Salivation is an innate behaviour and is adaptive because it facilitates digestion. Through natural selection, the neural circuitry that underlies salivation has become part of the genetic endowment of many species. Pavlov's experiments demonstrated that an innate reflexive behaviour, such as salivation, can be elicited by novel stimuli. Thus, a response that is naturally under the control of appropriate environmental stimuli, such as salivation caused by the presence of food in the mouth, can also come to be controlled by other kinds of stimuli.

Classical conditioning accomplishes two functions. First, the ability to learn to recognize stimuli that predict the occurrence of an important event allows the learner to make the appropriate response faster and more effectively. For example, the buzz of a wasp near your head may make you duck and thus avoid being stung. Seeing a rival increases an animal's heart rate and blood flow to its muscles, makes it assume a threatening posture, and causes the release of hormones that prepare it for vigorous exercise. Hollis (1982) found that male Siamese fighting fish were more likely to win fights if they were given a stimulus (CS) warning that an intruding male (UCS) would soon enter their territory. When male blue gouramis (another species of fish) received a stimulus (CS) signalling the approach of a female (UCS), they were more likely to mate sooner and produce more offspring (Hollis et al., 1997). The pairing between sweet tastes and calories (which occurs in the natural diets of many species) can provide a signal that one has eaten enough (Pierce et al., 2007; Swithers & Davidson, 2008) and prevent overeating. Significantly, the learning that occurs with a biologically relevant UCS is also more resistant to subsequent modifications (Savastano & Miller, 2003).

The second function of classical conditioning is even more significant. Through classical conditioning, stimuli that were previously unimportant acquire some of the properties of the important stimuli with which they have been associated and thus become able to modify behaviour. A neutral

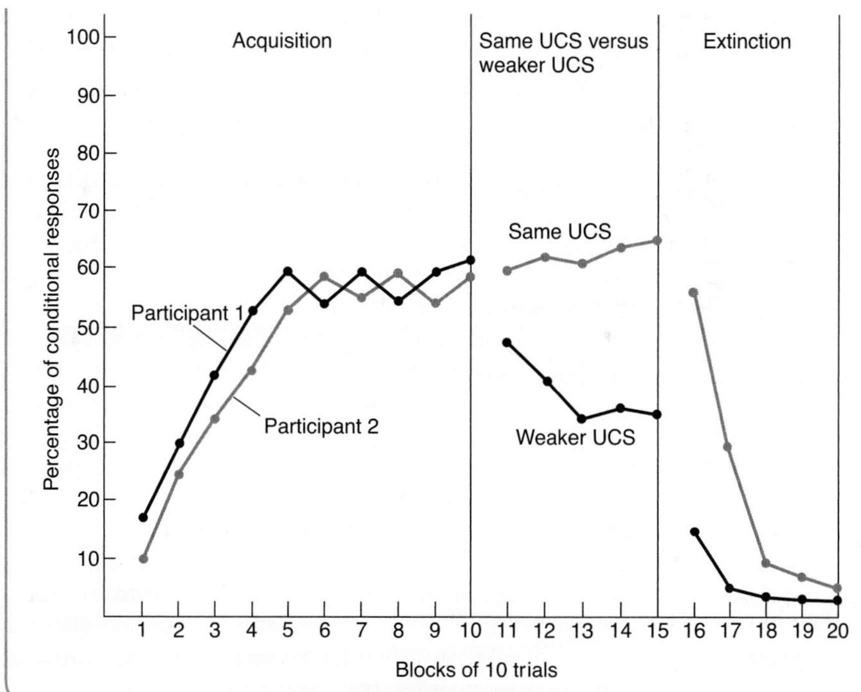


FIGURE 7•5 Acquisition and extinction of a conditional response. The left panel shows the learning curve for acquisition of an eyeblink response by two people. The middle panel shows a decrease in the percentage of CRs (eyeblinks) elicited by the CS (tone) when the intensity of the UCS (puff of air) was reduced. The right panel shows the extinction curves produced when the CS (tone) was no longer followed by the UCS (puff of air).

*(Adapted from Trapold, M. A., & Spence, K. W. (1960). Performance changes in eyelid conditioning as related to the motivational and reinforcing properties of the UCS.* Journal of Experimental Psychology, 59, *212. Published by APA. Used with permission.)*

stimulus becomes desirable when it is associated with a desirable stimulus or becomes undesirable when it is associated with an undesirable one. There is also some evidence that the specific sensory properties of the UCS become associated with the CS (Watt & Honey, 1997). In a sense, the stimulus takes on symbolic value. For example, we respond differently to the sight of a stack of money than to the sight of a stack of paper napkins. The reason for the special reaction to money is that money has, in the past, been associated with desirable commodities, such as food, clothing, automobiles, electronic devices, and so on. The symbolic value of money also seems to transfer to things associated with it, as shown by our culture's fascination with the wealthy and the famous. Ward-Robinson (2004) demonstrated how this transfer could occur in pigeons, using food. The pigeons were placed in a soundproof box. On one wall of the box there was a hole where the pigeons could be fed grain. The grain (UCS) was signalled by a sound (CS). Later, this sound was paired with a small light bulb located above the feeding door: The light would be turned on for five seconds, followed immediately by five seconds of the sound. Even though the light was never paired with the food, Ward-Robinson found that the pigeons would start pecking the light—behaving as if the light itself was grain. Krank and his colleagues found a similar type of behaviour in rats: When a small light was turned on just before rats were given a sip of alcohol, they would later approach and contact the light bulb whenever it lit up (Krank, O'Neill, Squarey, & Jacob, 2008).

The adaptive significance of classical conditioning is so general that even nematode worms exhibit it. Wen and colleagues (1997) placed worms in a solution of bacteria (a form of food for these worms). For some of the worms, the bacteria solution also contained a high number of salt ions; for others, it contained many chlorine ions. When later placed in a solution without bacteria, but with patches of either salt or chlorine ions, the worms migrated toward the ion source that had been paired with food. Clearly, the ion (CS) had become an attractant based on its previous pairing with food (UCS).

## Basic Principles of Classical Conditioning

Pavlov's research soon led to the discovery of several interesting phenomena that still bear the names he gave them 70 years ago (Pavlov, 1927). These include *acquisition, extinction, spontaneous recovery, stimulus generalization,* and *discrimination.*

**Acquisition** In laboratory experiments, a single pairing of the CS with the UCS is not usually sufficient for learning to take place. Only with repeated CS–UCS pairings does conditional responding gradually appear (although there are important exceptions, as we'll soon see). The learning phase of classical conditioning, during which the CR gradually increases in frequency or strength, is called **acquisition**. (During this phase, the CR is *acquired.*) The left side of **Figure 7•5** shows a learning curve that illustrates the course of acquisition of a conditional eyeblink response in two human participants. In this study, a tone (CS) was paired with a puff of air into the eye (UCS). The puff of air caused the participants' eyes to blink automatically (UCR). Conditioning was measured as the percentage of trials in which conditional eyeblinks

**acquisition** In classical conditioning, the time during which a CR first appears and increases in frequency.

**FIGURE 7•6** The timing of the CS and UCS in classical conditioning. The CS precedes the UCS by a brief interval of time, and both stimuli end simultaneously.

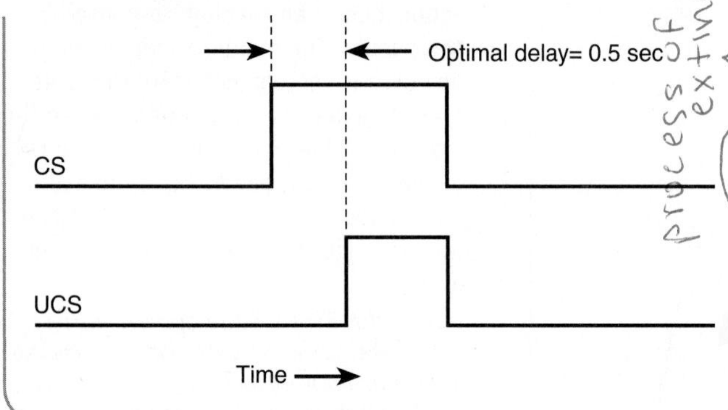


(CR) occurred. Note that at the beginning of the experiment, the tone elicited very few CRs. During the first 50 trials, the percentage of CRs increased rapidly but finally stabilized.

Two factors that influence the strength of the CR are the *intensity of the UCS* and the *timing of the CS and UCS*. The intensity of the UCS can determine how quickly the CR will be acquired: More intense UCSs usually produce more rapid learning.

Also, the more intense the UCS, the stronger the CR generally is. Look at the middle panel of Figure 7.5. After 100 conditioning trials, Participant 1 was given a less intense puff of air, while Participant 2 received the same UCS intensity as before. The percentage of CRs elicited from Participant 1 decreased soon after the intensity of the air puff was diminished, and levelled off at about 35 percent. This value represents the highest level of conditional responding that can be maintained by the weaker UCS.

The second factor affecting the acquisition of the CR is the timing of the CS and UCS. Classical conditioning occurs fastest when the CS occurs shortly before the UCS and both stimuli end at the same time. In many cases of classical conditioning, it has been found that 0.5 second is the optimal delay between the onset of the CS and the onset of the UCS. With shorter or longer delays, conditioning generally is slower and weaker. (See **Figure 7•6**.) And, as mentioned earlier, when the CS follows the UCS, there is generally little conditioning, although there are exceptions (see Spetch, Wilkie, & Pinel, 1981).

**Extinction and Spontaneous Recovery** What happens to a classically conditioned response if the CS continues to be presented but is no longer followed by the UCS? This procedure, called **extinction**, eventually eliminates the CR. Returning to our classically conditioned eyeblink response, suppose that after we reduce the intensity of the UCS, we stop presenting the UCS (the puff of air). However, we do continue to present the CS (the tone). The third panel of Figure 7.5 shows the results. CRs become less frequent, and eventually cease altogether. Note that extinction occurs more rapidly for Participant 1, which indicates that extinction is affected by the UCS intensity. Thus, once CRs are formed, they do not necessarily remain a part of an organism's behaviour.

It is important to realize that extinction occurs only when the CS no longer signals the UCS. For example, the eyeblink response will extinguish only if the tone is presented without the puff of air. If *neither* stimulus is presented, extinction will not occur. In other words, the participant must learn that the CS no longer predicts the occurrence of the UCS—and that cannot happen if neither stimulus is presented.

Once a CR has been extinguished, it may not disappear from the organism's behaviour permanently. Pavlov demonstrated that after responding had been extinguished, the CR would often suddenly reappear the next time the dog was placed in the experimental apparatus. Pavlov referred to the CR's reappearance after a "time out" period as **spontaneous recovery**. He also found that if he began presenting the CS and the UCS together again, the animals would acquire the conditional response very rapidly—much faster than they did in the first place.

**Stimulus Generalization and Discrimination** No two stimuli are exactly alike. Once a response has been conditioned to a CS, similar stimuli will also elicit that response. The more closely the other stimuli resemble the CS, the more likely they will elicit the CR. For example, Pavlov discovered that once a dog learned to salivate when it heard a bell, it would salivate when it heard a bell having a different tone or when it heard a buzzer. This phenomenon is called **generalization**: A response produced by a particular CS will also occur when a similar CS is presented. Of course, there are limits to generalization. A dog that learns to salivate when it hears a bell will probably not salivate when it hears a door close in the hallway.

In addition, an organism can be taught to distinguish between similar but different stimuli—a phenomenon called **discrimination**. (The term *discrimination* means "to distinguish.") Discrimination training is accomplished by using two different CSs during training. One CS is *always* followed by the UCS; the other CS is *never* followed by the UCS. For example, suppose that we regularly direct a puff of air at an animal's eye during each trial in which a low-pitched tone (CS+) is sounded, but on trials in which a high-pitched tone (CS–) is sounded, we present no air puff. At first, increased amounts of blinking will occur in response to both stimuli (generalization). Gradually, however, fewer and fewer blinks will occur after the CS–, but they will continue to be elicited by the CS+. (See **Figure 7•7**.) Discrimination, then, involves learning the difference between two or more stimuli. An animal

**extinction** In classical conditioning, the elimination of a response that occurs when the CS is repeatedly presented without being followed by the UCS.
**spontaneous recovery** After an interval of time, the reappearance of a response that had previously been extinguished.
**generalization** In classical conditioning, CRs elicited by stimuli that resemble the CS used in training.
**discrimination** In classical conditioning, the appearance of a CR when one stimulus is presented (the CS+) but not another (the CS–).

**FIGURE 7•7** Behaviour produced through discrimination training. The CS+ is always followed by the UCS (a puff of air directed at the eye); the CS– is always presented without the UCS.

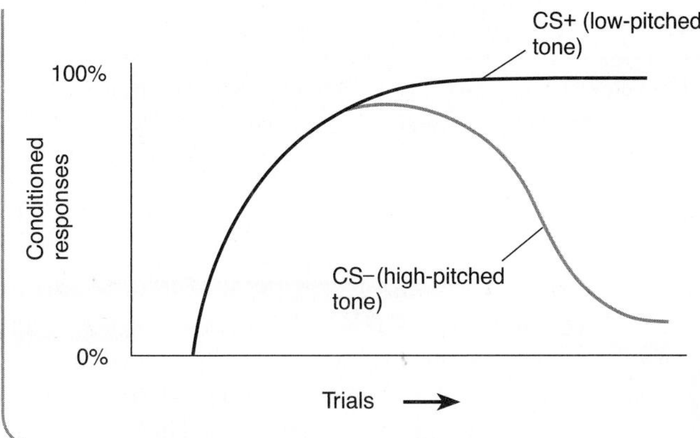


learns that differences among stimuli are important—it learns when to respond to one stimulus and when not to respond to a different stimulus.

## Conditional Emotional Responses

Many stimuli are able to arouse emotional responses, such as feelings of disgust, contempt, fear, anger, sadness, tenderness, longing, or sexual desire. Many of these stimuli, such as a place, a phrase, a song, or someone's voice and face, originally had no special significance. However, because these stimuli were paired with other stimuli that elicited strong emotional reactions, they acquired, as in the example of music from horror films, emotional or evaluative significance.

Todrank, Byrnes, Wrzesniewski, and Rozin (1995) showed a clear example of how this might happen. They asked people to sort through a number of photographs showing individuals of European origin and to consider whether they would like the individual in the photograph. Taking three pictures of people who were rated as "neutral" in attractiveness, Todrank and her colleagues then asked the participants of their study to look at the pictures and to smell a cloth impregnated with an odour such as baby powder or shampoo. One of these pictures was paired with an odour that people said they liked, one was paired with an odour people disliked, and the third picture was paired with a neutral odour. Todrank and her colleagues found that subsequent ratings of attractiveness for the individuals in the pictures shifted toward their preference for the odours. Pictures associated with a disliked odour were now rated as less attractive than those paired with a liked odour. Thus, classical conditioning may play a role in the development of personal likes and dislikes or in the emotional reaction to other stimuli, including those that produce pain (Wunsch, Philippot, & Plaghki, 2003).

Many people are troubled by behaviours that they wish they could stop or by bothersome thoughts and fears. **Phobias** are unreasonable fears of specific objects or situations, such as spiders, automobiles, or enclosed spaces. Presumably, at some time early in life, the person with the phobia was exposed to the now-fearsome object in conjunction with a stimulus that elicited pain or fear. For example, being stuck in a hot, overcrowded elevator with a group of frightened and sweating fellow passengers might be expected to lead to a fear of elevators or perhaps even to produce a full-fledged phobia.

Classical conditioning can occur even without direct experience with the conditional and unconditional stimuli. For example, a child of a parent who has a snake phobia can develop the same fear simply by observing signs of fear in the parent. The child need not be attacked or menaced by a snake. In addition, people can develop phobias vicariously—by hearing about or reading stories that vividly describe unpleasant episodes. The imaginary episode that we picture as we hear or read a story (UCS) can provide imaginary stimuli (CSs) that lead to *real* conditional emotional responses (CRs).

If classical conditioning is responsible for the development of phobias, then perhaps knowledge of the principles of learning can be used to eliminate them. In fact, therapists have done exactly that; we will discuss the therapeutic procedures they have devised in Chapter 18. There have also been suggestions (reviewed by LoLordo & Drougas, 1989) that biologically relevant stimuli (such as the sight of a snake) are especially prone to classically conditioned emotional responses. Later in this chapter, we will look at these biological connections.

## What Is Learned in Classical Conditioning?

At an influential meeting at Dalhousie University, many learning theorists pointed out the importance of information in classical conditioning (Macintosh & Honig, 1969). The different lines of research showed that, for classical conditioning to occur, the CS must be a reliable predictor of the UCS. Let's consider my horror film example again. The change in tempo of the music precedes some surprise threat. But think about all of the other stimuli in the theatre at that moment: the sight of people around you, the smell of popcorn, and so on. Why don't any of these become a CS for anxiety? What prevents you from forming an instant phobia to the new boyfriend or girlfriend who accompanied you to the horror movie? The answer is that only the change in music accompanied the really frightful parts of the movie. All of the other stimuli were less reliable predictors of the UCS. A neutral stimulus becomes a CS only when the following conditions are satisfied:

- The CS regularly occurs prior to the presentation of the UCS.
- The CS does not regularly occur when the UCS is absent.

**phobia** Unreasonable fear of specific objects or situations, such as insects, animals, or enclosed spaces, learned through classical conditioning.

**FIGURE 7•8** A blocking design. The experimental group is first conditioned to respond to $CS_1$. Then, after CRs are acquired to $CS_1$, $CS_2$ is presented at the same times as $CS_1$ and conditioning continues. Finally, $CS_1$ and $CS_2$ are tested separately. In the experimental group, only $CS_1$ evokes a CR. In the control group, both $CS_1$ and $CS_2$ evoked CRs when they were presented.

| | Experimental (blocking) group | Control group |
|---|---|---|
| Conditioning phase 1 | $CS_1$ (tone) → UCS (food) | $CS_3$ (click) → UCS (food) |
| Conditioning phase 2 | $CS_1$ (tone) plus $CS_2$ (light) → UCS (food) | $CS_1$ (tone) plus $CS_2$ (light) → UCS (food) |
| Test phase | $CS_1$ (tone) presented alone—CR<br>$CS_2$ (light) presented alone—**no CR** | $CS_1$ (tone) presented alone—CR<br>$CS_2$ (light) presented alone—CR |

This is just another way of saying what I've said before: The key factor in classical conditioning is the reliability of the CS in predicting the presentation of the UCS (Rescorla, 1966).

This principle has been clearly established by a conditioning phenomenon known as **blocking**, wherein a previously conditioned CS can attenuate the conditioning of a neutral CS if the two are presented together. In a demonstration of blocking (see **Figure 7•8**), one stimulus ($CS_1$) is paired with the UCS. Then, a new stimulus ($CS_2$) is presented together with $CS_1$ and the compound of two stimuli is followed by the UCS. Compared to a condition where $CS_1$ has not been previously trained, $CS_2$ acquires little, if any, CR (Pearce & Bouton, 2001).

You might think of blocking in the following way: The new stimulus, $CS_2$, adds no new information about the occurrence of the UCS; it is already predicted by the presentation of $CS_1$. Only if something about the UCS had changed at the time $CS_2$ was introduced would it provide new information (Rescorla, 1999).

These examples raise the further question as to what the information is about. Classical conditioning would seem to provide two types of information: the *what* and the *when* of future events.

The first type of information, the *what*, allows animals to learn that a particular event is about to occur. It has been suggested (e.g., Rescorla, 1973) that their behaviour is determined by their memory of the event. An experiment by Hollis, Langworthy-Lam, Blouin, and Romano (2004) using the fish we discussed earlier—blue gouramis—demonstrates Rescorla's idea. Male gouramis show a dominance hierarchy, in which one fish will defer to another, more dominant fish when they are both feeding. Typically, the less dominant male will swim in a "submissive" posture in the presence of food, which prevents him from being attacked by his hungry and aggressive rival. Hollis and her colleagues isolated subordinate male gouramis and conditioned them by pairing a light with the delivery of food. These fish rapidly learned the relationship between light and food and showed feeding behaviours whenever the light was turned on. Then, they were placed in a tank with a more dominant male. When the light was turned on, the first behaviour that the conditioned fish showed was not a feeding response, but the submissive response. It was as if the light activated an expectation that food was about to appear; the conditioned males reacted as they would when they encountered food in the presence of a more dominant rival. The results show that it is not, strictly speaking, the unconditioned response that determines the CR, but rather the memory of what the CS predicts.

In a test of this idea, Hilliard and Domjan (1995) examined the conditioning of sexual behaviours in male Japanese quail. The researchers showed the male birds a block of grey foam (CS) and then allowed the birds to interact with a female bird (UCS) for five minutes. After several such pairings of the foam and the female, the males showed a large increase in the time they interacted with the CS object. Behaviour to the CS was presumably determined by the males' memory of the female. Hilliard and Domjan then undertook to alter the sexual connotation of this memory. For example, in one condition (the satiated condition), males were given access to eight female birds over the course of 40 minutes. In another (the deprived condition), a different group of males was not given this opportunity. When all birds were later shown the CS, the satiated birds made fewer sexual responses. This implies that what was learned involved a memory of the UCS, a memory that could be altered by subsequent experience such as satiation.

The second type of information, the *when*, is about the timing of events. Consider the case of backward conditioning that I discussed earlier. In backward conditioning, the UCS precedes the CS. If animals only learned that the two stimuli "went together," you might expect some conditioning. However, because the CS follows the UCS, and therefore signals a long period of time without another UCS, the animal could learn that the CS predicts the absence of the UCS. Indeed, under some conditions, animals will show a little conditioning after a few backward trials, but will show the opposite (known as an **inhibitory conditional response**, as contrasted with an **excitatory conditional response**) after many trials (Heth, 1976). Indeed, they may learn something about the specific

**blocking** The prevention of or attenuation in learning that occurs to a neutral CS when it is conditioned in the presence of a previously conditioned stimulus.

**inhibitory conditional response** A response tendency conditioned to a signal that predicts the absence of the UCS; generally not observed directly but assessed though other tests.

**excitatory conditional response** A response tendency conditioned to a signal that the UCS is about to occur. This is the type of CR exemplified by Pavlov's salivation response.

**BACKWARDS CONDITIONING**

Presumed First-Order Backwards Conditioning Memory Representation

Phase 1 — UCS, $CS_B$

Presumed Second-Order Conditioning Memory Representation

Phase 2 — $CS_F$, $CS_B$

Presumed Integrated Memory Representation

Hypothesized Temporal Integration — $CS_F$, $CS_B$, UCS

**FIGURE 7•9** Experimental procedure and hypothesis of the Cole and Miller study. In Phase 1, rats were trained using a backward conditioning procedure. In Phase 1, rats were given backward conditioning trials in which $CS_B$ followed the UCS. In Phase 2, a new stimulus, $CS_F$, was presented before $CS_B$. Note, however, that the UCS was not given. The experimental hypothesis was that the rats would "fill in" the temporal sequence and behave as if $CS_F$ was a forward conditional stimulus.

*(Reprinted from* Learning and Motivation, 30*(2), Cole, R. P. & Miller R. R., Conditioned excitation and conditioned inhibition acquired through backward conditioning, 129–156, (1999) with permission from Elsevier. http://www.sciencedirect.com/science/journal/00239690)*

timing of events during the conditioning trial. Cole and Miller (1999) trained rats in a conditioned procedure in which a backward CS ($CS_B$) followed a UCS. Then, after substantial training, the UCS was eliminated, and a forward CS ($CS_F$) was presented just before $CS_B$. (See **Figure 7•9**.) Cole and Miller speculated that a form of temporal integration would occur, and that the rats would demonstrate an excitatory CR. Their experiment confirmed this: Even though $CS_F$ had never been presented prior to a UCS, the rats behaved as though it signalled an upcoming UCS.

## Interim Summary

### Habituation and Classical Conditioning

So far, we have considered two forms of learning: habituation and classical conditioning. Habituation screens out stimuli that experience has shown to be unimportant. This form of learning allows organisms to respond to more important stimuli, such as those related to survival and reproduction.

Classical conditioning occurs when a neutral stimulus occurs just before an unconditional stimulus—one that automatically elicits a behaviour. The response that an organism makes in response to the unconditional stimulus (the UCR) is already a natural part of its behaviour; what the organism learns to do is to make it in response to a new stimulus (the conditional stimulus, or CS). When the response is made to the CS, it is called the conditional response, or CR.

The relationship between the CS and UCS determines the nature of the CR. Acquisition of the CR is influenced by the intensity of the UCS and the delay between the CS and the UCS. Extinction occurs when the CS is still presented but is no longer followed by the UCS. However, the CR may show spontaneous recovery later, even after a delay. Generalization occurs when stimuli similar to the CS used in training elicit the CR. Discrimination involves training the organism to make a CR only after a particular CS occurs.

Through classical conditioning, stimuli that were previously neutral with respect to an organism's behaviour can be made important. This importance can have profound effects on a limitless variety of behaviours. For example, the importance of money, established through classical conditioning, affects a broad range of our behaviour. Many of the emotions we feel when we encounter a person, place, or object that previously has been associated with a pleasant or unpleasant situation are acquired through classical conditioning. This phenomenon explains why we sometimes feel a touch of nostalgia when we hear a song that reminds us of a friend we have not seen in a long time. Classical conditioning can also establish various classes of stimuli as objects of fear (phobia). For classical conditioning to occur, the CS not only must occur immediately before the UCS, but also must reliably predict the UCS. The memory of the UCS plays a strong role in the determination of the strength of the CR, and the timing of the events determines whether an excitatory or inhibitory CR is observed.

**QUESTIONS TO CONSIDER**

1. Can you think of a personal situation in which you might *not* become habituated to an orienting response? Describe this situation.

2. Do you think it would take longer to become habituated to a stimulus associated with danger (for example, the lights and sounds signalling an approaching train) or to a stimulus associated with a non-dangerous situation, such as the hourly chiming of a grandfather clock? Explain.
3. Reflect for a few moments on a recent situation in which you felt a strong emotion. What aspects of the situation contributed to this emotion? Can you describe the situation in terms of the elements of the classical conditioning paradigm?
4. Under what set of conditions might the emotion you just described be generalized to other situations? Under what set of conditions would this emotion not be generalized to other situations?

## Operant Conditioning

Habituation and classical conditioning teach us about stimuli in the environment: We learn to ignore unimportant stimuli, and we learn about those that predict the occurrence of important ones. These forms of learning deal with relations between one stimulus and another. In contrast, **operant conditioning** teaches us the relations between environmental stimuli and our own behaviour. (The term *operant* refers to the fact that an organism learns through responding—through *operating* on the environment.) The principle behind operant conditioning is already familiar to you: When a particular action has good consequences, the action will tend to be repeated; when a particular action has bad consequences, the action will tend not to be repeated.

### The Law of Effect

Operant conditioning was first discovered in the basement of a house in Cambridge, Massachusetts, by a 24-year-old man who would later become one of the twentieth century's most influential educational psychologists, Edward L. Thorndike. The house belonged to William James, whom you'll remember from Chapter 1, and Thorndike had persuaded him to give up the use of the basement in the interests of science.

Thorndike placed a hungry cat inside a "puzzle box." The animal could escape and eat some food only after it operated a latch that opened the door. (See **Figure 7•10**.) At first, the cat engaged in random behaviour: meowing, scratching, hissing, pacing, and so on. Eventually, the cat would accidentally activate the latch and open the door. On successive trials, the animal's behaviour would become more and more efficient until it was operating the latch without hesitation. Thorndike called this process "learning by trial and accidental success."

**FIGURE 7•10** Thorndike's original conditioning procedure. A cat placed in the puzzle box had to pull the ring of wire inside the box to operate the latch. The door would then open, and the cat could escape from the puzzle box and gain access to food. The graph shows the reduction in the time one cat needed to operate the latch over repeated trials.

*(Adapted from Thorndike, E. L. (1898). Animal intelligence.* Psychological Review Monograph Supplement, 2 *[whole No. 8].)*

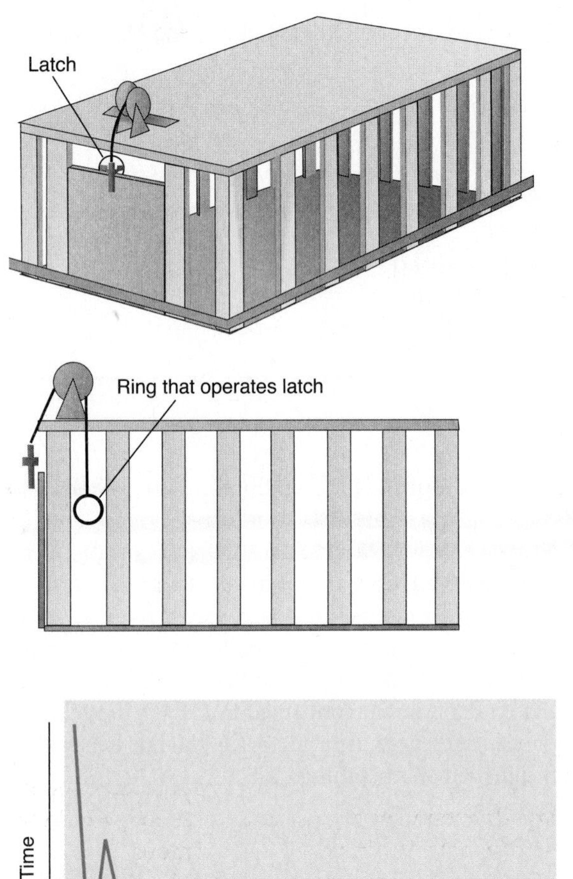


Thorndike explained that the cat learned to make the correct response because only the correct response was followed by a favourable outcome: escape from the box and the opportunity to eat some food. The occurrence of the favourable outcome strengthens the response that produced it. Thorndike called this relation between a response and its consequences the **law of effect.**

As you can see, the law of effect is analogous to the concept of natural selection, a point made by Thorndike himself. Natural selection determines which members of a species will

**operant conditioning** A form of learning in which behaviour is affected by its consequences. Favourable consequences strengthen the behaviour and unfavourable consequences weaken the behaviour.

**law of effect** Thorndike's idea that the consequences of a behaviour determine whether it is likely to be repeated.

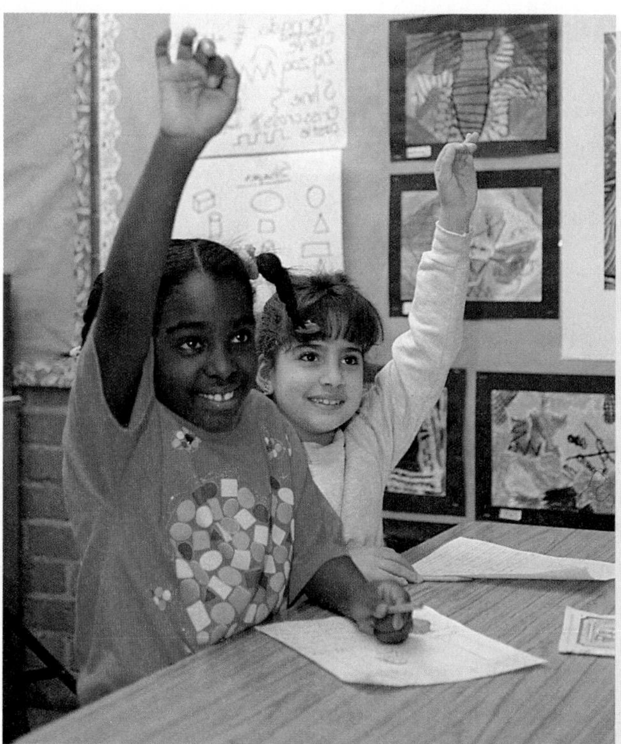

▲ *Students' raising of their hands in response to their teacher's questions is reinforced by the opportunity to speak and receive attention from their teacher.*

survive and reproduce. The law of effect determines which responses will survive and become part of the organism's behavioural repertoire. As Skinner (1981, 1990) noted, it is a sort of selection by consequences. The ability to adjust behaviour to fit changes in the environment is highly adaptive.

The impact of Thorndike's discovery of the law of effect on the early development of scientific psychology would be difficult to overstate. It stimulated an enormous number of experimental studies aimed at understanding behaviour–environment interactions, a line of research known today as *behaviour analysis*. Nowhere was this effect more evident than in the work of B. F. Skinner, to which we now turn.

## Skinner and Operant Behaviour

Although Thorndike discovered the law of effect, Harvard psychologist Burrhus Frederic Skinner championed the laboratory study of the law of effect and advocated the application of behaviour analysis and its methods to solving human problems (Skinner, 1953, 1971; Mazur, 1998). He devised objective methods for studying behaviour, invented apparatus and methods for observing it, and created his own philosophy for interpreting it. Moreover, he wrote several books for the general public, including a novel, *Walden Two*, that showed how his discoveries might be used to better society.

Skinner devised the **operant chamber**, an apparatus in which an animal's behaviour can be easily observed, manipulated, and automatically recorded. (See **Figure 7•11**.) For

**FIGURE 7•11** An operant chamber. (This operant chamber is used for lever pressing in rats.)

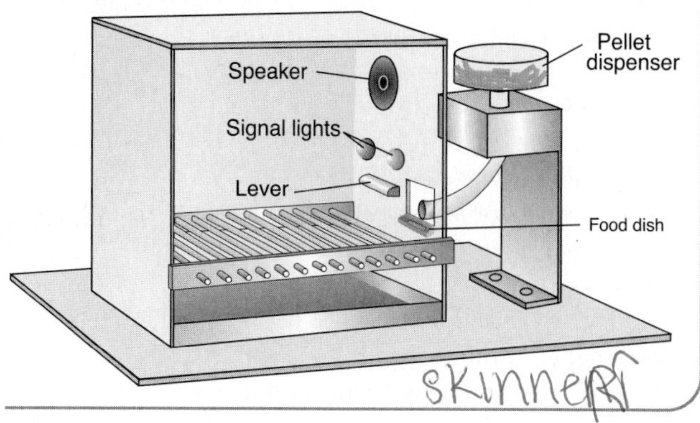


example, an operant chamber used for rats is constructed so that a particular behaviour, such as pressing on a lever, will occasionally cause a pellet of food to be delivered. An operant chamber used for pigeons is built so that a peck at a plastic disc on the front wall will occasionally open a drawer that contains some grain. In each instance, the operant chamber provides an unconstrained opportunity for a simple response to be performed by the animal.

Behaviour analysts manipulate environmental events to determine their effects on *response rate*, the number of responses emitted during a given amount of time. Events that increase response rate are said to *strengthen* responding; events that decrease response rate weaken responding. To measure response rate, Skinner devised the **cumulative recorder**, a device that records each response as it occurs in time.

Skinner's development of the operant chamber and the cumulative recorder represent clear advances over Thorndike's research methods because participants can (1) emit responses more freely over a greater time period, and (2) be studied for longer periods of time without interference produced by the researcher handling or otherwise interacting with them between trials. Under highly controlled conditions such as these, behaviour analysts have been able to discover a wide range of important behavioural principles.

### The Three-Term Contingency

Behaviour does not occur in a vacuum. Sometimes a response will have certain consequences; sometimes it will not. Suppose that you want to teach your dog to bark whenever you say the word *speak*. You get a few pieces of food that the dog likes. Then you attract his attention and say, "Speak!" while waving a piece of food in front of him. The dog begins to show excitement at the sight of the food and finally lets out a bark. Immediately, you give him the food. Then you bring

**operant chamber** An apparatus in which an animal's behaviour can be easily observed, manipulated, and automatically recorded.
**cumulative recorder** A mechanical device connected to an operant chamber for the purpose of recording operant responses as they occur in time.

out another piece of food and again say, "Speak!" This time the dog probably barks a little sooner. After several trials, the dog will bark whenever you say "Speak!" even if no food is visible. You do not give your dog a piece of food whenever he barks. You only do so if you have just said "Speak!" If the dog barks at other times, you ignore him or even tell him to be quiet. Your dog learns to discriminate between times when barking will get him a piece of food and times when it will not. The word *speak* serves as a **discriminative stimulus**—a stimulus that indicates that behaviour will have certain consequences and thus sets the occasion for responding.

Our daily behaviour is guided by many different kinds of discriminative stimuli. For example, consider answering the telephone. The phone rings, you pick it up and say "Hello" into the receiver. Most of the time, someone on the other end of the line begins to speak. Have you ever picked up a telephone when it was not ringing and said "Hello"? Doing so would be absurd, because there would be no one on the other end of the line with whom to speak. We answer the phone (make a response) only when the phone rings (the preceding event) because, in the past, someone with whom we enjoy talking has been at the other end of the line (the following event).

Skinner referred formally to the relationship among these three items—the preceding event, the response, and the following event—as the **three-term contingency**. He distinguished these components in the following ways. (See **Figure 7•12**.)

- The preceding event—the *discriminative stimulus*—sets the occasion for responding because, in the past, when that stimulus occurred, the response was followed by certain consequences. If the phone rings, we are likely to answer it because we have learned that doing so has particular (and generally favourable) consequences.
- The *response* we make—in this case, picking up the phone and saying "Hello" when it rings—is called an *operant behaviour*.
- The *following event*—the voice on the other end of the line—is the consequence of the operant behaviour.

The three-term contingency specifies that, in the presence of a discriminative stimulus, certain consequences follow the operant behaviour. These consequences are *contingent* upon behaviour; that is, they are produced by that behaviour. In the presence of discriminative stimuli, a consequence will occur *if and only if* an operant behaviour occurs. In the absence of a discriminative stimulus, the operant behaviour will have no effect. Once an operant behaviour is established, it tends to persist whenever the discriminative stimulus occurs, even if other aspects of the environment change (Mace et al., 1990; Nevin, 1988). Of course, motivational factors can affect a response. For example, if your dog is not hungry, it might not bother to bark when you say "Speak!" and you might not bother to answer the telephone if you are doing something you do not want to interrupt. We will look at the role of motivation in behaviour in Chapter 13.

**FIGURE 7•12** The three-term contingency.

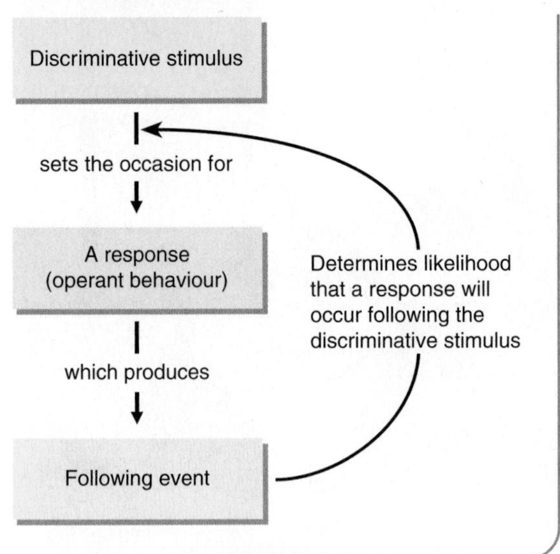


## Reinforcement, Punishment, and Extinction

Behaviour analysts study behaviour–environment interactions by manipulating the relations among components of the three-term contingency. Of the three elements, the consequence is the most frequently manipulated variable. In general, operant behaviours can be followed by five different kinds of consequences: positive reinforcement, negative reinforcement, punishment, response cost, and extinction. These consequences are always defined in terms of their effect on responding.

**Positive Reinforcement** **Positive reinforcement** is an increase in the frequency of a response that is regularly and reliably followed by an appetitive stimulus. An *appetitive stimulus* is any stimulus that an organism seeks out. If an appetitive stimulus follows a response and increases the frequency of that response, we call it a *positive reinforcer*. Suppose that you visit a new restaurant and really enjoy your meal. You are likely to visit the restaurant several more times because you had this experience. This example illustrates positive reinforcement. Your enjoyment of the food (the appetitive stimulus) reinforces your going to the restaurant and ordering dinner (the response).

**Negative Reinforcement** **Negative reinforcement** is an increase in the frequency of a response that is regularly and

**discriminative stimulus** In operant conditioning, the stimulus that sets the occasion for responding because, in the past, a behaviour has produced certain consequences in the presence of that stimulus.

**three-term contingency** The relation among discriminative stimuli, behaviour, and the consequences of that behaviour. A motivated organism emits a specific response in the presence of a discriminative stimulus because, in the past, that response has been reinforced only when the discriminative stimulus is present.

**positive reinforcement** An increase in the frequency of a response that is regularly and reliably followed by an appetitive stimulus.

**negative reinforcement** An increase in the frequency of a response that is regularly and reliably followed by the termination of an aversive stimulus.

▲ *Our use of umbrellas when it is raining is a negatively reinforced behaviour. Opening an umbrella blocks the rain that would otherwise fall on us.*

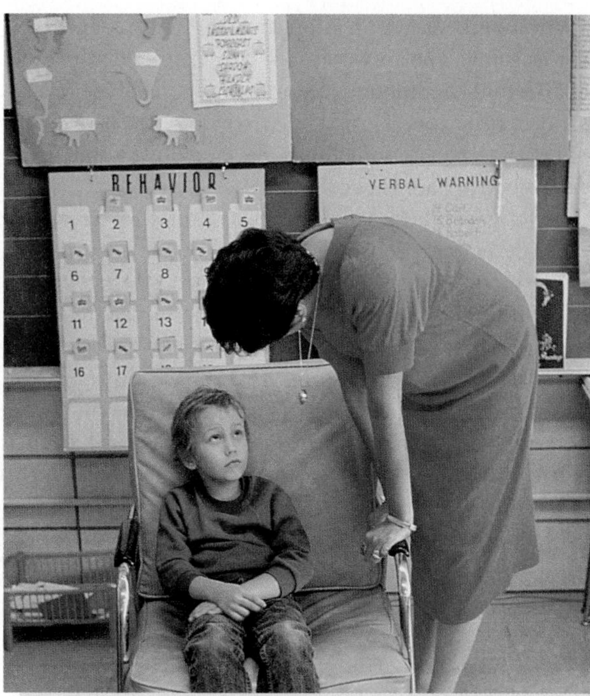


▲ *Punishment occurs when a punishing stimulus immediately follows a response. Punishment need not involve something physically aversive; social disapproval can also be punishing. However, punishment tends to elicit undesirable emotional side effects and must be used carefully.*

reliably followed by the termination of an *aversive stimulus*. An aversive stimulus is unpleasant or painful. If an aversive stimulus is terminated (ends or is turned off) as soon as a response occurs and thus increases the frequency of that response, we call it a *negative reinforcer*. For example, after you have walked barefoot across a stretch of hot pavement, the termination of the painful burning sensation negatively reinforces your response of sticking your feet into a puddle of cool water. Or suppose that a woman staying in a rented house cannot get to sleep because of the unpleasant screeching noise that the furnace makes. She goes to the basement to discover the source of the noise and finally kicks the side of the oil burner. The noise ceases. The next time the furnace screeches, she immediately goes to the basement and kicks the side of the oil burner. This example, too, illustrates negative reinforcement. The unpleasant noise (the aversive stimulus) is terminated when the woman kicks the side of the oil burner (the response).

Both positive and negative reinforcement increase the likelihood that a given response will occur again. However, positive reinforcement involves the *occurrence* of an *appetitive* stimulus, whereas negative reinforcement involves the *termination* of an *aversive* stimulus. Negative reinforcement is thus not the same as punishment (which we'll look at next).

**Punishment** **Punishment** is a decrease in the frequency of a response that is regularly and reliably followed by an aversive stimulus. If an aversive stimulus follows a response and decreases the frequency of that response, we call it a *punisher*. For example, receiving a painful bite would punish the response of sticking your finger into a parrot's cage.

Although punishment is effective in reducing or suppressing undesirable behaviour, it can also produce several negative side effects:

- Unrestrained use of physical force may cause serious bodily injury.
- Punishment often induces fear, hostility, and other undesirable emotions in people receiving punishment. It may result in retaliation against the punisher.
- Through punishment, organisms learn only which response *not* to make. Punishment does not teach the organism desirable responses.

Reinforcement and punishment are most effective in maintaining or changing behaviour when a stimulus *immediately* follows the behaviour. Consider a woman who returns home from work and discovers that her dog has soiled the carpet. The dog runs to greet her and she says, "Bad dog," and slaps it. When she comes home the next day, she calls her dog but it stays where it is, hiding under the bed. Why do you think the dog hides?

This example illustrates punishment, but not of the response that the woman intends. The response she punishes is the one that the dog has just made: running up to her when she enters the door. Because the dog soiled the rug some time ago, that response is not punished.

It may occur to you that many organisms—particularly humans—can tolerate a long delay between their work and its reward. This ability appears to contradict the principle that reinforcement must occur immediately. However, the apparent contradiction can be explained by a phenomenon called *conditioned reinforcement*, which we will examine later in this chapter.

**punishment** A decrease in the frequency of a response that is regularly and reliably followed by an aversive stimulus.

Why is immediacy of reinforcement or punishment essential for learning? The answer is found by examining the function of operant conditioning: learning about the consequences of our own behaviour. Normally, causes and effects are closely related in time; you do something and something immediately happens, good or bad. The consequences of our actions teach us whether to repeat those actions. Events that follow a response by a long delay were probably not caused by that response.

**Response Cost** **Response cost** is a decrease in the frequency of a response that is regularly and reliably followed by the termination of an appetitive stimulus. Response cost is a form of punishment. For example, suppose that you are enjoying a conversation with an attractive person that you have just met. You make a disparaging remark about a well-known politician. Your new friend's smile suddenly disappears. You quickly change the topic and never bring it up again. The behaviour (disparaging remark) is followed by the removal of an appetitive stimulus (your new friend's smile). The removal of the smile punishes the disparaging remark.

The procedure that produces response cost is often referred to as *time out from positive reinforcement* (or, more generally, *omission*) when it is used to remove a person physically from an activity that is reinforcing to that person. For example, suppose that a young boy is tormenting his little sister while they are watching television. Their mother might say to him, "That's enough! No more television for you today! Go to your room!" The boy can no longer engage in the activity he enjoys (watching television) after he is sent out of the room.

Do not confuse response cost with negative reinforcement. As a type of punishment, response cost causes a behaviour to *decrease,* whereas negative reinforcement causes a behaviour to *increase.* (This is probably a good rule to memorize.)

As we have just seen, there are four types of operant conditioning—two kinds of reinforcement and two kinds of punishment—caused by the occurrence or termination of appetitive or aversive stimuli. (See **Figure 7•13**.) These procedures extend Thorndike's law of effect. However, there is another way to change behaviour through operant conditioning that involves no consequences at all. It is called *extinction.*

**Extinction** **Extinction** is a decrease in the frequency of a previously reinforced response because it is no longer followed by a reinforcer. Behaviour that is no longer reinforced decreases in frequency—it is said to *extinguish.* For example, a rat whose lever pressing was reinforced previously with food will eventually stop pressing the lever when food is no longer delivered. People soon learn to stop dropping money into vending machines that don't work. A young boy will stop telling his favourite "knock-knock" joke if no one laughs at it anymore.

**response cost** A decrease in the frequency of a response that is regularly and reliably followed by the termination of an appetitive stimulus.
**extinction** A decrease in the frequency of a previously reinforced response because it is no longer followed by a reinforcer.
**shaping** The reinforcement of behaviour that successively approximates the desired response until that response is fully acquired.

**FIGURE 7•13** Reinforcement, punishment, and extinction produced by the onset, termination, or omission of appetitive or aversive stimuli. The upward-pointing arrows indicate the occurrence of a response.

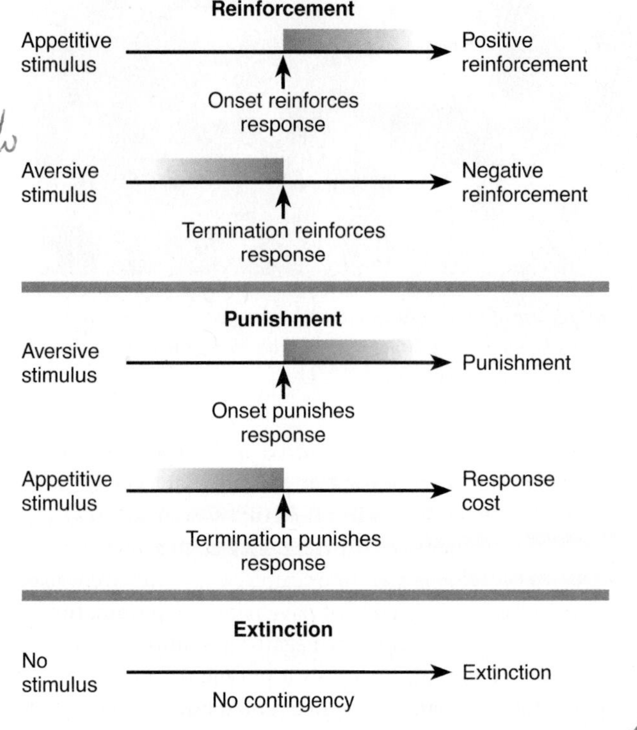


Extinction is not the same as forgetting. Forgetting takes place when a behaviour is not rehearsed (or a person does not think about a particular memory) for a long time. Extinction takes place when an organism makes a response that is no longer reinforced. If the organism does not have an opportunity to make that response, it will not extinguish. For example, if you go out of town for a few weeks, you will not forget how to operate the vending machine where you often buy a candy bar. But if you put money in the machine and do not receive anything in return, your response will extinguish.

Extinction makes good sense. If a response no longer "works," there is no point in persisting in making it. In fact, doing so expends energy unnecessarily and keeps an organism from discovering a different response that will work.

## Other Operant Procedures and Phenomena

The basic principles of reinforcement, punishment, and extinction described above are used in other operant procedures to teach an organism a new response, to teach it when to or when not to respond, or to teach it how to respond in a particular way. Let's examine some of these other operant procedures.

**Shaping** Most behaviour is acquired through an organism's interaction with reinforcing and punishing events in its environment. In fact, Skinner developed a technique, called **shaping**, to teach new behaviours to his participants. Shaping involves reinforcing any behaviour that *successively approximates* the

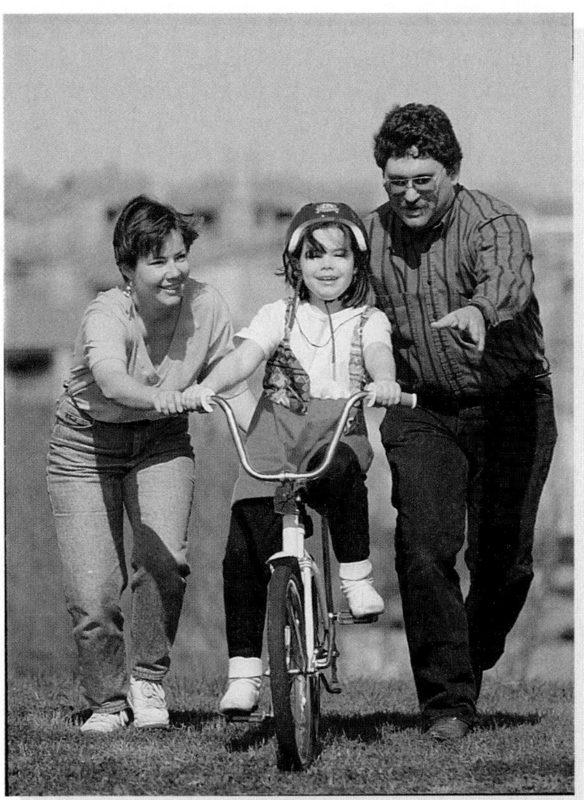

▲ *Complex behaviours, such as riding a bicycle, are not learned all at once. Instead, they are shaped; that is, we first learn behaviours that only approximate the level of skill ultimately needed to perform the behaviour properly.*

desired response. Suppose we want to train a rat to press a lever when a red light is lit (the discriminative stimulus) in an operant chamber. Although the rat has used its paws to manipulate many things in its lifetime, it has never before pressed a lever in an operant chamber. And when first placed in the chamber, it is unlikely to press the lever even once on its own.

We construct the chamber so that the delivery of a food pellet can be made dependent on the rat's pressing the lever. The lever on the wall of the chamber is attached to an electrical switch that is wired to electronic control equipment or to a computer. A mechanical dispenser can automatically drop moulded pellets of food, about the size of a very small pea, into a dish in the chamber.

Before we can shape lever pressing, we must make the rat hungry. We do so by feeding the rat once a day at the same time. When that time comes around, we know that it is hungry. We place the animal in the operant chamber and then train it to eat the food pellets as they are dispensed from the pellet dispenser. As each pellet is delivered, the dispenser makes a clicking sound. This sound is important. No matter where the rat is in the operant chamber, it can hear the sound, which indicates that the food pellet has been dispensed. Once the rat is hungry and has learned where to obtain food, we are ready to shape the desired response. We make the operation of the pellet dispenser contingent on the rat's behaviour. We start by giving the rat a food pellet for simply facing in the direction of the lever. Next, we wait until the rat makes a move toward the lever. Finally, we give the rat a piece of food only if it actually touches the lever. Soon, our rat performs like Thorndike's cats: It makes the same response again and again.

Behaviour analysts use shaping as a formal training procedure in the laboratory, but it is also a common procedure in the world outside. A teacher praises poorly formed letters produced by a child who is just beginning to print. As time goes on, only more accurately drawn letters bring approval. The method of successive approximations can also be self-administered. Consider the acquisition of skills through trial and error. To begin with, you must be able to recognize the *target behaviour*—the behaviour displayed by a person having the appropriate skill. Your first attempts produce behaviours that vaguely resemble those of a skilled performer, and you are satisfied by the results of these attempts. In other words, the stimuli that are produced by your behaviour serve as reinforcers for that behaviour. As your skill develops, you become less satisfied with crude approximations to the final behaviour; you are satisfied only when your behaviour improves so that it more closely resembles the target behaviour. Your own criteria change as you become more skilled. Skills such as learning to draw a picture, catch a baseball, or make a bed are all behaviours that are acquired through shaping. After all, when a child learns these skills, he or she first learns behaviours that only approximate the final level of skill that he or she will eventually obtain. This process is perfectly analogous to the use of changing criteria in training an animal to perform a complex behaviour.

**Intermittent Reinforcement** In the examples so far, we have considered situations in which a reinforcing stimulus is presented after each response (or, in the case of extinction, not at all). But usually, not every response is reinforced. Sometimes a kind word is ignored; sometimes it is appreciated. Not every fishing trip is rewarded with a catch, but some are, and that is enough to keep a person trying. As we'll see, the effects of intermittent reinforcement on behaviour are very different from those of continuous reinforcement.

The term **intermittent reinforcement** refers to situations in which not every occurrence of a response is reinforced. The relation between responding and reinforcement usually follows one of two patterns: Each response has a certain probability of being reinforced, or responses are reinforced after particular intervals of time have elapsed.

*Probability-based patterns* require a variable number of responses for each reinforcer. Consider the performance of an archer shooting arrows at a target. Suppose that the archer hits the bull's eye one-fifth of the time. On average, he will have to make five responses for every reinforcement (hitting

**intermittent reinforcement** The occasional reinforcement of a particular behaviour; produces responding that is more resistant to extinction.

the bull's eye); the ratio of responding to reinforcement is five to one. The number of reinforcers the archer receives is directly proportional to the number of responses he makes. If he shoots more arrows (that is, if his rate of responding increases), he will receive more reinforcers—assuming that he does not become tired or careless.

Behaviour analysts refer to this pattern of intermittent reinforcement as a *ratio schedule of reinforcement*. In the laboratory, the apparatus controlling the operant chamber may be programmed to deliver a reinforcer after every fifth response (a ratio of five to one), after every tenth response, after every two hundredth, or after any desired number. If the ratio is constant—for example, if a reinforcer is delivered following every tenth response—the animal will respond rapidly, receive the reinforcer, pause a little while, and then begin responding again. This type of ratio schedule is called a **fixed-ratio schedule** (specifically, in this case, a *fixed-ratio 10 schedule*).

If the ratio is variable, averaging a particular number of responses but varying from trial to trial, the animal will respond at a steady, rapid pace. For example, we might program a reinforcer to be delivered, on average, after every 50 responses. This type of ratio schedule is called a **variable-ratio schedule** (specifically, a *variable-ratio 50 schedule*). A slot machine is programmed to deliver money on a variable-ratio schedule of reinforcement. Variable in this instance means that the person cannot predict how many responses will be needed for the next payoff.

The second type of pattern of reinforcement involves time. A response is reinforced, but only after a particular time interval has elapsed. A good example is fishing. One form of fishing consists of casting a lure into the water and retrieving it in such a way that it resembles a minnow (the bait). If no fish are present, none will be caught; during these times responses will not be reinforced. However, every now and then, a hungry, eager-to-bite fish will swim by. If a lure is moving through the water at the same time, the angler may get a fish. After a fish is caught, another may come by soon or not for a long time. The only way to find out is to cast the lure. Clearly, the number of reinforcers that anglers receive is *not* proportional to the number of casts made. Casting the lure more often will not necessarily mean catching more fish because the opportunities for catching one come only now and then. Of course, if the angler waits too long between casts, he or she may miss catching a fish when it swims by.

This second pattern of intermittent reinforcement is called an *interval schedule of reinforcement*. After various intervals of time, a response will be reinforced. If the time intervals are fixed, the animal will stop responding after each reinforcement. It learns that responses made immediately after reinforcement are never reinforced. Then it will begin responding a little while before the next reinforcer is available. This type of interval schedule is called a **fixed-interval schedule**.

If the time intervals are variable, the animal (like the angler) will respond at a slow, steady rate. That way, it will not waste energy on useless responses, but it will not miss any opportunities for reinforcement either. This type of interval schedule is called a **variable-interval schedule**. In a variable-interval 60-second schedule of reinforcement, a reinforcer would be delivered immediately following the first response after different time intervals had elapsed. The interval might be 30 seconds at one time, and 90 seconds at another, but, on average, it will be 60 seconds. An animal whose behaviour is reinforced by this schedule would learn not to pause immediately after a reinforcer was delivered. Instead, it would steadily respond throughout the interval, regardless of the length of the interval.

Schedules of reinforcement are important because they show us that different reinforcement contingencies affect the pattern and rate of responding. (See **Figure 7•14**.) Think about your own behaviour. How would you perform in classes in which your grades were determined by a mid-term and a final, or by weekly quizzes, or by unannounced quizzes that occur at variable intervals? What kind of schedule of reinforcement is a salesperson on while waiting on potential customers? Some people work at a slow, steady rate, but

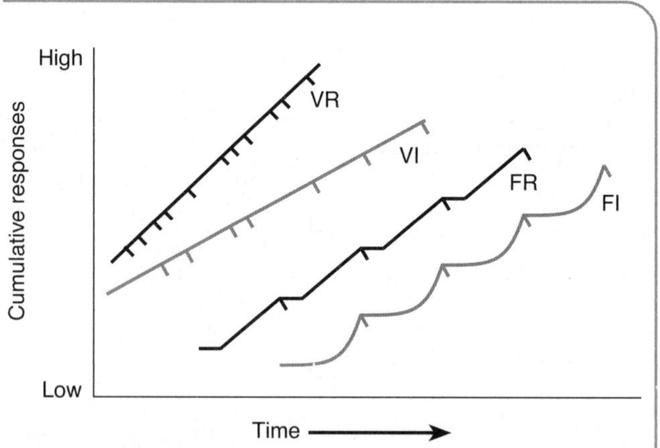


**FIGURE 7•14** Rate of responding as controlled by each of the following schedules: variable-ratio (VR), variable-interval (VI), fixed-ratio (FR), and fixed-interval (FI). The steepness of each curve represents speed of responding: The steeper the curve, the faster the responding. A pause in responding is represented by a horizontal line. The tick marks under each line represent delivery of a reinforcer.

**fixed-ratio schedule** A schedule of reinforcement in which reinforcement occurs only after a fixed number of responses have been made since the previous reinforcement (or the start of the session).
**variable-ratio schedule** A schedule of reinforcement similar to a fixed-ratio schedule but characterized by a variable response requirement having a particular mean.
**fixed-interval schedule** A schedule of reinforcement in which the first response that is made after a fixed interval of time since the previous reinforcement (or the start of the session) is reinforced.
**variable-interval schedule** A schedule of reinforcement similar to a fixed-interval schedule but characterized by a variable time requirement having a particular mean.

▲ *Highly skilled professional athletes make complicated movements seem easy. The thousands of hours of practice that make such graceful behaviours possible, however, come at the cost of intense effort and only intermittent reinforcement. Does the pattern of reinforcement make the difference between an athlete who perseveres and one who does not?*

others work furiously after long periods of inactivity. Can it be that in the past their work habits were shaped by different schedules of reinforcement?

### Resistance to Extinction and Intermittent Reinforcement

Suppose that we train two pigeons to peck at a plastic disc mounted on the wall of an operant chamber by reinforcing these responses with the opportunity to eat a small amount of food. We train the animals for 20 daily sessions of 30 minutes each, but we train the two animals differently. We give the first bird some food every time it pecks the disc. We train the second bird the same way at first, but then we begin reinforcing every third response on average—that is, we institute a variable-ratio three schedule. Each day, we increase the number of responses required for reinforcement until the bird is making an average of 50 responses for each reinforcer.

Now, suppose that we stop reinforcing responding altogether; we put both birds on an extinction schedule. We find that the behaviour of the first bird, accustomed to receiving food each time it responds, soon extinguishes. However, the second bird persists and makes thousands of responses before it finally quits. Why?

The difference in behaviour of the two birds illustrates the following rule: A response that has been reinforced intermittently is more resistant to extinction. The more responses an organism has had to make for each reinforcement, the longer it will respond during extinction. Continuous reinforcement (that is, reinforcement after every response) is very different from extinction. The very first non-reinforced response signals that conditions have changed. In contrast, intermittent reinforcement and extinction are more similar. An organism whose behaviour has been reinforced intermittently has had a lot of experience making non-reinforced responses. The animal cannot readily detect the fact that responses are no longer being reinforced—that the contingencies have changed. Therefore, the behaviour extinguishes more slowly.

As you know, some people keep trying, even if they have difficulty succeeding. Other people seem to give up when they encounter the smallest difficulty. Perhaps one of the reasons for differences in people's perseverance is their past experience with different types of schedules of reinforcement. We will explore this possibility further in Chapter 13, which considers the variables that affect motivation.

**Generalization and Discrimination** In classical conditioning, generalization means that stimuli resembling the CS also elicit the CR. In operant conditioning, **generalization** means that stimuli resembling a discriminative stimulus also serve as discriminative stimuli for a particular response.

As was the case in classical conditioning, generalization of an operant behaviour can be reduced through discrimination training. In classical conditioning, discrimination means that CRs occur only in response to certain CSs and not to other similar stimuli. In operant conditioning, **discrimination** means that response occurs only when a particular discriminative stimulus is present—one that was present while response was reinforced in the past. Responding does *not* occur when discriminative stimuli associated with extinction or punishment are present.

Through discrimination training, organisms can be trained to recognize very complex similarities; that is, they can learn to recognize particular concepts. For example, Herrnstein and Loveland (1964) trained pigeons to respond to the concept of a human being. First, they trained the birds to peck at a translucent plastic disc. Then, they assembled a set of more than 1000 colour slides. Some of the slides contained photographs of humans, depicted in a wide variety of scenes and poses. Other slides did not contain human figures. Herrnstein and Loveland selected a group of slides, with and without human figures, from the larger set and projected them on the translucent disc, where the birds could see them. Then they started discrimination training. When a human figure was projected, pecking was reinforced; that is, food was presented only if the pigeon pecked the disc when a slide containing a human being was shown. When the projected image did not contain a human, pecking was not reinforced (no food was presented). Thus, a disc containing no human figure was the discriminative stimulus that signalled extinction.

The birds quickly learned to respond to the concept of a human being. Their performance on the original set of slides

**generalization** In operant conditioning, the occurrence of responding when a stimulus similar (but not identical) to the discriminative stimulus is present.
**discrimination** In operant conditioning, responding only when a specific discriminative stimulus is present but not when similar stimuli are present.

generalized to slides that they had not seen before. The birds became as good as the researchers at detecting whether a human figure was present in an image. In fact, in one instance, the birds outperformed the humans. They pecked when they saw a slide that supposedly did not contain a human. When the researchers looked at the slide more carefully, they discovered a tiny image of a person hidden in a corner that they had missed when they had first sorted the slides.

Does this mean that pigeons categorize the world in ways that we do? As we saw in Chapter 6, human perception is very sensitive to the relationship between individual elements. Jitsumori and Yoshihara (1997) found that, using procedures like those of Herrnstein and Loveland, they could train pigeons to form categories involving human facial expressions of happiness or anger. When they tested various components of the expression (by mixing up eyes and mouths of different expressions) they found that the pigeons were generally using individual elements to form their categories.

Naturally occurring categories may be a different matter, however. Consider a species of songbird common throughout much of Canada, the black-capped chickadee. Their songs and calls identify them to other members of their species. The components of these songs tend to show relative properties (e.g., in a chickadee song, the pitch of one note is a certain fraction of the pitch of another). Njegovan and Weisman (1997) trained chickadees to discriminate different "songs" consisting of pairs of notes. For some chickadees, the positive songs consisted of pairs of notes in which the frequency of the first note was always higher in pitch than the second note and always by a certain ratio. For other chickadees, the two notes were not related in this way. The chickadees of the first group learned the discrimination faster. Interestingly, chickadees raised in the wild learned this discrimination in relative pitch much faster than those raised in the laboratory in the absence of adult birds.

**Conditioned Reinforcement and Punishment** We have studied reinforcement mainly in terms of *primary reinforcers* and *primary punishers*. **Primary reinforcers** are biologically significant appetitive stimuli, such as food when one is hungry. **Primary punishers** are biologically significant aversive stimuli, such as those that produce pain. Behaviour can also be reinforced with a wide variety of other stimuli: money, a smile, a hug, kind words, a pat on the back, or prizes and awards. These stimuli, called **conditioned reinforcers** (or *secondary reinforcers*), acquire their reinforcing properties through association with primary reinforcers. Because it can be exchanged for so many different kinds of primary reinforcers in our society, money is the most common conditioned reinforcer among humans. That money is a conditioned reinforcer can be demonstrated by asking yourself whether you would continue to work if you could no longer exchange money for food, drink, shelter, and other items. Likewise, **conditioned punishers** acquire their punishing effects through association with aversive events. For example, the sight of a flashing light on top of a police car serves as a conditioned punisher to a person who is driving too fast because such a sight precedes an unpleasant set of stimuli: a lecture by a police officer and a speeding ticket.

A stimulus becomes a conditioned reinforcer or punisher by means of classical conditioning. That is, if a neutral stimulus occurs regularly just before an appetitive or aversive stimulus, then the neutral stimulus itself becomes an appetitive or aversive stimulus. The primary reinforcer or punisher serves as the UCS because it produces the UCR: good or bad feelings. After classical conditioning takes place, these good or bad feelings are produced by the CS: the conditioned reinforcer or punisher. Once that happens, the stimulus can reinforce or punish behaviours by itself. Thus, operant conditioning often involves aspects of classical conditioning.

Conditioned reinforcement and punishment are very important. They permit an organism's behaviour to be affected by stimuli that are not biologically important in themselves but that are regularly associated with the onset or termination of biologically important stimuli. Indeed, stimuli can even become conditioned reinforcers or punishers by being associated with other conditioned reinforcers or punishers. The speeding ticket is just such an example. If an organism's behaviour could be controlled only by primary reinforcers and punishers, its behaviour would not be very flexible. The organism would never learn to perform behaviours that had only long-range benefits. Instead, its behaviour would be controlled on a moment-to-moment basis by a very limited set of stimuli. Conditioned reinforcers and punishers, such as money, grades, smiles, and frowns, allow for behaviour to be altered by a wide variety of contingencies.

**primary reinforcer** A biologically significant appetitive stimulus, such as food or water.

**primary punisher** A biologically significant aversive stimulus, such as pain.

**conditioned (or secondary) reinforcer (or punisher)** A stimulus that acquires its reinforcing (or punishing) properties through association with a primary reinforcer (or punisher). Sometimes referred to as a secondary reinforcer (or punisher).

▲ *For most people, handshakes, smiles, awards, and other forms of social approval serve as important forms of conditioned reinforcement.*

## Then and Now

### Cellular Basis of Learning

Pavlov was a physiologist by training, and he naturally sought to find a physiological explanation for the conditioned reflex that he had discovered. Using the knowledge available to him, he speculated that classical conditioning produced a kind of channel in the brain that allowed "excitation" to flow from one part of it to another. Of course, this explanation no longer makes sense. However, because classical conditioning seems so similar to the process of association (see Chapter 1), physiological psychologists and others still look for ways that conditioning might produce a connection between neurons.

Hebb (1949) proposed one of the first modern accounts of how connections between neurons might form. He suggested that, when two adjacent neurons are active simultaneously, they will tend to create or strengthen a synaptic connection between them. So, neurons that are activated by a UCS will tend to become connected to neurons activated by a CS when the two stimuli are paired together.

Today, Hebb's suggestion is known as *Hebbian learning*, and it forms the basis of many computer programs that mimic human learning. You can see that it nicely explains the role of timing in the acquisition of a conditioned response, since it emphasizes the simultaneous activity of neurons. (It does, however, have trouble explaining why forward conditioning is better than backward conditioning and why blocking occurs.) But, when Hebb proposed it, there was little or no evidence to support his principle. How learned connections between neurons formed at the cellular level was a relative mystery. Solving this mystery could explain how classical conditioning occurs and, perhaps, how reinforcement of operant behaviour works as well.

Knowledge of the cellular basis of conditioning and reinforcement is now emerging, instigated in large part by the pioneering work of Eric Kandel (Pittenger & Kandel, 2003). Kandel began his work with a marine mollusc, *Aplysia*, whose nervous system was simple and whose neurons could be uniquely identified. A simple nervous system permitted the controlled conditions necessary to isolate basic cellular processes. Kandel's work on the cellular basis of learning began some 40 years ago (Kandel & Spencer, 1968) and was recognized with a Nobel Prize in 2000. With the development of new and more refined experimental techniques, most current work on the cellular mechanisms of reinforcement focuses on the mammalian nervous system. That is the work described here.

**Figure 7•15** depicts some of the cellular events that occur when learning increases the ability of a presynaptic

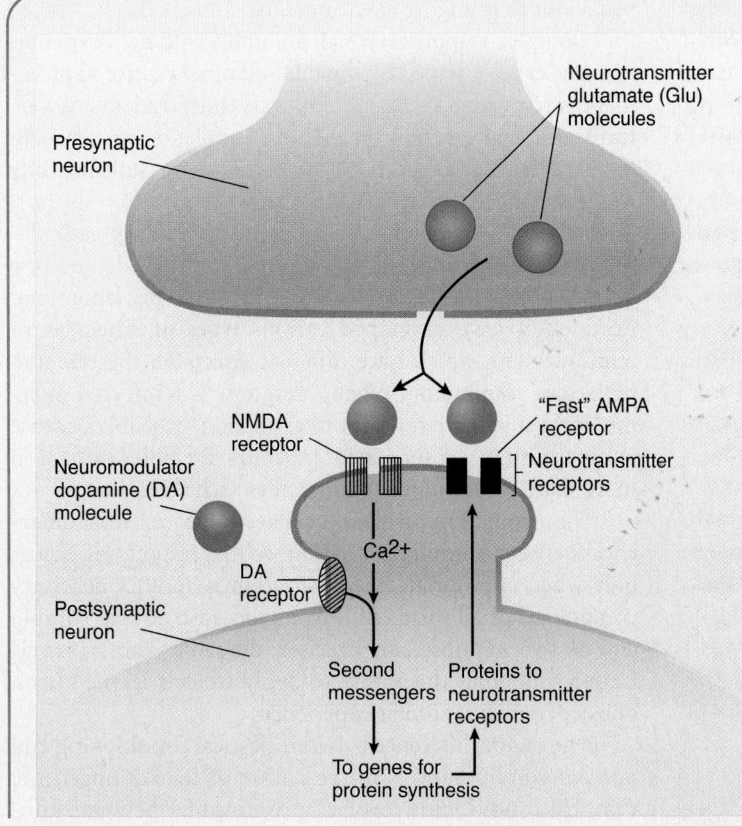


**FIGURE 7•15** Some of the cellular events that take place during learning. As a result of the process diagrammed here, the presynaptic neuron becomes more able to activate the postsynaptic neuron. This process occurs during long-term potentiation.

neuron to activate a postsynaptic neuron. Neurons affect one another though the liberation of compounds called neurotransmitters. The primary excitatory neurotransmitter in the brain is glutamate. An excitatory transmitter is a molecule that facilitates the initiation of an action potential in the postsynaptic neuron. Glutamate is liberated by the presynaptic neuron and acts upon two main types of glutamate receptors located in the cell membrane of the postsynaptic neuron. One glutamate receptor—the AMPA receptor—rapidly facilitates the initiation of action potentials in the postsynaptic neuron. A second glutamate receptor—the NMDA receptor—plays a different role. (AMPA and NMDA are acronyms for the chemical structures of these receptors.) The NMDA receptor plays a crucial role in producing learning, an increase in the ability of glutamate from the presynaptic neuron to activate the postsynaptic neuron. Normally, the channel in the NMDA receptor is blocked by a magnesium ion ($Mg^{2+}$). However, if the postsynaptic neuron is sufficiently stimulated through AMPA receptors, the electrical potential across the membrane of the postsynaptic neuron changes and the magnesium ion migrates out of the NMDA channel. The open NMDA channel now permits calcium ions ($Ca^{2+}$) to enter the cell. When calcium enters the postsynaptic neuron, a sequence of intracellular events occurs. A key event is the placement of a molecular "tag" on the AMPA receptors that have just been acted upon by glutamate. This tag lasts for several hours and marks those receptors as being recently stimulated (Bailey, Kandel, & Si, 2004; Frey & Morris, 1998).

If the neural pathways that have recently been activated are followed by behaviour that produces a reinforcer, dopaminergic neurons in midbrain nuclei are stimulated. When dopamine receptors on the postsynaptic neuron are engaged shortly after AMPA and NMDA receptors have been activated, a series of intracellular events (second messengers) are initiated. The second messengers activate genes that lead to the synthesis of new proteins. These new proteins migrate down the axon and produce long-lasting structural changes in tagged AMPA receptors and cause additional AMPA receptors to appear. At the conclusion of this process, when the presynaptic neuron next liberates glutamate, there is an increased chance of initiating an action potential in the postsynaptic neuron. Glutamate is able to open the channels in AMPA receptors for a longer time and activates more glutamate receptors in the postsynaptic membrane. The net result is that synaptic transmission is facilitated along the pathways by which environmental stimuli initiated neural activity that produced the reinforced response. Increase in neural transmission (synaptic efficacy) can be produced in the laboratory by electrically stimulating presynaptic neurons. This produces what is called long-term potentiation (LTP) (Bliss & Lomø, 1973). LTP is believed to be the cellular basis of learning (Whitlock, Heynan, Shuler, & Bear, 2006).

## Interim Summary

### Operant Conditioning

The law of effect specifies a relation between behaviour and its consequences. If a stimulus that follows a response makes that response become more likely, we say that the response was reinforced. If the stimulus makes the response become less likely, we say that it was punished. The reinforcing or punishing stimulus must follow the behaviour almost immediately if it is to be effective.

The process of operant conditioning helps adapt an organism's behaviour to its environment. Skinner described the relation between behaviour and environmental events as a three-term contingency: In the presence of discriminative stimuli, a consequence will occur if and only if an operant response occurs.

A reinforcer is an appetitive stimulus that follows an operant response and causes that response to occur more frequently in the future. A punisher is an aversive stimulus that follows an operant response and causes it to occur less frequently in the future. However, if an aversive stimulus is *terminated* after a response occurs, the response is reinforced through a process called negative reinforcement. And the termination of an appetitive stimulus can punish a response through a process called response cost. Extinction occurs when operant responses are emitted but not reinforced, which makes sense because organisms must be able to adapt their behaviour to changing environments.

Complex responses, which are unlikely to occur spontaneously, can be shaped by the method of successive approximations. Teachers use this process to train students to perform complex behaviours; something similar occurs when, in the course of learning a new skill, we become satisfied only when we detect signs of improvement.

Schedules of reinforcement, which were originally designed to study the principles of learning in the laboratory, have their counterparts in the world outside the laboratory. Researchers have developed various types of schedules of reinforcement, which have different effects on the rate and pattern of responding. When a response is reinforced intermittently, it is more resistant to extinction, probably because an intermittent reinforcement schedule resembles extinction more than a continuous reinforcement schedule does.

Discrimination involves the detection of essential differences between stimuli or situations so that responding occurs only when appropriate. Generalization is another necessary component of all forms of learning because no two stimuli, and no two responses, are precisely the same. Thus, generalization embodies the ability to apply what is learned from one experience to similar experiences.

The major difference between classical conditioning and operant conditioning is in the nature of the contingencies: Classical conditioning involves a contingency between stimuli (CS and UCS), whereas operant conditioning involves a contingency between the organism's behaviour and an appetitive or aversive stimulus. The two types of conditioning complement each other. The pairings of neutral stimuli with appetitive and aversive stimuli (classical conditioning) determine which stimuli become conditioned reinforcers and punishers. Long-term potentiation (LTP) is thought to involve the cellular processes that occur during learning. During LTP, changes in the receptors on the postsynaptic membrane allow the release of neurotransmitters by the presynaptic neuron to more effectively initiate action potentials in the postsynaptic neuron.

**QUESTIONS TO CONSIDER**

1. The law of effect is often extolled as a universal principle of behaviour. Can you think of an example in which the law of effect is not applicable to an instance of behaviour?
2. Suppose that you run into a friend while walking along the street. You stop and chat for a few minutes. How would you explain your interactions with your friend in terms of the three-term contingency?
3. Reflect for a moment on the activities in which you have engaged so far today. Where appropriate, explain how the principles of positive reinforcement, negative reinforcement, punishment, response cost, and extinction have operated to influence your behaviour today. Give specific, concrete examples and explain them using references to specific environmental events.
4. How might you (and the rest of your class) shape your psychology instructor's behaviour so that he or she stands at the far left side of the room while lecturing?
5. Many people have had the embarrassing experience of mistaking a stranger for a friend. For example, you may catch a glimpse of your "friend" walking down the other side of the street, call out her name, and wave rather excitedly only to discover as you look more closely that the person is not who you thought she was. How would you explain this event using the principles of behaviour discussed in this section?

# Conditioning of Complex Behaviours

So far, we have considered simple examples of reinforced behaviours. But people and many other animals are able to learn very complex behaviours. Consider the behaviour of a young girl learning to print letters. She sits at her school desk, producing long rows of letters. What kinds of reinforcing stimuli maintain her behaviour? Why is she devoting her time to a task that involves so much effort? Behaviour analysts would answer that her behaviour produces stimuli—printed letters—that serve as conditioned reinforcers. In previous class sessions, the teacher demonstrated how to print the letters and praised the girl for printing them herself. The act of printing was reinforced, and the printed letters that this act produces come to serve as conditioned reinforcers. The child prints a letter, sees that it looks close to the way it should, and the sight of the letter reinforces her efforts. Doing something correctly or making progress toward that goal can provide an effective reinforcer.

An everyday term for the conditioned reinforcement that shapes and maintains our behaviour when we perform a behaviour correctly is *satisfaction*. Usually, we work hard at some task because it "gives us satisfaction." An artist who produces a fine painting gains satisfaction from the image that emerges as she works on it and receives even stronger satisfaction from looking at the finished product. This satisfaction derives from experience. The artist has learned to recognize good pieces of art; when she produces one herself, she provides her own conditioned reinforcer.

## Aversive Control of Behaviour

Your own experience has probably taught you that punishment can be as effective as positive reinforcement in changing behaviour. Aversive control of behaviour seems to permeate our society. From penalties given for "unsportsmanlike behaviour" in a hockey game to the prison sentences given to criminals, our society uses punishment to try to control behaviour. Aversive control is common for two main reasons. First, it can be highly effective in inducing behaviour change, producing nearly immediate results. A person given a fine for running a stop sign is likely, at least for a short while, to heed the sign's instruction. The very effectiveness of punishment as a means of behaviour change can serve as an immediate reinforcer for the person doing the punishing.

Second, society cannot always control the positive reinforcers that shape and maintain the behaviour of its members. However, it can and does control aversive stimuli that may be used to punish misconduct. For example, suppose that a young person's peers encourage anti-social behaviours such as theft. Society has no control over reinforcers provided by the peer group, but it can control stimuli to punish the anti-social behaviours, such as fines and imprisonment.

**How Punishers Work** How does a punishing stimulus suppress behaviour? Punishment, like reinforcement, usually involves a discriminative stimulus. A child's shouting is usually punished in the classroom but not outdoors during recess. A dog chases a porcupine, gets stuck with quills, and never chases one again. However, it continues to chase the neighbour's cat.

Most aversive stimuli elicit some sort of protective or defensive response, such as cringing, freezing, hiding, or running away. The response depends on the species of animal and, of course, on the situation. If you slap your dog for a misdeed, it will cower and slink away, looking clearly "apologetic," because you are in a position of dominance. However,

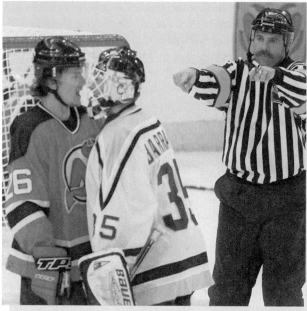

▲ *Punishment takes many forms. The aversive consequences of a penalty to one's team reduces the likelihood of an infraction.*

if the dog is struck by a stranger, it may very well react by attacking that person. Both types of behaviour are known as species-specific defence reactions (Bolles, 1970).

Suppose that a dog sees a porcupine for the first time. The sight of the animal elicits an approach response. The dog chases the porcupine, which stops and emits its own species-specific defence reactions: It bristles its quills and starts to swing its tail back and forth. The dog approaches and gets a face full of quills. The pain elicits a withdrawal response: The dog runs away. The next time the dog sees a porcupine, it runs toward it, seeing only a medium-sized animal that attracts its interest. But as soon as the dog gets close enough to see the porcupine clearly, it stops and turns away.

An analysis in terms of species-specific defence reactions would explain this episode in the following way. A stimulus (the sight of the porcupine) was present at the time the dog received a painful stimulus that elicited a species-specific defence reaction. Through the process of classical conditioning, the stimulus became linked to the response. The next time the dog spots the porcupine, the sight of it elicits the defensive withdrawal response. (See **Figure 7•16**.) In this analysis, punishment is the result of a classical conditioning process in which species-specific defence reactions are conditioned to a stimulus. The stimulus, in this example the sight of the porcupine, is one that occurs as a result of emitting the response (approaching the porcupine). Such stimuli are known as *feedback stimuli* because they are produced when a response is made. Punishment, according to this account, occurs because species-specific defence reactions are conditioned to feedback stimuli.

**escape response** An operant response acquired through negative reinforcement that terminates an aversive stimulus.

**avoidance response** An operant response acquired through negative reinforcement that prevents an aversive stimulus from occurring.

**FIGURE 7•16** A schematic diagram of the way an aversive stimulus may punish a behaviour by classical conditioning of a defensive withdrawal response.

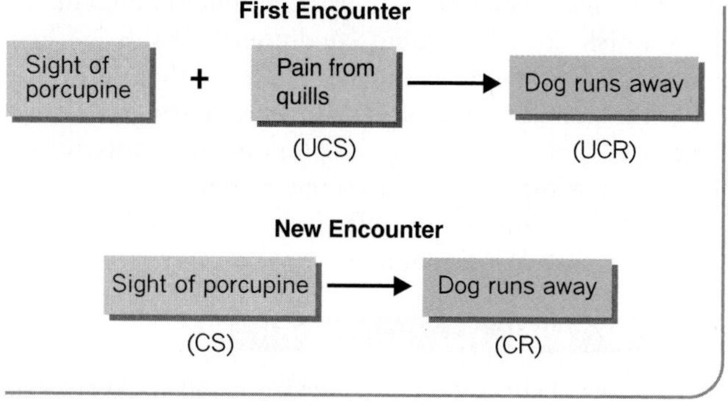


**Escape and Avoidance** Negative reinforcement teaches organisms to make responses that terminate aversive stimuli. These responses can make a stimulus cease (for example, the woman who kicked the oil burner and made the unpleasant noise stop), or the organism can simply run away. In either case, psychologists call the behaviour an **escape response**: The organism endures the effects of the aversive stimulus until its behaviour terminates the stimulus. In some cases, the animal can do more than escape the aversive stimulus; it can learn to do something to *prevent* it from occurring. This type of behaviour is known as an **avoidance response**.

Avoidance responses usually occur in response to some warning that the aversive stimulus is imminent. Suppose that you meet someone at a party who backs you against the wall and engages you in the most boring conversation you have ever had. In addition, this person's breath is so bad that you are afraid you will pass out. You finally manage to break away (an escape response). A few days later, you attend another party. You begin walking toward the buffet table and see the same person (discriminative stimulus) standing nearby. You decide that you will get some food later and turn away to talk with some friends at the other end of the room (an avoidance response).

As we saw earlier, phobias can be considered conditioned emotional responses—fears that are acquired through classical conditioning. But unlike most classically conditioned responses, phobias are especially resistant to extinction. If we classically condition an eyeblink response in a rabbit and then repeatedly present the CS alone, without the UCS (puff of air), the response will extinguish. However, if a person has a phobia for cockroaches, the phobia will not extinguish easily even if he or she encounters cockroaches and nothing bad happens. Why does the response persist?

Most psychologists believe that the answer lies in a subtle interaction between operant and classical conditioning. The

**FIGURE 7•17** Maintenance of a phobia through negative reinforcement—reduction of fear by an avoidance response.

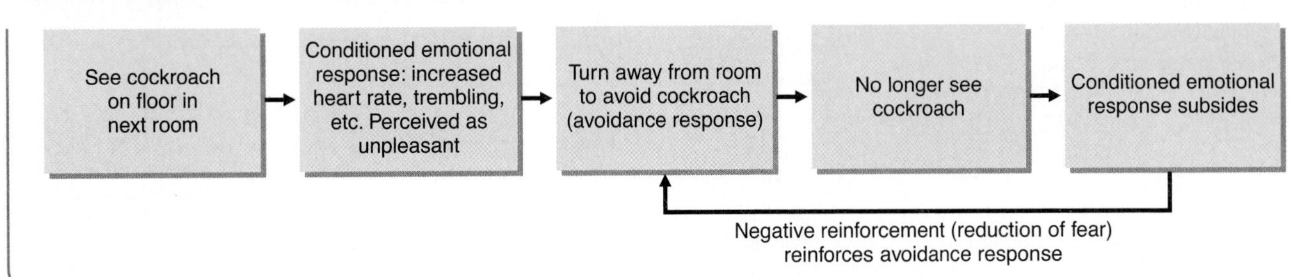


sight of a cockroach makes a person with a cockroach phobia feel frightened; that is, he or she experiences an unpleasant conditional emotional response. The person runs out of the room, leaving the cockroach behind and reducing the unpleasant feelings of fear. This reduction in an aversive stimulus reinforces the avoidance response and perpetuates the phobia. (See **Figure 7•17**.)

**Conditioning of Flavour Aversions** You have probably eaten foods that made you sick and now avoid them on the basis of the flavour alone. (Does any particular flavour come to mind?) The association of a substance's flavour with illness, often caused by eating that substance, leads to **conditioned flavour-aversion learning**.

Psychologists study flavour-aversion learning not only because it is a real-life experience, but also because it has taught them about unique relations that may exist between certain CSs and certain UCSs. As we just saw, punishment is a result of classical conditioning—a species-typical defensive response becomes classically conditioned to a feedback stimulus. This is exactly how conditioned flavour aversions are acquired. The flavour is followed by an unconditional stimulus (sickness) that elicits the unpleasant responses of the autonomic nervous system, such as cramping and retching. Then, when the animal encounters the flavour again, the experience triggers unpleasant internal reactions that cause the animal to stop eating the food.

Many learning researchers once believed that nearly any CS could be paired with nearly any UCS to produce nearly any CR. However, in a now-classic experiment, John Garcia and his colleague, Robert A. Koelling, showed that animals are more prepared to learn some types of relations among stimuli.

In the first phase of their experiment, Garcia and Koelling (1966) permitted rats to drink saccharin-flavoured water from a tube. Each lick from the tube produced three CSs: taste, noise, and bright lights. This phase ensured that the rats were equally familiar with each of the CSs. In the next phase, the rats were divided into four groups, each experiencing either "bright-noisy" water or "tasty" water. Each CS was paired with illness or electric shock. (See **Figure 7•18**.)

**conditioned flavour-aversion learning** A type of learning in which a substance is avoided because its flavour has been associated with illness.

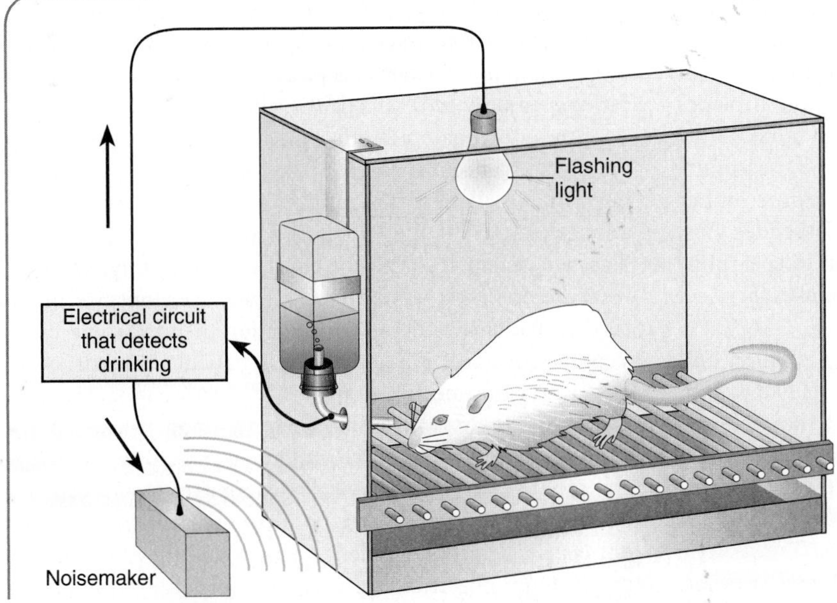


**FIGURE 7•18** Conditioned flavour aversion. A rat drinks "bright-noisy" water in the experiment conducted by Garcia and Koelling (1966). The light flashes and the noisemaker clatters each time the rat's tongue touches the waterspout.

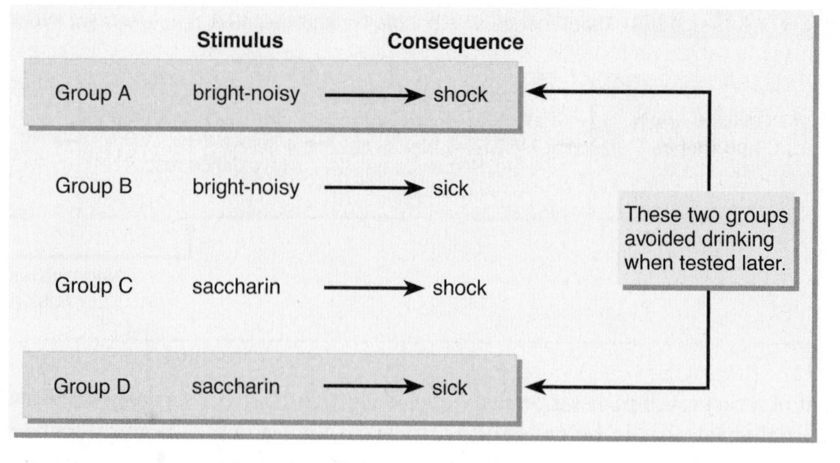


**FIGURE 7•19** The results of the experiment conducted by Garcia and Koelling (1966).

*(Adapted from Garcia, J., & Koelling, R. (1966). Relation of cue to consequence in avoidance learning.* Psychonomic Science, 4, *123–124.)*

After several trials, the researchers measured the amount of saccharin-flavoured water the rats consumed. They found that the rats learned the association between flavour and illness but not between flavour and pain produced by electric shock. Likewise, the rats learned the association between the "bright-noisy water" and shock-induced pain but not between the "bright-noisy water" and illness. (See **Figure 7•19**.) The results make sense; after all, an animal has to taste the flavour that makes it sick, not hear it, and in the world outside the laboratory a flavour does not usually indicate that you are about to receive an electric shock.

This experiment provides two important conclusions: (1) Rats can learn about associations between internal sensations (being sick) and novel tastes, and (2) the interval between the two stimuli can be very long (Revusky & Garcia, 1970). These facts suggest that the brain mechanisms responsible for a conditioned flavour aversion are different from the ones that mediate an aversion caused by stimuli applied to the outside of the body (such as a painful foot shock).

People can also acquire conditioned flavour aversions. A friend of mine, as a child, often took trips on airplanes with her parents. Unfortunately, she usually got airsick. Just before takeoff, her mother would give her some spearmint-flavoured chewing gum to help relieve the pressure on her eardrums that would occur when the plane ascended. Yes, she developed a conditioned flavour aversion to spearmint gum. In fact, the odour of the gum still makes her feel nauseated.

Conditioned flavour aversions show how classical and operant conditioning interact. For example, rats like to run. If you give them access to a rat-style treadmill, they will voluntarily exercise with the enthusiasm of a marathon runner. However, the running apparently has physiological effects that can also condition aversion. Salvy, Pierce, Heth, and Russell (2003) gave rats their daily meal just before providing them with an opportunity to run. The food, however, was mixed with a distinctive flavouring. Now, nothing compelled the rats to run, yet nevertheless they would enter the treadmill and spend an hour running. After several days, Salvy and her colleagues gave the rats an opportunity to eat either the flavoured food or another taste not associated with the opportunity to run. The rats avoided the flavour associated with running. Clearly, something about running was aversive and this conditioned an aversion to the flavoured food. Eating the now-aversive food was punished by its distinctive flavour. The rat could avoid this taste by switching to the other food—an operant behaviour. Interestingly, rats who are given a one-hour feeding session each day, and who are also allowed to run whenever they choose, often lose interest in eating and develop symptoms of severe weight loss. The food aversions that Salvy and her colleagues observed may play some role in this, and perhaps in the human eating disorders that will be discussed in Chapter 13.

As we just saw, conditioned flavour aversions occur when particular flavours are followed by feelings of nausea—even several hours later. This phenomenon has several implications for situations outside the laboratory.

An unfortunate side effect of chemotherapy or radiation therapy for cancer is nausea. Besides killing the rapidly dividing cells of malignant tumours, both chemotherapy and radiation therapy kill the rapidly dividing cells that line the digestive system, thus causing nausea and vomiting. Knowing what we do about conditioned flavour aversions, we might predict that chemotherapy or radiation therapy would cause a conditioned aversion to the foods a patient ate as part of his or her previous meal. Bernstein (1978) showed that this prediction is correct. She gave ice cream to some cancer patients who were about to receive chemotherapy and found that, several months later, 75 percent of these patients refused to eat ice cream of the same flavour. Control participants who did not taste it before their chemotherapy said they liked it very much. Only one trial was necessary to develop the conditioned flavour aversion.

Weight loss during chemotherapy can be a significant complication during cancer treatment, and food aversions are reported by patients as one reason they don't eat (Skolin et al., 2006). Consequently, a way of reducing food aversions would be beneficial. Remember our discussion of the role of information in classical conditioning? A CS must be a reliable predictor of the UCS to elicit a conditioned response. This concept suggests that a novel stimulus associated with an unexpected UCS may be more informative than more familiar ones. Broberg and Bernstein (1987) used this possibility to attach an aversion to a flavour other than one that cancer patients encounter in their normal diets. The researchers had cancer patients eat a coconut or root beer Lifesaver candy after the last meal before a chemotherapy session, hoping that the unique flavour would serve as a scapegoat, thus preventing a conditioned aversion to patients' normal foods. The procedure worked; the patients were much less likely to show an aversion to the food eaten during the last meal before the treatment.

## Observation and Imitation

Normally, we learn about the consequences of our own behaviour or about stimuli that directly affect us. But we can also learn by a less direct method: observing the behaviour of others. Video recorders come with written manuals that explain how to use them. However, it is much easier to learn how to program the recorder by watching someone who has had experience with it.

Nature provides clear examples that imitation does seem to be an innate tendency. Many species of birds must learn to sing the song of their species; if they are raised apart from other birds of their species, they will never sing, or they will sing a peculiar song that bears little resemblance to that of normally raised birds (Marler, 1961). However, if they hear the normal song played over a loudspeaker, they will sing it properly when they become adults. They have learned the song, but clearly there were no external reinforcement contingencies; nothing in the environment reinforced their singing of the song. This phenomenon also provides an excellent example of the distinction between learning and performance. A baby bird hears the proper song but does not sing it until adulthood. The changes that take place in its brain do not manifest in behaviour for many months (Bolhuis & Gahr, 2006).

Classically conditioned behaviours, as well as operantly conditioned behaviours, can be acquired through observation. For example, suppose a young girl sees her mother show signs of fear whenever she encounters a dog. The girl herself will likely develop a fear of dogs, even if she never sees another one. In fact, Bandura and Menlove (1968) reported that children who were afraid of animals—in this case, dogs—were likely to have a parent who feared dogs, but they usually could not remember any unpleasant direct experiences with them. As we will see in Chapter 15, we tend to imitate—and feel—the emotional responses of people we observe. Perhaps when we see someone we know well show signs of fear, we imitate these responses ourselves, and the responses become classically conditioned to the important stimulus present at the time.

## Spatial Learning and Navigation

The situations I have described so far tend to emphasize the temporal aspects of behaviour: reacting to a predicted event, repeating a reinforced response, and so on. However, behaviours are also organized in space. Animals learn to perform behaviours with reference to locations, such as where to look for food or where to find refuge at night. The image of a psychologist studying a rat in a maze is a bit of a cliché, but it does capture the fact that many important behaviours involve a decision that is spatially defined.

Psychologists who study learning first regarded spatial behaviours as examples of operant behaviour. That is, landmarks in space were like discriminative stimuli: They set the occasion for the reinforcement of simple responses such as left or right turns. When an animal navigated, say to a watering hole in its territory, these turns comprised the route.

Although this approach has the appeal of parsimony, it has been found inadequate to explain the many cases of complex navigation that animals naturally exhibit. Gallistel (1990) has described some compelling examples. One is that of a species of ant, *Cataglyphis fortis*, that lives in the Tunisian desert. The desert environment is a harsh one, and when an individual ant leaves its nest to forage, it must return quickly after finding food or it will die. *Cataglyphis fortis* has evolved an accurate means of keeping track of its whereabouts, so that when it finds food it is able to return directly home. (See **Figure 7•20**.)

Psychologists explain these cases by expanding the definition of what constitutes a response. In addition to simple responses of "left" or "right," it makes sense to think of animals learning to approach stimuli, or learning to travel with reference to a bearing (see Cornell and Heth, 2004, for a review). Routes consist of directional travel, in which both distance and direction are part of the behaviour. Animals learn to travel a certain distance along a route, and detect how far they've travelled to a goal (Cheng & Wehner, 2002).

Similarly, the nature of the discriminative stimulus has been re-evaluated. Landmarks are obviously relevant to any analysis of spatial behaviours. Because they are spatially defined, landmarks change their aspect as an organism moves: they become smaller with distance, they change position relative to each other, and so on. How an organism behaves relative to these dynamic changes is now a topic of interest to learning psychologists. For example, Spetch and colleagues (1997) examined how humans and pigeons search for a hidden target defined by a group of landmarks. They hid a target inside a geometric square defined by four corner landmarks. The pigeons searched within a small enclosure inside a room, while the human participants searched outdoors in a yard. Both rapidly learned to find the target, which was

**FIGURE 7•20** Foraging trip of an individual ant, *Cataglyphis fortis*. Outbound and inbound trajectories are depicted by solid and stippled lines, respectively. N indicates the ant's nest; F indicates the location of the food item found by the searching ant. The length of the outbound path is 354.5 metres; the maximal distance from the nest is 113.2 metres. Time marks (small filled circles) are given every 60 seconds.

*(From Müeller, M., & Wehner, R. (1988). Path integration in desert ants, Cataglyphis fortis.* Proceedings of the National Academy of Sciences of the United States of America, 85, *5287–5290. Reprinted with permission.)*

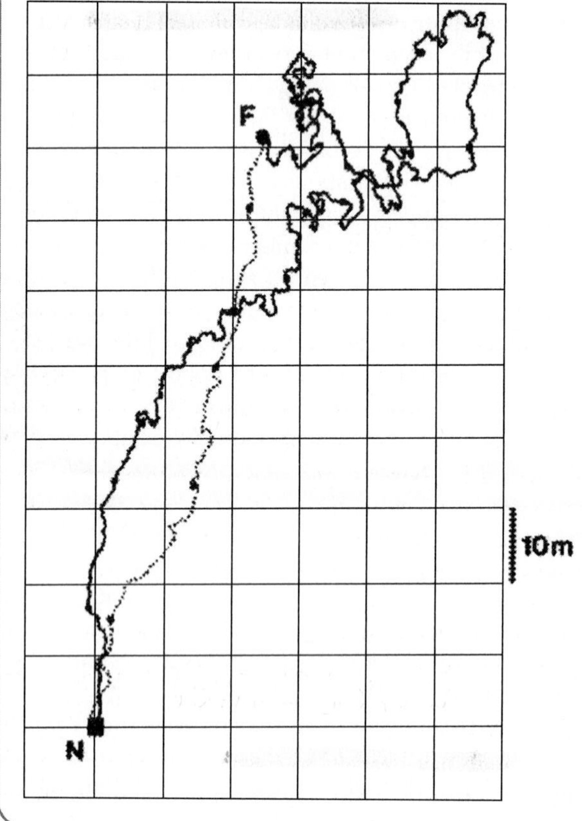


always hidden in the centre of the square. Then Spetch and her colleagues increased the size of the square. They wanted to see whether the research participants would search on the basis of the configuration of landmarks, or on the basis of absolute distance from some particular landmark. They found that humans tended still to search in the middle of the square, indicating that it was the geometric configuration that mattered. Pigeons, however, searched at an absolute distance from one of the landmarks, and not in the centre. These results indicate that different species may treat landmarks differently.

Many learning theorists now consider the concept of a *map* as a useful metaphor in thinking about spatial learning. Maps provide representations of directions and distances on paper. Perhaps the nervous system represents similar constructs to guide behaviour. Some people, such as my acquaintance Dave, the ranger in Alberta, may have excellent behavioural maps; others might have adequate maps, but, like the lost hiker, have them improperly oriented. It's not a perfect metaphor, but it provides a basis for thinking about what is learned in the case of spatial behaviours.

## Combining Behaviours: Insight

Many problems we have to solve in our daily lives require us to make responses that we have never made before and that we have never seen anyone else make, either. We often think about a problem, looking at the elements and trying to imagine various solutions. We try various responses in our heads, but none seems to work. Suddenly, we think of a new approach; maybe this one will work! We try it, and it does. We say that we have solved the problem through insight.

But what is insight? Some people see it as almost a magical process: a sudden flash of inspiration, a bolt from the blue, an answer coming from nowhere. Most people regard insight as a particularly human ability—or, at least, as an ability that belongs to our species and, perhaps, to some of the higher primates.

During the early part of this century, the German psychologist Wolfgang Köhler studied the problem-solving behaviours of chimpanzees. In one famous example (Köhler, 1927/1973), he hung some bananas from the ceiling of an animal's cage, just high enough to be out of reach. The cage also contained a large box. Sultan, one of the chimps, first tried to jump up to reach the bananas, then paced around the cage, stopped in front of the box, pushed it toward the bananas, climbed onto the box, and retrieved and ate the fruit. (See **Figure 7•21**.) Later, when the bananas were suspended even higher, he stacked several boxes, and on one occasion when no boxes were present, he grabbed Köhler by the hand, led him to the bananas, and climbed on top of him. (Sorry, but there doesn't seem to be a picture of that.)

Köhler believed that the insightful problem-solving behaviour shown by the chimpanzees was different from the behaviour of Thorndike's cats as they learned to escape the puzzle boxes. The cats clearly showed trial-and-error behaviour, coming upon the solution by accident. The escape from the box served as a reinforcing stimulus, and eventually the animals learned to operate the latch efficiently. But the behaviour of the chimpanzees seemed very different. They suddenly came upon a solution, often after looking at the situation (and, presumably, thinking about it). Köhler saw no accidental trial-and-error behaviour. Perhaps some processes other than operant conditioning are responsible for the kind of insight that primates can display. Perhaps insight is a behaviour that is not subject to the principles of learning outlined in this chapter.

More recent work suggests that insight may be less mysterious than it appears. Insight may actually be based on combinations of behaviours initially learned through trial

FIGURE 7•21 Insightful behaviour by a chimpanzee in an experiment similar to the one performed by Köhler. The chimpanzee piles boxes on top of each other to reach the bananas hanging overhead.

and error. In one study (Epstein, Kirshnit, Lanza, & Rubin, 1984), the researchers used operant procedures (with food as the reinforcer) to teach a pigeon two behaviours: (1) to push a box toward a target (a green spot placed at various locations on the floor) and (2) to climb onto a box and peck at a miniature model of a banana, which was suspended overhead. Once these behaviours had been learned, the researchers confronted the pigeon with a situation in which the box was in one part of the chamber and the banana was in another:

> At first, the bird appeared to be confused: It stretched toward the banana, turned back and forth from the banana to the box, and so on. Then, rather suddenly, it began to push the box toward the banana, sighting the banana and readjusting the path of the box as it pushed. Finally, it stopped pushing when the box was near the banana, climbed onto the box, and pecked the banana. (Epstein, 1985, p. 132)

The pigeon acted much the way that Sultan did. In a subsequent experiment, Epstein (1987) taught a pigeon to (1) peck at a model of a banana, (2) climb onto a box, (3) open a door, and (4) push a box toward a target. When the pigeon was confronted with a banana hanging above its head and a box behind a door, it combined all four behaviours: It opened the door, pushed the box out and moved it under the banana, climbed onto the box, and pecked the banana.

Insightful behaviour generally involves combining and adapting behaviours in a new context. We know from the experiments by Epstein and his colleagues that pigeons will show insightful behaviour only after they have learned the individual behaviours that must go together to solve a problem. For example, only if pigeons have learned to push a box toward a goal will they move it under a model banana. It is not enough to have learned to push a box; they must have learned to push it toward a goal. Presumably, the chimpanzees' experience with moving boxes around and climbing on them was necessary for them to solve the hanging banana problem.

## The Analysis of Human Behaviour

As I noted earlier, behaviour analysts study both humans and non-human animals. Although much research is still being done with non-humans, behaviour analysts have become increasingly interested in studying behaviour unique to humans, such as certain social and verbal behaviours. To provide you with an overview of the considerable breadth of research in this area, I will briefly describe two areas of operant research that focus on human behaviour: instructional control of behaviour, and drug use and abuse.

**Instructional Control** Human behaviour is influenced not only by reinforcement, but also by the interactions of reinforcement and rules—that is, by verbal descriptions of the relation between behaviour and reinforcement. In fact, much of our everyday behaviour involves following rules of one sort or another. Cooking from a recipe, following directions to a friend's house, and obeying the speed limit are common examples. Because rules have the potential to influence our behaviour in almost any situation, behaviour analysts are interested in learning more about how rules and reinforcement interact.

One way to investigate this interaction is to give participants rules that are false—that is, rules that are inaccurate descriptions of the behaviour required for reinforcement. In such experiments, people may behave in accordance with either the rule or the reinforcement requirement. For example, in one study (Buskist & Miller, 1986), a group of college students was told that the schedule in effect was a fixed-interval (FI) 15-second schedule, when in fact it was an FI 30-second schedule. Recall that in a fixed-interval schedule, a response will be reinforced only after a certain amount of time has passed since the last reinforcement. Another group was told the truth about the schedule.

At first, the misinformed students responded according to the instructions, making one response about every 15 seconds. However, because the rule directly contradicted the actual reinforcement schedule, they soon learned to respond about once every 30 seconds. The students abandoned the rule they had been given by the researchers in favour of the actual reinforcement contingency. The group of students who were told the truth responded accordingly.

A third group of students, also exposed to the FI 30 second schedule, was told that the schedule in effect was an FI 60-second schedule. The rule given to these students was ambiguous, but not exactly false. If the students made a response every 60 seconds, they would receive a reinforcer every time. These students could have received a reinforcer every 30 seconds, but they never learned to do so. The point is that rules can be influential in controlling behaviour not only when they are true, but also when they are ambiguous. The problem, of course, is that ambiguous instructions often lead to inefficient behaviour, as they did in this case.

**Drug Use and Abuse** Soon after Skinner outlined the principles of operant behaviour, others were quick to apply them to the study of drug action and drug taking (Thompson & Schuster, 1968). In fact, Skinner's three-term contingency is now partly the basis of an entirely separate discipline of pharmacology known as **behaviour pharmacology**, the study of how drugs influence behaviour. In this field, the terms *discriminative stimuli, responding,* and *consequences* translate into *drugs as discriminative stimuli, the direct effects of drugs on behaviour,* and *the reinforcing effects of drugs,* respectively.

Most psychoactive drugs function as reinforcers in both humans and animals. When administered as a consequence of responding, these drugs will induce and maintain high rates of responding (Griffiths, Bigelow, & Henningfield, 1980). Cocaine, for example, maintains very high rates of responding and drug consumption, to the point that food and water consumption decreases to life-threatening levels. (Unlimited access to cocaine in rhesus monkeys can sometimes lead to death.) These findings have allowed psychologists to study the abuse potential of newly available drugs. The realization that drugs are reinforcers has, in turn, led behaviour pharmacologists to treat cocaine dependence in people successfully by scheduling reinforcement for non-drug-taking behaviour (Higgins, Budney, & Bickel, 1994).

Perhaps even more startling, there is evidence that the reaction to the effects of a drug can also be conditioned. That is, after a drug produces its primary response, physiological mechanisms are activated that moderate or inhibit this response. These mechanisms are likely the body's way of maintaining a homeostatic balance. They also seem to be conditionable to the immediate environment, or context, in which the drug is taken (McDonald & Siegel, 1998). If the context, which now acts like a CS, is experienced without the drug, these compensatory responses may produce withdrawal symptoms. Conversely, if a strong dose of the drug is taken in a new environment, to which the compensatory response has not been conditioned, response may be largely unmoderated and a lethal overdose may occur.

**behaviour pharmacology** The study of how drugs influence behaviour; combines the principles of operant conditioning and the principles of drug action.

## Interim Summary

### Conditioning of Complex Behaviours

Much behaviour is under the control of aversive contingencies, which specify particular behaviours that are instrumental in either escaping or avoiding aversive stimuli. For instance, you may escape the clutches of a would-be mugger by running away, or you may avoid getting mugged altogether by staying in well-illuminated areas at night.

The phenomenon of conditioned flavour aversions illustrates how natural selection can affect the brain mechanisms involved in learning. Because there is a delay between tasting a poison and getting sick, the rule that a reinforcing or punishing stimulus must immediately follow the response cannot apply. Psychologists have used conditioned flavour aversions to help chemotherapy patients form aversions to foods that are not part of their normal diets. Psychologists have also applied conditioned flavour aversions to controlling wildlife predation on domestic animals.

Behaviour analysts study the behaviour of many species, but of late, behaviours especially important to our species have come under close scrutiny. How instructions control behaviour and how different classes of drugs, especially those most likely to be abused, affect behaviour are two areas of research receiving considerable attention.

The effects of reinforcing and punishing stimuli on behaviour can be complex and subtle. We can acquire both operantly and classically conditioned responses through observation and imitation. We learn directions and distances to spatial goals, usually in reference to landmarks. In addition, we can learn to modify and combine responses to solve new problems. The fact that pigeons, too, can exhibit insight suggests that insight learning does not always require "thinking" in the sense of imagining the behaviour before it is performed. Human behaviour is influenced not only by reinforcement, but also by the interactions of reinforcement and rules. Drug-taking behaviours can be analyzed through operant principles, and the effects of drugs on a user may be a consequence of classical conditioning.

**QUESTIONS TO CONSIDER**

1. Skinner might argue that many of the laws that govern behaviour in our culture are based more on aversive control of behaviour (punishment, response cost, negative reinforcement) than on positive reinforcement. Would you agree or disagree with this position? Why?
2. Negative reinforcement is often a difficult concept for students to grasp. Can you think of any examples of times when your behaviour was negatively reinforced? What stimuli in these examples served as the negative reinforcers? Which aspects of your behaviour were influenced by these stimuli?
3. What important behaviours have you learned, wholly or partially, by first observing them being performed by others? Would you have been able to learn these behaviours as well or as quickly without seeing them performed by someone else? Why or why not?

EPILOGUE

## What Do We Learn?

The couple in Dave's story were fortunate to be within cellphone range of the ranger's office. Being lost can be a traumatic experience; backcountry rangers often cite a sense of panic as the most dangerous reaction to feeling lost. Even mild cases of disorientation, such as taking the wrong turn in a large parking lot, is liable to leave you feeling uneasy. We seem to be much more comfortable when we can anticipate events and the consequences of our behaviours.

Learning is the process that allows us to anticipate events and adapt our behaviour to them. Pavlov and Thorndike worked with simple behaviours in highly constrained experiments, but their discoveries point to the way that learning operates in much more complex situations. Why were the couple willing to trust Dave's directions and follow his advice? Because, likely, throughout their lives they have experienced cases in which following the advice of an expert has been rewarded with success. How did Dave know where the couple was? Because the landmarks they described had been paired in his own hiking experience. How was he able to guide them out, remotely? Because behaviours, even if learned in isolation, can be combined.

Many psychologists have suggested that learning for an individual works like natural selection does for a species: It selects behaviours by increasing the likelihood of some and decreasing the likelihood of others. Reinforcers, therefore, function to adapt an individual's behaviour to the immediate environment. This raises the intriguing question of how natural selection might determine the things that can be reinforcing. In the case of things that satisfy basic needs, such as food, that answer seems clear. But other experiences, less connected to basic needs, also seem to affect learning. Why, for example, can the study of a map serve to increase the efficiency of a behaviour such as navigation of a forest trail? As well, other factors seem to constrain learning. Given the remarkable ability of the desert ant to find its way home, why weren't the couple in Dave's story able to use their experience of hiking in the morning to guide them on their way out? Clues to answering these questions will be provided in the next chapters.

## Canadian Connections to Research in This Chapter

Cornell, E. H., & Heth, C. D. (2004). Memories of travel: Dead reckoning within the cognitive map. In G. Allen (Ed.), *Remembering where: Advances in understanding spatial memory.* Mahwah, NJ: Lawrence Erlbaum Associates. (University of Alberta: www.ualberta.ca)

Giles, A. C., Rose, J. K., & Rankin, C. H. (2005). Investigations of learning and memory in *Caenorhabditis elegans. International Review of Neurobiology, 69,* 37–71. (University of British Columbia: www.ubc.ca)

Hebb, D. O. (1949). *The organization of behaviour.* New York: Wiley-Interscience. (McGill University: www.mcgill.ca)

Humphrey, G. (1933). *The nature of learning: In its relation to the living system.* London: Kegan, Paul, Trench, Trubner. (Queen's University: www.queensu.ca)

Krank, M. D., O'Neill, S., Squarey, K., & Jacob, J. (2008). Goal- and signal-directed incentive: Conditioned approach, seeing, and consumption established with unsweetened alcohol in rats. *Psychopharmacology, 196,* 397–405. (University of British Columbia: www.ubc.ca)

LoLordo, V. M., & Drougas, A. (1989). Selective associations and adaptive specializations: Taste aversions and phobias. In S. B. Klein and R. R. Mowrer (Eds.), *Contemporary learning theories: Instrumental conditioning theory and the impact of biological constraints on learning* (pp. 145–179). Hillsdale, NJ: Lawrence Erlbaum Associates. (Dalhousie University: www.dal.ca)

Macintosh, N. J., & Honig, V. R. (Eds.). (1969). *Fundamental issues in associative learning.* Halifax: Dalhousie University Press. (Dalhousie University: www.dal.ca)

McDonald, R. V., & Siegel, S. (1998). Environmental control of morphine withdrawal: Context specificity or stimulus novelty? *Psychobiology, 26,* 53–56. (McMaster University: www.mcmaster.ca)

Njegovan, M., & Weisman, R. (1997). Pitch discrimination in field- and isolation-reared black-capped chickadees (*Parus atricapillus*). *Journal of Comparative Psychology, 111,* 294–301. (Queen's University: www.queensu.ca)

Pierce, W. D., Heth, C. D., Owczarczyk, J. C., Russell, J. C., & Proctor, S. D. (2007). Overeating by young obesity-prone and lean rats caused by tastes associated with low energy foods. *Obesity, 15,* 1969–1979. (University of Alberta: www.ualberta.ca)

Revusky, S. H., & Garcia, J. (1970). Learned associations over long delays. In G. H. Bower & J. T. Spence (Eds.), *The psychology of learning and motivation: IV.* New York: Academic Press. (Memorial University: www.mun.ca)

Rose, J. K., & Rankin, C. H. (2001). Analyses of habituation in *Caenorhabditis elegans. Learning & Memory, 8,* 63–69. (University of British Columbia: www.ubc.ca)

Salvy, S.-J., Pierce, W. D., Heth, D. C., & Russell, J. C. (2003). Wheel running produces conditioned food aversion. *Physiology & Behavior, 80,* 89–94. (University of Alberta: www.ualberta.ca)

Spetch, M., Wilkie, D. M., & Pinel, J. P. J. (1981). Backward conditioning: A reevaluation of the empirical evidence. *Psychological Bulletin, 89,* 163–175. (University of British Columbia: www.ubc.ca)

Spetch, M. L., Cheng, K., MacDonald, S. E., Linkenhoker, B. A., Kelly, D. M., & Doerkson, S. R. (1997). Use of landmark configuration in pigeons and humans: II. Generality across search tasks. *Journal of Comparative Psychology, 111,* 14–24. (University of Alberta: www.ualberta.ca)

Wen, J. Y. M., Kumar, N., Morrison, G., Rambaldini, G., Runciman, S., Rousseau, J., & van der Kooy, D. (1997). Mutations that prevent associative learning in *C. elegans. Behavioral Neuroscience, 111,* 354–368. (University of Toronto: www.utoronto.ca)

Wicks, S. R., & Rankin, C. H. (1997). Effects of tap withdrawal response habituation on other withdrawal behaviors: The localization of habituation in the Nematode. *Behavioral Neuroscience, 111,* 342–353. (University of British Columbia: www.ubc.ca)

## Suggestions for Further Reading

Donahoe, J. W. & Palmer, D. C. (2005). *Learning and complex behavior.* Richmond, MA: Ledgetop Publishing. [Reprint of Donahoe, J. W. & Palmer, D. C. (1994). *Learning and complex behavior.* Boston: Allyn & Bacon. Supplementary additional material at www.LCB-online.org.]

An upper-level undergraduate and graduate text that describes basic behavioural and biological processes and their implications for complex human behaviour. The complex behaviour includes concept formation, attention, perception, memory, imagining, problem solving, and verbal behaviour with related findings from neuroscience and neuropsychology.

Mazur, J. E. (1999). *Learning and behavior.* Englewood Cliffs, NJ: Prentice-Hall.

An excellent book written for upper-division courses in behaviour analysis. This text presents an overview of classical and operant conditioning and is up to date on research and theoretical positions in behaviour analysis.

Skinner, B. F. (1953). *Science and human behavior.* New York: The Free Press.

This book, although originally published almost 50 years ago, is still a valuable interpretation of the behaviour-analytic position. The basic principles of operant conditioning and their application to understanding a wide range of behaviours are explained interestingly and clearly. This book is an excellent choice if you want to know more about Skinner's views.

Skinner, B. F. (1987). *Upon further reflection.* Englewood Cliffs, NJ: Prentice-Hall.

This anthology of Skinner's more recent ideas covers topics ranging from why we are not acting to save the world to cognitive science to behaviourism to education. This book, too, is thought-provoking and clearly written.

# 8

# MEMORY

# CHAPTER OUTLINE

## Overview and Sensory Memory

Iconic Memory • Echoic Memory

Memory involves the cognitive process of encoding, storage, and retrieval of information. Encoding involves putting stimulus information in a form that can be used by our memory system. Storage involves maintaining it in memory and retrieval involves locating and using it. Sensory memory stores newly perceived information for very brief periods. Although sensory memory appears to exist for all senses, visual (iconic) and auditory (echoic) memories have received the most empirical attention.

## Short-Term or Working Memory

Encoding of Information in the Short Term: Interaction with Long-Term Memory • Primacy and Recency Effects • The Limits of Working Memory • Varieties of Working Memory • Loss of Information from Short-Term Memory

Information may enter working memory (also called short-term memory) from both sensory memory and long-term memory. Working memory works very well for items at the beginning and end of lists. Working memory holds about 7 items and lasts for about 20 seconds, unless the information is rehearsed. Verbal and visual information in working memory appears to be represented both phonologically and acoustically and is subject to manipulation by thought processes. An important cause of loss of information in working memory is displacement of older information to make room for newer information.

## Learning and Encoding in Long-Term Memory

The Consolidation Hypothesis • *Then and Now: Consolidation and the "Genetic Action Potential"* • The Levels of Processing Hypothesis • Improving Long-Term Memory through Mnemonics

Long-term memory likely involves permanent structural changes in the brain. Our ability to retrieve information from long-term memory is often determined by how that information is learned or encoded. Rehearsal helps us store information permanently, although some types of rehearsal seem to be more effective than others. Special techniques, called mnemonics, improve storage and retrieval of information in long-term memory.

## The Organization of Long-Term Memory

Episodic and Semantic Memory • Explicit and Implicit Memory • The Biological Basis of Long-Term Memory

Research has distinguished among permanent memories for autobiographical information, conceptual information, information of which we are aware, and information of which we may be unaware. Studies involving amnesic people strongly suggest that the biological basis of long-term memory involves the hippocampus.

## Remembering, Recollecting, and Forgetting

How Long Does Memory Last? • Remembering and Recollecting • Forgetting and Interference • Reconstruction: Remembering as a Creative Process

Forgetting of information is greatest during the first few years after it is learned and decreases slowly afterwards. In some instances, remembering appears to be automatic—we do not have to put forth much conscious effort to retrieve a memory. In other cases, though, we must actively search for and use cues that aid our retrieval of a memory. Information contained in other memories may interfere with recall of a particular memory. Remembering complex information is often inaccurate because it involves reconstruction of information from existing memories.

PROLOGUE

## The Salem Witch Trials

In 1680, Juan, a slave to a New England farmer, testified in a court deposition that, about a month earlier, he had seen two black cats while eating dinner. Juan thought this strange since the farm housed only one cat. Stranger still, only the week before, the horses had startled and run away from him. He also remembered—and here Juan's testimony would take a turn down a deadly path—seeing his neighbour Bridget Oliver sitting in the barn that same afternoon with an egg in her hand. Juan saw her clearly, but, unaccountably, she was nowhere to be found a few seconds later.

Juan's testimony about events a month old must have been threatening to Bridget, for this was in Salem, Massachusetts, and Bridget was on trial for witchcraft. Manifestations of a sinister, invisible world were considered plausible, and testimony like Juan's was regarded as hard evidence of a capital crime. Fortunately for Bridget, the jurors weren't persuaded and she was acquitted of witchcraft. However, the suspicions lingered. A few years later, they would lead to her death.

In 1692, in a nearby village, a group of young girls began exhibiting mysterious ailments while remembering strange visitations. For reasons that are debated to this day, their stories touched off an unprecedented level of community hysteria and fear. Gossip about Bridget's earlier charges of witchcraft must have reached these girls, for they soon began to name her as one of the apparitions that afflicted them. By this time, Bridget had remarried following the death of her husband and was known as Bridget Bishop. Her remarriage (it was her third) and a penchant for clothing that was a bit too colourful by Puritan standards probably accelerated the gossip surrounding her. Whatever the cause, her neighbours began to remember other odd instances and to relate them to the grand jury. One recalled that, 14 years earlier, he had encountered Bridget on the way to his father's mill and, shortly thereafter, the wheel of his cart had fallen off. Another, relying on an eight-year-old memory, said that he had argued with Bridget and immediately thereafter had seen a black pig that vanished when he approached it. Two workmen claimed that, seven years earlier, they had seen some unusual dolls in a house that Bridget had lived in.

Bridget was hauled once again into court to defend herself against charges of witchcraft. This time she had no hope. To her plea that she didn't even know what a witch was, her interrogator snarled, "How do you know then that you are not a witch?" One has to admire the cool contempt in her answer to this verbal trap: "I do not know what you say." But such courage was no match for the hysteria swirling around her.

Bridget Bishop was put on trial for witchcraft on June 2, 1692. Within eight days, she would be tried, convicted, and executed.

Bridget Bishop was the first of the so-called "Salem witches" to be tried and executed. Although the legal charge against her related to an alleged spectral assault on the young girls of Salem Village, the case turned on whether there was evidence that Bridget had practised witchcraft before (Norton, 2003). Much of the testimony that convicted her concerned supposedly supernatural occurrences recollected many years later (remarkably, records of this testimony still exist; see Boyer & Nissenbaum, 1972). Bridget was condemned, in part, because the people of her time believed that a narrative recollection was a reliable mirror of the experience. To be sure, people could lie and they could forget, but a memory that was real to the recaller was considered plausible. (The only substantive debate about the veracity of the evidence was whether Satan was manipulating real events to make the innocent look guilty.) Yet notice the small twists of coincidence in the stories told against Bridget: If the argument had occurred after the pig sighting, would the incident have been so damning? If another cat had strayed into Juan's farm without his remembering it, would his dinnertime vision have seemed so mysterious? Notions of devilment aside, Bridget's fate rested on the assumption that her accusers could accurately reconstruct a sequence of events that occurred months or years in the past. This is a remarkable belief, yet it's an assumption that we make all the time.

## Overview of Memory

Recall from Chapter 7 that learning is the tendency for behaviour to change as a result of experience; learning reflects the brain's plasticity. Our ability to learn allows us to engage in an enormous variety of behaviours in response to different situations. However, a lapse of time may occur between the act of learning and a change in behaviour caused by that learning. For example, you may observe that a new restaurant has opened and then, some days later, decide that you want to eat out. Choosing the new restaurant is possible because you have retained information about it.

This chapter concerns **memory**—the cognitive processes of encoding, storing, and retrieving information. **Encoding** refers to the active process of putting stimulus information into a form that can be used by our memory system. **Storage** refers to the process of maintaining information in memory. **Retrieval** refers to the active processes of locating and using information stored in memory. Your choosing the restaurant, then, is a joint result of encoding the location, type of food, and its other attributes, storing this information, and retrieving it when you are later looking for a place to eat.

One of the first things to note about memory is that you are aware of these processes in different ways. Noticing the restaurant, judging its compatibility to your tastes, marking its location—all of these are activities that can be described; you are highly conscious of them. (Consciousness is the topic of Chapter 9.) In contrast, most of the time, the storage of information is not so directly available. You don't actively think of every restaurant you've seen every moment of the day; neither do you consciously think about every person you've met, every song you've heard, and every place you've been in such a continuous way. The information is latent and unactivated. Retrieval is a bit of a blend. Quickly now, what is the last line of the Christmas carol "Silent Night"? Normally, you need to think about earlier parts of the song before you can retrieve its ending. Retrieving the information is a progressive reactivation.

In 1949, Donald Hebb used this active/latent distinction to suggest that the brain remembered information in two different ways, a view known as dual trace theory (Hebb, 1949). Information that was active was in this state because neurons were firing continuously. Hebb thought that this activity was due to the feedback circuits of neurons. Repeated firing, in turn, strengthened the synaptic efficiency of the circuit, leading to structural changes in the neurons involved. This structural change would persist after the activity had ceased. The brain therefore retained traces of an experience either in an active state or in the latent structural state. The gist of Hebb's theory has been strikingly supported by the finding of long-term potentiation discussed in Chapter 7.

In the 1960s, Richard Atkinson and Richard Shiffrin suggested a way of thinking about memory that psychologists have found useful. They proposed that memory takes at least three forms: sensory memory, short-term memory, and long-term memory (Atkinson & Shiffrin, 1968). The first two roughly correspond to memory systems that retain active traces, while the last retains latent traces. **Sensory memory** is memory in which representations of the physical features of a stimulus are stored for a very brief time—perhaps for a second or less. This form of memory is difficult to distinguish from the act of perception. The information contained in sensory memory represents the original stimulus fairly accurately and contains all or most of the information that has just been perceived. For example, sensory memory contains a brief image of a sight we have just seen or a fleeting echo of a sound we have just heard. The function of sensory memory appears to be to hold information long enough for it to become part of the next form of memory: short-term memory.

**Short-term memory** is an immediate memory for stimuli that have just been perceived. As we will soon see, its capacity is limited in terms of the number of items it can store and its duration. If you go to the movies and the cashier says, "Your movie is playing in theatre six," you obviously need to remember this long enough to find the entrance. We can remember information like this by keeping it active, such as by repeating it once or twice. However, if you let the information become inactive (say, by stopping to talk with friends and buying some popcorn), you may not be able to remember it later. Information soon leaves short-term memory, and unless it is stored in long-term memory it will be lost forever.

**memory** The cognitive processes of encoding, storing, and retrieving information.
**encoding** The process by which sensory information is converted into a form that can be used by the brain's memory system.
**storage** The process of maintaining information in memory.
**retrieval** The active processes of locating and using stored information.
**sensory memory** Memory in which representations of the physical features of a stimulus are stored for very brief durations.
**short-term memory** An immediate memory for stimuli that have just been perceived. It is limited in terms of both capacity (7 ± 2 chunks of information) and duration (less than 20 seconds).

**FIGURE 8•1** A simplified model of information flow in human memory.

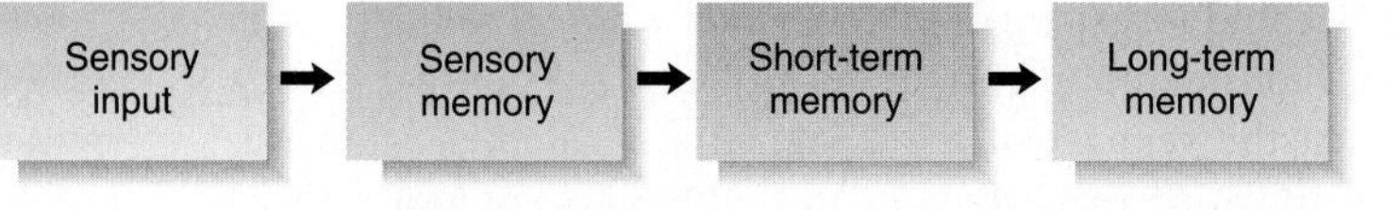


To demonstrate the fact that short-term memory can hold only a limited amount of information for a limited time, read the following numbers to yourself just once, and then close your eyes and recite them back.

1 4 9 2 3 0 7

You probably had no trouble remembering them. Now, try the following set of numbers, and go through them only once before you close your eyes.

7 2 5 2 3 9 1 6 5 8 4

Very few people can repeat 11 numbers; in fact, you may not have even bothered to try once you saw how many there were. Even if you practise, you will probably not be able to recite more than seven to nine independent pieces of information that you have seen only once. Thus, short-term memory has definite limits (Marois & Ivanoff, 2005).

If you wanted to, you could recite the 11 numbers again and again until you had memorized them. You could rehearse the information in short-term memory until it was eventually part of **long-term memory**—memory in which information is represented on a permanent or near-permanent basis. Unlike short-term memory, long-term memory has no known limits, and, as its name suggests, it is relatively durable. For example, Standing (1973) showed people 10 000 colour slides and found that they could recognize most of them weeks later, even though they had seen them just once. Presumably, long-term memory occurs because of physical changes that take place in the brain. If we stop thinking about something we have just perceived (that is, something contained in short-term memory), we may not remember the information later. However, information in long-term memory need not be continuously rehearsed. We can stop thinking about it until we need the information at a future time.

The implication that information flows from one type of memory to another has been termed the *modal model* of memory because it seems to be so widely assumed. (See **Figure 8•1**.) However, some cognitive psychologists argue that no real distinction exists between short-term and long-term memory; instead, they see them as different phases of a continuous process (Crowder, 1993). A loose analogy might be the way that cars could be manufactured in the global economy. One automaker might manufacture the car's frame in Japan, ship it to a factory in Canada to add the engine, and then finish the assembly at a factory in the United States. The different factories would have their own methods of operation, and the transfer of cars from one to another is a significant part of the story. The alternative method is to assemble the entire car in different stages within the same factory. The emphasis in the second method is on the way the car body changes as it moves through the process. The next few sections will follow the general outline of Figure 8.1, but you will see that psychologists have discovered that memory is more complex than this model would have us believe (Healy & McNamara, 1996).

## Sensory Memory

Information we have just perceived remains in sensory memory just long enough to be transferred to short-term memory. We become aware of sensory memory only when information is presented very briefly, so that we can perceive its after-effects. For example, a thunderstorm at night provides us with an opportunity to become aware of visual sensory memory. When a bright flash of lightning reveals a scene, we see things before we recognize them. That is, we see something first, then study the image it leaves behind. Although we probably have a sensory memory for each sense modality, research efforts so far have focused on the two most important forms: iconic (visual) and echoic (auditory) memory.

### Iconic Memory

Visual sensory memory, called **iconic memory** (icon means "image"), is a form of sensory memory that briefly holds a visual representation of a scene that has just been perceived. Because the representation is so closely tied to the perception, this form of memory is sometimes called "visible persistence." To study this form of memory, Sperling (1960) presented visual stimuli to people on a screen for extremely brief durations. He flashed a set of 9 letters on the screen for 50 milliseconds. (See **Figure 8•2**.) He then asked people to recall as many letters as they could, a method known as the whole-report procedure. On average, they could remember only four or five letters, but they insisted that, for a brief time, they could see more. However, the image of the letters faded too quickly for people to identify them all.

**long-term memory** Memory in which information is represented on a permanent or near-permanent basis.

**iconic memory** A form of sensory memory that holds a brief visual image of a scene that has just been perceived; also known as visible persistence.

▲ *Images to which we are briefly exposed, such as a bolt of lightning, linger momentarily in iconic memory.*

To determine whether the capacity of iconic memory accounted for this limitation, Sperling used a partial-report procedure. He sounded tones when presenting the stimuli, and asked people to name the letters in only one of the three horizontal rows: Depending on whether a high, middle, or low tone was sounded, they were to report the letters in the top, middle, or bottom line. When the participants were warned beforehand to which line they should attend, they had no difficulty naming all three letters correctly. However, Sperling then sounded the tone after he flashed the letters on the screen. The participants had to select the line from the mental image they still had: They could use only information from memory. With brief delays, they recalled the requested line of letters with high accuracy. For example, after seeing all nine letters flashed on the screen, they would hear the high tone, direct their attention to the top line of letters in their iconic memory, and "read them off" much as one might read the headlines in a newspaper. The participants' high level of performance indicated that there was little difference between having the letters physically present in front of them and having them present as a memory. However, Sperling also varied the delay between flashing the nine letters on the screen and sounding the high, medium, or low tone. If the delay was longer than one second, people could report only around 50 percent of the letters. Apparently, during the delay, the information had faded before all of it could be transferred to longer-lasting memory. This result indicated that the image of the visual stimulus fades quickly from iconic memory. It also explains why participants who were asked to report all nine letters failed to report more than four or five. They had to scan their iconic memory, identify each letter, and name it verbally. This process took time, and during this time the image of the letters was fading and the information becoming unreliable (Dixon, Gordon, Leung, & Di Lollo, 1997). Although their iconic memory originally contained all nine letters, participants had time to recognize and report only four or five before the mental image disappeared.

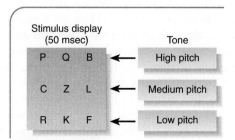

Stimulus display (50 msec)
Tone

| | | | | |
|---|---|---|---|---|
| P | Q | B | ← | High pitch |
| C | Z | L | ← | Medium pitch |
| R | K | F | ← | Low pitch |

**FIGURE 8•2** The critical features of Sperling's iconic memory study.

*(Adapted from Sperling, G. (1960). The information available in brief visual presentations.* Psychological Monographs, 74, *1–29.)*

## Echoic Memory

Auditory sensory memory, called **echoic memory**, is a form of sensory memory for sounds that have just been perceived. It is necessary for comprehending many sounds, particularly those that constitute speech. When we hear a word pronounced, we hear individual sounds, one at a time. We cannot identify the word until we have heard all of the sounds, so acoustical information must be stored temporarily until all sounds have been received. For example, if someone says "harbour," we may think of an anchorage for ships; but if someone says "harvest," we will think of something entirely different. The first syllable we hear—*har*—has no meaning by itself in English, so we do not identify it as a word. However, once the last syllable is uttered, we can put the two syllables together and recognize the word. At this point, the word enters short-term memory. Echoic memory holds a representation of the initial sounds until the entire word has been heard. Although early use of partial-report procedures suggested that echoic memory lasts less than 4 seconds (Darwin, Turvey, & Crowder, 1972), more recent evidence employing repeated patterns of random, or "white," noise indicates that echoic memory can last up to 20 seconds (Kaernbach, 2004). Indeed, if you consider your ability to recognize a friend's voice over the telephone, there's a sense in which we retain

**echoic memory** A form of sensory memory for sounds that have just been perceived.

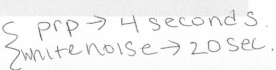

sound patterns for much longer (Winkler & Cowan, 2005). This everyday phenomenon presents a problem for the simplified model we've been discussing. To understand why, we need to consider the next stages in that model: short-term and long-term memory.

## Interim Summary

### Sensory Memory

Memory exists in three forms: sensory, short-term, and long-term. The characteristics of each differ, which suggests that they differ physiologically as well. Sensory memory is very limited; it provides temporary storage until the newly perceived information can be stored in short-term memory. Short-term memory contains a representation of information that has just been perceived, such as an item's name. Although the capacity of short-term memory is limited, we can rehearse the information as long as we choose, thus increasing the likelihood that we will remember it indefinitely (that is, that it will enter long-term memory).

Information in sensory memory lasts for only a short time. The partial-report procedure shows that when a visual stimulus is presented in a brief flash, all of the information is available for a short time. If the viewer's attention is directed to one line of information within a few hundred milliseconds of the flash, the information can be transferred into short-term memory. Echoic memory appears to operate similarly.

**QUESTIONS TO CONSIDER**

1. It is easy to understand how we can rehearse verbal information in short-term memory—we simply say the information to ourselves again and again. But much of the information we learn is not verbal. Can we rehearse non-verbal information in short-term memory? How do we do so?
2. Suppose that your iconic memory malfunctioned. Instead of holding information only briefly, your iconic memory retained information for longer periods of time. What complications or problems might follow from such a malfunction? Would there be any advantages to this sort of malfunction?

## Short-Term or Working Memory

Short-term memory has a limited capacity, and most of the information that enters it is subsequently forgotten. What, then, is its function? Before we can answer this question, let us examine its nature a little more closely.

### Encoding of Information in the Short Term: Interaction with Long-Term Memory

So far, the story I have been telling about memory has been simple: Information in sensory memory enters short-term memory, where it may be rehearsed for a while. The rehearsal process keeps the information in short-term memory long enough for it to be transferred into long-term memory. After that, a person can stop thinking about the information; it can be recalled later, when it is needed.

However, this simple story is incomplete. First of all, information does not simply "enter short-term memory." For example, read the letters below. Put them into your short-term memory, and keep them there for a few seconds while you look away from the book.

PXLMR

How did you keep the information in short-term memory? You would probably say that you repeated the letters to yourself. You may even have whispered or moved your lips. You are able to say the names of these letters because many years ago you learned them. But that knowledge is stored in long-term memory. Thus, when you see some letters, you retrieve information about their names from long-term memory, and then you hear yourself rehearse those names (out loud or silently, "within your head"). The five letters you looked at contain only visual information; their names came from your long-term memory, which means that the information put into short-term memory actually came from long-term memory.

To convince yourself that you used information stored in long-term memory to remember the five letters, study the symbols below, look away from the book, and try to keep them in short-term memory for a while.

ξ∩∂∋℘

Could you do so? I certainly can't. I never learned the names of these symbols, so I have no way of rehearsing them in short-term memory. Perhaps, then, **Figure 8•3** more accurately represents the successive stages of the memory process than does the diagram you saw in Figure 8.1.

You can see now that short-term memory is more than a simple way station between perception and long-term memory. Information can enter short-term memory from two directions: from sensory memory or from long-term memory. In Figure 8.3, this feature is represented by arrows pointing to short-term memory from both iconic memory and long-term memory. Perhaps another example will clarify the process further. When we are asked to multiply 7 by 19, information about the request enters our short-term memory from our sensory memory. Actually performing the task, though, requires that we retrieve some information from long-term memory. What does multiply mean? What is a 7 and a 19? At the moment of the request, such information is not being furnished through our senses; it is available only from

short term memory is a mixture of old + new information

**FIGURE 8•3** Relations between iconic memory, short-term memory, and long-term memory. Letters are read, transformed into their acoustic equivalents, and rehearsed as "sounds" in the head. Information can enter short-term memory from both iconic memory and long-term memory. Visual information enters short-term memory from iconic memory, but what is already known about that information (such as names of letters) is moved from long-term memory to short-term memory.

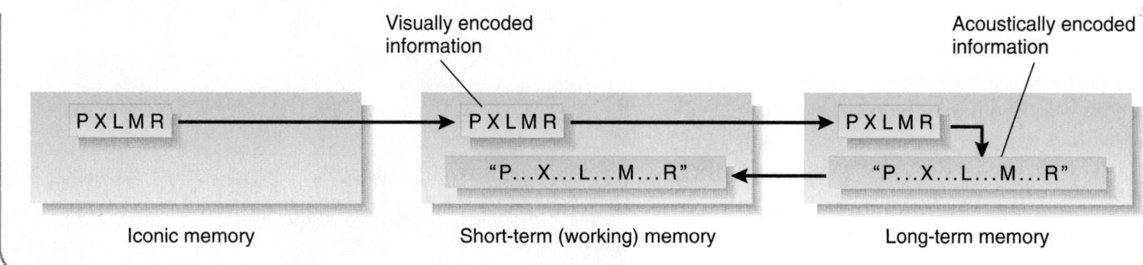


long-term memory. However, most versions of the model shown in Figure 8.1 assume that information is not recalled directly from long-term memory. Instead, it is first moved into short-term memory and then recalled. So short-term memory contains information when we are trying to encode that information and when we are trying to retrieve it.

The fact that short-term memory contains both new information and information retrieved from long-term memory has led some psychologists to prefer the term **working memory** (Baddeley, 1993). Working memory does seem to work on what we have just perceived. In fact, working memory represents a sort of behaviour that takes place within our heads. It represents our ability to remember what we have just perceived and to think about it in terms of what we already know (Haberlandt, 1994). We use it to remember what a person says at the beginning of a sentence until we finally hear the end. We use it to remember whether any cars are coming up the street after looking left and then right. We use it to think about what we already know and to come to conclusions on the basis of this knowledge. These behaviours are similar to what I have described as short-term memory and, from now on, the terms *short-term memory* and *working memory* will be used interchangeably. Some psychologists, however, prefer to distinguish the two forms of memory on the basis of the functions they serve (Kail & Hall, 2001).

## Primacy and Recency Effects

Imagine yourself as a participant in a memory study. You are asked to listen to the researcher as she slowly reads words, one at a time, off a long list. As soon as she finishes reading the list, you are asked to write down each word that you can remember. (This task is called a free-recall task.) Which words in the list do you think you are most likely to remember? If you are like most people in free-recall tasks like this one, you will remember the words at the beginning and the end of the list and forget the words in between. The tendency to remember the words at the beginning of the list is called the **primacy effect**; the tendency to remember words at the end of the list is called the **recency effect**.

What causes these effects? Research that has addressed this question points to two factors (Atkinson & Shiffrin, 1968). The primacy effect appears to be due to the fact that words earlier in a list have the opportunity to be rehearsed more than do words in other parts of a list. This makes good sense; the first words are rehearsed more because, at the experiment's outset, these are the only words available to rehearse. The rehearsal permits them to be stored in long-term memory. As more and more words on the list are presented, short-term memory becomes more and more full, so words that come later have more competition for rehearsal time. Because the first words on the list are rehearsed the most, they are remembered better.

What about the recency effect? As Atkinson and Shiffrin (1968) point out, because the words at the end of the list were the last to be heard, they are still available in short-term memory. Thus, when you are asked to write the words on the list, the last several words are still available in short-term memory, even though they did not undergo as much rehearsal as words at the beginning of the list.

Earlier, I said that working memory is a sort of behaviour—a type of behaviour that takes place inside the head. The primacy and recency effects are important because they show the consequence of this behaviour. Memory is not a random process that plucks information from the environment and stores it haphazardly in the brain. Instead, it follows predictable patterns and is dependent on the contributions of rehearsal and short-term memory. We cannot observe these behaviours directly, but we can observe their consequences.

**working memory** Memory for new information and information retrieved from long-term memory; used in this text as another name for short-term memory.

**primacy effect** The tendency to remember initial information. In the memorization of a list of words, the primacy effect is evidenced by better recall of the words early in the list.

**recency effect** The tendency to recall later information. In the memorization of a list of words, the recency effect is evidenced by better recall of the last words in the list.

## The Limits of Working Memory

How long does information remain in working memory? The answer to this question was provided in classic studies conducted by John Brown (1958) and Lloyd and Margaret Peterson (1959). The Petersons presented participants with a stimulus composed of three consonants, such as JRG. Not surprisingly, with rehearsal, people easily recalled it 30 seconds later. The Petersons then made the task a bit more challenging: They prevented the participants in their study from rehearsing. After they presented the participants with JRG, they asked them to count backward by three from a three-digit number they gave them immediately after they had presented the set of consonants. For example, they might present people with JRG, then say, "397." The participants would count out loud, "397 . . . 394 . . . 391 . . . 388 . . . 385," and so on until the researchers signalled them to recall the consonants. The accuracy of a participant's recall was determined by the length of the interval between presentation of the consonants and when recall was requested. (See **Figure 8•4**.) When rehearsal was disrupted by backward counting—which prevented participants from rehearsing information in short-term memory—the consonants remained accessible in memory for only a few seconds. After a 15- to 18-second delay between the presentation of the consonants and the recall signal, recall dropped to near zero. So, for now we can conclude that, once attended to, stimuli remain in working memory for less than 20 seconds unless they are rehearsed.

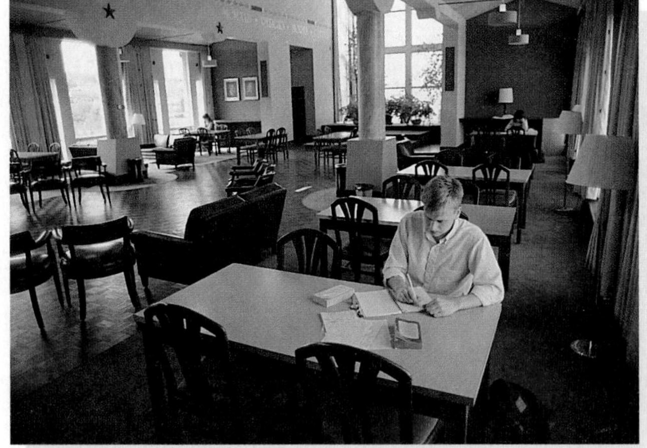

▲ *Unless we actively rehearse the material we are studying, we are unlikely to remember it for very long: It is relegated to short-term memory, in which information is stored for relatively short periods of time.*

As a matter of fact, working memory may be even more limited. Muter (1980) pointed out that in the procedure used by Brown and the Petersons, the counting task always appeared after the letters. Consequently, participants in their experiments would be expecting a distraction. What would happen if a distraction was unexpected? This would be like hearing a phone number you wanted to remember and then having the doorbell ring right afterwards. Muter examined this question by using the Peterson procedure, but with the counting task appearing only on a small proportion of trials, making it unexpected. He found that an unexpected distractor seriously disrupted working memory: Most people found it hard to recall three letters after only two seconds.

What is the capacity of working memory? A while ago, I asked you to try to repeat 11 numbers, which you were almost certainly unable to do. In fact, Miller (1956), in a paper entitled "The Magical Number Seven, Plus or Minus Two," demonstrated that people could retain, on average, about seven pieces of information in their short-term memories: seven numbers, seven letters, seven unrelated words, or seven tones of a particular pitch. If we can remember and think about only seven pieces of information at a time, how can we manage to write novels, design buildings, or even carry on simple conversations? The answer comes in a particular form of encoding of information that Miller called **chunking**, a process by which information is simplified by rules, which make it easily remembered once the rules are learned.

A simple demonstration illustrates this phenomenon. Read the 10 numbers printed below and see whether you have any trouble remembering them.

1 3 5 7 9 2 4 6 8 0

These numbers are easy to retain in short-term memory because we can remember a rule instead of 10 independent

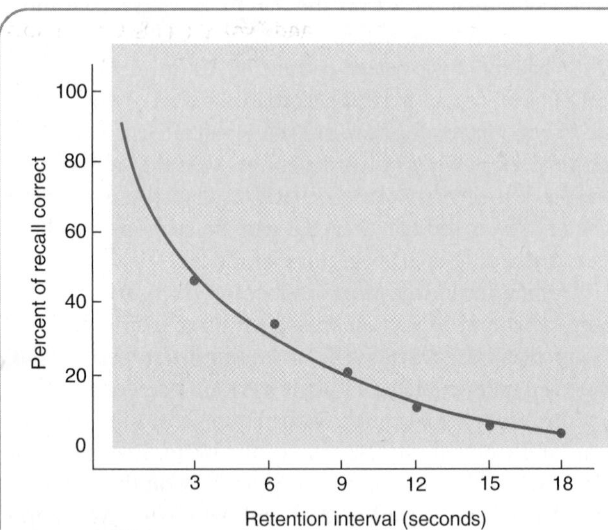


**FIGURE 8•4** Limits of recall from working memory. Percentage correct in the recall of the stimulus as a function of the duration of the distracter task used in the study by Peterson and Peterson.

*(Adapted from Peterson, L. M., & Peterson, M. J. (1959). Short-term retention of individual verbal items.* Journal of Experimental Psychology, 58, *193–198.)*

**chunking** A process by which information is simplified by rules, which make it easily remembered once the rules are learned. For example, the string of letters GSTCBCRCMP are easier to remember if a person learns the rule that organizes them into smaller "chunks": GST, CBC, and RCMP.

numbers. In this case, the rule concerns odd and even numbers. The actual limit of short-term memory is seven chunks, not necessarily seven individual items. Thus, the total amount of information we can store in short-term memory depends on the particular rules we use to organize it.

In life outside the laboratory (and away from the textbook), we are seldom required to remember a series of numbers. The rules that organize our short-term memories are much more complex than those that describe odd and even numbers. However, the principles of chunking apply to more realistic learning situations. For example, say the group of words below, look away from the page, and try to recite the words from memory.

> along got the was door crept locked slowly he until passage the he to which

No doubt you found the task hopeless; there was just too much information to store in short-term memory. Now try the following group of words:

> He slowly crept along the passage until he got to the door, which was locked.

This time you were probably much more successful. Once the same 15 words are arranged in a sequence that makes sense, they are not difficult to store in short-term memory.

The capacity of short-term memory for verbal material is not measured in letters, syllables, or words. Instead, the limit depends on how much meaning the information has. The first set of words above merely contains 15 different words. Because few people can immediately recite back more than 5 to 9 independent items, we are not surprised to find that we cannot store 15 jumbled words in short-term memory. However, when the items are related, we can store many more of them. We do not have to string 15 words together in a meaningless fashion. Instead, we can let the image of a man creeping down a passage toward a locked door organize the new information. Thus, we can read or hear a sentence such as the one above, understand what the sentence means, and remember that meaning.

This aspect of short-term memory suggests a way of making it more efficient in everyday use. If the information can be organized into a more meaningful sequence, there is less to be remembered. McNamara and Scott (2001) taught people to chain unrelated words together as they listened to them. The chaining technique was simple: People were to imagine a story involving these words. This technique sharply improved short-term memory. Later in this chapter we will discuss similar strategies to improve long-term memory.

## Varieties of Working Memory

So far, you have seen short-term or working memory referred to in the singular. But evidence suggests that working memory can contain a variety of sensory information: visual, auditory, somatosensory, gustatory, and olfactory. It can also contain information about movements that we have just made (motor memories), and it may provide the means by which we rehearse movements that we are thinking about making. Is all of this information contained in a single system, or do we have several independent working memories?

Baddeley (1993, 2000) has suggested that working memory consists of several components, all coordinated by a "central executive" function. One component maintains verbal information; another retains memories of visual stimuli. A third component might serve to store more general information, including memory for non-speech sounds (such as the sound of your friend's voice over the telephone), touch, odours, or other types of information.

**Phonological Working Memory** Although we receive information from different senses, much of it can be encoded verbally. For example, we can see or smell a rose and think the word *rose*; we can feel the prick of a thorn and think the word *sharp*; and so on. Thus, seeing a rose, smelling a rose, and feeling a thorn can all result in words running through our working memory. How is verbal information stored in working memory? Evidence suggests that the short-term storage of words, whether originally presented visually or acoustically, occurs in **phonological short-term memory**—short-term or working memory for verbal information. The Greek word *ph–on–e* means both "sound" and "voice"; as the name implies, phonological coding could involve either the auditory system of the brain or the system that controls speech. As we shall see, it involves both.

An experiment by Conrad (1964) showed how quickly visually presented information becomes encoded acoustically. He briefly showed people lists of six letters and then asked them to write the letters. The errors these people made were almost always acoustical rather than visual. For instance, they sometimes wrote B when they had seen V (these letters sound similar), but they rarely wrote F when they had seen T (these letters look similar). Keep in mind that Conrad presented the letters visually. The results suggest that people read the letters, encode them acoustically ("hear them in their minds"), and remember them by rehearsing the letters as sounds. During this process, they might easily mistake a V for a B.

The fact that the errors seem to be acoustical may reflect a form of acoustical coding in working memory. That is, phonological memory may be produced by activity in the auditory system—say, circuits of neurons in the auditory association cortex. However, people often talk to themselves. Sometimes, they talk aloud; sometimes, they whisper or simply move their lips. At other times, no movements can be

**phonological short-term memory** Short-term memory for verbal information.

detected, but people still report that they are thinking about saying something. They are engaging in **subvocal articulation**, an unvoiced speech utterance. Even though no actual movement may occur, it is still possible that activity occurs in the neural circuits in the brain that normally control speech. When we close our eyes and imagine seeing something, the mental image is undoubtedly caused by the activity of neurons in the visual association cortex. Similarly, when we imagine saying something, the "voice in our head" is probably controlled by the activity of neurons in the motor association cortex. Research suggests that even deaf children perform acoustical encoding in terms of the movements they would make to pronounce letters (Conrad, 1970). People may therefore use both acoustic and articulatory codes: They may simultaneously hear a word and feel themselves saying it in their heads. Phonological codes stored in long-term memory also may help to strengthen the rehearsed information (Roodenrys et al., 2002).

The best neurological evidence for the existence of phonological short-term memory comes from a disorder called conduction aphasia, which is usually caused by damage to a region of the left parietal lobe. **Conduction aphasia** appears as a profound deficit in phonological working memory. People who have conduction aphasia can talk and can comprehend what others are saying, but they are very poor at repeating precisely what they hear. When they attempt to repeat words that other people say, they often get the meaning correct but use different words. For example, if asked to repeat the sentence, "The cement truck ran over the bicycle," a person who has conduction aphasia may reply, "The concrete mixer got into an accident with a bike."

Most investigators believe that conduction aphasia is caused by brain damage that disrupts the connections between two regions of the cerebral cortex that play important roles in people's language ability. These two regions are Wernicke's area, which is concerned with the perception of speech, and Broca's area, which is concerned with the production of speech. (We'll look at these areas in more detail in Chapter 10.) As we saw, phonological working memory appears to involve both articulatory and acoustical coding. Because the brain damage that produces conduction aphasia disconnects regions of the brain involved in speech perception and production, perhaps the damage disrupts acoustical short-term memory by making such subvocal verbal rehearsal difficult or impossible. (See **Figure 8•5**.)

**FIGURE 8•5** A diagram showing how conduction aphasia is caused.

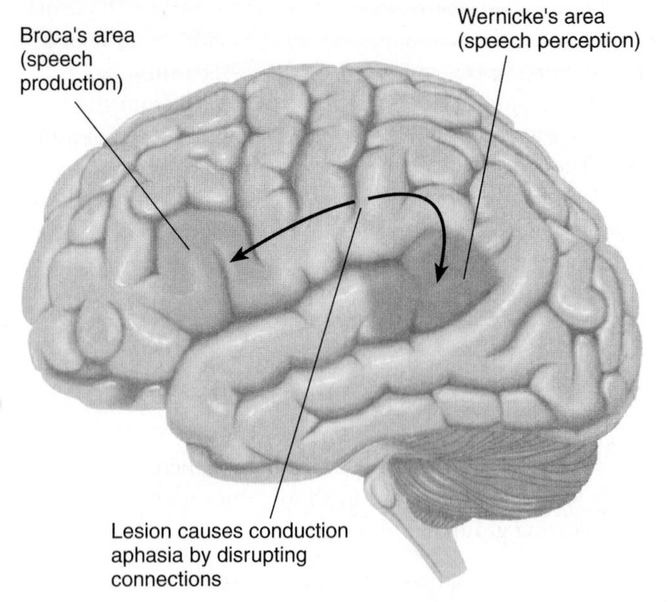


**Visual Working Memory** Verbal information can be received by means of the visual system or the auditory system—that is, we can hear words or read them. As we saw in the previous section, both forms of input produce acoustic and articulatory codes in phonological working memory. But much of the information we receive from the visual system is non-verbal. We recognize objects, perceive their locations, and find our way around the environment. We can look at objects, close our eyes, and then sketch or describe them. We can do the same with things we saw in the past. Thus, we apparently possess a working memory that contains visual information, either obtained from the immediate environment by means of the sense organs or retrieved from long-term memory.

Much of what we see is familiar; we have seen the particular items—or similar items—before. Thus, our visual working memory does not need to encode all of the details, the way a photograph copies all details in the scene gathered by the lens of a camera. For example, our short-term memory of the sight of a dog does not need to store every visual feature we saw, such as four legs, whiskers, ears, and a tail. Instead, we already have mental images of dogs in our long-term memory. When we see a dog, we can select a prototype that fits the bill, filling in a few features to represent the particular dog we just saw.

DeGroot (1965) performed an experiment that provides a nice example of the power of encoding visual information in working memory. He showed chessboards to expert players and to novices. If the positions of the pieces represented an actual game in progress, the experts could glance at the board for a few seconds and then look away and report the position of each piece; the novices could not. However, if the same number of pieces had been placed haphazardly on the board, the experts recognized immediately that their

**subvocal articulation** An unvoiced speech utterance.
**conduction aphasia** An inability to remember words that are heard, although they usually can be understood and responded to appropriately. This disability is caused by damage to Wernicke's and Broca's areas.

▲ *One advantage that experienced hockey players have over novice players is their superior long-term memory for different patterns of play on the ice. This information helps them anticipate the possible moves their opponent might make as well as plan their responses.*

positions made no sense, and they could not remember their positions any better than a non-expert could. Thus, their short-term memories for the positions of a large number of chess pieces depended on organizational rules stored in long-term memory as a result of years of playing chess. Novices could not remember the location of the pieces in either situation because they lacked long-term memories for patterns of chess pieces on a board and could not acquire the information as efficiently (Reingold, Charness, Pomplun, & Stampe, 2001).

Humans have a remarkable ability to manipulate visual information in working memory. For example, Shepard and Metzler (1971) presented people with pairs of drawings that could be perceived as three-dimensional constructions made of cubes. A person's task was to see whether the shape on the right was identical to the one on the left; some were, and some were not. Even when the shapes were identical, the one on the right was sometimes drawn as if it had been rotated. For example, in **Figure 8•6(a)** the shape on the right has been rotated clockwise 80 degrees, but in **Figure 8•6(b)** the two shapes are different.

Shepard and Metzler found that people were very accurate in judging whether the pairs of shapes were the same or different. However, they took longer to decide when the right-hand shape was rotated. (See **Figure 8•7**.) They reported that they formed an image of one of the drawings in their heads and rotated it until it was aligned the same way as the other one. (Mental manipulation of shapes is an important component of the ability to design and construct tools, buildings, bridges, and other useful objects.) If the participants' rotated images coincided with the other drawings, they recognized them as having the same shape. If they did not, they recognized them as being different (Shepard & Metzler, 1971).

**FIGURE 8•6** The mental rotation task. (a) The shape on the right is identical to the one on the left but rotated 80 degrees clockwise. (b) The two shapes are different.

*(Adapted from Shepard, R. N., & Metzler, J. (1971). Mental rotation of three-dimensional objects.* Science, 171, *701–703. Copyright 1971 by the American Association for the Advancement of Science.)*

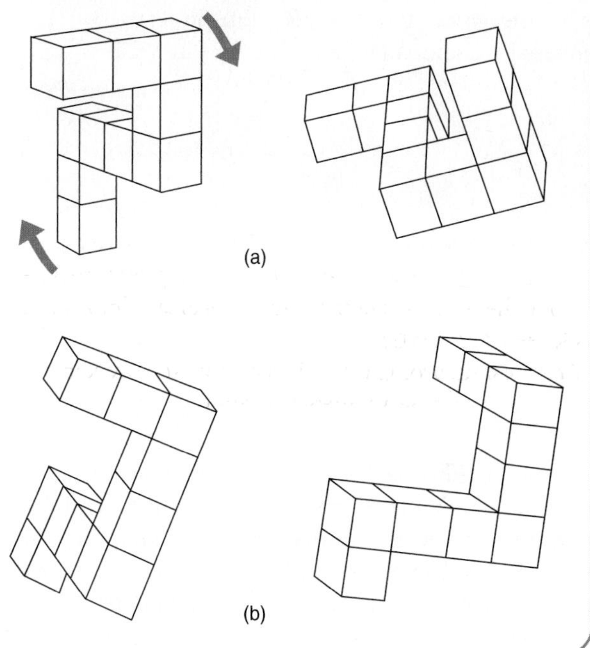


A two-dimensional rotation

Mean reaction time (seconds): 0, 1, 2, 3, 4

Angle of rotation (degrees): 0, 40, 80, 120, 160

**FIGURE 8•7** The results from the mental rotation task study. Mean reaction time is shown as a function of angle of rotation.

*(Adapted from Shepard, R. N., & Metzler, J. (1971). Mental rotation of three-dimensional objects.* Science, 171, *701–703. Copyright 1971 by the American Association for the Advancement of Science. Reprinted with permission from AAAS.)*

▲ *Working memory has been compared to juggling. With greater skill or effort, more items can be juggled—unless a distraction occurs.*

## Loss of Information from Short-Term Memory

The essence of short-term memory is its transience; hence, its name. Information enters from sensory memory and from long-term memory, is rehearsed, thought about, modified, and then leaves. Some of the information controls ongoing behaviour and some of it causes changes in long-term memory, but ultimately it is lost from short-term memory. What causes it to leave?

As mentioned earlier, psychologists have described working memory as a kind of behaviour that we use to maintain information over the short term. This way of thinking about working memory provides a useful framework to explain how we lose information, if we assume that information has a tendency to be degraded or to decay with time. Rehearsal activity of phonological short-term memory, such as subvocal articulation, prevents decay. Nairne (2002) has suggested a metaphor of how this might work. Working memory, Nairne says, is like a juggler trying to maintain several plates or balls in the air. As long as the juggler works actively at catching and throwing the plates, they don't fall and hit the ground (decay). With increased skill or more effort, the juggler can keep even more plates in the air. But any distraction or other competing behaviour will reduce the number of plates that can be juggled.

If you accept this metaphor, then consider this: Anything that makes the plates easier to handle should decrease the risk that they will be dropped. With respect to words, shorter words are easier to articulate and therefore should be easier to rehearse. Psychologists have shown that shorter words are remembered better under conditions of short-term memory (e.g., Tehan, Hendry, & Kocinski, 2001), a finding that supports the rehearsal-and-decay explanation.

However, as Nairne himself points out, "decay" is a nonspecific term and risks falling prey to the nominal fallacy discussed in Chapter 2. Why should information decay? Perhaps more active processes work to degrade the information or to make it more difficult to recall. Later in this chapter, after we have surveyed long-term memory, I will discuss one such possibility.

## Interim Summary

### Short-Term or Working Memory

Information in short-term memory is encoded according to previously learned rules. Information in long-term memory determines the nature of the encoding. Because short-term memory contains information retrieved from long-term memory as well as newly perceived information, many researchers conceive of it as working memory. Working memory is not simply a way station between sensory memory and long-term memory; it is where thinking occurs. When presented with a list of items, we tend to remember the items at the beginning of the list (the primacy effect) and at the end of the list (the recency effect) better than items in the middle of the list. The primacy effect presumably occurs because we have a greater opportunity to rehearse items early in the list and thus store them in long-term memory, and the recency effect occurs because we can retrieve items at the end of the list from short-term memory.

Working memory lasts for about 20 seconds and has a capacity of about 7 items—give or take 2. We often simplify large amounts of information by organizing it into "chunks" of information, which can then be more easily rehearsed and remembered.

Although each sensory system probably has a working memory associated with it, psychologists have devoted most of their attention to two kinds: phonological and visual working memory. The existence of acoustical errors (rather than visual ones) in the task of remembering visually presented letters suggests that information is represented phonologically in short-term memory. Because deaf people (but only those who can talk) also show this effect, the code appears to be articulatory. Phonological working memory is encoded acoustically as well. People who have conduction aphasia show a specific deficit in phonological short-term memory, apparently because their brain damage interrupts direct communication between Wernicke's area and Broca's area.

Visual working memory is also important and has been demonstrated in the laboratory by the ability of chess masters to remember a board and by the ability to perform mental rotation of shapes. Mental manipulation of shapes is an important component of our ability to design and construct tools, buildings, bridges, and other useful objects.

Information is maintained in working memory as long as it is rehearsed. Anything that interferes with rehearsal will lead to loss of short-term information, possibly through decay. However, that explanation requires a reason why information might decay.

**QUESTIONS TO CONSIDER**

1. Suppose that someone has sustained a brain injury that prohibits her from putting information into, and getting information out of, long-term memory. Would this injury affect only her long-term memory, or would her short-term memory be affected, too? Can you think of an experiment that you could perform that would answer this question? What would this person's life be like?
2. Take a few moments to imagine the shortest route you can take to get from your home to your favourite restaurant. In terms of how your short-term memory operates, explain how you are able to accomplish this bit of mental imagery.

# Learning and Encoding in Long-Term Memory

Information that is present in short-term memory may or may not be available later. But once information has successfully made its way into long-term memory, it remains relatively stable (Burt, Kemp, & Conway, 2001). Of course, we do forget things, but, nevertheless, our brains have the remarkable ability to store vast amounts of information and numerous experiences from our past.

What kinds of information can be stored in long-term memory? To answer this question, let us consider the kinds of things we can learn. First, we can learn to recognize things: objects, sounds, odours, textures, and tastes. Thus, we can remember perceptions received by all of our sensory systems, which means that we have visual memories, auditory memories, olfactory memories, somatosensory memories, and gustatory memories. These memories can be combined and interconnected, so that hearing a soft "meow" in the dark elicits an image of a cat. Perceptual memories can also contain information about the order in which events occurred, so that we can remember the plot of a movie we saw or hear the melody of a song in our heads.

We can also learn from experience. We can learn to make new responses—as when we learn to operate a new machine, ride a bicycle, or say a new word—or we can learn to make old responses in new situations. Perceptual memories presumably involve alterations in circuits of neurons in the sensory association cortex of the brain—visual memories in the visual cortex, auditory memories in the auditory cortex, and so on. Memories that involve combinations of perceptual information presumably involve the establishment of connections between different regions of the association cortex. Motor memories (memories for particular behaviours) presumably involve alterations in circuits of neurons in the motor association cortex of the frontal lobes. Thus, learning to perform particular behaviours in particular situations likely involves the establishment of connections between the appropriate regions of the sensory and motor cortexes.

Memory involves both active and passive processes. Sometimes, we use deliberate strategies to remember something (encode the information into long-term memory), as when we rehearse the lines of a poem or memorize famous dates for a history course. At other times, we simply observe and remember without any apparent effort, as when we tell a friend about an interesting experience we had. And memories can be formed even without our being aware of having learned something. What factors determine whether we can eventually remember an experience? Let's look at some hypotheses that have been proposed.

## The Consolidation Hypothesis

Hebb's dual trace theory was based on the distinction between active processing of information and latent retention due to structural changes in the brain. One way to think about the traditional view of memory is that sensory memory and short-term memory represent information in its active state. That is, these two memory systems do not represent places in the brain per se, but instead are the result of brain processes that keep the information active (Crowder, 1993). Once this activity subsides, the information can be retained only through longer-lasting structural changes.

The change of information from short-term memory into long-term memory has been called **consolidation.** These structural changes make the information stronger, easier to recall, and more resistant to forgetting. Consolidated information is long-term memory. Rehearsal itself is not consolidation; it is viewed as one of the mechanisms that allow consolidation to occur. In addition, consolidation may occur without awareness and could be a lengthy process.

Some of the best evidence in favour of the consolidation hypothesis comes from events that disrupt brain functioning. From the earliest times, people have observed that a blow to the head can affect memory. A blow to the head disrupts the balance in ions surrounding brain cells. The neurons' ion pumps increase as a result, causing large metabolic changes (Iverson, 2005). In such "closed-head injury" incidents, individuals' working memory seems to be strongly impaired (McAllister, Flashman, Sparling, & Saykin, 2004). For example, Dutch amateur boxers were given standard tests for memory ability before and after a boxing match and compared to non-boxers who simply exercised; the memory scores for the boxers showed significant impairments (Matser et al., 2000). In very severe cases, the injury produces a prolonged lack of memory for events, a condition called **retrograde amnesia** (*retro-* means

**consolidation** The process by which information in short-term memory changes to long-term memory, presumably because of physical changes that occur in neurons in the brain.

**retrograde amnesia** The loss of the ability to retrieve memories of one's past, particularly memories of episodic or autobiographical events.

"backward": in this case, backward in time). Consolidation theorists assume that this occurs because the brain centres for consolidation have been damaged. Significantly, retrograde amnesia shows a distinctive pattern: Recent memories are affected more strongly than older ones (Brown, 2002). This is the pattern that consolidation theory would predict: Recent memories have had less time to be consolidated and therefore are weaker, more difficult to retrieve, and more prone to forgetting.

## Then and Now

### Consolidation and the "Genetic Action Potential"

▲ *Songbirds, such as this male zebra finch, learn their species songs when they are young from an adult tutor and express them when they mature.*

In Chapter 7, we discussed Hebb's concept of learning: When two adjacent neurons are simultaneously active, a synaptic connection between them is created or strengthened. As we've seen, Hebb's framework provided a physiological explanation of consolidation as well as a way of thinking about short-term and long-term memory: Active circuits of neurons corresponded to short-term memory traces; their activity strengthened the connections among them, providing a basis for long-term memory (McGaugh, 1999).

The notion that consolidation involved the formation of synaptic structures was strengthened by research in the 1960s using chemicals that disrupt the synthesis of proteins. For example, Agranoff, Davis, and Brink (1965) injected puromycin, an antibiotic that also inhibits protein synthesis, into the skulls of goldfish after they had learned to swim from one end of a tank to the other to avoid an electric shock. When tested three days later, the fish showed strong deficits in what they had learned. Furthermore, injections given just before learning did not affect the ability to learn the avoidance response. Puromycin affected long-term retention of the response across days, but not the short-term trial-by-trial retention during the first day. Consolidation of the memory, in other words, required the synthesis of proteins.

Research such as this has helped illuminate some of the ways that long-term potentiation occurs (see Chapter 7). However, a key part of understanding consolidation requires knowing how the proteins are produced. Hebb's concept of learning suggested that it was in response to neural activity—that is, in response to an action potential. However, action potentials are brief relative to the time needed to form a synapse. Something must be able to bridge the gap between the electrochemical response of a neuron and its metabolic response.

In 2000, David Clayton suggested that the molecular activity of genes should be considered in information terms like the action potential. He coined the expression "genomic action potential" to describe the way that genes can be activated for periods of time spanning minutes or hours (Clayton, 2000). A key part of the genomic action potential are genes known as **immediate-early genes (IEGs)**, which can be activated, or induced, without the synthesis of proteins; hence, they are the first part of a chain triggered by events like an action potential.

A good example of the role that IEG might play in memory comes from songbirds. Many birds use songs to identify other members of their species—especially possible mates (e.g., Bloomfield, Farrell, & Sturdy, 2008). The calls are complex acoustically, and generally are learned when the bird is young by listening to an adult "tutor" (Bolhuis & Gahr, 2006). The song (which can have local variations or dialects) is stored in memory and then used, and fine-tuned, when the bird is an adult. This memory seems to be partly the result of a particular IEG with the unwieldy name ZENK (an acronym resulting from different names given to the gene by different investigators). Listening to birdsong has been found to increase genetic ZENK activity in adult birds (Avey, Kanyo, Irwin, & Sturdy, 2008; Mello, Vicario, & Clayton, 1992).

IEGs have been implicated in other situations that involve memory. For example, they may be involved in the perception of pain that underlies fear conditioning (see Zhuo, 2005). However, their precise role remains to be determined. Clayton (2000) has argued that the genomic action potential does more than just strengthen an isolated connection. It may strengthen secondary associations and thereby link an experience to a broader context. If so, then the consolidation envisioned by Hebb in a physiological sense would also provide the basis for the role of retrieval cues studied by cognitive psychologists.

**immediate-early genes (IEGs)** Genes that can be activated in the presence of chemicals that inhibit the synthesis of proteins. IEGs therefore do not rely on the previous activation of other genes.

## The Levels of Processing Hypothesis

The model discussed at the start of this chapter makes several assertions about the learning process. For one, it asserts that all information gets into long-term memory only after passing through short-term memory. Also, it asserts that the most important factor determining whether a particular piece of information reaches long-term memory is the amount of time it spends in short-term memory.

Craik and Lockhart (1972) developed a different approach. They pointed out that the act of rehearsal may effectively keep information in short-term memory but does not necessarily result in the establishment of long-term memories. They suggested that people engage in two different types of rehearsal: maintenance rehearsal and elaborative rehearsal. **Maintenance rehearsal** is the rote repetition of verbal information—simply repeating an item over and over. This behaviour serves to maintain the information in short-term memory but does not necessarily result in lasting changes. In contrast, when people engage in elaborative rehearsal, they think about the information and relate it to what they already know. **Elaborative rehearsal** involves more than new information. It involves deeper processing: forming associations, attending to the meaning of the information, thinking about that information, and so on. Thus, we elaborate on new information by recollecting related information already in long-term memory. Here's a practical example: You are more likely to remember information for a test by processing it deeply or meaningfully; simply rehearsing the material to be tested will not do.

This example suggests that a memory is more effectively established if the item is presented in a rich context—one that is likely to make us think about the item and imagine an action taking place. Consider the different images conjured up by these two sentences (from Craik & Tulving, 1975):

He dropped the watch.

The old man hobbled across the room and picked up the valuable watch.

The second sentence provides much more information. The image that is evoked by the more complex sentence provides the material for a more complex memory. This complexity makes the memory more distinctive and thus helps us pick it out from all the other memories we have.

In contrast with the traditional model of rehearsal, Craik and Lockhart (1972) proposed a levels-of-processing framework for understanding the way information enters long-term memory. They suggested that memory is a by-product of perceptual analysis. A central processor, analogous to the central processing unit of a computer, can analyze sensory information on several different levels. Craik and Lockhart conceived of the levels as being hierarchically arranged, from shallow (superficial) to deep (complex). A person can control the level of analysis by paying attention to different features of the stimulus. If a person focuses on the superficial sensory characteristics of a stimulus, then these features will be stored in memory. If the person focuses on the meaning of a stimulus and the ways in which it relates to other things the person already knows, then these features will be stored in memory. For example, consider the word written below.

tree

You can see that the word is written in black type, that the letters are lower case, that the bottom of the stem of the letter *t* curves upward to the right, and so on. Craik and Lockhart referred to these characteristics as surface features and to the analysis of these features as shallow processing. Maintenance rehearsal is an example of **shallow processing**. In contrast, consider the meaning of the word *tree*. You can think about how trees differ from other plants, what varieties of trees you have seen, what kinds of foods and what kinds of wood they provide, and so on. These features refer to a word's meaning and are called semantic features. Their analysis is called **deep processing**. Elaborative rehearsal is an example of deep processing. According to Craik and Lockhart, deep processing generally leads to better retention than surface processing does.

**Knowledge, Encoding, and Learning** You might think that memory is related to knowledge: As we gain more knowledge over time, our recall of that knowledge improves. That would explain why memories of adults are generally superior to those of children. However, merely possessing knowledge does not always facilitate recall; even the brightest people have problems with remembering things. What seems to be more important is what happens during the encoding of information. Remember, encoding involves getting material into memory. More than that, how we encode information is likely to affect our ability to remember it later. We have already seen that, to some degree, encoding information involves paying attention to it. We have also seen that if we can make material more meaningful during encoding, we may decrease the likelihood of forgetting that information later.

**Automatic versus Effortful Processing** Psychologists and educators have long known that retrieval is enhanced by practising or rehearsing information. Practising or rehearsing information, through either shallow or deep processing, is called **effortful processing**. As a student, you know

**maintenance rehearsal** The rote repetition of information; repeating a given item over and over again.
**elaborative rehearsal** The processing of information on a meaningful level, such as forming associations, attending to the meaning of the material, thinking about it, and so on.
**shallow processing** The analysis of the superficial characteristics of a stimulus, such as its size or shape.
**deep processing** The analysis of the complex characteristics of a stimulus, such as its meaning or its relationship to other stimuli.
**effortful processing** Practising or rehearsing information through either shallow or deep processing.

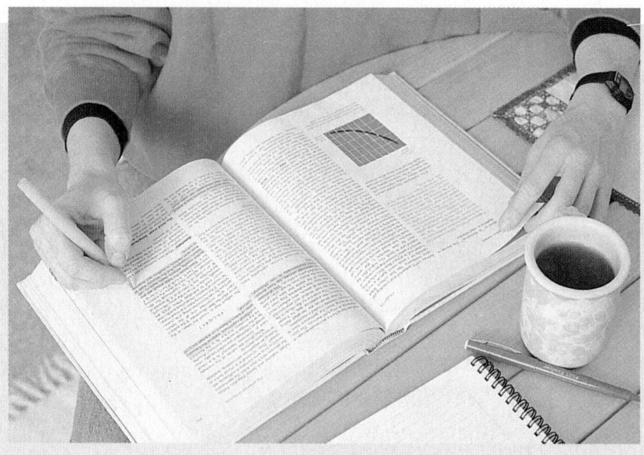

▲ *Taking notes while studying from a text (left) is a more active method of processing information than is merely highlighting important passages in the text (right). Note taking is a form of deep processing, and highlighting is a form of shallow processing.*

that the more you concentrate on your studies, the more likely it becomes that you will do well on an exam. But your experience also tells you that you have stored information in memory that you never rehearsed in the first place. Somehow, without any effort, information is encoded into your memory. This formation of memories of events and experiences with little or no attention or effort is called **automatic processing**.

Information that is automatically processed includes frequency (How many times have you read the word *encode* today?), time (When did you meet your best friend for the first time?), and place (Where in the textbook is the graph of Sperling's data located?). Automatic processing helps us learn things with relative ease, which makes life a lot less taxing than continually having to process information effortfully. Unfortunately, perhaps because of its complexity, most textbook learning is effortful, not automatic.

**Encoding Specificity** When encoding is not automatic, it is effortful, and the most useful effort we can expend would be an attempt to make the new material meaningful. We can think of making new or difficult material meaningful as elaborative encoding; you encountered this idea earlier as elaborative rehearsal. There are two conclusions that I'll offer concerning elaborative encoding. First, it seems clear that more rehearsal is better than less.

The second conclusion concerns **encoding specificity**, the principle that how we encode information determines our ability to retrieve it later. For example, suppose that someone reads you a list of words that you are to recall later. The list contains the word *beet*, along with a number of terms related to music, such as *melody*, *tune*, and *jazz*. When asked if the list contained the names of any vegetables, you might report that it did not. Because of the musical context, you encoded *beet* as *beat* and never thought of the tuberous vegetable while you were rehearsing the list (Flexser & Tulving, 1978).

Many experiments have made the point that meaningful elaboration during encoding is helpful and probably necessary for the formation of useful memories. Imagine, for example, trying to remember the following passage:

> With hocked gems financing him, our hero bravely defied all scornful laughter that tried to prevent his scheme. "Your eyes deceive," he had said. "An egg, not a table correctly typifies this unexplored planet." Now three sturdy sisters sought proof. Forging along, sometimes through calm vastness, yet more often over turbulent peaks and valleys, days became weeks as many doubters spread fearful rumors about the edge. At last, from nowhere welcomed winged creatures appeared, signifying momentous success.

How do you think you would have done on this task? Could you have remembered this passage very well? Probably not, for it is phrased rather oddly. However, what if, before you read the paragraph, you were told that it had a title: "Columbus Discovers America"? Do you think you might have encoded the story differently and so improved your recall? (Read the passage again and you will see that the "hocked gems" refer to the means by which Queen Isabella financed the expedition, the "sturdy sisters" refer to the three ships, and the "winged creatures" refer to the birds that signalled the proximity of land.) Dooling and Lachman (1971) found that people who were told the title of a story such as this one remembered the information much better. However, if they were given the title after they had read and processed the story, their recall was not improved (Bransford & Johnson, 1972). Apparently, the time to make information meaningful is during encoding.

**automatic processing** The formation of memories of events and experiences with little or no attention or effort.
**encoding specificity** The principle that how we encode information determines our ability to retrieve it later.

### Criticisms of the Levels of Processing Hypothesis

The concept of processing depth has been useful in guiding research efforts to understand how we learn and remember. However, many psychologists have noted that the distinction between shallow and deep processing has never been rigorously defined. The difference between looking at the shape of the letters of a word and thinking about its meaning is clear, but most instances of encoding cannot be so neatly categorized. The term *depth* seems to be a metaphor. It roughly describes the fact that information is more readily remembered when we think about it in relation to what we already know, but it is not exact and specific enough to satisfy most memory theorists.

Another problem with trying to understand exactly what is meant by terms such as *depth of processing* is that no matter what we may ask a person to do when we present a stimulus (for example, "Count the letters"), we have no way of knowing what else he or she may be doing that may aid recall of that item. In other words, researchers may not be able to control the depth to which a person processes information because they have no way of peering into his or her head and knowing exactly how the information is being manipulated. For each of us, our memory, its processes, and its contents are private. Memory, like all cognitive processes, is not an observable phenomenon.

Some psychologists have criticized the assertion that tasks that encourage people to focus on superficial features of stimuli inevitably lead to poorer memory than do tasks that encourage them to focus on deeper features. For example, after reading something new, people can often remember exactly where the information appeared on a page (Rothkopf, 1971). Despite such exceptions, however, the levels of processing approach has succeeded in showing that we deal with information in different ways depending on what we need to use it for. These ways provide a context for the way we later remember it.

## Improving Long-Term Memory through Mnemonics

When we can imagine information vividly and concretely, and when it fits into the context of what we already know, it is easy to remember later. Earlier, I described how working memory could be improved by chaining words together in a meaningful pattern. People have known for millennia that vividness and context can improve remembering and have devised mnemonic systems (from the Greek *mnemon*, meaning "mindful") that take advantage of this fact. **Mnemonic systems**—special techniques or strategies consciously used to improve memory—employ information already stored in long-term memory to make memorization an easier task.

Mnemonic systems do not simplify information; in fact, they make it more elaborate. More information is stored, not less. However, the additional information makes the material easier to recall. Furthermore, mnemonic systems organize new information into a cohesive whole so that retrieval of part of the information ensures retrieval of the rest of it. These facts suggest that the ease or difficulty with which we learn new information depends not on how much we must learn but on how well it fits with what we already know. The better it fits, the easier it is to retrieve.

**Method of Loci** In Greece before the sixth century B.C.E. few people knew how to write, and those who did had to use cumbersome clay tablets. Consequently, oratory skills and memory for long epic poems (running for several hours) were highly prized, and some people earned their livings by using them. Because people could not carry around several hundred kilograms of clay tablets, they had to keep important information in their heads. To do so, the Greeks devised the **method of loci**, a mnemonic system in which items to be remembered are mentally associated with specific physical locations. (The word *locus* means "place"; the plural is *loci*, pronounced "low sigh.")

To use the method of loci, would-be memory artists had to memorize the inside of a building. In Greece, they would wander through public buildings, stopping to study and memorize various locations and arranging them in order, usually starting with the door of the building. After memorizing the locations, they could make the tour mentally, just as you could make a mental tour of your house to count the rooms. To learn a list of words, they would visualize each word in a particular location in the memorized building and picture the association as vividly as possible. For example, for the word *love*, they might imagine an embracing couple leaning against a particular column in a hall of the building. To recall the list, they would imagine each of the locations in sequence, "see" each word, and say it. To store a speech, they would group the words into concepts and place a "note" for each concept at a particular location in the sequence.

Suppose that you wish to remember a short shopping list without writing it down. Your list consists of five items: cheese, milk, eggs, taco sauce, and lettuce. First, you would think of a familiar place, perhaps your house. Next, you would mentally walk through your house, visually placing different items from your list at locations—loci—in the house: a package of cheese hanging from a coat rack, milk dripping from the kitchen faucet, eggs lying in the hallway, a bottle of taco sauce on the kitchen chair, and a head of lettuce on the sofa. (See **Figure 8•8**.) Then, in the grocery store, you mentally retrace your path through the house and note what you have stored at the different loci. Any familiar location will do the trick as long as you can visually and vividly imagine the items to be remembered in the various landmarks.

**mnemonic system** A special technique or strategy consciously employed in an attempt to improve memory.

**method of loci** A mnemonic system in which items to be remembered are mentally associated with specific physical locations or landmarks.

**FIGURE 8•8** The method of loci. Items to be remembered are visualized in specific, well-known places.

**Peg-Word Method** A similar technique, the **peg-word method**, involves the association of items to be remembered with a set of mental pegs that are already stored in memory (Miller, Galanter, & Pribram, 1960). As with the method of loci, the goal involves visually associating the new with the familiar. In the peg-word method, the familiar material is a set of "mental pegs" that you already have in memory. One example is to take the numbers from 1 to 10 and rhyme each number with a peg word; for example, one is a bun, two is a shoe, three is a tree, four is a door, five is a hive, and so on. Returning to your grocery list, you might imagine the package of cheese in a hamburger bun, a shoe full of milk, eggs dangling from a tree, taco sauce on a door, and the lettuce on top of a beehive. (See **Figure 8•9**.) In the grocery store, you review

**peg-word method** A mnemonic system in which items to be remembered are associated with a set of mental pegs that one already has in memory, such as key words of a rhyme.

**FIGURE 8•9** The peg-word method. Items to be remembered are associated with nouns that rhyme with numbers.

each peg word in order and recall the item associated with it. At first, this technique may seem silly, but there is ample research suggesting that it actually works (Marshark, Richman, Yuille, & Hunt, 1987).

**Narrative Stories and Songs** Another useful aid to memory is to place information into a **narrative**, in which items to be remembered are linked together by a story. Bower and Clark (1969) showed that even inexperienced people can use this method. The investigators asked people to try to learn 12 lists of 10 concrete nouns each. They gave some of the people the following advice:

> A good way to learn the list of items is to make up a story relating the items to one another. Specifically, start with the first item and put it in a setting which will allow other items to be added to it. Then, add the other items to the story in the same order as the items appear. Make each story meaningful to yourself. Then, when you are asked to recall the items, you can simply go through your story and pull out the proper items in their correct order. (Bower & Clark, 1969, p. 181)

Here is a typical narrative, described by one of the participants (list words are italicized): "A *lumberjack dart*ed out of the forest, *skate*d around a *hedge* past a *colony* of *ducks*. He tripped on some *furniture*, tearing his *stocking* while hastening to the *pillow* where his *mistress* lay."

People in the control group were merely asked to learn the lists and were given the same amount of time as the people in the "narrative" group to study them. Both groups could remember a particular list equally well immediately afterwards. However, when all of the lists had been learned, recall of all 120 words was far superior in the group that had constructed narrative stories.

Music, like narrative, provides a structure for information. Songs that link melody to a sequence of words could serve the same role as the narrative elements of a story. Many advertisers use music with their messages, apparently believing that placing their slogan in a song will improve its memorability (Yalch, 1991). There is some evidence that supports this notion. Wallace (1994) asked people to learn the words to a ballad by listening to either a spoken or a sung version. She found that, provided people had a chance to learn the melody of the song, they learned the sung ballad more quickly than the spoken version. Changing the melody after each verse, in contrast, failed to improve learning.

Although hearing the melody of a song might improve your ability to learn its text, the effect might not be due to the structuring processes I noted when discussing the method of loci. A melody not only structures the text of a song but also alters the rate at which you hear the words. Using a sound editing program, Kilgour, Jakobson, and Cuddy (2000) found that, indeed, the rate of word presentation was important in determining the advantage that singing provides. When the words were spoken at the same rate that they were sung, there was no improvement in learning text from hearing it sung. The basis of this mnemonic, then, is that it slows the rate at which you hear information, allowing you to encode the information better.

▲ *Long-term memory has no known limits. Actors, like these from the Canadian Broadcast Corporation's production of* Canada: A People's History, *may remember their parts long after their performances are over. The historical narrative underlying their roles may help them encode their lines more easily too.*

Obviously, mnemonic systems have their limitations. They are useful for memorizing information that can be reduced to a list of words, but not all information can easily be converted to such a form. For example, if you were preparing to take an examination on the information in this chapter, figuring out how to encode it into lists would probably take you more time than studying and learning it by the more traditional methods suggested in the study guide.

## Interim Summary

### Learning and Encoding in Long-Term Memory

Long-term memory appears to consist of physical changes in the brain, probably within the sensory and motor association cortexes. Consolidation of memories is likely caused by rehearsal of information, which sustains particular neural activities and leads to permanent structural changes in the brain. Data from head injuries provide evidence that long-term and short-term memory are physiologically different: Short-term memories probably involve neural activity (which can be prolonged by rehearsal), whereas long-term memories probably involve permanent structural changes.

Craik and Lockhart's model of memory points out the importance of elaboration in learning. Maintenance

**narrative** A mnemonic system in which items to be remembered are linked together by a story.

rehearsal, or simple rote repetition, is usually less effective than elaborative rehearsal, which involves deeper, more meaningful processing. These theorists assert that long-term memory is a by-product of perceptual analysis. The level of processing can be shallow or deep and is controlled by changes in the amount of attention we pay to information.

Encoding of information to be stored in long-term memory may take place automatically or effortfully. Automatic processing of information is usually related to the frequency, timing, and place (location) of events. Textbook learning entails effortful processing, likely because of its complexity. The principle of encoding specificity—how we encode information into memory—determines the ease with which we can later retrieve that information. To produce the most durable and useful memories, information should be encoded in ways that are meaningful. However, critics of the levels of processing model point out that shallow processing sometimes produces very durable memories, and the distinction between shallow and deep has proved impossible to define explicitly.

Mnemonic systems are strategies used to enhance memory and usually employ information that is already contained in long-term memory and visual imagery. For example, to use the method of loci to remember a grocery list, you would simply imagine each item on the list appearing at a specific location—say, at various places in your home. Other mnemonic systems include the peg-word method, which involves visually associating items to be remembered with a specific set of "mental pegs," such as parts of a rhyme, and narrative stories, which involve weaving a story around the to-be-remembered items. Mnemonics are useful for remembering lists of items but are less useful for more complex material, such as textbook information.

**QUESTION TO CONSIDER**

1. Suppose that a friend comes to you for advice about studying for an upcoming English test. He explains to you that half of the test involves multiple-choice questions over key terms and the other half involves essay questions about the narrative of several short stories. Based on what you now know about encoding and memory, what suggestions might you offer him regarding how to prepare for the test? (Hints: Is there a difference between how rote information is best encoded and how more elaborate, complex information is best encoded? What role might the idea of levels of processing play in studying for a test?)

**episodic memory** A type of long-term memory that serves as a record of our life's experiences.

**semantic memory** A type of long-term memory that contains data, facts, and other information, including vocabulary.

## The Organization of Long-Term Memory

As we just saw, consolidation is not a simple, passive process. Many investigators believe that long-term memory consists of more than a simple pool of information. Instead, it is organized in terms of different systems—different kinds of information are encoded differently and stored in different ways, possibly in response to evolutionary pressures (Sherry & Schacter, 1987).

### Episodic and Semantic Memory

Endel Tulving suggested that there are two kinds of long-term memory: episodic memory and semantic memory (Tulving, 1972). **Episodic memory** provides us with a record of our life experiences. Events stored there are autobiographical; episodic memory consists of memory about specific things we have done, seen, heard, felt, tasted, and so on. They are tied to particular contexts: this morning's breakfast, my fifteenth birthday party, the first time I went skiing, and so forth. **Semantic memory** consists of conceptual information; it is a long-term store of data, facts, and information, including vocabulary. Your knowledge of what psychology is, how human sensory systems operate, and how behaviour is affected by its consequences is now part of your semantic memory. (If not, you need to review some of the material presented earlier in this book!) In other words, semantic memory contains information of the "academic" type. Semantic memories appear to interact with episodic ones. For example, when you go shopping, you undoubtedly remember the kinds of items you usually buy. Suppose you like yogurt for breakfast. Your preference is a fact about yourself that you recall from semantic memory. However, when you're trying to decide whether it's time to buy some more yogurt on this shopping trip, you'd probably try to think of the last time you looked in the refrigerator. Remembering whether you had eaten the last of the yogurt is a decision you would have to make from episodic memory.

The distinction between episodic and semantic memory reflects the fact that we make different uses of things we have learned: We describe things that happened to us or talk about facts we have learned. However, we cannot necessarily conclude that episodic memory and semantic memory are different memory systems. They may simply be different kinds of information stored in the same system. For example, I am a native English speaker, but I have also learned to speak French. Do I have an English memory system and a French memory system? Most likely not. Instead, my memory contains the information needed to recognize and speak both English and French words and to understand their meanings. The same system can handle both kinds of words. Nevertheless, many psychologists feel that episodic memory reflects a different system of the brain than that of semantic memory. They point to evidence like that supplied by K. C., a man now in his fifties

(a)

(b)

▲ *(a) Remembering the correct spelling of a word involves semantic memory—memory for academic-type information. (b) Remembering important life events, such as an important social event, involves episodic memory—memory for specific events that occurred at a specific time.*

who suffered a closed-head injury at age 30. As a result of the accident, K. C.'s ability to acquire new knowledge is severely impaired. His memory for things learned before the accident, however, shows a remarkable difference: general knowledge—the information of semantic memory—is relatively intact, while his knowledge about his life—the material that comprises episodic memory—has been completely obliterated. K. C. can recall knowledge about algebra and history that he learned at school, but cannot recall personal experiences such as the birthday parties he attended (Tulving, 2002).

## Explicit and Implicit Memory

For many years, most cognitive psychologists have studied memory as a conscious operation. People were presented with lists of words, facts, episodes, or other kinds of stimuli and were asked to recognize or recollect them later. In many cases, the response was a verbal one. More recently, psychologists have come to appreciate the fact that an unconscious memory system, which is capable of controlling complex behaviours, also exists (Squire, 1992). Psychologists use the terms *explicit memory* and *implicit memory* when making this distinction. **Explicit memory** is memory of which we are aware; we know that we have learned something, and we can talk about what we have learned with others. (For this reason, some psychologists prefer to use the term *declarative memory*.) **Implicit memory** is unconscious; we cannot talk directly about its contents. However, the contents of implicit memory can affect our behaviour—even our verbal behaviour. (Some psychologists use the term *procedural memory* because this system is responsible for remembering "how to" skills, such as bicycle riding; others use the term *non-declarative memory*.) The distinction between implicit and explicit memory is important because retrieval cues seem to influence implicit memory more than explicit memory, and the level of processing seems to influence explicit memory more than implicit memory (Blaxton, 1989; Roediger, 1990).

Implicit memory appears to operate automatically. It does not require deliberate attempts on the part of the learner to memorize something. It does not seem to contain facts; instead, it controls behaviours. For example, suppose we learn to ride a bicycle. We do so quite consciously and develop episodic memories about our attempts: who helped us learn, where we rode, how we felt, how many times we fell, and so on. But we also learn to ride. We learn to make automatic adjustments with our hands and bodies that keep our centre of gravity above the wheels. Most of us cannot describe the rules that govern our behaviour. For example, what do you think you must do if you start falling to the right while riding a bicycle? Many cyclists would say that they compensate by leaning to the left. But they are wrong; what they really do is turn the handlebars to the right. Leaning to the left would actually make them fall faster, because it would force the bicycle even farther to the right. The point is that although they have learned to make the appropriate movements, they cannot necessarily describe in words what these movements are.

## The Biological Basis of Long-Term Memory

Psychologists agree that long-term memory involves more or less permanent changes in the structure of the brain. Much of what we know about the biology of human memory has been derived from studies of people who suffer from memory loss—amnesia—or from studies of animals in which investigators use some of the methods described in Chapter 4 to learn more about the specific brain mechanisms involved in memory. In more recent years, functional imaging studies

**explicit memory** Memory that can be described verbally and of which a person is therefore aware.

**implicit memory** Memory that cannot be described verbally and of which a person is therefore not aware.

with humans help us determine which parts of the brain become active when we learn or remember particular kinds of memories.

**Human Anterograde Amnesia** Damage to particular parts of the brain can permanently impair people's ability to form new long-term memories, a phenomenon known as **anterograde amnesia.** The brain damage can be caused by the effects of long-term alcoholism, severe malnutrition, stroke, head trauma, or surgery (Parkin, Blunden, Rees, & Hunkin, 1991). In most cases, people with anterograde amnesia can still remember events that occurred prior to the damage, but they cannot remember what has happened since that time. They do not learn the names of people they subsequently meet, even if they see them daily for years. For these people, yesterday is always some time in the past, before they sustained their brain damage. (Yes, as time goes by, they are surprised to see such an old person looking back at them in the mirror.)

One of the most famous cases of anterograde amnesia is that of patient H. M. (Corkin, Sullivan, Twitchell, & Grove, 1981; Milner, 1970; Milner, Corkin, & Teuber, 1968). H. M.'s case is interesting because his amnesia is both severe and relatively uncontaminated by other serious neuropsychological deficits.

In 1953, when H. M. was 27, a neurosurgeon removed part of the temporal lobe on both sides of his brain. The surgery was performed to alleviate very severe epilepsy, which was not responding to drug treatment. The surgery cured the epilepsy, but it caused anterograde amnesia. (This type of operation is no longer performed.)

Since the operation, H. M. has been unable to learn anything new. He cannot identify by name people he has met since the operation. His family moved to a new house after his operation, and he never learned how to get around in the new neighbourhood. (His parents have since died, and he now lives in a nursing home where he can be cared for.) He is capable of remembering a small amount of verbal information as long as he is not distracted; constant rehearsal can maintain information in his short-term memory. However, rehearsal does not appear to have any long-term effects; if he is distracted for a moment, he will completely forget whatever he had been rehearsing. Indeed, because he so quickly forgets what previously happened, he does not easily become bored. He can endlessly reread the same magazine or laugh at the same jokes, finding them fresh and new each time.

H. M. is aware that he has a memory problem. For example, here is his response to an investigator's question.

> Every day is alone in itself, whatever enjoyment I've had, and whatever sorrow I've had. . . . Right now, I'm wondering. Have I done or said anything amiss? You see, at this moment everything looks clear to me, but what happened just before? That's what worries me. It's like waking from a dream; I just don't remember. (Milner, 1970, p. 37)

Given that H. M. cannot remember much of his past, it is relevant to ask whether he retains a sense of self. Suzanne Corkin, who has known H. M. for many years, has an interesting discussion on this issue (Corkin, 2002). She feels that the answer is definitely "yes." H. M. seems comfortable when he sees his image in a mirror (think of how you would feel if you saw yourself looking 50 years older than you remembered) and he exhibits strong moral and conscientious attitudes. Perhaps the most telling aspect is that he also has a sense of humour about his own condition. When once asked about how he remembers, he replied: "Well, that I don't know 'cause I don't remember (laugh) what I tried" (Corkin, 2002, p. 158).

Since the case of H. M. was reported, many investigators have described similar cases of people who acquired anterograde amnesia after sustaining damage to the temporal lobes. The critical site of damage appears to be the hippocampus, a structure located deep within the temporal lobe, and regions of the cortex of the medial temporal lobe with which the hippocampus is connected.

H. M.'s memory deficit is striking and dramatic. However, when he and other patients with anterograde amnesia are studied more carefully, it becomes apparent that the amnesia does not represent a total failure in learning ability. When the patients are appropriately trained and tested, we find that they are able to acquire new implicit (non-declarative) memories. For example, Cavaco and colleagues (2004) tested amnesic patients on a variety of tasks modelled on real-world activities, such as weaving, tracing figures, operating a stick that controlled a video display, and pouring water into small jars. Both amnesic patients and normal subjects did poorly on these tasks at first, but their performance improved through practice. Thus, as you can see, patients with anterograde amnesia are capable of a variety of tasks that require perceptual learning, stimulus–response learning, and motor learning.

The most remarkable thing is that although the patients can learn to perform these tasks, they do not remember anything about having learned them. They do not remember the experimenters, the room in which the training took place, the apparatus used, or any events that occurred during the training. As mentioned earlier, when we learn to ride a bicycle, we form two kinds of memories: explicit (episodic) memories—the details of who taught us and where the training took place—and implicit (non-declarative) memories—the skills required to successfully ride a bicycle. Clearly, the hippocampus is involved in forming new explicit memories, but is not necessary for the formation of new implicit memories.

After H. M.'s family moved, he was unable to learn how to get around in the new neighbourhood. Many studies have found that one of the features of anterograde amnesia is the inability to form new spatial memories—to learn to use spatial cues to navigate in a new environment. For example,

**anterograde amnesia** A disorder caused by brain damage that disrupts a person's ability to form new long-term memories of events that occur after the time of the brain damage.

Luzzi, Pucci, Di Bella, and Piccirilli (2000) reported the case of a man with temporal lobe damage who lost his ability to find his way around a new environment. The only way he could find his room was by counting doorways from the end of the hall or by seeing a red napkin that was located on top of his bedside table.

**The Roles of the Hippocampus and Basal Ganglia** Just what role does the hippocampus play in the consolidation of episodic memories? Through its connections with the medial temporal cortex, the hippocampus receives information from all association areas of the cerebral cortex and sends information back to them (Gluck & Myers, 1997). Thus, the hippocampal formation is in a position to know—and to influence—what is going on elsewhere in the brain. Most investigators believe that permanent long-term memories of episodes are stored in the cerebral cortex, not in the hippocampus. However, through its connections with the cerebral cortex, the hippocampus plays an essential role in consolidating these memories. The consolidation process takes time, but once it is completed, the hippocampus is no longer needed for retrieval of the memory of these episodes. Thus, people with anterograde amnesia are able to recall episodic memories of events that occurred before their brain damage occurred (Miyashita, 2004; Squire & Bayley, 2007).

If declarative memories are consolidated through the actions of the hippocampus, what brain regions are responsible for non-declarative memories? Evidence suggests that the basal ganglia play an essential role. Several experiments have shown that people with diseases of the basal ganglia have deficits that can be attributed to difficulty in learning automatic responses. For example, Owen and colleagues (1992) found that patients with Parkinson's disease were impaired on learning a visually cued instrumental conditioning task, and Willingham and Koroshetz (1993) found that patients with Huntington's disease failed to learn a sequence of button presses. (Parkinson's disease and Huntington's disease are both degenerative diseases of the basal ganglia.)

A series of experiments using both structural and functional brain imaging provide evidence for the role of the hippocampus in declarative learning and the role of the basal ganglia in non-declarative learning. Hartley, Maguire, Spiers, and Burgess (2003) trained people to find their way in a computerized virtual-reality town. Some people became acquainted with the town by exploring it, giving them the opportunity to learn where various landmarks (shops, cafés, etc.) were located with respect to each other. Other people were trained to follow a specific pathway from one landmark to the next, making a sequence of turns to get from a particular starting point to another. The investigators hypothesized that the first task, which involved spatial learning, would require the participation of the hippocampus, while the second task, which involved learning a set of specific responses to a set of specific stimuli, would require the participation of the basal ganglia. The results were as predicted: Functional MRI (fMRI) revealed that the spatial task activated the hippocampus and the response task activated the caudate nucleus (a component of the basal ganglia).

Iaria and colleagues (2003) used a similar task that permitted individuals to learn a maze either through distant spatial cues or through a series of turns. About half of the participants spontaneously used spatial cues, and the other half spontaneously learned to make a sequence of responses at specific locations. Again, fMRI showed that the hippocampus was activated in people who followed the spatial strategy and the caudate nucleus was activated in those who followed the response strategy. Even more remarkably, a structural MRI study by Bohbot and colleagues (2007) found that people who tended to follow a spatial strategy had a larger-than-average hippocampus, and people who tended to follow a response strategy had a larger-than-average caudate nucleus.

Are there areas of the brain that, when damaged, produce impairments of implicit memory? Parkinson's disease is a degenerative disease that destroys the striatum, an area of the midbrain. Recent evidence by Doyon and colleagues (1998) has demonstrated that bilateral damage to the striatum in an individual with Parkinson's disease interferes with that person's ability to learn to perform a visual-motor task efficiently and automatically. Interestingly, people in the early stages of the disease, with unilateral damage, did manage to learn the task to an automatic level. However, when they were tested on the task a year later, after the disease had damaged the striatum in both hemispheres, performance was poorer than among control participants. Explicit memory for the task (i.e., being able to verbalize what the task required) was the same, however, for both people with and those without Parkinson's disease. Similarly, people with damage to the cerebellum also had trouble learning and retrieving the implicit memory task, but did not show a decline in explicit memory.

**Explicit Memory in Animals** Although the words *explicit* and *declarative* cannot apply to non-human animals (after all, they cannot talk), the distinction between these two categories of memory systems is also seen in species besides our own. Although we cannot ask laboratory animals to tell us about episodes that occurred earlier in their lives, we can certainly determine whether they can perform spatial tasks similar to the ones just described.

In one common spatial learning task, rats are placed in a large circular tank filled with water mixed with an opaque white powder. This apparatus is known as the "Morris water maze," after the investigator who developed it (Morris, Garrud, Rawlins, & O'Keefe, 1982). The murky water hides the location of a small platform, situated just beneath the surface of the liquid. The experimenters put the rats into the water and let them swim until they encounter the hidden platform and climb onto it. They release the rats from a new position on each trial, which means that they cannot simply learn to swim in a particular direction. After a few trials, normal rats learn to swim directly to the hidden platform from wherever they were released.

The Morris water maze requires spatial learning; to navigate around the maze, the animals get their bearings from the relative locations of stimuli located outside the maze: furniture, windows, doors, and so on. But the maze can be used for stimulus–response learning too. If the animals are always released at the same place, they learn to head in a particular direction—say, toward a particular landmark they can see above the wall of the maze (Eichenbaum, Stewart, & Morris, 1990).

If rats with hippocampal lesions are always released from the same place, they learn this non-relational, stimulus–response task about as well as normal rats do. However, if they are released from a new position on each trial, they swim in what appears to be an aimless fashion until they finally encounter the platform. (See **Figure 8•10.**)

One of the most intriguing discoveries about the hippocampal formation was made by O'Keefe and Dostrovsky (1971), who recorded the activity of individual pyramidal cells in the hippocampus as an animal moved around the environment. The experimenters found that some neurons fired at a high rate only when the rat was in a particular location. Different neurons had different spatial receptive fields; that is, they responded when the animals were in different locations. A particular neuron might fire 20 times

**FIGURE 8•10** The Morris water maze. (a) Environmental cues present in the room provide information that permits the animals to orient themselves in space. (b) Variable and fixed start positions. Normally, rats are released from a different position on each trial. If they are released from the same position every time, the rats can learn to find the hidden platform through stimulus–response learning. (c) Performance of normal rats and rats with hippocampal lesions using variable (graph on left) or fixed start (graph on right) positions. Hippocampal lesions impair acquisition of the relational task. (d) Representative samples of the paths followed by normal rats and rats with hippocampal lesions on the relational task (variable start positions).

*(Adapted from Eichenbaum, H. (2000).* Nature Reviews: Neuroscience, 1, *41–50.* Data from Eichenbaum, *Stewart, & Morris, 1990.)*

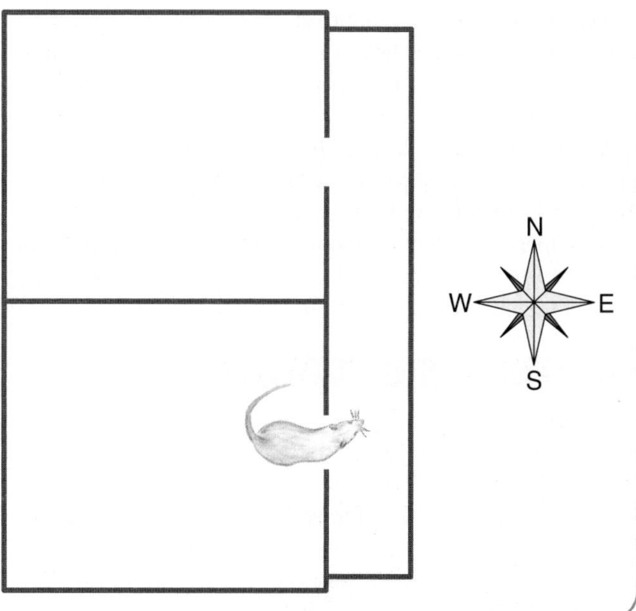


**FIGURE 8•11** The apparatus used in the study by Skaggs and McNaughton (1998). Place cells reflect the location where the animal "thinks" it is. Because the rat was normally placed in the north chamber, its hippocampal place cells responded as if it were there when it was placed in the south chamber one day. However, once it stuck its head into the corridor, it saw that the other chamber was located to its right, so it "realized" that it had just been in the south chamber. From then on, the pattern of firing of the hippocampal place cells accurately reflected the chamber in which the animal was located.

per second when the animal was in a particular location but only a few times per hour when the animal was located elsewhere. For obvious reasons these neurons were named **place cells.**

When a rat is placed in a symmetrical chamber, where there are few cues to distinguish one part of the apparatus from another, the animal must keep track of its location from objects it sees (or hears) in the environment outside the maze. Changes in these items affect the firing of the rats' place cells as well as their navigational ability. When experimenters move the stimuli as a group, maintaining their relative positions, the animals simply reorient their responses accordingly. However, when the experimenters interchange the stimuli so that they are arranged in a new order, the animals' performance (and the firing of their place cells) is disrupted. (Imagine how disoriented you might be if you entered a familiar room and found that the windows, doors, and furniture were in new positions.)

Evidence indicates that firing of hippocampal place cells appears to reflect the location where an animal "thinks" it is. Skaggs and McNaughton (1998) constructed an apparatus that contained two nearly identical chambers connected by a corridor. Each day, rats were placed in one of the chambers, and a cluster of electrodes in the animals' brains recorded the activity of hippocampal place cells. Each rat was always placed in the same chamber each day. Some of the place cells showed similar patterns of activity in each of the chambers, and some showed different patterns, which suggests that the hippocampus "realized" that there were two different compartments but also "recognized" the similarities between them. Then, on the last day of the experiment, the investigators placed the rats in the other chamber of the apparatus. For example, if a rat was usually placed in the north chamber, it was placed in the south chamber. The firing pattern of the place cells in at least half of the rats indicated that the hippocampus "thought" it was in the usual chamber—the one to the north. However, once the rat left the chamber and entered the corridor, it saw that it had to turn to the left to get to the other chamber and not to the right. The animal apparently realized its mistake, because for the rest of that session the neurons fired appropriately. They displayed the "north" pattern in the north chamber and the "south" pattern in the south chamber. (See **Figure 8•11**.)

## Interim Summary

### The Organization of Long-Term Memory

Episodic and semantic memory refer to different degrees of specificity in long-term memories: We can remember the time and place we learned an episodic memory but not a semantic memory. Most psychologists believe that the distinction is important but do not believe that episodic and semantic memories are parts of different systems. Another distinction—between explicit and implicit memory—has received much attention. We use explicit memory when we remember facts and events that we can consciously describe. Implicit memory, in contrast, is unconscious; it is, for example, the memory system that we use when we acquire specific behaviours and skills.

Much of what we have learned about the biological basis of memory comes from studies involving humans with brain damage and from laboratory studies in which animals undergo

**place cell** A neuron that becomes active when the animal is in a particular location in the environment; most typically found in the hippocampal formation.

surgical procedures that produce amnesia. Anterograde amnesia appears to reflect a deficit of explicit memory but not a major impairment of implicit memory. The deficit in explicit memory appears to be strongly related to normal functioning of the hippocampus; it may be that the hippocampus is involved in the consolidation of long-term explicit memory. On the other hand, the basal ganglia may be responsible for implicit memory. The behaviour of laboratory animals also demonstrates this distinction between episodic and other kinds of memories.

### QUESTIONS TO CONSIDER

1. Does it make sense to you to suppose that there are different kinds of memory for different kinds of information and that different kinds of information require different kinds of encoding to be remembered? Can you propose alternative ways to think about how long-term memory might be organized (in contrast to the system we have described in this chapter)? Try it. (You may find it helpful to compose a list of all categories of information people can remember—people, places, things, words, events, and so on—and all ways that remembering can take place—fast, slow, with or without much effort, with or without awareness, using or not using retrieval cues, and so on.)
2. What would it be like to lack, as H. M. does, the ability to form new explicit memories? If, as has been suggested, implicit memory systems preceded explicit systems in our evolutionary history, do you think our ancestors were capable of conscious awareness independent of memory?
3. In the past two decades, many researchers have wondered whether non-human animals can think. We learned in this chapter that animals can remember and forget information. Does this mean that they can also think? Donald Hebb described both thinking and working memory in terms of the activity of cell assemblies. Would this approach argue that because animals possess memory, they also can think?

# Remembering, Recollecting, and Forgetting

So far, we have looked at research on and theories about the act of learning and the nature of long-term memory. But what do we know about remembering, the process of retrieving information from long-term memory, and forgetting, the absence of this process?

## How Long Does Memory Last?

The question "How long does memory last?" has fascinated psychologists and other researchers for many years. In fact, a German psychologist, Hermann Ebbinghaus, reported the results of the first experiment to determine memory duration in 1885. Using himself as a participant, Ebbinghaus memorized 13 nonsense syllables such as *dax*, *wuj*, *lep*, and *pib*. He then studied how long it took him to relearn the original list after intervals varying from a few minutes up to 31 days. **Figure 8•12** shows what he found. Much of what he learned was forgotten very quickly—usually within a day or two. But even after 31 days he could still recall some of the original information.

**FIGURE 8•12** Ebbinghaus's (1885) forgetting curve. *(Adapted from Ebbinghaus, H. (1885/1913).* Memory: A contribution to experimental psychology. *(Translated by H. A. Ruger & C. E. Bussenius). New York: Teacher's College, Columbia University.)*

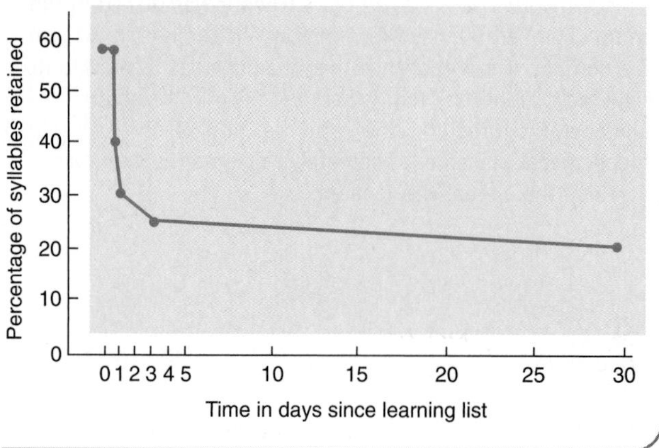


Ebbinghaus's research dealt with remembering nonsense syllables. What about remembering aspects of real life? For example, how long might you remember the important experiences of your youth? Schmidt, Peeck, Paas, and van Breukelen (2000) tried to answer this question by asking former students of an elementary school in the city of Heerlen in the Netherlands to recall the street names around the school. Dutch cities have many meandering streets, so the participants of this study would have had extensive experience trying to remember the many places of their childhood neighbourhood. Schmidt and colleagues found that, on average, participants who had moved away recalled about 60 percent of the street names that could be named by participants who still lived there. Plotted as a function of the number of years since they had last visited the neighbourhood, recall of street names showed a large drop in ability to recall for the first 4 years, followed by little further forgetting for the next 40 years. (See **Figure 8•13**.) Interestingly, recall declined with the number of times participants had moved between different cities, showing that another city's geography could interfere with their memory. We'll return to this possibility in the next section. In general, the rate of forgetting of this kind of information, which also includes knowledge of a second language, people's names, music, and special situations, is greatest in the first few years after it is learned and decreases slowly afterwards (Bahrick, 1984; Kausler, 1994).

**FIGURE 8•13** Observed number of street names recalled by former students of a Dutch elementary school as a function of the years they were not exposed to the neighbourhood.

*(From Schmidt, H. G., Peeck, V. H., Paas, F., & van Breukelen, G. J. P. (2000). Remembering the street names of one's childhood neighborhood: A study of very long-term retention.* Memory, 8, *37–49.)*

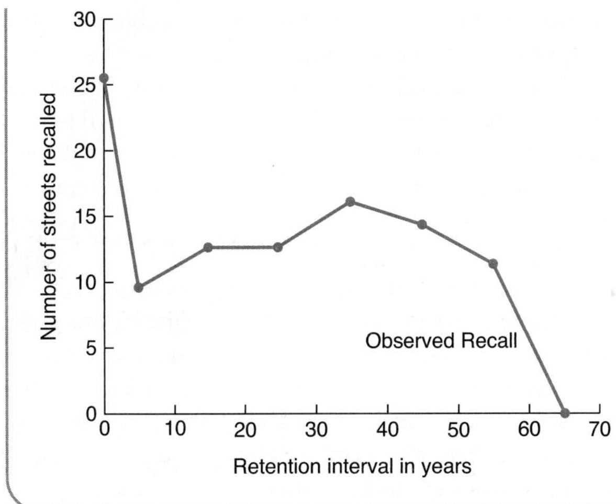


**FIGURE 8•14** The Stroop effect. Name the colour in which each word is printed as quickly as you can; you will find it difficult to ignore what the words say.

blue blue blue green
green yellow red
yellow yellow blue
red green yellow
yellow green yellow
yellow red yellow
green blue yellow
red blue green green
blue blue green red

## Remembering and Recollecting

Remembering is a process that seems enormously variable. Thinking about examinations you may have taken should help make that point. Sometimes the information you need comes to mind immediately; at other times, it's an effort to remember information you just studied. In these latter cases, what is effortful is the attempt to come up with the thoughts (the internal stimuli) that cause the information to be retrieved.

The retrieval of implicit memories seems automatic: When the appropriate stimulus occurs, it automatically evokes the appropriate response. For example, when I open my car door, I do not have to think about how the latch works; my hand goes to the appropriate place, my fingers arrange themselves in the proper positions, and I make the necessary movements. There are some cases where explicit memories, too, are retrieved automatically. Whisper your name to yourself. How did you manage to remember what your name is? How did you retrieve the information needed to move your lips in the proper sequence? Those questions cannot be answered by the method of introspection. The information simply pops out at us when the proper question is asked (or, more generally, when the appropriate stimulus is encountered).

Reading provides a particularly compelling example of the automatic nature of memory retrieval. When an experienced reader looks at a familiar word, the name of the word occurs immediately, and so does the meaning. In fact, it is difficult to look at a word and not think of its name. **Figure 8•14** contains a list of words that can be used to demonstrate a phenomenon known as the Stroop effect (Stroop, 1935; MacLeod, 1991). Look at the words and, as quickly as you can, say the names of the colours in which the words are printed; do not read the words themselves.

Most people cannot completely ignore the words and simply name the colours; the tendency to think of the words and pronounce them is difficult to resist. The Stroop effect indicates that even when we try to suppress a well-practised memory, it tends to be retrieved automatically when the appropriate stimulus occurs.

But what about the fact that some memories seem to be difficult to recall? For most people, remembering information is effortless and smooth. It is something we do unconsciously and automatically—most of the time. Occasionally, though, our memory of a name or a place or something else fails. The experience is often frustrating because we know that the information is "in there someplace," but we just cannot seem to get it out: "Oh, what is his name? I can see his face, he has a moustache, and he's skinny. It seems like his name starts with a D: Don? No. Dave? Nope. Dennis? No, that's not it either—what is his name?! Now I remember, his name is Doug. Doug Hoisington, a friend of mine in New York." This phenomenon is known as the **tip-of-the-tongue phenomenon** and has fascinated psychologists since the days of William James (1893). It was first studied carefully during the 1960s (Brown & McNeill, 1966), and since then we have learned a good deal about it (Brown, 1991). It is a common, if not universal, experience; it occurs about once a week and increases with age; it often involves proper names and

**tip-of-the-tongue phenomenon** An occasional problem with retrieval of information that we are sure we know but cannot immediately remember.

knowing the first letter of the word; and it is solved during the experience about 50 percent of the time.

The active search for stimuli that will evoke the appropriate memory, as exemplified in the tip-of-the-tongue phenomenon, has been called recollection (Baddeley, 1982). Recollection may be aided by contextual variables, including physical objects, suggestions, or other verbal stimuli. These contextual variables are called **retrieval cues**. For example, if you're trying to remember who gave you a particular gift at your last birthday party, you might find it helpful to look at photographs. The pictures of the people and the image of the scene provide retrieval cues for the information you're trying to recall.

As you might guess, the usefulness of retrieval cues often depends on encoding specificity. Encoding specificity is quite general in its impact on retrieval. In one rather strange example, skilled scuba divers served as participants and learned lists of words either under water or on land (Godden & Baddeley, 1975). Their ability to recall the lists was later tested in either the same or a different environment. The variable of interest was where the participants learned the list: in or out of the water. When lists were learned under water, they were recalled much better under water than on land, and lists learned on land were recalled better on land than in the water. The context in which information is learned or processed influences our ability to recollect that information. The implication for studying is clear: To improve recall of material to be tested, the best study strategy is to review the material under conditions similar to those that will prevail during the test. If you are going to take all of your psychology tests in a specific room, then you should study for those tests in that room.

Retrieval cues demonstrate that memory may be a response to internal stimuli. When we say we remember something, we are describing that response. But are we describing that response accurately?

Context and retrieval cues can be so powerful in recollection that they can elicit false memories. Suppose that you were asked to learn this list of words: *bed, rest, awake, tired, dream, wake, night, blanket, doze, slumber, snore, pillow, peace, yawn, drowsy*. Now, without looking back, ask yourself: was *sleep* one of the words? You might find it hard to be sure it wasn't, because the context evoked by the entire set of words suggests the core idea of sleep. In a now-classic article, Roediger and McDermott (1995) found that people would spontaneously recall words after listening to a list of closely associated words. That is, they fall prey to an illusion, thinking that they remember something that did not happen.

Marcia Johnson has argued that remembering is based on our ability to discriminate different responses to retrieval cues (Johnson, 2006). Her theory is known as the source monitoring framework and is based on the premise that remembering requires the ability to discriminate between different internal experiences. Experiences that are due to real episodes in our life must be differentiated from other experiences, based on vividness, plausibility, emotional context, and other factors.

For example, suppose you have a heated discussion with your mother. Later that day, you describe this to your brother, who takes your mother's side and repeats many of her arguments, adding some of his own. If you try to recall this incident months later, you now have a problem: Which of the arguments were hers and which were your brother's? Both are vivid and both elicit the emotion you felt at the time. Because they're so similar, you might find it hard to distinguish who said what. Indeed, you might even fail to distinguish that you had two separate arguments and "remember" that you were arguing with both your mother and your brother at the same time.

The source monitoring framework suggests that retrieval cues are supplemented by perceptual and cognitive processes that help us evaluate the accuracy of a memory. In the example we've been discussing, you might rely on logical clues to refine your memory, such as deducing that because your brother worked that day, he couldn't have been present when you argued with your mother. Johnson's approach to memory emphasizes the extent to which the subjective qualities of experience, our knowledge, and the social and motivational context of an episode are all factors that determine our ability to remember.

Like genuine retrieval, false recall depends on encoding specificity. Goodwin, Meissner, and Ericsson (2001) asked people to learn lists that could suggest a core word. For example, a list of words like *hard, pillow, light*, and so on, could suggest the word *soft*. And, indeed, people falsely recalled *soft* as a word that they had heard. However, if the associated words were paired with words that suggested an unrelated context, such as *hard hat, pillow case*, etc., then false recall was lower.

▲ *What do these famous lines have in common? "Beam me up, Scotty," "Me Tarzan, you Jane," "Play it again, Sam," "Elementary, my dear Watson"? Their fame, yes. But none of these lines, attributable to their characters, were actually said. The fact that people quote them may lead you to remember them incorrectly, as the source monitoring framework would suggest.*

**retrieval cues** Contextual variables, including physical objects or verbal stimuli, that improve the ability to recall information from memory.

## Forgetting and Interference

Although long-term memory appears to last for a long time, you have probably heard the notion that people forget some things they once knew because too much time has elapsed since the memory was last used and so it has decayed. Although psychologists argued in favour of this idea many years ago, most psychologists today hold that memory failure occurs for other reasons. One popular alternative explanation for memory failure is interference.

The finding that some memories may interfere with the retrieval of others is well established. An early study by Jenkins and Dallenbach (1924) showed that people are less likely to remember information after an interval of wakefulness than after an interval of sleep, presumably because of new memories that are formed when one is awake. (See **Figure 8•15**.)

Subsequent research soon showed that there are two types of interference in retrieval. Sometimes we experience **retroactive interference**—when we try to retrieve information, other information, which we have learned more recently, interferes. The top part of **Figure 8•16** charts how researchers test for the effects of retroactive interference. The experimental group first learns a list of words (we'll call the list "A"). Next, during the retention interval, the experimental group learns a second list of words, "B." Finally, the experimental group is asked to recall the first list of words ("A"). Meanwhile, the control group learns only the words in list "A"—the group is not asked to learn the words in list "B" during the retention interval. However, the control group is asked to recall the words in list "A" immediately following the retention interval. If the experimental group recalls fewer words during the test than does the control group, retroactive interference is said to have occurred in the people in that group.

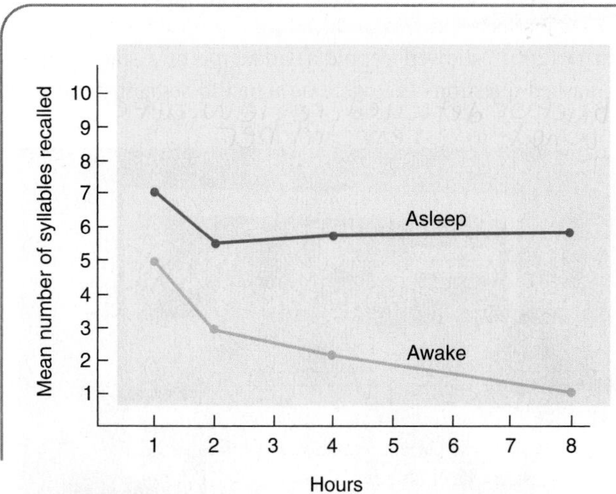


FIGURE 8•15 Interference in memory retrieval. The mean number of nonsense syllables recalled after sleeping or staying awake for varying intervals of time.

*(Adapted from Jenkins, J. G., & Dallenbach, K. M. (1924). Oblivescence during sleep and waking.* American Journal of Psychology, 35, *605–612.)*

FIGURE 8•16 Retroactive and proactive interference.

**Retroactive Interference**

| **Group** | Initial learning | Retention interval | Retention test |
|---|---|---|---|
| Experimental | Learn A | Learn B | Recall A |
| Control | Learn A | | Recall A |

**Proactive Interference**

| **Group** | Pre-learning | | Retention interval | Retention test |
|---|---|---|---|---|
| Experimental | Learn A | Learn B | | Recall B |
| Control | | Learn B | | Recall B |

You may have a hard time recalling the presents you received on your seventh birthday because you have had many birthdays since. If your seventh birthday had been just yesterday, you would likely show perfect recall. When memories that interfere with retrieval are formed after the learning that is being tested, we have retroactive interference.

At other times, retrieval is impaired by **proactive interference**, in which our ability to recall new information is reduced because of information we learned previously. The bottom part of Figure 8.16 illustrates the experimental procedure used to test for proactive interference. In this procedure, prior to learning a list (we'll call it list "B" in this procedure), the experimental group learns the words in another list, "A." The control group learns only the words in list "B." Both groups then experience a retention interval before they are asked to recall the words in list "B." If the experimental group recalls fewer words in list "B" during the test than does the control group, proactive interference is said to have occurred.

Let us assume that you took French for several years in high school, and that you are now taking a Spanish class in university. You find that some of the knowledge and study skills from high school are beneficial. But, occasionally, you discover that when you try to recall some Spanish, French pops up instead. Indeed, one reason that you may not be able to recall with certainty what birthday presents you received last year is that you have had so many birthdays before.

As reasonable and intuitive as the principle of interference may be, it has not gone unchallenged. Researchers agree that interference can affect retrieval, but some argue that the kinds of recall tasks people are asked to perform in the

**retroactive interference** Interference in recall that occurs when recently learned information disrupts our ability to remember older information.

**proactive interference** Interference in recall that occurs when previously learned information disrupts our ability to remember newer information.

laboratory are most likely to be affected by interference. In real life, such effects may not be so powerful. For example, meaningful prose, such as the kind found in novels, is resistant to interference. Laboratory studies most often use lists of nonsense syllables and unrelated words.

## Reconstruction: Remembering as a Creative Process

Much of what we recall from long-term memory is not an accurate representation of what actually happened. Many errors in memory, however, are not mere inaccuracies: They tend to show systematic patterns. Often, our recollection corresponds to what makes sense to us at the time we retrieve it. It becomes, in other words, a plausible account of what might have happened or even of what we think should have happened. Psychologists have long recognized that the context of remembering is a very important determinant of memory.

**The Role of Schemas** You'll recall from the discussion about encoding specificity earlier in the chapter that when a retrieval cue is understood to have a different meaning at the time of remembering than it did at the time of encoding, it loses its effectiveness. The framework that provides the meaning is called a schema. Schemas help us encode information in more meaningful ways, but they also can induce systematic errors. For example, thinking of living things as animals, plants, or fungi might help you classify organisms; however, your schema of "living things" might lead you to overlook the possibility that viruses could be a form of life.

An early experiment by Bartlett (1932) called attention to the way schemas affect memory. The experimenter had people read a story or essay or look at a picture. Then he asked them on several later occasions to retell the prose passage or draw the picture. Each time, the participants "remembered" the original a little differently. If the original story had contained peculiar and unexpected sequences of events, people tended to retell it in a more coherent and sensible fashion, as if their memories had been revised to make the information accord more closely with their own schema for what the story was about. Bartlett concluded that people remember only a few striking details of an experience and that, during recall, they reconstruct the missing portions in accordance with their own interpretation of what was likely.

**Eyewitness Testimony** Elizabeth Loftus (1979) has investigated a different set of variables that affect the recall of details from episodic memory. Her research indicates that the kinds of questions used to elicit information can have a major effect on what people remember. In courts of law, lawyers are not permitted to ask witnesses leading questions—questions phrased so as to suggest what the answer should be. Loftus's research showed that even subtle changes in a question can affect people's recollections. For example, Loftus and Palmer (1974) showed people films of car accidents and asked them to

**FIGURE 8•17** Leading questions and recall. Shown are the mean estimated speeds of vehicles as recalled by people in the study by Loftus and Palmer (1974).

*(Based on data from Loftus, E. F., & Palmer, J. C. (1974). Reconstruction of automobile destruction: An example of the interaction between language and memory.* Journal of Verbal Learning and Verbal Behaviour, 13, *585–589.)*

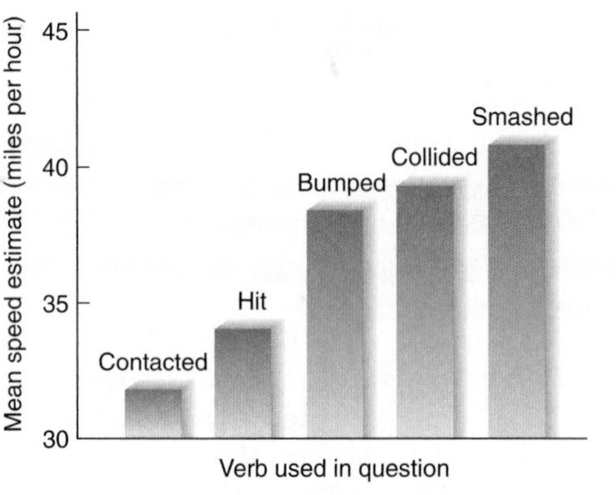


estimate vehicles' speeds when they *contacted, hit, bumped, collided,* or *smashed* each other. As **Figure 8•17** shows, the people's estimates of the vehicles' speeds were directly related to the force of the impact suggested by the verb, such as *hit*, that appeared in the question.

In a similar experiment, when people were asked a week after viewing the film whether they saw any broken glass (there was none), people in the *smashed* group were most likely to say yes. Thus, a leading question that encouraged them to remember the vehicles going faster also encouraged them to remember that they saw non-existent broken glass. The question appears to have modified the memory itself.

Another experiment indicates that how events are reviewed affects this suggestibility. Lane, Mather, Villa, and Morita (2001) showed people a videotape of a staged crime, then asked questions that were designed to suggest things that

▲ *The questions asked during a pretrial investigation may affect an eyewitness's later testimony.*

were not part of the video. For example, the witnesses might be asked, "At the beginning of the scene, a young man dressed in jeans, a T-shirt, and gloves entered the house. Did he enter through the door?" In the video, the thief did not wear gloves; the test was to see if witnesses would incorrectly include the gloves in their recall of the scene later on. Before recalling information about the scene, however, they were asked, as witnesses might reasonably be asked to do, to review the videotape mentally. Some were asked to review as much detail as possible; others were asked to review only the highlights. Instructions to focus on details led to an increased tendency to incorporate the suggested, and false, information, such as the presence of gloves. Apparently, after being asked to review details, eyewitnesses rehearse the suggestions and come to view these as true.

Experiments such as these have important implications for eyewitness testimony in courts of law (Yarmey, 2003). A judge can prevent a lawyer from asking leading questions during a trial, but he or she cannot undo the effects of leading questions put to the witness during pretrial investigations. Many experiments indicate that learning new information and recalling it later are active processes—we do not simply place an item of information in a mental filing cabinet and pick it up later (Roediger & McDermott, 1995). We organize and integrate information in terms of what we already know about life and have come to expect about particular experiences. Thus, when we recall the memory later, it may contain information that was not part of the original experience. Even more disturbing, our confidence in this new information may be quite high.

At first, this phenomenon may appear to be maladaptive because it means that we cannot always trust our own recollections, no matter how hard we try to be accurate. However, our tendency to reconstruct memories probably reflects the fact that information about an episode can be more efficiently stored by means of a few unique details. The portions of an episode that are common to other experiences, and hence resemble information already stored in long-term memory, need not be retained. If every detail of every experience had to be encoded uniquely in long-term memory, perhaps we would run out of storage space. Unfortunately, this process sometimes leads to instances of faulty remembering, both on the witness stand and in life in general.

**Flashbulb Memories** Are some memories immune to this reconstructive process? One possibility is that some episodic memories are acquired under such powerful personal experiences of emotion and surprise that they become especially vivid and long-lasting. Consider your personal memory of when you first heard about the attack on the World Trade Center on September 11, 2001. Can you recall where you were, what you were doing, and who gave you the news? Do you remember your personal feelings? The feelings of those around you? Can you recall what you did next?

Roger Brown and James Kulik provided a name for memories activated by events of extreme surprise and great personal consequence: **flashbulb memories.** Using the assassination of President John F. Kennedy as an example, Brown and Kulik (1977) suggested that surprising, traumatic events could result in the encoding of some (but not all) of the context surrounding the individual at the time. When they asked people in 1977 to recollect their personal situation at the time they heard of Kennedy's 1963 assassination, they discovered that most accounts included the information behind the six questions asked in the previous paragraph. Brown and Kulik speculated that flashbulb memories were not only especially vivid but also, possibly, especially long-lasting or even permanent.

However, other evidence suggests that flashbulb memories are not immune to the effects of distortion and modification discussed in the previous section. Schmolck, Buffalo, and Squire (2000) looked at an event that, although it was less consequential than the Kennedy assassination or September 11, nevertheless produced flashbulb memories in students at the University of California: the 1995 acquittal of O. J. Simpson for the murder of his wife, Nicole, and her friend Ron Goldman. The investigators asked the students to record their reactions to the event three days after it happened. Then, either 15 months or 32 months later, they asked them to recall the event again. In general, recollection after 15 months was accurate. After 32 months, however, more than 40 percent of the recollections were seriously distorted. Schmolck, Buffalo, and Squire found that among 50 individuals who could be described as having a flashbulb memory of the verdict, 38 percent could not remember it as they had originally described it three days after the event. A significant error made in the years after the event was recall of the source of the news, with many people misreporting that they had heard about the verdict from the media rather than from another person. Rather than saying that they couldn't remember, these individuals apparently assumed that because they get much of their news from the media, they must have heard about the Simpson verdict in the same way. This assumption was then incorporated into their memory of the event.

In this chapter's prologue, we saw how witnesses in the Salem witchcraft trials testified about fantastic episodes of supernatural occurrences. In reading some of these accusations, you might have immediately thought that the witnesses were lying; people could not possibly recall things so counter to actual fact. Or could they?

Daniel Schacter has suggested that memory can exhibit seven deficiencies or "sins." These sins of memory are transience, absent-mindedness, blocking, misattribution, suggestibility, bias, and persistence. The first three are deficiencies of omission: Transience is the weakening of memory over time; absent-mindedness is the failure to register information that needs to be memorized; and blocking is the failure to retrieve information we know we possess. The other four are deficiencies of commission and add wrong information to

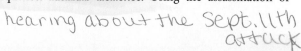

**flashbulb memories** Memories established by events that are highly surprising and personally of consequence.

our memory: Misattribution confuses different sources of memory; suggestibility embellishes memory under the influence of misleading questions or statements from others; bias creates errors because of our own beliefs; and persistence brings to mind information that we would rather forget (Schacter, 2001; Schacter & Dodson, 2002).

Schacter's "seven sins" have particular relevance to the criminal justice system. In many criminal investigations—particularly those in which little or no physical evidence is available—the memory of witnesses becomes especially important. Their ability to remember events and faces can determine the success or failure of the investigation—and of the subsequent prosecution, should a suspect be brought to trial. But memories of eyewitnesses are transient, especially when the events in question are fast-paced, confusing, and frightening. Elizabeth Loftus has explored some of the implications of memory deficiencies in her laboratory. However, it is relevant to consider how many of these deficiencies could occur outside the laboratory.

In 1996, inspired in part by Loftus's work, Crombag, Wagenaar, and van Koppen (1996) pushed the notion of an eyewitness to the limit. In 1992, a Boeing 747 had crashed into an Amsterdam apartment building, creating a blazing fire but, fortunately, with fewer casualties than first feared. Crombag, Wagenaar, and van Koppen subsequently circulated a questionnaire to college students and faculty asking whether they had seen the television footage of the moment when the plane hit the building. Despite the fact that no such footage existed, 55 percent of the respondents claimed to have personally seen it. Furthermore, among this group claiming to have seen the footage, 82 percent were so confident of what they had seen that they provided details about the crash. A group of law students tested later was even more prone to false memories of the crash: 66 percent of them claimed to have seen it.

"Crashing memories" (that is, pseudo-memories) have been found for other high-profile events. For example, Jelicic and colleagues (2006) asked undergraduates whether they had seen video of the murder of a prominent Dutch politician, Pim Fortuyn. Again, no such footage existed; yet 63 percent of respondents reported seeing it. Asked if they could describe details of what they had seen, 23 percent provided accounts.

What produces this tendency to confidently recall memories of things that cannot be? Jelicic and colleagues (2006) found evidence that it was associated with a tendency to fantasize. People reporting memories of the film were more likely to answer yes to questions such as "In general, I spend at least half of the day fantasizing or daydreaming" and "My fantasies are so vivid that they are like a good film." In another study, Smeets and colleagues (2006) found that crashing memories depend in part on the way the question is asked. Using the non-existent Pim Fortuyn assassination film as their example, Smeets and colleagues found that they received the highest number of false recollections when they asked about the film in an ambiguous way ("Did you see the amateur film about the Fortuyn shooting?") rather than in a highly specific manner ("Did you see the amateur film of the moment Fortuyn was shot by Volkert van der G.?"). Sixty-three percent answered yes to the ambiguous question; only 30 percent answered positively to the specific questions. So, as also shown in the work by Loftus and her colleagues, language plays an important role in how we evaluate our memories, leading us to commit Schacter's "sin" of suggestibility.

Suggestibility is not the sole cause of a crashing memory, however. Smeets and colleagues (2006) also asked about the film in a very neutral manner: "Do you remember whether there was a film of the moment Fortuyn was shot by Volkert van der G.?" Twenty-seven percent of participants could remember there being such a film. Crombag, Wagenaar, and van Koppen (1996) suggested that misattribution (another one of the sins) could play a strong role. Perhaps, since the event was such a prominent one for Dutch citizens, people imagined what the shooting was like and incorporated that image into memory of video that they did see.

If so, this possibility validates another legal principle. Crombag, Wagenaar, and van Koppen point out the principle of many Western legal traditions to prohibit "hearsay" testimony—testimony about what someone else has remembered. Far from being just a legal nicety, the prohibition against hearsay testimony emphasizes that evidence must have a clear source. Our memory system may not be best at keeping its sources straight.

## Interim Summary

### Remembering, Recollecting, and Forgetting

Remembering sometimes requires the generation of thoughts that are associated with the information and the discrimination of their source. As research of childhood memories shows, the forgetting of information occurs primarily in the first few years after it is learned, and the rate of forgetting decreases slowly thereafter. Once we have learned something and retained it for a few years, chances are that we will remember it for a long time afterwards.

Sometimes, retrieval of one memory is made more difficult by the information contained in another memory, a phenomenon known as interference. In retroactive interference, information that we have recently learned interferes with our recollection of information learned earlier. In proactive interference, information that we learned a while ago interferes with information we have learned more recently. Although interference has been demonstrated in the laboratory, interference may not operate so obviously in real life. Prose and other forms of everyday language appear to be more resistant to interference than the nonsense syllables often used in memory experiments.

Recalling a memory of a complex event entails a process of reconstruction that uses old information. And, as Loftus's research has established, our ability to recall information from episodic memory is influenced by retrieval cues, such as the questions lawyers ask people in courts of law to establish how an event occurred. Sometimes the reconstruction introduces new "facts" that we consider memories of what we previously perceived. Reconstructions also affect the recollection of flashbulb memories—especially vivid memories of surprising and consequential events. This reconstructive process undoubtedly makes more efficient use of the resources we have available for storage of long-term memories.

Reconstructions can be so strong that people may even claim to have witnessed impossible events. Schacter has suggested seven "sins of memory." Two of these, suggestibility and misattribution, might be responsible for memories of events that did not happen.

**QUESTION TO CONSIDER**

1. Recall a particularly important event in your life. Think about the activities that led up to this event and how it has affected your life since. How much of the information you recall about this event is accurate? How many of the details surrounding this event have you reconstructed? How would you go about finding the answers to these questions?

# EPILOGUE

## The Salem Testimony Reconsidered

Reading the transcripts of the Salem Witch Trials is a sobering experience. The charges sound preposterous, the evidence seems flimsy, and the sentences were harsh. One man, who refused to enter a plea at his trial, was placed under heavy rocks and crushed to death over two days. Before the trials ended, 15 women and 6 men had been executed. One quickly gains an appreciation for what the term *witch hunt* really means.

Many theories have been advanced to explain the accusations. It's conceivable that some of the young girls whose stories started the witch hunt suffered from a mental illness; however, it seems unlikely that all of them did. Perhaps they became frightened about what they had started and couldn't find a way to admit it. From this distance in time, the answer will probably never be fully known.

What is startling, even now, is the credulity of the investigators, judges, and jurors for testimony that was based on fantasy. One incident brings this home: Early in the investigation, the young girls accused a four-year-old child of haunting them. The authorities promptly jailed this unfortunate girl. Undoubtedly confused and terrified, and relying on a child's imagination, she told her inquisitors that she had been given a black snake that sucked her blood. The investigators noted for the record that they then found a small wound, "the size of a flea bite," on the child's finger. Given that she had been housed in the town jail, it probably was, indeed, a flea bite. Asked who had given her the snake, she mentioned her mother. Because of testimony like that, her mother, Sarah Good, was hanged nine days after Bridget Bishop.

Now that you've learned about the work of Elizabeth Loftus and others, you can better appreciate how much the interrogators contributed to the whole episode. The witnesses must have also received some strong coaching, implicit or not, from their neighbours in the village—each with their own agenda. The prologue also hinted that subtle matters of timing may have played a role. A sighting of a mysterious black pig after an argument with a presumed witch makes for a much better schema than a random encounter. Similarly, remembering that he lost some coins right after she gave them to him probably seemed like a more plausible scenario to one of Bridget's accusers than admitting his own absent-mindedness. Finally, one cannot help but wonder how many of the encounters with apparitions in the middle of the night were merely dreams confused as reality.

As the research with Dutch street names shows, we are capable of recalling information from our past to a surprising extent. Yet memory is not a DVD recorder. Rather, it is the outcome of brain processes that evolved for special functions; we weren't designed by natural selection to be perfect courtroom witnesses. As Schacter has put it, our memory is prone to seven deadly sins. In all likelihood, that was the real devil at work in Salem.

## Canadian Connections to Research in This Chapter


Avey, M. T., Kanyo, R. A., Irwin, E. L., & Sturdy, C. B. (2008). Differential effects of vocalization type, singer and listener on ZENK immediate early gene response in black-capped chickadees (*Poecile atricapillus*). *Behavioural Brain Research, 188,* 201–208. (University of Alberta: www.ualberta.ca).

Bloomfield, L. L., Farrell, T. M., & Sturdy, C. B. (2008). Categorization and discrimination of "chick-a-dee" calls by wild-caught and hand-reared chickadees. *Behavioural Processes, 77,* 166–176. (University of Alberta: www.ualberta.ca)

Craik, F. I. M., & Lockhart, R. S. (1972). Levels of processing: A framework for memory research. *Journal of Verbal Learning and Verbal Behavior, 11,* 671–684. (University of Toronto: www.utoronto.ca)

Fergus Craik was the 1987 winner of the Donald O. Hebb Award of the Canadian Psychological Association.

Craik, F. I. M., & Tulving, E. (1975). Depth of processing and the retention of words in episodic memory. *Journal of Experimental Psychology: General, 104,* 268–294. (University of Toronto: www.utoronto.ca)

Endel Tulving was the 1983 winner of the Donald O. Hebb Award of the Canadian Psychological Association and the 1983 winner of the American Psychological Association's Award for Distinguished Scientific Contributions.

Dixon, P., Gordon, R. D., Leung, A., & Di Lollo, V. (1997). Attentional components of partial report. *Journal of Experimental Psychology, 23,* 1253–1271. (University of Alberta: www.ualberta.ca)

Doyon, J., LaForce, R. Jr., Bouchard, G., Gaudreau, D., Roy, J., Poirier, M., Bédard, P. J., Bédard, F., & Bouchard, J.-P. (1998). Role of the striatum, cerebellum and frontal lobes in the automatization of a repeated visuomotor sequence of movements. *Neuropsychologia, 36,* 625–641. (Université Laval: www.ulaval.ca)

Flexser, A. J., & Tulving, E. (1978). Retrieval independence in recognition and recall. *Psychological Review, 85,* 153–171. (University of Toronto: www.utoronto.ca)

Hebb, D. O. (1949). *The organization of behavior.* New York: Wiley-Interscience. (McGill University: www.mcgill.ca)

Donald Hebb was the first winner (in 1980) of the Donald O. Hebb Award of the Canadian Psychological Association and the 1961 winner of the American Psychological Association's Award for Distinguished Scientific Contributions.

Kilgour, A. R., Jakobson, L. S., and Cuddy, L. L. (2000). Music training and rate of presentation as mediators of text and song recall. *Memory & Cognition, 28,* 700–710. (Queen's University: www.queensu.ca)

MacLeod, C. M. (1991). Half a century of research on the Stroop effect: An integrative review. *Psychological Bulletin, 109,* 163–203. (University of Toronto: www.utoronto.ca)

Milner, B. (1970). Memory and the temporal regions of the brain. In K. H. Pribram & D. E. Broadbent (Eds.), *Biology of memory.* New York: Academic. (McGill University: www.mcgill.ca)

Brenda Milner was the 1981 winner of the Donald O. Hebb Award of the Canadian Psychological Association and the 1973 winner of the American Psychological Association's Award for Distinguished Scientific Contributions.

Muter, P. (1980). Very rapid forgetting. *Memory & Cognition, 8,* 174–179. (University of Toronto: www.utoronto.ca)

Reingold, E. M., Charness, N., Pomplun, M., & Stampe, D. M. (2001). Visual span in expert chess players: Evidence from eye movements. *Psychological Science, 12,* 48–55. (University of Toronto: www.utoronto.ca)

Sherry, D. F., & Schacter, D. L. (1987). The evolution of multiple memory systems. *Psychological Review, 94,* 439–454. (University of Toronto: www.utoronto.ca)

Standing, L. (1973). Learning 10,000 pictures. *Quarterly Journal of Experimental Psychology, 25,* 207–222. (Bishop's University: www.ubishops.ca)

Tulving, E. (2002). Episodic memory: From mind to brain. *Annual Review of Psychology, 53,* 1–25. (University of Toronto: www.utoronto.ca)

Yarmey, A. D. (2003). Eyewitness identification: Guidelines and recommendations for identification procedures in the United States and in Canada. *Canadian Psychology, 44,* 181–189. (University of Guelph: www.uoguelph.ca)

Zhuo, M. (2005). Targeting central plasticity: A new direction of finding painkillers. *Current Pharmaceutical Design, 11,* 2797–2807. (University of Toronto: www.utoronto.ca)

## Suggestions for Further Reading

Luria, A. R. (1968). *The mind of a mnemonist.* New York: Basic Books.

Given the importance of learning and forgetting in almost everyone's life, it is not surprising that many popular books have been written about human memory. This book is the great Russian neurologist's account of a man with an extraordinary memory.

Loftus, E. F., & Ketcham, K. (1994). *The myth of repressed memory: False memories and allegations of sexual abuse.* New York: St. Martin's.

Elizabeth Loftus is an internationally recognized authority on remembering. She has researched and written extensively on the errors people make in recalling events. This book deals with case studies of individuals who purportedly were able to recall significant events that had been "repressed" because of their traumatic nature. As Loftus and Ketcham note, such repressed memories likely never existed in the first place.

Ormrod, J. E. (2008). *Human learning* (5th ed.). Upper Saddle River, NJ: Pearson.

Schacter, D. L. (2001). *The seven sins of memory.* Boston: Houghton Mifflin.

The Ormrod book is an upper-level undergraduate text that contains a well-written and thoughtful consideration of memory and its processes. The book's discussion of memory is placed in the larger context of learning processes, such as those discussed in Chapter 7. The Schacter book is an engaging overview of memory errors.



Deficiencies of omission:

1. transience → weakening of memory in time
2. absent-mindedness → failure to memorize.
3. blocking → failure to gather info that we possess

Deficiencies of commission: (adding wrong info to memory)

1. Misattribution → confusion of sources of memory.
2. suggestibility → changes memory under influence of misleading questions/statements.
3. bias → errors due to own beliefs.
4. persistence → constantly thinking about info we want to forget

# 9

# Consciousness

# CHAPTER OUTLINE

## Consciousness as a Social Phenomenon

Can We Understand Consciousness? • The Adaptive Significance of Consciousness • Consciousness and the Ability to Communicate • Consciousness and the Control of Behaviour

Although consciousness is a subjective phenomenon, it is a natural phenomenon that can be studied scientifically. Consciousness may be explained as a product of our ability to communicate symbolically with other people.

## Selective Attention

Auditory Information • Visual Information • Brain Mechanisms of Selective Attention

Our ability to focus on particular categories of stimuli or stimuli in particular locations is called selective attention. The ability to detect changes in visual information depends on its location, nature, and meaningfulness. PET studies show that attention to a particular characteristic of a visual stimulus increases the activity of particular regions of the visual association cortex involved in the analysis of that characteristic.

## Consciousness and the Brain

Isolation Aphasia: A Case of Global Unawareness • Visual Agnosia: Lack of Awareness of Visual Perceptions • *Then and Now: Perception without Awareness* • The Split-Brain Syndrome

Studies of people with brain damage show that some mental processes can be lost from awareness. It is sometimes possible for people to perceive objects they are unaware of or to lose the ability to understand words while retaining the ability to recognize and repeat them. People with split brains (those whose corpus callosum has been cut) cannot talk about perceptions or other mental processes that occur in their right hemispheres.

## Hypnosis

Characteristics of Hypnosis • Theories of Hypnosis

Hypnotic phenomena include hallucinations and other changes in consciousness, post-hypnotic suggestibility, and post-hypnotic amnesia. The behaviour of a hypnotized participant depends on the suggestions of the hypnotist and the participant's expectations. Hypnosis is related to people's ability to participate actively in a story that interests them and may be related to their ability to empathize with other people. It may also involve a special state in which awareness is dissociated from the mechanisms that control behaviour.

## Sleep

The Stages of Sleep • The Functions of Sleep • Dreaming • Brain Mechanisms of Sleep

Sleep consists of slow-wave sleep and REM sleep. One of the most important functions of slow-wave sleep may be to permit the cerebral cortex to rest. In adults, REM sleep may be involved in learning. Dreaming occurs during REM sleep. The brain contains two biological clocks that control circadian rhythms and rhythms of slow-wave sleep and REM sleep.

PROLOGUE

## A Trial

The case was as strange as any of the novels or screenplays he had written. William Deverell, well known as a lawyer and as the author of popular thrillers, had time to reflect on this irony as he waited with his client, Robert Frisbee, for the jury to return to the courtroom and announce its verdict. Frisbee was on trial for murder—accused of a brutal slaying made all the more salacious by the fact that it had occurred in the luxury penthouse of a cruise ship travelling through Canadian waters. The victim, Muriel Barnett, was a wealthy widow from San Francisco. She had been discovered in her blood-spattered stateroom bludgeoned to death with a bottle of scotch. Frisbee, who served as her chauffeur and private secretary and who shared her stateroom, had been found confused and disoriented in the room with her body. His bathrobe was soaked with Barnett's blood, yet he had answered the butler's knock on the door as if nothing had happened.

For weeks, attorney Deverell had sought to explain to the jury how these facts could be reconciled with Frisbee's innocence. Deverell based his defence on the concept of non-insane automatism—a concept of Canadian jurisprudence that can exonerate a person who commits a crime while involuntarily unconscious of the action. As Deverell describes it, the doctrine is that "the person commits no offence if the mind was not with the body when the crime was committed." A person who kills while sleepwalking, for example, could be acquitted of deliberate murder. Deverell needed to demonstrate that Frisbee was in an unconscious state of mind at the time of the murder. What arguments could he make that would convince the jury?

For one, there was Frisbee's temperament. He had had a troubled childhood, and had grown up to be a passive and unassuming adult. Deverell introduced testimony from a psychiatrist that Frisbee was "morbidly dependent" on others and had constructed a personality for himself based largely on what others wanted him to be. Violence toward others was completely foreign to this "constructed" personality.

Deverell also pointed out that Frisbee's past behaviour toward his employer seemed far from murderous. He was slavishly devoted to Barnett and to her late husband, catering to their capricious and sometimes degrading whims. Meek and subservient, he rarely if ever asserted himself in Barnett's presence.

Finally, Deverell pointed to external influences. Two hours before the murder, Frisbee had apparently consumed a considerable amount of drugs: six ounces of vodka, ten ounces of champagne, and two tranquilizers. He had, he said, fallen asleep until woken up by the butler. He could remember nothing since he had carefully tucked his employer into bed for her afternoon nap.

The Crown prosecutor, of course, had tried to destroy these arguments. He had argued that the murder, despicable as it was, was nevertheless Frisbee's rational response to a financial opportunity. Barnett was about to change her will, and Frisbee had reason to believe he would be cut out of it.

It was up to the jury now. The jurors had to decide whether it was reasonable to conclude that Frisbee had acted without conscious control of his behaviour. Deverell had pointed to all of those factors that we see as important in the moment-to-moment integrity of human consciousness, arguing that Frisbee's amnesia was evidence that his mind had temporarily ceased its controlling role over the body's actions. Now he could only wait.

The jury filed in, and Deverell's unassuming client rose to hear how it would judge his state of mind at the time of the murder. The Registrar of the Court asked for the verdict . . .

On January 10, 1987, Robert Frisbee was convicted of first-degree murder in a Victoria, British Columbia, courtroom. In rendering its verdict, the jury had to consider profound issues of human psychology. Frisbee's legal team, as I described in the prologue, had argued that consuming alcohol and drugs had turned him into an automaton no longer under the control of his mind. The legal arguments, vividly related by Deverell (1991), were complex and, in this particular case at least, failed to persuade the jury that there was a reasonable doubt of Frisbee's guilt. But the issues are as old as the discipline of psychology itself: Is it possible to behave purposely, but without voluntary control? Can we perform actions and not be aware of them? And most important for a science based on objective data, can we rely on verbal reports, such as Frisbee's self-proclaimed amnesia, to decide these issues? These questions bring us to consider the role of consciousness in the control of behaviour. (Frisbee's conviction, by the way, was reduced to second-degree murder after his lawyers appealed the verdict. The appellate court held that the jury had not been properly instructed regarding evidence of intentionality.)

## Consciousness as a Social Phenomenon

Why are we aware of ourselves: of our thoughts, our perceptions, our actions, our memories, and our feelings? Is some purpose served by our ability to realize that we exist, that events occur, that we are doing things, and that we have memories? Philosophers have puzzled over this question for centuries without finding a convincing answer. Psychologists neglected the problem of consciousness for many years. Early behaviourists denied that there was anything to explain. The only subject matter for psychological investigation was behaviour, and consciousness was not behaviour. More recently, investigators have begun to apply the methods of inquiry developed by psychology and neuroscience and, finally, we seem to be making some progress.

▲ *When do we become aware of our own existence?*

### Can We Understand Consciousness?

Historically, people have taken three philosophical positions about the nature of consciousness (Flanagan, 1992). The first, and earliest, position is that consciousness is not a natural phenomenon. (Natural phenomena are those subject to the laws of nature that all scientists attempt to discover: laws involving matter and purely physical forces.) This position says that consciousness is something supernatural and miraculous, not to be understood by the human mind.

The second position is that consciousness is a natural phenomenon but also that, for various reasons, we cannot understand it. Consciousness exists because of the nature of the human brain, but just how this occurs is not known. Some people say that we can never understand consciousness because our brains are simply not capable of doing so; it would take a more complex brain than ours to understand the biology of subjective awareness. Others say that we are probably capable of understanding consciousness but that at present we lack the means to study it scientifically. Still others say that, in principle, everything can be explained—including all aspects of the human brain—but that *consciousness* is a vague, poorly defined term. Before we can hope to study it with any success, we must define just what it is we want to study.

The third position is that people are indeed conscious, that this consciousness is produced by the activity of the human brain, and that there is every reason for us to be optimistic about our ability to understand this phenomenon. This was the position advocated for many years by Donald Hebb, who stated that "consciousness, a variable state, is a present activity of thought processes in some form; and thought itself is an activity of the brain" (Hebb, 1980, p. 3). However, Hebb rejected the notion that concepts like consciousness were "nothing but" neural impulses. For him, the psychological concepts were at a different level; understanding the neural level would enrich and enhance our understanding of the psychological.

### The Adaptive Significance of Consciousness

To discover the functions of consciousness, we must not confuse consciousness with complex mental processes such as perceiving, remembering, or thinking. Consciousness is the *awareness* of these processes, not the processes themselves. Thus, consciousness is a characteristic that exists *in addition* to functions such as perception, memory, thinking, and planning.

It is difficult to see why a living organism having elaborate behavioural abilities plus consciousness would have any advantages over one that possessed the same abilities but lacked consciousness. If the behaviour of these two types of organisms were identical in all situations, they should be equally successful. So let us put aside the search for useful functions of consciousness itself. A more fruitful approach might be to conceive of consciousness as a by-product of another characteristic of the human brain that does have useful functions. The factors of natural selection that favour this other characteristic would also be the factors that favour consciousness. But what might this characteristic be?

Let us consider what we know about consciousness. First, although the word *consciousness* is a noun, it does not refer to a thing. The word *life* is a noun, too, but modern biologists know better than to look for "life." Instead, they study the characteristics of living organisms. Similarly, "consciousness" does not exist. What exists are humans having the ability to do something in particular: be conscious. So, then, what does it mean to be conscious? Consciousness is a private experience, which cannot be shared directly. We experience our own consciousness but not that of others. We conclude that other people are conscious because they are like us and because they can tell us that they, too, are conscious.

Another clue to the functions of consciousness is that we are not conscious of everything about ourselves, nor are we equally conscious of the same thing all the time. That is, *consciousness is not a general property of all parts of the brain.* A phenomenon known as **blindsight** is one example (see Chapter 6). Blindsight is the ability to reach for objects accurately while remaining unaware of seeing them. It is caused by damage to the visual cortex, or to some of the pathways leading into or from that area. A person with blindsight will, for example, be able to reach for a walking cane, all the while maintaining that he or she doesn't see it. Apparently, a part of the visual system can control our ability to react to the presence of objects, directing our eye movement, our limbs, and other behaviours, but without necessarily giving the information needed for us to describe or to think about the objects. For other parts of our brain, awareness comes about with a special effort, as when we concentrate on or attend to certain experiences. With concentration, we can then describe these activities of the brain so as to convey them to other people.

In my opinion, it is no coincidence that the principal evidence we have of consciousness in other people comes through the use of language. I believe that the most likely explanation for consciousness lies in its relation to deliberate, symbolic communication. Our ability to communicate (through words, signs, or other symbolic means) provides us with self-awareness. Self-awareness, then, is built on *inner speech,* which allows us to describe our behaviours and compare them to others (Morin, 2003). Thus, consciousness—like communication—is, I believe, primarily a social phenomenon.

**blindsight** The ability to interact behaviourally with objects while remaining consciously unaware of them.

## Consciousness and the Ability to Communicate

How does the ability to communicate symbolically give rise to consciousness? To answer this question, let us consider what can be accomplished through verbal communication. We can ask other people to help us get something we need. We can share our knowledge with others by describing our past experiences. We can make plans with other people to accomplish tasks that are beyond the abilities of a single person. We can warn other people of our intentions and in so doing avoid potential conflicts. In other words, we can express our needs, thoughts, perceptions, memories, intentions, and feelings to other people.

All of these accomplishments require two general capacities. First, we must be able to translate private events—our needs, thoughts, and other processes—into symbolic expressions. This means that the brain mechanisms we employ for communicating with others must receive input from the systems of the brain involved in perceiving, thinking, remembering, and so on. Second, our words (or other symbols) must have an effect on the person listening. Once the words are decoded in the listener's brain, they must affect the listener's own thoughts, perceptions, memories, and—ultimately—behaviour. For example, if we describe an event that we witnessed, our listener will be able to imagine that event, too. The episode will become part of our listener's memory.

Of course, the world is not divided into talkers and listeners. We are all capable of expressing our thoughts symbolically and of decoding the symbols that other people express. Having both of these capabilities enables us to communicate with ourselves, privately. We can make plans in words, think about the consequences of these plans in words, and use words to produce behaviours—all without actually *saying* the words. We *think* them.

As we saw in Chapter 8, thinking in words appears to involve subvocal articulation. Thus, the brain mechanisms that permit us to understand words and produce speech are the same ones we use to think in words. Similarly, investigators have noted that when deaf people are thinking to themselves, they often make small movements with their hands, just as those of us who can hear and speak sometimes talk to ourselves under our breath. Apparently, we exercise our expressive language mechanisms, whatever they may be, when we think.

So what does all of this have to do with consciousness? My thesis is this: The ability to communicate with ourselves symbolically gives rise to consciousness. We are conscious of those private events we can talk about, to ourselves or to other people: our perceptions, needs, intentions, memories, and feelings.

For example, consider an experiment by Cheesman and Merikle (1986). They presented people with a word (the prime) that was either congruent or incongruent with the colour of a subsequent patch of colour (the target). Participants in this study were asked to name the colour of the target, a task that is more difficult when the prime is incongruent. (By now, you should recognize, from Chapter 8, that this is an example of the Stroop effect.) In Cheesman and Merikle's study, however, a random jumble of letters (a mask) was sometimes presented after the prime, before the target. When the mask was presented right after the prime, people were unable to identify the prime (that is, they were not concious of what the prime was); when the mask was presented after a suitable delay, consciousness was not impaired. Cheesman and Merikle found that incongruent primes produce a Stroop-like interference even when the mask interfered with the concious ability to identify the meaning of the prime.

Now, by itself, this may not be evidence of a role for consciousness. After all, the fact that the primes have a Stroop-like effect whether or not people are conscious of their meaning does not show that consciousness adds anything to our ability to process information. However, Cheesman and Merikle included a special condition in which there were many more congruent than incongruent primes. In other words, if the word *green* appeared, it was much more likely to be followed by a green patch than any other colour. So, by using the prime, one could predict what colour was about to come. Now, when the prime was consciously perceivable, people used the predictive information of the prime. However, when it was not consciously perceivable, they failed to exploit this predictive arrangement. Conscious awareness, I suggest, has this property: We become able to describe, and thereby use, the psychological events that are private to ourselves.

Are humans the only living organisms having self-awareness? Probably not. The evolutionary process is incremental: New traits and abilities, including the ability of humans to communicate symbolically, build on ones that already exist. Most forms of communication among animals other than humans—for example, mating displays and alarm calls—are automatic and probably do not involve consciousness. However, other forms of communications can be learned, just as we learn our own language. Certainly, your dog can learn to communicate with you. The fact that it can learn to tell you when it wants to eat, go for a walk, or play suggests that it, too, may be conscious. Obviously, our ability to communicate symbolically far surpasses that of any other species; thus, our consciousness is much more highly developed. But the underlying brain mechanisms, such as those of the explicit memory system we discussed in Chapter 8, may be present in species closely related to ours (Moscovitch, 1995). Studies looking at the behaviour of animals viewing mirror images suggest that some primates may have a concept of self-awareness (see Boysen and Himes, 1999, for a review).

Could a computer ever be conscious? In principle, I do not see any reason to reject this possibility. I think most people would admit that alien species from another planetary system could be conscious. Their brains would be different from ours, so the design of our brain is not the only one capable of consciousness. Perhaps, then, the thought of a conscious computer is not far-fetched, either. The computer would have to possess devices that enabled it to perceive events in its environment, think about these events, remember them, and so on. It would also have to communicate symbolically with us (or with other computers), describing its perceptions, thoughts, and memories. Furthermore, when we described our own mental events, our words would have to evoke thoughts and perceptions in the computer, just as they do in the brain of a human. In an abstract sense, at least, many of the functions of computers can serve as metaphors for self-awareness. (Pinker, 1997, provides some good examples.)

## Consciousness and the Control of Behaviour

In the past, psychologists have found fault with using consciousness to explain behaviour. Many found it pointless to explain something that we could observe (behaviour) in terms of something that we could not (consciousness). However, this view has lately been reconsidered, largely because of the techniques of brain study I have described in earlier chapters. Now, psychologists are more willing to address some of the deeper issues that figured in the discipline's early history.

In Chapter 1, we discussed René Descartes's view of human nature. Descartes believed that human actions were controlled by a non-material mind. Although his dualism is not a productive way of explaining behaviour, his idea that our conscious thoughts control our movements seems like common sense. But is it?

William James proposed a contrasting idea. As you will see in Chapter 13, he suggested that our emotional awareness comes after a reaction. James wrote: "We feel sorry because we cry, angry because we strike, afraid because we tremble" (James, 1890, p. 449). James was speaking of emotion, but his theory is an alternative way of thinking about consciousness.

Recent evidence from cognitive psychology and neuropsychology provides a way of thinking about the issue of conscious control of behaviour. Some of this evidence uses the phenomenon of visual illusions that was discussed in Chapter 6. For example, consider the two crayons in **Figure 9•1**. Although they are both the same size, the horizontal crayon tends to look shorter—a visual illusion known as the "top hat illusion" because it is often demonstrated using judgments about the crown versus brim of a hat. Suppose, now, that I ask you to pick up each crayon by grasping the ends. Would you reach for the horizontal crayon with your fingers closer together?

Goodale and his colleagues have evidence that our actions are little affected by such visual illusions. In one experiment, Ganel and Goodale (2003) compared perceptual judgments of object shape with the ability to pick up the object. They simply showed people a wooden block on a table and asked them whether the block was wide or narrow. They then replaced the block with another and again asked for a judgment of width; this trial was repeated several times. It is easy to judge width under these conditions if the blocks all have the same length. However, if the blocks vary in length, the task is more difficult. Shape, in other words, is holistic, in the sense meant by the Gestaltists discussed in Chapter 6. However, when Ganel and Goodale asked the participants of their study to grasp the blocks across the middle, their grasping action was not affected by variation in length.

**FIGURE 9•1** The "top hat illusion" depicted with naturalistic objects. The two crayons are the same lengths. However, the vertically positioned crayon looks longer.

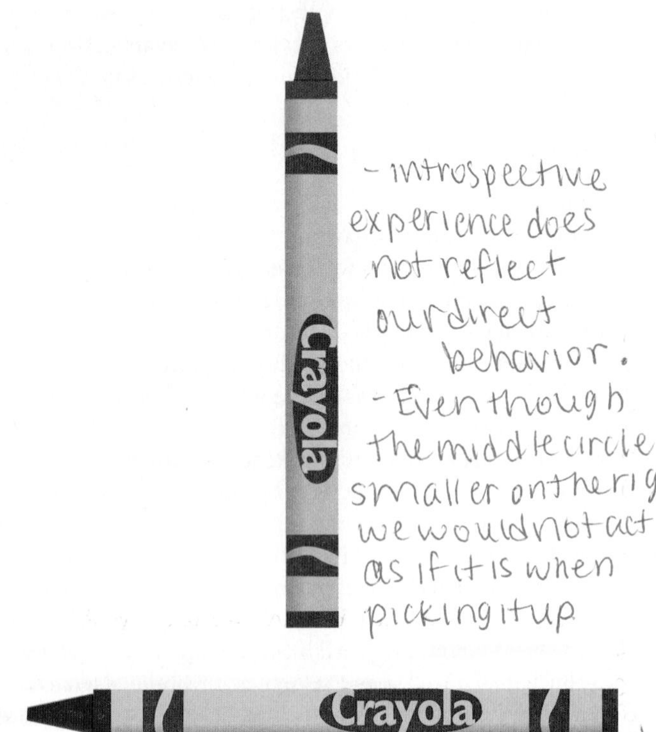


**FIGURE 9•2** The Ebbinghaus illusion. The circles in the centre of each array are of equal sizes.

*(Adapted from Haffenden, A. M., Schiff, K. C., & Goodale, M. A. (2001). The dissociation between perception and action in the Ebbinghaus illusion: Non illusory effects of pictorial cues on grasp.* Current Biology, 11, *177–181, portion of Figure 1. Reprinted with permission.)*

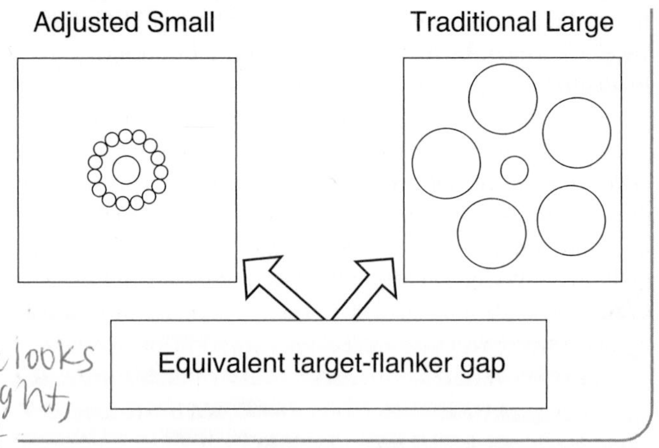


Our perceptual awareness of objects, then, may be based on a different visual system than the one we use for actions. For example, look at **Figure 9•2**, which shows an effect known as the Ebbinghaus illusion. The central circle on the left looks larger than the one on the right, because our perception reacts to differences in relative size. However, if these circles were objects (think of a quarter surrounded by pennies or by loonies) and you were to reach for the centre, your behaviour would be unaffected by the difference in relative size: The distance between your thumb and index finger, for example, would not be different if you reached for the object on the right rather than the one on the left (Haffenden, Schiff, & Goodale, 2001). Our introspective experiences might tell us that the two circles are different, but our behaviour would reflect otherwise.

If our perceptual awareness differs from our actions, then what does this say about consciousness and behaviour? When you reach for the coffee cup on your desk, is your action controlled by your conscious thoughts of picking it up? Certainly, the thought and the action go together. But remember the lesson from Chapter 2: Correlation does not necessarily imply causation. It could be that the conscious thought and the action are both caused by a third action of the brain (Wegner, 2003).

Some of the brain recording techniques discussed in Chapter 4 may provide insight into this possibility. In a set of experiments performed in 1983, Libet and his colleagues asked people to make a hand motion while watching a rapidly moving clock hand. They were to report where the clock hand was at the time they became aware of an intention to move. Their reports indicated that they experienced awareness of the intention about three-tenths of a second before the motion. However, Libet also measured the "readiness potential," the electrical brain activity of the motor cortex prior to the movement. This potential occurred about seven-tenths of a second before the motion—even earlier than the intention. The brain seemed to be starting the movement before there was awareness of "willing" the motion. Libet (2002) describes some of his interpretation of these observations.

There is considerable controversy over what these observations mean. Much of it concerns how to interpret the readiness potential. Recall that it precedes a person's awareness of the intention to act. Does it reflect the brain's "decision" to initiate a movement? Haggard and Eimer (1999) reasoned that if the readiness potential was the cause of movement, it should show covariation in time with awareness. They asked the participants in their study to move either their left hands or their right hands on a trial, and to report when they were aware of the intention to move. Haggard and Eimer looked at those occasions in which the report of awareness was "late" (that is, closer in time to the actual movement) to see if the readiness potential was also late. It was not. However, they also looked at another brain activity, the "lateralized readiness potential." Remember from Chapter 4 that motor control of the body is contralateral, with the left motor cortex controlling the right side of the body; the lateralized readiness potential measures activity specific to the side where the movement occurs. This potential did covary with the report of awareness. When awareness was late, the lateralized readiness potential was also late; when awareness was early, the potential occurred earlier.

So the lateralized readiness potential may reflect brain activity that leads to awareness about action. But it is specific to the side of the body that moves, which presumably means that it must follow a more general decision to make any movement. It may be only a part of a sequence of brain activity leading up to conscious awareness. To explore this sequence further, Haggard, Clark, and Kalogeras (2002) looked at awareness of both voluntary and involuntary movements. It is possible to induce muscle twitches by magnetic impulses delivered through the surface of the scalp. Haggard and his colleagues used this technique to produce involuntary movements of the hand and compared trials with stimulation to those in which a participant moved a hand voluntarily. As in the Libet experiment, each person watched a clock hand spinning around a dial and reported where the hand was when he or she felt either the intention to move or the involuntary movement produced by stimulation. On some trials, called "operant" trials, a tone came a quarter of a second after a movement and the person was asked to report the time of the tone.

An interesting pattern occurred. On the operant trials, reported times of voluntary movement were late, and reported times of the following tone were early. This was opposite to the involuntary trials, where the reported time of the movement was early and the reported time of the tone was late. In other words, people's subjective experience of the sequence was that, on voluntary trials, the movement and the tone were close together. On involuntary trials, the perception was that they were further apart. Our brain, therefore, must "bind together" the experience of voluntary movement with its external consequences. Perhaps this binding process helps us recognize those external events that are the consequences of our behaviours.

Obhi (2007) provides a clue as to the kind of information that might be used. In Obhi's experiment, participants rested their index fingers above one of the keys on a computer keyboard. On some trials, the experimenter pressed the finger onto the key, either softly, or more forcefully. On other trials, the participant pressed the key without assistance—either softly or forcefully. Using the rotating clock procedure, participants were asked after each trial when the keypress movement had started. In general, they reported that the movement had occurred earlier than it really had. Whether it was made actively or passively made no difference in the amount of this error. However, the amount of error was less for the forceful movements. Consequently, it seems as if awareness of the movement, even when it was intentional, was based on sensory feedback from the finger. This is in line with James's notion that a large part of our subjective experience arises with sensations from the body.

Perhaps you've noticed that this discussion is somewhat different from others. Consciousness is a difficult topic for scientific research, since the underlying behaviour is not directly observable. Perhaps we will not be able to answer the question of whether conscious thought controls behaviour. But the techniques of neuroscience have certainly advanced our understanding of the way in which brain activity is linked to our verbal reports (Rees, 2001). The result may help us understand cases in which consciousness departs from our normal experiences—for example, in the case of hallucinations and psychological disorders (Rees, Kreiman, & Koch, 2002).

## Interim Summary

### Consciousness as a Social Phenomenon

Consciousness, as it is defined here, can be viewed as a by-product of our ability to communicate symbolically by using words or other signs. Its physiological basis is the activity of language mechanisms of the brain. The private use of language (thinking to oneself) is clearly conscious. Private nonverbal processes are conscious if we can describe them—that is, if their activities are available to the neural mechanisms of language. In the same way, we are conscious of *external* events only if we can think (and verbalize) about our perceptions of them. These perceptions may be different from the actions we take to interact with the external events. Even our awareness of "voluntary" movements may reflect a by-product of other brain activities that initiate behaviour.

This view of human self-awareness is only one of several, and it may finally be proved wrong. However, it does help present a unified picture of a variety of phenomena related to consciousness. Its primary value is that it relates a private and mysterious phenomenon to a set of behaviours that can be observed and studied.

**QUESTIONS TO CONSIDER**

1. What do you think about the possibility that members of other species may be conscious? What evidence would you look for to answer this question?
2. If my thesis is correct, babies acquire consciousness as they acquire language. Do you think this conclusion is somehow related to the fact that we cannot remember what happened to us when we were very young?
3. What would happen if a person were raised in isolation and never came in contact with (or communicated with) another person? That person would not be able to talk. What would that person's mental life be like? Would he or she be conscious?

# Selective Attention

We do not become conscious of all of the stimuli detected by our sensory organs. For example, if an angler is watching a large trout circling underneath an artificial fly she has gently cast on the water, she probably will not notice the chirping of birds in the woods behind her or the temperature of the water surrounding her legs or the floating twigs drifting by with the current. Her attention is completely devoted to the behaviour of the fish, and she is poised to respond with the appropriate movements of her fly rod if the fish takes the bait. The process that controls our awareness of particular categories of events in the environment is called **selective attention.**

As we saw in Chapter 8, sensory memory receives more information than it can transfer into short-term (working) memory. For example, Sperling (1960) found that although people could remember only about four or five of the nine letters he flashed on the screen if they tried to remember them all, they could *direct their attention* to any of the three lines of letters contained in sensory memory and identify them with perfect accuracy. The topic of Chapter 8 was memory; that chapter discussed the nature of sensory memory and the fate of information that entered short-term memory. In this chapter, we will look at the nature of the process of attention and the fate of information that does not enter short-term memory.

The process of selective attention determines which events we become conscious of. Attention may be controlled automatically, as when an intense stimulus (such as a loud sound) captures our attention. It may be controlled by instructions ("Pay attention to that one over there!"). Or it may be controlled by the demands of the particular task we are performing. (For example, when we are driving a car, we pay special attention to other cars, pedestrians, road signs, and so on.) Attention to visual events in particular tends to act like a spotlight, or perhaps a zoom lens, that highlights the events within some spatially contained area (McCormick, Klein, & Johnston, 1998). Our attentional mechanisms serve to enhance our responsiveness to certain stimuli and to tune out irrelevant information.

Attention plays an important role in memory. By exerting control over the information that reaches short-term memory, it determines what information ultimately becomes stored in explicit long-term memory. But the storage of information in *implicit memory* does not require conscious attention. Not all of the information we do not pay attention to is lost.

Why does selective attention exist? Why do we not simply process *all* of the information that is being gathered by our sensory receptors—after all, it sometimes happens that we miss something important because our attention is occupied elsewhere. According to Broadbent (1958), the answer is that the brain mechanisms responsible for conscious processing of this information have a limited capacity. There is only so much information that these mechanisms can handle at one particular moment. Thus, we need some system to serve as a gatekeeper, controlling the flow of information to this system. The nature of this gatekeeper—selective attention—is still the subject of ongoing research.

**selective attention** The process that controls our awareness of, and readiness to respond to, particular categories of stimuli or stimuli in a particular location.
**dichotic listening** A task that requires a person to listen to one of two different messages being presented simultaneously, one to each ear, through headphones.
**shadowing** The act of continuously repeating verbal material as soon as it is heard.

## Auditory Information

The first experiments that investigated the nature of attention took advantage of the fact that we have two ears. Cherry (1953) devised a test of selective attention called **dichotic listening**, a task that requires a person to listen to one of two messages presented simultaneously, one to each ear. (*Dichotic* means "divided into two parts.") He placed headphones on his participants and presented recordings of different spoken messages to each ear. He asked the participants to **shadow** the message presented to one ear—to continuously repeat back what that voice was saying. Shadowing ensured that they would pay attention to only that message.

What happened to the information that entered the unattended ear? In general, it appeared to be lost. When questioned about what that ear had heard, participants responded that they had heard something, but they could not say what it was. Even if the voice presented to the unshadowed ear began to talk in a foreign language, they did not notice the change.

These results suggest that a channel of sensory input (in this case, one ear) can simply be turned off. Perhaps neurons in the auditory system that detect sound from the unattended ear are inhibited so that they cannot respond to sounds presented to that ear. (See **Figure 9•3(a)**.)

The story is not so simple. Other evidence shows that selective attention is not achieved by simply closing a sensory channel. Some information, by its very nature, can break through into consciousness. For example, if a person's name is presented to the unattended ear, he or she will very likely hear it and remember it later (Moray, 1959). Or if the message presented to the unattended ear contains sexually explicit words, people tend to notice them immediately (Nielsen & Sarason, 1981). The fact that some kinds of information presented to the unattended ear can grab our attention indicates that even unattended information undergoes some verbal analysis. If the unattended information is "filtered out" at some level, this filtration appears to occur *after* the sounds are identified as words. (See **Figure 9•3(b)**.)

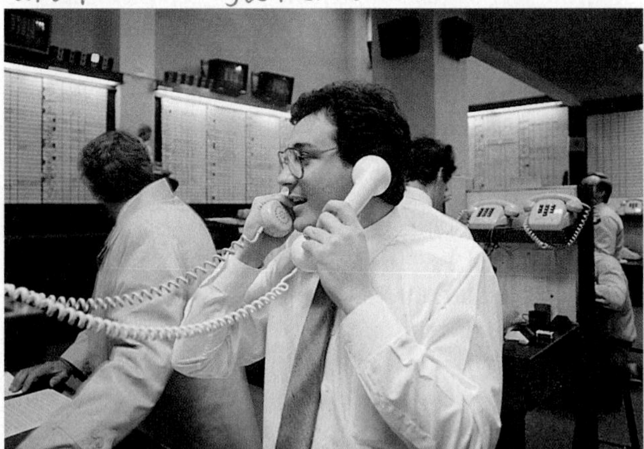

▲ *This stock exchange broker must keep track of several different conversations and selectively attend to each of them, one after the other.*

**FIGURE 9•3** Models of selective attention in the dichotic listening task. (a) Filtering of unattended sensory information immediately after it is received by the sensory receptors. This model cannot explain the fact that some information presented to the unattended ear enters consciousness. (b) Filtering of unattended sensory information after some preliminary analysis.

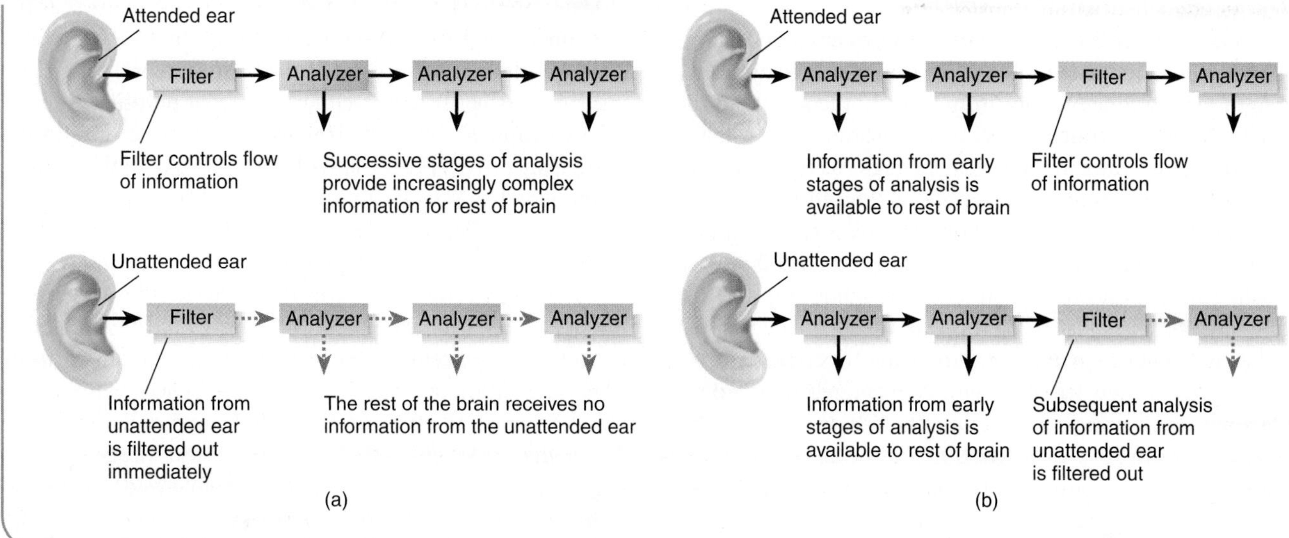


McKay (1973) showed that information presented to the unattended ear can influence verbal processing even when the listener is not conscious of this information. In the attended ear, participants heard sentences such as the following:

They threw stones toward the bank yesterday.

While this sentence was being presented, the participants heard the word *river* or *money* in the unattended ear. Later, they were asked which of the following sentences they had heard:

They threw stones toward the side of the river yesterday.

They threw stones toward the savings and loan association yesterday.

Of course, the participants had heard neither of these sentences. McKay found that the participants' choices were determined by whether the word *river* or *money* was presented to the unattended ear. They did not specifically recall hearing the words presented to the unattended ear, but obviously these words had affected their perception of the meaning of the word *bank*.

Besides being able to notice and remember some characteristics of information received by the unattended sensory channel, we are able to store information temporarily as it comes in. No doubt you have had the following sort of experience. You are intently reading or thinking about something, when you become aware that someone has asked you a question. You look up and say, "What?" but then answer the question before the other person has had a chance to repeat it. You first became aware that you had just been asked a question, but you did not know what had been asked. However, when you thought for a moment, you remembered what the question was—you heard it again in your mind's ear, so to speak. The information, held in temporary storage, was made accessible to your verbal system.

Treisman (1960) showed that people can follow a message that is being shadowed even if it switches from one ear to the other. Suppose a person is shadowing a message presented to the left ear, while the message to the right ear is unshadowed. (See **Figure 9•4**.) In the example given in Figure 9.4, the person will probably say "crept out of the swamp" and not "crept out of flowers." Apparently, the switch occurs when the message begins to make no sense. However, by the time the person realizes that "crept out of flowers" makes no sense, the rest of the message, "the swamp," has already been presented to the right ear. Because the person is able to continue

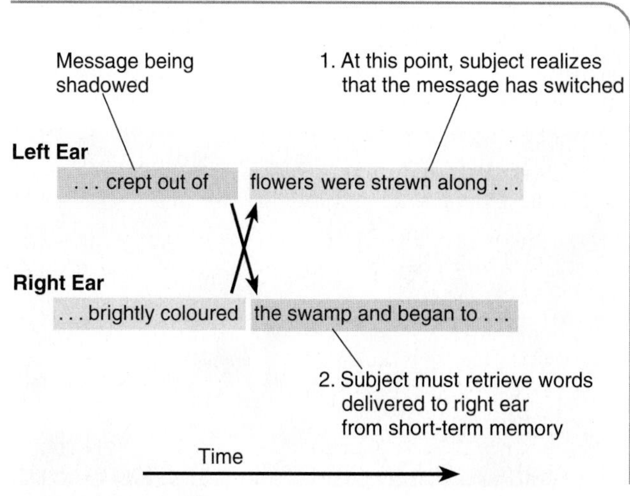


**FIGURE 9•4** Shadowing a message that switches ears. When the message switches, the person must retrieve some words from memory that were heard by the unattended ear.

eg → reading and looking up to some one waiting for an answer to a question — you ask 'what' but answer the question before they repeat b/c it is accessed in temporary storage the message without missing any words, he or she must be able to retrieve some words from memory. Thus, even though an unshadowed message cannot be remembered later, it produces some trace that can be retrieved if attention is directed to it soon after the words are presented.

Selective attention to auditory messages has practical significance outside the laboratory. For example, sometimes we have to sort out one message from several others without the benefit of such a distinct cue; we seldom hear one voice in one ear and another voice in the other. We might be trying to converse with one person while we are in a room with several other people who are carrying on their own conversations. Even in a situation like the one shown in **Figure 9•5** we can usually sort out one voice from another—an example of the *cocktail-party phenomenon.* In this case, we are trying to listen to the person opposite us and to ignore the cross-conversation of the people to our left and right. Our ears receive a jumble of sounds, but we are able to pick out the ones we want, stringing them together into a meaningful message and ignoring the rest. This task takes some effort; following one person's conversation in such circumstances is more difficult when what he or she is saying is not very interesting. If we overhear a few words of another conversation that seems more interesting, it is hard to strain out the cross-conversation.

## Visual Information

More recent experiments have studied the nature of visual attention. These experiments have shown that we can successfully attend to the *location* of the information, to the *nature* of the information (revealed by its physical features, such as form or colour), and to the *meaningfulness* of the information (its relevance to our interpretation of what we're seeing).

**Location of the Information** Let us consider location first. Sperling's studies on sensory memory were probably the first to demonstrate the role of attention in selectively transferring visual information into verbal short-term memory (or, for our purposes, into consciousness). Other psychologists have studied this phenomenon in more detail. For example, Posner, Snyder, and Davidson (1980) had people watch a computer-controlled video display screen. A small mark in the centre of the screen served as a fixation point for the participants' gaze. They were shown a warning stimulus near the fixation point followed by a target stimulus—a letter displayed to the left or the right of the fixation point. The warning stimulus consisted of either an arrow pointing right or left or simply a plus sign. The arrows served as cues to the participants to expect the letter to occur either to the right or to the left. The plus sign served as a neutral stimulus, containing no spatial information. The participants' task was to press a button as soon as they detected the letter.

Eighty percent of the time, the arrow accurately pointed toward the location in which the letter would be presented. However, 20 percent of the time, the arrow pointed *away from* the location in which it would occur. The advance warning clearly had an effect on the participants' response times: When they were correctly informed of the location of the letter, they responded faster; when they were incorrectly informed, they responded more slowly. (See **Figure 9•6**.)

This study shows that selective attention can affect the detection of visual stimuli: If a stimulus occurs where we expect it, we perceive it more quickly; if it occurs where we do *not* expect it, we perceive it more slowly. Thus, people can follow instructions to direct their attention to particular locations in the visual field. Because the participants' gaze remained fixed on the centre of the screen in this study, this movement of attention was independent of eye movement. How does this focusing of attention work neurologically? The most likely explanation seems to be that neural circuits that detect a particular kind of stimulus are somehow sensitized, so that they can more easily detect that stimulus. In this case,

FIGURE 9•5 The cocktail-party phenomenon. We can follow a particular conversation even when other conversations are going on around us.

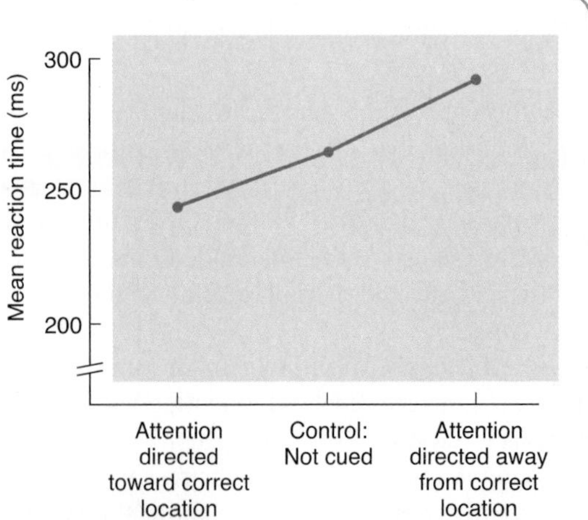


FIGURE 9•6 Location as a cue for selective attention. Mean reaction time, in response to a letter displayed on a screen after participants received a cue directing attention toward the location in which the letter appears, was less than when no cue or an incorrect cue was received.
*(Based on data from Posner, Snyder, & Davidson (1980).)*

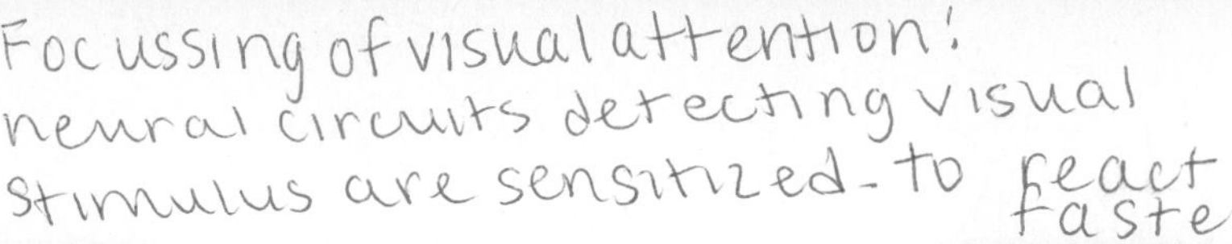



**FIGURE 9•7** Drawings of the scenes from the videotapes in Neisser and Becklen's study. (a) The hand game. (b) The basketball game. (c) The two games superimposed.

*(From Neisser, U., & Becklen, R. (1975).* Cognitive Psychology, 7, *480–494. Reprinted with permission.)*

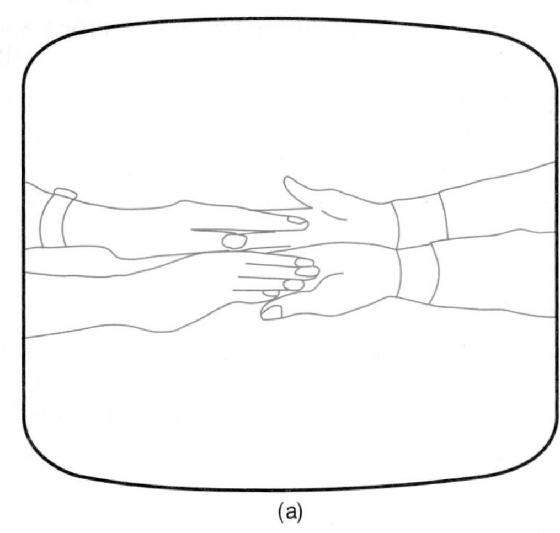

(a)

(b)

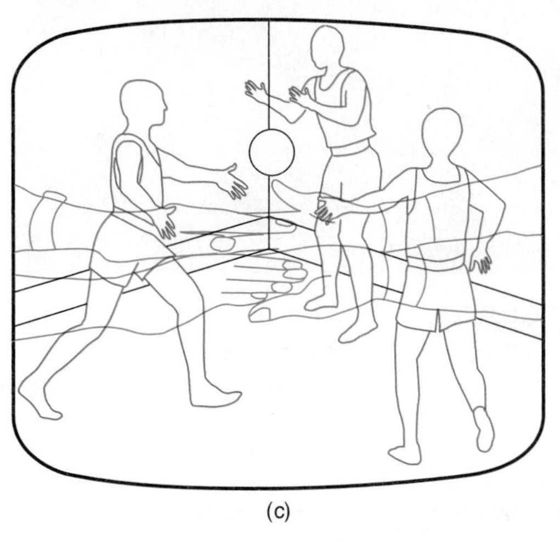

(c)

**FIGURE 9•8** First image in change blindness test. Study this picture for about 10 seconds.

*(Figure 1 from Pearson, P. M., & Schaefer, E. G. (2005). Toupee or not toupee? The role of instructional set, centrality, and relevance in change blindness.* Visual Cognition, 12, *1528–1543.)*

the mechanism of selective attention sensitized the neural circuits that detect visual stimuli in a particular region.

**The Nature of the Information** The second dimension of visual attention is the nature of the object being attended to (Desimone & Duncan, 1995; Vecera & Farah, 1994). Sometimes, two events happen in close proximity, but we can watch one of them while ignoring the other. For example, Neisser and Becklen (1975) showed people a videotape that presented a situation similar to the one confronted by a person trying to listen to the voice of one person at a cocktail party. The videotape contained two different actions presented one on top of the other: a basketball game and a hand game, in which people try to slap their opponents' hands, which are resting on top of theirs. The participants could easily follow one scene and remember what had happened in it; however, they could not attend simultaneously to both scenes. (See **Figure 9•7**.)

**The Meaningfulness of the Information** Simons (2000) makes the general point that while our visual experience is rich with information, our ability to represent it in memory may be limited. We saw such limitations in the case of memory in Chapter 8. Perhaps when we focus our attention on a part of the external world, our consciousness relies on the stability of the rest of it. After all, people don't spontaneously change hair colour or the clothes they're wearing just because we look away. Would we notice it if they did?

Surprisingly, the answer seems to be no under some circumstances. If visual displays are artificially changed during a saccade or other disruption, **change blindness** often results: People often fail to notice significant changes in the picture (O'Regan, Rensink, & Clark, 1999; Rensink, 2002). For example, look at the scene in **Figure 9•8**. Spend about 10 seconds

**change blindness** Failure to detect a change when vision is interrupted by a saccade or an artificially produced obstruction.

**FIGURE 9•9** How does this photograph differ from Figure 9.8?

*(Figure 1 from Pearson, P. M., & Schaefer, E. G. (2005). Toupee or not toupee? The role of instructional set, centrality, and relevance in change blindness.* Visual Cognition, 12, *1528–1543.)*

examining it. Now, turn the page and look at **Figure 9•9**. Can you name the difference between the two? (It's mentioned in the next paragraph.) If you don't spot it, try flipping back and forth between the two, spending 10 seconds on each view. That way, you can compare your performance to a friend's (should you wish to see if he or she is better than you at this type of task).

Change blindness seems to reflect our inability to remember a scene in its entirety. When we fail to attend to a feature, we don't encode it and can't recognize when it changes. So, for example, if you didn't attend to the fact that the people in Figure 9.8 were walking in a crosswalk, you probably wouldn't recognize that the crosswalk has moved in Figure 9.9. The presence or absence of change blindness can therefore tell us something about the features that draw our attention.

Pearson and Schaefer (2005) employed this logic and explored the role of meaningfulness in change blindness. They used photographs like the one in Figure 9.8, which depicted a scene as it might be seen by a person driving a car. With a graphics editing program, they then changed one feature. Some of these features were relevant to driving while others were not. When they asked people to spot the difference between the original photograph and the changed version, pictures in which the driving-relevant features changed were spotted more quickly than those in which the driving-irrelevant feature changed. In other words, a feature that is more meaningful to the overall scene is attended to. Masuda and Nisbett (2006) have found that cultural background can also affect attention in a change blindness task. Japanese people were more sensitive than Americans to changes in the part of a picture that describes context, suggesting that they attend to more holistic aspects of a scene.

Simons and Levin (1998) showed how powerful the effect of meaningfulness may be. If someone stopped and asked you for directions, you'd probably be attending to the question at hand, and not necessarily to the physical appearance of the person. For this kind of casual encounter on the street, physical appearance is usually not important. Simons and Levin showed that people who were giving a construction worker directions failed to notice when the worker himself changed during a brief distraction. What happens to information that is not attended to? Recent evidence suggests that the visual system is prone to surprising cases of **inattentional blindness**, a failure to perceive an event when attention is diverted elsewhere. We've probably all had the experience of attending an event like a hockey game and being so engrossed in the action that we "looked right through" and failed to notice a good friend across the aisle. But suppose you were watching a basketball game and a woman in a gorilla suit walked right through the action, stopping in the middle of it to pound her chest? (See **Figure 9•10**.) You probably feel you would definitely notice that, right? Remarkably, half of the people who observed this action in a film sequence designed by Simons and Chabris (1999) failed to notice the gorilla. This was despite the fact that the unusual event occurred in

**inattentional blindness** Failure to perceive an event when attention is diverted elsewhere.

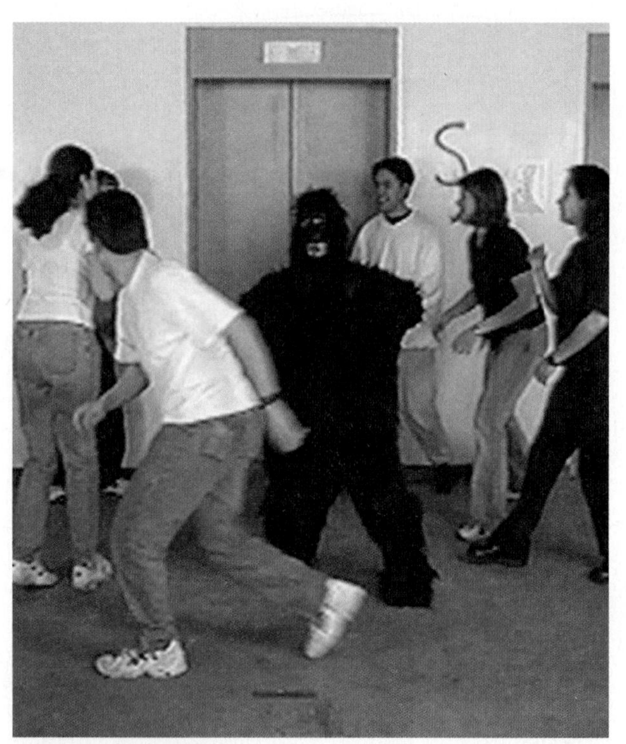

**FIGURE 9•10** A frame from the film constructed by Simons and Chabris for their study of inattentional blindness. Observers were asked to watch a basketball game being played by two teams, and to count the passes between members of either the white or black team. As they watched, a woman wearing a gorilla suit walked in from the right, paused in the middle of the game facing the camera, and then walked out to the left. Half of the observers failed to notice this unusual event. To learn more about the "gorilla" study or to view the original video, go to http://viscog/beckman.uiuc.edu/media/carlson.html.

*(From Simons, D. J., & Chabris, C. F. (1999). Gorillas in our midst: Sustained inattentional blindness for dynamic events.* Perception, 28, *1059–1074, Figure 3. Reprinted with permission.)*

the centre of the action. Interestingly, the unusual nature of the event seemed to make it more likely to be missed: When a game was interrupted by a woman carrying an umbrella, more people noticed her. That suggests it is the similarity of the unexpected event with the things we attend to that determines inattentional blindness (Koivisto & Revonsuo, 2008).

## Brain Mechanisms of Selective Attention

As we saw, one possible explanation for selective attention is that some components of the brain's sensory system are temporarily sensitized, which enhances their ability to detect particular categories of stimuli. For example, if a person were watching for changes in shapes, colours, or movements (that is, if the person's attention were focused on one of these attributes), we might expect to see increased activity in the portions of the visual cortex devoted to the analysis of shapes, colours, or movements.

This result is exactly what Corbetta and colleagues (1991) found. These investigators had people look at a computerized display containing 30 coloured rectangles, which could change in shape, colour, or speed of movement. The participants were asked to say whether they detected a change. On some trials, they were told to pay attention only to one attribute: shape, colour, or speed of movement. The stimuli were counterbalanced so that the same set of displays was presented during each condition. Thus, the only difference between the conditions was the type of stimulus change the participants were watching for.

The investigators used a PET scanner to measure brain activity while these people were watching the display. They found that paying attention to shape, colour, or speed of movement caused activation of different regions of the visual association cortex. The locations corresponded almost precisely to the regions other studies have shown to be activated by shapes, colours, or movements. Thus, selective attention toward different attributes of visual stimuli is accompanied by activation of the appropriate regions of the visual association cortex.

Luck, Chelazzi, Hillyard, and Desimone (1993) obtained similar results in a study using monkeys. They recorded the activity of single neurons in the visual association cortex. When a cue indicated that the monkey should be watching for a stimulus to be presented in a particular location, neurons that received input from the appropriate part of the visual field began firing more rapidly, even before the stimulus was presented. These neurons seemed to be "primed" for detecting a stimulus in their part of the visual field.

## Interim Summary

### Selective Attention

As we saw in the first section of this chapter, consciousness can be analyzed as a social phenomenon derived through evolution of the brain mechanisms responsible for our ability to communicate with each other (and, in addition, with ourselves). However, because our verbal mechanisms can contain only a limited amount of information at one time, we cannot be conscious of all the events that take place in our environment. The process of selective attention determines which stimuli will be noticed and which will be ignored. The factors that control our attention include novelty, verbal instructions, and our own assessment of the significance of what we are perceiving.

Dichotic listening experiments show that what is received by the unattended ear is lost within a few seconds unless something causes us to take heed of it; after those few seconds, we cannot say what that ear heard. Possibly because visual stimulation is so complex, distractions can produce inattentional blindness to certain kinds of visual experiences.

Studies using visually presented information indicate that attention can focus on location, on form or other physical attribute, and on the relevance of the information. We can pay attention to particular objects or to stimuli that occur in a particular place. Change blindness studies show that we are more sensitive to relevant stimuli than to irrelevant ones, suggesting that meaningfulness is an important factor in attention. Brain imaging techniques have found that when people pay attention to particular characteristics of visual stimuli, the activity of particular regions of the brain is enhanced.

**QUESTIONS TO CONSIDER**

1. Have you ever had an experience similar to the one described in this section, in which someone asks you a question that you weren't paying attention to, and then, before it can be repeated, you realize what it was? How long do you think the unattended information lasts before it is eventually lost? Can you think of an experiment that would permit you to find out?
2. Let's reconsider the cocktail-party phenomenon. Suppose that someone is carrying on a conversation and then happens to overhear a word or two from another conversation that seems much more interesting than the present one. Wanting to be polite, the person tries to ignore the other conversation, but finds it difficult. Should we regard this example as a failure of the person's attentional mechanism, or is it actually useful that we usually don't become so absorbed in one thing that we miss out on potentially interesting information?
3. Why do we feel that paying attention to something not very interesting takes some effort—that it requires work? And if we concentrate on something for a long time, we feel tired. Where does this tiredness take place? Do some circuits of neurons become "weary"? Why, then, do we not become tired when we are concentrating just as hard on something that interests us?

# Consciousness and the Brain

As we have already seen, brain damage can alter human consciousness. For example, Chapter 8 described the phenomenon of anterograde amnesia, caused by brain damage—particularly, to the hippocampus. Although people with this defect cannot form new verbal memories, they can learn some kinds of tasks. However, they remain unaware that they have learned something, even when their behaviour indicates that they have. The brain damage does not prevent all kinds of learning, but it does prevent conscious awareness of what has been learned.

If human consciousness is related to speech, then it is probably related to the brain mechanisms that control comprehension and production of speech. This hypothesis suggests that for us to be aware of a piece of information, the information must be transmitted to neural circuits in the brain responsible for our communicative behaviour. Several reports of cases of human brain damage support this suggestion.

## Isolation Aphasia: A Case of Global Unawareness

Geschwind, Quadfasel, and Segarra (1968) described the case of a woman who had suffered severe brain damage from inhaling carbon monoxide from a faulty water heater. The damage spared the primary auditory cortex, the speech areas of the brain, and the connections between these areas. However, the damage destroyed large parts of the visual association cortex and isolated the speech mechanisms from other parts of the brain. In fact, the syndrome they reported is referred to as **isolation aphasia**, a language disturbance that includes an inability to comprehend speech or to produce meaningful speech, but also an ability to repeat speech and to learn new sequences of words. Thus, although the woman's speech mechanisms could receive auditory input and could control the muscles used for speech, they received no information from the other senses or from the neural circuits that contain memories concerning past experiences and the meanings of words.

The woman remained in the hospital for nine years, until she died. During this time, she made few movements except with her eyes, which were able to follow moving objects. She gave no evidence of recognizing objects or people in her environment. She did not spontaneously say anything, answer questions, or give any signs that she understood what other people said to her. By all available criteria, she was not conscious of anything that was going on. However, the woman could *repeat* words that were spoken to her. And if someone started a poem she knew, she would finish it. For example, if someone said, "Roses are red, violets are blue," she would respond, "Sugar is sweet, and so are you." She even learned new poems and songs and would sing along with the radio. Her case suggests that consciousness is not simply activity of the brain's speech mechanisms; it is activity prompted by information received from other parts of the brain concerning memories or events presently occurring in the environment.

## Visual Agnosia: Lack of Awareness of Visual Perceptions

The case I just described was of a woman who appeared to have completely lost her awareness of herself and her environment. In other instances, people have become unaware of particular kinds of information. For example, in the case of blindsight, people with a particular kind of brain damage can point to objects they cannot see—or rather, that they are not aware of seeing. Two colleagues and I studied a young man with a different kind of disconnection between perception and awareness. His brain had been damaged by an inflammation of the blood vessels and he consequently suffered from **visual agnosia**, the inability to recognize the identity of an object visually (Margolin, Friedrich, & Carlson, 1985). The man had great difficulty identifying common objects by sight. For example, he could not say what a hammer was by looking at it, but he quickly identified it when he was permitted to pick it up and feel it. He was not blind; he could walk around without bumping into things, and he had no trouble making visually guided movements to pick up an object that he wanted to identify. The simplest conclusion was that his disease had damaged the neural circuits responsible for visual perception.

However, the simplest conclusion was not the correct one. Although the patient had great difficulty visually recognizing objects or pictures of objects, he often made hand movements that appeared to be related to the object he could not identify. For example, when we showed him a picture of a pistol, he stared at it with a puzzled look, then shook his head and said that he couldn't tell what it was. While continuing to study the picture, he clenched his right hand into a fist and began making movements with his index finger. When we asked him what he was doing, he looked at his hand, made a few tentative movements with his finger, then raised his hand in the air and moved it forward each time he moved his finger. He was unmistakably miming the way a person holds and fires a pistol. "Oh!" he said. "It's a gun. No, a pistol." Clearly, he was not aware of what the picture was until he paid attention to what his hand was doing. On another occasion, he looked at a picture of a belt and said it was a pair of pants. We asked him to show us where the legs and other parts of the pants were. When he tried to do so, he became puzzled. His hands

**isolation aphasia** A language disturbance that includes an inability to comprehend speech or to produce meaningful speech without affecting the ability to repeat speech and to learn new sequences of words; caused by brain damage that isolates the brain's speech mechanisms from other parts of the brain.

**visual agnosia** The inability of a person who is not blind to recognize the identity of an object visually; caused by damage to the visual association cortex.

**FIGURE 9•11** Hypothetical exchanges of information within the brain of a patient with visual agnosia.

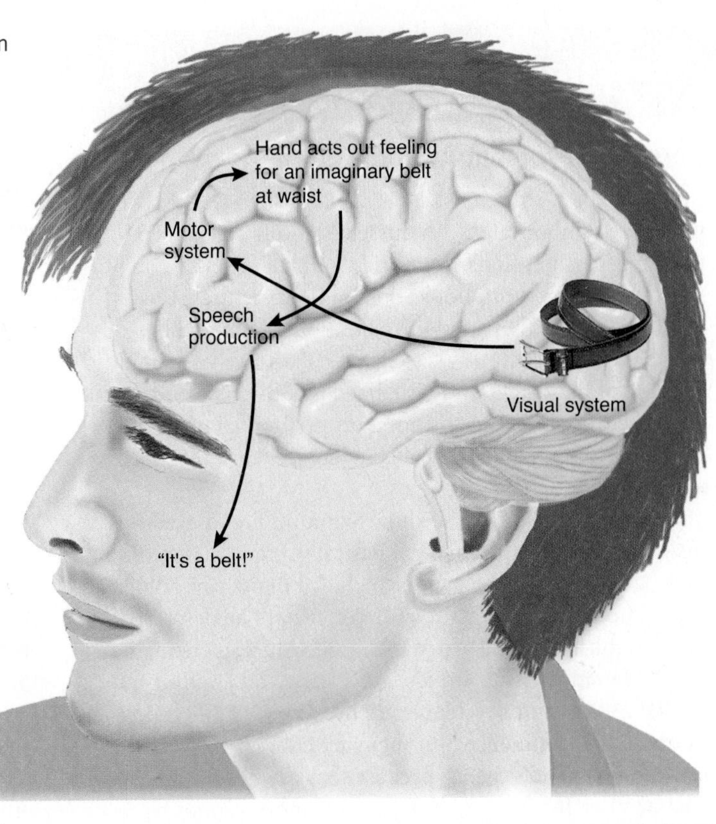


went to the place where his belt buckle would be (he was wearing hospital pyjamas) and moved as if he were feeling one. "No," he said. "It's not a pair of pants—it's a belt!"

The patient's visual system was not normal, yet it functioned better than we could infer from only his verbal behaviour. That is, his perceptions were much more accurate than his words indicated. The fact that he could mime the use of a pistol or feel an imaginary belt buckle with his hands indicated that his visual system worked well enough to initiate appropriate non-verbal behaviours, though not the appropriate words. Once he felt what he was doing, he could name the object. The process might involve steps such as those shown in **Figure 9•11**.

Although the patient had lost his ability to read, speech therapists were able to teach him to use finger spelling to read. He could not say what a particular letter was, but he could learn to make a particular hand movement when he saw it. After he had learned the finger-spelling alphabet used by deaf people, he could read slowly and laboriously by making hand movements for each letter and feeling the words that his hand was spelling out.

This case supports the conclusion that consciousness is synonymous with a person's ability to talk about his or her perceptions or memories. In this particular situation, disruption of the normal interchange between the visual perceptual system and the verbal system prevented the patient from being directly aware of his own visual perceptions. Instead, it was as if his hands talked to him, telling him what he had just seen.

## The Split-Brain Syndrome

One surgical procedure demonstrates dramatically how various brain functions can be disconnected from each other and from verbal mechanisms. It is used for people who have severe epilepsy that cannot be controlled by drugs. In these people, violent storms of neural activity begin in one hemisphere and are transmitted to the other by the corpus callosum, the large bundle of axons that connects corresponding parts of the cortex on one side of the brain with those on the other. Both sides of the brain then engage in wild neural firing and stimulate each other, causing an epileptic seizure. These seizures can occur many times each day, preventing the patient from leading a normal life. Neurosurgeons discovered that the **split-brain operation**—cutting the corpus callosum to disconnect the two cerebral hemispheres—greatly reduces the frequency of the epileptic seizures.

Sperry (1966) and Gazzaniga and his associates (Gazzaniga, 1970; Gazzaniga & LeDoux, 1978) have studied split-brain patients extensively. Normally, the cerebral cortexes of the left and right hemispheres exchange information through the corpus callosum. With one exception (described later), each hemisphere receives sensory information from

**split-brain operation** A surgical procedure that severs the corpus callosum, thus abolishing the direct connections between the cortex of the two cerebral hemispheres.

## Then and Now

### Perception without Awareness

In this chapter, consciousness is present when we can communicate symbolically with ourselves about our perceptions, needs, intentions, memories, and feelings. This ability was one of the assumptions adopted by structuralist psychologists when they used introspection as a method to describe mental structures (see Chapter 1). As we've seen in the case of blindsight and visual agnosia, this assumption is faulty because awareness is not a property of all parts of the brain. Perceptions can cause behaviours, even when we are not aware of them.

In Chapter 14, we'll see how Sigmund Freud used this insight to describe personality. Basically, Freud believed that the causal factors of behaviour included many psychological experiences that we are not aware of, factors he described as unconscious. In Freud's theory, an individual's personality is shaped by unconscious needs, memories, and emotions; special methods of psychiatry are necessary, said Freud, to examine their influence. But many psychologists reject the specifics of Freud's theory because they are not testable (see Chapter 14). If a particular need or memory cannot be communicated, it is difficult to use it as a causal factor in any meaningful way.

However, Freud's speculation might be approached in a different way: It is useful to ask what parts of the brain, or which of its activities, do not give rise to awareness even though they control behaviour in some other way. In this section, we'll consider the extent to which perception can occur without awareness.

The structuralist psychologists believed that the investigation of non-conscious psychological experience was a matter of training. Introspection was intended to be a rigorous method in which observers were trained to detect aspects of their subjective experiences and then describe them. However, the key limitation of introspection is that it is subjective. Consequently, there is no way to verify whether an introspective report truly corresponds to a person's state of awareness. Objective criteria are necessary.

One approach is to show, using the same stimulus, that a perceptual judgment produces an outcome different than one based on awareness (Tsuchiya & Adolphs, 2007). For example, suppose we play two tones with different pitches to a person. On some trials we play the high pitch, on others the low, and on still others, we play no tone at all. We lower their loudness to a level that makes it impossible for the person in the experiment to say with any accuracy when a tone was presented. Therefore, at that level of loudness, our person is not aware of the tone. However, on each trial we ask whether it was high or low. If our person could still accurately identify the pitch, we would have shown a degree of independence between awareness and perception.

Psychologists have looked for evidence of dissociation since the late 1800s and have found many cases in which it occurs (Merikle, Smilek, & Eastwood, 2001). The study described in the previous section by Cheesman and Merikle (1986) using primes is one such example; Cheesman and Merikle found a Stroop effect even when the prime was obscured by a mask that prevented its recognition. Hence, there was dissociation between awareness and perception. But in that experiment, as we saw, awareness of the prime did help people predict the colour of the patch they were about to see. So, the Stroop effect was not dependent on awareness, but the use of predictive information was.

With the development of brain scanning technology like fMRI (see Chapter 4) psychologists have begun to use this method to explore the relationship between awareness and perception at the level of different brain structures. Pessoa, Japee, Sturman, and Ungerleider (2006), for example, looked at the way images of people with fearful expressions would affect the amygdala. The amygdala is located in the temporal lobe, just in front of the hippocampus (refer to Figure 4.32 on page 122), and is a region of convergence between sensory systems and systems responsible for emotional responses. As we'll see in Chapter 13, the amygdala appears to be involved when we respond to stimuli that are associated with learned emotional reactions. Pessoa and colleagues looked at whether activity of the amygdala depended on awareness of an emotional stimulus.

They used a procedure similar to Cheesman and Merikle's, except that it involved faces. A picture of a person with a fearful, happy, or neutral expression was shown to participants for a short time (either 33 or 67 milliseconds) and then followed immediately by a face with a neutral expression. After viewing this second face, the participants were asked what kind of face was seen, and how confident they were about their answer (see **Figure 9•12**). The second, neutral, face was designed to interfere, or mask, the first face. Pessola and colleagues tested this masking using a signal detection analysis (see Chapter 5). They found that, for most people, the mask made the preceding face undetectable when it was presented for 33 milliseconds, but not when it was presented for 67 milliseconds. That is, these people were unaware of which face had been presented when it was a short presentation, but were aware when it was a longer one. The question is, would the amygdala respond to faces without awareness?

The answer was no. The fMRI response showed amygdala activity to fearful stimuli presented for 67 milliseconds, but not to fearful stimuli presented for 33 milliseconds. **Figure 9•13** shows the region tested and the difference between faces that people were aware of, and those that they were not aware of. In this case, the combination of signal detection analysis and brain scanning techniques showed that awareness of the fearful image and the amygdala's response were linked.

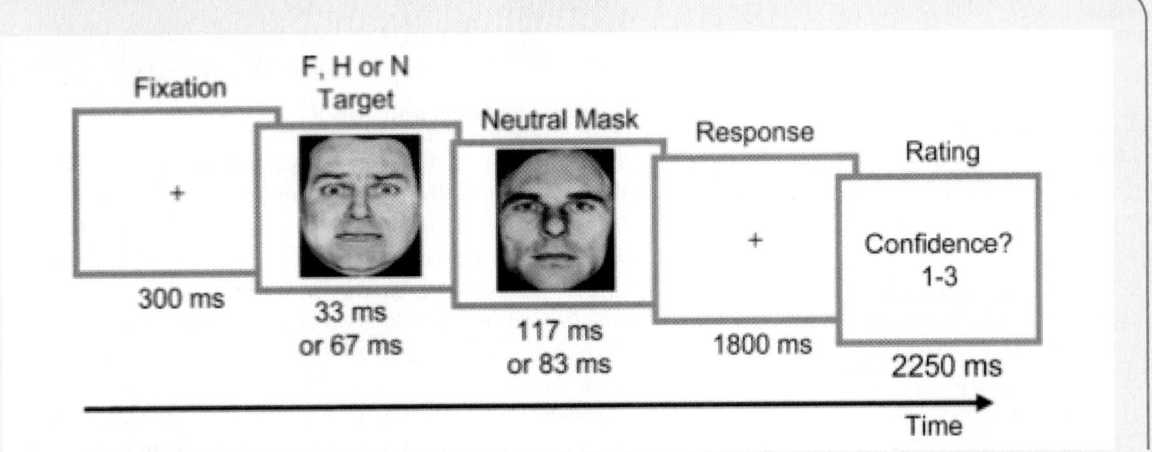


**FIGURE 9•12** The sequence of images in the Pessoa, Japee, Sturman, and Ungerleider (2006) study. The first face shown had a fearful, happy, or neutral expression. The second face shown always had a neutral expression.

*(Figure 1 from Pessoa, L., Japee, S., Sturman, D., & Ungerleider, L. G. (2006). Target visibility and visual awareness modulate amygdala responses to fearful faces.* Cerebral Cortex, 16, *366–375. Used by permission of Oxford University Press.)*

**FIGURE 9•13** Differences in amygdala activity when people see a fearful expression relative to when they see a neutral expression. When faces are presented for a duration that allows awareness of the face, the amygdala is active in both hemispheres (upper photograph). When faces are presented too briefly for awareness, there is no amygdala activity in either hemisphere.

*(Figure 3 of Pessoa, L., Japee, S., Sturman, D., & Ungerleider, L. G. (2006). Target visibility and visual awareness modulate amygdala responses to fearful faces.* Cerebral Cortex, 16, *366–375.)*

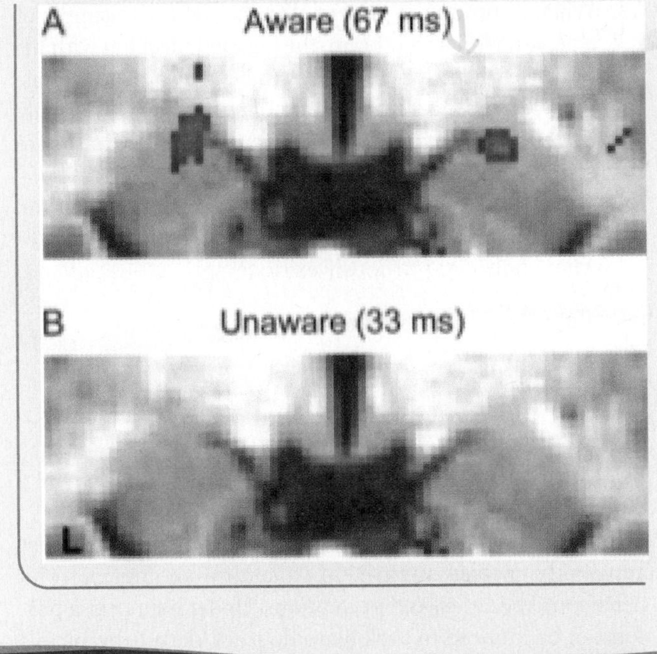


the opposite side of the body and controls muscle movements on that side. The corpus callosum permits these activities to be coordinated, so that each hemisphere knows what is going on in the other hemisphere. After the two hemispheres are disconnected, they operate independently; their sensory mechanisms, memories, and motor systems can no longer exchange information. The effects of these disconnections are not obvious to a casual observer, for the simple reason that only one hemisphere—in most people, the left—controls speech. The right hemisphere of an epileptic person with a split brain can understand speech reasonably well, but it is poor at reading and spelling. As well, because Broca's speech area is located in the left hemisphere, the right hemisphere is totally incapable of producing speech.

Because only one side of the brain can talk about what it is experiencing, a casual observer will not detect the independent operations of the right side of a split brain. Even the patient's left brain has to learn about the independent existence of the right brain. One of the first things that these patients say they notice after the operation is that their left hand seems to have a mind of its own. For example, patients may find themselves putting down a book held in the left hand, even if they are reading it with great interest. At other times, they surprise themselves by making obscene gestures with the left hand. Because the right hemisphere controls the movements of the left hand, these unexpected movements puzzle the left hemisphere, the side of the brain that controls speech.

One exception to the crossed representation of sensory information is the olfactory system. When a person sniffs a flower through the left nostril, only the left brain receives a sensation of the odour. Thus, if the right nostril of a patient with a split brain is closed and the left nostril is open, the patient will accurately identify odours verbally. If the odour enters the right nostril, the patient will say that he or she smells nothing. But, in fact, the right brain has perceived the odour and can identify it. This ability is demonstrated by an experiment in which the patient is told to reach for some objects

**FIGURE 9•14** Identification of an object by a person with a split brain in response to an olfactory stimulus.

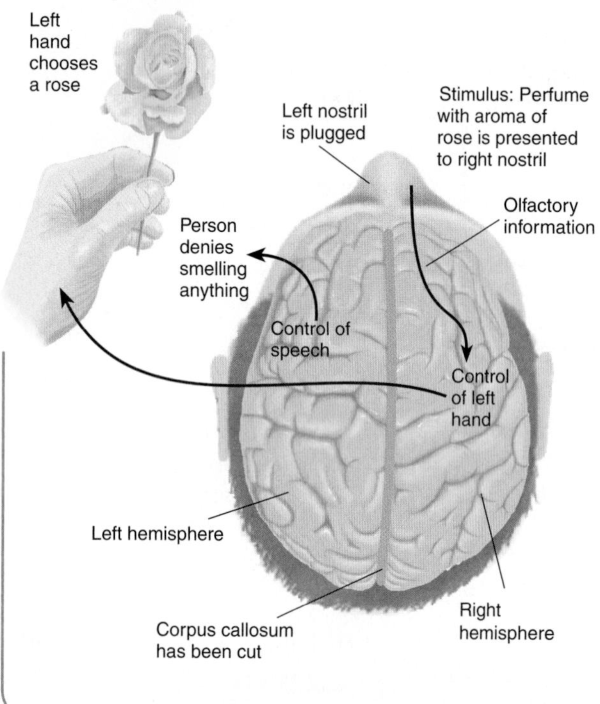
Left hand chooses a rose
Left nostril is plugged
Stimulus: Perfume with aroma of rose is presented to right nostril
Olfactory information
Person denies smelling anything
Control of speech
Control of left hand
Left hemisphere
Right hemisphere
Corpus callosum has been cut

hidden from view by a partition. If asked to use the left hand, with the left nostril closed, he or she will select the object that corresponds to the odour: a plastic flower for a floral odour, a toy fish for a fishy odour, a model tree for the odour of pine, and so forth. But if the left nostril is closed, the right hand fails this test, because it is connected to the left hemisphere, which did not smell the odour. (See **Figure 9•14**.)

Sometimes, the hands conflict and attempt to do different things—or even to fight one another. One study even reported that a man with a split brain attempted to beat his wife with one hand and protect her with the other. Did he really want to hurt her? Perhaps the answer depends on which hemisphere should be regarded as the "real" person.

As we saw in Chapter 4, the left hemisphere, besides giving us the ability to read, write, and speak, is good at other tasks that require verbal abilities, such as mathematics and logic. The right hemisphere excels at tasks of perception and has a much greater artistic ability. If a patient with a split brain tries to use his or her right hand to arrange blocks to duplicate a geometrical design provided by the researcher, the hand will hopelessly fumble around with the blocks. Often, the left hand (controlled by the right hemisphere) will brush the right hand aside and easily complete the task. It is as if the right hemisphere becomes impatient with the clumsy ineptitude of the hand controlled by the left hemisphere.

The effects of cutting the corpus callosum reinforce the conclusion that consciousness depends on the ability of speech mechanisms in the left hemisphere to receive information from other regions of the brain. If such communication is interrupted, then some kinds of information can never reach consciousness.

## Interim Summary

### Consciousness and the Brain

The suggestion that consciousness is a function of our ability to communicate with each other receives support from some cases of human brain damage. As we saw, people with certain kinds of damage can point to objects they say they cannot see; people with isolation aphasia can perceive speech and talk without apparent awareness; and a patient with a particular form of visual agnosia can make appropriate hand movements when looking at objects that cannot be consciously recognized. Thus, brain damage can disrupt a person's awareness of perceptual mechanisms without disrupting other functions performed by these mechanisms. In other cases, such as the recognition of fearful expressions, the amygdala seems to be linked to conscious processes. And although a person whose corpus callosum has been severed can make perceptual judgments with the right hemisphere, he or she cannot talk about them and appears to be unaware of them.

**QUESTIONS TO CONSIDER**

1. Some people with split brains have reported that they can use only one hand to hold a book while reading. If they use the other hand, they find themselves putting the book down even though they want to continue reading. Which hand puts the book down? Why does it do so?
2. When a stimulus is presented to the right hemisphere of a person with a split brain, the person (speaking with his or her left hemisphere) claims to be unaware of it. Thus, the left hemisphere is unaware of stimuli perceived only by the right hemisphere. Because the right hemisphere cannot talk to us, should we conclude that it lacks conscious self-awareness? If you think it is conscious, has the surgery produced two independent consciousnesses where only one previously existed?

## Hypnosis / mesmerism

Hypnosis is a specific and unusual form of verbal control that apparently enables one person to control another person's behaviour, thoughts, and perceptions. Under hypnosis, a person can be induced to bark like a dog, act like a baby, or tolerate being pierced with needles. Although these examples are interesting and amusing, hypnosis is important to psychology because it provides insights about the nature of consciousness and has applications in the fields of medicine and psychotherapy (Green, Barabasz, Barrett, & Montgomery, 2005; Laurence & Perry, 1988; Patterson & Jensen, 2003).

Although hypnosis may have been used by religious cults in the times of classical Greece (Spanos & Chaves, 1991), the modern phenomenon of hypnosis, or *mesmerism,* was discovered by Franz Anton Mesmer (1734–1815), an Austrian physician. He found that when he passed magnets back and forth over people's bodies (in an attempt to restore their "magnetic fluxes" and cure them of disease), they would often have convulsions and enter a trancelike state during which almost miraculous cures could be achieved. As Mesmer discovered later, the patients were not affected directly by the magnetism of the iron rods; they were responding to his undoubtedly persuasive and compelling personality. We now know that convulsions and trancelike states do not necessarily accompany hypnosis, and we also know that hypnosis does not cure physical illnesses. Mesmer's patients apparently had psychologically produced symptoms that were alleviated by suggestions made while they were hypnotized.

## Characteristics of Hypnosis

A person undergoing hypnosis can be alert, relaxed, tense, lying quietly, or exercising vigorously. There is no need to move an object in front of someone's face or to say "You are getting sleepy"; an enormous variety of techniques can be used to induce hypnosis in a susceptible person. The only essential feature seems to be the participant's understanding that he or she is to be hypnotized.

Hypnotized people are very suggestible; their behaviour will conform to what the hypnotist suggests, even to the extent that they may appear to misperceive reality. Generally, hypnotic suggestions are one of three types (Kirsch & Lynn, 1998):

- *Ideomotor* suggestions are those in which the hypnotist suggests that a particular action will occur without awareness of voluntary action, such as raising an arm.
- *Challenge* suggestions are suggestions that the hypnotized individual will be unable to perform a normally voluntary action.
- *Cognitive* suggestions are suggestions that the hypnotized person is undergoing distortions of sensory or cognitive experiences, such as not feeling pain or not being able to remember something.

▲ *Is a hypnotized person really under the control of the hypnotist, or is the person simply acting out a social role?*

**FIGURE 9•15** The Ponzo illusion and hypnotic blindness. The short horizontal lines are actually the same length. Even when a hypnotic suggestion made the slanted lines disappear, the visual system still perceived the illusion.

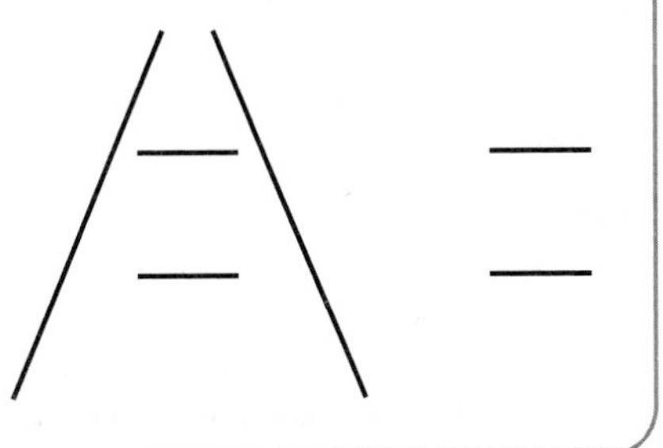

One of the most dramatic phenomena of hypnosis is **post-hypnotic suggestibility**, in which a person is given instructions under hypnosis and follows those instructions after returning to a non-hypnotized state. For example, a hypnotist might tell a man that he will become unbearably thirsty when he sees the hypnotist look at her watch. She might also admonish him not to remember anything upon leaving the hypnotic state, so that **post-hypnotic amnesia** is also achieved. After leaving the hypnotic state, the man acts normally and professes ignorance of what he perceived and did during hypnosis, perhaps even apologizing for not having succumbed to hypnosis. The hypnotist later looks at her watch, and the man suddenly leaves the room to get a drink of water.

Studies indicate that when changes in perception are induced through cognitive suggestions, the changes occur not in people's actual perceptions but in their verbal reports about their perceptions. For example, Miller, Hennessy, and Leibowitz (1973) used the *Ponzo illusion* to test the effects of hypnotically induced blindness. Although the two parallel horizontal lines in the left portion of Figure 9.15 are the same length, the top one looks longer than the bottom one. This effect is produced by the presence of the slanted lines to the left and right of the horizontal ones; if these lines are not present, the horizontal lines appear to be the same length. (See **Figure 9•15**.) Through hypnotic suggestion, the researchers made the slanted lines "disappear." But even though the participants reported that they could not see the slanted lines, they still perceived the upper line as longer

**post-hypnotic suggestibility** The tendency of a person to perform a behaviour suggested by the hypnotist some time after the person has left the hypnotic state.

**post-hypnotic amnesia** A failure to remember what occurred during hypnosis; induced by suggestions made during hypnosis.

than the lower one. This result indicates that the visual system continues to process sensory information during hypnotically induced blindness; otherwise, the participants would have perceived the lines as equal in length. The reported blindness appears to occur not because of altered activity in the visual system but because of altered activity in the verbal system (and in consciousness).

## Theories of Hypnosis

Hypnosis has been called a special case of learning, a transference of the superego, a goal-directed behaviour shaped by the hypnotist, a role-playing situation, and a restructuring of perceptual-cognitive functioning. In other words, no one yet knows exactly what it is. Hypnosis has been described as a state of enhanced suggestibility, but that is simply a description, not an explanation. Several investigators have advanced theories of hypnosis. We will look at two general views.

**The Sociocognitive Approach** All of the behavioural and perceptual phenomena discussed so far in this book have obvious survival value for the organism; that is, functional analysis of a behavioural phenomenon usually points to a plausible reason for the occurrence of the behaviour. Therefore, if hypnotic phenomena occurred only when a person was hypnotized, it would be difficult to understand why the brain happened to evolve in such a way that it is susceptible to hypnosis. Does it seem plausible that this susceptibility first manifested itself in the eighteenth century when Mesmer discovered the phenomenon of hypnosis? The *sociocognitive* view of hypnosis developed by Spanos (1991) and others proposes that at least some aspects of hypnosis are related to events that can happen every day.

Spanos argues that hypnosis should not be viewed as a special state of consciousness, in the way that sleep is a state of consciousness that differs from waking. Rather, "hypnotic behaviours" are social actions that reflect what the hypnotized individual believes to be characteristic of a hypnotized trance. The hypnotized person willingly adopts a role, and enacts that role according to rules as he or she understands them. Some of the rules governing this role are supplied by the direct instructions of the hypnotist, others are indirectly implied by what the hypnotist says and does, and still others consist of expectations that the people already have about what hypnotized people do.

People's expectations about hypnosis do indeed play an important role in their behaviour while under hypnosis. In lectures to two sections of an introductory psychology class, Orne (1959) told one section (falsely) that one of the most prominent features of hypnosis was rigidity of the preferred (that is, dominant) hand. Later, he arranged a demonstration of hypnosis during a meeting of students from both sections. Several of the students who had heard that the dominant hand became rigid showed this phenomenon when hypnotized, but none of the students who had not heard this myth developed a rigid hand. Similarly, if people become willing to follow a hypnotist's suggestions, perhaps they do so because they believe that this suggested behaviour is what is supposed to happen. Perhaps people willingly follow a hypnotist's suggestion to do something silly (such as bark like a dog) because they know that hypnotized people are not responsible for their behaviour.

If hypnosis can be described as role playing, then why are so many people willing to play this role? Barber (1975) submits that the suspension of self-control that occurs during hypnosis is very similar to our "participation" in the story of a movie or novel. When we go to a movie or read a book, we generally do so with the intent of being swept up in the story. We willingly let the filmmaker or author lead us through a fantasy. When we hear a story or read a book, we even imagine the scenes and the events that occur in them. We feel happy when good things happen to characters that we identify with and like, and we feel sad when bad things happen to them. Certainly, we express a full range of emotions while watching a good movie or reading a good book. In fact, one of the criteria we use to judge a movie or book is whether it causes us to enter this fantasy world; if it does not, we regard the work as a poor one. Perhaps these imagined events are similar to the hallucinations experienced during hypnosis.

**The Dissociation Approach** Other psychologists have adopted an approach to hypnosis based on the distinction between a psychological process and our *awareness* of that process. We have examined the distinction between explicit and implicit memory and have considered extraordinary cases, such as visual agnosia, where perception may occur without explicit awareness. *Dissociation* theories of hypnosis use this distinction. Basically, a hypnotized individual is assumed to be unaware of events and experiences that he or she would ordinarily be conscious of. Hypnotic induction is presumed to separate or isolate some psychological processes from conscious perception or control.

One version of this approach, developed by Hilgard (1991), places particular attention on the dissociation of sensory experiences from conscious awareness. Most of us have had episodes of "absent-mindedness," where we suddenly catch ourselves with no clear awareness of events in the immediate past (Cheyne, Carriere, & Smilek, 2006). Now consider how this might relate to cognitive suggestions that distort perceptions, such as the perception of pain. (Psychologists can, under appropriate ethical guidelines, administer non-injurious pain, such as placing an arm in cold water. Under hypnosis, the individual would be given suggestions that the pain is not perceived.) Hilgard suggests that hypnosis is a particularly extreme example of "absent-minded" episodes, where conscious awareness of ongoing stimulation—even pain—is suppressed by the suggestions of the hypnotist.

Other versions of this approach (Bowers & Davidson, 1991; Kihlstrom, 1998) have suggested that this dissociation may extend to conscious *control* of actions. I once received a call from my wife while I was at work; her first words to me were "What are *you* doing at Virginia's house?" She had consciously intended to dial her friend Virginia but, out of long habit, had dialed my university number instead. For this brief moment, her conscious intention was dissociated from her actions (see Koch and Crick, 2001, for some similar examples). Dissociated control theories of hypnosis interpret response to ideomotor and challenge suggestions in terms of similar states. The key assumption is that behaviour may have a hierarchy of control centres; under hypnosis, higher levels of control become isolated from lower levels (Wagstaff, Cole, & Brynas-Wagstaff, 2007).

Psychologists who study hypnosis disagree as to whether the sociocognitive or the dissociative approach is better suited to what we know about hypnosis. Neither seems complete. The dissociative explanation, for example, does not provide a clear mechanism by which hypnotic induction can produce dissociation. It may be that, ultimately, some synthesis of the two approaches will provide a better account (Woody & Sadler, 1998). Regardless, some psychologists have adopted the position that, whatever its explanation, hypnosis can provide a tool for exploring issues related to brain functioning (Rainville et al., 1997). Advances in our knowledge of brain function might also help us understand the specific neural pathways that produce some of the effects of hypnosis (Sandrini et al., 2000).

## Interim Summary

### Hypnosis

Hypnosis is a form of verbal control over a person's consciousness in which the hypnotist's suggestions affect some of the person's perceptions and behaviours. Although some people have viewed hypnosis as a mysterious, trancelike state, investigations have shown it to be similar to many phenomena of normal consciousness. There is no single way to induce hypnosis, and the responses depend very much on what the hypnotist says.

The sociocognitive approach to explaining hypnosis asserts that being hypnotized is similar to participating vicariously in a narrative, which is something we do whenever we become engrossed in a novel, a movie, a drama, or even the recounting of a friend's experience. When we are engrossed in this way, we experience genuine feelings of emotion, even though the situation is not "real." The dissociative theories of hypnosis, in contrast, consider it a specialized state in which awareness and conscious control centres of the brain become isolated from those controlling behaviour.

**QUESTION TO CONSIDER**

1. Some people prefer explanations that demystify puzzling phenomena such as hypnosis. Others resist such explanations; for them, an interesting phenomenon is spoiled by an explanation that places it in the realm of physics and biology. How do you feel about these two viewpoints?

# Sleep

Sleep is not a state of unconsciousness. Sleep is a behaviour characterized by an *altered* consciousness. During sleep, we have dreams that can be just as vivid as the experiences of behaviour when we are awake. However, we forget most of them as soon as they are over. Our amnesia leads us to think—incorrectly—that we were unconscious while we were asleep. In fact, there are two distinct kinds of sleep—and thus, two states of altered consciousness.

We spend approximately one-third of our lives sleeping—or trying to. You might therefore think that the reason we sleep is clearly understood by scientists who study this phenomenon. And yet, despite the efforts of many talented researchers, we are still not sure why we sleep. Many people are preoccupied with sleep—or with the lack of it—and report dissatisfaction with the quality of their sleep (Samuels, 2008). Collectively, they consume large amounts of drugs each year in an attempt to get to sleep. Advertisements for non-prescription sleep medications imply that a night without a full eight hours of sleep is a physiological and psychological disaster. Is this worry justified? Does missing a few hours—or even a full night—of sleep actually harm us? As we will see, the answer seems to be no.

## The Stages of Sleep

Sleep is not uniform. We can sleep lightly or deeply; we can be restless or still; we can have vivid dreams, or our consciousness can be relatively blank. Researchers who have studied sleep have found that its stages usually follow an orderly, predictable sequence.

Most sleep research takes place in sleep laboratories. Because a person's sleep is affected by his or her surroundings, a sleep laboratory contains one or more small bedrooms, furnished and decorated to be as homelike and comfortable as possible. The most important apparatus of the sleep laboratory is the **polygraph**, a machine located in a separate room that records on paper the output of various devices that can be attached to the sleeper. For example, the polygraph can record the electrical activity of the brain through small metal discs pasted to the scalp, producing an **electroencephalogram (EEG)**. It can record electrical signals from muscles, producing an **electromyogram (EMG)** or from the heart, producing an **electrocardiogram (EKG)**. Or it can record eye movements

**polygraph** An instrument that records changes in physiological processes such as brain activity, heart rate, and breathing.

**electroencephalogram (EEG)** The measurement and graphical presentation of the electrical activity of the brain, recorded by means of electrodes attached to the scalp.

**electromyogram (EMG)** The measurement and graphical presentation of the electrical activity of muscles, recorded by means of electrodes attached to the skin above them.

**electrocardiogram (EKG)** The measurement and graphical presentation of the electrical activity of the heart, recorded by means of electrodes attached to the skin.

**FIGURE 9•16** A participant prepared for a night's sleep in a sleep laboratory.

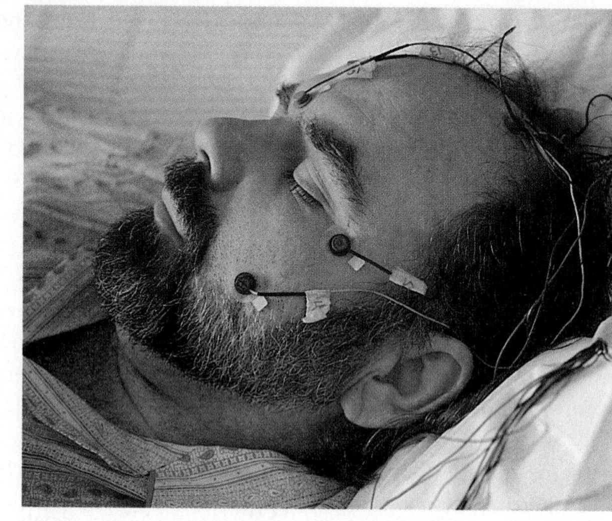

through small metal discs attached to the skin around the eyes, producing an **electro-oculogram (EOG)**. Other special transducers can detect respiration, sweating, skin or body temperature, and a variety of other physiological states.

Let us look at a typical night's sleep of a male university student on his third night in the laboratory. (Of course, we would obtain similar results from a female, with one exception, which I will note later.) The EEG electrodes are attached to his scalp, EMG electrodes to his chin, EKG electrodes to his chest, and EOG electrodes to the skin around his eyes. (See **Figure 9•16**.) Wires connected to these electrodes are plugged into the amplifiers of the polygraph. The output of each amplifier causes a pen on the polygraph to move up and down while a long, continuous sheet of paper moves by.

The EEG record distinguishes between alert and relaxed wakefulness. When a person is alert, the tracing looks rather irregular, and the pens do not move very far up or down. The EEG in this case shows high-frequency (15–30 Hz), low-amplitude electrical activity called **beta activity**. When a person is relaxed and perhaps somewhat drowsy, the record shows **alpha activity**, a medium-frequency (8–12 Hz), medium-amplitude rhythm. (See **Figure 9•17**.)

**electro-oculogram (EOG)** The measurement and graphical presentation of the electrical activity caused by movements of the eye, recorded by means of electrodes attached to the skin adjacent to the eye.

**beta activity** The irregular, high-frequency activity of the electroencephalogram, usually indicating a state of alertness or arousal.

**alpha activity** Rhythmical, medium-frequency activity of the electroencephalogram, usually indicating a state of quiet relaxation.

**theta activity** EEG activity of 3.5–7.5 Hz; occurs during the transition between sleep and wakefulness.

**delta activity** The rhythmical activity of the electroencephalogram, having a frequency of less than 3.5 Hz, indicating deep (slow-wave) sleep.

**FIGURE 9•17** An EEG recording of the stages of sleep.

*(From Horne, J. A. (1989).* Why we sleep: The functions of sleep in humans and other mammals. *Oxford, UK: Oxford University Press. Copyright 1988 Oxford University Press. By permission of Oxford University Press.)*

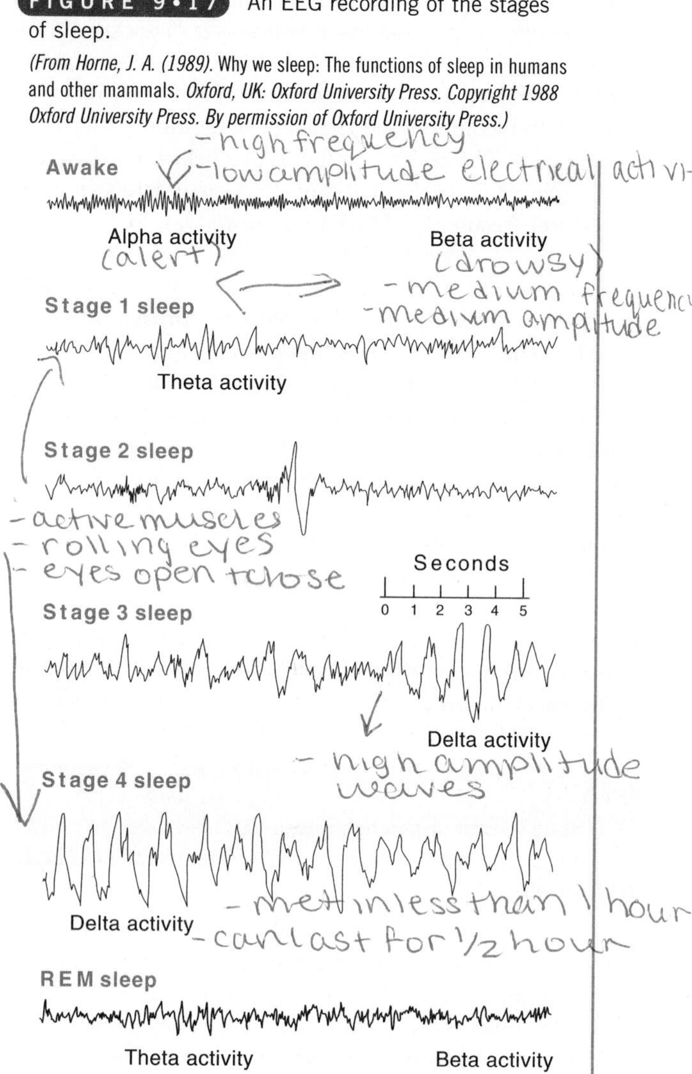


The technician leaves the room, the lights are turned off, and the student closes his eyes. As he relaxes and grows drowsy, his EEG changes from beta activity to alpha activity. The first stage of sleep (stage 1) is marked by the presence of some **theta activity**, EEG activity of 3.5 to 7.5 Hz. This stage is actually a transition between sleep and wakefulness; the EMG shows that the student's muscles are still active, and his EOG indicates slow, gentle, rolling eye movements. The eyes slowly open and close from time to time. Soon, the student is fully asleep. As sleep progresses, it gets deeper and deeper, moving through stages 2, 3, and 4. The EEG gets progressively lower in frequency and higher in amplitude. (See Figure 9.17.) This pattern is interrupted between two and five times a minute by short bursts of waves of 12 to 14 Hz, known as *sleep spindles*. It has been suggested that sleep spindles represent the activity of a mechanism that is involved in keeping a person asleep (Nicolas, Petit, Rompre, & Montplaisir, 2001). Stage 4 consists mainly of **delta activity**, characterized by relatively high-amplitude waves occurring at less than 3.5 Hz. Our sleeper

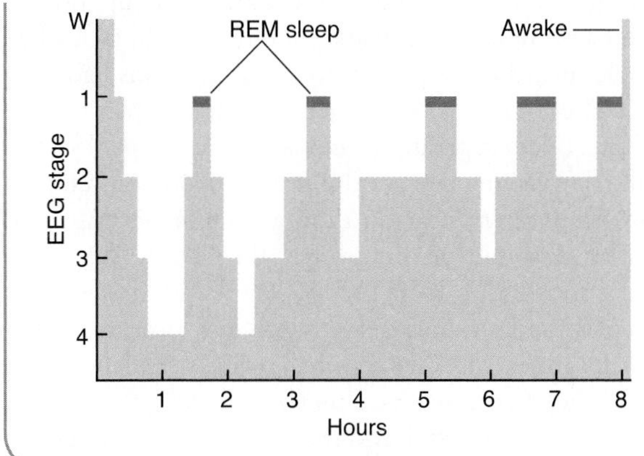


**FIGURE 9•18** Typical progression of stages from wakefulness (W) to Stage 4 during a night's sleep. The dark blue shading indicates REM sleep.

*(From Hartmann, E. (1967).* The biology of dreaming. *Courtesy of Charles C. Thomas, Publisher, Springfield, Illinois.)*

becomes less responsive to the environment, and it becomes more difficult to awaken him. Environmental stimuli that caused him to stir during stage 1 produce little or no reaction during stage 4. The sleep of stages 3 and 4 is called **slow-wave sleep.**

Stage 4 sleep is reached in less than an hour and continues for as long as a half-hour. Then, suddenly, the EEG begins to indicate lighter levels of sleep, back through stages 3 and 2 to the activity characteristic of stage 1. The sleeper's heartbeat becomes irregular and his respiration alternates between shallow breaths and sudden gasps. The EOG shows that the participant's eyes dart rapidly back and forth, up and down. The EEG record looks like that of a person who is awake and active. Yet the sleeper is fast asleep. Although his EMG is generally quiet, indicating muscular relaxation, his hands and feet twitch occasionally.

At this point, the sleeper is dreaming. He has entered another stage of sleep, called **rapid eye movement (REM) sleep.** The first episode of REM sleep lasts about 20 to 30 minutes and is followed by approximately one hour of slow-wave sleep. As the night goes on, the episodes of REM sleep get longer and the episodes of slow-wave sleep get shorter, but the total cycle remains at approximately 90 minutes. A typical night's sleep consists of four or five of these cycles. **Figure 9•18** shows a record of a person's stages of sleep; the dark blue shading indicates REM sleep.

As I noted, although a person in REM sleep exhibits rapid eye movements and brief twitches of the hands and feet, the EMG shows that the facial muscles are still. In fact, physiological studies have shown that, aside from occasional twitching, a person actually becomes paralyzed during REM sleep. Males are observed to have partial or full erections. In addition, women's vaginal secretions increase at this time. These genital changes are usually not associated with sexual arousal or dreams of a sexual nature. **Table 9•1** lists the principal characteristics of REM sleep and slow-wave sleep.

**TABLE 9•1 Principal Characteristics of REM Sleep and Slow-Wave Sleep**

| REM Sleep | Slow-Wave Sleep |
|---|---|
| Rapid EEG waves | Slow EEG waves |
| Muscular paralysis | Lack of muscular paralysis |
| Rapid eye movements | Slow or absent eye movements |
| Penile erection or vaginal secretion | Lack of genital activity |
| Dreams | |

## The Functions of Sleep

Sleep is one of the few universal behaviours. All mammals, all birds, and some cold-blooded vertebrates spend part of each day sleeping. Sleep is seen even in species that would seem to be better off without sleep. For example, the Indus dolphin (*Platanista indi*) lives in the muddy waters of the Indus estuary in Pakistan (Pilleri, 1979). Over the ages, it has become blind, presumably because vision is not useful in the animal's environment. (It has an excellent sonar system, which it uses to navigate and find prey.) However, despite the dangers caused by sleeping, sleep has not disappeared. The Indus dolphin never stops swimming; doing so would result in injury, because of the dangerous currents and the vast quantities of debris carried by the river during the monsoon season. Pilleri captured two Indus dolphins and studied their habits. He found that they slept a total of seven hours a day, in very brief naps of 4 to 60 seconds each. If sleep did not perform an important function, we might expect that it, like vision, would have been eliminated in this species through the process of natural selection.

The universal nature of sleep suggests that it performs some important functions. But just what are they? The simplest explanation for sleep is that it serves to repair the wear and tear on our bodies caused by moving and exercising. Perhaps our bodies just get worn out by performing waking activities for 16 hours or so.

One approach to discovering the functions of sleep is the deprivation study. Consider, for example, the function of eating. The effects of starvation are easy to detect: The person loses weight, becomes fatigued, and will eventually die if he or she does not eat again. By analogy, it should be easy to

**slow-wave sleep** Sleep other than REM sleep, characterized by regular, slow waves on the electroencephalograph.

**rapid eye movement (REM) sleep** A period of sleep during which dreaming, rapid eye movements, and muscular paralysis occur and the EEG shows beta activity.

discover why we sleep by seeing what happens to a person who goes without sleep.

Unfortunately, deprivation studies have not obtained persuasive evidence that sleep is needed to keep the body functioning normally. Horne (1978) reviewed more than 50 experiments in which humans had been deprived of sleep. He reported that most of them found that sleep deprivation did not interfere with people's ability to perform physical exercise. In addition, they found no evidence of a physiological stress response to sleep deprivation. If people encounter stressful situations that cause illness or damage to various organ systems, changes can be seen in such physiological measures as blood levels of cortisol and epinephrine. (The physiology of stress is described in more detail in Chapter 16.) Generally, these changes did not occur.

Although sleep deprivation does not seem to damage the body, and sleep does not seem to be necessary for athletic exercise, sleep may be required for normal brain functioning. Several studies suggest that sleep-deprived people are able to perform normally on most intellectual tasks, as long as the tasks are short. They perform more poorly on tasks that require a high level of cortical functioning after two days of sleep deprivation (Horne & Petit, 1985). In particular, they perform poorly on tasks that require them to be watchful, alert, and vigilant. Conversely, an afternoon nap of between 20 and 60 minutes has been found to decrease sleepiness and improve cognitive ability (Milner & Cote, 2008).

During stage 4 sleep, the metabolic activity of the brain decreases to about 75 percent of the waking level (Sakai et al., 1979). Thus, stage 4 sleep appears to give the brain a chance to rest. In fact, people are unreactive to all but intense stimuli during slow-wave sleep and, if awakened, act groggy and confused—as if their cerebral cortex has been shut down and has not yet resumed its functioning. These observations suggest that during stage 4 sleep the brain is, indeed, resting.

Sleep deprivation studies of humans suggest that although the brain may need slow-wave sleep in order to recover from the day's activities, the rest of the body does not. Another way to determine whether sleep is needed for restoration of physiological functioning is to look at the effects of daytime activity on nighttime sleep. If the function of sleep is to repair the effects of activity during waking hours, then we should expect that sleep and exercise are related. That is, we should sleep more after a day of vigorous exercise than after a day spent quietly at an office desk.

In fact, the relation between sleep and exercise is not very compelling. For example, Ryback and Lewis (1971) found no changes in slow-wave or REM sleep of healthy participants who spent six weeks resting in bed. If sleep repairs wear and tear, we would expect these people to sleep less. Adey, Bors, and Porter (1968) studied the sleep of *completely* immobile quadriplegics and paraplegics and found only a small decrease in slow-wave sleep as compared to uninjured people.

Although bodily exercise has little effect on sleep, *mental* exercise seems to increase the demand for slow-wave sleep. In an ingenious study, Horne and Minard (1985) found a way to increase mental activity without affecting physical activity and without causing stress. The investigators told volunteers to show up for an experiment in which they were supposed to take some tests designed to assess reading skills. In fact, when the people turned up, they were told that the plans had been changed. They were invited for a day out, at the expense of the researchers. (Not surprisingly, they willingly accepted.) They spent the day visiting an art exhibition, a shopping centre, a museum, an amusement park, a zoo, and an interesting mansion. After a scenic drive through the countryside, they watched a movie in a local theatre. They were driven from place to place and certainly did not become overheated by exercise. After the movie, they returned to the sleep laboratory. They said they were tired, and they readily fell asleep. Their sleep duration was normal, and they awoke feeling refreshed. However, their slow-wave sleep—particularly stage 4 sleep—was increased.

## Dreaming

One of the most fascinating aspects of sleep is the fact that we enter a fantasy world several times each night during which we perceive imaginary events and perform imaginary behaviours. Why do we do so?

**States of Consciousness During Sleep** A person who is awakened during REM sleep and asked whether anything was happening will almost always report a dream. The typical REM sleep dream resembles a play or movie; it has a narrative form. Conversely, reports of narrative, story-like dreams are rare among people awakened from slow-wave sleep. In general, mental activity during slow-wave sleep is more nearly static; it involves situations rather than stories, and generally unpleasant ones. For example, a person awakened from slow-wave sleep might report a sensation of being crushed or suffocated.

Unless the sleeper is heavily drugged, almost everyone has four or five bouts of REM sleep each night, with accompanying dreams. Yet if the dreamer does not happen to awaken while the dream is in progress, it is lost forever. Some people who claimed not to have had a dream for many years slept in a sleep laboratory and found that, in fact, they did dream. They were able to remember their dreams because the investigator awakened them during REM sleep.

The reports of people awakened from REM and slow-wave sleep clearly show that people are conscious during sleep, even though they may not remember any of their sleeping experiences. Lack of memory for an event does not mean that it never happened; it only means that there is no permanent record accessible to conscious thought during wakefulness. Thus, we can say that slow-wave sleep and REM sleep reflect two different states of consciousness.

**Functions of Dreams** There are two major approaches to the study of dreaming: a psychological analysis of the contents of dreams, and psychobiological research on the nature and functions of REM sleep. Let us consider the psychological analysis first.

**Symbolism in Dreams** Since ancient times, people have regarded dreams as important, using them to prophesy the future, decide whether to go to war, or determine the guilt or innocence of a person accused of a crime. In the twentieth century, Sigmund Freud proposed a very influential theory about dreaming. He said that dreams arise out of inner conflicts between unconscious desires (primarily sexual ones) and prohibitions against acting out these desires, which we learn from society. According to Freud, although all dreams represent unfulfilled wishes, their contents are disguised and expressed symbolically. The *latent content* of the dream (from the Latin word for "hidden") is transformed into the *manifest content* (the actual storyline or plot). Taken at face value, the manifest content is innocuous, but a knowledgeable psychoanalyst can supposedly recognize unconscious desires disguised as symbols in the dream. For example, climbing a set of stairs or shooting a gun might represent sexual intercourse. The problem with Freud's theory is that it is not disprovable; even if it is wrong, a psychoanalyst can always provide a plausible interpretation of a dream that reveals hidden conflicts disguised in obscure symbols.

Hobson and Pace-Schott (2002) have developed a model of brain activity during sleep that explains dreaming without relying on unconscious conflicts or desires. As we will see later, research using laboratory animals has shown that REM sleep occurs when a circuit of acetylcholine-secreting neurons in the pons becomes active, stimulating rapid eye movements, activation of the cerebral cortex, and muscular paralysis. (Yes, other animals engage in REM sleep, and they appear to dream, too.) The activation of the visual system produces both eye movements and images. In fact, several experiments have found that the particular eye movements that a person makes during a dream correspond reasonably well with the content of a dream; that is, the eye movements are those that one would expect a person to make if the imaginary events were really occurring (Dement, 1974). The images evoked by the cortical activation often incorporate memories of episodes that have occurred recently or of things that a person has been thinking about lately. Presumably, the circuits responsible for these memories are more excitable because they have recently been active. Hobson and Pace-Schott suggest that slow-wave sleep and REM sleep work together. Memories that are consolidated during slow-wave sleep are reactivated during REM sleep and consolidated with other memories. The activation of these brain mechanisms produces fragmentary images; our brains try to tie these images together and make sense of them by creating a more or less plausible story.

▲ *Marc Chagall's painting depicts images and symbols that could occur in a dream. Freud's assertion that dreams provide an opportunity for unconscious desires to be expressed symbolically is challenged by many psychologists today.*
*Marc Chagall,* Winter Night in Vitebsk, *1948, Private Collection, USA/SuperStock. © Estate of Marc Chagall/SODRAC (2008).*

**Effects of REM Sleep Deprivation** As we saw, total sleep deprivation impairs people's ability to perform tasks that require them to be alert and vigilant. What happens when only REM sleep is disrupted? People who are sleeping in a laboratory can be selectively deprived of REM sleep. An investigator awakens them whenever their polygraph records indicate that they have entered REM sleep. The investigator must also awaken control participants just as often at random intervals to eliminate any effects produced by being awakened several times.

If someone is deprived of REM sleep for several nights and is then allowed to sleep without interruption, the onset of REM sleep becomes more frequent. The person engages in many more bouts of REM sleep than normal during the next night or two, as if catching up on something important that was missed.

Researchers have discovered that the effects of REM sleep deprivation are not very striking. In fact, medical journals contain reports of several patients who showed little or no REM sleep after sustaining damage to the brain stem (Gironell, de la Calzada, Sagales, & Barraquer-Bordas, 1995; Lavie et al., 1984). The lack of REM sleep did not appear to cause serious side effects. One of the patients, after receiving his injury, completed high school, attended law school, and began practising law.

Several investigators have suggested that REM sleep may play a role in learning, a view consistent with the explanation for dreaming suggested by Hobson and Pace-Schott (2002). Many studies using laboratory animals have shown that deprivation of REM sleep does impair the ability to learn a complex task. However, although the animals learn the task more slowly, they still manage to learn it. Thus, REM sleep is not necessary for learning. If REM sleep does play a role in learning, it appears to be a subtle one—at least, in the adult.

▲ *Late-term fetuses and newborn infants spend much time in REM sleep, which has led some investigators to hypothesize that this activity plays a role in brain development.*

## Brain Mechanisms of Sleep

If sleep is a behaviour, then some parts of the brain must be responsible for its occurrence. In fact, researchers have discovered several brain regions that have special roles in sleep and biological rhythms.

Let us first consider biological rhythms. All living organisms show rhythmic changes in their physiological processes and behaviour. Some of these rhythms are simply responses to environmental changes. For example, the growth rate of plants is controlled by daily rhythms of light and darkness. In animals, some rhythms are controlled by internal "clocks" located in the brain. Mammals have two biological clocks that play a role in sleep. One of these controls **circadian rhythms**—rhythms that oscillate once a day (*circa,* about; *dies,* day). The second clock, which controls the cycles of slow-wave and REM sleep, oscillates several times a day.

The clock that controls circadian rhythms is located in a small pair of structures located at the bottom of the hypothalamus: the *suprachiasmatic nuclei (SCN).* The activity of neurons in the SCN oscillates once each day; the neurons are active during the day and inactive at night. These changes in activity control daily cycles of sleep and wakefulness. If people are placed in a windowless room with constant lighting, they will continue to show circadian rhythms, controlled by the oscillations of their suprachiasmatic nuclei. However, because this biological clock is not very accurate, people's circadian rhythms will eventually get out of synchrony with the day/night cycles outside the building. But within a few days after leaving the building, their rhythms will be resynchronized with those of the sun. This resynchronization is accomplished by a direct connection between the eyes and the SCN. Each morning, when we see the light of the sun (or turn on the room lights), our biological clock resets and begins ticking off the next day.

The second biological clock in the mammalian brain runs considerably faster, and it runs continuously, unaffected by periods of light and darkness. In humans, this clock cycles with a 90-minute period. The first suggestion that a 90-minute cycle occurs throughout the day came from the observation that infants who are fed on demand show regular feeding patterns (Kleitman, 1961). Later studies found 90-minute cycles of rest and activity, including such activities as eating, drinking, smoking, heart rate, oxygen consumption, stomach motility, urine production, and performance on various tasks that make demands on a person's ability to pay attention. Kleitman termed this phenomenon the **basic rest-activity cycle (BRAC)**. (See Kleitman, 1982, for a review.) During the night, the clock responsible for the BRAC controls the alternating periods of REM sleep and slow-wave sleep.

Studies using laboratory animals have found that the clock responsible for the BRAC is located somewhere in the pons. The pons also contains neural circuits that are responsible for REM sleep. The neurons that begin a period of REM sleep release acetylcholine. The release of this transmitter substance activates several other circuits of neurons. One of these circuits activates the cerebral cortex and causes dreaming. Another activates neurons in the midbrain and causes rapid eye movements. Yet another activates a set of inhibitory neurons that paralyzes us and prevents us from acting out our dreams. The location of the two biological clocks is shown in **Figure 9•19**.

The first hint that REM sleep was turned on by acetylcholine-secreting neurons came from the observation that overdoses of insecticides that excite such neurons also cause visual hallucinations, like those of dreaming. Subsequent research using laboratory animals confirmed this suspicion. These acetylcholine-secreting neurons (referred



**FIGURE 9•19** Two biological clocks in the human brain. The suprachiasmatic nucleus (SCN) of the hypothalamus is responsible for circadian rhythms. The clock in the pons is responsible for the basic rest-activity cycle (BRAC) and cycles of REM sleep and slow-wave sleep.

**circadian rhythm** A daily rhythmical change in behaviour or physiological process.

**basic rest-activity cycle (BRAC)** A 90-minute cycle (in humans) of waxing and waning alertness controlled by a biological clock in the pons; during sleep, it controls cycles of REM sleep and slow-wave sleep.

**FIGURE 9•20** Control of REM sleep. REM sleep is produced by activation of the acetylcholine-secreting REM-ON neurons located in the pons. These neurons are normally inhibited by serotonin-secreting neurons.

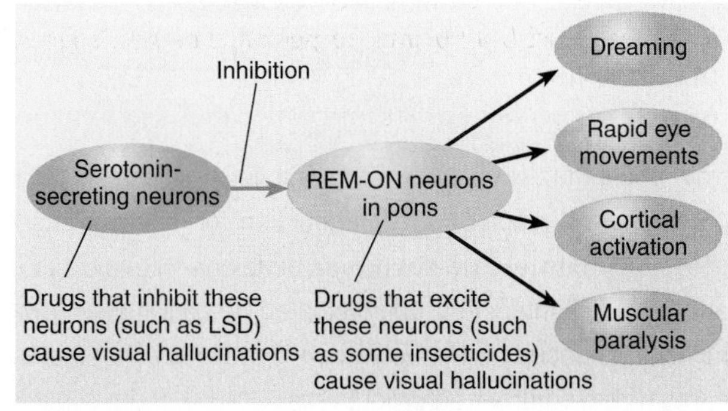


to as *REM-ON* neurons) are normally inhibited by neurons that secrete another transmitter substance, serotonin. Thus, drugs that decrease the activity of serotonin-secreting neurons will permit the REM-ON neurons to become active. LSD is one of these drugs, and this fact explains why people who take LSD experience visual hallucinations similar to the ones that occur during dreams. On the other hand, drugs that increase the activity of serotonin-secreting neurons will suppress REM sleep. All antidepressant drugs have this effect, which suggests that excessive amounts of REM sleep may play a role in mood disorders. This hypothesis will be explored in more detail in Chapter 17. (See **Figure 9•20**.)

What about the brain mechanisms responsible for slow-wave sleep? The most important brain region seems to be the **preoptic area**, located just in front of the hypothalamus, at the base of the brain. (This region is named for the fact that it is located anterior to the point where some axons in the optic nerves cross to the other side of the brain.) If the preoptic area is destroyed, an animal will sleep much less (McGinty & Sterman, 1968; Szymusiak & McGinty, 1986). If it is electrically stimulated, an animal will become drowsy and fall asleep (Sterman & Clemente, 1962a, 1962b).

## Interim Summary

### Sleep

Sleep consists of several stages of slow-wave sleep, characterized by increasing amounts of delta activity in the EEG, and REM sleep. REM sleep is characterized by beta activity in the EEG, rapid eye movements, general paralysis (with twitching movements of the hands and feet), and dreaming. Sleep is a behaviour, not simply an altered state of consciousness. Although evidence suggests that sleep is not necessary for repairing the wear and tear caused by physical exercise, it may play an important role in providing an opportunity for the brain to rest.

Although narrative dreams occur only during REM sleep, people often are conscious of static situations during slow-wave sleep. Freud suggested that dreams provide the opportunity for unconscious conflicts to express themselves through symbolism in dreams. Hobson suggested that dreams are the attempts of the brain to make sense of hallucinations produced by the activation of the cerebral cortex. The function of REM sleep in adults is uncertain, but it may be involved somehow in learning. The brain contains two biological clocks. One, located in the suprachiasmatic nucleus of the hypothalamus, controls circadian (daily) rhythms. This clock is reset when light strikes the retina in the morning. The second clock, located in the pons, controls the basic rest-activity cycle, which manifests itself in changes in activity during the day and alternating periods of slow-wave sleep and REM sleep during the night. A circuit of acetylcholine-secreting neurons in the pons, normally inhibited by serotonin-secreting neurons, turns on REM sleep. Slow-wave sleep is controlled by neurons in the preoptic area.

#### QUESTIONS TO CONSIDER

1. What is accomplished by dreaming? Some researchers believe that the subject matter of a dream does not matter—it is the REM sleep itself that is important. Others believe that the subject matter does count. Some researchers believe that if we remember a dream, the dream failed to accomplish all of its functions; others say that remembering is useful because it can give us some insights into our problems. What do you think of these controversies?
2. Some people report that they are "in control" of some of their dreams—that they feel as if they decide what comes next and are not simply swept along passively. Have you ever had this experience? And have you ever had a "lucid dream," in which you were aware of the fact that you were dreaming?
3. Until recently (that is, in terms of the evolution of our species), our ancestors tended to go to sleep when the sun set and wake up when it rose. Once our ancestors learned how to control fire, they undoubtedly stayed up somewhat later, sitting in front of a fire. But it was only with the development of cheap, effective lighting that many members of our species adopted the habit of staying up late and waking several hours after sunrise. Considering that the neural mechanisms of sleep evolved long ago, do you think the changes in our daily rhythms affect any of our physical and intellectual abilities?

**preoptic area** A region at the base of the brain just in front of the hypothalamus; contains neurons that appear to control the occurrence of slow-wave sleep.

EPILOGUE

## Guilty State of Mind

The point of law behind Robert Frisbee's defence was to play a significant role in another murder trial. One morning in May 1987, a Toronto man by the name of Kenneth Parks, under stress from lack of work and from gambling debts, drove 23 kilometres to the home of his parents-in-law and stabbed his mother-in-law to death. He then drove to the police station and, in a state of confusion, confessed that he might have killed someone. At trial, his defence team argued successfully that Parks had committed the assault while in a state of automatism—sleepwalking—and that his actions were not the result of a conscious desire to injure his parents-in-law. The Supreme Court of Canada upheld his acquittal, ruling that Parks was not mentally disordered in a legal sense and that his lack of conscious intent meant that his actions were not voluntary. This was part of the defence used in Frisbee's trial and, in essence, it remains part of Canadian jurisprudence to this day.

The doctrine that someone could admittedly commit an act of murder yet still be found not guilty may strike you as odd. Judges and lawyers must consider what makes a person truly accountable for an action. Our legal system considers guilt to be the result of deliberate action (or inaction, in some cases) and hence does not punish as felonies behaviours that are truly involuntary and unanticipated. In allowing sleepwalking as a defence, the Canadian courts recognize that there are cases where complex behaviours may occur without conscious awareness. As we've seen in this chapter, such cases can occur under laboratory conditions. In addition, the dissociation theory of hypnosis implies that very complex behaviours could occur in this state as well.

The Kenneth Parks decision struck many people as preposterous. William Deverell, Frisbee's lawyer, admitted that it was a difficult defence to present to a jury. Yet much of our new knowledge of cognitive neuroscience has laid the foundation for understanding how awareness and action interact; in the years ahead, we may find many instances of the "zombie within," as Koch and Crick (2001) describe it. It may be that our ancient principles and traditions of law have correctly foreseen the future.

## Canadian Connections to Research in This Chapter


Bowers, K. S., & Davidson, T. M. (1991). A neodissociative critique of Spanos's social-psychological model of hypnosis. In S. J. Lynn and J. W. Rhue (Eds.), *Theories of hypnosis: Current models and perspectives* (pp. 105–143). New York: Guilford Press. (University of Waterloo: www.uwaterloo.ca)

Cheesman, J., & Merikle, P. M. (1986). Distinguishing conscious from unconscious perceptual processes. *Canadian Journal of Psychology, 40,* 343–367. (University of Saskatchewan: www.usask.ca)

Cheyne, J. A., Carriere, J. S. A., & Smilek, D. (2006). Absent-mindedness: lapses of conscious awareness and everyday cognitive failures. *Consciousness and Cognition, 15,* 578–592. (University of Waterloo: www.uwaterloo.ca)

Ganel, T., & Goodale, M. A. (2003). Visual control of action but not perception requires analytical processing of object shape. *Nature, 426,* 664–667. (University of Western Ontario: www.uwo.ca)

Haffenden, A. M., Schiff, K. C., & Goodale, M. A. (2001). The dissociation between perception and action in the Ebbinghaus illusion: Non illusory effects of pictorial cues on grasp. *Current Biology, 11,* 177–181. (University of Western Ontario: www.uwo.ca)

Hebb, D. O. (1980). *Essay on mind.* Hillsdale, NJ: Erlbaum. (Dalhousie University: www.dal.ca)

Donald Hebb was the first winner (in 1980) of the Donald O. Hebb Award of the Canadian Psychological Association and the 1961 winner of the American Psychological Association's Award for Distinguished Scientific Contributions.

Laurence, J. R., & Perry, C. (1988). *Hypnosis, will and memory: A psycho-legal history.* New York: Guilford Press. (Concordia University: www.concordia.ca)

Masuda, T., & Nisbett, R.E. (2006). Culture and change blindness. *Cognitive Science, 30,* 381–399. (University of Alberta: www.ualberta.ca)

McCormick, P. A., Klein, R. M., & Johnston, S. (1998). Splitting versus sharing focal attention: Comment on Castiello and Umilt (1992). *Journal of Experimental Psychology: Human Perception and Performance, 24,* 350–357. (St. Francis Xavier University: www.stfx.ca)

Merikle, P. M., Smilek, D., & Eastwood, J. D. (2001). Perception without awareness: Perspectives from cognitive psychology. *Cognition, 79,* 115–134. (University of Waterloo: www.uwaterloo.ca)

Milner, C. E., & Cote, K. A. (2008). A dose-response investigation of the benefits of napping in healthy young, middle-aged and older adults. *Sleep and Biological Rhythms, 6*, 2–15. (Brock University: www.brocku.ca)

Morin, A. (2003). Inner speech and conscious experience. *Science & Consciousness Review*, April. (Mount Royal College: www.mtroyal.ab.ca)

Moscovitch, M. (1995). Recovered consciousness: A hypothesis concerning modularity and episodic memory. *Journal of Clinical and Experimental Neuropsychology, 17*, 276–290. (University of Toronto: www.utoronto.ca)

Obhi, S. S. (2007). Evidence for feedback dependent conscious awareness of action. *Brain Research, 1161*, 88–94. (Wilfrid Laurier University: www.wlu.ca)

Pearson, P. M., & Schaefer, E. G. (2005). Toupee or not toupee? The role of instructional set, centrality, and relevance in change blindness. *Visual Cognition, 12*, 1528–1543. (University of Winnipeg: www.uwinnipeg.ca)

Rainville, P., Duncan, G. H., Price, D. D., Carrier, B., & Bushnell, M. C. (1997). Pain affect encoded in human anterior cingulate but not somatosensory cortex. *Science, 277*, 968–971. (Université de Montréal: www.umontreal.ca)

Samuels, C. (2008). Sleep, recovery, and performance: The new frontier in high-performance athletics. *Neurologic Clinics, 26*, 169–180. (University of Calgary: www.ucalgary.ca)

Spanos, N. P. (1991). A sociocognitive approach to hypnosis. In S. J. Lynn and J. W. Rhue (Eds.), *Theories of hypnosis: Current models and perspectives* (pp. 324–361). New York: Guilford Press. (Carleton University: www.carleton.ca)

Spanos, N. P., & Chaves, J. F. (1991). History and historiography of hypnosis. In S. J. Lynn and J. W. Rhue (Eds.), *Theories of hypnosis: Current models and perspectives* (pp. 43–78). New York: Guilford Press. (Carleton University: www.carleton.ca)

Woody, E., & Sadler, P. (1998). On reintegrating dissociated theories: Comment on Kirsch and Lynn (1998). *Psychological Bulletin, 123*, 192–197. (University of Waterloo: www.uwaterloo.ca)

## Suggestions for Further Reading

Damasio, A. (1999). *The feeling of what happens: Body and emotion in the making of consciousness.* New York: Harcourt Brace.

A leading neuroscientist looks at the topic of consciousness, with an unconventional suggestion regarding its origins.

Dennett, D. C. (1991). *Consciousness explained.* Boston: Little, Brown.

This book provides a provocative look at consciousness from a philosophical, psychological, and computational viewpoint.

Jaynes, J. (1976). The origin of consciousness in the breakdown of the bicameral mind. Boston: Houghton Mifflin.

Jaynes' book presents the provocative hypothesis that human consciousness is a recent phenomenon that emerged long after the evolution of the human brain, as we know it now. You do not need to agree with Jaynes' thesis to enjoy reading this scholarly book.

Baker, R. A. (1990). *They call it hypnosis.* Buffalo, NY: Prometheus Books.

Laurence, J. R., & Perry, C. (1988). *Hypnosis, will, and memory: A psycho-legal history.* New York: Guilford Press.

Sheehan, P. W., & McConkey, K. M. (1982). *Hypnosis and experience: The exploration of phenomena and process.* Hillsdale, NJ: Lawrence Erlbaum Associates.

If you would like to learn more about hypnosis, you will enjoy reading any of these books. The Sheehan and McConkey book provides a more advanced, scholarly approach.

Horne, J. (1988). *Why we sleep: The functions of sleep in humans and other mammals.* Oxford, UK: Oxford University Press.

Horne's book about sleep is excellent and interesting.

PEARSON mypsychlab To access more tests and your own personalized study plan that will help you focus on the areas you need to master before your next class test, be sure to go to **www.MyPsychLab.com**, Pearson Education Canada's online Psychology website available with the access code packaged with your book.

# 10

# Language

## CHAPTER OUTLINE

### Speech and Comprehension



Language permits us to communicate perceptions, thoughts, and memories. Words have meanings (semantics), and they are arranged into sentences that follow specific rules (syntax). Context plays an important role in the complex task of identifying individual words from continuous speech. Both semantics and syntax provide meaning. Studies of patients with brain damage and PET studies of people engaging in verbal behaviour suggest that some parts of the brain play special roles in language-related behaviours.

### Reading



Reading allows words to be transmitted anywhere in the world and to be preserved for future generations. The eye-tracking device allows researchers to study people's eye movements during reading. Reading is accomplished by whole-word recognition and by decoding the sounds that are represented by letters and groups of letters. Brain damage can produce acquired dyslexias, disrupting one or both of these processes. Developmental dyslexias may involve abnormal development of parts of the left hemisphere that play a special role in language abilities. The phenomenon of semantic priming has permitted researchers to investigate the interactions of neural circuits responsible for recognizing and understanding spoken and written words.

### Language Acquisition by Children



By the time babies are born, they have already learned something about language from what they have heard while in their mothers' uteruses. Language is very much a social behaviour; babies learn to carry on "conversations" with caregivers even before they can utter real words, and they use movements, facial expressions, and sounds to communicate. During the two-word stage, children begin to combine words creatively, saying things they have never heard. Infants learn how to communicate verbally from adults and older children, who use a special form of address known as child-directed speech. Some researchers believe that the human brain contains a language acquisition device that already contains universal rules of grammar. The question of whether language abilities are uniquely human is being addressed by researchers who have succeeded in teaching other primates some aspects of language.

## PROLOGUE

### Do Animals Have Language?

When I discuss language with my students, I begin by asking, "Can animals understand language?"

One student answered, "My dog Shadow knows his name and he understands when I tell him to sit or stay. Sure, he may not be able follow a Shakespearean play, but he knows what I'm talking about."

"How do you know?"

"When I tell my dog that he's been a good boy, he seems happy!" she answered.

Her response was typical. Many people believe that animals have a basic understanding of language, at least enough to understand commands such as "sit" and "stay." Is it true? Can animals really understand language or do we just like to think that they do?

*A chimp named Kanzi communicates using a special keyboard. Look for more information on Kanzi in this chapter's epilogue.*

Although still controversial, many researchers believe that some animals can learn language. Washoe, a female chimpanzee, was one year old when she began to learn sign language; by the time she was four, she had a vocabulary of more than 130 signs. Previous attempts to teach chimps to learn and use human language failed because they focused on speech. Washoe, like all chimpanzees, lacks the control of the tongue, lips, palate, and vocal cords that humans have and cannot produce the variety of complex sounds that characterize human speech. Like children, she used single signs at first; then she began to produce two-word sentences such as *Washoe sorry, gimme flower, more fruit,* and *Roger tickle.* Sometimes she strung three or more words together, using the concept of agent and object: *You tickle me.* She asked and answered questions, apologized, made assertions—in short, did the kinds of things that children would do while learning to talk. Occasionally, she even made correct generalizations by herself. After learning the sign for the verb *open* (as in *open box, open cupboard*), she used it to say *open faucet,* when requesting a drink. She made signs to herself when she was alone and used them to "talk" to cats and dogs, just as children will do. Although it is difficult to compare her progress with that of human children (the fairest comparison would be with that of a child learning to sign), humans clearly learn language much more readily than chimpanzees do.

It was not long ago that humans were the only species that were considered to have *languages*—flexible systems that use symbols to express many meanings. It has been long known that most species can communicate with one another, but this does not mean that they have language. For example, even insects communicate: A female moth that is ready to mate can release a chemical that will bring male moths from miles away. You would be hard pressed to find anyone who would say that the moth understands language.

Inspired by Project Washoe's (Gardner & Gardner, 1969, 1978) success, several other investigators have taught primate species to use sign language. One conclusion that has emerged from the studies of primates is that true verbal ability is a social behaviour. Throughout this chapter you will see how language is a social behaviour for humans as well. This chapter focuses on how we begin learning language in the earliest stages of life and how our language develops as we reach adulthood.

Language obviously plays a crucial role in our day-to-day communication, but we also use language as a tool in our remembering and thinking. As we saw in Chapter 8, we often encode information in memory verbally. In addition, we can extend our long-term memory for information by writing notes and consulting them later. Language also enables us to think about very complex and abstract issues by encoding them as words and then manipulating the words according to logical rules.

Speaking, listening, writing, and reading are behaviours that, like other behaviours, we can study. Linguists have studied the "rules" of language and have described precisely what we do when we speak or write. In contrast, researchers in **psycholinguistics**, a branch of psychology devoted to the study of verbal behaviour, are more concerned with human

**psycholinguistics** A branch of psychology devoted to the study of verbal behaviour.

cognition than with the particular rules that describe language. Psycholinguists are interested in how children acquire language: how verbal behaviour develops and how children learn to speak from their interactions with adults. They also study how adults use language and how verbal abilities interact with other cognitive abilities. These issues, rather than the concerns of linguists, are the focus of this chapter.

# Speech and Comprehension

The ability to engage in verbal behaviour confers decided advantages on our species. Through listening and reading, we can profit from the experiences of others, even from those of people who died long ago. Through talking and writing, we can share the results of our own experiences. We can request from other people specific behaviours and information that are helpful to us. We can give information to other people so that their behaviour will change in a way that benefits them (or us).

## Perception of Speech

When we speak to someone, we produce a series of sounds in a continuous stream, punctuated by pauses and modulated by stress and changes in pitch. We write sentences as sets of words, with spaces between them. But we say sentences as a string of sounds, emphasizing (stressing) some, quickly sliding over others, raising the pitch of our voice on some, lowering it on others. We maintain a regular rhythmic pattern of stress. We pause at appropriate times—for example, between phrases—but we do not pause after pronouncing each word. Thus, speech does not come to us as a series of individual words; we must extract the words from a stream of speech (Liberman, 1996; Miller & Eimas, 1995).

▲ *People's earliest attempts at written communication took the form of stylized pictures. These petroglyphs are located in Writing-On-Stone Provincial Park in Alberta.* (Jack Brink, Courtesy of The Provincial Museum of Alberta, Edmonton, Alberta)

**Recognition of Speech Sounds** The auditory system performs a formidably complex task in enabling us to recognize speech sounds. Human vocalizations are clearly distinguished from other sounds around us. They contain enough information that we can recognize individuals from the sounds of their speech. Furthermore, we can filter out the non-speech sounds, such as coughs or chuckles, within an individual's vocalization. We do this despite the fact that the underlying sounds of speech vary according to the sounds that precede and follow them, the speaker's accent, and the stress placed on the syllables in which they occur. Like our ability to recognize faces visually, the auditory system recognizes the *patterns* underlying speech rather than just the sounds themselves (Sinha, 2002).

The use of functional imaging technologies described in Chapter 4 has provided researchers with valuable information to help us better understand how language is processed in the brain (e.g., Myers & Blumstein, 2008). Using fMRI scans, Belin, Zatorre, and Ahad (2002) found that some regions of the brain responded more when people heard human vocalizations (both speech and non-speech) than when they heard only natural sounds. Regions in which there was a large difference were located in the temporal lobe, on the auditory cortex. (Refer to Figure 4.24 on page 113). Interestingly, given what we have seen in Chapter 9 regarding the results of the split-brain operation, both the left and right hemispheres showed this contrast between vocalizations and other sounds. However, when Belin, Zatorre, and Ahad studied the way the brain reacted to either natural speech or speech that had been scrambled in frequency, the auditory area on the left hemisphere showed a greater contrast in response. This suggests that when it comes to analyzing the detailed information of speech, the left hemisphere plays a larger role.

What is this detailed information? The analysis of speech usually begins with its elements, or **phonemes.** Phonemes are the elements of speech—the smallest units of sound that allow us to distiguish the meaning of a spoken word. For example, the word *pin* consists of three phonemes: /p/ + /i/ + /n/.

Many experiments have investigated how we discriminate among phonemes ranging from auditory preferences in children with autism (Constantino et al., 2007) to how different types of auditory training programs affect reading and phonemic awareness (Valentine, Hedrick, & Swanson, 2006).

**phoneme** The minimum unit of sound that conveys meaning in a particular language, such as /p/.

Let us consider just one distinction that we can detect: **voice-onset time**, the delay between the initial sound of a consonant and the onset of vibration of the vocal cords. Voicing is the vibration of your vocal cords. The distinction between voiced and unvoiced consonants permits us to distinguish between /p/ and /b/, between /k/ and /g/, and between /t/ and /d/. Try to figure out the difference yourself by saying *pa* and *ba*. Pay attention to what the sounds are like, not to how you move your lips to make them.

The difference is very subtle. When you say *pa*, you first build up a little pressure in your mouth. When you open your lips, a puff of air comes out. The *ah* sound does not occur immediately, because the air pressure in your mouth and throat keeps air from leaving your lungs for a brief time. Your vocal cords do not vibrate until air from your lungs passes through them. When you say *ba*, you do not first build up pressure. Your vocal cords start vibrating as soon as your lips open. The delay in voicing that occurs when you say *pa* is very slight: only 0.06 second. Try saying *pa* and *ba* aloud a few more times and note the difference. Your vocal cords will start to vibrate just a little later when you say *pa*.

Phonemic discriminations begin with auditory processing of the sensory differences, and this occurs in both hemispheres (Binder et al., 2004). However, regions of the left auditory cortex seem to specialize in recognizing the special aspects of speech. Scott, Blank, Rosen, and Wise (2000) identified some of these areas using PET scans. They played recordings of either natural speech, speech that was computer-distorted and unintelligible but contained the phonemic complexity of the sounds, or speech that was intelligible but lacked the normal frequencies of human speakers. Some areas responded to both natural and unintelligible speech, while others responded only to speech that was intelligible—even if it was highly distorted. (See **Figure 10•1**.)

These latter regions of the auditory cortex must rely on information that transcends the distortions of individual phonemes. Perhaps this information is based on larger segments of speech, such as that provided by syllables. A behavioural experiment conducted by Ganong (1980) supports this suggestion. He found that the perception of a phoneme is affected by the sounds that follow it. He used a computer to synthesize a novel sound that fell between those of the phonemes /g/ and /k/. When the sound was followed by *ift*, the participants heard the word *gift*, but when it was followed by *iss*, they heard *kiss*. These results suggest that we recognize speech sounds in pieces larger than individual phonemes.

Phonemes are combined to form **morphemes**, which are the smallest units of meaning in language. The syntax of a particular language determines how phonemes can be combined to form morphemes. For example, the word *fastest* contains two morphemes, /fast/, which is a free morpheme, because it can stand on its own and still have meaning, and /ist/, which is a bound morpheme. Bound morphemes cannot stand on their own and must be attached to other morphemes to provide meaning. Morphemes are an important component in language. In Chapter 8, you learned about the Stroop effect. MacNevin and Besner (2002) found that morphemic priming affects how well people perform on the Stroop test.

**voice-onset time** The delay between the initial sound of a consonant (such as the puffing sound of the phoneme /p/) and the onset of vibration of the vocal cords.
**morpheme** The smallest unit of meaning in language.

## Recognition of Words in Continuous Speech: The Importance of Learning and Context

These larger units of speech are established by learning and experience. Sanders, Newport, and Neville (2002) examined brain wave activity when people listened to a continuous string of sounds. The sounds were composed of short syllabic sounds spliced together, such as the string

babupudutabatutibubabupubu

Sanders and her colleagues then took some of the sounds from the continuous stream (such as the sequence *dutaba*) and designated them as "words." They asked their participants to study these nonsense words carefully. A special electrical signal, called the N100 wave, appears shortly after people hear the onset of a word. Sanders and her co-workers found that when people learned these nonsense sounds as words,

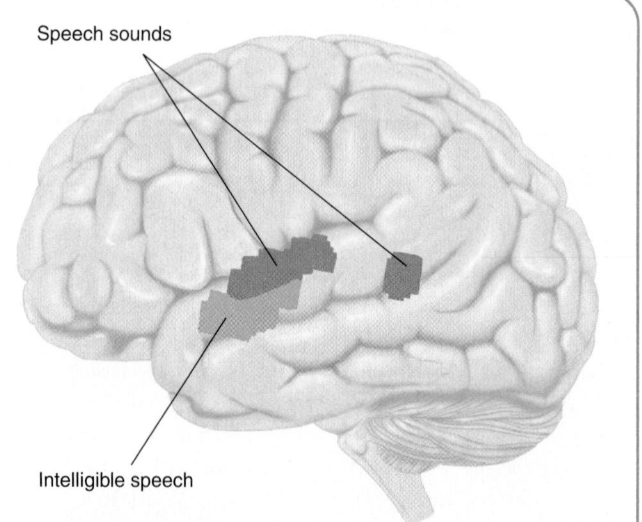


**FIGURE 10•1** Results of PET scans indicating regions of the superior temporal lobe that respond to speech sounds. Dark brown: Regions that responded to phonetic information (normal speech sounds or a computerized transformation speech that preserved the complexity of the speech sounds but rendered it unintelligible). Light brown: Region that responded only to intelligible speech (normal speech sounds or a computerized transformation that removed most normal frequencies but preserved intelligibility).

*(Adapted from Scott, S. K., Blank, C. C., Rosen, S., and Wise, R. J. S. (2000).* Brain, *123, 2400–2406.)*

they showed the N100 response—despite the fact that there were no additional auditory cues to segment the string of sounds.

In addition to learning the units of speech, we also learn its content. Even though speech is filled with hesitations, muffled sounds, and sloppy pronunciations, we are able to recognize the sounds because of the context. Context affects the perception of words through top-down processing. (This concept was discussed in Chapter 6.) Other contexts also affect word perception. For example, although we tend to think of a conversation as involving only sounds, we also use other types of cues present in the environment to help us understand what someone is saying. If we are standing at a snack shop at a beach and someone says, "I scream," we are likely to hear it as "ice cream" (Reynolds & Flagg, 1983). These same cues also play a role in written speech. We take advantage of context when reading just as we do when speaking (Musseler, Niblein, & Koriat, 2005).

## Understanding the Meaning of Speech

The meaning of a sentence (or of a group of connected sentences that are telling a story) is conveyed by the words that are chosen, the order in which they are combined, the affixes attached to the beginnings or ends of the words, the pattern of rhythm and emphasis of the speaker, and knowledge about the world shared by the speaker and the listener. Let us examine some of these features.

**Syntax** If we want a listener to understand our speech, we must follow the "rules" of language. We must use words with which the listener is familiar and combine them in specific ways. For example, if we say, "The two boys looked at the heavy box," we can expect to be understood; but if we say, "Boys the two looking heavily the box at," we will not be. Only the first sentence follows the rules of English grammar.

All languages have a *syntax*, or *grammar*. They all follow certain principles, which linguists call **syntactical rules**, for combining words to form phrases, clauses, or sentences. (*Syntax*, like *synthesis*, comes from the Greek *syntassein*, "to put together.") Syntax provides important information. Consider the following sentence: *A little girl picked the pretty flowers*. A linguist (or an English teacher) can analyze the sentence and identify the part of speech for each word. However, linguists and English teachers could *understand* sentences like this one while they were still children—even before they learned the names *articles, noun phrases*, and so on. Our understanding of syntax is automatic, we are no more conscious of this process than a child is conscious of the laws of physics when he or she learns to ride a bicycle. Although our understanding is perceived automatically, our brains behave differently when we encounter more difficult syntax. fMRI studies have shown that as syntax becomes more complex or ambiguous, our brains become more active (Mason, Just, Keller, & Carpenter, 2003).

In Chapter 8, we saw that some memories (*implicit memories*) cannot be described verbally, whereas others (*explicit memories*) can. Apparently, the syntactical rules are learned implicitly. Later, we can be taught to talk about these rules and to recognize their application (and, for example, construct diagrams of sentences), but this ability is not needed to speak and understand the speech of others. In fact, Knowlton, Ramus, and Squire (1991) found that patients with anterograde amnesia were able to learn an artificial grammar even though they had lost the ability to form explicit memories. In contrast, as Gabrieli, Cohen, and Corkin (1988) observed, such patients are unable to learn the meanings of new words. Thus, learning syntax and word meaning appears to involve different types of memory—and, consequently, different brain mechanisms.

The syntactical rules of the English language are very complicated and by themselves do not tell us much about the psychology of verbal behaviour. However, becoming acquainted with the types of cues we attend to in trying to understand things people say (or write) is useful. Syntactical cues are signalled by *word order, word class, function and content words, affixes, word meanings*, and *prosody*.

*Word order* is important in English. For example, if we say, "The A Xs the B," we are indicating that the agent is A, the object is B, and the thing being done is X. For example, in the sentences *The boy hit the ball* and *The ball hit the boy*, word order tells us who does what to whom. (Word order, however, does not play the same role in all languages. For example, in classical Latin, word order can imply a particular emphasis, but the meaning of a sentence is conveyed by other syntactical cues.)

*Word class* refers to the grammatical categories (such as noun, pronoun, verb, adjective) that we learn about in school. But a person need not learn to categorize these words deliberately in order to recognize them and use them appropriately. For example, when we hear a sentence containing the word *beautiful*, we recognize that it refers to a person or a thing. Consider these two sentences: *The beautiful girl picked the strawberries* and *The tablecloth was beautiful*. Although the word *beautiful* is used in two different ways, at the beginning or end of the sentence, we have no trouble identifying what the word refers to.

Words can be classified as function words or content words. **Function words** include determiners, quantifiers, prepositions, and words in similar categories: *a, the, to, some, and, but, when*, and so on. **Content words** include nouns, verbs, and most adjectives and adverbs: *apple, rug, went, caught, heavy, mysterious, thoroughly, sadly*. Content words express

**syntactical rule** A grammatical rule of a particular language for combining words to form phrases, clauses, and sentences.

**function word** A preposition, article, or other word that conveys little of the meaning of a sentence but is important in specifying its grammatical structure.

**content word** A noun, verb, adjective, or adverb that conveys meaning.

meaning; function words express the relations between content words and thus are very important syntactical cues. As we shall see later, people with a particular type of brain damage lose the ability to comprehend syntax. Included with this deficit is the inability to understand function words or to use them correctly in speech.

**Affixes** are sounds that we add to the beginning (*prefixes*) or end (*suffixes*) of words to alter their grammatical function. For example, we add the suffix *-ed* to the end of a regular verb to indicate the past tense (*drop/dropped*); we add *-ing* to a verb to indicate its use as a noun (*sing/singing*); and we add *-ly* to an adjective to indicate its use as an adverb (*bright/brightly*). We are very quick to recognize the syntactical function of words with affixes like these. For example, Epstein (1961) presented people with word strings such as the following:

> a vap koob desak the citar molent um glox nerf
> A vapy koob desaked the citar molently um glox nerfs.

People could more easily remember the second string than the first, even though letters had been added to some of the words. Apparently, the addition of the affixes *-y*, *-ed*, and *-ly* made the words seem more like a sentence and they thus became easier to categorize and recall.

*Word meanings,* or **semantics**, also provide important cues to the syntax of a sentence. (*Semantics* comes from the Greek *sema*, "sign.") For example, consider the following set of words: *Frank discovered a louse combing his beard.* The *syntax* of this sentence is ambiguous. Is Frank combing Frank's beard? Is the louse combing Frank's beard? Is the louse combing the louse's beard? According to the rules of formal grammar, the louse is doing the combing. But our knowledge of the world and of the usual meanings of words tells us that Frank was doing the combing, because people, not lice, have beards and combs.

Just as function words help us determine the syntax of a sentence, so content words help us determine its meaning. For example, even with its function words removed, the following set of words still makes pretty good sense: *man placed wooden ladder tree climbed picked apples.* You can probably fill in the function words yourself and get *The man placed the wooden ladder against the tree, climbed it, and picked some apples.* We can often guess at function words, which is fortunate, because they are normally spoken quickly and without emphasis and are therefore the most likely to be poorly pronounced.

The final syntactical cue is called prosody. **Prosody** refers to the use of stress, rhythm, and changes in pitch that accompany speech. Prosody can emphasize the syntax of a word or group of words or even serve as the primary source of syntactic information. Prosody is extremely important in language comprehension, because so much of our communication relies on spoken forms. Consider the following two sentences discussed by Steinhauer, Alter, and Friederici (1999):

> Since Jay always jogs five miles seems like a short distance to him.
> Since Jay always jogs five miles this seems like a short distance to him.

The first sentence probably seemed a bit harder to comprehend. That's because we lack the prosody cues conveyed by normal speech. A person speaking that sentence would normally slightly elongate the word *jogs*, lower the pitch of the voice at the end of the word, and pause briefly. These cues signal that the words *five miles* belong with *seems* rather than with *jogs*. Putting a comma between *jogs* and *miles* would accomplish in print what we would normally do in speech.

Although we don't normally notice these cues as we process spoken language, they are certainly part of our ability to segment speech and understand it. Using phrases in German that approximate the two English sentences above, Steinhauer and colleagues placed a verbal pause between *jogs* and *five* in the second sentence. In this case, the syntactic cues to meaning conflict with the prosody. People who heard this hybrid sentence were virtually unanimous in detecting the mismatch. Furthermore, electrical activity of the brain, recorded from exterior electrodes placed on the scalp, showed the kind of brain activity that accompanies unexpected experiences.

**Relation between Semantics and Syntax** There is more than one way to say something, and sometimes a particular sentence can mean more than one thing. In Chapter 8, we looked at an experiment by Sachs that showed that we soon forget the particular form a sentence takes but remember its meaning much longer. Noam Chomsky (1957, 1965), a noted linguist, suggested that newly formed sentences are represented in the brain in terms of their meaning, which he called their **deep structure.** The deep structure represents the kernel of what the person intended to say. In order to say the sentence, the brain must transform the deep structure into the appropriate **surface structure:** the particular form the sentence takes.

An example of a "slip of the tongue" recorded by Fromkin (1973) gives us some clues about the way a sentence's deep structure can be transformed into a particular surface structure.

> Rosa always date shranks.

**affix** A sound or group of letters that is added to the beginning of a word (prefix) or to its end (suffix).
**semantics** The meanings and the study of the meanings represented by words.
**prosody** The use of changes in intonation and emphasis to convey meaning in speech besides that specified by the particular words; an important means of communication of emotion.
**deep structure** The essential meaning of a sentence, without regard to the grammatical features (surface structure) of the sentence that are needed to express it in words.
**surface structure** The grammatical features of a sentence.

**FIGURE 10•2** Deep structure and surface structure. A possible explanation for the error in the sentence *Rosa always date shranks.*

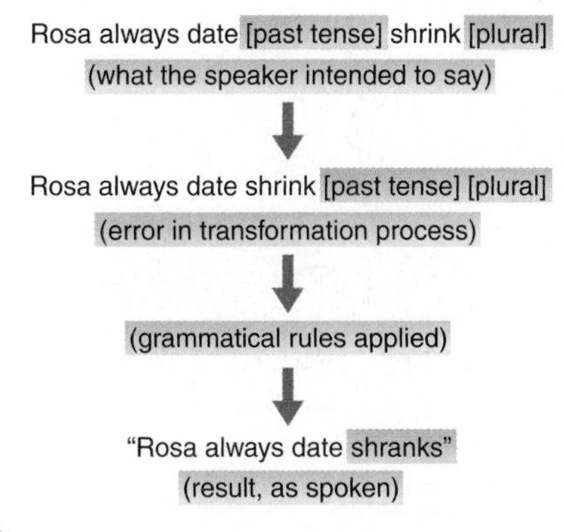


The speaker actually intended to say, "Rosa always dated shrinks" (meaning psychiatrists or clinical psychologists). We can speculate that the deep structure of the sentence's verb phrase was something like this: *date* [past tense] + *shrink* [plural]. The words in brackets represent the names of the syntactical rules that are to be used in forming the surface structure of the sentence. Obviously, the past tense of *date* is *dated*, and the plural of *shrink* is *shrinks*. However, something went wrong during the transformation of the deep structure (meaning) into the surface structure (words and syntax). Apparently, the past tense rule was applied to the word *shrink*, resulting in *shrank*. The plural rule also was applied, making the nonsense word *shranks*. (See **Figure 10•2**.) Following Fromkin's lead, Erard (2007a, 2007b) has compiled a long list of slips of the tongue that illustrate their root in the linearity of language. For example, there's the usher who asked politely, "May I sew you to your sheet?" Or the minister who asked God to fill the congregation with "fresh veal and new zigor." Or the politicians and commentators who switched the names Osama and Obama. In each case, what might be considered errors in translation from deep to surface structure are imposed by the requirement that words necessarily follow one another.

Most psychologists agree that the distinction between surface structure and deep structure is important. As we saw in Chapter 8, people with a language disorder known as conduction aphasia have difficulty repeating words and phrases, but they can *understand* them. In other words, they can retain the deep structure, but not surface structure, of other people's speech. Later in this chapter we will encounter more neuropsychological evidence in favour of the distinction. However, most psychologists disagree with Chomsky about the particular nature of the cognitive mechanisms through which deep structure is translated into surface structure (Hulit & Howard, 2004; Tanenhaus, 1988).

**Knowledge of the World** Comprehension of speech also involves knowledge about the world and about particular situations that we may encounter (Anderson, Budiu & Reder, 2001; Carpenter, Miyake, & Just, 1995). Schank and Abelson (1977) suggested that this knowledge is organized into **scripts**, which specify various kinds of events and interactions that people have witnessed or have learned about from others. Once the speaker has established which script is being referred to, the listener can fill in the details. For example, consider the following sentences (Hunt, 1985): *I learned a lot about the bars in town yesterday. Do you have an aspirin?* To understand what the speaker means, you must be able to do more than simply understand the words and analyze the sentence structure. You must know something about bars; for example, that they serve alcoholic beverages and that "learning about them" probably involves some drinking. You must also realize that drinking these beverages can lead to a headache and that aspirin is a remedy for headaches.

## Brain Mechanisms of Verbal Behaviour

Studies of people with brain damage and PET studies of people engaged in verbal behaviour suggest that mechanisms involved in perceiving, comprehending, and producing speech are located in different areas of the cerebral cortex. These studies have furthered our understanding of the processes of normal verbal behaviour. Let us examine some of these mechanisms.

### Speech Production: Evidence from Broca's Aphasia

To produce meaningful speech, we must convert perceptions, memories, and thoughts into speech. The neural mechanisms that control speech production appear to be located in the frontal lobes. Damage to a region of the motor association cortex in the left frontal lobe (Broca's area) disrupts the ability to speak: It causes **Broca's aphasia**, a language disorder characterized by slow, laborious, non-fluent speech. (See **Figure 10•3**.) As mentioned in earlier chapters, Broca made this discovery while studying a patient named "Tan." The patient was given the name "Tan" as this was the only word he was able to say. When trying to talk with patients who have Broca's aphasia, most people find it hard to resist supplying the words the patients are obviously groping for. But although these patients often mispronounce words, the ones they manage to come out with are meaningful. They have something to say, but the damage to the frontal lobe makes it difficult for them to express these thoughts.

"Tan" likely had damage that extended beyond Broca's area (Selnes & Hillis, 2000). Although people who have Broca's aphasia have great difficulty with speech, the vast majority can say more than a single word. Here is a sample of

**script** The characteristics (events, rules, and so on) that are typical of a particular situation; assists the comprehension of verbal discourse.
**Broca's aphasia** Severe difficulty in articulating words, especially function words, caused by damage that includes Broca's area, a region of the frontal cortex on the left (speech-dominant) side of the brain.

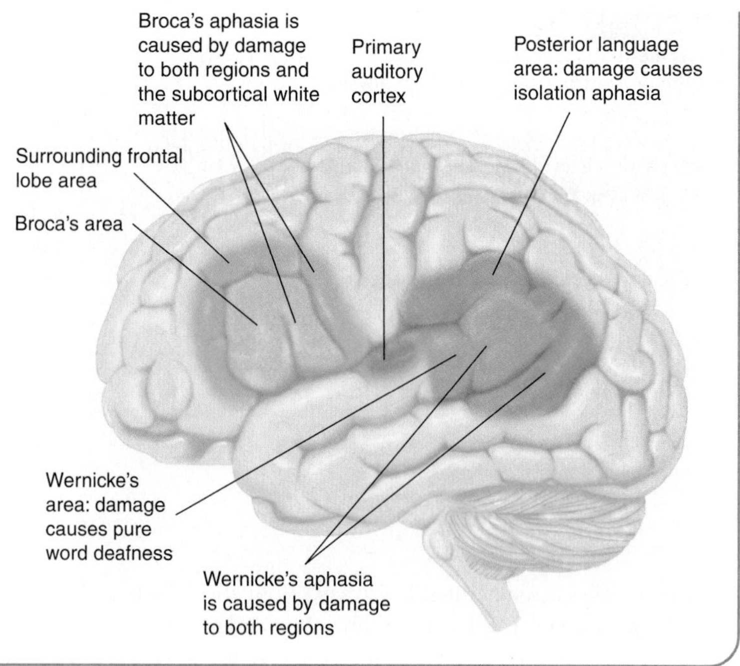
Broca's aphasia is caused by damage to both regions and the subcortical white matter
Primary auditory cortex
Posterior language area: damage causes isolation aphasia
Surrounding frontal lobe area
Broca's area
Wernicke's area: damage causes pure word deafness
Wernicke's aphasia is caused by damage to both regions

**FIGURE 10•3** The locations of Broca's area and Wernicke's area, and associated areas involved in language deficits.

speech from a man with Broca's aphasia, who is telling the examiner why he has come to the hospital. As you will see, his words are meaningful, but what he says is certainly not grammatical. The dots indicate long pauses.

> Ah . . . Monday . . . ah Dad and Paul [patient's name] . . . and Dad . . . hospital. Two . . . ah doctors . . . and ah . . . thirty minutes . . . and yes . . . ah . . . hospital. And, er Wednesday . . . nine o'clock. And er Thursday, ten o'clock . . . doctors. Two doctors . . . and ah . . . teeth. Yeah, . . . fine. (Goodglass, 1976, p. 278)

Lesions that produce Broca's aphasia must be centred in the vicinity of Broca's area. However, damage restricted to the cortex of Broca's area does not appear to produce Broca's aphasia; the damage must extend to surrounding regions of the frontal lobe and to the underlying subcortical white matter (Damasio, 1989; Naeser et al., 1989).

Wernicke (1874) suggested that Broca's area contains motor memories—in particular, memories of the sequences of muscle movements that are needed to articulate words. Talking involves rapid movements of the tongue, lips, and jaw, and these movements must be coordinated with each other and with those of the vocal cords; thus, talking requires some very sophisticated motor control mechanisms. Obviously, circuits of neurons somewhere in our brain will, when properly activated, cause these sequences of movements to be executed. The mechanisms that control these movements do not rely only on the sounds that we produce when we speak, but also adjust to somatosensory feedback (Tremblay, Shiller, & Ostry, 2003). Because damage to the lower left frontal lobe (including Broca's area) disrupts the ability to articulate words, this region is the most likely candidate for the location of these "programs." The fact that this region is located just in front of the part of the primary motor cortex that controls the muscles used for speech certainly supports this conclusion.

**agrammatism** A language disturbance; difficulty in the production and comprehension of grammatical features, such as proper use of function words, word endings, and word order. Often seen in cases of Broca's aphasia.

In addition to their role in the production of words, neural circuits located in the lower left frontal lobe appear to perform some more complex functions. Damage to Broca's area often produces **agrammatism**: loss of the ability to produce or comprehend speech that employs complex syntactical rules. For example, people with Broca's aphasia rarely use function words. In addition, they rarely use grammatical markers such as *-ed* or auxiliaries such as *have* (as in *I have gone*). A study by Saffran, Schwartz, and Marin (1980) illustrates this difficulty. The following quotations are from agrammatic patients attempting to describe pictures:

> *Picture of a boy being hit in the head by a baseball*
>
> The boy is catch . . . the boy is hitch . . . the boy is hit the ball. (p. 229)
>
> *Picture of a girl giving flowers to her teacher*
>
> Girl . . . wants to . . . flowers . . . flowers and wants to . . . The woman . . . wants to . . . The girl wants to . . . the flowers and the woman. (p. 234)

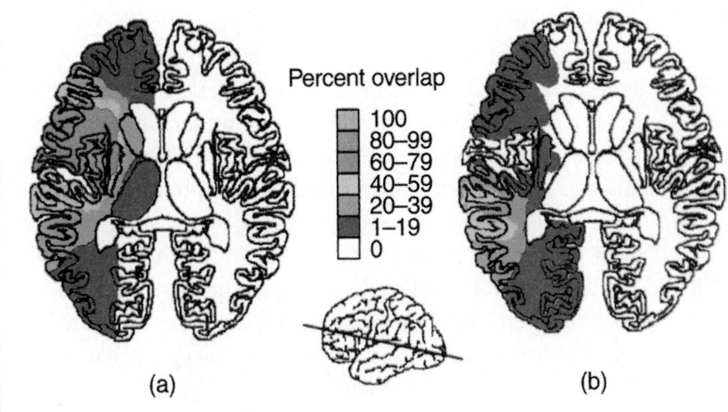


**FIGURE 10•4** Evidence for involvement of the insular cortex in speech articulation. Percentage overlap in the lesions of 25 patients (a) with difficulties in speech articulation and (b) without speech articulation difficulties. The only region common to all lesions that produced speech articulation difficulties was the precentral gyrus of the insular cortex.

*(Reprinted with permission from Dronkers, N. F. (1996).* Nature, 384, *159–161. Copyright 1996 Macmillan Magazines Limited.)*

So far, I have described Broca's aphasia as a disorder in speech *production*. In an ordinary conversation, Broca's aphasics seem to understand everything that is said to them. They appear to be irritated and annoyed by their inability to express their thoughts well, and they often make gestures to supplement their scanty speech. The striking disparity between their speech and their comprehension often leads people to assume that their comprehension is normal. However, their comprehension is *not* normal. To test agrammatic people for speech comprehension, Schwartz, Saffran, and Marin (1980) showed them a pair of drawings, read a sentence aloud, and then asked them to point to the appropriate picture. The patients heard 48 sentences such as *The clown applauds the dancer* and *The robber is shot by the cop*. For the first sample sentence, one picture showed a clown applauding a dancer, and the other showed a dancer applauding a clown. On average, the brain-damaged people responded correctly to only 62 percent of the pictures (chance would be 50 percent). In contrast, the performance of normal people is close to 100 percent on such a simple task.

The correct picture in the study by Schwartz and her colleagues was specified by a particular aspect of grammar: word order. The agrammatism that accompanies Broca's aphasia appears to disrupt patients' ability to use grammatical information, including word order, to decode the meaning of a sentence. Thus, their deficit in comprehension parallels their deficit in production. If they heard a sentence such as *The mosquito was swatted by the man*, they would understand that it concerns a man and a mosquito and the action of swatting. Because of their knowledge of men and mosquitoes, they would have no trouble figuring out who is doing what to whom. But a sentence such as *The cow was kicked by the horse* does not provide any extra cues; if the grammar is not understood, neither is the meaning of the sentence (e.g., Zurif, 1990).

Damage to Broca's area seems to affect a hierarchy of language functions, leading to difficulty in sequencing the muscles of speech that produces articulation problems. At a higher level would be the ability to sequence speech into appropriate grammatical sequences. We might expect brain areas critical to the former function to be located closer to the motor areas of the frontal cortex.

Recent evidence supports this possibility. Dronkers (1996) examined MRI and CT scans of 25 individuals with severe problems of speech articulation. More than half of these were also diagnosed with Broca's aphasia. Depicted in **Figure 10•4(a)** are the areas in which damage overlapped among the different patients. You can see that all of the patients had damage in an area deep within the frontal cortex, in a region known as the *insula*. Compare this to Figure 4.24 (page 113) and you will see how close this region is to the motor areas of the lips and face. In contrast, Dronkers found no damage to this area among a group of individuals without speech articulation problems. (See **Figure 10•4(b)**.) The strong pattern shown has helped revise thinking about the function of this part of the brain (Donnan, Darbey, & Saling, 1997). More recently, Dronkers and colleagues (2004) used neuroimaging and lesion analysis to show that middle-temporal regions outside Broca's area are important for the comprehension of words and other areas of the brain are important for the comprehension of sentences.

The agrammatism that accompanies Broca's aphasia may be a consequence of damage to a different area. Caplan, Alpert, and Waters (1999) examined PET scans of individuals who were asked to decide whether various sentences made sense. Some of these sentences were syntactically more complex than others. Interpreting the more difficult syntactic sentences produced greater activity in the frontal cortex just in front of the motor centre, coinciding with the area identified by Broca.

In the hierarchy of language functions, this area in front of the motor centre might be responsible for grammatical sequences that transcend speech. For example, consider the sign language systems used by many people in the Deaf community, such as American Sign Language used in many parts of Canada and the United States or Langue des Signes Québécoise used in francophone Canada. Although they do not require verbal articulation, these languages depend on grammatical structure just as spoken languages do. In a remarkable comparison, Petitto and colleagues (2000) examined cerebral blood circulation (using PET scans) of both vocal and sign language users when they were asked to produce verbs in response to nouns. Both groups showed activation of the area identified by Caplan, Alpert, and Waters (1999) as important to syntactical processing.

**Speech Comprehension: Evidence from Wernicke's Aphasia** Comprehension of speech obviously begins in the auditory system, which is needed to analyze sequences of sounds and to recognize them as words. Recognition is the first step in comprehension. Recognizing a spoken word is a complex perceptual task that relies on memories of sequences of sounds. This task appears to be accomplished by neural circuits in the upper part of the left temporal lobe, a region that has come to be known as **Wernicke's area**. (Refer to Figure 10.3.)

Brain damage in the left hemisphere that invades Wernicke's area as well as the surrounding region of the temporal and parietal lobes produces a disorder known as Wernicke's aphasia. (See Figure 10.3.) The symptoms of **Wernicke's aphasia** are poor speech comprehension and production of meaningless speech. Unlike Broca's aphasia, the speech associated with Wernicke's aphasia is fluent and unlaboured; the person does not strain to articulate words and does not appear to be searching for them. The patient maintains a melodic line, with the voice rising and falling normally. When you listen to the speech of a person with Wernicke's aphasia, it appears to be grammatical. That is, the person uses function words such as *the* and *but* and employs complex verb tenses and subordinate clauses. However, the person uses few content words, and the words that he or she strings together just do not make sense. In the extreme, speech deteriorates into a meaningless jumble, illustrated by the following example:

> *Examiner*: What kind of work did you do before you came into the hospital?
>
> *Patient*: Never, now mista oyge I wanna tell you this happened when happened when he rent. His—his kell come down here and is—he got ren something. It happened. In thesse ropiers were with him for hi—is friend—like was. And it just happened so I don't know, he did not bring around anything. And he did not pay it. And he roden all o these arranjen from the pedis on from iss pescid. In these floors now and so. He hadn't had em round here. (Kertesz, 1981, p. 73)

**Wernicke's area** A region of the auditory association cortex located in the upper part of the left temporal lobe; involved in the recognition of spoken words.

**Wernicke's aphasia** A disorder caused by damage to the left temporal and parietal cortex, including Wernicke's area; characterized by deficits in the perception of speech and by the production of fluent but rather meaningless speech.

Because of the speech deficit of people with Wernicke's aphasia, when we try to assess their ability to comprehend speech, we must ask them to use non-verbal responses. That is, we cannot assume that they do not understand what other people say to them just because they do not give the proper answer. A commonly used test of comprehension assesses their ability to understand questions by pointing to objects on a table in front of them. For example, they are asked to "Point to the one with ink." If they point to an object other than the pen, they have not understood the request. When tested this way, people with severe Wernicke's aphasia do indeed show poor comprehension.

Because Wernicke's area is a region of the auditory association cortex and because a comprehension deficit is so prominent in Wernicke's aphasia, this disorder has been characterized as a *receptive* aphasia. Wernicke suggested that the region that now bears his name is the location of memories of the sequences of sounds that constitute words. This hypothesis is reasonable; it suggests that the auditory association cortex of Wernicke's area recognizes the sounds of words, just as the visual association cortex in the lower part of the temporal lobe recognizes the sight of objects.

But why should damage to an area responsible for the ability to recognize spoken words disrupt people's ability to speak? Wernicke's aphasia, like Broca's aphasia, actually

▲ *Recognition is not the same as comprehension. If you encounter a foreign word several times you will learn to recognize it, but you will need additional information to learn to comprehend it.*

appears to consist of several deficits. The abilities that are disrupted include recognition of spoken words, comprehension of the meaning of words, and the ability to convert thoughts into words (Basso, 2003). Let us consider each of these abilities in turn.

Remember, *recognizing* a word is not the same as *comprehending* it. If you hear a foreign word several times, you will learn to recognize it; however, unless someone tells you what it means, you will not comprehend it. Recognition is a perceptual task; comprehension involves retrieval of additional information from long-term memory. Damage to Wernicke's area produces a deficit in *recognition*; damage to the surrounding temporal and parietal cortex produces a deficit in production of meaningful speech and comprehension of the speech of others.

Brain damage that is restricted to Wernicke's area produces an interesting syndrome known as **pure word deafness**—a disorder of auditory word recognition, uncontaminated by other problems. Although people with pure word deafness are not deaf, they cannot understand speech. As one patient put it, "I can hear you talking, I just can't understand what you're saying." Another said, "It's as if there were a bypass somewhere, and my ears were not connected to my voice" (Saffran, Marin, & Yeni-Komshian, 1976, p. 211). These patients can recognize non-speech sounds such as the barking of a dog, the sound of a doorbell, the chirping of a bird, and so on. Often, they can recognize the emotion expressed by the intonation of speech even though they cannot understand what is being said. More significantly, their own speech is excellent. They can often understand what other people are saying by reading their lips. They can also read and write, and sometimes they ask people to communicate with them in writing. Clearly, pure word deafness is not an inability to comprehend the meaning of words; if it were, people with this disorder would not be able to read people's lips or read words written on paper.

What happens if the region around Wernicke's area is damaged, but Wernicke's area itself is spared? The person will exhibit all of the symptoms of Wernicke's aphasia *except* a deficit in auditory word recognition. (We already encountered this disorder in Chapter 9.) Damage to the region surrounding Wernicke's area (which I will henceforth refer to as the *posterior language area*) produces a disorder known as **isolation aphasia**, an inability to comprehend speech or to produce meaningful speech accompanied by the ability to repeat speech and learn new sequences of words. (See Figure 10.3.) The difference between isolation aphasia and Wernicke's aphasia is that patients with isolation aphasia can repeat what other people say to them; thus, they obviously can recognize words. However, they cannot comprehend the meaning of what they hear and repeat; nor can they produce meaningful speech of their own. Apparently, the sounds of words are recognized by neural circuits in Wernicke's area, and this information is transmitted to Broca's area so that the words can be repeated. (In fact, a bundle of axons does directly connect these two regions.) But because the posterior language area is destroyed, the meaning of the words cannot be comprehended. (See **Figure 10•5**.)

**FIGURE 10•5** Connections among regions of the brain that play a special role in language. The arrows provide an explanation of the ability of people with isolation aphasia to repeat words without being able to understand them.

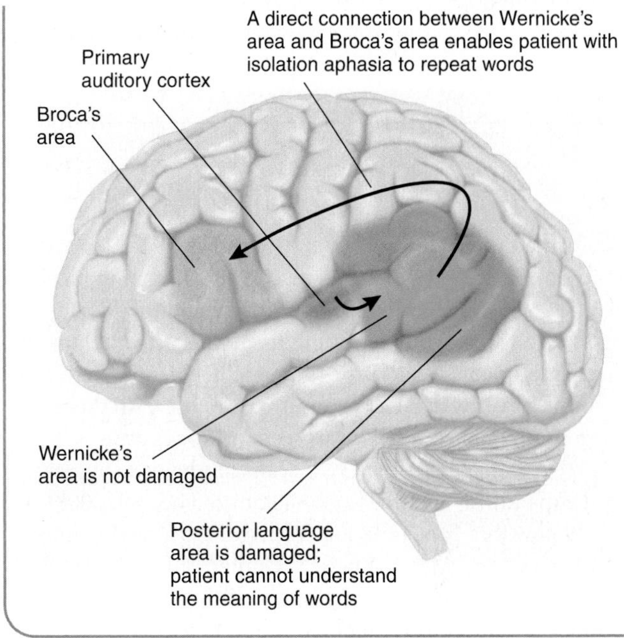
A direct connection between Wernicke's area and Broca's area enables patient with isolation aphasia to repeat words
Primary auditory cortex
Broca's area
Wernicke's area is not damaged
Posterior language area is damaged; patient cannot understand the meaning of words

### Word Recognition and Production: PET and fMRI Studies

The results of studies using the PET-scanning method are generally consistent with the results of studies of language-impaired patients with brain damage. First, several studies have found that patients with Broca's aphasia show abnormally low activity in the lower left frontal lobe, while patients with Wernicke's aphasia show low activity in the temporal/parietal area of the brain (Davis & Johnsrude, 2007; Karbe et al., 1989; Karbe, Szelies, Herholz, & Heiss, 1990; Metter, 1991). These results explain the fact that lesions in the depths of the brain can sometimes produce aphasia; these lesions disrupt the activity of the frontal or temporal/parietal cortex and produce language disturbances.

Other studies have used PET scanners to investigate the neural activity of people without cerebral damage while they

**pure word deafness** The ability to hear, to speak, and (usually) to write, without being able to comprehend the meaning of speech; caused by bilateral temporal lobe damage.

**isolation aphasia** A language disturbance that includes an inability to comprehend speech or to produce meaningful speech, accompanied by the ability to repeat speech and to learn new sequences of words; caused by brain damage to the left temporal/parietal cortex that spares Wernicke's area.

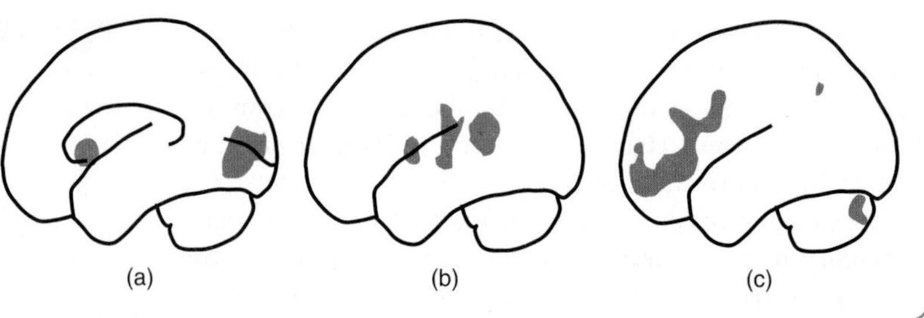


**FIGURE 10•6** PET scans of participants from the study by Petersen and colleagues (1988). (a) Listening passively to a list of nouns. (b) Silently reading a list of nouns. (c) Thinking of verbs related to a list of nouns.

performed verbal tasks. **Figure 10•6** shows PET scans from a study by Petersen and colleagues (1988). Listening passively to a list of nouns activated the primary auditory cortex and Wernicke's area, while repeating the nouns activated the primary motor cortex and Broca's area. When people were asked to think of verbs that were appropriate to use with the nouns, even more intense activity was seen in Broca's area.

Brain imaging using fMRI scans has helped supplement and expand this picture (e.g., Shalom & Poeppel, 2008). We know now that Broca's area is involved in processing musical sequences (e.g., Maess, Koelsch, Gunter, & Friederici, 2001) and in perceiving the rhythm and imagery of motion (Binkofski, Amunts, & Stephan, 2000). Binder and colleagues (1997) produced comprehensive scans of individuals processing the semantic characteristics of spoken words. Their results showed activation of Wernicke's area, which supports the traditional model we have been examining. But semantic decisions also activated large areas of the temporal and parietal areas outside Wernicke's area, as well as frontal lobe regions around Broca's area. Processing the *meaning* of words must involve other areas of the cortex as well.

**What Is Meaning?** As we have seen, Wernicke's area is involved in the analysis of speech sounds and, thus, in the recognition of words. Brain damage to the posterior language area that surrounds Wernicke's area does not disrupt people's ability to recognize words, but it does disrupt their ability to understand them or to produce meaningful speech of their own. What, exactly, do we mean by *meaning*? And what types of brain mechanisms are involved?

Words refer to objects, actions, or relations in the world. Thus, the meaning of a word (its *semantics*) is defined by particular memories associated with it. For example, knowing the meaning of the word *tree* means being able to imagine the physical characteristics of trees: what they look like, what the wind sounds like blowing through their leaves, what the bark feels like, and so on. It also means knowing facts about trees: about their roots, buds, flowers, nuts, wood, and the chlorophyll in their leaves. These memories are not stored in the primary speech areas but in other parts of the brain, especially regions of the association cortex. Different categories of memories may be stored in particular regions of the brain, but they are somehow tied together, so that hearing the word *tree* activates all of them.

In thinking about the brain's verbal mechanisms involved in recognizing words and comprehending their meaning, I find that the concept of a dictionary serves as a useful analogy. Dictionaries contain entries (the words) and definitions (the meanings of the words). In the brain, there are at least two types of entries: auditory and visual. That is, we can look up a word according to how it sounds or looks (in writing). Consider just one type of entry: the sound of a word. We hear a familiar word and understand its meaning. How do we do so?

First, we must recognize the sequence of sounds that constitute the word; we find the auditory entry for the word in our "dictionary." As we saw, this entry appears to be located in Wernicke's area. Next, the memories that constitute the meaning of the word must be activated. Presumably, Wernicke's area is connected—through the posterior language area—with the neural circuits that contain these memories. (See **Figure 10•7**.)

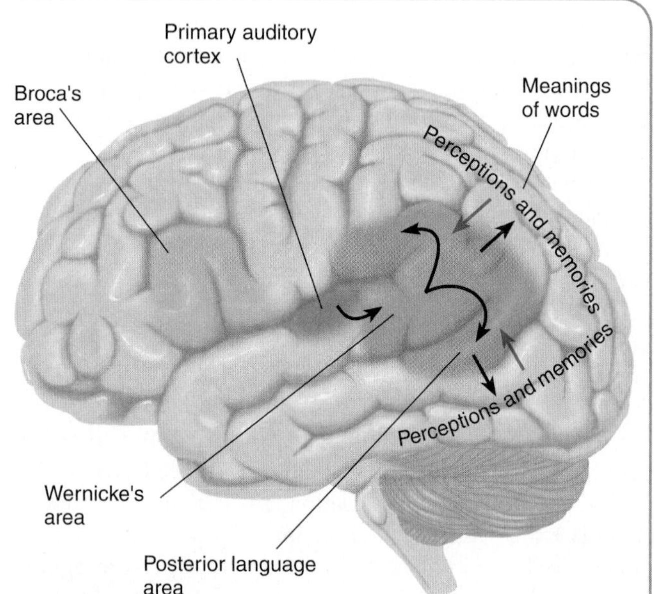


**FIGURE 10•7** Words into thoughts and thoughts into words. The "dictionary" in the brain relates the sounds of words to their meanings and permits us to comprehend the meanings of words and translate our own thoughts into words. Black arrows represent comprehension of words; red arrows represent translation of thoughts or perceptions into words.

The process works in reverse when we describe our thoughts or perceptions in words. Suppose that we want to tell someone about a tree that we just planted. Thoughts about the tree (for example, a visual image of it) occur in our association cortex—the visual association cortex, in this example. Information about the activity of these circuits is sent first to the posterior language area and then to Broca's area, which causes the words to be set into a grammatical sentence and pronounced.

What evidence do we have that meanings of words are represented by neural circuits in various regions of the association cortex? The best evidence comes from the fact that damage to particular regions of the sensory association cortex can damage particular kinds of information and thus abolish particular kinds of meanings. For example, I met a patient who had recently sustained a stroke that had damaged a part of her right parietal lobe that plays a role in spatial perception. She was alert and intelligent and showed no signs of aphasia. However, she was confused about directions and other spatial relations. Although she could point to the ceiling and to the floor if I asked her to, she could not say which was above the other. Similarly, although her perception of other people appeared to be normal, she could not say whether a person's head was at the top or bottom of the body. I wrote a set of multiple-choice questions that evening, and the next day I gave her a test. When a question contained a word that dealt with space, she failed to understand what it meant. For example, she chose the following statements:

> A tree's branches are *under* its roots.
>
> The sky is *down*.

But when a question did not deal with space, she had no trouble choosing the correct alternative. For example, she chose the following statements:

> After exchanging pleasantries, they got *down* to business.
>
> He got sick and threw *up*.

Consider the use of the word *up* in the last sentence. It does not refer to a direction (actually, when we vomit, we usually point our mouths *down*, for obvious reasons). Instead, the word is simply part of a phrase. Similarly, getting *down* to business does not imply that the business has just gotten closer to the floor.

Damage to other regions of the brain can disrupt particular categories of meaning in speech. For example, damage to part of the association cortex of the *left* parietal lobe can produce an inability to name the body parts. This disorder is called autotopagnosia, or "poor knowledge of one's own topography." (A better name would have been *autotopanomia*, "poor *naming* of one's own topography.") People who can otherwise converse normally cannot reliably point to their elbows, knees, or cheeks when asked to do so, and they cannot name body parts when the examiner points to them. However, they have no difficulty understanding the meaning of other words.

## Interim Summary

### Speech and Comprehension

Language is an orderly system of communication. The recognition of words in continuous speech is a complex process. Phonemes are recognized even though their pronunciation is affected by neighbouring sounds, by accents and speech peculiarities, and by stress. Studies have shown that we distinguish between voiced and unvoiced consonant phonemes by means of voice-onset time. Research has also shown that the primary unit of analysis is not individual phonemes but groups of phonemes—perhaps syllables. We use learning and contextual information in recognizing what we hear.

Meaning is a joint function of syntax and semantics. All users of a particular language observe syntactical rules that establish the relations of the words in a sentence to one another. These rules are not learned explicitly. In fact, research indicates that people can learn to apply rules of an artificial grammar without being able to say just what these rules are. The most important features that we use to understand syntax are word order, word class, function and content words, affixes, word meanings, and prosody. Content words refer to objects, actions, and the characteristics of objects and actions and thus can express meaning even in some sentences having ambiguous syntax.

Chomsky has suggested that speech production entails the transformation of deep structure into surface structure. Most psychologists disagree with the details of Chomsky's explanation but consider the distinction between deep and surface structure to be an interesting and important insight.

Speech comprehension requires more than an understanding of syntax and semantics; it also requires knowledge of the world. We must share some common knowledge about the world with a speaker if we are to understand what the speaker is referring to.

The effects of brain damage suggest that memories of the sounds of words are located in Wernicke's area and that memories of the muscular movements needed to produce them are located near Broca's area. Thus, Wernicke's area is necessary for speech perception, and Broca's area is necessary for its production. Wernicke's aphasia (caused by damage that extends beyond the boundaries of Wernicke's area) is characterized by fluent but meaningless speech that is scarce in content words but rich in function words. Presumably, function words and other syntactical features of speech related to motor operations involve mechanisms in the frontal lobes; as we saw, Broca's aphasia (caused by damage that extends beyond the boundaries of Broca's area) is characterized by non-fluent but meaningful speech that is scarce in function words but rich in content words.

Damage restricted to Wernicke's area does not produce aphasia; instead, it produces pure word deafness, a deficit in speech comprehension unaccompanied by other language difficulties. Damage to the temporal/parietal region surrounding Wernicke's area produces isolation aphasia—loss of the ability to produce meaningful speech or to comprehend the speech of others but retention of the ability to repeat speech. The results of studies of patients with brain damage have been supported by PET studies. Understanding the meaning of words requires other areas of the cortex, which contain memories of the relations between words and the concepts they denote.

**QUESTIONS TO CONSIDER**

1. Suppose that you were asked to determine the abilities and deficits of people with aphasia. What tasks would you include in your examination to test for the presence of particular deficits?
2. What are the thoughts of a person with severe Wernicke's aphasia like? These people produce speech having very little meaning. Can you think of any ways that you could test these people to see if their thoughts were any more coherent than their words?

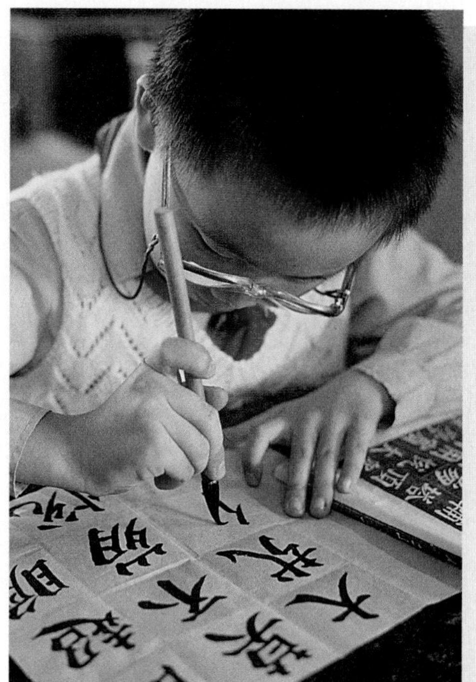

▲ *When people read Chinese, the amount of time they fixate on each character is proportional to its complexity—the number of brush strokes used to make it.*

# Reading

With the notable exception of Chinese (and other Asian writing systems based on Chinese), most modern languages use alphabetic writing systems in which a small number of symbols represent (more or less) the sounds used to pronounce words. For example, most European languages are represented by the Roman alphabet, originally developed to represent the sounds of Latin and subsequently adopted by peoples ruled or influenced by the Roman Empire. The Roman alphabet was adapted from the Greek alphabet, which in turn was adapted from the Phoenician alphabet. For example, the letter *D* has its origin in the Phoenician symbol *daleth*, which meant "door." At first, the symbol literally indicated a door, but it later came to represent the phoneme /d/. The Greeks adopted the symbol and its pronunciation but changed its name to *delta*. Finally, the Romans took it, altering its shape into the one we use in our own language today.

**fixation** A brief interval between saccadic eye movements during which the eye does not move; visual information is gathered during this time.

## Scanning of Text

As we saw in Chapter 5, our eyes make rapid jumps, called *saccades*, as we scan a scene. These same rapid movements occur while we read. In fact, a French ophthalmologist discovered saccadic eye movements while watching people read (Javal, 1879).

We do not perceive things while the eyes are actually moving but during the brief **fixations** that occur between saccades. The average fixation lasts about 250 milliseconds (ms, 1/1000 of a second), but duration can vary considerably. **Figure 10•8** shows the pattern of fixations made by good and poor readers. The ovals above the text indicate the location of the fixations (which occur just below the ovals, on the text itself), and the numbers indicate their duration (in milliseconds). All of the good reader's saccades were in the forward direction, whereas the poor reader looked back and examined previously read words several times (indicated by the arrows). In addition, the good reader's fixations were, on average, considerably shorter.

What do we look at when we read? University students fixate on most words when they are asked to read text carefully enough to understand its meaning. They fixate on 80 percent of the content words but on only 40 percent of the function words (Reichle, Pollatsek, Fisher, & Rayner, 1998). Of course, function words are generally shorter than content words, but the difference is not simply a matter of size.

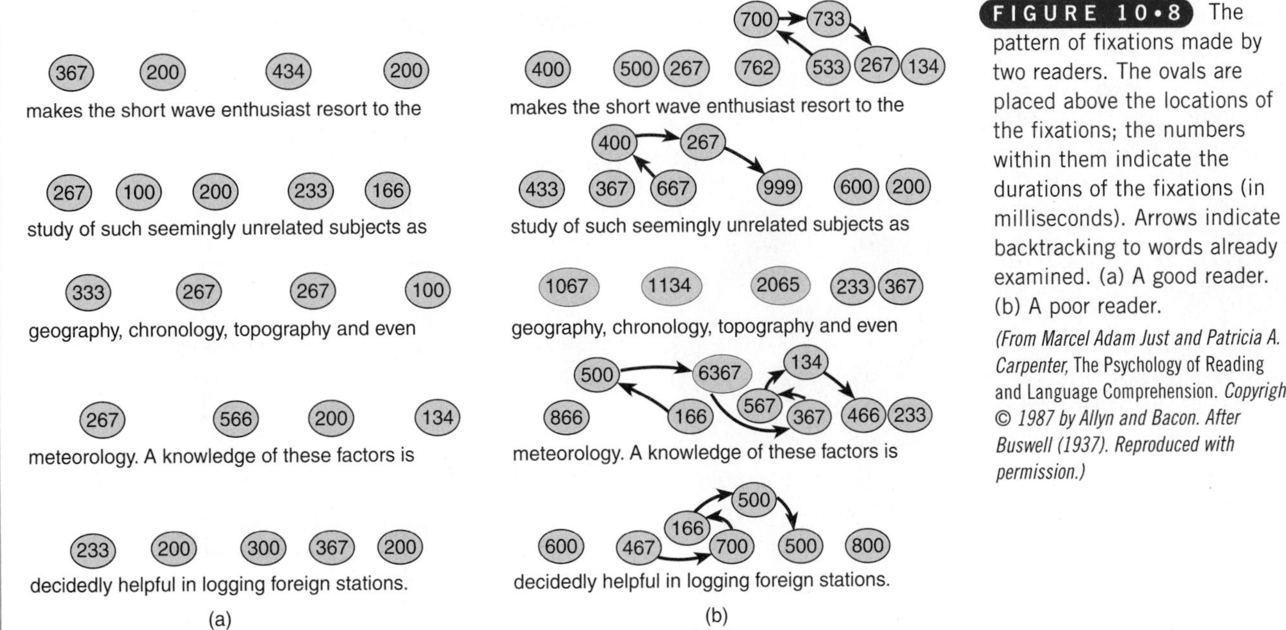


**FIGURE 10•8** The pattern of fixations made by two readers. The ovals are placed above the locations of the fixations; the numbers within them indicate the durations of the fixations (in milliseconds). Arrows indicate backtracking to words already examined. (a) A good reader. (b) A poor reader.

*(From Marcel Adam Just and Patricia A. Carpenter,* The Psychology of Reading and Language Comprehension. *Copyright © 1987 by Allyn and Bacon. After Buswell (1937). Reproduced with permission.)*

Readers are more likely to skip over short function words such as *and* or *the* than over short content words such as *ant* or *run* (Carpenter & Just, 1983).

Eye movements provide an excellent window into the dynamics of the reading process. Apparently, as we read a sentence, we analyze it word by word (Rayner & Pollatsek, 1989). Of course, some words contribute more to our understanding than do others. And sometimes we must wait to see how a sentence turns out to understand the beginning. The less frequently a word occurs in normal usage, the greater the fixation time (e.g., Rayner, Sereno, & Raney, 1996); presumably, we take longer to recognize and understand unusual words. For example, the word *sable* receives a longer fixation than the word *table*. The word that follows an unusual word does not receive a longer-than-usual fixation, which indicates that the reader finishes processing the word before initiating the next saccade (Thibadeau, Just, & Carpenter, 1982). Fixation time is also influenced by predictability of words in text, as measured by readers' ability to guess a missing word that should come after a few introductory words. Gaze time is longer for unpredictable than for predictable words, even when comparison words in experiments are matched for word length and frequency of usage (Reichle, Pollatsek, Fisher, & Rayner, 1998).

Besides spending a longer time fixating on unusual words, readers spend more time fixating on *longer* words. In fact, if word familiarity is held constant, the amount of time a word receives is proportional to its length (Carpenter & Just, 1983). In addition, Just, Carpenter, and Wu (1983) found that the amount of time that Chinese readers spent fixating on a character in the traditional Chinese writing system was proportional to the number of brush strokes used to make it. All Chinese characters are of approximately the same size, so the increased fixation time appears to reflect the complexity of a word rather than the amount of space it occupies.

## Phonetic and Whole-Word Recognition: Evidence from Neuropsychology

Most psychologists who study the reading process believe that readers have two basic ways to recognize words: phonetic and whole-word recognition (McGuinness, 2004; Rayner et al., 2002; Snowling & Hulme, 2005). **Phonetic reading** involves the decoding of the sounds that letters or groups of letters make. For example, I suspect that you and I would pronounce *praglet* in approximately the same way. Our ability to pronounce this nonsense word depends on our knowledge of the relation between letters and sounds in the English language. We use such knowledge to "sound the word out." But do we have to "sound out" familiar, reasonably short words such as *table* or *grass*? It appears that we do not; we recognize each of these words as a whole. We engage in **whole-word reading**—reading by recognizing a word as a whole.

If a reader is relatively inexperienced, he or she will have to sound out most words and, consequently, will read rather slowly. Experienced readers will have had so much practice looking at words that they will quickly recognize most of them as individual units. In other words, during reading, phonetic and whole-word reading are engaged in a race. If

**phonetic reading** Reading by decoding the phonetic significance of letter strings; "sound reading."
**whole-word reading** Reading by recognizing a word as a whole; "sight reading."

▲ *Most school systems teach children phonetic reading skills so that they can sound out words they do not recognize.*

the word is familiar, the whole-word method will win. If the word is unfamiliar, the whole-word method will fail, and the phonetic method will have enough time to come to completion.

**Figure 10•9** illustrates some elements of the reading process. The diagram is an oversimplification of a very complex process, but it helps organize some of the facts that investigators have obtained. It considers only reading and pronouncing single words, not understanding the meaning of text. When we see a familiar word, we normally recognize it as a whole and say it aloud. If we see an unfamiliar word or a pronounceable non-word, we must try to read it phonetically. We recognize each letter and then sound it out, based on our knowledge of phonetics.

Whole-word recognition is not only faster than phonetic decoding, but also absolutely necessary in a language (such as English) in which spelling is not completely phonetic. Consider the following pairs of words: *cow/blow, bone/one, post/cost, limb/climb*. Obviously, no single set of phonological rules can account for the pronunciation of both members of each pair. (*Phonology*—loosely translated as "laws of sound"—refers to the relation between letters and the sounds they represent in a particular language.) Yet all of these words are familiar and easy to read. If we did not have the ability to recognize words as wholes, we would not be able to read irregularly spelled words, which are rather common in our language. Some languages, such as Italian, are more closely tied to phonetics. Speakers of these languages apparently process speech in different areas than speakers of less phonetic languages (Paulesu et al., 2000).

**surface dyslexia** A reading disorder in which people can read words phonetically but have difficulty reading irregularly spelled words by the whole-word method.

**phonological dyslexia** A reading disorder in which people can read familiar words but have difficulty reading unfamiliar words or pronounceable non-words because they cannot sound out words.

**FIGURE 10•9** A simplified model of the reading process, showing whole-word and phonetic reading. The model considers only reading a single word aloud. Whole-word reading is used for most familiar words; phonetic reading is used for unfamiliar words and for non-words such as *glab, trisk*, or *chint*.

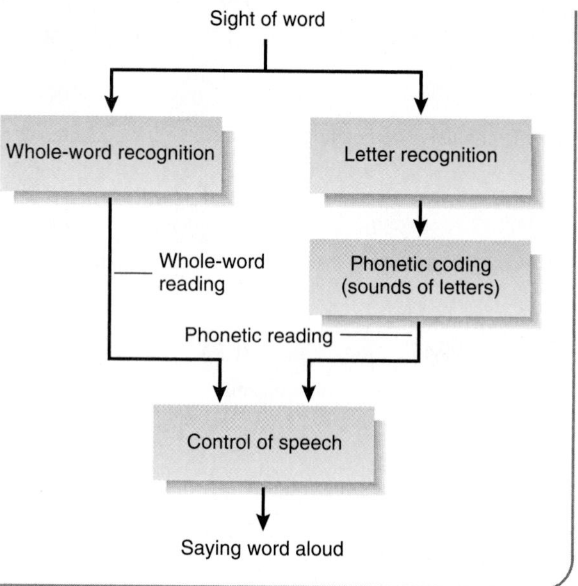


The best evidence that proves that people can read words without sounding them out comes from studies of patients with acquired dyslexias. *Dyslexia* means "faulty reading." *Acquired* dyslexias are those caused by damage to the brains of people who already know how to read. In contrast, *developmental* dyslexias are reading difficulties that become apparent when children are learning to read. Developmental dyslexias may involve anomalies in brain circuitry, and I will discuss them later.

Although investigators have reported several types of acquired dyslexias, we will look at just three of them here. All of these disorders are caused by damage to the left parietal lobe or left temporal lobe, but the anatomy of dyslexias is not well understood. **Surface dyslexia** is a deficit in whole-word reading (Marshall & Newcombe, 1973; McCarthy & Warrington, 1990). The term *surface* reflects the fact that people with this disorder make errors related to the visual appearance of the words and to pronunciation rules, not to the meaning of the words, which is metaphorically "deeper" than the appearance. Because patients with surface dyslexia have difficulty recognizing words as wholes, they are obliged to sound them out. Thus, they can easily read words with regular spelling, such as *hand, table*, or *chin*. However, they have difficulty reading words with irregular spelling, such as *sew, pint*, and *yacht*. In fact, they may read these words as *sue, pinnt*, and *yatchet*. They have no difficulty reading pronounceable non-words, such as *glab, trisk*, and *chint*. (See **Figure 10•10**.)

Patients with **phonological dyslexia** have the opposite problem; they can read by the whole-word method but

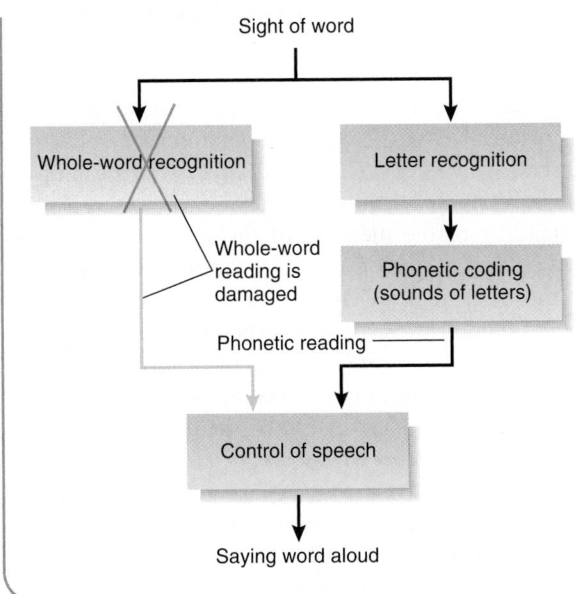


**FIGURE 10•10** A hypothetical explanation of surface dyslexia. Only phonetic reading remains.

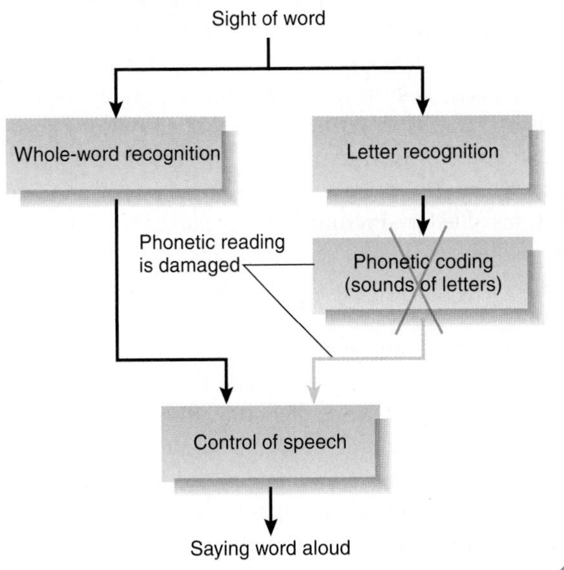


**FIGURE 10•11** A hypothetical explanation of phonological dyslexia. Only whole-word reading remains.

cannot sound out words. Thus, they can read words that they are already familiar with, but they have great difficulty figuring out how to read unfamiliar words or pronounceable non-words (Beauvois & Dérouesné, 1979; Dérouesné & Beauvois, 1979). People with phonological dyslexia may be excellent readers if they have already acquired a good reading vocabulary before their brain damage occurs. (See **Figure 10•11**.)

Phonological dyslexia provides evidence that whole-word reading and phonological reading involve different brain mechanisms. Phonetic reading, which is the only way we can read non-words or words we have not yet learned, entails some sort of letter-to-sound decoding. It also requires more than decoding of the sounds produced by single letters, because, for example, some sounds are transcribed as two-letter sequences (such as *th* or *sh*) and the addition of the letter *e* to the end of a word lengthens an internal vowel (*can* becomes *cane*). Further, there is evidence from PET scans (Fiez, Balota, Raichle, & Petersen, 1999) and fMRI scans (Gaillard et al., 2001) that phonetic reading activates the left frontal lobe in the area associated with Broca's aphasia.

As we saw earlier in this chapter, recognizing a spoken word is different from understanding it. For example, patients with transcortical sensory aphasia can repeat what is said to them even though they show no signs of understanding what they hear or say. Another language disorder resembles isolation aphasia, except that the words in question are written, not spoken (Lytton & Brust, 1989; Schwartz, Marin, & Saffran, 1979). People with this disorder, called **direct dyslexia**, can read words aloud *even though they cannot understand the words they are saying*. After sustaining a stroke that damaged his left frontal and temporal lobes, Lytton and Brust's patient lost the ability to communicate verbally; his speech was meaningless and he was unable to comprehend what other people said to him. However, he could read words with which he was already familiar. He could *not* read pronounceable non-words; thus, he had lost the ability to read phonetically. His comprehension deficit seemed complete; when the investigators presented him with a word and several pictures, one of which corresponded to the word, he read the word correctly but had no idea which picture went with it.

The symptoms of developmental dyslexias resemble those of acquired dyslexias (Vellutino & Fletcher, 2005). They first manifest themselves in childhood and tend to occur in families, which suggests the presence of a genetic (and hence developmental) component. Grigorenko (2001) reported studies of the prevalence of developmental dyslexias, ranging from 1 percent in Japan and China to 33 percent in Venezuela, with a 26-nation mean of 7 percent. Several studies have found evidence that brain abnormalities in a portion of Wernicke's area may be responsible for developmental dyslexias (Galaburda, 1993; Galaburda & Kemper, 1979; Galaburda et al., 1985). In addition, Galaburda, Menard, and Rosen (1994) found evidence that structural differences in the auditory system of the brain may play a role in this disorder. Brain imaging data indicate that people with developmental dyslexias can use both Broca's area and Wernicke's area for language processing. However, these individuals lack the degree of synchrony of neural activity in the two areas shown by people without dyslexia (Paulesu et al., 1996). In other words, dyslexic patients may not be able to combine the activity of the two areas.

As we saw earlier, PET studies have shown that the auditory association cortex is activated by the sound of words but

**direct dyslexia** A language disorder caused by brain damage in which people can read words aloud without understanding them.

not by other sounds. Petersen, Fox, Snyder, and Raichle (1990) obtained similar results using visual stimuli. These investigators presented people with four types of visual stimuli: unfamiliar letter-like forms, strings of consonants, pronounceable non-words, and real words. They found that although all visual stimuli activated the primary visual cortex, one region of the visual association cortex was activated only by pronounceable non-words or by real words. Their finding suggests that this region plays a role in recognition of familiar combinations of letters. Presumably, damage to this region, or faulty development of the neural circuits located there, is responsible for some forms of dyslexia. (See **Figure 10•12**.)

A more recent study involving Finnish participants found temporal but not anatomical differences in the responses of developmentally dyslexic and non-dyslexic adults (Helenius, Salmelin, Service, & Connolly, 1999). The participants viewed sentences presented one word at a time. The final word in the sentence was manipulated to be expected, unexpected but meaningful, sharing the same first letters as the expected word but non-meaningful, and unexpected as well as non-meaningful. Though no differences in the spatial distribution of cortical responses were observed between the two groups, cortical activation by word meaning began later in dyslexic participants, and their cortical responses were significantly weaker than those of normal readers.

Reduced cerebral activity in the left occipitotemporal area of developmentally dyslexic adults was reported by McCrory, Mechelli, Frith, and Price (2005). PET scanning occurred as participants were asked to read words and name pictures consisting of line drawings. The lower activity appeared for both tasks, prompting the authors to conclude that deficits in reading words and naming pictures may have a common neurological basis. The failure to properly integrate phonology and visual information may characterize developmental dyslexia.

## Understanding the Meanings of Words and Sentences

Recognizing a word is a matter of perception. The primary task is a visual one. But as we saw in the previous section, when we encounter an unfamiliar word we use phonological codes to "sound it out." Once we recognize a word, the next step in the reading process is understanding its meaning.

We learn the meanings of words through experience. The meanings of content words involve memories of objects, actions, and their characteristics; thus, the meanings of content words involve visual, auditory, somatosensory, olfactory, and gustatory memories. These memories of the meanings of words are distributed throughout the brain. For example, our understanding of the meaning of the word *apple* involves memories of the sight of an apple, the way it feels in our hands, the crunching sound we hear when we bite into it, and the taste and odour we experience when we chew it. Our understanding of the meanings of adjectives, such as the word *heavy*, involves memories of objects that are difficult or impossible to lift. The image evoked by the phrase *heavy package* undoubtedly involves memories of our own experience with heavy packages, whereas the one evoked by the phrase *heavy rocket* (with which we have had no personal experience) is understood in terms of visual size and bulk.

What about the understanding of abstract content words, such as the nouns *honesty* and *justice*? These words are probably first understood as adjectives: An *honest student* is one who does not cheat on exams or plagiarize while writing papers, an *honest bank clerk* does not steal money, and so on. Our understanding of these words depends on our direct experience with such people or our vicarious experience with them through stories we read or hear about. By itself, the word *honesty* is abstract; it does not refer to anything concrete.

The understanding of most function words is also abstract. For example, the word *and* serves to link two or more things being discussed; the word *or* indicates a choice; the word *but* indicates that a contradiction will be expressed in the next phrase. The meanings of such words are difficult to imagine or verbalize, rather like the rules of grammar. The meanings of prepositions, such as *in*, *under*, or *through*, are more concrete and are probably represented by images of objects in relation to each other.

As we read (or hear) a sentence, the words and phrases we encounter activate memories that permit us to understand their meanings. Unless we deliberately pause to figure

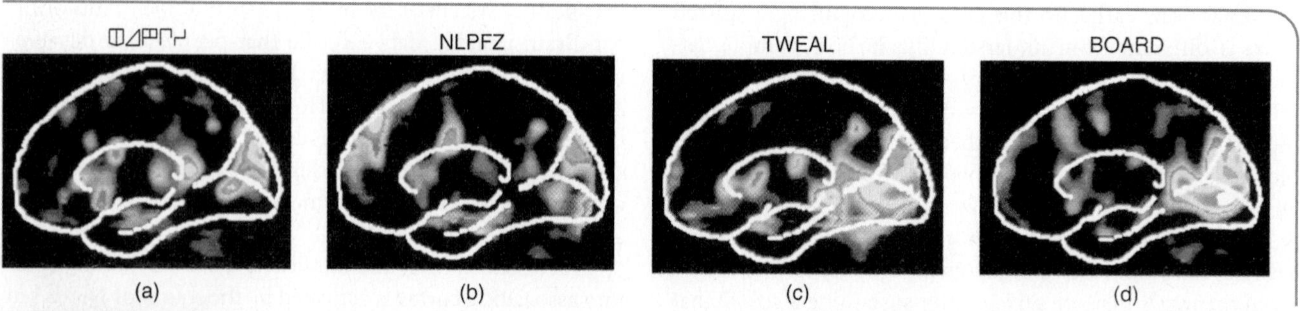


**FIGURE 10•12** PET scans of the medial surface of the brains of people who read (a) letter-like forms, (b) strings of consonants, (c) pronounceable non-words, and (d) real words.

*(From Petersen, S. E., Fox, P. T., Snyder, A. Z., & Raichle, M. E. (1990).* Science, 249, *1041–1044. Reprinted with permission.)*

out an obscure allusion (which should not happen very often in the case of good writing and speaking), this activation is an automatic, unconscious process. When we read the sentence *She opened her mouth to let the dentist examine her aching tooth*, we very quickly picture a specific scene. Our understanding depends not only on comprehension of the specific words, but also on our knowledge of dental chairs, dentists, toothaches and their treatment, and so on.

A phenomenon known as **semantic priming** gives us some hints about the nature of activation of memories triggered by the perception of words and phrases. Semantic priming is a facilitating effect on the recognition of words having meanings related to a word encountered earlier (Tulving & Schacter, 1990). It involves similarities in the *meanings* of words. If a person reads a particular word, he or she can more easily read a second word that is related in meaning to the first. For example, if a person sees the word *bread*, he or she will be more likely to successfully recognize a fuzzy image of the word *butter* or an image that is presented very briefly by means of a tachistoscope (Johnston & Dark, 1986). Presumably, the brain contains circuits of neurons that serve as "word detectors" involved in visual recognition of particular words (McClelland & Rumelhart, 1981; Morton, 1979). Reading the word *bread* activates word detectors and other neural circuits involved in memories of the word's meaning. Apparently, the activation spreads to circuits denoting related concepts, such as butter. Thus, our memories must be linked according to our experience regarding the relations between specific concepts.

**Figure 10•13** suggests how neural representations of concepts may be linked together. The concept "piano" has many different features, including the sounds a piano makes, its size, the shapes it can have, its components, the people who interact with it, and so on. Depending on the context in which it is perceived, the word *piano* can activate various subsets of these features. For example, the sentences *The piano was tuned* and *The piano was lifted* activate neural representations of different features.

Context effects, an example of top-down processing, have been demonstrated through semantic priming. For example, Zola (1984) asked people to read sentences such as the following while he recorded their eye movements with an eye tracker.

1. Movie theaters must have adequate popcorn to serve their patrons.
2. Movie theaters must have buttered popcorn to serve their patrons.

Zola found that people made a significantly shorter fixation on the word *popcorn* in sentence 2. Let us consider why they did so. The word *adequate* is not normally associated with the word *popcorn*, so the people who read sentence 1 were unprepared for this word when they got to it. However, *buttered* certainly goes with *popcorn*, especially in the context of a movie theatre. Thus, the context of the sentence must have provided some activation of the word detector for *popcorn*, making it easier for people to recognize the word.

Semantic priming studies have also shed some light on another aspect of the reading process—the development of a

**semantic priming** A facilitating effect on the recognition of words having meanings related to a word that was presented previously.

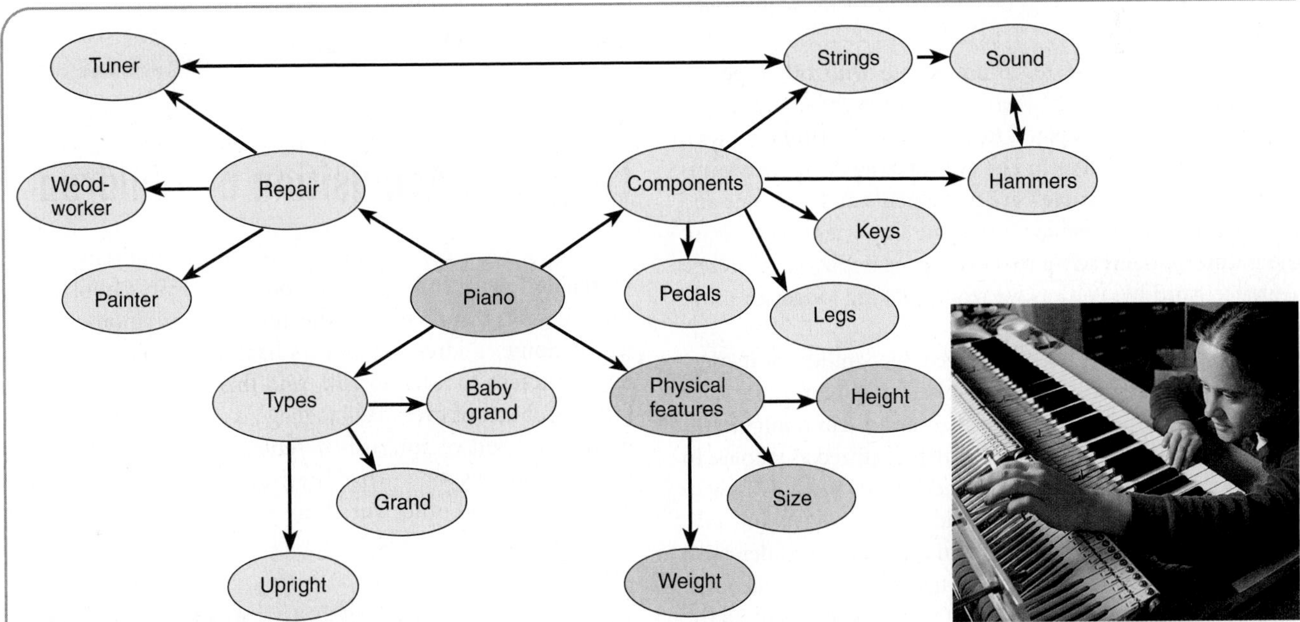


**FIGURE 10•13** Linking neural representations of concepts. Recognizing the word *piano* activates neural representations of features related to pianos. The blue ovals indicate the concepts activated by the sentence *The piano was lifted.*

*(From Marcel Adam Just and Patricia A. Carpenter,* The Psychology of Reading and Language Comprehension. *Copyright © 1987 by Allyn and Bacon. Reproduced with permission.)*

*mental model.* Many investigators believe that as a person reads some text, he or she generates a mental model of what the text is describing (see Johnson-Laird, 1985, for a discussion of mental models). For example, if the text contains a narrative, the reader will imagine the scenes and actions that are being recounted. Glenberg, Meyer, and Lindem (1987) had participants read the following sentences. Some participants were shown the following text with the words *put on*; others were shown it with the words *took off*:

> John was preparing for a marathon in August. After doing a few warm-up exercises, he *put on/took off* his sweatshirt and went jogging. He jogged halfway around the lake without too much difficulty.

After the participants had read the last sentences, the researchers flashed the word *sweatshirt* on a screen and measured the participants' reaction times. Those participants who had read *put on* recognized the word faster than did those who had read *took off*. Presumably, the mental model of the first group of participants contained a man wearing a sweatshirt; thus, the word detector for *sweatshirt* was primed.

Reading may therefore involve two types of memory. As we scan text, we use memory for the words in the sentences to discern the meanings of other words, as in the *buttered popcorn* example. But we also retain a memory for the mental model we construct from the narrative. Singer and Ritchot (1996) suggest that these are two different abilities, and that they make independent contributions to reading efficiency.

## Interim Summary

### Reading

Writing allows people to communicate with other people they have never met—and who may not even be alive at the time the writing takes place. Recognition of written words is a complex perceptual task. The eye-tracking device allows researchers to study people's eye movements and fixations and to learn from these behaviours some important facts about the nature of the reading process. For example, we analyze a sentence word by word as we read it, taking longer to move on from long or unusual words.

Once a word has been perceived, recognition of its pronunciation and meaning takes place. Long or unfamiliar words are sounded out—that is, they are read phonologically. In contrast, short, familiar words are recognized as wholes. In fact, only whole-word reading will enable us to know how to pronounce words such as *cow* and *blow*, or *bone* and *one*, which have irregular spellings. In an experienced reader, both whole-word and phonetic reading take place simultaneously. If a word is recognized as a whole, the reader moves on to the next one; if not, he or she continues to decode it phonologically. The distinction between these two forms of recognition is supported by behavioural data and by studies of people with acquired dyslexias. People with surface dyslexia have difficulty with whole-word reading, while people with phonological dyslexia have difficulty sounding out unfamiliar words or pronounceable non-words. In addition, people with direct dyslexia can read words but cannot understand their meaning. Developmental dyslexias appear to be caused by abnormal development of parts of the left hemisphere, and may reflect an inability to combine information from Broca's area and Wernicke's area.

The meanings of words are learned through experience. Concrete content words are represented by memories of objects, actions, and their characteristics. Abstract content words are probably first understood as adjectives that refer to properties of concrete concepts. Function words are understood by their grammatical roles or by the relations they represent. The phenomenon of semantic priming suggests that some neural circuits (word detectors) recognize the visual form of words, while other circuits encode various aspects of the meanings of words. Connections between these circuits are responsible for our ability to recognize associations in meaning. Thus, semantic priming has been used to study the processes of word recognition and comprehension of meaning.

**QUESTIONS TO CONSIDER**

1. Suppose someone close to you received a head injury that caused phonological dyslexia. What would you do to try to help her read better? (It would probably be best to build on her remaining abilities.) Suppose she needed to learn to read some words she had never seen before. How would you help her do so?
2. Young children often move their lips while they read. Why do you think they do so?

## Language Acquisition by Children

The linguistic accomplishments of young children are remarkable. Even a child who later does poorly in school learns the rules of grammar and the meanings of thousands of words. Some children fail to work hard at school, but no normal child fails to learn to talk. And this happens despite the fact that much of everyday language is ungrammatical, hesitating, and full of unfinished sentences. What shapes this learning process, and what motivates it? This section addresses these and other questions related to children's verbal development.

### How and Why Do Children Learn to Speak Grammatically?

Many linguists have concluded that the ability to learn language is innate. A child must only live in the company of speakers of a language to acquire that language. To explain how this happens, linguists have proposed that a child's brain contains a "language acquisition device," which embodies rules of "universal grammar"; because each language expresses these rules in slightly different ways, the child must learn the details, but the basics are already there in the brain (Chomsky, 1965; Lennenberg, 1967; McNeill, 1970).

The assertion that an innate language acquisition device guides children's acquisition of a language is part of a general theory about the cognitive structures responsible for language and its acquisitions (Pinker, 1990, 1994). The most important components are as follows:

1. Children who are learning a language make hypotheses about the grammatical rules they need to follow. These hypotheses are confirmed or disconfirmed by the speech they hear.
2. An innate language acquisition device (a part of the brain) guides children's hypothesis formation. Because they have this device, there are certain types of hypothetical rules they will never entertain and certain types of sentences they will never utter.
3. The language acquisition device makes reinforcement unnecessary; the device provides the motivation for the child to learn a language.
4. There is a critical period for learning a language. The language acquisition device works best during childhood; after childhood, languages are difficult to learn and almost impossible to master.

The presence of a language acquisition device is controversial, and researchers are still debating these points. In one sense, a language acquisition device does exist. The human brain is a language acquisition device; without it, languages are not acquired. The real controversy is over the characteristics of this language acquisition device. Is it specialized for universal rules of grammar, and does it provide innate motivation that makes reinforcement unnecessary?

The answer may be emerging in the increased resolution of the techniques of functional brain imaging. An fMRI study by Musso and colleagues (2003) shows what is now possible. Musso and colleagues examined the brain activity of native German speakers as they learned two types of language: a real but unfamiliar language (such as Italian or Japanese) or an artificial language that used Italian or Japanese words but violated grammatical principles common to both languages. Of course, German and, say, Italian differ in a number of ways. For example, when saying "I eat a pizza," the "I" is explicitly stated in German ("*Ich esse ein Pizza*") but not in Italian ("*Mangio una pizza*"). However, the variation is within the range of universal rules of grammar that recognize the deeper structure of the meaning. In contrast, Musso and colleagues constructed their artificial languages to contain arbitrary and bizarre grammatical conventions based solely on linear word order. For example, to construct a question, the word order of a sentence simply would be reversed. To ask whether Paolo is eating the pizza, the artificial language would read *Pizza la mangia Paolo?* Or to construct a negative statement, the word *no* would be added after the third word of a sentence, as in *Paolo mangia la no pizza* ("Paolo eats the no pizza").

As you might imagine, it can be difficult as an adult to learn any language, let alone one that violates what we might regard as conventional grammatical rules. But which areas of the brain control this learning? Musso and colleagues found that only the real languages triggered activity in a definite region: Broca's area. Learning the artificial grammar produced only non-specific activity across large areas of the brain. Apparently, when we learn the hierarchical rules of grammar we rely specifically on the regions of the brain around Broca's area.

The ease with which young children learn a language is an area of research that is still the focus of much debate. It may be that our evolutionary history shaped some regions of our brain so that they were well equipped to handle the special characteristics of linguistic behaviours (see Dunbar, 2004, for a short commentary). But the precise nature of the brain mechanisms and the environmental contributions remain for us to discover.

## Perception of Speech Sounds by Infants

To begin to understand how children learn language, we must look at how language development starts before birth. Although the sounds that reach a fetus are somewhat muffled, speech sounds can still be heard. And some learning appears to take place prenatally. The voice that a fetus hears best and most often is obviously that of its mother. DeCasper and Spence (1986) found that newborn infants preferred hearing their mothers reading a passage they had read aloud several times before the babies were born to hearing them read a passage they had never read before. Presumably, the infants had learned something about the rhythm and intonation of the passage they had heard in utero. There is also some evidence that newborns can learn to discriminate speech sounds while they sleep (Cheour et al., 2002).

Psychologists have developed a clever technique to determine what sounds a very young infant can perceive. A special pacifier nipple is placed in the baby's mouth. The nipple is connected by a plastic tube to a pressure-sensitive switch that converts the infant's sucking movements into electrical signals. These signals can be used to turn on auditory stimuli. Each time the baby sucks, a particular sound is presented. If the auditory stimulus is novel, the baby usually begins to suck at a high rate. If the stimulus remains the same, its novelty wears off (habituation occurs) and the rate of sucking decreases. With another new stimulus, the rate of sucking again suddenly increases, unless the baby cannot discriminate the difference. If the stimuli sound the same to the infant, the rate of sucking remains low after the change.

Using this technique, Eimas, Siqueland, Jusczyk, and Vigorito (1971) found that one-month-old infants could tell

**TABLE 10.1 Examples of Responses Infants Make to Various Speech Sounds**

| First Age of Occurrence | Response |
|---|---|
| Newborn | Is startled by a loud noise |
| | Turns head to look in the direction of sound |
| | Is calmed by the sound of a voice |
| | Prefers mother's voice to a stranger's |
| | Discriminates among many speech sounds |
| 1–2 mo | Smiles when spoken to |
| 3–7 mo | Responds differently to different intonations (e.g., friendly, angry) |
| 8–12 mo | Responds to name |
| | Responds to "no" |
| | Recognizes phrases from games (e.g., "Peekaboo," "How big is baby?") |
| | Recognizes words from routines (e.g., waves to "bye-bye") |
| | Recognizes some words |

*Source: Berko Gleason, J. (1993).* The development of language. *New York: Macmillan Publishing Company. Used by permission.*

the difference between the sounds of the consonants *b* and *p*. They presented the sounds *ba* and *pa*, synthesized by a computer. The infants discriminated between speech sounds having voice-onset times that differed by only 0.02 second. Even very early during postnatal development, the human auditory system is ready to make very fine discriminations.

**Table 10•1** lists some of the responses infants make to various types of speech sounds.

## The Prespeech Period and the First Words

Kaplan and Kaplan (1970) have outlined the progression of early vocalizations in infants. The first sound that a baby makes is crying. As we will see in Chapter 12, this aversive stimulus serves a useful function. It is important in obtaining behaviours from the baby's caregivers. At about one month of age, infants start making other sounds, including one that is called *cooing* because of the prevalence of the *oo* sound. Often during this period, babies also make a series of sounds that resemble a half-hearted attempt to mimic the sound of crying.

At around six months, a baby's sounds begin to resemble those that occur in speech. Even though their babbling does not contain words—and does not appear to involve attempts to communicate verbally—the sounds infants make, and the rhythm in which they are articulated, reflect the adult speech that babies hear. Infants of this age also show evidence of long-term memory for the sound patterns of words read to them (Jusczyk & Hohne, 1997).

A study by Kuhl and colleagues (1992) provides further evidence of the effect of children's environment on their language development. Native speakers learn not to distinguish between slight variations of sounds present in their language. In fact, they do not even *hear* the differences. For example, Japanese contains a sound that comes midway between /l/ and /r/. Different native speakers pronounce the sound differently, but all pronunciations are recognized as examples of the same phoneme. When native speakers of Japanese learn English, they have great difficulty distinguishing the sounds /l/ and /r/; for example, *right* and *light* sound to them like the same word. Presumably, the speech sounds a child hears alter the brain mechanisms responsible for analyzing them so that minor variations are not even perceived. The question is, When does this alteration occur? Most researchers have supposed that it happens after children begin to learn the meanings of words at around 10 to 12 months of age.

Kuhl and her colleagues found, however, that this learning takes place much earlier. They studied six-month-old infants in the United States and Sweden. The infants were seated in their mothers' laps, where they watched a researcher sitting nearby, playing with a silent toy. Every two seconds, a loudspeaker located to the infant's left presented the sound of a vowel. From time to time, the sound was altered. If the infant noticed the change and looked at the loudspeaker, the researcher reinforced the response by activating a toy figure that pounded on a miniature drum. Thus, the procedure provided a test of infants' ability to distinguish slight differences in vowel sounds. (See **Figure 10•14**.)

The researchers presented two different vowel sounds, one found in English but not in Swedish and the other found in Swedish but not in English. From time to time, they varied the sound slightly. The reactions of the Swedish infants and the American infants were strikingly different. Swedish infants noticed when the English vowel changed but not when

**FIGURE 10•14** A child being tested in the experiment by Kuhl and her colleagues.

the Swedish vowel changed; American infants did the opposite. In other words, by the age of six months, the infants had learned not to pay attention to slight differences in speech sounds of their own language, but were still able to distinguish slight differences in speech sounds they had never heard. Even though they were too young to understand the *meaning* of what they heard, the speech of people around them had affected the development of their perceptual mechanisms.

The experiment by Kuhl and her colleagues used synthetic sounds to produce changes from either the English or the Swedish vowel. Does this effect generalize to actual vowels that differ in sound? Using a similar procedure with infants raised in English-speaking households, Polka and Werker (1994) looked at the ability of infants to distinguish between two English vowels or between two German vowels. They found that the ability to distinguish vowels in both languages is present in four-month-old infants. By six months of age, however, the infants had become more language-specific, showing little ability to distinguish between the German vowels. Thus, language acquisition seems to be a matter of becoming *less* discriminating of speech sounds—when they do not form part of one's native language. Furthermore, this tuning seems to occur very early in life.

Brain activity shows the effects of this tuning. Cheour and colleagues (1998) examined how an infant's brain responds to changes in vowels that are either part of their native language or not. Using Finnish and Estonian vowels with one-year-old babies from both linguistic groups, Cheour and colleagues found that the brain showed a special change in electrical pattern when a native vowel was changed to another native vowel; the change is elicited by events that are discrepant from a repetitive pattern. These mismatch signals were not elicited by changes from a native vowel to a nonnative vowel sound.

These results are, in a sense, puzzling. Very young infants seem highly sensitive to sound differences in speech. However, as an infant begins to learn words from sound patterns, and to associate those words with objects, he or she becomes less discriminating between sounds. Perhaps acute sensitivity to sound differences is necessary in the early stages of language acquisition, to provide the brain with the means of organizing speech experiences. As the infant begins to represent speech in new ways, this sensitivity is either no longer necessary or perhaps even detrimental (Stager & Werker, 1997).

Infants babble before they talk. They often engage in serious "conversations" with their caregivers, taking turns "talking" with them. Infants' voices are modulated, and the stream of sounds they make sounds as though they are using a secret language (Menn & Stoel-Gammon, 1993). They are also able to categorize sounds with respect to rhythm and tempo (Trehub & Thorpe, 1989).

At about one year of age, a child begins to produce words. The first sounds children use to produce speech appear to be similar across all languages and cultures: The first vowel is usually the soft *a* sound of *father*, and the first consonant is a *stop consonant* produced with the lips—*p* or *b*. Thus, the first word is often *papa* or *baba*. The next feature to be added is *nasality*, which converts the consonants *p* or *b* into *m*. Thus, the next word is *mama*. Naturally, mothers and fathers all over the world recognize these sounds as their children's attempts to address them.

The first sounds of a child's true speech contain the same phonemes that are found in the babbling sounds the child is already making; thus, speech emerges from prespeech sounds. While learning words from their caregivers and from older children, infants often invent their own **protowords**, unique strings of phonemes that serve word-like functions. The infants use these protowords consistently in particular situations (Menn & Stoel-Gammon, 1993). For example, Halliday (1975) reported that when his son Nigel wanted something, he would reach for it with an intent facial expression and say, "Na! Na!" until he was given the desired object.

The development of speech sounds continues for many years. Some sequences are added very late. For example, the *str* of *string* and the *bl* of *blink* are difficult for young children to produce; they usually say *tring* and *link*, omitting the first consonant. Most children recognize sounds in adult speech before they can produce them. Consider this conversation (Dale, 1976):

> *Adult*: Johnny, I'm going to say a word two times and you tell me which time I say it right and which time I say it wrong: *rabbit, wabbit.*
> *Child*: *Wabbit* is *wight* and *wabbit* is *wong.*

Although the child could not pronounce the *r* sound, he clearly could recognize it.

Early language acquisition, then, takes place within a context of changing perceptual, motor, and cognitive abilities. Werker and Tees (1999) have suggested that humans are born with a perceptual system that is especially attuned to the requirements of speech, but that also interacts with the infant's linguistic environment and other developmental changes. Speech perception, word comprehension, and babbling work in concert to establish the foundation of more sophisticated speech.

## The Two-Word Stage

At around 18 to 20 months of age, children start putting two words together, and their linguistic development takes a leap forward. It is at this stage that linguistic creativity really begins. Consider the creativity in *allgone outside*, said by a child when the door was closed.

Like first sounds, children's two-word utterances are remarkably consistent across all cultures that have been observed. Children use words in the same way, no matter what language their parents speak. Even deaf children who learn sign language from their parents put two words together in the same way as children who can hear (Bellugi & Klima,

**protoword** A unique string of phonemes that an infant invents and uses as a word.

1972). And deaf children whose parents do not know sign language invent their own signs and use them in orderly, "rule-governed" ways (Goldin-Meadow & Feldman, 1977). Thus, the grammar of children's language at the two-word stage appears to be universal (Owens, 1992).

For many years, investigators described the speech of young children in terms of adult grammar, but researchers now recognize that children's speech simply follows different rules. Young children are incapable of forming complex sentences—partly because their vocabulary is small, partly because their short-term "working" memory is limited (they cannot yet encode a long string of words), and partly because their cognitive development has not yet reached a stage at which they can learn complex rules of syntax (Locke, 1993).

## How Adults Talk to Children

Parents do not talk to children the way they talk to adults; they use only short, simple, well-formed, repetitive sentences and phrases (Brown & Bellugi, 1964). In fact, such speech deserves its own label: **child-directed speech** (Snow, 1986). In a comprehensive review of the literature, deVilliers and deVilliers (1978) found that adults' speech to children is characterized by clear pronunciation, exaggerated intonations, careful distinctions between similar-sounding phonemes, relatively few abstract words and function words, and a tendency to isolate constituents that undoubtedly enables young children to recognize them as units of speech.

Another important characteristic of child-directed speech is that it tends to refer to tangible objects the child can see, to what the child is doing, and to what is happening around the child (Snow et al., 1976). Words are paired with objects the child is familiar with, which is the easiest way to learn them. For example, caregivers make statements and ask questions about what things are called, what noises they make, what colour they are, what actions they are engaging in, whom they belong to, and where they are located. Their speech contains more content words, and fewer verbs, modifiers, and function words (Newport, 1975; Snow, 1977).

Adults often expand children's speech by imitating it but putting it into more complex forms, which undoubtedly helps the child learn about syntactical structure (Brown & Bellugi, 1964):

*Child*: Baby highchair.
*Adult*: Baby is in the highchair.
*Child*: Eve lunch.
*Adult*: Eve is having lunch.
*Child*: Throw daddy.
*Adult*: Throw it to daddy.

**child-directed speech** The speech of an adult directed toward a child; differs in important features from adult-directed speech and tends to facilitate learning of language by children.
**inflection** A change in the form of a word (usually by adding a suffix) to denote a grammatical feature such as tense or number.

The most important factor controlling adults' speech to children is the child's attentiveness. Both adults and children are very sensitive to whether another person is paying attention to them. As Snow (1986) notes, people do not talk *at* children, they talk *with* them. When a child looks interested, we continue with what we are doing. When we notice signs of inattention, we advance or simplify our level of speech until we regain the child's attention. Stine and Bohannon (1983) found that when children give signs that they do not understand what an adult is saying, the adult adjusts his or her speech, making it simpler.

Infants also exert control over what their caregivers talk about. The topic of conversation usually involves what the infant is playing with or is guided by what the infant is gazing at (Bohannon, 1993). This practice means that infants hear speech that concerns what they are already paying attention to, which undoubtedly facilitates learning. In fact, Tomasello and Farrar (1986) found that infants of mothers who talked mostly about the objects of their infants' gazes uttered their first words earlier than other infants and also developed larger vocabularies early in life. Werker, Pegg, and McLeod (1994) found that when infants were shown a video of a Cantonese speaker talking to either an infant or to an adult, babies from both Cantonese-speaking and English-speaking homes preferred to look at the infant-directed communication.

## Acquisition of Adult Rules of Grammar

The first words children use tend to be content words, probably because these words are emphasized in adult speech and because they refer to objects and actions that children can directly observe (Brown & Fraser, 1964). As children develop past the two-word stage, they begin to learn and use more and more of the grammatical rules that adults use. The first form of sentence lengthening appears to be the expansion of object nouns into noun phrases (Bloom, 1970). For example, *That ball* becomes *That a big ball.* Next, verbs get used more often, articles are added, prepositional phrases are mastered, and sentences become more complex. These results involve the use of inflections and function words. Function words, you recall, are the little words (*the, to, and*, and so on) that help shape the syntax of a sentence. **Inflections** are special suffixes we add to words to change their syntactical or semantic function. For example, the inflection *-ed* changes most verbs into the past tense (*change* becomes *changed*), *-ing* makes a verb into a noun (*make* becomes *making*), and *-'s* indicates possession (*Paul's truck*).

The rules that govern the use of inflections or function words are rarely made explicit. A parent seldom says, "When you want to use the past tense, add *-ed* to the verb"—nor would a young child understand such a pronouncement. Instead, children must listen to speech and figure out how to express such concepts as the past tense. Studies of children's speech have told us something about this process.

The most frequently used verbs in most languages are *irregular*. Forming the past tense of such verbs in English does *not* involve adding *-ed.* (Examples are *go/went, throw/threw, buy/bought, see/saw,* and *can/could.*) The past tense of such verbs must be learned individually. Because irregular verbs get more use than do regular ones, children learn them first, producing the past tense easily in sentences such as *I came, I fell down,* and *She hit me.* Soon afterwards, they discover the regular past tense inflection and expand their vocabulary, producing sentences such as *He dropped the ball.* But they also begin to say *I runned, I falled down,* and *She hitted me*—all examples of **overgeneralization errors.** Having formed a syntactical rule from their experience, they apply it to all verbs, including the irregular ones that they were previously using correctly. In fact, it takes children several years to learn to use the irregular past tense correctly again (Pinker, 1999).

One function of grammar is to convey the relationships between objects. Some languages, such as English, also convey this information through compound nouns, such as *police car,* meaning "a car for police." But the relationships can be quite varied. Once, when visiting my daughter in Calgary, we spotted a stretch limousine with a large pair of horns as a hood ornament. We both spontaneously labelled it the "longhorn limo," although, of course, we knew it was not a limo for longhorns.

English-speaking children as young as three years of age know how to combine nouns to describe these interactive relationships. Nicoladis (2003) showed children pictures that could be described by compound nouns. (See **Figure 10•15**.) She would ask: "What is this?" Three- and four-year-old children generally gave three types of responses: Compound nouns such as "fish shoes" were the most frequent, followed by more rare instances of preposition phrases (e.g., "fish on shoes") or single words (e.g., "shoes"). Three-year-olds were just as likely as four-year-olds to create such compound words, although somewhat surprisingly they were less likely to comprehend compound names and choose them from a set of alternatives.

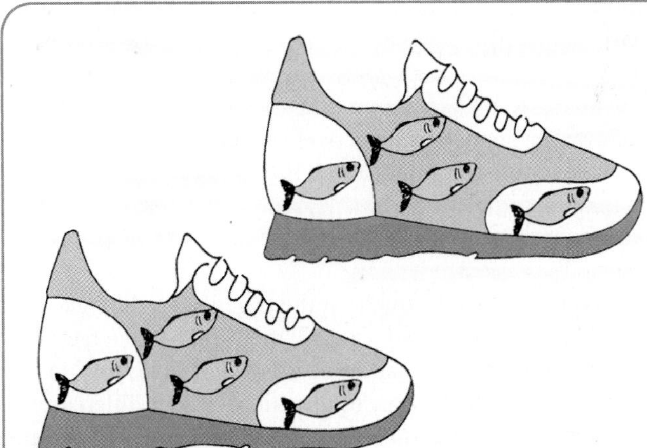

**FIGURE 10•15** An object that could be described by a compound noun.

*(From Nicoladis, E. (2003). What compound nouns mean to preschool children.* Brain and Language, 84, *38–49.)*

In his book *Crazy English,* Richard Lederer provides a whimsical sample of the puzzles that irregularities in English pose:

> If adults commit adultery, do infants commit infantry? If olive oil is made from olives, what do they make baby oil from? If a vegetarian eats vegetables, what does a humanitarian consume? A writer is someone who writes, and a stinger is something that stings. But fingers don't fing, grocers don't groce, hammers don't ham, humdingers don't humding, ushers don't ush, and haberdashers do not haberdash. . . .
>
> . . . If the plural of *tooth* is *teeth,* so shouldn't the plural of *booth* be *beeth*? One goose, two geese—so one moose, two meese? If people ring a bell today and rang a bell yesterday, why don't we say that they flang a ball? If they wrote a letter, perhaps they also bote their tongue. (Quoted in Pinker, 2007, p. 40)

## Acquisition of Meaning

How do children learn to use and understand words? The simplest explanation is that they hear a word spoken at the same time that they see (or hear, or touch) the object to which the word refers. After several such pairings, they add a word to their vocabulary. In fact, children first learn the names of things with which they interact, or things that change (and thus attract their attention). For example, they are quick to learn words like *cookie* or *blanket,* but are slow to learn words like *wall* or *window* (Pease, Gleason, & Pan, 1993; Ross, Nelson, Wetstone, & Tanouye, 1986).

Suppose that we give a boy a small red plastic ball and say "ball." After a while, the child says "ball" when he sees it. Yet we cannot conclude from this behaviour that the child knows the meaning of *ball.* So far, he has encountered only one referent for the word: a small one made of red plastic. If he says "ball" when he sees an apple or an orange, or even the moon, we must conclude that he does not know the meaning of *ball.* This type of error is called **overextension**—the use of a word to denote a larger class of items than is appropriate. If he uses the word to refer only to the small red plastic ball, his error is called an **underextension**—the use of a word to denote a smaller class of items than is appropriate.

Both overextensions and underextensions are normal; a single pairing of a word with the object does not provide enough information for accurate generalization. Suppose that someone is teaching you a foreign language. She points to a penny and says "pengar." Does the word mean "penny," "money," "coin," or "round"? You cannot decide from this one

**overgeneralization errors** Errors in language that occur when learners produce incorrect words or statements based on other rules of language.

**overextension** The use of a word to denote a larger class of items than is appropriate; for example, referring to the moon as a ball.

**underextension** The use of a word to denote a smaller class of items than is appropriate; for example, referring only to one particular animal as a dog.

example. Without further information, you may overextend or underextend the meaning of the word if you try to use it. If your teacher then points to a dollar bill and again says "pengar," you will deduce (correctly) that the word means "money."

Caregivers often correct children's overextensions. The most effective type of instruction occurs when an adult provides the correct label and points out the features that distinguish the object from the one with which the child has confused it (Chapman, Leonard, & Mervis, 1986). For example, if a child calls a yo-yo a "ball," the caregiver might say, "That's a yo-yo. See? It goes up and down" (Pease, Gleason, & Pan, 1993, p. 130).

Graham, Baker, and Poulin-Dubois (1998) looked at how children 16 to 19 months of age interpret these adult utterances. They provided artificial labels to objects, and then observed whether children would gaze at another object that matched it in a categorical sense or in a thematic sense. For example, an infant would be shown a baby stroller while the researcher said, "This is a wug." Then a picture of another stroller would appear on one side of the infant and a picture of a baby would appear on the other. At the same time, the researcher would say, "Find the wug." Looking at the picture of the second stroller was more prolonged when the artificial label was used than when no label was used. In contrast, the amount of looking at the baby was not affected by the use of a label. Graham and her colleagues interpreted these results as showing an assumption on the part of infants that language labels spoken by adults refer to basic categorical membership rather than other kinds of links. Infants' assumptions of categorical references, and their ability to use them, seem to underlie a large part of their rapid acquisition of vocabulary between the ages of two and six years (Poulin-Dubois, Graham, & Sippola, 1995).

## Then and Now

### Gender and Language

Think about the last text message you sent. Did you include an emoticon (e.g., a "smiley-face")? Do you think you would have been less likely to include that emoticon if the receiver of the message was male? Current research on gender differences in communication style indicates that you might have sent that emoticon to Pam, but not to Jim.

As you've seen throughout the text, the differences between men and women have been extensively studied throughout all areas of psychology. Language is no exception. Researchers have found that even children as young as five years of age have noticeable gender differences in speech (Maltz & Borker, 1982). Early investigations into the impact of gender on language indicated that males tend to use more assertive speech, more crude language, and ask less clarifying questions than females (Lakoff, 1975). The past 30 years of research have not consistently confirmed all of the findings of these gender differences in language, but it appears that males tend to be more straightforward, succinct, and less emotional than females when they communicate (Mulac, Bradac, & Gibbons, 2001). In a literature review looking at the empirical research on gender and language, Mulac, Bradac, and Gibbons found that men used more judgmental adjectives, such as *good* and *dumb*; were more directive in their speech than women; and were more likely to focus their speech on themselves with many references to *I*. Females had more references to emotion words, such as *happy* and *hurt*, and had more uncertainty in their speech (e.g., phrases like *It seems to be . . .* ).

Most research conducted on the impact of gender on language has focused on traditional written or spoken language. As the popularity of BlackBerries, iPods, instant messaging, and social networking sites such as Facebook and MySpace continue to increase, we can see that modern communication is changing. Researchers have started to investigate the impact of these types of media on how we communicate. Since electronic communication lacks many of the cues found in spoken language (e.g., pitch, tone of voice, appearance of speaker, etc.), researchers initially believed that online interactions were essentially gender-neutral (Herring, 2003). It appears that this is not the case. Researchers are learning that regardless of the type of media used to communicate, gender differences remain. For example, consistent with previous research, males tend to be more direct in their online text and use more foul language than females (Guiller & Durndell, 2006).

Fox, Bukatko, Hallahan, and Crawford (2007) were interested in gender differences when people communicated using instant messaging. Fox and colleagues had participants engage in several online conversations. Each conversation had to last at least five minutes and involve ten exchanges of text. The researchers then coded the information and investigated the impact of gender on how people sent instant messages. Consistent with earlier research on gender and language, their results showed that women were more expressive in their communications than men. Expressiveness in instant messaging was measured by the use of emoticons and adjectives and the number of topics discussed. The gender of the person receiving the message also affected online communication. If the receiver of the instant message was male, the messages sent to him tended to contain more words. Messages sent to females tended to contain more references to emotion.

As mentioned throughout the text, gender differences should not be overstated. Overall, men and women tend to communicate in a similar fashion. Fox and colleagues' research demonstrates some of the minor gender differences in communication and is an interesting example of the type of work that is conducted as changing technology continues to affect the way people interact.

## Interim Summary

### Language Acquisition by Children

Studies using the habituation of a baby's sucking response have shown that the human auditory system is capable of discriminating among speech sounds soon after birth. Human vocalization begins with crying, then develops into cooing and babbling, and finally results in patterned speech. During the two-word stage, children begin to combine words creatively, expressing things in a way that they have never heard.

Child-directed speech is very different from that directed toward adults; it is simpler, clearer, and generally refers to items and events in the present environment. As young children gain more experience with the world and with the speech of adults and older children, their vocabulary grows and they learn to use adult rules of grammar. Although the first verbs they learn tend to have irregular past tenses, once they learn the regular past tense rule (add *-ed*), they apply this rule even to irregular verbs that they previously used correctly.

Some researchers believe that a child learns language by means of a brain mechanism called a language acquisition device, which contains universal grammatical rules and motivates language acquisition. Although children's verbal performance can be described by complex rules, it is possible that simpler rules—which children could reasonably be expected to learn—can also be devised. Everyone agrees that deliberate reinforcement is not necessary for language learning, but a controversy exists about just how important child-directed behaviour is. A critical period for language learning may exist, but the evidence is not yet conclusive.

**QUESTIONS TO CONSIDER**

1. Can you think of any examples of child-directed speech that you may have overheard (or engaged in yourself while talking with a young child)? How would you feel if you were talking with a baby who suddenly lost interest in you? Would you be motivated to do something to regain the baby's attention? What would you do?
2. Do you think it is easier for a young child to learn a language than it is for an adult? How could we make a fair comparison of the tutoring young children and adults receive from people with whom they talk? Do you think that a modified form of child-directed language could be developed as an effective way of tutoring adults who want to learn a second language?
3. Would you like to talk with a chimpanzee? If so, what would you like to talk about? What would it take to convince you that the animal was using something like a simplified human language, as opposed to simply repeating words and phrases learned by rote? Some people seem to be uncomfortable with the idea that the difference in the ability of humans and other primates to communicate may be a matter of degree and not an all-or-nothing matter. How do you feel about this issue? Finally, does teaching a chimpanzee a human language incur special responsibilities on the part of the investigator?

## EPILOGUE

### The Controversy of Animal Language

At the beginning of the chapter, you read about the controversy surrounding animal language. Some researchers argue that humans are unique and, as such, make unique errors in speech. Which of us has not caught herself or himself in such a gaffe—calling out, "Let me get the door," only to discover that you are pointing your remote-control car-door opener at the still-locked door to your apartment.

Highly regarded scholars have argued that such difficulty should be uniquely human, as *Homo sapiens sapiens* is the only species endowed with language. Hauser, Chomsky, and Fitch (2002) have pointed to the property of recursion (as illustrated by the multi-layered sentence *I just got back from the class taught by the professor who was at the pizza restaurant where my friend and his roommate ate last night*) as dividing language from all other forms of communication that have been observed in other species. According to Pinker and Jackendoff (2005), the list of unique properties is longer and includes phonological rules, syntactical rules, and speech perception.

Despite such weight of argument, there are those who continue to chip away at the assertion of uniqueness, looking for evidence in the unexpected actions of other, particularly primate, species. Recently Lyn (2007) has focused on the errors made by a pair of bonobos (one of them Kanzi, shown in the prologue). The data were recorded over a 10-year period and consisted of vocabulary tests given to the animals by means of an extensive keyboard consisting of lexigrams. Kanzi and the female bonobo, Panbanisha, had lexigraphic vocabularies of nearly 400 symbols and could combine them in complex, language-like sequences.

Lyn found that the patterns of errors in tests, in which the animal was shown a photo or listened to a spoken word and had to press the correct lexigram, were not random. For example, if the photo featured a blackberry, the errors were likely to involve lexigrams that had the same sound, belonged to the same semantic categories (edible, fruit), or had a similar appearance. Errors were especially likely to involve combinations of these categories. Thus, the lexigram for *cherry* was a perfect candidate. Lyn's analysis pointed to the similarity between the bonobos' errors and those typical of children in similar conditions. However, there was a notable exception. Children typically make errors within syntactic categories (e.g., mistaking *tree* for *cherry*—both nouns), but the bonobos did not, prompting Lyn to speculate that, unlike children, they do not discriminate between semantic and syntactic categories.

A parallel between the errors made by bonobos and by children exists in the linguistic slips made by adult speakers and adult users of sign language. German linguists Hohenberger, Happ, and Leuninger (cited by Erard, 2007) used an experimental method for inducing slips in their participants. They found that the errors produced by German speakers ("slips of the tongue") were also produced by deaf persons who used German Sign Language ("slips of the hand"), though not necessarily with the same frequencies. Also, participants using sign language were more likely to correct their errors, presumably because signing occurs more slowly than speaking and therefore may be more readily self-monitored. (See Thompson, Emmorey, and Gollan, 2005, for an analysis of the "tip of the fingers" phenomenon in deaf users of American Sign Language comparable to the "tip-of-the-tongue" phenomenon in English speakers that was described in Chapter 8.)

These findings suggest a linguistic production system that does not necessarily respect species differences nor whether the language produced is spoken or manual. Further studies of patterns of errors in linguistic production may reveal its specific neural substrates and bring us closer to understanding this complex issue.

## Canadian Connections to Research in This Chapter


Belin, P., Zatorre, R. J., & Ahad, P. (2002). Human temporal-lobe response to vocal sounds. *Cognitive Brain Research, 13,* 17–26. (McGill University: www.mcgill.ca)

Furrow, D., & Nelson, K. (1986). A further look at the motherese hypothesis: A reply to Gleitman, Newport & Gleitman. *Journal of Child Language, 13,* 163–176. (Mount Saint Vincent University: www.msvu.ca)

Graham, S. A., Baker, R. K., & Poulin-Dubois, D. (1998). Infants' expectations about object label reference. *Canadian Journal of Experimental Psychology, 52,* 103–112. (University of Calgary: www.ucalgary.ca)

Hebb, D. O., Lambert, W. E., & Tucker, G. R. (1973, April). A DMZ in the language war. *Psychology Today,* 55–62. (McGill University: www.mcgill.ca)

Donald Hebb was the first winner (in 1980) of the Donald O. Hebb Award of the Canadian Psychological Association and the 1961 winner of the American Psychological Association's Award for Distinguished Scientific Contributions.

Kertesz, A. (1981). Anatomy of jargon. In J. Brown (Ed.), *Jargonaphasia.* New York: Academic Press. (University of Western Ontario: www.uwo.ca)

Nicoladis, E. (2003). What compound nouns mean to preschool children. *Brain and Language, 84,* 38–49. (University of Alberta: www.ualberta.ca)

Petitto, L. A., Zatorre, R. J., Gauna, K., Nikelski, E. J., Dostie, D., & Evans, A. C. (2000). Speech-like cerebral activity in profoundly deaf people processing signed languages: Implications for the neural basis of human language. *Proceedings of the National Academy of Sciences, USA, 97,* 13 961–13 966. (McGill University: www.mcgill.ca)

Polka, L., & Werker, J. (1994). Developmental changes in perception of nonnative vowel contrasts. *Journal of Experimental Psychology: Human Perception and Performance, 20,* 421–435 (McGill University: www.mcgill.ca)

Poulin-Dubois, D., Graham, S., & Sippola, L. (1995). Early lexical development: The contribution of parental labelling and infants' categorization abilities. *Journal of Child Language, 22,* 325–343. (Concordia University: www.concordia.ca)

Singer, M., & Ritchot, K. F. M. (1996). The role of working memory capacity and knowledge access in text inference processing. *Memory & Cognition, 24,* 733–743. (University of Manitoba: www.umanitoba.ca)

Snow, C. E. (1972). Mother's speech to children learning language. *Child Development, 43,* 540–565. (McGill University: www.mcgill.ca)

Stager, C. L., & Werker, J. F. (1997). Infants listen for more phonetic detail in speech perception than in word-learning tasks. *Nature, 388,* 381–382. (University of British Columbia: www.ubc.ca)

Treheb, S. E., & Thorpe, L. A. (1989). Infants' perception of rhythm: Categorization of auditory sequences by temporal structure. *Canadian Journal of Psychology, 43*, 217–229. (University of Toronto: www.utoronto.ca)

Tremblay, S., Shiller, D. M., & Ostry, D. J. (2003). Somatosensory basis of speech production. *Nature, 423*, 866–869. (McGill University: www.mcgill.ca)

Tulving, E., & Schacter, D. L. (1990). Priming and human memory systems. *Science, 247*, 301–306. (University of Toronto: www.utoronto.ca)

Endel Tulving was the 1983 winner of the Donald O. Hebb Award of the Canadian Psychological Association and the 1983 winner of the American Psychological Association's Award for Distinguished Scientific Contributions.

Werker, J. F., Pegg, J. E., & McLeod, P. J. (1994). A cross-language investigation of infant preference for infant-directed communication. *Infant Behavior and Development, 17*, 323–333. (University of British Columbia: www.ubc.ca)

Werker, J. F., & Tees, R. C. (1999). Influences on infant speech processing: Toward a new synthesis. *Annual Review of Psychology, 50*, 509–535. (University of British Columbia: www.ubc.ca)

## Suggestions for Further Reading

Carter, R. (1998). *Mapping the mind.* London: Weidenfeld & Nicolson.

Although not exclusively about language, this book is a beautifully illustrated book describing the "geography" of the brain's functional areas.

Just, M. A., & Carpenter, P. A. (1987). *The psychology of reading and language comprehension.* Boston, MA: Allyn and Bacon.

Pinker, S. (1994). *The language instinct: How the mind creates language.* New York: William Morrow.

The book by Pinker provides a general overview on cognitive science research regarding language. The book by Just and Carpenter focuses on written language.

Berko Gleason, J. (1993). *The development of language.* New York: Macmillan.

This book does an excellent job of describing language acquisition in infants and children.

Calvin, W. H. (2004). *A brief history of the mind: From apes to intellect and beyond.* New York: Oxford University Press.

De Luce, J., & Wilder, H. T. (1983). *Language in primates: Perspectives and implications.* New York: Springer-Verlag.

Calvin's book has received favourable reviews for its speculative, but well-presented, suggestions regarding the origins of human language and cognition. De Luce and Wilder's book describes attempts to teach language to non-human primates. It also describes the controversies about the success and significance of these attempts.

PEARSON mypsychlab To access more tests and your own personalized study plan that will help you focus on the areas you need to master before your next class test, be sure to go to **www.MyPsychLab.com**, Pearson Education Canada's online Psychology website available with the access code packaged with your book.

# 11

# INTELLIGENCE AND THINKING

# CHAPTER OUTLINE

## Theories of Intelligence

Spearman's Two-Factor Theory • Evidence from Factor Analysis • An Information Processing Theory of Intelligence • Neuropsychological Theories of Intelligence

Spearman's two-factor theory proposes that intelligence consists of a global general factor and specific task-related factors. Factor analysis suggests that one or two general factors of intelligence may exist. Sternberg's triarchic theory of intelligence is an application of the information processing approach that emphasizes the importance of adaptive behaviour in a natural environment. Gardner's theory emphasizes the categories of aptitudes and skills (physical as well as cognitive) that permit people to thrive in their cultures. Researchers are coming to recognize that different environments require different types of skills; thus, different cultures have different definitions of intelligence.

## Intelligence Testing

From Mandarins to Galton • Intelligence Tests • Reliability and Validity of Intelligence Tests • The Use and Abuse of Intelligence Tests

Binet's attempts to identify schoolchildren who needed special attention led him to develop a series of tests that eventually became the Stanford-Binet Scale. Binet and his colleague Simon developed the concept of norms with which to compare a particular individual and formulated the concept of mental age. Wechsler developed an intelligence test that could be applied to adults (the WAIS) and another for children (the WISC). The reliability of modern intelligence tests is excellent. Their validity is difficult to assess because we have no single criterion of intelligence. One way intelligence tests may be used is to identify gifted students and students with special needs so that they may be enrolled in appropriate educational programs. Intelligence tests may be abused if teachers and administrators expect little from students labelled as "unintelligent" and so fail to encourage them to achieve the most that they can.

## The Roles of Heredity and Environment

The Meaning of Heritability • Sources of Environmental and Genetic Effects during Development • Results of Heritability Studies • *Then and Now: The Issue of Race and Intelligence*

Variability in people's intellectual abilities is produced by three sources: environmental variability, genetic variability, and an interaction between the two. Environmental variability has its origins even before birth; it is influenced by factors that affect prenatal development and physical development during childhood as well as sources of formal education and intellectual stimulation. Genetic variability affects the structure and development of the brain and also affects people's resistance to diseases and other environmental events that can affect the development and functioning of the brain. The topic of race and intelligence has been the subject of considerable passion and debate, much of which has been illogical and misinformed. Environmental factors appear to play a larger role than hereditary ones in racial differences in performance on intelligence tests.

## Thinking

Classifying • Formal and Natural Concepts • Deductive Reasoning • Inductive Reasoning • Problem Solving

Psychologists interested in the process of thinking have studied the formation and recognition of concepts, deductive reasoning, inductive reasoning, and problem solving. Concepts exist at the basic, subordinate, and superordinate level, but we mostly think about basic-level concepts. Concepts are more than simple collections of essential features; they can involve complex relationships. Deductive reasoning consists of applying general principles to specific instances and requires the ability to construct and manipulate mental models that represent a problem. Inductive reasoning consists of inferring general principles from particular facts; people use various forms of hypothesis testing to infer general principles. Problem solving requires a concept of a goal and an evaluation of the ability of particular behaviours to bring us closer to that goal.

PROLOGUE

## Multiplicity of Intelligence? A Case Study of Brain Damage

Mr. V. was a 72-year-old man who had suffered a massive stroke in his right hemisphere that paralyzed the left side of his body.

When I first met Mr. V., he was seated in a wheelchair equipped with a large tray on which his right arm rested; his left arm was immobilized in a sling. He would greet his doctor politely, almost formally, articulating his words carefully with a slight European accent.

Mr. V. seemed intelligent, and this impression was confirmed when his doctor returned the results of some of the subtests of the Wechsler Adult Intelligence Test (WAIS-III) that had been administered by a psychologist. The subtests showed that Mr. V. could define rather obscure words, provide the meanings of proverbs, supply information, and do mental arithmetic. In fact, his verbal intelligence appeared to be in the upper 5 percent of the population. The fact that English was not his first language made his performance even more remarkable. However, he did poorly on simple tasks that required him to deal with shapes and geometry. He could not solve even the sample problem for the block design subtest, in which coloured blocks must be put together to duplicate a pattern shown in a drawing.

An interesting aspect of Mr. V.'s behaviour was the lack of reaction he had to his symptoms. One day, Mr. V.'s doctor asked him some simple questions about himself and his lifestyle. He began by asking Mr. V. about his favourite pastime.

"I like to walk," said Mr. V. "I walk at least two hours each day around the city, but mostly I like to walk in the woods. I have maps of most of the nearby provincial parks on the walls of my study, and I mark all the trails I've taken. I figure that in about six months I will have walked all of the trails that are short enough to do in a day. I'm too old to camp out in the woods."

"You're going to finish up those trails in the next six months?" said his doctor.

"Yes, and then I'll start over again!" Mr. V. replied.

"Mr. V., are you having any trouble?" asked the doctor.

"Trouble? What do you mean?"

"I mean physical, medical, difficulties."

"No." Mr. V. said with a slightly puzzled look.

"Well, what are you sitting in?"

Mr. V. gave his doctor a look that indicated he thought the question was rather stupid—or perhaps insulting. "A wheelchair, of course," he answered.

"Why are you in a wheelchair?"

Mr. V. looked exasperated; he obviously did not like to answer foolish questions. "Because my left leg is paralyzed!" he snapped.

I asked Mr. V.'s doctor why Mr. V. talks about continuing his walking schedule when he obviously knows that he cannot walk. Does he think that he will recover soon?

"No, that's not it," said Mr. V.'s doctor. "He knows what his problem is, but he doesn't really understand it. The people at the rehabilitation hospital are finding it difficult because he keeps trying to go outside for a walk.

"The problem Mr. V. experiences stems from the fact that intelligence is made up of a variety of skills that must be coordinated and the results of their use must be synthesized. The right hemisphere is specialized in seeing many things at once: in seeing all parts of a geometric shape and grasping its form or in seeing all elements of a situation and understanding what they mean. That is what's wrong. He can tell you about his paralyzed leg, about the fact that he is in a wheelchair, and so on, but he does not put these facts together and realize that his days of walking are over. Mr. V. is very intelligent, but his judgment can be lacking because of the stroke damage."

Do you consider Mr. V. to be intelligent? Your answer likely depends on how you define intelligence. What is it? We acknowledge that some people are more intelligent than others, but just what do we mean by that? In general, if people do well academically or succeed at tasks that involve their heads, we consider them to be intelligent. Thus, a critic who writes a witty, articulate review of an artist's exhibition of paintings is said to demonstrate intelligence, whereas the painter is said to show talent. Most psychologists would define **intelligence** as a person's ability to learn and remember information, to recognize concepts and their relations, and to apply the information to their own behaviour in an adaptive way. Recently, psychologists have pointed out that any definition of intelligence depends on cultural judgments (e.g., Berry, 2001; Sternberg & Grigorenko, 2001). Analyses of the types of skills that enable people to survive and flourish in different cultures suggest that we may need to broaden the generally accepted definition to include a wider range of abilities.

The study of intelligence is dominated by three main approaches. The **differential approach** favours the development of tests that identify and measure individual differences in people's abilities to solve problems, particularly those that use skills important in the classroom. For example, these tests ask people to define words, explain proverbs, solve arithmetic problems, discover similarities in shapes and patterns, and answer questions about a passage of prose. There is a good chance that you may have taken one of the tests if you have recently applied for a job, or if you are applying to graduate school.

The **developmental approach** studies the ways in which children learn to perceive, manipulate, and think about the world. The most influential proponent of this approach was the Swiss psychologist Jean Piaget (1896–1980). We will consider Piaget's work in detail in Chapter 12, which focuses on development over the lifespan. The third approach, the **information processing approach**, focuses on the types of skills people use to think and to solve various types of problems. We will focus on Robert Sternberg's influential theory of successful intelligence, which focuses on people's ability to analyze and manage personal strengths and weaknesses.

# Theories of Intelligence

People vary in many ways, such as in their abilities to learn and use words, to solve arithmetic problems, and to perceive and remember spatial information. The differential approach assumes that we can best investigate the nature of intelligence by studying the ways in which people differ on tests of such intellectual abilities. But is intelligence a global trait or is it a composite of separate, independent abilities?

Psychologists have devised intelligence tests that yield a single number, usually called an IQ score. But the fact that these tests provide a single score does not itself mean that intelligence is a single, general characteristic. For example, suppose that we wanted to devise a test of athletic ability. We would have people run, jump, throw and catch a ball, lift weights, balance on a narrow beam, and perform other athletic feats. We would measure their performance on each task and add these numbers up, yielding a total score that we would call the *AQ*, or *athletic quotient.* But would this single measure be useful in predicting who would be the best skier, or baseball player, or swimmer, or gymnast? Obviously not. Athletic ability consists of a variety of skills, and different sports require different combinations of skills. For example, if Mark Messier's 2005 retirement from the NHL had been based on his desire to try out for shortstop of the Toronto Blue Jays, we would have advised caution: Baseball requires different skills than hockey. Just ask Michael Jordan, whose attempt to move from professional basketball to professional baseball was not the success that he had hoped for.

**intelligence** The general term used to refer to a person's ability to learn and remember information, to recognize concepts and their relations, and to apply the information to their own behaviour in an adaptive way.
**differential approach** An approach to the study of intelligence that involves the creation of tests that identify and measure individual differences in people's knowledge and abilities to solve problems.
**developmental approach** An approach to the study of intelligence based on the way children learn to perceive, manipulate, and think about the world.
**information processing approach** An approach to the study of intelligence that focuses on the types of skills people use to think and to solve problems.

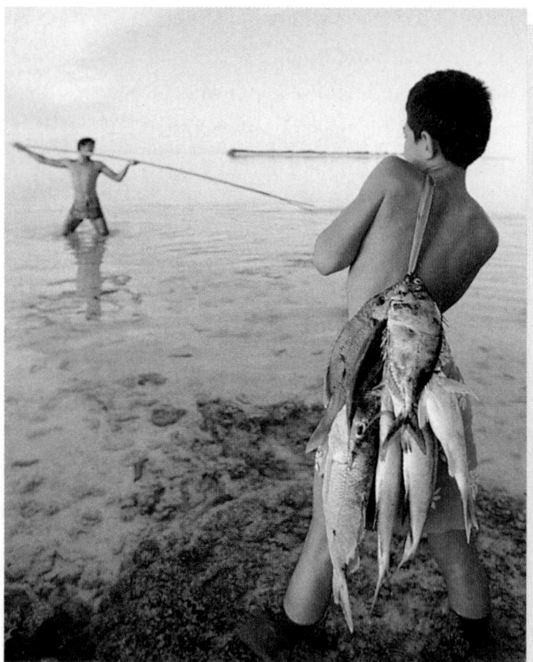

▲ *Different cultures have different definitions of intelligence. Members of the Aitutaki tribe from the Cook Islands respect a person's ability to obtain food from the sea.*

Some researchers promote the idea that some intellectual abilities are completely independent of one another. For example, a person can be excellent at spatial reasoning but poor at solving verbal analogies. Even those who believe that intelligence is a global trait acknowledge that people also have specific intellectual abilities and that these abilities are at least somewhat independent. But psychologists disagree over whether specific abilities are totally independent or whether one general factor influences all abilities. We will look at three theories of intelligence: a two-factor theory, an information processing theory, and a neuropsychological theory.

## Spearman's Two-Factor Theory

Charles Spearman (1927) proposed that a person's performance on a test of intellectual ability is determined by two factors: the ***g* factor**, which is a general factor, and the ***s* factor**, which is a factor specific to a particular test. Spearman did not call his *g* factor "intelligence"; he considered that term too vague. He defined the *g* factor as comprising three "qualitative principles of cognition": apprehension of experience, eduction of relations, and eduction of correlates. (*Eduction,* not "edu*ca*tion," is the process of drawing or bringing out—that is, of figuring out from given facts.) A common task on tests of intellectual abilities—solving analogies—requires all three principles (Sternberg, 1988a, 1997). For example, consider the following analogy:

LAWYER:CLIENT::DOCTOR:_______

This analogy problem is read as "LAWYER is to CLIENT as DOCTOR is to _____." *Apprehension of experience* refers to people's ability to perceive and understand what they experience; thus, reading and understanding each of the words in the analogy requires apprehension of experience. In this context, *eduction of relations* refers to the ability to perceive the relation between LAWYER and CLIENT; namely, that the lawyer works for the client. *Eduction of correlates* refers to the ability to apply a rule inferred from one case to a similar case. Thus, the person whom a doctor works for is obviously a PATIENT. Because analogy problems require all three of Spearman's principles of cognition, he advocated their use in intelligence testing.

Correlations among various tests of particular intellectual abilities have provided empirical evidence for Spearman's two-factor theory. The governing logic is as follows: Suppose that we administer 10 different tests of intellectual abilities to a group of people. If each test measures a separate, independent ability, the scores these people make on any one test will be unrelated to their scores on any other; the correlations among the tests will be approximately zero. However, if the tests measure abilities that are simply different manifestations of a single trait, the scores will be perfectly related; the intercorrelations will be close to 1.0. In fact, the intercorrelations among a group of tests of intellectual abilities are neither zero nor 1.0. Instead, most of these tests are at least moderately correlated, so that a person who scores well on a vocabulary test also tends to score better than average on other tests, such as arithmetic or spatial reasoning. The correlations among various tests of intellectual ability usually range from .30 to .70.

Spearman concluded that a general factor (*g*) accounted for the moderate correlations among different tests of ability. Thus, a person's score on a particular test depends on two things: the person's specific ability (*s*) on the particular test (such as spatial reasoning) and his or her level of the *g* factor, or general reasoning ability.

## Evidence from Factor Analysis

With Karl Pearson, Spearman developed a statistical procedure known as **factor analysis**. This procedure permits researchers to identify underlying commonalities among groups of tests. In the case of intelligence tests, these *common factors* would be particular abilities that affect people's performance on more than one test. Suppose that a group of people takes several different tests of intellectual ability. If

***g* factor** According to Spearman, a factor of intelligence that is common to all intellectual tasks; includes apprehension of experience, eduction of relations, and eduction of correlates.
***s* factor** According to Spearman, a factor of intelligence that is specific to a particular task.
**factor analysis** A statistical procedure that identifies common factors among groups of tests.

**TABLE 11•1 Three Factors Derived by Factor Analysis of Scores on WAIS Subtests**

| | Factors | | |
|---|---|---|---|
| **Subtest** | **A** | **B** | **C** |
| Information | .70 | .18 | .25 |
| Digit span | .16 | .84 | .13 |
| Vocabulary | .84 | .16 | .18 |
| Arithmetic | .38 | .35 | .28 |
| Comprehension | .63 | .12 | .24 |
| Similarities | .57 | .12 | .27 |
| Picture completion | .41 | .15 | .53 |
| Picture arrangement | .35 | .18 | .41 |
| Block design | .20 | .14 | .73 |
| Object assembly | .16 | .06 | .59 |
| Digit symbol | .24 | .22 | .29 |

*Source: Adapted from* Multivariate Statistical Methods, *4th edition by D.F. Morrison.* 

each person's scores on several of these tests correlate well with one another, we would conclude that the tests or subtests (at least partly) measure the same factor. A factor analysis determines which sets of tests form groups. For example, Birren and Morrison (1961) administered the Wechsler Adult Intelligence Scale (WAIS, described in the next section) to 933 people. This test consisted of 11 different subtests (all still present in the newer, expanded scale). Birren and Morrison calculated the correlations each subtest had with every other subtest and then subjected these correlations to a factor analysis.

**Table 11•1** lists the results of a factor analysis on Birren and Morrison's data. The analysis revealed three factors, labelled A, B, and C. The numbers in the three columns in the table are called *factor loadings*; they are somewhat like correlation coefficients in that they express the degree to which a particular test is related to a particular factor. For the various subtests on factor A, the largest factor loading is for vocabulary, followed by information, comprehension, and similarities. In the middle range are picture completion, arithmetic, picture arrangement, and digit symbol. Digit span, object assembly, and block design are the smallest. Verbal subtests make the most important contribution to factor A, so we might be tempted to call this factor *verbal ability*. However, almost all tests make at least a moderate contribution, so some people may prefer to call this factor *general intelligence*. Digit span has a heavy loading on factor B (.84), and arithmetic and digit symbol have moderate loadings. Perhaps factor B is related to *maintaining information in short-term memory* and *manipulating numbers*. Factor C appears to be determined mainly by block design, object assembly, picture completion, and picture arrangement. A good name for this factor might be *spatial ability*.

Factor analysis provides clues about the nature of intelligence, but it cannot provide a theory of intelligence. The names given to the factors are up to the investigator and therefore include a degree of subjective judgment. Furthermore, factor analysis can never be more meaningful than the individual tests on which it is performed. To identify the relevant factors in human intelligence, one must include an extensive variety of tests in the factor analysis, and be assured there are many (Daniel, 1997). For example, experience has shown that the WAIS is a useful predictor of scholastic performance and (to a lesser extent) of vocational success. Thus, it appears to measure some important abilities. But a factor analysis can be informative only about tests to which it is applied. It will never reveal other important abilities that are *not* measured by the tests it is used to investigate. For example, the WAIS does not contain a test of musical ability. If it did, a factor analysis would undoubtedly yield an additional factor related to that ability.

Many factor analyses have been performed on tests of intellectual abilities. For example, Louis Thurstone (1938) administered a battery of 56 tests to 218 college students and then performed a factor analysis. He extracted seven factors, which he labelled *verbal comprehension, verbal fluency, number, spatial visualization, memory, reasoning*, and *perceptual speed*. At first, Thurstone thought that his results contradicted Spearman's hypothesized *g* factor. However, Eysenck suggested a few years later that a second factor analysis could be performed on Thurstone's factors. If the analysis found one common factor among the factors, then Spearman's *g* factor would receive support. In other words, if Thurstone's seven factors themselves had a second-order factor in common, this factor might be conceived of as general intelligence.

Cattell performed just such a second-order factor analysis and found not one but two major factors. Horn and Cattell (1966) called these factors *fluid intelligence* ($g_f$) and *crystallized intelligence* ($g_c$). Fluid intelligence is defined by relatively culture-free tasks, such as those that measure the ability to see relations among objects or the ability to see patterns in a repeating series of items. Crystallized intelligence is defined by tasks that require people to have acquired information from their culture, such as vocabulary and the kind of information learned in schools. Cattell regards fluid intelligence as closely related to a person's native capacity for intellectual performance; in other words, it represents a potential ability to learn and solve problems. In contrast, he regards crystallized intelligence as what a person has accomplished through the use of his or her fluid intelligence—what he or she has learned. Horn differs with Cattell; he cites evidence suggesting that both factors are learned but are also based to a degree on heredity. He says that $g_f$ is based on casual learning and $g_c$ is based on cultural, school-type learning (Horn, 1994).

Word analogies and vocabulary, general information, and use of language tests load heavily on the crystallized intelligence factor. According to Cattell, $g_c$ depends on $g_f$. Fluid intelligence supplies the native ability, whereas experience with language and exposure to books, school, and other learning opportunities develop crystallized intelligence.

**TABLE 11•2 Summary of Tests with Large Factor Loadings on $g_f$ or $g_c$**

| Test | $g_f$ | $g_c$ |
|---|---|---|
| *Figural relations:* Deduction of a relation when this is shown among common figures | .57 | .01 |
| *Memory span:* Reproduction of several numbers or letters presented briefly | .50 | .00 |
| *Induction:* Deduction of a correlate from relations shown in a series of letters, numbers, or figures, as in a letter series test | .41 | .06 |
| *General reasoning:* Solving problems of area, rate, finance, and the like, as in an arithmetic reasoning test | .31 | .34 |
| *Semantic relations:* Deduction of a relation when this is shown among words, as in an analogies test | .37 | .43 |
| *Formal reasoning:* Arriving at a conclusion in accordance with a formal reasoning process, as in a syllogistic reasoning test | .31 | .41 |
| *Number facility:* Quick and accurate use of arithmetical operations such as addition, subtraction, and multiplication | .21 | .29 |
| *Experiential evaluation:* Solving problems involving protocol and requiring diplomacy, as in a social relations test | .08 | .43 |
| *Verbal comprehension:* Advanced understanding of language, as in a vocabulary reading test | .08 | .68 |

*Source: Adapted from Horn, J. L. (1968). Organization of abilities and the development of intelligence.* Psychological Review, 75, *249. Copyright 1968 by the American Psychological Association. Adapted by permission of the author.*

If two people have the same experiences, the one with the greater fluid intelligence will develop the greater crystallized intelligence. However, a person with a high fluid intelligence exposed to an intellectually impoverished environment will develop a poor or mediocre crystallized intelligence. **Table 11•2** presents a summary of tests that load on $g_f$ and $g_c$.

## An Information Processing Theory of Intelligence

According to Robert Sternberg, the degree of success that people achieve in life is strongly affected by the extent to which they effectively analyze and manage their unique combinations of strengths and weaknesses. Sternberg (1996, 1997, 2003a, 2003b) has devised a *triarchic* ("ruled by three") theory of intelligence that derives from the information processing approach used by many cognitive psychologists. The three parts of the theory deal with three aspects of intelligence: analytic intelligence, creative intelligence, and practical intelligence. As you will see, these three components go beyond the abilities measured by most common tests of intelligence. Taken together, these three aspects contribute to what Sternberg (1996, 1999, 2002) calls **successful intelligence**. Successful intelligence is the ability to (a) analyze one's strengths and weaknesses, (b) use the strengths to greatest advantage, and (c) minimize the impact of weaknesses by overcoming or compensating for them.

**Analytic intelligence** consists of the mental mechanisms people use to plan and execute tasks. The components revealed by the factor analyses of verbal ability and deductive reasoning that we just described are facets of analytic intelligence. Sternberg suggests that these components of analytic intelligence serve three functions. *Metacomponents* (transcending components) are the processes by which people decide the nature of an intellectual problem, select a strategy for solving it, and allocate their resources. For example, good readers vary the amount of time they spend on a passage according to how much information they need to extract from it (Wagner & Sternberg, 1983). This decision is controlled by a metacomponent of intelligence. *Performance components* are the processes actually used to perform the task—for example, word recognition and working memory. *Knowledge acquisition components* are those that the person uses to gain new knowledge by sifting out relevant information and integrating it with what he or she already knows.

The second part of Sternberg's theory deals with creative intelligence (Sternberg, 2003b). **Creative intelligence** is the ability to deal effectively with novel situations and to solve familiar problems automatically. According to Sternberg's theory, a person with high creative intelligence is able to deal more effectively with novel situations than is a person with low creative intelligence. The person is better able to analyze the situation and to bring mental resources to bear on the problem, even if he or she has never encountered one like it before. After encountering a particular type of problem several times, the person with good creative intelligence is also able to "automate" the procedure so that similar problems can be solved without much thought, freeing mental resources for more demanding work. A person who has to reason out the solution to repetitive problems every time they occur will be left behind by people who can give the answer quickly and automatically. Sternberg suggests that this distinction is closely related to the distinction between fluid and crystallized intelligence (Carroll, 1993; Horn, 1994; Horn & Cattell, 1966). According to Sternberg, tasks that use fluid intelligence demand novel approaches, whereas tasks that use crystallized intelligence demand mental processes that have become automatic. There is another interesting dimension of creative intelligence that demonstrates why we should not

**successful intelligence** According to Sternberg, the ability to effectively analyze and manage personal strengths and weaknesses.
**analytic intelligence** According to Sternberg, the mental mechanisms people use to plan and execute tasks; includes metacomponents, performance components, and knowledge acquisition components.
**creative intelligence** According to Sternberg, the ability to deal effectively with novel situations and to solve problems automatically that have been encountered previously.

by others. You will see in an upcoming section that each of these three abilities is assessed to a greater or lesser extent by intelligence tests that were developed independent of Gardner's work. You might also notice that there is some overlap with Sternberg's notion of *practical intelligence*. For example, Gardner's *naturalist intelligence* fits well with Sternberg's adaptation form of practical intelligence when applied to the specific example of being able to distinguish edible and poisonous plants. The difference is that Sternberg's adaptation form of practical intelligence is a quality broadly associated with practical abilities, whereas Gardner affords naturalist intelligence its own independent status among other intelligences.

The remainder of Gardner's intelligences generally have not been recognized in psychology as distinct facilities. For example, we have tended not to consider skill at moving one's body as a measure of intelligence, although this talent was undoubtedly selected during the evolution of our species. Individuals who could more skilfully prepare tools, hunt animals, climb trees, scale cliffs, and perform other tasks requiring physical skills were more likely to survive and reproduce. Psychologists have developed mechanical aptitude tests, primarily to help employers select skilled prospective employees, but such skills have generally been regarded as representing something less than intelligence. If a person has good verbal skills, most people in Western cultures will not regard the person as less intelligent if he or she is also clumsy. But they will not credit a person who has poor verbal skills with much intelligence even if he or she has highly honed physical skills.

Gardner's theory also has the advantage of recognizing views of intelligence held by some non-Western cultures. Consider that the **syllogism**, a tool for measuring deductive logic, is often found in tests of intelligence. A syllogism is a logical construction that consists of a major premise (e.g., *All birds have feathers*), a minor premise (e.g., *A Canada goose is a bird*), and a conclusion (e.g., *A Canada goose has feathers*). The major and minor premises are assumed to be true. The problem is to decide whether the conclusion is true or false. Although Gardner would not agree, several studies suggested that unschooled people in remote villages in various parts of the world were unable to solve syllogistic problems. Scribner (1977) visited two tribes of people in Liberia, West Africa: the Kpelle and the Vai. She found that, indeed, the tribespeople gave what Westerners would consider wrong answers.

This is not to say, however, that the people were not able to reason logically. They simply approached problems differently. For example, Scribner presented the following problem to a Kpelle farmer. At first glance, the problem appears to be a reasonable one even for a person without formal schooling because it refers to his own tribe and to an occupation he is familiar with.

> All Kpelle men are rice farmers. Mr. Smith is not a rice farmer. Is he a Kpelle man?

The man replied:

> *Subject*: I don't know the man in person. I have not laid eyes on the man himself.
>
> *Experimenter*: Just think about the statement.
>
> *Subject*: If I know him in person, I can answer that question, but since I do not know him in person, I cannot answer that question.
>
> *Experimenter*: Try and answer from your Kpelle sense.
>
> *Subject*: If you know a person, if a question comes up about him you are able to answer. But if you do not know the person, if a question comes up about him it's hard for you to answer. (Scribner, 1977, p. 490)

The farmer's response did not show that he was unable to solve a problem in deductive logic. Instead, it indicated that as far as he was concerned, the question was unreasonable. In fact, his response contained an example of logical reasoning: "If you know a person . . . you are able to answer."

Clearly, we cannot measure the intellectual ability of people in other cultures against our own standards. In the world of traditional tribal people, problems are solved by application of logical reasoning to facts gained through direct experience. Their deductive-reasoning ability is not necessarily inferior to ours; it is simply different. The theory of multiple intelligences allows for the recognition of different types of intelligence. Gardner would recognize the ability of a member of the Puluwat culture of the Caroline Islands to navigate across the sea by the stars as an example of intelligence (Gardner, 1999; Gladwin, 1970). As Gardner's theory gains recognition, social and cultural attitudes toward what constitutes intelligence may change accordingly.

Gardner himself prefers not to be involved in the development of formal measures that reflect elements of his intelligences (Gardner, 1999). That has not deterred others. The Bar-On Emotional Intelligence Inventory (Bar-On, 1997), for example, draws on elements of Gardner's interpersonal and intrapersonal intelligences and on complementary work by Salovey and Mayer (e.g., Mayer & Salovey, 1993; Salovey & Mayer, 1989–90). Dawda and Hart (2000) have reported initial research suggesting that the scale may indeed be useful for measuring differences among people on the interpersonal and intrapersonal dimensions. The possibility that emotional intelligence may have a unique status of its own is being investigated by a number of researchers with promising results (e.g., Caruso, Mayer, & Salovey, 2002; Casey, Garrett, Brackett, & Rivers, 2008; Saklofske, Austin, & Minski, 2003).

**syllogism** A logical construction that contains a major premise, a minor premise, and a conclusion. The major and minor premises are assumed to be true, and the truth of the conclusion is to be evaluated by deductive reasoning.

## Interim Summary

### Theories of Intelligence

Although intelligence is often represented by a single score, the IQ, modern investigators do not deny the existence of specific abilities. What is controversial is whether a general factor also exists. Spearman thought so; he named the factor *g* and demonstrated that people's scores on a variety of specific tests of ability were correlated. However, he believed that specific factors (*s* factors) also existed. Thurstone performed a factor analysis on 56 individual tests that revealed the existence of 7 factors, not a single *g* factor. Eysenck reasoned that because these factors were themselves correlated, a factor analysis on them was justified. Cattell performed such an analysis and obtained two factors, and he confirmed this result with factor analyses of tests of his own. The nature of the tests that loaded heavily on these two factors suggested the names fluid intelligence ($g_f$) and crystallized intelligence ($g_c$), with the former representing a person's native ability and the latter representing what a person learns.

Sternberg's triarchic theory of intelligence attempts to integrate laboratory research using the information processing approach and an analysis of intelligent behaviour in the natural environment. According to Sternberg, we use analytic intelligence to plan and execute tasks. We use creative intelligence to apply past strategies to new problems. Finally, we use practical intelligence to adapt to, select, or shape our environment. Gardner's neuropsychological theory of intelligence is based primarily on the types of skills that can be selectively lost due to brain damage. His definition of intelligence includes many abilities that are commonly regarded as "skills" or "talents." Like Sternberg's theory, Gardner's theory emphasizes the significance of behaviours to the culture in which they occur.

The concept of intelligence is determined by culture. Most Western societies include academic skills such as verbal ability and formal reasoning in their definitions of intelligence and regard non-academic abilities as talents. People in pre-industrial societies are less likely to approach a logical problem abstractly. Instead, they tend to base their conclusions on what they know to be true—and not on the hypothetical situations proposed by the person questioning them. In their societies, such an approach is more likely than an academic approach to solve the kinds of problems they encounter.

#### QUESTIONS TO CONSIDER

1. How do you define intelligence in your everyday life? Would your definition work equally well for someone from a preliterate society as for someone from the culture in which you live?
2. How do you rate your own fluid and crystallized intelligence? Can you think of instances of your own behaviour (for example, answering questions, solving problems, working out a strategy) that illustrate each type of intelligence?
3. Gardner has considered the possibility of a "spiritual" intelligence. What do you think? What criteria would Gardner use to decide whether to grant spiritual intelligence entry to his list?

# Intelligence Testing

Many employers use specialized aptitude tests to help them select employees. Because the scores achieved on these tests have major implications for the quality of people's adult lives, testing has become one of the most important and controversial areas of applied psychology (e.g., Hough & Oswald, 2000). Today, there are hundreds of tests of specific abilities, such as manual dexterity, spatial reasoning, vocabulary, mathematical aptitude, musical ability, creativity, and memory. There are also general tests of scholastic aptitude, some of which you have probably taken yourself. All of these tests vary widely in reliability, validity, and ease of administration.

## From Mandarins to Galton

Undoubtedly, humans have been aware of individual differences in abilities since our species first evolved.

Some people were more efficient hunters, some were more skilful at constructing tools and weapons, and some were more daring and clever warriors. As early as 2200 B.C., Chinese administrators tested civil servants (mandarins) periodically to be sure that their abilities qualified them for their jobs. But in Western cultures, differences in social class were far more important than individual differences in ability until the Renaissance, when the modern concept of individualism came into being.

Sir Francis Galton (1822–1911), a biologist and statistician, was the most important early investigator of individual differences in ability. He was strongly influenced by his cousin Charles Darwin, who stressed the importance of inherited differences in physical and behavioural traits related to a species' survival. Galton observed that there were family differences in ability and concluded that intellectual abilities were heritable. Having noted that people with low ability were poor at making sensory discriminations, he decided that tests involving such discriminations would provide valid measures of intelligence.

In 1884, Galton established the Anthropometric ("human-measuring") Laboratory at the International Health Exhibition in London. His exhibit was so popular that afterwards his laboratory became part of the South Kensington Museum. He tested more than 9000 people on 17 variables, including height and weight, muscular strength, and the ability to perform sensory discriminations. One task involved detecting small differences in the weights of objects of the same size and shape. The use of simple tests of sensory discrimination fell into disfavour among subsequent researchers in the field of intelligence, so Galton's program was not continued after his death.

Nevertheless, Galton made some important contributions to science and mathematics. His systematic evaluation of various large numbers of people and the methods of population statistics he developed served as models for the statistical tests now used in all branches of science. His observation that the distribution of most human traits closely resembles the normal curve (developed by the Belgian statistician Lambert Quételet, 1796–1874) is the foundation for many modern tests of statistical significance. (See **Figure 11•1**.)

Galton also outlined the logic of a measure he called *correlation*: the degree to which variability in one measure is related to variability in another. From this analysis, Karl Pearson derived the correlation coefficient ($r$) used today to assess the degree of statistical relation between variables. In addition, Galton developed the logic of *twin studies* and *adoptive parent studies* to assess the heritability of a human trait. We will discuss these methods later in the chapter. (You also read about them in Chapter 3.)

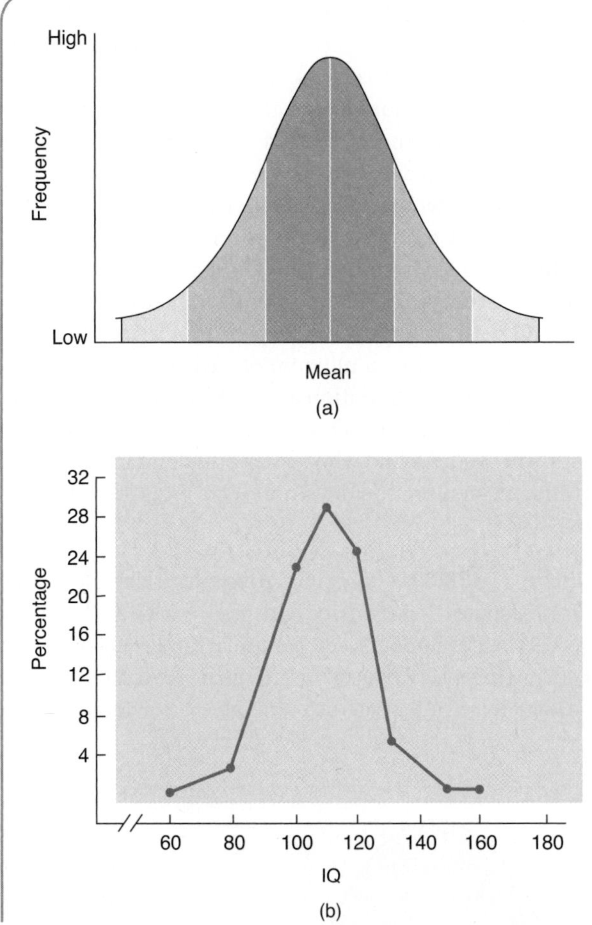


**FIGURE 11•1** The normal curve and data from intelligence testing. (a) A mathematically derived normal curve. (b) A curve showing the distribution of IQ scores of 850 children 2.5 years of age.

*(From Terman, L. M., & Merrill, M. A. (1960).* Stanford-Binet Intelligence Scale. *Boston: Houghton Mifflin; material cited pertains to the 1960 edition and not to the fourth edition, published in 1996. Reproduced by permission of the Riverside Publishing Company.)*

## Intelligence Tests

In the early 1920s, Gilbert (1921) proposed that you could measure intelligence simply by placing a ruler perpendicular against your face. He stated that "if your forehead recedes from the ruler, it is an indication that you are weak in reasoning and deductive facilities." On the other hand, "should the forehead and chin project over the vertical, you not only have highly-developed reasoning power, but great will power." This simplistic approach, and others like it, used to be considered a reasonable strategy to assess cognitive capabilities. Fortunately, many years of research have led to a greater understanding of how we can better measure intelligence.

Modern intelligence tests began in France, with the work of Alfred Binet (1857–1911). His test, since adapted by North American psychologists, is still used today. Another psychologist, David Wechsler, devised two intelligence tests, one for adults and another for children.

**The Binet-Simon Scale** Alfred Binet, a French psychologist, disagreed with Galton's conception of human intelligence. He and a colleague (Binet & Henri, 1896) suggested that a group of simple sensory tests could not adequately determine a person's intelligence. They recommended measuring a variety of psychological abilities (such as imagery, attention, comprehension, imagination, judgments of visual space, and memory for various stimuli) that appeared to be more representative of the traits that distinguished people of high and low intelligence.

The French government asked Binet to look into problems associated with teaching children with learning difficulties. To identify children who were unable to profit from normal classroom instruction and who therefore needed special attention and programs, Binet and a colleague, Theodore Simon, assembled a collection of tests, many of which had been developed by other investigators, and published the **Binet-Simon Scale** in 1905. The tests were arranged in order of difficulty, and the researchers obtained norms for each test. **Norms** are data concerning comparison groups that permit the score of an individual to be assessed relative to his or her peers. In this case, the norms consisted of distributions of scores obtained from children of various ages. Binet and Simon also provided a detailed description of the testing procedure,

**Binet-Simon Scale** An intelligence test developed by Binet and Simon in 1905; the precursor of the Stanford-Binet Scale.

**norms** Data concerning comparison groups that permit the score of an individual to be assessed relative to his or her peers.

which was essential for obtaining reliable scores. Without a standardized procedure for administering a test, different testers can obtain different scores from the same child.

Binet revised the 1905 test to assess the intellectual abilities of both normal children and those with learning problems. The revised versions provided a procedure for estimating a child's **mental age**—the level of intellectual development that could be expected for an average child of a particular age. For example, if a child of 8 scores as well as average 10-year-old children, his or her mental age is 10 years. Binet did not develop the concept of IQ (intelligence quotient), nor did he believe that the mental age derived from the test scores expressed a simple trait called "intelligence." Instead, he conceived of the overall score as the average of several different abilities.

**The Stanford-Binet Scale** Lewis Terman, of Stanford University in the United States, translated and revised the Binet-Simon Scale. The revised group of tests, published in 1916, became known as the **Stanford-Binet Scale.** Revisions by Terman and Maud Merrill were published in 1937 and 1960. In 1996, an entirely new version was published. The Stanford-Binet Scale, which is widely used in North America, consists of various tasks grouped according to mental age. Simple tests include identifying parts of the body and remembering which of three small cardboard boxes contains a marble. Intermediate tests include tracing a simple maze with a pencil and repeating five digits orally. Advanced tests include explaining the difference between two abstract words that are close in meaning (such as *fame* and *notoriety*) and completing complex sentences.

The 1916 Stanford-Binet Scale contained a formula for computing the intelligence quotient (IQ), a measure devised by Stern (1914). The **intelligence quotient (IQ)** represents the idea that if test scores indicate that a child's mental age is equal to his or her chronological age (that is, calendar age), the child's intelligence is average; if the child's mental age is above or below his or her chronological age, the child is more or less intelligent than average. This relation is expressed as the quotient of mental age (MA) and chronological age (CA). The result is called the **ratio IQ**:

$$IQ = \frac{MA}{CA} \times 100$$

The quotient is multiplied by 100 to eliminate fractions. For example, if a child's mental age is 10 and the child's chronological age is 8, then his or her IQ is $(10 \div 8) \times 100 = 125$.

The 1960 version of the Stanford-Binet Scale replaced the ratio IQ with the **deviation IQ.** Instead of using the ratio of mental age to chronological age, the deviation IQ compares a child's score with those received by other children of the same chronological age. (The deviation IQ was invented by David Wechsler, whose work is described in the next section.) Suppose that a child's score is one standard deviation above the mean for his or her age. The standard deviation of the ratio IQ scores is 16 points, and the score assigned to the average IQ is 100 points. (See Chapter 2 for a description of the standard deviation, a measure of variability.) If a child's score is one standard deviation above the mean for his or her age, the child's deviation IQ score is 100 + 16 (the standard deviation) = 116. A child who scores one standard deviation below the mean receives a deviation IQ of 84 (100 – 16). (See **Figure 11•2.**)

**mental age** A measure of a person's intellectual development; the level of intellectual development that could be expected for an average child of a particular age.
**Stanford-Binet Scale** An intelligence test that consists of various tasks grouped according to mental age; provides the standard measure of the intelligence quotient.
**intelligence quotient (IQ)** A simplified single measure of general intelligence; by definition, the ratio of a person's mental age to his or her chronological age, multiplied by 100; often derived by other formulas.
**ratio IQ** A formula for computing the intelligence quotient; mental age divided by chronological age, multiplied by 100.
**deviation IQ** A procedure for computing the intelligence quotient; compares a child's score with those received by other children of the same chronological age.

**Wechsler's Tests** While chief psychologist at New York City's Bellevue Psychiatric Hospital, David Wechsler (1896–1981) developed several popular and well-respected tests of intelligence. His goals were to devise tests of intelligence that were not limited to a single performance index,

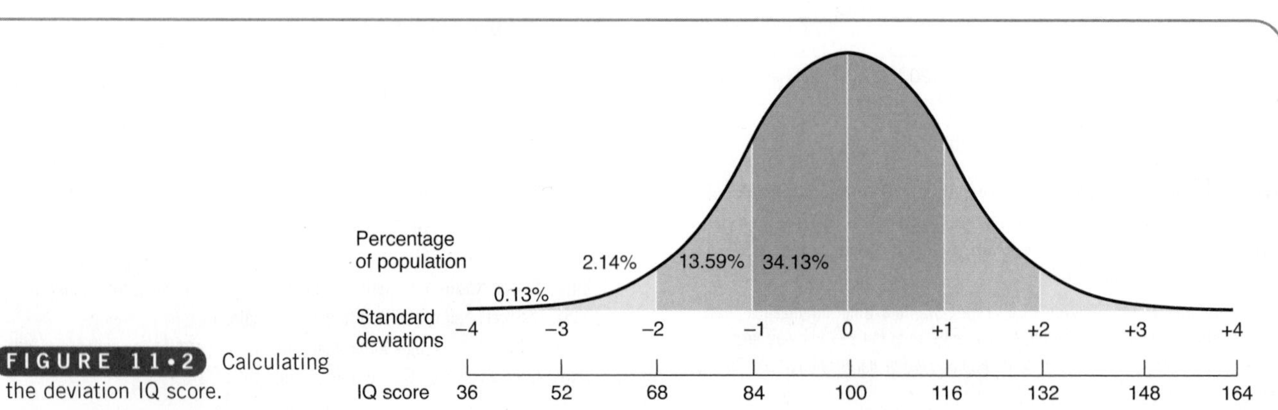


**FIGURE 11•2** Calculating the deviation IQ score.

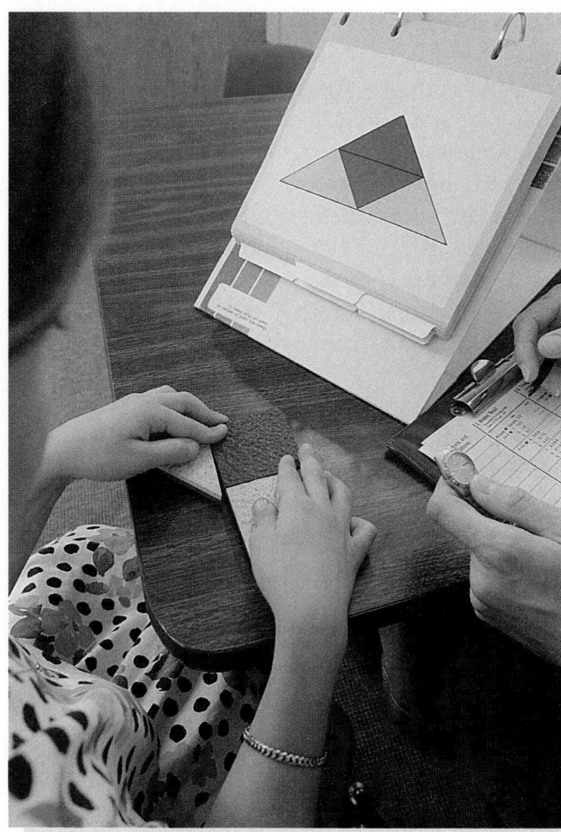

▲ *A block design subtest, like the one shown above, is part of both of Wechsler's scales, the WISC for children and the WAIS for adults.*

**FIGURE 11•3** WAIS-IV sample questions.

(Wechsler Adult Intelligence Scale-Fourth Edition (WAIS-IV). *Copyright © 2008 by NCS Pearson, Inc. Reproduced with permission. All rights reserved. "Wechsler Adult Intelligence Scale" and "WAIS" are trademarks, in the US and/or other countries, of Pearson Education, Inc. or its affiliates(s).)*

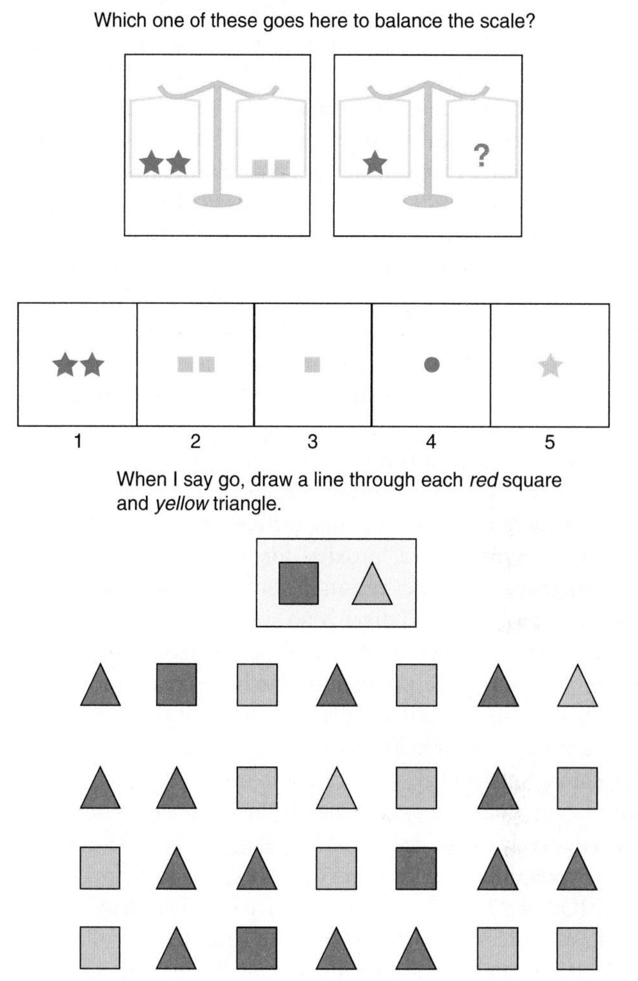


that were not limited to verbal content, and that avoided cultural and linguistic biases. The Wechsler-Bellevue Scale, published in 1939, was revised in 1942 for use in the armed forces and was superseded in 1955 by the **Wechsler Adult Intelligence Scale (WAIS).** This test was revised in 1981 (the WAIS-R) and again in 2008 (the WAIS-IV). The **Wechsler Intelligence Scale for Children (WISC),** first published in 1949 and revised most recently in 2003 (the WISC-IV), closely resembles the WAIS. Wechsler also devised an intelligence test for preschool children, a memory scale, and other measures of ability.

The WAIS-IV consists of several subtests, including measures of fluid intelligence and perceptual organization, which are new to this latest edition of the scale. **Figure 11•3** shows three examples of the types of questions found on the WAIS-IV. The norms obtained for the WAIS-IV permit the tester to calculate a deviation IQ score.

The WAIS has become the most popular individually administered adult intelligence test. An important advantage is that it tests verbal and performance abilities separately. Neuropsychologists often use it because people with brain damage tend to score very differently on the performance and verbal tests; thus, comparisons of performance and verbal test scores suggest the presence of undiagnosed brain damage. Because people who have had few educational and cultural opportunities often do worse on the verbal tests than on the performance tests, the WAIS is useful in estimating what their score might have been had they been raised in a more favourable environment.

## Reliability and Validity of Intelligence Tests

As you will recall from Chapter 2, the adequacy of a measure is represented by its reliability and validity. In the case of intelligence testing, reliability is assessed by the correlation between the scores people receive on the same measurement

**Wechsler Adult Intelligence Scale (WAIS)** An intelligence test for adults devised by David Wechsler; contains subtests divided into the categories of verbal and performance.

**Wechsler Intelligence Scale for Children (WISC)** An intelligence test for children devised by David Wechsler; similar in form to the Wechsler Adult Intelligence Scale.

on two different occasions; perfect reliability is 1.0. High reliability is achieved by means of standardized test administration and objective scoring: All test takers are exposed to the same conditions during testing, and all test givers score responses in the same way. The acceptable reliability of a modern test of intellectual ability should be at least .85.

The validity of an intelligence test is assessed by the strength of the correlation between test scores and the **criterion**—an independent measure of the variable that is being assessed. An interesting example of the importance of criterion validity comes from the research literature on self-reported intelligence. One question addressed by researchers is the validity of people's self-reports of their own intelligence. The typical research approach to this question is to obtain self-ratings of intelligence and formal scores for the same people from established IQ tests. The IQ test scores provide the *criterion* against which the self-report measures of intelligence are assessed. Paulhus, Lysy, and Yik (1998), for example, asked university students to estimate their own intelligence, but failed to find correlations greater than .30 between the self-report scores and the criterion IQ scores. Their conclusion: At least for university students, self-reports of intelligence cannot stand in as valid "proxies" for formal IQ test results.

There is no single criterion measure with which to assess validity, simply because there is no single definition of intelligence. We can, however, look at Binet's original goal of intelligence testing: the prediction of scholastic aptitude. The evidence about this criterion is reasonably clear. School performance, as measured by grades, correlates at about .50 with IQ scores (Neisser et al., 1996). Keep in mind, though, that this correlation does not mean that IQ *determines* school performance. Given the size of this correlation, about 75 percent of the variability in school performance is due to factors other than IQ. The list of potential influences other than IQ on scholastic success is a lengthy one, but consider the following likely candidates: quality of instruction, family emphasis on education, personal interest and motivation, effort and persistence, and peer group attitudes toward school. Many of us know students who obtained stellar IQ scores, but who performed wretchedly in school because they were uninterested or lacked motivation. Likewise, we know people who never posted more than average aptitude scores, but who through hard work and perseverance have achieved remarkable success in school. The same pattern of variability occurs for other potential criterion measures. For example, IQ scores account for less than half of the variability on income and job performance measures (Neisser et al., 1996). Once again, motivation and social variables will account for at least as much as raw IQ.

## The Use and Abuse of Intelligence Tests

Schools that group students according to ability usually do so on the basis of test scores. Schools also administer tests to students who appear to have learning disabilities in order to assess needs that may require special programs. At selective academic institutions, test scores usually serve as an important criterion for admission. Similarly, many business organizations use ability tests to screen job candidates. Because test scores have such important consequences for people's opportunities, we must know whether intelligence tests are valid and whether they are being used appropriately. You have seen that much of the variability on grades and job performance is due to factors other than IQ. The best and fairest practice is to consider IQ as just one of many predictors relevant to such decisions.

**criterion** An independent measure of a variable being assessed.

**The Problem of Bias** Critics of intelligence testing have argued that the results of some tests are strongly affected by what people have learned (e.g., Miller-Jones, 1989), not just by their inherent abilities. Consider the effects of a person's family background and culture on his or her ability to answer questions such as "Who wrote *Romeo and Juliet*?" "What is a hieroglyph?" and "What is the meaning of *catacomb*?" (Vernon, 1979, p. 22). Obviously, a child from a family with a strong educational background is much more likely to be able to answer these questions than is an equally intelligent child from a less well-educated family. The worst form of this bias occurs when entire groups of people are disadvantaged because the content of the test material is foreign to their own cultural contexts. Test constructors have responded to the criticism of cultural bias, and modern tests are now less likely to contain questions that are obviously biased (see Helms, 1997).

This is not to say that problems of cultural bias do not still occur. It is hard to make bias-free tests, because the test makers (like the rest of us) are strongly socialized in their cultures to see what they themselves know as ubiquitous knowledge. For example, the 2002–2003 Miller Analogies Test sample set includes the following analogy:

_____:SHADE::INOCULATION:PARASOL

Knowledge of the meaning of "parasol" likely varies by cultural background. Cultural bias in intelligence testing is not limited to issues of surface vocabulary. (The keyed answer to this problem is "immunity." A parasol produces shade, and an inoculation produces immunity.) Darou (1992) tells a story of presenting a standard analogy question to a First Nations counsellor in the North: "Saw is to whine, as snake is to . . ." (p. 97), for which the scored correct answer would be "hiss." The person questioned could not generate the correct answer. The reason? Most saws that people in the region had experience with were handsaws and chainsaws, neither of which whine. Clinching the inappropriateness of the question was the fact that there were no snakes in the area. In short, the people did not have first-hand knowledge with which to appreciate the question. Even when questions having obvious cultural bias are excluded from tests, different experiences can lead to different test-taking strategies in subtler ways (e.g., Helms, 1992). For example, as we saw earlier,

Kpelle tribespeople approach hypothetical logical problems very differently from people in literate societies. Their "failure" to solve such problems indicates cultural differences, not intellectual differences.

**The Problem of Self-Fulfilling Prophecies** There are ways in which intelligence testing can potentially be harmful even if the tests are free of bias. There is good reason to believe that knowledge about children's intelligence scores can set in motion *self-fulfilling prophecy* phenomena. A self-fulfilling prophecy occurs when people's expectations about what will happen lead them to act in ways that make the expectations come true, even if the expectations were unfounded in the first place (Merton, 1948). In short, if teachers learn that a child has a low intelligence test score, they may see encouragement and special attention as a waste of time—time perhaps better spent with students who have greater native ability. Likewise, parents who learn that their child has scored low on an intelligence test may try to channel the child away from academic pursuits. The reactions of both teachers and parents would be ill-advised, because we know that intelligence scores are just part of the overall picture of a child's intellectual growth and functioning. Failure to provide the child with special attention and encouragement could in fact seal the child's fate, and produce just the poor academic performance that was expected on the basis of the intelligence test scores. The prophecy (i.e., the expectation) of academic failure would be fulfilled, even though the child could have been able to do well academically, given proper support. Although ethical considerations prevent direct testing of this possibility, related research strongly suggests that these concerns are well placed (e.g., Madon et al., 2001; Rosenthal, 1985).

Should children be told their intelligence test scores? You can imagine the discouraging and demotivating effects on children of learning that they have not achieved high intelligence test scores. Here again, we see the opportunity for self-fulfilling prophecy. Expecting not to perform well academically could bring about performance below the child's actual capacity.

**Identifying Specific Learning Needs** Intelligence testing does have potential benefits when it is used in accordance with Binet's original purpose: to identify students who require special instruction. Children with severe learning problems may develop a sense of inferiority if they are placed in mainstream classes without appropriate specialized teaching support. These tests can also identify exceptionally bright students who are performing poorly because they are bored with the pace of instruction or who have been labelled as "troublemakers" by their teachers.

Many otherwise bright children have various learning disabilities. Some have trouble learning to read or write; some perform poorly at arithmetic or motor skills. For example, some children have developmental dyslexias that make learning to read difficult for them. Children with dyslexia are often frustrated by the contrast between their inability to read and their other more competent abilities. They may act out this frustration through disruptive behaviour at school and at home, or they may simply stop trying to excel at anything. As a result, they are sometimes labelled as having mental retardation and are placed in inappropriate education programs. In this situation, tests of intellectual abilities can be useful. By identifying a specific learning disability in an otherwise bright child, testing helps ensure remedial action and prevents mislabelling. It is very important to keep in mind that environment matters. Many deficits can be overcome.

**Identifying Degrees of Mental Retardation** Binet's original use of intelligence tests—to identify children who learn more slowly than most others and who therefore need special educational opportunities—is still important. Intelligence tests are an accepted means of evaluating the extent of a child's disabilities and, thus, of indicating the most appropriate remedial program.

The term **mental retardation** was originally applied to children with severe learning problems because they appeared to achieve intellectual skills and competencies at a significantly later age than children typically do. People with mental retardation were formerly relegated to a bleak and hopeless existence in institutions. Fortunately, there are many more options today for people with intellectual deficiencies. I will discuss the causes of mental retardation later in this chapter.

People with mental retardation face a double problem. Because they have a greater or lesser degree of intellectual disability, they will have at least some, and in some cases extreme, difficulty with the usual tasks of living. They also must deal with prejudice and discrimination. Being intelligent is a highly valued quality in our society, and people with intellectual deficits often are the target of derision. Unfortunately, being different often translates into being "bad." Many people also believe that if a person has an intellectual disability, he or she lacks normal emotions, desires, and needs. These beliefs are, of course, false. Because of the stigma attached to mental retardation, and the very use of the term as an insult, we hesitated over the use of the designation in this section. Nevertheless, the term *mental retardation* is still the professionally accepted label, and we use it here for purposes of describing the degrees of this disability. In other contexts, we think *cognitive disability* or *intellectual disability* is the better choice of terms.

According to the American Psychological Association, degrees of mental retardation are defined jointly by IQ scores and adaptive limitations in everyday living (Jacobson & Mulick, 1996). The most severe classification, *profound mental retardation*, is applied when a person has an IQ score below the range of 20. This is a very rare level of disability that

**mental retardation** Mental development that is substantially below normal; often caused by some form of brain damage or abnormal brain development.

▲ *With appropriate education, most people with mild mental retardation can lead independent lives and perform well at jobs.*

involves problems in all domains of life and is also associated with motor difficulties. The person shows little cognitive development during his or her early years. People with this degree of disability require total supervision and care. The next category is *severe mental retardation*, which is used when a person's IQ score is between 20 and 34. This degree of disability includes difficulty with speech development during the early years. People with severe mental retardation can profit from special education programs, and can contribute to their own care, although they almost always need total supervision. People with *moderate mental retardation* have IQ scores between 35 and 54, are able to learn most basic life skills, are able to hold well-supervised jobs, and can live semi-independently with some supervision and assistance. The vast majority of people (about 90 percent) with mental retardation are classified as having *mild mental retardation*. IQ scores for this level fall between 55 and 70. Although people with mild mental retardation may need assistance and support from time to time, they generally are able to live independently and to learn the skills and responsibilities needed to maintain employment. It is important to recall again that IQ does not itself determine achievement and satisfaction in life. Families, neighbours, schools, communities, and special programs are all significant contributors to the well-being of people with intellectual disabilities.

## Interim Summary

### Intelligence Testing

Although the earliest known instance of ability testing was carried out by the ancient Chinese, modern intelligence testing dates from the efforts of Francis Galton to measure individual differences. Galton made an important contribution to the field of measurement, but his tests of simple perceptual abilities were abandoned in favour of tests that attempt to assess more complex abilities, such as memory, logical reasoning, and vocabulary.

Binet developed a test that was designed to assess students' intellectual abilities in order to identify children with special educational needs. Although the test that superseded his, the Stanford-Binet Scale, provided for calculation of IQ, Binet believed that "intelligence" was actually a composite of several specific abilities. For him, the concept of mental age was a convenience, not a biological reality. Wechsler's two intelligence tests, the WAIS-III for adults and the WISC-IV for children, are widely used today. The information provided by the verbal and performance scores helps neuropsychologists diagnose brain damage and can provide at least a rough estimate of the innate ability of poorly educated people.

The reliability of modern intelligence tests is excellent, but assessing their validity is still difficult. Because no single criterion measure of intelligence exists, intelligence tests are validated by comparing the scores with measures of achievement, such as scholastic success.

Intelligence tests can have both good and bad effects on the people who take them. The principal benefit is derived by identifying children with special needs (or special talents) who will profit from special programs. The principal danger lies in stigmatizing those who score poorly and depriving them of the opportunity for good jobs or further education.

**QUESTIONS TO CONSIDER**

1. Would you like to know your own IQ score? Why? Do you think knowing your IQ score would make a difference in your life? How would you feel if your IQ score were "average"?
2. Suppose you wanted to devise an intelligence test of your own. What kinds of problems would you include? What abilities would these problems measure?

# The Roles of Heredity and Environment

Abilities of various kinds—intellectual, athletic, musical, and artistic—appear to run in families. Why? Are the similarities due to heredity, or are they solely the result of a common environment, which includes similar educational opportunities and exposure to people having similar kinds of interests? We considered this problem briefly in Chapter 3; now we will examine it in more detail. As you will see, both hereditary and environmental factors play a role.

## The Meaning of Heritability

When we ask how much influence heredity has on a given trait, we are usually asking what the heritability of the trait is.

**Heritability** is a statistical measure that expresses the proportion of the observed variability in a trait within a population that is a direct result of genetic variability. The value of this measure can vary from 0 to 1.0. The heritability of many physical traits in most cultures is very high; for example, eye colour is affected almost entirely by hereditary factors and little, if at all, by the environment. Thus, the heritability of eye colour is close to 1.0.

Heritability is a concept that many people misunderstand. It does not describe the extent to which the inherited genes are responsible for producing a particular trait; it measures the relative contributions of differences in genes and differences in environmental factors to the overall observed variability of the trait in a particular population. An example may make this distinction clear. Consider the heritability of hair colour among Inuit. Assume that all young Inuit have black hair. Because all members of this population possess the same versions of the genes that determine hair colour, there is no genetic variability. Therefore, the heritability of hair colour among Inuit is zero. This may sound odd to you, because you know that hair colour is genetically determined. So, how can a trait be genetically determined, indeed inherited, but have zero heritability? The key is that genetic influence or determination and heritability are not the same thing. Heritability refers only to the genetic influence on the dispersion of differences on a trait (whether hair colour or IQ) in a population. If there are no differences among individuals in the population in a trait, then there is no heritability for that trait. As with hair colour, we infer the heritability of a person's intelligence through observation of the trait within a population. By measuring the correlation between IQ scores and various genetic and environmental factors, we can arrive at an estimate of heritability. Clearly, even if hereditary factors do influence intelligence, the heritability of this trait must be considerably less than 1.0 because so many environmental factors (the mother's prenatal health and nutrition, the child's nutrition, the educational level of the child's parents, and the quality of the child's school) can influence it.

Keep in mind as you read along that a person does not inherit a certain number of IQ points. Rather than IQ, you inherit genes that influence the development of intelligence. The life you experience early in the womb, in your family, schools, and neighbourhood, all influence your IQ in conjunction with your genes. Most importantly, remember that heritability estimates do not apply to individuals (see Sternberg & Grigorenko, 1999, for an interesting discussion of this point). These estimates apply only to populations of people. Also keep in mind that knowing that heritability for a trait is .50 does not mean that 50 percent of the trait is inherited in an individual. Again, heritability refers to populations, not to individuals.

When we consider studies that assess the heritability of intellectual abilities, we should be aware of the following considerations:

1. The heritability of a trait depends on the amount of variability of genetic factors in a given population. If there is little genetic variability, genetic factors will appear to be unimportant. Because the ancestors of people living in developed Western nations came from all over the world, genetic variability is likely to be much higher there than in an isolated community of people in a remote part of the world. Therefore, if a person's IQ score is at all affected by genetic factors, the measured heritability of IQ will be higher in, say, North American culture than in an isolated community.
2. The relative importance of environmental factors in intelligence depends on the amount of environmental variability (EV) that occurs in the population. If environmental variability is low, then environmental factors will appear to be unimportant. That is, if everyone is exposed to the same environment, there is logically no opportunity to observe how that environment might affect people compared to other environments. In a society with a low variability in environmental factors relevant to intellectual development—one in which all children are raised in the same way by equally skilled and conscientious caregivers, all schools are equally good, all teachers have equally effective personalities and teaching skills, and no one is discriminated against—the effects of EV would be small and those of GV (genetic variability) would be large. In contrast, in a society where only a few privileged people receive a good education, environmental factors would be responsible for much of the variability in intelligence: The effects of EV would be large relative to those of GV.
3. Heritability is affected by the degree to which genetic inheritance and environment interact. Genetic factors and environmental factors often affect each other. For example, suppose that because of genetic differences some children are calm and others are excitable. Suppose that the excitable children will profit most from a classroom in which distractions are kept to a minimum and teachers are themselves calm and soothing. Further suppose that the calm students will profit most from an exciting classroom that motivates them to work their hardest. In this situation, the actual performance of the students would be based on an interaction between heredity and environment. If all students were taught in a calm classroom, the excitable children would learn more and obtain better IQ scores. If all students were taught in an exciting classroom, the calm children would do better and obtain the higher scores. (Ideally, a child's learning environment should match his or her hereditary predispositions.)

## Sources of Environmental and Genetic Effects during Development

Donald Hebb (1949) set the stage for our current understanding of how genetics and environment contribute to intelligence. In his neuropsychological theory of behaviour, he

**heritability** The degree to which the variability of a particular trait in a particular population of organisms is a result of genetic differences among those organisms.

explains that both biological and environmental factors occurring before and after birth can affect intellectual abilities. Hebb's (1949, 1966) view was that the term *intelligence*, as used by psychologists, reflects two components. The first component (*Intelligence A*) is the hereditary, biological potential for intellectual development. The second component (*Intelligence B*) reveals the effect of biological development coupled with environmental influences on functioning. Intelligence B, then, is what we measure with IQ tests. From this perspective, newborn infants cannot be said to possess any substantial intellectual abilities; rather, they are more or less capable of developing these abilities during their lives. Therefore, prenatal influences affect a child's potential intelligence by affecting the development of the brain. Factors that impair brain development will necessarily also impair the child's potential intelligence.

The factors that control the development of a human organism are incredibly complex. For example, the most complicated organ—the brain—consists of many billions of interconnected neurons, all of which are connected to other neurons. In addition, many of these neurons are connected to sensory receptors, muscles, or glands. During development, these billions of neurons must establish the proper connections so that the eyes send their information to the visual cortex, the ears send theirs to the auditory cortex, and the nerve cells controlling movement connect with the appropriate muscles.

As the axons of developing neurons grow, they thread their way through a tangle of other growing cells, responding to physical and chemical signals along the way, much as a salmon swims upriver to the tributary in which it was spawned. During this stage of prenatal development, differentiating cells can be misguided by false signals. For example, if a woman contracts rubella during early pregnancy, toxic chemicals produced by the disease virus may adversely affect the development of the fetus. Sometimes, these chemicals can misdirect the interconnections of brain cells and produce mental retardation. Thus, although development of a human organism is programmed genetically, environmental factors can affect development even before a person is born.

Harmful prenatal environmental factors include physical trauma (for instance, through injury to the mother in an automobile accident) and toxins. A developing fetus can be exposed to toxins from diseases contracted by the mother during pregnancy (such as rubella) or from other sources. A pregnant woman's intake of various drugs can have disastrous effects on fetal development. For example, alcohol, opiates, cocaine, and the chemicals present in cigarettes can harm fetuses. There is some evidence that even low levels of alcohol use, such as a single alcoholic "binge," during a critical stage of pregnancy can cause permanent damage to the fetus (Bailey & Sokol, 2008). One of the most common drug-induced abnormalities, fetal alcohol syndrome, is seen in many offspring of women who are chronic alcoholics. Children with **fetal alcohol syndrome** are much smaller than average, have characteristic facial abnormalities, and, more significantly, have mental retardation.

**fetal alcohol syndrome** A disorder that adversely affects an offspring's brain development and is caused by the mother's alcohol intake during pregnancy.

Genetic abnormalities can also harm development. Some of these abnormalities cause brain damage and consequently produce mental retardation. The best-known example of these abnormalities is Down syndrome, which is described in Chapter 3. Although Down syndrome is a genetic disorder, it is not hereditary; it results from imperfect division of the 23 pairs of chromosomes during the development of an ovum or (rarely) a sperm. Chapter 3 also described phenylketonuria (PKU), an inherited metabolic disorder that disrupts normal brain development. If left untreated, PKU can result in severe mental retardation. Note that although PKU is a genetic disease, its effects on development can be eliminated by limiting dietary intake of phenylalanine, bringing home the point that environment (in this case, eliminating phenylalanine from food) can completely overcome even very strong genetic influences.

A child's brain continues to develop from birth onward. Environmental factors can either promote or impede that development. Postnatal factors such as birth trauma, diseases, or toxic chemicals can prevent optimum development and thereby affect the child's potential intelligence. For example, encephalitis (inflammation of the brain), when contracted during childhood, can result in mental retardation. So can the ingestion of poisons such as mercury or lead.

Educational influences in the environment, including (but not limited to) home life and schooling, enable a child to attain his or her potential intelligence. By contrast, a less-than-optimum environment prevents the fullest possible realization of potential intelligence. Experience with people who have mental retardation demonstrates this point. Known causes account for only about 25 percent of observed instances of mental retardation. In addition, people with mental retardation that has no obvious physical cause are likely to have close relatives who also have mental retardation. These findings strongly suggest that some of the remaining 75 percent are hereditary. However, environmental causes (such as poor nutrition or the presence of environmental toxins) can produce brain damage in members of the same family; thus, not all cases of mental retardation within families are necessarily hereditary.

The interactive effects of environmental and genetic factors are complex. The effects of hereditary factors on adult intellectual ability are necessarily indirect, and many environmental factors exert their effects throughout a person's life. Because an adult's intellectual abilities are the product of a long chain of events, we cannot isolate the effects of the earliest factors. The types of genetic and environmental factors that influence potential intelligence at each stage of development are summarized below.

*Conception.* A person's genetic endowment sets in place the biological component, or potential, for the development of intellectual abilities.

*Prenatal development.* Good nutrition and a normal pregnancy result in optimum brain development and optimum potential intelligence. Drugs, toxic substances, poor nutrition, and physical accidents can impair brain development, thus lowering potential intelligence. Genetic disorders such as phenylketonuria and Down syndrome can impair brain development, thus lowering potential intelligence.

*Birth.* Anoxia (lack of oxygen) or head trauma can cause brain damage, thus lowering potential intelligence.

*Infancy.* The brain continues to develop and grow. Good nutrition continues to be important. Sensory stimulation and interaction with a responsive environment are important for cognitive development. An infant's environment and brain structure jointly determine his or her intelligence.

*Later life.* A person's intelligence continues to be jointly determined by environmental factors and brain structure and chemistry. Aging brings with it an increased chance of developing senile dementia, a class of diseases characterized by the progressive loss of cortical tissue and a corresponding loss of mental functions. (*Senile* means "old"; *dementia* literally means "an undoing of the mind.") The most common causes of *dementia* are Alzheimer's disease (discussed in Chapter 12) and *multiple infarcts*—the occurrence of a large number of small strokes, each of which damages a small amount of brain tissue. In addition, as we will see in Chapter 12, mental deterioration can also be produced by depression, a psychological disorder. Unlike Alzheimer's disease or multiple infarcts, depression can be treated with drugs and with psychotherapy.

## Results of Heritability Studies

Estimates of the degree to which heredity influences a person's intellectual ability come from several sources. As we saw in Chapter 3, the two most powerful methods are comparisons between identical and fraternal twins and comparisons between adoptive and biological relatives. As you read the evidence about heritability, remember what heritability *does* and *does not* mean. If we find that heritability for a trait is .50, it does not mean that 50 percent of the trait was inherited. It means that 50 percent of the variance for that trait in a population is influenced by genetics. A very high heritability estimate does not mean that environmental influences are unimportant. Rather, it means that under environmental conditions favourable to the expression of the trait, a great deal of variability in the population will be attributable to genetics. But environments themselves are variable, and in the real world some environments will promote the genetic expression of the trait and some will inhibit that expression.

**General Intelligence** **Table 11•5** presents correlations for general intelligence between people of varying degrees of kinship and estimates based on these data of the relative contributions of genetic and environmental factors. The data in the table were obtained from a summary of several studies by Henderson (1982). As you can see, the correlation between two people is indeed related to their genetic similarity. For example, the correlation between identical twins is larger than that between fraternal twins. The correlation between parent and child is approximately the same regardless of whether or not the child is raised by the parent (.35 versus .31). The correlation, in turn, is higher than that between an adopted child and the parent who raises him or her (.16). Genetics clearly makes a difference, but how much?

**TABLE 11•5 Correlations between IQ Scores for Members of Various Kinship Pairs**

| Relationship | Rearing | Percentage of Genetic Similarity | Correlation |
|---|---|---|---|
| Same individual | — | 100 | .87[a] |
| Identical twins | Together | 100 | .86 |
| Fraternal twins | Together | 50 | .62 |
| Siblings | Together | 50 | .41 |
| Siblings | Apart | 50 | .24 |
| Parent–child | Together | 50 | .35 |
| Parent–child | Apart | 50 | .31 |
| Adoptive parent–child | Together | ? | .16 |

[a] The correlation is not 1.0 because a person's score may vary from one test to another due to tiredness, distraction, etc. Nevertheless, such a high correlation shows the high reliability of IQ tests.

*Source: Adapted from Henderson, N. D.* Human behavior genetics, *pp. 403–440. Reproduced, with permission from the* Annual Review of Psychology, *Volume 33. © 1982 by Annual Reviews Inc.*

Neisser and colleagues (1996) summarize the evidence on heritability of IQ by placing it at about .45 in childhood and about .75 in late adolescence. In other words, it appears that heritability of IQ increases with age. Recent studies with people in their eighth and ninth decades likewise show higher IQ heritability estimates than typically seen for children (McClearn et al., 1997). How could this be? The answer that Neisser and colleagues and other researchers (e.g., Sternberg & Grigorenko, 1999) suggest is that until early adulthood, people are subject to the authority and decisions of many other people and institutions. The environment therefore stands to play a relatively important role in the development of intellectual abilities. When people become independent, however, they can begin to choose their own environments. To the extent that those choices reflect the heritable component of intelligence, the influence of the chosen environments becomes less distinct from genetic influence.

**Specific Abilities** So far, we have looked at the effects of genetic factors on tests of general intelligence. Scarr and Weinberg (1978) compared some specific intellectual abilities of parents and their adopted and biological children and of children and their biological and adopted siblings. To do so, they administered four of the subtests of the Wechsler Adult Intelligence Scale: arithmetic, vocabulary, block design, and

**TABLE 11•6 Correlations between IQ Scores for Members of Various Kinship Pairs**

| WAIS Subscale | Relationship | | |
|---|---|---|---|
| | Father–Offspring | Mother–Offspring | Sibling |
| ***Adoptive family correlations*** | | | |
| Arithmetic | .07 | –.03 | –.03 |
| Vocabulary | .24 | .23 | .11 |
| Block design | .02 | .13 | .09 |
| Picture arrangement | –.04 | –.01 | .04 |
| ***Biological family correlations*** | | | |
| Arithmetic | .30 | .24 | .24 |
| Vocabulary | .39 | .33 | .22 |
| Block design | .32 | .29 | .25 |
| Picture arrangement | .06 | .19 | .16 |

*Source: Adapted from Scarr, S., & Weinberg, R. A. (1978).* American Sociological Review, 43, *674–692. Adapted with permission.*

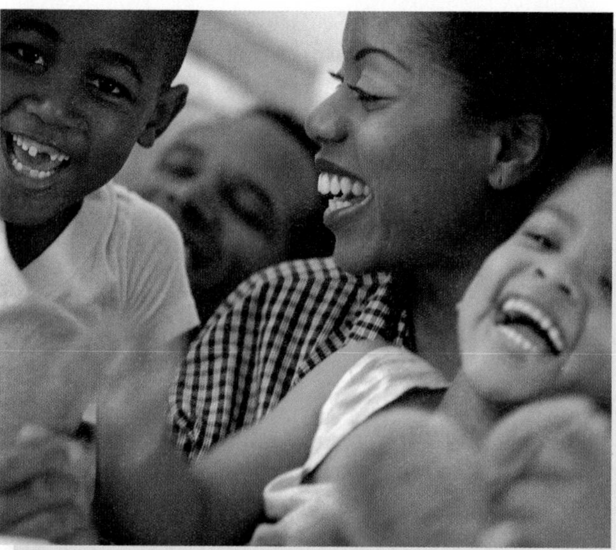

▲ *Although heredity plays some role in the development of intelligence, children's home environments can determine the extent to which they achieve their full potential.*

picture arrangement. **Table 11•6** shows the results. As you can see, the correlations between biological relatives were considerably higher than those between adoptive relatives, indicating that genetic factors played a more significant role than shared environmental factors. In fact, with the exception of vocabulary, adopted children showed little resemblance to other members of their family.

These results suggest that a person's vocabulary is more sensitive to his or her home environment than are other specific intellectual abilities. Presumably, such factors as the availability of books, parental interests in reading, and the complexity of vocabulary used by the parents have a significant effect on the verbal skills of all members of the household, whether or not they are biologically related.

## Then and Now

### The Issue of Race and Intelligence

As you have seen throughout this chapter, intelligence tests have a long history of use and misuse. The fact that heredity plays an important role in people's intellectual capacities raises the question of whether people of some races are generally more intelligent than those of other races. A variety of intelligence tests have been used to look at differences in cognitive abilities due to race. Because of the harmful effects that racism has had on the lives of so many people, this question is not simply an academic one.

Many studies have claimed to establish that race predicts intelligence. One of the earliest tests of racial differences and intelligence was conducted in 1897. One thousand children were tested by having to repeat a section of poetry that was read aloud to them. In this study, the "black" children outperformed the "white" children (Stetson, 1897). This study received little publicity, and the majority of research that followed found opposite results (Guthrie, 1998). Sadly, much of the research conducted in the early 1900s through to the 1960s had a racist agenda (e.g., Ferguson, 1916; McGurk, 1959; Tanser, 1939). Researchers in the 1960s began to realize that many of the earlier studies were flawed, and that differences in IQ score were due to differences other than genetics (e.g., culturally insensitive tests).

Although researchers recognized that the work of the past was biased by prejudice, examination of differences in intelligence continued to produce an effect for race. For example, people in the United States who are identified as "black" generally score an average of 85 on IQ tests, whereas people who are identified as "white" score an average of 100 (Jensen, 1985; Lynn, 1978). Remember from Chapter 2, however, that mean differences do not tell us about variability of scores. This is an especially important point in the socially significant context of differences between races. What the means fail to tell us is that the variation of scores *within* each race is far greater than the variation *between* the two races. In other words, IQ scores of the two races overlap much more than they differentiate. Some whites score higher than blacks, and some blacks score higher than whites. However, there is a seemingly reliable difference, on average.

The issue is not the difference in average scores themselves but what those differences *mean*. The simplest explanation, and the one most widely accepted, has been that the historical and continuing disadvantaged status of black people in the United States suppresses intellectual development of a sufficient proportion of them so that a mean difference in test scores is predictable and understandable.

A more provocative stance that has gained a degree of popular currency is that the racial differences in scores on intelligence tests are caused by heredity. *The Bell Curve*, a book written by American social scientists Herrnstein and Murray (1994), provoked a furor among psychologists and in the news media. The book asserted that psychologists agree that a single general factor corresponding to intelligence exists, that IQ is for all intents and purposes genetically determined, that racial differences in IQ are the result of heredity, and that IQ is almost impossible to modify through education and special programs. In fact, many influential Americans (e.g., Horn, 2002; Sternberg, 1995) and Canadians (Wahlsten, 1997b) vehemently disagree with these conclusions.

Sternberg (1995) examined *The Bell Curve* claims and found that there is scientific evidence against all of them. As we have already seen in this chapter, most psychologists believe that intelligence cannot be accounted for by a single factor. As well, if you ask people what they mean by the word *intelligence*, three factors rather than one will emerge from their responses: verbal ability, practical problem-solving ability, and social competence (Sternberg, Conway, Ketron, & Bernstein, 1981). Different cultures weight these factors differently; some think that social competence is more important, while others value competence on cognitive tasks (Berry, 1984, 2001; Okagaki & Sternberg, 1993; Ruzgis & Grigorenko, 1994). Even the statistical methods used to estimate the percentage of variance of intelligence attributable to genetics is questionable (Wahlsten, 1997b).

What about the assertions that IQ is almost impossible to modify? In fact, special programs *have* been successful in raising children's IQ scores—on the order of 8 to 20 points (see Ramey, 1994; Wahlsten, 1997b). Herrnstein and Murray (1994) went further by claiming that there are diminishing returns for advanced education for black people. The data show otherwise (Myerson, Rank, Raines, & Schnitzler, 1998). The gain in general cognitive ability from university education is actually greater for blacks than for whites.

And what about genetics? There are many reasons why we *cannot* conclude that the observed racial differences in average test scores are the result of heredity. We will examine the two most important ones here: the definition of race and the role of the environment.

First, let's examine the concept of *race*. A biologist uses the term to identify a population of plants or animals that has some degree of reproductive isolation from other members of the species, with which it is perfectly capable of interbreeding. For example, collies, cocker spaniels, and beagles constitute different races of dogs (although we usually refer to them as breeds). In this case, reproductive isolation is imposed by humans.

Any isolated group of organisms will, as a result of chance alterations in genetic factors and differences in local environment, become genetically different over time. Groups of humans whose ancestors mated only with other people who lived in a restricted geographical region tend to differ from other groups on a variety of hereditary traits, including stature, hair colour, skin pigmentation, and blood type. However, subsequent migrations and conquests caused mating between many different groups of people. As a result, human racial groups are much more similar than they are different.

Many researchers have used the trait of skin pigmentation to classify people by race. Two chemicals, melanin and keratin, cause skin to be black and yellow, respectively; a combination produces brown skin, while lighter-coloured skin contains little of either substance. Evidence suggests that the selective value of differing amounts of skin pigmentation is related to its ability to protect against the effects of sunlight (Loomis, 1967). Such protection was important near the equator, where the sun is intense all year, but was less important in temperate zones. Because vitamin D is synthesized primarily through the action of sunlight on deep layers of the skin, lack of pigmentation was advantageous to residents of northern latitudes, except to those living in Arctic regions, where vitamin D was readily available from fish and seal meat. The selective advantage of differences in skin pigmentation is obvious, but there is no plausible reason to expect these differences to be correlated with intellectual ability.

The second reason why we cannot conclude that racial differences in test scores are caused by heredity is the existence of environmental differences. Most of the data used in such studies as those cited in *The Bell Curve* come from the United States. In the U.S. (and to varying degrees, in many other countries), racial membership is a cultural phenomenon, not a biological one. A man with three grandparents of European origin and one grandparent of African origin is defined as "black" unless he hides this fact and defines himself as "white." Black people and white people are treated differently: The average American black family is poorer than the average white one; American blacks usually attend schools of lesser academic quality than whites; pregnant black women in the U.S. typically receive poorer medical care than their white counterparts, and their diet tends to be not as well balanced; and so on. In these circumstances, we would expect people's IQ scores to differ in accordance with whether they had been raised as average blacks or as average whites—in other words, independent of their genetic backgrounds.

Some investigators have attempted to use statistical methods to remove the effects of environmental variables, such as socio-economic status, that account for differences in performance between American blacks and whites. However, these methods are controversial, and many statisticians question their validity. On the other hand, a study by Scarr and Weinberg (1976) provides unambiguous evidence that environmental factors can substantially increase the measured IQ of an American black child. Scarr and Weinberg studied 99 black children who were adopted while they were young into white families of higher-than-average educational and socio-economic status. The expected average IQ of black children in the same area who were raised in black families was approximately 90. The average IQ of the adopted group was observed to be 105.

Some authors have flatly stated that there are no racial differences in biologically determined intellectual capacity. But this claim, like the one asserting that blacks are inherently less intelligent than whites, has not been scientifically verified. Although we know that American blacks and whites have different environments and that a black child raised in an environment similar to that of a white child will receive a similar IQ score, the question of whether any racial hereditary differences exist has not been answered. However, given that there is at least as much variability in intelligence between two people selected at random as there is between the average black and the average white, knowing a person's race tells us very little about how intelligent he or she may be.

The more interesting and more valid questions concerning race are those addressed by social psychologists and anthropologists—questions concerning issues such as the prevalence of prejudice, ethnic identification and cohesiveness, fear of strangers, and the tendency to judge something (or someone) that is different as inferior. In fact, Chapter 15 discusses the topic of prejudice from the perspective of social psychology.

## Interim Summary

### The Roles of Heredity and Environment

Variability in all physical traits is determined by a certain amount of genetic variability and environmental variability, and an interaction between genetic and environmental factors. The degree to which genetic variability is responsible for the observed variability of a particular trait in a particular population is called heritability. Heritability is not an indication of the degree to which the trait is determined by biological factors; rather, it reflects the relative proportions of genetic and environmental variability found in a particular population.

Intellectual development is affected by many factors, both prenatal and postnatal. A person's heredity, because of its effect on brain development, affects his or her potential intelligence. This potential intelligence can be permanently reduced during prenatal or postnatal development by injury, toxic chemicals, poor nutrition, or disease. In order for a person to achieve his or her potential intelligence, the person must have an environment that will foster the learning of facts and skills needed to function well in society.

Twin studies and studies comparing biological and adoptive relatives indicate that both genetic and environmental factors affect intellectual ability, which is probably not surprising.

Some people have suggested that racial differences in intellectual ability are the result of differences in heredity. However, the available data do not support this conclusion. First, race is almost always defined culturally, not genetically. Second, we cannot rule out the effects of environmental differences. It is impossible to measure people's inherited intellectual ability directly; all we can do is measure their *performance*—on tests, in school, or on the job. Because performance is determined by what people have learned, it reflects environmental factors as well as genetic ones. Because members of some racial groups have unequal opportunities to use their innate biological capacities to develop intellectual skills, no conclusions can be drawn about whether the racial differences are hereditary. The little evidence we do have suggests that when educational opportunities are equalized, so are intelligence test scores.

#### QUESTIONS TO CONSIDER

1. Can you think of any types of environments that may have favoured natural selection for particular kinds of abilities—for example, mathematical ability, spatial ability, perceptual ability, or ability to memorize stories?
2. One of the most hotly contested issues in education today is that of "tracking"—assigning students having different levels of academic ability to different classes. Take the point of view of students who have high and low academic levels of ability, and try to think of some arguments for and against this practice.

# Thinking

One of the most important components of intelligence is thinking: categorizing, reasoning, and solving problems. Thinking is an activity that takes place where no one can see it—inside our heads. Because it is hidden, we can only infer its existence from people's behaviour. When we think, we perceive, classify, manipulate, and combine information. When we are through, we know something we did not know before (although our "knowledge" may be incorrect).

The purpose of thinking is, in general, to solve problems. These problems may be simple classifications (*What is that, a bird or a bat?*). They may involve decisions about courses of action (*Should I buy a new car or pay to fix the old one?*). Or they may require the construction, testing, and evaluations of complex plans of action (*How am I going to manage to earn money to support my family, help raise our children, and continue my education so that I can get out of this dead-end job—and still be able to enjoy life?*). Much, but not all, of our thinking involves language. We certainly think to ourselves in words, but we also think in shapes and images. And some of the mental processes that affect our decisions and plans take place without our being conscious of them. Thus, we will have to consider non-verbal processes as well as verbal ones (Holyoak & Spellman, 1993; Reber, 1992).

This section discusses the important elements and goals of thinking: classification and concept formation, logical reasoning, and problem solving.

## Classifying

When we think, we do not consider each object or each event as a completely independent entity. Instead, we classify things—categorize them according to their characteristics. Then, when we have to solve a problem involving a particular object or situation, we can use information that we have already learned about similar objects or situations. To take a very simple example, when we enter someone's house for the first time, we recognize chairs, tables, couches, lamps, and other pieces of furniture even though we may have never seen these particular versions before. Because we recognize these categories of objects, we know where to sit, how to increase the level of illumination, and so on.

**Concepts** are categories of objects, actions, or states of being that share some attributes: cat, comet, team, destroying, playing, forgetting, happiness, truth, justice. Most thinking deals with the relations and interactions among concepts. For example, *The hawk caught the sparrow* describes an interaction between two birds; *Studying for an examination is fun* describes an attribute of a particular action; and *Youth is a carefree time of life* describes an attribute of a state of being. (There is no rule that says that thoughts have to be true!) Let us examine some features of concepts and concept formation.

Concepts exist because the characteristics of objects have consequences for us. For example, *mean dogs* may hurt us, whereas *friendly dogs* may give us pleasure. *Mean dogs* tend to growl, bare their teeth, and bite, whereas *friendly dogs* tend to prance around, wag their tails, and solicit our attention. Thus, when we see a dog that growls and bares its teeth, we avoid it because it might bite us; but if we see one prancing around and wagging its tail, we may try to pet it. We have learned to avoid or approach dogs that display different sorts of behaviour through direct experience with dogs or through the vicarious experience of watching other people interact with them. The point is, we can learn the concepts of mean and friendly dogs from the behaviour of one set of dogs while we are young and respond appropriately to other dogs later in life. Our experiences with particular dogs *generalize* to others.

### Formal and Natural Concepts

**Formal concepts** are defined by listing their essential characteristics, as a dictionary definition does (or as this textbook does). For example, dogs have four legs, a tail, fur, and wet noses; are carnivores; can bark, growl, whine, and howl; pant when they are hot; bear live young; and so on. Thus, a formal concept is a sort of category that has rules about membership and non-membership.

Psychologists have studied the nature of formally defined concepts, such as species of animals. Collins and Quillian (1969) suggested that such concepts are organized hierarchically in semantic memory. Each concept has associated with it a set of characteristics. Consider the hierarchy of concepts relating to animals shown in **Figure 11•4**. At the top is the concept *animal*, with which are associated the characteristics common to all animals, such as *has skin, can move around, eats, breathes*, and so on. Linked to the concept *animal* are groups of animals, such as *birds, fish*, and *mammals*, along with their characteristics.

Collins and Quillian assumed that the characteristics common to all members of a group of related concepts (such as all birds) were attached to the general concept (in this case, *bird*) rather than to all of the members. Such an arrangement would produce an efficient and economical organization of memory. For example, all birds have wings. Thus, we need not remember that a canary, a blue jay, a robin, and an ostrich all have wings; we need only remember that each of these concepts belongs to the category of *bird* and that birds have wings.

Collins and Quillian tested the validity of their model by asking people questions about the characteristics of various concepts. Consider the concept *canary*. The investigators asked people to say "true" or "false" to statements such as *A canary eats*. When the question dealt with characteristics that were specific to the concept (such as *can sing* or *is yellow*), the participants responded quickly. If the question dealt with a

**concept** A category of objects or situations that share some common attributes.

**formal concept** A category of objects or situations defined by listing their common essential characteristics, as dictionary definitions do.

FIGURE 11•4 Collins and Quillian's model of the hierarchical organization of concepts in semantic memory.
*(From Robert L. Solso,* Cognitive Psychology, *Second Edition. Copyright © 1988 by Allyn and Bacon. After Collins and Quillian (1969). Reproduced with permission.)*

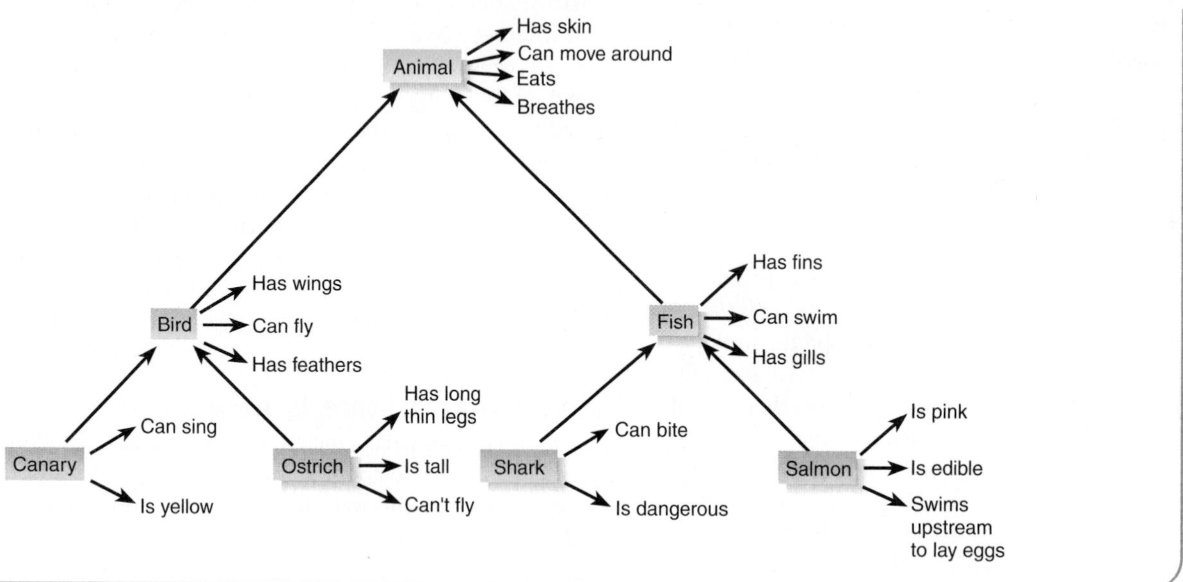


characteristic that was common to a more general concept (such as *has skin* or *breathes*), the participants took a longer time in answering. Presumably, when asked a question about a characteristic that applied to all birds or to all animals, the participants had to "travel up the tree" from the entry for *canary* until they found the level that provided the answer. The farther they had to go, the longer the process took.

The model just presented has an appealing simplicity and logic to it, but it turns out that people's brains do not follow such tidy, logical schemes in classifying concepts and their characteristics. For example, although people may indeed conceive of objects in terms of a hierarchy, a particular person's hierarchy of animals need not resemble that compiled by a zoologist. For example, Rips, Shoben, and Smith (1973) found that people said "yes" to *A collie is an animal* faster than they did to *A collie is a mammal.* According to Collins and Quillian's model, *animal* comes above *mammal* in the hierarchy, so the results should have been just the opposite.

Although some organization undoubtedly exists between categories and subcategories, it appears not to be perfectly logical and systematic. For example, Roth and Mervis (1983) found that people judged *Chablis* to be a better example of *wine* than of *drink*, but they judged *champagne* to be a better example of *drink* than of *wine.* This inconsistency clearly reflects people's experience with the concepts. Chablis is obviously a wine: It is sold in bottles that resemble those used for other wines, it looks and tastes similar to other white wines, the word *wine* is found on the label, and so on. By these standards, champagne appears to stand apart. A wine expert would categorize champagne as a particular type of wine. However, the average person, not being particularly well acquainted with the fact that champagne is made of fermented grape juice, encounters champagne in the context of something to drink on a special occasion, something to christen ships with, and so on. Thus, its characteristics are perceived as being rather different from those of Chablis.

**natural concept** A category of objects or situations based on people's perceptions and interactions with things in the world; based on exemplars.
**exemplar** A memory of particular examples of objects or situations that are used as the basis of classifying objects or situations into concepts.

The concepts we use in everyday life are *natural concepts*, not formal ones discovered by experts who have examined characteristics we are not aware of (Mervis & Rosch, 1981; Rosch, 1975, 1999, 2002). That is, people do not look up the meanings of concepts in their heads the way they seek definitions in dictionaries. **Natural concepts** are based on our own perceptions and interactions with things in the world. For example, some things have wings, beaks, and feathers, and they fly, build nests, lay eggs, and make high-pitched noises. Other things are furry, have four legs and tails, and run around on the ground. Formal concepts consist of carefully defined sets of rules governing membership in a particular category; natural concepts are collections of memories of particular examples that share some similarities. Formal concepts are used primarily by experts (and by people studying to become experts), whereas natural concepts are used by ordinary people in their daily lives.

Rosch suggests that people's natural concepts consist of collections of memories of *particular examples*, called **exemplars** that share some similarities. The boundaries between formal concepts are precise, whereas those between natural concepts are fuzzy—the distinction between a member and a nonmember is not always clear. Thus, to a non-expert, not all members of a concept are equally good examples of that concept. A robin is a good example of *bird*; a penguin or ostrich is a poor one. We may acknowledge that a penguin is a bird because we have been taught that it is, but we often qualify the category membership by making statements such as "*Strictly speaking*, a penguin is a bird." Exemplars represent the important characteristics of a category—characteristics that we can easily perceive or that we encounter when we interact with its members.

According to Rosch, natural concepts vary in their level of precision and detail. They are arranged in a hierarchy from very detailed to very general. When we think about concepts and talk about them, we usually deal with **basic-level concepts**—those that make important distinctions between different categories—but do not waste time and effort with those that do not matter. For example, *chair* and *apple* are basic-level concepts. Concepts that refer to collections of basic-level concepts, such as *furniture* and *fruit*, are called **superordinate concepts.** Concepts that refer to types of items within a basic-level category, such as *lawn chair* and *Granny Smith apple*, are called **subordinate concepts.** (See **Figure 11•5**.)

The basic-level concept tends to be the one that people spontaneously name when they see a member of the category. That is, all types of chairs tend to be called "chair," unless there is a special reason to use a more precise label (for example, if you wanted to buy a particular kind of chair). People tend to use basic-level concepts for a very good reason: *cognitive economy*. The use of subordinate concepts wastes time and effort on meaningless distinctions, and the use of superordinate concepts loses important information. Rosch and colleagues (1976) presented people with various concepts and gave them 90 seconds to list as many attributes as they could for each of them. The participants supplied few attributes for superordinate concepts but were able to think of many for basic-level concepts. Subordinate concepts evoked no more responses than basic-level concepts did. Thus, because they deal with a large number of individual items and their characteristics, basic-level concepts represent the most information in the most efficient manner. When people think about basic-level concepts, they do not have to travel up or down a tree to find the attributes that belong to the concept. The attributes are directly attached to the exemplars that constitute each concept.

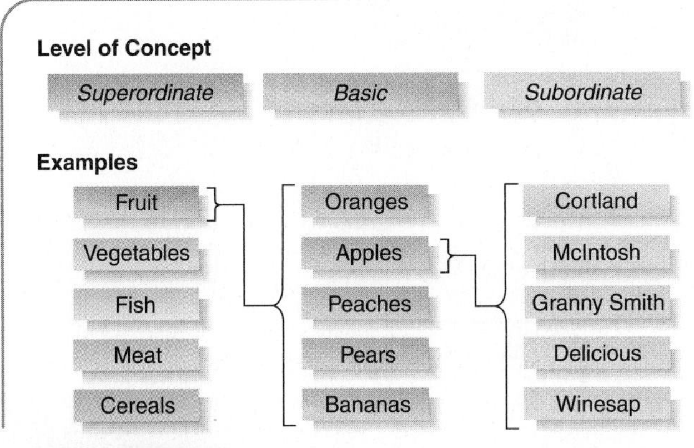


**FIGURE 11•5** Examples of basic-level, subordinate, and superordinate concepts.

**FIGURE 11•6** Concept formation. Participants were asked which of the groups of shapes were most similar. (a) Three pairs of geometrical shapes. (b) The same shapes with the addition of squares.

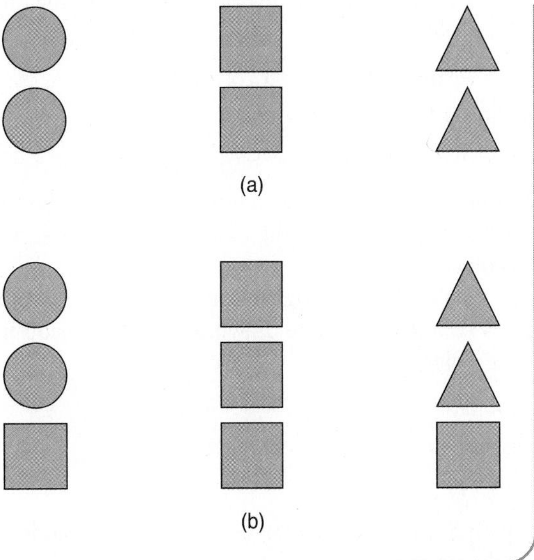


It is important to recognize that concepts can represent something more complex than simple exemplars or collections of attributes. Goldstone, Medink, and Gentner (1991) showed participants groups of figures and asked them to indicate which were most similar to each other. When they showed the participants two triangles, two squares, and two circles, the participants said that the squares and triangles were most similar, presumably because both contained straight lines and angles. However, when they added a square to each of the pairs, the participants said that the two most similar groups were the triangles plus square and the circles plus square. (See **Figure 11•6**.) The concept this time was "two things and a square." If the participants were simply counting attributes, then the addition of a square to the pairs should not have changed their decision. As this study shows very clearly, concepts can include relations among elements that cannot be described by counting attributes.

Concepts are the raw material of thinking; they are what we think about. But thinking itself involves the manipulation and combination of concepts. Such thinking can take several forms, but the most common forms are deductive reasoning and inductive reasoning.

**basic-level concept** A concept that makes important distinctions between different categories.

**superordinate concept** A concept that refers to collections of basic-level concepts.

**subordinate concept** A concept that refers to types of items within a basic-level category.

## Deductive Reasoning

**Deductive reasoning** consists of inferring specific truths from general principles or rules. Series problems and syllogisms are often used to study deductive reasoning. Consider the following series problem:

John is taller than Phil.
Sue is shorter than Phil.
Therefore, John is taller than Sue.

Application of simple mathematical principles should have led you to recognize that the conclusion to this series problem is correct.

Let's try a syllogism. A syllogism consists of two premises from which a conclusion can be drawn. Is the conclusion in the following syllogism correct?

All mammals have fur.
A bat is a mammal.
Therefore, a bat has fur.

Most people understand that the conclusion is indeed justified by the premises, but now look at these two:

All Xs are Y.
Z is an X.
Therefore, all Xs are Z
*and*
All nemots have some hair.
A zilgid has some hair.
Therefore, all zilgids are nemots.

Although the conclusions are not warranted on logical grounds for these latter syllogisms, many people will endorse them as true. For the first of these, try replacing *X* with "planet," *Y* with "round," and *Z* with "Jupiter." The last syllogism is just as dense, but here is the solution: The first premise says only that all nemots have hair—it leaves open the possibility that not a single nemot is a zilgid. Still not clear? Try substituting "cat" for *nemot* and "dog" for *zilgid*. How is it possible that we make such mistakes when the answers are so clear after we make the concrete substitutions?

### Mental Models

Psychologists used to believe that people dealt with deductive reasoning problems by applying formal rules of logic. If people did so, however, it would not matter whether they dealt with letters of the alphabet, cats and dogs, numbers or planets. They would identify the underlying structure of the problem and solve it forthwith. In response to the problem posed by exceptions to logical problem solving, Johnson-Laird and his colleagues (Johnson-Laird, 1995, 1999, 2001; Johnson-Laird, Byrne, & Schaeken, 1992) suggest that people approach problems involving logical deduction by creating **mental models.**

You can think of a mental model of a situation as a construction of a *possibility* (Johnson-Laird, 1999)—that is, of what might be true given a number of premises. A mental model includes semantic information because most problems involve meaningful content, specify relations among elements of the problem, and rely more or less on knowledge about the world. Spatial arrangements also play a central role in Johnson-Laird's theory of mental models. Johnson-Laird (1985) notes that syllogistic reasoning is much more highly correlated with spatial ability than with verbal ability. Spatial ability includes the ability to visualize shapes and to manipulate them mentally. For example, read the following problem and answer it. *A is less than C. B is greater than C. Is B greater than A?* In order to compare *A* with *B*, you must remember the order of the three elements. One kind of mental model is an imaginary line going from small to large in which you mentally place each item on the line as you encounter it. Then, with all three elements in a row, the possibilities are mentally arrayed before you, and you can answer the question. (See **Figure 11•7**.) Although this example is short on meaningful content, it is manageable if you devoted enough time to constructing a spatial mental model. Now let's attach some more meaningful content. *The pie is sweeter than the cake. The custard is not as sweet as the cake. Is the custard sweeter than the pie?* You should have found it easier to produce a mental model in which the pastries were arrayed and consequently found it easier to answer the question. Having concrete objects to array on your mental line probably made

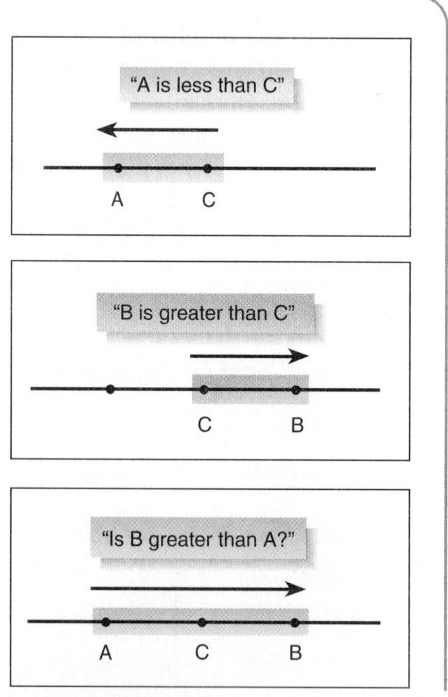


FIGURE 11•7 A mental model. Logical problems are often solved by imagining a physical representation of the facts.

**deductive reasoning** Inferring specific instances from general principles or rules.
**mental model** A mental construction based on physical reality that is used to solve problems of logical deduction.

this example easier for you. You can now see the problem with the nemods and zilgids in the syllogism. You cannot visualize something that does not exist, and it thus becomes very difficult to construct mental models with which to solve the syllogism. (Of course, knowing something about the plausibility of dogs being cats also influenced your reaction.)

An interesting feature of solving problems with mental models involving comparisons of series of items is that we seem to attend more to our mental models than to the facts on which we base those models. For example, read the following passage:

> Although the four craftsmen were brothers, they varied enormously in height. The electrician was the very tallest, and the plumber was shorter than him. The plumber was taller than the carpenter, who, in turn, was taller than the painter. (Just & Carpenter, 1987, p. 202)

After reading this passage, people more easily answer questions about differences in heights within pairings of brothers. For example, they are faster to answer the question "Who is taller, the electrician or the painter?" than the question "Who is taller, the plumber or the carpenter?" This finding is particularly important because the passage explicitly states that the plumber is taller than the carpenter. Answering this question only requires accessing memory for that specific bit of information. Answering the question about the electrician and painter, however, *requires an inference* and therefore should take more time than just repeating what you were told. Just and Carpenter's study shows that the result of an inference can be more readily available than information explicitly given. How can this be? The most plausible explanation is that when people read the passage, they construct a mental model that represents the four brothers arranged in order of height. The painter is clearly the shortest and the electrician is clearly the tallest. Thus, a comparison between the extremes can be made very quickly. (See **Figure 11•8**.)

**FIGURE 11•8** A "mental model" of the craftsmen experiment. Participants could judge the relative heights of the electrician and the painter faster than those of the plumber and the carpenter. Although the passage describing the craftsmen explicitly compared the heights of the plumber and the carpenter, people had to infer that the electrician was taller than the painter.

**FIGURE 11•9** A spatial model of reasoning: "What do you call your mother's sister's son?"

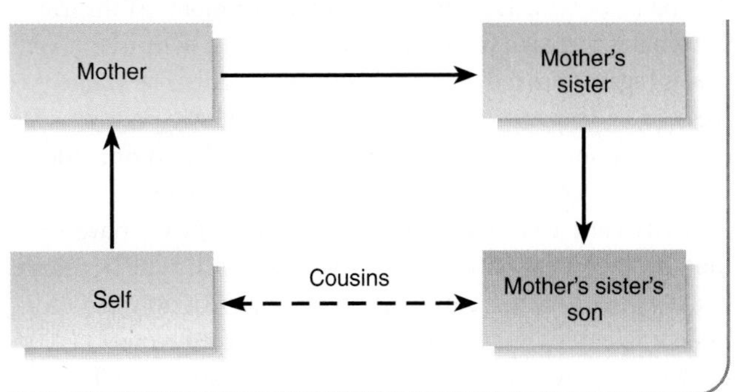


Here is a different type of problem to illustrate the point: *What do you call your mother's sister's son?* Most people report that they answer this question by constructing a mental family tree, with their mother above them, their mother's sister to the side, and her son below her. Then, comparing that location with their own, they can easily see that the answer is "cousin." (See **Figure 11•9**.) Consistent with the idea that spatial representation is a significant feature of mental models, Luria (1973) found that people with damage to the parietal lobes had difficulty answering such questions. As you learned in Chapter 4, the parietal lobes are involved with somatosensation and spatial abilities.

Finally, let's consider another complex problem, adapted from an experiment by Wason and Johnson-Laird (1972), that is known as a *selection task*.

> Your job is to determine which of the hidden parts of these cards you need to see in order to answer the following question decisively:
>
> Is it true that if there is a vowel on one side of a card, there is an even number on the other side?
>
> You have only one opportunity to make this decision; you must not assume that you can inspect the cards one at a time. Name the card or cards which you absolutely must see to correctly answer the question.

The participants were shown four cards like those illustrated in **Figure 11•10**. Read the problem again, look at the cards, and decide which card or cards you would have to see.

Most people say that they would need to see card (a), and they are correct. If there was *not* an even number on the back of

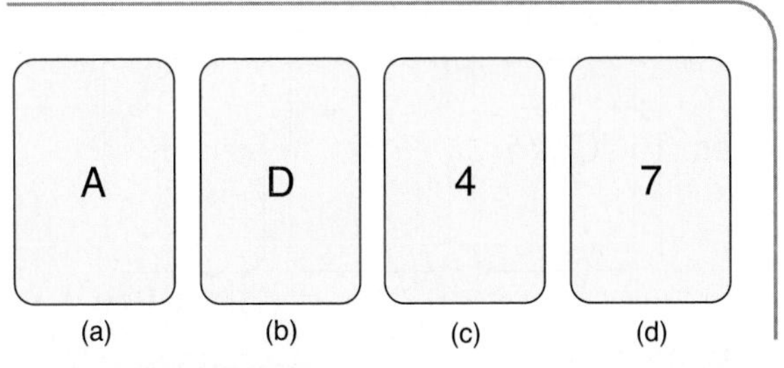


**FIGURE 11•10** Cards used in a formal test of problem solving.

card (a), then the rule is not correct. However, many participants failed to realize that card (a) is not enough. Card (d) must also be inspected. True, there is no even number on this card, but what if there is a vowel on the other side? If there is, then the rule is (again) proved wrong. Many participants also wanted to see card (c), but there is no need to do so. The hypothesis says nothing about whether an even number can be on one side of the card without there being a vowel on the other side.

The card task is a very abstract one, and we have seen that concreteness can increase the ease with which people reach "logical" conclusions, even if they do not do so in a formally logical manner. Would relating the card–vowel task to familiar, concrete, content make it more transparent? The answer comes from studies like one conducted by Griggs and Cox (1982). They asked people to decide which cards should be checked to see whether the following statement was true: "If a person is drinking beer, she must be over age nineteen." The cards represented people; their age was on one side and their beverage (beer or Coke) was on the other. Which card(s) would you check? (See **Figure 11•11**.)

Most participants correctly chose cards (a) and (d). They knew that if someone were drinking beer (a), they had to check that she was over the age of 19 in order for the rule to be true. Similarly, if someone were 16 years old (d), they knew that they needed to check the card to see that she was not drinking beer in order for the rule to be correct. The participants readily recognized the fact that they did not need to know the age of someone drinking Coke, and that someone 22 years old can drink whatever beverage she prefers. One explanation for the increased ease of this problem with concrete content comes from the mental model perspective. It would seem to be much easier to construct and mentally manipulate representations of Coke, beer, and teenagers than to think about vowels and card suits. There are, however, other explanations. Cheng and Holyoak (1985), for example, proposed that people have sets of helpful mental rules ("pragmatic reasoning schemas") that centre on issues of causality, permission, and obligation. According to Cheng and Holyoak, these schemas are more likely to be evoked with the meaningful beer–age task, which requires consideration of whether an action (drinking) is permitted, than in the more spartan vowel–card task. The jury is still out on a generally accepted explanation of the selection task, which, as Johnson-Laird (1999) commented, "has launched a thousand studies."

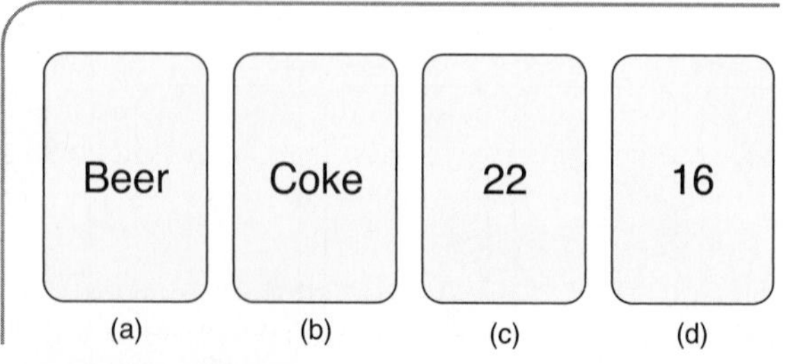


**FIGURE 11•11** Cards used in a more realistic version of the problem-solving test.

▲ *The late Nobel laureate Richard Feynman, who solved complex problems by inventing bizarre mental models.*

Many creative scientists and engineers report that they use mental models to reason logically and solve practical and theoretical problems (Krueger, 1976). For example, the American physicist and Nobel laureate Richard Feynman said that he used rather bizarre mental models to keep track of characteristics of complex mathematical theorems to see whether they were logical and consistent. Here is how Feynman described his thought processes:

> When I'm trying to understand . . . I keep making up examples. For instance, the mathematicians would come in with a . . . theorem. As they're telling me the conditions of the theorem, I construct something that fits all the conditions. You know, you have a set (one ball)—disjoint (two balls). Then the balls turn colors, grow hairs, or whatever, in my head as they [the mathematicians] put more conditions on. Finally, they state the theorem, which is some . . . thing about the ball which isn't true for my hairy green ball thing, so I say "False!" (Feynman, 1985, p. 70)

Such use of mental models by a talented and gifted scientist strengthens the conclusion that being able to convert abstract problems into tangible mental models is an important aspect of intelligent thinking.

## Inductive Reasoning

As we saw, deductive reasoning involves applying the rules of logic to infer specific instances from general principles or rules. This type of reasoning works well when general principles or rules have already been worked out. But how do we accumulate new knowledge and formulate new general principles or rules? Having read Chapter 2 of this book, you already know the answer—by following the scientific method. But few people know the rules of the scientific method, and even those who do seldom follow them in their daily lives.

**FIGURE 11•12** Examples of the type of cards used in a test of inductive reasoning.

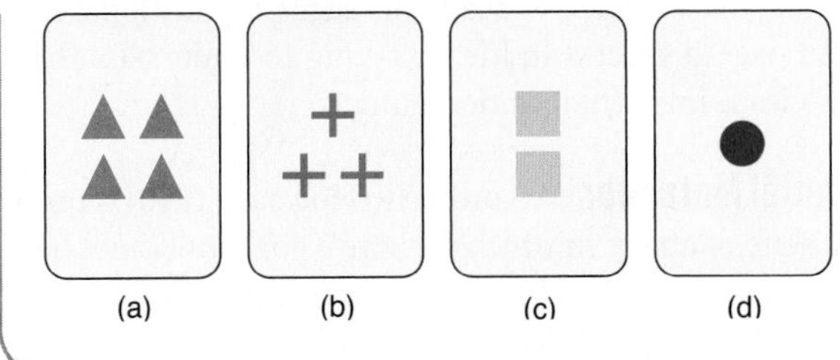


**Inductive reasoning** is just the opposite of deductive reasoning; it consists of inferring general principles or rules from specific facts. A well-known laboratory example of inductive reasoning works like a guessing game. The participants are shown cards that contain figures differing in several dimensions, such as shape, number, and colour. On each trial, they are given two cards and asked to choose the one that represents a particular concept. After they choose a card, the researcher says "right" or "wrong." (See **Figure 11•12**.)

One trial is not enough to recognize the concept. For example, if the first trial reveals that card (a) is correct, then the concept could be *red*, or *four*, or *triangle*, or some combination of these, such as *red triangle, four red shapes*, or even *four red triangles*. Information gained from the second trial permits the participant to rule out some of these hypotheses—for example, if on the second trial four red squares is a correct card choice, it appears that shape does not matter, but colour and number do. The participant uses steps to solve the problem much the way a scientist does: Form a hypothesis on the basis of the available evidence and test that hypothesis on subsequent trials. If it is proven false, abandon it, try to think of a hypothesis consistent with what went before, and test the new hypothesis.

**Logical Errors in Inductive Reasoning** Obviously, people can be trained to follow the rules of the scientific method. However, without special training, they follow common-sense rules, some of which work and some of which do not. Psychologists interested in people's inductive reasoning ability have identified several tendencies that lead them astray. It is precisely because of such tendencies that we need to learn specific rules (such as those of the scientific method) so that we can have confidence in our conclusions.

Psychologists have identified several tendencies that interfere with people's ability to reason inductively. These include the failure to seek information that would be provided by a comparison group and the disinclination to seek evidence that would indicate whether a hypothesis is false. (In Chapter 15, we discuss two others: the representativeness and availability heuristics.)

**Failure to Consider a Comparison Group** A tendency that interferes with people's ability to reason inductively is their failure to consider a comparison group. Suppose that you learn that 79 percent of the people with a particular disease get well within a month after taking a new, experimental drug (Stich, 1990). What would you conclude? Is the drug effective? The correct answer to this question is "We cannot conclude anything—we need more information." What we need to know is what happens to people with the disease if they do not take the drug. If we find that only 22 percent of these people recover within a month, we would conclude that the drug is effective; 79 percent is much greater than 22 percent. On the other hand, if we find that 98 percent recover without taking the drug, we would conclude that the drug is worse than useless—it actually interferes with recovery. In other words, we need a control group. However, most people are perfectly willing to conclude that, because 79 percent seems like a high figure, the drug must work. Seeing the necessity for a control group does not come naturally; unless people are deliberately taught about control groups, they will not recognize the need for them.

Failure to seek or use information that would be provided by a control group has been called *ignoring the base rate*. As several researchers have suggested, the problem here may be that we engage in two types of reasoning (Reber, 1992). One type of reasoning is deliberate and conscious and involves explicit memories of roles that we can describe verbally. The other type of reasoning is unconscious and uses information we have learned implicitly. (The distinction between explicit and implicit memories and their relation to consciousness was discussed in Chapters 8 and 9.) Because the explicit and implicit memory systems involve at least some different brain mechanisms, information from one system cannot easily interact with information from the other system. In fact, if people are allowed to observe actual occurrences of certain events (that is, acquire the information about the base rate of occurrence automatically and implicitly), they do consider information about event frequency (Holyoak & Spellman, 1993).

**Confirmation Bias** Have you ever looked at the horoscope in the daily paper and been shocked to find that it is reasonably accurate? If you have, you may have fallen prey to the confirmation bias. The confirmation bias is a disinclination to seek evidence that would indicate whether a hypothesis is false. Instead, people tend to seek evidence that might confirm their hypothesis. People's belief in the paranormal can be partially explained by the confirmation bias. For example, Wiseman and Smith (2002) asked college students to evaluate four fictional horoscopes that had been created by the researchers. The students were told which two of the four horoscopes were based on their own astrological sign, and which two were not. The students in this study reliably indicated that the horoscopes that were supposedly associated with their own astrological sign were more accurate. The reason the students thought this was that they were looking for evidence to confirm their belief that the information presented in the horoscope somehow applied to them, rather than looking for contradictory evidence.

Another example of the confirmation bias is Wason's (1968) classic research in which people were presented with the

**inductive reasoning** Inferring general principles or rules from specific facts.

series of numbers "two, four, six" and asked to try to figure out the rule to which they conformed. The person was to test his or her hypothesis by making up series of numbers and saying them to the researcher, who would reply "yes" or "no." Then, whenever the person decided that enough information had been gathered, he or she could say what the hypothesis was. If the answer was correct, the problem was solved. If it was not, the person was to think of a new hypothesis and test that one.

Several rules could explain the series "two, four, six." The rule could be "even numbers," or "each number is two more than the preceding one," or "the middle number is the mean of the first and third number." When people tested their hypotheses, they almost always did so by presenting several sets of numbers, *all of which were consistent with their hypotheses.* For example, if they thought that each number was two more than the preceding one, they might say "ten, twelve, fourteen" or "sixty-one, sixty-three, sixty-five." *Very few* participants tried to test their hypotheses by choosing a set of numbers that did *not* conform to the hypothesized rule, such as "twelve, fifteen, twenty-two." In fact, the series "twelve, fifteen, twenty-two" does conform to the rule. The rule was so simple that few people figured it out: Each number must be larger than the preceding one.

The confirmation bias is very strong. Unless people are taught to do so, they tend not to think of possible non-examples of their hypotheses and to see whether they might be true—the way that scientists do. But, in fact, evidence that disconfirms a hypothesis is conclusive, whereas evidence that confirms it is not. Suppose that you thought the answer to the problem I just described was "even numbers." You could give ascending lists of three even numbers hundreds of times, and each list would be correct. Nevertheless, your rule would still be wrong. If you gave just one non-example—say, "five, six, seven," the researcher would say "yes" and you would immediately know that the answer was not "even numbers."

The confirmation bias in inductive reasoning has a counterpart in deductive reasoning. For example, consider the following sentences (Johnson-Laird, 1985):

All the pilots are artists.
All the skiers are artists.
True or false: All the pilots are skiers.

Many people say "true." They test the truth of the conclusion by imagining a person who is a pilot and an artist and a skier—and that person complies with the rules. Therefore, they decide that the conclusion is true. However, if they would try to disconfirm the conclusion—to look for an example that would fit the first two sentences but not the conclusion—they would easily find one. Could a person be a pilot but not a skier? Of course; the first two sentences say nothing to rule out that possibility. There are artist-pilots and there are artist-skiers, but nothing says that there must be artist-pilot-skiers.

## Problem Solving

The ultimate function of thinking is to solve problems. We are faced with an enormous variety of them in our daily lives: fixing a television set, planning a picnic, choosing a spouse, navigating across the ocean, solving a math problem, tracking some game, designing a bridge, finding a job. The ability to solve problems is related to academic success, vocational success, and overall success in life, so trying to understand how we do so is an important undertaking.

**The Spatial Metaphor** According to Holyoak (1990), a problem is a state of affairs in which we have a goal but do not have a clear understanding of how it can be attained. As he notes, when we talk about problems, we often use spatial metaphors to describe them (Lakoff & Turner, 1989). We think of the solving of a problem as *finding a path to the solution.* We may have to *get around roadblocks* that we encounter or *backtrack* when we *hit a dead end.* If we *get lost*, we may try to *approach the problem from a different angle.* If we have experience with particular types of problems, we may know some *shortcuts.*

In fact, Newell and Simon (1972) have used the spatial metaphor to characterize the problem-solving process. At the beginning of a person's attempt to solve a problem, the *initial state* is different from the *goal state*—if it were not, there would be no problem. The person solving the problem has a number of *operators* available. Operators are actions that can be taken to change the current state of the problem; metaphorically, operators move the current state from one position to another. Not all people will be aware of the operators that are available. Knowledge of operators depends on education and experience. In addition, there may be various costs associated with different operators; some may be more difficult, expensive, or time consuming than others. The *problem space* consists of all possible states that can be achieved if all possible operators are applied. A *solution* is a sequence of operators (a "path") that moves from the initial state to the goal state.

**Figure 11•13** illustrates this process schematically. The circles represent the current or possible states of affairs while the problem is being solved. The arrows represent the operators—the actions that can be taken. Some actions are reversible (double arrows); others are not. A solution follows a path from the initial state to the goal state.

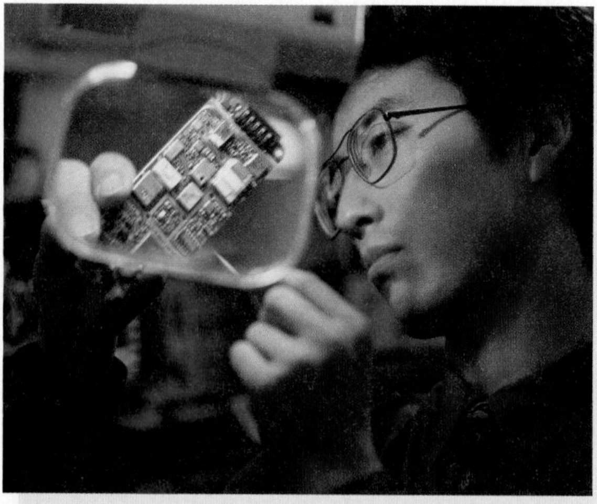

▲ *Problem solving takes many forms. An engineer examines a micro-electronic chip of a cellular phone.*

**FIGURE 11•13** Newell and Simon's spatial metaphor of the problem-solving process.

*(Adapted from Holyoak, K. J. (1990). In D. N. Osherson & E. E. Smith (Eds.),* An invitation to cognitive science. Volume 3: Thinking. *Cambridge, MA: MIT Press.)*

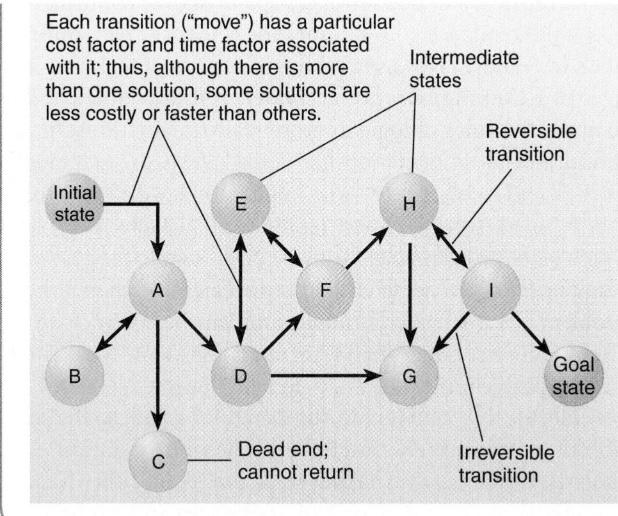


**Algorithms and Heuristics** Some kinds of problems can be solved by following a sequence of operators known as an algorithm. **Algorithms** are procedures that consist of series of steps that, if followed in the correct sequence, will provide a solution. For example, you are undoubtedly familiar with an algorithm known as "long division." If you properly apply the steps of this algorithm to divide one number by another, you will obtain the correct answer. However, many problems are not as tidy as math problems, nor as easy to solve. When there is no algorithm to follow, we must follow a heuristic to guide our search for a path to the solution. **Heuristics** (pronounced *hyoo-ris-tiks*, derived from the Greek *heuriskein*, "to discover") are general rules that are useful in guiding our search for a path to the solution of a problem. Heuristics tell us what to pay attention to, what to ignore, and what strategy to take.

Heuristic methods can be very specific, or they can be quite general, applying to large categories of problems. For example, management courses try to teach students problem-solving methods they can use in a wide variety of contexts. Newell and Simon (1972) suggest a general heuristic method that can be used to solve any problem: means-ends analysis. The principle behind **means-ends analysis** is that a person should look for differences between the current state and the goal state and seek ways to reduce these differences. The steps of this method are as follows (Holyoak, 1990, p. 121):

1. Compare the current state to the goal state and identify differences between the two. If there are none, the problem is solved; otherwise, proceed.
2. Select an operator that would reduce one of the differences.
3. If the operator can be applied, do so; if not, set a new subgoal of reaching a state at which the operator could be applied. Means-ends analysis is then applied to this new subgoal until the operator can be applied or the attempt to use it is abandoned.
4. Return to step 1.

Suppose that the problem is to clear snow off my driveway. Rejecting several possible operators because they are too time consuming or too costly (*dig the snow off with my hands* or *melt the snow with a propane torch*), I decide to apply the operator *start the snowblower and run it up and down the driveway*. Unfortunately, I find that the snowblower will not start, which means that the operator I have chosen cannot be applied. Thus, I set up a subgoal: *Fix* the snowblower.

One possible operator that will get me toward that subgoal is *put the snowblower in the car and take it to a mechanic*, but the snow on my driveway precludes that option. Therefore, I decide to fix it myself. In order to fix the snowblower, I have to know what the problem is. I consider some possible actions, including *take the engine apart to see whether something inside is broken*, but I decide to try some simpler ones, such as *see whether the wire is attached to the spark plug* or *see whether there is gasoline in the tank*. I find the wire attached but the gas tank empty. The only operator that will get me to my subgoal is *fill the tank with gasoline*. But I have no gasoline. Therefore, I construct another subgoal: *Get some gasoline*.

What are the possible sources of gasoline? A gas station? No, I can't move the car. A neighbour? The snow is so deep that I do not want to fight my way through the drifts. The tank of my car? That's it. New subgoal: *Remove some gasoline from the car's fuel tank*. How do I get it out? New subgoal: *Find rubber hose to siphon the gasoline into the tank of the snowblower*. I do so, I start the engine, and I clear the snow off the driveway. The problem is solved.

The example I have just cited is obviously not very challenging, but it does illustrate the use of means-ends analysis. At all times, the person's activity is oriented toward reducing the distance between the current state and the goal state. If problems are encountered along the way (that is, if operators cannot be applied), then subgoals are created and means-ends analysis is applied to solving that problem—and so on, until the goal is reached.

Of course, there may be more than one solution to a particular problem, and some solutions may be better than others. A good solution is one that uses the smallest number of actions while minimizing the associated costs. The relative importance of cost and speed determines which solution is best. For example, if the problem is to rescue a child who is up to her neck in quicksand, the best solution may be the most expensive one: Drive your $125 000 Mercedes into the pool of quicksand, climb onto the roof, jump down to the hood, reach over the front of the car, pull her out, and then

**algorithm** A procedure that consists of a series of steps that will solve a specific type of problem.
**heuristic** A general rule that guides decision making.
**means-ends analysis** A general heuristic method of problem solving that involves looking for differences between the current state and the goal state and seeking ways to reduce the differences.

climb back over the top of the car and get to dry land before the car sinks. Finding a large object other than your valuable car would be cheaper, but it would take too much time.

Intelligent problem solving involves more than trying out various actions (applying various operators) to see whether they bring us closer to the goal. It also involves *planning*. When we plan, we act vicariously, "trying out" various actions in our heads. Obviously, planning requires that we know something about the consequences of the actions we are considering. Experts are better at planning than novices are. If we do *not* know the consequences of particular actions, we will be obliged to try each action (apply each operator) and see what happens. Planning is especially important when many possible operators are present, when they are costly or time consuming, or when they are irreversible. If we take an irreversible action that brings us to a dead end, we have failed to solve the problem.

## Interim Summary

### Thinking

Formal concepts are defined as lists of essential characteristics of objects and events. In everyday life, we use natural concepts—collections of memories of particular examples, called exemplars. Concepts exist at the basic, subordinate, and superordinate level. We do most of our thinking about concepts at the basic level.

Deductive reasoning consists of inferring specific instances from general principles. That is, we take information that is already known and see whether particular occurrences are consistent with that information. One of the most important skills in deductive reasoning is the ability to construct mental models that represent problems.

Inductive reasoning involves inferring general principles from particular facts. This form of thinking involves generating and testing hypotheses. Without special training (such as learning the rules of the scientific method), people often ignore the necessity of control groups, or show a confirmation bias—the tendency to look only for evidence that confirms one's hypothesis. However, performance on some puzzle-like tests of reasoning may not accurately reflect people's ability to apply the rules of logic in more realistic situations. In addition, not all information has equal effects on judgments; explicit and implicit memories appear to play different roles.

Problem solving is best represented spatially: We follow a path in the problem space from the initial state to the goal state, using operators to get to each intermediate state. Sometimes a problem fits a particular mould and can be solved with an algorithm—a cut-and-dried set of operations. However, in most cases, a problem must be attacked by following a heuristic—a general rule that helps guide our search for a path to the solution of a problem. The most general heuristic is means-ends analysis, which involves taking steps that reduce the distance from the current state to the goal. If obstacles are encountered, subgoals are created and attempts are made to reach them.

**QUESTIONS TO CONSIDER**

1. Try to think of a new concept you have learned recently. Can you describe its features, or is it easier to think of an exemplar?
2. Chapter 2 described the scientific method. Some of the rules and procedures you learned there were designed to avoid the errors in logical thinking that were described in this chapter. Try to relate the scientific method to these errors.

## EPILOGUE

### Measuring Intelligence

In the beginning of the chapter, you read about Mr. V. and were asked to think about whether you considered him intelligent. Your answer depends on which theory of intelligence you believe is most accurate. As we've seen, intelligence is a broad term that has gone through many revisions over the years. Mr. V. would probably score high on a standard IQ test, but would perform poorly on some tests of Gardner's multiple intelligences and would not have the elements necessary to meet Sternberg's concept of successful intelligence.

The debate regarding what intelligence is and how it should be measured continues today. Even across cultures, the concept of intelligence varies (e.g., Swami et al., 2008). Researchers, such as Sternberg and Gardner, are expanding the aspects of behaviour and thought that need to be assessed when considering intelligence. Other researchers believe that the notion of intelligence is becoming so broad that it is almost meaningless. (For an interesting critique of Gardner's theory, see Klein, 1997.) In regards to measuring intelligence, there is evidence that IQ tests are of value and predict academic achievement (e.g., Lynn & Mikk, 2007), but controversy remains about the predictive validity of some tests, such as entrance exams for graduate school (e.g., Brown, 2007). Clearly, psychologists still have much work to do in this fascinating and important field.

## Canadian Connections to Research in This Chapter

Berry, J. W. (1984). Towards a universal psychology of cognitive competence. In P. S. Fry (Ed.), *Changing conceptions of intelligence and intellectual functioning*. Amsterdam, Holland: North-Holland. (Queen's University: www.queensu.ca)

Berry, J. W. (2001). Contextual studies of cognitive adaptation. In J. M. Collis & S. Messick (Eds.), *Intelligence and personality: Bridging the gap in theory and measurement*. Mahwah, NJ: Lawrence Erlbaum Associates. (Queen's University: www.queensu.ca)

Professor Berry received the Donald O. Hebb Award of the Canadian Psychological Association in 1998.

Darou, W. G. (1992). Native Canadians and intelligence testing. *Canadian Journal of Counselling, 26*, 96–99. (Canadian International Development Agency: www.acdi-cida.gc.ca)

Dawda, D., & Hart, S. D. (2000). Assessing emotional intelligence: Reliability and validity of the Bar-On Emotional Quotient Inventory (EQ-i) in university students. *Personality and Individual Differences, 28*, 797–812. (Simon Fraser University: www.sfu.ca)

Hebb, D. O. (1949). *The organization of behavior*. New York: Wiley. (McGill University: www.mcgill.ca)

Hebb, D. O. (1966). *A textbook of psychology*. Philadelphia, PA: W. B. Saunders Company. (McGill University: www.mcgill.ca)

Donald Hebb was the first winner (in 1980) of the Donald O. Hebb Award of the Canadian Psychological Association and the 1961 winner of the American Psychological Association's Award for Distinguished Scientific Contributions.

Paulhus, D. L., Lysy, D. C., & Yik, M. S. M. (1998). Self-report measures of intelligence: Are they useful as proxy IQ tests? *Journal of Personality, 66*, 525–554. (University of British Columbia: www.ubc.ca)

Saklofske, D. H., Austin, E. J., & Minski, P. S. (2003). Factor structure and validity of a trait emotional intelligence measure. *Personality and Individual Differences, 34*, 707–721. (University of Saskatchewan: www.usask.ca)

Vernon, P. E. (1979). *Intelligence: Heredity and environment*. San Francisco, CA: W. H. Freeman. (University of Calgary: www.ucalgary.ca)

Wahlsten, D. (1997b). The malleability of intelligence is not constrained by heritability. In B. Devlin, S. E. Fienberg, D. P. Resnick, & K. Roeder (Eds.), *Intelligence, genes, and success*. New York: Copernicus. (University of Alberta: www.ualberta.ca)

## Suggestions for Further Reading

Aiken, L. (2003). *Psychological testing and assessment* (11th ed.). Boston, MA: Allyn and Bacon.

Gardner, H. (1999). *Intelligence reframed: Multiple intelligences for the 21st century*. New York: Basic Books.

Kaplan, R. M., & Saccuzzo, D. P. (2001). *Psychological testing: Principles, application, and issues* (5th ed.). Pacific Grove, CA: Brooks/Cole.

Sternberg, R. J. (2003). *Wisdom, intelligence, and creativity synthesized*. New York: Cambridge University Press.

Gardner's book describes his theory, which is based on the existence of specific brain functions related to talents often overlooked by traditional tests of intelligence. The books by Aiken and by Kaplan and Saccuzzo provide excellent discussions of the differential, or psychometric, approach to intelligence. Sternberg's book describes his information processing theory of intelligence.

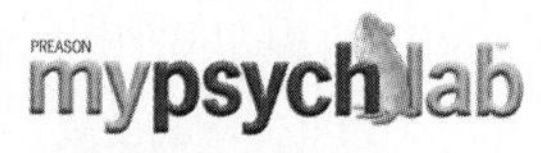


To access more tests and your own personalized study plan that will help you focus on the areas you need to master before your next class test, be sure to go to **www.MyPsychLab.com**, Pearson Education Canada's online Psychology website available with the access code packaged with your book.

# 12

# Lifespan Development

# CHAPTER OUTLINE

## Prenatal Development

Stages of Prenatal Development • Threats to Normal Prenatal Development

During the prenatal period, the fertilized ovum develops into a fetus, a human in miniature. The crucial factors in the fetus's development are the mother's diet and physical health; the presence of toxins in the prenatal environment can cause the fetus to be born with physical and cognitive defects.

## Physical and Perceptual Development in Infancy and Childhood

Motor Development • Perceptual Development

Timing and experience are two key elements in normal motor and perceptual development. For normal development to occur, a child must encounter stimulation from the environment during a specific time interval. If stimulation does not occur during this period, normal development is impeded, perhaps permanently.

## Cognitive Development in Infancy and Childhood

The Importance of a Responsive Environment • The Work of Jean Piaget • Vygotsky's Sociocultural Theory of Cognitive Development • Applying Information Processing Models to Cognitive Development • *Then and Now: Detecting the Strange*

In Piaget's view, a child passes through four distinct intellectual changes, which coincide with changes in a child's nervous system and with a child's experience, on his or her way to becoming an adult. According to Vygotsky, a child's cognitive development is strongly influenced by sociocultural variables, especially language. Information processing models of cognitive development centre on how brain maturation influences the development of cognitive processes. The violation-of-expectation procedure has helped us understand early cognition.

## Social Development in Infancy and Childhood

Behaviours of the Infant That Foster Attachment • The Nature and Quality of Attachment • Approaches to Child Rearing

Attachment is the social and emotional bond that develops between an infant and caregiver during infancy. The quality of attachment depends largely on the nature of infants' relationships with their caregivers. Social development during childhood is influenced by the parent's style of child rearing.

## Development of Gender Roles

The Nature of Gender Differences • The Causes of Gender Role Differences

Evolution appears to have shaped differences in brain development for males and females: Males tend to have better spatial abilities and females tend to have better communication skills. Socialization processes, such as parenting, are involved in shaping gender-appropriate behaviour. However, most gender differences in behaviour are small.

## Moral Development

Piaget's Theory of Moral Development • Kohlberg's Theory of Moral Development • Evaluation of Piaget's and Kohlberg's Theories of Moral Development

Piaget concluded that people pass through two stages of moral development. The first is marked by egocentrism and adherence to rules and the second is marked by empathy. Kohlberg argued that moral development ascends through three levels: externally defining morality, considering how the social system relates to morality, and, finally, understanding the principles on which moral rules are based.

## Adolescence

Physical Development • Cognitive Development • Social Development • Identity and Self-Perception

Adolescence begins with sexual maturation, which brings with it marked changes in social behaviour and the ability to reason. Females tend to build relationships based on trust, while males tend to seek social support in becoming more independent. A key aspect of adolescent social development involves forming an identity.

## Adulthood and Old Age

Physical Development • Cognitive Development • Social Development

Our physical abilities peak in early adulthood and decline gradually thereafter, although adopting a healthy lifestyle can retard loss of these abilities. Compared to young adults, older adults perform worse on tests of abstract reasoning but better on tests related to general knowledge and abilities related to experience. Success in love, family, and work is the yardstick by which most people measure their satisfaction in life.

PROLOGUE

## A Rescue Mission

On December 25, 1989, furious at the way he had ruled their country, Romanian revolutionaries executed Nicolae Ceauşescu and his wife, Elena. In the subsequent months, the outside world learned that, among the horrors of their regime, the Ceauşescus had perpetrated a terrible ordeal on the nation's young children. Anxious to increase the country's birth rate and, at the same time, pay off the national debt with food exports, Ceauşescu had restricted access to birth control and confiscated farm harvests. Thousands of families had no choice but to consign their infant children to state-run orphanages.

Collectively, these orphanages were warehouses for children. Many orphanages were unheated, with poor sanitation, few trained staff, and inadequate resources. Westerners who visited the orphanages after the coup found many children left naked and forgotten in crowded wards. By almost any comparison, the children in these orphanages had suffered extreme neglect and deprivation of adult company.

Anxious to help, many foreign couples sought to adopt these children. Thousands of orphans found foster homes in other countries, with parents who had made a special effort to rescue them and to provide a nurturing environment. Although complaints about bureaucratic corruption forced the Romanian government to suspend international adoptions in 2001, for a time it seemed that adoption had allowed some of these children to escape the ravages of the orphanage system.

Elinor Ames, a Canadian psychologist who spearheaded an effort to rescue some of the orphans, soon found that there were troubling aftermaths (Fisher, Ames, Chisholm, & Savoie, 1997). When Ames and her colleagues interviewed the parents who had adopted these children, she discovered that even though the children were still young, they showed significant difficulties in adjusting to their new lives. The parents reported eating problems (usually voracious appetites), medical problems, and frequent bouts of repetitive and robotic movements. Compared to Canadian children, the Romanian orphans also had more problems related to siblings and peers. They seemed unable to adapt to new social situations and to adjust their behaviour to life outside an institution. At the time, the children were about two to three years of age.

To Ames and her colleagues, the future of these children looked deeply uncertain in 1997. How extensive was the psychological damage caused by the neglect experienced early in life? How broad were its effects? The children's bodies responded quickly to improvements in their environment. Could psychological damage be likewise repaired by the efforts of the foster parents who had adopted them? What would the future hold for these children?

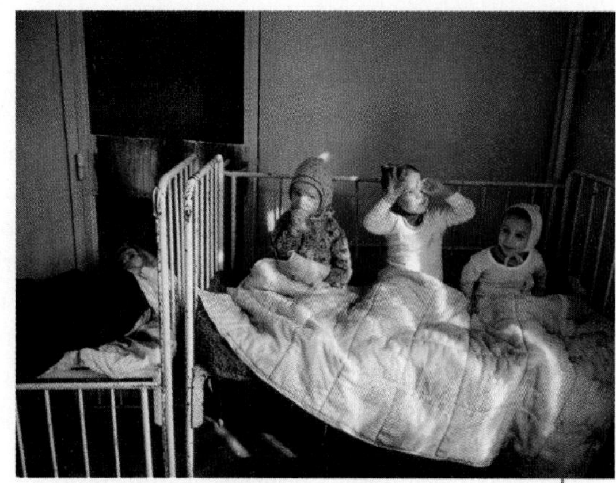

▲ *As a result of state policies, many Romanian children were abandoned to large state orphanages.*

In this chapter, we will discuss the physical, intellectual, and social changes we go through as we age, and some problems associated with abnormal development, similar to those described in the chapter's prologue. We will examine each of the major developmental periods of a person's life—prenatal development, infancy and childhood, adolescence, adulthood, and old age—and will look at the psychological processes that change over these periods.

Psychologists used to limit their study of development to the period encompassing birth through childhood. We recognize now that development does not stop at the end of childhood (Baltes & Carstensen, 2003). Growing older is a matter not only of aging, but also of changing—personally, intellectually, and socially. (See **Table 12•1**.) Developmental psychologists study both the similarities and the differences among people as they develop and change.

Because they study change, developmental psychologists employ special strategies of research. In a **cross-sectional study**, individuals of different ages are simultaneously compared with respect to some test or observation. For example, a developmental psychologist might present mathematical problems to groups of five-, seven-, and nine-year-olds to measure the children's grasp of the concept of negative numbers. In contrast, a **longitudinal study** compares observations of the same individuals at different times of their lives. A longitudinal study of children's grasp of negative numbers might test a group of children when they were five years of age, and then repeat the test on the same children at seven and then at nine.

Cross-sectional studies are usually more convenient to carry out, and they avoid the problems associated with repeatedly testing or observing the same individuals. However, they contain a subtle problem in interpretation. We will examine this problem in connection with a concrete issue later in this chapter. Meanwhile, let's begin our consideration of lifespan development by exploring the prenatal period.

**cross-sectional study** A study of development in which individuals of different ages are compared at the same time.
**longitudinal study** A study of development in which observations of the same individuals are compared at different times of their lives.

**TABLE 12•1 Phases of the Lifespan**

| Phase | Approximate Age | Highlights |
|---|---|---|
| 1. Prenatal | Conception through birth | Rapid physical development of both nervous system and body |
| 2. Infancy | Birth to 2 years | Motor development; attachment to primary caregiver |
| 3. Childhood | 18 months to 12 years | Increasing ability to think logically and reason abstractly; refinement of motor skills; peer influences |
| 4. Adolescence | 13 years to about 20 years | Thinking and reasoning becomes more adultlike; identity crisis; continued peer influences |
| 5. Adulthood | 20 years to 65 years | Love, committed relationship; career; stability and then decrease in physical abilities |
| 6. Old age | 65 years and older to death | Reflection on life's work and accomplishments; physical health deteriorates; prepare for death; death |

# Prenatal Development

The **prenatal period** extends over the approximately nine months between conception and birth. The length of a normal pregnancy is 266 days, or 38 weeks. During this time, development depends on two factors whose effects characterize themes of this chapter. First, there is the genetic contribution from egg and sperm that determines the genotype of the new individual. We saw in Chapter 3 how this genetic material can replicate, producing descendants that are genetic copies of this single cell. A child develops from this single source of genetic "instructions."

Prenatal development, however, is not simply a matter of cellular replication producing copies of the original fertilized egg. Although all cells of an individual (with the exception of reproductive cells) have the same genetic content, they obviously differ; for example, blood cells are not the same as neurons and muscle cells are not the same as those that produce bone. In mammals, there are about 200 different types of cells, all of which develop from the same union of sperm and egg (Allis, Jenuwein, & Reinberg, 2007). Some factor must direct the mechanisms of replication during the prenatal period so that cells that are genetically identical will develop along different paths.

X chromosome inactivation (see Chapter 3) is one example of this factor at work (Brockdorff & Turner, 2007). As discussed in Chapter 3, one of the two X chromosomes that women bear is "silenced" early in development, such that most of its genes do not synthesize the proteins they normally would. Inactivation of one X chromosome is important because it limits the total amount of proteins produced by genes located on the X chromosome. Without this limit, the metabolism of a developing female would be very different from that of a developing male (who has only one X chromosome). X chromosome inactivation occurs early in the development of females and affects all subsequent cellular reproduction—the "silenced" chromosome is passed along to descendant cells, but it remains silenced. The mechanism by which one of the two X chromosomes is selected to be inactivated is not known, but it obviously has an important influence on a woman's development since it determines whether the chromosome inherited from her mother or her father will be active.

**prenatal period** The nine months between conception and birth. This period is divided into three developmental stages: the zygotic, the embryonic, and the fetal.
**zygote stage** The first stage of prenatal development, during which the zygote divides many times and the internal organs begin to form.
**embryonic stage** The second stage of prenatal development, beginning at about two weeks and ending about eight weeks after conception, during which the heart begins to beat, the brain starts to function, and most of the major body structures begin to form.
**teratogens** Substances, agents, and events that can cause birth defects.

X chromosome inactivation is one example of an epigenetic modification, a modification of cell inheritance that is not due to alterations of the DNA sequence itself (see Chapter 3). Epigenetic changes include the way the DNA molecule is folded within other proteins, chemical changes in the structure of the nucleotide cytosine, and complex modifications in the way DNA information is mapped into protein synthesis (Allis, Jenuwein, & Reinberg, 2007). Epigenetic modifications form a second factor of early development, and illustrate the important point that the cell's chemical environment moderates the expression of its genetic code. So, while the genetic information contained within the individual remains the same throughout development, the reproducing cells become specialized as blood cells, neurons, and muscle cells.

## Stages of Prenatal Development

The union of the ovum (egg) and sperm, conception, is the starting point for prenatal development. During the **zygote stage**, which lasts about two weeks, the *zygote*, or the single new cell that is formed at conception, divides many times, and the internal organs begin to form. By the end of the first week, the zygote consists of about a hundred cells. Many of the cells are arranged in two layers, one for the skin, hair, nervous system, and sensory organs and the other for the digestive and respiratory systems and glands. Near the end of this stage, a third layer of cells appears that will eventually develop into muscles and the circulatory and excretory systems.

The **embryonic stage** of prenatal development, the second stage, begins at about two weeks and ends about eight weeks after conception. During this stage, the zygote is transformed into an embryo and development occurs at an incredibly rapid pace. By a month after conception, a heart has begun to beat, a brain and spinal cord have started to function, and most of the major body structures are beginning to form. By the end of this stage, the major features that define the human body—arms, hands, fingers, legs, toes, shoulders, head, and eyes—are discernible. Behaviourally, the embryo can react reflexively to stimulation. For example, if the mouth is stimulated, the embryo moves its upper body and neck. Because so many changes depend on a delicate chemical balance, the embryo at this stage is most susceptible to external chemical influences, including alcohol and other drugs, or toxins produced by diseases such as rubella (German measles). These substances are **teratogens** (from the Greek *teras*, meaning "malformation"). The term refers to any substance, agent, or event that can cause birth defects.

The beginning of sexual development occurs during the embryonic stage. The twenty-third chromosome pair determines the sex of the embryo. The female partner contributes an X chromosome to this pair at conception, whereas the male partner contributes either an X or a Y chromosome. If the male partner contributes a Y chromosome, the embryo will become a male (XY); if he contributes an X, the embryo will become a female (XX). Early in prenatal development,

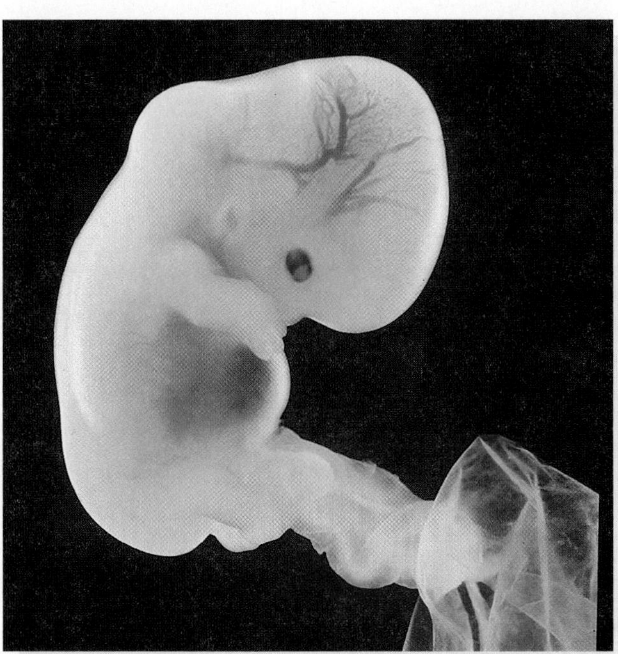

▲ *As this photograph of a six-week-old fetus illustrates, most of the major features that define the human body are present near the end of the embryonic stage of development (which starts at about two weeks and ends about eight weeks after conception).*

the embryo develops a pair of gonads that will become either ovaries or testes. (The word *gonad* comes from the Greek *gonos*, "procreation.") If a Y chromosome is present, a gene located on it causes the production of a chemical signal that makes the gonads develop into testes. Otherwise, the gonads become ovaries.

The presence or absence of testes determines the development of the other sex organs. If testes are present, they begin to secrete a class of sex hormones known as **androgens** (*andros* means "man"; *gennan* means "to produce"). The most important androgen is *testosterone*. Androgens bring about the development of the male internal sex organs, the penis, and the scrotum. These hormones are therefore absolutely necessary for the development of a male. The development of female sex organs (uterus, vagina, and labia) occurs naturally; it does not need to be stimulated by a hormone. (See **Figure 12•1**.)

The **fetal stage** is the final period of prenatal development and lasts about seven months. It officially begins with the appearance of bone cells and ends with birth. At the end of the second month of pregnancy, the fetus is about 4 cm long and weighs about 30 g. By the end of the third month, the development of major organs is completed and the bones and muscles are beginning to develop. The fetus is now 8 cm long and weighs about 90 g. The fetus may show some movement, especially kicking.

By the end of the fourth month, the fetus is about 15 cm long and weighs about 170 g. It is also now sleeping and waking regularly. Fetal movements also become strong enough to be felt by the mother, and the heartbeat is loud enough to be heard through a stethoscope. Sound and light sensitivity will emerge within a few weeks. During the sixth month, the fetus grows to more than 30 cm long and weighs about 700 g. The seventh month is a critical month because if the fetus is born prematurely at this point, it has a fair chance of surviving. A newborn at this age would almost certainly require help breathing. However, fetuses mature at different rates, and some seven-month-old fetuses may be mature enough to survive premature birth while others may not.

During the last two months of prenatal development, the fetus gains weight at the rate of about 250 g per week. On average, the fetus is about 50 cm long and weighs about 3.5 kg at the end of this period. The fetus is ready to be born.

## Threats to Normal Prenatal Development

The prenatal environment normally provides the correct supply of nutrients to the fetus. Probably the single most important factor in the fetus's development is the mother's diet: The food she eats is the fetus's only source of nutrition. If the mother is extremely malnourished, the fetus's nervous system develops abnormally, and intellectual deficits may result.

Teratogens can also cause birth defects. Psychologists who study birth defects are very interested in how drugs affect the fetus, because taking drugs is a behaviour that is directly under the control of the mother. Certain antibiotics, especially when taken in large quantities over long periods, can produce fetal defects. For example, tetracycline, a common antibiotic, can cause irregularities in the bones and discoloration of the teeth. Cocaine use by mothers during pregnancy produces dramatic effects. If a pregnant woman uses cocaine, there is an increased risk of premature birth, low birth weight, and a smaller-than-normal head circumference. One study showed that growth deficits attributable to prenatal cocaine exposure were still remarkable in children at age seven (Covington et al., 2002). Research evidence also suggests that prenatal exposure to cocaine interferes with neural development, and that there may be long-term consequences in the areas of arousal and attention (Bard, Coles, Plaatzman, & Lynch, 2000; Mayes, Cicchetti, Acharyya, & Zhang, 2003; Potter, Zelazo, Stack, & Papageorgiou, 2000; Singer et al., 2002). Further, some babies are born addicted and show withdrawal symptoms such as hyperactivity, irritability, tremors, and vomiting (Zuckerman & Brown, 1993).

A pregnant woman's cigarette smoking is another behaviour that can affect the fetus. The carbon monoxide contained in cigarette smoke reduces the supply of oxygen to the fetus. Reduced oxygen levels are particularly harmful to the fetus during the last half of pregnancy when the fetus is

**androgens** The primary class of sex hormones in males. The most important androgen is testosterone.

**fetal stage** The third and final stage of prenatal development, which lasts for about seven months, beginning with the appearance of bone tissue and ending with birth.

FIGURE 12•1 Differentiation and development of the sex organs.

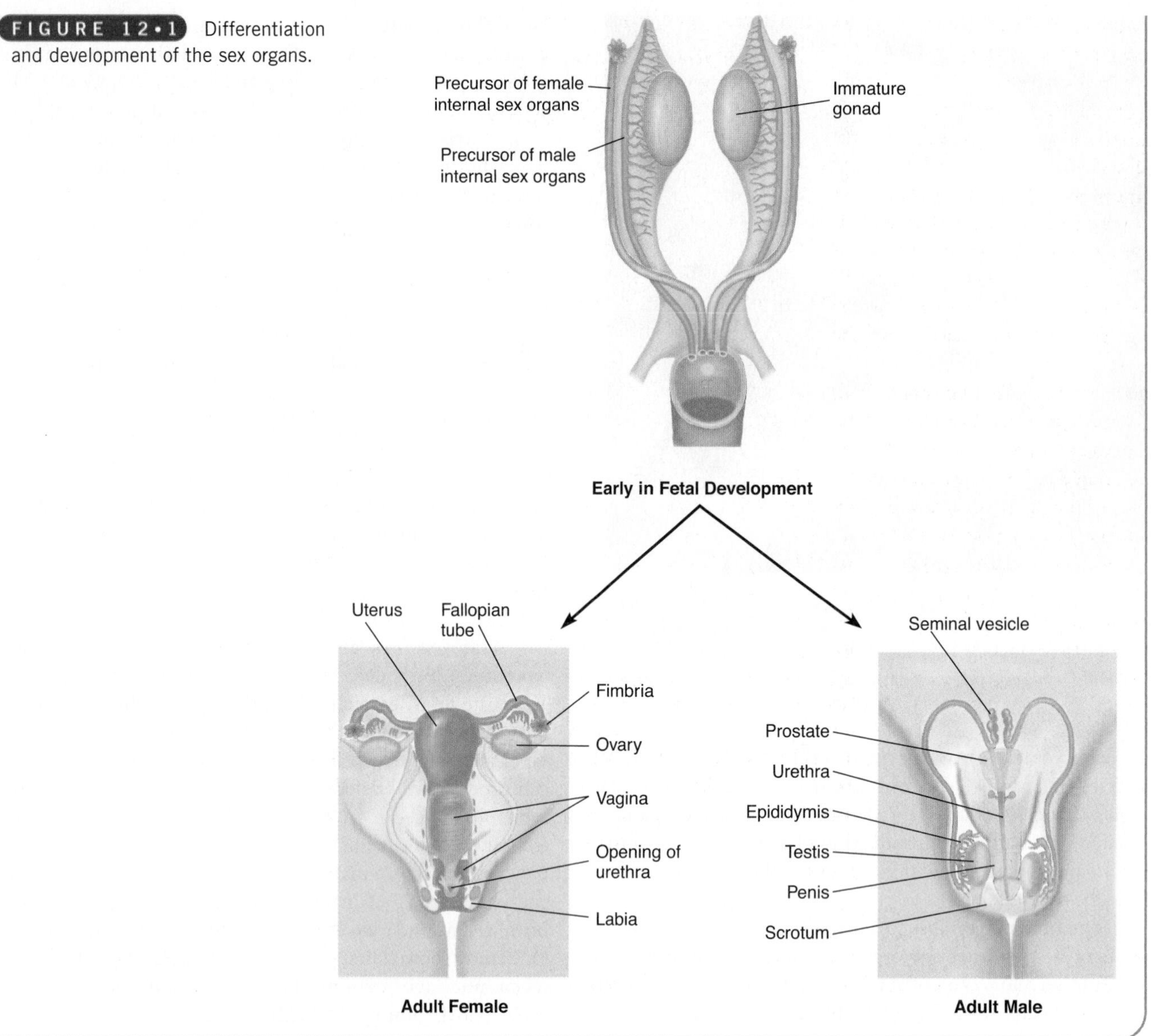


developing most rapidly and its demand for oxygen is greatest. The main physical effects of mothers' smoking are increased rate of miscarriages, low–birth weight babies, an increased chance of premature birth, and more births by Caesarean section (Floyd et al., 1993; Kirchengast & Hartmann, 2003). One recent study suggests that prenatal exposure to cigarette smoking may produce lowered arousal levels in newborns (Franco et al., 2000), and there are indications of relatively uncommon but statistically related birth defects, such as cleft palate (e.g., Chung, Kowalski, Kim, & Buchman, 2000). Maternal smoking is associated with deficits in the ability of a newborn baby's brain to process speech sounds (Key et al., 2007) and may be related to behaviour problems in adolescence (Weissman, Warner, Wickramaratne, & Kandel, 1999).

The damaging effects of alcohol use during pregnancy have been most widely studied (Habbick et al., 1996; Henderson, Kesmodel, & Gray, 2007; Kelly, Day, & Streissguth, 2000; Steinhausen & Spohr, 1998; Streissguth, 2001). These effects can include both pre- and postnatal growth deficits, deformations of the eyes and mouth, low brain mass, other brain and central nervous system abnormalities, and heart deformation—the problems collectively known as fetal alcohol syndrome, or FAS (Niccols, 2007). Even if children with FAS are reared in healthy environments with regular, nutritious meals, their physical and intellectual development still falls short of that of normal children. Drinking as little as two ounces of alcohol a day early in pregnancy can produce some symptoms of FAS (Astley et al., 1992). That's just a bit more than is contained in an airline-type miniature bottle. The best advice should be clear: Don't drink during pregnancy.

Tragically, some teratogens are much more difficult to avoid. Among these are the chemicals that occur in our environment because of industrial or agricultural pollution. For example, many pesticides use a class of chemicals based on phosphorus. Sánchez-Peña and colleagues (2004) found that Mexican agricultural workers exposed to such organophosphorus pesticides had a much larger risk of damage to the chromosome structure of their sperm cells than those without such exposure. Of course, pesticides are just one of the many contaminants that we may be exposed to; lead, mercury, and polychlorinated biphenyls (PCBs) are other environmental teratogens. The prevalence of teratogens in our environment has led some researchers to seek "anti-teratogens" that could reduce these risks (e.g., Guna Sherlin & Verma, 2001).

## Interim Summary

### Prenatal Development

The three stages of prenatal development span the time between conception and birth. In just nine months, the zygote grows from a single cell, void of human resemblance, into a fully developed fetus, complete with physical features that look much like yours and mine, except in miniature. Gender is determined by the sex chromosomes. Male sex organs are produced by the action of a gene on the Y chromosome that causes the gonads to develop into testes. The testes secrete androgens, which stimulate the development of male sex organs. If testes are not present, the fetus develops as a female. The most important factor in normal fetal development is the mother's nutrition. Normal fetal development can be disrupted by the presence of teratogens, which can cause intellectual deficits and physical deformities. One well-studied teratogen is alcohol, which, when consumed by a pregnant woman, may lead to fetal alcohol syndrome.

**QUESTIONS TO CONSIDER**

1. Each of us experiences similar prenatal developmental stages and processes, so why do differences among people start to emerge in this very early period?
2. Suppose that you are a psychologist working in a pediatric clinic. A woman, pregnant with her first child, asks you for advice on what she can do to care for her unborn child. Based on what you now know about prenatal development, what advice would you give her?

# Physical and Perceptual Development in Infancy and Childhood

The terms *infant* and *toddler* apply to babies up to the age of two years. A newborn human infant is helpless and absolutely dependent on adult care. Recent research has shown, however, that newborns do not passively await the ministrations of their caregivers (Gartstein, Crawford, & Robertson, 2008). They quickly develop skills that shape the behaviour of the adults with whom they interact. This section will look at motor development and perceptual development in infancy and early childhood; in the next section, we'll examine some influential theories of cognitive development.

## Motor Development

Normal motor development follows a distinct pattern, which appears to be dictated by maturation of the muscles and the nervous system. The term **maturation** refers to any relatively stable change in thought, behaviour, or physical growth that is due to the aging process and not to experience. Although individual children progress at different rates, their development follows the same basic maturational pattern (see **Figure 12•2**).

At birth, the infant's most important movements are reflexes—automatic movements in response to specific stimuli. The most important reflexes are the rooting, sucking, and swallowing responses. If a baby's cheek is touched lightly, the baby will turn its head in the direction of the touch (the rooting response). If the object makes contact with the baby's lips, the baby will open its mouth and begin sucking. When milk or any other liquid enters the mouth, the baby will automatically make swallowing movements. Obviously, these reflexes are important for the baby's survival. As we will see later in this chapter, these behaviours are important for an infant's social development as well.

Development of motor skills requires two ingredients: maturation of the child's nervous system and practice. Development of the nervous system is not complete at birth; considerable growth occurs during the first several months, and the amount of this growth seems to be associated with IQ in later childhood (Gale et al., 2004). In fact, important changes in brain structure occur throughout the lifespan as a result of experience (Kolb, Gibb, & Robinson, 2003; Kolb & Whishaw, 1998).

Particular kinds of movements must await the development of the necessary neuromuscular systems. However, motor development is not merely a matter of using these systems once they develop. Instead, physical development of the nervous system depends to a large extent on the ways in which the baby moves while interacting with the environment. In turn, more complex movements depend on further development of the nervous system, creating an interplay between motor and neural development. Thus, different steps in motor development are both an effect of previous development and a cause of further development (Thelen & Corbetta, 2002).

## Perceptual Development

We have known for a long time that fetal experience with sensory stimuli can prepare the way for the newborn's experience. Kisilevsky and colleagues (2003) found that playing a

**maturation** Any relatively stable change in thought, behaviour, or physical growth that is due to the aging process and not to experience.

FIGURE 12•2 Milestones in a child's motor development.
*(Adapted from Shirley, M. M. (1933).* The first two years. Vol. 2: Intellectual development. *Minneapolis: University of Minnesota Press.)*

recording of the mother's voice outside her abdomen increased the heart rate of her fetus, while playing a stranger's voice did not. At the time of birth, a child's senses are already functioning, at least to a certain extent (e.g., Maurer & Maurer, 1988). We know that the newborn's auditory system can detect sounds, because the baby will show a startle reaction when presented with a sudden loud noise. Similarly, a bright light will elicit eye closing and squinting. A cold object or a pinch will produce crying, so the sense of touch must be present. If held firmly and tilted backward, a baby will stiffen and flail his or her arms and legs, indicating that babies have a sense of balance. We also know that newborn infants have a sense of taste, because they indicate their taste preferences by facial expression and by choosing to swallow or not to swallow different liquids. Infants have an early-developing ability to distinguish odours, an ability that can be seen as an element of mother–infant bonding. For example, infants at two weeks can distinguish their own mother from other lactating women by breast odour (Porter, Makin, Davis, & Christensen, 1992). We also know that infants very early on can recognize and prefer their mother's voice (e.g., DeCasper & Fifer, 1980; Purhonen et al., 2005). Research shows that preference and discrimination likely develop before birth as a result of the fetus's in utero exposure to the mother's voice (Kisilevsky et al., 2003).

Observations such as these establish the sensory abilities of infants. But when do infants develop the capacity to interpret sensory signals? Is perception present at birth? Developmental psychologists have looked at many perceptual systems to answer this question. We'll consider two systems: the perception of forms and the perception of distance.

**Form Perception** Researchers study the visual perceptual abilities of infants by observing their eye movements with an eye-tracking device while showing them visual stimuli. A harmless spot of infrared light, invisible to humans, is directed onto the baby's eyes. A special television camera, sensitive to infrared light, records the spot and superimposes it on an image of the display that the baby is looking at. The technique is precise enough to enable experimenters to tell which parts of a stimulus the baby is scanning. For example, Salapatek (1975) reported that a one-month-old infant tends not to look at the inside of a figure. Instead, the baby's gaze seems to be "trapped" by the edges. By the age of two months, the baby scans across the border to investigate the interior of a figure. **Figure 12•3** shows a reconstruction of the paths followed by the eye scans of infants of these ages. (The babies were looking at real faces, not the drawings shown in the figure.)

The work by Salapatek and his colleagues suggests that at the age of one or two months, babies do not perceive complete shapes; their scanning strategy is limited to fixations on a few parts of the object at which they are looking. By three months, however, babies show clear signs of

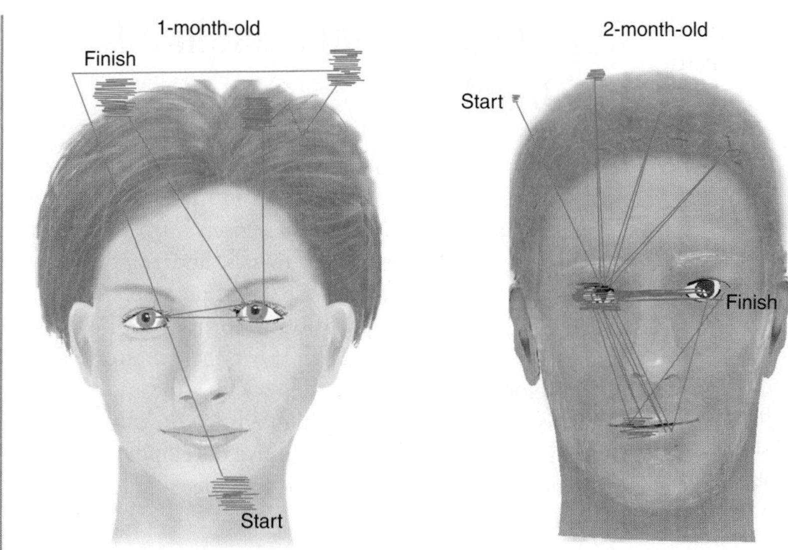


**FIGURE 12•3** The scanning sequence used by infants when viewing faces.

*(From Salapatek, P. (1975). Pattern perception in early infancy. In L. B. Cohen and P. Salapatek (Eds.),* Infant perception: From sensation to cognition. Vol. 1: Basic visual processes. *New York: Academic Press. Used with permission from Copyright Clearance Center.)*

pattern recognition. For example, by this age they prefer to look at stimuli that resemble the human face (Rosser, 1994), and by four or five months they can discriminate between even very similar faces (Bornstein & Arterberry, 2003; Fagan & Singer, 1979).

**Distance Perception** The ability to perceive three-dimensional space comes at an early age. Gibson and Walk (1960) placed six-month-old babies on what they called a visual cliff. On one side of this apparatus is a platform containing a checkerboard pattern. The platform adjoins a glass shelf mounted three or four feet over a floor that also is covered by the checkerboard pattern. Most babies who could crawl would not venture onto the glass shelf. The infants acted as if they were afraid of falling; that is, they could perceive the distance between themselves and the floor.

Remember from Chapter 6 that several different types of cues in the environment contribute to depth perception. One cue arises from retinal disparity. As explained in Chapter 6, under normal circumstances points on objects that are different distances from the viewer fall on slightly different points of the two retinas. The perception of depth occurs when the two images are fused through visual processing. This form of depth perception, stereopsis ("solid vision"), will not develop unless animals have experience viewing objects with both eyes during a period early in life.

The dependence of stereopsis on retinal disparity has important implications for the development of normal vision. If an infant's eyes are crossed, the same points on the two retinas receive the same information, producing no disparity and no depth perception through stereopsis. Crossed vision can be corrected through surgery or through special glasses, but an infant requires disparity at a particular age to experience depth perception through stereopsis. Fawcett, Wang, and Birch (2005) examined children who had experienced crossed vision in infancy to see when loss of disparity most affects stereopsis. There are different reasons why crossed vision occurs, but overall, it has its worst influence at 3.5 months after birth, although its influence can affect stereopsis even at 4 years of age (see **Figure 12•4**).

**Critical and Sensitive Periods in Perceptual Development** Psychologists use the term **critical period** to denote a specific time during which certain experiences must occur if an individual is to develop normally. Many perceptual, behavioural, and cognitive abilities are subject to critical periods. For example, as we saw in the prologue and as we shall see later in this chapter, if infants are not exposed to a

**critical period** A specific time in development during which certain experiences must occur for normal development to occur.

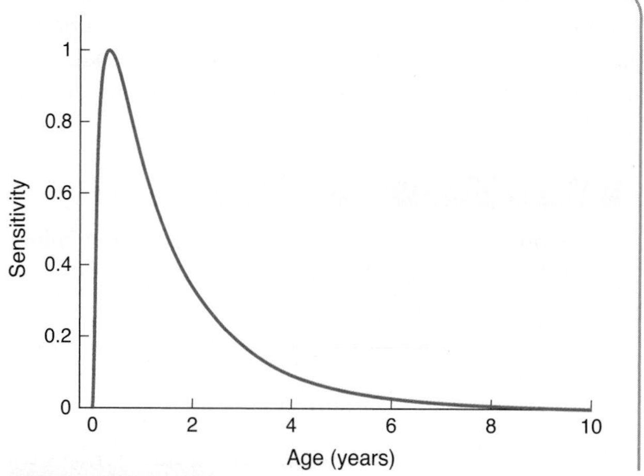


**FIGURE 12•4** Sensitivity of stereopsis development to disruption in retinal disparity.

*(Adapted from Fawcett, S. L., Wang, Y.-Z., & Birch, E. E. (2005). The critical period for susceptibility of human stereopsis.* Investigative Ophthalmology & Visual Science, 46, *521–525.)*

stimulating environment and do not have the opportunity to interact with caregivers during the first two years of their lives, their cognitive development will be impaired.

Other abilities may show a weaker dependence on experience: The ability in question may develop in response to experience that occurs at any time within a broad range, but the effect may be stronger during some periods than during others. This weaker form of dependency is often referred to as a **sensitive period.** Acquisition of a second language seems to be such a case. A person can learn a second language throughout life, but (as discussed in Chapter 10) a second language is learned more easily in childhood than later.

Critical periods and sensitive periods demonstrate that human development is more than an unfolding of a genetically determined program. It consists of a continuous interaction between physical maturation and environmental stimulation.

## Interim Summary

### Physical and Perceptual Development in Infancy and Childhood

A newborn infant's first movements are actually reflexes that are crucial to its survival. For example, the rooting, sucking, and swallowing reflexes are important in finding and consuming food. More sophisticated movements, such as crawling and standing, develop and are refined through natural maturation and practice.

A newborn's senses appear to be at least partially functional at birth. However, normal development of the senses, like that of motor abilities, depends on experience. Genetically, an infant has the potential to develop motor and sensory abilities that coincide with the maturation of its nervous system. However, in order for this potential to be realized, the infant's environment must supply the opportunity to test and practise these skills. If an infant is deprived of the opportunity to practise them during a critical period, these skills may fail to develop, which will affect the infant's performance as an adult.

#### QUESTION TO CONSIDER

1. Suppose you are expecting your first child. How might you design your child's room (or nursery) to facilitate motor and perceptual development? What kinds of toys would you include in the room? What sorts of experiences might you wish to have with your child to promote normal motor and sensory development?

**sensitive period** A period of time during which certain experiences have more of an effect on development than they would have if they occurred at another time.

# Cognitive Development in Infancy and Childhood

As children grow, their nervous systems mature and they undergo new experiences. Perceptual and motor skills develop in complexity and competency. Children learn to recognize people and their voices, begin to talk and respond to the speech of others, and learn how to solve problems. Infants as young as 12 months are even able to form memories of specific events (see Bauer, 2002). In short, their cognitive capacities develop.

This section will begin by highlighting the importance of a responsive environment to cognitive development; then we will turn to Piaget's theory, Vygotsky's theory, and the information processing model.

## The Importance of a Responsive Environment

Cognitive development is the process by which infants get to know things about themselves and their world. One of the first steps in a baby's cognitive development is for the baby to learn that events in the environment can be dependent on its own behaviour. It appears, in fact, that the type of setting that is most effective in promoting cognitive development is an environment in which the infant's behaviour has tangible effects.

In an experimental test of this hypothesis, Watson and Ramey (1972) presented three groups of infants with a mobile 10 minutes per day for 14 days. A pillow containing a pressure-sensitive switch was placed under each baby's head, and the mobile was suspended above the baby's face. For one group, the mobile automatically rotated whenever the infant moved its head and activated the switch. For another group, the mobile remained stationary. For a third group, the mobile intermittently moved on its own (but not in response to infant head movements). So the first group of infants had experience controlling the mobile's movements, whereas the other two groups experienced no association between their own actions and the mobile's movement.

The babies were tested again. This time, the mobile was connected to the pillow switch for infants in all three of the experimental groups. Infants who had learned the contingency between head turning and mobile movement again turned their heads when they saw the mobile. They seemed to have learned that they could control its movements. In contrast, when the babies in the second and third groups were given the opportunity to make the mobile move by turning their heads, they did *not* learn to do so. It was as if they had learned from their prior experience that they could not affect whether the mobile would move. Research using similar methods found that infants were visibly pleased when they controlled the onset of a Sesame Street music video (Lewis, Alessandri, & Sullivan, 1990). Losing this type of contingent control, on the other

▲ *Watson and Ramey's experiment using mobiles demonstrated the importance of a responsive environment in promoting cognitive development.*

hand, produces facial expressions of anger (Lewis, Alessandri, & Sullivan, 1990; Sullivan & Lewis, 2003).

Findings from research on infant control of stimuli in their environments are consistent with a great deal of other evidence about adults (as you will see in later chapters). Being able to extend oneself and affect objects and other people are important aspects of personal and social functioning. There are implications here for infant-rearing practices. In some tragic cases, babies have been raised in unresponsive, unstimulating institutions. One such child, whom I'll call J. F. to respect her privacy, was one of the orphans described in the prologue to this chapter. J. F. spent the first three years of her life in a Romanian orphanage and, in all that time, had only once been outside for fresh air and sunshine. When her prospective foster parents first saw her, sores and dirt covered her skin, and her fingernails were so long they curled under. One of her legs was so disfigured by injections of tranquilizing drugs that it would later need surgery to help her walk. Although three years old, she looked less than half that age. A Canadian woman who was visiting was so touched by the child's plight that she dropped her plans to adopt a younger child and adopted J. F. instead.

J. F.'s new mother and father tried hard to provide the care that the child had been denied for the first three years of her life. However, J. F. seemed incapable of accepting the typical attachment between a child and her parents. As described by Faulder (2006), J. F.'s emotional maturity was that of an 18-month-old. Her mother described her as always in "spin cycle"—unable to focus on any behaviour, even on play. The problems of adjustment that Elinor Ames observed in her research sample (discussed in the prologue) had, in J. F.'s case, led to a downward spiral.

By the time she was 10, J. F.'s behaviour had turned her household into a "living hell." She had been diagnosed with autism, attention deficit disorder, and hyperactivity. Other suspected conditions included attachment disorder and Tourette's syndrome. One day, overwhelmed by J. F.'s behaviour, her mother phoned a local social agency screaming for help. To this point, a stable home life and the love of two parents had not been enough. J. F. would spend the next six years living in a group home in another town.

The experience of J. F.'s parents is not unique. Le Mare, Audet, and Kurytnik (2007) studied the frequency with which the foster parents of Romanian adoptees used social support agencies and found that those parents requested help more often than parents of non-adopted children. The group differences were especially pronounced when the adopted children were between 10 and 11 years of age, when parents typically sought assistance for behavioural and academic problems.

Nelson (2007) has suggested that, at key times, the brain's development requires the stimulation that normal childhood provides; without this stimulation, regions of the brain lack directions for further development. Cognitive and social development might be characterized as a sequence. If earlier periods in the sequence are disrupted, development is delayed. This notion of sequence, with distinct and ordered stages, was suggested by early observers of child development, such as Baldwin and Montessori (see Chapter 1). Nowadays, it is most closely associated with the theories of Jean Piaget.

## The Work of Jean Piaget

Jean Piaget (1896–1980) was a Swiss researcher who viewed cognitive development as a maturational process. Piaget considered himself a philosopher concerned with the development of knowledge rather than a developmental psychologist. Piaget's work began with observations he made of his own children. He noticed that they tended to engage in behaviours that were distinctive to their age and to make related mistakes in problem solving. Other children of similar ages tended to engage in similar behaviours and to make the same kinds of mistakes. He concluded that these similarities are the result of a sequence of development that all normal children follow. Completion of each period, with its corresponding abilities, is the prerequisite for entering the next period.

An important component of Piaget's theory is the notion of an **operation**. In the field of both logic and mathematics, an operation is a transformation of an object or thing. For example, multiplication by 2 transforms 6 into 12. Similarly, hearing someone say "Rhonda is my sister" transforms your conception of "Rhonda" into another conception, that of the speaker's sister. For Piaget, an important logical characteristic of an operation is that it is invertible—that is, it can be reversed. By inverting the operation of multiplication

**operation** In Piaget's theory, a logical or mathematical rule that transforms an object or concept into something else.

▲ *According to Piaget, children develop schemata, such as grasping objects or putting them into their mouths, that become the basis for understanding current and future experiences.*

into division, we can transform 12 back to 6. According to Piaget, an important aspect of cognitive development is whether a child possesses the ability to use operations of different types.

As children develop, Piaget suggested, they acquire mental representations or frameworks that are used for understanding and dealing with the world and for thinking about and solving problems. As Chapter 8 explained, a mental framework that organizes and synthesizes information about a person, place, or thing is known as a schema. Piaget proposed that schemata are first defined in terms of objects and actions but that later they become the basis of the concrete and abstract concepts that constitute adult knowledge. For example, a baby girl is said to have a "grasping schema" when she is able to grasp a rattle in her hand. Once she has learned how to grasp a rattle, she can apply the same schema to other objects. Later, she can incorporate the "grasping schema" with others to accomplish the behaviour of picking up an object. At that point, she will possess a "picking up schema."

Let us consider schemata further. Infants acquire schemata by interacting with their environment. According to Piaget, two processes help a child adapt to his or her environment: assimilation and accommodation. **Assimilation** is the process by which new information is incorporated into existing schemata. For example, suppose that a young boy has schemata for what adults are like and for what children are like. Adults are tall and drive cars. Children are short and ride bikes. When this child meets new children and adults, they will usually fit, or be assimilated, into his existing schemata and will be properly categorized. But our child will be challenged when he meets his mother's older sister Marge, who is no taller than the average 12-year-old and rides a bike. The child will need to account for the fact that Aunt Marge is nevertheless identifiably an adult. The process by which existing schemata are changed by new experiences is called **accommodation.** Our child's schemata for children and adults will have to change to include the possibility that some short people are adults rather than children. As you continue in this chapter, keep in mind that assimilation and accommodation apply not just to categorization of people and objects, but to methods of doing things and even to abstract concepts.

## Piaget's Four Periods of Cognitive Development

Although development is a continuous process, Piaget argued that at key points in an individual's life, the two processes of assimilation and accommodation fail to adjust adequately to the child's knowledge of the world. At these points, through a process that Piaget labelled **equilibration**, the individual's schemas are radically reorganized. According to Piaget, these key points in a child's life divided cognitive development into four periods: sensorimotor, preoperational, concrete operational, and formal operational. (See **Table 12•2.**) What a child learns in one period enables him or her to progress to the next period. Crucially, it matters whether the schemata of an earlier period can be reorganized in a way that will permit operations to occur in the next. The periods in Piaget's theory are more than just intervals of time; they are necessary stages in a progression from primitive sensory knowledge to abstract reasoning.

**TABLE 12•2 The Four Periods of Piaget's Theory of Cognitive Development**

| Period | Approximate Age | Major Features |
|---|---|---|
| Sensorimotor | Birth to 2 years | Object permanence; deferred imitation; rudimentary symbolic thinking |
| Preoperational | 2 to 6 or 7 years | Increased ability to think symbolically and logically; egocentrism; cannot yet master conservation problems |
| Concrete operational | 6 or 7 years to 11 years | Can master conservation problems; can understand categorization; cannot think abstractly |
| Formal operational | 11 years upward | Can think abstractly and hypothetically |

**assimilation** The process by which new information about the world is incorporated into existing schemata.
**accommodation** The process by which existing schemata are modified or changed by new experiences.
**equilibration** A process within Piaget's theory that reorganizes schemata.

**FIGURE 12•5** Object permanence. An infant will not realize that the object has been left under the cloth.
*(Adapted from Bower, T. G. R. (1972).* Perception in infancy (2nd ed.). *San Francisco: W. H. Freeman.)*

**The Sensorimotor Period** The **sensorimotor period**, which lasts for approximately the first two years of life, is the first stage in Piaget's theory of cognitive development. It is marked by an orderly progression of increasingly complex cognitive development ranging from reflexes to symbolic thinking. During this period, cognition is closely tied to external stimulation, including that produced by physical objects and people (see Muller & Carpendale, 2000).

An important feature of the sensorimotor period is the development of **object permanence**—the realization that objects do not cease to exist when they are out of sight. Until about six months of age, children appear to lose all interest in an object that disappears from sight; the saying "out of sight, out of mind" seems particularly appropriate. In addition, cognition is inseparable from action or behaviour: Thinking is doing.

During the last half of the first year, infants develop much more complex concepts concerning the nature of physical objects. They grasp objects, turn them over, and investigate their properties. By looking at an object from various angles, they learn that the object can change its visual shape and still be the same object. In addition, if an object is hidden, infants will actively search for it; their object concept now contains the rule of object permanence. For infants at this stage of development, a hidden object still exists. Out of sight is no longer out of mind. In the game of peekaboo, babies laugh because they know that after momentarily disappearing, you will suddenly reappear and say, "Peekaboo!"

By early in the second year, awareness of object permanence is well enough developed that infants will search for an object in the last place they saw it hidden. However, at this stage, infants can keep track of changes only in a hiding place they can see. For example, if an adult picks up an object, puts it under a cloth, drops the object while his or her hand is hidden, closes the hand again, and removes the hand from the cloth, infants will look for the object in the adult's hand. When they do not find the object there, they look puzzled or upset and do not search for the object under the cloth. (See **Figure 12•5**.)

**The Preoperational Period** Piaget's second period of cognitive development, the **preoperational period**, lasts from approximately age two to age seven and involves the ability to think logically as well as symbolically. This period is characterized by rapid development of language ability and

**sensorimotor period** The first period in Piaget's theory of cognitive development, lasting from birth to two years. It is marked by an orderly progression of increasingly complex cognitive development: reflexes, permanence, a rough approximation of causality, imitation, and symbolic thinking.
**object permanence** The idea that objects do not disappear when they are out of sight.
**preoperational period** The second of Piaget's periods, which represents a four- to five-year transitional period between first being able to think symbolically and then being able to think logically. During this stage, children become increasingly capable of speaking meaningful sentences.

**FIGURE 12•6** Conservation. Early in the preoperational period, a child does not have the ability to understand that a liquid quantity is conserved.

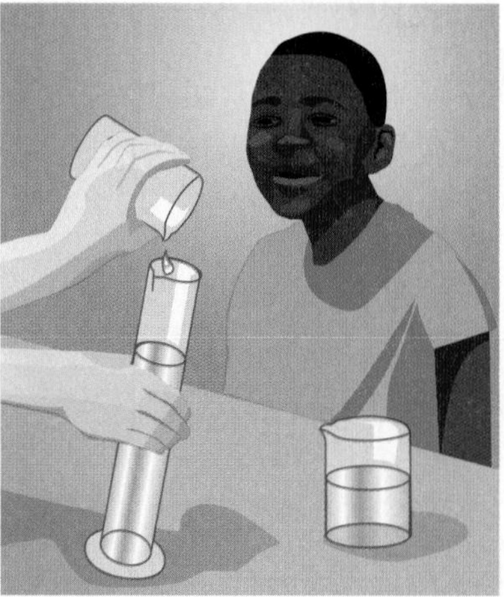

of the ability to represent things symbolically. The child arranges toys in new ways to represent other objects (for example, a row of blocks can represent a train), begins to classify and categorize objects, and starts learning to count and to manipulate numbers. During the preoperational period, schemas are reorganized around words. Words are symbols that have no physical resemblance to the concept they represent; Piaget referred to such abstract symbols as signs. Signs are social conventions. They are understood by all members of a culture. A child who is able to use words to think about reality has made an important step in cognitive development.

**Egocentrism**, a child's belief that others see the world in precisely the way he or she does, is another important characteristic of the preoperational period. A preoperational child sees the world only from his or her own point of view. For example, a preoperational child playing hide-and-seek may run to a corner, turn his back to you, and "hide" by covering his eyes. Although in plain sight of you, he believes that because he cannot see you, you must not be able to see him.

A third important characteristic of the preoperational period—and the reason for its name—is that the child's schemas do not permit invertible operations. For example, if I take a stack of pennies on a table and spread them out all over the tabletop, they have been transformed into a different array. A child in the preoperational period cannot conceptualize that this operation can be reversed. Instead, he or she believes that I have radically changed something about the pennies.

Piaget's work demonstrated this belief quite clearly and, in doing so, showed that a child's representation of the world is strikingly different from that of an adult. For example, most adults realize that the volume of water remains constant when the water is poured from a short, wide container into a taller, narrower container, even though its level is now higher. However, early in the preoperational period, children will fail to recognize this fact; they will say that the taller container contains more water. (See **Figure 12•6**.) The ability to realize that an object retains volume, mass, length, or number when it undergoes various transformations is referred to as a grasp of **conservation**; the transformed object conserves its original properties. **Figure 12•7** depicts three additional tests of children's understanding of conservation.

**egocentrism** Self-centredness; preoperational children can see the world only from their own perspective.
**conservation** Understanding that specific properties of objects (height, weight, volume, length) remain the same despite apparent changes in the shape or arrangement of those objects.
**period of concrete operations** The third period in Piaget's theory of cognitive development, during which children come to understand the conservation principle and other concepts, such as categorization.

**The Period of Concrete Operations** Piaget's third stage of cognitive development, the **period of concrete operations**, spans approximately ages 7 to 11 and involves children's developing understanding of the conservation principle and other concepts, such as categorization. Its end marks the transition from childhood to adolescence. This period is characterized by the emergence of the ability to perform logical analysis, by an increased ability to empathize with the feelings and attitudes of others, and by an understanding of more complex cause-and-effect relations.

The child becomes much more skilled at the use of symbolic thought. For example, even before the period of concrete operations, children can arrange a series of objects in order of size and can compare any two objects and say which is larger. However, if they are shown that stick A is larger than stick B and that stick B is larger than stick C, they cannot infer that stick A is larger than stick C. Children become capable of making such inferences during the early part of this period. At this stage, however, although they can reason with respect to concrete objects, such as sticks that they have seen,

**FIGURE 12•7** Various tests of conservation.

*(Adapted from* Of children, An introduction to child development, *4th ed. by Guy R. Lefrancois. © 1983, 1980 by Wadsworth, Inc. Reprinted by permission of Wadsworth Publishing Company, Belmont, California, 94002.)*

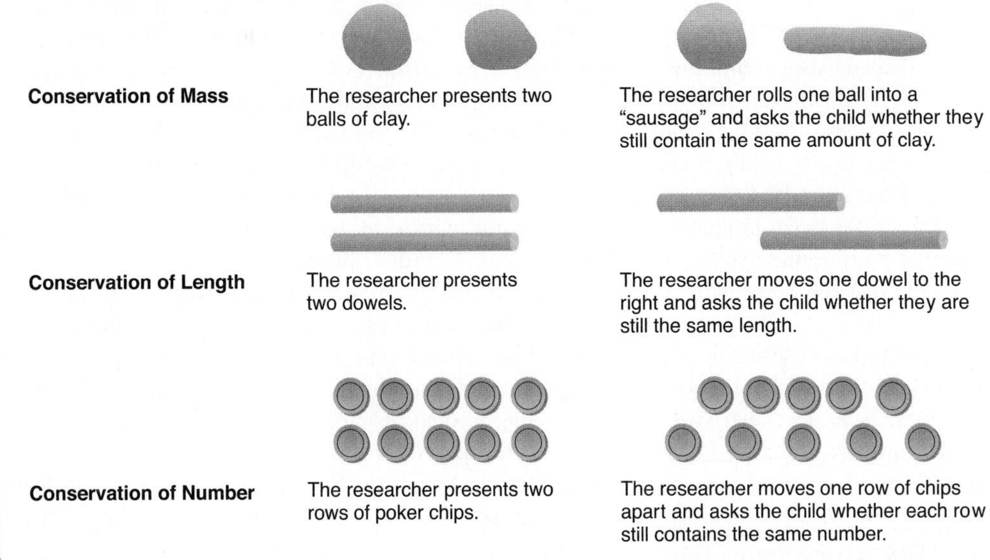


they cannot do so with hypothetical objects. For example, they cannot solve the following problem: "Judy is taller than Frank and Frank is taller than Carl. Who is taller, Judy or Carl?" The ability to solve such problems awaits the next period of cognitive development.

Conservation of Mass
The researcher presents two balls of clay.
The researcher rolls one ball into a "sausage" and asks the child whether they still contain the same amount of clay.
Conservation of Length
The researcher presents two dowels.
The researcher moves one dowel to the right and asks the child whether they are still the same length.
Conservation of Number
The researcher presents two rows of poker chips.
The researcher moves one row of chips apart and asks the child whether each row still contains the same number.

**The Period of Formal Operations** During the **period of formal operations**, which begins at about age 11, children first become capable of abstract reasoning. They can now think and reason about hypothetical objects and events. They also begin to understand that under different conditions, their behaviour can have different consequences. Formal operational thinking is not "culture free"—it is influenced by cultural variables, especially formal schooling (Piaget, 1972; Rogoff & Chavajay, 1995). Without exposure to the principles of scientific thinking, such as those taught in junior high school and high school science classes, people do not develop formal operational thinking.

According to Piaget, not all people pass through all four stages and reach the formal operational period, even as physically mature adults. In some cases, adults show formal operational thought only in their areas of expertise. Thus, a mechanic may be able to think abstractly while repairing an engine but not while solving math or physics problems. A physicist may be able to reason abstractly when solving physics problems but not while reading poetry. However, once an individual reaches that level of thinking, he or she will always, except in the case of brain disease or injury, perform intellectually at that level.

## Evaluation of Piaget's Contributions

Piaget's theory has had an enormously positive impact, stimulating interest and research in developmental psychology and educational psychology (e.g., Brainerd, 2003; Voyat, 1998). Not all of Piaget's conclusions have been accepted uncritically, however. One criticism levelled at Piaget is that he did not always define his terms operationally. Consequently, it is difficult for others to interpret the significance of his generalizations. Many of his studies lack the proper controls discussed in Chapter 2. Thus, much of his work was not experimental, which means that cause-and-effect relations among variables cannot be identified with certainty.

Research evidence suggests that a child's ability to understand conservation of various physical attributes occurs even

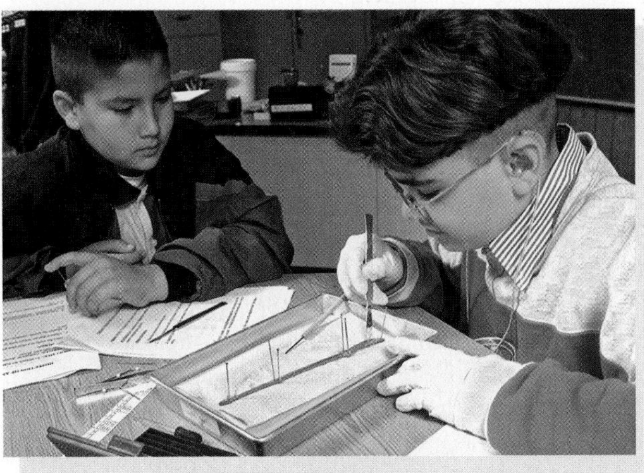

▲ *Formal operational thinking is influenced by cultural variables, especially formal schooling.*

**period of formal operations** The fourth period in Piaget's theory of cognitive development, during which individuals first become capable of more formal kinds of abstract thinking and hypothetical reasoning.

earlier than Piaget supposed. For example, Gelman (1972) found that when the appropriate task is used, even three-year-old children are able to demonstrate a grasp of conservation of number. Also, some children are able to anticipate conservation (for example, by predicting what will happen if a liquid is poured into a differently shaped glass) even if they fail the actual test (Caroff, 2002). Piaget also appears to have underestimated the ability of young children to understand another person's point of view. In other words, children are less egocentric at early ages than Piaget thought (Flavell, 1992). Children as young as two years old make inferences about other people's knowledge that require understanding what the others could or could not have seen happen (O'Neill, 1996).

Despite the fact that Piaget's method of observation led him to underestimate some important abilities, his meticulous observations of child behaviour have been extremely important to the field of child development and have had a great influence on educational practice.

## Vygotsky's Sociocultural Theory of Cognitive Development

Another important contributor to our understanding of cognitive development was the Russian psychologist Lev Vygotsky (1896–1934). Although Vygotsky's work was conducted during the 1920s and early 1930s, his writings continue to influence present-day conceptualizations of cognitive development during childhood (Kozulin & Falik, 1995).

Vygotsky agreed with Piaget that experience with the physical world is an important factor. However, he disagreed that this is the whole story. He argued that the culture in which a child lives also plays a significant role in the child's cognitive development (Vygotsky, 1934/1987). Vygotsky argued that children do not learn to think about the physical world in a vacuum. The cultural context—what they hear others say about the world and how they see others interact with physical aspects of the world—matters (Behrend, Rosengren, & Perlmutter, 1992; Thomas, 1996). Thus parents, teachers, friends, and many others help children acquire ideas about how the world works. We would expect, then, that the development of children raised in non-stimulating environments devoid of interesting interactions with other people, with books, and, yes, with television would lag behind that of children raised in more stimulating environments.

Vygotsky further believed that children's use of speech influences their cognitive development. Children up to about age seven often talk to themselves. When drawing in a colouring book, a child may say, "I'll colour her arms and face green and her pants black." Piaget would focus on such talk as reflecting egocentrism. Vygotsky's focus would be different. He would say that the child's talk reflects a cognitive developmental process—the child is developing a mental plan that will serve as a guide to subsequent behaviour. According to Vygotsky, language is the basis for cognitive development, including the ability to remember, solve problems, make decisions, and formulate plans.

After about age seven, children stop vocalizing their thoughts and instead carry on what Vygotsky labelled *inner speech*. Inner speech represents the internalization of words and the mental manipulation of them as symbols for objects in the environment. As children interact with their parents, teachers, and peers, they learn new words to represent new objects. Given Vygotsky's linking of language and thought, this increased facility with language would imply better cognitive skill as well.

These two themes of Vygotsky's theory—the interconnection between thought and language, and the importance of society and culture—led him to propose a developmental distinction important to educational psychologists. The skills and problem-solving abilities that a child can show on his or her own indicate the level of development that the child has mastered. Vygotsky called this the **actual developmental level.** For Piaget, this level would represent the limit of the child's cognitive skill. However, Vygotsky argued that a patient parent or a skilled mentor could assist a child to achieve a potentially higher level. Perhaps you've had the experience of studying for a test and being stumped by a particular kind of problem. That would, loosely, define your actual developmental level. But now suppose that a teacher shows you a method for solving the problem that not only makes perfect sense to you but also helps you solve similar problems. Vygotsky called that increased capacity for problem solving resulting from guided help the **zone of proximal development.** Indeed, as the "expertise" of the people they interact with increases, so do the children's cognitive skills. For example, Rogoff and her colleagues have shown that children become better problem solvers if they practise solving problems with their parents or with more experienced children than if they practise the problems alone or with children of similar cognitive ability (e.g., Rogoff, 1990).

**actual developmental level** In Vygotsky's theory, the stage of cognitive development reached by a child, as demonstrated by the child's ability to solve problems on his or her own.

**zone of proximal development** In Vygotsky's theory, the increased potential for problem solving and conceptual ability that exists for a child if expert mentoring and guidance are available.

## Applying Information Processing Models to Cognitive Development

As our knowledge about human memory has expanded since the time of Piaget and Vygotsky, developmental psychologists have examined how an information processing perspective on human sensation, perception, and memory might fit within an account of human development. One approach is to consider how processes of memory might change during development, and what effects these changes might have. Another approach has looked not at the processes of cognition per se, but rather at the knowledge base that children have at different ages. Presumably, if we knew how a child understood the world, we would be able to know how he or she would encode, store, and retrieve the semantic information required to adjust to it.

**Memory** Can infants remember? Piaget's observations on the concept of object permanence seemed to indicate that infants younger than six months do not encode objects; therefore, they cannot remember them. Rovee-Collier and her colleagues, however, have challenged this conclusion using a variation of the mobile task I described at the start of this section (e.g., Rovee-Collier, 1999). Infants from two to six months of age were shown a mobile that they could move by means of a ribbon attached to one of their legs. After varying amounts of time they would be shown the mobile again, but with the ribbon disconnected. If the infant kicked at a rate higher than normal, Rovee-Collier would conclude that that infant recognized the mobile on the second presentation. Infants 6 to 18 months of age were tested in a similar way using a mechanical switch to operate a toy train.

Rovee-Collier proved not only that memory is present in infants, but also that the retention span increases systematically over the 2- to 18-month period of life (Rovee-Collier, 1999). **Figure 12•8** shows data from both the mobile and train test situations; the maximum delay over which the infants show retention is plotted against their age. Using a similar procedure, Rovee-Collier and her colleagues have shown that retrieval cues increase retrieval in infants—and that infants apparently demonstrate an implicit/explicit differentiation similar to that discussed in Chapter 8.

**FIGURE 12•8** Retention of memory of the sight of an infant mobile or a toy train by infants 2 to 18 months of age. Blue circles depict data from infants tested with a mobile that they could move by leg motions. Orange circles depict data from infants trained with the toy train. Six-month-old infants were tested with both the mobile and the train.

*(From Rovee-Collier, C. (1999). The development of infant memory.* Current Directions in Psychological Science, 8, *80–85. © 1978 American Psychological Society.)*

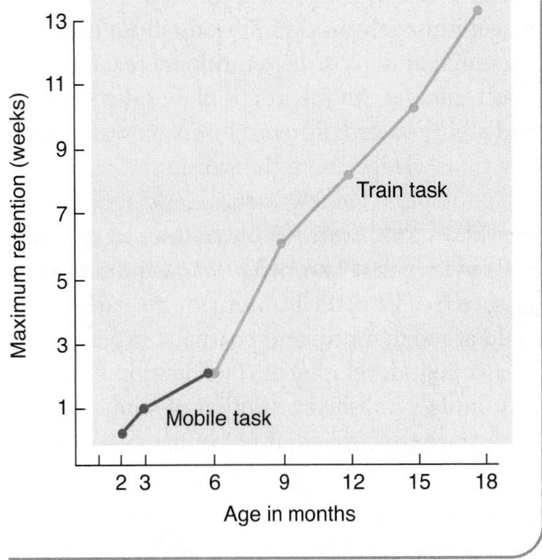


**The M-Space Model** Case (1998) suggested that cognitive development is a matter of a child's becoming more efficient in using mental strategies. The heart of Case's model is **mental space (M-space)**—a hypothetical construct, similar to short-term or working memory, whose chief function is the processing of information from the external world. M-space expands, or a child's information processing capacity increases, as a result of a combination of three variables.

First, as the brain matures, so does its capacity to process greater amounts of information. Maturation of the brain, specifically the increasing number of networks of neural connections and increasing myelinization of neurons, also enhances more efficient processing of information. Second, as children become more practised at using schemata, less demand is placed on cognitive resources, which can now be devoted to other, more complex cognitive tasks. For example, when children first learn to ride a bicycle, they must focus entirely on keeping their balance and steering the bike in a straight line. However, once they have acquired these skills, they no longer have to devote so much attention to steering the bike and not falling off. Now they can look around, talk to other bike riders, and so on. Third, schemata for different objects and events become integrated so that children now think in novel ways about these objects and events. The net result of such integration is the acquisition of central conceptual structures—networks of schemata that allow children to understand the relationships among the objects and events represented by schemata. As increasingly complex central conceptual structures are formed, children advance to higher levels of cognitive development, as represented in Piaget's stages. Each of the milestones in Piaget's theory, such as deferred imitation and conservation, requires increasing amounts of M-space.

The M-space model essentially rephrases Piaget's theory of cognitive development in information processing terms. The purpose of the model has not been to discredit Piaget's theory. On the contrary, one important function of the model, and others like it, has been to reinterpret the theory in the language of modern cognitive psychology.

**mental space (M-space)** A hypothetical construct in Case's model of cognitive development, similar to working memory, whose primary function is to process information from the external world.

## Then and Now

### Detecting the Strange

Psychologists who study early cognitive development face the obvious difficulty that infants and young children have limited behaviours and language. For example, the object permanence task depicted in Figure 12.5 depends on the infant's searching in the adult's hand, and then reacting to the object's absence. Even an investigator as gifted in observation as Jean Piaget must rely on assumptions about the infant's ability to search and his or her emotional reaction to finding the object missing. An infant's or child's dexterity, motivation, and ability to verbalize put limits on our capacity to detect early knowledge about the world.

Because psychologists had few ways to "ask" infants about what they know, they were unable to test fully the assumption of empiricism that knowledge was acquired only through experience (see Chapter 1). Many of the early behaviourists could argue that pre- and postnatal experience could shape subsequent development. The developmentalist Z. Y. Kuo, for example, published a number of studies in which he tried to trace the behaviour of young chicks to the movements induced by heartbeats while they were still in the egg (Kuo, 1932). If they could test human infants in the first few months of life, psychologists could evaluate the claims of empiricists in more detail.

Sometimes, a science such as psychology progresses because, as in the case of the human genome, technology advances and permits new observations. Other times, progress occurs because observations from one area of psychology inspire a new method of insight. In the case of the study of cognitive development, knowledge of habituation (see Chapter 7) has provided a new tool for the study of early cognition in human infants.

As we saw, habituation is a reduction in the response to a stimulus that occurs from repeated presentation. So, for example, we might habituate to the sound of the classroom clock when it "ticks" at each minute. However, if the ticks were suddenly to change to some other sound (such as a bell), we would probably dishabituate and look at the clock. Our sudden attention to the clock shows that we can perceive the difference between the tick sound and the bell sound. Dishabituation can reveal our ability to discriminate.

The logic of this argument was used by some developmental psychologists to examine questions of perception and memory in young infants, because it involved very simple behaviours; an infant shown a picture of a face that had changed would dishabituate by looking at the changed face for a longer time than previously. In the 1980s, this technique began to be applied to broader questions of cognition.

For example, Baillargeon, Spelke, and Wasserman (1985) applied this technique to the question of object permanence. We've seen that, before six months of age, children have an "out of sight, out of mind" approach to objects. As they enter the next six months of life, they explore objects, manipulate them, and see them from different angles. They also demonstrate the evidence of object permanence seen in Figure 12.5. Piaget interpreted these observations to mean that object permanence occurred later in this period. Baillargeon and her colleagues looked to see if it might occur sooner.

They reasoned that, even within the first six months of life, an infant would have seen many cases in which something solid hits another solid object. In the physical world, such collisions reflect the solidity of an object, since the first object doesn't pass through the second one. Watching a violation of that solidity principle would be dishabituating: We'd expect the child (or anyone) to stare at it. That was the premise of their experiment. Accordingly, they sat 5.5-month-old children in front of a display in which the children could watch a screen move, in drawbridge-like fashion, from being flat on the table, to being vertical, to being flipped over 180 degrees. The movement would then reverse. The top panel of **Figure 12•9** shows a schematic of what the infants saw.

Then the infants were shown the same scene, but with a yellow box right behind the screen. Again, the screen would swing up and start to flip over, but now it would collide with the box. At that point, through a visual trick with mirrors, Baillargeon and her colleagues arranged for one of two events to happen. In the "possible event," the screen would stop when it collided with the box and return to its original position (see the top panel of Figure 12.9). This is what one would expect of normal, solid objects and represents an experience that infants have presumably seen before. In the "impossible event," however, the screen would appear to continue to move through the object (which would now vanish) to the flipped position and then return, with the yellow box magically reappearing (see the bottom panel of Figure 12.9). Since permanent objects do not vanish like this, this event would be different from experience. The question was whether infants less than six months of age

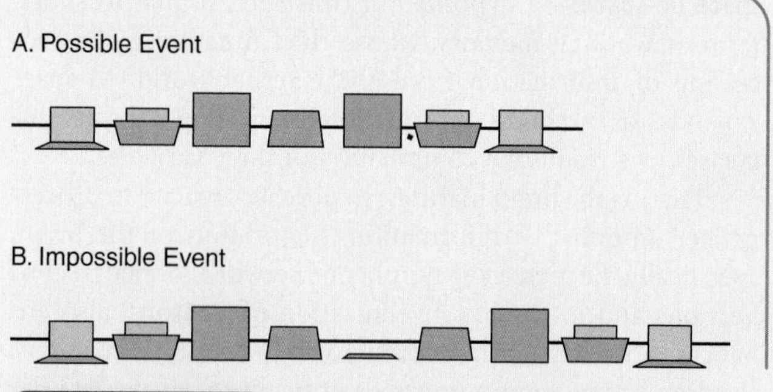


**FIGURE 12•9** The two types of events in the Baillargeon, Spelke, and Wasserman (1985) experiment.
*(Reprinted from* Cognition, *20(3), Baillargeon, R., Spelke, E. S., & Wasserman, S., Object permanence in five-month-old infants, 191–208, (1985) with permission from Elsevier. http://www.sciencedirect.com/science/journal/00100277)*

would discriminate this difference, showing a knowledge of object permanence.

They clearly did. An observer noted how long an infant would look at either the possible or impossible event; watching was longer in the latter case. That is, the infants expected the yellow box to be there, even when their view of it was blocked by the screen. Seeing the screen stop was also expected. However, having the yellow box vanish was not expected—even when it was occluded. As a result, the behaviour of looking dishabituated, and the infants stared at the scene. Notice, by the way, that this is a pretty strong test, because the impossible event is more similar to the training event. If the infants were responding only to the visual aspects of the display, and not to their knowledge of object permanence, they might have been expected to show dishabituation to the possible event.

This type of procedure is known as the "violation-of-expectation" test, and it has produced evidence that has proven to be very revealing about how infants develop knowledge of the physical world, especially those rules and laws that govern objects in that world. One very simple law is an optical one: When one object passes behind another, it is occluded, or blocked from view. But where there is a gap in the occluding object, the object should be visible. Luo and Baillargeon (2005) found that infants develop this knowledge piece by piece. They discovered this using the violation-of-expectation procedure.

To understand Luo and Baillargeon's experiment, think of an old-fashioned theatre stage with a main curtain across the front and side curtains on the left and right. If I were to wave at you, walk behind the left side curtain, and later emerge at the edge of the right side curtain, you would find nothing unusual about that sequence. But if the central curtain was raised and you saw me enter one side and exit the other without seeing me cross the open stage, you'd be pretty surprised, right? It would appear that I had teleported from behind the left curtain to the right curtain. When Luo and Baillargeon (2005) used a bit of stage magic to accomplish what I just described, infants of less than six months spent a lot of time looking at the scene.

However, this knowledge about occlusion is only partially present in infants. Luo and Baillargeon performed another test, similar to what the stage would be like if the central curtain were only half raised. Now, you would expect to see my legs as I walked across the stage. Infants 2.5 months of age, however, are not surprised if they fail to see this partial occlusion (although infants of three months are). Rather, the younger infants are surprised if they do see the partial occlusion. They seem to treat a partial gap as if it were no gap at all. Apparently, knowledge about optical occlusion develops incrementally, as infants acquire an understanding of the solidity and continuity of occluding objects.

The violation-of-expectation procedure has been a useful tool for the study of cognitive development, although there has been some criticism (e.g., Haith, 1998; see also Slaughter & Suddendorf, 2007, for an evaluation of a methodological issue). It has proven useful, however, in identifying aspects of visual experience that infants find unusual and in stimulating theoretical arguments as to why that might be so.

**Knowledge of Cognition** Another important area of growth, especially as the infant or child encounters social settings, is knowledge about others' beliefs or state of mind. For example, suppose you notice that your professor keeps a whiteboard marker in a drawer of the classroom podium. One day, you come to the classroom early, before your professor, and see someone from the class before yours reach into the drawer, pick up the marker, and leave with it. You would still expect your professor to look for the marker in the drawer. You recognize that your knowledge about the marker can be different from your professor's. You have developed expectations about how experiences relate to beliefs, something that developmental psychologists describe as **theory of mind.**

Four-year-olds seem capable of correctly inferring how events can shape the state of mind or beliefs of another. But three-year-olds do not: They use their own beliefs to predict the beliefs and actions of others. Developmental psychologists have observed this difference in a procedure sometimes called the "Sally-Anne" test (e.g., Baron-Cohen, Leslie, & Frith, 1985). A child is shown two dolls—Sally and Anne. The Sally doll is shown placing a marble in a basket within a dollhouse and then shown leaving the house. While she is away, the Anne doll takes the marble and places it in a box. The Sally doll returns to the house, and the child is asked: "Where will Sally look for her marble?" A three-year-old girl watching this drama would think that, since she knows where the marble is, another, such as Sally, would also know that. In other words, she has not differentiated her own beliefs from another's. By the following year, however, she will have developed a type of "naive psychology" by which she will recognize that other people's behaviours follow patterns based on their own beliefs (Kail, 2001; Slaughter & Repacholi, 2003).

The term *naive psychology* is not meant to imply anything negative. When a child develops a theory of mind, he or she acquires a sophisticated tool for predicting the actions of others. Think of your own ability to understand a friend's nuanced reaction to a forgotten birthday greeting and you'll recognize the significance of this developmental change. Indeed, it's been suggested that the lack of a theory of mind may underlie some severe developmental disorders, such as autism (Baron-Cohen, Leslie, & Frith, 1985).

**theory of mind** Expectations concerning how experience affects mental states, especially those of another.

## Interim Summary

### Cognitive Development in Infancy and Childhood

The first step in a child's cognitive development is learning that many events are contingent on his or her own behaviour. This understanding occurs gradually and is controlled by the development of the nervous system and by increasingly complex interactions with the environment.

Piaget hypothesized that a child's cognitive development is divided into four periods—a system that is widely, if not universally, accepted. The periods are determined by the joint influences of the child's experiences with the physical and social environment and the maturation of the child's nervous system. An infant's earliest cognitive abilities are closely tied to the external stimuli in the immediate environment; objects exist for the infant only when they are present. Gradually, infants learn that objects exist even when hidden. The development of object permanence leads to the ability to represent things symbolically, which is a prerequisite for the use of language. Next, the ability to perform logical analysis and to understand more complex cause-and-effect relations develops. Around the age of 11, a child develops more adult-like cognitive abilities—ones that may allow the child to solve difficult problems by means of abstract reasoning.

Critics point out that, in some cases, Piaget's tests of cognitive development underestimate children's abilities. For example, if tested appropriately, it is evident that children conserve various properties earlier than Piaget thought, and that their egocentrism is less pronounced than his tests indicated. Nevertheless, his conclusions continue to have a profound impact on the field of child development. Vygotsky's writings and the research they have stimulated have showed that the sociocultural context in which children are raised has a significant impact on their cognitive development. In particular, language appears to influence how children learn to think, solve problems, formulate plans, make decisions, and contemplate ideas.

Information processing accounts of cognitive development that focus, for example, on the memory of infants and children have been developed recently. One of these, Case's M-space model, argues that cognitive development proceeds according to expansion of mental space, or the brain's information processing capacity. M-space expands due to three causes: brain maturation, practice using schemata, and the integration of schemata for different objects and events. Such models essentially reinterpret Piaget's theory in the language of information processing. The violation-of-expectation procedure has demonstrated that object permanence can occur early in infancy. Other results from this procedure have helped describe how infants view the physical laws of the world around them. The Sally-Anne task has shown the stage at which they understand the psychological world by acquiring a theory of mind.

**QUESTIONS TO CONSIDER**

1. Earlier, in another Question to Consider, we asked you to design a home environment that would facilitate your child's motor and perceptual development. How might you also construct that environment to facilitate your child's cognitive development? What types of toys would you give your child and what kinds of personal interactions would you want to have with him or her?
2. Suppose that you want to develop a test to determine which of Piaget's periods of cognitive development a child is in. What kinds of activities would you include in such a test, and how would the child's behaviour with respect to those activities indicate his or her stage of development?

**attachment** A social and emotional bond between infant and caregiver that spans both time and space.

# Social Development in Infancy and Childhood

The first adults with whom infants interact are usually their parents. In most cases, one parent serves as the primary caregiver. As many studies have shown, a close relationship called *attachment* is extremely important for infants' social development. **Attachment** is a social and emotional bond between infant and caregiver that spans both time and space. It involves both the warm feelings that the parent and child have for each other and the comfort and support they provide for each other, which becomes especially important during times of fear or stress. This interaction must work both ways, with each participant fulfilling certain needs of the other. According to theorist John Bowlby (1907–1990), the innate capacity for the development of attachment is a part of the native endowment of many organisms (Bowlby, 1969, 1988). Bowlby and Mary Ainsworth have developed an approach that has succeeded in identifying many of the variables that influence attachment in humans (Ainsworth & Bowlby, 1991). We will look at what Bowlby, Ainsworth, and other researchers have learned about human attachment.

Be mindful that cultural variables strongly influence the development of attachment. Interactions between infant and parent produce different sorts of attachment behaviours that vary from culture to culture. For example, in an extensive comparison of cross-cultural attachment patterns, Harwood (Harwood, Miller, & Irizarry, 1995; Miller & Harwood, 2002) found that white American mothers want their children to be self-sustaining individuals and so emphasize independence, self-reliance, and self-confidence in their interactions with their children. In contrast, Puerto Rican mothers want their

▲ *Attachment is the cornerstone of an infant's social development and it has important implications for the parent's social behaviour as well.*

children to be polite and law-abiding persons and thus stress the importance of respect, courtesy, interdependence, and tact in interacting with their children.

## Behaviours of the Infant That Foster Attachment

What factors cause attachment to occur? Evidence suggests that human infants are innately able to produce special behaviours that shape and even control the behaviour of their caregivers. As Bowlby (1969) noted, the most important of these behaviours are sucking, cuddling, looking, smiling, and crying.

**Sucking** A baby must be able to suck in order to obtain milk. But not all sucking is related to nourishment. Piaget (1952) noted that infants often suck on objects even when they are not hungry. Non-nutritive sucking appears to be an innate behavioural tendency in infants that serves to inhibit a baby's distress. In modern societies, most mothers cover their breasts between feedings or feed with a bottle, so a baby's non-nutritive sucking must involve inanimate objects or the baby's own thumb.

**Cuddling** Infants of all species of primates have special reflexes that encourage front-to-front contact with their mothers. For example, a baby monkey clings to its mother shortly after birth. This clinging leaves the mother free to use her hands and feet. Human infants are carried by their parents and do not hold on by themselves. However, infants do adjust their posture to mould themselves to the contours of the parent's body. This cuddling response plays an important role in reinforcing the behaviour of the caregiver.

Harry Harlow (1974) conducted a series of experiments on infant monkeys and showed that clinging to a soft, cuddly form appears to be an innate response. Harlow and his colleagues isolated baby monkeys from their mothers immediately after birth and raised them alone in cages containing two mechanical surrogate mothers. One surrogate mother was made of bare wire mesh but contained a bottle that provided milk. The other surrogate mother was padded and covered with terry cloth but provided no nourishment.

The babies preferred to cling to the cuddly surrogate and went to the wire model only to eat. If they were frightened, they would rush to the cloth-covered model for comfort. These results suggest that close physical contact with a cuddly object is a biological need for a baby monkey, just as food and drink are. A baby monkey clings to and cuddles with its mother because the contact is innately reinforcing, not simply because she provides it with food.

Undoubtedly, physical contact with soft objects is also inherently reinforcing for human infants. The term *security blanket* suggests that these objects are comforting during times of distress. Indeed, children are most likely to ask for their special blankets or stuffed animals before going to bed, when they are ill, or when they are in an unfamiliar situation.

**Looking** For infants, looking serves as a signal to parents: Even a very young infant seeks eye-to-eye contact with his or her parents. If a parent does not respond when eye contact is made, the baby usually shows signs of distress. Tronick and colleagues (1978) observed face-to-face interactions between mothers and their infants. When the mothers approached their babies, they typically smiled and began talking in a gentle, high-pitched voice. In return, infants smiled and stretched their arms and legs. The mothers poked and gently jiggled their babies, making faces at them. The babies responded with facial expressions, wiggles, and noises of their own.

To determine whether the interaction was really two-sided, the researchers had each mother approach her baby while keeping her face expressionless or mask-like. At first, the infant made the usual greetings, but when the mother did not respond, the infant turned away. (See **Figure 12•10.**) From time to time, the infant looked at her again, giving a brief smile, but again turned away when the mother continued to stare without changing her expression. These interactions were recorded on videotape and were scored by raters who did not know the purpose of the experiment, so the results were not biased by the researchers' expectations.

Every mother found it difficult to resist her baby's invitation to interact. In fact, some of the mothers broke down and smiled back. Most of the mothers who managed to hold out (for three minutes) later apologized to their babies, saying something like, "I am real again. It's all right. You can trust me again. Come back to me" (Tronick et al., 1978, p. 10). This study clearly shows that the looking behaviour of an infant is an invitation for the mother to respond.

**Smiling** By the time an infant is five weeks old, visual stimuli begin to dominate as elicitors for smiling. A face (especially a moving one) is a more reliable elicitor of a baby's smile than a voice is; even a moving mask will cause an infant

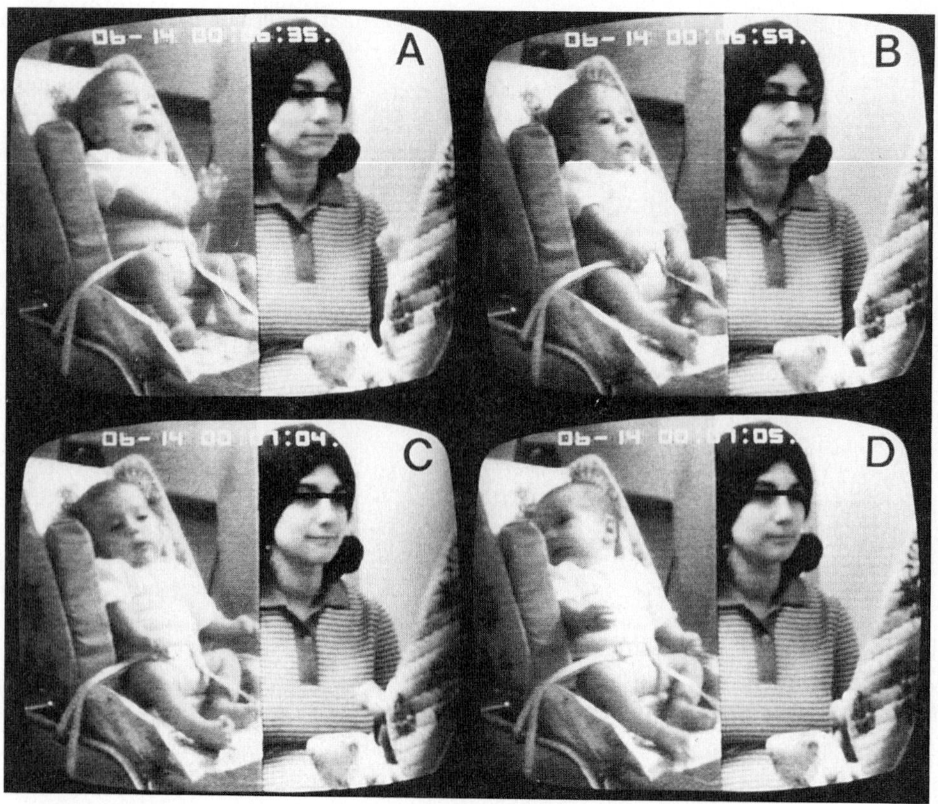


FIGURE 12•10
Reaction of an infant to its mother's expressionless face. Although each panel shows mother and infant side by side, they actually faced each other. The infant greets the mother with a smile and, getting no response, eventually turns away from her.

*(From Tronick, E., Als, H., Adamson, L., Wise, S., & Brazelton, T. B. (1978). The infant's response to entrapment between contradictory messages in face-to-face interaction.* Journal of the American Academy of Child Psychiatry, 17, *1–13. © 1978 American Academy of Child Psychiatry.)*

to smile. At approximately three months of age, specific faces—those of people to whom the infant has become attached—will elicit smiles. Furthermore, newborns and infants will often repeat the facial movements of another, suggesting the presence of an early mechanism for imitation (Lepage & Théoret, 2007). The significance of these observations should be obvious. An infant's smile is very rewarding. Almost every parent reports that parenting becomes a real joy when the baby starts to smile as the parent approaches—the infant is now a "person."

**Crying** For almost any adult, the sound of an infant's crying is intensely distressing or irritating. For a baby, the event that most effectively terminates crying is being picked up and cuddled, although unless the baby is fed and made more comfortable, he or she will soon begin crying again. Because picking up the baby stops the crying, the parent learns through negative reinforcement (see Chapter 7) to pick up the infant when he or she cries. Thus, crying serves as a useful means for a cold, hungry, colicky, or wet child to obtain assistance.

Individual differences in how caregivers perceive distress in an infant's crying is an important quality that determines adult reactions and is influenced by context and expectations. Wood and Gustafson (2001), for example, found that adults responded more quickly to infant cries that they personally interpreted as communicating distress; they somewhat inhibited their response to the same cries if they believed the infant needed sleep.

Although an infant's behavioural repertoire is limited, it is apparent that a complex process is at work. At a very early age, perhaps through innate mechanisms, infants perform behaviours that their adult caregivers find reinforcing. The baby, in other words, is partially teaching the parent. From the baby's perspective, what is the object of this? Evolutionary psychologists would respond that the baby is teaching the parent to behave in ways that enhance the baby's chances of surviving and eventually reproducing.

**stranger anxiety** The wariness and fearful responses, such as crying and clinging to their caregivers, that infants exhibit in the presence of strangers.

## The Nature and Quality of Attachment

For an infant, the world can be a frightening place. The presence of a primary caregiver provides a baby with considerable reassurance when he or she first becomes able to explore the environment. Although the unfamiliar environment produces fear, the caregiver provides a secure base that the infant can leave from time to time to see what the world is like. Let's look at two issues that develop as infants explore their world: stranger anxiety and separation anxiety, and reactions to strange situations.

**Stranger Anxiety and Separation Anxiety** Attachment partially reveals itself in two specific forms of infant behaviour: stranger anxiety and separation anxiety. **Stranger anxiety**, which usually appears in infants between the ages of 6 and 12 months, consists of wariness and sometimes fearful responses, such as crying and clinging to their caregivers, that infants exhibit in the presence of strangers. **Separation anxiety** is a set of fearful responses, such as crying, arousal, and clinging to the caregiver, that an infant exhibits when the caregiver attempts to leave the infant. It first appears in infants when they are about 6 months old and generally peaks at about 15 months—a finding consistent among many cultures (Kagan, Kearsley, & Zelazo, 1978). Like stranger anxiety, separation anxiety can occur under different conditions and with different degrees of intensity. For example, if an infant is used to being left in a certain environment, say a daycare centre, he or she may show little or no separation anxiety (Maccoby, 1980). The same holds true for situations in which the infant is left with a sibling or other familiar person (Bowlby, 1969). However, if the same infant is left in an unfamiliar setting with unfamiliar people, he or she is likely to show separation anxiety (Bowlby, 1982). Familiarity, then, at least for infants, breeds attachment.

**Ainsworth's Strange Situation** Ainsworth and her colleagues (Ainsworth, Blehar, Waters, & Wall, 1978) have developed a test of attachment called the **Strange Situation**. The Strange Situation consists of a series of eight episodes, during which the baby is exposed to various events that might cause some distress related to attachment and security. In different episodes, the researcher introduces the infant and its parent to an unfamiliar playroom and then leaves, the parent leaves and later is reunited with the infant, or a stranger enters the playroom with or without the parent present. The Strange Situation is based on the idea that if the attachment process has been successful, an infant should use his or her mother as a secure base from which to explore an unfamiliar environment. The episodes permit the observation of separation anxiety, stranger anxiety, and the baby's reactions to comforting by both the parent and the stranger.

The use of the Strange Situation led Ainsworth and her colleagues to identify three patterns of attachment; a fourth was identified later by Main and Solomon (1990).

- **Secure attachment** is the ideal pattern: The infants show a distinct preference for their caregiver over the stranger. Infants may cry when their caregiver leaves, but they stop crying and seek contact when she returns. The majority of babies form a secure attachment. Babies may also form three types of insecure attachments.
- Babies with **resistant attachment** show tension in their relations with their caregiver. Infants stay close to their caregiver before the caregiver leaves but show both approach and avoidance behaviours when the caregiver returns. Infants continue to cry for a while after their caregiver returns and may even push them away.
- Infants with **avoidant attachment** generally do not cry when they are left alone, and they tend to react to strangers much as they react to their caregiver. When their caregiver returns, these infants are likely to avoid or ignore her. They tend not to cling and cuddle when they are picked up.
- Babies with **disoriented attachment** have low quality attachment and appear to be the most troubled. They react to their caregiver in confused and contradictory ways. They may stop crying when held, but they may show no emotion on their faces, turn their heads away from their caregiver, or become rigid. A common way of describing the emotional tone of such infants is that they appear dazed.

Although infants' personalities certainly affect the nature of their interactions with their caregivers and hence the nature of their attachment, mothers' behaviour appears to be the most important factor in establishing a secure or insecure attachment (Ainsworth, Blehar, Waters, & Wall, 1978; Pederson, Gleason, Moran, & Bento, 1998; Pederson & Moran, 1996). Mothers of securely attached infants tend to be those who respond promptly to their crying and who are adept at handling them and responding to their needs (Moran et al., 2008). The babies apparently learn that their mothers can be trusted to react sensitively and appropriately. Mothers who do not modulate their responses according to their infants' own behaviour—who appear insensitive to their infants' changing needs—are most likely to foster avoidant attachment. Mothers who are impatient with their infants and who seem more interested in their own activities than in interacting with their offspring tend to foster resistant attachment. There is some evidence that mothers who interfere with their infants' behaviours, but without sensitivity to their infants' needs, and who exhibit fearful and disoriented responses are likely to foster disoriented attachment (Carlson, 1998; Madigan, Moran, & Pederson, 2006). Of course, mothers are not the only people who can form close attachments with infants; so do fathers (see Parke, 2000) and other adults who interact with them.

In our culture, secure attachment would seem to be more adaptive in terms of getting along with both peers and adults than would insecure attachment. It is becoming

**separation anxiety** A set of fearful responses, such as crying, arousal, and clinging to the caregiver, that the infant exhibits when the caregiver attempts to leave the infant.

**Strange Situation** A test of attachment in which an infant is exposed to different stimuli that may cause distress.

**secure attachment** A kind of attachment in which infants use their caregivers as a base for exploring a new environment. They will venture out from their caregivers to explore a Strange Situation but return periodically.

**resistant attachment** A kind of attachment in which infants show mixed reactions to their caregivers. They may approach their caregivers upon their return but at the same time continue to cry or even push their caregivers away.

**avoidant attachment** A kind of attachment in which infants avoid or ignore their caregivers and often do not cuddle when held.

**disoriented attachment** A kind of attachment in which infants behave in confused and contradictory ways toward their caregivers.

▲ *Notwithstanding the importance of attachment, high-quality daycare can benefit social development.*

increasingly clear that attachment plays an influential role in social relationships, including those found in adolescence and adulthood, such as romantic love (Feeney & Noller, 1991). Among women, insecure attachment seems to be correlated with clinical depression and difficulties in coping with stress (Barnas, Pollina, & Cummings, 1991).

**Effects of Child Daycare** This recognition of the importance of attachment inevitably leads to the question of whether child daycare has deleterious effects on a child's development. In recent decades, many families have entrusted their infants to daycare because both parents work. In 2005, 69 percent of Canadian families with dependent children reported that both parents worked (Marshall, 2006). Thus, because so many infants spend many of their waking hours away from their families, the question of the effects of daycare is not simply academic.

Without question, the quality of care provided in a daycare setting is critical (Zaslow, 1991). High-quality daycare either produces no impairment of attachment or actually benefits social development (Broberg, Wessels, Lamb, & Hwang, 1997; Field, 1994; National Institute of Child Health and Human Development, 1997), although it is difficult to generalize this conclusion across the full range of daycare programs available, because the latter issue is measured by correlational methods (NICHD Early Child Care Research Network, 2003). Nevertheless, high-quality daycare is expensive, and there are not enough subsidized spaces available for all of the families that need them. Worldwide, the daycare available to low-income families is generally of lower quality than that available to middle- or upper-income families. Regrettably, the infants who receive the poorest daycare tend to be members of unstable households, often headed by single mothers. Thus, they are at risk of receiving a double dose of less-than-optimal care.

## Approaches to Child Rearing

Our consideration of social development has emphasized the way in which the child and the parents affect each other. A family, in other words, is a type of system in which the members have interacting roles. The parents provide the support for the child's attachment. However, the child also controls much of the parent's behaviour through reactions that are intrinsically reinforcing. It is a developmental partnership.

As Vygotsky recognized, the child–parent partnership works best when the parent provides scaffolding for the child's development. Scaffolding is the matching of the mentor's efforts to the child's developmental level. For example, when teaching a child the motor skills of riding a bicycle, a mother might run alongside the child, taking her hands off the bicycle during straight segments, but helping her child to steer. As she becomes more confident in her child's ability to steer, she can reduce this help. When well practised, scaffolding is generally the most effective form of parent–child instruction or mentoring (Meadows, 1996).

Social adjustment is a type of skill, and it is interesting to consider what type of child-rearing practices best support its development. The notion of scaffolding implies that certain approaches to parenting will work best in the child–parent partnership. What might those approaches be?

Parents seem to adopt one of four approaches when raising their children: authoritarian, permissive, authoritative, or indifferent (Baumrind, 1983, 1991). Authoritarian parents establish firm rules and expect them to be obeyed without question. Disobedience is met with punishment. Permissive parents adopt the opposite strategy: They impose few rules and do little to influence their children's behaviour. Authoritative parents also establish rules and enforce them, but not merely through punishment. Instead, they seek to explain the relationship between the rules and punishment. Authoritative parents also allow for exceptions to the rules. They set rules not as absolute or inflexible laws, but rather as general behavioural guidelines. Indifferent parents exhibit a lack of interest in their children's behaviour, to the point of possible neglect.

Not surprisingly, authoritarian parents tend to have children who are more unhappy and distrustful than are children of permissive or authoritative parents. You might imagine that children of permissive parents would be the most likely to be self-reliant and curious. Not so. In fact, they appear to be the least self-reliant and curious, probably because they never received parental encouragement and guidance for developing these sorts of behaviours. Rather, they are left on their own without the benefit of learning directly from an adult's experience and without the guidance needed to learn self-control. Authoritative parents bring up their children in an environment in which individuality and personal responsibility are encouraged, and so they tend to rear children who are self-controlled, independent, and socially competent. Psychologically, then, one important element in raising happy and independent children is an open line of communication between parent and child. As you might expect, children of indifferent parents tend to be the least competent (Baumrind, 1991).

Cultural differences also seem to play a role in child rearing, as Vygotsky suggested. Mejia-Arauz, Rogoff, Dexter, and Najafi (2007) studied how children living in the United States from three cultural backgrounds would perform a task when they had to work together. Children from Mexican families with mothers who had received limited schooling were compared with children of Mexican families with mothers who had extensive, European-influnced schooling and with children of European descent whose mothers had extensive schooling. The task was to follow instructions for origami.

Children from Mexican families with mothers who had received limited schooling not strongly influenced by U.S. or European influences were more likely to work on the task together than were the other two groups. The American children of European heritage in particular were more likely to work individually or in pairs. They were also more likely to chat more while interacting than to interact non-verbally (which was the common form of interaction among the Mexican children). The results seem to confirm studies showing that certain cultures (even children from those cultures)—such as those in Mexico—are more likely to show evidence of collaboration on a shared task.

## Interim Summary

### Social Development in Infancy and Childhood

Because babies are totally dependent on their parents, the development of attachment between parent and infant is crucial to the infant's survival. A baby has the innate ability to shape and reinforce the behaviour of the parent. To a large extent, the baby is the parent's teacher. In turn, parents reinforce the baby's behaviour, which facilitates the development of a durable attachment between them.

Some of the behaviours that babies possess innately are sucking, cuddling, looking, smiling, and crying. These behaviours promote parental responses and are instrumental in satisfying physiological needs.

Normally, infants are afraid of novel stimuli, but the presence of their caregivers provides a secure base from which they can explore new environments. Ainsworth's Strange Situation allows a researcher to determine the nature of the attachment between infant and caregiver. By using this test, several investigators have identified some of the variables—some involving infants and some involving mothers—that influence attachment. Fathers, as well as mothers, can form close attachments with infants. Excellent child care by outsiders will not harm a child's social development, but less-than-excellent child care, especially if it begins in the child's first year of life, can adversely affect attachment.

A caregiver's style of parenting can have strong effects on the social development of children and adolescents. Authoritative parents, compared to authoritarian and permissive parents, tend to rear competent, self-reliant, and independent children.

#### QUESTION TO CONSIDER

1. We know that attachment occurs in humans and other primates. Do you think it occurs in other species, especially other mammalian species, as well? What kind of evidence would you need to collect to say that it does? Could you develop a test like Harlow's for researching attachment in other species? Develop your answer with a specific species in mind—for example, cats or dogs.

# Development of Gender Roles

Physical development as a male or a female is only one aspect of sexual development (Bostwick & Martin, 2007). Social development is also important. **Gender identity** is one's private sense of being a male or a female and consists primarily of the acceptance of membership in a particular group of people: males or females. Acceptance of this membership does not necessarily indicate acceptance of the gender roles or gender stereotypes that may accompany it. For example, a dedicated feminist may fight to change the role of women in her society but still clearly identify herself as a woman. **Gender roles** are cultural expectations about the ways in which men and women should think and behave. Closely related to them are **gender stereotypes**, beliefs about differences in the behaviours, abilities, and personality traits of males and females. Society's gender stereotypes have an important influence on the behaviour of its members. In fact, many people unconsciously develop their gender identity and gender roles based on gender stereotypes they learned as children. This section considers the role of gender stereotypes in influencing the nature and development of gender roles.

Berk (2005) notes that by age three many children perceive themselves as being a boy or a girl. At that same age, boys and girls (though girls more than boys) have a fairly good grasp of gender roles and stereotypes (e.g., O'Brien et al., 2000). Later, in the process of learning what it means to be boys or girls, children associate some attitudes, abilities, and behaviours with one gender or the other (e.g., Jacklin & Maccoby, 1983). For example, Meelissen and Drent (2008) found that, in a sample of Dutch elementary school children, most boys felt that boys, in general, know more about computers than girls. About a third of the girls felt the same way.

Where do children learn gender stereotypes? Although a child's peer group and teachers are important, parents play an especially important role in the development of gender

**gender identity** One's private sense of being male or female.
**gender role** Cultural expectations about the ways in which men and women should think and behave.
**gender stereotypes** Beliefs about differences in the behaviours, abilities, and personality traits of males and females.

stereotypes (Deaux, 1999). In the study of attitudes about computers, the encouragement of their parents to use computers was a strong influence on both boys and girls. However, boys perceived that their parents encouraged them more (Meelissen & Drent, 2008).

## The Nature of Gender Differences

The origin and nature of gender differences continues to be a controversial topic in psychology (Eagly & Wood, 1999; Shibley Hyde & Plant, 1995; Wood & Eagly, 2002). A well-known case, that of D. R., a boy born in Winnipeg, illustrates how complex the issue is (Colapinto, 2000).

D. R. was born as the elder of two identical twin boys. At eight months old, he underwent what should have been a routine circumcision to correct a urinary problem. Tragically, the surgery went wrong and D. R.'s penis was destroyed. He would not be able to live as a normal boy.

In an effort to come to grips with this accident, D. R.'s parents sought medical and psychological advice on how best to raise their son. In the end, they accepted the rather controversial advice that D. R.'s sex should be reassigned by removing his testes and raising him as a girl. This program of surgical and psychological therapy had been performed on intersex individuals (those with sexual characteristics that are not phenotypically male or female), but its use on an unambiguous boy was experimental.

For 14 years, D. R.'s parents tried to raise him as a girl. The physicians and therapists who had recommended this protocol were able to compare D. R.'s development to that of his twin brother. Many of their reports were interpreted as showing that D. R.'s upbringing had successfully acculturated him to be, psychologically, a girl.

The reality, apparently, was quite different. As a child, D. R. was not told of what had been done to him, but he remembers never feeling comfortable as a girl. He was teased in school, and reacted strongly with physical aggression. Although he wore feminine clothing to please his mother, he never felt comfortable in it. When asked by his therapists to envision his future, he imagined himself as an adult male. He prided himself on being able to dominate his twin brother, and adopted the role of the protector. As well, throughout his childhood, he preferred to urinate while standing up.

D. R.'s childhood and early adolescence were marked by his steadfast resistance to act out the gender role of a girl. Faced with his obvious unhappiness, his parents told him the truth when he was 14. The news actually came as a relief to D. R., since he had been dreading the demands that puberty would bring; he decided immediately to revert to the sex of his birth. In subsequent years, he became popular, as a young man, with peers of both sexes. Within 10 years, D. R. married and became a stepfather with three children. Like many of us, though, he struggled with other challenges in life.

Part of the controversy over gender differences stems from the way in which differences between males and females are measured and the apparent magnitude of those differences, and part of it stems from the sociopolitical implications of the differences (for example, sexism). Berk (2005) reviewed the research on gender differences and concluded that the most reliable differences are the following: Girls show earlier verbal development, more effective expression and interpretation of emotional cues, and a higher tendency to comply with adults and peers. Boys show stronger spatial abilities, more aggression, and greater tendency toward risk taking. Boys are also more likely to show developmental problems such as language disorders, behaviour problems, or physical impairments.

These differences are unlikely to be wholly biologically determined. In fact, socialization undoubtedly has a strong influence. Gender differences for many psychological characteristics are small. For example, after reviewing scores obtained from the Wechsler Intelligence Scales and the California Achievement Tests between 1949 and 1985, Feingold (1993) concluded that cognitive gender differences were small or non-existent in children and small in adolescents. Deaux (1985) reports that, on average, only 5 percent of the variability in individual differences among children can be attributed to gender; the other 95 percent is due to individual genetic and environmental factors. Therefore, gender, by itself, is not a very good predictor of a person's talents, personality, or behaviour.

## The Causes of Gender Role Differences

Children readily learn gender stereotypes and adopt the roles deemed appropriate for their gender. Two causes—biology and culture—may be responsible for this acceptance.

**Biological Causes** A likely site of biologically determined gender differences is the brain. Studies using laboratory animals have shown that the exposure of a developing brain to male sex hormones has long-term effects. The hormones alter the development of the brain and produce changes in the animals' behaviour, even in adulthood (Bostwick & Martin, 2007; Carlson, 2005). In addition, the human brain shows some structural gender differences, which are probably also caused by exposure to different patterns of hormones during development (Kolb & Stewart, 1995), although the precise effects of these differences on the behaviour of males and females are not well understood at present. As well, investigations using fMRI techniques show neural activation differences between men and women during navigation in a virtual maze; men show greater activation of the left hippocampus, and women show greater involvement of right hemispheric structures (Grön et al., 2000).

Gender differences in two types of cognitive ability—verbal ability and spatial ability—may be at least partly caused by differences in the brain. Girls tend to learn to speak and to read sooner than boys, and boys tend to be better at tasks requiring spatial perception. Kimura (1999) suggests possible reasons for these sex differences. When the

▲ *Many people acquire their gender identities and gender roles as a result of the gender stereotypes they learn as children.*

human brain was evolving into its present form, our ancestors were hunter-gatherers, and men and women probably had different roles. Women, due to restrictions on their movements imposed by child-bearing, were more likely to work near the home, performing fine manual skills with small, nearby objects. Men were more likely to range farther from home, engaging in activities that involved coordination of body movements with respect to distant objects, such as throwing rocks or spears or launching darts toward animals. In addition, men had to be able to keep track of where they were so they could return home after following animals for long distances.

If Kimura's (1999) reasoning is correct, it is easy to see why, on average, men's spatial abilities are better than those of women. But why do girls learn to speak and read sooner than boys? Many researchers believe that our ancestors used hand gestures long before verbal communication developed. Kimura suggests that fine motor control and speech production are closely related—that the neural circuits that control the muscles we use for speech may be closely related to those we use to move our hands. Presumably, then, women would be better at both.

Buss (1995) argues that other differences in the adaptive problems that men and women have faced in the course of evolution have also led to gender differences. As we learned in Chapter 3, chief among these adaptive problems are issues tied to reproduction. For women, these problems include identifying and attracting a mate who is willing to invest his resources (time, energy, property, food, and so on) in her and her children. For men, these problems include identifying and attracting a fertile mate who is willing to copulate with him. Buss argues that over the course of evolution, men and women have come to differ because the problems posed by reproduction and child rearing require different strategies for their successful resolution.

Kimura's and Buss's accounts are based on evolutionary arguments that can be tested only indirectly. However, they provide a good example of the biological approach—in particular, the functional, evolutionary approach—to an understanding of human behaviour.

**Cultural Causes** Although evolutionary forces may have laid the groundwork for gender differences in brain mechanisms associated with verbal ability and spatial ability, practice at and training in tasks involving these abilities can improve people's performance at them (Hoyenga & Hoyenga, 1993). In fact, most psychologists believe that socialization plays the most significant role in the establishment of gender role differences. First adults and then peers teach, by direct instruction and by example, what is expected of boys and girls. These expectations are deeply ingrained in our culture and unconsciously affect our perceptions and our behaviour.

The effect of gender on an adult's *perception* of infants is clear and has been confirmed in many studies. What about differences in the behaviours directed toward boys and girls? The strongest difference in the way parents socialize their sons and daughters appears to be their encouragement of gender-typed play and the choice of "gender-appropriate" toys. Many parents encourage their boys to play with trucks, blocks, and other toys that can be manipulated and encourage their girls to play with dolls. However, a cross-cultural review of 172 studies conducted in North America, Australia, and Western Europe concluded that parents do not consistently treat their sons and daughters differently in any other important ways (Lytton & Romney, 1991).

Although parents do encourage "sex-appropriate" play, there is evidence that biological factors may play an initial role in children's preferences. Although fathers are less likely to give dolls to one-year-old boys than to one-year-old girls, the boys who do receive the dolls are less likely to play with them (Snow, Jacklin, & Maccoby, 1983). Perhaps, as Lytton and Romney (1991) suggest, adults' expectations and encouragement build on children's preferences, producing an amplifying effect. Then, because boys' toys provide more opportunity for developing motor skills, visuo-spatial skills, and inventiveness, and girls' toys provide more opportunity for nurturance and social exchange, some important differences in gender roles may become established.

Once children begin to play with other children outside the home, peers have a significant influence on the development of their gender roles. In fact, Stern and Karraker (1989) found that the behaviour of two- to six-year-old children was even more influenced by the knowledge of a baby's gender than was the behaviour of adults. By the time children are three years old, they reinforce gender-typed play by praising, imitating, or joining in the behaviour. In contrast, they criticize gender-inappropriate behaviour (Langlois & Downs, 1980).

Of course, all of the research I have cited in this section describes *tendencies* of parents and children to act in a particular way. Some parents make a deliberate attempt to encourage their children's interest in both "masculine" and "feminine" activities, with the hope that doing so will help keep all opportunities for achievement and self-expression open to them, regardless of their gender.

## Interim Summary

### Development of Gender Roles

Children's gender roles tend to conform to their society's gender stereotypes. Very few real differences exist between the sexes, and those that do are relatively small. Females tend to show earlier verbal development, are better at expressing emotion and interpreting emotional cues, and show more compliance with adults and peers. Males tend to have better spatial abilities, are more aggressive, and tend to take more risks.

Some of these differences may have biological roots. Kimura suggests that the different tasks performed by our ancestors shaped brain development and favoured men with better spatial skills and women with better communication skills. Buss argues that problems related to reproduction and child rearing have caused gender differences in how these problems are solved. However, most gender differences in abilities and behaviours are small, and socialization undoubtedly plays a significant part in gender role differences.

Research has shown that both parents and peers tend to encourage children to behave in sex-appropriate ways—especially with regard to play activities and toys. However, scientific studies have revealed few other reliable differences in the ways parents treat young boys versus young girls.

**QUESTIONS TO CONSIDER**

1. Can you imagine an alternative course of human evolution in which gender roles would have developed along different lines? What events in the course of human evolution could have happened (but did not, of course) that would have changed the nature of gender roles as we know them today?
2. Imagine that you were born the opposite gender—instead of being a male, you are a female, or vice versa. In what significant ways would your life be different? For example, in what important ways would your social, emotional, and intellectual experiences be different? (Be careful not to base your answer on stereotypes you have of the other gender.)

# Moral Development

The word *morality* comes from a Latin word that means "custom." Moral behaviour is behaviour that conforms to a generally accepted set of rules. With very few exceptions, by the time a person reaches adulthood, he or she has accepted a set of rules about personal and social behaviour. These rules vary in different cultures and may take the form of codified laws or informally accepted taboos (Chasdi, 1994). Let us begin by considering the way a child acquires a concept of morality. The pioneer in this field, as in cognitive development, was Jean Piaget.

## Piaget's Theory of Moral Development

According to Piaget, the first stage of moral development (ages 5 to 10 years) is **moral realism**, which is characterized by egocentrism, or "self-centredness," and blind adherence to rules. Egocentric children can evaluate events only in terms of their personal consequences. The behaviour of children at this stage is not guided by the effects it might have on someone else, because young children are not capable of imagining themselves in the other person's place. Thus, in Piaget's view, young children do not consider whether an act is right or wrong but only whether it is likely to have good or bad consequences for them personally. Punishment is a bad consequence, and the fear of punishment is the only real moral force at this age. A young child also believes that rules come from parents (or other authority figures, such as older children or God) and that rules cannot be changed.

**moral realism** The first stage of Piaget's model of moral development, which includes egocentrism and blind adherence to rules.

**TABLE 12•3 Levels and Stages of Kohlberg's Theory of Moral Development**

| Level and Stage | Highlights |
|---|---|
| ***Preconventional Level*** | |
| Stage 1: Morality of punishment and obedience | Avoidance of punishment |
| Stage 2: Morality of naive instrumental hedonism | Egocentric perspective; weighing of potential risks and benefits |
| ***Conventional Level*** | |
| Stage 3: Morality of maintaining good relations | Morality based on approval from others |
| Stage 4: Morality of maintaining social order | Rules and laws define morality |
| ***Postconventional Level*** | |
| Stage 5: Morality of social contracts | Obey societal rules for the common good, although individual rights sometimes outweigh laws |
| Stage 6: Morality of universal ethical principles | Societal laws and rules based on ethical values |
| Stage 7: Morality of cosmic orientation | Adoption of values that transcend societal norms |

As children mature, however, two changes occur. First, older children judge an act by the intentions of the actor as well as by the consequences of the act—unlike young children, who consider only an act's objective outcomes, not the subjective intent that lay behind the act. For example, Piaget told children two stories, one about John, who accidentally broke 15 cups, and another about Henry, who broke one cup while trying to do something that was forbidden to him. When young children were asked which of the two boys was the naughtiest, they said that John was, because he broke 15 cups. They did not take into account the fact that the act was entirely accidental, as more mature individuals would.

Second, as children mature cognitively, they become less egocentric. Their lack of egocentrism makes them more capable of empathy. Children who are no longer egocentric (older than age seven) can imagine how another person feels. This shift away from egocentrism means that children's behaviour may be guided not merely by the effects their actions have on the children themselves but also by the effects they have on others. At around 10 years of age, children enter Piaget's second stage of moral development, **morality of co-operation**. During this stage, rules become more flexible; the child is more empathic but also understands that many rules (such as those that govern games) are social conventions that may be altered by mutual consent.

## Kohlberg's Theory of Moral Development

Piaget's description of moral development has been considerably elaborated on by Lawrence Kohlberg (1927–1987). Kohlberg studied boys between 10 and 17 years of age, and he studied the same boys over the course of several years. He presented the children with stories involving moral dilemmas. For example, one story described a man called Heinz whose wife was dying of a cancer that could only be treated by a medication discovered by a druggist living in the same town. The man could not afford the price demanded by the druggist, so the distraught man broke into the druggist's store and stole enough of the drug to save his wife's life. The boys were asked what Heinz should have done and why he should have done it. On the basis of his research, Kohlberg decided that moral development consisted of three levels and seven stages. (See **Table 12•3**.) These stages are closely linked to children's cognitive development as outlined by Piaget.

Although Kohlberg's theory is a stage theory like Piaget's, it is less tied to specific ages. Moral development involves a sequence, so that early stages are more characteristic of children and later stages tend to characterize adults. However, what is important is the progression of stages rather than any particular age at which a stage might appear. Kohlberg's first two stages belong to the **preconventional level**, during which morality is externally defined. During stage 1, *morality of punishment and obedience*, children blindly obey authority and avoid punishment. When asked to decide what Heinz should do, children at this stage base their decisions on fears about Heinz's being punished for letting his wife die or for committing a crime. During stage 2, *morality of naive instrumental hedonism*, children make moral choices egocentrically, guided by the pleasantness or unpleasantness of the consequences of a behaviour. Heinz's dilemma is reduced to a weighing of the probable risks and benefits of stealing the drug.

The next two stages belong to the **conventional level**, which includes an understanding that the social system has an interest in people's behaviour. During stage 3, *morality of maintaining good relations*, children want to be regarded by

**morality of co-operation** The second stage of Piaget's model of moral development, which involves the recognition of rules as social conventions.

**preconventional level** Kohlberg's first level of moral development, which bases moral behaviour on external sanctions, such as authority and punishment.

**conventional level** Kohlberg's second level of moral development, in which people realize that society has instituted moral rules to maintain order and to serve the best interests of its citizenry.

people who know them as good and well behaved. Moral decisions are based on perceived social pressure. Either Heinz should steal the drug because people would otherwise regard him as heartless, or he should not steal it because they would regard him as a criminal. During stage 4, *morality of maintaining social order*, laws and moral rules are perceived as instruments used to maintain social order and, as such, must be obeyed. Thus, both protecting a life and respecting people's property are seen as rules that help maintain social order.

Kohlberg also described a final level of moral development, the **postconventional level**, during which people realize that moral rules have some underlying principles that apply to all situations and societies. During stage 5, *morality of social contracts*, people recognize that rules are social contracts, that not all authority figures are infallible, and that individual rights can sometimes take precedence over laws. During stage 6, *morality of universal ethical principles*, people perceive rules and laws as being justified by abstract ethical values, such as the value of human life and the value of dignity. In stage 7, *morality of cosmic orientation*, people adopt values that transcend societal norms as they grapple with issues such as "Why be moral at all?" This stage represents the zenith of moral development. As Kohlberg noted, only a very few people—perhaps the prophets of major religions—ever reach stage 7. In fact, Kohlberg believed that not all people reach the postconventional level of moral development.

## Evaluation of Piaget's and Kohlberg's Theories of Moral Development

Piaget's and Kohlberg's theories have greatly influenced research on moral development, but they have received some criticism. For example, Piaget's research indicated that children in the first stage (moral realism) respond to the magnitude of a transgression rather than to the intent behind it. But even adults respond to the magnitude of a transgression, and rightly so. The theft of a few postage stamps by an office worker is not treated in the same way as the embezzlement of thousands of dollars.

Kohlberg's conclusions have also been challenged. For example, Carpendale (2000) points out that it is not uncommon for people to perform at less than their highest level of achieved moral reasoning, although Kohlberg believed that people would use lower than achieved levels only under extreme conditions that undermined higher levels of moral reasoning. Many researchers agree with Rest (1979), who concluded that Kohlberg's "stages" are not coherent entities but do describe a progression in the ability of children to consider more and more complex reasons for moral rules.

**postconventional level** Kohlberg's third and final level of moral development, in which people come to understand that moral rules include principles that apply across all situations and societies.

## Interim Summary

### Moral Development

Piaget suggested that moral development consists of two principal stages: moral realism, characterized by egocentrism and blind adherence to rules, and morality of co-operation, characterized by empathy and a realization that behaviour is judged by the effects it has on others. Kohlberg suggested that moral development consists of three levels, further divided into stages. During the preconventional level, morality is based on the personal consequences of an act. During the conventional level, morality is based on the need to be well regarded and on sharing a common interest in social order. During the postconventional level, which is achieved by only a few people, morality becomes an abstract, philosophical virtue.

Critics of Piaget and Kohlberg point out that the stages of moral development are not necessarily fixed. Aspects of one stage can appear at another. Subtle changes in the way that moral dilemmas are posed can produce very different answers.

### QUESTION TO CONSIDER

1. Laticia's parents are going away for the weekend and ask her to go with them. Laticia, who is 15 years old, says that she can't go because she has a special soccer practice on Saturday. Disappointed, her parents accept her answer; they agree to let her stay home, because they know how important soccer is to her. Later, after they return, they learn that Laticia lied to them about the practice. When they confront her, she tells them that she knows she lied to them but that she did it so as not to hurt their feelings—she really did not want to go away with them for the weekend. Laticia's parents say that they understand her dilemma but feel they must punish her regardless for breaking an important family rule. How do you suppose that Piaget and Kohlberg would explain Laticia's level of morality? How would they explain her parents' level of morality?

# Adolescence

After childhood comes adolescence, the threshold to adulthood. (In Latin, *adolescere* means "to grow up.") The transition between childhood and adulthood is as much social as it is biological. In some societies, people are considered to be adults as soon as they are sexually mature, at which time they may assume adult rights and responsibilities, including marriage. In most industrialized societies, where formal education often continues into the late teens and early twenties, adulthood officially comes several years later. The end of adolescence is difficult to judge because the line between adolescence and young adulthood is fuzzy: There are no distinct physical changes that mark this transition.

## Physical Development

**Puberty** (from the Latin *puber*, meaning "adult"), the period during which people's reproductive systems mature, marks the beginning of the transition from childhood to adulthood. Many physical changes occur during this stage: People reach their ultimate height, develop increased muscle size and body hair, and become capable of reproduction. There is also a change in social roles. As a child, a person is dependent on parents, teachers, and other adults. As an adolescent, he or she is expected to assume more responsibility. Relations with peers also suddenly change; members of one's own sex become potential rivals for the attention of members of the other sex.

**Sexual Maturation** The internal sex organs and genitalia do not change much for several years after birth, but they begin to develop again at puberty. When boys and girls reach about 11 to 14 years of age, their testes or ovaries secrete hormones that begin the process of sexual maturation. This activity of the gonads is initiated by the hypothalamus, the part of the brain to which the pituitary gland is attached. The hypothalamus instructs the pituitary gland to secrete hormones that stimulate the gonads to secrete sex hormones. These sex hormones act on various organs of the body and initiate the changes that accompany sexual maturation.

The sex hormones secreted by the gonads cause growth and maturation of the external genitalia and of the gonads themselves. In addition, these hormones cause the maturation of ova and the production of sperm. All of these developments are considered primary sex characteristics, because they are essential to the ability to reproduce. The sex hormones also stimulate the development of secondary sex characteristics, the physical changes that distinguish males from females. Before puberty, boys and girls look much the same—except, perhaps, for their hairstyles and clothing. At puberty, young men's testes begin to secrete testosterone; this hormone causes their muscles to develop, their facial hair to grow, and their voices to deepen. Young women's ovaries secrete estradiol, the most important estrogen, or female sex hormone. Estradiol causes women's breasts to grow and their pelvises to widen, and it produces changes in the layer of fat beneath the skin and in the texture of the skin itself.

Development of the adult secondary sex characteristics takes several years, and not all characteristics develop at the same time. The process begins in girls at around age 11. The first visible change is the accumulation of fatty tissue around the nipples, followed shortly by the growth of pubic hair. The spurt of growth in height commences, and the uterus and vagina begin to enlarge. The first menstrual period begins at around age 12, just about the time the rate of growth in height begins to decline. In boys, sexual maturation begins slightly later. The first visible event is the growth of the testes and scrotum, followed by the appearance of pubic hair. A few months later, the penis begins to grow, and the spurt of growth in height starts. The larynx grows larger, which causes the voice to become lower. Sexual maturity—the ability to father a child—occurs at around age 15. The growth of facial hair usually occurs later; often a full beard does not grow until the late teens or early twenties.

In industrialized societies, the average age at the onset of puberty has been declining. For example, the average age at the onset of menstruation was between 14 and 15 years in 1900 but is between 11 and 13 years today. The most important reason for this decline is better childhood nutrition. It appears that this decline is levelling off in industrialized societies, but in many developing countries, the age of the onset of puberty is beginning to fall as these countries enjoy increasing prosperity.

**Behavioural Effects of Puberty** The changes that accompany sexual maturation have a profound effect on young people's behaviour and self-concept. They become more sensitive about their appearance. Many girls worry about their weight and the size of their breasts and hips. Many boys worry about their height, the size of their genitals, their muscular development, and the growth of their beards. In addition, most adolescents display a particular form of egocentrism that develops early in the transition into the stage of formal operations: *self-consciousness.* Some developmental psychologists believe that self-consciousness results from teenagers' difficulty in distinguishing their own self-perceptions from the views other people have of them, although the evidence for this is not conclusive (Vartanian, 2000).

Because the onset of puberty occurs at different times in different individuals, young adolescents can find themselves more or less mature than some of their friends, and this difference can have important social consequences. An early study by Jones and Bayley (1950) found that early-maturing boys tended also to become more socially mature and were most likely to be perceived as leaders by their peers. Late-maturing boys tended to become hostile and withdrawn and often engaged in negative attention-getting behaviour. Later studies have generally confirmed these findings (Brooks-Gunn, 1988; Peterson, 1985). The effect of age of maturity in girls is less clear. Some studies indicate that early-maturing girls may benefit from higher status and prestige, but they are also more likely to engage in norm-breaking behaviours such as stealing, cheating on exams, staying out late, and using alcohol (Brooks-Gunn, 1989). Brooks-Gunn suggests that the

**puberty** The period during which people's reproductive systems mature, marking the beginning of the transition from childhood to adulthood.

primary cause of the norm-breaking behaviours is the fact that early-maturing girls are more likely to become friends with older girls.

## Cognitive Development

Early in adolescence, an individual's brain begins a period of growth of structures in the frontal lobe (Sowell et al., 1999). As we saw in Chapter 4, the frontal lobe is associated with regions related to control and planning. These are also the areas that most distinguish *Homo sapiens* from other primates. So, in a way, the changes in the brain during adolescence are the changes that especially define us as human (Keating, 2004). What are these changes?

As Piaget saw it, adolescents' cognitive changes were based on the logical power of abstract reasoning. In late childhood, according to Piaget, a child entered the stage of formal operations. Adolescence, then, should be characterized as a sort of Sherlock Holmes phase in which adolescents apply deductive skills to problems. There is certainly evidence that this period of development is marked by increased facility with the tools of formal reasoning (Morris & Sloutsky, 2002). However, as we saw in Chapter 11, formal logic does not necessarily dominate adult thinking, let alone that of adolescents. We use heuristics, biases, and mental models in place of, or as supplements to, formal logic. The prevalence of these strategies for reasoning has led some investigators (e.g., Klaczynski, 2004) to suggest that there are two reasoning systems: an analytic processing system and an experiential processing system. The **analytic processing system** is the basis of deliberate, abstract, and higher-order reasoning. It provides the capacity to remove a problem from its context and to apply logical rules to solve it. The **experiential processing system**, on the other hand, is rapid, mostly unconscious, and heuristic. It provides the memories for particular solutions to problems and forms the basis for the biases and stereotypes that we may apply to problems.

Adolescence may be the time during which we not only develop our analytic abilities but also become good at knowing when they must be used. The two systems give us a large number of reasoning tools, which work in some cases but not in all. Thus, cognitive development during adolescence is marked by choice: The individual shows increased capacity to select consciously the mode of reasoning appropriate to the context (Keating, 2004).

## Social Development

During adolescence, a person's behaviour and social roles change dramatically. Adolescence is not simply a continuation of childhood; it marks a real transition from the dependency of childhood to the relative independence of adulthood. The social roles they exhibit begin to resemble the patterns of adults. Based on self-reports, the greater involvement of girls, as compared to boys, in domestic work within the home approaches the large difference between men and women (Hilbrecht, Zuzanek, & Mannell, 2008). Adolescence is also a period during which many people seek out new experiences and engage in reckless behaviour—behaviour that involves psychological, physical, and legal risks for them as well as for others (for example, having sexual relations and using illegal drugs) (Galambos & Tilton-Weaver, 1998; Smylie, Medaglia, & Maticka-Tyndale, 2006).

**Forming an Identity** Erik Erikson, a psychoanalyst who studied with Anna Freud, Sigmund Freud's daughter, developed a theory of psychosocial development that divides human development into eight stages. Erikson proposed that people encounter a series of crises or conflicts in their social relations with other people and that the way these conflicts are resolved determines the nature of development. In fact, according to Erikson, the resolution of these conflicts *is* development. If the conflict is resolved positively, the outcome is a happy one; if it is not resolved or is resolved negatively, the outcome is unhealthy and impairs development. Because the nature of people's social relations changes throughout life, their psychosocial development does not end when they become adults. **Table 12•4** lists Erikson's eight stages of development, the nature of the crises, and the possible consequences.

Erikson argued that the primary crisis faced by adolescents is identity versus role confusion. If they are able to develop plans for accomplishing career and personal goals and to decide which social groups they belong to, they have formed a personal identity. Failure to form an identity leaves a teenager confused about his or her role in life. You have probably heard the term *identity crisis*, as in "She's having an identity crisis." Erikson coined this phrase.

Erikson's concept of the identity crisis has been researched extensively by Marcia (1980, 1994; Bradley & Marcia, 1998), who has asserted that developing an identity consists of two components: crisis and commitment. A *crisis* is a period during which an adolescent struggles intellectually to resolve issues related to personal values and goals. For example, a teenager who questions his or her parents' religious and moral values is experiencing a crisis. *Commitment* is a decision based on consideration of alternative values and goals that leads to a specific course of action. For instance, a teenager who decides to go to a different church than his or her parents is said to make a commitment. In this case, he or she also is said to identify with the beliefs of that church.

Marcia hypothesized that adolescents experience different degrees of crisis and commitment. Some teenagers never experience crises, and others do but may never resolve them. Marcia developed four main possibilities, which he called

**analytic processing system** The basis of deliberate, abstract, and higher-order reasoning.
**experiential processing system** The basis of rapid, mostly unconscious, and heuristic reasoning.

**TABLE 12•4 Erikson's Eight Stages of Psychosocial Development**

| Period | Conflict | Outcome: Positive Resolution | Outcome: Negative Resolution |
|---|---|---|---|
| Childhood | Trust vs. mistrust<br>Autonomy vs. self-doubt<br>Initiative vs. guilt<br>Competence vs. inferiority | Trust, security, confidence, independence, curiosity, competence, industry | Insecurity, doubt, guilt, low self-esteem, sense of failure |
| Adolescence | Identity vs. role confusion | Strong sense of self-identity | Weak sense of self |
| Adulthood | Intimacy vs. isolation<br>Generativity vs. stagnation<br>Integrity vs. despair | Capacity to develop deep and meaningful relationships and care for others; consideration for future generations; personal sense of worth and satisfaction | Isolation, unhappiness, selfishness, stagnancy, sense of failure and regret |

*identity statuses.* (See **Figure 12•11**.) As shown in the figure, in Marcia's model, adolescents who experience a crisis, consider alternative solutions to it, and are committed to a course of action based on personal values are said to be identity achievers. Identity achievers are self-confident and have a high level of moral development (Dellas & Jernigan, 1990). Adolescents who experience a crisis but do not resolve it and therefore cannot become committed are said to be in *moratorium*. Teenagers who have not experienced a crisis but who are nonetheless committed to a course of action are said to be in *foreclosure*. Teenagers in foreclosure are typically adolescents who identify strongly with people such as their parents and never consider alternatives to those identities. They can be dogmatic in their views and feel threatened by others who challenge their identities (Frank, Pirsch, & Wright, 1990). Adolescents who do not experience a crisis and who do not become committed are said to experience *identity diffusion*. Because they have not considered alternative courses of action and made a decision, teenagers who are identity diffused, especially over a long period, tend to be immature and impulsive and to have a sense of hopelessness about the future (Archer & Waterman, 1990). Erikson would probably have considered these people identity-confused.

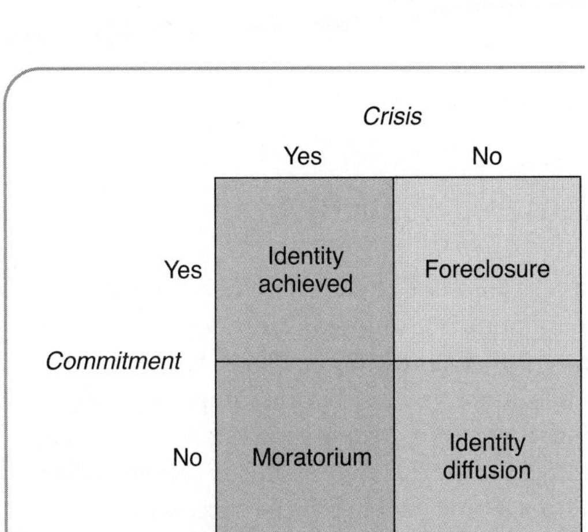

Marcia's research has shown that adolescents move in and out of the different statuses as they experience new situations and crises. A teenager does not necessarily move progressively from one status to another. For example, after thinking about whether to major in business or engineering, a university student may decide on engineering because she thinks that she will like the work and earn good money. In terms of this decision, she is an identity achiever. However, after taking several engineering courses, she may decide that she really doesn't like engineering after all. Now she must decide whether to keep her major or to change it. She is now no longer committed; she is in moratorium.

Marcia's research is interesting for two reasons. First, it shows that most adolescents do indeed experience crises in their search for an identity. Second, it shows that a teenager's psychological reaction to a crisis depends on the time at which he or she is dealing with the crisis. That there are four possible avenues that can be involved in achieving an identity testifies to the complexity of "finding oneself."

| Commitment \ Crisis | Yes | No |
|---|---|---|
| Yes | Identity achieved | Foreclosure |
| No | Moratorium | Identity diffusion |

**FIGURE 12•11** Marcia's four identity statuses. Different combinations of crises and commitment yield four different identity statuses.

## Identity and Self-Perception

The search for a personal identity brings with it changes in self-concept and self-esteem (Berk, 2005). During childhood, children tend to perceive themselves in terms of both physical traits, such as "I am a boy and have brown hair and blue eyes" and individual personality characteristics, such as "I am honest" or "I am smart" (Damon & Hart, 1992). During adolescence, teenagers become more focused on their social relationships and tend to perceive themselves more in terms of their interactions with others. They may use phrases such as "I am outgoing" or "I am trustworthy" to describe themselves. In late adolescence, teenagers begin to perceive themselves more in terms of the values that they hold. They may now describe themselves in terms of their political, social, or philosophical views, such as "I am a conservative" or "I am an environmentalist." As a teenager strives to develop an identity, earlier self-perceptions, including those held during childhood, are incorporated into his or her emerging self-concept. Newer self-perceptions do not merely replace older ones. Instead, the newer ones augment the older ones.

**Sexuality** Sexuality has become a very evident component of modern culture in most industrialized societies. Displays of sexual attractiveness play an important role in advertisements in magazines and on television; sexual activities are portrayed in books and films; personal sexual practices are discussed in print and during talk shows on radio and television. Sexuality was always a part of life (after all, our species has managed to propagate during all periods of history), but since the latter part of the twentieth century, it has become much more open and evident than it was previously. In Canada, slightly less than half of all males and females are sexually active by grade 11 (McKay, 2004).

**Friendships and Relations with Parents** As adolescents begin to define their new roles and to assert them, they almost inevitably come into conflict with their parents. However, research indicates that most of the differences between people of different generations are in style rather than in substance. Adolescents and their parents tend to have similar values and personal ideals (Zentner & Renaud, 2007). Unless serious problems occur, family conflicts tend to be provoked by relatively minor issues, such as messy rooms, loud music, clothes, curfews, and household chores. These problems tend to begin around the time of puberty; if puberty occurs particularly early or late, so does the conflict (Paikoff & Brooks-Gunn, 1991).

## Interim Summary

### Adolescence

Adolescence is the transitional stage between childhood and adulthood. Puberty is initiated by the hypothalamus, which causes the pituitary gland to secrete hormones that stimulate maturation of the reproductive system.

Puberty marks a significant transition, both physically and socially. Early maturity appears to be socially beneficial to boys, because early maturers are more likely to be perceived as leaders. The effects of early maturity in girls are mixed; although their advanced physical development may help them acquire some prestige, early-maturing girls are more likely to engage in norm-breaking behaviour.

Conflict may underlie cognitive development in adolescence. Just before adolescence, children develop the tools of logical reasoning. However, adult reasoning uses a variety of reasoning strategies, of which logic is just one. Adolescence may be a period of growth in our capacity to choose among these strategies.

A focal point in adolescent development is the formation of an identity. Both Erikson and Marcia argue that adolescents face identity crises, the outcome of which determines the nature and level of identity that teenagers will form. Marcia argues that forming an identity has two primary components: the crisis itself and the commitment or decision regarding a specific course of action after consideration of possible alternatives. The extent to which a teenager experiences a crisis and how he or she resolves it lead to identity achievement, moratorium, foreclosure, or identity diffusion. An adolescent's identity may also be influenced by social roles, such as females' greater tendency to desire to form close relationships with other, and later, by values.

Sexuality becomes important and many people engage in sexual intercourse in their teens. Although adolescence brings conflicts between parents and children, these conflicts tend to centre on relatively minor issues. Most adolescents hold the same values and attitudes concerning important issues as their parents do.

#### QUESTIONS TO CONSIDER

1. What important behavioural effects did you experience as a result of your own sexual maturation? In what ways did your social and emotional lives change? How does your experience compare to those of your friends who underwent puberty before or after you did?
2. It is often said (by adults) that adolescents act as if they are incapable of properly judging risk. Do you think this is true? Could this be related to the different types of identity resolutions discussed by Marcia?

# Adulthood and Old Age

It is much easier to outline child or adolescent development than adult development; children and adolescents change faster, and the changes are closely related to age. Adult development is much more variable because physical changes in adults are more gradual. Mental and emotional changes during adulthood are more closely related to individual experience than to age. Some people achieve success and satisfaction with their careers, while some hate their jobs. Some marry and have happy family lives, while others never adjust to the roles of spouse and parent. No single description of adult development will fit everyone.

## Physical Development

As we grow older, there is one set of changes that we can count on: physical ones. Our physical abilities peak at around age 30 and decline gradually thereafter. By maintaining a well-balanced diet, exercising regularly, and not smoking, drinking, or using drugs, we can, in large measure, help our bodies maintain some of their physical vigour even into old age. This is not to say that good diet and exercise habits can make a 70-year-old look and feel like a 25-year-old. But if we don't eat well and exercise regularly, we will have less physical energy and poorer muscle tone than if we do. And apparently, staying in shape as a younger adult pays off in one's later years. Older people who were physically fit as younger adults are generally in better health and feel better about themselves than those who were not physically fit (Perlmutter & Hall, 1992).

Unfortunately, though, prudent diets and exercising cannot reverse the physical changes that accompany aging. People in their later forties, fifties, and sixties often experience decreases in visual acuity and the ability to perceive depth, hearing, sensitivity to odours and flavours, reaction time, agility, physical mobility, and physical strength.

Muscular strength peaks during the late twenties or early thirties and then declines slowly thereafter as muscle tissue gradually deteriorates. By age 70, strength has declined by approximately 30 percent in both men and women (Young, Stokes, & Crowe, 1984). However, age has much less effect on *endurance* than on strength. Both laboratory tests and athletic records reveal that older people who remain physically fit show remarkably little decline in the ability to exercise for extended periods of time (Spirduso & MacRae, 1990).

Although it is easy to measure a decline in the sensory systems (such as vision or hearing), older people often show very little *functional* change in these systems. Most of them learn to make adjustments for their sensory losses, using additional cues to help them decode sensory information. For example, people with a hearing loss can learn to attend more carefully to other people's gestures and lip movements; they can also profitably use their experience to infer what is said.

Functional changes with age are also minimal in highly developed skills. For example, Salthouse (1984, 1988) found that experienced older typists continued to perform as well as younger ones, despite the fact that they performed less well on standard laboratory tests of sensory and motor skills, including the types of skills that one would expect to be important in typing. The continuous practice they received enabled them to develop strategies to compensate for their physical decline.

## Cognitive Development

Psychologists have studied the effects of education and experience on intellectual abilities and have questioned whether intelligence inevitably declines with age. Most of us can conceive of a future when we can no longer run as fast as we do now or perform well in a strenuous sport, but we do not like to think of being outperformed intellectually by younger people. In fact, research indicates that people can get old without losing their intellectual skills.

**Cognitive Development and Brain Disease** Before we discuss the normal effects of aging in a healthy individual, we should consider some changes caused by disease. As people get older, they have a greater risk of developing *dementia* (literally "an undoing of the mind")—a class of diseases characterized by the progressive loss of cortical tissue and a corresponding loss of mental functions. The most prevalent form of dementia is **Alzheimer's disease**. About 2 to 3 percent of Americans between the ages of 71 and 79 show diagnostic evidence of Alzheimer's disease; the prevalence increases rapidly with age, such that 30 percent of people 90 years of age or older show evidence of the disease (Plassman et al., 2007). Canadian rates, although measured over different age ranges, show a similar pattern (Chertkow, 2008). There appear to be three relatively distinct subgroups of Alzheimer's patients (Fisher, Rourke, & Bieliauskas, 1999). The disease may manifest itself through (1) global deficits, or may be most evident in functions identified with (2) the left hemisphere (deficits in word knowledge) or (3) the right hemisphere (deficits in the ability to copy geometric forms). In general, though, Alzheimer's disease is characterized by progressive loss of memory and other mental functions (Ashford, Schmitt, & Kumar, 1996). At first, the patient may have difficulty remembering appointments and sometimes fail to think of words or people's names. As time passes, he or she shows increasing confusion and increasing difficulty with tasks such as balancing a chequebook. In the early stages of the disease, memory deficit involves recent events; but as the disease progresses, even old memories are affected. If the person ventures outside alone during the advanced stages of the disease, he or she is likely to get lost. Eventually, the person becomes bedridden, becomes completely helpless, and, finally, dies (Khachaturian & Blass, 1992; Terry & Davies, 1980).

Geneticists have discovered an association between defects on chromosomes 14, 19, and 21, and at least one kind of Alzheimer's disease, which seems to reduce levels of the neurotransmitter acetylcholine (Cruts & Van Broeckhoven, 1996; Gottfries, 1985; Poduslo & Yin, 2001; Selkoe, 1989; Shellenberg, 1997). Alzheimer's disease produces severe degeneration of the hippocampus and cerebral cortex, especially the association cortex of the frontal and temporal lobes. **Figure 12•12** shows a computer-enhanced photograph of a slice through a normal brain (right) and the brain of a

**Alzheimer's disease** A fatal degenerative disease in which neurons of the brain progressively die, causing loss of memory and other cognitive processes.

**FIGURE 12•12** Alzheimer's disease. A computer-enhanced photograph of a slice through the brain of a person who died of Alzheimer's disease (left) and a normal brain (right). Note that the grooves (sulci and fissures) are especially wide in the Alzheimer's brain, indicating degeneration of the brain.

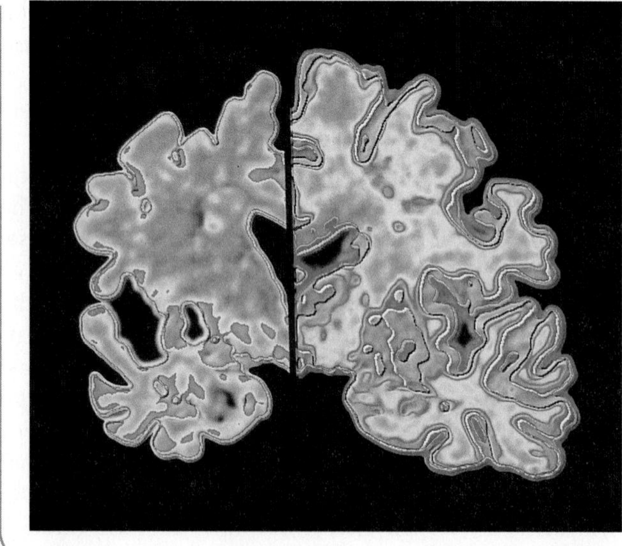

patient who died of Alzheimer's disease (left). You can see that much of the tissue of the Alzheimer's brain has been lost; the grooves in the brain (sulci and fissures) are much wider.

**Cognitive Development and Normal Aging** Aging affects different intellectual abilities to different degrees. Schaie (1990), describing the results of the Seattle Longitudinal Study of Aging, reports that, on average, people's scores on five tests of intellectual abilities showed an increase until their late thirties or early forties, then a period of stability until their mid-fifties or early sixties, followed by a gradual decline. **Figure 12•13** shows the participants who maintained stable levels of performance on each of the tests over a seven-year period. As you can see, the performance of most participants—even the oldest—remained stable, although there were some reductions. Subsequent results from the Seattle Longitudinal Study of Aging (Schaie, 1996) suggest that these declines are due to the way different intellectual abilities change with age. Some abilities, such as the ability to perform rapid numerical or perceptual tasks, decline markedly as age increases. Verbal ability, as measured by vocabulary, shows little change. Other abilities, such as verbal memory, show a moderate decline at advanced age.

Related research by Kirasic (1991) has shown that, at least for performance on spatial tasks, deficits in short-term memory may coincide with aging. For example, Kirasic and Bernicki (1990) showed young and older adults 66 slides of a walk through a real neighbourhood. Sometimes the slides were in the correct order; at other times, they were mixed up. All participants were then asked to make distance estimates between some of the scenes shown in the slides. Both younger and older participants performed equally well in estimating distances for the slides presented in logical order. But older participants performed less well than younger participants when the slides were scrambled. Kirasic and Bernicki concluded that information from the slides presented in normal order was encoded into short-term memory similarly for both sets of participants. However, the scrambled presentation of slides taxed available resources in the older participants' short-term memory, resulting in performance decline.

If memory shows wear with age, one might reasonably suspect that intelligence, too, would show a similar decline. This was once thought to be true based on results from cross-sectional studies (studies that compare different age groups on the same task). However, we now know that this is not the case,

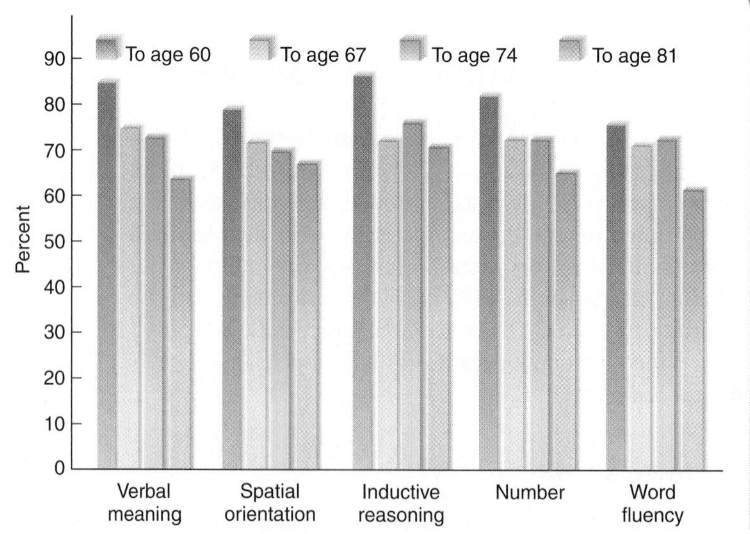


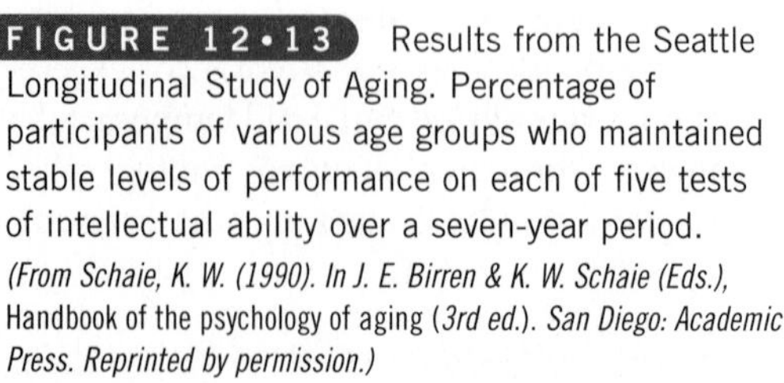

**FIGURE 12•13** Results from the Seattle Longitudinal Study of Aging. Percentage of participants of various age groups who maintained stable levels of performance on each of five tests of intellectual ability over a seven-year period. *(From Schaie, K. W. (1990). In J. E. Birren & K. W. Schaie (Eds.),* Handbook of the psychology of aging *(3rd ed.). San Diego: Academic Press. Reprinted by permission.)*

**FIGURE 12•14** A comparison of cross-sectional and longitudinal data concerning changes in verbal ability with age. In contrast to the cross-sectional data, the longitudinal data show that verbal ability increased gradually to about age 55 and then decreased gradually.

*(Based on Schaie, K. W., & Strother, C. R. (1968). A cross-sequential study of age changes in cognitive behaviour.* Psychological Bulletin, 70, *675.)*

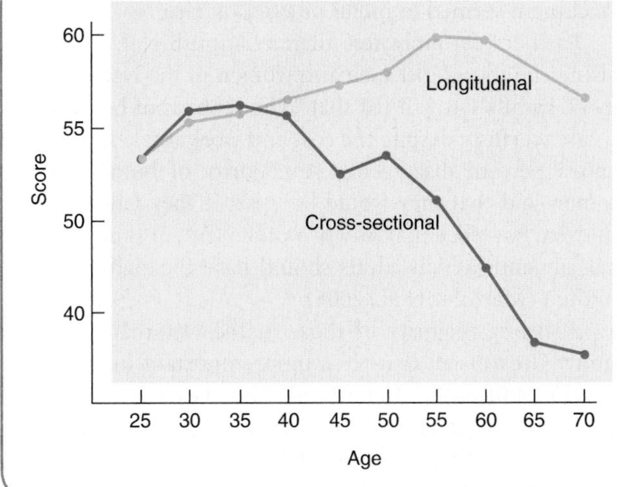


largely due to the work of Schaie and Strother (1968), who compared results from a cross-sectional approach with results from a longitudinal approach (a study in which a group of participants is followed over some period in order to identify developmental changes that occur over time). For example, look at **Figure 12•14**, which shows performance on a verbal abilities subsection of an intelligence test plotted as a function of age. (Here, verbal abilities means the ability to understand ideas represented by words.) The cross-sectional data show that intelligence scores decrease—and rather precipitously so—after age 50. The longitudinal data paint a different picture: Scores increase until about age 55 and then decline gradually.

▲ *Studies of aging must take into account the possibility that people of different ages were reared in different time periods and may have had different educational experiences.*

Why would different methods produce these different patterns of results? Cross-sectional studies do not take into account the fact that the people being tested were reared in different time periods. Thus, one explanation for these disparate results is that older people did not have the same educational and career opportunities as their younger counterparts taking the test might have had. The longitudinal method takes this possibility into consideration by testing the same people at regular intervals spanning many years. In doing so, it gives a more accurate picture of the relationship between age and intelligence.

Many investigators believe that intelligence can be divided into two broad categories. In general, older people in good health do well on tests of *crystallized intelligence*—abilities that depend on knowledge and experience, the "seat of the pants" learning that comes from everyday life. Vocabulary, the ability to see similarities between objects and situations, and general information are all aspects of crystallized intelligence. On the other hand, *fluid intelligence*—the capacity for abstract reasoning—appears to decline with age (Baltes & Schaie, 1974; Horn, 1982). The ability to solve puzzles, to memorize a series of arbitrary items such as unrelated words or letters, to classify figures into categories, and to change problem-solving strategies easily and flexibly are aspects of fluid intelligence.

The fact that older people excel in crystallized intelligence and younger people excel in fluid intelligence is reflected in the kinds of intellectual endeavours for which the two age groups seem to be best suited. For example, great mathematicians usually make their most important contributions during their twenties or early thirties; apparently, the ability to break out of the traditional ways of thinking and to conceive new strategies is crucial in such achievements. In contrast, great contributions to literature and philosophy, in which success depends heavily on knowledge and experience, tend to be made by older people. There is evidence, too, that mental activity pursued in the first two decades of life can increase cognitive functioning later (Fritsch et al., 2007).

## Social Development

Recall that Erikson believed that the adult years consist of three psychosocial stages: intimacy versus isolation, during which people succeed or fail in loving others; generativity versus stagnation, during which people either withdraw inwardly and focus on their problems or reach out to help others; and integrity versus despair, during which life is reviewed with either a sense of satisfaction or despair (see Table 12.4).

Adult development occurs against the backdrop of what many developmental psychologists consider to be the two most important aspects of life: love and work. For most of us, falling in love is more than just a compelling feeling of wanting to be with someone. It often brings with it major responsibilities, such as marriage and children. Work, too, is more than just a way to pass time. It involves setting and achieving goals related to income, status among peers, and accomplishments outside the family. For most adults, overall satisfaction with life reflects the degree to which they have been successful in marriage, raising a family, and achieving goals. With this in mind, let's look briefly at how love and work ebb and flow over the course of adult development.

**Marriage and Family** Most young people envision themselves falling in love and getting married. Fifty-one percent of women and 66 percent of men agreed with the statement "It is better to get married than to go through life being single" (Martinez et al., 2006). Whether or not men and women actually encounter that life, statistics indicate that one's path can take many turns. The most comprehensive description of marriage and family patterns is the National Survey of Family Growth, completed in 2002. Among women 15 to 44 years of age, 46 percent were currently married. Cohabitation with a male, however, was a common pattern reported by 43 percent of women—either before marriage or as an arrangement for women who had never married. Among surveyed women ages 15 to 44, 48 percent had had one husband or cohabiting male partner in their lifetime, while 27 percent had never married or cohabited (Chandra et al., 2005). Among men, 42 percent were currently in a marriage, while 49 percent had cohabited with a woman. In contrast to women, only 37 percent of men had had a marriage or cohabiting female partner during their lifetime (Martinez et al., 2006).

Romantic relationships, whether they lead to marriage or cohabitation, need not involve a member of the opposite sex. Roisman and colleagues (2008) have looked at the quality of the relationship between engaged, married, gay male, and lesbian couples. They found that positive views of their relationship were expressed similarly by married woman, married men, gay males, and lesbians. Relative to those in longer-term relationships, dating heterosexual couples and engaged women have more positive evaluations of their relationships. When individuals interacted with each other, committed couples—either opposite sex or same sex—were judged as having a higher quality of interaction than heterosexual dating couples. In other words, same-sex partnerships were indistinguishable from opposite-sex relationships in terms of perceived and actual quality.

What produces a positive relationship? Of course, romantic partners wrestle with that issue all the time. One intriguing hint may be found in the early experience we had with the romantic partners we observed in our childhood: our caregivers. Earlier, we discussed how different caregiver behaviours could result in secure or insecure attachment personalities. Simpson, Winterheld, Rholes, and Oriña (2007) examined how attachment issues—assessed in adulthood—could affect the kind of care one would want to receive from a romantic partner. They assessed the attachment state of men and women who were dating and classified them as exhibiting either secure or insecure attachment attitudes toward their childhood caregivers. They then looked to see how, as a couple, each partner would react to different kinds of support given by the other when they were discussing relationship problems. A person with secure attachment responded best when his or her romantic partner offered emotional support; in contrast, someone with insecure attachment seemed to prefer practical advice.

Partners certainly test their relationship if it involves raising children. Most men and women in the National Survey of Family Growth felt that "The rewards of being a parent are worth it, despite the cost and work it takes," with less than 5 percent disagreeing. A majority of both men and women said that they would be upset if they failed to have children. As well, a majority of women (but not men) agreed that gay and lesbian adults should have the right to adopt children (Martinez et al., 2006).

A strong majority of those in the National Survey of Family Growth felt that "It is more important for a man to spend a lot of time with his family than to be a success at his career" (Martinez et al., 2006). Of course, the care of young children is a difficult responsibility. But as children grow older and become more self-sufficient, the day-to-day burdens of raising a family lessen, and spouses are able to spend more time with each other. However, adolescents pose new problems for their parents: Teenage offspring may question parental authority, and their burgeoning social agendas may put a wrinkle in their parents' personal and social calendars. For many parents, rearing adolescents, particularly during the years just before young people leave home, represents the low point of marital happiness (Cavanaugh, 1990).

Generally speaking, once a family's youngest child has left home, marital happiness increases and continues to do so throughout the remainder of the couple's life together. It was once thought that the "empty nest" posed problems for the middle-aged couple, particularly the mother, who was thought to define her role solely around her children. Although parents may miss daily contact with their children, they also feel happy (not to mention relieved) that a major responsibility of life—raising self-reliant children who will become responsible members of society—has been completed successfully. Just as importantly, the parents now have time for each other and the freedom to pursue their own interests. It may be true that an empty nest is a happy nest. Research tends to support this statement. In one study, only 6 percent of empty-nest couples reported that life prior to their last child leaving home was better than their empty-nest experience. More than 50 percent of the couples interviewed said that their lives were better now than before their children had left home (Deutscher, 1968; Neugarten, 1974).

**Work** The task of raising a family is balanced with one or both parents having a career. In fact, events that occur in the workplace often affect the quality of home life. A promotion and a raise may mean that the family can now do things that they could not before—they can now pursue a new hobby or travel together. Working long hours to get that raise, however, can decrease the amount of time that a couple can spend together with their children.

With the dramatic increase in the number of women entering the workforce in the past 25 years, many psychologists have focused their research efforts on understanding *dual-earner marriages*—those in which both parents work full-time or part-time. In 2006, 52 percent of married-couple families had two wage earners (Bureau of Labor Statistics, May 9, 2007), making this an important area of future study.

**Death** Death is the final event of life. It is a biological and social event, as family and friends are emotionally affected by the death of a loved one. Although a death may claim a life at any time, most people die when they are old. One question that developmental psychologists have asked about death and dying among the elderly is, How do old people view the inevitability of their own deaths?

At one time or another, most of us contemplate our own deaths. Some of us may contemplate death more than others but, to be sure, the thought of death crosses our minds at least occasionally. As you might expect, elderly people contemplate their deaths more often than do younger people. Generally speaking, they fear death less than their younger counterparts do (Kalish, 1976). Why? No one knows for sure, but a tentative explanation may be that older people have had more time to review the past and to plan for the future knowing that death is close at hand. Thus, they are able to prepare themselves psychologically (and financially) for death.

Contemplating and preparing for death, though, is not like knowing that you are actually dying. The changes in attitudes that terminally ill people experience have been studied by Kübler-Ross (1969, 1981). After interviewing hundreds of dying people, she concluded that people undergo five distinct phases of coping psychologically with death. The first stage is *denial*. When terminally ill people learn of their condition, they generally try to deny it. *Anger* comes next: now they resent the certainty of death. In the third stage, *bargaining*, people attempt to negotiate their fate with God or others, pleading that their lives might be spared. While bargaining, they realize that they are, in fact, going to die. This leads to *depression*, the fourth stage, which is characterized by a sense of hopelessness and loss. The fifth and final stage, *acceptance*, is marked by a more peaceful resignation to the facts.

Kübler-Ross's work points to the psychological factors involved in dying and has provided an initial theory about how the dying come to grips with their fate. Her work, though, has not been accepted uncritically. Her research was not scientific: Her method of interviewing people was not systematic, and her results are largely anecdotal. Moreover, of the five stages, denial is the only one that appears to be universal. Apparently, not all terminally ill people have the same psychological response to the fact that they are dying.

However, despite its flaws, Kübler-Ross's work is important because it has prompted an awareness, both scientific and public, of the plight of the terminally ill. The scientific response, as you might guess, has been to do more medical research in the hope of prolonging the lives of people with cancer and other terminal illnesses. The public response has involved the attempt to provide support for the dying and their families through *hospice services* (Aiken, 2001). In the past, hospices were places where strangers and pilgrims could find rest and shelter. Today, hospices are special places that provide medical and psychological support for the dying and their families. Nationally, Health Canada has established a Secretariat on Palliative and End-of-Life Care. The Secretariat is charged with developing a national strategy for end-of-life care. This initiative was motivated in part by a Senate report that stated that the fundamental Canadian values of human worth and dignity create a right of every person to quality end-of-life care.

## Interim Summary

### Adulthood and Old Age

Up to the time of young adulthood, human development can reasonably be described as a series of stages: a regular sequence of changes that occur in most members of our species. However, development in adulthood is much more variable and few generalizations apply. Aging brings with it a gradual deterioration in people's sensory capacities and changes in physical appearance that many people regard as unattractive. The effects of these changes can be minimized by vigorous participation in life's activities.

Although older people are more likely than young people to develop dementia because of illnesses such as Alzheimer's disease, severe intellectual deterioration is not the normal outcome of aging. Rather than undergoing sudden intellectual deterioration, older people are more likely to exhibit gradual changes, especially in abilities that require flexibility and the learning of new behaviours. Intellectual abilities that depend heavily on crystallized intelligence—an accumulated body of knowledge—are much less likely to decline than are those based on fluid intelligence—the capacity for abstract reasoning.

Erikson has proposed that people encounter a series of crises that serve as turning points in development. Erikson's stages span the entire life cycle, from infancy to old age. Adult social development occurs within the context of love, marriage, family, and work. Marriages seem to be happiest just after the birth of children and after the children have left home. They appear to be unhappiest just before the children leave home, possibly due to the emotional and time demands that adolescents place on their parents. Many families have parents who both work, which helps ease the financial burdens of raising a family and long-term financial obligations. Although the woman who works gains respect outside the home, she is often faced with also having to manage most household responsibilities.

Older people have less fear of death than younger people have, perhaps because they have had more time to contemplate and prepare for it. Kübler-Ross's interviews with terminally ill people have revealed that many of them seem to experience a five-stage process in facing the reality that they are going to die. Although her research has been found to have some methodological flaws, it has drawn both scientific and public attention to the plight of the terminally ill and the necessity of properly caring for them.

**QUESTION TO CONSIDER**

1. Imagine that you are the director of a new community mental health program for adults. The focus of this program is on prevention: minimizing the negative effects of the aging process on adults who participate in the program. Your first task is to design a comprehensive plan to maximize adults' physical, social, emotional, and intellectual capacities. What activities would you include in such a plan? Why?

## EPILOGUE

### Life's Span

It may have occurred to you that the two individuals described in this chapter, J. F. and D. R., provide different perspectives on the topic of development. D. R.'s biological constitution dominated his rearing conditions. As much as can be determined, his family genuinely tried to raise him as a girl. Nevertheless, D. R. did not think of himself as a girl, and, when given the choice, decided to life his live as a man. Nature seems to have trumped nurture.

J. F.'s genetic history isn't known, and it is possible that the trouble she experienced with her foster family originated with a congenital disorder. However, her case is not that different from a large number of Romanian orphans, and the common factor in all of them is the neglect they suffered during their early institutionalization. Nurture (or, rather, lack of it) seems to have predominated in her case.

How can we make sense of these two disparate outcomes? The concept of a critical period may provide a clue. Charles A. Nelson of Harvard Medical School, who has studied the effect of institutional neglect on brain development (e.g., Nelson, 2007), suggests that early cognitive and social growth depend on genetic and environmental influences in two ways: There are experience-expectant mechanisms, and experience-dependent ones. The first responds to the kind of environment that should be common to all of us as members of our species. It includes nutrition, shelter, and parental care. Our genetic mechanisms rely on these features, since they have been reliably part of our evolutionary history. When they fail to occur, as they did for the children caught in the Ceauşescu regime, the normal sequences of development lack the necessary foundations. It would be like expecting an automobile to operate on the surface of the moon; its design

▲ *J. F., at the age of 18, with her adoptive parents.*

is based on assumptions that do not apply in the other environment.

Experience-dependent mechanisms provide the fine-tuning of development. If the expectancies of the environment are met, these mechanisms respond to the normal variation of rearing conditions. D. R.'s basic psychological needs were met by a concerned and loving family from birth—the surgical accident notwithstanding—and he does not seem to have exhibited the attachment deficits that many of the Romanian orphans suffer from. If his past had not been disclosed to him, he may well have been able to live as an adult female. However, his genetic background had prepared him for life as a male, and it seems likely that he would not have fit a conventional gender role in those circumstances. It seems clear that he would have had a much happier childhood if his nurturing had matched his nature.

Liane Faulder (2006), the reporter who described J. F.'s story, called it "one of the most emotionally difficult stories I have witnessed in my career." Anyone who reads her account would have to concur. Even as an adult, J. F. exhibits an emotional detachment that she herself finds hard to comprehend. Nevertheless, it is gratifying to end this story by saying that, when she was 18 and could make the decision as an adult, J. F. returned to live with her foster parents, who never stopped giving her the love she was denied as a baby.

## Canadian Connections to Research in This Chapter


Bradley, C. L., & Marcia, J. E. (1998). Generativity-stagnation: A five-category model. *Journal of Personality, 66,* 39–64. (Simon Fraser University: www.sfu.ca)

Carpendale, J. I. M. (2000). Kohlberg and Piaget on stages and moral reasoning. *Developmental Review, 20,* 181–205. (Simon Fraser University: www.sfu.ca)

Case, R. (1998). The development of conceptual structures. In W. Damon (Ed.), *Handbook of child psychology: Vol. 2. Cognition, perception, and language.* New York: Wiley. (Ontario Institute for Studies in Education: www.oise.utoronto.ca)

Chertkow, H. (2008). Diagnosis and treatment of dementia: Introduction—Introducing a series based on the Third Canadian Consensus Conference on the Diagnosis and Treatment of Dementia, *Canadian Medical Association Journal, 178,* 316–321. (McGill University: www.mcgill.ca)

Fisher, L., Ames, E., Chisholm, K., & Savoie, L. (1997). Problems reported by parents of Romanian orphans adopted to British Columbia. *International Journal of Behavioral Development, 20,* 67–82. (Simon Fraser University: www.sfu.ca)

Fisher, N. J., Rourke, B. P., & Bieliauskas, L. A. (1999). Neuropsychological subgroups of patients with Alzheimer's disease: An examination of the first 10 years of CERAD data. *Journal of Clinical and Experimental Neuropsychology, 21,* 488–518. (University of Toronto: www.utoronto.ca)

Professor Fisher received a President's New Researcher Award from the Canadian Psychological Association in 2000.

Galambos, N. L., & Tilton-Weaver, L. C. (1998). Multiple-risk behaviour in adolescents and young adults. *Health Reports* (Statistics Canada, Catalogue 82–003), *10,* 9–20. (University of Victoria: www.uvic.ca)

Habbick, B. F., Nanson, J. L., Snyder, R. E., Cassey, R. E., & Schulman, A. L. (1996). Foetal alcohol syndrome in Saskatchewan: Unchanged incidence in a 20-year period. *Canadian Journal of Public Health, 87,* 204–207. (Royal University Hospital, University of Saskatchewan: www.usask.ca)

Hilbrecht, M., Zuzanek, J., & Mannell, R. C. (2008). Time use, time pressure, and gendered behavior in early and late adolescence. *Sex Roles, 58,* 342–357. (University of Waterloo: www.uwaterloo.ca)

Keating, D. (2004). Cognitive and brain development. In R. M. Lerner & L. Steinberg (Eds.), *Handbook of adolescent psychology* (2nd ed.), pp. 45–84. Hoboken, NJ: John Wiley and Sons. (University of Toronto: www.utoronto.ca)

Kimura, D. (1999). *Sex and cognition.* Cambridge, MA: The MIT Press. (University of Western Ontario: www.uwo.ca)

Professor Kimura received the Donald O. Hebb Award of the Canadian Psychological Association in 1985.

Kisilevsky, B. S., Hains, S. M. J., Lee, K., Xie, X., Huang, H., Ye, H. H., Zhang, K., & Wang, Z. (2003). Effects of experience on fetal voice recognition. *Psychological Science, 14,* 220–224. (Queen's University: www.queensu.ca)

Kolb, B., Gibb, R., & Robinson, T. E. (2003). Brain plasticity and behavior. *Current Directions in Psychological Science, 12,* 1–5. (University of Lethbridge: www.uleth.ca)

Kolb, B., & Stewart, J. (1995). Changes in the neonatal gonadal hormonal environment prevent behavioral sparing and alter cortical morphogenesis after early female frontal cortex lesions in male and female rats. *Behavioral Neuroscience, 109,* 285–294. (University of Lethbridge: www.uleth.ca)

Kolb, B., & Wishaw, I. Q. (1998). Brain plasticity and behavior. *Annual Review of Psychology, 49,* 43–64. (University of Lethbridge: www.uleth.ca)

Professor Kolb was awarded the Donald O. Hebb Award of the Canadian Psychological Association in 2000 and became a member of the Royal Society of Canada in the same year.

Lepage, J.-F., & Théoret, J. (2007). The mirror neuron system: Grasping others' actions from birth? *Developmental Science, 10,* 513–523. (Université de Montréal: www.umontreal.ca)

Lytton, H., & Romney, D. M. (1991). Parents' sex-related differential socialization of boys and girls: A meta-analysis. *Psychological Bulletin, 109,* 267–296. (University of Calgary: www.ucalgary.ca)

Madigan, S., Moran, G., & Pederson, D. R. (2006). Unresolved states of mind, disorganized attachment relationships, and disrupted interactions of adolescent mothers and their infants. *Developmental Psychology, 42,* 293–304. (University of Western Ontario: www.uwo.ca)

Marcia, J. E. (1980). Identity in adolescence. In I. Adelson (Ed.), *Handbook of adolescence.* New York: Wiley. (Simon Fraser University: www.sfu.ca)

Marcia, J. E. (1994). The empirical study of ego identity. In H. A. Bosma & T. L. G. Graafsma (Eds.), *Identity and development: An interdisciplinary approach* (Vol. 172). Thousand Oaks, CA: Sage Publications, Inc. (Simon Fraser University: www.sfu.ca)

Marshall, K. (2006, July). Converging gender roles. *Perspectives* (Statistics Canada, Catalogue 75–001–XIE), 5–17. (Statistics Canada, Labour and Household Surveys Analysis Division: www.statcan.ca)

Maurer, D., & Maurer, C. (1988). *The world of the newborn.* New York: Basic Books. (McMaster University: www.mcmaster.ca)

McKay, A. (2004). Adolescent sexual and reproductive health in Canada: A report card in 2004. *Canadian Journal of Human Sexuality, 13,* 67–81. (Sex Information and Education Council of Canada: www.sieccan.org)

Moran, G., Forbes, L., Evans, E., Tarabulsy, G. M., & Madigan, S. (2008). Both maternal sensitivity and atypical maternal behavior independently predict attachment security and disorganization in adolescent mother–infant relationships. *Infant Behavior and Development, 31,* 321–325. (University of Western Ontario: www.uwo.ca)

Muller, U., & Carpendale, J. I. M. (2000). The role of social interaction in Piaget's theory: Language for social cooperation and social cooperation for language. *New Ideas in Psychology, 18,* 139–156. (University of Toronto: www.utoronto.ca)

Pederson, D. R., Gleason, K. E., Moran, G., & Bento, S. (1998). Maternal attachment representations, maternal sensitivity, and the infant–mother attachment relationship. *Developmental Psychology, 34,* 925–933. (University of Western Ontario: www.uwo.ca)

Pederson, D. R., & Moran, G. (1996). Expressions of the attachment relationship outside the strange situation. *Child Development, 67,* 915–927. (University of Western Ontario: www.uwo.ca)

Potter, S. M., Zelazo, P. R., Stack, D. M., & Papageorgiou, A. N. (2000). Adverse effects of fetal cocaine exposure on neonatal auditory information processing. *Pediatrics, 105,* e40. (McGill University and Montreal Children's Hospital: www.mcgill.ca)

Smylie, L., Medaglia, S., & Maticka-Tyndale, E. (2006). The effect of social capital and socio-demographics on adolescent risk and sexual health behaviours. *Canadian Journal of Human Sexuality, 15,* 95–112. (University of Windsor: www.uwindsor.ca)

## Suggestions for Further Reading

Lemme, B. H. (2006). *Development in adulthood* (4th ed.). Boston: Allyn and Bacon.

A well-written and thorough introduction to the major issues involved in the study of adult development.

Hoyenga, K. B., & Hoyenga, K. T. (1993). *Gender-related differences: Origins and outcomes.* Boston: Allyn and Bacon.

This book examines gender differences from evolutionary, physiological, and cultural perspectives.

Harwood, R. L., Miller, J. G., & Irizarry, N. L. (1997). *Culture and attachment: Perceptions of the child in context.* New York: Guilford Press.

As its title implies, this book considers cultural variables that influence the development of attachment between infants and their caregivers, including socio-economic status, perceptions of different attachment behaviours, and perceptions of children themselves.

Colapinto, J. (2000). *As nature made him: The boy who was raised as a girl.* Toronto: HarperCollins.

Colapinto's book is an excellent description of the case of D. R., described in the text. D. R. did reveal his full identity for the sake of Colapinto's book in an effort to make his story known and to change medical thinking about the value of sexual reassignment after genital trauma. Sadly, D. R.'s life became increasingly unhappy; he died in 2004.

13

# Motivation and Emotion

# CHAPTER OUTLINE

## What Is Motivation?

Biological Needs • Physiology of Reinforcement • Optimum-Level Theory • Perseverance

Motivation refers to a group of phenomena that affect the nature, strength, and persistence of an individual's behaviour. One important category of motivated behaviours involves internal regulation—the maintenance of homeostasis. Motivation is closely related to the processes of reinforcement and punishment. All reinforcing stimuli (including addictive drugs) appear to cause the release of dopamine in the brain. The optimum-level theory suggests that we are motivated to approach stimuli that bring our level of arousal closer to its optimum level. Superfluous use of extrinsic rewards can actually decrease intrinsic motivation.

## Eating

What Starts a Meal? • What Stops a Meal? • Obesity • Anorexia Nervosa and Bulimia Nervosa

Eating is caused by both social and physiological factors. The most important physiological factor is the detection of a fall in the level of nutrients available in the blood. Short-term control of eating involves detectors in the stomach that monitor the level of nutrients received during a meal. Long-term control appears to involve a chemical released by overnourished fat cells. Both genetic and environmental factors are responsible for obesity. Anorexia nervosa is a serious, often life-threatening disorder whose causes are not well understood.

## Sexual Behaviour

Effects of Sex Hormones on Behaviour • Sexual Orientation

Hormones play an important role in motivating sexual behaviour. Sex hormones have organizational effects on prenatal development and activational effects in adulthood. Although testosterone is the most important male sex hormone, it stimulates sexual desire in both men and women. The development of sexual orientation appears to have biological roots, both hormonal and genetic.

## Aggressive Behaviour

Ethological Studies of Aggression • Hormones and Aggression • Environmental Variables That Affect Human Aggression

Ethological studies show that aggression serves useful purposes in most species of animals. In males of most species, male sex hormones have both organizational and activational effects on aggressive behaviour. Field studies suggest that violence in the mass media may promote aggression.

## The Nature of Emotion

Emotions as Response Patterns • Social Judgments: Role of the Orbitofrontal Cortex

An emotion is a particular pattern of behaviours, physiological responses, and feelings evoked by a situation that has motivational relevance. Emotional response patterns have three components: behavioural, autonomic, and hormonal.

## Expression and Recognition of Emotions

The Social Nature of Emotional Expressions in Humans • Universality of Emotional Expressions • Situations That Produce Emotions: The Role of Cognition • Feelings of Emotions • *Then and Now: The James-Lange Theory*

Expressions of emotion are largely innate social behaviours that communicate important information between individuals. Although emotional reactions are automatic responses that are seen in many species, cognition plays an important role in recognition of emotion-inducing situations. Cross-cultural studies show that people in all cultures show similar facial expressions, although cultural rules determine under what circumstances people should let their feelings show. According to the James-Lange theory, feelings of emotion are caused by feedback from the body when a situation causes an emotional reaction. This feedback comes from behaviours and from responses controlled by the autonomic nervous system. The effects of spinal cord injury on feelings of emotion tend to support the James-Lange theory, but recent evidence indicates that some emotions may be felt without sensations from the body.

PROLOGUE

## "Robotic" Behaviour? Or Something Else?

Malaysians have a word, *latah*, that describes a very unusual condition. People susceptible to *latah* react to unexpected or startling stimuli with elaborate and fitful reactions lasting several minutes. During this time, a *latah* person will sometimes shout, imitate another, or blindly follow instructions. Robert Bartholomew, an anthropologist who married into an extended Malay family, describes an episode involving his wife's aunt:

> I first observed S. as this timid, decrepit, wizen-faced woman was intentionally startled by S.'s elderly uncle, who walked near her and slapped his hands together. She responded with a short vulgar phrase, stood up, lost all inhibition, and began following each of her teaser's commands and mimicking his every gesture. During the ensuing 10-minute episode, S. was "made to" cry like a baby, perform silat (Malay self-defense), dance vigorously, and partially disrobe, all to the obvious amusement of the entire wedding party, who crowded around her inside the bride's parents' home. She would occasionally improvise gestures, such as lifting her sarong in a sexually suggestive manner and utter the most vile words and phrases. (Bartholomew, 1984, p. 333)

This hyper-reactivity to unexpected sounds and events has been a puzzle since it was first described by Western observers. The *latah* behaviours occur as a result of a powerful stimulus, in the same way that any of us might jump or startle when a balloon pops. However, unlike a reflexive startle, the behaviours are elaborate. Tanner and Chamberland (2001) studied a group of 15 Indonesian women with this condition, and noted that, as in the case of S., a *latah* state is marked by vulgar speech, imitation of sounds and gesture, and automatic obedience. Most reflexes are quick, short, and simple responses directly elicited by specific stimuli. Are the elaborate behaviours of *latah* similar to reflexes?

Within Malay culture, the answer is yes. A person in a *latah* state is considered to be acting involuntarily. Behaviours that would normally be regarded as scandalous are excused or even, as in the case of S., considered amusing. Persons in *latah* are not held responsible for their actions. Instead, a relative or a friend will assume responsibility to make sure a *latah* woman doesn't harm herself or anyone else during that state (Winzeler, 1999), and the person provoking the *latah* state is considered to be in control (Bartholomew, 1984).

On the other hand, much of a *latah* person's behaviour seems like a performance, designed to attract attention to someone who might otherwise be ignored. Bartholomew (1984) found that S.'s startle response was much more muted when nobody other than him was present. As well, despite her claims of not liking the "teasing," S. never asked her relatives to desist. Therefore, the curious collection of *latah* behaviours could be a deception.

Are the behaviors of a *latah* state unconscious and involuntary? Or are they deliberate and wilful?

Human behaviour is notoriously inconsistent. In a given situation, different people act differently, and even a single individual acts differently at different times. There are many reasons for inconsistent behaviour. A person eats or does not eat, depending on how recent the last meal was and how tasty the available food is. A person who usually picks up hitchhikers does not do so after hearing that a convict has just escaped from a nearby prison. A person who likes to play tennis will probably turn down a game if suffering from a severe headache. These reasons for inconsistent behaviour are aspects of *motivation* (derived from a Latin word meaning "to move"). Of course, once the reasons are known, the behaviours are no longer considered "inconsistent." In common usage, motivation refers to a driving force that moves us to a particular action. More formally, **motivation** is a general term for a group of phenomena that affect the *nature* of an individual's behaviour, the *strength* of the behaviour, and the *persistence* of the behaviour.

The first part of this chapter describes the nature of motivation and its relation to reinforcement. There are many approaches to motivation: physiological, behavioural, cognitive, and social. The emphasis here is on behavioural and physiological aspects of motivation—the external stimuli and internal changes that affect a person's behaviour. Motivation affects all categories of behaviour, so a complete discussion of motivation would have to consider everything we do. Rather than say too little about too many things, the first part of this chapter considers three important categories of motivated behaviours: eating, sexual behaviour, and aggression. These behaviours are particularly important to the survival of the individual and of the species. The discussion of motivation will not end with this chapter. As you will see, motivation plays an especially important role in social behaviour; thus, we will look at some topics dealing with social motivation in Chapter 15.

The second part of this chapter describes research on emotion. Motivation and emotion are often discussed together and in that order. There is a good reason for this pairing. Our behaviour is motivated by situations that we tend to approach or to avoid—situations that are important to us. Besides motivating us to do something, these situations evoke behaviours that other people can recognize, including facial expressions, changes in posture, and alterations in tone of voice. They also affect how we *feel*. In other words, situations that motivate our behaviour also provoke emotions.

# What Is Motivation?

When we speak casually of motivation, we tend to describe it in terms of goals. We go to the kitchen fridge because we remember there's some leftover banana cream pie in there. The driver doesn't pick up hitchhikers to avoid being robbed. That is, we behave in a particular way to get something (or to avoid something, in the case of a possible criminal hitchhiker). In that sense, motivation is *proactive*, or forward-looking. However, in the case of the tennis player with the headache, motivation is also *reactive*, or in response to conditions present at the time. The passage of time since dinner makes that pie seem all the more attractive.

The proactive sense of motivation is very similar to concepts of reinforcement. We are motivated to perform a behaviour to gain (or avoid losing) a reinforcer or to avoid (or escape from) an aversive event. Some events that proactively motivate, such as food or pain, are obvious; others, such as smiles or frowns, are subtle. But the reactive sense of motivation applies to why reinforcers might have their effects. This section describes the attempts that psychologists have made to identify the nature of reinforcement and to relate the process of reinforcement to motivation.

## Biological Needs

People have killed others for food. And you can imagine how hard you would struggle to breathe if something obstructed your windpipe. Biological needs can be very potent motivators. To survive, we all need air, food, water, various vitamins and minerals, and protection from extremes in temperature. Complex organisms possess physiological mechanisms that detect deficits or imbalances associated with these needs and related **regulatory behaviours** that bring physiological conditions back to normal. Examples of regulatory behaviours include eating, drinking, hunting, shivering, building a fire, and putting on a warm coat. This process of detection and correction, which maintains physiological systems at their optimum value, is called **homeostasis** ("stable state"). Deficits or imbalances motivate us because they cause us to perform the appropriate regulatory behaviours.

A regulatory system has four essential features: the **system variable** (the characteristic to be regulated), a **set point** (the optimum value of the system variable), a **detector** that monitors the value of the system variable, and a **correctional mechanism** that restores the system variable to the set point. A simple example of such a regulatory system is a room whose

**motivation** A general term for a group of phenomena that affect the nature, strength, and persistence of an individual's behaviour.

**regulatory behaviour** A behaviour that tends to bring physiological conditions back to normal, thus restoring the condition of homeostasis.

**homeostasis** The process by which important physiological characteristics (such as body temperature and blood pressure) are regulated so that they remain at their optimum level.

**system variable** The variable controlled by a regulatory mechanism; for example, temperature in a heating system.

**set point** The optimum value of the system variable in a regulatory mechanism. The set point for human body temperature, recorded orally, is approximately 37°C.

**detector** In a regulatory process, a mechanism that signals when the system variable deviates from its set point.

**correctional mechanism** In a regulatory process, the mechanism that is capable of restoring the system variable to the set point.

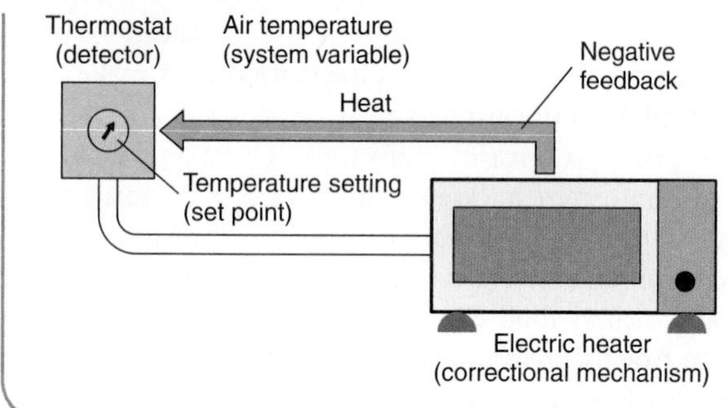


FIGURE 13•1 An example of a regulatory system.

temperature is regulated by a thermostatically controlled heater. The system variable is the air temperature of the room, and the detector for this variable is a thermostat. The thermostat can be adjusted so that contacts of a switch will close when the temperature falls below a preset value (the set point). Closing of the contacts turns on the correctional mechanism: the coils of the heater. (See **Figure 13•1**.)

If the room cools below the set point, the thermostat turns the heater on, which warms the room. The rise in room temperature causes the thermostat to turn the heater off. Because the activity of the correctional mechanism (heat production) feeds back to the thermostat and causes it to turn the heater off, this process is called **negative feedback**. Negative feedback is an essential characteristic of all regulatory systems.

The earliest systematic attempt to explain the nature of motivation and reinforcement was the **drive reduction hypothesis**. This theory stated that biological needs, caused by deprivation of the necessities of life, are unpleasant. The physiological changes associated with, say, going without food for several hours, produce an unpleasant state called *hunger*. Hunger serves as a **drive**, energizing an organism's behaviour. The organism then engages in behaviours that in the past have obtained food. The act of eating reduces hunger, and this drive reduction is reinforcing. (See **Figure 13•2**.)

**negative feedback** A process whereby the effect produced by an action serves to diminish or terminate that action. Regulatory systems are characterized by negative feedback loops.
**drive reduction hypothesis** The hypothesis that a drive (resulting from physiological need or deprivation) produces an unpleasant state that causes an organism to engage in motivated behaviours. Reduction of drive is assumed to be reinforcing.
**drive** A condition, often caused by physiological changes or homeostatic disequilibrium, that energizes an organism's behaviour.

Not all drives are based on homeostasis—on biological needs like the ones for food and water. The most obvious example is the drive associated with sexual behaviour. An individual can survive without sexual behaviour, but the sex drive is certainly motivating, and sexual contact is certainly reinforcing. Similarly, most organisms placed in a featureless environment will soon become motivated to seek something new; they will work at a task that gives them a view of the world outside.

The drive reduction hypothesis of reinforcement has fallen into disfavour for two primary reasons. The first is that drive is almost always impossible to measure. For example, suppose you obtain pleasure from looking at photographs taken by a friend while on vacation. According to the drive reduction hypothesis, your "exploratory drive" or "curiosity drive" is high, and looking at vacation photos reduces it, providing reinforcement. Or, consider a woman who very much enjoys listening to music. What drive induces her to turn on her music system? What drive is reduced by this activity? There is no way to measure "drive" in either of these examples and confirm that it actually exists; thus, the hypothesis cannot be experimentally tested.

The second problem is that if we examine our own behaviour, we find that many events we experience as reinforcing are also exciting, or drive *increasing*. The reason a roller coaster ride is fun is certainly not because it *reduces* drive. The same is true for skiing, cycling, or viewing a horror film. Likewise, an interesting, reinforcing conversation is one that is exciting, not one that puts you to sleep. As well, people who engage in prolonged foreplay and sexual intercourse do not view these activities as unpleasant even though they are accompanied by such a high level of drive. In general, the experiences we really want to repeat (that is, the ones we find reinforcing) are those that increase, rather than decrease, our level of arousal.

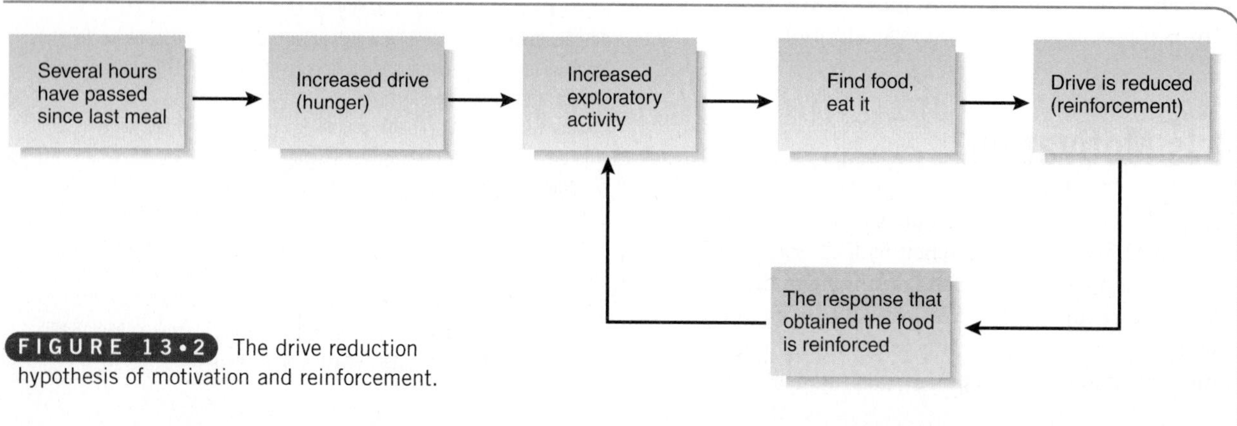


FIGURE 13•2 The drive reduction hypothesis of motivation and reinforcement.

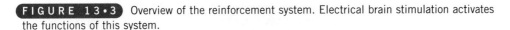

FIGURE 13•3 Overview of the reinforcement system. Electrical brain stimulation activates the functions of this system.

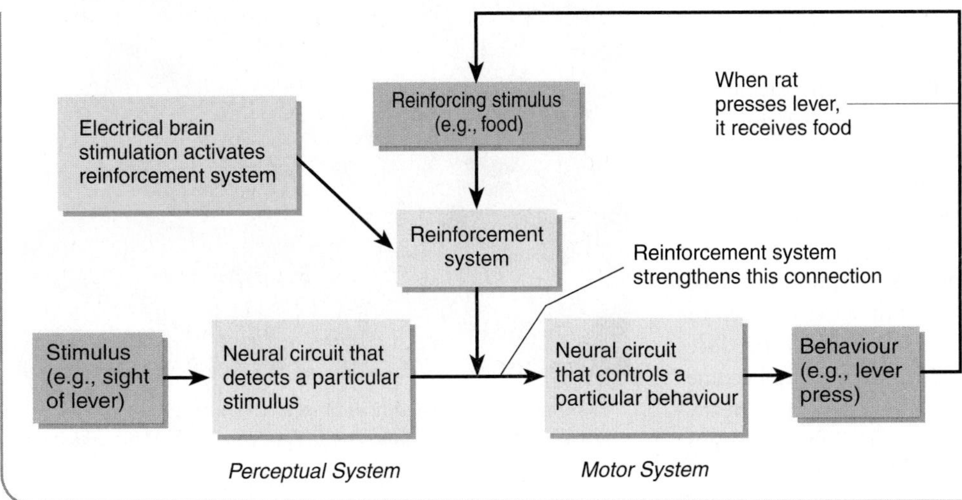


## Physiology of Reinforcement

To understand the nature of reinforcement, we must understand something about its physiological basis. In an important, although somewhat accidental, finding, Olds and Milner (1954) showed that electrical stimulation of the brain could be reinforcing to rats (see Chapter 4). Almost all investigators believe that electrical stimulation of the brain is reinforcing because it activates the same system that is activated by natural reinforcers and by drugs that people commonly abuse. The normal function of this system is to strengthen the connections between the neurons that detect the discriminative stimulus (such as the sight of a lever in Olds and Milner's research) and the neurons that produce the operant response (such as a rat's lever press). The electrical brain stimulation activates this system directly. (See **Figure 13•3**.)

Researchers have discovered that an essential component of the reinforcement system consists of neurons that release dopamine as their transmitter substance. Thus, all reinforcing stimuli appear to trigger the release of dopamine in the brain. **Figure 13•4** illustrates the effects of sexually related stimuli and sexual activity on the release of dopamine in a part of the brain known to be associated with reinforcement.

## Optimum-Level Theory

Although events that increase our level of arousal are often reinforcing, there are times when a person wants nothing more than some peace and quiet. In this case, avoidance of exciting stimuli motivates us. As we saw in Chapter 7, the removal (or avoidance) of an aversive stimulus produces *negative reinforcement*. In an attempt to find a common explanation for both positive and negative reinforcement, some psychologists have proposed the **optimum-level hypothesis** of reinforcement and punishment: When an individual's arousal level is too high, less stimulation is reinforcing; when it is too low, more stimulation is desired (Berlyne, 1966; Hebb, 1955). Berlyne hypothesized two forms of exploration related to arousal. *Diversive exploration* is a response to understimulation (boredom) that increases the diversity of the stimuli the organism tries to come in contact with. *Specific exploration* is a response to overstimulation (usually because

**optimum-level hypothesis** The hypothesis that organisms will perform behaviour that restores the level of arousal to an optimum level.

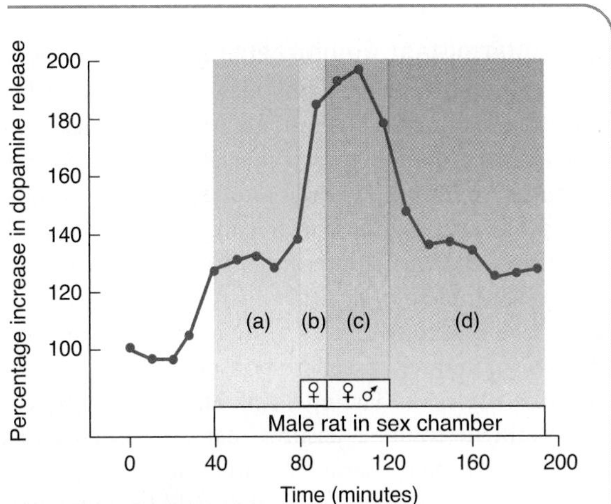


FIGURE 13•4 Release of dopamine produced by reinforcing stimuli. The graph indicates levels of dopamine in a region of a male rat's forebrain.
(a) Rat is placed in apparatus in which it has mated before.
(b) Receptive female is placed behind a wire-mesh partition.
(c) Partition is removed; the animals copulate.
(d) The female is removed.

of a specific need, such as lack of food or water) that leads to the needed item, thereby decreasing the organism's drive level. Hebb focused on how arousal affects the effectiveness of behaviour. At the optimum level of arousal, the mid-range behaviour is organized and effective. Within that optimum range, in fact, increasing arousal will produce increasingly effective behaviour. Too little arousal, in the suboptimum range, leads to ineffective behaviour because the person is not sufficiently motivated. Too much arousal, again, outside the optimum range, leads to disorganized, and therefore ineffective, behaviour.

The hypothesis that organisms seek an optimum level of arousal is certainly plausible. Any kind of activity—even the most interesting and exciting ones—eventually produces satiety, where something that was once reinforcing becomes bothersome. Presumably, participation in an exciting behaviour gradually raises an organism's arousal above its optimum level. However, the logical problem that plagues the drive-reduction hypothesis also applies to the optimum-level hypothesis. Because we cannot measure an organism's drive or arousal, we cannot say what its optimum level is. Thus, the optimum-level hypothesis remains without much empirical support.

## Perseverance

Some people work hard even though the rewards for their work seem to occur infrequently; in everyday language, we refer to these people as highly motivated. They exhibit **perseverance**. Their behaviour shows persistence; they continue to perform even though their work is not regularly reinforced. Other people give up easily or perhaps never really try. Understanding the effects of reinforcement helps us explain why some people persevere and others do not.

**Effects of Intermittent Reinforcement** Perseverance is studied in various ways: by the withholding of reinforcers, by reinforcement of competing behaviour, and so on (Nevin & Grace, 2000). In Chapter 7, we saw that behaviour acquired with intermittent reinforcement was more resistant to extinction than behaviour acquired with continuous reinforcement. What happens during intermittent reinforcement that makes behaviour more persistent?

Among the important factors is the particular sequence of reinforced and unreinforced responses during training (Capaldi, Haas, Miller, & Martins, 2005). Studies have shown that if intermittent training ensures that a reinforced response occurs only after a series of unreinforced responses, resistance to extinction is greatly enhanced. Training that consists of the same number of unreinforced responses, but in which the reinforcers do not occur even after long series of unreinforced responses, does not produce behaviour that is nearly as resistant to extinction. In other words, succeeding after several failures causes the learner to resist the effects of subsequent failure. As applied to human behaviour outside the laboratory, these findings suggest that experiencing failure in our past facilitates persistence of later performance, but only if failure is eventually followed by success. The "school of hard knocks" does not by itself teach us to endure in the face of adversity. On the contrary, experiencing tough times can lead us to give up unless we sometimes experience success.

**perseverance** The tendency to continue to perform a behaviour even when it is not being reinforced.

▲ *One meaning of motivation is perseverance—working steadily on projects that take much time and effort to complete.*

In studies of extinction, psychologists discovered another motivational effect: Environmental stimuli that are present during extinction become aversive. The aversive properties of these stimuli are evident in several ways. First, it has long been known that laboratory animals acquire responses if they allow them to escape environments in which extinction is scheduled. The motivational effects of extinction are called frustration (Amsel, 1962). Second, if another animal is present when the learner's responses undergo extinction, the other animal may be attacked—a finding that has been observed in humans (Kelly & Hake, 1970; Lerman, Iwata, & Wallace, 1999). This phenomenon is called extinction-induced aggression. Extinction causes other members of the species to become eliciting stimuli for aggressive behaviour and thereby establishes the opportunity to aggress as a reinforcing stimulus. For obvious reasons, most studies on frustration and extinction-induced aggression have been conducted with non-humans; however, frustration in response to extinction is widely prevalent in mammals (Papini, 2003) and the applicability to human behaviour seems clear. The quiet office worker who pounds on the candy machine when it fails to dispense a purchase is probably displaying extinction-induced aggression. A similar phenomenon also may occur when groups within society who are not prospering blame other groups for their misfortune, as in scapegoating.

**Overjustification Hypothesis** Some psychologists have hypothesized that providing extrinsic rewards for behaviour that is already maintained by intrinsic rewards may actually weaken the target behaviour (e.g., Oliver & Williams, 2006; Ryan & Deci, 2002; Vallerand & Ratelle, 2002). This is called the **overjustification hypothesis.** The general idea behind the concept of overjustification is that the superfluous application of extrinsic rewards for behaviour that is intrinsically motivated creates a shift to extrinsic rewards, the net result being a loss of intrinsic motivation. As long as the extrinsic rewards are available, an observer may not notice a difference. But what happens when extrinsic rewards are no longer provided? The overjustification theory predicts that after a shift occurs from intrinsic to extrinsic motivation and extrinsic rewards disappear, the person will lose interest in the activity. That is, if the behaviour has become maintained by the extrinsic rewards, the behaviour will weaken when these rewards are no longer available.

A study by Lepper, Greene, and Nisbett (1973) was among the first of many to demonstrate the overjustification effect. The investigators first carefully documented the free-play activities preferred by a large number of children in a daycare setting. Among the favourite activities was drawing with large felt markers on sheets of newsprint. Drawing, therefore, showed behavioural evidence of intrinsic motivation. The children did not need to play with the art materials, but they did so without any extrinsic consequences. Two weeks after this preliminary assessment, the researchers returned and for one day randomly assigned the children to one of three conditions. In one condition, each child was asked to produce a drawing to win a prize. Thus, the prize was contingent on the children's performing the requested behaviour. Moreover, the children expected to receive prizes for drawing. Children in a second condition also were asked to make a drawing but were not offered the extrinsic reward. However, they unexpectedly received the same prize as children in the first condition when they had completed drawing. In a third condition, the children were neither offered nor given the prize.

After a delay of one or two weeks, the researchers returned and unobtrusively observed children during their normal free playtime. Remember that during free-play periods, no one was present who might offer or give extrinsic rewards to the children—they were on their own. The results of these observations revealed a strong overjustification effect. Children who had previously received an expected prize played with the drawing materials less than did children in the other two groups. In terms of overjustification, they showed less intrinsic motivation during their free-play period. The children who received an unexpected prize in the prior session showed no evidence that their intrinsic motivation had been undermined. They spent about the same amount of time drawing as before. When the prize was unexpected, no shift from intrinsic to extrinsic motivation occurred. Although this finding has been replicated (see Ryan & Deci, 2000), its effects may be limited. When rewards are used to challenge and to benefit the learner, they are effective motivators (Cameron & Pierce, 2005).

**Learned Helplessness** Organisms with a history in which their behaviour has been ineffective in determining its consequences become less sensitive to the consequences of their behaviour. That is, they lose motivation, because they have learned that they are powerless to affect their own destinies. Maier and Seligman (1976) reported a series of animal experiments that demonstrated this effect, which is called learned helplessness. **Learned helplessness** involves learning that the consequences of behaviour are independent of one's behaviour—that an aversive outcome cannot be avoided or escaped or that an appetitive outcome cannot be achieved.

The basic experiment in this area was conducted by Overmier and Seligman (1967). These researchers placed dogs in an apparatus in which unavoidable shocks were given. Next, they placed each dog in another apparatus in which the animal underwent a series of trials that provided a warning stimulus before an electrical shock. In this second situation, the animals could avoid the shocks by stepping over a small barrier to the other side of the apparatus. Dogs in a control group quickly learned to step over the barrier and avoid the shock. However, dogs that had previously received inescapable shocks in the other apparatus failed to learn. They just squatted in the corner and took the shock as if they had learned that it made no difference what they did. They had learned to be helpless. A related effect was found with appetitive stimuli: Acquisition of a learned response is impaired if animals receive food regardless of their behaviour before experimenters make food contingent on the response (Engberg, Hansen, Welker, & Thomas, 1972).

Some psychologists believe that learned helplessness has important implications for human motivation (Job, 2002; Seligman, 1975; Seligman & Nolen-Hoeksema, 1987). When people have experiences in which they are powerless to control the events that happen to them, they may become depressed, and their motivational level may decrease. The change in motivation occurs because the helplessness training reduces their expectation that performing a task will bring success. Learned helplessness has also been likened to a personality trait; that is, people who have had major experiences with unsolvable dilemmas may not try to succeed in other types of tasks, including problems they could solve (Overmier, 1998).

**overjustification hypothesis** The superfluous application of extrinsic rewards to intrinsically motivated behaviour will undermine intrinsic motivation.

**learned helplessness** A response to exposure to an inescapable aversive stimulus, characterized by reduced ability to learn a solvable avoidance task; thought to play a role in the development of some psychological disturbances.

## Interim Summary

### What Is Motivation?

*Motivation* is a general term for a group of phenomena that affect the *nature, strength,* and *persistence* of an individual's behaviour. It includes a tendency to perform behaviours that bring an individual into contact with an appetitive stimulus or that move it away from an aversive one. One important category of motivated behaviours involves internal regulation—the maintenance of homeostasis. Regulatory systems include four features: a system variable (the variable that is regulated), a set point (the optimum value of the system variable), a detector to measure the system variable, and a correctional mechanism to change it.

The discovery that electrical stimulation of parts of the brain could reinforce behaviour led to the study of the role of brain mechanisms involved in reinforcement. Apparently, all reinforcing stimuli (including addictive drugs) cause the release of dopamine in the brain.

Because high levels of drive or arousal can be aversive, several investigators proposed the optimum-level theory of motivation and reinforcement. This theory suggests that organisms strive to attain optimum levels of arousal; thus, reinforcement and punishment are produced by the same drive. However, a problem remains: Because drive cannot be directly measured, we cannot determine whether an individual's drive is above or below its optimum level.

Perseverance is the tendency to continue performing a behaviour that is no longer being externally reinforced. An important factor that affects perseverance is the organism's previous history with intermittent reinforcement.

Some experiences can diminish an organism's perseverance. The application of extrinsically controlling rewards to already intrinsically motivated behaviour can lead to reduced perseverance. Other experiences can interfere with the ability to cope with new situations. Learned helplessness involves learning that an aversive event cannot be avoided or escaped.

#### QUESTIONS TO CONSIDER

1. Have you ever been working hard on a problem and suddenly thought of a possible solution? Did the thought make you feel excited and happy? What do you think we would find if we could measure the release of dopamine in your brain?
2. A child keeps asking his parents to take him out to play even after the parents say that they are busy and will go out to play later. What are some of the ways you might seek to explain the child's behaviour, given what you know about schedules of reinforcement?

# Eating

In this section, we shall see that the regulation and expression of eating is one of the most complex motivated behaviours. As a matter of fact, all other motivations are dependent on it. If life were not sustained by eating, other motivations would be irrelevant.

Simply put, motivation to eat is aroused when there is a deficit in the body's supply of stored nutrients, and it is satisfied by a meal that replenishes this supply. A person who exercises vigorously uses up the stored nutrients more rapidly and consequently must eat more food. Thus, the amount of food a person normally eats is regulated by physiological need. But what, exactly, causes a person to start eating, and what brings the meal to an end? These are simple questions, yet the answers are complex. There is no single physiological measure that can tell us reliably whether a person should be hungry; hunger is determined by a variety of conditions. So, instead of asking what the cause of hunger is, we must ask what the *causes* are.

## What Starts a Meal?

Although hunger and satiety appear to be two sides of the same coin, investigations have shown that the factors that cause a meal to begin are different from the ones that end it. Therefore, we will look at these two sets of factors separately.

**Physiological Factors** The reasons for beginning a meal must somehow be related to the fact that the body needs nourishment: Physiological factors clearly are involved in eating. But how do physiological factors help determine when to eat?

Cannon and Washburn (1912) proposed that eating begins when we have an empty stomach. They suggested that the walls of an empty stomach rub against each other to produce what are commonly called "hunger pangs." Some skeptics called Cannon's explanation of hunger "the rumble theory." However, observations of surgical patients indicated that there was more to the onset of eating than hunger pangs. Removal of the stomach did not abolish hunger pangs, and these patients reported the same feelings of hunger and satiety that they had experienced before surgery (Inglefinger, 1944). (The patients had their stomachs removed because of cancer or large ulcers, and their esophagi had been attached directly to their small intestines.) Although the patients ate small, frequent meals because they had no stomachs to hold food, their reports of feelings of hunger and their total food intake were essentially normal.

Depletion of the body's store of nutrients is a more likely cause of hunger. The primary fuels for the cells of our body are glucose (a simple sugar) and fatty acids (compounds produced by the breakdown of fats). If the digestive system contains food, these nutrients are absorbed into the blood and nourish our cells. But the digestive tract is sometimes empty;

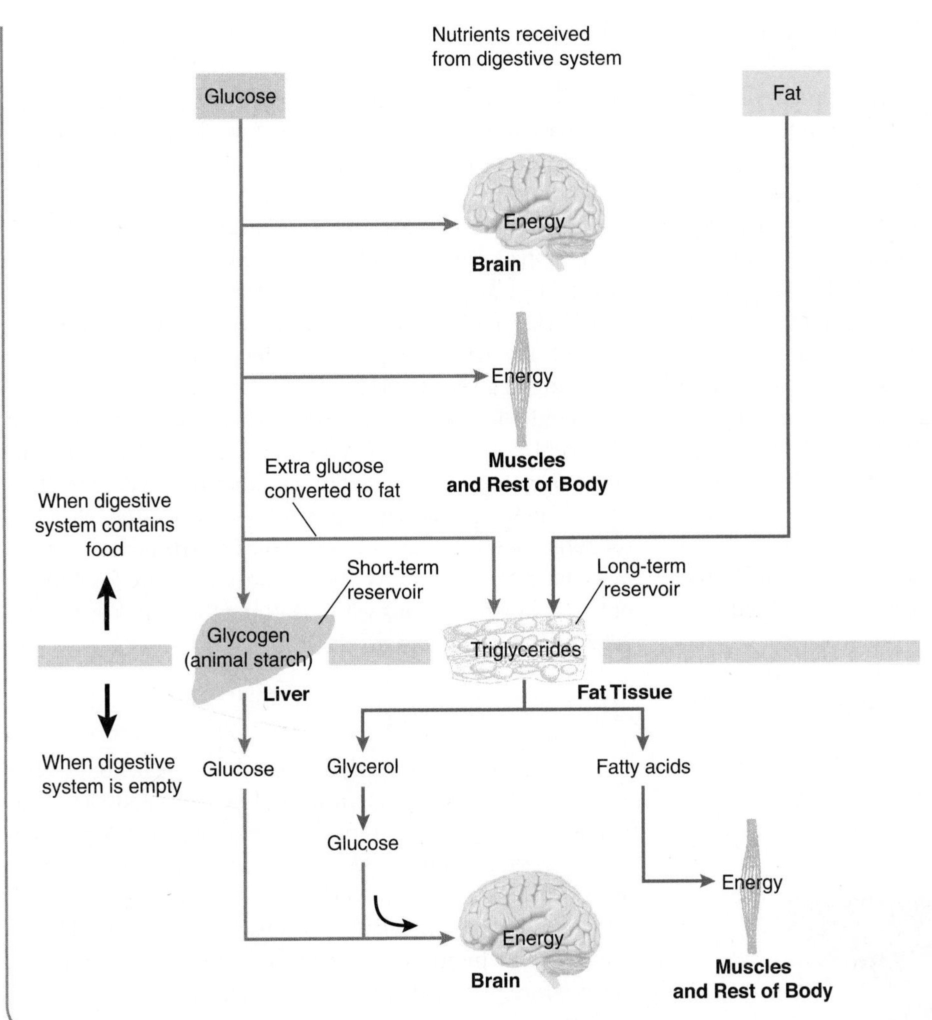


**FIGURE 13•5** Overview of food metabolism. When the digestive system contains food, glucose nourishes the brain and muscles. Extra glucose is stored in the liver and converted to fat. When the digestive system is empty, glucose obtained from glycogen stored in the liver nourishes the brain until this short-term reservoir is used up. Fatty acids from fat tissue nourish the muscles, and glycerol is converted to glucose to nourish the brain.

in fact, it is empty when we wake up every morning. There must be a reservoir that stores nutrients to keep the cells of the body nourished when the gut is empty. Indeed, there are two reservoirs: a short-term reservoir and a long-term reservoir. The short-term reservoir stores carbohydrates and the long-term reservoir stores fats.

The short-term reservoir is located in the cells of the muscles and the liver, and it is filled with a carbohydrate—a form of animal starch called **glycogen**. When glucose is present in the bloodstream after the digestion of a meal, some glucose is used for fuel, but some is converted into glycogen and stored in the liver. The long-term reservoir is the adipose tissue (fat tissue) found beneath the skin and in various locations in the abdomen. Adipose tissue consists of cells capable of absorbing nutrients from the blood, converting them to triglycerides (fats), and storing them. Fat cells can expand enormously in size to store triglycerides. In fact, the primary difference between obese and normal-weight persons is the size of their fat cells, not the number.

The long-term reservoir keeps us alive during prolonged fasting. Once the level of glycogen in our short-term reservoir of carbohydrates is depleted, fat cells release fatty acids and a carbohydrate called glycerol. Brain cells metabolize glucose exclusively, whereas the other cells of the body can metabolize fatty acids. Because glycerol converts into glucose, the brain is nourished even after the short-term reservoir has been depleted. (See **Figure 13•5**.)

Because of the importance of glucose as a fuel, Mayer (1955) proposed the glucostatic hypothesis of hunger. According to the **glucostatic hypothesis**, hunger occurs when the level of glucose in the blood falls below a set point, which occurs when the glycogen in the short-term reservoir has been depleted. Mayer proposed that the decrease in blood sugar was detected by receptors on glucose-sensitive neurons in the brain, called glucostats. (The term *glucostat* is analogous to thermostat but refers to the detection of glucose rather than of temperature.) Mayer suggested that these detectors

**glycogen** An insoluble carbohydrate that can be synthesized from glucose or converted to it; used to store nutrients.

**glucostatic hypothesis** The hypothesis that hunger is caused by a low level or availability of glucose, a condition that is monitored by specialized sensory neurons.

activate neural circuits that make a person hungry and stimulate the correctional mechanism of eating.

Subsequent research with both rats and humans demonstrated that the glucostatic hypothesis was too simple. Eating can be instigated in a number of different ways. An empty stomach causes a hormone, ghrelin, to be secreted. This hormone is a potent simulator of eating (Ariyasu et al., 2001; Kojima et al., 1999). Also, the liver contains two different types of nutrient receptors, one that detects the level of glucose and the other that detects the level of fatty acids (see Langhans, 1996). Both sets of receptors activate pathways that project to the brain; these pathways, in turn, activate neural circuits that initiate eating. For example, if a drug that blocks glucose receptors is injected into the vein that brings blood from the intestines to the liver, eating occurs immediately (Novin, VanderWeele, & Rezek, 1973). Moreover, if the nerves (vagus nerves) that carry information from these receptors to the brain are cut, eating fails to occur. Finally, the brain itself contains receptors that detect the level of glucose, and blocking these receptors also induces eating (Ritter, Dinh, & Zhang, 2000). Because the control of eating is so important to survival, natural selection has produced multiple interrelated mechanisms whereby eating is initiated.

**Cultural and Social Factors** Most of us in Western society eat three times a day. When the time for a meal comes, we get hungry and eat, consuming a relatively constant amount of food. The regular pattern of eating is not determined solely by biological need; it is at least partially determined by habit. For many of us, most of the time, eating is initiated not by deprivation of nutrients but by environmental stimuli, such as the time shown by the clock on the wall.

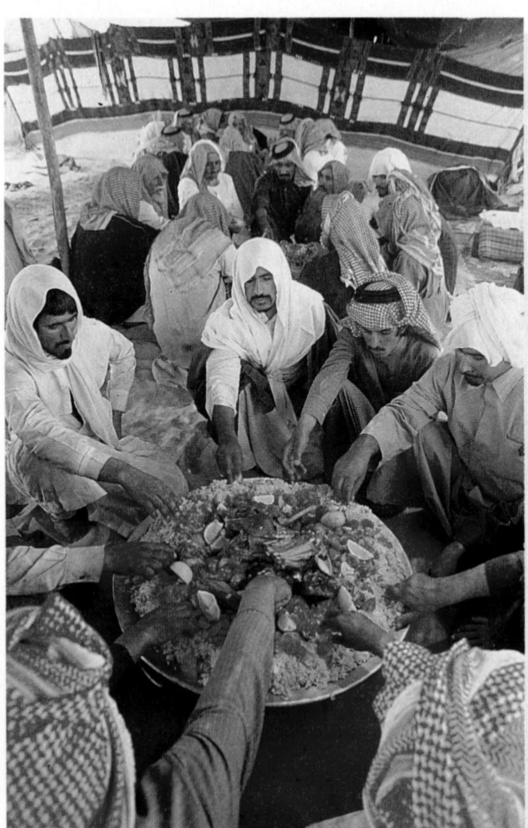

▲ *What we eat and how we eat are determined by cultural factors.*

If you have ever had to miss a meal, you might have noticed that your hunger did not continue to grow indefinitely. Instead, it subsided some time after the meal would normally have been eaten only to grow again just before the scheduled time of the next one. Hunger, then, can wax and wane according to a learned schedule.

Besides learning when to eat, we learn what to eat. What we accept as food depends on our culture and location. Our tastes also are shaped by habits acquired early in life. A child whose family exclusively eats a meat-and-potatoes diet will probably not become a venturesome gastronome. We are more likely to feel hungry and to consume more food in the presence of companions who are doing the same (de Castro, 2002; Lumeng & Hillman, 2007).

## What Stops a Meal?

We have seen that several factors—both behavioural and physiological—can initiate a meal, but what ends it? What brings a meal to a conclusion? Consider what happens when you eat. Your stomach fills with food, and the digestive process begins. However, about an hour passes before significant amounts of nutrients are absorbed into the bloodstream from the intestines. Therefore, the body's supply of fuel is not replenished until a considerable time after the meal begins. If you were to continue to eat until the nutrients actually entered the bloodstream, your stomach would burst. Other factors must be responsible for stopping the meal.

The physiological factors that stop a meal are divided into two groups: those that arise from the immediate effects of eating a meal and those that are produced by the longer-term consequences. The primary immediate cause of satiety is the stimulation of receptors by a distended stomach. In experiments with rats, eating does not occur if food is directly introduced into the stomach, even though the food was neither tasted nor smelled. Also, if procedures are used to remove food from the stomach after it has been eaten, eating continues unabated (Deutsch & Gonzalez, 1980). The stomach rather precisely measures the volume of its contents. Food-deprived rats were allowed to eat their fill and then some of the contents of the stomach were removed via a tube. When the rats were again allowed to eat, they ate almost exactly as much as had been taken out (Davis & Campbell, 1973).

The stomach appears to contain detectors that inform the brain about the chemical nature of its contents as well as the quantity. The ability to detect the chemical nature of food that has entered the stomach is important, because eating should stop relatively soon if the food is very nutritious but should continue for a longer time if it is not. Deutsch, Young, and Kalogeris (1978) injected either milk or a dilute salt solution into hungry rats' stomachs and 30 minutes later allowed them to eat. The rats that had received injections of milk ate less than the ones that had received the salt solution. Because the rats could not taste what was put in their stomachs, the effect had to come from detectors there. The nature of these detectors is not known, but they must respond to some chemicals present in food. You can try an experiment of your own: Drink two glasses of water when you are very hungry and see whether they satisfy your appetite.

The intestines also contain receptors that detect the presence of nutrients. The duodenum, the portion of the intestines into which the stomach empties, secretes a hormone called CCK that suppresses eating (Smith & Gibbs, 1992). And, further along the sequence of events that occur after a meal, the liver also has receptors that detect nutrients. After nutrients have been absorbed from the stomach and intestines, they enter the bloodstream and stimulate the receptors in the liver. If investigators stimulate these receptors by directly injecting nutrients into the veins supplying the liver of a rat, the rat's eating is reduced even though its stomach is empty (Langhans, Grossmann, & Geary, 2001; Tordoff & Friedman, 1988).

Even longer-term signals for satiety are produced by the adipose tissue that stores fat. The discovery of this signal came after studies with a strain of genetically obese mice. The ob mouse (as the strain is called) has a low metabolism, overeats, and becomes extremely fat. As these mice age, they develop diabetes, as do many obese humans both young and old. Researchers in several laboratories have discovered a genetic basis for the obesity of these animals (Campfield et al., 1995; Halaas, Gajiwala, Maffei, & Cohen, 1995; Pelleymounter et al., 1997). These animals have a mutation in a gene called OB that normally produces a protein known as leptin (from the Greek word *leptos,* meaning "thin"). Leptin is secreted by fat cells that have absorbed a large amount of triglyceride and acts on receptors in the hypothalamus to inhibit hunger. However, because of their mutant OB gene, ob mice are unable to synthesize leptin.

Leptin has profound effects on metabolism and eating, acting as an anti-obesity hormone. If ob mice are given daily injections of leptin, their metabolic rates increase, their body temperatures rise, they become more active, and they eat less. As a result, their weight returns to normal. The treatment works even when the leptin is injected directly into the brain, indicating that the chemical acts directly on the neural circuits that control eating and metabolism (see Woods, Seeley, Porte, & Schwartz, 1998). **Figure 13•6** shows an untreated ob mouse and an ob mouse that has received injections of leptin.

Maffei and colleagues (1995) found that leptin is secreted in humans and that the level of leptin in the blood is correlated with obesity. However, if normal levels of leptin are produced by human fat cells, why do some people nevertheless overeat and become obese? Much ongoing research continues to be devoted to the puzzle of obesity, to which we now turn.

**FIGURE 13•6** The effects of leptin on obesity in mice of the ob (obese) strain. The ob mouse on the left is untreated; the one on the right received daily injections of leptin.
*(Photo courtesy of Dr. J. Sholtis, The Rockefeller University. Copyright © 1995 Amgen, Inc.)*

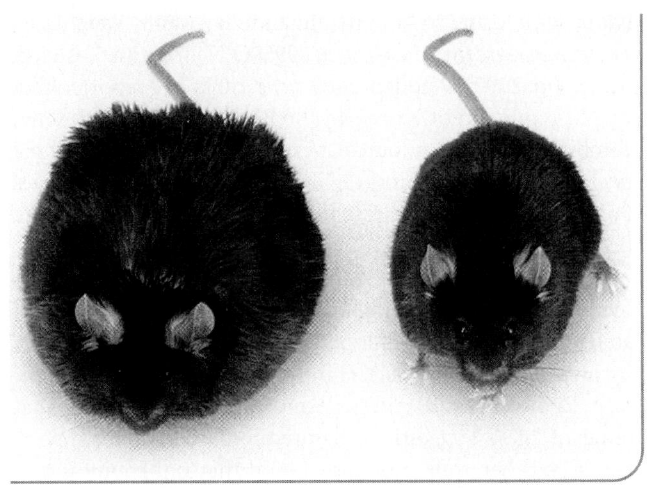

## Obesity

The mechanisms that control eating generally do a good job. However, some people do *not* control their eating habits and become too fat or too thin. Does what we have learned about the normal regulation of food intake help us understand these disorders?

The 2003 Canadian Community Health Survey (Statistics Canada, 2004) showed that 14.9 percent of Canadian adults between the ages of 20 and 64 were obese. (Obesity is defined as having a Body Mass Index (BMI) of 30 or greater.) The BMI is calculated as a person's weight divided by the square of his or her height (kg/m$^2$); it varies with a person's age, height, and weight but is associated with risk of death from various causes. In an extensive review of these risks, Wadden, Brownell, and Foster (2002) suggested some of the benefits resulting from interventions for obesity. They reviewed studies suggesting that the risk of mortality increases by around 30 percent in people with a moderately high BMI; this percentage continues upward to 40 percent when BMI is very high (Manson et al., 1995). The causes of death in obese people include stroke, diabetes, and cancer (all of which correlate with obesity). Obese people also suffer social and physical complications. Obese girls complete fewer years of schooling, despite having grades just as good as those who remain; are less likely to marry; and earn less than their non-obese counterparts. Obese people also elicit negative aesthetic judgments from others.

Obesity is extremely difficult to treat. Success at weight loss depends on the goals of the person losing the weight. First, people need to be motivated to lose weight. Second, they need to realize that weight reduction programs are designed for health reasons rather than aesthetic reasons. For example, until recently, interventions were guided toward helping people achieve their ideal weight (rather than a weight that would reduce the risk of ill health). Current emphasis, however, is on reducing health complications; a weight loss of 5 to 15 percent can be effective in producing this reduction, even though the obese person may not be happy with losing so little weight and may want a weight loss of 20 to 35 percent (Blackburn, 1995; O'Neil, Smith, Foster, & Anderson, 2000). Wadden, Brownell, and Foster reported that weight reduction of 7 units of the Body Mass Index (kg/m$^2$) combined with 150 minutes of exercise per week reduced the likelihood of developing diabetes by 58 percent (Diabetes Prevention Program Research Group, 2002, cited in Wadden, Brownell, & Foster, 2002).

Many psychological variables have been suggested as causes of obesity, including relatively low impulse control, inability to delay gratification, and maladaptive eating styles (primarily eating too fast). However, in a review of the literature, Rodin, Schank, and Striegel-Moore (1989) found that none of these suggestions has received empirical support. Rodin and her colleagues also found that unhappiness and depression seem to be the *effects* of obesity, not its causes, and that dieting behaviour seems to make the problem worse. Repeated bouts of weight loss and weight gain make subsequent weight loss more difficult to achieve.

There is no single, all-inclusive explanation for obesity, but there are many partial ones. Habit plays an important role in the control of food intake. Early in life, when we are most active, we form ideas about how much food constitutes a meal. Later in life, we become less active, but we do not always reduce our food intake accordingly. We fill our plates according to what we think is a proper-sized meal (or perhaps the plate is filled for us), and we eat everything, ignoring the satiety signals that might tell us to stop before the plate is empty. This analysis may also partly explain why people have so much difficulty losing weight.

Metabolic factors also play an important role in obesity. (The word *metabolism* refers to the physiological processes that produce energy from nutrients.) Just as cars differ in their fuel efficiency, so do people. Rose and Williams (1961) studied pairs of individuals who were matched for weight, height, age, and activity. One member of a pair might consume twice as many calories per day as their partner but nevertheless maintains the same weight. People with an efficient metabolism deposit excess calories in the long-term nutrient reservoir: fat cells. Over time, the reservoir grows, and the individuals become obese. In contrast, people with an inefficient metabolism can eat large meals without getting fat. All of their calories are spent to maintain muscles and heat production. Whereas a fuel-efficient automobile is desirable, a fuel-efficient body runs the risk of becoming obese in many modern-day environments in which calories are plentiful.

There may well be an evolutionary basis for high metabolic efficiency—whatever the factors that produce it. Food was only intermittently available during human prehistory. The ability to store extra nutrients in the form of fat when food was available would therefore have been a highly adaptive trait (e.g., Assanand, Pinel, & Lehman, 1998). In addition, the known variability in metabolism among people today may reflect the specific environments in which their ancestors lived (e.g., James & Trayhurn, 1981). A relative scarcity of food would promote the evolution of efficient metabolisms that would allow people to function on a relatively small number of calories per day.

Another evolutionary consideration in the origins of obesity has been developed by Pinel, Assanand, and Lehman (2000). They observe that the evolutionary response to intermittently available food was fat storage during periods of high food availability and fat use during periods of food scarcity. Today, therefore, high rates of obesity are occurring in many countries because we regularly store energy in the form of fat but do not suffer the scarcities that would cause us to draw on those stores. In other words, our biological heritage promotes overeating and excess storage of fat because the present environments differ from the past environments in which natural selection took place. Research has shown that animals will eat more when they experience a taste that has been associated with few calories in the past (Pierce et al., 2007). Nowadays, with so many foods on the market that vary in caloric content (e.g., low-fat but artificially sweetened snacks), our ability to learn the relationship between the foods we need and their tastes may be hampered (Davidson & Swithers, 2004).

We saw earlier that large fat cells secrete a protein, leptin, that lowers weight by increasing metabolic rate (that is, by making the metabolism less efficient) and decreasing food intake. Why, then, do some people become fat? Are they like ob mice, with defective OB genes? In most cases, the answer is no (Maffei et al., 1995). The fat cells of most obese people do secrete leptin; the receptors in the brain that normally detect leptin, however, may be deficient. For leptin to reduce weight, the brain must contain functioning leptin receptors. However, it is too soon to know whether the discovery of leptin and leptin receptors will aid in the treatment of obesity (de Luis et al., 2008).

## Anorexia Nervosa and Bulimia Nervosa

Overeating is the most common eating problem in Western societies today. However, some people have the opposite problem: They suffer from **anorexia nervosa**, a disorder characterized by a severe decrease in eating (Uyeda, Tyler, Pinzon, & Birmingham, 2002). Both males and females can be afflicted with anorexia nervosa, but the disorder is about three to four times more common in women. The literal meaning of the word *anorexia* is "loss of appetite," but people with this disorder generally do not lose their appetites. Instead, they limit their intake of food despite intense preoccupation with

**anorexia nervosa** An eating disorder characterized by attempts to lose weight, sometimes to the point of starvation.

▲ *The fashion industry's emphasis on thinness has been cited as a possible contribution to the prevalence of anorexia nervosa in Western cultures.*

food and its preparation. They may enjoy thinking about food and preparing meals for others to consume; they may even hoard food that they do not eat. However, they have an intense fear of becoming obese, and this fear continues even if they become dangerously thin. Many reduce their weight by cycling, running, or almost constant walking and pacing. When the weight loss becomes severe, menstruation stops. Anorexia nervosa is difficult to treat; as many as 6 percent of people with the disorder die from causes related to it (Neumarker, 1997).

The fact that anorexia nervosa is seen primarily in young women has prompted both biological and social explanations. The disorder sometimes runs in families, and current studies estimate that more than 50 percent of the variation in its occurrence is affected by genetic factors (Klein & Walsh, 2004). Many psychologists believe that the emphasis that Western cultures place on slimness—especially in women—is largely responsible for this disorder (see Pinhas et al., 1999). One account states that if a young person responds to this pressure with excessive dieting and exercise, a complex biological and behavioural pattern emerges that produces self-starvation (Pierce & Epling, 1997). Södersten and colleagues (e.g., Zandian, Ioakimidis, Bergh, & Södersten, 2007) have suggested that activity and starvation activate systems of reward and attention that reinforce dieting; effective treatment depends on re-establishing reinforcement for normal eating behaviours.

Another eating disorder, **bulimia nervosa**, is characterized by a loss of control of food intake and is again more common in women. (The term *bulimia* comes from the Greek words *bous,* meaning "ox," and *limos,* meaning "hunger.") People with bulimia nervosa periodically gorge themselves with food, especially desserts and snack foods, and especially in the afternoons or evenings. These binges are usually followed by self-induced vomiting or the use of laxatives accompanied by feelings of depression and guilt (Halmi, 1996; Steiger, Lehoux, & Gauvin, 1999). With this combination of bingeing and purging, the net nutrient intake of bulimics varies considerably. Weltzin, Hsu, Pollice, & Kaye (1991) report that 19 percent of bulimics undereat, 37 percent eat a normal amount, and 44 percent overeat. Episodes of bulimia are sometimes seen in patients with anorexia nervosa. Bulimia nervosa is seldom fatal, but it can result in poor health outcomes. Its causes are as uncertain as those of anorexia nervosa.

## Interim Summary

### Eating

Hunger is the feeling that precedes and accompanies an important regulatory behaviour: eating. Eating begins for both social and physiological reasons. Physiologically, the most important event appears to be the detection of a lowered supply of nutrients available in the blood. Detectors in the liver measure glucose and fatty acid levels, and detectors elsewhere in the body measure the level of fatty acids. Both sets of detectors inform the brain of the need for food and arouse hunger. This process seems to be important mainly under extreme conditions of deprivation. Social factors and habit are the most likely day-to-day instigators of hunger and eating. We stop eating for different reasons. Detectors responsible for satiety, which appear to be located in the walls of the stomach, monitor both the quality and the quantity of the food that has just been eaten. Long-term control of eating appears to be regulated by a chemical known as leptin, which is released by overnourished fat tissue and detected by cells in the brain. The effects of this chemical are to decrease meal size and increase metabolic rate, thus helping the body burn up its supply of triglycerides.

Sometimes, normal control mechanisms fail, and people gain too much weight. For any individual, genetic and environmental factors may interact to cause the person's weight to deviate from the norm. People differ in the efficiency of their metabolisms, and this efficiency can easily lead to obesity. Experiences such as repeated fasting and refeeding are often accompanied by overeating. More research on the causes of obesity may lead to ways of determining which factors are responsible for an individual's excessive weight. It is too soon to know how the discovery of leptin and the leptin receptor will aid in the treatment of obesity.

Anorexia nervosa is a serious, even life-threatening, disorder. Most anorexic patients are young women. Although they avoid eating, they often remain preoccupied with food.

**bulimia nervosa** A loss of control over food intake characterized by gorging binges followed by self-induced vomiting or use of laxatives; also accompanied by feelings of guilt and depression.

Psychologists believe that a social emphasis on thinness is an underlying factor that contributes to the development of the disorder. Bulimia nervosa is characterized by bingeing followed by self-induced vomiting, and can result in poor health outcomes.

**QUESTIONS TO CONSIDER**

1. In some cultures and times (such as Europe in the Baroque era), it was desirable to be overweight. Why might that have been? Why might thinness be desirable in our culture?
2. Do you think that the fact that most people with anorexia nervosa are female is caused entirely by social factors (such as the emphasis on thinness in our society), or do you think that biological factors (such as hormonal differences) also play a role? Can you think of any ways to answer these questions experimentally?

# Sexual Behaviour

Sexual behaviour is not motivated by a physiological need, the way that eating is. Because we must perform certain behaviours in order to reproduce, the process of natural selection has ensured that our brains are constructed in such a way as to cause enough of us to mate with each other that the species will survive.

## Effects of Sex Hormones on Behaviour

Sex hormones—hormones secreted by the testes and ovaries—have effects on cells throughout the body. In general, these effects promote reproduction. For example, they cause the production of sperm, build up the lining of the uterus, trigger ovulation, and stimulate the production of milk. Sex hormones also affect nerve cells in the brain, thereby affecting behaviour.

Sex hormones do not *cause* behaviours. Behaviours are responses to particular situations and are affected by people's experiences in the past. What sex hormones do is affect people's *motivation* to perform particular classes of reproductive behaviours. We therefore start our exploration of sexual behaviour with the motivational effects of sex hormones.

**organizational effect** An effect of a hormone that usually occurs during prenatal development and produces permanent changes that alter the subsequent development of the organism. An example is androgenization.
**activational effect** The effect of a hormone on a physiological system that has already developed. If the effect involves the brain, it can influence behaviour. An example is facilitation of sexual arousal and performance.
**estrous cycle** The ovulatory cycle in mammals other than primates; the sequence of physical and hormonal changes that accompany the ripening and disintegration of ova.

**Effects of Androgens** As we saw in Chapter 12, androgens such as testosterone are necessary for male sexual development. During prenatal development, the testes of male fetuses secrete testosterone, which causes the male sex organs to develop. This hormone also affects the development of the brain. The prenatal effects of sex hormones are called **organizational effects** because they alter the organization of the sex organs and the brain. Studies using laboratory animals have shown that if the organizational effects of androgens on brain development are prevented, the animal later fails to exhibit male sexual behaviour. In addition, males cannot have an erection and engage in sexual intercourse unless testosterone is present in adulthood. These effects are called **activational effects** because the hormone activates sex organs and brain circuits that have already developed.

One of the effects of androgens on men is increased interest in sexual behaviour. When levels of testosterone decline in adult men (which can occur due to aging, disease, or other factors), they report decreased interest in sex, along with other changes such as increased irritability and depression (Tenover, 1998). Providing artificial testosterone supplements to men with this problem increases their interest in sex, their ability to have erections, and their frequency of sexual intercourse (Seftel, Mack, Secrest, & Smith, 2004). Thus, we may conclude that testosterone definitely affects male sexual performance.

Interestingly, this last study showed that a placebo—a non-active chemical that a participant couldn't distinguish from the drug treatment—produced some of the same changes (although not to the same degree). Therefore, interest in sex, and even the physiological changes that accompany it, is also affected by psychological factors (see Rupp & Wallen, 2008). For example, men's interest in sexually explicit photographs will vary with their level of testosterone, but the effect seems to be at least partially due to the hormone's preventing the habituation of sexual interest after the novelty of the sexual aspects of the pictures had declined (Rupp & Wallen, 2007).

Although testosterone affects sexual motivation, it does not determine the *object* of sexual desire. A homosexual man who receives injections of testosterone will not suddenly become interested in women. If the testosterone has any effect, it will be to increase his interest in sexual contact with other men. Sexual orientation is discussed in a later section.

**Effects of Progesterone and Estradiol** In most species of mammals, the hormones estradiol and progesterone have strong effects on female sexual behaviour. The levels of these two sex hormones fluctuate during the menstrual cycle of primates and the **estrous cycle** of other female mammals. The difference between these two cycles is primarily that the lining of the primate uterus—but not that of other mammals—builds up during the first part of the cycle and sloughs off at the end. A female mammal of a non-primate species will receive the advances of a male only when the levels of estradiol and progesterone in her blood are high. This condition

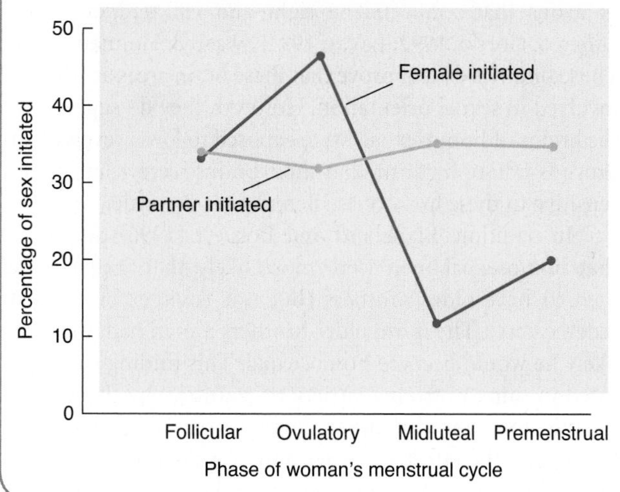


**FIGURE 13•7** Mean percentage of sexual activity initiated by women or their partners during the woman's menstrual cycle.

*(Van Goozen, S. H. M., Wiegant, V. M., Endert, E., Helmond, F. A., & Van de Poll, N. E. (1997). Psychoendocrinological assessment of the menstrual cycle: The relationship between hormones, sexuality, and mood.* Archives of Sexual Behavior, 26, *359–382.)*

occurs around the time of ovulation, when copulation is likely to make her become pregnant.

Although ovarian hormones do not control women's sexual activity, they may still have an influence on women's sexual interest. A study by Van Goozen and colleagues (1997) found that the sexual activity initiated by men and women showed very different relations to the woman's menstrual cycle (and hence to her level of ovarian hormones). Men initiated sexual activity at about the same rate throughout the woman's cycle, whereas sexual activity initiated by women showed a distinct peak around the time of ovulation, when estradiol levels are highest. (See **Figure 13•7**.)

Laeng and Falkenberg (2007) obtained evidence that estradiol can affect a woman's interest in a romantic partner. When people look at an emotionally significant stimulus, changes in their autonomic nervous system cause their pupils to dilate. This response is automatic and unintentional. Laeng and Falkenberg found that when women looked at pictures of their boyfriends around the time of ovulation, their pupils dilated more than they did at other times in their menstrual cycles. These differences were not seen in women taking birth control pills, which suppress the secretion of estradiol. (See **Figure 13•8**.)

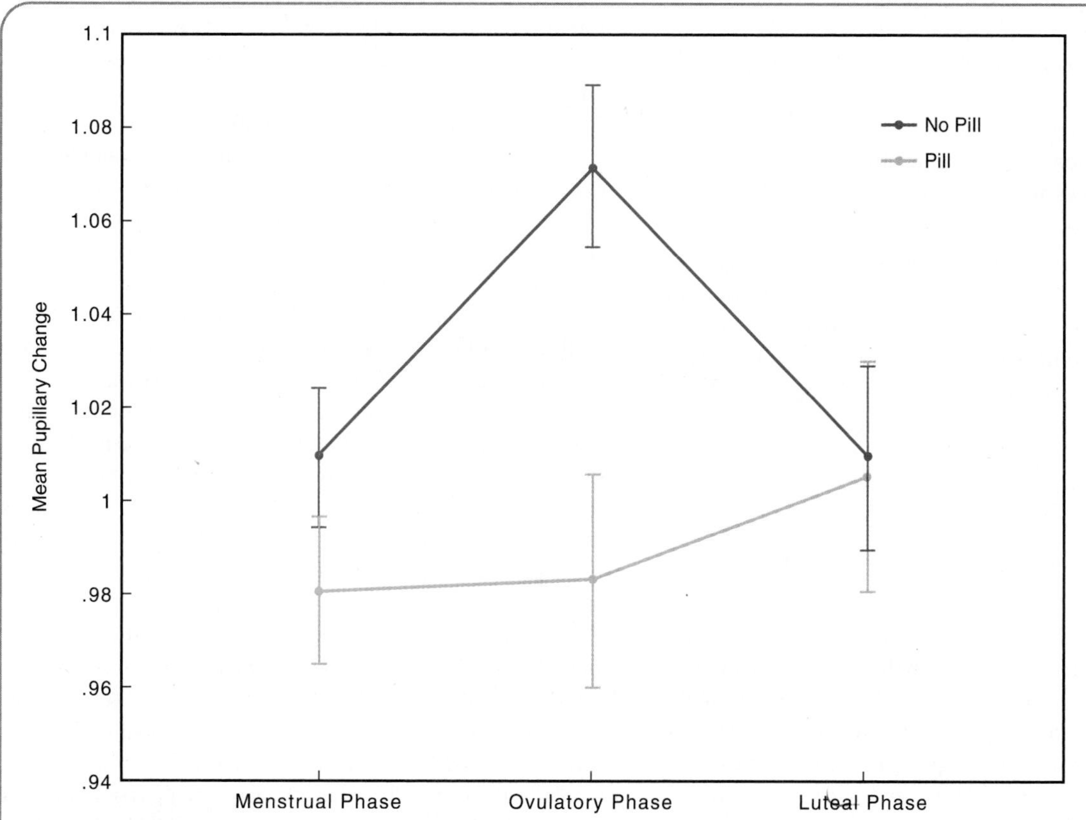


**FIGURE 13•8** Mean change in pupil diameter of women (either using oral contraceptives or not) when viewing photographs of their boyfriends, plotted over the phases of their hormonal cycles.

*(Laeng, B., & Falkenberg, L. (2007). Women's pupillary response to sexually significant others during the hormonal cycle.* Hormones and Behavior, 52, *520–530.)*

## Sexual Orientation

Homosexual behaviour (engaging in sexual activity with members of the same sex; from the Greek *homos,* meaning "the same") is seen in male and female animals of many different species. When humans reach puberty, the effects of sex hormones on their maturing bodies and on their brains increase their interest in sexual activity. As sexual interest increases, people develop a special interest in members of either the other sex or the same sex. Why does opposite-sex attraction occur? And why does same-sex attraction sometimes occur? As we shall see, research has not yet provided definite answers to these questions, but it has provided some hints.

An ambitious project reported by Bell, Weinberg, and Hammersmith (1981) studied a large number of male and female homosexuals. The participants were asked about their relationships with their parents, siblings, and peers and about their feelings, gender identification, and sexual activity. The results provided little or no support for traditional theories of homosexuality, which stress the importance of a person's early environment. The major conclusions of the study follow:

1. Sexual orientation appears to be determined prior to adolescence and prior to homosexual or heterosexual activity. The most important single predictor of adult homosexuality was a self-report of homosexual feelings, which usually occurred three years before first genital homosexual activity. This finding suggests that homosexuality is a deep-seated tendency. It also tends to rule out the suggestion that seduction by an older person of the same sex plays an important role in the development of homosexuality.
2. Most homosexual men and women have engaged in some heterosexual experiences during childhood and adolescence, but in contrast to their heterosexual counterparts, they found these experiences unrewarding. This pattern is also consistent with the existence of a deep-seated predisposition prior to adulthood.
3. There is a strong relation between gender non-conformity in childhood and the development of homosexuality. Gender non-conformity is characterized by an aversion in boys to "masculine" behaviours and in girls to "feminine" behaviours.

The results of the study are consistent with the hypothesis that homosexuality is at least partly determined by biological factors. That is, biological variables predispose a child to behaviour that is more typical of the other sex and eventually to sexual arousal by members of his or her own sex.

Is there evidence of what these biological causes of homosexuality may be? We can immediately eliminate the possibility that male homosexuals have insufficient levels of testosterone; well-adjusted male homosexuals have normal levels of testosterone (Garnets & Kimmel, 1991). Prenatal exposure to hormones and chemicals plays a large role in the development of homosexuality in both sexes (Swaab, 2007). Additional evidence comes from post-mortem studies of the brains of deceased homosexual men. Compared to the brains of heterosexual males, these brains show differences in the size of two sub-regions of the hypothalamus and of a bundle of axons that connects the right and left temporal lobes (Allen & Gorski, 1992; LeVay, 1991; Swaab & Hofman, 1990). These findings do not prove that these brain areas are directly involved in sexual orientation. However, they do suggest that the brains of homosexuals were exposed to lower levels of androgens before birth or that their brains were relatively insensitive to these hormones (Berenbaum & Snyder, 1995).

In addition, Blanchard and Bogaert (1996) discovered that homosexual men were more likely than heterosexual men to have older brothers (but not younger brothers or older sisters). The more older brothers a man had, the more likely he would become homosexual. This finding was replicated in samples from a variety of countries by the original investigators and by other investigators. Bogaert (2006) found that the effect was seen only if a man had older biological brothers, born to the same mother. The likelihood of homosexuality was not related to the presence of older adoptive brothers, or older brothers with the same father. So far, the most plausible explanation is that each time a woman carries a male fetus, her immune system becomes exposed to proteins that occur only in males. This exposure leads to development of maternal antibodies against these proteins that affect brain development of subsequent male fetuses (Blanchard & Ellis, 2001; Bogaert, 2003).

A final factor that may play a role in sexual orientation is heredity. Twin studies take advantage of the fact that identical twins have identical genes, whereas the genetic similarity between fraternal twins is, on average, 50 percent. Bailey and his colleagues (Bailey & Pillard, 1991; Bailey, Pillard, Neale, & Agyei, 1993) studied pairs of twins in which at least one member identified himself or herself as homosexual. If both twins are homosexual, they are said to be concordant for this trait. If only one is homosexual, the twins are said to be discordant. Thus, if homosexuality has a genetic basis, the percentage of monozygotic twins who are concordant for homosexuality should be higher than that for dizygotic twins. This is exactly what the investigators found: The concordance rate was 52 percent versus 22 percent for male twins, and 48 versus 16 percent for female twins.

Although less research has been done on the origins of female homosexuality, Cohen-Bendahan, van de Beek, and Berenbaum (2005) found that the incidence of homosexuality was several times higher than the national average in women who had been exposed to high levels of androgens prenatally. (The exposure was due to a genetic condition that causes the adrenal glands to secrete abnormally high levels of androgens, an event that begins prenatally.) Thus, sexual orientation in females may indeed be affected by biological factors, including prenatal hormones.

To summarize, evidence suggests that two major biological factors—heredity and the prenatal environment (exposure to hormones and maternal antibodies)—affect a person's sexual orientation. These research findings certainly contradict the suggestion that a person's sexual orientation is a matter of choice in adulthood. It appears that homosexuals are no more responsible for their sexual orientation than heterosexuals are. Ernulf, Innala, and Whitam (1989) found that people who believed that homosexuals were "born that way" expressed more positive attitudes toward them than did people who believed that they "chose to be" or "learned to be" that way. Thus, we can hope that research on the origins of homosexuality will reduce prejudice based on a person's sexual orientation. The question "Why does someone become homosexual?" will probably be answered when we discover why someone else becomes heterosexual.

### Transsexualism and Androgen Insensitivity Syndrome

As we saw, when the organizational effects of androgens are blocked in male laboratory animals, the animals fail to develop normal male sexual behaviour. In humans, male sexual behaviour also appears to depend on prenatal androgens (MacLean, Warne, & Zajac, 1995; Money & Ehrhardt, 1972). Some people are insensitive to androgens. They have androgen insensitivity syndrome, caused by a genetic mutation that prevents the formation of androgen receptors. Because the cells of the body cannot respond to androgens, the person develops female external genitalia instead of a penis and scrotum. The person does not develop ovaries or a uterus.

When an individual with one X chromosome and one Y chromosome is born with androgen insensitivity syndrome, the parents must choose whether to raise the child as a boy or a girl. (This situation is different from the case of D. R., described in Chapter 12, whose gender assignment resulted from genital trauma.) If the individual will be raised as a girl, the testes (which remain in the abdomen) are removed and, at the appropriate time, the person is given estrogen pills to induce puberty. Subsequently, the individual will function sexually as a woman. However, whether the adult is comfortable with this gender identity is a complex issue, depending on the degree of androgen insensitivity and the amount of psychological support received (see Hughes, Houk, Ahmed, & Lee, 2006, for a review).

Prenatal androgens also appear to have an effect on certain regions of the brain, including one region in the forebrain known as the *bed nucleus of the stria terminalis* (BNST). The BNST is larger in men than in women (Zhou, Hofman, Gooren, & Swaab, 1995). This difference is not present in childhood, but rather appears later in life, around the time of puberty (Chung, De Vries, & Swaab, 2002). The region is the same size in both heterosexual and homosexual men, suggesting that, although this region may differentiate male sexuality from female, it is not involved in male homosexuality.

The BNST, however, may be related to sexual identification rather than sexual orientation. Some individuals, typically described as **transsexual**, see themselves as belonging to a sex different than the one they were assigned at birth. A transsexual person, for example, may feel herself to be a female trapped inside a male body. Post-mortem studies of people born as males but identifying as females have found that the size of the BNST in these individuals is, indeed, similar to that of females (Zhou, Hofman, Gooren, & Swaab, 1995). Based on when they seek medical consultation regarding it, transsexual people recognize their condition sometime after puberty (van Kesteren, Gooren, & Megens, 1996)—about the time that the BNST begins to show a size difference between males and females.

## Interim Summary

### Sexual Behaviour

Testosterone has two major effects on male sexual behaviour: organizational and activational. In the fetus, testosterone organizes the development of male sex organs and of some neural circuits in the brain. Testosterone, an androgen, increases sexual motivation in men but does not, in itself, determine the object of sexual desire. In women, the hormones estradiol and progesterone fluctuate during the menstrual cycle. Ovarian hormones do not control women's sexual activity, but sexual interest seems to increase in response to high levels of estradiol.

At puberty, the effects of sex hormones on a person's maturing body and brain increase interest in sexual activity. Most people develop a special interest in members of the opposite sex, but some develop same-sex attractions. Although homosexuality was once regarded as a disorder, there is no evidence to support this. There are hints that homosexuality develops at least partly in response to biological factors. These factors are not as simple as a difference in hormonal levels but may involve the organizing effects of sex hormones on the developing embryo. Studies of homosexuality in twins show a higher concordance of homosexuality within identical twins than within pairs of non-identical twins. Thus, there may be both experiential effects of the prenatal environment and genetic effects that influence the development of same-sex attraction. Prenatal exposure to androgens can have a significant effect on the development of the sex organs and on a region of the forebrain. Transsexuality in males may reflect the fact that, in these individuals, this region looks more female-like than male-like.

**transsexual** Identifying with a sex different than the one assigned at birth.

**QUESTIONS TO CONSIDER**

1. Whatever the relative roles played by biological and environmental factors may be, most investigators believe that a person's sexual orientation is not a matter of choice. Why do you think so many people consider sexual orientation to be a moral issue?
2. Given the rapid pace of scientific and technical advances in genetics and allied fields, consider the possibility that one day parents may have the means to control the sex and sexual orientation of their offspring through in utero treatments. Do you think that such control should be exercised? In answering this question, consider what the benefits and dangers of exercising such control might be.

# Aggressive Behaviour

Aggression is a serious problem in human society. Every day, we hear of incidents involving violence and cruelty. If we are to live in a safer world, we must learn about the causes of aggressive behaviour. Many factors influence a person's tendency to commit acts of aggression, including frustration when behaviour is no longer reinforced, childhood experiences, exposure to violence in the media, and physiological factors. Various aspects of aggressive behaviour have been studied by biological, behavioural, and social scientists. We will examine some of the key variables that affect human aggression; but first, let's look at research on non-human animals in their natural environments.

## Ethological Studies of Aggression

Violence and aggression are seen in many species other than our own. If aggression were harmful to the survival of a population, we would not expect it to be so prevalent in nature. Ethologists—zoologists who study the behaviour of animals in their natural environments—have analyzed the causes of aggression and have shown that in many cases aggressive behaviour does, in fact, have value for the survival of species.

**Intraspecific aggression** is aggression by one animal against a member of its own species. Ethologists have shown that intraspecific aggression has several biological advantages. First, it tends to disperse a population of animals, forcing some into new territories. The adaptations required by these new environments increase the flexibility of the species. Second, rivalry among males for mating opportunities perpetuates the genes of the healthier, more vigorous animals. The human situation, of course, is somewhat different from that of other species because of culture. Culture, through learning, provides a means whereby the selecting effects of previous environments may be transmitted to the next generation by means other than genetics. Perhaps intraspecific aggression has outlived whatever usefulness it may have had for humans.

**intraspecific aggression** Aggression by one animal against a member of its own species.
**threat gesture** A stereotyped gesture that signifies that one animal is likely to attack another member of the species.
**appeasement gesture** A stereotyped gesture made by a submissive animal in response to a threat gesture by a dominant animal; tends to inhibit an attack.

Ethologists studying aggression have discovered a related set of behaviours in many species: ritualized threat gestures and appeasement gestures. **Threat gestures** communicate an animal's aggressive intent to other members of the species before actual violence begins. For example, if one dog intrudes on another's territory, the defender growls and bares its teeth, raises the fur on its back (presumably making it look larger to its opponent), and stares at the intruder. Almost always, the dog defending its territory drives the intruder away. Threat gestures are particularly important in species whose members are able to kill one another. For example, wolves often threaten each other with growls and bared teeth but rarely bite each other. To forestall an impending attack, one of the animals must show that it does not want to fight—that it admits defeat. The submissive animal makes an **appeasement gesture.** If a pair of wolves gets into a fight, one animal usually submits to the other by lying down and exposing its throat. The sight of a helpless and vulnerable opponent apparently terminates the victor's hostility, and the fight ceases. The aggression of the dominant animal is appeased. Because an all-out battle between two wolves would probably end in the death of one and serious injury to the other, the tendency to perform ritualized displays has an obvious advantage to the survival of both individuals. These rituals also can provide information to both participants as to which is the stronger (Hurd, 1997).

## Hormones and Aggression

In birds and most mammals, male sex hormones (androgens, such as testosterone) exert a strong effect on aggressiveness. In non-human species, testosterone exerts an organizational effect on the brain, altering the development of both the brain and the sex organs, and an activational effect on some forms of aggressive behaviour during adulthood. As shown in **Figure 13•9**, for example, a normal adult male mouse will fiercely attack other male mice that intrude on its territory; however, if a male mouse is castrated early in life, before its brain has matured, it will not attack another male later, even if given injections of testosterone (Conner & Levine, 1969). As always, natural selection and learning interact to determine behaviour. As an illustration, pigeons establish literal pecking orders that determine the ranks of birds in the colony. In one study, low-ranking male pigeons increased their rank after they had been injected with testosterone and

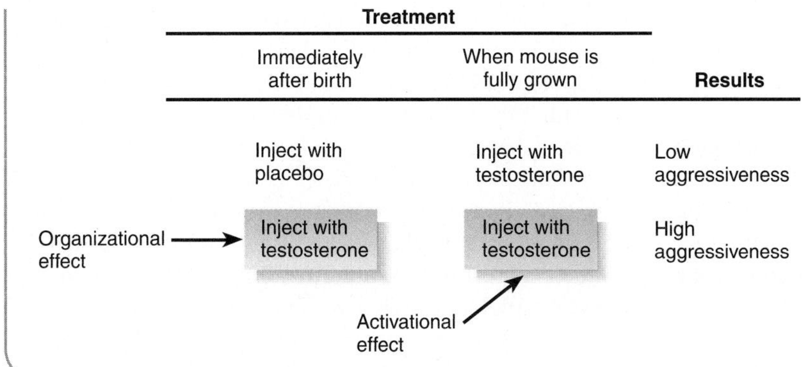


FIGURE 13•9 Organizational and activational effects of testosterone on aggressive behaviour of male mice that were castrated immediately after birth.

their aggressive behaviour (pecking another pigeon) had been reinforced with food in another situation. However, neither testosterone alone nor reinforcing aggressive behaviour alone had a similar effect (Lumia, 1972).

Do hormones also influence aggressive behaviour in humans? It has been shown that persons of either sex with higher testosterone levels appear to be more aggressive (Starzyk & Quinsey, 2001). Some male perpetrators of sexual assault have been treated with drugs that block androgen receptors and thus prevent androgens from exerting their normal effects. The rationale for this treatment is based on animal research that indicates that androgens promote both sexual behaviour and aggression in males. The efficacy of such treatment in humans, either for aggression or for the resolution of sexual problems, has yet to be established (Brett, Roberts, Johnson, & Wassersug, 2007; Lehne & Money, 2000).

We must remember that correlation does not necessarily indicate causation. A person's environment can affect his or her testosterone level. For example, one very thorough study found that the blood testosterone levels of a group of five men confined on a boat for 14 days changed as the men established a dominance–aggression ranking among themselves: The higher the rank, the higher the testosterone level (Jeffcoate, Lincoln, Selby, & Herbert, 1986). Yet, in a correlational study such as this, we cannot be sure that high testosterone levels cause people to become dominant or violent; perhaps their success in establishing a position of dominance increases their testosterone levels relative to those of the people they dominate.

Some athletes have taken anabolic steroids to increase their muscle mass and strength and, supposedly, their competitiveness. Anabolic steroids include natural androgens and synthetic hormones that have androgenic effects. This would lead us to expect increases in aggressiveness among these athletes. And indeed, several studies have found exactly that effect. For example, male weightlifters who were taking anabolic steroids were found to be more aggressive and hostile than those who were not (Yates, Perry, & Murray, 1992). Again, bear in mind that we cannot be certain that the steroid was responsible for the increased aggressiveness: Perhaps the men who were already more competitive and aggressive chose to take the steroids. Taken together, however, the research findings strongly suggest (although they do not prove) that androgens stimulate aggression in humans as they do in other animals.

## Environmental Variables That Affect Human Aggression

Environmental variables, including the behaviour of family members and peers as well as the impact of the media, can play a part in human aggression.

**Imitation of Aggression** Many parents discipline their children through physical methods, such as spanking, or verbal methods, such as scolding. The discomfort that these methods produce is used by the parent as an aversive stimulus that will either punish a behaviour that the parent wants to suppress or increase through negative reinforcement a behaviour that the parent wants to encourage (see Chapter 7). However, another possibility exists: The child may learn to imitate the parent's actions and show an increase in physical or verbal aggression. Bandura, Ross, and Ross (1961) showed that this could occur even when the aggression is produced by a relative stranger. They brought children into a playroom with several toys. Some of the children were accompanied by an adult role model who, after a few minutes, began to punch a large plastic doll. (The doll was a popular toy at the time, marketed under the name "Bobo"; the experiment is often referred to as the "Bobo study.") Other children either had no role model, or a role model who played quietly and non-aggressively with other toys. Later, all of the children encountered a mildly frustrating experience (the experimenter took away some of their toys) in the presence of the Bobo doll and their reactions were noted. Children who had seen an adult punch and kick the doll responded in the same way, even repeating some of the verbally aggressive shouts that the adult had used. As a group, these children were much more aggressive toward the doll than children in the other groups.

The Bandura, Ross, and Ross study raised the disturbing possibility that physical methods of discipline may actually increase aggression through imitation learning (Widom, 1989). A large percentage of non-violent people may have been spanked when they were children with no obvious harm. However, when parents habitually resort to aggression, their children may learn to do the same. To take an extreme example, many (though by no means all) parents who beat their children have themselves been victims of child abuse (Proeve & Reilly, 2007). It is important to note, however, that most adults who were physically abused as children manage to avoid repeating the pattern with their own children (Salter et al., 2003).

Most parents do not beat their children, or even spank them frequently. However, there is another source for imitation learning in our society: violent behaviour on television and in movies, comic books, and video games. Does the continued observation of violence in the mass media lead children to choose aggressive means to solve their problems? Or are the television networks and movie studios correct when they argue that children have no trouble separating fact from fantasy and that the mass media only give us what we want as viewers?

Psychologists and sociologists have shown keen interest in this question. Numerous researchers have studied the possible effects of media violence using correlational methods in both real-life environments and the laboratory. What can be concluded from the hundreds of investigations? Generally, there is a positive correlation between the amount of violent media programming that children watch and subsequent aggressive behaviour, although the strength of the correlation depends on many factors, such as whether behaviour is studied in the laboratory or in actual home settings (see Bushman & Huesmann, 2001; Huesmann, Moise-Titus, Podolski, & Eron, 2003). The relationship holds even when people are tracked from childhood to adulthood (Huesmann, Moise-Titus, Podolski, & Eron, 2003; Johnson et al., 2002). The obvious conclusion would seem to be that violent media programming causes increased violence among those who watch it. Yet, as suggestive as such studies are, we must be careful to remember the fundamental problem with correlational studies (see Chapter 2): Correlation does not prove causation. Any effort at reducing violence in society requires that we make the right decisions about where to put our resources and attention. If media violence is a major culprit, then that is where a great deal of our attention and efforts should go. However, another possibility is that causation flows in the opposite direction. We must ask whether the results of the media violence studies might simply show that the degree to which people are predisposed to violence causally affects the amount of violent programming they choose to watch (e.g., Freedman, 2002). For example, it would not be surprising if aggressive boys choose to watch more aggressive programming than non-aggressive boys do. People watch programs that interest them. Thus, the alternative hypothesis about causal directionality is plausible. It may be that violent programming does substantially increase violence and aggression in our society, but the research carried out to date has not established this beyond a doubt. We'll return to this issue in Chapter 15.

▲ *Does the continued observation of violence in mass media, such as video games, lead children to choose aggressive means to solve their problems? This is an active area of research.*

## Interim Summary

### Aggressive Behaviour

Aggression serves useful purposes in the majority of species. Ethological studies of other species reveal the presence of mechanisms to avert violence: Threat gestures warn of an impending attack, and appeasement gestures propitiate the potential aggressor. In males of most species of animals, androgens have both organizational and activational effects on aggressive behaviour. The same may be true for humans.

Aggressive behaviours can be imitated by children who view an adult behaving aggressively, which suggests that aggression may be at least partly based on observation. Violence in the media could therefore be a possible source of violence in our society. However, correlational data cannot distinguish between whether violent programming affects aggressiveness or aggressiveness affects choosing to watch violent programming.

#### QUESTIONS TO CONSIDER

1. From an evolutionary perspective, aggressive behaviour and a tendency to establish dominance have useful functions. In particular, they increase the likelihood that only the healthiest and most vigorous animals will reproduce. Can you think of examples of good and bad effects of these tendencies among humans?

2. Given what you know about the psychology of aggression, how would you make a person less aggressive? If a person is aggressive because he or she secretes more of a particular hormone, does this excuse his or her behaviour?

# The Nature of Emotion

Until this point, we have focused on forms of behaviour that are most intimately related to motivation: operant behaviour instigated by reinforcement, eating; aggressive behaviour instigated by aversive stimuli; and reproductive behaviour instigated by sexual stimuli. However, these same stimuli also elicit other important effects. These effects fall under the heading of emotion. The word **emotion** refers to the behaviour, physiological reactions, and subjective feelings that accompany motivated behaviour. When we are motivated, we display a wide range of emotional reactions: happiness, sadness, fear, and so forth. Different emotions are evoked by specific kinds of situations and provide distinctive stimuli that affect both the subsequent behaviour of the person experiencing the emotion and the behaviour of others who detect the emotion. For example, we communicate emotions to others by means of postural changes, facial expressions, and non-verbal sounds (such as sighs, moans, and laughs). These expressions serve useful social functions: They tell other people how we feel and—more to the point—what we are likely to do. For example, they warn a rival that we are angry or tell friends that we are sad and would like some comfort and reassurance. They can also indicate that a danger might be present or that something interesting seems to be happening.

## Emotions as Response Patterns

If you ask people to define the word *emotion,* they will probably talk about feelings. However, the ultimate reason for the existence of emotions is to provide patterns of behaviour appropriate to particular situations. Evolution has selected for patterns of emotional responses that are useful to the individual making them.

Emotional reactions have three components: behavioural, autonomic, and hormonal. The *behavioural* component consists of muscular movements appropriate to the situation that elicits them. For example, if a father sees his toddler venture onto a busy street, he will run to prevent the child from being hurt. In addition, his autonomic nervous system and the secretion of hormones by his adrenal glands will facilitate the behavioural component by mobilizing energy for vigorous movement. The father's heart rate will increase, the arteries that supply blood to his muscles will dilate, and his rate of respiration will increase.

**Conditioned Emotional Responses** Like other behaviour, emotional responses can be modified by experience. For example, once we have learned that a particular situation is dangerous, we become frightened when we next encounter that situation. This type of response, acquired through a classical procedure, is called a conditioned emotional response (see Chapter 7). A **conditioned emotional response** is produced when a neutral stimulus is paired with an emotion-producing stimulus. An early demonstration that emotions can be conditioned was made by Watson and Rayner (1920). They were able to study a nine-month-old boy whom they named "Albert B." Albert was a healthy child who seemed to Watson and Rayner "on the whole stolid and unemotional." However, they discovered that a loud noise, made by striking a steel bar with a hammer, could startle Albert and make him cry. A little later, when Albert was 11 months old, they showed him a live white rat—an animal that Albert had shown no fear of previously—and then, when Albert reached for it, they struck the bar. After two pairings of the white rat and the sound, Watson and Rayner observed that Albert was much more hesitant to touch the rat. After five pairings, he showed definite signs of fear, crying and crawling away from the rat. Watson and Rayner's conditioning procedure had produced an acquired fear.

Research by physiological psychologists indicates that a particular brain region plays an important role in the expression of conditioned emotional responses. This region is the amygdala, which is located in the temporal lobe, just in front of the hippocampus (refer to Figure 4.32 on page 122). The amygdala is a region of convergence for sensory systems and systems responsible for behavioural, autonomic, and hormonal components of conditioned emotional responses (Amaral, Price, Pitkänen, & Carmichael, 1992; Pitkänen, Savander, & LeDoux, 1997; Stefanacci & Amaral, 2000).

Studies conducted with animals have found that damage to the amygdala disrupts components of conditioned emotional responses. If this region is destroyed, animals no longer show signs of fear when confronted with stimuli that have been paired with aversive events. In addition, they act tame when handled by humans, their blood levels of stress hormones are lower, and they are less likely to develop stress-induced illnesses (Coover, Murison, & Jellestad, 1992; Davis, 1992; LeDoux, 1992). These effects are also seen in people who have sustained damage to the amygdala through stroke or disease (Bechara et al., 1995). Conversely, when the amygdala is stimulated by means of electrodes or by the injection of an excitatory drug, animals show physiological and behavioural signs of fear and agitation (Davis, 1992) and humans

**emotion** A relatively brief display of a feeling made in response to environmental events having motivational significance or in response to memories of such events.

**conditioned emotional response** A classically conditioned response produced by a stimulus that evokes an emotional response—in most cases, including behavioural and physiological components.

report feelings of fear. Such findings indicate that the autonomic and hormonal components of emotional responses are under the control of the amygdala and may contribute to the harmful effects of long-term stress. (We will examine the topic of stress in Chapter 16.)

## Social Judgments: Role of the Orbitofrontal Cortex

Earlier, we looked at aggression as it related to motivational stimuli, such as threats or appeasement gestures. Aggression in humans is often accompanied by emotions such as anger and fear, so it is appropriate to consider it in connection with emotions.

The muscular movements made during aggression are programmed by neural circuits in the brain stem. The activity of the brain stem circuits appears to be controlled by the hypothalamus and the amygdala, which also influence many other species-typical behaviours. And, of course, the activity of these structures is controlled by perceptual systems that detect the status of the environment, including the presence of other animals. Aggression, and the emotions that accompany it, is therefore the result of a number of brain processes.

**Role of Serotonin** Several studies have found that serotonergic neurons play an inhibitory role in human aggression. For example, a depressed rate of serotonin release in the brain (indicated by low levels of the breakdown products of serotonin in the cerebrospinal fluid) is associated with aggression and other forms of anti-social behaviour, including assault, arson, murder, and child beating (Lidberg, Asberg, & Sundqvist-Stensman, 1984; Lidberg et al., 1985; Virkkunen, De Jong, Bartko, & Linnoila, 1989). Coccaro and colleagues (1994) studied a group of men with personality disorders (including a history of impulsive aggression). They found that the men with the lowest serotonergic activity were most likely to have close relatives with a history of similar behaviour problems.

If low levels of serotonin release contribute to aggression, perhaps drugs that act as serotonin agonists might help to reduce anti-social behaviour. In fact, a study by Coccaro and Kavoussi (1997) found that fluoxetine (Prozac), a serotonin agonist, decreased irritability and aggressiveness, as measured by a psychological test.

**Role of the Ventral Prefrontal Cortex** Many investigators believe that impulsive violence is a consequence of faulty emotional regulation. For most of us, frustrations may elicit an urge to respond emotionally, but we usually manage to calm ourselves and suppress these urges. The ventral prefrontal cortex plays a special role in control of emotional behaviours, especially anger and aggression.

**ventral prefrontal cortex** The region of the prefrontal cortex at the base of the anterior frontal lobes, involved in control of emotional behaviour.

The **ventral prefrontal cortex** is located at the base of the anterior frontal lobes. Its inputs provide it with information about what is happening in the environment and what plans are being made by the rest of the frontal lobes; its outputs permit it to affect a variety of behaviours and physiological responses, including emotional responses organized by the amygdala. Evidence suggests that the ventral prefrontal cortex serves as an interface between brain mechanisms involved in automatic emotional responses (both learned and unlearned) and those involved in the control of complex behaviours. This role includes using our emotional reactions to guide our behaviour and controlling the occurrence of emotional reactions in various social situations. The fact that the ventral prefrontal cortex plays an important role in control of emotional behaviour is shown by the effects of damage to this region.

The first—and most famous—case comes from the mid-nineteenth century. Phineas Gage, a dynamite worker, was using a steel rod to ram a charge of dynamite into a hole drilled in solid rock. The charge exploded and sent the rod into his left cheek, through his brain, and out the top of his head. (See **Figure 13•10**.) The accident severely damaged his ventral prefrontal cortex (Damasio et al., 1994). He survived, but was a different man. Before his injury, he was serious, industrious, and energetic. Afterwards, he became childish, irresponsible, and thoughtless of others. He was unable to make or carry out plans, and his actions appeared to be capricious and whimsical.

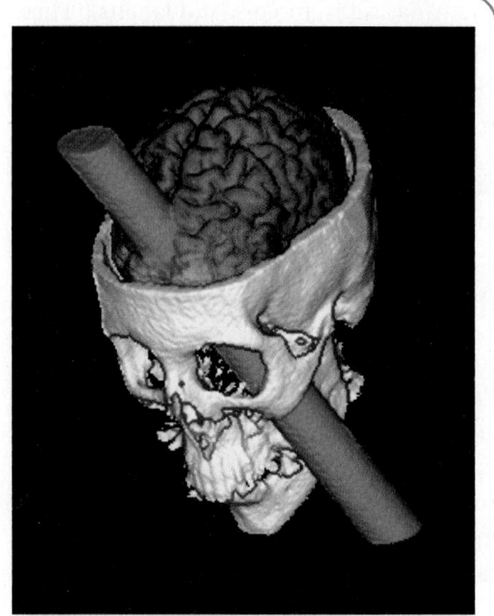

**FIGURE 13•10** A reconstruction of the skull of Phineas Gage and the rod that passed through his head. The steel rod entered his left cheek and exited through the top of his head.

*(From Damasio, H., Grabowski, T., Frank, R., Galaburda, A. M., and Damasio, A. R. (1994). The return of Phineas Gage: Clues about the brain from the skull of a famous patient.* Science, *264, 1102–1105. Copyright 1994 American Association for the Advancement of Science.)*

**Moral Judgment** Evidence suggests that emotional reactions guide moral judgments as well as decisions involving personal risks and rewards and that the prefrontal cortex plays a role in these judgments as well. Consider the following moral dilemma: You see a runaway trolley with five people aboard hurtling down a track leading to a cliff. Without your intervention, these people will soon die. However, you are standing near a switch that will shunt the trolley onto another track, where the vehicle will stop safely. Unfortunately, a worker is standing on that track, and he will be killed if you throw the switch to save the five helpless passengers. Should you stand by and watch the trolley go off the cliff, or should you save them—and kill the man on the track?

Most people conclude that the better choice would be to throw the switch; saving five people justifies the sacrifice of one man. But consider a variation of this dilemma. As before, the trolley is hurtling toward doom, but there is no switch at hand to shunt it onto another track. Instead, you are standing on a bridge over the track. An obese man is also standing there, and if you give him a push, his body will fall onto the track and stop the trolley. (You are too small to stop the trolley, so cannot save the five people by sacrificing yourself.) What should you do?

Most people balk at pushing the man off the bridge, even though the end result would be the same as in the first dilemma: one person lost, five people saved. Whether we kill someone by sending a trolley in his direction or by pushing him off a bridge into the path of the trolley, he dies when the trolley strikes him. But, somehow, pushing a person's body and causing his death seems more emotionally wrenching than throwing a switch that changes the course of a runaway trolley. Thus, moral judgments appear to be guided by emotional reactions and are not simply the products of rational, logical decision-making processes.

In a functional imaging study, Greene and colleagues (2001) presented people with moral dilemmas such as the one just described and found that thinking about them activated several brain regions involved in emotional reactions, including the medial prefrontal cortex. Making innocuous decisions, such as whether to take a bus or a train to some destination, did not activate these regions. Perhaps, then, our reluctance to push someone to his death is guided by the unpleasant emotional reaction we feel when we contemplate this action.

If the prefrontal cortex helps to mediate the role of emotions in moral judgments, then damage to this area should impair such judgments. In fact, tendencies toward anti-social behaviour are apparently associated with decreased volume of the prefrontal cortex and a lack of prefrontal activation during an aversive conditioning procedure (Birbaumer et al., 2005; Raine et al., 2002).

Raine and colleagues (1998) found evidence of decreased prefrontal activity and increased subcortical activity (including the amygdala) in the brains of convicted murderers. These changes were primarily seen in impulsive, emotional murderers. The prefrontal activity of cold-blooded, calculating, predatory murderers—whose crimes were not accompanied by anger and rage—was closer to normal. Presumably, increased activation of the amygdala reflected an increased tendency for display of negative emotions, and the decreased activation of the prefrontal cortex reflected a decreased ability to inhibit the activity of the amygdala and thus control people's emotions.

Earlier in this section, we saw that decreased activity of serotonergic neurons is associated with aggression, violence, and risk taking. As we have just seen, decreased activity of the prefrontal cortex is also associated with anti-social behaviour. These two facts appear to be linked. The prefrontal cortex receives a major projection of serotonergic axons. Research indicates that serotonergic input to the prefrontal cortex activates this region. In addition, several studies have found evidence for deficits in serotonergic innervation of the medial prefrontal cortex in people with a history of impulsive violence. For example, a PET study found evidence of decreased serotonergic input to the medial prefrontal cortex of such people (Frankle et al., 2005).

As we saw earlier, impulsive aggression has been successfully treated with specific serotonin reuptake inhibitors such as fluoxetine (Prozac). New and colleagues (2004) used a PET scanner to measure regional brain activity of people with histories of impulsive aggression before and after 12 weeks of treatment with fluoxetine. They found that the drug increased the activity of the orbitofrontal cortex and reduced aggressiveness.

## Interim Summary

### The Nature of Emotion

Emotion refers to the behaviour, physiological reactions, and subjective feelings that accompany motivated responses. Emotions provide patterns of behaviour that help us respond appropriately to situations. Emotional reactions have three components: behavioural, autonomic, and hormonal. The behavioural component of emotion is particularly evident in conditioned emotional responses, which are learned when a neutral stimulus is paired with an emotion-producing stimulus. Research has shown that the autonomic and hormonal components of emotional responses are under the control of the amygdala.

The muscular movements that an animal makes when engaged in aggressive behaviours are programmed by neural circuits in the brain stem. Serotonergic neurons have been implicated in the inhibition of human aggression. Low levels of serotonin release may contribute to this aggression, and serotonin agonists decrease irritability and aggressiveness.

The ventral prefrontal cortex plays a crucial role in the regulation of emotion, by integrating information from regions that control automatic emotional responses with other areas that control more complex behaviours. Moral decision making also seems to be controlled by the prefrontal cortex. This area of the brain receives major projections of serotonergic axons. Serotonin reuptake inhibitors increase the activity of this region, which may enhance its ability to control other regions involved in aggression, such as the amygdala.

**QUESTIONS TO CONSIDER**

1. Phobias are dramatic examples of conditioned emotional responses. We can acquire these responses without direct experience with an aversive stimulus. For example, a child who sees a parent show signs of fright in the presence of a dog may also develop a fear reaction to the dog. Do you think that some prejudices might be learned in this way as well?
2. If you were falsely accused of a crime, would you want to submit to a lie detector test to try to prove your innocence? Why or why not?

# Expression and Recognition of Emotions

We have considered emotions as organized response patterns (behavioural, autonomic, and hormonal) that are produced by environmental stimuli that are motivating. For example, being confronted with a threat not only motivates escape behaviour but also evokes various emotional responses. At the same time, emotions exist, in part, because expressions of emotion communicate important information to other members of the species. Members of many species (including humans) convey their emotions to others by means of postural changes and facial expressions. Such responses tell other individuals how we feel and—more to the point—what we are likely to do. For example, they warn when we are angry and should be left alone or when we are sad and would welcome comfort. This section reviews research on the expression and recognition of emotions.

## The Social Nature of Emotional Expressions in Humans

The expression of emotions is significantly social. For example, Lee and Wagner (2002) asked women to recount a positive and a negative emotional event that had happened to them in the past year. They were given a microphone to speak into but, unbeknownst to them, were also being videotaped. (This concealment required special justification on the basis of the ethical issues discussed in Chapter 2; Lee and Wagner provide a good account of how they resolved this dilemma.) Half of the women had a female acquaintance sit across from them as they described these experiences; the other participants spoke only into the microphone. Later, the videotapes were watched to determine when a participant showed positive or negative facial expressions.

When participants described their experiences alone, there was a good correspondence between the emotional experience they were describing and their facial expressions: positive experiences were accompanied by positive expressions and negative experiences were accompanied by negative expressions. However, the physical presence of another person affected facial expressions. Individuals showed significantly more positive facial expressions when they were talking about a positive experience to an acquaintance than when they were alone. Therefore, a social setting seemed to amplify the expression of positive feelings. However, negative facial expressions were fewer in the presence of another. Therefore, social context can depress the expression of negative emotions.

We tend to think that our facial expressions are closely linked to our emotional experiences. However, as we saw in the case of other emotional behaviours, facial expressions also serve as communication. We use them to manage others' impressions of our own state, which breaks down the link between our experience of emotion and our external expression of it.

## Universality of Emotional Expressions

The social content of emotional expression raises the question of culture. Different cultures and communities possess their own languages. Do they possess their own emotional expressions? Charles Darwin felt that emotions had evolved, and, based on information he received from anthropologists, suggested that they were expressed the same way in different cultures.

In the late 1960s, Ekman and Friesen undertook a series of cross-cultural observations that validated Darwin's hypothesis (Ekman, Friesen, & Ellsworth, 1972). They visited an isolated tribe in a remote area of New Guinea—the South Fore tribe, a group of 319 adults and children who had never been exposed to Western culture. If the tribespeople could identify the emotional expressions of Westerners as accurately as they could identify those of members of their own tribe, and if their own facial expressions matched those of Westerners, then the researchers could conclude that these expressions were not culturally determined.

Because translations of single words from one language to another are not always accurate, Ekman and colleagues told little stories to describe an emotion instead of presenting a single word. They told the story to a subject, presented three photographs of Westerners (each depicting a different emotion), and asked the subject to choose the appropriate one. The tribespeople were able to do this. In a second study, Ekman and colleagues asked South Fore tribespeople to imagine how they would feel in situations that would produce various emotions, and then videotaped the subjects' facial expressions. They showed photographs of the videotapes to American college students, who had no trouble identifying the emotions. Four of them are shown in **Figure 13•11**. The figure's caption describes the story that was used to elicit each

FIGURE 13•11 Portraying emotions. Ekman and Friesen asked South Fore tribespeople to make faces (shown in the photographs) when they were told stories. (a) "Your friend has come and you are happy." (b) "Your child had died." (c) "You are angry and about to fight." (d) "You see a dead pig that has been lying there a long time."

*(From Ekman, P. (1980).* The face of man: Expressions of universal emotions in a New Guinea village. *New York: Garland STPM Press. Photos © Paul Ekman 1972–2004. Reprinted with permission.)*

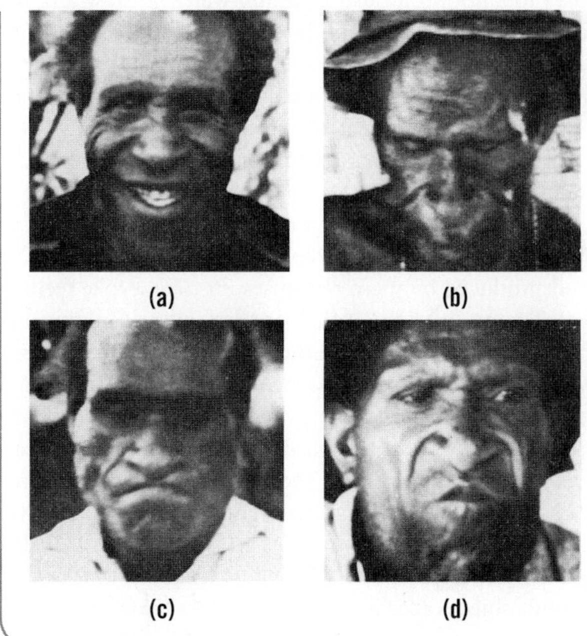

expression. **Table 13•1** shows the degree of accuracy of various cultures at recognizing facial expressions of emotion.

However, not all psychologists have agreed with Ekman's conclusions. While the finding that facial expressions can be identified cross-culturally is robust, there is little agreement on what these findings mean. Critics such as Fridlund (1992, 1994) have argued that all facial expressions are communicative and that to single out a group of emotional facial expressions ignores their fundamental social nature. Expressions may not be emotional signals but social tools used for communication: We can communicate happiness or approval via a smile, but this smile may not be generated by genuine emotion but rather by social cues or needs. This objection is difficult to counter, in part because facial expressions may sometimes be used for non-emotional purposes. Smiling may indeed be an expression of joy, but it can also be an expression of sarcasm or even, in sinister contexts, threat. What critics suggest is that facial expressions do not reflect the emotion but the social signalling of the emotion; the two are different.

TABLE 13•1 **Cross-Cultural Accuracy in Recognizing Emotion**

| Expression | U.S. | Chile | Brazil | Argentina | Japan |
|---|---|---|---|---|---|
| Happiness | 97 | 90 | 92 | 94 | 87 |
| Fear | 88 | 78 | 77 | 68 | 71 |
| Disgust | 84 | 85 | 86 | 79 | 82 |
| Anger | 68 | 76 | 82 | 72 | 63 |
| Surprise | 91 | 88 | 81 | 93 | 87 |
| Sadness | 87 | 91 | 82 | 88 | 80 |
| Average | 86 | 85 | 83 | 82 | 78 |

*Adapted from: Elfenbein, H. A. and Ambady, N. (2003). Universals and cultural differences in recognizing emotions.* Current Directions in Psychological Science, 12, *5, 159–164. Reproduced with permission of Blackwell Publishing Ltd.*

Other critics, such as Russell (1991, 1994), have even questioned whether the cross-cultural findings are robust. Russell has argued in some detail that the faults in the methodology in these experiments, particularly the method of presenting each emotion sequentially and asking respondents to choose the expression they have seen from a list of alternative descriptions, make the conclusions of these studies impossible to interpret.

It has been suggested that people are better at recognizing emotions within their own cultural group. However, Beaupré and Hess (2005) have challenged this notion. They measured emotional recognition in a sample of French-Canadian, sub-Saharan-African, and Chinese participants living in Canada. All samples performed similarly when asked to recognize expressions of emotion on the in-group and outgroup faces, but some groups were better at this task in general (regardless of nationality of the face). French Canadians recognized sadness more accurately than did the other two cultures, and recognized shame more accurately than did the Chinese. The researchers argue, however, that because the stimuli used in the experiment derive from North American investigations, this benefited the French Canadians, hence their better accuracy.

**Cultural Differences** Perhaps members of some cultures recognize certain emotions more accurately because these emotions are more important to them. Researchers from the University of Illinois asked European-American, Asian-American, Japanese, Indian, and Hispanic students to report their emotional experiences over a one-week period and note how many pleasant and unpleasant emotions they generally experienced (Scollon, Diener, Oishi, & Biswas-Diener, 2004). Individuals from Asian cultures reported less life satisfaction and fewer pleasant emotions than did North Americans. Asian Americans appear to show this pattern more than do European Americans (Diener, Suh, Smith, & Shao, 1995; Okazaki, 2000).

The researchers also found that Hispanic Americans reported the greatest levels of pride, whereas the three Asian samples reported the lowest levels. Among the Asian samples, Indians reported the lowest level of pride (suggesting that pride is not a greatly valued emotion in Indian culture and may be perceived negatively rather than positively). No cultural differences were found for sadness, but differences were found for guilt: Japanese and Asian Americans reported greater levels of guilt than did European Americans and Hispanics. The Indian sample reported the lowest level of guilt.

## Situations That Produce Emotions: The Role of Cognition

Emotions rarely occur spontaneously; they are provoked by particular stimuli, as we saw with conditioned emotional responses, and are affected by social context, as you just read. Emotions are the products of cognitive processes as well. For humans, the emotions evoked by eliciting stimuli can recur in later situations if they engage cognitive processes such as memory. Like memory, our emotions can be affected by the circumstances of retrieval. For example, Italian students who had recently participated in a large, peaceful demonstration recalled it as being more violent than it was when they saw altered photographs implying violence; they also rated it significantly more negative and said that they were unlikely to attend another (Sacchi, Agnoli, & Loftus, 2007).

Humans often experience emotions on the basis of their judgments about the significance of particular situations. For example, a pianist who is satisfied with her performance may perceive applause as praise for outstanding artistry, judging it to be a positive evaluation of her own worth. She will feel pride and gratification. In this case, her emotional state is produced by social reinforcement—the expression of approval and admiration by other people. However, if the pianist believes that she has performed poorly, she may judge the applause as the mindless enthusiasm of people who have no taste and for whom she feels only contempt. The page-turner is also present on the stage and thus also perceives the applause. However, because he does not evaluate the applause as praise for anything he did, he does not experience the emotions that the pianist feels. The applause may even make him feel jealous. Clearly, a given set of stimuli does not always elicit the same emotion. Judgments about the significance of the stimuli determine the emotion that the person feels.

## Feelings of Emotions

Emotions are accompanied by physiological reactions, and these reactions can evoke feelings of emotion. We can easily understand why. Strong emotions increase the heart rate and can produce irregular breathing, queasy feelings in the internal organs, trembling, sweating, reddening of the face, or even fainting. We may ask whether these physiological reactions constitute the emotion or are merely symptoms of some other underlying process.

The theory developed by physiologists Walter Cannon and Phillip Bard, and an earlier theory proposed by psychologist William James and physiologist Carl Lange, are two somewhat different approaches to feelings of emotion. The James-Lange theory proposed that the physiological and behavioural responses to emotion-arousing stimuli produced feelings of emotion (James, 1884; Lange, 1887). The Cannon-Bard theory contended that feelings of emotion were relatively independent of the physiological and behavioural responses to emotion-arousing stimuli (Cannon, 1927).

Based on the evidence available at the time, Cannon and Bard incorrectly believed that autonomic and behavioural responses to emotion-arousing stimuli were too slow and too indistinct to affect the rapidly occurring and often subtle differences in feelings of emotion. As an illustration of the difference between the theories, Cannon and Bard took the position that the sight of an approaching bear evokes both physiological/behavioural responses and, largely independently, feelings of fear.

In contrast, James and Lange believed that the sight of the bear evokes physiological/behavioural responses and that stimuli produced by these responses, in turn, evoke feelings of fear. That is, the sight of the bear first evokes running and increases in heart rate and then, after these changes are sensed, feelings of fear. In essence, the James-Lange theory states that emotion-producing situations elicit an appropriate set of physiological responses, such as trembling, sweating, and increased heart rate. The situations also elicit behaviours, such as clenching of fists or fighting. The brain receives sensory feedback from the muscles and from the organs that produce these responses, and it is this feedback that constitutes our subjective feelings of emotion. As James put it:

> The bodily changes follow directly the perception of the exciting fact, and . . . our feelings of the same changes as they occur is the emotion. Common sense says we lose our fortune, are sorry, and weep; we meet a bear, are frightened, and run. . . . The hypothesis here to be defended says that this order of sequence is incorrect. . . . The more rational statement is that we feel sorry because we cry, angry because we strike, afraid because we tremble, and not that we cry, strike, or tremble because we are sorry, angry or fearful, as the case may be. (James, 1890, p. 449)

James's approach is closely related to a process called attribution, which we will encounter in Chapter 15. Attribution theory, an area of social psychology, is concerned with how we draw conclusions about the causes of other people's behaviour. The James-Lange theory says that we go through much the same process when we draw conclusions about our own behaviour. We observe our own physiological and behavioural responses and, based on that information, attribute feelings to ourselves. Our emotional feelings are based on what we find ourselves doing and on the sensory feedback we receive from the activity of our muscles and internal organs. Where feelings of emotions are concerned, we are self-observers. Thus, patterns of emotional responses and expressions of emotions give rise to feelings of emotion. By this reasoning, emotional feelings are the products of emotional responses. (See **Figure 13•12.**)

**FIGURE 13•12** A diagrammatic representation of the James-Lange theory of emotion. An event in the environment triggers behavioural, autonomic, and endocrine responses. Feedback from these responses produces feelings of emotions.

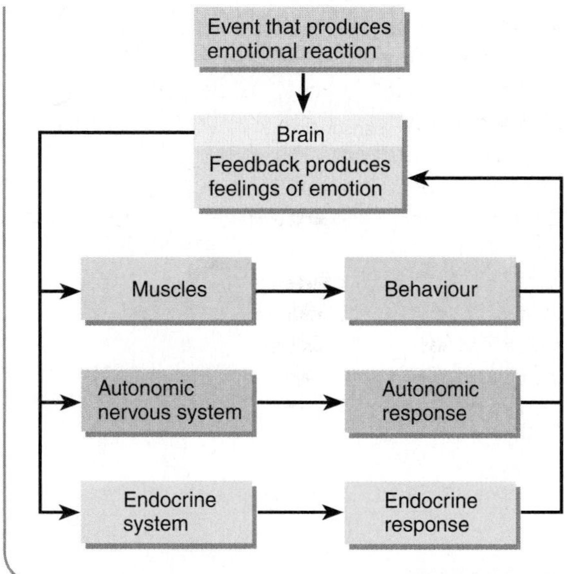


James's description of the process by which emotional feelings are produced may seem odd. We usually believe that we directly experience feelings without physiological or behavioural intermediaries. We tend to see the outward manifestations of emotions as secondary events. But have you ever found yourself in an unpleasant confrontation with someone and discovered that you were trembling, even though you did not think that you were so upset by the encounter? Or were you ever surprised to find yourself blushing in response to some remark? Or did tears ever come to your eyes while watching a film that you did not think was affecting you? What might you conclude about the causes of your emotional feelings in situations like these? Would you ignore the evidence of your own physiological and behavioural reactions?

## Interim Summary

### Expression and Recognition of Emotions

Expressive behaviour communicates important information about emotions to other people. An observational study of humans indicated that smiles appear to occur most often when someone is there to see the smile. This finding supports the social nature of emotional expression.

Emotions are provoked by particular motivational stimuli, and in humans these stimuli include those from cognitive processes as well as observable behaviour. For example, emotions can be produced by memories of previous emotion-arousing situations.

Emotions are accompanied by feelings that come from inside the body. James and Lange suggested that the physiological and behavioural reactions to emotion-producing situations were perceived as feelings. Thus, feelings of emotion were not the causes but rather the results of these reactions. Hohmann's early study of people with spinal cord damage was consistent with the James-Lange theory, but subsequent research has found that people who can no longer feel reactions from most of the body reported emotional feelings similar to people without such deficits.

**QUESTIONS TO CONSIDER**

1. As you know, we tend to become accustomed to our present circumstances. If we finally achieve a goal we have been striving for—a car, a well-paying job, a romantic attachment with a wonderful person—we find that the happiness it brings us is not permanent. But if we then lose what we have gained, we are even less happy than we were in the first place. Is it ever possible for a person to be happy all of the time?
2. We can control the display of our emotions, but can we control our feelings? Can you think of any ways to make yourself feel happy or stop feeling angry?

## Then and Now

### The James-Lange Theory

It is important to recognize that the James-Lange theory is a theory regarding the *feeling* of emotion. Emotions are the behavioural, autonomic, and hormonal responses to situations; feelings of emotion are the subjective component—our conscious experience of the emotion. In Chapter 9, we saw that consciousness could be considered a form of communication. Considered this way, the James-Lange theory is basically a theory about the way emotion is communicated. James and Lange thought that this communication begins with peripheral responses communicating a quality of the emotion to the brain, which then interprets it.

The clearest test of this theory, then, would be to see how emotion is experienced when this peripheral communication is blocked. The classic study in this regard was conducted by Hohmann (1966), who questioned people who had suffered damage to the spinal cord about the intensity of their emotional feelings. If feedback from the body is important, one would expect that emotional feelings would be less intense if the injury was high (that is, close to the brain) than if it was low, because a high spinal cord injury would make the person insensitive to a larger part of the body. In fact, Hohmann found precisely this result: The higher the injury, the less intense the feeling was. (See **Figure 13•13.**)

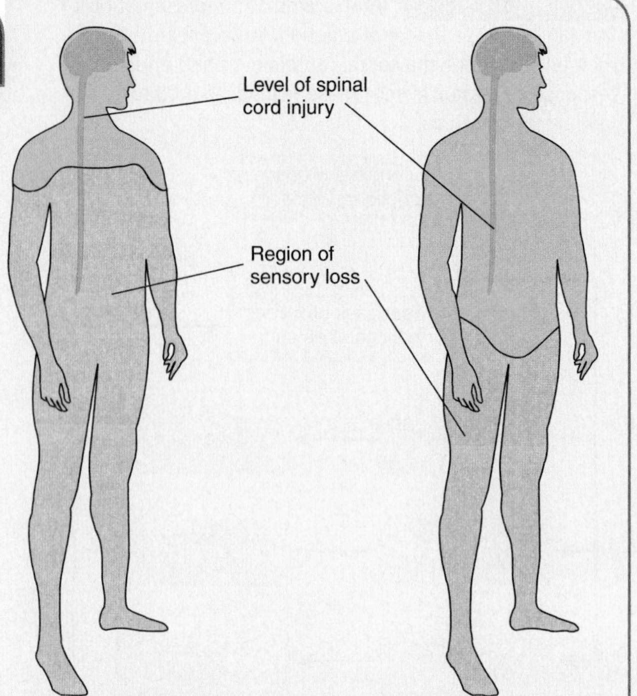


**FIGURE 13•13** Hohmann's investigation of emotion in people with spinal cord damage. The higher the spinal cord damage, the less intense was the person's feeling.

The comments of patients with high spinal cord injuries also suggested that the severely diminished feedback does change their feelings, but not necessarily their behaviour.

> I was at home alone in bed one day and dropped a cigarette where I couldn't reach it. I finally managed to . . . put it out. I could have burned up right there, but the funny thing is, I didn't get all shook up about it. I just didn't feel afraid at all. . . . (Hohman, 1966, pp. 150–151)

Hohmann's results support the James-Lange theory. However, with new advances in measuring brain function, such as fMRI (see Chapter 4), neuroscientists are finding that the story is more complex. Some of this research has re-examined, in the way Hohmann did, how spinal cord damage affects feelings of emotion. For example, Nicotra, Critchley, Mathias, and Dolan (2006) tested whether patients with spinal cord injuries would show a conditioned emotional response to pictures of faces that had been paired with electric shock. Although they could report the sensation of pain, these patients did not show a conditioned emotional response relative to people without spinal cord injury. Significantly, when a face paired with electric shock was shown to patients with spinal cord injuries, fMRI images showed less activity in the ventral prefrontal cortex compared to people without injury. These findings, like Hohmann's, support the James-Lange theory: Intact communication with the periphery is necessary for the brain, particularly the ventral prefrontal cortex, to register fear.

Other results, however, are less kind to the theory. Cobos and colleagues (2002) examined how people reacted to photographs that elicit emotions. They showed the participants in their study images that evoked positive or negative feelings and measured several behavioural reactions. Some of the participants in this study were people with spinal cord injuries. In general, their reactions were very similar to the reactions of people without injuries. Importantly, when asked to judge their ability to feel different kinds of emotion, there was no clear difference related to the level of the spinal cord injury.

A picture is emerging that there may be several systems related to feelings of emotion (Dalgleish, 2004). Our feelings of emotion may also be a matter of timing. Tsuchiya and Adolphs (2007) have suggested that connections within the brain may give us an initial, quick, emotional feeling, while slower bodily sensations influence our feelings in later stages. As they note, this is a detail about the brain that James himself would never have imagined.

EPILOGUE

## What's the Reason?

The people of Malaysia excuse the actions of a person in a *latah* state because they attribute her behaviour to the provocation of the teaser. Although the behaviours might be deeply scandalous, the person performing them is not held accountable. It's the teaser—an external agent—who has caused the action. If a woman acted the same way without provocation, however, that would be a different matter.

Unless you are Malay yourself, *latah* is not part of your culture; yet, our culture's attitudes toward motivation are not that much different. Suppose you were having a meal with an acquaintance and someone jostled your arm, causing you to spill water on your friend. Any reasonable observer would excuse you and blame the incident on the person who jostled you. However, if you were suddenly to pour water on your friend of your own volition, then the *motive* for your action becomes the issue and you are blamed. That same reasonable observer might conclude that you are angry or hostile, or, perhaps, that you harbour some deep resentments that bubbled to the surface, causing you to take them out on your friend. The irony is that, as we hold ourselves accountable for our actions, we also tend to use internal causes as explanations. When we do this, we attribute our own or another person's actions to causes that we cannot see and may not even be able to understand.

Many psychologists in the early 1900s viewed the central questions of psychology in motivational terms and used concepts such as drives, instincts, and impulses. Sigmund Freud, whose theories we'll discuss in the next chapter, was one such scholar. As our knowledge of psychology has increased, however, we've been able to replace these unobservable explanations with descriptions that relate either to an individual's past (such as learned coping strategies) or to our ancestral history (such as evolved homeostatic mechanisms). The result has been not only a more integrated view of motivation, but also one that is more adaptable to solving the issues people face in dealing with problems of health.

Robert Bartholomew, who has personal experience with *latah*, has suggested that the paradox of *latah* behaviour might be understood from non-mysterious and observable factors. Simply put, he has suggested that *latah* is a form of deception: The behaviours are performances in which the actor knows very well what she is doing. Why are they done? There may be many cultural reasons, but it's not hard to see how the attention a *latah* performance brings could be reinforcing to someone who is typically ignored at family functions and generally overlooked. The motivation for *latah* behaviours is therefore in the past experiences of its practitioners.

Bartholomew's explanation is not without its critics, who feel that deception is too strong a word for something that may be neurologically or culturally determined. However, nature presents us with puzzles about behaviour all the time, and can be infinitely more deceptive about the solutions. We need to resist the tendency to interpret motivated behaviour in terms of amorphous causes. Our understanding of people—and our ability to help them—presupposes a clearer understanding of the causes of their actions.

## Canadian Connections to Research in This Chapter

Assanand, S., Pinel, J. P. J., & Lehman, D. R. (1998). Personal theories of hunger and eating. *Journal of Applied Social Psychology, 28*, 998–1015. (University of British Columbia: www.ubc.ca)

Beaupré, M. G., & Hess, U. (2005). Cross-cultural emotion recognition among Canadian ethnic groups. *Journal of Cross-Cultural Psychology, 36*, 355–370. (Université du Québec, Montréal: www.uquebec.ca)

Blanchard, R., & Bogaert, A. F. (1996). Homosexuality in men and number of older brothers. *American Journal of Psychiatry, 153*, 27–31. (Clarke Institute of Psychiatry: www.camh.net)

Bogaert, A. F. (2004). The interaction of fraternal birth order and body size in male sexual orientation. *Behavioral Neuroscience, 117*, 381–384. (Brock University: www.brocku.ca)

Bogaert, A. F. (2006). Biological versus nonbiological older brothers and men's sexual orientation. *Proceedings of the National Academy of Science (USA), 103,* 10771–10774. (Brock University: www.brocku.ca)

Brett, M. A., Roberts, L. F., Johnson, T. W., & Wassersug, R. J. (2007). Eunuchs in contemporary society: Expectations, consequences, and adjustments to castration (Part II). *Journal of Sexual Medicine, 4,* 946–955. (Dalhousie University: www.dal.ca)

Cameron, J., & Pierce, W. D. (2005). Rewards and motivation in the classroom. *Academics Exchange Quarterly, 9*(2), 67–70. (University of Alberta: www.ualberta.ca)

Freedman, J. L. (2002). *Media violence and its effect on aggression: Assessing the scientific evidence.* Toronto: University of Toronto Press. (University of Toronto: www.utoronto.ca)

Hebb, D. O. (1955). Drives and the C.N.S. (conceptual nervous system). *Psychological Review, 62,* 243–254. (McGill University: www.mcgill.ca)

Donald Hebb was the first winner (in 1980) of the Donald O. Hebb Award of the Canadian Psychological Association and the 1961 winner of the American Psychological Association's Award for Distinguished Scientific Contributions.

Olds, J., & Milner, P. (1954). Positive reinforcement produced by electrical stimulation of septal areas and other regions of rat brains. *Journal of Comparative and Physiological Psychology, 47,* 419–427. (McGill University: www.mcgill.ca)

Pierce, W. D., & Epling, W. F. (1997). Activity anorexia: The interplay of culture, behavior, and biology. In P. Lamal (Ed.), *Cultural contingencies: Behavior analytic perspectives on cultural practices.* Westport, CT: Prager Publishers/Greenwood Publishing Group, Inc. (University of Alberta: www.ualberta.ca)

Pierce, W. D., Heth, C. D., Owczarczyk, J. C., Russell, J. C., & Proctor, S. D. (2007). Overeating by young obesity-prone and lean rats caused by tastes associated with low energy foods. *Obesity, 15,* 1969–1979. (University of Alberta: www.ualberta.ca)

Pinel, J. P. J., Assanand, S., & Lehman, D. R. (2000). Hunger, eating, and ill health. *American Psychologist, 55,* 1105–1116. (University of British Columbia: www.ubc.ca)

Pinhas, L., Toner, B. B., Ali, A., Garfinkel, P. E., & Stuckless, N. (1999). The effects of the ideal of female beauty on mood and body satisfaction. *Eating Disorders, 25,* 223–226. (University of Toronto: www.utoronto.ca)

Statistics Canada. (2004, June 15). *The Daily.* (Statistics Canada: www.statcan.ca/Daily/English/040615/d040615b.htm)

Steiger, H., Lehoux, P. M., & Gauvin, L. (1999). Impulsivity, dietary control and the urge to binge in bulimic syndromes. *International Journal of Eating Disorders, 26,* 261–274. (McGill University: www.mcgill.ca)

Uyeda, L., Tyler, I., Pinzon, J., & Birmingham, C. L. (2002). Identification of patients with eating disorders: The signs and symptoms of anorexia nervosa and bulimia nervosa. *Eating & Weight Disorders, 7,* 116–123. (University of British Columbia: www.ubc.ca)

Vallerand, R. J., & Ratelle, C. F. (2002). Intrinsic and extrinsic motivation: A hierarchical model. In E. L. Deci & R. M. Ryan (Eds.), *Handbook of self-determination research.* Rochester, NY: University of Rochester Press. (Université du Québec à Montréal: www.uqam.ca)

## Suggestions for Further Reading

Carlson, N. R. (2006). *Physiology of behavior* (9th ed.). Boston: Allyn and Bacon.

This is a good intermediate-level text that describes in detail the physiological bases of motivation and emotion.

Ekman, P. (2003). *Emotions revealed: Recognizing faces and feelings to improve communication and emotional life.* New York: Times Books/Henry Holt and Co.

Ekman offers a very readable account of his work on facial expressions of emotion.

Franken, R. E. (2002). *Human motivation* (5th ed.). Pacific Grove, CA: Brooks/Cole Publishing.

This book examines the general principles of motivation as well as specific types of motivated behaviour.

Logue, A. W. (2005). *The psychology of eating and drinking* (3rd ed.). New York: W. H. Freeman.

This book covers alcohol abuse as well as eating and eating disorders.

LeVay, S. (1993). *The sexual brain.* Cambridge, MA: MIT Press.

A well-written book on sexual behaviour and the social and biological variables that affect it.

Jenkins, J. M., Catley, K., & Stein, N. L. (Eds.). (1998). *Human emotions: A reader.* Malden, MA: Blackwell Publishers.

Bauby, J.-D. (1997). *The diving bell and the butterfly* (tran. J. Leggatt). New York: Knopf.

The book by Jenkins, Catley, and Stein contains chapters by many experts in the field of emotion. Bauby's book is probably one of the most unusual ever written. Its author was the senior editor of a French fashion magazine when a stroke left him with "locked-in syndrome," a horrifying condition that leaves a person completely paralyzed yet also fully conscious. Bauby wrote the book using the only movement he could make: blinking his eye to choose individual letters, one after the other. It is moving to read his descriptions of his emotional experience. The book also provides new insight into the subjective evidence behind the James-Lange theory.

Bartholomew, R. E. (2000). *Exotic deviance: Medicalizing cultural idioms from strangeness to illness.* Boulder, CO: University Press of Colorado.

Bartholomew describes the *latah* experience and many other interesting behaviours motivated by cultural factors.

# 14

# PERSONALITY

# CHAPTER OUTLINE

## Trait Theories of Personality

Personality Types and Traits • Identification of Personality Traits

Trait theories of personality stress that personality consists of enduring characteristics evident in behaviour in many situations. Several researchers have identified traits that appear to form the core of personality, including extroversion, neuroticism, psychoticism, openness, agreeableness, and conscientiousness. Others have added three "darker" traits of psychopathy, machiavellianism, and narcissism. Comparisons across cultures must recognize differences in language, but when people describe someone known to them, they generally use traits from the core factors.

## Psychobiological Approaches

Heritability of Personality Traits • *Then and Now: Twin Differences and the Genome* • Brain Mechanisms in Personality

Psychobiological approaches to the study of personality focus on the role of inherited factors and brain mechanisms in personality development. Although most of the variability in personality traits is due to heredity, a substantial portion is also due to the interaction of heredity and environment. Our increasing understanding of the human genome may help us unravel how this interaction occurs.The neural systems responsible for reinforcement, punishment, and arousal appear to underlie the personality traits of extroversion, neuroticism, and psychoticism. Other research shows that shyness may have its roots in a neural mechanism that includes the amygdala.

## Social Cognitive Approaches

Expectancies and Observational Learning • Reciprocal Determinism and Self-Efficacy • Person Variables • Locus of Control • Positive Psychology

The social cognitive approach to the study of personality represents a mixture of behaviour-analytic and cognitive concepts. Bandura asserts that personality development involves the imitation of others' behaviour and expectations about potential reinforcing and punishing contingencies. Bandura also argues that the interaction of behavioural, environmental, and personal (cognitive) variables ultimately determines personality. Prominent among these variables is self-efficacy, or one's expectations of success in a given situation. Mischel extended Bandura's emphasis on personal variables to include five other factors: competencies, encoding strategies and personal constructs, expectancies, subjective values, and self-regulatory systems and plans. This extension stresses that behaviour results from the interaction of dispositional and situational variables. Rotter's work has shown that the extent to which people perceive that the outcomes they experience are controlled by internal variables or external variables also plays an important role in personality. Positive psychology studies the beneficial aspects of personality that make life rewarding and fulfilling

## The Psychodynamic Approach

The Development of Freud's Theory • Structures of the Mind: Id, Ego, and Superego • Defence Mechanisms • Freud's Psychosexual Theory of Personality Development • Further Development of Freud's Theory: The Neo-Freudians • Some Observations on Psychodynamic Theory and Research

The psychodynamic approach to the study of personality began with the work of Freud, who proposed that personality development is based on psychosexual tensions that are present from birth. Freud theorized that personality develops as psychosexual tensions express themselves during different stages of development. Defence mechanisms reduce the anxiety produced by conflicts among the id, ego, and superego. The neo-Freudians accepted parts of Freud's theory but rejected others. Although Freud's theory influenced many Western conceptions of human nature, it has not been subjected to extensive scientific examination, largely because the theory itself is difficult to test.

## The Humanistic Approach

Maslow and Self-Actualization • Rogers and Conditions of Worth • Some Observations on the Humanistic Approach

Humanistic psychologists are interested in personal growth, satisfaction with life, and positive human values. Maslow argued that reaching one's potential first requires satisfaction of basic needs, such as food, safety, love, and esteem. Rogers maintained that self-actualization is best realized in circumstances characterized by unconditional positive regard. The humanistic approach remains empirically untested.

## Assessment of Personality

Objective Tests of Personality • Projective Tests of Personality • Evaluation of Projective Tests

Two types of tests have been developed with which to assess personality. Objective tests, such as the MMPI and the NEO-PI-R, contain multiple-choice and true–false questions that are aimed at revealing the extent to which the test taker possesses specific traits. Projective tests, such as the Rorschach Inkblot Test and the Thematic Apperception Test, present the test taker with ambiguous stimuli; it is assumed that test takers will "project" aspects of their personalities into their responses to these stimuli. Although projective tests are widely used, they have relatively low reliability and validity.

# PROLOGUE

## The Case of Robert Dziekanski

On October 13, 2007, Robert Dziekanski arrived at Vancouver International Airport, in British Columbia, after an 11-hour flight from his native Poland. This was the first airplane trip for the 40-year-old construction worker, and he may have been very nervous. He would have been filled with anticipation as well, for Robert was coming to British Columbia to join his mother and to fulfill a lifelong desire to travel. Indeed, his suitcases contained not clothes but books about his passion, geography. His mother describes him as a polite man who always listened to her. Despite the fact that she had lived in North America for the last 10 years of Robert's life, they had remained close and talked by telephone every night. By all accounts, he was looking forward to seeing his mother at the airport and starting a new life in a new country.

There was another side to Robert Dziekanski, however, and it would trigger events that, sadly, denied him that chance at a new life. As a teenager in the Polish city of Gliwice, according to news reports, he had been troubled. He had been jailed for robbery, had failed to keep a steady job, and had lived with an alcoholic girlfriend in a shabby apartment. A neighbour admitted that he was "no angel." Notwithstanding these conflicting descriptions of his personality, it is undeniable that Robert faced considerable stress upon his arrival. He had recently given up smoking, and had just finished an 11-hour flight. He spoke no English and had considerable trouble negotiating the immigration procedures. His mother had not alerted him to the fact that the international arrivals area would be off-limits to her, and her absence must have confused him greatly. Meanwhile, she had been told that he was not at the airport and had left.

Alone, with no one who understood Polish, Robert spent the next 10 hours in the immigration, customs, and waiting areas. By that time, he had become confused and erratic. A cell-phone video taken by another traveller shows Robert strangely carrying a small table in front of him. Although breathing heavily, he seems meek and mild at that moment; however, a later shot shows him throwing an object at a wall. Then he began to pick up chairs and move them from place to place. Airport security was called.

▲ *Robert Dziekanski, shortly before airport security shot him with a stun gun.*

When the security officers arrived, they introduced themselves and were immediately faced with judging whether Robert was a threat to himself or to others. What happened in the next 26 seconds is still disputed. In the video, Robert seems co-operative, but his motions are jerky and sudden. He moved away from the officers and said something in a loud voice. A split second later, one of the officers fired an electric stun gun at Robert, who screamed and dropped to the floor, convulsing. Robert lost consciousness soon after these events, either from the effects of the electric shock or from some other medical condition. A few minutes later, he died.

Common experience tells us that there is no one else exactly like us. But how do we describe these differences? If you were asked "How does your best friend differ from you?" you probably would use descriptions that generalize that person's behaviours, such as "He tends to see only the good in people, while I'm more realistic" or "She's a bit of a neat freak compared to me." We try to convey something about our friend that covers more than just the here and now.

Everyday observations like these provide a starting point for psychology's study of personality. But psychology's approach to studying personality is more than informal generalizations. To psychologists, the concept generally has a much more specific definition: **Personality** is a particular pattern of behaviour and thinking that prevails across time and situations and differentiates one person from another. The goal of psychologists who study personality is to discover the causes of individual differences in behaviour.

What types of research efforts are necessary to study personality? Some psychologists devote their efforts to the development of tests that can reliably measure differences in personality. Others try to identify the events—biological and environmental—that cause people to behave as they do. Thus, research on human personality requires two kinds of effort: identifying personality characteristics and determining the variables that produce and control them (Buss, 1995). Keep in mind that in the study of personality, we must be careful to avoid the nominal fallacy. As you'll recall from Chapter 2, the nominal fallacy is the false belief that the causes of an event are explained by simply naming and identifying them. Merely identifying and describing a personality characteristic is not the same as explaining it.

# Trait Theories of Personality

Among the first categorizations of personality was one based on the concept of personality traits. Personality theorists who study traits use the term much in the way we often think of personality in everyday life—to denote a set of personal characteristics that determine the different ways we act and react in a variety of situations (Sneed, McCrae, & Funder, 1998). However, as you will see, trait theorists do not all agree on exactly which characteristics to include. Let's begin by differentiating personality types from personality traits.

## Personality Types and Traits

The earliest known explanation for individual differences in personality was proposed by the Greek physician Hippocrates in the fourth century B.C.E. and refined by his successor Galen in the second century C.E. The theory was based on then-common medical beliefs that originated with the ancient

**personality** A particular pattern of behaviour and thinking that prevails across time and situations and differentiates one person from another.

FIGURE 14•1 Characteristics of the four humours, according to a medieval artist: (a) choleric—violent and aggressive temperament; (b) melancholic—gloomy and pessimistic temperament; (c) phlegmatic—sluggish, relaxed, and dull temperament; and (d) sanguine—outgoing, passionate, and fun-loving temperament.

(a)

(b)

(c)

(d)

Greeks. The body was thought to contain four humours, or fluids: yellow bile, black bile, phlegm, and blood. People were classified according to the disposition supposedly produced by the predominance of one of these humours in their systems. Choleric people, who had an excess of yellow bile, were bad-tempered and irritable. Melancholic people, who had an excess of black bile, had gloomy and pessimistic temperaments. Phlegmatic people, whose bodies contained an excessive amount of phlegm, were sluggish, calm, and unexcitable. Sanguine people had a preponderance of blood (*sanguis*), which made them cheerful and passionate. (See **Figure 14•1**.)

Later biological investigations, of course, discredited the humoral theory. But the notion that people could be divided into different **personality types**—different categories into which personality characteristics can be assigned based on factors such as developmental experiences—persisted long afterwards. Indeed, our casual descriptions of people may correspond to these notions. Someone who witnessed Robert Dziekanski's reactions to questioning by airport security may have considered him "volatile" or "aggressive." But historical precedent and common-sense labels aren't enough. After identifying and defining personality types, theorists must determine whether these types actually exist and whether knowing an individual's personality type can lead to valid predictions about his or her behaviour in different situations. Someone who observed Dziekanski in the waiting area hours earlier—when he apparently waited without causing any incident—may have characterized him in entirely different ways.

Most investigators today reject the idea that people can be assigned to discrete categories. Instead, they generally conceive of individual differences in personality as differences in degree, not kind. Rather than focusing on types, many current investigators prefer to measure the degree to which an individual expresses a particular personality trait. A **personality trait** is an enduring personal characteristic that reveals itself in a particular pattern of behaviour in different situations. A simple example illustrates the difference between types and traits. We could classify people into two different types: tall people and short people. Note that this is an either/or categorization. Indeed, we do use these categorical terms in everyday language. But we all recognize that height is best conceived of as a trait—a dimension on which people differ along a wide range of values. If we measure the heights of a large sample of people, we will find instances all along the distribution, from very short to very tall, with most people falling in between the extremes. (See **Figure 14•2**.) It is not that people are only either tall or short (analogous to personality types) but that people vary in the extent to which they show tallness or shortness (analogous to personality traits).

**personality types** Different categories into which personality characteristics can be assigned based on factors such as developmental experiences or physical characteristics.

**personality trait** An enduring personal characteristic that reveals itself in a particular pattern of behaviour in a variety of situations.

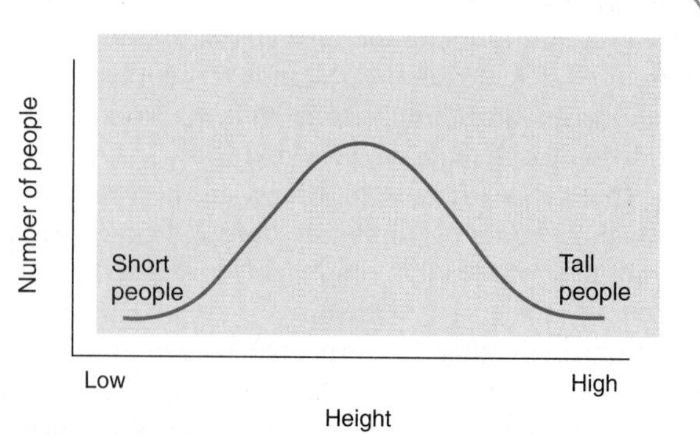


FIGURE 14•2 The distribution of height. We can measure people's heights, a trait, on a continuous scale. We can also look at the extremes and divide people into the categories of short and tall types.

We've all had experiences with people who behave in different characteristic ways: Some are friendly, some are mean, some are lazy, some are timid, and some are reckless. Trait theories of personality fit this common-sense view. However, personality traits are not simply patterns of behaviour: They are factors that underlie these patterns and are responsible for them. Once our personality traits are developed, they reside in our brains. This does not mean that the acquisition of personality traits is strictly biological and that learning is not involved. However, if our personality traits are changed through learning, those changes must have a neurological basis in the brain. In other words, we carry our personality traits around with us in our heads—or more exactly, in our brains.

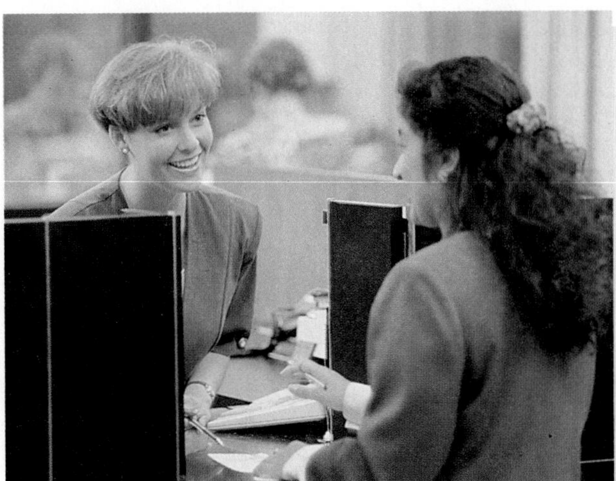

▲ *Surface traits, such as friendliness, are those traits that are obvious to others.*

## Identification of Personality Traits

In this section, we introduce several influential trait categorization models: the theories of Gordon Allport, Raymond Cattell, and Hans Eysenck as well as the five-factor model and related frameworks proposed by other trait psychologists.

**Allport's Search for Traits** Gordon Allport (1897–1967) was one of the first psychologists to search systematically for a basic core of personality traits. He began his work by identifying all words in an unabridged dictionary of the English language that described aspects of personality (Allport & Odbert, 1936), and found approximately 18 000 such entries. Allport then conducted analyses that identified those words that described only stable personality characteristics. Words that represented temporary states, such as *flustered*, or evaluations, such as *admirable*, were eliminated.

Why did Allport undertake this exercise? He believed that the considerable extent to which trait labels appear in English attests to the importance of traits in how people think about themselves and others. Indirectly, then, the wealth of trait terms helped confirm his belief that a well-developed trait theory would have value in understanding human functioning. In fact, he believed that traits were neuropsychological properties that led to behavioural consistency over time and contexts by producing functional similarity in the way a given person interprets and experiences events. That is, people with a particular trait react similarly across situations because they experience a unique sense of similarity across those situations that guides their feelings, thoughts, and behaviour. There is evidence that some traits are consistent over time. In a 44-year longitudinal study, researchers found that creativity and some aspects of personality remained consistent over time (Feist & Barron, 2003).

According to Allport, not all traits have equal influence on their possessors. The most powerful of them are those he termed *cardinal traits.* Cardinal traits characterize a strong unifying influence on a person's behaviour. Allport believed that these traits were rare, but that people characterized by them clearly stand out from the crowd. Examples include Adolf Hitler's relentless exercise of oppressive power, Nelson Mandela's commitment to justice, and Mother Teresa's altruism. *Central traits* are less singular in their influence than cardinal traits, but capture important characteristics of an individual. When we say that someone is honest and warm to distinguish him or her from others, we capture Allport's meaning of central traits. Finally, Allport's category of *secondary traits* includes characteristics that have minor influence on consistency of behaviour. An example would be a person's tendency to frequently change jobs.

Allport's research stimulated other psychologists to think about personality in terms of traits or dispositions. In fact, most modern trait theories can be traced to Allport's earlier theoretical work. Like Allport, modern trait theorists maintain that only when we know how to describe an individual's personality will we be able to explain it.

**Cattell: Sixteen Personality Factors** Raymond Cattell (1905–1998) used Allport's list of 18 000 trait words as a starting point for his theory of central traits. Cattell winnowed this large word set down to 171 adjectives that he believed made up a relatively complete set of distinct surface traits (those that refer to observable behaviours). He then used the process of factor analysis (see Chapter 11) to identify clusters of these traits that he believed in turn represented underlying traits. Cattell analyzed questionnaire responses from thousands of people in this manner, and eventually identified 16 personality factors. He referred to these 16 traits as source traits because, in his view, they were the cornerstones upon which personality is built. **Figure 14•3** illustrates a personality profile of a hypothetical individual rated on Cattell's 16 factors. Think of someone you know well. Do you think you would be able to predict how they would score on these factors? Do you think these factors would help you predict the behaviour of someone you did not know?

**Eysenck: Three Factors** Hans Eysenck (1916–1997) also used factor analysis to devise a theory of personality (Eysenck, 1970; Eysenck & Eysenck, 1985). His research

**FIGURE 14•3** A hypothetical personality profile using Cattell's 16 personality factors.

*(Adapted from the 16PF® Practitioner Report. Copyright 2005 by the Institute for Personality and Ability Testing, Inc., Champaign, Illinois, USA. Reproduced with permission. All rights reserved.)*

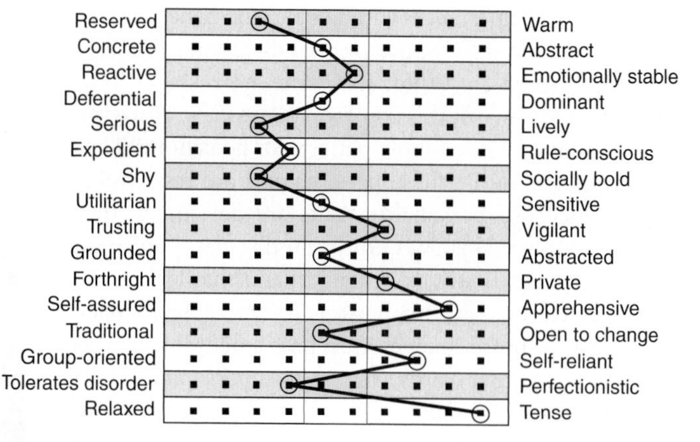


identified three important factors: extroversion, neuroticism, and psychoticism. These factors are bipolar dimensions. Extroversion is the opposite of introversion, neuroticism is the opposite of emotional stability, and psychoticism is the opposite of self-control. **Extroversion** refers to an outgoing nature and a high level of activity. In general, extroverts like people and socializing, are spontaneous, and take risks. **Introversion** refers to the opposites of these characteristics. Introverts are shy, reserved, and careful. People at the high end of **neuroticism** are fraught with worry and guilt, and are moody and unstable. Those who score low on neuroticism are even-tempered and are characterized by **emotional stability. Psychoticism** refers to an aggressive, egocentric, and anti-social nature; **self-control** refers to a kind and considerate nature, obedient of rules and laws. Eysenck's use of the term *psychoticism* is different from its use by most clinical psychologists; his term refers to anti-social tendencies and not to a mental illness. A person at the extreme end of the distribution of psychoticism would receive the diagnosis of anti-social personality disorder. (We'll look at this disorder in more detail in Chapter 17.)

**Table 14•1** lists some questions that have high correlations or factor loadings on Eysenck's three factors. The best way to understand the meaning of these traits is to read the questions and to imagine the kinds of people who would answer "yes" or "no" to each group. If a factor loading is preceded by a minus sign, it means that people who say "no" receive high scores on the trait; otherwise, high scores are obtained by those who answer "yes."

**extroversion** The tendency to seek the company of other people, to be spontaneous, and to engage in conversation and other social behaviours with them.
**introversion** The tendency to avoid the company of other people, to be inhibited and cautious; shyness.
**neuroticism** The tendency to be anxious, worried, and full of guilt.
**emotional stability** The tendency to be relaxed and at peace with oneself.
**psychoticism** The tendency to be aggressive, egocentric, and anti-social.
**self-control** The tendency to be kind, considerate, and obedient of laws and rules.

Eysenck argued that the most important aspects of a person's temperament are determined by the combination of the three dimensions of extroversion, neuroticism, and psychoticism—just as colours are produced by the combinations of the three dimensions of hue, saturation, and brightness. **Figure 14•4** illustrates the effects of various combinations of the first two of these dimensions—extroversion and neuroticism—and relates them to the four temperaments described by Galen.

More than most other trait theorists, Eysenck emphasizes the biological nature of personality (Eysenck, 1998). Eysenck believes that the functioning of a neural system located in the brain stem produces different levels of arousal of the cerebral cortex. Consider the introversion–extroversion dimension, which, according to Eysenck, is based on an optimum arousal level of the brain. Introverts have relatively high levels of cortical excitation, while extroverts have relatively low levels. Thus, in order to maintain the optimum arousal level, the extrovert requires more external stimulation than does the introvert. The extrovert seeks stimulation from external sources by interacting with others or by pursuing novel and highly stimulating experiences. The introvert avoids external stimulation in order to maintain his or her arousal level at an optimum state. Different states of arousal are hypothesized to lead to different values of the extroversion trait for different people.

Eysenck's theory has received considerable support, especially from his own laboratory, which has been highly productive. Most trait theorists accept the existence of his three factors because they have emerged in factor analyses performed by many different researchers.

**The Five-Factor Model** Recall that Allport attempted to discover personality traits through an analysis of the words we use in everyday language to talk about personality. Languages reflect the observations of a culture; that is, people invent words to describe distinctions they notice. An analysis of such distinctions by Tupes and Christal (1961), replicated by Norman (1963), has led to the five-factor model (Costa &

**TABLE 14•1 Some Items from Eysenck's Tests of Extroversion, Neuroticism, and Psychoticism**

| Factor | Loading |
|---|---|
| ***Extroversion*** | |
| Do you like mixing with people? | .70 |
| Do you like plenty of bustle and excitement around you? | .65 |
| Are you rather lively? | .63 |
| ***Neuroticism*** | |
| Do you often feel "fed up"? | .67 |
| Do you often feel lonely? | .60 |
| Does your mood often go up and down? | .59 |
| ***Psychoticism*** | |
| Do good manners and cleanliness matter much to you? | −.55 |
| Does it worry you if you know there are mistakes in your work? | −.53 |
| Do you like taking risks for fun? | .51 |

*Source: Adapted from Eysenck, H. J., & Eysenck, M. W. (1985).* Personality and individual differences: A natural science approach. *New York: Plenum Press.*

**FIGURE 14•4** Eysenck's theory illustrated for two factors. According to Eysenck, the two dimensions of neuroticism (stable versus unstable) and introversion–extroversion combine to form a variety of personality characteristics. The four personality types based on the Greek theory of humours are shown in the centre.

*(From Eysenck, H. J. (1973).* The inequality of man. *London: Temple Smith. Reprinted with permission.)*

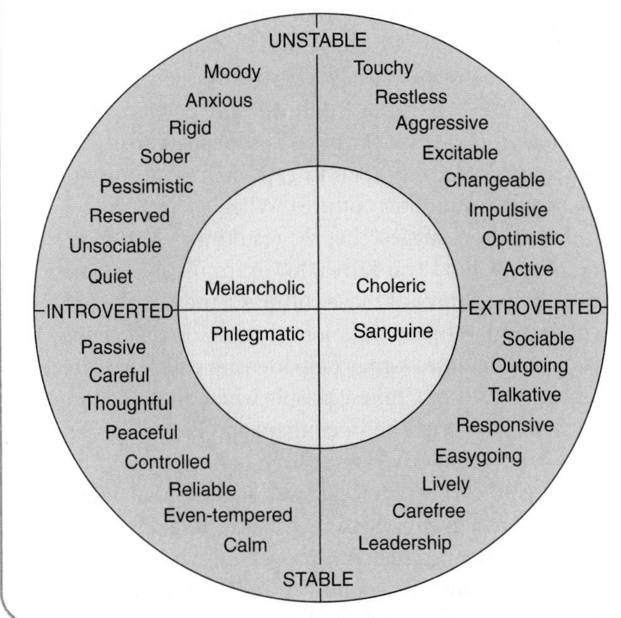


McCrae, 1998a; McCrae & Costa, 1997, 1999, 2004). The **five-factor model** proposes that personality is composed of five primary dimensions: neuroticism, extroversion, openness, agreeableness, and conscientiousness. These factors are measured by the **Neuroticism, Extraversion, and Openness Personality Inventory**, or **NEO-PI-R**. (The name was chosen before the factors of agreeableness and conscientiousness were added, and the *R* stands for *revised*. If you want a more useful mnemonic to remember the dimensions, think of the acronym OCEAN for openness, conscientiousness, extroversion, agreeableness, and neuroticism.)

The NEO-PI-R consists of 240 items that can potentially be used to describe the person being evaluated. The test items can be answered by the participant or by someone he or she knows well (Costa & McCrae, 1998b). (Studies have shown that self-ratings agree well with ratings of spouses and other people who know a person well.) The test items are brief sentences, such as "I really like most people I meet" and (for ratings by someone else) "She has a very active imagination." The person completing the test rates the accuracy of each item on a scale of 1 to 5, from strong disagreement to strong agreement. The sums of the answers to different sets of items represent scores on each of the five factors.

The five-factor model is regarded by many personality psychologists as a robust model of personality (Paunonen, 2003; Wiggins & Pincus, 2002; Wiggins & Trapnell, 1997). Although it originated in the factor analysis tradition of Cattell, it seems to incorporate some of the traits suggested by Eysenck, especially neuroticism and extroversion (Goldberg, 1993). It has considerable cross-cultural applicability (e.g., Allik & McCrae, 2002, 2004; McCrae et al., 1998). Self-ratings on the NEO-PI-R agree closely with ratings by family members (García, Antón, García, & Colom, 2007). Furthermore, it predicts other aspects that seem related to personality. DeNeve and Cooper (1998) showed that the five factors can be used to predict subjective well-being, and Vollrath (2000) found moderate predictability for responses to "daily hassles" experienced by college students. Barrick, Mount, and Judge (2001) reported a meta-analysis of studies measuring job performance relative to the five personality dimensions. Generally speaking, extroversion seems to predict success in jobs that require leadership (managerial positions) or in jobs that demand the ability to improvise in order to reach goals (sales positions). Not surprisingly, conscientiousness predicts success across job classifications.

**five-factor model** A theory stating that personality is composed of five primary dimensions: neuroticism, extroversion, openness, agreeableness, and conscientiousness. This theory was developed using factor analyses of ratings of the words people use to describe personality characteristics.
**Neuroticism, Extraversion, and Openness Personality Inventory (NEO-PI-R)** The instrument used to measure the elements described in the five-factor model (neuroticism, extroversion, openness, agreeableness, and conscientiousness).

Is there a biological basis for these five factors? A rapidly accumulating body of evidence points to a very strong degree of heritability (Jang, Livesley, & Vernon, 1996; Livesley, Jang, & Vernon, 2003; Loehlin, McCrae, Costa, & John, 1998; McCrae et al., 2000). Correlations in traits are higher within monozygotic twins than dizygotic twins (Vernon, Villani, Vickers, & Harris, 2008). The data suggest that environmental factors pale beside genetic influences.

Finally, five is not necessarily the final number of fundamental personality dimensions. Jackson (Jackson & Tremblay, 2002) argues that a six-factor model may be more appropriate. According to Jackson, the conscientiousness factor in the traditional five-factor model actually represents two distinct dimensions. One of these component dimensions, methodicalness, reflects planfulness and a need for orderliness. The other, industriousness, is characterized by perseverance and achievement orientation.

**The Dark Triad** Some personality psychologists have suggested that a special cluster of traits may underlie socially offensive personalities. For example, it has been noted that habitual criminals sometimes exhibit great skill in manipulating individuals, while exhibiting little sign of the regret that most people feel when their actions harm or offend others. This skill at manipulation has been called **machiavellianism** after an Italian political theorist and writer of the Renaissance period. A pronounced lack of empathy and a high degree of impulsivity has been identified with a trait known as **psychopathy**. Paulhus and Williams (2002) suggested that these two traits, together with a trait called **narcissism**, which leads to grandiosity and feelings of superiority, formed a "Dark Triad" of overlapping negative traits. The Dark Triad is considered distinct from the five factors, although there are low to moderate correlations between them (Egan & McCorkindale, 2007; Jakobwitz & Egan, 2006). Males tend to score higher on tests that measure Dark Triad traits, although the intercorrelations between the traits are similar across the sexes. So, although women may not exhibit Dark Triad traits as much as men do, women who have this personality manifest it in the same general way that men would. Vernon, Villani, Vickers, and Harris (2008) have also measured the correlation of Dark Triad traits between twins, and find considerable genetic influence on these traits.

At its extreme, the Dark Triad personality seems to epitomize the notion of a cold, calculating, domineering, and remorseless criminal. It may be that this represents a "criminal personality type." However, it's probably a mistake to label these traits as intrinsically maladaptive. Traits are collective descriptions for certain behaviours, and behaviours are adaptive or not depending on the context. The increasing social isolation of the modern world may reward many of the milder aspects of the Dark Triad.

**machiavellianism** A trait characterized by skill at manipulating others socially.

**psychopathy** A trait describing a lack of empathy for others and a high degree of impulsivity.

**narcissism** A trait characterized by grandiosity and feelings of superiority.

**Traits across Cultures** Any comprehensive theory of personality must be able to encompass all cultures, countries, and languages. If personality comprises a standard set of factors, which we all exhibit to a lesser or greater extent, then these factors should be exhibited or reported cross-culturally. If not, then the theory is culture-specific and describes personality only within a limited number of cultures.

With regards to the study of personality, problems in demonstrating universality lie in taxonomy. Do the same words mean the same things across cultures? For example, various cultures attribute different meanings to conscientiousness, from the five-factor model (Caprara & Perugini, 1994). It means something different to the Dutch, Hungarians, and Italians, and to Americans, Germans, Czechs, and Poles. In a review of the evidence for the universality of a collection of basic personality traits, Boele de Raad (1998), from the University of Groningen in the Netherlands, suggests that the best one can do is to find acceptable counterparts of the five factors in all cultures; the first three factors of the model (neuroticism, extroversion, and openness) can be found in most cultures, but the cross-cultural validity of the others may be questionable.

McCrae and Terracciano (2005) asked college students from 50 cultures, including Arabic and black African cultures, to identify a man or woman they knew well and rate him or her using the third-person version of the NEO-PI-R. The five-factor model was replicated in almost all cultures (Morocco and Nigeria were two of a half-dozen or so cultures that did not show this pattern). Women were more positive than men in rating others, especially when rating other women.

In a separate study of the geography of personality traits, Allik and McRae (2004) examined whether respondents from 36 cultures differed according to the five-factor model. They found that the culture's temperature or its distance from the equator was not related to personality. However, cultures that were geographically close appeared to share similar personality traits: the greatest geographical distinction was between European and American cultures, and between Asian and African cultures. Americans and Europeans were significantly more extroverted and open to experience but less agreeable than people from other cultures. Why?

The authors suggest that the results may be due to shared gene pools (China and Korea, for example, share genetic ancestry) or to features of those cultures. Studying the process of acculturation—the assimilation of a person's behaviour with that person's culture—may help identify which is correct. For example, a study of Chinese people who emigrated to Canada found that differences between them and European Canadians lessened the longer the Chinese lived in Canada (McCrae et al., 1998). Openness and agreeableness, in particular, increased in the immigrant group, but introversion remained stable and did not match levels seen in European Canadians. These data suggest that some personality traits might be adopted or enhanced by acculturation, but others may not.

▲ *Studies of the five-factor model have found that cultures that are geographically close appear to exhibit similar personality traits.*

Can cultures also differ according to what they believe about personality? Implicit trait theories describe whether people ascribed differences in personality to stable traits or, instead, to the immediate context or situation of an individual. In a later section of this chapter, we'll look at how personality theorists approach this question. Here, we consider what the layperson believes. Church and colleagues (2005) investigated cross-cultural beliefs about personality in what they called two individualistic cultures (the United States and Australia) and two collectivistic cultures (Mexico and the Philippines). They hypothesized that the more individualistic the culture, the greater or stronger that culture's beliefs in traits, rather than situations, as determinants of behaviour. Trait beliefs were stronger among Americans than among Mexicans or Filipinos, but contextual beliefs were weaker.

## Interim Summary

### Trait Theories of Personality

We can conceive of personality characteristics as types or traits. The earliest theory of personality classified people into types according to their predominant humour, or body fluid. Today, most psychologists conceive of personality differences as being represented by degree, not kind.

Personality traits are the factors that underlie patterns of behaviour. Presumably, these factors are biological in nature, although they may be the products of learning as well as heredity. The search for core personality traits began with Allport, who studied how everyday words are used to describe personality characteristics. Although he never isolated a core set of traits, his work inspired others to continue the search for such traits. Several researchers developed their theories of personality through factor analysis. Cattell's analyses indicated the existence of 16 personality factors and Eysenck's research suggested that personality is determined by three dimensions: extroversion (versus introversion), neuroticism (versus emotional stability), and psychoticism (versus self-control). McCrae and Costa's five-factor model, based on an analysis of words used to describe people's behavioural traits, includes extroversion, neuroticism, agreeableness, openness, and conscientiousness. Ongoing research may identify additional fundamental personality dimensions, including socially negative traits such as the "Dark Triad" of machiavellianism, psychopathy, and narcissism. Studies of similarities in traits across different cultures have found that the first three traits of the five-factor model can be found in most cultures, and that, when people describe someone known to them, they generally use traits from the five-factor model. There are some differences between cultures, however, and people who immigrate to another culture exhibit changes in some specific traits.

#### QUESTIONS TO CONSIDER

1. Think of one personality trait that you are sure you possess. How did you come to possess this trait? To what extent does possessing this trait explain the kind of person you are?
2. Consider the culture you have been raised in. Are some of the traits we've discussed more valued than others within your culture? Do you think this might have an impact on the likelihood that you would show such traits?
3. Make a list of all of the personality traits that you feel describe you. Which approach to personality—Cattell's, Eysenck's, or the five-factor model—do you feel best represents the personality traits you possess? What are the reasons for your answer?

# Psychobiological Approaches

The statistical evidence from factor analysis provides a description of consistent patterns of behaviours that we can identify as traits. At the beginning of the chapter, it was noted that we carry our personality traits around in our brains. That is, personality traits are the result of actions of the brain. Although we are far from understanding the psychobiology of personality, some progress has been made.

## Heritability of Personality Traits

Cattell and Eysenck, among other trait theorists, have asserted that a person's genetic history has a strong influence on his or her personality. Many studies have shown that some personality traits are strongly heritable (e.g., Bouchard & Hur, 1998; Krueger, Markon, & Bouchard, 2003).

**FIGURE 14•5** Correlation of personality traits of identical and fraternal twins. These data show the degree to which the scores of identical and fraternal twins are correlated on each of the five-factor personality traits. The correlations for identical twins are approximately double those of fraternal twins on each trait. This indicates that genes we receive from our parents do influence personality structure.

*(Adapted from Bouchard, T. J. Jr. (1997). The genetics of personality. In K. Blum & E. P. Noble (Eds.),* The handbook of psychiatric genetics *(pp. 273–296). Boca Raton, FL: CRC Press Inc.)*

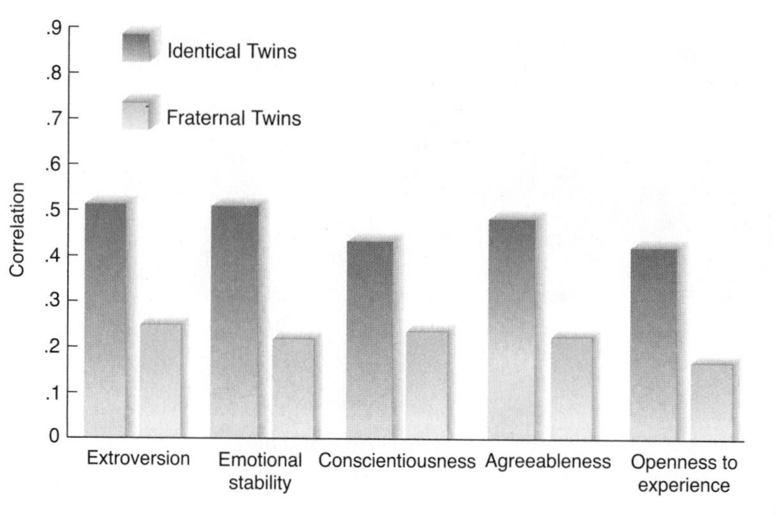


Psychologists assess the heritability of a trait by comparing identical and fraternal twins, comparing twins raised together and twins raised apart, and comparing twins raised by biological and adoptive relatives (see Chapter 3). Many studies have found that identical twins are more similar to each other than are fraternal twins on a variety of personality measures, which indicates that these characteristics are heritable (e.g., Jang et al., 2002; Livesley, Jang, & Vernon, 2003; McCrae et al., 2000; Vernon, Villani, Vickers, & Harris, 2008). **Figure 14•5** shows correlations for the five-factor personality traits between pair members of identical and fraternal twin sets. Identical twins' personality traits correlate much higher than those of fraternal twins. In fact, Bouchard (1997) found that the correlations for identical twins' personality traits were approximately double those of fraternal twins.

Zuckerman (1991) compiled the results of 11 studies using various tests of Eysenck's factors of extroversion, neuroticism, and psychoticism. Every study found that identical twins were more similar than fraternal twins on every measure. According to Zuckerman's calculations, the best estimates of the heritability of these three traits are extroversion, 70 percent; psychoticism, 59 percent; and neuroticism, 48 percent. The results of these studies suggest that heredity is responsible for between 50 and 70 percent of the variability in these three personality traits. Thus, it would appear that the remaining 30 to 50 percent of the variability is caused by differences in environment. In other words, some family environments should tend to produce extroverts, others should tend to produce introverts, and so on.

However, research indicates that the matter is not so simple. If family environment has a significant effect on personality characteristics, then identical twins raised together should be more similar than those raised apart. But in the studies reviewed by Zuckerman (1991), they were not. Several of those studies measured the correlation in personality traits of pairs of identical twins raised together and apart. Taken as a group, these studies found no differences—indicating that differences in family environment seem to account for none of the variability of personality traits in the twins who were tested. Researchers are now developing more sensitive measures of family environment variables (e.g., Keltikangas-Järvinen & Heinonen, 2003; Vernon, Jang, Harris, & McCarthy, 1997). As these techniques evolve, we should be better able to examine the relative contributions of genetics and experience to personality.

As we saw in Chapter 3, heredity and environment can interact. In fact, the major source of the interaction seems to be the effect that people's heredity has on their family environments (Plomin & Asbury, 2001; Plomin & Bergeman, 1991). That is, people's genetic endowment plays an important role in determining how family members interact with them. There are two possible explanations for these results: The family environments could have been more similar for identical twins than for fraternal twins, or the family environments could have been the same in all cases but were *perceived* as different by the fraternal twins. Evidence suggests that the first possibility is correct. That is, the family environments really were more similar for identical twins (Loehlin, 1992).

▲ *Research into the genetic basis of personality suggests that traits such as extroversion may be inherited.*

## Then and Now

### Twin Differences and the Genome

One of the most significant scientific events of our time is the completion of the Human Genome Project in 2003. The "finished sequence" describes about 99 percent of the code-bearing part of the human genome with an accuracy of 99.99 percent (International Human Genome Sequencing Consortium, 2004). However, the project cost about $3.7 billion, so it's reasonable to ask what the possible benefit might be.

Of course, having the human genetic code available allows us to compare individuals with respect to the genes they possess. As we've seen, there are many suggestions that personality traits may be genetic in origin. Therefore, you might think that the Human Genome Project would be especially useful to personality psychologists seeking the genetic bases of different traits. That may be so, but another useful role of human genome knowledge may be to help us understand the *non-genetic* sources of personality.

As you can appreciate from this chapter, personality measurement is based on individual differences. Variation among individuals defines the different dimensions of personality, such as in the five-factor model. When identical twins co-vary in personality measures, genetic factors are implicated. We've seen that, depending on the trait in question, 50 to 70 percent of its variation may be due to heredity. But that evidence is statistical: It involves looking at the correlations between identical twins on personality measures and comparing them to fraternal twins. As we've also seen, it has been difficult, using statistical measures, to determine where the non-genetic component comes from.

As a concrete example, consider two women, born as identical twins, interviewed by Kaminsky and his colleagues (Kaminsky et al., 2008). When these twins were young, their parents dressed them identically, making them physically indistinguishable. As girls, they were the best of friends and, as adults, they remain emotionally close. Yet they followed very different paths in life: One twin left home when she was 17, travelled, learned languages, and eventually became a war correspondent. She covered many of the world's hotspots, saw people killed, and in her forties married a cameraman who also worked on war assignments. They have no children. Her twin, who had no interest in learning a second language, stayed home, married a lawyer while young, had two children, and now works in a law office. When tested on various personality measures, such as the MMPI described later in this chapter, they showed many differences. For example, the second twin, who worked in the law office, showed traits reflecting anxiety, tension, and discomfort, while the twin who worked as a war correspondent did not. Basically, in several measures, the twin who was a war correspondent showed traits that seemed risk seeking, while her twin sister seemed risk averse.

Given that their parents seemingly made an effort to treat the two girls identically, it's hard to identify where the differences in personality arose. Prior to the completion of the Human Genome Project, this question would have been approached largely in a statistical fashion. However, in the first study of its kind, Kaminsky and his colleagues were able to approach it directly, by comparing the epigenetic factors that distinguished the twins.

Epigenetics describes mechanisms of cell inheritance that do not involve modifications of the genetic code (see Chapter 3). Therefore, an epigenetic change in a cell at one point in an individual's life will be inherited by daughter cells thereafter. Thus, two people who begin life as identical twins could show epigenetic differences later in life. The human genome tells us where to look for such epigenetic modifications. One such modification can occur in places on the DNA molecule where cytosine is followed by guanine. This change, known as *DNA methylation*, makes the genetic code less accessible to the mechanisms that synthesize proteins, reducing the expression of the gene that contains it.

Using their knowledge of the twins' genome, Kaminsky and his colleagues (2008) searched for such modifications and found 38 places where the twins differed. Then, knowing the human genome sequence, they examined the genes that might be affected. One of these was a gene known as DLX1, which is critical for the production of neurons that can regulate the stress response. Kaminsky and his colleagues speculate that the twin who chose to be a war correspondent may have managed her stress and adapted to the risks involved because of this epigenetic change. What might produce DNA methylation in this region of the genome, of course, is still an open question.

As Kaminsky and his colleague note, this is just a single observation that needs to be replicated. However, with the human genome now transcribed, our knowledge of personality differences due to non-genetic sources is certain to accelerate.

How can this be? One might think that each family has a certain environment and that everyone in the household would come under its influence equally. But even within a family, each member experiences different social interactions. Although there are aspects of a family that are shared by the entire household, the factors that play the largest role in shaping personality development appear to come from unique social interactions between an individual and other family members. Because of hereditary differences, one child may be more sociable; this child will be the recipient of more social interactions. Another child may be abrasive and disagreeable; this child will be treated more coldly. In the case of identical twins, who have no hereditary differences, the amount of social interaction with each twin is likely to be similar. Thus, although a child's environment plays an important part in his or her personality development, hereditary factors play a large role in determining the nature of this environment.

One caution about this interpretation is in order. Although the studies we have cited have been replicated in several cultures, none of them has investigated the effects of the full range of cultural differences in family lives. That is, when comparisons have been made between twins raised together and those raised apart, almost all have involved family environments *within* the same culture. It is possible that cultural differences in family environments could be even more important than the differences produced by a person's heredity. Hur (2005) found that the shared environment of Korean families affected aspects of self-perception more than it did in American families.

Should we assume that all personality traits are products, direct or indirect, of a person's heredity? The answer is no. Some personality characteristics show a strong effect of shared environment but almost no effect of genetics. For example, twin studies have found a strong influence of family environment, but not of heredity, on belief in God, involvement in religion, masculinity/femininity, attitudes toward racial integration, and intellectual interests (Loehlin & Nichols, 1976; Rose, 1995). Thus, people tend to *learn* some important social attitudes from their family environments.

Another way of examining the question of heredity is to look at personality early in life, in infancy. The NEO-PI-R was not designed to be administered to infants, but there is a related concept that psychologists use to describe the behaviours of infants: temperament, or each infant's individual pattern of behaviours and emotional reactions. Parents often will characterize their infants in terms of temperament (as when your mother recalls you as a "fussy" or "quiet" baby), and there are several scales for measuring temperaments in infants and preschool children. For example, in one assessment questionnaire, caregivers are asked a variety of questions, such as "When your child was being approached by an unfamiliar adult while shopping or out walking, how often did your child show distress or cry?" Unlike with personality, there is as yet no commonly agreed-on description of temperament; however, one measure, the Toddler Behaviour Assessment Questionnaire, proposes that temperament can be measured with respect to five dimensions: activity level, pleasure, social fearfulness, anger proneness, and interest/persistence.

The environmental factors of the family that affect temperament seem to be the unique social influences we just discussed. Correlations between infant siblings who are adopted and not related are very low (Saudino, 2005). The different temperaments of children within a family seem to be based on their individual interactions with other family members. In addition, as children develop, their temperaments show some change. Generally, the changed aspects of temperament seem to be the result of environmental factors, while the stable aspects are controlled by genetics (Saudino, 2005).

## Brain Mechanisms in Personality

We know that brain damage can produce permanent changes in personality, and drugs that affect particular neurotransmitters can alter people's moods and anxiety levels. Brain mechanisms are clearly implicated in personality traits, but what particular brain mechanisms are involved, and what personality traits do they affect? Several psychologists have attempted to relate extroversion, neuroticism, and psychoticism to underlying physiological mechanisms (Eysenck & Eysenck, 1985; Gray, 1991; Zuckerman, 1991).

Zuckerman (1991) suggests that the personality dimensions of extroversion, neuroticism, and psychoticism are determined by the neural systems responsible for reinforcement, punishment, and arousal. People who score high on extroversion are particularly sensitive to reinforcement; perhaps their neural reinforcement systems are especially active. People who score high on neuroticism are anxious and fearful. If they also score high on psychoticism, they are hostile as well. People who score high on psychoticism have difficulty learning when not to do something. As Zuckerman suggests, they have a low sensitivity to punishment. They also have a high tolerance for arousal and excitation; in other words, we could say that their optimum level of arousal is abnormally high. **Table 14•2** summarizes Zuckerman's hypothetical explanations for the three major personality dimensions.

**Biological Basis for Shyness** Kagan, Reznick, and Snidman (1988) investigated the possibility that timidity in social situations (shyness) has a biological basis in humans. They noted that about 10 to 15 percent of normal children between the ages of two and three become quiet, watchful, and subdued when they encounter an unfamiliar situation. In other words, they are shy and cautious when approaching novel stimuli. Childhood shyness seems to be related to two personality dimensions: a low level of extroversion and a high level of neuroticism (Briggs, 1988).

Kagan and his colleagues selected two groups of 21-month-old and 31-month-old children according to their reactions to unfamiliar people and situations. The shy group consisted of children who showed signs of inhibition, such as clinging to their mothers or remaining close to them, remaining silent, and failing to approach strangers or other novel stimuli. The non-shy group showed no such inhibition; these children approached the strangers and explored the

**TABLE 14•2 Zuckerman's (1991) Hypothetical Biological Characteristics That Correspond to Personality Dimensions**

| Personality Trait | Biological Characteristics |
|---|---|
| Extroversion | High sensitivity to reinforcement |
| Neuroticism | High sensitivity to punishment |
| Psychoticism | Low sensitivity to punishment; high optimum level of arousal |

novel environment. The children were similarly tested for shyness several more times, up to the age of 7.5 years.

The investigators found shyness to be an enduring trait; children who were shy at the ages of 21 or 31 months continued to be shy at the age of 7.5 years. In addition, the two groups of children showed differences in their physiological reactions to the test situation. Shy children were more likely to show increases in heart rate, their pupils tended to be more dilated, their urine contained more norepinephrine, and their saliva contained more cortisol. (Norepinephrine and cortisol are two hormones secreted during times of stress. Furthermore, their secretion in fearful situations is controlled by the amygdala.) Obviously, the shy children found the situation stressful, whereas the non-shy children did not.

This study suggests that the biological basis of an important personality characteristic during childhood—shyness—may be the excitability of neural circuits that control avoidance behaviours. When Kagan and his colleagues first raised this possibility, functional brain imaging was not available. However, 20 years later, they had a chance to test, as adults, some of the children who had been classified as either shy or not shy at the age of two years. Indeed, people who had shown signs of inhibition and shyness as two-year-olds showed greater activity in the amygdala when they viewed pictures of unfamiliar faces than when they viewed familiar faces. Adults who had not shown inhibition as infants did not exhibit this difference (Schwartz et al., 2003).

## Interim Summary

### Psychobiological Approaches

Studies of twins and adopted children indicate that personality factors, especially extroversion, neuroticism, and psychoticism, are affected strongly by genetic factors. However, there is little evidence of an effect of common family environment, largely because an individual's environment is strongly affected by heredity factors, such as personality and physical attributes.

Important personality traits are likely to be the products of neural systems responsible for reinforcement, punishment, and arousal. Zuckerman believes that extroversion is caused by a sensitive reinforcement system, neuroticism is caused by a sensitive punishment system (which includes the amygdala), and psychoticism is caused by the combination of a deficient punishment system and an abnormally high optimum level of arousal.

Few studies have directly tested the hypothesis that personality differences can be accounted for by biological differences, although there are indications that epigenetic effects may play a partial role. One experiment, however, indicates that childhood shyness is a relatively stable trait that can be seen in the way children react to strangers and to strange situations. The differences between shy and non-shy children manifest themselves in physiological responses controlled by the amygdala that indicate the presence of stress.

**QUESTIONS TO CONSIDER**

1. I have identical twin boys. One is much more outgoing than the other. If personality traits are heritable, how would you explain this difference? How can they share 100 percent of their genes, yet have different "personalities"?
2. Are you a thrill seeker? To what extent do you seek out situations that might be considered risky or at least mildly exciting? Depending on your answers to these questions, what might Zuckerman say about your personality (in terms of psychoticism)?

## Social Cognitive Approaches

Some psychologists view personality as the result of a behavioural learning process in which environmental variables act on the individual to produce behaviours. We might interpret certain behaviours in terms of traits like "extroversion," but the key question is why "extrovert behaviours" are frequently emitted by a particular person, and why that person might emit them in one situation but not in another.

Models that interpret personality as behaviour stem partially from B. F. Skinner's experimental analysis of behaviour (see Chapter 7). Although Skinner's work has influenced contemporary personality theory, he should not be mistaken for a personality theorist. Personality was definitely not Skinner's focus. However, his ideas have relevance when we consider personality as a description for a certain set of behaviours.

Skinner believed that the consequences of behaviour were important causal factors. Environmental variables, therefore, are those that define the contingencies between stimuli, behaviours, and outcomes. Behaviour is consistent from one situation to the next if it is maintained by similar kinds of consequences across those situations. Behaviour changes only when the consequences change.

Behaviourists influenced by Skinner's approach have attempted to apply the experimental analysis of behaviour to social contingencies and social behaviours. However, many choose to apply a behavioural approach by blending it with cognitive theory. The result is **social cognitive theory**, which embodies the idea that both the consequences of behaviour and an individual's beliefs about those consequences determine personality. Since many of the consequences we receive for our behaviours come from others, social behaviours are important sources for the behaviours and thoughts that distinguish us as individuals. One such researcher is Albert

**social cognitive theory** The idea that both the consequences of behaviour and an individual's beliefs about those consequences determine personality.

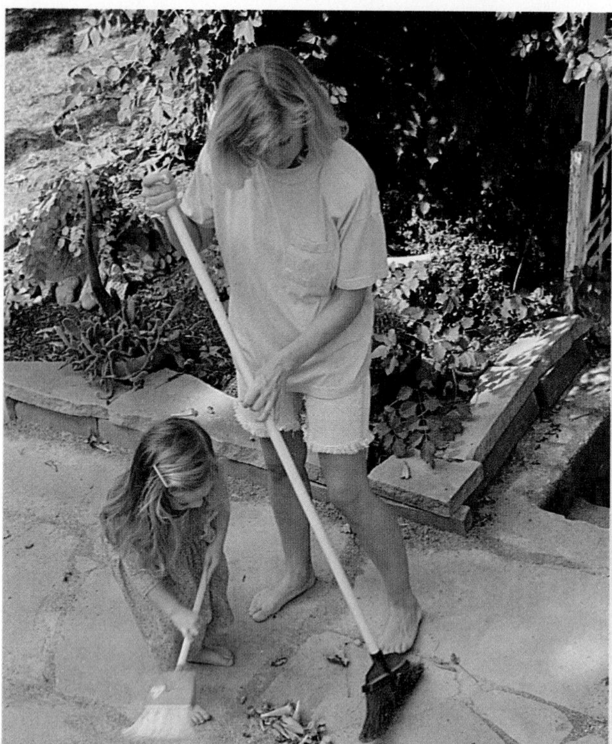

▲ *At the heart of the social cognitive theory account of personality is the idea that personality is the result of observing and imitating the actions of others.*

Bandura (b. 1925) who combined elements of learning theory with cognitive concepts to explain social behaviour.

## Expectancies and Observational Learning

Bandura's theory is based on **observational learning**, which is learning through observation of the consequences that others (usually called models) experience as a result of their behaviours. Observational learning is undoubtedly important in animal species whose young must learn a behaviour before they are physically able to perform it. Your own experience is no doubt filled with examples of observational learning, as it is partly through observation that we learn to dance, to make a paper airplane, to write in cursive, and to engage in many other activities. The more complex the behaviour, the more times we must observe its being executed, and practise what we have observed, before we can learn it well. Learning to tie a shoelace requires more attention to details than learning to roll a ball across the floor.

Observational learning is more than just imitation. It also depends on reinforcement, as in other forms of learning.

**observational learning** Learning through observation of the kinds of consequences others (called models) experience as a result of their behaviour.
**expectancy** The belief that a certain consequence will follow a certain action.
**reciprocal determinism** The idea that behaviour, environment, and person variables interact to determine personality.

The nature of the reinforcement differs, however, in that it is the model who is reinforced. In other words, reinforcement is vicarious, and not directly experienced by the observer. The vicarious nature of some learning experiences is obvious in children as they imitate the actions of others. A three-year-old who applies deodorant to herself does so not because this behaviour has been reinforced in the past, but rather because after watching her mother do it, she expects it would be "fun" for her to do so as well.

In Bandura's theory, vicarious reinforcement is made possible through cognition (Bandura, 1986, 1995, 2002; Bandura & Locke, 2003). In particular, individuals can form an expectancy based on their behaviours. An **expectancy** is an individual's belief that a specific consequence will follow a specific action. To put it another way, expectancy has to do with how someone perceives the contingencies of reinforcement for his or her own behaviour. If a person does something, it may be because he or she expects to be rewarded or punished. In different situations, expectancies may vary. For example, a young boy may learn that he can get what he wants from his younger sister by hitting her. However, on one occasion, his parents may catch him hitting his sister and punish him. His expectancy may now change: He may still get what he wants by behaving aggressively, but if he is caught, he'll be punished. This new expectancy may influence how he behaves toward his sister in the future, especially when his parents are present.

## Reciprocal Determinism and Self-Efficacy

Bandura, unlike many other theorists, does not believe that either personal characteristics (traits) or the environment alone determines personality (Bandura, 1978). Rather, he argues for **reciprocal determinism**, the idea that behaviour, environment, and person variables interact to determine personality. (See **Figure 14•6**.) We know that our actions can affect the environment. We also know that the environment can affect our behaviour. Likewise, our thoughts may affect the ways in which we behave to change the environment, and in turn those changes can influence our thoughts. When our acts of kindness are met with kindness in return, we perceive the environment as friendly and are apt to show kindness under other, similar circumstances. Likewise, when we are treated rudely, we perceive the environment as unfriendly (perhaps hostile) and will likely attempt to avoid or change similar environments in the future.

**Self-efficacy** refers to a person's beliefs about his or her ability to act as required in a particular situation to experience satisfying outcomes (Bandura, 1982, 1997). According to Bandura, our degree of self-efficacy is an important determinant of whether we will attempt to make changes in our environment. Each day, we make many decisions based on our perceptions of the extent to which our actions will produce reinforcement. Our actions are based on our evaluation of our competency. Moreover, self-efficacy determines not only whether we will engage in a particular behaviour, but

**FIGURE 14•6** Patterns of interaction in reciprocal determinism. According to Bandura's theory, behaviour, environment, and person variables, such as cognitions and expectations, interact to determine personality.

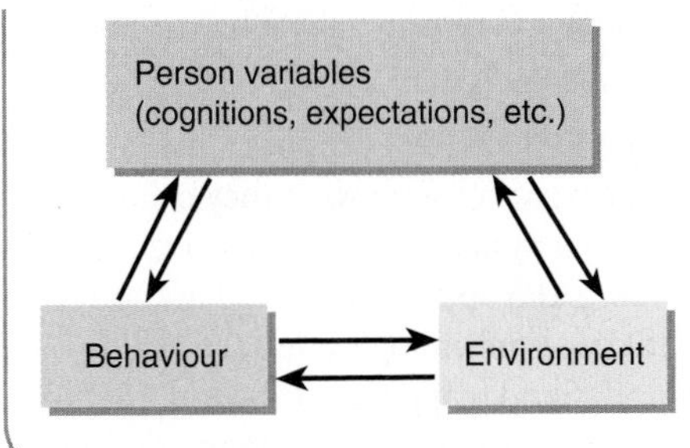


also the extent to which we will maintain that behaviour in the face of adversity. For example, if you believe that you are underqualified for a job at the Fairmont Banff Springs hotel, even though you really want the job, you are not apt to apply for an interview; nothing good could come of the effort. However, if you are confident of your qualifications, you will surely attempt to get an interview. Even if you are turned down for that job, you might interview for a position at another resort hotel because you are sure of your abilities. Eventually, your abilities will produce the outcomes you desire. Low self-efficacy can hamper both the frequency and the quality of behaviour–environment interactions, and high self-efficacy can facilitate both.

## Person Variables

Earlier, we saw that trait theorists seek to explain two aspects of personality: the distinctiveness of any one individual, and the aspects of personality that stay the same within that individual. But is this second objective reasonable? Is there stability to personality? Can the introverted high school student become a social star in college?

One extreme position, consistent with the behaviour approach, is to assume that the behaviours that make up our personality are specific to a given situation and not the result of any persevering traits. This position is known as **situationism**. In Chapter 7, we examined how discriminative stimuli control behaviours; perhaps personality is likewise dependent on the stimuli that control behaviours. Would a person high in conscientiousness stop at a red light at 3 a.m. with no one around and no chance of being caught? If you think the answer is "no," then you probably see the point.

This question is amenable to empirical testing and has been the subject of much research. In response to this research, some personality psychologists have argued for theories that represent the situation as part of the rules that govern behaviour. Stability in personality, in this view, is a consequence of stability in the underlying rules. Variation results from the way the situation activates those rules. For example, social cognitive theory might say that your behaviour while approaching an amber traffic light is controlled by the reactions of your passengers. Perhaps your parents are more conscientious than your friends about stopping at an amber light. Consequently, your driving would be more conservative when your parents are in the car than when your friends are there. If you're often with your friends, your personality as a driver might be seen as aggressive. On the few occasions when you're driving your parents, however, your driving personality might be considered cautious.

One possible scheme that makes these factors explicit is the model proposed by Walter Mischel, whose early work was strongly based on situationism but who has modified that position since then. Mischel, like Bandura, believes that much of personality is learned through interaction with the environment. Also like Bandura, Mischel emphasizes the role of cognition in determining how people learn the relationship between their behaviour and its consequences. In addition, though, Mischel argues that individual differences in cognition, or **person variables** as he calls them, account for differences in personality. Five person variables, as follows, figure prominently in this version of social cognitive theory (Mischel, 1990, 2003; Mischel, Cantor, & Feldman, 1996):

- *Competencies.* We each have different skills, abilities, and capacities. What we know and the kinds of behaviours that have been reinforced in the past influence the kinds of actions in which we will likely engage in the future.
- *Encoding strategies and personal constructs.* We also differ in our ability to process information. The way we process information determines how we perceive different situations. One person may perceive going on a date as fun, and so look forward to it; another person may perceive going on a date as potentially boring, and so dread it.
- *Expectancies.* On the basis of our past behaviour and our knowledge of current situations, we form expectancies about the effects of our behaviour on the environment. Expecting our behaviour to affect the environment positively leads to one action; expecting our behaviour to affect it negatively leads to another.
- *Subjective values.* The degree to which we value certain reinforcers over others influences our behaviour. We seek those outcomes that we value most.
- *Self-regulatory systems and plans.* We monitor our progress toward achieving goals and subject ourselves to either self-punishment or self-reinforcement, depending on our progress. We also modify and formulate plans regarding how we feel a goal can best be achieved.

**self-efficacy** People's beliefs about how well or badly they will perform tasks.
**situationism** The view that the behaviours defining a certain personality are determined solely by the current situation rather than by any persevering traits.
**person variables** Individual differences in cognition, which, according to Mischel, include competencies, encoding strategies and personal constructs, expectancies, subjective values, and self-regulatory systems and plans.

Mischel's view is a dynamic one: People's thoughts and behaviours are undergoing constant change as they interact with the environment. New plans are made and old ones are reformulated; people adjust their actions in accordance with their competencies, subjective values, and expectancies of behaviour–environment interactions.

Despite his skepticism about the value of the concept of personality traits, Mischel has acknowledged that some personality traits may be important predictors of behaviour (Mischel, 1977, 1979). He has also pointed out that some situations by their very nature severely constrain a person's behaviour, whereas others permit a wide variety of responses. For example, red traffic lights cause almost all motorists to stop their cars. In this case, knowing the particular situation (the colour of the traffic light) predicts behaviour better than knowing something about the personality characteristics of the drivers. Conversely, some situations are weak and have little control over people's behaviour. As Zuckerman (1991) points out, an amber traffic light is such a situation; when drivers see an amber light, some will stop if they possibly can and others will accelerate and rush through the intersection. The difference between the two behaviours is likely determined by individual personality traits.

Mischel and Shoda (1998) characterized the debate between supporters of the trait approach and social cognitive approaches in the following way:

> The uneasy, often even antagonistic relationship between these two approaches over the many decades in part reflects that their advocates tend to be committed passionately to different goals that seem to be in intrinsic conflict and even mutually preemptive. Consequently, the field has long been divided into two subdisciplines, pursuing two distinct sets of goals—either personality processes or personality dispositions—with different agendas and strategies that often seem in conflict. . . . (p. 231)

**locus of control** An individual's beliefs that the consequences of his or her actions are controlled by internal, person variables or by external, environmental variables.

Mischel and Shoda (1995, 1998) propose a move toward reconciliation of the approaches with what they call the cognitive-affective processing system (CAPS) approach. Still in its formative stage, the CAPS approach would have to recognize the multiple influences of biology, affect, cognition, and learning. Mischel and Shoda appear to extend the olive branch. The next few years of theory development and research in personality could be a very interesting time in the history of psychology.

## Locus of Control

Julian Rotter (1966, 1990) has focused on the extent to which people perceive themselves to be in control of the consequences of their behaviour. **Locus of control** refers to whether one believes that the consequences of one's actions are controlled by internal, person variables or by external, environmental variables. A person who expects to control his or her own fate—or, more technically, who perceives that rewards are dependent on his or her own behaviour—has an *internal locus of control*. A person who sees his or her life as being controlled by external forces unaffected by his or her own behaviour has an *external locus of control*. (See **Figure 14•7**.)

Rotter developed the *I-E Scale*, which assesses the degree to which people perceive the consequences of their behaviour to be under the control of internal or external variables. The

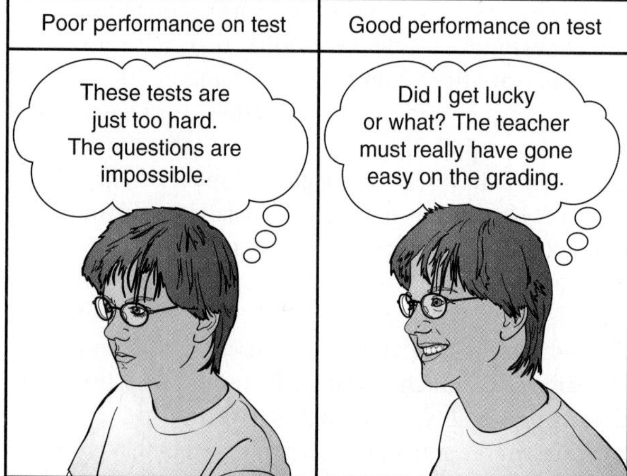


FIGURE 14•7 Internal and external loci of control. People having internal loci of control perceive themselves as able to determine the outcomes of the events in their lives. People having external loci of control perceive the events in their lives as determined by environmental variables.

I-E Scale contains 29 pairs of statements to which a person indicates his or her degree of agreement. A typical item on the scale might look something like this:

> The grades that I get depend on my abilities and how hard I work to get them.
>
> The grades that I get depend mostly on my teacher and his or her tests.

The scale is scored by counting the number of choices consistent with either the internal or the external locus of control orientation. Scores may range from 0 to 23, with lower scores indicative of greater internal locus of control. The highest possible score is 23 because 6 of the choice pairs are non-scored "filler" items. Of all the populations Rotter has assessed with the I-E Scale, the highest level of internal locus of control was obtained from a group of U.S. Peace Corps volunteers (Rotter, 1966).

Rotter's scale captured the imaginations of researchers because it seemed to be an antidote to what was perceived in the 1960s as an overemphasis on drive and motivational concepts (Lefcourt, 1992). The attraction has been a long-lived one, and the scale has been used in hundreds if not thousands of studies of social behaviour in a wide variety of situations. Consider some of the findings obtained from research using the I-E Scale:

- People who have internal locus of control orientation will work harder to obtain a goal if they believe that they can control the outcome in a specific situation. Even when told that a goal could be obtained through their own skill and effort, those who have external orientations tend not to try as hard as those who have internal orientations.
- People who have internal orientations are also more likely to be aware of and to engage in good health practices. They are more apt to take preventive medicines, to exercise regularly, to diet when appropriate, and to quit smoking than are people who have external orientations.
- People who have high internal locus of control tend to have strong academic achievement goals and to do well in school. However, they are also likely to blame themselves when they fail, even when failure is not their fault. People with an external locus of control tend to blame others for their failures (Lefcourt, 1966, 1992).

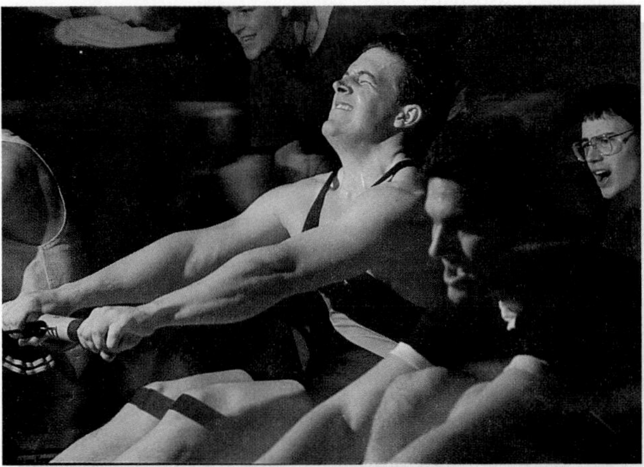

▲ *People with an internal locus of control believe that achievement of their goals depends on their personal efforts toward accomplishing those goals.*

## Positive Psychology

As you saw in Chapter 1, psychology has for many years concerned itself with improving human welfare and with healing psychological disorders. In the course of that history, psychologists have often looked to those instances where personality factors have impeded or limited the potential of an individual. Negative factors are often stronger than positive ones (e.g., Rozin & Royzman, 2001), so in this respect psychologists may be repeating an inherent bias for negativity.

Martin Seligman has suggested that psychology should concern itself with the beneficial aspects of personality that make life rewarding and fulfilling (e.g., Seligman & Csikszentmihalyi, 2000). Positive psychology is a psychological program that examines optimal human functioning (Linley, Joseph, Harrington, & Wood, 2006). It is an agenda that many psychologists have adopted to study the origins, processes, and mechanisms that lead to psychological well-being, satisfaction, and fulfillment. Like humanistic psychology, which will be discussed later in this chapter, positive psychology concerns the valued aspects of personality. It is, however, more closely identified with the scientific methods of biological, behavioural, cognitive, and social research.

As one example of positive psychology, Fincham and Beach (2007) looked at forgiveness as a factor in the quality of a marriage. Forgiveness is an active process by which an individual voluntarily reduces the negative emotions felt toward a transgressor. Married life (or any close partnered relationship, for that matter) produces many opportunities for forgiveness. Fincham and Beach asked married individuals to consider an instance when their partners had said or done something to hurt them. They then looked at whether a tendency to forgive that act was correlated with the quality and happiness of marriage, either at the time or 12 months later. It turned out that, for both husbands and wives, a tendency to forgive was correlated with the quality of the marriage at the time. (Interestingly, wives' tendency to forgive their husbands did not correlate with their husbands' tendency to forgive them.)

It's worth noting that the social roles for women (see Chapter 12) place a strong emphasis on social skills, and this may encourage them to view forgiveness as an active strategy to maintain a strong marital bond. Positive psychology would seek to understand the interplay between personality variables that promotes a valued relationship. The cognitive and behavioural approaches discussed in this section would be helpful in achieving this understanding.

## Interim Summary

### Social Cognitive Approaches

Social cognitive theory blends Skinner's notion of reinforcement with cognitive concepts such as expectancy to explain social interaction and personality. According to Bandura, people learn the relation between their behaviour and its consequences by observing how others' behaviour is rewarded and punished. Bandura also believes that personality is the result of reciprocal determinism—the interaction of behaviour, environment, and person variables. The extent to which a person is likely to attempt to change his or her environment is related to self-efficacy, the expectation that he or she will be successful in producing the change. People with low self-efficacy tend not to try to alter their environments; just the opposite is true for people with high self-efficacy.

Mischel has argued that personality differences are due largely to individual differences in cognition. These variables include competencies, encoding strategies and personal constructs, expectancies, subjective values, and self-regulatory systems and plans.

In the past, psychologists disagreed about the relative importance of situations and personality traits in determining a person's behaviour. It now appears that personality traits are correlated with behaviour, especially when multiple observations of particular behaviours are made. In addition, some situations (such as a funeral or a stoplight) are more powerful than others, exerting more control on people's behaviour. Traits and situations interact: Some people are affected more than others by a particular situation, and people tend to choose the types of situations in which they find themselves.

Rotter's research has shown that locus of control—the extent to which people believe that their behaviour is controlled by person variables or by environmental variables—is also an important determinant of personality. Positive psychology seeks to integrate knowledge of social and cognitive psychology to explain valued aspects of life, such as happiness and satisfaction.

#### QUESTIONS TO CONSIDER

1. Think of a situation in which you modelled your behaviour on someone else's. What factors led you to imitate this behaviour? To what extent did you form an expectancy that imitating this behaviour would lead to a particular consequence?
2. Provide a personal example of reciprocal determinism. Explain the interaction of behaviour, environment, and person variables in this example.
3. Do you feel that you have an internal or external locus of control? As an example, describe a recent decision that you made or a social interaction that you had. How would your life be different if you adopted the opposite locus of control?

## The Psychodynamic Approach

For many people, the name Sigmund Freud is synonymous with psychology. Indeed, his work has had profound and lasting effects on our society. Terms such as *ego, libido, repression, rationalization*, and *fixation* are as familiar to many Western lay people as to clinicians. Before Freud formulated his theory, people believed that most behaviour was determined by rational, conscious processes. Freud was the first to claim that what we do is often irrational and that the reasons for our behaviour are seldom conscious. The mind, to Freud, was a battleground for the warring factions of instinct, reason, and conscience; the term **psychodynamic** refers to this struggle. As you will soon see, although Freud's work began with the clinical treatment of patients with psychological problems, it later provided a framework for explaining how psychodynamic factors determine personality.

### The Development of Freud's Theory

Sigmund Freud (1856–1939) was a Viennese physician who acquired his early training in neurology in the laboratory of Ernst Wilhelm von Brücke, an eminent physiologist and neuroanatomist. Freud's work in the laboratory consisted mostly of careful anatomical observation rather than experimentation. Careful observation also characterized his later work with human behaviour; he made detailed observations of individual patients and drew inferences about the structure of the human mind from these cases.

After studying in Paris with Jean Martin Charcot, who was investigating the usefulness of hypnosis as a treatment for hysteria, Freud opened his own medical practice in Vienna. He began an association with the prominent physician Josef Breuer. They published a seminal book called *Studies on Hysteria*, and one of the cases cited in it, that of Anna O., provided the evidence that led to some of the most important tenets of Freud's theory. Anna O. suffered from a staggering number of symptoms, including loss of speech, disturbances in vision, headaches, and paralysis and loss of feeling in her right arm. Under hypnosis, Anna was asked to think about the time when her symptoms had started. Each of her symptoms appeared to have begun just when she was unable to express a strongly felt emotion. While under hypnosis, she experienced these emotions again, and the experience gave her relief from her symptoms. It was as if the emotions had been bottled up, and reliving the original experiences had

**psychodynamic** A term used to describe the Freudian notion that the mind is in a state of conflict among instincts, reason, and conscience.

uncorked them. This release of energy (which Breuer and Freud called catharsis) presumably eliminated her symptoms.

Apparently, the woman was not cured, however. Ellenberger (1972) discovered hospital records indicating that Anna O. continued to take morphine for the distress caused by the disorders Breuer had supposedly cured. Freud appears to have eventually learned the truth, but this fact did not become generally known until recently. Breuer's failure to help Anna O. with her problems does not really undermine Freud's approach, however. The Freudian theory of personality must stand or fall on its own merits, despite the fact that one of its prime teaching examples appears to be largely fiction.

Freud concluded from his observations of patients that all human behaviour is motivated by instinctual drives, which, when activated, supply "psychic energy." This energy is aversive, because the nervous system seeks a state of quiet equilibrium. According to Freud, if something prevents the psychic energy caused by activation of a drive from being discharged, psychological disturbances will result.

Freud believed that instinctual drives are triggered by events in a person's life. Many of these events, and the reactions they cause, will be mundane and part of the normal fabric of life. Traumatic events, however, may seriously threaten the desired state of psychic energy equilibrium. During a traumatic event, a person may try to deny or hide his or her strong emotional reaction rather than express it. Indeed, sometimes we must hide and not act on strong emotions, according to Freud. Strong anger, for example, could lead to murder. There is a cost to hiding emotional reactions and suppressing the psychic energy that fuels them: the emotion may be expressed neurotically—that is, with excessive anxiety. The individual will not be able to recall his or her extreme emotional reactions because they will be embedded in the **unconscious**, the inaccessible part of the mind. Unconscious emotions, however, still exert control over conscious thoughts and actions. As we will see later, the ways in which those emotions eventually find a degree of release will help define our unique personalities, according to Freud.

Freud also believed that the mind actively prevents unconscious memories of traumatic events from reaching conscious awareness. That is, the mind *represses* the memories of traumatic events, most of which are potentially anxiety-provoking, from being consciously discovered. Freud used the idea of an iceberg as a metaphor to describe the mind. Only the tip is visible above water; the much larger and more important part of it is submerged. Likewise, the conscious mind hides a larger and more important part of the mind: the unconscious. To understand an individual's personality, we must tap into his or her unconscious.

Freud, then, argued that our personalities are determined by both conscious and unconscious powers, with the unconscious exerting considerable influence on the conscious. To understand how the unconscious exerts its control over conscious thought and action, we need to explore Freud's view of the structure of personality.

**FIGURE 14•8** Freud's conception of the structure of the mind. Freud compared the conscious portion of the mind to the tip of an iceberg and the unconscious portion to the larger part of the iceberg below the water's surface. While the id is completely unconscious, both the ego and superego may be partially conscious and partially unconscious. In addition, Freud argued that part of the mind is preconscious (not shown in this figure), containing information that may be brought into consciousness through effort.

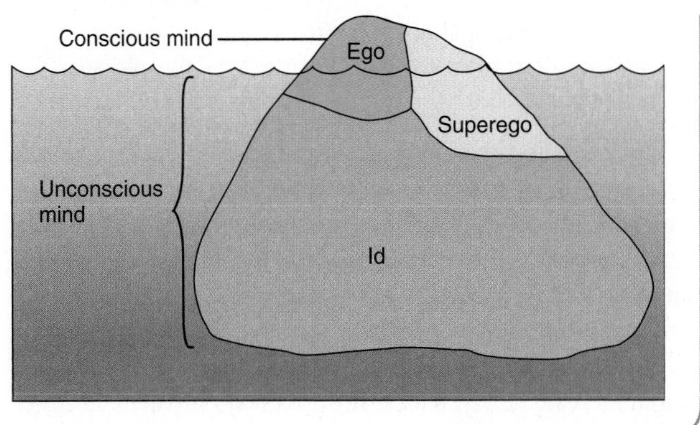


## Structures of the Mind: Id, Ego, and Superego

Freud was struck by the fact that psychological disturbances could stem from events that a person apparently could no longer consciously recall, although they could be revealed during hypnosis. This phenomenon led him to conclude that the mind consists of unconscious, preconscious, and conscious elements. The *unconscious* includes mental events of which we are not aware, the *conscious* entails mental events of which we are aware, and the *preconscious* involves mental events that may become conscious through effort.

Freud divided the mind into three structures: the id, the ego, and the superego. (See **Figure 14•8.**) The operations of the **id** are completely unconscious. The id contains the **libido**, which is the primary source of instinctual motivation for all psychic forces; this force is insistent and is unresponsive to the demands of reality. The id obeys only one rule—to obtain immediate gratification in whatever form it may take—called the **pleasure principle.** If you are hungry, the id compels you to eat; if you are angry, the id prompts you to strike out or to seek revenge or to destroy something; if you are sexually

**unconscious** The inaccessible part of the mind.
**id** The unconscious reservoir of libido, the psychic energy that fuels instincts and psychic processes.
**libido** An insistent, instinctual force that is unresponsive to the demands of reality; the primary source of motivation.
**pleasure principle** The rule that the id obeys: Obtain immediate gratification, whatever form it may take.

aroused, the id presses for immediate sexual gratification. It is important to understand that, for Freud, the id was a source of unrestrained, uncivilized, and ultimately harmful behaviour. Freud (1933) conceived of the id as

> . . . the dark, inaccessible part of our personality. . . . We approach the id with analogies: we call it a chaos, a cauldron full of seething excitations. . . . It is filled with energy reaching it from the instincts, but it has no organization, produces no collective will, but only a striving to bring about the satisfaction of the instinctual needs subject to the observance of the pleasure principle. (p. 65)

The **ego** is the thinking, planning, and protective self; it controls and integrates behaviour. It acts as a mediator, negotiating a compromise among the pressures of the id, the counterpressures of the superego (to be discussed), and the demands of reality. The ego's functions of perception, cognition, and memory perform this mediation. The ego is driven by the **reality principle**, the tendency to satisfy the id's demands realistically, which almost always involves compromising the demands of the id and superego. It involves the ability to delay gratification of a drive until an appropriate goal is located. To ward off the demands of the id when these demands cannot be gratified, the ego uses defence mechanisms (described later). Some of the functions of the ego are unconscious.

The **superego** is subdivided into the conscience and the ego-ideal. The **conscience** is the internalization of the rules and restrictions of society. It determines which behaviours are permissible and punishes wrongdoing with feelings of guilt. The **ego-ideal** is the internalization of what society values and what the person will strive to achieve.

**ego** The ego also serves as the general manager of personality, making decisions regarding the pleasures that will be pursued at the id's demand, the person's safety requirements, and the moral dictates of the superego that will be followed.

**reality principle** The tendency to satisfy the id's demands realistically, which almost always involves compromising the demands of the id and superego.

**superego** The repository of an individual's moral values, divided into the conscience—the internalization of a society's rules and regulations—and the ego-ideal—the internalization of one's goals.

**conscience** The internalization of the rules and restrictions of society; it determines which behaviours are permissible and punishes wrongdoing with feelings of guilt.

**ego-ideal** The internalization of what a person would like to be—his or her goals and ambitions.

**manifest content** The apparent storyline of a dream.

**latent content** The hidden message of a dream, produced by the unconscious.

**free association** A method of Freudian analysis in which an individual is asked to relax, clear his or her mind of current thoughts, and then report all thoughts, images, perceptions, and feelings that come to mind.

Freud believed the mind to be full of conflicts. A conflict might begin when one of the two primary drives, the sexual instinctual drive or the aggressive instinctual drive, is aroused. The id demands gratification of these drives but is often held in check by the superego's internalized prohibitions against the behaviours the drives tend to produce. *Internalized prohibitions* are rules of behaviour learned in childhood that protect the person from the guilt he or she would feel if the instinctual drives were allowed to express themselves. The result of the conflict is compromise formation, in which a compromise is reached between the demands of the id and the suppressive effects of the superego. According to Freud, phenomena such as dreams, artistic creations, and slips of the tongue (we now call them Freudian slips) are examples of compromise formation.

In what many consider to be his greatest work, *The Interpretation of Dreams*, Freud wrote, "The interpretation of dreams is the royal road to a knowledge of the unconscious activities of the mind" (Freud, 1900, p. 647). To Freud, dreams were motivated by repressed wishes and urges. By analyzing dreams, Freud thought that repressed wishes and memories could be rediscovered. For example, Freud believed that the **manifest content** of a dream—its actual storyline—is only a disguised version of its **latent content**—its hidden message, which is produced by the unconscious. The latent content usually will be related to unexpressed wishes generated by instinctual drives.

For example, a person may want to hurt or injure another person, perhaps a competitor for a job promotion. However, acting out this scenario in a dream would lead to guilt and anxiety. Therefore, the aggressive wishes of the unconscious are transformed into a more palatable form—the manifest content of the dream might be that the co-worker accepts a different job offer, removing any competition for the promotion. The manifest content of this dream manages to express, at least partly, the latent content supplied by the unconscious.

In addition to analyzing his patients' dreams, Freud also developed the technique of free association to probe the unconscious mind for clues of intrapsychic conflict. **Free association** is a method of analysis in which an individual is asked to relax, clear his or her mind of what he or she is currently thinking, and then report all thoughts, images, perceptions, and feelings that come to mind. During free association, Freud looked for particular patterns in the patient's report that might reveal wishes, fears, and worries that the patient's mind might be keeping hidden. For example, free association might reveal, among other things, the thought of beating someone up, an image of a knife, and perhaps a feeling of relief. Recognizing a pattern in his patient's report, Freud then might develop hypotheses about the client's hidden desire to harm someone and about the reasons motivating both that desire and the relief experienced once the aggressive urge is satisfied. These hypotheses then guide the therapy.

**TABLE 14•3 Freudian Defence Mechanisms**

| Defence Mechanism | Description | Example |
|---|---|---|
| Repression | The mind's active attempt to prevent memories of traumatic experiences from reaching conscious awareness. | Being unable to remember childhood sexual abuse or other traumatic events that occurred earlier in life. |
| Reaction formation | Replacing an anxiety-provoking idea with its opposite. | Having intense feelings of dislike for a person, but acting friendly and kind toward him or her. |
| Projection | Denial of one's unacceptable feelings and desires and finding them in others. | Denying your negative feelings toward a person, but believing that that person has negative feelings toward you. |
| Sublimation | Channelling psychic energy from an unacceptable drive into a more acceptable one. | Diverting energy from the sex drive to produce a work of art. |
| Rationalization | Creating an acceptable reason for a behaviour that is actually performed for a less acceptable reason. | Asserting that your reason for viewing pornographic material is to understand its social implications, when in fact you are doing so for sexual gratification. |
| Conversion | The manifestation of a psychic conflict in terms of physical symptoms. | A psychic conflict, perhaps aroused by a particular person, causes you to develop symptoms of deafness or blindness to avoid contact with him or her. |

## Defence Mechanisms

According to Freud, the ego contains **defence mechanisms**—mental systems that become active whenever the id's unconscious instinctual drives come into conflict with the superego's internalized prohibitions. The signal for the ego to use one of its defences is the state of anxiety produced by an intrapsychic conflict, which motivates the ego to apply a defence mechanism and thus reduce the anxiety. Let's look at six of the most frequently used defence mechanisms. (See **Table 14•3**.)

**Repression** is responsible for keeping threatening or anxiety-provoking memories from our conscious awareness. For example, repression of memories of a childhood sexual assault might provide the child with periods of freedom from otherwise paralyzing fear of future assaults. Freud believed that repression was perhaps the most powerful of the defence mechanisms.

**Reaction formation** involves replacing an anxiety-provoking idea with its opposite. An often-cited example of a reaction formation is that of a person who is aroused and fascinated by pornographic material but whose superego will not permit this enjoyment. He or she becomes a militant crusader against pornography. Reaction formation can be a very useful defence mechanism in this situation, permitting acceptable interaction with the forbidden sexual material. The crusader against pornography often studies the salacious material to see just how vile it is so that he or she can better educate others about its harmful nature. Thus, enjoyment becomes possible without feelings of guilt.

**Projection** involves denying one's own unacceptable id-based desires and finding evidence of these desires in others' behaviour. For example, a man who is experiencing a great deal of repressed hostility may perceive the world as being full of people who are hostile to him. In this way, he can blame someone else for his own aggression when he strikes out. That is, it would be unacceptable to the superego to initiate aggression, but perfectly acceptable to take pre-emptive action in self-defence.

**Sublimation** is the diversion of psychic energy from an unacceptable drive to an acceptable one. For example, a person may feel strong sexual desire but find its outlet unacceptable because of internalized prohibitions. Despite dismissal of the originally desired outlet for the drive, the psychic energy

**defence mechanisms** Mental systems that become active whenever unconscious instinctual drives of the id come into conflict with internalized prohibitions of the superego.
**repression** The mental force responsible for actively keeping potentially threatening or anxiety-provoking memories from being consciously discovered.
**reaction formation** A defence mechanism that involves behaving in a way that is the opposite of how one really feels because the true feelings produce anxiety.
**projection** A defence mechanism in which one's unacceptable behaviours or thoughts are attributed to someone else.
**sublimation** A defence mechanism that involves redirecting pleasure-seeking or aggressive instincts toward socially acceptable goals.

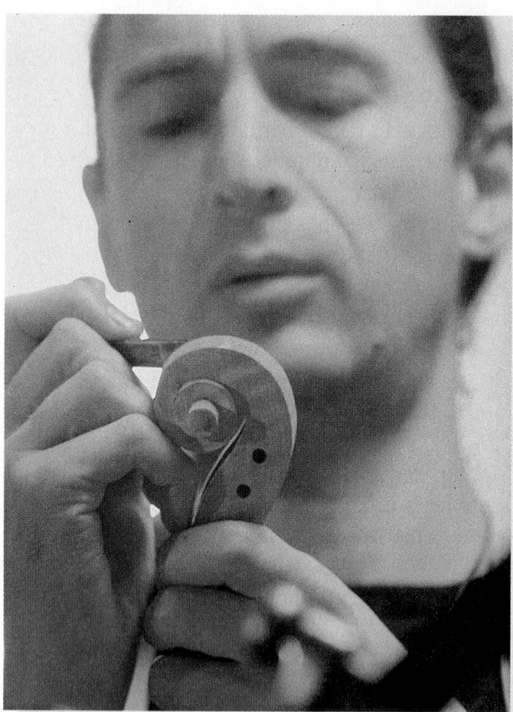

▲ *Freud argued that creativity was often the result of sublimation—the redirection of psychic energy from unacceptable actions, such as unrestrained sexual behaviour, to acceptable actions, such as the jointly sensual and creative work shown here.*

remains and finds another outlet, such as artistic or other creative activities. Freud considered sublimation an important factor in artistic and intellectual creativity. He believed that people have a fixed amount of drive available for motivating all activities; therefore, surplus sexual instinctual drive that is not expended in its most direct fashion can be used to increase a person's potential for creative achievement.

**Rationalization** is the process of inventing an acceptable reason for a behaviour that is really being performed for another, less acceptable reason. For example, a man who feels guilty about his real reasons for purchasing a magazine containing pictures of naked men or women may say, "I don't buy the magazine for the pictures. I buy it to read the interesting and enlightening articles it contains."

**Conversion** is the provision of an outlet for intrapsychic conflict in the form of a physical symptom. The conflict is transformed into blindness, deafness, paralysis, or numbness. (This phenomenon has also been called *hysteria*, which should not be confused with the common use of the term to mean "running around and shouting and generally acting out of control.") For example, a person might develop blindness so that he or she will no longer be able to see a situation that arouses a strong, painful intrapsychic conflict. Anna O.'s problem would be described as a conversion reaction.

Interestingly, researchers have found that the use of defence mechanisms predicts personality changes in later adulthood (Cramer, 2003). In this study, participants' personality traits were measured over a 24-year period using the five-factor model. Although most personality traits remained reasonably stable, the use of defence mechanisms such as denial and projection correlated with an increase in neuroticism, decreased extroversion, and decreased agreeableness. The use of these defence mechanisms was not found to be negative in all cases, though. For participants who used defence mechanisms, low scores on IQ tests were found to correlate with positive personality traits.

## Freud's Psychosexual Theory of Personality Development

Freud believed that personality development involves passing through several *psychosexual stages* of development—stages that involve seeking pleasure from specific parts of the body called *erogenous zones*. As we will see, each stage of personality development involves deriving physical pleasure from a different erogenous zone. (Freud used the term *sexual* to refer to physical pleasures and the many ways an individual might seek to gratify an urge for such pleasure. When referring to children, he did not use the term to refer to adult sexual feelings or orgasmic pleasure.)

Freud's theory of personality development has been extremely influential because of its ability to explain personality disorders in terms of whole or partial **fixation**—arrested development due to failure to pass completely through an earlier stage of development. Freud believed that a person becomes fixated at a particular stage of development when he or she becomes strongly attached to the erogenous zone involved in that stage. Although ideal personality development involves passing successfully through all of the psychosexual stages, Freud maintained that most people develop some degree of fixation during their early development. Let's take a closer look at Freud's psychosexual stages and the kinds of fixation that may develop in them.

Because newborn babies can do little more than suck and swallow, their sexual instinctual drive finds an outlet in these activities. Even as babies become able to engage in more complex behaviours, they continue to receive most of their sexual gratification orally. (Remember that by "sexual" in this context, Freud meant the physical pleasure derived from reducing the hunger drive.) We can think of infants at this stage as being dominated by the id. Over- or undergratification of the hunger drive during this **oral stage** can result in fixation.

**rationalization** A defence mechanism that justifies an unacceptable action with a more acceptable, but false, excuse.
**conversion** A defence mechanism that involves converting an intrapsychic conflict into a physical form, such as blindness, deafness, paralysis, or numbness.
**fixation** The continued attachment of psychic energy to an erogenous zone due to incomplete passage through one of the psychosexual stages.
**oral stage** The first of Freud's psychosexual stages, during which the mouth is the major erogenous zone due to reduction of the hunger drive.

Undergratification might result from early weaning and overgratification from too zealous attempts by parents to feed the infant. According to Freud, too little gratification during the oral stage will set in motion the development of personality traits related to dependency, what we commonly refer to as a "clinging vine" type. Too much gratification, or overstimulation, will lay the groundwork for the development of aggressive personality characteristics. Other oral stage fixation activities include habits such as smoking, hoarding, and excessive eating.

The **anal stage** of personality development begins during the second year of life (*anal* is derived from *anus*, the opening of the large intestine). According to Freud, sensual pleasure derives from emptying the bowels. But most parents place demands on their infants around this time to control their bowels, to delay their gratification, through toilet training. The stage is set for the early development of ego functions—the deliberate management of id impulses (in this case, the desire to vacate the bowels as soon as the urge arises). The way that parents toilet train their infants will again have a stage-setting effect on later personality development. Harsh toilet training characterized by punishment for failing to reach the toilet may lead to fixation at this stage. The personality characteristics that start to develop will centre on orderliness and a need for control. In adult form, we would refer to these characteristics as compulsiveness and, at an extreme, megalomania (a single-minded need for power and control). Mild toilet training, the preferred method, involves encouraging and praising the infant for successfully producing the bowel movement at the right place and time. The stage is set for pride in the expression of id needs coupled with appropriate ego control. Personality characteristics that should evolve include creativity and emotional expressiveness.

At around age three, a child discovers that it is pleasurable to play with his penis or her clitoris (again, an immature sexuality), and enters the **phallic stage.** (*Phallus* means "penis," but Freud used the term *phallic stage* for children of both sexes.) Children during this stage form strong, immature sexual attachments to the parent of the opposite sex. They do so, according to Freud, because mothers predominantly nurture male children and fathers predominantly nurture female children. In other words, opposite-sex parents become the focus of sensual pleasure for children during this stage. These attachments become the focus of psychological and interpersonal conflicts that Freud called *complexes.* According to Freud, children experience jealousy of their same-sex parent's close relationship with the opposite-sex parent—the one that children want exclusively for themselves. The process diverges for boys and girls beyond this point.

A boy's love of his mother is mixed with hostility toward his rival father and, importantly, fear of his father. Freud believed that boys unconsciously fear being punished by their fathers over their desire for their mother, including the ultimate punishment: castration. These elements constitute the *Oedipus complex* (after the king of Greek mythology who unknowingly married his mother after killing his father). This rich mix of emotions demands resolution.

▲ *Does toilet training affect personality development? Freud thought so: He asserted that improper toilet training caused personality development to become fixated during the anal stage of psychosexual development.*

A girl's love of her father and envy of her mother, Freud said, is complicated by her discovery that she does not have a penis. This discovery, Freud theorized, leads to penis envy and girls' magical belief that they can acquire a penis through their attachment to their father. They then gravitate even more strongly toward their fathers, who have the organ they do not, in order to associate with power and compensate for their self-perceived weakness. These powerful emotions are what Freud called the *Electra complex.* (In Greek mythology, Electra, aided by her brother, killed her mother and her mother's lover to avenge her father's death.)

The conflict for both girls and boys is resolved through a process called *identification.* According to Freud, children of both sexes turn their attention to their same-sex parent—the father for boys and the mother for girls. They begin to imitate their same-sex parent in many ways and, in a sense, idolize them. The effect of this imitation is to build a strong bond between the flattered and approving parent and the attentive, hero-worshipping son and heroine-worshipping daughter. Fear and envy are resolved. Gender roles are learned and anxiety over the genitals is resolved. This process of identification is also the initial source of *superego* development. Through

**anal stage** The second of Freud's psychosexual stages, during which the primary erogenous zone is the anus due to pleasure derived from vacating a full bowel.

**phallic stage** The third psychosexual stage. During this stage, the primary erogenous zone is the genital area, and pleasure derives from both direct genital stimulation and general physical contact.

their admiration and imitation of their same-sex parent, children learn society's fundamental principles of right and wrong (as interpreted by the parents, of course).

After the phallic stage comes a **latency period** of several years, during which the child's sexual instinctual drive is mostly submerged. Following this period is the onset of puberty. The child, now an adolescent, begins to form adult sexual attachments to young people of the opposite sex. Because the sexual instinctual drive now finds its outlet in heterosexual genital contact, this stage is known as the **genital stage**.

The results of psychosexual development amount to the building blocks of personality and general psychological functioning. Children develop basic ego and superego functions and gender role identities. Their own special mixes of fixations will follow them through life and manifest themselves as unique personality traits.

## Further Development of Freud's Theory: The Neo-Freudians

As you might imagine, Freud's theory created quite a controversy in the Victorian era when it was unveiled. Its emphasis on childhood sexuality and seething internal conflicts seemed preposterous and offensive to many. Yet the theory's proposal that our thoughts and behaviour as adults stem from unconscious forces as well as from our early childhood experiences was revolutionary, and was recognized by many scholars as a genuinely original idea. Freud attracted a number of followers who studied his work closely but who did not accept it completely. Each of these people agreed with Freud's view on the dynamic forces operating within the psyche. Each of them disagreed with Freud, though, on how much importance to place on the role of unconscious sexual and aggressive instincts in shaping personality. Five psychodynamic theorists—Carl Jung, Alfred Adler, Karen Horney, Erik Erikson, and Melanie Klein—have been particularly influential in elaborating psychodynamic theory.

**Carl Jung** Early in the twentieth century, several students of psychoanalysis met with Freud to further the development of the field. One of these people was Carl Jung (1875–1961). Freud called Jung "his adopted eldest son, his crown prince and successor" (Hall & Nordby, 1973, p. 23). However, Jung developed his own version of psychodynamic theory that deemphasized the importance of sexuality. He also disagreed with his mentor on the structure of the unconscious. Freud had little tolerance for those who disagreed with him. After 1913, he and Jung never saw each other again. Jung continued to develop his theory after the split by drawing ideas from mythology, anthropology, history, and religion, as well as from an active clinical practice in which he saw people with psychological disorders.

To Jung, libido was a positive creative force that propels people toward personal growth. He also believed that forces other than the id, ego, and superego, such as the collective unconscious, form the core of personality. To Jung, the ego was totally conscious, and contained the ideas, perceptions, emotions, thoughts, and memories of which we are aware. One of Jung's more important contributions to psychodynamic theory was his idea of the **collective unconscious**, which contains memories and ideas inherited from our ancestors. Stored in the collective unconscious are **archetypes**, inherited and universal thought forms and patterns that allow us to notice particular aspects of our world. From the dawn of our species, all humans have had roughly similar experiences with things such as mothers, evil, masculinity, and femininity. Each one of these is represented by an archetype. For example, the *shadow* is the archetype containing basic instincts that allow us to recognize aspects of the world such as evil, sin, and carnality. Archetypes are not stored images or ideas—we are not born with a picture of evil stored somewhere in our brains—but inherited dispositions to behave, perceive, and think in certain ways.

**Alfred Adler** Alfred Adler (1870–1937), like Jung, studied with Freud. Also like Jung, Adler felt that Freud had overemphasized sexuality. Adler argued that feelings of inferiority play the key role in personality development. At birth, we are dependent on others for survival. Early in our development, we encounter older, more experienced people who are more capable than we are in almost every aspect of life. The inferiority we feel may be social, intellectual, physical, or athletic. These feelings create tension that motivates us to compensate for the deficiency. Emerging from this need to compensate is a **striving for superiority**, which Adler believed to be the major motivational force in life. In Adler's theory, superiority connotes a "personal best" approach rather than defining achievement merely in terms of outperforming others. Our unique experiences with inferiority, and our consequent strivings for superiority, become organizing principles in our lives, and therefore define our personalities.

According to Adler (1939), striving for superiority is affected by another force, *social interest*, which is an innate desire to contribute to society. Social interest is not wholly instinctual, though, because it can be influenced by experience. Although individuals have a need to seek personal superiority, they have a greater desire to sacrifice for causes that benefit the society as a whole. Thus, while Freud believed that

**latency period** The period between the phallic stage and the genital stage during which sexual urges are submerged.
**genital stage** The final of Freud's psychosexual stages (from puberty through adolescence). During this stage, the adolescent develops adult sexual desires.
**collective unconscious** According to Jung, the part of the unconscious that contains memories and ideas inherited from our ancestors over the course of evolution.
**archetypes** Universal thought forms and patterns that Jung believed resided in the collective unconscious.
**striving for superiority** The motivation to achieve one's potential. Adler argued that striving for superiority is born from our need to compensate for our inferiority.

people act in their own self-interests, motivated by the id, Adler believed that people desire to help others, directed by social interest. This is a sea change. Positive motives, not negative ones, direct personality.

**Karen Horney** Karen Horney (pronounced "Horn-eye"; 1885–1952), like other Freudian dissenters, did not believe that sex and aggression are the primary determinants of personality. She did agree with Freud, though, that anxiety is a basic problem that people must address and overcome.

According to Horney, individuals suffer from basic anxiety caused by insecurities in relationships. People often feel alone, helpless, or uncomfortable in their interactions with others. For example, a person who begins a new job is often unsure of how to perform his or her duties, whom to ask for help, and how to approach his or her new co-workers. Horney theorized that to deal with basic anxiety, the individual has three options (Horney, 1950):

- *Moving toward others.* Accept the situation and become dependent on others. This strategy may entail an exaggerated desire for approval or affection.
- *Moving against others.* Resist the situation and become aggressive. This strategy may involve an exaggerated need for power, exploitation of others, recognition, or achievement.
- *Moving away from others.* Withdraw from others and become isolated. This strategy may involve an exaggerated need for self-sufficiency, privacy, or independence.

Horney believed that these three strategies corresponded to three **basic orientations** with which people approach their lives. These basic orientations reflect different personality characteristics. The *self-effacing solution* corresponds to the moving-toward-others strategy and involves the desire to be loved. The *self-expansive solution* corresponds to the moving-against-others strategy and involves the desire to master oneself. The *resignation solution* corresponds to the moving-away-from-others strategy and involves striving to be independent of others. For Horney, personality is a mixture of these three strategies and basic orientations. As the source of anxiety varies from one situation to the next, so may the strategy and basic orientation used to cope with it. From her view, to understand personality, one must consider not only psychodynamic forces within the mind, but also the environmental conditions to which those forces are reacting.

**Erik Erikson** Erik Erikson (1902–1994) studied with Anna Freud, Sigmund Freud's daughter. He emphasized social aspects of personality development rather than biological factors. He also differed with Freud about the timing of personality development. According to Freud, the most important development occurs during early childhood. Erikson emphasized the ongoing process of development throughout the lifespan. As we saw in Chapter 12, Erikson proposed that people's personality traits develop as a result of a series of crises they encounter in their social relations with other people. Because these crises continue throughout life, psychosocial development does not end when people become adults. Erikson's theory of lifelong development has been very influential, and his term *identity crisis* has become a familiar one.

**Melanie Klein and Object-Relations Theory** Yet another dissenter from Freud's ideas was Melanie Klein (1882–1960). Klein felt that the psychodynamic battleground that Freud proposed occurs very early in life, during infancy. Furthermore, its origins are different from those Freud proposed. An infant begins life utterly dependent on another. That other person, of course, is the infant's mother. The interactions between infant and mother are so deep and intense that they form the focus of the infant's structure of drives. Some of these interactions provoke anger and frustration (as when the mother withdraws the feeding infant from her breast); others provoke strong emotions of dependence as the child begins to recognize that the mother is more than a breast from which to feed. These reactions threaten to overwhelm the individuality of the infant. The way in which the infant resolves the conflict, Klein believed, is reflected in the adult's personality (Gomez, 1997).

Klein's work stimulated a contrasting school of psychodynamic theory called **object-relations theory**. According to object-relations theory, adult personality reflects the relationships that the individual establishes with others while an infant. The term *object* is not confined to inanimate things; rather, it includes the people—especially the mother—with whom the infant must relate. For object-relations theorists, relationships are the key to personality development. An individual forms a mental representation of his or her self, of others, and of the relationships that bind them. For many object-relations theorists, the need that drives the development of personality is not sexual gratification, as Freud believed, but rather the need for other human beings (Westen, 1998).

## Some Observations on Psychodynamic Theory and Research

Sigmund Freud's theory has profoundly affected psychological theory, psychotherapy, and literature. His writing, although sexist and outmoded in some respects, is lively and stimulating in others. His ideas have provided many people with food for thought. However, his theory has received little empirical support, mainly because he used concepts that are difficult to operationalize. How is one to study the ego, the

**basic orientations** Horney's sets of personality characteristics that correspond to the strategies of moving toward others, moving against others, and moving away from others.

**object-relations theory** The theory that personality is the reflection of relationships that the individual establishes with others as an infant.

superego, or the id? How can one prove (or disprove) through research that an artist's creativity is the result of a displaced aggressive or sexual instinctual drive? On the other hand, some of Freud's ideas are alive and well today. In later chapters, you will read about evidence for unconscious processing of social information and about the power that discussing traumatic events has on one's well-being. Although the theories of Jung, Adler, Horney, Erikson, and Klein have their followers, they have not led to much in the way of scientific research.

## Interim Summary

### The Psychodynamic Approach

Freud proposed that the mind is full of conflicts between the primitive urges of the id, the practical concerns of the ego, and the internalized prohibitions of the superego. According to Freud, these conflicts tend to be resolved through compromise formation and through ego defences such as repression, sublimation, and reaction formation. His theory of psychosexual development, a progression through the oral, anal, phallic, and genital stages, provided the basis for a theory of personality and personality disorders.

Freud's followers, most notably Jung, Adler, Horney, Erikson, and Klein, embraced different aspects of Freud's theory, disagreed with other aspects of it, and embellished still other aspects. Jung disagreed with Freud about the structure of the unconscious and the role of sexuality in personality development, and saw libido as a positive life force. Adler also disagreed with Freud on the importance of sexuality. Instead, Adler emphasized the need to compensate for our inferiority and our innate desire to help others as the major forces in personality development. Horney argued that personality is the result of the strategies and behaviours people use to cope with anxiety, which she believed is the fundamental problem that all people must overcome in the course of normal personality development. Erikson maintained that personality development is more a matter of psychosocial processes than of psychosexual processes. He viewed personality development as involving eight stages, each of which involves coping with a major conflict or crisis. Resolution of the conflict allows the person to pass to the next stage; failure to resolve it inhibits normal personality development. Klein suggested that psychodynamic conflict occurs early in infancy and centres on the relation between the infant and the mother. Her work formed the basis for object-relations theory, which posits that relationships with others constitute the fundamental basis of personality.

**QUESTIONS TO CONSIDER**

1. Have you ever found yourself using any of the Freudian defence mechanisms discussed in this chapter? If so, under what circumstances do you tend to use them, and what unconscious conflict do you suppose you might be protecting yourself from?
2. Do you possess any behaviours that might represent a fixation? If so, what are they and what fixations do they represent?
3. Which neo-Freudian view on personality development makes the most sense to you? Why do you feel this way? What is your rationale for concluding that one view is more sensible than the others? Which of the theories best explains your own personality development? Provide an example.

**humanistic approach** An approach to the study of personality in which emphasis is placed on the positive, fulfilling aspects of life.
**self-actualization** The realization of one's true intellectual and emotional potential.

# The Humanistic Approach

The **humanistic approach** to the study of personality emphasizes the positive, fulfilling elements of life. Humanistic psychologists are interested in nurturing personal growth, life satisfaction, and positive human values. They believe that people are innately good and have an internal drive for **self-actualization**—the realization of one's true intellectual and emotional potential. The two most influential humanistic theorists have been Abraham Maslow and Carl Rogers.

## Maslow and Self-Actualization

For both Freud and Abraham Maslow (1908–1970), motivation is one of the central aspects of personality. However, where Freud saw strong instinctual urges generating tensions that could not be completely resolved, Maslow saw positive impulses that could be easily overwhelmed by negative forces within one's culture. According to Maslow (1970), human motivation is based on a hierarchy of needs. Our motivation for different activities passes through several levels, with entrance to subsequent levels dependent on first satisfying needs in previous levels. (See **Figure 14•9**.) If an individual's needs are not met, he or she cannot scale the hierarchy and so will fail to attain his or her true potential.

In Maslow's view, understanding personality requires understanding this hierarchy. Our most basic needs are *physiological needs*, including the need for food, water, oxygen, rest, and so on. Until these needs are met, we cannot be motivated by needs found in the next level (or any other level). If our physiological needs are met, we find ourselves motivated

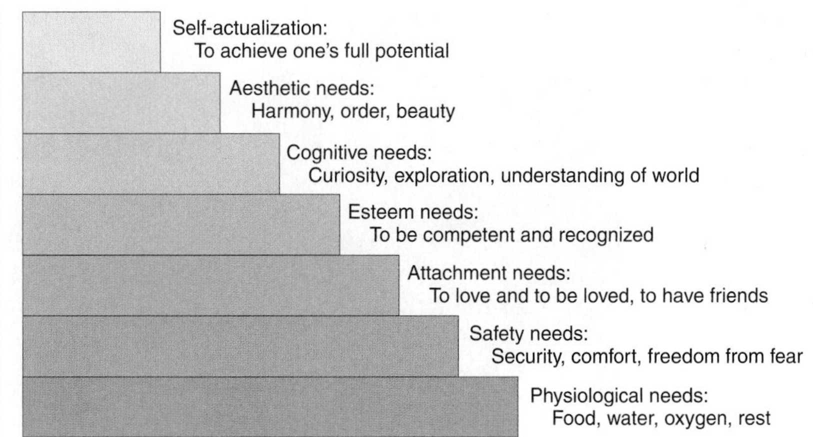


FIGURE 14•9 Maslow's hierarchy of needs. According to Maslow, every person's goal is to become self-actualized. To achieve this goal, individuals must first satisfy several basic needs.

by *safety needs*, including the need for security and comfort, as well as for peace and freedom from fear. Once the basic survival and safety needs are met, we can become motivated by *attachment needs*, the need to love and to be loved, to have friends and to be a friend. Next, we seek to satisfy *esteem needs*—to be competent and recognized as such. You are probably beginning to get the picture: We are motivated to achieve needs higher in the hierarchy only after first satisfying lower needs. If we are able to lead a life in which we have been able to provide ourselves with food and shelter and surround ourselves with love, we are free to pursue self-actualization.

Maslow based his theory partially on his own assumptions about human potential and partially on his case studies of historical figures whom he believed to be self-actualized, including Albert Einstein and Henry David Thoreau. Maslow examined the lives of each of these people in order to assess the common qualities that led each to become self-actualized. In general, he found that these individuals were very accepting of themselves and of their life circumstances; were focused on finding solutions to pressing cultural problems rather than to personal problems; were open to others' opinions and ideas; were spontaneous in their emotional reactions to events in their lives; had strong senses of privacy, autonomy, human values, and appreciation of life; and had a few intimate friendships rather than many superficial ones.

Maslow (1964) believed that the innate drive for self-actualization is not specific to any particular culture. He viewed it as a fundamental part of human nature. In his words, "Man has a higher and transcendent nature, and this is part of his essence . . . his biological nature of a species which has evolved" (p. xvi).

## Rogers and Conditions of Worth

Carl Rogers (1902–1987) also believed that people are motivated to grow psychologically, aspiring to higher levels of fulfillment as they progress toward self-actualization (Rogers, 1961). Like Maslow, Rogers believed that people are inherently good and have an innate desire to become better. Rogers, though, did not view personality development in terms of satisfying a hierarchy of needs. Instead, he believed that personality development centres on one's *self-concept*, or one's opinion of oneself, and on the way one is treated by others.

Rogers argued that all people have a need for *positive regard*, or approval, warmth, love, respect, and affection flowing from others. Young children, in particular, show this need when they seek approval for their actions from parents and siblings. In Rogers' view, children often want others to like

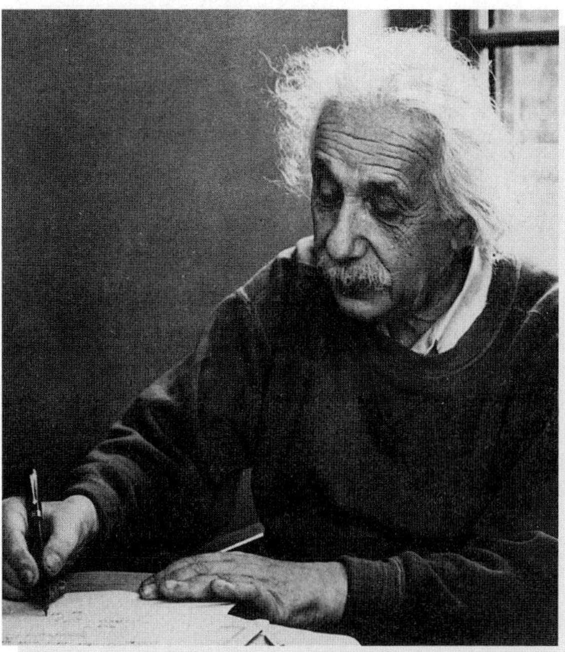

▲ *Abraham Maslow considered Albert Einstein (above) to possess those qualities representative of self-actualization, including self-acceptance, a focus on finding solutions to cultural problems, open-mindedness, and spontaneity.*

them to the extent that gaining positive regard is a major focus of their lives. The key to developing a psychologically healthy personality, though, is to develop a positive self-concept or image of oneself. How does one do this? Rogers' answer is that we are happy if we feel that others are happy with us. Likewise, we are unhappy with ourselves when others are disappointed in or unsatisfied with us.

Thus, our feelings toward ourselves depend to a large extent on what others think of us. As children, we learn that there exist certain conditions or criteria that must be met before others give us positive regard. Rogers called these criteria **conditions of worth.**

Positive regard is often conditional. For example, parents may act approvingly toward their young child when he helps in the kitchen or in the yard but not when he pinches his younger sister or tells a fib about how many cookies he has taken from the cookie jar. The boy learns that what others think of him depends on his actions. Soon, too, he may come to view himself as others view him and his behaviour: "People like me when I do something good and they don't like me when I do something bad."

Although conditions of worth are a necessary part of the socialization process, they can have negative effects on personality development if satisfying them becomes the individual's major ambition. So long as the individual focuses chiefly on seeking positive regard from others, he or she may ignore other aspects of life, especially those that lead to positive personality growth. In Rogers' view, then, conditions of worth may stand in the way of self-actualization. An individual may devote her life to satisfying the expectations and demands of others in lieu of working toward realizing her potential. In this sense, the need for positive regard may smother an individual's progress toward self-actualization.

According to Rogers, the solution to this problem is **unconditional positive regard**, or love and acceptance that has no strings attached. In a family setting, this means that parents may establish rules and expect their children to obey them, but not through methods that compromise the children's feelings of worth and self-respect. For example, if a child misbehaves, the parents should focus on the child's behaviour and not the child. The parent is free to stop destructive behaviour, for example, but should not implicitly undermine the child's self-concept through negative labelling ("What a stupid thing to do," "You're such a bad girl," "You must want to hurt Mummy"). By distinguishing between behaviour and the child herself, parents help the child learn that her behaviour is unacceptable but that her parents still love her. Implementing unconditional regard in this way permits children to explore life within reasonable bounds and thereby to realize their inherent potential. Parents have an enormous responsibility.

**conditions of worth** Conditions that others place on us for receiving their positive regard.
**unconditional positive regard** Unconditional love and acceptance of an individual by another person.

▲ *According to Rogers, all people have a basic need for approval, warmth, and love from others. This need is best met through unconditional positive regard: love and acceptance with no strings attached.*

Rogers would say that parents need to understand and believe that their children are intrinsically good. Bad behaviour results only when the child's positive potential is being undermined or constrained by the social environment.

In developing his theory, Rogers used unstructured interviews in which the client, not the therapist, directed the course of the conversation. He believed that if the therapist provided an atmosphere of unconditional positive regard, a client would eventually reveal her *true self*, the kind of person she now is, as well as her *ideal self*, the kind of person she would like to become. Rogers also gave the *Q sort test* to many of his clients. This test consists of a variety of cards, each of which contains a statement such as "I am generally an optimistic person" or "I am generally an intolerant person." The client's task is to sort the cards into several piles that vary in degree from "least like me" to "most like me." The client sorts the cards twice, first on the basis of his real self and next in terms of his ideal self. The difference between the arrangement of the cards in the piles is taken as an index of how close the client is to reaching his ideal self. Rogers' goal as a therapist was to facilitate the client's becoming his ideal self. We will examine Rogers' approach to therapy in more detail in Chapter 18.

## Some Observations on the Humanistic Approach

The humanistic approach is impressive because of its emphasis on people seeking a healthy and positive life for themselves and others. Indeed, the approach has wide appeal to those who seek an alternative to the more mechanistic and strictly biologically or environmentally determined views of human nature. However, critics point out two closely related problems with this approach.

**TABLE 14•4 A Summary of the Major Personality Theories**

| Theory | Primary Figures | Primary Emphases | Primary Strengths | Primary Limitations |
|---|---|---|---|---|
| Trait | Allport, Cattell, Eysenck | An individual's traits determine personality. | Focuses on stability of behaviour over long periods. Attempts to measure traits objectively. | Largely descriptive; ignores situational variables that may affect behaviour. |
| Psychobiological | Eysenck, Zuckerman | The role of genetics and the brain and nervous system in personality development. | Emphasis on the interaction of biology and environment in determining personality; rigorous empirical approach. | Reliance on correlational methods in determining the role of genetics in personality. |
| Social cognitive | Bandura, Mischel, Rotter | Personality is determined by both the consequences of behaviour and our perception of them. | Focuses on direct study of behaviour and stresses rigorous experimentation. | Ignores biological influences on personality development. Often more descriptive than explanatory. |
| Psychodynamic | Freud, Jung, Adler, Horney, Erikson, Klein | Unconscious psychic conflicts; repression of anxiety-provoking ideas and desires. | The idea that behaviour may be influenced by forces outside conscious awareness. | Basic concepts are not empirically testable. |
| Humanistic | Maslow, Rogers | Stresses the positive aspects of human nature and how to become a better person. | Useful in therapeutic settings. | Contains untestable concepts; primarily descriptive. |

First, many of the concepts used by humanistic psychologists are defined subjectively and so are difficult to test empirically. For example, how might we empirically examine the nature of self-actualization? Few published studies have even attempted to answer this question. By now, you know the hallmark of a good scientific theory: the amount of research it generates. On this count, the humanistic approach comes up short by scientific standards. Keep in mind, though, that humanistic theorists are aware that the structure of their theories hinders the use of scientific research methods. Maslow, for instance, simply did not care; in fact, he believed that the scientific approach was a hindrance to the development of psychology.

A second criticism of the humanistic approach is that it cannot account for the origins of personality. It is subject to the nominal fallacy; it describes personality, but it does not explain it. Humanistic psychologists believe that self-actualization is an innate tendency, but there is no research that shows this to be so. Conditions of worth are said to hamper a child's quest for self-actualization and thus alter the course of personality development away from positive psychological growth. However, the humanistic approach provides no objective explanation of this process.

Before moving on to the next section, take a few moments to examine **Table 14•4**, which reviews each of the major theories of personality we have discussed.

## Interim Summary

### The Humanistic Approach

The humanistic approach attempts to understand personality and its development by focusing on the positive side of human nature and people's attempts to reach their full potential: self-actualization.

Maslow argued that self-actualization is achieved only after the satisfaction of several other important but lesser needs—for example, physiological, safety, and attachment needs. Maslow's case study analysis of people whom he believed to be self-actualized revealed several common personality characteristics, including self-acceptance, a focus on addressing cultural problems rather than personal ones, spontaneity, preservation of privacy, an appreciation for life, and possession of a few very close, intimate friendships.

According to Rogers, the key to becoming self-actualized is developing a healthy self-concept. The primary roadblocks in this quest are conditions of worth—criteria that we must meet to win the positive regard of others. Rogers maintained that too often people value themselves only to the extent that they believe other people do. As a result, they spend their lives seeking the acceptance of others instead of striving to become self-actualized. Rogers proposed that only by treating others with unconditional positive regard could we help people to realize their true potentials.

Although the humanistic approach emphasizes the positive dimensions of human experience and the potential that each of us has for personal growth, it has been faulted for being unscientific. Critics argue that its concepts are vague and untestable and that it is more descriptive than explanatory.

**QUESTIONS TO CONSIDER**

1. Are you a self-actualized person? If not, what obstacles might be standing in the way of your reaching your true potential?
2. Describe some of the conditions of worth that others have placed on you as you have developed into an adult. Explain how your experience confirms or disconfirms Rogers' idea that conditions of worth are impediments to personal growth and to the development of a healthy self-concept.

# Assessment of Personality

One of the best ways to get to know people—what they are like and how they react in certain situations—is to spend time with them. Obviously, psychologists do not have the luxury of spending large amounts of time with people in order to learn about their personalities. Generally, in fact, they have only a short period to accomplish this goal. From this necessity, personality tests were first developed. The underlying assumption of any personality test is that personality characteristics can be measured. This final section of the chapter describes the two primary types of personality tests—objective tests and projective tests—and discusses the three tests most frequently used by clinical psychologists (Watkins, Campbell, Nieberding, & Hallmark, 1995).

## Objective Tests of Personality

**Objective personality tests** are similar in structure to classroom tests. Most contain multiple-choice and true–false items, although some allow the person taking the test to indicate the extent to which he or she agrees or disagrees with an item. The responses that participants can make on objective tests are constrained by the test design. The questions asked are unambiguous, and explicit rules for scoring the participants' responses can be specified in advance.

One of the oldest and most widely used objective tests of personality is the **Minnesota Multiphasic Personality Inventory (MMPI)**, originally devised by Hathaway and McKinley in 1939. The purpose for developing the test was to produce an objective, reliable method for identifying various personality traits that were related to a person's mental health. The developers believed that this test would be valuable in assessing people for a variety of purposes. For instance, it would provide a specific means of determining how effective psychotherapy was. Improvement in people's scores over the course of treatment would indicate that the treatment was successful.

In devising this test, Hathaway and McKinley wrote several hundred true–false items and administered the test to several groups of people in mental institutions in Minnesota who had been diagnosed as having certain psychological disorders. These diagnoses had been arrived at through psychiatric interviews with the patients. Such interviews are expensive, so a simple paper-and-pencil test that accomplished the same result would be valuable. The control group consisted of relatives and friends of the patients, who were tested when they came to visit them. (Whether these people constituted the best possible group of normal participants is questionable.) The responses were analyzed empirically, and the questions that correlated with various diagnostic labels were included in various scales. For example, if people who had been diagnosed as paranoid tended to answer "true" to "I believe I am being plotted against," this statement would become part of the paranoia scale.

The current, revised version of this test, the MMPI-2, has norms based on a sample of people that is much more representative ethnically and geographically than the original sample was (Butcher et al., 2000; Graham, 1990). It includes 567 questions, grouped into 10 clinical scales and several validity scales. A particular item can be used on more than one scale. For example, both people who are depressed and people who are hypochondriacal tend to agree that they have gastrointestinal problems. The clinical scales include terms traditionally used to label psychiatric patients, such as hypochondriasis, depression, and paranoia.

Four validity scales were devised to provide the tester with some assurance that participants are answering questions reliably and accurately and that they can read the questions and pay attention to them. The ? scale ("cannot say") is simply the number of questions not answered. A high score on this scale indicates either that the person finds some questions irrelevant or that the person is evading issues he or she finds painful.

The L scale ("lie") contains items such as "I do not read every editorial in the newspaper every day" and "My table manners are not quite as good at home as when I am out in company." A person who disagrees with questions like these is almost certainly not telling the truth. A high score on the L scale suggests the need for caution in interpreting other

**objective personality tests** Tests for measuring personality that can be scored objectively, such as a multiple-choice or true–false test.

**Minnesota Multiphasic Personality Inventory (MMPI)** An objective test originally designed to distinguish individuals with different psychological problems from normal individuals. It has since become popular as a means of attempting to identify personality characteristics of people in many everyday settings.

scales and also reveals something about the participant's personality.

The F scale ("frequency") consists of items that are answered one way by at least 90 percent of the normal population. The usual responses are "false" to items such as "I can easily make other people afraid of me, and sometimes do it for the fun of it" and "true" to items such as "I am liked by most people who know me." A high score on this scale indicates carelessness, poor reading ability, or very unusual personality traits.

The K scale ("defensiveness") was devised to identify people who are trying to hide their feelings to guard against internal conflicts that might cause them emotional distress. A person receives a high value on the K scale by answering "false" to statements such as "Criticism or scolding hurts me terribly" and "At periods, my mind seems to work more slowly than usual."

As well as being used in clinical assessment, the MMPI has been employed extensively in personality research, and a number of other tests, including the California Psychological Inventory and the Taylor Manifest Anxiety Scale, are based on it. However, the MMPI was developed as a way of assessing clinical states. A clinical psychologist is faced with a very different task than that of a personality theorist describing general traits of personality. Thus, the factors that might be important to the five-factor explanation of behaviour may not be relevant to questions of therapy or to the classification of psychological disorders.

A recent development in personality assessment has been a movement to produce an "open source" set of personality tests that can be used by researchers around the world. One such project is the International Personality Item Pool. The items included in this set are specifically designed to be readily translated into other languages, facilitating cross-cultural comparisons. The project is still under development, but does promise to have a large impact on personality research (Goldberg et al., 2006). You can examine the current status of this project at www.ipip.ori.org.

## Projective Tests of Personality

Projective tests of personality are different in form from objective ones and are derived from psychodynamic theories of personality. Psychoanalytically oriented psychologists believe that behaviour is determined by unconscious processes more than by conscious ones. Thus, they believe that a test that asks straightforward questions is unlikely to tap the real roots of an individual's personality characteristics. **Projective tests** are designed to be ambiguous so that the person's answers will be more revealing than simple agreement or disagreement with statements provided by objective tests. The assumption of projective tests is that an individual will "project" his or her personality into the ambiguous situation and thus make responses that give clues to this personality. In addition, the ambiguity of the test makes it unlikely that participants will have preconceived notions about which answers are socially desirable. Thus, it will be difficult for a participant to give biased answers in an attempt to look better (or worse) than he or she actually is.

**The Rorschach Inkblot Test** One of the oldest projective tests of personality is the Rorschach Inkblot Test, published in 1921 by Hermann Rorschach, a Swiss psychiatrist. The **Rorschach Inkblot Test** consists of 10 pictures of inkblots, originally made by spilling ink on a piece of paper that was subsequently folded in half, producing an image that is symmetrical in relation to the line of the fold. Five of the inkblots are black and white, and five are coloured. (See **Figure 14•10**.)

**projective tests** Unstructured personality measures in which a person is shown a series of ambiguous stimuli, such as pictures, inkblots, or incomplete drawings. The person is asked to describe what he or she "sees" in each stimulus or to create stories that reflect the theme of the drawing or picture.
**Rorschach Inkblot Test** A projective test in which a person is shown a series of symmetrical inkblots and asked to describe what he or she thinks they represent.

FIGURE 14•10 An inkblot similar to one that appears in the Rorschach Inkblot Test.

The participant is shown each card and asked to describe what it looks like. Then the cards are shown again, and the participant is asked to point out the features he or she used to determine what was seen. The responses and the nature of the features the participant uses to make them are scored on several dimensions.

In the following example described by Pervin (1975), a person's response to a particular inkblot (a real one, not the one shown in Figure 14.10) might be "Two bears with their paws touching one another playing pattycake or could be they are fighting and the red is the blood from the fighting." The classification of this response, also described by Pervin, would be: large detail of the blot was used, good form was used, movement was noted, colour was used in the response about blood, an animal was seen, and a popular response (two bears) was made. A possible interpretation of the response might be:

> Subject starts off with popular response and animals expressing playful, "childish" behaviour. Response is then given in terms of hostile act with accompanying inquiry. Pure color response and blood content suggest he may have difficulty controlling his response to the environment. Is a playful, childlike exterior used by him to disguise hostile, destructive feelings that threaten to break out in his dealings with the environment? (Pervin, 1975, p. 37)

Although the interpretation of people's responses to the Rorschach Inkblot Test was originally based on psychoanalytical theory, many investigators have used it in an empirical fashion. That is, a variety of different scoring methods have been devised, and the scores obtained by these methods have been correlated with clinical diagnoses, just as investigators have done with people's scores on the MMPI. When this test is used empirically, the style and content of the responses are not interpreted in terms of a theory (as Rorschach interpreted them) but are simply correlated with other measures of personality.

**The Thematic Apperception Test** Another popular projective test, the **Thematic Apperception Test (TAT)**, was developed in 1938 by psychologists Henry Murray and C. D. Morgan to measure various psychological needs. People are shown a picture of a very ambiguous situation and are asked to tell a story about what is happening in the picture, explaining the situation, what led up to it, what the characters are thinking and saying, and what the final outcome will be. Presumably, the participants will "project" themselves into the scene, and their stories will reflect their own needs. As you might imagine, scoring is difficult and requires a great deal of practice and skill. The tester attempts to infer the psychological needs expressed in the stories.

**Thematic Apperception Test (TAT)** A projective test in which a person is shown a series of ambiguous pictures that involve people. The person is asked to make up a story about what the people are doing or thinking. The person's responses are believed to reflect aspects of his or her personality.

Consider the responses of one woman to several TAT cards, along with a clinician's interpretation of these responses (Phares, 1979). The questions asked by the examiner are in parentheses.

> Card 3BM. Looks like a little boy crying for something he can't have. (Why is he crying?) Probably because he can't go somewhere. (How will it turn out?) Probably sit there and sob hisself to sleep. Card 3GF. Looks like her boyfriend might have let her down. She hurt his feelings. He's closed the door on her. (What did he say?) I don't know. Card 10. Looks like there's sorrow here. Grieving about something. (About what?) Looks like maybe one of the children's passed away.
>
> Interpretation: The TAT produced responses that were uniformly indicative of unhappiness, threat, misfortune, a lack of control over environmental forces. None of the test responses were indicative of satisfaction, happy endings, etc. . . . In summary, the test results point to an individual who is anxious and, at the same time, depressed. (Phares, 1979, p. 273)

The pattern of responses in this case is quite consistent; few people would disagree with the conclusion that the woman is sad and depressed. However, not all people provide such clear-cut responses. As you might expect, interpreting differences in the stories of people who are relatively well adjusted is much more difficult. As a result, distinguishing among people with different but normal personality traits is hard.

## Evaluation of Projective Tests

Most empirical studies have found that projective tests such as the Rorschach Inkblot Test and the TAT have poor reliability and little validity. For example, Eron (1950) found no differences between the scores of people who were in mental hospitals and university students. (You can supply your own joke about that.) Entwisle (1972) reported that "recent studies . . . yield few positive relationships between need achievement [measured by the TAT] and other variables" (p. 179). In a review of more than 300 studies, Lundy (1985) found that the validity of the TAT appears to be lower when it is administered by an authority figure, in a classroom setting, or when it is represented as a test. Lundy (1988) suggests that, in such situations, participants are likely to realize that they are talking about themselves when they tell a story about the cards and may be careful about what they say.

Even if people taking the TAT are not on their guard, their scores are especially sensitive to their moods (Masling, 1960, 1998). Therefore, the scores they receive on one day are often very different from those they receive on another day. But a test of personality is supposed to measure enduring traits that persist over time and in a variety of situations. The TAT has also been criticized for potential gender bias, mostly because of male-dominated themes, such as power, ambition, and status, used to score the test (Worchel, Aaron, & Yates, 1990).

The reliability and validity of the Rorschach Inkblot Test are also rather low. One study that used the most reliable scoring method found little or no correlation between participants' scores on the Rorschach and their scores on six objective tests of personality (Greenwald, 1990, 1999).

If projective tests such as the Rorschach and the TAT have been found to be of low reliability and validity, why do many clinical psychologists and psychiatrists continue to use them? The primary reason seems to be tradition. The use of these tests has a long history and the rationale for the tests is consistent with psychodynamic explanations of personality. Many psychodynamic and clinical psychologists still argue that the tests are valuable for discovering and evaluating inner determinants of personality (Watkins, 2000).

## Interim Summary

### Assessment of Personality

Objective tests contain items that can be answered and scored objectively, such as true–false or multiple-choice questions. One of the most important objective personality tests is the Minnesota Multiphasic Personality Inventory, which was empirically devised to discriminate among people who had been assigned various psychiatric diagnoses. It has since been used widely in research on personality. Its validity scales have been challenged by researchers who suggest that most people's responses can be taken at face value. More recently, researchers interested in personality have turned to tests not based on people with psychological disorders, such as the NEO-PI-R.

Projective tests, such as the Rorschach Inkblot Test and the Thematic Apperception Test, contain ambiguous items that elicit answers that presumably reveal aspects of personality. Because answers can vary widely, test administrators must receive special training to interpret them. Unfortunately, evidence suggests that the reliability and validity of such tests are not particularly high.

**QUESTIONS TO CONSIDER**

1. Which kind of personality inventory—objective tests or projective tests—do you suppose would be more effective in revealing the more important aspects of your personality? Why?
2. If your results on a personality inventory revealed that you possess a personality trait that you didn't think you had (especially if it is a negative trait), how would you react? Would you tend to disparage the test, or would you admit that, in fact, this trait is part of your personality?
3. What kinds of personality differences between males and females have you noticed? Are these differences genuine or are they a product of the stereotypes you hold of the sexes? How do you know?

## EPILOGUE

### Assessing Personality

Robert Dziekanski could not have known this, but from the time the airport security officers first spoke to him, he had only a few seconds to show—through his behaviour, since he couldn't speak their language—that he was not a threat. His death occurred because he could not do this.

The investigations that were launched after this incident will probably tell us a lot about the procedures that were followed and whether they were adequate for such a situation. But they will probably never tell us exactly why Robert responded the way he did. Why did his behaviour change from confusion to aggression so erratically? Why did he pick up a table, of all things, and carry it around?

In this chapter, we examined a number of frameworks that might be used to understand Robert's behaviour. There is the historical notion that people fall into certain "types," such as choleric, making them prone to react generally. Other approaches are more particular. The cognitive-affective processing system approach, for example, might point to memories that Robert could have had of his arrest as a teenager. Perhaps, for a split second, he saw the security officers as a threat and reacted with fear. Perhaps, too, the nicotine and food deprivation he experienced during his 10-hour wait in the customs area inhibited his normal emotional and cognitive reactions.

Situational approaches to personality would seem to be especially relevant to this case.

Now consider the case from the opposite perspective. The security officers had only seconds to assess Robert's personality. Was he aggressive? Would his behaviour turn from violence against the furniture to violence against other passengers? Now imagine that you were forced to make that same judgment every time you met someone, whether a friend or a stranger. Suppose you had no way of predicting whether an acquaintance you bump into would smile in greeting or shout at you to get out of the way. A world without any stability in personality traits would be socially chaotic. Perhaps this is why some personality traits show strong genetic indications. Our evolutionary history has selected us partly on the basis of our social skills, and these require the ability to anticipate what others will do. So our social origins require stable and predictable traits.

But not too predictable. Remember that, among those stable traits, are the Dark Triad. Persons with strong machiavellian tendencies could all too easily predict and exploit our behaviour if it were too regular. The fact that unique experiences shape our individual personalities is probably a source of social protection. Evolution has shaped us to be different, despite our similarities. In a world where mistrust or misperception can lead to drastic consequences such as what happened to Robert Dziekanski, it's best to remember that.

## Canadian Connections to Research in This Chapter


Ellenberger, H. F. (1972). The story of "Anna O": A critical review with new data. *Journal of the History of the Behavioral Sciences, 8,* 267–279. (Université de Montréal: www.umontreal.ca)

Jackson, D. N., Ashton, M. E., & Tomes, J. L. (1996). The six-factor model of personality: Facets from the Big Five. *Personality and Individual Differences, 21,* 391–402. (University of Western Ontario: www.uwo.ca)

Jackson, D. N., Paunonen, S. V., Fraboni, M., & Goffin, R. D. (1996). A five-factor versus six-factor model of personality structure. *Personality and Individual Differences, 20,* 33–45. (University of Western Ontario: www.uwo.ca)

Jackson, D. N., & Tremblay, P. F. (2002). The six factor personality questionnaire. In B. de Raad (Ed.), *Big Five assessment.* Ashland, OH: Hogrefe & Huber Publishers. (University of Western Ontario: www.uwo.ca)

Professor Jackson received the Canadian Psychological Association Award for Outstanding Contribution to the Application of Psychology to Human Problems in 1986.

Kaminsky, Z., Petronis, A., Wang, S-C., Levine, B., Ghaffar, O., Floden, D., & Feinstein, A. (2008). Epigenetics of personality traits: An illustrative study of identical twins discordant for risk-taking behavior. *Twin Research and Human Genetics, 11,* 1–11. (University of Toronto: www.utoronto.ca)

Lefcourt, H. M. (1966). Internal versus external control of reinforcement: A review. *Psychological Bulletin, 65,* 206–220. (University of Waterloo: www.uwaterloo.ca)

Lefcourt, H. M. (1992). Durability and impact of the locus of control construct. *Psychological Bulletin, 112,* 411–414. (University of Waterloo: www.uwaterloo.ca)

Livesley, W. J., Jang, K. L., & Vernon, P. A. (2003). Genetic basis of personality structure. In T. Millon & M. J. Lerner (Eds.), *Handbook of psychology: Personality and social psychology, Vol. 5.* New York: John Wiley & Sons, Inc. (University of British Columbia: www.ubc.ca)

Professor Jang received the President's New Researcher Award from the Canadian Psychological Association in 1998.

Paunonen, S. V. (2003). Big Five factors of personality and replicated predictions of behavior. *Journal of Personality & Social Psychology, 84*(2), 411–422. (University of Western Ontario: www.uwo.ca)

Snow, W. G., & Weinstock, J. (1990). Sex differences among non-brain-damaged adults on the Wechsler Adult Intelligence Scales: A review of the literature. *Journal of Clinical and Experimental Neuropsychology, 12,* 873–886. (Sunnybrook and Women's College Health Sciences Centre, Toronto: www.surg.med.utoronto.ca/AnnRep/AR05_06/sunnybrook.html)

Vernon, P. A., Jang, K. L., Harris, J. A., & McCarthy, J. M. (1997). Environmental predictors of personality differences: A twin and sibling study. *Journal of Personality and Social Psychology, 72,* 177–183. (University of Western Ontario: www.uwo.ca)

Wiggins, J. S. (Ed.). (1996). *The five-factor model of personality: Theoretical perspectives.* New York: Guilford Press. (University of British Columbia: www.ubc.ca)

Wiggins, J. S., & Pincus, A. L. (2002). Personality structure and the structure of personality disorders. In P. T. Costa, Jr. & T. A. Widiger (Eds.), *Personality disorders and the five-factor model of personality* (2nd ed.). Washington, DC: American Psychological Association. (University of British Columbia: www.ubc.ca)

Wiggins, J. S., & Trapnell, P. D. (1997). Personality structure: The return of the Big Five. In R. Hogan, J. A. Johnson, & S. Briggs (Eds.), *Handbook of personality psychology.* San Diego, CA: Academic Press. (University of British Columbia: www.ubc.ca)

## Suggestions for Further Reading

Buss, A. H. (1995). *Personality: Temperament, social behaviour, and the self.* Boston, MA: Allyn and Bacon.

Carver, C. S., & Scheier, M. F. (2000). *Perspectives on personality* (5th ed.). Boston, MA: Allyn and Bacon.

Wiggins, J. S. (Ed.). (1996). *The five-factor model of personality: Theoretical perspectives.* New York: Guilford.

Theories of personality, personality testing, and research on the determinants of personality receive thorough coverage in these three texts.

Bandura, A. (1986). *Social foundations of thought and action: A social cognitive theory.* Englewood Cliffs, NJ: Prentice-Hall.

In this book, Bandura presents his account of social cognition and social behaviour, which is derived from the behaviour-analytic tradition and cognitive psychology.

Freud, S. (1957). *General introduction to psychoanalysis* (J. Riviere, Trans.). New York: Permabooks.

Jones, E. (1953). *The life and work of Sigmund Freud.* New York: Basic Books.

The best resource on Freud's theories of personality is Freud himself. Jones provides an interesting discussion of Freud's life as well as of his writings.

15

# SOCIAL PSYCHOLOGY

# CHAPTER OUTLINE

## Social Cognition

Schemata and Social Cognition • The Self • Culture and Social Psychology • Attribution • Attributional Biases • Attribution, Heuristics, and Social Cognition • Social Cognition and Neuroscience

Our thoughts, feelings, perceptions, and beliefs about the world are organized into mental frameworks, or within schemata, that help us manage and synthesize information about our social world. Our self-concept is based on schemata that organize and synthesize personal knowledge and feelings we have about ourselves. In making attributions about the causes of another person's behaviour, we consider the relative contributions of dispositional and situational factors. However, we tend to overestimate the role of dispositional factors and underestimate the role of situational factors—a phenomenon called the fundamental attribution error. We also often misapply heuristics or mental shortcuts when making attributions.

## Attitudes and Their Formation

Formation of Attitudes • Attitude Change and Persuasion • Cognitive Dissonance • Self-Perception

Attitudes have affective, behavioural, and cognitive components and may be learned through mere exposure to the object of the attitude, classical conditioning processes, and imitation. To understand explicit attempts to change a person's attitude, we must consider both the source of the intended persuasive message and the message itself. A message tends to be persuasive if its source is credible or attractive and if it is pitched correctly at its intended audience. How critically we consider persuasive arguments determines the impact of attempts to change our attitudes. Cognitive dissonance is an aversive state that occurs when our attitudes and behaviour are inconsistent.

## Prejudice

The Origins of Prejudice • Self-Fulfilling Prophecies • Hope for Change

A prejudice is an attitude toward a particular group based on characteristics of that group. A self-fulfilling prophecy is a stereotype that influences a person to act in ways congruent with that stereotype of the group to which he or she belongs. Teaching people to think about members of other groups as individuals and to consider them in terms of their personal situations and characteristics can reduce prejudices and tendencies toward stereotyping.

## Social Influences and Group Behaviour

Imitation • Social Facilitation • Social Loafing • Commitment • Attractive People • Authority • Group Decision Making • Resisting Social Influences • *Then and Now: The Impact of Media Violence*

Conformity and bystander intervention are two instances in which we tend to imitate the actions of others. The presence of others enhances the performance of a well-learned behaviour but interferes with the performance of complex or not-well-learned behaviour. When a group of people must collectively perform a task, the effort of any one individual is often less than we would predict had the individual attempted the task alone, a behaviour known as social loafing. We tend to honour commitments we make to others, respond positively to requests made of us by attractive people and authority figures, and identify with group values and goals. Unscrupulous persons often exploit these tendencies for their own gain. Effective group decision making can be hampered by elements of the discussion leading to the decision. Recognizing how people may try to exploit the rules of social influence is helpful in reducing the effectiveness of such exploitation.

## Interpersonal Attraction and Loving

Interpersonal Attraction • Loving

We are attracted to others who think positively of us, who are similar to us, who are physically attractive, and who live, work, or play near us. Sternberg's theory of love describes how the elements of intimacy, passion, and commitment are involved in the different kinds of love. Interpersonal attraction occurs under many conditions, not just those that are ideal.

PROLOGUE

## Social Psychology and Salespeople

A few years ago, it was time for me to buy a new car. I did background research, and had a good idea of what the dealer cost was for the model I wanted and what would be a decent commission for a salesperson. I went to a dealer near my home, took a test drive, and settled down with my salesman, Greg, to negotiate the deal.

Greg quoted an unbelievably low price. I had to ask him to repeat himself. Even with factory-to-dealer discounts and incentives, I couldn't imagine how they were going to make any money. "Deal!" I said. We completed the formal offer, I gave Greg a cheque for several thousand dollars to seal the agreement, and then from Greg came the dreaded salesperson phrase, "I'll have to go get the manager to approve this."

I knew then that I was in the middle of a process called "lowballing," a technique whereby a salesperson quotes a very low price, only to find a reason (for example, a mistake while reading the invoice) to raise the price later. The downpayment cheque is meant to commit the buyer to the deal (more about this later in the chapter). I was supposed to sit in the salesperson's office, happily daydreaming about my new car, psychologically developing a sense of ownership. Being a psychologist, though, I knew better, and in fact sat there getting more and more irritable while Greg had a cup of coffee or whatever he did other than talking to the manager.

Sure enough, Greg returned and said, "Geez, I really messed this up. I usually work in used cars. I'm not up on these prices. My manager really blew a gasket. Your car is $8000 more than I told you. You're going to have to come close to that. I can knock off maybe $500."

"No," I said, "I'm only willing to pay what we agreed on."

Greg countered with, "No, the car is worth way more than that. You have to up your offer."

"No," I said again, "you need to stand behind your first offer to me, or I'm going home. I teach about lowballing in my class at university. I know what you're doing, and you can stop it now."

To my surprise, Greg immediately caved in and I got the car for the price he quoted originally. While I was signing the final papers, two other salespeople teased Greg in front of me about blowing the deal and needing to spend more time on the used car lot.

Most human activities are social: We spend many of our waking hours interacting with other people. Our behaviour affects the way others act and, in turn, their behaviour affects our actions. The field of psychology that studies our social nature is called **social psychology**. It is, in the words of Gordon Allport (1968), the examination of "how the thoughts, feelings, and behaviour of individuals are influenced by the actual, imagined, or implied presence of others" (p. 3).

**social psychology** The branch of psychology that studies our social nature—how the actual, imagined, or implied presence of others influences our thoughts, feelings, and behaviours.

This chapter examines the effects that people have on each other's behaviour. Interactions with other people affect all aspects of human behaviour from infancy through old age. The important people in our lives shape our emotions, thoughts, and personalities. Our perceptions—which we think of as private, solitary events—are affected by our interactions with others. Social psychologists have found that even the most personal and seemingly subjective aspects of our lives, such as interpersonal attraction, can be studied with an impressive degree of scientific rigour.

# Social Cognition

Understanding social behaviour requires considerable attention to a person's environment, both physical and social. Sizing up a social situation depends on many cognitive processes, including memory for people, places, and events; concept formation skills; and, more fundamentally, sensory and perceptual abilities (Bodenhausen, Macrae, & Hugenberg, 2003; Fiske & Taylor, 1991; Kunda, 1999). Social psychologists are successfully applying our knowledge of these basic psychological processes to the understanding of **social cognition**—how people attend to, perceive, interpret, and respond to the social world.

## Schemata and Social Cognition

All of us form impressions of others: friends, neighbours, supervisors, or teachers—virtually everyone we meet as well as many people we have not met and know only through casual observation or the reports of others. We assign all sorts of characteristics to people. We may, for example, think of someone as friendly or hostile, helpful or selfish. A major task of social psychology is to understand how we form these impressions. In Solomon Asch's (1952) words, "How do the perceptions, thoughts, and motives of one person become known to other persons?" (p. 143). To answer questions like this, psychologists study **impression formation**, the way in which we integrate information about another's traits into a coherent sense of who the person is. As noted by Asch more than half a century ago, our impressions of others are formed by more complex rules than just a simple sum of the characteristics that we use to describe people.

**Schema** A central theme of cognitive psychology is the concept of **schema** (*schemata* is the plural form), a mental framework or body of knowledge that organizes and synthesizes information about a person, place, or thing (Markus, 1977; Olson, Roese, & Zanna, 1996; Wyer & Srull, 1994). Schemata aid us in interpreting the world. The first time you visited a professor in his or her office, for example, there were probably few surprises. The schema that you have of "professor" guided your interactions with him or her. However, you would probably be surprised if you saw that your professor's office was filled with soccer trophies, autographed photos of rock stars, or rare Elvis posters. Such possessions are probably inconsistent with your impression of professors.

To grasp how schemata guide our interpretations, try to understand the following passage:

> The procedure is actually quite simple. First you arrange things into different groups. Of course, one pile may be sufficient depending on how much there is to do.... It is important not to overdo things. That is, it is better to do too few things at once than too many. In the short run this may not seem important, but complications can easily arise. A mistake can be expensive as well. At first the whole procedure will seem complicated. Soon, however, it will become just another facet of life. (Bransford & Johnson, 1972, p. 722)

Does this passage make sense to you? What if I tell you that the title of the passage is "Washing Clothes"? Now you can interpret the passage easily, for the sentences make perfect sense within the context of your schema for washing clothes. Not surprisingly, research has demonstrated that understanding is greater when people know the title of the passage before it is read (Bransford & Johnson, 1972).

**Central Traits** How does information about specific types of traits affect our overall sense of what a person is like? If I described an acquaintance of mine to you as "witty, smart, and warm," your general sense of the person probably would be quite positive. But imagine your reaction if I described my acquaintance as being "witty, smart, and cold." Your reaction probably would be much less positive. Why? Asch (1946) proposed that certain traits, called **central traits**, organize and influence our understanding of other traits a person possesses to a greater extent than do other traits. Central traits impart meaning to other known traits and suggest the presence of yet other traits that have yet to be revealed. Asch's (1946) tests of this idea focused on the warm–cold trait dimension. In one study, he provided all participants with the same basic list of traits that were said to describe a hypothetical person: intelligent, skilful, industrious, determined, practical, and cautious. Some participants were told that the person was also "warm," whereas others were told that the person was also "cold." Overall, those who heard the list with "warm" formed more positive impressions about the character of the imaginary person than did those who heard the trait "cold." Participants in the "warm" condition were also more likely to speculate that the person was also generous, happy, and altruistic. When the words *polite* and *blunt* were substituted for *warm* and *cold* in the trait list, no differences were observed in impressions. Traits such as "polite" and "blunt" thus are known as peripheral traits. Parallel results to Asch's findings for the warm–cold variable were found in a natural setting where a real person was described privately to some people as "warm" and to others as "cold," although the person's actions and demeanour were identical in both cases (Kelley, 1950). More recent work suggests that the negative influence of the "cold" trait is stronger than the positive influence of the "warm" trait (Singh, Onglatco, Sriram, & Tay, 1997; Singh & Teoh, 2000).

**social cognition** The processes involved in perceiving, interpreting, and acting on social information.
**impression formation** The way in which we integrate information about another's traits into a coherent sense of who the person is.
**schema** A mental framework or body of knowledge that organizes and synthesizes information about a person, place, or thing.
**central traits** Personality attributes that organize and influence the interpretation of other traits.

This imbalance may occur because there is already a bias toward positivity in impressions of people (e.g., Heyman & Giles, 2004; Sears, 1983). Negative information, such as that conveyed by a negative central trait description, might be more discrepant and salient in the context of a generally positive impression than just another piece of positive information about the person would be (Skowronski & Carlston, 1989). Gender differences have also been found. For example, Reich and Ray (2006) found that "foolish" females were scored higher on ratings of social desirability than "foolish" males.

**The Primacy Effect** Getting to know someone takes time because it requires many interactions. Perhaps the first time you saw someone was at a party when he was loud and boisterous, having a good time with his friends. But later, you learned that he is a math major with excellent grades who is actually generally reserved. What is your general impression of this person: loud and boisterous, or bright and shy? To determine whether first impressions might overpower later impressions, Asch (1946) presented one of the following lists of words to each of two groups of people:

> Intelligent, industrious, impulsive, critical, stubborn, envious
>
> Envious, stubborn, critical, impulsive, industrious, intelligent

Notice that these lists contain the same traits but in reverse order. After they heard the list, Asch asked the participants to describe the personality of the person having these characteristics. People who heard the first list thought of the person as someone who was able and productive but who possessed some shortcomings. The person described by the second list, however, was seen as someone who had serious problems. The tendency to form an impression of a person based on the initial information we learn about him or her is called the **primacy effect.** To some extent, the primacy effect reflects greater attention to trait information presented early than to that presented late (Belmore, 1987; Park, 1986). Consistent with this attentional interpretation, Webster, Richter, and Kruglanski (1996) found that the primacy effect was more pronounced for participants who were mentally fatigued than for those who were relatively alert.

We seldom receive lists of traits about people in the way that Asch and others provided them to research participants. Somehow, we develop these lists ourselves. How? Perhaps the most intuitively appealing answer is that as we observe what a person does and says, we purposefully think about what those behaviours reveal about his or her personal qualities (e.g., Carlston & Skowronski, 1994). In a later section in this chapter, titled "Attribution," you will learn about one theory of this kind of explicit inferential person perception (Kelley, 1967). There are other, simpler views. For example, Brown and Bassili (2002) suggested that people may generate trait-like labels from observing a person's behaviour. These labels then become automatically associated in memory with whatever stimulus happens to have been around at the same time. For example, if you are talking to a firefighter who describes a heroic rescue, you may associate the trait of "bravery" with the firefighter. When you think about that person in the future, you will also recall the trait information—bravery. Brown and Bassili (2002) showed that trait labels from behavioural descriptions may become associated with almost any stimulus, including inanimate ones. For example, they found evidence that people had associated personality traits with bananas. This means that if a firefighter were discussing his or her heroic actions with you while eating a banana, you may later associate the banana with the trait "brave." This outcome is both "illogical and nonsensical" from a person-perception point of view, because people presumably do not consider bananas to be persons. Clearly, this is not a spontaneous, purposeful attempt to decipher what a person or object is like.

**primacy effect** The tendency to form impressions of people based on the first information we receive about them.

**self-concept** Self-identity. One's knowledge, feelings, and ideas about oneself.

**self** A person's distinct individuality.

**self-schema** A mental framework that represents and synthesizes information about oneself; a cognitive structure that organizes the knowledge, feelings, and ideas that constitute the self-concept.

## The Self

If I asked you who you are, how would you respond? You might tell me your name, that you are a student, and perhaps that you are also an athlete or have a part-time job. Alternatively, you could tell me about your family, nationality, ethnicity, or religion. There are many ways you could potentially describe yourself to me, all of which would reflect your **self-concept**—your knowledge, feelings, and ideas about yourself. The **self** is a person's distinct individuality. Your self-concept, then, is your self-identity—how you perceive yourself and interpret events that are relevant to defining who you are. At the core of the self-concept is the **self-schema**—a mental framework that represents and synthesizes information about yourself (Markus, 1977). The self-schema, then, is a cognitive structure that organizes the knowledge, feelings, and ideas that constitute the self-concept.

The self-concept is dynamic; it changes with experience. Some researchers, such as Markus and Nurius (1986), argue that we should think of ourselves in terms of a working self-concept that changes as we have new experiences or receive feedback about our behaviour. That is, each of us has many potential selves that we might become, depending on experience. Can you imagine the different twists and turns your life might take and how your self-concept might be affected as a result? Can you imagine the circumstances that might lead you to change your major, drop out of school, or get married or divorced, and how your self-concept might be affected? Consider how people who had experienced a traumatic life event (for example, the death of a family member or friend) responded when they were asked to describe their current and possible future selves (Markus & Nurius, 1986; Ruvolo & Markus, 1992). They all reported that they were worried, upset, depressed, and lacked control over their lives. That is, everyone described similar *current* selves. Nonetheless, some people described different sorts of possible *future* selves. The people who had not yet recovered from the traumatic event predicted that they would be unhappy and lonely. The people in the recovered group predicted just the opposite: They saw themselves as happy, self-confident, and having many friends. Thus, thinking of ourselves only in terms of who we are at present does not accurately reflect how we will think of ourselves in the future or the kind of person we might become.

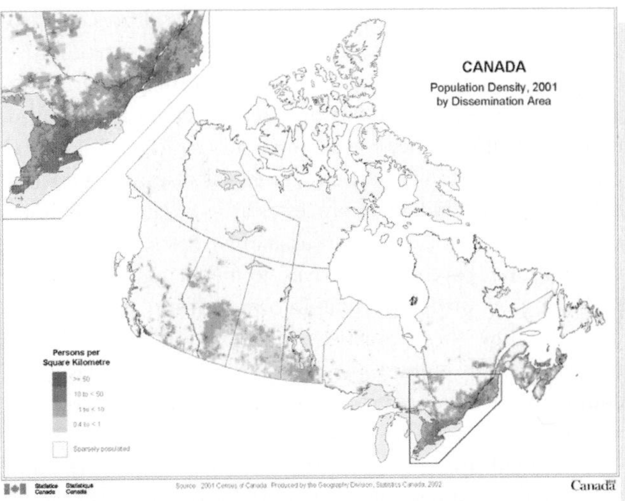


▲ *Population density, revealed by a population density map of Canada here, is an important ecological cultural variable.*

## Culture and Social Psychology

Throughout the text, you have learned how culture plays a powerful role in individual and social development. Identifying the complex interchange between biological, familial, social, and cultural influences on the self is a daunting challenge, but one that has been taken up with a considerable degree of enthusiasm in social psychology (e.g., see Berry, 2003; Lehman, Chiu, & Schaller, 2004; Matsumoto, 2003).

Although most psychologists study members of their own cultures, **cross-cultural psychologists** are interested in the effects of cultures on behaviour (Berry, Poortinga, Segall, & Dasen, 2002). The term *culture* traditionally referred to a group of people who live together in a common environment, who share customs and religious beliefs and practices, and who often resemble each other genetically. However, definitions of culture now vary widely. For example, "North American culture" includes people of diverse ethnic and religious backgrounds, political beliefs, and economic statuses, while "Fore people" includes a small, fairly homogeneous group of people living in the highlands of Papua New Guinea. Within a broadly defined culture, we can identify subcultures based on ethnicity, age, political beliefs, and other characteristics by which people define themselves. Keep in mind that "culture" is not synonymous with country or continent. Many cultures can exist within a single geographic zone.

▲ *Some cultures are small and relatively homogeneous, such as these Maori people living in New Zealand's North Island, dressed for a festival.*

Cross-cultural research provides an opportunity for psychologists to test the generality of the results of a study performed with members of a particular culture. If similar studies performed with members of different cultures produce similar results, we can be more confident that we have discovered a general principle that applies broadly to members of our species. On the other hand, if the studies yield different results in different cultures, we need to carry out further research. Obviously, differences among cultures affect the variables we are interested in. We need to perform further cross-cultural research to identify these differences. The cross-cultural approach lends itself to questions of immense political and economic importance. For example, think of the many issues that arise from immigration from one culture to another (Berry, 2001).

Cultures differ with respect to two major classes of variables: biological and ecological. Biological variables include such factors as diet, genetics, and endemic diseases. Ecological variables include such factors as geography, climate, political systems, population density, religion, cultural myths, and education. Behavioural differences among people of different cultures result from differences in biological and ecological variables.

Identifying the cultural variables responsible for behavioural differences is a difficult process, as it can be viewed as affecting behaviour in different ways (Lonner & Adamopoulos, 1997). In cross-cultural research, culture is considered to be a treatment variable—something like an independent variable

**cross-cultural psychology** A branch of psychology that studies the effects of culture on behaviour.

(Berry, Poortinga, Segall, & Dasen, 2002). But cultures, like people, differ in many ways, and people are born into their cultures, not assigned to them by psychologists performing experiments. Thus, cross-cultural comparisons are subject to the same limitations that affect other correlational studies.

Psychologists who do cross-cultural research stress that culture and psychological processes are fundamentally intertwined. Fiske, Kitayama, Markus, and Nisbett (1998) propose that cultural psychology strives to better understand the psychological principles that inform cultural practice and, in turn, how these practices affect various psychological processes. Many cultural psychologists believe that basic psychological processes may be universal, but that these processes are informed by culture.

Sociocultural psychologists have investigated the interplay of culture and social behaviours, personality differences, problem solving, intellectual abilities, perceptual abilities, and aesthetics. (Segall, Dasen, Berry, and Poortinga, 1999, provide an engaging overview.) One particularly fruitful question from the cultural perspective focuses on the formation of the self-concept, the perceptions one forms of others, and the extent to which others may influence the development of one's self-concept (Heine, 2001; Markus & Kitayama, 2003). For example, in North America, parents sometimes encourage their children to eat all of their dinner by admonishing them to "think about all the starving children in the world and how lucky you are not to have to go hungry," while in Japan, parents often urge their finicky children to "think of the farmer who worked so hard to produce this rice for you; if you don't eat it he will feel bad, for his efforts will have been in vain" (Markus & Kitayama, 1991). Western cultures often emphasize the uniqueness of the individual and an appreciation of being different from others. In contrast, Japanese and other Eastern cultures often emphasize paying attention to others and the relatedness of the individual and others.

Markus and Kitayama (1991) have conceptualized two construals of the self that reflect such cultural differences. (To *construe* something is to interpret it or to explain its meaning.) The *independent construal* emphasizes the uniqueness of the self, its autonomy from others, and self-reliance. Although other people have an influence on a person's behaviour, a person's self-concept is largely defined independently of others. The *interdependent construal* emphasizes the interconnectedness of people and the role that others play in developing an individual's self-concept. In the interdependent construal, what others think of the individual or do to the individual matter—the person is extremely sensitive to others and strives to form strong social bonds with them.

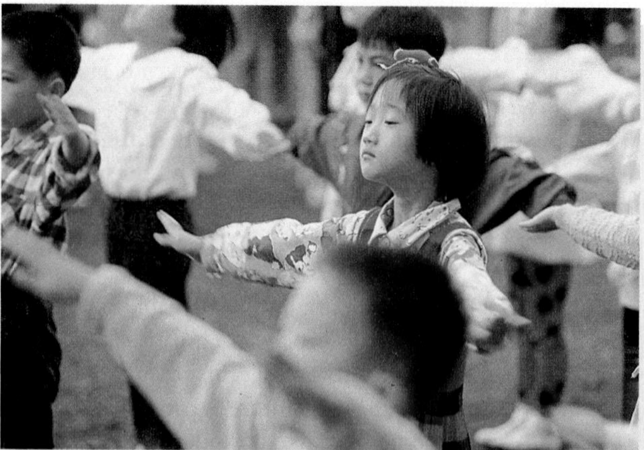

▲ *People in many Eastern cultures are more likely to construe their self-concepts in terms of the social interactions they have with others than are people in Western cultures.*

Researchers have reported convincing evidence for the construal model. For example, Markus and Kitayama (1991) found that students from India judge the self as more similar to others, whereas American students judge the self as more dissimilar to others. Campbell and colleagues (1996) suggested on the basis of similar reasoning that clarity of self-concept might also differ between Eastern and Western cultures. *Clarity* refers to how confident people are that they possess particular attributes, how sharply defined they believe those attributes are, and how internally and temporally consistent they think their attributes are. Campbell and colleagues proposed that high self-concept clarity more closely matches an independent construal of self than an interdependent construal. As expected, Campbell and colleagues found that Canadian university students expressed greater self-concept clarity than did Japanese students.

Consider one of the implications of these different construals for the common experiences of temporary successes and failures in life. Heine and colleagues (2001) reasoned that the independent construal of self corresponds to a self-view of one's traits and abilities as relatively stable and difficult to change. The interdependent construal of self, on the other hand, should yield a self-view of traits and abilities as relatively malleable to the extent that they must be responsive to relationship demands. Research findings by Heine and colleagues (2001) are consistent with this analysis. Canadian students of European descent were more likely to persist on a task after a successful experience than after failure, whereas Japanese students from Kyoto University were more likely to persist following a failure than a success. If you believe that abilities are difficult to change, then perhaps you focus on your strengths and push for more successes. If you believe that change is possible, then perhaps you work to correct your perceived deficiencies in the hope of becoming more successful.

If you are from a Western culture, you may have interpreted the theory and research results in this section to mean: "People from Western cultures have better self-concepts and approaches to life than do people from Eastern cultures." Your conclusion would follow from the way your culture values and encourages independence and stability of the self. A reader from an Eastern culture could well read these same paragraphs and conclude: "People from Eastern cultures have better self-concepts and approaches to life than do people from Western cultures." Those cultures tend to value and emphasize the changing nature and demands of interpersonal relations. Indeed, well-being and satisfaction among Eastern students have been found to be strongly associated with interpersonal behaviours and socially engaged emotions such as friendliness (Kitayama, Markus, & Kurakawa, 2000; Markus & Kitayama, 1991). In contrast, well-being and satisfaction among Western students are more strongly associated with individual achievement and self-reflective emotions such as pride.

## Attribution

We are all, in some ways at least, practising social psychologists (Jones, 1990). Each of us uses certain principles to construct theories about the nature and causes of other people's behaviour. We are confronted each day by many thousands of individual acts performed by other people. Some acts are important to us because they provide clues about people's personality characteristics, how they are likely to interact with us, and how they are perceiving us. If we had to pay careful attention to each of these acts—to classify them, to think about their significance, and to compare them with other observations—we would be immobilized in thought. Instead, we use schemata that often lead us to the correct conclusions. In doing so, we save much time and effort. The process by which people infer the causes of other people's behaviour is called **attribution**.

**Disposition versus Situation** According to attribution theorists, the primary classification that we make concerning the causes of a person's behaviour is the relative importance of situational (or *external*) and dispositional (or *internal*) factors (Heider, 1958). **External factors** are stimuli in the physical and social environment, such as living conditions, other people, societal norms, and laws. **Internal factors** are a person's traits, needs, and intentions. One of the tasks of socialization is to learn what behaviours are expected in various kinds of situations. Once we learn that in certain situations most people act in a specific way, we develop schemata for how we expect people to act in those situations. For example, when people are introduced, they are expected to look at each other, smile, say something like "How do you do?" or "It's nice to meet you," and perhaps offer to shake the other person's hand. If people act in conventional ways in given situations, we are not surprised. Their behaviour appears to be dictated by social custom—by the characteristics of the situation.

As we get to know other people, we also learn what to expect from them as individuals. We learn to characterize people as friendly, generous, suspicious, pessimistic, or greedy by observing their behaviour in a variety of situations. Sometimes, we even make inferences from a single observation (Krull & Erickson, 1995). If someone's behaviour is very different from the way most people would act in a particular situation, we attribute his or her behaviour to internal causes. For example, if we see a person refuse to hold a door open for someone in a wheelchair, we assign that person some negative personal characteristics.

**Kelley's Theory of Attribution** Kelley (1967) suggested that we attribute the behaviour of other people to external (situational) or internal (personal) causes on the basis of three types of information: consensus, distinctiveness, and consistency.

**Consensual behaviour**—behaviour enacted in common by a large number of people in a particular situation—is usually attributed to external causes. For example, if you hear Bill praise a new off-campus club and have heard many other people say the same things (high consensus), you will be tempted to understand Bill's praise as caused by the qualities of the club (an external attribution). In other words, the club is a great place. What if everyone else disagrees with Bill's evaluation (low consensus)? You will be tempted to see Bill's review as reflecting something personal about him (an internal attribution). Maybe Bill has no taste, or maybe some unique need of his makes him like the club.

We also base our attributions on **distinctiveness**—the extent to which a person performs a particular behaviour only during a particular type of event or toward a particular person or thing. If you have never heard Bill praise a club as highly as he praises the new one, his behaviour is high in distinctiveness. Behaviours that are distinctively associated with a particular situation are attributed to that external cause. In this case, you would understand Bill's praise for the new club to reflect the quality of the club itself (an external attribution). If Bill praises every club he's ever visited as highly as he praises the new one, though, you would attribute his evaluation to something internal to Bill. Again, maybe he is unperceptive or is very easily entertained.

Finally, we base our attributions on **consistency** information—on whether a person's behaviour occurs reliably over time. Consistency is an unusual category of information within the theory, because consistency must be high in order to support both internal and external attributions. Suppose that Bill's behaviour is characterized by high distinctiveness and high consensus. Both signs point to an attribution to the external entity—the club. Bill likes this new club more than he likes any others, and most other people rave about the new club. If Bill likes the club every time he goes (high consistency), then your conclusion is clear: It's a great club. Now

**attribution** The process by which people infer the causes of other people's behaviour.
**external factors** People, events, and other stimuli in an individual's environment that can affect his or her thoughts, feelings, attitudes, and behaviours.
**internal factors** An individual's traits, needs, and intentions, which can affect his or her thoughts, feelings, attitudes, and behaviours.
**consensual behaviour** Behaviour that is shared by many people; behaviour that is similar from one person to the next. To the extent that people engage in the same behaviour, their behaviour is consensual.
**distinctiveness** The extent to which a person behaves differently toward different people, events, or other stimuli.
**consistency** The extent to which a person's behaviour is consistent across time toward another person, an event, or a stimulus.

**TABLE 15•1 Kelley's Theory of Attribution**

| | Attribution of Internal Causality | Attribution of External Causality |
|---|---|---|
| ***Consensus*** | Low. Mike is smiling broadly while talking with Helen; most people do not smile while talking with her. | High. Mike is smiling broadly while talking with Helen; most other people do as well. |
| ***Distinctiveness*** | Low. Mike smiles like this while talking with most people. | High. Mike does not smile like this when talking with most other people. |
| ***Consistency*** | High. Mike always smiles like this when he talks with Helen. | High. Mike always smiles like this when he talks with Helen. |
| ***Conclusion (Attribution)*** | Mike is smiling at Helen because he is a happy person who enjoys talking with people. | Mike is smiling at Helen because there is something about her that makes him happy. |

Kelley's theory is based on the principles of consensus, distinctiveness, and consistency.

consider the consequences of low consistency with high distinctiveness and high consensus: The next time Bill goes to the club, he tells you that he hates it, but then he goes again, and tells you it's the best place he's ever been. The result of low consistency is confusion. Is there something that sometimes does and sometimes does not happen at the club or is there something strange about Bill? You can see that low consistency creates the same type of confusion when consensus and distinctiveness information point to an internal attribution. If Bill's assessment of the club were low in consensus and low in distinctiveness, high consistency would make great sense. Bill truly seems to have fun at clubs no matter what or when. Low consistency produces difficulties. The first time Bill went to the new club, he said he loved it. Nobody else likes the new club, but then Bill loves all clubs. Despite these facts, Bill goes to the new club again, and reports that he hates it. We can only imagine that an odd confluence of circumstances is responsible for his pattern of enjoyment. **Table 15•1** summarizes Kelley's ideas about causal attributions by means of another example.

Do we engage in this somewhat difficult process as a matter of course? The research evidence certainly shows that we are *able* to do so. When people are presented with episodes of social behaviour that include consensus, distinctiveness, and consistency information, they answer questions about internal and external causes as Kelley's attribution theory predicts (e.g., Hazelwood & Olson, 1986; McArthur, 1972). But such results do not mean that we always engage in this type of explicit processing (e.g., Brown & Bassili, 2002). Overall, the evidence suggests that people are more likely to engage in complex inferential processes like those described by Kelley when they are asked questions directly about why someone behaved as he or she did (e.g., Enzle & Schopflocher, 1978), when the events they are exposed to are unexpected or abnormal (Hilton & Slugoski, 1986), and when they believe it is important for the advancement of their personal interests to understand the cause of others' behaviours (e.g., Burger & Hemans, 1988; Kunda, 1990).

**fundamental attribution error** The tendency to overestimate the significance of internal factors and underestimate the significance of external factors in explaining other people's behaviour.

## Attributional Biases

When we make attributions, we do not function as impartial, dispassionate observers. There are biases in the attribution process that affect our conclusions about the actor (the person performing the behaviour). Let's look at two kinds of bias: the fundamental attribution error and the false consensus.

**The Fundamental Attribution Error** When attributing an actor's behaviour to possible causes, an observer tends to *overestimate* the significance of dispositional factors and *underestimate* the significance of situational factors. This bias is called the **fundamental attribution error** (Ross, 1977). For example, when we see a goalie miss a save, we are more likely to conclude that the goalie lacks skill than to consider the possibility that his sightlines were blocked.

This bias toward dispositional attribution is remarkably potent. Even when evidence indicates otherwise, people seem to prefer internal or dispositional explanations to situational ones. For example, consider a study by Jones and Harris (1967). University students read essays that had supposedly been written by another student. The topic of the essay was Fidel Castro's rule of Cuba. Half of the students read an essay that was very positive toward Castro (the "pro" version), and the other half read a very negative account of Castro's leadership (the "con" version). The key manipulation in the experiment was information about the circumstances under which the writer supposedly composed the essay. Half of the students who read the pro and con versions of the essay were told that the writer had been *assigned* a position (i.e., pro or con) to take when writing the essay. The remaining students were told that the writer *chose* the orientation. After reading the essay, all participants were asked to estimate the essay writer's *true* attitudes toward Castro. Amazingly, people reported that the essay writer's attitudes matched the pro or con stance of the essay regardless of whether the stance in the essay had been assigned to or chosen by the writer. For example, if the writer's statements about Castro were positive, people took those statements to match the writer's beliefs, even though the writer had been ordered to produce those statements. Thus, people did not take into account the situational demands on the writer who was assigned a position.

Subsequent research has replicated this fundamental attribution error with many different methods and across cultures (e.g., Krull et al., 1999; Miyamoto & Kitayama, 2002); in fact, it is extremely difficult to eliminate this error.

Victim-blaming is another example of the fundamental attribution error, particularly when the victim truly is not responsible for his or her misfortune. According to Lerner (1980), people generally subscribe to a **belief in a just world**. That is, people believe that the world is a fair place in which people get what they deserve. One result of this belief is that people tend to blame the victim when misfortune or tragedy strikes. Why? An innocent victim threatens the stability of the perceiver's just world belief system (see Hafer, 2000a). Blaming the victim establishes a just outcome (bad things happen to bad people) and therefore protects and maintains the belief that the world, and life, is fair (and safe).

Belief in the world as a just place may also help motivate people to persist in the pursuit of their goals. According to Hafer (2000b, 2002), just world beliefs assure people that their efforts toward reaching long-term goals will ultimately be rewarded. In order to happily work hard on writing this textbook, for example, I need to be confident that there will be just outcomes—that the book will be published as promised and that students will have an opportunity to learn from it. If I believed that the world was unjust, that any number of random events might prevent publication of the textbook, it would be difficult for me to continue this work. Hafer's (2000b) research supports this view by showing that focusing university students on their long-term (post-graduation) goals increased the extent to which they blamed innocent victims for their trials and tribulations. Thus, participants who were sensitized to long-term fairness concerns seemed especially motivated to maintain their belief in justice by insisting that an innocent victim was not innocent but deserved to be harmed.

Crown prosecutors and mental health practitioners are all too familiar with victim-blaming. Innocent victims of crime are often blamed for their misfortunes. People who are raped, for example, often must cope with being blamed for their own assault (Bell, Kuriloff, & Lottes, 1994; Wakelin & Long, 2003). Complex social problems, such as poverty (e.g., Guimond & Dube, 1989), seem prone to the same self-defensive blaming phenomenon. By blaming the poor for their own predicament, we can maintain a sense of justice and avoid having to deal with the difficult underlying causes of poverty. Interestingly, in a study of people from 12 different countries, Furnham (1992) discovered that the tendency to blame victims was positively correlated with status and wealth.

When trying to explain our own behaviour, we are much more likely to attribute it to characteristics of the situation than to our own personal characteristics, a phenomenon called the **actor-observer effect**. In other words, we tend to see our own behaviour as relatively variable and strongly influenced by the situation, while we see the behaviour of others as more stable and due to personal causes. When we try to explain our own behaviour, we are not likely to make the fundamental attribution error (Sande, Goethals, & Radloff, 1988).

A study of university-age male–female couples demonstrates the actor-observer effect (Orvis, Kelley, & Butler, 1976). Each partner was asked separately to describe disagreements in the relationship, such as arguments and criticism. Each partner was also asked to explain his or her attribution of the underlying causes of the disagreements. When describing his or her own behaviour, each person tended to refer to environmental factors, such as financial problems or not getting enough sleep. However, when describing their partners' behaviour, people often referred to specific negative personality characteristics, such as selfishness or low commitment to the relationship.

Why do we tend to commit the fundamental attribution error when we observe the behaviour of others but not when we explain the causes of our own behaviour? Jones and Nisbett (1971) suggested two possible reasons. First, we have a different focus of attention when we view ourselves. When we ourselves are doing something, we see the world around us more clearly than we see our own behaviour. However, when we observe someone else doing something, we focus our attention on what is most salient and relevant: that person's behaviour, not the situation in which he or she is placed.

A second possible reason is that different types of information are available to us about our own behaviour and that of other people. We have more information about our own behaviour and we are thus more likely to realize that our own behaviour is often inconsistent. We also have a better notion of which stimuli we are attending to in a given situation. This difference in information leads us to conclude that the behaviour of other people is consistent and thus is a product of their personalities, whereas ours is affected by the situation in which we find ourselves.

There is a partial exception to the preference for external self-attributions. When we attempt to attribute our behaviour to causes—to explain the reasons for our actions—we tend to attribute our accomplishments and successes to internal causes and our failures and mistakes to external causes, a phenomenon called the **self-serving bias** (Miller & Ross, 1975). Suppose that you receive an outstanding test score. If you are like most people, you will think that the high score is well deserved. After all, you are a smart individual who studied hard. Your attributions reflect internal causes. You are bright and a hard worker. Now suppose that you receive a failing score on the test—what sorts of attributions do you tend to make? Again, if you are like most people, you may blame your low score on the fact that it was a difficult, even "unfair," test or on the teacher for being so picky about the answers he or she considered wrong. Your attributions in this case blame external

**belief in a just world** The belief that people get what they deserve in life; a fundamental attribution error.

**actor-observer effect** The tendency to attribute one's own behaviour to external factors but others' behaviour to internal factors.

**self-serving bias** The tendency to attribute our accomplishments and successes to internal causes and our failures and mistakes to external causes.

causes for the low score—the test's difficulty and the picky grading of your teacher. One possible explanation for the self-serving bias is that people are motivated to protect and enhance their self-esteem (Brown & Rogers, 1991; Robins & Beer, 2001). Simply put, we protect our self-esteem when we blame failure on the environment and we enhance it when we give ourselves credit for our successes. Not coincidentally, self-enhancement has at least the short-term effect of promoting positive mood (Robins & Beer, 2001).

**False Consensus** Another attribution error is the tendency of an observer to perceive his or her own response as representative of a general consensus—an error called **false consensus** (Gilovich, 1990). For example, McFarland and Miller (1990) asked psychology students to indicate in which of two unpleasant experiments they would prefer to participate. Regardless of their choice, participants believed that the majority of other students would select the same experiment they had. Overall, then, people overestimated the similarity of others' preferences.

One explanation accounts for false consensus in terms of self-esteem. Presumably, people do not like to think of themselves as being too different from other people, so they prefer to think that most other people will act the way they do. Another possible explanation is that people tend to place themselves in the company of others who are similar to themselves (Ross, 1977).

## Attribution, Heuristics, and Social Cognition

We tend to follow general rules, or heuristics, when making decisions. This tendency is especially evident when we make social judgments. Most of the time, these rules serve us well. However, they sometimes lead us astray. When they do, we refer to them as biases or fallacies. The two most important kinds of heuristics are representativeness and availability.

**The Representativeness Heuristic** When we meet someone for the first time, we notice his or her clothes, hairstyle, posture, manner of speaking, hand gestures, and many other characteristics. Based on our previous experience, we use this information to make tentative conclusions about other characteristics that we cannot immediately discover. In doing so, we attempt to match the characteristics we can observe with stereotypes we have of different types of people. If the person seems representative of one of these stereotypes, we conclude that he or she fits that particular category (Lupfer, Clark, & Hutcherson, 1990). In reaching this conclusion, we use the **representativeness heuristic**—we classify an object into the category to which it appears to be the most similar.

The representativeness heuristic is based on our ability to categorize information. We observe that some characteristics tend to go together (or we are taught that they do). When we observe some of these characteristics, we conclude that the others are also present. Most of the time, this strategy works; we are able to predict people's behaviour fairly accurately.

Sometimes, the representativeness heuristic can mislead us. Consider the following example: I, a professor of psychology, have a friend who is also a professor. He likes to swim laps in the pool every lunch hour. He also likes to play tennis; if he can find a willing opponent, he will play in the dead of winter if the court can be swept clear of snow. Which of the following is his field: sports medicine or psychology?

If you said "psychology," the odds are you most likely would be right, because there are many more professors of psychology than of sports medicine. Simply considering the actual base-rate frequency of professors in these two fields enhances the likelihood that your guess is correct. Yet you might have chosen sports medicine, or at least seriously considered it. The *image* of an athletic, tennis-playing person is such a distinctive cue that it is difficult not to conclude that my friend works in sports medicine. The image of the tennis player seems to be more representative of a person professionally involved in sports than of one involved in psychology. Paying too much attention to the image is an example of the **base-rate fallacy**—not considering the likelihood that a person is a member of a particular category on the basis of mathematical probabilities.

**The Availability Heuristic** When people attempt to assess the importance or the frequency of an event, they tend to be guided by the ease with which examples of that event come to mind—by how available these examples are to the imagination. This mental shortcut is called the **availability heuristic**. In general, the things we are able to think of most easily are more important and occur more frequently than things that are difficult to imagine. Thus, the availability heuristic works well—most of the time. But it can lead to mistakes as well.

Tversky and Kahneman (1982) demonstrated how the availability heuristic can cause errors by asking people to estimate whether English words starting with *k* were more or less common than words with *k* in the third position (for example, *kiss* versus *lake*). Most people said that there were more words starting with *k*. In fact, there are more than twice as many words having *k* in the third position as those having *k* in the first. But because thinking of words that start with a particular letter is easier than thinking of words that contain the letter in another position, people are misled. **Table 15•2** shows another example, based on a study by Tversky and Kahneman (1974), of how the availability heuristic works. Read the names in the table first and then read the explanation.

**false consensus** The tendency of a person to perceive his or her own response as representative of a general consensus.

**representativeness heuristic** A general rule for decision making by which people classify a person, place, or thing into the category to which it appears to be the most similar.

**base-rate fallacy** The failure to consider the likelihood that a person, place, or thing is a member of a particular category on the basis of mathematical probabilities.

**availability heuristic** A general rule for decision making by which a person judges the likelihood or importance of an event by the ease with which examples of that event come to mind.

**TABLE 15•2 The Availability Heuristic in Operation**

Does this list contain more men's or women's names? The answer may surprise you: The number of male and female names is equal. Because of the availability heuristic, however, most people tend to guess that female names are more numerous. Since the women listed are more famous than the men, it is easier to bring their names to mind, and this leads to overestimates of their frequency on the list.

| | | |
|---|---|---|
| Margaret Atwood | Arthur Hutchinson | Cliff Newman |
| Anne Murray | Sarah McLachlan | Edward Palmer |
| Shania Twain | Margaret Laurence | Robert Porter |
| Céline Dion | Edward Lytton | Sheila Copps |
| Michael Drayton | Jack Lindsay | Henry Vaughan |
| Larry Schneider | Elizabeth Manley | Pamela Wallin |
| Pamela Anderson | Roberta Bondar | |
| Charles Fisher | Alannah Myles | |
| Ron Fisher | Peter Mitchell | |
| Bruce Holliday | Mary Walsh | |

*Source: Baron, R., Earhard, B., & Ozier, M. (2001).* Psychology *(3rd Canadian ed.), p. 269. Toronto: Allyn & Bacon. Reprinted with permission by Pearson Canada Inc.*

Many variables can affect the availability of an event or a concept and thus increase its effect on our decision making. For example, having recently seen a particular type of event makes it easier for us to think of other examples of that event. This phenomenon is called *priming*. Many first-year medical students fall prey to this process when, after learning the symptoms of various diseases, they start to "discover" these very symptoms in their own bodies. Rather than imagining the symptoms, they become overly attentive to normal physiological processes in their bodies and misinterpret them as symptoms of illness. Beware that this often happens to psychology students when they read the forthcoming chapters on psychological disorders. Although this *medical student syndrome* is superficially similar to the persistent disorder known as *hypochondriasis* (see Chapter 17), most medical students quickly learn to avoid the problem.

The availability heuristic also explains why personal encounters tend to have an especially strong effect on our decision making. For example, suppose that you have decided to transfer to another university for your last two undergraduate years. You have narrowed your choices down to two schools. You read the latest instalment of the *Maclean's Guide to Canadian Universities*, and the evaluations clearly favour one of your two chosen universities. You decide to apply to that school, and mention the fact to an acquaintance you happen to meet later that day. She says, "Oh, no! Don't go there! I went there for two terms. The profs are distant. Badly prepared TAs do all the lectures. The grading system is unfair and way too competitive. The general atmosphere is appalling. I couldn't wait to leave." Would your acquaintance's experience affect your decision about where to transfer?

Many people would take this personal encounter very seriously. Even though it consists of the experiences of only one person, whereas the *Maclean's* evaluations are based on many interviews and summaries of data, a vivid personal encounter is much more available and memorable than a set of statistics and tends to have a disproportionate effect on people's behaviour (Borgida & Nisbett, 1977).

## Social Cognition and Neuroscience

There is a growing intersection between social psychology and cognitive neuroscience. It has been christened officially as *social neuroscience* (sometimes *social cognitive neuroscience*) and now sports a journal by that title and a growing cadre of researchers and theorists (e.g., Azar, 2002; Cacioppo, 2002; Decety & Keenan, 2006; Harmon-Jones & Winkielman, 2007). As you might expect, this new discipline seeks the neurophysiological substrates for social psychological concepts and theories, including attribution, stereotyping, prejudice, attitudes, cognitive dissonance, and interpersonal attraction. Social psychologists and cognitive neuroscientists collaborate to design and conduct research using electrophysiological recording procedures (event-related potential, for example) and brain imaging (especially fMRI), among other methods.

For example, the discovery of *mirror neurons* in the inferior prefrontal cortex of monkeys by Italian researchers in the early 1990s (di Pellegrino et al., 1992) has prompted models of social cognition. Specific mirror neurons fire when the individual performs a specific action (such as grasping a peanut) but also when the individual observes another individual performing a similar action. McGovern (2007) has argued that mirror neurons constitute the substrate for the child's acquisition of a *theory of mind* by which she or he learns to discriminate others' intentions and their cognitive states more generally. Mundy and Newell (2007) have proposed that social cognition begins to develop as the anterior and posterior attention systems become integrated so as to allow the child to monitor her or his own attention and that of others (what the authors call *joint attention*). They argue that this ability is critical for the formation and maintenance of social relationships and that impaired relationships (such as those in autistic spectrum disorders) result when joint attention fails to develop.

At the same time that social psychology is turning to cognitive neuroscience, there are those in its ranks who question whether it is guilty of an overreliance on certain methodologies that neglect the direct observation of behaviour. In other words, has social psychology become insufficiently behavioural? To remedy the situation, social psychologists can look to the example of the classic studies cited throughout this chapter, many of which paid direct attention to the behaviour of the participant and his or her relation to situational variables. The challenge will be to revise existing methodologies and develop new ones that are explicitly behavioural while assuring a precision of experimental control that will expose in clear relief the social variables of which behaviour is a function.

## Interim Summary

### Social Cognition

Social cognition involves our perception and interpretation of information about our social environment and our behaviour with respect to changes in that environment. Our experiences give rise to schemata, the mental frameworks with which we organize and synthesize information about our interactions with others. Central traits function as schemata and help us form impressions of others. The initial information we learn about someone figures prominently in forming an impression about that person—a tendency called the primacy effect.

A person's self-concept represents his or her knowledge, feelings, and ideas about himself or herself. At the centre of the self-concept is the self-schema, a mental framework for processing and interpreting information about the self. Our self-concepts change with our personal experiences and are influenced by the culture in which we live. In fact, different cultures often have different ways of conceptualizing the self. Western cultures emphasize the uniqueness of the self. In contrast, Eastern cultures emphasize the interdependence of the self and others.

We attribute particular instances of behaviour to two types of causes: internal and external. A behaviour that is high in consensus (many other people act the same way), high in distinctiveness (occurs only in the particular situation), and consistent over time is usually attributed to an external cause. A behaviour low in consensus, low in distinctiveness, and consistent over time is usually attributed to an internal cause.

The fundamental attribution error is an overreliance on internal factors and an underreliance on situational factors in judging the causes of someone else's behaviour. We are most likely to make the fundamental attribution error when trying to understand the causes of other people's behaviour because we are more aware of the situational factors that affect our own behaviour. One example of the fundamental attribution error is the belief that people get exactly what they deserve in life, a phenomenon called belief in a just world. When comparing our behaviour to that of others, we tend to see our own behaviour as being more influenced by situational than personal factors and others' behaviour as being more due to personal factors than to situational factors—a phenomenon called the actor-observer effect. However, when it comes to accepting credit for our successes or blame for our failures, we tend to show the self-serving bias: We tend to attribute our successes to internal causes and our failures to external causes. False consensus refers to the tendency to believe that others act and believe much as we do, even when they do not.

We use mental shortcuts called heuristics in perceiving, in making decisions, and in determining what is going on around us. The representativeness heuristic describes our tendency to seize on a few especially salient characteristics of a person or situation. Thus, we sometimes ignore other evidence and commit the base-rate error. The availability heuristic describes our tendency to judge the importance or the frequency of events by the ease with which examples come to mind. If we have recently been exposed to a particular concept, that concept becomes more available (through the phenomenon of priming) and thus biases our decisions. Personal encounters give rise to vivid memories of particular episodes, and the availability of these episodes, too, tends to outweigh less vivid—but more representative—evidence.

#### QUESTIONS TO CONSIDER

1. What factors do you feel have been most influential in the development of your self-concept? What sorts of experiences do you think will influence continued development of your self-concept during your university career, and how?
2. How much of our social behaviour do we engage in unconsciously—that is, without our awareness? What effect do you suppose being more conscious of our social interaction would have on that interaction?
3. Imagine you are the first person on the scene of an auto accident in which several people have been injured badly. What factors—external, internal, or some combination of them—would guide your behaviour?

# Attitudes and Their Formation

The study of **attitudes**—evaluations of persons, places, and things—and their formation constitutes an important part of the field of social psychology (Petty, Wegener, & Fabrigar, 1997; Wood, 2000).

## Formation of Attitudes

Attitudes are generally represented as having three components: affect, cognition, and behaviour (Eagly & Chaiken, 1998; Zanna & Rempel, 1988). The affective component consists of the kinds of feelings that a particular topic arouses. The cognitive component consists of a set of beliefs about a topic. The behavioural component consists of a tendency to act in a particular way with respect to a particular topic. (See **Figure 15•1**.) Social psychologists have studied all three aspects of attitudes, and we will examine their findings in this section.

**Affective Components of Attitudes** Affective components of attitudes can be very strong and pervasive. The bigot feels uneasy in the presence of people from a certain religious, racial, or ethnic group; the nature lover feels exhilaration from a pleasant walk through the woods. Like other emotional

**attitude** An evaluation of persons, places, and things.

FIGURE 15•1 The three components of attitude: affect, behaviour, and cognition. (a) Affective component (feelings): Enjoys kayaking. (b) Behavioural component (actions): Pursues kayaking as a hobby. (c) Cognitive component (beliefs): Believes that kayaking has an element of risk but is fun.

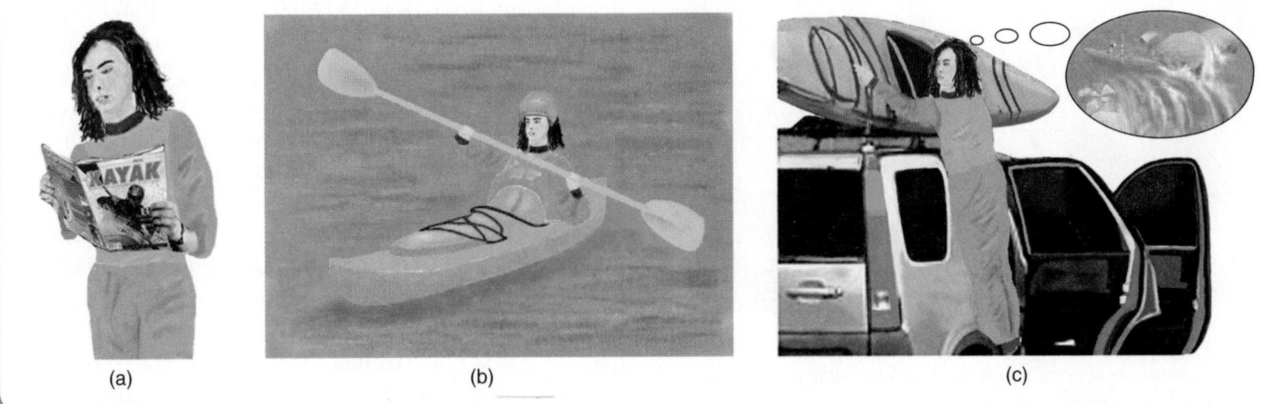


reactions, these feelings are strongly influenced by direct or vicarious classical conditioning (Rajecki, 1990).

*Direct classical conditioning* is straightforward. Suppose that you meet someone who seems to take delight in embarrassing you. She makes clever, sarcastic remarks that disparage your intelligence, looks, and personality. Unfortunately, her remarks are so clever that your attempts to defend yourself make you appear even more foolish. After a few encounters with this person, the sight of her or the sound of her voice is likely to elicit feelings of dislike and fear. Your attitude toward her will be negative.

*Vicarious classical conditioning* undoubtedly plays a major role in transmitting parents' attitudes to their children. People are skilled at detecting even subtle signs of fear, hatred, and other negative emotional states in other people, especially when they know them well. Thus, children often perceive their parents' prejudices and fears even if these feelings are unspoken. Children who see their parents showing distaste at the sight of members of some ethnic group are likely to learn to react in the same way. We have a strong tendency to acquire classically conditioned behaviours when we observe them being elicited in other people by the conditional stimulus.

Simply being exposed repeatedly to an otherwise neutral object or issue over time may influence our attitude toward it. This attraction for the familiar is called the **mere exposure effect** (Zajonc, 1968). One of the first studies to demonstrate this effect used several neutral stimuli—toward which there were no positive or negative feelings—such as nonsense words, photographs of the faces of unknown people, and Chinese characters (Zajonc, 1968). The more the participants saw the stimuli, the more they liked the stimuli later. Research also shows that the mere exposure effect is stronger when stimuli are presented below participants' threshold of awareness (e.g., Murphy, Monahan, & Zajonc, 1995) and that the positive affect produced in this way generalizes to other similar stimuli (Monahan, Murphy, & Zajonc, 2000).

Note that the effect of mere exposure is limited to initially neutral stimuli. The effect of mere exposure does not apply to stimuli that are initially disliked. Repeated exposure to things or people we do not like seems only to confirm that we do not like them (Perlman & Oskamp, 1971).

**Cognitive Components of Attitudes** The cognitive components of attitudes include conscious beliefs (Ajzen, 2001). We acquire most beliefs about a particular topic quite directly: We hear or read a fact or opinion, or other people reinforce our statements expressing a particular attitude. Someone may say to a child, "Latinos are not very smart," or "Whites will take advantage of you." A group of racially prejudiced people will probably ostracize a person who makes positive statements about the group or groups against which they are prejudiced. Conversely, conscientious parents may applaud their child's positive statements about other ethnic groups or about social issues such as environmental conservation.

**Behavioural Components of Attitudes** People do not always behave as their expressed attitudes and beliefs would lead us to expect. In a classic example, LaPiere (1934) drove through the United States with a Chinese couple. They stopped at more than 250 restaurants and lodging places and were refused service only once. Several months after their trip, LaPiere wrote to the owners of the places they had visited and asked whether they would serve Chinese people. The response was overwhelmingly negative; 92 percent of those who responded said that they would not. Clearly, their behaviour gave less evidence of racial bias than their expressed attitudes did. This study has been cited as proof that attitudes do not always influence behaviour. However, more recent research indicates that there is a relation between attitudes and behaviour but that the relation is influenced by several factors.

**mere exposure effect** The formation of a positive attitude toward a person, place, or thing based solely on repeated exposure to that person, place, or thing.

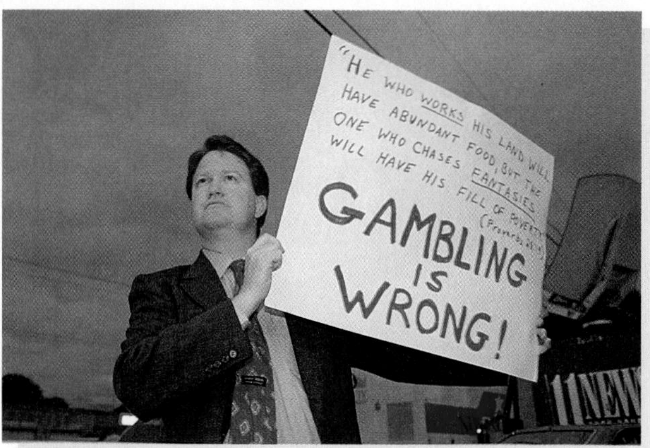


▲ *A protest is one example of a situation in which a person's attitude on an issue corresponds to his or her behaviour, in this case, demonstrating against legalized gambling.*

**Degree of Specificity** If you measure only a person's general attitude toward a topic, you will be less likely to be able to predict his or her behaviour (e.g., Haddock, Zanna, & Esses, 1994).

Behaviours, unlike attitudes, are specific events. As the attitude being measured becomes more specific, the person's behaviour becomes more predictable. For example, Weigel, Vernon, and Tognacci (1974) measured people's attitudes toward a series of topics that increased in specificity from "a pure environment" to "the Sierra Club" (a North American organization that supports environmental causes). They used the participants' attitudes to predict whether they would volunteer for various activities to benefit the Sierra Club. A person's attitude toward environmentalism was a poor predictor of whether he or she would volunteer; his or her attitude toward the Sierra Club itself was a much better predictor. (See **Table 15•3.**) For example, a person might favour a pure environment but also dislike organized clubs or have little time to spare for meetings. This person would express a positive attitude toward a pure environment but would not join the club or volunteer for any activities to support it.

**Motivational Relevance** Expressing a particular attitude toward a topic takes less effort than demonstrating that commitment with a time-consuming behaviour. As the old saying goes, "Talk is cheap." Sivacek and Crano (1982) demonstrated this phenomenon by asking students to volunteer their time to help campaign against a pending law that would raise the drinking age from 18 to 20. Although almost all of the students were opposed to the new drinking law, younger students, who would be affected by its passage, were much more likely to volunteer their time and effort. Thus, attitudes are more likely to be accompanied by behaviours if the effects of the behaviours have motivational relevance for the individual.

**TABLE 15•3 Correlation between Willingness to Join or Work for the Sierra Club and Various Measures of Related Attitudes**

| Attitude Scale | Correlation |
|---|---|
| Importance of a pure environment | .06 |
| Concern about pollution | .32 |
| Support for conservation | .24 |
| Positive attitude toward the Sierra Club | .68 |

*Source: Based on Weigel, R. H., Vernon, D. T. A., & Tognacci, L. N. (1974). Specificity of the attitude as a determinant of attitude-behavior congruence.* Journal of Personality and Social Psychology, 30, *724–728.*

**Accessibility** Another variable that affects the relation between attitude and behaviour is whether the attitude is activated in the context where behavioural consistency is an issue. If you have a negative attitude toward forest clear-cutting, but that attitude is not activated, when you are asked to support a forest-preservation group it is unlikely that your behaviour (making a donation, for instance) will be consistent with your attitude (e.g., Fazio & Roskos-Ewoldsen, 1994). An important quality of accessibility of an attitude is how quickly it comes to mind when activated. Some theorists consider this period of time between a situational stimulus relevant to the attitude and a person's statement of his or her attitude to be a good predictor of attitude-response consistency. For example, Bassili found that each one-second delay in an interviewee's response to pre-election questions about whom he or she favoured in the 1990 Ontario election (Bassili, 1993) and the 1993 federal election (Bassili, 1995) translated into an 8 percent mismatch with whom he or she actually voted for in the elections. The longer the latency, the greater the inconsistency between attitudes and behaviour.

**Constraints on Behaviour** Other more obvious factors, such as existing circumstances, also produce discrepancies between attitudes and behaviours. For example, a young man might have a very positive attitude toward a certain young woman. If he were asked, he might express a very positive attitude toward kissing her. However, he never kisses her because she has plainly shown that she is not interested in him. No matter how carefully we measure the young man's attitudes, we cannot predict his behaviour without additional information (in this case, from the young woman).

## Attitude Change and Persuasion

People often attempt to persuade us to change our attitudes. Two aspects of the persuasion process have received special attention: the source of the message and the message itself.

Messages tend to be more persuasive if the source is credible. Source credibility is high when the source is perceived as knowledgeable and is trusted to communicate this knowledge accurately. For example, in one study, people developed a more favourable attitude toward different types of medicine when the information appeared in the prestigious *New England Journal of Medicine* than when it appeared in a mass-circulation tabloid (Hovland & Weiss, 1951).

Messages also seem to have more impact when the source is attractive. For example, physically attractive people are more likely than physically unattractive people to persuade others to sign a petition (Chaiken, 1979). Individuals who are asked to endorse products for advertisers are almost always physically attractive or appealing in other ways. Likeability of the communicator, independent of physical attractiveness, has a similar effect on persuasion (Roskos-Ewoldsen & Fazio, 1992).

As you would expect, aspects of the message itself are important in determining its persuasive appeal. For example, is an argument that provides only one side of an issue more effective than one that presents both sides? The answer depends on the audience. If the audience either knows very little about the issue or already holds a strong position with respect to it, one-sided arguments tend to be more effective. If the audience is well informed about the issue, however, a two-sided argument tends to be more persuasive (McAlister et al., 1980).

How effective are scare tactics embedded in the message in changing someone's attitude? This question was addressed when a program called Scared Straight was implemented in New Jersey to persuade youthful offenders to abandon their delinquent lifestyles. The program entailed an afternoon visit to Rahway State Prison and a very distressing, intimidating encounter with some prison inmates. Although the program initially appeared successful, the majority of the offenders exposed to the program eventually returned to delinquent activities (Hagan, 1982). Other research has shown that scare tactics may be effective in bringing about change, but only when combined with instructive information about how to change one's behaviour (Gleicher & Petty, 1992). Messages appear most effective in changing attitudes when they contain both emotional and informative (cognitive) components.

Petty and his colleagues have developed the **elaboration likelihood model** to account for attitude change through persuasion (Cacioppo, Petty, & Crites, 1993; Petty & Wegener, 1999; Petty, Wheeler, & Tormala, 2003). (See **Figure 15•2**.)

| | Persuasive Message | |
|---|---|---|
| | *Central Route* | *Peripheral Route* |
| Elaboration (consideration of strengths and weaknesses of argument) | Yes | Little or none |
| Association with positive stimuli | Little or none | Yes |
| Cause of attitude change | Quality of argument | Emotional appeal |

**FIGURE 15•2** The elaboration likelihood model of attitude change. A persuasive message may centre either on a substantive argument that requires an individual to think critically about its strengths and weaknesses (the central route) or on a superficial argument that is associated with positive stimuli (the peripheral route).

According to this model, persuasion can take either a central or a peripheral route. The central route requires a person to think critically about the argument or arguments being presented, to weigh their relative strengths and weaknesses, and to elaborate on the relevant themes. At issue is the actual substance of the argument, not its emotional or superficial appeal. The peripheral route, on the other hand, refers to attempts at persuasion in which the change is associated with positive stimuli—a professional athlete, a millionaire, or an attractive model—that actually may have nothing to do with the substance of the argument. Selling products by associating them with attractive people or implying that buying the product will result in emotional, social, or financial benefits are examples of the use of peripheral attitude change techniques.

## Cognitive Dissonance

In 1954, Leon Festinger came across a newspaper headline that stated: "Prophecy from Planet Clarion to City: Flee that flood. It'll swamp us on Dec. 21, outer space tells suburbanite." Festinger decided to investigate this headline and contacted the "suburbanite" mentioned in the article. She was a homemaker from Chicago whose name was Marion Keech. Keech believed that she was receiving messages from outer space through her left arm in the form of "automatic writing." These writings revealed to Keech that the world would end in a flood on December 21. Fortunately for Keech and her group of believers, the messages from outer space noted that a spaceship was going to come to Earth before the great flood and save their group. Keech had a few followers, but generally disliked the media and did not try to draw much attention to her group.

Festinger and his colleagues Stanley Schachter and Henry Riecken joined Keech's group to observe what would happen in the highly likely event that the world would *not* end on December 21. They wanted to know how the members would react.

As December 21 approached, the group members exhibited strong commitment to their belief in Keech's prophecy. Some quit their jobs; others stopped attending university; others even left their spouses. Money and possessions were given away, as they would have no value during space travel.

On the fateful day, the members prepared for the arrival of the spaceship. They even removed all metal, such as zippers, from their clothing because they had been told, through Keech, that the ship would be very hot and could melt metal (apparently the group members were not concerned about what this heat could do to their skin). The spaceship would arrive at midnight. The group waited anxiously. As the clock passed twelve, and with no spaceship in

**elaboration likelihood model** A model that explains the effectiveness of persuasion. The central route requires the person to think critically about an argument and the peripheral route entails the association of the argument with something positive.

sight, the members grew nervous. Initially, they thought the clock was running fast. They waited longer. By 4 a.m., the members were distraught. Then, Keech received another message from outer space stating that the belief of the group had been so strong that they saved the world!

What happened next surprised Festinger, Riecken, and Schachter (1956). The group members, who had previously avoided the public eye, began to spread the word the next day. They contacted media outlets and told anyone who would listen about their group and the messages that had been received from outer space. What caused this group, which had been proven wrong, to believe more strongly and try to tell others about their belief? The answer can be explained by cognitive dissonance theory.

Although we usually regard our attitudes as causes of our behaviour, our behaviour also affects our attitudes. Two major theories attempt to explain the effects of behaviour on attitude formation. The oldest theory is cognitive dissonance theory, developed by Leon Festinger (1957; see also Cooper, 2007). According to **cognitive dissonance theory**, when we experience a discrepancy between our attitudes and behaviour, between our behaviour and self-image, or between two attitudes, an aversive state of tension called *dissonance* results. For example, a person may believe that he has overcome his racial prejudices only to find himself disapproving of a racially mixed couple he sees in a shop. According to cognitive dissonance theory, the person should experience an aversive conflict between his belief in his own lack of prejudice and the simultaneous evidence of prejudice from his reaction to the couple. McGregor, Newby-Clark, and Zanna (1999) argue that simultaneity of awareness of the dissonant ideas and representations maximizes the degree of dissonance we feel. To some extent, we must be focused on the discrepancy for the full aversive weight of dissonance to be experienced.

In Festinger's view, an important source of human motivation is *dissonance reduction*: The aversive state of dissonance motivates a person to reduce it. A person can achieve dissonance reduction by (1) reducing the importance of one of the dissonant elements, (2) adding consonant elements, or (3) changing one of the dissonant elements.

Suppose that a student believes he is very intelligent but he receives a failing mark in an important course. Because the obvious prediction is that intelligent people get good grades, the discrepancy causes the student to experience dissonance. To reduce this dissonance, he may decide that grades are not important and that intelligence is not very closely related to grades. He is using strategy 1, reducing the importance of one of the dissonant elements—the fact that he received a poor mark in one of his courses. Or he can dwell on the belief that his professor was unfair or that his job left him little time to study for the exam. In this case, he is using strategy 2, reducing dissonance by adding consonant elements—those factors that can account for his poor performance and hence explain the discrepancy between his perceived intelligence and grades. Finally, he can use strategy 3 to change one of the dissonant elements. He can either start getting good grades in the course or revise his opinion of his own intelligence.

**cognitive dissonance theory** The theory that changes in attitude can be motivated by an unpleasant state of tension caused by a disparity between a person's beliefs or attitudes and his or her behaviour.

**compliance** Engaging in a particular behaviour at another person's request.

**Induced Compliance** Cognitive dissonance theoretically occurs when a person's behaviour is inconsistent with his or her beliefs or knowledge. But the degree of dissonance a person experiences will depend on whether other factors can justify one of the dissonant elements (i.e., the behaviour, beliefs, or knowledge). Being paid handsomely for doing something you dislike can justify your behaviour and, on balance, reduce the dissonance between doing one thing and believing the other. Being paid a very small amount, on the other hand, may not justify your behaviour and can leave you with considerable cognitive dissonance. In such cases, the act of **compliance**—engaging in a particular behaviour at another person's request—can cause a change in attitudes. For example, an executive of a commercial television network may know that the programs she produces are sleazy, mindless drivel, but she is so well paid that she experiences little or no dissonance as a result of producing them. Her high salary justifies her job and the programs she creates, making the inconsistency between her evaluation of the programs and her continued creation of them bearable. But consider a poorly paid vacuum cleaner sales representative who constantly tells prospective customers that the merchandise he knows to be shoddy is marvellous. The absence of a strong financial incentive leaves room for a great deal of dissonance to result from the inconsistency between his verbal behaviour (saying that the merchandise is great) and his knowledge (that the merchandise is crummy). One way for the salesperson to reduce the dissonance is to come to believe that the merchandise really is as good as he says (keeping in mind that the other option is to quit his job and therefore end the lying).

In a classic study in the field of psychology, Festinger and Carlsmith (1959) experimentally tested this analysis of how justification affects the strength of cognitive dissonance and resultant attitude change. Their study began with students performing very boring tasks, such as putting spools on a tray, dumping them out, putting them on the tray again, dumping them out again, and so on. After the students had spent an hour on exercises such as these, the researchers asked each student in two experimental conditions whether he or she would help out by trying to convince the next participant that the boring tasks actually were enjoyable. Some students were offered the paltry sum of $1 for lying to the next participant (a very low justification for saying the tasks were enjoyable); others were offered $20 for doing so (a very high justification, in 1959 dollars, for lying). The next "participant" was actually a paid confederate of the researchers who listened attentively to the real participants' claims about how interesting the tasks were. Following this phase of the experiment, the researcher paid the participants the agreed-upon amount. No mention of deceiving another participant or of payment was made to the participants in a third, control condition.

At the end of the experiment, all participants were asked to rate how much they really had enjoyed the tasks they had engaged in at the beginning of the session. Festinger and Carlsmith predicted that those who were paid only $1 would come to perceive the task as being relatively interesting. Those who had been induced to praise the tasks to another person without a psychologically sufficient justification should have experienced strong cognitive dissonance. Their original attitude about the tasks and their oral behaviour were inconsistent. Because the participants could not take back their oral behaviour, the only thing left to change was their attitude toward the tasks. The well-paid participants, on the other hand, had a perfect justification for their oral behaviour and should not have experienced much cognitive dissonance. As predicted, the poorly paid participants did in fact rate the tasks as more enjoyable than did those who were well paid. (See **Figure 15•3**.) You can see in Figure 15.3 that being paid a lot left people with about the same attitude toward the boring tasks as those participants in the control condition who experienced no dissonance because they never told anyone the tasks were enjoyable.

**Arousal and Attitude Change** Festinger hypothesized that dissonance reduction is motivated by an aversive drive. A study by Croyle and Cooper (1983) obtained physiological evidence to support this hypothesis. The researchers chose as their participants university students who *disagreed* with the assertion that alcohol should be banned at campus clubs and eating establishments. Each student was induced to write an essay, and was instructed whether to write one containing strong arguments in favour of the assertion or one in opposition to it. While the participants were writing the essay, the researchers measured the electrical conductance of their skin, which is known to be a good indicator of the physiological arousal that accompanies stress. Some participants were made to feel as though they had no choice but to write the essay. Other participants were told that their participation was completely voluntary and that they were free to leave at any time; they even signed a form emphasizing the voluntary nature of the task. Of course, there was sufficient social pressure so that everyone in this "free choice" condition did volunteer to stay. Those who were instructed to write the essay should have perceived a sufficient justification for the content of their essays because they were following the researcher's demands. They would thus be expected to experience less dissonance than those who believed that they had exercised free choice in deciding to participate.

Students in the "free choice" condition who had written essays contradicting their original opinions showed both a change in opinion and evidence of physiological arousal. Those who were simply told to write the essay or who wrote arguments that they had originally agreed with showed little sign of arousal or attitude change. (See **Figure 15•4**.)

**Attitudes and Expenditures** Festinger's theory of cognitive dissonance accounts for another relation between behaviour and attitudes: our tendency to value an item more if it costs us

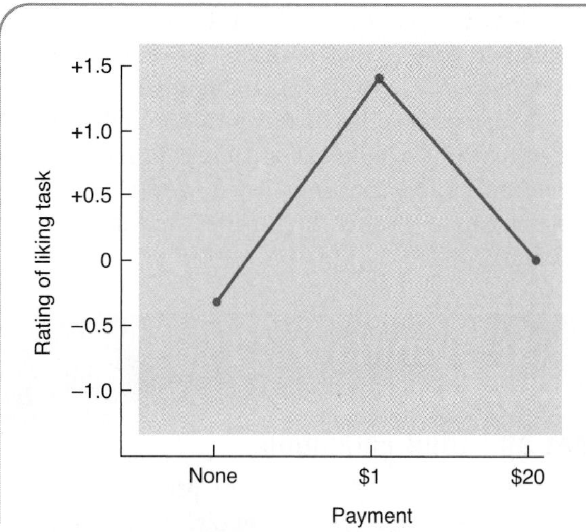


**FIGURE 15•3** Effects of induced compliance. People who received $1 to lie about a boring task later indicated that they liked the task more than did people who received $20.

*(Based on data from Festinger, L., & Carlsmith, J. M. (1959). Cognitive consequences of forced compliance.* Journal of Abnormal and Social Psychology, 58, *203–210.)*

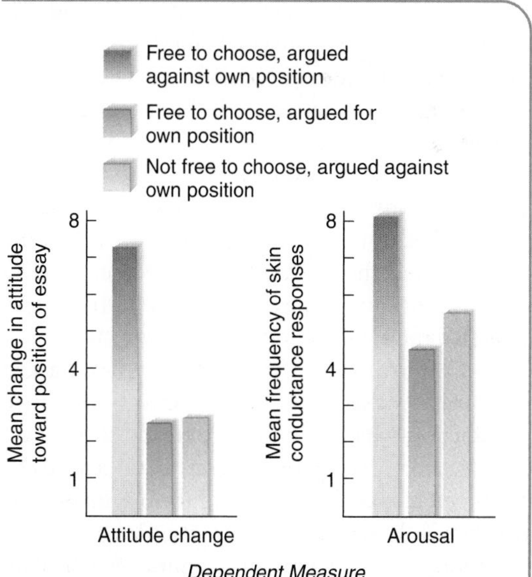


**FIGURE 15•4** Physiological evidence for cognitive dissonance. Mean change in attitude toward the position advocated by the essay and mean frequency of skin conductance responses (a physiological index of arousal) for people who argued for or against their own positions.

*(Based on data from Croyle, R. T., & Cooper, J. (1983). Dissonance arousal: Physical evidence.* Journal of Personality and Social Psychology, 45, *782–791.)*

something in time, effort, or other resources such as money. For example, some people buy extremely expensive brands of cosmetics even though the same ingredients are used in much cheaper brands. Presumably, they believe that if an item costs more, it must work better. Following the same rationale, most animal shelters sell their stray animals to prospective pet owners, not only because the money helps defray their operating costs, but also because they assume that a purchased pet will be valued more, and treated better, than a free pet.

Egan, Santos, and Bloom (2007) addressed the possible evolutionary significance of cognitive dissonance using a procedure they presented to both preschool children and capuchin monkeys. The procedure involved a choice between two alternatives that the children (coloured stickers) and the monkeys (coloured M&Ms) had prejudged to be equally preferable. Then they were required to choose between the alternatives. Consistent with the authors' predictions, when offered a choice between the non-chosen sticker and a sticker that was originally as attractive as the two stickers used in the choice procedure, the children chose the new sticker. Similarly, the capuchins chose a novel M&M over the one they had rejected in the choice procedure. These changes of preference did not occur following a control (no-choice) condition. The authors reasoned that making the choice induced cognitive dissonance and that it had been reduced subsequently by altering the valuation of the non-selected option.

These findings suggest that the resolution of dissonance occasioned by discrepancies between belief and action does not require complex decision making. Additional evidence was provided by Lieberman, Ochsner, Gilbert, and Schacter (2001), who studied amnesic adults and age-matched control participants. The amnesic patients exhibited anterograde amnesia (see Chapter 8) associated with hippocampal or diencephalic damage. Each participant examined two sets of 15 art prints before ranking the prints in each set according to how much they liked them, from most to least. After the rankings were obtained, the participants were presented with pairs of prints. In some pairs, one print was taken from those the participant had ranked high and the other was taken from those ranked low. Sometime later, the participants were asked to re-rank the prints in each pair. Consistent with cognitive dissonance reduction, the re-rankings were more extreme than the original rankings—that is, the participants liked the originally preferred prints even more and the originally less-preferred prints even less. However, this attitude change was no different among the amnesic participants, who had no memory of the prints they had previously seen, than it was among the control participants. Thus, the changes in preference characteristic of cognitive dissonance may be achieved more simply than is typically assumed.

**self-perception theory** The theory that we come to understand our attitudes and emotions by observing our own behaviour and the circumstances under which it occurs.

## Self-Perception

Daryl Bem (1972) proposed an alternative to the theory of cognitive dissonance. He defined **self-perception theory** in the following way:

> Individuals come to "know" their own attitudes, emotions, and other internal states partially by inferring them from observations of their own overt behavior and/or the circumstances in which this behavior occurs. Thus, to the extent that internal cues are weak, ambiguous, or uninterpretable, the individual is functionally in the same position as an outside observer, an observer who must necessarily rely on those same external cues to infer the individual's inner states. (Bem, 1972, p. 2)

Bem noted that an observer who attempts to make judgments about someone's attitudes, emotions, or other internal states must examine the person's behaviour for clues. For example, if you cannot ask someone why he or she is doing something, you must analyze the situation in which the behaviour occurs to try to determine the motivation. Bem suggested that people analyze their own internal states in a similar way, making attributions about the causes of their own behaviour.

Think about how Bem would explain Festinger and Carlsmith's results in which students who were paid only $1 later rated a boring task as more interesting than did those who were paid $20. Suppose that an observer watches a person who has been paid $1 to deliver a convincing speech about how interesting a task was. Because being paid such a small sum is not a subjectively sufficient reason for calling a dull task interesting, the observer will probably conclude that the speaker actually enjoyed the task. Lacking good evidence for external causes, the observer will attribute the behaviour to an internal factor: interest in the task. Bem argued that the speaker makes the same inference about himself or herself. Because the speaker was not paid enough to justify lying, he or she must have enjoyed the task. The principal advantage of self-perception theory is that it makes fewer assumptions than does dissonance theory; it does not postulate a motivating aversive-drive state. Perhaps self-perception and cognitive dissonance occur under different situations, producing attitude changes for different reasons. Further evidence will be needed to determine whether the theories are competing or complementary.

## Interim Summary

### Attitudes and Their Formation

Attitudes have affective components, primarily formed through direct or vicarious classical conditioning, and cognitive components, formed through direct instruction, reinforcement, imitation, or mere exposure.

We now understand the principal reasons for poor correspondence between attitudes and behaviour: differences in degree of specificity of the attitude and behaviour, motivational relevance, accessibility of the relevant attitude, and external constraints that prevent a person's acting on his or her attitudes.

Explicit attempts at changing our attitudes often involve persuasion. We tend to be persuaded by arguments that have a credible source, such as an expert on a particular topic, or an attractive source, such as a handsome or beautiful model. Aspects of the message being delivered in a persuasive appeal are also important. If you know little about an issue or hold a strong opinion about it, then you are likely to be persuaded by a one-sided appeal. However, if you are already well informed about the issue, then you are likely to find a two-sided appeal more persuasive. Scare tactics appear to work best when they include information that is instructive (that is, that explains how to change one's behaviour) as well as emotional.

Festinger's theory of cognitive dissonance suggests reasons for interactions between attitudes and behaviour. It proposes that discrepancies between attitudes and behaviour, or between one attitude and another, lead to the unpleasant state of cognitive dissonance. This dissonance can be reduced by changing the importance of dissonant elements, adding consonant ones, or changing one of the dissonant elements.

Bem's alternative to cognitive dissonance—self-perception theory—suggests that many of our attitudes are based on self-observation. When our attitudes are ambiguous, we look to the situation for the stimuli and probable reinforcers and punishers that cause us to act as we do.

**QUESTIONS TO CONSIDER**

1. Attitudes have sometimes been described as "predispositions to act." What does this phrase mean? Do you believe this statement is an accurate description of attitudes? Why or why not?
2. What kinds of arguments would be effective in persuading you to change your attitude toward a prominent political figure? How would you describe these arguments in psychological terms?
3. Have you ever experienced cognitive dissonance? If so, what factors made you feel this way and how did you eventually reduce the dissonance?

# Prejudice

A **prejudice** is a particular form of attitude. The dictionary definition of *prejudice* is a preconceived opinion, a bias, or a partiality toward a person or group, which may be favourable or unfavourable. However, people usually use the term to describe an unfavourable bias, and that's the sort of prejudice we're concerned with in this section: a negative evaluation of a group of people defined by their racial, ethnic, or religious heritage or by their gender, language, occupation, sexual orientation, level of education, or place of residence. A prejudice (literally, a "prejudgment") is a sort of mental shortcut through which people focus on a few salient features of a person (such as skin colour, accent, family name, or manner of dressing) and assume that the person possesses other, mainly negative, characteristics as well. As you can see, a prejudice is an insidious example of the representativeness heuristic.

Stereotypes are an important component of prejudice. In fact, the meanings of the two terms overlap somewhat. But strictly speaking, a prejudice describes a negative evaluation of members of a particular group, whereas a **stereotype** describes an overgeneralized, and therefore potentially false, belief about their characteristics. (Occasionally, stereotypes can include favourable beliefs, but again we usually think of negative examples.) Many of the regional political differences in Canada are expressed through stereotypes. Sometimes Easterners are characterized as self-centred by Westerners, and sometimes Westerners are called rednecks by Easterners. Both stereotypes communicate beliefs about characteristics that, although they may well be true in some specific instances, are overgeneralized to entire groups of people.

Stereotypes may be used to exert control over others and to justify and maintain others in their present social standings (Fiske, 1993). For example, a male employer who holds a stereotype of women as "followers" rather than "leaders" effectively ensures that women in his business will not be promoted to management positions.

Prejudice often leads to discrimination. Discrimination refers to behaviours, not to attitudes. In other contexts, the word *discrimination* simply means "to distinguish." In the present context, **discrimination** means treating people differently because of their membership in a particular group (K. L. Dion, 2003). Thus, we can discriminate favourably or unfavourably according to the nature of our attitudes and beliefs about the relative value of a particular group. Prejudice occurs any time members in one group, the *in-group*, exhibit negative attitudes toward members of another group, called the *outgroup*. Discrimination occurs any time members of the in-group display behaviour intended to prevent members of the outgroup from having or getting something, such as a promotion, a raise, or a home in a particular neighbourhood.

Although we most often think of prejudice, stereotypes, and discrimination at the level of the individual, we often see these phenomena operating at the level of groups, even nations. At this level, they give rise to *ethnocentrism*, which is

**prejudice** A preconceived opinion or bias; especially, a negative attitude or evaluation toward a group of people defined by their racial, ethnic, or religious heritage or by their gender, occupation, sexual orientation, level of education, place of residence, or membership in a particular group.

**stereotype** An overgeneralized and false belief about the characteristics of members of a particular group.

**discrimination** The differential treatment of people based on their membership in a particular group.

the notion that one's own cultural, national, racial, or religious group is superior to or more deserving than others. Conflict—international conflict, civil war or unrest, and gang violence—often results from ethnocentric beliefs and behaviours. Understanding prejudice, stereotyping, and discrimination, then, are important aspects of understanding social interactions, especially conflict, across all levels of culture.

▲ *Members of in-groups often demonstrate similarities that distinguish them from members of outgroups.*

## The Origins of Prejudice

Unfortunately, prejudice seems to be an enduring characteristic of the human species and may be observed in education, business, athletics, and politics. History has shown that even groups of people who have been oppressed go on to commit their own type of ethnocentric exploitation if they manage to overthrow their oppressors. Why is prejudice such a widespread trait?

**The Roots of Prejudice in Competition** Affiliation and prejudice are two sides of the same coin. That is, along with the tendency to identify with and feel close to members of our own group or clan goes the tendency to be suspicious of others. A classic experiment by Sherif and colleagues (1961) demonstrated just how easily intergroup mistrust and conflict can arise. The study took place at a remote summer camp. The participants, 11-year-old boys, were assigned to one of two cabins, isolated from each other. During the first week, the boys in each cabin spent their time together as a group, fishing, hiking, swimming, and otherwise enjoying themselves. The boys formed two cohesive groups, which they named the Rattlers and the Eagles. They became attached to their groups and identified strongly with them.

Next, the researchers sowed the seeds of dissension. They set up a series of competitive events between the two groups. The best team would win a trophy for the group and individual prizes for its members. As the competition progressed, the boys began to taunt and insult each other. Then the Eagles burned the Rattlers' flag, and in retaliation the Rattlers broke into the Eagles' cabin and scattered or stole their belongings. Although further physical conflict was prevented by the researchers, the two groups continued to abuse each other verbally and seemed to have developed a genuine hatred for each other.

Finally, the researchers arranged for the boys to work together. The researchers sabotaged the water supply for the camp and had the boys fix it; they had the boys repair a truck that had broken down; and they induced the boys to pool their money to rent a movie. After the boys worked on co-operative ventures, rather than competitive ones, the intergroup conflicts diminished.

The findings of this experiment suggest that when groups of people compete with each other, they tend to view their rivals negatively. Note that the boys at the summer camp were racially and ethnically mixed; the assignment to one cabin or the other was arbitrary. Thus, a particular boy could have been either a Rattler-hating Eagle or an Eagle-hating Rattler, depending on chance assignment to one group or the other.

**The Role of Self-Esteem in Prejudice** Most social psychologists believe that competition is an important factor in the development of prejudice. The competition need not be for tangible goods; it can be motivated by a desire for social superiority. As we have seen many times in this book, the concept of self-esteem helps explain many different types of behaviour. The tendency to perceive one's own group (the in-group) as superior and that of others (the outgroup) as inferior may be based on a need to enhance one's own self-esteem. Thus, people who belong to groups that preach racial hatred tend to be those whose own social status is rather low.

An experiment by Meindl and Lerner (1985) supports this conclusion. The researchers exposed English-speaking Canadians to a situation designed to threaten their self-esteem. They asked participants to walk across the room to get a chair. For those in the experimental group, the chair was rigged so that a pile of old-style computer data cards would be knocked over and scattered on the floor. In a situation like this, most people feel clumsy and foolish—and a bit guilty about making trouble for the person who has to put the cards back in order. After this experience, the participants were asked about their attitudes toward French-speaking Canadians. Participants in the experimental group, who had toppled the cards, rated the "others" more negatively than did those in the control group, who had not toppled the cards in retrieving the chair. Presumably, by viewing the francophones as members of a group inferior to their own, the participants partially compensated for the loss of their own self-esteem. We should note that levels of self-esteem have been shown to vary from culture to culture (e.g., Feather & McKee, 1993). We might therefore suspect that the effects found by Meindl and Lerner (1985) in Canada might not occur in more collectivist societies.

**The Role of Social Cognition in Prejudice** Research on social cognition has also provided us with information about the origins of prejudice. When we follow heuristics or mental shortcuts, we sometimes make errors of judgment. These mental shortcuts also play a role in the development of prejudice.

As we saw, stereotypes are overgeneralized, usually negative, beliefs about the members of an outgroup. These beliefs are convenient to the believer because they provide a way for a person to classify others quickly. When a person finds himself using group labels together with traits or other personal qualities, he is using stereotypes. Doing so is seductive because making a general point about a group is often more powerful, and cognitively easier, than dealing with the actual complexities of the problem the person is trying to explain (Macrae, Milne, & Bodenhausen, 1994). Attributing slow traffic movement to older drivers as a group, for example, is easier than analyzing the truly complex effects of roadway engineering, traffic flow patterns, and differences among all people in driving skills. The problem is that stereotypes are usually false in their application to all members of the outgroup.

Stereotypes are often learned from communications by family members, friends, and acquaintances. Research reveals that stereotypical information becomes more and more stereotypical as it passes from one person to another and to another (Ruscher, 1998). The mass media are another prominent means by which stereotypes are disseminated. Thompson, Judd, and Park (2000) have shown that stereotypes are more extreme when acquired through social communication than through direct contact with the outgroup. The media are a particularly dangerous source because they are both insidious and widespread. When members of ethnic or regional groups are portrayed in television shows or in movies as criminals, as having low-status jobs, as prone to substance abuse, or as being rather comic and stupid, people acquire stereotypes without being aware that they have done so. Such beliefs are unlikely to be examined, challenged, and changed to reflect reality. Even when faced with contradictory evidence, people seem to resist changing their general stereotype. For example, Kunda and Oleson (1997) gave people information that challenged their stereotypes and found that people maintained their original stereotypes by creating special subcategories for the exceptions that proved the rule. Other work suggests that people use stereotypes selectively to support and maintain desired impressions of others (Kunda & Sinclair, 1999).

Recall that the availability heuristic involves making the assumption that distinctive, easily imagined items occur more frequently than less distinctive and less easily imagined items. This phenomenon probably explains why people overestimate the rate of violent crime and overestimate the relative numbers of violent crimes committed by members of identifiable minority groups. Violent acts are certainly distinctive events, and identifiable minority group members are by definition conspicuous when depicted in the media. Both the crimes and the minority members stand out, and as a result seem to be causally related—members of the minority group are incorrectly seen to be especially prone to criminal acts. This tendency is an example of an **illusory correlation**—an apparent relation between two distinctive elements that does not actually exist (see Spears & Haslam, 1997).

Another fallacy that promotes the formation of stereotypes is the **illusion of outgroup homogeneity**: People tend to assume that members of other groups are much more similar than are members of their own group (Ostrom & Sedikides, 1992). This tendency is even seen between the sexes: Men tend to perceive women as being more alike than men are, and women do the opposite (Park & Rothbart, 1982). The same is true for young and old people (Linville, Fischer, & Salovey, 1989). Most of us resist being stereotyped but nevertheless practise this activity when thinking about members of other groups.

In a study of attitudes toward racial equality, Dixon, Durrheim, and Tredoux (2007) asked nearly 2000 South African adults contacted at random to estimate the frequency of their contact with members of the predominate ethnic groups: black and white. The researchers also asked the participants' attitudes regarding racial equality and government policies designed to produce such equality. The researchers' interest was the extent to which contact predicted attitudes. The results showed that, although increased contact improves whites' attitudes, there remains a "stubborn kernel" of opposition to government-mandated efforts to achieve racial equality. Interestingly, the results for blacks were the opposite: The greater their contact with whites, the less supportive they were of government efforts, such as those seeking restitution for blacks. The authors concluded that greater contact between in-group and outgroup may produce asymmetrical effects on attitudes.

**The Role of Evolution in Prejudice** Finally, a very different explanation of in-group biases toward outgroups (including prejudice, stereotypes, and discrimination) has been devised by Krebs and Denton (1997). These authors propose that cognitive structures that are biased in favour of the in-group, and against outgroups, were selected in the course of early human evolution because those structures had adaptive value.

The basic argument will be familiar to you by now. Early humans are usually characterized as living in small co-operative groups that were in competition with each other for scarce resources. Making rough and ready characterizations of others as belonging to one's own group or to another group presumably would facilitate both in-group co-operation and competitive effectiveness against outgroups. A positive bias toward our own in-group would contribute to cohesiveness

**illusory correlation** An apparent correlation between two distinctive elements that does not actually exist.
**illusion of outgroup homogeneity** A belief that members of groups to which one does not belong are very similar to one another.

among the members of our group. A negative bias against other groups would motivate us to keep outgroups under close scrutiny in order to detect dangers to ourselves.

Krebs and Denton (1997) point out that, in modern life, these once-adaptive biases can produce difficulties by perpetuating conflict where co-operative solutions are now possible. And, of course, our contemporary sense of humanity and justice is offended by undeserved negative evaluation and treatment of others simply because they belong to other groups.

## Self-Fulfilling Prophecies

A **stereotype self-fulfilling prophecy** is an expectancy, based on a stereotype, that induces a person to act in a manner consistent with that stereotype. Such a tendency is especially insidious because the behaviour of the person who is the target of the stereotype-based expectancy then tends to confirm the stereotype.

One of the most memorable examples of the self-fulfilling prophecy was demonstrated in an experiment by Snyder, Tanke, and Berscheid (1977). The researchers had male participants carry on telephone conversations with female participants. Just before each conversation took place, the male participants were shown a photograph of the young woman to whom they would talk. In fact, the pictures were not those of the partner but were photographs of attractive or unattractive women chosen by the researchers. The conversations that took place were recorded, and the voices of the female participants were played to independent observers, who rated their impressions of the young women.

Based on the sound of the female participants' voices and what they said, the independent observers rated the women whose partners believed them to be attractive as being more friendly, likeable, and sociable than when the partners thought they were unattractive. Obviously, the male participants talked differently to women they thought were attractive or unattractive. Their words had either a positive or a negative effect on the young women, which could be detected by the observers.

## Hope for Change

One of the primary reasons for prejudice is that it can serve to justify exploitation of the outgroup by the in-group. If the outgroup can be portrayed as "stupid," "dependent," and "irresponsible," the in-group can justify the exploitation of that outgroup as being in the outgroup's own best interest or at least conclude that its treatment of the outgroup is the best that the outgroup can reasonably expect. When ethnocentric practices lead to material advantages in the form of cheap labour or unequal sharing of resources, the injustices will tend to persist. Such situations are not easily altered by the discoveries of social psychologists.

**stereotype self-fulfilling prophecy** A stereotype-based expectancy that causes a person to act in a manner consistent with the stereotype.

However, many instances of personal prejudice are inadvertent. Many people are unaware of their stereotypes and preconceptions about members of other groups; or, if they are aware of them, they can be persuaded (though with difficulty) that their beliefs are unjustified. The best solution in these cases is to teach people to become cognitively less lazy and to take time to reflect on their biases. For example, Langer, Bashner, and Chanowitz (1985) gave a group of grade six children specific training in thinking about the problems of people with disabilities. They thought about such problems as the way in which a person with disabilities might drive a car and the reasons a blind person might make a good newscaster. After this training, they were found more willing to go on a picnic with a person with disabilities than were children who did not receive the training. They were also more likely to see the specific consequences of particular disabilities than to view people with disabilities as "less fit." Thus, at the individual level, people can learn to recognize their biases and to overcome their prejudices.

## Interim Summary

### Prejudice

Prejudice is a negative evaluation of a group of people defined by such characteristics as race, ethnicity, religion, gender, socio-economic status, or sexual orientation. An important component of prejudice is the existence of a stereotype—a false belief about the characteristics possessed by members of a particular group. Prejudices often lead to discrimination—actual behaviours injurious to the members of the group. Intergroup conflict, such as war or gang violence, often has at its core ethnocentrism, or the belief that one's own group is superior to or more deserving than another group.

One of the important causes of prejudice appears to be competition between groups for limited resources and the increased self-esteem that results from affiliating with a group perceived to be better than other groups. The study at the boys' camp by Sherif and his colleagues indicates just how easily prejudices can form, even when the groups consist of similar types of individuals.

Stereotypes are examples of the heuristics that guide us through many of our social encounters. One reason we tend to view outgroup members negatively is our use of the availability heuristic: Negative behaviours are often more vivid than positive ones, and outgroup members are more noticeable. Thus, when outgroup members commit an illegal act, we are more likely to notice it and to remember it. We then incorrectly conclude that the behaviour is a characteristic of the outgroup as a whole.

People also tend to apply the illusion of outgroup homogeneity. Although they realize that their own group contains members who are very different from each other, they tend to view members of other groups as rather similar. Obviously, this tendency contributes to the formation of stereotypes.

Some social psychologists suggest an evolutionary explanation of in-group and outgroup biases. They propose that competitive needs during early human history favoured mental structures that quickly categorized in-group and outgroup members.

Prejudices have many harmful effects, such as the self-fulfilling prophecy in which being perceived and treated as inferior leads the target of the prejudice to act that way. And even when the person does not, the observer may misperceive—or at least selectively perceive—the behaviour. However, there is hope for the future. Many instances of prejudice are inadvertent. When people are taught to think about members of other groups as individuals having specific characteristics, they can learn to avoid relying on some of their injurious mental shortcuts.

**QUESTIONS TO CONSIDER**

1. Think about a prejudice that you have. (It could be toward a place or a thing; it doesn't have to be directed toward a particular group of people.) What factors have caused this prejudice? To what extent are stereotypes involved in this prejudice?
2. How different are the members of your family compared to those of another family that you know? Describe how the illusion of outgroup homogeneity may or may not apply in this instance.

▲ *Our manner of dress and grooming often reflects the prevailing norms of the group or groups with which we most strongly identify ourselves.*

# Social Influences and Group Behaviour

Human beings are unmistakably social creatures: A great deal of our lives is spent in the company of others. By itself, this is not an especially profound observation, but it leads to some interesting implications, particularly for social psychologists. We do not merely occupy physical space with other people. We affiliate and form groups with each other. A **group** is a collection of individuals who generally have common interests and goals. For example, the members of Canada's Association for the 50Plus (CARP) have a different set of interests and goals than do members of the Canadian Diabetes Association, although some of their interests and goals may overlap.

The emotions, cognitions, and behaviours that define each of us as individuals are strongly influenced, often without our awareness, by those with whom we interact. Frequently, this influence is unintentional: Other people may be equally unaware of how they are influencing us. At other times, this influence is intended to manipulate us in some way (Santos, Leve, & Pratkanis, 1994). In this section we will consider the means by which we influence, and are influenced by, others.

## Imitation

Probably the most powerful social influence on our behaviour and attitudes is the behaviour of other people. If we see people act in a particular way, we tend to act in that way, too. Sometimes, we observe that people are not performing a particular behaviour; if so, we, too, tend not to perform that behaviour.

**Conformity** Most of us cherish our independence and like to think that we do what we do because we want to do it, not because others decree that we should. But none of us is immune to social influences, and most instances of conformity benefit us all. If we see someone whose face has been disfigured by an accident or disease, we do not stare at the person or comment on his or her appearance. If someone drops a valuable item, we do not try to pick it up and keep it for ourselves.

Many of the rules that govern our social behaviour are formally codified as laws that we are legally obligated to follow. However, many other rules that influence our behaviour are not formal laws but, instead, unwritten agreements. These

**group** A collection of individuals who generally have common interests and goals.

informal rules that define the expected and appropriate behaviour in specific situations are called **social norms**, or, when applied to members of a particular group, *group norms*. How we look at strangers, the way we talk to our friends or our supervisors at work, and the kind of food that we eat are all influenced by the norms of the society in which we live. Despite the fact that they do not develop from a conspicuous formal or legal process, norms are very powerful sources of social influence, as we will see next.

Sherif (1936) conducted a study that provided an empirical demonstration of the power of social influence in establishing group norms. The study was based on a perceptual illusion, originally discovered by astronomers, called the *autokinetic effect*: A small stationary light, when projected in an otherwise completely darkened room, appears to move. The illusion is so strong that even if someone is aware of the effect, the apparent movement often still persists.

Sherif first placed people in the room individually and asked each of them how far the light was moving at different times. The answers were quite variable; one person might see the light move 6 cm on average, while another might see it move an average of 300 cm. Next, Sherif had groups of three people observe the light together and make a joint decision about the extent of the movement. Finally, all of the participants observed the light individually. The most interesting result of the study was that once people had taken part in the group decision, their individual judgments tended to resemble those that the group had made. That is, the group established what Sherif called a *collective frame of reference*. The changing of one's thoughts or behaviour to be similar to those of a social group is called **conformity**. Even when tested by themselves on a different day, the group members still conformed to this frame of reference.

Sherif's findings are not too surprising if we consider that the participants found themselves in an uncertain situation. It makes sense to use others' opinions or judgments as a frame of reference when you are not sure what is going on. But just how strongly do group norms influence individual behaviour when the situation is unambiguous—when we are certain that we perceive things as they really are? The answer to this question was provided in a series of elegant studies conducted by Solomon Asch (1951, 1952, 1955).

Asch asked several groups of seven to nine students to estimate the lengths of lines presented on a screen. A sample line was shown at the left, and the students were asked to choose which of the three lines to the right matched it. (See **Figure 15•5**.) The participants gave their answers orally.

In fact, there was only one real student in each group; all other participants were confederates of the researcher. The seating was arranged so that the real student answered last.

**social norms** Informal rules defining the expected and appropriate behaviour in specific situations.

**conformity** The adoption of attitudes and behaviours shared by a particular group of people.

**FIGURE 15•5** An example of the stimuli used by Asch (1951).

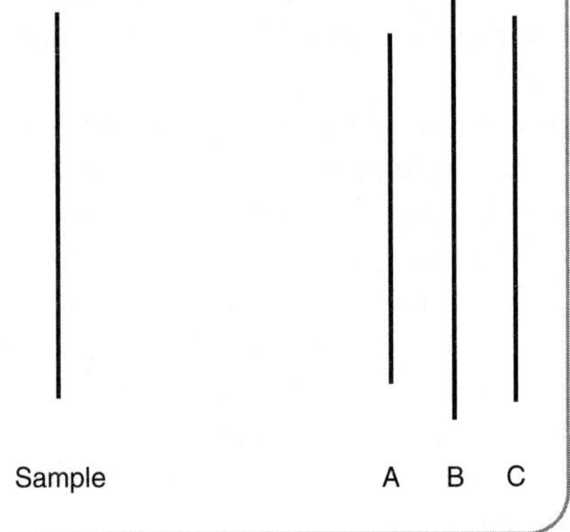


Under some conditions, the confederates made incorrect responses. When they made incorrect responses on 6 of the 12 trials in an experiment, 76 percent of the students went along with the group on at least one trial. Under control conditions, when the confederates responded accurately, only 5 percent of the participants made an error.

Group pressure did not affect the students' perceptions; it affected their behaviour. That is, they went along with the group decision even though the choice still looked wrong to them—and even though the other people were complete strangers. When they were questioned later, they said that they had started doubting their own eyesight or had thought that perhaps they had misunderstood the instructions. The students who did not conform felt uncomfortable about disagreeing with the other members of the group. The Asch effect shows how strong the tendency to conform can be.

We might ask why people so readily conform. Two of the most important reasons are the desire to be liked and the desire to be right (Baron, Vandello, & Brunsman, 1996; Cialdini & Goldstein, 2004). As we will see later, people tend to like other people who are similar to themselves, especially those who act like them and share their attitudes and opinions. Because most of us prefer to be liked, we tend to conform to the expectations of others. In addition, most of us prefer to be right rather than wrong.

**Bystander Intervention** Conformity can sometimes have disastrous consequences. In 1964, in New York City, a woman named Kitty Genovese was chased and repeatedly stabbed by an assailant, who took 35 minutes to kill her. The woman's screams went unheeded by at least 38 people who watched from their windows. No one tried to stop the attacker; no one even made a quick, anonymous telephone call to the police until after the attacker had left. When the bystanders were questioned later, they could not explain their inaction.

As you can imagine, people were appalled and shocked by the bystanders' response to the Genovese murder. Commentators said that the apparent indifference of the bystanders demonstrated that society, especially in urban areas, had become cold and apathetic. But the interviews with the bystanders suggested otherwise. They were not uncaring. Rather, they were distressed and confused by what happened and by their failure to intervene.

Experiments performed by social psychologists suggest that the apathy explanation is wrong—people in cities are not generally indifferent to the needs of other people. The fact that Kitty Genovese's attack went unreported is not remarkable because 38 were present; it is precisely *because* so many people were present that the attack was not reported.

Darley and Latané have extensively studied the phenomenon of **bystander intervention**—the actions of people witnessing a situation in which someone appears to require assistance. Their experiments have shown that, in such situations, the presence of other people who are doing nothing inhibits others from giving aid. For example, Darley and Latané (1968) staged an "emergency" during a psychology experiment. Each student participant took part in a discussion about personal problems associated with university life with one, two, or five other people by means of an intercom. The researcher explained that the participants would sit in individual rooms so that they would be anonymous and hence more likely to speak frankly. The researcher would not listen in but would get their reactions later in a questionnaire. Actually, only one real student was present; the other voices were very convincing tape recordings. During the discussion, one of the people, who had previously said that he sometimes had seizures, apparently had one. His speech became incoherent, and he stammered out a request for help.

Almost everyone left the room to help the victim when they were the only witness to the seizure. (This finding has been replicated in dozens of experiments. When people are alone and an emergency occurs, they are very responsible, not apathetic.) However, when there appeared to be other witnesses, the participants were much less likely to try to help. In addition, those who did try to help reacted more slowly if other people were thought to be present. (See **Figure 15•6**.)

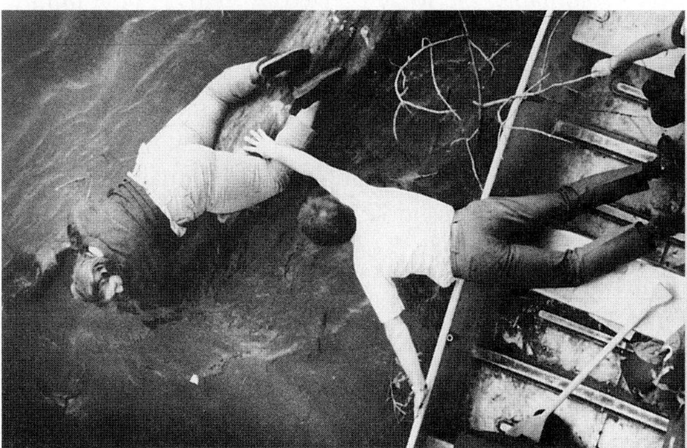

▲ *Not all bystanders are indifferent to the plight of people in danger. The man shown in this photograph rescued a woman who had been stranded for 40 minutes on a log floating in a river.*

**FIGURE 15•6** Bystander intervention. Percentage of participants attempting to help as a function of the number of other people the participant believed to be present.

*(Based on data from Darley, J. M., & Latané, B. (1968). Bystander intervention in emergencies: Diffusion of responsibility.* Journal of Personality and Social Psychology, 8, *377–383.)*

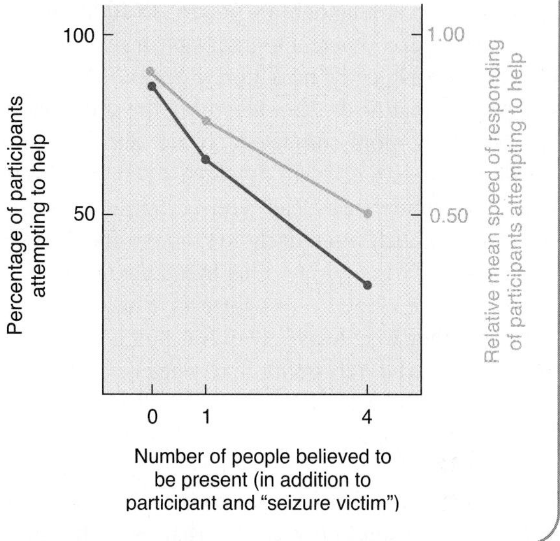


Darley and Latané reported that the students who did not respond were not indifferent to the plight of their fellow student. Indeed, when the researcher entered the room, they usually appeared nervous and emotionally aroused, and they asked whether someone was helping the victim. The researchers did not receive the impression that these students had decided not to act; rather, they were still in conflict, trying to decide whether they should do something.

Thus, it seems that whether bystanders will intervene in an emergency depends, at least in part, on how they perceive the situation and on whether people witness the event alone or in the presence of others. Latané and Darley (1970) have proposed a model describing a sequence of steps that bystanders face when confronted with a potential emergency:

They must notice and correctly interpret the event.

They must assume responsibility for helping the victim.

They must consider the possible courses of action and conclude that the costs of intervening are not prohibitively high.

Finally, they must actually implement the chosen course of action.

Of course, this sequence takes place rapidly and without much awareness on the bystander's part, as is true of many situations to which we respond daily.

**bystander intervention** The intervention of a person in a situation that appears to require his or her aid.

Unfortunately, at least from the perspective of the victim, obstacles may arise at any stage in this decision-making process that make it unlikely that a bystander will intervene. In many cases, the bystander who is aware that others are available to help may not feel any personal responsibility to do so, a phenomenon called **diffusion of responsibility**. This factor is considered to be responsible for the finding that help is less likely to be offered when several bystanders are present. In addition, the bystander may not feel competent to intervene or may be fearful of doing so; consequently, no action is taken because the person may believe that he or she will worsen the situation or that someone else is more competent to act. Shotland and Heinold (1985) staged an accident in which a person seemed to be bleeding. Bystanders who had received training in first-aid treatment were much more likely to come to the victim's aid, and they did so whether or not other bystanders were present. Because they knew how to recognize an emergency and knew what to do, they were less likely to fear doing the wrong thing and did not need to rely on more competent others.

## Social Facilitation

As we just saw, the behaviour of other people has a powerful effect on our own. Studies have shown that even the mere presence of other people can affect a person's behaviour. Triplett (1898) published the first experimental study on **social facilitation**—the enhancement of a person's performance by the presence of other people. He had people perform simple tasks, such as turning the crank of a fishing reel. He found that his participants turned the crank faster and for a longer time if other people were present. Although many other studies found the same effect, some investigators reported just the opposite phenomenon: If the task was difficult and complex, the presence of an audience impaired the people's performance. You yourself have probably noticed that you have difficulty performing certain tasks if someone is watching you.

Robert Zajonc (pronounced "zi-onze"; 1965) suggested a persuasive explanation for social facilitation. He claims that the presence of people who are watching a performer (or of people whom the performer perceives as watching) raises that person's arousal level. Presumably, the increase in arousal has the effect of increasing the probability of performing dominant responses—responses that are most likely to occur in a particular situation. When the task is simple, the dominant response is generally the correct one, so an audience improves performance. When the task is complex, a person can perform many different responses and must decide which one is appropriate. The presence of the audience makes the selection of the appropriate behaviour more difficult because the increased arousal tends to cause the person to perform the dominant response, which may not be the correct one.

Subsequent experiments have supported Zajonc's explanation. For example, Martens (1969) tested the prediction that the presence of a group increases a person's level of arousal. While participants performed a complex motor task alone or in the presence of 10 people, the researcher determined physiological arousal by measuring the amount of sweat present on the participants' palms. The presence of an audience produced a clear-cut effect: The participants who performed in front of other people had sweatier palms.

Such arousal may contribute to the making of costly mistakes—at least from the perspective of the aroused person. For example, in their study of residential burglars, Cromwell, Marks, Olson, and Avery (1991) found that burglars who work in groups are five times more likely to get caught than are burglars who work alone. The researchers argue that burglary is a complex task that cannot be "well learned" because each burglary is different. The complexity of the burglary combined with high levels of arousal produced by the group presence may contribute to errors in "professional" judgment in both planning and carrying out the crime. The result would be a higher apprehension rate for groups of criminals than for individuals. You will see in the next section that another explanation for this group burglar effect is *social loafing*.

## Social Loafing

As mentioned, people usually try harder when other people are watching them. However, when the other people are co-workers rather than observers, the presence of a group sometimes results in a decrease in effort, or **social loafing**. Thus, a group is often less than the sum of its individual members. Many years ago, Ringelmann (cited by Dashiell, 1935) measured the effort that people made when pulling a rope in a mock tug-of-war contest against a device that measured the exerted force. Presumably, the force exerted by eight people pulling together in a simple task would be at least the sum of their individual efforts or even somewhat greater than the sum because of social facilitation. However, Ringelmann found that the total force exerted was only about half what would be predicted by the simple combination of individual efforts. His participants exerted less force when they worked in a group.

Modern studies have confirmed these results and have extended them to other behaviours. Several variables have been found to determine whether the presence of a group will produce social facilitation or social loafing. One of the most important of them is individual identifiability.

Williams, Harkins, and Latané (1981) asked people to shout as loud as they could, individually or in groups. (You should know that people in the group condition could not see or hear the others.) People in groups shouted less loudly than individuals when they believed that the recording equipment could measure only *the total group effort*. However, when

**diffusion of responsibility** An explanation of the failure of bystander intervention stating that when several bystanders are present, no one person assumes responsibility for helping.
**social facilitation** The enhancement of task performance caused by the mere presence of others.
**social loafing** The decreased effort put forth by individuals when performing a task with other people.

they believed that the equipment would measure *individual effort*, people in groups shouted just as loudly as individuals. These results suggest that a person's efforts in a group activity are affected by whether his or her individual efforts can be observed. If they can, social facilitation is likely to occur; if they cannot, social loafing is more likely.

Two interpersonal variables that affect social loafing are *group cohesiveness* and *individual responsibility*. For example, Karau and Hart (1998) showed that groups that share a common position on an issue (and therefore are *cohesive*) do not exhibit social loafing compared to individuals. Non-cohesive groups do show the social loafing phenomenon. Harkins and Petty (1982) tested the hypothesis that if a person's efforts are duplicated by those of another person (and if his or her individual efforts are not identifiable), the person is likely to exert less-than-maximum effort. These researchers had people work in groups of four on a task that required them to report whenever a dot appeared in a particular quadrant of a video screen. In one condition, each person watched an individual quadrant and was solely responsible for detecting dots that appeared there. In the other condition, all four participants watched the same quadrant; thus, the responsibility for detecting dots was shared. People did not loaf when they were responsible for their own quadrants.

Karau and Williams (1995) noted that gender and culture also appear to moderate people's tendency to become social loafers. Although all people in different cultures are susceptible to social loafing, the effect is smaller for women than for men and for people living in Eastern cultures than for those living in Western cultures. Karau and Williams offer a reasonable explanation for this finding. First, women across cultures tend to be more group-oriented than men across cultures. Second, people of both genders living in Eastern cultures tend to be more group-oriented in their thinking and behaviour than people of both genders living in Western cultures. So, it seems that people living in Eastern cultures, and women in general, tend to place greater importance on participating in group activities, which partially buffers them from social loafing effects.

## Commitment

Once people commit themselves by making a decision and acting on it, they are reluctant to renounce their commitment. For example, have you ever joined one side of an argument on an issue that you do not really care about, only to find yourself vehemently defending a position that until then meant almost nothing to you? This phenomenon was demonstrated in a clever study by Knox and Inkster (1968). The researchers asked people at the betting windows of a racetrack how confident they were that their horses would win. They questioned half of the people just before they had made their bets, the other half just afterwards. The people who had already made their bets were more confident than were those who had not yet paid. Their commitment increased the perceived value of their decision.

An experiment by Freedman and Fraser (1966) showed that commitment has a long-lasting effect on people's tendency to comply with requests. Imagine that you answer a knock on your door to find a person who explains that he is a volunteer for Canadians for Safe Driving. He asks if you will place a 7.5-cm-square sign in your window to encourage responsible driving, and you agree to this small request. Then, two weeks later, the same person returns and asks if you would allow workers from Canadians for Safe Driving to visit your home and install a billboard on your front lawn. He shows you a photograph of an attractive house that is almost completely hidden by a huge, ugly, poorly lettered sign that reads "DRIVE CAREFULLY." Do you think you would agree to this second request? Freedman and Fraser (1966) revealed powerful effects of just this type of approach. Fully 76 percent of participants who had been asked earlier to display a small sign agreed to the second, large request! In a control condition where no initial small request was made, only 17 percent of participants agreed to have the billboard installed. Freedman and Fraser referred to the sequence of a small request followed by a large one as the *foot-in-the-door technique* of gaining compliance.

Commitment increases people's compliance even when the reason for the original commitment is removed. For example, recall the chapter prologue in which I described my experience while negotiating the price of a new car. I made a commitment for the car—I had signed a formal offer to purchase the car at the proposed price and handed the salesperson a large cheque to show my good-faith intention to buy it. However, when the salesperson returned, supposedly after talking with his manager, he said that he had made a mistake on the price and then quoted a new price many thousands of dollars higher. I confronted the salesperson about his underhanded technique, and was very fortunate to get my new car for the originally quoted low price. All too often, though, the customer is taken in by this ruse and agrees to the higher price. As I noted in the prologue, this technique is called *lowballing*.

Commitment probably increases compliance for several reasons. First, the act of complying with a request in a particular category may change a person's self-image. Through the process of self-attribution, people who accept a small sign to support safe driving may come to regard themselves as public-spirited individuals—what sensible person is not for safe driving? Thus, when they hear the billboard request, they find it difficult to refuse. After all, they are public spirited, so how can they say no? Saying no would imply that they did not have the courage of their convictions. Thus, this reason has at its root self-image; to maintain a good self-image, the person must say yes to the larger request.

## Attractive People

People also tend to be influenced by requests or persuasive messages from attractive people. As we will see in a later section, physical good looks are one of the most important factors in determining whether we find someone likeable.

Kulka and Kessler (1978) demonstrated the effect of good looks on people's behaviour in a controlled experiment. They staged mock trials of a negligence suit in which someone was suing another person for damages. The participants served as jury members and decided how much money the plaintiffs should be awarded. Physically attractive plaintiffs received an average of $10051, but physically unattractive plaintiffs received only $5623. Justice may not be so blind after all.

Why is attractiveness such a potent influence on people's behaviour? The most likely explanation involves classical conditioning and—again—self-image. Classical conditioning holds that when people have positive or negative reactions to some stimuli, they begin to have positive or negative reactions to other stimuli associated with those stimuli. Advertisers regularly pay tribute to the effectiveness of association when they use attractive models and celebrities to endorse their products.

Besides making products or opinions more attractive by being associated with them, attractive people are better able to get others to comply with their requests. This phenomenon, like so many others, probably has self-esteem at its root. One of the reasons people tend to comply with the requests of attractive people is that they want to be liked by attractive people; in their minds, being liked by attractive people makes them more desirable, too. People tend to emphasize their associations with attractive and important people. We have all encountered name-droppers who want us to think that they are part of a privileged circle of friends.

## Authority

People tend to comply with the requests of people in authority and to be swayed by their persuasive arguments. Such obedience is generally approved by societies when its authority figures are respected and trustworthy, and it is usually the case that authority figures are relatively benign in their intentions. We are all aware of exceptions to this generality, however, including the induced suicides and murders at Jonestown and the atrocities committed by those who were "just following orders" during the Nazi regime in Germany.

A disturbing example of commonplace obedience to illegitimate demands was obtained in a series of experiments performed by Stanley Milgram (1963). He advertised for participants in local newspapers to obtain as representative a sample of lay people as possible. These participants served as "teachers" in what they were told was a learning experiment. A confederate (a middle-aged accountant) serving as the "learner" was strapped into a chair "to prevent excessive movements when he was shocked," and electrodes were attached to his wrist. The participants were told that "although the shocks can be extremely painful, they cause no permanent tissue damage."

The participant was then brought to a separate room that housed an apparatus with dials, buttons, and a series of switches that supposedly delivered shocks ranging from 15 to 450 volts. The participant was instructed to use this apparatus to deliver shocks, in increments of 15 volts for each "mistake," to the learner in the other room. Beneath the switches were descriptive labels ranging from "Slight Shock" to "Danger: Severe Shock."

The learner gave his answers by pressing the appropriate lever on the table in front of him. Each time he made an incorrect response, the researcher told the participant to throw another switch and give a larger shock. The learner became increasingly agitated as the level of shock increased. At 75 volts, the learner began to complain and moan. At 150 volts, he demanded that he be allowed to stop the experiment. At 180 volts, the learner said that he could not stand the pain any longer and demanded to be set free. At the 300-volt level, the learner pounded on the wall and then stopped responding to questions. The researcher told the participant to consider "no answer" as an incorrect answer. At the 315-volt level, the learner pounded on the wall again. If the participant hesitated in delivering a shock, the researcher said, "Please go on." If this admonition was not enough, the researcher said, "The experiment requires that you continue," then, "It is absolutely essential that you continue," and finally, "You have no other choice; you must go on." The factor of interest was how long people would continue to administer shocks to the hapless victim. A majority of people gave the learner what they believed to be the 450-volt shock, despite the fact that he had pounded on the wall twice and then stopped responding altogether. (See **Figure 15•7**.)

In a later experiment, when the confederate was placed in the same room as the participant and his struggling and apparent pain could be observed, 37.5 percent of the participants obeyed the order to administer further shocks (Milgram, 1974). Thirty percent were even willing to hold his hand against a metal plate to force him to receive the shock.

Milgram's experiments indicate that a significant percentage of people will follow the orders of authority figures, no matter what the effects are on other people. Milgram had originally designed his experimental procedure to understand why ordinary people in Germany had participated in the murders of millions of innocent people during the Second World War. He had planned to perfect the technique in the United States and then travel to Germany to continue his studies. The results he obtained made it clear that he did not have to leave home.

Most people find the results of Milgram's studies surprising. They cannot believe that for such a large proportion of people the social pressure to conform to the researcher's orders is stronger than the participant's own desire not to hurt someone else. As Ross (1977) points out, this misperception is an example of the fundamental attribution error. People tend to *underestimate* the effectiveness of situational factors and to *overestimate* the effectiveness of dispositional ones. Clearly, the tendency to obey an authority figure is amazingly strong.

A great deal of attention has been paid to the ethical questions raised by Milgram's research (e.g., Elms, 1995). Psychologists and non-psychologists alike have questioned

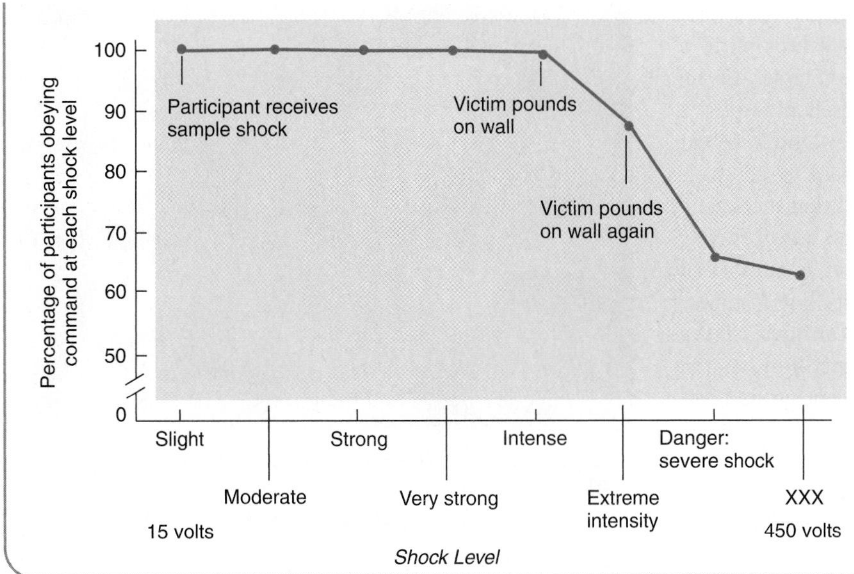


FIGURE 15•7 Data from one of Milgram's studies of obedience.

*(After Milgram, 1963. From Baron, R. A., & Byrne, D. Social Psychology, 8/e. Published by Allyn and Bacon, Boston, MA. Copyright 1997 by Pearson Education. Reprinted by permission of the publisher.)*

whether he should have conducted his research. For example, some critics point out that Milgram's studies revealed extremely negative information to participants about themselves (their capacity for harmful obedience)—information they might never have learned had it not been for their participation in the research. In his defence, it must be stressed that Milgram exercised a high degree of care with his participants that still affects social psychologists today. He conducted an extensive debriefing at the end of each experimental session in which the true purpose of the experiment was explained to the participants. He made sure that participants understood that they were not deviant, and that the situation had been very powerful. Interestingly, at least some people considered the enhanced insight into their own behaviour to be a positive aspect of their participation. In addition, participants were later sent a detailed written report of the experimental procedure and a follow-up questionnaire asking them about their feelings regarding their participation. Eighty-four percent said they were glad to have participated in the experiment, and only 1.3 percent indicated that they wished they had not participated.

## Group Decision Making

The process by which members of a group reach a decision is different from the process involved in individual decision making, if only because decisions in groups are usually preceded by discussion. However, discussing issues relevant to a decision does not always guarantee that the best decision will be made. Two examples of problems associated with group decision making are group polarization and groupthink.

**Group Polarization** In some group decision-making situations, discussion of alternative choices leads to decisions that are either riskier or more conservative than the group's initial position on the issue at hand. In general, if the initial position of group members is to make a risky decision, group discussion will lead to making an even riskier decision. In contrast, if the initial position of group members is to make a conservative decision, group discussion will usually lead to an even more conservative decision. The tendency for the initial position of a group to become exaggerated during the discussion preceding a decision is called **group polarization.**

One important consequence of group polarization is attitude change. For example, suppose that you join a local environmental group because you have a desire to protect the environment. After attending several meetings and discussing environmental issues with other group members, you may find that your pro-environment attitude has become even stronger: You are more of an environmentalist than you thought you were! That group discussion can affect attitude change so powerfully has been documented in many psychology experiments. For example, Myers and Bishop (1970) found that initial levels of racial prejudice voiced by groups were altered through group discussion. Discussion caused the group with an initially low level of prejudice to become even less prejudiced and the group with an initially high level of prejudice to become even more prejudiced.

What causes group discussion to lead to polarization? Although several explanations have been offered, three seem plausible: those concerning informational influence, repeated exposure, and normative influence (Isenberg, 1986). *Informational influence* involves learning new information germane to the decision to be made. Information that favours a particular decision is often repeated; thus, the discussion becomes slanted toward that decision, increasing the likelihood that more and more members of the group will become convinced that this is the best decision. In addition, people also

**group polarization** The tendency for the initial position of a group to become exaggerated during the discussion preceding a decision.

learn of information of which they were previously unaware, which makes them even more convinced that moving to a more extreme position is the best thing to do (Stasser, 1991).

*Repeated exposure* to information by itself may play a role. When group members discuss issues, they tend to repeat the points that have been identified as relevant to the decision. Brauer, Judd, and Gliner (1995) showed that increasing repetition of attitudes during group discussion was positively related to the extremity of group polarization. A number of mechanisms could produce this relationship. For instance, we have seen that repeated mere exposure can increase the strength of attitudes. It may also be that repetition has the effect of increasing group cohesiveness and the in-group positivity bias.

*Normative influence* involves comparison of one's individual views with the group norm. People in groups receive social reinforcement for agreeing with the views of others. The more that group members wish to achieve group cohesion in decision making, the greater the tendency for individual group members to embrace the logic underlying the group's decisions—no matter how extreme those decisions might be. Thus, the more that groups of people square off to debate important issues, such as abortion, gun control, welfare, and so on, the more likely it is that they will become convinced of the credibility of their own positions—not because they are the correct positions but because of the mutual support that group members give each other for holding those positions.

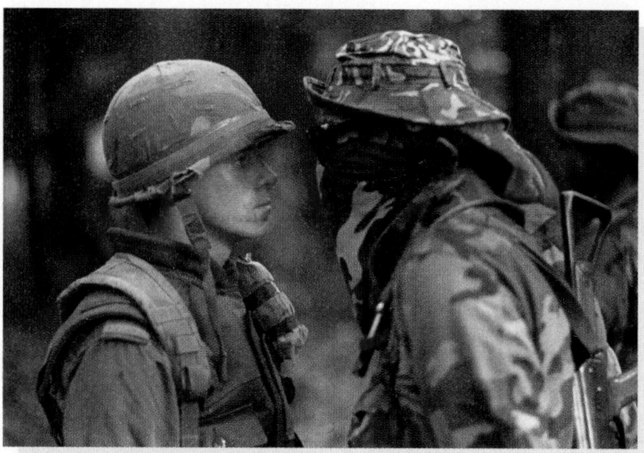

▲ *What group decision-making processes do you suppose led to the standoff that took place in 1990 at a blockade in the small town of Oka, Quebec, between Mohawk warriors and Canadian troops?*

**Groupthink** Irving Janis has studied a related phenomenon that sometimes occurs in group decision making—**groupthink**, the tendency to avoid dissent in the attempt to achieve group consensus (Janis, 1972, 1982). Janis developed the notion of groupthink after studying the ineffective decision making that led U.S. President John F. Kennedy to order an ill-fated attempt to overthrow Fidel Castro's regime in Cuba in 1961. The decision to embark on the Bay of Pigs invasion was made by Kennedy and a small group of advisers. After studying the conditions that led to this decision as well as other important group decisions that altered the course of twentieth-century history, Janis proposed his theory of groupthink.

The theory specifies the conditions necessary for groupthink as well as its symptoms and consequences. (See **Figure 15•8**.) The conditions that foster groupthink include a stressful situation in which the stakes are very high, a group of people who already tend to think alike and who are isolated from others who could offer criticism of the decision, and a strong group leader who makes his or her position well known to the group. In the Bay of Pigs example, the overthrow of one of America's arch-enemies was at stake, Kennedy's advisers were like-minded regarding the invasion and met in secret, and Kennedy was a forceful and charismatic leader who made his intentions to invade Cuba known to the group.

**groupthink** The tendency to avoid dissent in the attempt to achieve group consensus in the course of decision making.

Janis also notes five symptoms of groupthink, all of which were present during the decision to invade Cuba. First, group members share the illusion that their decision is sound, moral, and right—in a word, invulnerable. Second, dissent from the leader's views is discouraged, further supporting the illusion that the group's decision is the right one. Third, instead of assessing the strengths and weaknesses of the decision, group members rationalize their decision, looking only for reasons that support it. Fourth, group members are closed-minded—they are not willing to listen to alternative suggestions and ideas. And fifth, self-appointed "mindguards" exist within the group who actively discourage dissent from the group norm.

Combined, these symptoms lead to flawed decision making. They contribute to the tendency to conduct only incomplete or no research on the issue at hand, to fail to examine alternative courses of action specified by the decision, and, finally, to fail to consider potential risks inherent in the decision. For example, the U.S. invasion of Iraq may have been due to the influence of groupthink, as the information regarding weapons of mass destruction was not adequate to justify the invasion (Rodrigues, Assmar, & Jablonski, 2005).

Some observers of Canadian politics believe that the government's advertising sponsorship program preceding the 1995 referendum on Quebec separation, and the ensuing financial scandal, was the result of groupthink. Baker (2004), for instance, says that "those involved with the operation and execution of the sponsorship program succumbed to groupthink. No doubt they thought they were motivated by the highest goal, the unity of the country. But they became blind to their responsibility to ensure that the money set aside for the promotion of Canada in Quebec was effectively used." As we have learned through the investigation of the sponsorship program, it appears that a combination of corruption and groupthink is to blame for the scandal.

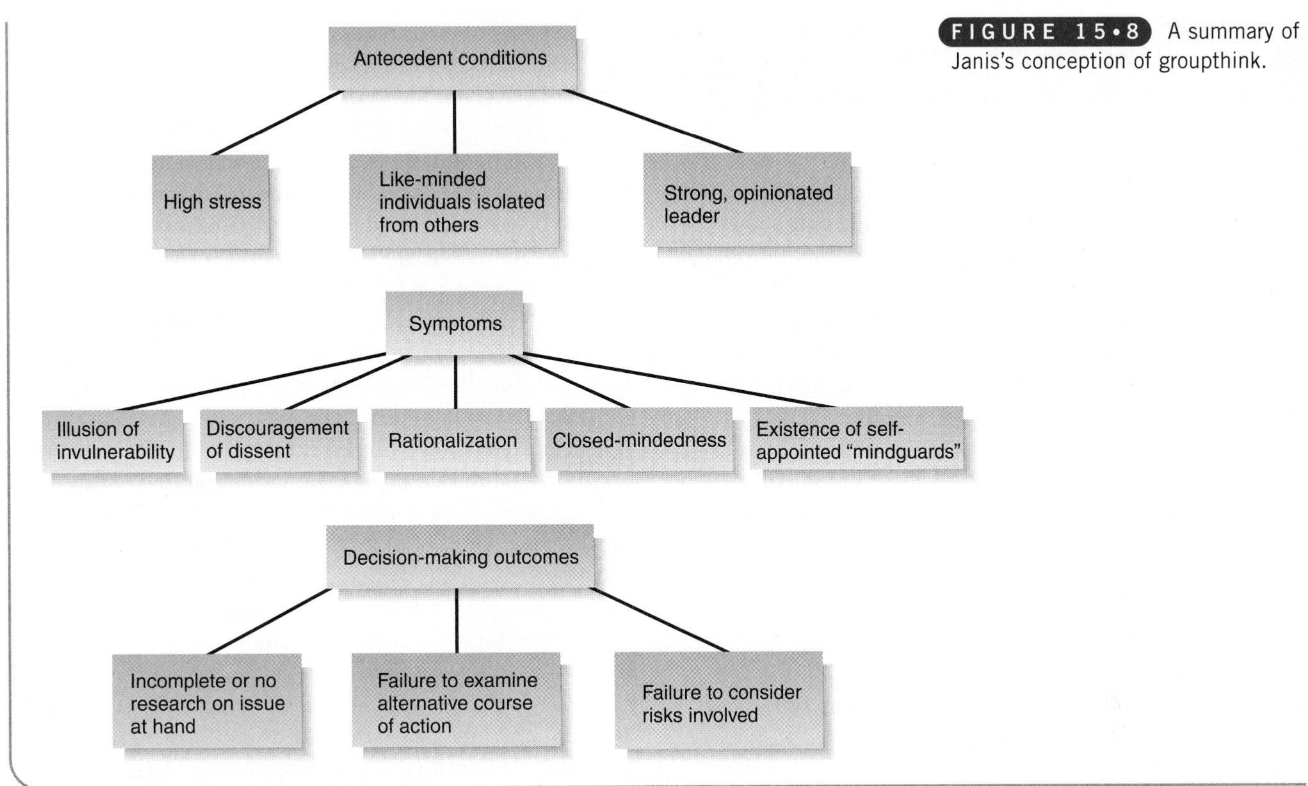


FIGURE 15•8 A summary of Janis's conception of groupthink.

Janis argues that groupthink may be avoided by taking several precautions. First, criticism by group members should be encouraged. Second, relevant input should be sought from appropriate people who are not members of the group. Third, the group should be broken into smaller subgroups in which different ideas and opinions are generated and developed. And fourth, the group leader should not overstate his or her position on the matter and should be on guard for rationalization, closed-mindedness, and illusions of invulnerability.

## Resisting Social Influences

At first glance, social influence may appear to be negative; perhaps we would be better off if all our behaviour was under rational, conscious control. But as Cialdini (1993) points out, this conclusion is not warranted. Most of the time, our species profits from our tendencies to be fair in our interactions with others, to take our cues for acting from each other, to honour our commitments, and to obey authority figures. If we had to expend time and effort in consciously deciding what to do in every situation we encountered in our lives, we would be exhausted at the end of each day and get hardly anything done. For most normal people in most situations, the automatic, unconscious reaction is the best and most efficient one. We should save our cognitive efforts for the times when they count the most. However, no general rule works all of the time; exceptions can occur that have bad effects. For example, an authority figure can order us to do things that hurt ourselves or others, and advertisers and sales representatives who know the rules of social influence can induce us to purchase items we do not need.

Cialdini suggests that the best way to defend ourselves from the unscrupulous use of social influences is to be sensitive to ourselves and to the situation. Whenever we are spending money or committing ourselves to do something that will cost us time and effort, we should ask ourselves whether we feel any discomfort. Do we feel pressured? Do we feel tense? Do we wish we were somewhere else? If so, someone is probably trying to manipulate us. We should try to relax and step back from the situation. Does the other person stand to profit from what he or she is trying to get us to do? If we could go back to the time just before we got into this situation, would we put ourselves where we are now or would we avoid this situation? If we would avoid it, then now is the time to leave. The feeling that we have to keep going, that we have to live up to our commitment, is exactly what the other person is counting on.

We must realize that when someone is trying to manipulate us, the rules that govern normal social interchanges are off. Of course, we should be polite and honest—just as we want other people to be with us—but we are not obliged to return "favours" from someone trying to sell us something. If he or she tricks us into making a commitment, we should feel no compunction about breaking it. If someone tries to abuse our natural tendencies to be fair in our interactions with others, we should fight back. Otherwise, we run the risk of becoming cynical in our dealings with other people who are not trying to take advantage of us. Forewarned is forearmed.

## Then and Now

### The Impact of Media Violence

As you will recall from Chapter 13, psychologists are strongly motivated to understand how media violence affects real-world behaviour. Tragedies such as the Columbine High School killings, the Montreal Massacre, the school shooting in Taber, Alberta, and the more recent mass murder at Virginia Tech have led to conclusions in the news media that violent media may be partially responsible for these horrific events. The killers in Columbine played *Doom*, a violent but popular video game, and there has been speculation in the news media that violent video games also may have played a role in the Virgina Tech murders. Does violence in television, music, or video games really lead to tragedy? Social psychologists have spent decades trying to answer this important question.

An analysis of more than 1500 films revealed that nearly one-quarter of them had crime as their central subject matter and that an average of four criminal acts were committed in each film. What's surprising about these statistics is that they are from a review of films made in the 1920s (Dale, 1935). Concern about the impact of the violent content in the media is clearly nothing new. Social psychologists have been studying the impact of media content on behaviour since the inception of the field of social psychology. The early work in this area focused on film and radio. With the popularity of television increasing steadily since the 1950s, research on violent media has focused on television. Signorielli, Gerbner, and Morgan (1995) estimated that children witness more than 100 000 acts of violence before the age of 12. More recently, researchers have investigated the impact of violent lyrics in music and violent imagery in video games. Video games are a more active medium than television, and some psychologists argue that violent video games such as *Doom* contain many of the same psychological techniques that are used to desensitize soldiers to commit acts of violence against enemies (Grossman, 2000).

One of the classic studies investigating the impact of observed aggression on children's behaviour is Bandura's research on social learning (Bandura, 1963; Bandura, Ross, & Ross, 1961). Bandura had children observe adults playing with a "Bobo" doll (an inflatable doll that pops back up after it's pushed down; see Chapter 13). In one condition, children observed adults playing aggressively with the doll. These children watched as the adults smacked the doll with an open hand, hit it with a mallet, kicked it, and yelled at it. In another condition, a different group of children did not observe any aggression toward the doll. Bandura found that children who watched an adult acting aggressively toward the Bobo doll were themselves more aggressive. They were more likely to hit the doll, and showed increased play with aggressive toys, such as guns, even though this had not been modelled by the adults.

Bandura's groundbreaking research demonstrated that, at least in some situations, children model violent behaviour. Hundreds of studies have been conducted following Bandura's work to better understand the role of violent media on aggressive behaviour. In the early 1970s, government-funded inquiries into the link between media violence and violent behaviour led some researchers to conclude that there is a relationship between violence on film and real-world acts of aggression (Gunter, 2008). These findings spurred more empirical research, some of which indicated that exposure to violence in television in the lab increases aggressive behaviour in children. For example, Liebert and Baron (1972) exposed children to a violent police drama. When these children were allowed free play with other children who had not seen the violent program, they behaved far more aggressively than a separate group of children who had watched only a nonviolent sporting event. Follow-up studies were conducted and most conclusions were similar—violent portrayals in the media can increase the likelihood of aggressive acts, especially in children. While the results are intriguing, there is growing criticism that they do not generalize outside the laboratory and do not apply to all situations.

A **meta-analysis**—a statistical procedure for estimating the magnitude of experimental effects reported by published studies—looking at the effect of violent video games on behaviour failed to find any reliable indication that playing a violent video game actually leads to real-world violence. In fact, Ferguson (2007) found not only that violent video games had little impact on actual behaviour, but also that these games actually improved visuo-spatial cognition. Ferguson's conclusions suggest that playing violent video games may be associated with some positive effects, but does not appear to be associated with any negative effects.

How do children themselves perceive their own use of video games? Olson, Kutner, and Warner (2008) conducted interviews with boys between the ages of 12 and 14. The boys reported that they play video games because they are exciting and that the games help them work through feelings of anger and reduce stress. The boys recognized that the games were removed from reality, and did not believe that the violent content had any negative impact on their behaviour. Interestingly, the boys had concerns that younger children who played the same video games may be prone to imitate the violent actions in them.

What are we left to conclude after decades of research by social psychologists on this critically important topic? Recent research warns that we should not accept a global conclusion about the harmful effects of violent media; rather, we need to recognize that while not everyone is affected by violence in the media, there are some people under some conditions that can be susceptible (Gunter, 2008). Social psychologists are still at work on this complex issue.

**meta-analysis** A statistical procedure by which the results of many studies are combined to estimate the magnitude of a particular effect.

## Interim Summary

### Social Influences and Group Behaviour

You probably did not need to be told that one of the most important influences on our behaviour is provided by other humans, but the experiments of social psychologists have shown us just how potent these social influences are. We tend to imitate the behaviour of other people, conforming to social norms and preferring not to disagree with attitudes and judgments expressed by others. This tendency undoubtedly serves us well most of the time, but the fact that people are less likely to assist someone if other bystanders are present shows that imitation can also have unfortunate effects.

When they are part of a group or are observed by others, people act differently than when alone. In general, the presence of observers increases the likelihood that the performer will make the dominant response; depending on the complexity of the task, this effect can either facilitate or inhibit performance. When performing as part of a group, a person's efforts will often be less vigorous if individual contribution cannot be measured. Three important interpersonal variables that affect social loafing are group cohesiveness, identifiability, and individual responsibility. Members of cohesive groups do not fall prey to social loafing. If our efforts can be detected by others, the contingencies of social reinforcement and punishment come into play, and we tend not to loaf. Also, if we have a particular responsibility that is not duplicated by other people—if our contribution is a unique and important one—we tend to continue to work hard in support of the group effort.

When we commit ourselves to a course of action, we tend to honour this commitment. As the study with the billboards showed, we act consistently with prior commitments even when we are not conscious of having made them. As well, not everyone is treated equally by other people. Attractive people tend to get what they want from others; we find it difficult to say no to them. And, as Milgram's research showed, people will obey outlandish, even inhumane, requests from those perceived as authority figures.

Effective group decision making may be hampered by both group polarization and groupthink. In group polarization, the initial position of the group is exaggerated to one extreme or the other for three reasons: informational influence, repeated exposure, and normative influence. Informational influence involves the presentation of new and specific information that slants the opinion of the group toward either a riskier or a more conservative decision. Repeated exposure seems to have an effect on its own, even when the information is not new. Normative influence involves group members acting to obtain mutual reinforcement—they make the decision that is most likely to contribute to group cohesiveness. Groupthink develops in situations that are highly stressful when the group making a decision involves an opinionated group leader and like-minded individuals who are isolated from others. It is characterized by feelings that the group's decision is invulnerable, by lack of dissent, by rationalization, by closed-mindedness, and by "mindguards" who actively discourage differences of opinion. When steps are taken to avoid these symptoms, better, more effective decisions become possible.

Although our tendency to be influenced socially is generally in our best interests, sometimes unscrupulous persons take advantage of this tendency in attempts to exploit others. The best way to protect ourselves from such persons is to become more aware of situations in which such exploitation is likely to occur.

**QUESTIONS TO CONSIDER**

1. How would social life be different if people tended not to conform to certain social norms? Think of an instance in which your behaviour conformed to a social norm. How might the outcome of this social interaction have been different had you not conformed?
2. In life-saving and CPR classes, students are taught to take control in emergency situations. For example, in a situation in which a person appears to be drowning, they assign onlookers specific responsibilities, such as calling 911, fetching rescue equipment, and so on. To what extent does taking control in this manner enhance bystander intervention? What effect might it have on the onlookers' tendency toward diffusion of responsibility?
3. Suppose that you have been asked by your psychology professor to organize a small group of class members to prepare a presentation. As the leader of the group, what steps might you take to prevent the individual members of your group from becoming social loafers?

# Interpersonal Attraction and Loving

When an individual conforms to a group norm, it is the individual, not the group, who is being influenced. When you comply with the request of a car salesperson or obey the dictates of an authority figure, the influence flows in one direction; it is your behaviour that is being influenced. However, many cases of social influence are reciprocal. As we shall see in this section, the behaviour of two individuals may have mutual, although not necessarily equal, influences on each other.

## Interpersonal Attraction

Many factors determine **interpersonal attraction**, or people's tendency to approach each other and evaluate each other positively. Some factors are characteristics of the individuals

**interpersonal attraction** People's tendency to approach each other and to evaluate each other positively.

themselves; others are determined by the socially reinforcing aspects of the environment.

**Positive Evaluation** Humans like to be evaluated positively—to be held in high regard by other people. This tendency is expressed in interpersonal attraction. There is no surprise in the fact that we like those who treat us well and dislike those who punish us.

**Familiarity** We have learned that attractiveness plays an important role in social influence. Fortunately for the majority of us who are not especially beautiful or handsome, the variable of *exposure* also influences people's attitudes toward others. The more frequent the exposure, the more positive the attitude is.

In order for an attachment to form between people, they must meet each other. Festinger, Schachter, and Back (1959) found that the likelihood of friendships between people who lived in an apartment house was related to the distance between the apartments in which they lived; the closer the apartments, the more likely the friendship was. People were also unlikely to have friends who lived on a different floor unless their apartments were next to a stairway, where they would meet people going up or down the stairs.

Repetition generally increases our preference for a stimulus (the mere exposure effect). This phenomenon applies to people as well. Even in the brief time it takes to participate in an experiment, familiarity affects interpersonal attraction. Saegert, Swap, and Zajonc (1973) had university women participate in an experiment supposedly involving the sense of taste. Groups of two students entered booths, where they tasted and rated various liquids. The movements of the students from booth to booth were choreographed so that pairs of women were together from zero to 10 times. Afterwards, the participants rated their attraction to each of the other people in the experiment. The amount of attraction the participants felt toward a given person was directly related to the number of interactions they had had—the more interactions they had had with others, the more attracted they were. (See **Figure 15•9**.)

**FIGURE 15•9** Familiarity, exposure, and attraction. The rated likeability of a fellow participant as a function of the number of interactions.

*(Based on data from Saegert, S. C., Swap, W., & Zajonc, R. B. (1973). Exposure, context, and interpersonal attraction.* Journal of Personality and Social Psychology, 25, *234–242.)*

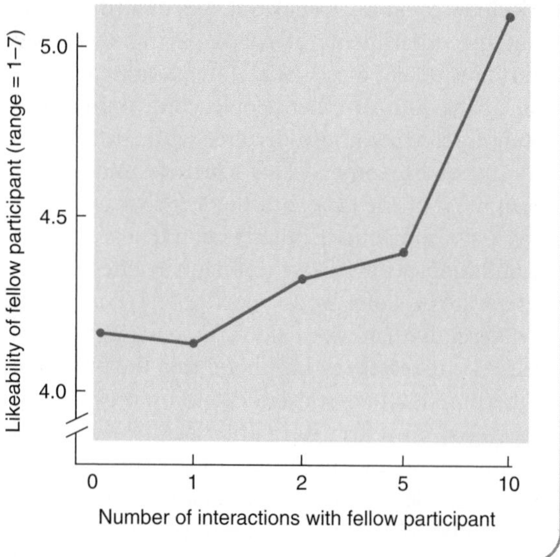


**Similarity** Another factor that influences interpersonal attraction is similarity—similarity in looks, interests, and attitudes (e.g., Byrne, 1997). There is a tendency for people in close relationships to be similar in physical attractiveness. Some research indicates that couples who are mismatched in this respect are the most likely to break up (White, 1980). Although we might think that people would seek the most attractive partners that they could find, people tend to fear rejection and ridicule. Men especially tend to be afraid of approaching attractive women (Bernstein, Stephenson, Snyder, & Wicklund, 1983).

Couples also tend to be similar in personality, attitudes, and intelligence (Brehm, 1992), and the greater the similarity between the partners, the more enduring their relationship (Hatfield & Rapson, 1993). Presumably, a person who shares our attitudes is likely to approve of us when we express them. Also, having friends who have similar attitudes guarantees that our opinions are likely to find a consensus; we will not often find ourselves in the unpleasant position of saying something that brings disapproval from other people.

Similarity of attitudes is not the only factor determining the strength of interpersonal attraction. Other kinds of similarities are also important, such as age, occupational status, and ethnic background. Friends tend to have similar backgrounds as well as similar attitudes.

**Physical Appearance** People commonly judge each other to some extent on the basis of a characteristic that is supposed to be only skin deep—physical appearance. In general, we are more attracted to good-looking people than to people who are not so good-looking (Albright, Kenny, & Malloy, 1988). In fact, there is a very strong stereotype favouring the beautiful among us (e.g., K. K. Dion, 1986; Dion, Berscheid, & Walster, 1972). This is known as the "what is beautiful is good" stereotype. In Canada and the United States, for example, beautiful people are seen as happier, more intelligent, and more socially skilled than those who are less physically attractive (e.g., Eagly, Ashmore, Makhijani, & Longo, 1991).

This bias extends to at least one Eastern culture, although there are interesting differences. Wheeler and Kim (1997) found that university students in Korea shared most of the biases shown by North Americans, but also saw beautiful people as more trustworthy and concerned for others, differences not found in North America. In addition, Korean students did not share the North American bias toward perceiving beautiful people as more self-assertive and dominant than plainer people. Recall our earlier discussions that in collectivist cultures (such as Korea), great value is placed on the interconnectedness of people, whereas independence and personal achievement are more valued in individualist cultures (such as Canada and the United States). The differences in beauty stereotype between cultures lines up rather well with these differences in orientation.

Walster, Aronson, Abrahams, and Rottman (1966) studied the behavioural effects of physical appearance at a dance at which university students were paired by a computer. Midway through the evening, the researchers asked the students to rate the attraction they felt toward their partners and to say whether they thought they would like to see them in the future. For both sexes, the only characteristic that correlated with attraction was physical appearance. Intelligence, grades, and personality variables seemed to have no significant effect.

When we publicly discuss the factors important to us in dating partners, we usually do not dwell on physical attractiveness. Why? One important possibility is that we are perfectly aware that physical attractiveness strongly affects our choices and desires, but social norms and common wisdom (e.g., "beauty is only skin deep") inhibit us from dwelling on the importance of beauty. We do not want to appear to be superficial. Another possibility is that although we are aware of the beauty stereotype, we do not believe that it affects our own decisions and behaviour—it's just something that influences other people. Hadjistavropoulos and Genest (1994) examined these possibilities by comparing normal questioning techniques with a special measurement system that encourages honest answering. Participants who answered in the face of a device that supposedly could detect honest responding admitted a stronger influence of physical attractiveness on their reactions to others than did participants who answered under normal circumstances.

Physically attractive people seem to benefit in many ways from this stereotype. Being good-looking can open many doors. But would it surprise you to know that most elements of the stereotype are wrong? Being beautiful guarantees none of the correspondingly beautiful qualities (Feingold, 1992).

**Physiological Arousal** People may become attracted to one another under almost any circumstances. Hollywood often idealizes romantic relationships by showing us how they unfold under the most dire situations. Against a backdrop of war, earthquake, shipwreck, alien invasion, or jealous rivals, the spark of love ignites between the hero and heroine, who will then brave all difficulties to keep their love alive. Melodramatic, perhaps . . . yet, as Walster and Berscheid (1971) have put it, "Passion sometimes develops in conditions that would seem more likely to provoke aggression and hatred" (p. 47). How is it that love can spring forth from a less-than-optimal beginning?

Consider a study conducted by Dutton and Aron (1974), who had an attractive young woman briefly interview male university students as they walked across North Vancouver's Capilano suspension bridge. The bridge is about 1.5 m wide, 137 m long, and 70 m high; it sways and wobbles impressively as you walk across it. The same woman interviewed control participants on a more conventional, sturdy bridge spanning a 3 m drop. The interviewer gave her telephone number to all participants with the suggestion that they call her if they wanted to discuss the experiment further.

The men who were interviewed on the suspension bridge appeared to find the woman more attractive than did those who were interviewed on the ordinary bridge—they were much more likely to telephone her later. These results suggest that the anxiety produced by walking across the suspension bridge increased the men's attraction toward the woman. Dutton and Aron (1974) explained their findings using attribution theory: A man experiences increased arousal in the presence of a woman; he attributes it to the most obvious stimulus—the woman—and concludes that he is attracted to her. Later, he acts on this conclusion by telephoning her. Arousal—pleasant or aversive—tends to increase interpersonal attraction between men and women. This is not a new idea. An ancient Roman expert advised men to take their women to the Colosseum to see the gladiators fight because the experience would increase their romantic ardour.

Interpersonal attraction is very complex. It develops under many different conditions—not always under ideal conditions and not just when one person helps reduce the other's fear or anxiety. In between these two extremes lies a vast middle ground, which awaits more research. As we will see next, there is also much to learn about how interpersonal attraction is transformed into love.

## Loving

The relationships we have with others are generally marked by two different kinds of emotion: **liking**, a feeling of personal regard, intimacy, and esteem toward another person, and **loving**, a combination of liking and a deep sense of attachment to another person. Loving someone does not necessarily entail romance. You may have several close friends whom you love dearly yet have no desire to be involved with romantically.

Romantic love, also called **passionate love**, is an emotionally intense desire for sexual union with another person (Hatfield, 1988). Feeling romantic love generally involves experiencing five closely intertwined elements: a desire for intimacy with another, feeling passion for that person, preoccupation with thoughts of that person, emotional dependence on that person, and feeling wonderful if that person feels romantic love toward you and dejected if not.

**liking** A feeling of personal regard, intimacy, and esteem toward another person.

**loving** A combination of liking and a deep sense of attachment to, intimacy with, and caring for another person.

**passionate love** An emotional, intense desire for sexual union with another person; also called romantic love.

**TABLE 15•4 Sternberg's Theory of Love**

According to Sternberg, love is based on different combinations of intimacy, passion, and commitment. These elements may combine to form eight different kinds of relationships.

| | Intimacy | Passion | Commitment |
|---|---|---|---|
| Non-love | | | |
| Liking | ***** | | |
| Infatuated love | | ***** | |
| Empty love | | | ***** |
| Romantic love | ***** | ***** | |
| Companionate love | ***** | | ***** |
| Fatuous love | | ***** | ***** |
| Consummate love | ***** | ***** | ***** |

*Source: After Sternberg, R. J. (1986). A triangular theory of love.* Psychological Bulletin, 93, *119–135.*

***** indicates that element is present in the relationship; a blank space ( ) indicates that element is not present or is present in low quantities in the relationship.

▲ *Growing older need not be a barrier to interpersonal attraction.*

"Falling in love" and "being in love" are common expressions that people use to describe their passionate desires for one another. Passionate love may occur at almost any time during the life cycle, although people involved in long-term cohabitation or marriages seem to experience a qualitatively different kind of love. The partners may still make passionate love to one another, but passion is no longer the defining characteristic of the relationship. This kind of love is called **companionate love** and is characterized by a deep, enduring affection and caring for another. Companionate love is also marked by a mutual sense of *commitment*, or a strong desire to maintain the relationship. This desire manifests itself in many ways. For example, people will downplay the attractiveness of other members of the opposite sex (Gonzaga et al., 2008). How passionate love develops into companionate love is presently an unanswered question, although odds are that the sort of intimacy that punctuates romantic love is still a major force in the relationship. An important feature of intimacy is *self-disclosure*, or the ability to share deeply private feelings and thoughts with another. Indeed, part of loving another is feeling comfortable sharing deeply personal aspects of yourself with that person.

Robert Sternberg has developed a theory of how intimacy, passion, and commitment may combine to produce liking and several different forms of love (Barnes & Sternberg, 1997; Sternberg, 1988b). (See **Table 15•4**.) According to this theory, liking involves only intimacy, infatuation involves only passion, and empty love involves only commitment. Combining any two of these elements produces still other kinds of love. Romantic love entails both intimacy and passion but no commitment. Companionate love entails both intimacy and commitment but no passion. Fatuous love (a kind of love marked by complacency in the relationship) entails both passion and commitment but no intimacy. The highest form of love, consummate love, contains all three elements.

Sternberg's theory, of course, is descriptive. It characterizes different kinds of love, but it does not explain the origins of love. What function has love served in the evolution of our species? The answer can be summed up very succinctly: procreation and child rearing. Although love of any kind for another person is not a necessary requirement for sexual intercourse, a man and a woman who passionately love each other are more likely to have sex than are a man and a woman who do not. If their union produces a child, then love serves another function—it increases the likelihood that both parents will share in the responsibilities of child rearing. Our capacity for loving, then, contributes in very practical ways to the continued existence of our species.

**companionate love** Love that is characterized by a deep, enduring affection and caring for another person, accompanied by a strong desire to maintain the relationship.

## Interim Summary

### Interpersonal Attraction and Loving

Although the factors that influence interpersonal attraction are complex and not yet fully understood, they all appear to involve social reinforcement. People learn to act in ways that reinforce friends and lovers in order to maintain and strengthen their ties with them. Attraction is increased by positive evaluation of oneself by the other person, familiarity, similarity, shared opinions, and physical good looks.

Attribution also undoubtedly plays an important role in interpersonal attraction. For example, our beliefs about why other people act as they do affect how much we like them and are attracted to them. Early research seemed to indicate that anxiety could influence interpersonal attraction through the attribution process. Yet a careful analysis suggests that the reason romantic bonds can be strengthened by adversity involves negative reinforcement. The presence of another person makes an unpleasant situation more tolerable, and this reduction in strength of an aversive stimulus is reinforcing.

Loving someone entails a combination of liking and strong feelings of attachment. Sternberg's theory of love describes how different combinations of intimacy, passion, and commitment give rise to liking and to different kinds of love. For example, romantic love involves both intimacy and passion, but infatuation involves only passion.

From an evolutionary standpoint, love serves both procreative and child-rearing functions. Sociobiologists have observed that men and women differ with respect to the social-cognitive cues they use when selecting potential mates. Men prefer potential mates to be young and physically attractive because young, attractive women tend to be fertile. Women prefer potential mates to control socio-economic resources because these resources are important to supporting the family unit.

**QUESTIONS TO CONSIDER**

1. To what kinds of people are you most attracted? What factors, internal or external, appear to be most important in your relationships?
2. Is Sternberg's theory of love an accurate account of your own experience with different kinds of love? Are there kinds of love that you have experienced that are not included in his theory?

E P I L O G U E

## Lowballing Revisited

If you are like most students, you probably found this chapter highly engaging because social cognition, presentation, and social interaction—not to mention interpersonal attraction and, possibly, mate selection—are predominant aspects of your everyday life. In addition, the application of social psychological principles will help you make informed decisions as a consumer and help you avoid the common tricks and traps used by salespeople.

The chapter began with a first-person account of an application of a social psychological concept—in this case, lowballing. The technique takes a number of forms, and therefore another example of lowballing is a fitting way to end our discussion of social psychology.

My friend recently went to buy out her lease at a car dealership. As she was about to pay, she noticed an additional $300 "administrative" charge on top of the previously agreed-upon price. When she asked about this charge, the salesperson said that it was to cover paperwork and the bill of sale. My friend knew that the bill of sale would cost roughly $12 and asked the salesperson to explain the other $288. He replied, "Well, it covers our administrative costs. It's something that everyone has to pay; there is nothing I can do." She refused to pay, decided to do some research, and found that other car dealerships were charging an administrative fee that ranged anywhere from $168 to $400. She called the dealership's head office to ask for an explanation and was told that she did not have to pay the $300 fee. The person she spoke with at head office apologized and said that the company tried to monitor individual dealerships as best as it could.

When she returned to the dealership, one last attempt was made to have her pay the administrative charge. A new salesperson greeted her and said that he would take care of her account. He presented her with the buy-out paperwork and it still included the $300 fee. My friend patiently explained the situation and said that, again, she was not going to pay this amount. At that point, the salesperson became agitated and insisted that all of their customers must pay the administrative fee and that she had been misinformed by head office. He said that he would personally call head office and get to the bottom of it—which, of course, he didn't. After much hassle, my friend was finally able to buy out her lease at the originally agreed-upon price.

Hopefully, the lessons learned in this chapter can help you with your next major purchase, and you will remember to be highly skeptical of any administrative fees!

## Canadian Connections to Research in This Chapter


Baker, C. (2004, February 22). Groupthink at the core of AdScam. *Winnipeg Free Press.* (Winnipeg Free Press: www.winnipegfreepress.com)

Bassili, J. N. (1995). Response latency and the accessibility of voting intentions: What contributes to accessibility and how it affects vote choice. *Personality and Social Psychology Bulletin, 21*, 686–695. (University of Toronto: www.utoronto.ca)

Berry, J. W. (2003). Origins of cross-cultural similarities and differences in human behavior: An ecocultural perspective. In A. Toomela (Ed.), *Cultural guidance in the development of the human mind: Advances in child development within culturally structured environments.* Westport, CT: Ablex Publishing. (Queen's University: www.queensu.ca)

Brown, R. D., & Bassili, J. N. (2002). Spontaneous trait associations and the case of the superstitious banana. *Journal of Experimental Social Psychology, 38*, 87–92. (University of Toronto: www.utoronto.ca)

Campbell, J. D., Trapnell, P. D., Heine, S. J., Katz, I. M., Lavalee, L. F., & Lehman, D. R. (1996). Self-concept clarity: Measurement, personality correlates and cultural boundaries. *Journal of Personality and Social Psychology, 70*, 141–156. (University of British Columbia: www.ubc.ca)

Chaiken, S. (1979). Communicator's physical attractiveness and persuasion. *Journal of Personality and Social Psychology, 37*, 1387–1397. (University of Toronto: www.utoronto.ca)

Dion, K. K. (1986). Stereotyping based on physical attractiveness: Issues and conceptual perspectives. In C. P. Herman, M. P. Zanna, & E. T. Higgins (Eds.), *Physical appearance, stigma, and social behavior: The Ontario symposium.* Hillsdale, NJ: Lawrence Erlbaum Press. (University of Toronto: www.utoronto.ca)

Dion, K. K., Berscheid, E., & Walster, E. (1972). What is beautiful is good. *Journal of Personality and Social Psychology, 24*, 285–290. (University of Toronto: www.utoronto.ca)

Dion, K. L. (2003). Prejudice, racism, and discrimination. In T. Millon & M. J. Lerner (Eds.), *Handbook of psychology: Personality and social psychology* (Vol. 5). New York: John Wiley & Sons, Inc. (University of Toronto: www.utoronto.ca)

Kenneth Dion received the Donald O. Hebb Award for Distinguished Contributions to Psychology as a Science from the Canadian Psychological Association in 2001.

Dutton, D. G., & Aron, A. P. (1974). Some evidence of heightened sexual attraction under conditions of high anxiety. *Journal of Personality and Social Psychology, 30*, 510–517. (University of British Columbia: www.ubc.ca)

Enzle, M. E., & Schopflocher, D. (1978). Instigation of attribution processes by attribution questions. *Personality and Social Psychology Bulletin, 4*, 595–599. (University of Alberta: www.ualberta.ca)

Guimond, S., & Dube, L. (1989). Representation of the causes of economic inferiority of French-speaking Canadians from Quebec. *Canadian Journal of Behavioural Science, 21*, 28–39. (Royal Military College of Canada: www.rmc.ca)

Haddock, G., Zanna, M. P., & Esses, V. M. (1994). The (limited) role of trait-laden stereotypes in predicting attitudes toward native peoples. *British Journal of Social Psychology, 33*, 83–106. (University of Waterloo: www.uwaterloo.ca)

Hadjistavropoulos, T., & Genest, M. (1994). The underestimation of the role of physical attractiveness in dating preferences: Ignorance or taboo? *Canadian Journal of Behavioural Science, 26*, 298–318. (University of British Columbia: www.ubc.ca)

Hafer, C. L. (2000a). Do innocent victims threaten the belief in a just world? Evidence from a modified Stroop Task. *Journal of Personality and Social Psychology, 79*, 165–173. (Brock University: www.brocku.ca)

Hafer, C. L. (2000b). Investment in long-term goals and commitment to just means drive the need to believe in a just world. *Personality and Social Psychology Bulletin, 26*, 1059–1073. (Brock University: www.brocku.ca)

Hafer, C. L. (2002). Why we reject innocent victims. In M. Ross & D. T. Miller (Eds.), *The justice motive in everyday life.* New York: Cambridge University Press. (Brock University: www.brocku.ca)

Hazelwood, J. D., & Olson, J. M. (1986). Covariation information, causal questioning, and interpersonal behavior. *Journal of Experimental Social Psychology, 22*, 276–291. (University of Western Ontario: www.uwo.ca)

Heine, S. J. (2001). Self as cultural product: An examination of East Asian and North American selves. *Journal of Personality, 69*, 881–906. (University of British Columbia: www.ubc.ca)

Heine, S. J., Kitayama, S., Lehman, D. R., Takata, T., Ide, E., Leung, C., & Matsumoto, H. (2001). Divergent consequences of success and failure in Japan and North America: An investigation of self-improving motivations and malleable selves. *Journal of Personality and Social Psychology, 81*, 599–615. (University of British Columbia: www.ubc.ca)

Knox, R. E., & Inkster, J. A. (1968). Postdecision dissonance at post time. *Journal of Personality and Social Psychology, 8*, 310–323. (University of British Columbia: www.ubc.ca)

Krebs, D. L., & Denton, K. (1997). Social illusions and self-deception: The evolution of biases in person perception. In J. A. Simpson & D. T. Kenrick (Eds.), *Evolutionary social psychology.* Mahway, NJ: Lawrence Erlbaum Associates, Publishers. (Simon Fraser University: www.sfu.ca)

Kunda, Z. (1990). The case for motivated reasoning. *Psychological Bulletin, 108*, 480–498. (University of Waterloo: www.uwaterloo.ca)

Kunda, Z. (1999). *Social cognition: Making sense of people.* Cambridge, MA: The MIT Press. (University of Waterloo: www.uwaterloo.ca)

Kunda, Z., & Oleson, K. (1997). When exceptions prove the rule: How extremity of deviance determines deviants' impact on stereotypes. *Journal of Personality and Social Psychology, 72*, 965–979. (University of Waterloo: www.uwaterloo.ca)

Kunda, Z., & Sinclair, L. (1999). Motivated reasoning with stereotypes: Activation, application, and inhibition. *Psychological Inquiry, 10*, 12–22. (University of Waterloo: www.uwaterloo.ca)

Lehman, D. R., Chiu, C.-Y., & Schaller, M. (2004). Psychology and culture. *Annual Review of Psychology, 55*, 689–714. (University of British Columbia: www.ubc.ca)

Lerner, M. J. (1980). *The belief in a just world.* New York: Plenum Press. (University of Waterloo: www.uwaterloo.ca)

McFarland, C., & Miller, D. T. (1990). Judgments of self-other similarity: Just like other people, only more so. *Personality and Social Psychology Bulletin, 16,* 475–484. (Simon Fraser University: www.sfu.ca)

McGregor, I., Newby-Clark, I. R., & Zanna, M. P. (1999). "Remembering" dissonance: Simultaneous accessibility of inconsistent cognitive elements moderates epistemic discomfort. In E. Harmon-Jones & J. Mills (Eds.), *Cognitive dissonance: Progress on a pivotal theory in social psychology.* Washington, DC: American Psychological Association. (University of Waterloo: www.uwaterloo.ca)

Miller, D. T., & Ross, M. (1975). Self-serving biases in the attribution of causality: Fact or fiction? *Psychological Bulletin, 82,* 213–225. (University of Waterloo: www.uwaterloo.ca)

Olson, J. M., Roese, N. J., & Zanna, M. P. (1996). Expectancies. In E. T. Higgins & A. W. Kruglanski (Eds.), *Social psychology: Handbook of basic principles.* New York: Guilford Press. (University of Waterloo: www.uwaterloo.ca)

Sande, G. N., Goethals, G. R., & Radloff, C. E. (1988). Perceiving one's own traits and others: The multifaceted self. *Journal of Personality and Social Psychology, 54,* 13–20. (University of Manitoba: www.umanitoba.ca)

Zanna, M. P., & Rempel, J. K. (1988). Attitudes: A new look at an old concept. In D. Bar-Tal & A. W. Kruglanski (Eds.), *The social psychology of knowledge.* Cambridge, UK: Cambridge University Press. (University of Waterloo: www.uwaterloo.ca)

Professor Zanna received the Donald O. Hebb Award for Distinguished Contributions to Psychology as a Science from the Canadian Psychological Association in 1993 and was elected Fellow of the Royal Society of Canada in 1999.

## Suggestions for Further Reading

Baron, R. A., Byrne, D., & Watson, G. (1998). *Exploring social psychology* (2nd Canadian ed.). Scarborough, ON: Allyn and Bacon Canada.

This excellent and very readable text describes all aspects of social psychology.

Ross, L., & Nisbett, R. E. (1991). *The person and the situation: Perspectives of social psychology.* New York: McGraw-Hill.

This book describes the variables that influence our causal attributions and the interaction between persons and situations.

Smith, P. B., & Bond, M. H. (1999). *Social psychology across cultures: Analysis and perspectives* (2nd ed.). Boston, MA: Allyn and Bacon.

This short paperback presents cross-cultural perspectives on many of the topics discussed in this chapter. The book is written clearly and contains interesting insights into how cultural variables influence social behaviour.

Cialdini, R. B. (1993). *Influence: Science and practice* (3rd ed.). New York: HarperCollins.

Cialdini's book is written for a general audience. It provides a fascinating, well-written, and often humorous account of the ways in which people influence each other.

Milgram, S. (1974). *Obedience to authority.* New York: Harper & Row.

In this book, Milgram explains his rationale for conducting his controversial obedience research, describes in detail the research itself, and, finally, ponders its significance in light of moral and ethical considerations.

16

# Lifestyle, Stress, and Health

# CHAPTER OUTLINE

## Cultural Evolution: Lifestyle Choices and Consequences

Our lifestyles have been shaped by environmental changes and influenced by cultural evolution and our biology. Lifestyles significantly affect individual survival.

## Healthy and Unhealthy Lifestyles

Nutrition • Physical Fitness • Cigarette Smoking • *Then and Now: Selling Smoking* • Drinking Alcoholic Beverages • Sexually Transmitted Diseases and AIDS

In the long run, healthy behaviours enhance longevity and quality of life. Unhealthy behaviours, such as eating poorly, smoking, excessive use of alcohol, and practising unsafe sex, tend to affect our lives negatively in the long run but can affect them "positively" in the short run. Unhealthy behaviours are acquired and maintained because of their immediately reinforcing effects.

## Unhealthy Lifestyles Are Preventable: Self-Control

We are often faced with a choice between an immediate, small reward and a delayed, but larger reward. Prior commitment to a course of action that allows us to obtain the delayed but larger reward constitutes self-control.

## Stress and Health

The Biological Basis of Stress • Cognitive Appraisal and Stress • Stressful Lifestyles and Impaired Health

Our responses to stressful stimuli are governed by the autonomic nervous system, which produces changes in the activity of many organs, and by our perception of the extent to which a stimulus poses a threat to our physical or psychological well-being. Prolonged stress can lead to chronic heart disease, a breakdown of the immune system, which increases our susceptibility to infectious diseases, and, in some cases, an anxiety disorder called post-traumatic stress disorder. Personality variables, especially those involved in coping with stress, appear to be related to the development of cancer.

## Coping with Everyday Stress

Sources of Stress • Coping Styles and Strategies • Stress Inoculation Training

Stress can be caused by a wide variety of sources—positive experiences as well as negative ones. The levels of stress that we experience can be controlled by the use of specific coping strategies. Stress inoculation training is a form of stress management that teaches people how to develop and implement effective coping strategies for handling stressful situations before they occur.

# PROLOGUE

## Dealing with Alcohol Abuse

My future wife (let's call her "FW") lived in an up-down duplex when I met her. During an early visit to her place, she introduced me to the upstairs tenant, Leif. Leif was about 30, looked at times like he was 18, and much of the time acted like he was 15. But he could be totally engaging. He bounced around on the balls of his feet, and anytime he came downstairs to visit, a party threatened to break out.

Leif was a freelance interior designer who, through dumpster diving and much talent, had transformed his flat into a place of magic and fantasy. I have vivid images of billowing fabric, mosaic surfaces, golden highlights, and stars on the ceiling. He asked my opinion about a few of the projects he was working on for clients. By and large, I thought his ideas were wonderful.

Leif had problems, though. That first time I met him, he was sporting a nasty abrasion on his forehead. He had tripped, he said. He might have, but I soon became familiar with a pattern of injuries. Leif would go to the bar, get loaded, and eventually someone would feel obliged to beat him up. His eyes were blackened several times during the few months I knew him. Leif drank too much. He drank all the time.

Leif lost most of his contract jobs because of his drinking. He drank late, slept late, and was late at best with his work. Although his clients liked his ideas, they had to cut him loose in order to meet their own deadlines.

Slowly but surely, Leif's circle of friends narrowed. In the long run, his positive qualities could not fully compensate for his alcohol-induced irresponsibility, unpredictability, and neediness.

When all of this gelled for FW and me, we decided to do an "intervention." We chose a time when Leif was sober, and engaged him in straight talk. We told him how much we liked him and cared for him and how talented and valuable he was. We told him that he suffered from alcoholism and that there were choices to be made that only he could make. He could continue on the path he was on and be doomed to a lifetime of unhappiness, ill health, trouble, and disappointment. FW was even more specific—she told him that his very life was in danger. We discussed with him the common underpinnings of alcoholism, the resources available to him in our city, the first steps he needed to take, and how we would support him in that direction. We assured him that he could succeed. He passed on our advice and declined our help. We tried again later, with the same result.

After FW moved to my house, new tenants moved into her flat, and we lost track of Leif for a period of time. We stopped by FW's old place one day, though, to visit neighbours. We learned that Leif had recently endangered the lives of everyone in the house by turning on his gas oven without lighting it. An apparent suicide attempt. He had then disappeared into the night. Several months later we learned that he had been found dead on the side of a road, 1000 kilometres from friends and family, of a drug and alcohol overdose.

Throughout this book, we have seen that human behaviour and thought are the result of the interaction of biological and environmental variables. Psychology encompasses the study of this interaction and the application of the resulting knowledge to improving our lives. In this chapter, we wish to emphasize these points again with issues that may be closer to home for you—personal behaviours that have serious implications for your long-term physical health and your psychological well-being. The central theme of this chapter is that the particular behaviours that make up an individual's lifestyle have important consequences for that person's quality of life. As illustrated in the prologue, these consequences go beyond the individual; they also affect the lives of many others.

We will look first at how cultural evolution shapes our lives, especially in terms of the sorts of lifestyle choices we make. Next, we will study these choices as they relate to our personal health and safety. We will also discuss stress, its biological and psychological effects, and how to cope with it.

**cultural evolution** The adaptive change of a culture to recurrent environmental pressures.

# Cultural Evolution: Lifestyle Choices and Consequences

**Cultural evolution** is a culture's adaptive change to recurrent environmental pressures. Unlike biological evolution, which is driven by biological forces, cultural evolution is driven mainly by psychological forces. Cultural evolution is a product of human intellect and physical capacity, both of which have strong genetic components. As you may recall from Chapter 3, cultural evolution has been the guiding force behind social, cultural, and technical innovation in such areas as law, the arts, science, medicine, and engineering. As a culture faces new problems, solutions are proposed and tested. Solutions that work are passed from generation to generation through imitation, books, oral histories, and, most recently, in electronic forms—bits of information stored on computer chips. Some solutions are modified by future generations so that they work more effectively. Those that don't work are abandoned.

Cultural evolution has been the primary agent involved in shaping **lifestyle**, the aggregate behaviour of a person, or the way a person leads his or her life. The ways in which we interact with others, the kinds of work we pursue, the hobbies and personal interests we enjoy, the habits we develop, and the decision to marry and raise a family or remain single are characteristics of our lifestyles.

For our prehistoric ancestors, lifestyle was pretty much the same for everyone. When they were hungry, they hunted and gathered food; they walked or ran to get from one place to another; they worked hard to stay alive. Options about how to accomplish these tasks arose only as the pace of cultural evolution increased. That is, our ancestors learned more about creating more effective means of transportation, growing and storing food, and building homes from durable materials. Today, there is no predominant lifestyle; cultural evolution has afforded us the luxury of choosing among many alternatives. We can hunt or gather food if we want, but we can also buy it in grocery stores or go to restaurants. When we want to go somewhere, we can walk or run, but more often we ride on planes, trains, and automobiles. Most of us in Western cultures no longer worry only about how to stay alive; we now worry about how to spend our spare time, or about how to have more of it. Grocery stores, transportation, medicine, and leisure time are innovations spawned through cultural evolution.

Cultural evolution has resulted in a much higher standard of living than that of our prehistoric or even our relatively modern ancestors. However, cultural evolution has also produced threats to our health and safety. People can be hit and killed by cars and trucks. The manufacture of foods and other goods contributes to pollution, which may cause disease. Many of the chemical agents we use for lubrication and cleaning are poisonous. It falls as a personal responsibility to each of us to avoid these threats. Failure to do so carries the risk of injury or death.

Our contemporary lifestyles contain many threats to survival with which our ancestors did not have to deal. For example, the amount and kinds of food we eat and the excessive use of alcohol can lead to illness and, in some cases, premature death. In contrast, a healthy lifestyle can be viewed as one that ensures an individual's physical and psychological well-being. Typically, a healthy lifestyle includes, among other things, a nutritious diet, regular exercise, no use of tobacco, moderate use of alcohol, practice of safe sex, and even using seat belts in automobiles.

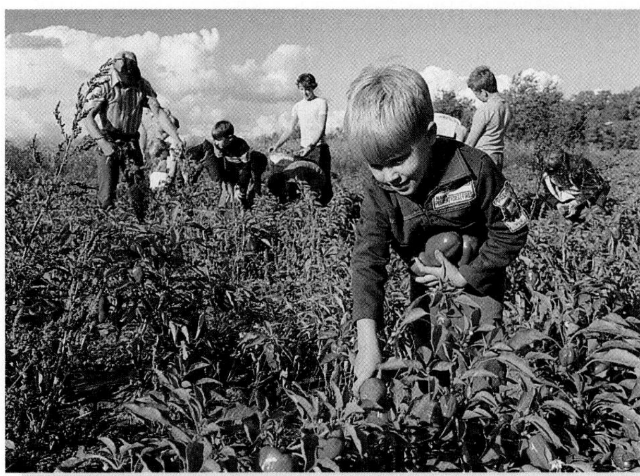

▲ *Cultural evolution affords us many choices in matters related to our survival. Although most of us prefer to buy our food at the supermarket, some people prefer to pick their food fresh from the field.*

Why do some of us maintain unhealthy lifestyles if doing so diminishes our physical and psychological well-being? How do we acquire those unhealthy behaviours in the first place? After all, they appear to work against the process of natural selection. The answer to this question is a complicated one, so I will offer only a general response here. Although the consequences of unhealthy lifestyle behaviours have obvious negative *biological* implications, the behaviours themselves can be acquired and maintained by both *biological* and *psychological* factors.

It is easy to misinterpret biological evolutionary theory and argue that genes that give rise to unhealthy lifestyles should eventually become extinct. Remember that natural selection operates on traits that affect the ability to reproduce. Most adaptations resulting from biological evolution concern only those relevant to surviving to sexual maturity, reproducing, and rearing offspring until they become self-sufficient. Many, if not most, of the consequences of unhealthy lifestyles—heart disease, cancer, and the other negative effects of poor nutrition, alcoholism, and smoking—do not appear until people are well beyond reproductive age. Thus, it may be that genes that promote many unhealthy lifestyles functionally are overlooked by biological evolution—they are just not relevant to reproduction.

The law of effect (see Chapter 7) undoubtedly plays a powerful role in cultural evolution, too: one that appears to be analogous to the role of natural selection in biological evolution. The law of effect states that behaviours that produce favourable consequences tend to be repeated, and those that produce unfavourable consequences tend not to be repeated. Cultural practices and customs that result in reinforcement tend to be maintained, if not elaborated. Exercising, eating

**lifestyle** The aggregate behaviour of a person; the way in which a person leads his or her life.

nutritious foods, getting sufficient rest, and other healthy behaviours are acquired and maintained because of the reinforcing consequences enjoyed by the people who practise them. How does the law of effect apply if unhealthy lifestyles have negative consequences?

Unfortunately, many unhealthy behaviours have *reinforcing consequences in the short run* and *damaging consequences in the long run*. Many unhealthy behaviours are maintained because they tend to be available on a version of revolving credit—instead of "buy now, pay later," it takes the form of "enjoy now, suffer later." Teens who smoke cigarettes receive immediate rewards—physiological and psychological pleasure and perhaps perceived acceptance from their peers. It is only many years later, when they are in their forties or fifties, that the life-threatening effects of smoking may appear. In the meantime, they have become physiologically addicted to the nicotine contained in the cigarette smoke. The law of effect partially accounts for why those who adopt unhealthy lifestyles are not weeded out through cultural evolution. As we've seen, the law of effect can actually work against us sometimes.

## Interim Summary

### Cultural Evolution: Lifestyle Choices and Consequences

Our lifestyles—the ways in which we interact with others; the kinds of work, hobbies, habits, and personal interests we pursue; and our decision to marry or remain single—are the results of the cumulative effects of cultural evolution on our society. Cultural evolution includes advances in technology and medicine and changes in social and cultural customs that are passed from one generation to the next. Although cultural evolution has improved our standard of living relative to that of our ancestors, it has also produced threats to our health and safety. These threats manifest themselves in particular lifestyle choices we make regarding our diet, physical activity, use of tobacco, alcohol and other drugs, sexual behaviour, and personal safety.

Biological evolution cannot weed out individuals who adopt unhealthy lifestyles because the consequences are not usually experienced until after people have passed their childbearing years. Many of the consequences of unhealthy behaviours are reinforcing in the short run but life threatening in the long run. Thus, unhealthy behaviours are acquired and maintained because of their immediately reinforcing effects. It is usually only after many years that the cumulative negative effects of these lifestyles threaten one's health.

**QUESTIONS TO CONSIDER**

1. What kinds of lifestyle choices have you made? Have they been generally healthy ones or unhealthy ones? What personal, social, and cultural factors influenced you to make the decisions you have?
2. How has the law of effect operated in lifestyle decisions you have made? Can you explain some of your habits—good, bad, or otherwise—in terms of their immediately reinforcing effects? If you have an unhealthy habit, and you know it is unhealthy, why do you continue to engage in it? What steps might you take to break this habit?

## Healthy and Unhealthy Lifestyles

A healthy lifestyle, you will recall, is one that enhances an individual's well-being—both physical and psychological—and an unhealthy lifestyle is one that diminishes physical and psychological well-being. Let's look at several elements that affect well-being: nutrition, physical fitness, tobacco use, alcohol abuse, and sexual practices.

### Nutrition

Until very recently, our species lived on a low-fat, high-fibre diet. Our ancestors lived mainly on fruits, vegetables, nuts, and lean meats. In the last 150 years or so, though, our diets have changed; they are now considerably higher in fats and lower in fibre, largely because of the consumption of processed foods, fried foods, and sweets. Although we eat foods like bananas, broccoli, and lean beef, we also consume foods like hot fudge sundaes, doughnuts, and fried chicken. Diets too high in saturated fats (those fats found in animal products and a few vegetable oils) and too low in fibre have been linked with specific health disorders, such as **coronary heart disease (CHD)**, the narrowing of blood vessels that supply nutrients to the heart, and **cancer**, a malignant and intrusive tumour that destroys body organs and tissue. Heart disease and stroke are the leading causes of death in developed countries (World Health Organization, 2003). Recent estimates indicate that approximately 36 percent of annual deaths in Canada are attributable to CHD, with cancer not far behind at 29 percent (Health Canada, 2000).

The chief culprit in CHD is **serum cholesterol**, a chemical that occurs naturally in the bloodstream, where it serves as a detoxifier. Cholesterol is also the source of lipid membranes of cells and steroid hormones. Thus, it is a vital substance. Cholesterol has two major forms: *HDL* (high-density lipoprotein) and *LDL* (low-density lipoprotein). HDL is sometimes

**coronary heart disease (CHD)** The narrowing of blood vessels that supply nutrients to the heart.
**cancer** A malignant, uncontrolled growth of cells that destroys surrounding tissue.
**serum cholesterol** A fat-like chemical found in the blood. One form (LDL) promotes the formation of atherosclerotic plaques. Another form (HDL) may protect against coronary heart disease.

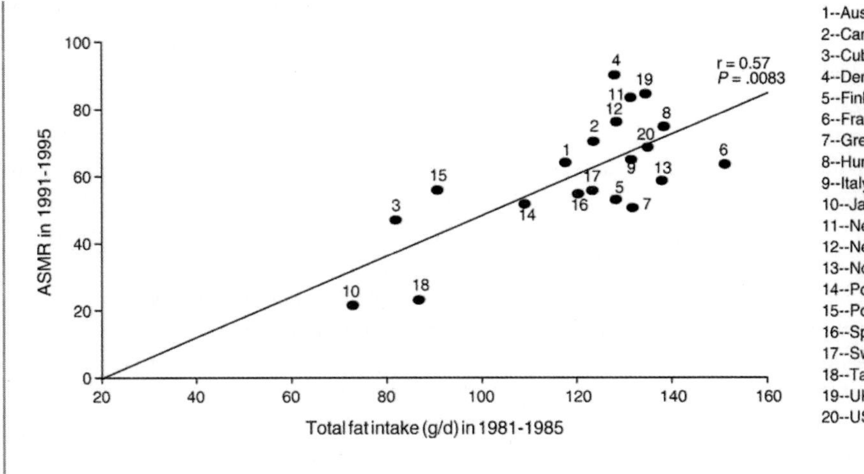


**FIGURE 16•1** The correlation between diet and breast cancer in women between the ages of 45 and 79. Nations whose citizens live on diets rich in fats face increased risk of death due to breast cancer (ASMR = age-standardized mortality rates).

*(Adapted from Liaw, Y. P., Chen, H. L., Cheng, C. W., & Huang, H. L. (2005). An international epidemiological study of breast cancer mortality and total fat intake in postmenopausal women.* Nutrition Research, *26(1), 68–73. Reprinted with permission from Elsevier. http://www.sciencedirect.com/science/journal/02715317)*

called "good" cholesterol because high levels are inversely associated with CHD; it seems to play a protective role. LDL is often called "bad" cholesterol because high levels are associated with the formation of atherosclerotic plaques, which clog arteries. It has been estimated that lowering serum cholesterol to acceptable levels by reducing fat intake would reduce adult deaths by 2 percent per year (Tosteson et al., 1997).

Cultures having the highest death rates due to breast cancer are those whose citizens consume relatively large amounts of fats (Cohen, 1987; Liaw, Chen, Cheng, & Huang, 2005). Research by Cohen (1987) indicated a strong correlation between mortality rates of breast cancer and fat consumption. Recent follow-up research by Liaw, Chen, Cheng, and Huang (2005) replicated Cohen's findings using post-menopausal women. **Figure 16•1** shows the correlation between death due to breast cancer and daily fat consumption for women between the ages of 45 and 79. As you can see, people in countries such as Canada and the United States have both relatively high fat intake and relatively high death rates due to breast cancer. In contrast, people in countries such as Japan and Thailand have both relatively low fat intake and relatively low death rates due to breast cancer. Remember, these data are correlational. We know there is a relationship between high fat intake and breast cancer, but with these data we cannot prove that high fat intake is the cause of the cancer.

Nutrition plays an important role in good health and is pivotal to a healthy lifestyle. Based on Cohen's work, we would seem likely to decrease our risk for both CHD and cancer by *choosing* to eat foods that are not only low in fat but also high in fibre. Fibre is an important dietary component that may help reduce LDL cholesterol levels. Which foods are low in fat but high in fibre? **Figure 16•2** provides the answer by showing the classes of foods and their recommended daily servings.

**FIGURE 16•2** Eating Well with Canada's Food Guide. The high and low numbers represent the appropriate range of servings per day for each food group. The amount of food you need every day falls somewhere within this range depending on a variety of factors such as sex, age, and activity level.

*(*Eating Well with Canada's Food Guide *(2007). Health Canada. Reproduced with the permission of the Minister of Public Works and Government Services Canada. http://www.hc-sc.gc.ca/fn-an/food-guide-aliment/index-eng.php)*

***Recommended Number of Food Guide Servings per Day***

| | Children | | | Teens | | Adults | | | |
|---|---|---|---|---|---|---|---|---|---|
| Age in Years | 2-3 | 4-8 | 9-13 | 14-18 | | 19-50 | | 51+ | |
| Sex | Girls and Boys | | | Females | Males | Females | Males | Females | Males |
| *Vegetables and Fruit* | 4 | 5 | 6 | 7 | 8 | 7-8 | 8-10 | 7 | 7 |
| *Grain Products* | 3 | 4 | 6 | 6 | 7 | 6-7 | 8 | 6 | 7 |
| *Milk and Alternatives* | 2 | 2 | 3-4 | 3-4 | 3-4 | 2 | 2 | 3 | 3 |
| *Meat and Alternatives* | 1 | 1 | 1-2 | 2 | 3 | 2 | 3 | 2 | 3 |

The chart above shows how many Food Guide Servings you need from each of the four food groups every day.

Having the amount and type of food recommended and following the tips in *Canada's Food Guide* will help:

- Meet your needs for vitamins, minerals and other nutrients.
- Reduce your risk of obesity, type 2 diabetes, heart disease, certain types of cancer and osteoporosis.
- Contribute to your overall health and vitality.

Many of our favourite foods are high in fat and low in fibre. The immediate effect of eating these foods is to delight the palate, but in the long run more serious consequences may occur: poor health, obesity, and possibly even death. Why might we prefer high-fat foods and sweets? In the past, our ancestors who faced starvation would be best served by eating fat, which provides high caloric value. In addition, sweet tastes usually indicate that food is safe, not poisonous. Thus, preferences for high-fat foods and for sweets were adaptive. These preferences have been passed genetically along to us, although because our living conditions differ from those of our ancestors, they are not always adaptive now. For example, to many people, the appeal of a nice snack of poutine and a few doughnuts is far greater than that of a less risky tofu burger and an apple. In the long run, a diet centred on sweet and fatty foods is unhealthy.

## Physical Fitness

Our ancestors were probably in better physical shape than most of us are today. Hunting, gathering, and a nomadic existence ensured plenty of exercise. Most people today lead more sedentary lives. They may get little exercise other than walking to and from their cars. Like high-fat, low-fibre diets, lack of exercise is correlated with increased risk of CHD (Peters et al., 1983; Powell, Thompson, Caspersen, & Kendrick, 1987). In fact, people who engage in exercise at least twice a week are 41 percent less likely to develop CHD than people who do not exercise at all (Sundquist, Qvist, Johansson, & Sundquist, 2005). People who exercise regularly appear to accumulate less body fat and to be less vulnerable to the negative effects of stress (Brown, 1991; Hoffman, 1997).

Kaplan (2000) has summarized the extensive research literature as showing that physical fitness decreases the risk of death due to a wide variety of causes, including diabetes mellitus, CHD, and cystic fibrosis. According to Ralph Paffenbarger, a noted epidemiologist who has devoted his career to studying CHD and cancer, people who exercise regularly are likely to live longer (Paffenbarger, Hyde, Wing, & Hsieh, 1986). His evidence comes from a long-term longitudinal study of the lifestyles of 17 000 Harvard University alumni. He periodically questioned his participants about their exercise patterns (type of exercise, frequency, and so on) and physical health. Here is a sample of his results:

1. During the first 16 years of surveillance, 1413 of the original 17 000 participants died, 45 percent from CHD and 32 percent from cancer. Significantly more of these deaths occurred in participants who had led sedentary lives.
2. Alumni who reported that they exercised the equivalent of 50 to 55 km of running or walking per week faced *half* the risk of dying prematurely as that faced by those who reported exercising the equivalent of 10 or fewer km per week.
3. On average, those who exercised moderately (an equivalent of 30 km running or walking per week) lived about two years longer than those who exercised less than the equivalent of 10 km.

**aerobic exercise** Physical activity that expends considerable energy, increases blood flow and respiration, and thereby stimulates and strengthens the heart and lungs and increases the body's efficient use of oxygen.

Of course, these results do not mean that everyone who exercises regularly will live an extra two years. However, because regular exercise reduces high blood pressure, increases lung capacity, and decreases the ratio of bad (LDL) cholesterol to good (HDL) cholesterol, Paffenbarger's results suggest that regular exercise engenders good health. Moreover, recent research indicates that prolonged exercise activates dopamine (Hoffman, 1997), an endorphin that helps reduce negative emotions and promote positive ones (DePue et al., 1994).

According to Kenneth Cooper, aerobic exercises such as running, walking, bicycling, and swimming are superior to other forms of exercise for improving cardiovascular health (Cooper, 1968, 1985). **Aerobic exercises** are those that expend considerable energy, increase blood flow and respiration, and thereby stimulate and strengthen the heart and lungs and increase the body's efficiency in using oxygen. According to Cooper (1985), running at least 5 km in less than 20 minutes 4 times a week (or any equivalent aerobic exercise) significantly increases cardiovascular health. One study showed that aerobic exercise had an additional benefit: reduced heart response to mental stress (Kubitz & Landers, 1993). Two groups of students who had not exercised for at least three months prior to the study were divided into two groups. One group rode an exercycle 3 times a week for 40 minutes for 8 weeks; the other group did not perform any aerobic exercises. At the end of the eight-week period, both groups were given timed colour perception and math tests in order to provoke moderate stress reactions. Students who participated in the aerobic exercise program showed lower absolute heart rates in response to the tests than did the students who did not exercise. Bray and Born (2004) provided further evidence that exercise is beneficial for students. The researchers found that students who reported lower levels of physical activity also reported higher levels of fatigue and tension. Further research indicates that low physical activity is associated with increased stress levels and increased perceived hassles (Nguyen-Michel, Unger, Hamilton, & Spruijt-Metz, 2006). In contrast, students who exercise report an increase in self-esteem and well-being (Ensel & Lin, 2004). Unfortunately, while nearly two-thirds of high school students reported adequate levels of exercise, this figure drops to less than half during the first eight weeks of university. Does this ring a bell with you? If it does, keep in mind that students who do not exercise are twice as likely to be off to the doctor's office than active students (Bray & Kwan, 2006).

Although exercise levels tend to decline for students in their first year of university, aerobic exercise has become a common activity for millions of people throughout the world. People are much more likely to walk, jog, cycle, and take part in other aerobic forms of exercise than they were prior to research that demonstrated the many health benefits of aerobic activity. It is important to continue to keep physically fit later in life. Starkweather (2007) found that people between the ages of 60 and 90 who exercised reported improvements in mood, stress levels, and overall quality of life. The fact that work like Cooper's could have such a profound effect on the everyday activities of people testifies to the power of scientific research in producing positive changes in lifestyle. In the next section, we will see similar results: Recent research on the hazards of cigarette smoking has helped reduce the number of people who smoke.

## Cigarette Smoking

Although tobacco products have been used in one form or another for many years, only in the last few decades have we discovered just how harmful they can be to one's health. In Canada, the expected number of premature deaths among lifelong smokers was found to be nearly twice that expected among people who have never smoked (Health Canada, 2007). In addition to these health risks, people who use tobacco also face increased risks of bronchitis, emphysema, and strokes. We know that the severity of these risks is directly related to the amount of carbon monoxide and tars contained in cigarette smoke. Non-smokers share the health risks created by cigarette smoking. By now, almost everyone is familiar with the problem of *passive smoking*, the inhalation of smoke from others' cigarettes. In 1981, Hirayama showed that non-smoking wives of husbands who smoked cigarettes were more at risk of developing lung cancer than were non-smoking wives of non-smoking husbands. Since that time, scores of studies have replicated this effect (e.g., Brennan et al., 2004; Hackshaw, Law, & Wald, 1997; Zhong, Goldberg, Parent, & Hanley, 2000) and have documented many other health risks attributable to breathing others' smoke (Steenland, 1999). We know, for example, that passive smoking is related to coronary heart disease (He et al., 1999; Leone et al., 2004; Steenland, Thun, Lally, & Heath, 1997), to an increased risk of brain hemorrhage (Anderson et al., 2004), and to nasal and sinus cancer (Benninger, 1999). Children are particularly susceptible to the effects of second-hand smoke. In addition to the risks of cancer and heart disease, children who live in homes where adults smoke are more likely to develop middle-ear disease (Adair-Bischoff & Sauve, 1998), lower respiratory tract infections (Li, Peat, Xuan, & Berry, 1999), and an increase in sensitivity to allergies (Kramer et al., 2004). And let's not forget Fido and Fluffy. Pets are at risk from passive smoking, too (Bertone, Snyder, & Moore, 2003; Rief, Bruns, & Lower, 1998). Given the health risks of smoking and the fact that people today are more knowledgeable about these risks, it is surprising that smoking is still as popular as it is. **Table 16•1** shows the prevalence of cigarette smoking by age and sex in Canada for 2007. Despite some encouraging declines in the rate of smoking over the last decade, the death toll from tobacco products continues to overshadow that caused by automobile accidents and other premature causes of death.

**TABLE 16•1 Prevalence of Smoking by Age and Sex in Canada**

| Age Range | Males (%) | Females (%) |
|---|---|---|
| 15–19 | 14.8 | 15.2 |
| 20–24 | 27.4 | 21.4 |
| 25–34 | 24.5 | 18.6 |
| 35–44 | 23.5 | 18.7 |
| 45–54 | 23.3 | 21.1 |
| 55+ | 14.9 | 10.3 |

*Source: Health Canada (2007).* Canadian Tobacco Use Monitoring Survey, 2007. *http://www.hc-sc.gc.ca/hl-vs/tobac-tabac/research-recherche/stat/ctums-esutc_2007_e.html*

Why do people—especially adolescents—begin smoking? We know that peer pressure strongly contributes to the acquisition of the smoking habit during adolescence (Hall & Valente, 2007; Harakeh, 2007; Hayes & Plowfield, 2007). As well, adolescents who have favourable impressions of a smoker are likely to imitate that person's actions, including smoking. Smoking uptake among adolescents is strongly affected by having a best friend who smokes (e.g., Aloise-Young, Graham, & Hansen, 1994; Hirschman, Leventhal, & Glynn, 1984). There is also good evidence of intergenerational transmission of smoking, particularly of a positive relationship between mother and child smoking patterns (Chassin, Presson, Rose, & Sherman, 1998; Nichols, Graber, Brooks-Gunn, & Botvin, 2004).

Cigarette manufacturers in the United States capitalize on the propensity to imitate respected others: They portray smoking as a glamorous, mature, independent, and sometimes rebellious behaviour. Billboard and magazine advertisements generally portray cigarette smokers as young, healthy, attractive, and exciting people. It is difficult to assess the impact of such advertising on smoking uptake. Perhaps the best indicator available comes from work by J. P. Pierce and his colleagues. These researchers have found a strong positive relationship between amount of exposure to cigarette advertising and smoking among adolescents in the United States (Pierce et al., 1998). Pierce has also found another interesting relationship between advertising and smoking in the United States. Smoking uptake among male youths increases after major cigarette marketing campaigns directed toward males, and uptake among female youths increases after campaigns directed toward females (Pierce & Gilpin, 1995). Not surprising, perhaps, but such findings are inconsistent with the tobacco industry's claim that advertising affects brand choice but not smoking uptake. If smoking among adolescents were merely experimentation, little harm would be done. But adolescents who try smoking are twice as likely to smoke when they become adults, and 7 of 10 adolescents who smoke regularly maintain the habit into adulthood (Chassin, Presson, Sherman, & Edwards, 1990).

Cigarette smoking, like other forms of drug use, is addictive. To say that a person is addicted to a drug means two things. First, it means that a person's nervous system may have developed a tolerance to the drug (for some drugs, such as cocaine, sensitization, not tolerance, occurs). Second, it means that a person has become physically dependent on the drug. *Tolerance* simply means that the neurons in the central nervous system (CNS) respond progressively less and less to the presence of the drug; larger doses of the drug therefore are required to produce the same CNS effects that smaller doses produced earlier. *Physical dependence* means that CNS neurons now require the presence of the drug to function normally. Without the drug in the CNS, the individual will experience *withdrawal symptoms*, or uncomfortable physical conditions such as sweating, tremors, and anxiety. In addition to tolerance and physical dependence, many drugs, including the nicotine in cigarette smoke, produce *psychological dependence*, a craving to use the drug for its pleasurable effects. In other words, obtaining and using the drug become focal points of an individual's life. You may have been around people who have "needed" a cigarette but were unable to get one at that moment. You likely noticed how getting a cigarette or thoughts of smoking preoccupied their attention. Another, perhaps more objective, way of describing psychological dependence is to say that it involves behaviour that is acquired and maintained through positive reinforcement. A reinforcing drug is one that strengthens or maintains the behaviour that constitutes seeking, acquiring, and using the drug.

Nicotine from cigarette smoke exerts powerful effects on the central nervous system and heart by stimulating postsynaptic receptors sensitive to acetylcholine, a neurotransmitter. This stimulation produces temporary increases in heart rate and blood pressure, decreases in body temperature, changes in hormones released by the pituitary gland, and the release of adrenaline from the adrenal glands. And, in common with all reinforcers, natural and artificial, it also causes dopamine to be secreted in the brain. As we saw in Chapters 4 and 13, the release of dopamine in the brain is reinforcing, so this effect contributes to the maintenance of cigarette smoking. Cigarette smoking also may be maintained by *negative reinforcement*. People who try to quit smoking usually suffer from withdrawal symptoms, including headaches, insomnia, anxiety, and irritability. These symptoms are relieved by smoking another cigarette. Such negative reinforcement appears to be extremely powerful. More than 60 percent of all smokers have tried to quit smoking at least once, but have lit up again to escape the unpleasant withdrawal symptoms.

Nicotine alone cannot be blamed for the health risks posed by cigarette smoking. These risks are caused by the combination of nicotine and other toxic substances, such as the carbon monoxide and tars found in cigarette smoke. For example, while nicotine causes an increase in heart rate, the carbon monoxide in smoke deprives the heart of the oxygen needed to perform its work properly. The smoker's heart undergoes stress because it is working harder with fewer nutrients than normal. Over a period of years, this continued stress weakens the heart, making it more susceptible to disease than is the heart of a non-smoker.

Many smokers believe that they can diminish the health risks posed by their habit by switching to low-nicotine cigarettes. Unfortunately, this strategy is undermined by the fact that smokers develop a tolerance to nicotine and typically smoke more low-nicotine cigarettes and inhale more deeply to make up for the decreased nicotine content of their new brand. The only worthwhile approach is to cease smoking.

Most people who quit smoking try to do so on their own (Schachter, 1982). A survey of more than 4000 adults who smoked (Zhu et al., 2000) revealed that only about one-fifth of those trying to quit used any form of assistance (e.g., counselling, nicotine replacement therapy, etc.). Measured one year later, the researchers found that people who used assistance were more than twice as likely to have abstained from smoking than those who did not use any form of assistance. Although underused, there are many programs available to help people stop smoking. A popular medical approach to smoking cessation is the *transdermal nicotine patch*, a bandage-like patch that allows nicotine to be absorbed through the skin. The patch was developed by a behavioural psychologist, Frank Etscorn. Over several months, the nicotine levels of the patches are reduced, and the individual is weaned from nicotine altogether. This treatment is sometimes combined with the drug bupropion hydrochloride (marketed as *Zyban*), which reduces the desire for cigarettes in some people. Success rates are reasonably high, with 20 to 30 percent of those who quit still not smoking after six months. You may think this rate low until you consider that the long-run success rate of helping people quit smoking using other treatment approaches is only about 12 percent (Pomerleau, 1992).

Quitting smoking has both immediate and long-term positive effects, even if the individual has been smoking for a long time. **Table 16•2** shows the time frame of the body's recovery from cigarette smoking. Even after as few as 20 minutes have passed since smoking a cigarette, the body begins to

**TABLE 16•2 The Body's Response to Stopping Cigarette Smoking**

*Within 20 minutes of last puff*
Blood pressure and pulse decrease to normal levels.
Body temperature of extremities increases to normal levels.

*Within 1 day*
Risk of heart attacks decreases.

*Within 2 days*
Nerve endings begin regenerating.
Taste and smell acuity increases.

*Within 3 days*
Breathing becomes easier due to relaxing of bronchial tubes.
Lung capacity increases.

*From 2 weeks to 3 months*
Blood circulation improves.
Walking and other exercises begin to seem easier.
Lung efficiency increases as much as 30 percent.

*After 5 years*
Risk of death due to lung cancer decreases by 47 percent.

*Source: It's never too late to quit. (1989).* Living Well, IX*(4). Kalamazoo, MI: Bob Hope International Heart Research Institute.*

## Then and Now

### Selling Smoking

"That's it! Winston is the one filter cigarette that delivers flavour twenty times a pack!" was Fred Flintstone's reply to Barney Rubble's suggestion of taking a "Winston break" in an early 1960s commercial. *The Flintstones*, a popular cartoon program, was one of many television shows sponsored by a tobacco company in the 1950s and 1960s. Tobacco companies have been advertising cigarettes for more than a hundred years in North America. As restrictions on tobacco advertising have become increasingly stringent, the style of advertising has changed.

In the late 1800s, cigarettes were advertised primarily in newspapers, but also with promotional giveaways such as clocks and trading cards. The cards were similar to sports trading cards that are sold today, except that they were sold with cigarettes instead of a stick of gum and featured pictures of models, actresses, and war heroes. As radio programs became more popular, listeners heard ads promoting how brands like Chesterfield would leave a "clean, fresh taste in your mouth."

In the 1960s, more than 80 percent of tobacco advertising was found on television. Not only were the airwaves filled with tobacco ads, but child-friendly programs such as *I Love Lucy* were sponsored by tobacco companies. Ads featuring stars such as John Wayne (who developed lung cancer and died of stomach cancer) promoted the mild and smooth taste of a variety of cigarette brands. As concerns about public health increased, the tobacco industry agreed to cease television ads. In return, it asked that cigarette warning labels not include the word *cancer*. The last television ad for cigarettes aired on December 31, 1970 (Parker-Pope, 2002).

The end of television advertising did not slow down the marketing of smoking. Rather than advertise directly on television, tobacco companies started to sponsor films, and ensure that the stars of the films smoked their brand of cigarette. As restrictions on cigarette advertising increased throughout the 1990s, more feature films had primary characters who smoked (Sargent et al., 2001).

Although restrictions on cigarette advertising continue to increase, the tobacco industry still finds ways to sell its products. Canada has charted a different course than the United States insofar as tobacco advertising is concerned. Since 1988, most forms of direct cigarette advertising have been banned in Canada in a conscious effort to discourage smoking. As of 2003, displaying cigarette company logos at cultural and sporting events is banned. Tobacco advertising is allowed only in places where young people are not permitted by law. Beginning in 2001, federal legislation required that at least half of what is displayed on cigarette packages must include pictorial and written warnings about the hazards of smoking. Cigarette packs must also contain explicit information about how to quit smoking.

There is some debate about the effectiveness of these warning labels. In the United States, the warning labels only contain text, whereas in Canada there are graphic pictures along with text warning consumers about the potential harm associated with cigarette smoking. Peters and colleagues (2007) brought smokers and non-smokers into the lab and measured how they reacted to these different types of ads. What they found was that regardless of whether you smoked, the labels that contained pictorial warnings produced more negative emotional response to both smoking cues and to the image of smokers. These researchers recommend that the use of pictorial warning labels should continue in Canada and also be adopted in the United States.

show recovery, including a return to normal blood pressure, pulse rate, and body temperature in the extremities. After 72 hours, breathing becomes easier, partially because of increased lung capacity. After five years, the risk of death by lung cancer is reduced by almost 50 percent.

Although smoking cessation is a positive change in lifestyle, it is better never to have started in the first place. (Nearly half of the 6 764 000 Canadians who smoke say that they intend to quit within the next 6 months.) Quitting can be very difficult, although some behavioural and pharmacological treatments have been shown to be effective (Shiffman, Brockwell, Pillitteri, & Gitchell, 2008). As mentioned, most people try to quit without the use of these treatments. Psychologists and other health researchers are therefore interested not only in designing treatment programs to help people quit smoking, but also in developing prevention programs to help people, especially adolescents, resist the temptation to start smoking. Prevention programs are generally aimed at mitigating social factors such as imitation, peer pressure, and influence from advertisements that can initially induce people to light up. Such programs involve educating adolescents about the health risks related to cigarette smoking and teaching them how to respond negatively to people who encourage them to smoke. On a positive note, there is evidence that these programs may be having an impact. Chassin, Presson, Sherman, and Kim (2003) compared samples of grade 7 and grade 11 students in 1980 and 2001. The researchers found that smoking among adolescents has decreased, and that beliefs about smoking have generally become more negative. In comparison to the 1980 sample of adolescents, the sample from 2001 viewed smoking not only more negatively, but also as more addictive and as having more negative social consequences.

One Canadian anti-smoking program, the Waterloo Smoking Prevention Project (Flay et al., 1985), originally appeared especially effective in reducing the number of adolescents who experimented with smoking. Grade 6 students were first asked to seek out information about smoking and to think about their beliefs regarding smoking. Next, the students were taught about the social pressures involved in smoking and were given explicit training in how to resist those pressures. This training also included role playing such resistance strategies and asking each student to make a commitment regarding whether he or she would start smoking. The students were monitored five times over the next two years to see how many of them had experimented with smoking. By the end of the two-year period, fewer than 8 percent of the students who had been involved in the prevention program were experimenting with smoking. In contrast, almost 19 percent of the students who had not gone through the program had experimented with smoking. The program obviously had a very positive initial impact. What happened in the longer run? Flay and colleagues obtained information about smoking behaviour at grades 11 and 12 for more than 80 percent of the original participants. Unfortunately, the initial gains had been lost (Flay et al., 1989). This is not a rare outcome. Murray, Pirie, Leupker, and Pallonen (1989) contacted more than 7000 students who had participated in studies of smoking prevention. The researchers found no differences in smoking patterns between those who had and had not been exposed to smoking prevention programs. One promising suggestion (Murray, Pirie, Leupker, & Pallonen, 1989) is that occasional "booster" sessions may be necessary to maintain the effects of initial prevention exercises. This makes sense. After a prevention program for adolescents ends, peer pressure and smoking by family members can continue to be important sources of temptation to smoke, whereas resistance strategies may be forgotten over time or become inappropriate to contemporary circumstances as the adolescent ages. Booster sessions could be helpful in upgrading and strengthening the original resistance strategies.

## Drinking Alcoholic Beverages

The psychological effects of alcohol (and other drugs) have been known to humanity longer than have those of nicotine. Alcohol has been used for thousands of years for its euphoria-inducing properties.

Alcohol is widely abused today. To abuse a substance means to use it in a way that poses a threat to the safety and well-being of the user, society, or both. Most people who use alcohol do not abuse it, and not all people who abuse alcohol are alcoholics. For example, people who drive under the influence of alcohol pose a serious threat to both themselves and others, but they may not be alcoholics.

**Alcoholism** is an addiction to ethanol, the psychoactive agent in alcoholic beverages. A psychoactive substance is any substance that affects brain and CNS functioning.

**alcoholism** An addiction to ethanol, the psychoactive agent in alcoholic beverages.

**TABLE 16•3 The Negative Physical, Psychological, and Cultural Consequences of Alcohol Abuse**

| |
|---|
| *Physical* |
| Cirrhosis, which results in death |
| Poor nutrition |
| Impaired sexual functioning |
| *Psychological* |
| Gradual deterioration of cognitive functioning |
| Increased feelings of anxiety and irritability |
| Aggressive behaviour |
| *Cultural* |
| Impaired social skills and interpersonal functioning |
| Divorce |
| Employee absenteeism and decreased productivity |
| Death in alcohol-related traffic accidents |

Alcoholism is a serious problem in Canada. For example, about 5 percent of adults living in Ontario can be classified as alcoholic (Addiction Research Foundation, 1999). About 60 percent of the national population consumes some alcohol, about 26 percent currently do not drink but have done so in the past, and about 13 percent have never consumed alcohol (Kelner, 1997). Among the heaviest drinkers in the country, males outnumber females by a ratio of about five to one (Kelner, 1997). **Table 16•3** describes some of the very real and serious physical, psychological, and social consequences of alcohol abuse. In regards to social consequences, researchers found that alcohol can play a role in relationship conflicts (MacDonald, Zanna, & Holmes, 2000). When asked to think about a past conflict in a romantic relationship, people who were intoxicated felt more negatively about the incident, and believed that their partners were more upset. As well, an analysis of partner violence revealed a strong correlation between increased alcohol consumption and violent relationship conflicts (Murphy et al., 2005).

Because neuronal activity of the brain becomes suppressed and reduces inhibitory controls on behaviour when moderate to heavy amounts of alcohol are consumed, individuals become more relaxed and more outgoing, show impaired motor coordination, and have difficulty thinking clearly. As more alcohol is consumed, neuronal activity in the brain is depressed further, producing distortions in perception, slurred speech, memory loss, impaired judgment, and poor control of movement. Unconsciousness and death may result from ingesting large amounts of alcohol over a relatively short period of time.

Alcohol is rapidly absorbed from the stomach and intestinal tract. Because alcohol is a small fat- and water-soluble molecule, it is quickly and evenly distributed throughout the body via the circulatory system. Blood alcohol levels are affected by body mass and muscularity. Generally speaking, a large person would have to consume more alcohol than a smaller person to attain the same level of intoxication; but, at a given weight, a muscular person would have to consume more than a person with a higher proportion of body fat. In addition, regardless of body characteristics, blood levels of alcohol increase more slowly in people who drink on a full stomach than in those having little or no food in their stomach. Food in the stomach impairs absorption of substances through the gastrointestinal tract.

Degree of inebriation is related to the manner in which alcohol is metabolized by the body. Unlike most other drugs, alcohol is metabolized by the liver at a constant rate, regardless of how much alcohol has been consumed. For example, in one hour, the body will metabolize the alcohol in about 8.5 grams of alcohol—that is, about two-thirds of a regular beer or about 30 grams of liquor. Hence, if a person consumes more than one beer or one shot of liquor per hour, his or her blood alcohol level rises beyond that level caused by the first drink, and he or she may begin to become intoxicated. When blood alcohol levels reach 0.3 to 0.4 percent (roughly the effect of 10 drinks consumed over a short period), people lose consciousness, and at 0.5 percent, neurons in the brain that control the respiratory and circulatory systems stop functioning, causing death. Driving under the influence of alcohol is defined by blood alcohol concentration (BAC); in Canada, it is illegal to drive with a BAC greater than 0.08 percent. Research has shown that even at "safe" legal levels, alcohol consumption may increase risk-taking behaviours while driving and increase the likelihood of an accident (Burian, Liguori, & Robinson, 2002). Consuming alcohol can also make people more tolerant in their attitudes toward drinking and driving (MacDonald, Zanna, & Fong, 1995), a truly lethal combination. Although national statistics are not available on deaths due to drinking and driving, Transport Canada (2002) reports that in 2000 more than one-third of drivers who died in traffic accidents had consumed alcohol, and most were legally impaired. Nearly 90 percent of those killed in alcohol-related collisions were male.

Although you have probably heard the oft-quoted phrase that "drinking and driving don't mix," you may or may not have heard that "drinking and using other drugs don't mix." Drinking and using other drugs can be deadly. **Table 16•4** describes some of the dangerous consequences of mixing alcohol with other drugs, including over-the-counter medications.

Heavy drinkers sometimes suffer *delirium tremens*—the DTs—a pattern of withdrawal symptoms that includes trembling, irritability, hallucinations, sleeplessness, and confusion when they attempt to quit drinking. In many cases, alcoholics become so physically dependent on the drug that abrupt cessation of drinking produces convulsions and sometimes death.

As you learned in Chapter 3, an individual's tendency to develop alcoholism may have a genetic basis (McKim, 1991; Vaillant, 2002). Vaillant and Milofsky (1982), in a long-term study of adopted boys, found that sons of chronic alcoholics had a greater tendency to become alcoholics themselves, despite the fact that their adoptive parents were non-alcoholics. Cloninger (1987) found that children of alcoholic parents adopted at birth into normal (non-alcoholic) homes were about four times more likely to abuse alcohol than were other adopted children whose biological parents were non-alcoholics. A review of family, twin, and adoption studies suggests that more than 50 percent of the development of alcoholism is due to genetic factors (Köhnke, 2008; Quickfall & el-Guebaly, 2006).

As pointed out in Chapter 12, women who drink moderate to heavy quantities of alcohol during pregnancy risk giving birth to children who suffer from *fetal alcohol syndrome*. Alcohol crosses the placental barrier and enters the fetal blood supply, where it retards the development of the fetus's nervous system. Fetal alcohol syndrome is characterized by decreased birth weight and physical malformations. It is the third leading

**TABLE 16•4 The Effects of Mixing Alcohol with Other Drugs**

| Drug | Example | Possible Consequences of Using Simultaneously with Alcohol |
|---|---|---|
| Narcotics | Codeine or Percodan | Increased suppression of CNS functions and possible death due to respiratory failure |
| Minor pain relievers | Aspirin or Tylenol | Stomach irritation and bleeding; increased likelihood of liver damage from acetaminophen |
| Antihistamines | Actifed | Increased drowsiness, making operation of motor vehicles and power equipment more dangerous |
| CNS stimulants | Caffeine, Dexedrine | Reverses some of the depressive effects of alcohol; however, they do not produce increases in sobriety if consumed while one is drunk |
| Antipsychotics | Largactil | Impaired control of motor movements and possible death due to respiratory failure |
| Antianxiety drugs | Valium, Librium | Decreased arousal; impaired judgment, which can lead to accidents in the home or on the road |

*Source: Based on Palfai, T., & Jankiewicz, H. (1991).* Drugs and human behaviour. *Dubuque, IA: Wm. C. Brown; and data from the National Institute for Alcohol Abuse and Alcoholism Clearinghouse for Alcohol Information (1982).*

cause of birth defects involving mental retardation, and it is completely preventable. Simply put, a woman will not give birth to a child with fetal alcohol syndrome if she does not drink during her pregnancy.

Alcohol use and cigarette smoking are prompted by many of the same factors: imitation and peer pressure. Many young people view drinking as the thing to do because it seemingly represents maturity, independence, and rebelliousness, and because it is associated with having fun. For example, in their advertisements, brewers portray people using their products at the end of a hard day's work, at festive parties, and to celebrate special occasions. To their credit, some brewers are now using their advertisements also to inform consumers of the potential dangers of alcohol abuse.

Treatment programs for drug abuse, including smoking and drinking, take several forms. In some cases, aversion therapy (see Chapter 18) is used; in others, less intrusive forms of therapy involving extensive counselling are used. In the latter case, the psychologist's or counsellor's general aim is to teach the individual to

1. identify environmental cues or circumstances that may cause the addictive behaviour to occur or recur;
2. learn to behave in ways that are incompatible with the undesirable behaviour;
3. have confidence that he or she can overcome the addiction; and
4. view setbacks in overcoming the addiction as temporary and as learning experiences in which new coping skills can be acquired.

Prevention programs for people with addictive behaviours are only moderately successful. For example, many alcohol management programs have about a 30 to 50 percent success rate. Recall that smoking cessation programs (not including those that use the nicotine patch) fare even worse: They have about a 12 percent success rate (Pomerleau, 1992). As you might guess, an important goal for psychologists in the twenty-first century is to develop more effective programs for treating addictive behaviours.

## Sexually Transmitted Diseases and AIDS

The most life-threatening illness that can be transmitted sexually is acquired immune deficiency syndrome (AIDS), which can also be spread through tainted blood transfusions and the sharing of hypodermic needles among intravenous drug users. (See **Table 16•5**.) AIDS is the last stage of the illness triggered by the human immunodeficiency virus (HIV).

Once prevalent mainly among homosexual men in the Western hemisphere, AIDS has spread among heterosexuals as well. The World Health Organization (2007) estimated that more than 33 million people were living with HIV in 2007. As well, there were nearly 2.5 million new cases of HIV infection, and approximately 2 million people died from AIDS in 2007 alone. According to the World Health Organization (2007), unprotected sex between males accounts for 45 percent of new HIV infections in Canada, while 37 percent of new infections can be attributed to unprotected heterosexual sex.

Changes in lifestyle, *safe sex practices*, can reduce the risk of contracting an STD, including HIV and consequent AIDS.

**TABLE 16•5 Four STDs, Their Causes, Symptomatology, and Treatment**

| STD | Cause | Symptoms | Treatment |
|---|---|---|---|
| Gonorrhea | *Gonococcus* bacterium | Appear 3 to 5 days after sexual contact with afflicted person. In both sexes, discharges of pus. Urination accompanied by a burning sensation. In female, pelvic inflammatory disease. If untreated, fevers, headaches, backaches, and abdominal pain develop. | Penicillin and other antibiotics can cure this disease. |
| Genital herpes | Herpes simplex type I and II virus | Small blisters around point of sexual contact. Blisters burst, causing pain. Symptoms recur every 1 to 2 weeks. | Acyclovir and similar drugs can suppress but do not cure this condition. |
| Syphilis | *Treponema pallidum* bacterium | Chancre or lesion where bacteria first entered body. If untreated, the bacteria penetrate body tissue, including the brain. May result in death. | Penicillin and other antibiotics can cure this disease. |
| AIDS | Human immunodeficiency virus (HIV) | Destruction of body's immune system allowing diseases like cancer and pneumonia to infect the body. | A combination of protease-inhibiting drugs can suppress the HIV load and improve immunologic functioning, lessen symptoms, and reduce the risk of transmission to newborns. There is no cure for the syndrome, however. |

These practices include limiting the number of sexual partners, finding out the sexual history of partners before engaging in sexual relations, and using a condom during sex; or even abstaining from sexual intercourse altogether. In the case of AIDS, these lifestyle changes must involve not only safe sex practices, but also behaviours that will prevent non-sexual transmission of the AIDS virus, such as refusal to share hypodermic needles.

If everyone engaged in safe sex practices, and if injection drug users refused to share hypodermic needles, the AIDS threat would be reduced significantly. The problem, of course, is that it is one thing to talk about safe sex and clean needles but another thing actually to act. Why is this so? For the intravenous drug user, the answer is clear: The most important thing in life is getting high. Nothing else really matters. For the couple about to engage in casual sex, the issue is less clear. Although each individual's behaviour is motivated by sexual gratification, the social awkwardness involved in discussing each other's sexual history may lead to a failure to engage in safe sex behaviours.

One way to reduce this problem may be to establish prevention programs in which people role-play safe sex practices in an attempt to help them overcome the feelings of uneasiness involved in asking another about his or her sexual history (Bosarge, 1989). Most importantly, prevention programs must accomplish four main goals (e.g., Fisher & Fisher, 1992, 2000):

1. teach people the relationship between their behaviour and contracting STDs and AIDS;
2. familiarize people with safe sex behaviours, such as the proper way to use a condom;
3. break down barriers to using safe sex practices, such as refusal to inquire about a partner's sexual history, the idea that one is invulnerable to STD or HIV infection, and myths about using condoms (such as that only "wimps" use them);
4. provide encouragement and support in order to motivate behaviours that reduce STD and AIDS risks.

Although prevention programs have been successful in reducing high-risk sexual behaviours, they are least successful in situations in which a person's personal or cultural values prevent him or her from engaging in safe sex practices (Herdt, 2001; Herdt & Lindenbaum, 1992). These values generally involve misperceptions of what practising safe sex means. Some males refuse to wear condoms because doing so would detract from their conception of what it means to be a man. These individuals perceive that practising safe sex robs them of their masculinity. Many people, especially young people, have the mistaken belief that they are invulnerable to any type of misfortune, including contracting an STD. They believe, in essence, that these things "happen to other people, not me." The illusion of control seems to play a role as well. Some people falsely believe that they can tell by looking at another person whether he or she is infected, and therefore whether safe sex practices are necessary (e.g., Thompson, Kent, Thomas, & Vrungos, 1999). Other research shows that familiarity breeds a false sense of safety. Misovich, Fisher, and Fisher (1996) found that university students believed that simply knowing a partner well reduced the need to use condoms. The situation worsens with alcohol consumption. Alcohol consumption can create what Steele and Josephs (1990) call *alcohol myopia*. In the context of sex, alcohol myopia means that the salient attractions of sexual activity remain clear to the drinker, but the more distant risks of fatal infection recede to the blurry horizon (MacDonald, MacDonald, Zanna, & Fong, 2000; MacDonald, Zanna, & Fong, 1998). One result is the failure to use condoms, thus increasing the risk of HIV and other STD infection. Brown & Vanable (2007) surveyed more than 300 college students and found that alcohol use was correlated with unprotected sex with non-steady partners. The challenge for psychologists and counsellors is to reorient these types of thinking so that people learn the connection between their sexual behaviour and its possible negative consequences.

**Reactions to Contagious Diseases** Although knowledge of the routes of possible infection of HIV and AIDS is improving, there is still a segment of the population that will not sit next to a person if they know that he or she has AIDS (Bishop, 1994; Rushing, 1995). But why? Perhaps you know that AIDS is a contagious disease and that heart disease is not. If you know that, perhaps you also know that there is absolutely no evidence that AIDS can be transmitted through casual contact, such as by sitting next to an HIV-infected person on a bench at the mall. Yet many people would not feel comfortable sitting next to the person with AIDS for fear that they could catch the disease somehow.

Unfortunately, segments of our culture have reacted with disdain, calling for quarantines (for example, refusing to let children with AIDS attend school), ostracizing people with AIDS, or physically assaulting them and others who belong to high-risk groups (such as gay people). It is true that some segments of our culture have reacted sympathetically to people with AIDS—they have learned about the disease, what causes it, and how it spreads. These people would not feel particularly uncomfortable sitting on the bench next to the person with AIDS. Despite widespread media coverage of the AIDS epidemic throughout the world and instructional programs designed to educate the general public about AIDS, it remains the most feared, stigmatized, and publicly misunderstood contagious disease of our time (Rushing, 1995). When negative behaviour of this sort occurs, especially on a collective, widespread social basis, it is referred to as *fear of contagion*. Historical analyses of previous epidemics, such as the Black Death, or bubonic plague, that struck Europe during the fourteenth century have shown that fear of contagion is only likely to occur when four conditions are met. The disease must be deadly, it must appear suddenly, it must have no apparent explanation, and people must believe that many people are at risk of contracting it (Rushing, 1995).

The AIDS epidemic meets these four conditions. It is deadly and it appeared suddenly: AIDS still is not completely understood. We know that a virus causes it, but we don't know how to completely eradicate it—there is no equivalent of penicillin for this disease as yet. And, finally, as AIDS makes strong inroads into heterosexual populations, more and more people now see themselves and others like them at risk of contracting the disease. Many people still hold the false belief that AIDS is transmitted through casual contact (Bishop, 1991a, 1991b).

## Interim Summary

### Healthy and Unhealthy Lifestyles

The kinds of food we eat, how much exercise we get, the extent to which we use tobacco and alcohol, and our sexual practices have profound implications for our health and longevity. Eating right, exercising regularly, not smoking, consuming alcohol moderately, and practising safe sex do not guarantee that one will live a long life, but they do improve one's chances.

People who eat high-fat, low-fibre diets tend to be more susceptible to CHD and cancer than are people who eat low-fat, high-fibre diets. But many of the foods we like the most are high in fat and low in fibre. In the short run, eating these foods may delight our palate, but over the long run, eating these foods may lead to weight gain and increased LDL cholesterol levels, both risk factors for CHD and cancer. A well-balanced diet in combination with exercising regularly reduces the risk of CHD and cancer.

Poor eating habits and sedentary living are not the only lifestyle aspects that put people at risk for developing CHD and cancer. Cigarette smoking and consuming alcohol have similar effects. Although we now know a great deal about how cigarette smoking and alcohol consumption negatively affect the body and lead to disease, many people continue to smoke and drink. Why do people start and continue to do these things? Once again, the answer is to be found in the immediate pleasure derived from engaging in these behaviours. In everyday language, these behaviours can make people feel good. In addition to being reinforcing, these behaviours are addictive—the body may become dependent on the chemicals contained in cigarette smoke and alcohol for normal, day-to-day functioning.

Another threat to health and longevity is sexually transmitted diseases. People have been advised to take precautionary measures against contracting any STD by practising safe sex. In the case of AIDS, people who inject themselves with drugs are also advised not to share hypodermic needles. Programs aimed at preventing the spread of STDs and AIDS focus on teaching people the relationship between their behaviour and the likelihood of contracting one or more of these diseases and on how to use safe sex strategies.

Fear of contagion is influenced by four factors: The disease must be deadly, it must appear suddenly, it must have no apparent explanation, and people must believe that many are at risk of contracting it. Despite education efforts to inform the public about AIDS, fear of contagion with respect to AIDS remains a serious problem.

**QUESTIONS TO CONSIDER**

1. In what kinds of unhealthy lifestyle behaviours do you engage? What psychological processes influenced how these behaviours developed? Why do you keep engaging in them?
2. Have you thought much about changing your lifestyle behaviours? Do you have any bad habits you would like to break or any good habits (such as exercising more) you would like to begin? If so, why haven't you done so—what is preventing you from altering your behaviour?

**self-control** Behaviour that produces a larger, long-term reward when people are faced with the choice between it and a smaller, short-term reward.

## Unhealthy Lifestyles Are Preventable: Self-Control

Our lifestyles are not always wholly adaptive; some aspects of our lifestyles are detrimental to both our longevity and our quality of life. We have seen that unhealthy aspects of our lifestyles include poor nutrition, physical inactivity, cigarette smoking, alcohol abuse, and failure to use safe sex practices. Behaviours that make up our lifestyles are partly a consequence of the environmental conditions created by cultural evolution and partly a result of our genetic and physiological constitution.

Unhealthy lifestyles can be avoided. The problem, of course, is getting people to substitute healthy behaviours for unhealthy ones and to make positive lifestyle changes. Cultural evolution, or, more specifically, advances in technology, have afforded us choices: to use a condom or not, to eat foods rich in vitamins and minerals or to follow a poor diet, to smoke or not, and so forth.

How do we decide whether we should eat fattening and unhealthy foods now or follow a prudent diet and lose weight and become healthier over the long run? The essence of each of these choices is whether to opt for the *small, short-term reward* produced by one action or the *larger, longer-term reward* produced by another, necessarily incompatible action. You can have unprotected sex now with a partner you do not know very well and run the risk of getting an STD or AIDS or you can practise safe sex and enhance the likelihood that you will remain healthy. What is at issue here is **self-control**, behaviour that produces a larger, long-term reward when one is faced with the choice between it and a small, short-term reward.

Psychologists Howard Rachlin (1970) and George Ainslie (1975) proposed a clear and conceptually useful model of self-control. This model, based on laboratory research using animals, captures well the essence of most self-control decisions that we face. Look at **Figure 16•3(a)**. The vertical axis represents the value of a reward to us; the horizontal axis represents the passage of time. The curve represents a large, long-term reward—for example, acquiring and maintaining good physical health. Let us assume either that we are not in very good physical health (we have a high level of blood cholesterol because we eat a lot of high-fat, low-fibre foods, we smoke and drink more than we would like, and we don't get much exercise) or that we are in good condition and wish to remain that way. That is, the curve in Figure 16.3(a) represents a goal we wish to achieve or a condition we wish to maintain *in the long run*. Now look at **Figure 16•3(b)**. This curve represents a smaller, short-term reward—for example, the pleasure derived from eating a hot fudge sundae or fried chicken, smoking a cigarette, drinking a beer, or being sedentary. The curve representing the value of the short-term reward in (b) looks smaller than the curve representing the long-term reward in (a), and it is—some of the time. But now look at what happens when the two curves are placed in the same graph in **Figure 16•3(c)**: There comes a point in time at which the value of the small, short-term reward becomes greater than that of the larger, long-term reward.

How can that be? Suppose that you are dieting. Further suppose that your roommate or spouse is baking cookies (imagine your favourite kind of cookie to make this example more compelling). You are drawn to the kitchen, where a dozen freshly baked cookies, giving off a tantalizing aroma, are sitting on the counter. Your roommate (or spouse) says, "Have one." Now you are faced with a choice: Do you eat a cookie or two (or perhaps more) and consume more calories than your diet calls for, or do you say, "No, thanks"? The temptation you face here is captured in Figure 16.3(c). At this moment, the value of the small, short-term reward, the cookies, exceeds that of the larger, long-term reward, maintaining or losing weight. You cannot regularly consume more calories than your diet calls for *and* maintain or lose weight. Many psychologists argue that if you wait until you are faced with the choice between the small, short-term reward and the larger, long-term reward (*the moment of decision*), you will most likely opt for the small, short-term reward. The most effective way to exercise self-control is to somehow avoid having to make that choice in the first place. (See **Figure 16•3(d)**.) Self-control is a *prior commitment to a course of action that precludes making this decision*. According to this model, the best way to exercise self-control is to move the moment of decision to some time *before* you are confronted with the choice between the two rewards. That way, the value of the long-term reward is higher than the value of the short-term reward at the moment of decision. Setting your alarm clock the night before you have to get up early (as

▲ *These three men have learned the benefits of self-control—in this case, choosing the long-term benefits of weight loss over the short-term rewards of overeating.*

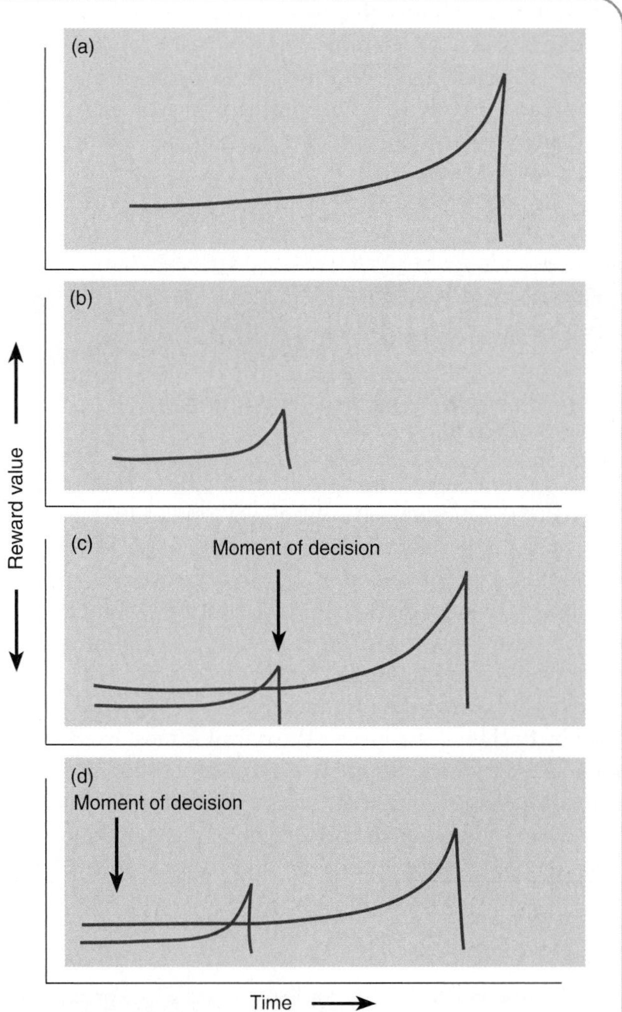


**FIGURE 16•3** The relationship between commitment and self-control. (a) Value of the long-term, delayed reward. (b) Value of the short-term, immediate reward. (c) No commitment, no self-control. (d) Self-control and commitment.

opposed to making the decision to get up the next morning when you are groggy) and enrolling in a payroll savings plan (as opposed to getting your paycheque and deciding then to put some of it in savings) are forms of prior commitment. Without setting your alarm clock or enrolling in the savings plan, future events (the larger, long-term reward) may have little influence on your behaviour. In the case of dieting, prior commitment may include avoiding being home at times when your roommate or spouse is baking cookies or entering a contract with that person stating that he or she will not offer you any goodies. Other possible self-control strategies also exist for coping with situations like this. For example, you might imagine yourself saying "no" over and over again to such a temptation and feeling happy about your answer, and then following this model when actually faced with the temptation.

As we have seen, many treatment programs are unsuccessful at getting people to make lasting commitments to changes in their lifestyles. What is sorely needed is the development of effective commitment strategies that encourage people to make choices that benefit their health. Developing these strategies is a pre-eminent goal of **health psychology**, the branch of psychology concerned with the promotion and maintenance of sound health practices such as eating well, exercising regularly, not smoking or drinking, and engaging in safe sex practices.

## Interim Summary

### Unhealthy Lifestyles Are Preventable: Self-Control

The negative consequences of unhealthy behaviours can be avoided by exercising self-control—by opting to engage in behaviour that produces the larger, but often delayed, reward when one is confronted with the choice between it and the smaller, more immediate reward. For example, you may opt to turn down dessert tonight (the smaller, more immediate reward) in the attempt to lose weight (the larger, less immediate reward). According to the model of self-control developed by Rachlin and Ainslie, self-control is most likely when you make a prior commitment to a course of action that leads only to the larger, long-term reward. For example, you may turn down a dinner invitation tonight because you know that when the server brings the dessert tray to your table you will be unable to resist ordering dessert. Not placing yourself in that situation by declining the dinner invitation is a commitment to the larger, long-term reward of losing weight.

Once you begin viewing life as consisting of a series of choices between small, short-term rewards and larger, long-term rewards, you can begin to see clearly how the choices you make now influence the consequences you will face later.

**QUESTIONS TO CONSIDER**

1. Think of an aspect of your life in which you would like to exercise more self-control. Explain how you might implement the model of self-control described in this section to help you with this aspect of your life. What barriers might prevent you from implementing this model in your life?
2. Many people believe that exercising self-control is a matter of "willpower." What is willpower, and how does it differ from the model of self-control about which you have just finished reading? From your point of view, is self-control due to willpower? Why or why not?

**health psychology** The branch of psychology involved in the promotion and maintenance of sound health practices.
**stress** A pattern of physiological, behavioural, and cognitive responses to stimuli (real or imagined) that are perceived as endangering one's well-being.
**stressors** Stimuli that are perceived as endangering one's well-being.

## Stress and Health

At some point, we've all experienced stress, whether it was writing a difficult exam or coping with the loss of a friend. **Stress** is a pattern of physiological, behavioural, emotional, and cognitive responses to real or imagined stimuli that are perceived as blocking a goal or endangering or otherwise threatening our well-being. These stimuli are generally aversive and are called **stressors**. Stress is a product of natural

▲ *Stressors, such as the inundation of one's home by flood waters, threaten one's normal life routine and well-being.*

selection. It is a behavioural adaptation that helped our ancestors fight or flee from wild animals and enemies. Likewise, stress often helps us confront or escape threatening situations (Linsky, Bachman, & Straus, 1995; Roelofs et al., 2007). While stress is not a direct product of cultural evolution, the changes in the environment wrought by cultural evolution have helped make stress commonplace.

Stressors come in many forms. They may be catastrophic in nature (see Meichenbaum, 1995) or they may belong to the class of trivial, everyday irritations. Stressors are not always bad. Some stressors, such as athletic competition and class exams, can affect behaviour in positive ways. However, when stress is extended over long periods, it can have negative effects on both a person's psychological health and a person's physical health (Peavy et al., 2007; Selye, 1991).

## The Biological Basis of Stress

Our physical response to stressors is governed by the autonomic nervous system, which is controlled by the hypothalamus. Stress is a biological response that is experienced as an *emotion*, although the form it takes varies depending on the nature of the stressor. In some situations, we may feel frightened, and in others we may feel inspired or exhilarated.

When an individual senses a stressor, the hypothalamus sends signals to the autonomic nervous system and to the pituitary gland, both of which respond by stimulating body organs to change their normal activities:

1. Heart rate increases, blood pressure rises, blood vessels constrict, blood sugar levels rise, and blood flow is directed away from extremities and toward major organs.
2. Breathing becomes deeper and faster and air passages dilate, which permits more air to enter the lungs.
3. Digestion stops and perspiration increases.
4. The adrenal glands secrete adrenaline (epinephrine), which stimulates the heart and other organs.

It is easy to see why these changes are adaptive. They each prepare the body to deal with the stressor—collectively, these physiological responses produce a heightened psychological and physical state of alertness and readiness for action. Whether we confront the stressor or run from it, the biological response is generally the same. Likewise, regardless of the nature of the stressor, the biological response is the same. Whether you find yourself in a dark alley confronted by a man with a knife or facing your next psychology exam, the autonomic nervous system and the pituitary gland stimulate the body to respond to the stressor.

There are two cases in which such responses can be maladaptive. First, stress can produce anxiety, which may impair one's ability to perform a task. As you may have experienced yourself, anxiety can hinder performance on class tests, speaking in public, competition during athletic events, and remembering lines in a play.

The second case involves the effects of prolonged and severe stress. Many people's lifestyles place them in situations in which they are confronted with stressors daily. As we will see shortly, such lifestyles place these people at increased risk of illness.

**Selye's General Adaptation Syndrome** Much of what we know about the effects of dealing with prolonged and severe stressors on the body stems from the work of endocrinologist Hans Selye. Through his work with laboratory animals, he found that chronic exposure to severe stressors produces a sequence of three physiological stages: *alarm, resistance*, and *exhaustion*. (See **Figure 16•4**.) Selye (1956/1976, 1993) referred to these stages collectively as the **general adaptation syndrome (GAS)**.

The responses in the *alarm reaction* involve arousal of the autonomic nervous system and occur when the organism is first confronted with a stressor. During this stage, the organism's resistance to the stressor temporarily drops below normal, and the organism may experience shock—impairment of normal physiological functioning. With continued exposure to the stressor, the organism enters the *stage of resistance*, during which its autonomic nervous system returns to normal functioning. Resistance to the stressor increases and eventually plateaus at above-normal levels. The stage of resistance, then, reflects the organism's adaptation to environmental stressors. However, with continued exposure to the stressor, the organism enters the *stage of exhaustion*. During this stage, the organism loses its ability to adapt, and resistance plummets to below-normal levels, leaving the organism susceptible to illness and even death.

Biologically speaking, we are able to adapt to the presence of environmental stressors for only so long before we become susceptible to exhaustion and illness. The extent to

**general adaptation syndrome (GAS)** The model proposed by Selye to describe the body's adaptation to chronic exposure to severe stressors. The body passes through an orderly sequence of three physiological stages: alarm, resistance, and exhaustion.

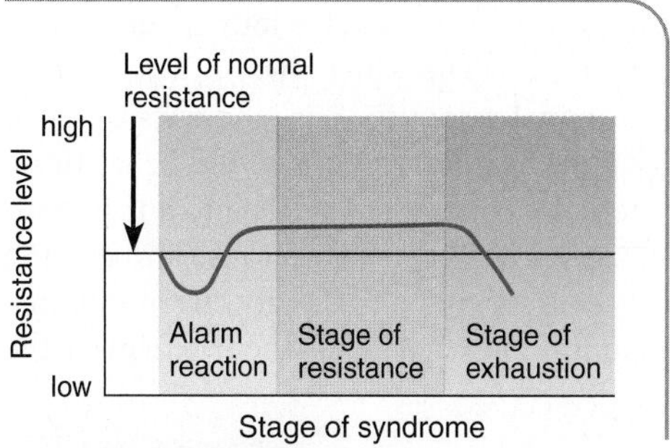


**FIGURE 16•4** The general adaptation syndrome as proposed by Hans Selye.

*(Selye, H. (1974).* Stress without distress. *New York: Harper & Row. Reprinted by permission.)*

which people can adapt varies across individuals and depends on how the stressor is perceived.

Chapter 13 pointed out that emotional responses evolved because they are useful and adaptive. Why, then, can they harm our health? The answer appears to be that our emotional responses are designed primarily to cope with short-term events. The physiological responses that accompany the negative emotions prepare us to threaten or fight rivals or to run away from dangerous situations. Walter Cannon coined the phrase **fight-or-flight response**, which refers to the physiological reactions that prepare us for the strenuous efforts required by fighting or running away. Normally, once we have bluffed or fought with an adversary or run away from a dangerous situation, the threat is over and our physiological condition can return to normal. The fact that the physiological responses may have adverse long-term effects on our health is unimportant as long as the responses are brief. But when the threatening situations are continuous rather than episodic, they produce a more or less continuous stress response. This continued state of arousal can lead to CHD and other physical problems.

Several studies have demonstrated the deleterious effects of stress on health. For example, survivors of concentration camps, who were obviously subjected to long-term stress, have generally poorer health later in life than do other people of the same age (Cohen et al., 1953). Holocaust survivors who were children during the Second World War are more likely to display psychosocial and post-traumatic symptoms today (Cohen, Brom, & Dasberg, 2001). Air traffic controllers—especially those who work at busy airports where the danger of collisions is greatest—show a greater incidence of high blood pressure, which gets worse as they grow older (Cobb & Rose, 1973). (See **Figure 16•5.**) Researchers have developed strategies to help air traffic controllers reduce stress. Vogt, Hagemann, and Kastner (2006) tested air traffic controllers using flight simulations and found that stress levels were reduced significantly when the number of planes being monitored dropped from 12 to 6. This type of research has been used to promote changes in the work environment for air traffic controllers.

**FIGURE 16•5** Stress and hypertension in air traffic controllers. Incidence of hypertension in various age groups of air traffic controllers at high-stress and low-stress airports.

*(Based on data from Cobb, S., & Rose, R. M. (1973). Hypertension, peptic ulcer, and diabetes in air traffic controllers.* Journal of the American Medical Association, 82, *476–482.)*

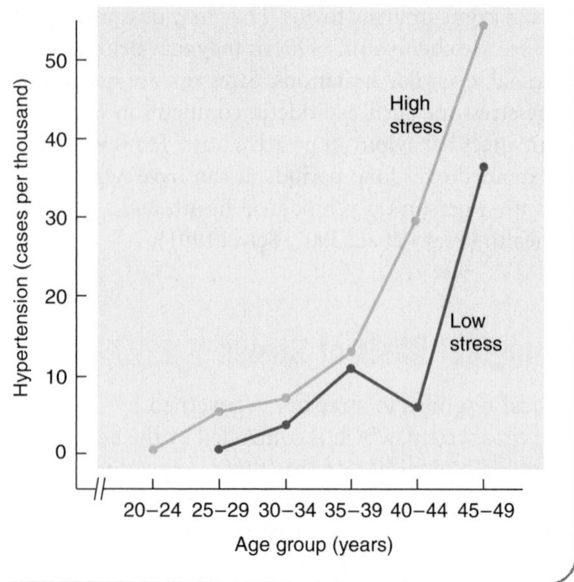


## Physiological Mechanisms Involved in Stress

As we saw in Chapter 13, emotions consist of behavioural, autonomic, and hormonal responses. The latter two components—autonomic and hormonal responses—are the ones that can have adverse effects on health. (Of course, the behavioural components can, too, if a person rashly gets into a fight with someone much bigger and stronger.) Because threatening situations generally call for vigorous activity, the autonomic and hormonal responses that accompany them help make the body's energy resources available. The sympathetic branch of the autonomic nervous system is active, and the adrenal glands secrete epinephrine, norepinephrine, and steroid stress hormones. Because the effects of sympathetic activity are similar to those of the adrenal hormones, we will limit our discussion to the hormonal responses.

Epinephrine releases the stored form of glucose that is present in the muscles, thus providing energy for strenuous exercise. Along with norepinephrine, it also increases blood flow to the muscles by increasing the output of the heart, which also increases blood pressure. Over the long term, these changes contribute to CHD. The other stress-related hormone is *cortisol*, a steroid secreted by the cortex of the adrenal gland. Cortisol is called a **glucocorticoid** because it has profound effects on glucose metabolism, effects similar to those of epinephrine. In addition, glucocorticoids help break down protein and convert it to glucose, help make fats available for energy, increase blood flow, and stimulate behavioural responsiveness, presumably by affecting the brain. They have other physiological effects, too, some of which are only poorly understood. Almost every cell in the body contains glucocorticoid receptors, which means that few parts of the body are unaffected by these hormones. (See **Figure 16•6.**)

Glucocorticoids do more than help an animal react to a stressful situation—they help it survive. When a rat's adrenal glands are removed, it becomes much more susceptible to the negative effects of stress. A stressful situation that a normal rat would take in its stride may kill one whose adrenal glands

**fight-or-flight response** Physiological reactions that help ready us to fight or to flee a dangerous situation.

**glucocorticoid** A chemical, such as cortisol, that influences the metabolism of glucose, the main energy source of the body.

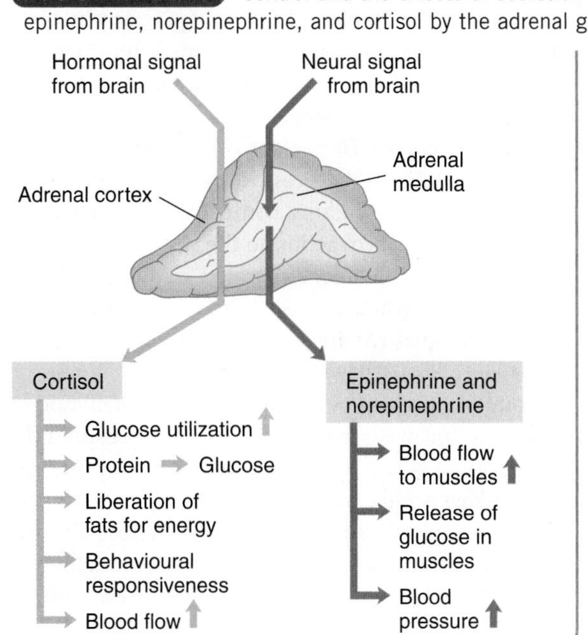


FIGURE 16•6 Control and the effects of secretion of epinephrine, norepinephrine, and cortisol by the adrenal gland.

have been removed. Physicians know they must provide additional amounts of glucocorticoid when treating people whose adrenal glands have been damaged or removed if these individuals are subjected to stress (Tyrell & Baxter, 1981).

The most harmful effects of stress are caused by the prolonged secretion of glucocorticoids (Selye, 1956/1976). Although the short-term effects of glucocorticoids are essential, the long-term effects are damaging. These effects include increased blood pressure, damage to muscle tissue, one form of diabetes, infertility, stunted growth, inhibition of the inflammatory responses, and suppression of the immune system. High blood pressure can lead to heart attacks and stroke. Children subjected to prolonged stress may not attain their full height. Inhibition of the inflammatory response makes it more difficult for the body to heal itself after an injury, and suppression of the immune system makes an individual vulnerable to disease.

Not only does chronic stress lead to health-impairing behaviours (such as smoking, loss of sleep, and excessive alcohol consumption), it can also negatively affect the brain itself (McEwen, 2008). Extreme stress has been shown to cause brain damage in young primates (Uno et al., 1989). The investigators studied a colony of vervet monkeys housed in a primate centre in Kenya. They found that some monkeys died, apparently as a result of stress. Vervet monkeys have a hierarchical society, and monkeys near the bottom of the hierarchy are picked on by the others; thus, they are almost continuously subjected to stress. (Ours is not the only species with social structures that cause stress in some of its members.) The deceased monkeys had enlarged adrenal glands, a sign of chronic stress. In addition, neurons in a particular region of their hippocampal formations were completely destroyed. Stress-induced damage of this nature is especially worrying because the hippocampus plays a vital role in learning and memory (Sapolsky, 1996). Severe stress appears to cause brain damage in humans as well. Jensen, Genefke, and Hyldebrandt (1982) found evidence of brain degeneration in CT scans of people who had been tortured. Victims of mass violence show similar results (van der Hal-van Raalte, Van Ijzendoorn, Bakermans-Kranenburg, 2007; Weinstein, Fucetola, & Mollica, 2001).

## Cognitive Appraisal and Stress

We have seen that many of the harmful effects of long-term stress are caused by our own reactions—primarily the secretion of stress hormones. Some events that cause stress, such as prolonged exertion or extreme cold, cause damage directly. These stressors will affect everyone; their severity will depend on each person's physical capacity. Selye's model has been useful for understanding the biological components involved in stress, but it does not explain the role of psychological components in stress. The effects of other stressors, such as situations that cause fear or anxiety, depend on people's perceptions and emotional reactivity. That is, because of individual differences in temperament or experience with a particular situation, some people may find a situation stressful and others may not. In these cases, it is the *perception* that counts.

Richard Lazarus argues that our *perception* of the stressor determines, to a large extent, the stress we experience (Lazarus, 2000; Lazarus & Folkman, 1984). According to Lazarus, an individual's stress levels are affected by his or her **cognitive appraisal**, or perception, of the stressful situation. Cognitive appraisal is a two-stage process. In the first stage, we evaluate the threat: We attempt to judge the seriousness of the perceived threat posed by the stressor. If we decide that the threat is real, we pass to the second stage, during which we assess whether we have the resources necessary to cope adequately with the threat. The extent to which we believe both that the stressor is a serious one and that we *do not* have the resources necessary to deal with it determines the level of stress we will experience. The belief that we cannot deal effectively with a stressor perceived as extremely dangerous leads to the highest levels of stress. Because different people may evaluate differently both the stressor and their ability to cope with it, they are likely to show different levels of stress when faced with the same stressor. We know from common experience that this is true. For example, people vary tremendously in their reactions to snakes: A harmless garter snake will arouse intense fear in some people and none in others.

Selye's findings, then, do not apply to all people; there are individual differences in how people react to prolonged exposure to stress. Some people, in fact, show little, if any, risk of becoming ill during or after chronic stress. Psychologist Susan Kobasa (1979; Kobasa, Maddi, Puccetti, & Zola, 1994)

**cognitive appraisal** One's perception of a stressful situation.

refers to these people as *hardy* individuals. In a study of how business executives coped with long-term stress, she found that some became ill and some did not. What she wanted to know is what caused this difference. Through detailed analyses of her participants' responses to different psychological inventories, she found that the hardy executives viewed the stressors in their lives as challenges and that they met these challenges head-on—they did not avoid them or become anxious about them. They also felt that they had control over the challenges (stressors) rather than that the challenges had control over them.

In other words, Kobasa's findings support Lazarus's idea of the importance of cognitive appraisal in dealing with stress: How we initially size up the stressor, how we tackle it, and the extent to which we believe that we can control the stressor seem to influence whether we become at risk for illnesses related to being chronically stressed.

Kobasa and her colleague, Salvatore Maddi, argue that the nature of early family home life is the cornerstone of hardiness (Maddi, 2002; Maddi & Kobasa, 1991). The development of a hardy personality is correlated with the combination of parental warmth, a stimulating home environment, and family support.

## Stressful Lifestyles and Impaired Health

Selye's research involved exposing laboratory animals to chronic and intense stressors under controlled conditions. In addition to showing that resistance to stressors appears to involve three stages, his results also showed that animals became seriously ill during the stage of exhaustion. Can prolonged exposure to severe stressors produce similar risks for humans? Many studies investigating the relationship of lifestyle to health have shown that the answer to this question is yes. Specifically, stressful lifestyles have been shown to be related to increased risk of CHD, cancer, impaired immune system functioning, and high blood pressure.

**Stress and CHD** One of the leading causes of death in Western societies is CHD—diseases of the heart and the blood vessels. CHD can cause heart attacks and strokes. Heart attacks occur when the blood vessels that serve the heart become blocked, while strokes involve the blood vessels in the brain. The two most important risk factors in CHD are high blood pressure and, as we learned earlier, a high level of cholesterol in the blood.

The likelihood that people will suffer from CHD may depend on how they react to stress. For example, Wood, Sheps, Elveback, and Schirder (1984) examined the blood pressure of people who had been subjected to a cold pressor test when they were children. The cold pressor test reveals how people's blood pressure reacts to the stress caused when their hand is placed in a container of ice water for one minute. Wood and his colleagues found that 70 percent of their study participants who hyperreacted to the stress when they were children had high blood pressure as adults, compared with 19 percent of those who showed little reaction to the stress as children.

Research on primates demonstrated individual differences in emotional reactivity as a risk factor for CHD. Manuck and colleagues (Manuck, Kaplan, & Clarkson, 1983; Manuck, Kaplan, & Matthews, 1986) fed a high-cholesterol diet to a group of monkeys, which increases the likelihood of their developing coronary artery disease. They measured the animals' emotional reactivity by threatening to capture the animals. (Monkeys avoid contact with humans, and they perceive being captured as a stressful situation.) Those animals that showed the strongest negative reactions eventually developed the highest rates of CHD. Presumably, these animals reacted more strongly to all types of stress, and their reactions had detrimental effects on their health.

Friedman and Rosenman (1959, 1974) identified a behaviour pattern that appeared to be related to a person's susceptibility to CHD. They characterized the disease-prone **type A pattern** as one of excessive competitive drive, an intense disposition, impatience, hostility, fast movements, and rapid speech. People with the **type B pattern** were less competitive; less hostile; more patient, easygoing, and tolerant; and they moved and talked more slowly; they were also less likely to suffer from CHD. Friedman and Rosenman developed a questionnaire that distinguished between these two types of people. The test is rather interesting, because the person who administers it is not a passive participant. The interviewer asks questions in an abrupt, impatient manner, interrupting the test taker if he or she takes too much time to answer a question. The point of such behaviour is to try to elicit type A behaviour.

The possibility of a relation between type A personality and CHD has generated a great deal of research. For example, the Western Collaborative Group Study (Rosenman et al., 1975, 1994) examined 3154 healthy men for 8.5 years. Among many other results, the Group found that the type A behaviour pattern was associated with twice the rate of CHD relative to non–type A behaviour patterns. Findings such as these led an independent review panel to classify the type A behaviour pattern as a risk factor for CHD (Review Panel, 1981). However, contradictory results have sometimes been obtained since then, and it is important to disentangle them.

An emerging understanding of these inconsistent results focuses on how the type A personality is measured. Positive links between the type A pattern and CHD tend to emerge when type A individuals are identified through observation and evaluation of their behaviours during interviews, but not when self-report questionnaires are used (e.g., Pitts & Phillips, 1998). There are many plausible explanations for the

**type A pattern** A behaviour pattern characterized by high levels of competitiveness and hostility, impatience, and an intense disposition; supposedly associated with an increased risk of CHD.

**type B pattern** A behaviour pattern characterized by lower levels of competitiveness and hostility, patience, and an easygoing disposition; supposedly associated with a decreased risk of CHD.

conflicting evidence, then. For example, identification of type A personality through direct observation of the related behaviours simply may be a better measure of type A style than the self-descriptive method of classification. Or perhaps the two measurement methods each identify somewhat non-overlapping components of type A style, but only the behavioural component is related strongly to CHD risk.

Although the relation between CHD and the type A behaviour pattern remains unresolved, several studies have found relationships between personality variables and particular risk factors, as distinct from a direct connection between type A personality and CHD. For example, Howard, Cunningham, and Rechnitzer (1976) found that people who exhibited extreme type A behaviour were more likely to smoke and to have high blood pressure and high blood levels of cholesterol. Weidner and colleagues (1987) confirmed the high level of cholesterol in a sample of men and women with the type A behaviour pattern, and Irvine, Garner, Craig, and Logan (1991) confirmed the association between type A behaviour and high blood pressure. Lombardo and Carreno (1987) found that type A smokers held the smoke in their lungs longer, leading to a high level of carbon monoxide in their blood.

Beyond CHD, there is further evidence that people with a type A personality have an increased risk of poor health. Yang, Sheng, and Bao (2003) found that type A personality traits were found in 80 percent of patients who had suffered a cerebral hemorrhage, compared to only 34 percent in a control group that did not have any cerebrovascular disease. How can we understand these research findings? The generally agreed-upon conclusion is that personality variables are involved in susceptibility to heart attack and other diseases, but that we need a better definition of just what these variables are. In addition, it is possible that different personality variables are associated with different risk factors, which makes it difficult to tease out the relevant variables. Personality factors certainly play an important role in CHD, but the precise nature of this role is still emerging through ongoing research.

**Post-traumatic Stress Disorder** The aftermath of traumatic events, such as those that accompany wars or natural disasters, often includes psychological symptoms that persist long after the stressful events are over. **Post-traumatic stress disorder (PTSD)** is an anxiety disorder in which the individual has feelings of social withdrawal accompanied by atypically low levels of emotion, caused by prolonged exposure to a stressor, such as a catastrophe. The symptoms produced by such exposure include recurrent dreams or recollections of the event, feelings that the traumatic event is recurring ("flashback" episodes), and intense psychological distress. These dreams, recollections, or flashback episodes lead the person to avoid thinking about the traumatic event, which often results in diminished interest in social activities, feelings of detachment from others, suppressed emotional feelings, and a sense that the future is bleak and empty. Psychological symptoms of PTSD include outbursts of anger, heightened reactions to sudden noises, sleep problems, and general difficulty concentrating, while physiological symptoms include increased cortisol and norepinephrine responses to stress (Bremner, 2006).

▲ *Canadian peacekeepers face most of the same stressors as those who engage in conflict, and are just as susceptible to post-traumatic stress disorder (Lamerson & Kelloway, 1996).*

Although PTSD is commonly associated with war, the disorder can be caused by many events. For example, many victims of rape, torture, natural disasters, and motor accidents suffer from PTSD (e.g., Korol, Kramer, Grace, & Green, 2002; Pulcino et al., 2003; Rheingold, Acierno, & Resnick, 2004). The severity of PTSD depends on factors such as sex, severity of the event, past psychiatric illness, and level of educational achievement (Basoglu, Salclogle, & Livanou, 2002). Post-traumatic stress disorder can strike people at any age. Children may show symptoms not usually seen in adulthood, including loss of recently acquired language skills or toilet training and somatic complaints such as stomach aches and headaches. Usually, the symptoms begin immediately after the traumatic event, but they are sometimes delayed for several months or years (Andrews, Brewin, Philpott, & Stewart, 2007; Pelcovitz & Kaplan, 1996). Whatever the context, increasing severity of the trauma increases the risk of developing PTSD (Berwin, Andrews, & Valentine, 2000).

The social support that people receive (or do not receive) after being exposed to an unusually stressful situation can also affect the likelihood of their developing post-traumatic stress disorder (Berwin, Andrews, & Valentine, 2000). As a result, mental health professionals try to seek out victims of natural disasters and crimes such as rapes or shooting sprees

**post-traumatic stress disorder (PTSD)** An anxiety disorder in which the individual has feelings of social withdrawal accompanied by atypically low levels of emotion caused by prolonged exposure to a stressor, such as a catastrophe.

to provide them with treatment that might prevent future psychological disorders (e.g., Flannery, 1999; Mitchell, 1999).

Research has shown that excessive use of alcohol tends to co-occur with PTSD (e.g., Driessen et al., 2008; Stewart, Mitchell, Wright, & Loba, 2004). One possibility for this association is that people with PTSD try to treat their own disorder with alcohol. People might use alcohol to manage negative moods and to block terrifying memories of the traumatic event(s). The problem, of course, is that such tactics will not work well in the long run, and excessive alcohol use itself will generate additional mental and physical health problems. The far better alternative is professional assistance.

**Psychoneuroimmunology** As we have seen, long-term stress can be harmful to one's health and can even result in brain damage. The most important causes are elevated levels of glucocorticoids, epinephrine, and norepinephrine. But, in addition, stress can impair the functions of the immune system, which protects us from assault by viruses, microbes, fungi, and other types of parasites. Study of the interactions between the immune system and behaviour (mediated by the nervous system, of course) is called **psychoneuroimmunology**.

**The Immune System** The **immune system**, a network of organs and cells that protects the body from invading bacteria, viruses, and other foreign substances, is one of the most complex systems of the body. Its function is to protect us from infection. Because infectious organisms have developed devious tricks through the process of evolution, our immune system has evolved devious tricks of its own. The description we provide here is abbreviated and simplified, but it presents some of the important elements of the system.

The immune system derives from white blood cells that develop in the bone marrow and in the thymus gland. Some of the cells roam through the blood or lymph glands and sinuses; others reside permanently in one place. The immune reaction occurs when the body is invaded by foreign organisms.

There are two types of specific immune reactions: chemically mediated and cell mediated. Chemically mediated immune reactions involve antibodies. All bacteria have unique proteins on their surfaces, called **antigens**. These proteins serve as the invaders' calling cards, identifying them to the immune system. Through exposure to the bacteria, the immune system learns to recognize these proteins. The result of this learning is the development of special lines of cells that produce specific **antibodies**—proteins that recognize antigens and help kill the invading micro-organism. One type of antibody is released into the circulation by **B lymphocytes**, which receive their name from the fact that they develop in bone marrow. These antibodies, called **immunoglobulins**, are chains of protein. Each of five different types of immunoglobulin is identical except for one end, which contains a unique receptor. A particular receptor binds with a particular antigen, just as a molecule of a hormone or a transmitter substance binds with its receptor. When the appropriate line of B lymphocytes detects the presence of an invading bacterium, the cells release their antibodies, which bind with the bacterial antigens. The antibodies either kill the invaders directly or attract other white blood cells, which then destroy the invaders. (See **Figure 16•7(a)**.)

The other type of defence mounted by the immune system, a cell-mediated immune reaction, is produced by

**psychoneuroimmunology** Study of the interactions between the immune system and behaviour as mediated by the nervous system.

**immune system** A network of organs and cells that protects the body from invading bacteria, viruses, and other foreign substances.

**antigens** The unique proteins found on the surface of bacteria; these proteins are what enable the immune system to recognize the bacteria as foreign substances.

**antibodies** Proteins in the immune system that recognize antigens and help kill invading micro-organisms.

**B lymphocytes** Cells that develop in bone marrow and release immunoglobulins to defend the body against antigens.

**immunoglobulins** The antibodies that are released by B lymphocytes.

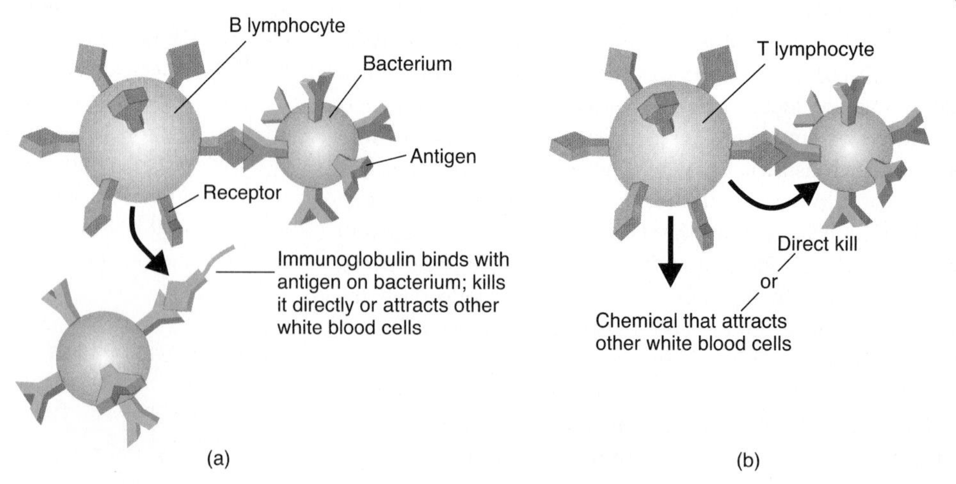


**FIGURE 16•7** Immune reactions. (a) Chemically mediated reaction. The B lymphocyte detects an antigen on a bacterium and releases a specific immunoglobulin. (b) Cell-mediated reaction. The T lymphocyte detects an antigen on a bacterium and kills it directly or releases a chemical that attracts other white blood cells.

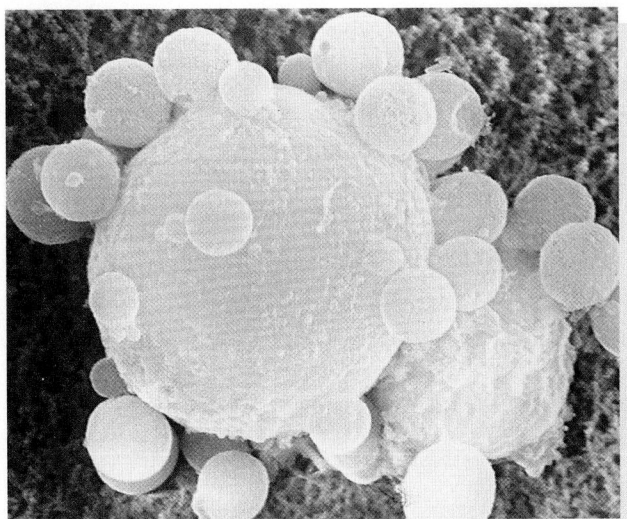

▲ *A T lymphocyte at work destroying tumour cells.*

**T lymphocytes**, which originally develop in the thymus gland. These cells also produce antibodies, but the antibodies remain attached to the outside of their membranes. T lymphocytes primarily defend the body against fungi, viruses, and multicellular parasites. When antigens bind with their surface antibodies, the cells either directly kill the invaders or signal other white blood cells to come and kill them. (See **Figure 16•7(b)**.)

In addition to the immune reactions produced by lymphocytes, natural killer cells continuously prowl through tissue. When they encounter a cell that has been infected by a virus or that has become transformed into a cancer cell, they engulf and destroy it. Thus, natural killer cells constitute an important defence against viral infections and the development of malignant tumours.

Our immune system normally protects us; however, there are times when it can cause us harm. Allergic reactions occur when an antigen causes cells of the immune system to overreact, releasing a particular immunoglobulin that produces a localized inflammatory response. The chemicals released during this reaction can enter general circulation and cause life-threatening complications. Allergic responses are harmful, and why they occur is unknown.

The immune system can do something else that harms the body—it can attack its own cells. **Autoimmune diseases** occur when the immune system becomes sensitized to a protein present in the body and attacks the tissue that contains this protein. Exactly what causes the protein to be so targeted is not known. What is known is that autoimmune diseases often follow viral or bacterial infections. Presumably, in learning to recognize antigens that belong to the infectious agent, the immune system develops a line of cells that treat one of the body's own proteins as foreign. Some common autoimmune diseases include rheumatoid arthritis, diabetes, lupus, and multiple sclerosis.

**Neural Control of the Immune System** Stress can suppress the immune system, resulting in a greater likelihood of infectious diseases, and it can also aggravate autoimmune diseases. It may even affect the growth of cancers. What is the physiological explanation for these effects? One answer, and probably the most important one, is that stress increases the secretion of glucocorticoids, and these hormones directly suppress the activity of the immune system. All types of white blood cells have glucocorticoid receptors, and suppression of the immune system is presumably mediated by these receptors (Cole & Mollard, 2007; Solomon, 1987).

Because the secretion of glucocorticoids is controlled by the brain, the brain is obviously responsible for the suppressing effect of these hormones on the immune system. For example, in a study of rats, Keller and colleagues (1983) found that the stress of inescapable shock decreased the number of lymphocytes found in the blood. This effect was abolished by removal of the adrenal gland. Thus, the decrease in lymphocytes appears to have been caused by the release of glucocorticoids triggered by the stress. (See **Figure 16•8(a)**.) However, the same authors found that removal of the adrenal glands did not abolish the effects of stress on another type of immune response: stimulation of lymphocytes by an antigen. (See **Figure 16•8(b)**.) Thus, not all effects of stress on the immune system are mediated by glucocorticoids; there must be additional mechanisms.

These other mechanisms may involve direct neural control. The bone marrow, the thymus gland, and the lymph nodes all receive neural input. Although researchers have not yet obtained direct proof that this input modulates immune function, it would be surprising if it did not.

The immune system also appears to be sensitive to chemicals produced by the nervous system. The best evidence comes from studies of the opioids produced by the brain. Shavit and colleagues (1984) found that inescapable intermittent shock produced both analgesia (decreased sensitivity to pain) and suppression of the production of natural killer cells. These effects both seem to have been mediated by brain opioids, because both effects were abolished when the researchers administered a drug that blocks opiate receptors. Shavit and colleagues (1986) found that natural killer cell activity could be suppressed by injecting morphine directly into the brain; thus, the effect of the opiates appears to take place in the brain. We do not yet understand the mechanism by which the brain affects the natural killer cells. As you can see, the links between stress and the immune system are complex and involve a number of mechanisms (Moynihan, 2003; Saurer, Ijames, Carrigan, & Lysle, 2008; Schleifer, Keller, & Stein, 1985).

**T lymphocytes** Cells that develop in the thymus gland that produce antibodies, which defend the body against fungi, viruses, and multicellular parasites.

**autoimmune diseases** Diseases such as rheumatoid arthritis, diabetes, lupus, and multiple sclerosis, in which the immune system attacks and destroys some of the body's own tissue.

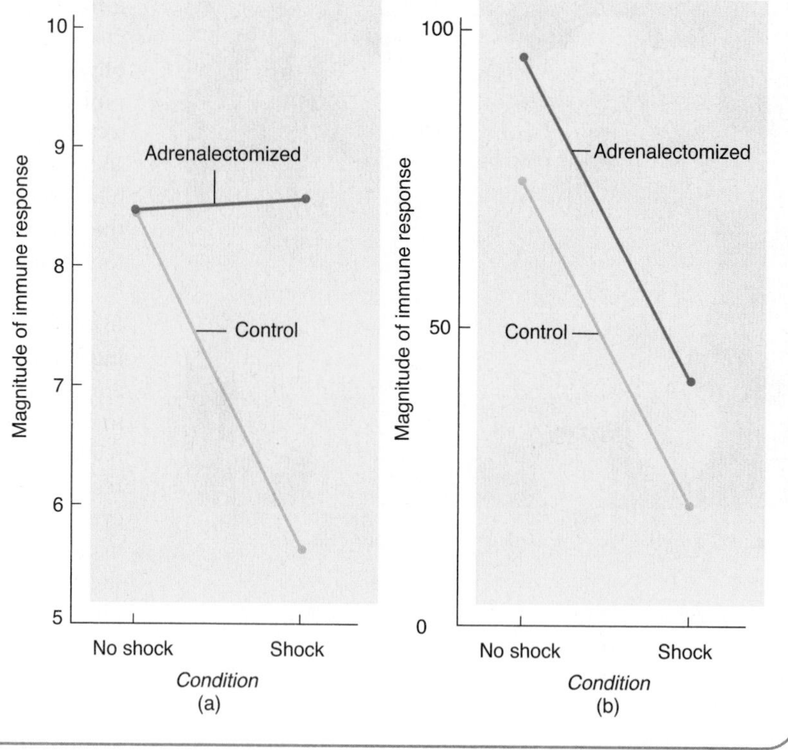


**FIGURE 16•8** Effects of the removal of rats' adrenal glands on suppression of the immune system produced by inescapable shocks. (a) Number of white blood cells (lymphocytes) found in the blood. (b) Lymphocyte production after exposure to an antigen.

*(Based on data from Keller, S. E., Weiss, J. M., Schleifer, S. J., Miller, N. E., & Stein, M. (1983). Stress-induced suppression of immunity in adrenalectomized rats.* Science, 221, *1301–1304.)*

**Infectious Diseases** You may have noticed that when a married person dies, his or her spouse often dies soon afterwards. The cause frequently is an infection. In fact, a wide variety of stress-producing events in a person's life can increase the susceptibility to infectious diseases. Even in childhood, stress caused by family and school can decrease immune system functioning. Caserta and colleagues (2008) found that stress caused by school and family had a negative impact on the health of children. If stress in grade school can affect health, it stands to reason that stressful college programs should lead to decreased health. Glaser and colleagues (1987) found that medical students were more likely to contract acute infections—and to show evidence of suppression of the immune system—during the time that final examinations were given. In addition, autoimmune diseases often get worse when a person is subjected to stress, as Feigenbaum, Masi, and Kaplan (1979) found for rheumatoid arthritis. In a laboratory study, Rogers and colleagues (1980) found that when rats were stressed by handling them or exposing them to a cat, they developed a more severe case of an artificially induced autoimmune disease than did control rats who were not exposed to the same stressors.

Stone, Reed, and Neale (1987) attempted to see whether stressful events in people's daily lives might predispose them to upper respiratory infection. If a person is exposed to a micro-organism that might cause such a disease, the symptoms do not occur for several days; that is, there is an incubation period between exposure and signs of the actual illness. The researchers therefore reasoned that if stressful events suppressed the immune system, there should be a higher likelihood of respiratory infections several days after such stress. To test their hypothesis, they had volunteers keep daily records of desirable and undesirable events in their lives for 12 weeks. The volunteers also kept a daily record of any discomfort and illness symptoms.

The researchers found that during the three- to five-day period just before showing symptoms of an upper respiratory infection, people experienced an increased number of undesirable events and a decreased number of desirable events in their lives. (See **Figure 16•9**.) The researchers suggest that this effect is caused by decreased production of a particular immunoglobulin that is present in the secretions of mucous membranes, including those in the nose, mouth, throat, and lungs. This immunoglobulin serves as the first defence against infectious micro-organisms that enter the nose or mouth. They found that this immunoglobulin (known as IgA) is associated with mood. When people are unhappy or depressed, their IgA levels are lower than normal. In a parallel fashion, desirable events appear to increase levels of IgA (Stone et al., 1996). These results suggest that relatively chronic stress caused by undesirable life events, by suppressing the production of IgA, may lead to a rise in the likelihood of upper respiratory infections (e.g., Cohen & Hamrick, 2003). Other work shows that pre-existing stress also exacerbates the severity of symptoms once a viral infection (influenza A) is already contracted (Cohen, Doyle, & Skoner, 1999).

Wu and colleagues (1999) demonstrated a direct association between stress and the immune system. These investigators found that caregivers of family members with Alzheimer's disease—who certainly underwent considerable

**FIGURE 16•9** Mean percentage change in frequency of undesirable and desirable events during the 10-day period preceding the onset of symptoms of upper respiratory infections.

*(Based on data from Stone, A. A., Reed, B. R., & Neale, J. M. (1987). Changes in daily event frequency precede episodes of physical symptoms.* Journal of Human Stress, 13, *70–74.)*

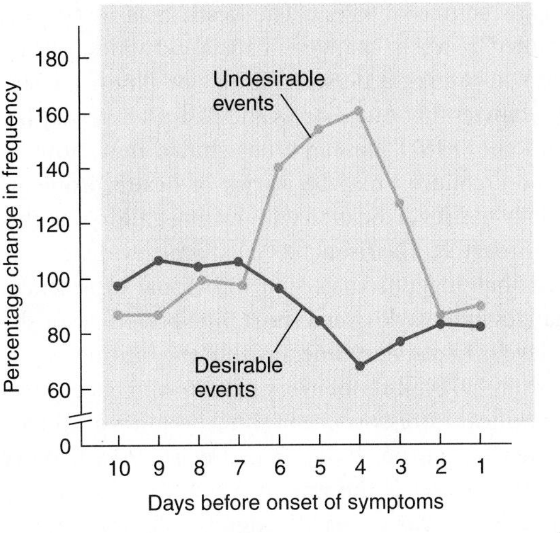


**FIGURE 16.10** Stimulation of white blood cell (lymphocyte) production by an antigen in the blood of husbands before and after their wives' deaths.

*(Adapted from Schleifer, S. J., Keller, S. E., Camerino, M., Thornton, J. C., & Stein, M. (1983). Suppression of lymphocyte stimulation following bereavement.* Journal of the American Medical Association, 250, *374–377.)*

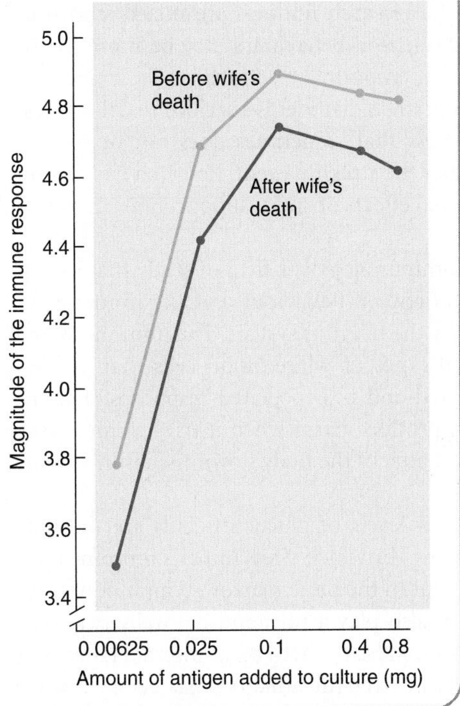


stress—showed weaker immune systems, based on several different laboratory tests. Similar research shows that the effect of stress on the immune system can last years after the stressor is no longer present (Esterling, Kiecolt-Glaser, Bodnar, & Glaser, 1994; Vitaliano, Zhang, & Scanlan, 2003).

People who are widowed have higher-than-average rates of cancer and other illnesses. To investigate the possibility that bereavement suppresses the immune system, Schleifer and several other researchers (1983) drew blood samples from 15 men whose wives were dying of terminal breast cancer. Two blood samples were drawn, the first before the spouse's death and the second within two months afterwards. Both times, an agent that normally stimulates blood lymphocyte activity was mixed with the lymphocytes, and the resultant level of activity was measured. On average, the activity level of blood lymphocytes after the spouse's death was less than before her death, which meant that the bereaved spouses were more susceptible to illness. (See **Figure 16•10**.) Follow-up research indicates that there may be gender differences in how the death of a loved one affects our health. Vahtera and colleagues (2006) sampled more than 25 000 people and found that stress due to the death of a family member or spouse has a negative impact on health across gender, but women tended to be more vulnerable to illness than men. The researchers measured health after the loss of a loved one and found that men's health declined only in the first months after the tragic event, whereas women's health was still negatively affected a year after their loss. Taken together, the results of these studies (and many other similar studies) suggest a strong link between stress and weakening of the immune system.

## Interim Summary

### Stress and Health

Stress is defined in terms of our physiological and psychological response to stimuli that either prevent us from obtaining a goal or endanger our well-being. People's emotional reactions to aversive stimuli can harm their health. Selye's well-known model describes how prolonged exposure to stress leads to illness and sometimes death. The stress response, which Cannon called the fight-or-flight response, is useful as a short-term response to threatening stimuli but is harmful in the long term. This response includes increased activity of the sympathetic branch of the autonomic nervous system and increased secretion of epinephrine, norepinephrine, and glucocorticoids by the adrenal gland.

Although increased levels of epinephrine and norepinephrine can raise blood pressure, most of the harm to health comes from glucocorticoids. Prolonged exposure to high levels of these hormones can increase blood pressure, damage muscle tissue, lead to infertility, inhibit growth, inhibit the inflammatory response, and suppress the immune system. It can also damage the hippocampus, and some investigators believe that glucocorticoids accelerate the aging process.

Because the harm of most forms of stress comes from our own response to it, individual differences in personality variables can alter the effects of stressful situations. The most important variable is the nature of a person's coping response. Research on the type A behaviour pattern suggests that some of these variables can predict the likelihood of CHD. However, the research findings are mixed, and some suggest that health-related behaviours may be more important than patterns of emotional reactions.

Post-traumatic stress disorder is a serious reaction to unusually intense stress that sometimes does not occur until several months after the stressful event. Research has demonstrated the beneficial effects of social support after the stressful event.

Psychoneuroimmunology is a field of study that investigates interactions between behaviour and the immune system as mediated by the nervous system. The immune system consists of several types of white blood cells that produce chemically mediated and cell-mediated responses. The immune system can produce harm when it triggers an allergic reaction or when it attacks the body's own tissues in autoimmune diseases.

Increased blood levels of glucocorticoids are the most important mechanism by which stress impairs immune functioning. Neural input to the bone marrow, lymph nodes, and thymus gland may also play a role, and naturally occurring opioids appear to suppress the activity of internal killer cells.

A wide variety of stressful situations has been shown to increase people's susceptibility to infectious diseases. For example, the stress associated with the loss of a spouse appears to contribute to upper respiratory infections in some people.

**QUESTIONS TO CONSIDER**

1. What kinds of stressors do you face in your life? When confronted with a stressor, what kinds of physiological, emotional, cognitive, and behavioural reactions do you experience? What makes some stressors more aversive to you than others?
2. Has the stress response outlived its usefulness to our species? It seems as though this response was more useful to our prehistoric ancestors in avoiding predators and finding food than it is to us in our work and play. In your opinion, would our lives be better off without this response? Explain.

# Coping with Everyday Stress

Regardless of one's lifestyle, stress is a fact of everyday life. How much stress we experience and the degree to which stress impairs our health depends to a large extent on our perception of the threat posed by the stressor. Depending on the individual, almost any aspect of the environment can be perceived as a stressor.

## Sources of Stress

Life changes that threaten or otherwise complicate life constitute a major source of stress. The death of a loved one, being promoted at work, changes in social activities, getting married, and sustaining a personal injury or illness are significant life changes that cause stress and disrupt everyday life (Holmes & Rahe, 1967). Research has shown that mothers of grade school children may be at risk of health problems due to the daily hassles associated with raising children in this age group (Stuart & Garrison, 2002). Some evidence has accumulated that suggests that if an individual experiences enough changes in lifestyle over a short time period, he or she is likely to develop a physical illness within the next two years (Rahe & Arthur, 1978). But not every person who encounters a series of significant stressors over a short period is at risk for illness (DePue & Monroe, 1986; Santed et al., 2003). Why? Once again, the answer is the way in which people perceive stressors. Recall Lazarus's idea of cognitive appraisal: The amount of stress induced by a stimulus perceived to be a stressor is determined by how significant we *believe* its threat to be and whether we feel able to cope with it.

Stressors do not have to be catastrophic or cause significant changes in lifestyle to induce stress. Often the everyday hassles we experience are enough to leave us feeling stressed out. Locking our keys in the car, being late for an appointment, and having a disagreement with a friend are examples of stressful everyday events. Researchers have found that there is a strong correlation between well-being and the amount of daily hassles a person experiences (Landreville & Veazina, 1992).

A common source of daily stress comes simply from making routine choices about what to do, how to do it, or when to do it. Consider, for example, a choice between studying tonight for a test you have tomorrow or going to a party with some friends. You want to do both, but you can do only one (you are back into the classic self-control situation again—the choice between a small, short-term reward and a larger, long-term reward). Psychologists refer to this as an *approach-approach conflict* because the choice involves two desirable outcomes. Other choices involve *approach-avoidance conflicts*—one outcome is desirable and the other is not. For example, you want to visit England and decide to travel by ship because you are afraid of flying. Still other choices involve *avoidance-avoidance conflicts* in which both outcomes are undesirable. For instance, choosing between having a root canal procedure or having a tooth extracted creates stress because you do not want to have either one of them, yet you must submit to one or the other in order to maintain your health. People appear to have favoured methods of dealing with such conflicts. Some people tend to deal with stressful conflicts through approach whereas others tend to use avoidance strategies (e.g., Rutherford & Endler, 1999).

Holmes and Rahe (1967) developed one of the first measures of life stressors, the Social Readjustment Rating Scale (SRRS). The SRRS was constructed on the assumption that any *change* in a person's life—for better or worse—is a stressor. The test asks people to rate the amount of change or adjustment caused by recent events in their lives, such as getting married or divorced, getting a new job or being fired, moving to a new location, and losing a loved one. Responses are given in terms of life-change units (LCUs)—how much change or adjustment is caused by specific events. Once a person completes the SRRS, the LCUs are summed, resulting in a single score. High scores indicate high levels of stress and low scores represent low levels of stress. People who score high on the SRRS have been shown to have more health-related illnesses and adjustment problems than those who score low (Holmes & Rahe, 1967; Monroe & Hadjiyannakis, 2002).

The Daily Hassles and Uplifts Scale (DeLongis, Folkman, & Lazarus, 1988), another commonly used scale, measures daily events that are either troublesome (hassles) or pleasant (uplifts). This scale has people rate, at each day's end, the extent to which an event—such as the weather, deadlines, family, and physical appearance—served as a hassle or uplift for them on that day. This scale may be filled out daily over extended periods to provide a picture of how the routine events of everyday life create stress for people. Daily hassles yield a more accurate prediction of physical illness and adjustment problems than do daily uplifts (DeLongis, Folkman, & Lazarus, 1988; Stuart & Garrison, 2002) and major life events (Garrett, Brantley, Jones, & McKnight, 1991).

## Coping Styles and Strategies

Our discussion thus far has focused on the bad news about stress: its damaging effects on the body and mind. Let's consider some good news: Each of us can learn to control stress. We may not always be able to predict when and where we will encounter stressors or to control their intensity, but we can mitigate their damaging effects by adopting coping strategies that are consistent with our lifestyles. A **coping strategy** is simply a plan of action that we follow, either in anticipation of encountering a stressor or as a direct response to stress as it occurs, which is effective in reducing the level of stress we experience.

According to Lazarus and Folkman (1984; Folkman & Lazarus, 1991), there are two types of coping responses: problem-focused and emotion-focused. **Problem-focused coping** is directed toward the source of the stress. For example, if the stress is job-related, a person might try to change conditions at the job site or take courses to acquire skills that will enable him or her to obtain a different job. **Emotion-focused coping** is directed toward a person's own personal reaction to the stressor. For example, a person might try to relax and forget about the problem or find solace in the company of friends.

▲ *Aerobic exercise, such as jogging, not only has positive effects on physical health but also reduces stress and promotes feelings of well-being.*

Obviously, if the source of a stress-producing problem has a potential solution, problem-focused coping is the best strategy. If it does not, then emotion-focused coping is the only option.

Health psychologists have shown that several common emotion-focused coping techniques are effective in controlling stress—namely, aerobic exercise, cognitive reappraisal, progressive relaxation training, and social support.

**Aerobic Exercise** As we have seen, aerobic exercise has many benefits. People who engage regularly in aerobic exercise are likely to live longer than people who do not exercise regularly (Paffenbarger, Hyde, Wing, & Hsieh, 1986). Those who consistently make time for aerobic exercise also tend to report reduced stress. Consider the results of an experiment involving mildly depressed female university students (McCann & Holmes, 1984). The students were assigned to one of three groups: a control group that received no treatment for depression, a group that received relaxation training, and a group that engaged in aerobic exercise (jogging and dancing). The students rated their depression levels at the beginning of the experiment and then again 10 weeks later. As expected, self-reported levels of depression in the control condition showed no change. Students given relaxation training showed a slight decrease in depression. Those who participated in aerobic exercise showed a large decrease in depression. Further

**coping strategy** A plan of action that a person follows to reduce the perceived level of stress, either in anticipation of encountering a stressor or in response to its occurrence.
**problem-focused coping** Any coping behaviour that is directed at reducing or eliminating a stressor.
**emotion-focused coping** Any coping behaviour that is directed toward changing one's own emotional reaction to a stressor.

research has shown that aerobic exercise, such as jogging, is associated with improved hormonal responses to stress and a decrease in depressive mood states (Nabkasorn et al., 2007).

Although we know that aerobic exercise is effective in reducing stress, we do not yet know exactly how it reduces stress. One possibility is that increased heart and lung efficiency coupled with the lower blood pressure that results from aerobic exercise simply makes people feel better. Another possibility is that people who can adjust their schedules to make room for regular workouts have a sense of control that those who cannot find the time for exercise lack. People who make exercise a priority in their schedules have to control other aspects of their lives to ensure that they do, indeed, exercise. As we saw in Chapter 14, people who have an internal locus of control take responsibility for the course of their lives. One possibility, then, is that internals, more than externals, will attend to threats to their health and initiate steps to prevent illness (Avison & Cairney, 2003; Lefcourt & Davidson-Katz, 1991). A special locus of control scale, developed by Wallston, Wallston, and DeVellis (1978), focuses on health behaviours. People with a strong internal locus of health control have been found to engage in more health-promoting behaviours, including exercise, than do those with external orientations (e.g., Norman, Bennett, Smith, & Murphy, 1998).

**Cognitive Reappraisal** Aerobic exercise is not the coping strategy of choice for everyone. Some people find that simply altering their perceptions of the threat posed by stressors reduces stress. This coping strategy is called **cognitive reappraisal** (or *cognitive restructuring*) and is an extension of Lazarus and Folkman's (1984) idea of cognitive appraisal. The rationale underlying this strategy is easy to grasp: If our cognitive appraisal of a stressor is a determining factor in producing stress, then by *reappraising* that stressor as less threatening, stress should be reduced. Sometimes simply learning to substitute an incompatible response, such as replacing a negative statement with a positive one, is sufficient to reduce stress (Lazarus, 1971; Meichenbaum, 1977). For example, students who suffer from test anxiety perceive tests as extremely threatening. They may say to themselves "I am going to flunk the test tomorrow" or "That test is going to be so hard." To reappraise the stressor in this case would involve replacing these statements with ones such as "I'm going to pass that test tomorrow" or "Sure, that test will be hard, but I'm ready for it."

Cognitive reappraisal is an effective coping strategy because it is often a more realistic approach to interpreting the threat posed by stressors than is the original appraisal. We have good reason to appraise a charging bear as a real threat, but not a university examination. After all, we may not be able to deal well with the bear, but we can always learn how to take tests and improve our study habits. An additional benefit of cognitive reappraisal is that it teaches the individual that he or she can take control of stressful situations.

**Relaxation Training** A third coping strategy is simply learning to relax when confronted with a stressor. Relaxing is based on the same principle as cognitive reappraisal: Substitute an incompatible response for the stress reaction. Consider the following example. You are anxious to get home, but you are caught in rush-hour traffic. Your blood pressure rises, you begin to perspire, and you feel a knot forming in your stomach. What would happen if you were to relax? First, these physical responses would gradually recede, and second, you would feel less stress.

One procedure for producing relaxation is the **progressive relaxation technique.** It involves three steps: (1) recognizing your body's signals informing you that you are experiencing stress; (2) using those signals as a cue to begin relaxing; and (3) relaxing by focusing your attention on different groups of muscles, beginning with those in the head and neck and then those in the arms and legs. Here is an example of how relaxation may be used to reduce feelings of stress. Suppose that when confronted by a stressor—for example, a test—you respond by tensing certain muscles: those in your hand and fingers that you use to hold your pen or pencil and those around your mouth that you use to clench your teeth. Once you become aware of these responses, you can use them as cues to relax the muscle groups involved.

**Social Support** Although all of us experience stress, the experience is a subjective and private matter. Nobody else can truly know what we feel inside. However, being confronted by a stressor and coping with stress are often social matters. We learn as children to seek others—parents, siblings, and friends—when we need help. This is a pattern of coping that continues over the lifespan. *Social support*, the help that we receive from others in times of stress, is an important coping strategy for many people. We can benefit from the experience of others in dealing with the same or similar stressors.

We may also learn how to reappraise the situation if others show us how to cope. As well, other people can provide encouragement and incentives to overcome the stressor when we might otherwise fail to cope with the stressful situation.

## Stress Inoculation Training

According to psychologist Donald Meichenbaum, the best way to cope with stress is to take the offensive—to have a plan in mind for dealing with stressors before you are actually confronted by them. In other words, people should not wait until they are faced with a stressor to cope with it. Instead, they should anticipate the kinds of stressors most likely to

**cognitive reappraisal** Any coping strategy in which one alters one's perception of the threat posed by a stressor to reduce stress.

**progressive relaxation technique** A relaxation technique involving three steps: (1) recognizing the body's signals that indicate the presence of stress; (2) using those signals as a cue to begin relaxing; and (3) relaxing groups of muscles, beginning with those in the head and neck and then those in the arms and legs.

affect them and develop the most effective coping plan for dealing with specific stressors. Meichenbaum (1985, 1993), in fact, has devised a problem-focused coping method, called **stress inoculation training**, which focuses on helping people develop coping skills that will decrease their susceptibility to the negative effects of stress. Stress inoculation training (SIT) has been found to be effective in reducing stress levels among people working in a variety of settings, including nurses, teachers, police trainees (Bishop, 1994), military personnel (Armfield, 1994), bankers (Cambronne, Shih, & Harri, 1999), social workers (Keyes, 1995), and athletes (Newcomer & Perna, 2003). Law students, who face a great deal of stress in their first year of school, showed a decrease in personal, emotional, and general stress if they had participated in a SIT program (Sheehy & Horan, 2004).

In Meichenbaum's words, stress inoculation training

> is analogous to the concept of medical inoculation against biological diseases. . . . Analogous to medical inoculation, [stress inoculation training] is designed to build "psychological antibodies," or coping skills, and to enhance resistance through exposure to stimuli that are strong enough to arouse defenses without being so powerful as to overcome them. (1985, p. 21)

Stress inoculation training usually occurs in a clinical setting involving a therapist and a client and takes place over three phases aimed at achieving seven goals. (See **Table 16•6.**)

**TABLE 16•6 Summary of the Phases and Goals of Meichenbaum's (1985) Stress Inoculation Training Program**

| | |
|---|---|
| **Conceptualization Phase** | |
| *Goal 1:* | Learning the transactional nature of stress and coping. |
| *Goal 2:* | Learning to become better at realistically appraising stressful situations by learning self-monitoring skills with respect to negative or maladaptive thoughts, emotions, and behaviours. |
| **Skills Acquisition and Rehearsal Phase** | |
| *Goal 3:* | Learning problem-solving skills specific to the stressor. |
| *Goal 4:* | Learning and rehearsing emotion-regulation and self-control skills. |
| *Goal 5:* | Learning how to use maladaptive responses as cues to implement the new coping strategy. |
| **Application and Follow-Through Phase** | |
| *Goal 6:* | Learning to practise imagery rehearsal using progressively more difficult or stressful situations. |
| *Goal 7:* | Learning to apply new coping skills to other, perhaps unexpected, stressors. |

*Source: Adapted from Meichenbaum, D. (1985).* Stress inoculation training. *New York: Pergamon Press, pp. 21–26.*

The first phase is called the *conceptualization phase* and involves two basic goals. Goal 1 involves learning about the *transactional* nature of stress and coping. Stress and coping are strongly influenced by the interaction of cognitive and environmental variables. A person experiences stress to the extent that he or she appraises the stressor—an environmental variable—as taxing or overwhelming his or her ability to cope with it—a cognitive variable. In Meichenbaum's view, coping is any behavioural-cognitive attempt to overcome, eliminate, or otherwise control the negative effects caused by the stressor (see also Lazarus & Folkman, 1984).

Goal 2 involves becoming better at realistically appraising stressful situations by taking stock of, or self-monitoring, patterns in maladaptive thinking, feeling, and behaving. A person may keep a diary, or a "stress log," to record stressful events, the conditions under which these events occur, and his or her reactions to these events.

The second phase is called the *skills acquisition and rehearsal phase* and involves Goals 3 through 5. Goal 3 involves learning specific problem-solving skills aimed at reducing stress. For example, a person may learn to identify and define a specific stressor and outline a plan for dealing with it in behavioural terms. The plan should include developing alternative ideas for dealing with the stressor and considering the possible consequences that correspond to each alternative. At this point, a person may find it helpful to undergo relaxation training and self-instructional training, in which he or she learns to make positive self-statements when confronted by a stressor.

Goal 4 involves learning and rehearsing emotion-regulation and self-control skills. These skills help people remain calm and rational when confronted with a stressor. Goal 5 involves learning how to use maladaptive responses as a cue to invoke the new coping strategy. For example, when faced with a stressor, you may feel yourself getting tense. This feeling of tension is your cue to implement specific aspects of your inoculation training, which presumably would reduce your level of stress.

The *application and follow-through phase* is the third and final phase of Meichenbaum's program and includes Goals 6 and 7. Goal 6 involves *imagery rehearsal*, in which a person practises coping with the stressor by imagining being confronted by that stressor in progressively more difficult situations. The purpose of rehearsing the coping skills is to build confidence in the ability to use the new coping strategy. Goal 7 involves learning to apply new coping abilities to both expected and unexpected stressors. This might be accomplished by imagining several situations in which you feel anxious, imagining implementing the coping strategy in response to the anxiety, and, finally, imagining feeling relieved as a result of coping with the stressor.

**stress inoculation training** The stress management program developed by Meichenbaum for teaching people to develop coping skills that increase their resistance to the negative effects of stress.

Suppose that, like many people, you are uncomfortable in new social situations. You feel comfortable around friends and people whom you know well, but you become anxious or nervous when you meet people for the first time. In fact, you become so nervous that it interferes with your ability to function socially—you may even begin to avoid social situations where you would meet new people. How might you use Meichenbaum's system to deal with this stressor?

*Goal 1: Understanding the transactional nature of stress.* In this case, you perceive meeting new people as stressful. You may avoid going to parties and other social functions, which makes you feel better because the anxiety goes away. Although you really want to become more outgoing, you become anxious when you find yourself in such social situations: Your stomach tenses, your palms sweat, and you worry about what to say and how to act. In other words, specific environmental variables—social functions, meeting new people, and so on—cause cognitive and emotional discomfort, such as anxiety and nervousness. You feel inadequate in coping with these types of social situations.

*Goal 2: Learning to appraise these social situations realistically through self-monitoring.* Which social situations make you feel the most nervous? Do you feel more anxious meeting same-sex or opposite-sex people? Are there instances when meeting new people is not anxiety-provoking? Do you feel less anxious when you are forced to meet people on your own or when a friend introduces you to others? By answering questions such as these, you learn more about the specific elements of the social situation that are stressful. And, through such self-monitoring (which also includes keeping a record of specific social situations and how you respond to them), you become more likely to look at the situation more objectively, which facilitates your ability to appraise the situation realistically. You may find, in fact, that only specific social situations, such as meeting people of the opposite sex, make you nervous.

*Goal 3: Acquiring specific problem-solving behaviours targeted at reducing stress.* What advice might you offer someone who experiences anxiety in social situations? What behaviours might you engage in that would be effective in reducing the amount of stress that you experience when meeting new people? What are the drawbacks to these different behaviours? By exploring these sorts of questions, you begin to think about which actions on your part might be effective at reducing stress in social situations. Let us assume that you have identified the stressor as being meeting people of the opposite sex. The next step is to outline a plan of action for coping with this stressor. You decide that you will tackle your problem by first thinking about how you might best engage in the following behaviours and then actually implementing them (questions in parentheses are examples of questions you might ask yourself while thinking about how you will implement a course of action):

1. You will go to a party that a friend of yours is having next Friday night. (Should I go alone or with another friend for support? Should I arrive early or late?)
2. You will introduce yourself to the first member of the opposite sex that you meet by stating your name and asking the other person his or her name—"Hi, My name is ________; what's yours?" You will then ask this person where he or she is from, who he or she knows at the party, and what he or she is studying or does for a living. (What should I do if this person turns away at some point? Should I take it as a rejection or should I just forget about it and introduce myself to someone else?)
3. If the person responds to your questions, you will attempt to extend the conversation for at least another minute before you politely excuse yourself to talk with people that you know well. (If the conversation is going well, should I keep it going for as long as I can?)
4. You will meet at least three new people using this strategy before the party ends.

Outlining the problem and the steps toward resolving the problem in this fashion will allow you to develop a plan of action, to critique it (for example, what should I do if the person I have introduced myself to won't respond to my questions or is just as nervous about meeting people as I am?), and to reconsider the problem in light of your strategy.

*Goal 4: Learning to control emotions and developing self-control in the face of the stressor.* You may feel extremely anxious when meeting new people, even to the point that you feel as though you cannot control your anxiety—you want to run away from the situation. To overcome the stressor, though, you must learn to subordinate these feelings to more rational thinking. For example, when meeting new people, try to focus on what you must do to meet people rather than on your own anxiety. That is, concentrate on what it is you must do—the specific behaviours you need to execute in order to meet someone and carry on a conversation with him or her—rather than on feeling nervous. It is with this goal, more than any of the others, that a therapist is likely to be of help. A therapist would offer you advice on the step-by-step behaviours you would engage in to replace maladaptive emotions and responses with adaptive ones.

*Goal 5: Using maladaptive responses as cues to implement the plan of action.* The key to confronting stressors using stress inoculation training is to change how you respond to the symptoms of stress that the stressors elicit from you. Rather than panicking when you feel stressed, you use the symptoms of stress as a cue to implement what you have learned in your inoculation training. You may, for example, tell yourself, "I can handle the situation" or "I'll relax and just be myself" or "Now is the time for me to introduce myself and ask this person his or her name" when you feel that first tinge of butterflies in your stomach. Goal 6 prepares you mentally for taking this step in reality.

*Goal 6: Practising the plan of action.* Once you have decided the behaviours you need to adopt to reduce your stress, practise them mentally and with someone else. Picture yourself meeting someone whom you have seen before but do not know. Imagine how you will respond if he or she asks you a particular question. Do a rehearsal as well. Ask one of your close friends to pretend that he or she is someone to whom you will introduce yourself. Ask your friend to respond to your questions the way he or she would if meeting you for the first time.

*Goal 7: Applying new coping abilities in expected and unexpected socially stressful situations.* Because you now better understand the nature of your stress and have acquired and practised problem-solving skills and coping strategies, you are ready to imagine confronting the stressor in real-life situations. For example, imagine going to a party and meeting new people. Imagine the conversation you may carry on with the people you imagine to be there. After such imagery rehearsal, going to a real party and meeting new people should be less stressful. You may not become the life of the party, but you should be more comfortable mingling with your fellow partygoers.

Stress is an inevitable consequence of environmental change. Both large changes, such as a natural disaster or changing jobs, and small changes, such as remembering that you have a quiz tomorrow, contribute to the overall level of stress that we experience at any one time. Whether stress impairs our health depends on three variables: the extent to which we appraise the stressor as threatening, whether we engage in good health practices, and the extent to which we use coping strategies effectively.

## Interim Summary

### Coping with Everyday Stress

Stress may stem from a wide variety of sources. Even positive events, such as the birth of a child or the marriage of a son or daughter, can produce stress. Stress may lead to physical illness when a person undergoes several stressful events over a short period of time. However, the extent to which people become ill appears to depend on the extent to which they perceive a stressor as a threat to their well-being and the extent to which they believe they can cope with that threat.

Lazarus and Folkman (1984) have identified two types of coping. Problem-focused coping represents any attempt to reduce stress by attempting to change the event or situation producing the stress. Emotion-focused coping centres on changing one's personal reaction to the stressful event or situation. Emotion-focused coping may involve activities such as aerobic exercise, cognitive reappraisal, relaxation training, and seeking social support.

Meichenbaum's stress inoculation training program is a problem-focused coping strategy that prepares people to cope with anticipated stressors. The program involves three phases and seven goals. The first phase involves learning how to conceptualize the transactional nature of stress. The second phase entails learning coping skills specific to the stressors in their lives and practising or rehearsing these skills in hypothetical situations. The third phase involves preparing people to implement these coping skills in real-life situations. The seven goals of stress inoculation training focus on specific kinds of knowledge, behaviour, and coping strategies central to preparing people to anticipate, confront, and reduce the threat posed by stressful situations.

#### QUESTIONS TO CONSIDER

1. Which general approach do you take to coping with the stress in your life: problem-focused or emotion-focused? What led you to develop this style of coping? How effective are you at coping with stress?
2. What stressors do you seem to be able to handle better than your friends? What stressors are some of your friends better at handling than you are? To what extent do differences in perception of the threat posed by these stressors account for these differences in being able to cope with them?
3. Think of a stressor that is especially difficult for you to deal with. Develop an outline for coping with it based on Meichenbaum's stress inoculation training program. Explain why your program may or may not be effective.

## EPILOGUE

### Personality and Health

Leif's death left a lasting impact on his friends, family, and me. As you have read, personal loss, or anything that creates stress in our life, affects not only our well-being, but also our physical health. After Leif passed away, my wife fell ill with the flu. At the time, I was going through a stressful period at the office while trying to console her. Considering what we know about the correlation between stress and suppressed immune functioning, it was not a surprise that I developed a nasty cold. This is not to say that I would not have had a cold otherwise, but the news of Leif's passing and a heavy workload likely made me more susceptible to illness.

Psychologists continue to study the complex interplay between psychological and physical health. For example, many people—both professionals and lay people—believe that psychological factors play a role in determining whether people develop cancers or, if they do, whether the cancers can be "beaten." Several investigators have suggested that a type C (cancer-prone) personality exists. Although the evidence is mixed, some careful, long-term studies suggest that cancerous tumours may develop faster in passive people who suppress the expression of negative emotions. A study on the effects of psychotherapy suggests that learning to cope with the pain and stress of cancer can increase survival rates. We do not know whether personality variables affect the growth of cancer directly, through internal physiological processes, or whether they affect people's health-related behaviour, such as exercise, avoidance of smoking, and compliance with medical treatment.

## Canadian Connections to Research in This Chapter


Adair-Bischoff, C. E., & Sauve, R. S. (1998). Environmental tobacco smoke and middle ear disease in preschool-age children. *Archives of Pediatrics and Adolescent Medicine, 152*, 127–133. (University of Calgary, Faculty of Medicine: www.ucalgary.ca)

Bray, S. R., & Born, H. A. (2004). Transition to university and vigorous physical activity: Implications for health and psychological well-being. *Journal of American College Health, 52*(4), 181–188. (University of Lethbridge: www.uleth.ca)

Fisher, J. D., & Fisher, W. A. (1992). Changing AIDS-risk behavior. *Psychological Bulletin, 111*, 455–474. (University of Western Ontario: www.uwo.ca)

Fisher, W. A. (1997). A theory-based framework for intervention and evaluation in STD/HIV prevention. *The Canadian Journal of Human Sexuality, 6*, 105–111. (University of Western Ontario: www.uwo.ca)

Howard, J. H., Cunningham, D. A., & Rechnitzer, P. A. (1976). Health patterns associated with type A behavior: A managerial population. *Journal of Human Stress, 2*, 24–31. (University of Western Ontario: www.uwo.ca)

Irvine, J., Garner, D. M., Craig, H. M., & Logan, A. G. (1991). Prevalence of type A behavior in untreated hyptertensive individuals. *Hypertension, 18*, 72–78. (University of Toronto: www.utoronto.ca)

Lamerson, C. D., & Kelloway, E. K. (1996). Towards a model of peacekeeping stress: Traumatic and contextual influences. *Canadian Psychology, 37*, 195–204. (University of Guelph: www.uoguelph.ca)

Lefcourt, H. M., & Davidson-Katz, K. (1991). Locus of control and health. In C. R. Snyder & D. R. Forsyth (Eds.), *Handbook of social and clinical psychology: The health perspective.* Elmsford, NY: Pergamon Press, Inc. (University of Waterloo: www.uwaterloo.ca)

MacDonald, G., Zanna, M. P., & Holmes, J. G. (2000). An experimental test of the role of alcohol in relationship conflict. *Journal of Experimental Social Psychology, 36*, 182–193. (University of Waterloo: www.uwaterloo.ca)

Professor Zanna received the Donald O. Hebb Award for Distinguished Contributions to Psychology as a Science from the Canadian Psychological Association in 1993 and was elected Fellow of the Royal Society of Canada in 1999.

MacDonald, T., Zanna, M., & Fong, G. T. (1998). Alcohol and intentions to engage in risky health-related behaviors: Experimental evidence for a causal relationship. In J. G. Adair & D. Belanger (Eds.), *Advances in psychological science* (Vol. 1). Hove, UK: Psychology Press/Erlbaum (UK) Taylor and Francis. (University of Lethbridge: www.uleth.ca)

MacDonald, T. K., MacDonald, G., Zanna, M. P., & Fong, G. T. (2000). Alcohol, sexual arousal, and intentions to use condoms in young men: Applying alcohol myopia theory to risky sexual behavior. *Health Psychology, 19*(3), 290–298. (Queen's University: www.queensu.ca)

MacDonald, T. K., Zanna, M. P., & Fong, G. T. (1995). Decision making in altered states: Effects of alcohol on attitudes toward drinking and driving. *Journal of Personality and Social Psychology, 68*, 973–985. (University of Waterloo: www.uwaterloo.ca)

McKim, W. A. (1991). *Drugs and behavior: An introduction to behavior pharmacology* (2nd ed.). Englewood Cliffs, NJ: Prentice-Hall. (Memorial University of Newfoundland: www.mun.ca)

Meichenbaum, D. (1977). *Cognitive-behavior modification: An integrative approach.* New York: Plenum Press. (University of Waterloo: www.uwaterloo.ca)

Professor Meichenbaum received the 1989 Professional Award from the Canadian Psychological Association.

Meichenbaum, D. (1985). *Stress inoculation training.* New York: Pergamon Press. (University of Waterloo: www.uwaterloo.ca)

Meichenbaum, D. (1993). Changing conceptions of cognitive behavior modification: Retrospect and prospect. *Journal of Consulting and Clinical Psychology, 61*, 202–204. (University of Waterloo: www.uwaterloo.ca)

Meichenbaum, D. (1995). Disasters, stress, and cognition. In S. E. Hobfoll & M. W. deVries (Eds.), *Extreme stress and communities: Impact and intervention.* Dordrecht, Netherlands: Kluwer Academic Publishers. (University of Waterloo: www.uwaterloo.ca)

Misovich, S. J., Fisher, J. D., & Fisher, W. A. (1996). The perceived AIDS-preventative utility of knowing one's partner well: A public health dictum and individuals' risky sexual behavior. *The Canadian Journal of Human Sexuality, 5*, 83–90. (University of Western Ontario: www.uwo.ca)

Rutherford, A., & Endler, N. S. (1999). Predicting approach-avoidance: The roles of coping styles, state anxiety, and situational appraisal. *Anxiety, Stress & Coping: An International Journal, 12*, 63–84. (York University: www.yorku.ca)

Professor Endler is the recipient of many awards for his work. He received the Canadian Silver Jubilee Medal (Queen Elizabeth II) in 1978, was elected fellow of the Royal Society of Canada in 1986 and received the Canadian Psychological Association's Donald O. Hebb Award for Distinguished Contributions to Psychology as a Science in 1997.

Schleifer, S. J., Keller, S. E., & Stein, M. (1985). Stress effects on immunity. *Psychiatric Journal of the University of Ottawa, 10*(3), 125–131. (University of Ottawa: www.uottawa.ca)

Selye, H. (1956/1976). *The stress of life.* New York: McGraw-Hill. (Université de Montréal: www.umontreal.ca)

Selye, H. (1974). *Stress without distress.* New York: Harper & Row. (Université de Montréal: www.umontreal.ca)

Selye, H. (1993). History of the stress concept. In L. Goldberger & S. Breznitz (Eds.), *Handbook of stress: Theoretical and clinical aspects* (2nd ed.). New York: Free Press. (Université de Montréal: www.umontreal.ca)

Stewart, S. H. (1996). Alcohol abuse in individuals exposed to trauma: A critical review. *Psychological Bulletin, 120*, 83–112. (Dalhousie University: www.dal.ca)

Professor Stewart received the 1998 President's New Researcher Award from the Canadian Psychological Association.

## Suggestions for Further Reading

Poole, G., Matheson, D. H., & Cox, D. N. (2001). *The psychology of health and health care: A Canadian perspective.* Toronto: Prentice-Hall.

This book covers all aspects of health psychology. It contains specific chapters devoted to health promotion, stress, illness, and coping with stress and illness.

Meichenbaum, D. (1985). *Stress inoculation training.* New York: Pergamon Press.

This brief book outlines Meichenbaum's program for managing stress. Although intended for practitioners, it is written plainly enough for everyone to understand.

Monat, A., & Lazarus, R. S. (Eds.). (1991). *Stress and coping: An anthology.* New York: Columbia University Press.

This collection of highly readable articles by the foremost experts on stress and coping focuses on both biological and psychological components of stress and methods of coping.

Rushing, W. A. (1995). *The AIDS epidemic: Social dimensions of an infectious disease.* Boulder, CO: Westview Press.

This book provides an overview of the impact of AIDS on social behaviour. It explores both the social causes of the disease and the cultural reactions to it.

PEARSON mypsychlab To access more tests and your own personalized study plan that will help you focus on the areas you need to master before your next class test, be sure to go to **www.MyPsychLab.com**, Pearson Education Canada's online Psychology website available with the access code packaged with your book.

17

# The Nature and Causes of Psychological Disorders

# CHAPTER OUTLINE

## Classification and Diagnosis of Psychological Disorders

What Is "Abnormal"? • Perspectives on the Causes of Psychological Disorders • The DSM-IV-TR Classification Scheme • Some Problems with DSM-IV-TR Classification • The Need for Classification • Prevalence of Psychological Disorders • Clinical versus Actuarial Diagnosis • Disorders Usually Diagnosed in Childhood • *Then and Now: Autistic Disorder*

Abnormal behaviour is any behaviour that departs from the norm. Several perspectives on the causes of psychological disorders exist. The DSM-IV-TR is a classification system that describes an individual's psychological condition on the basis of criteria that must be met before he or she should be diagnosed as having a psychological disorder. Because it is based on the medical model of abnormal behaviour, the DSM-IV-TR may overlook environmental and cognitive causes of abnormal behaviour. However, some form of classification of abnormal behaviour is necessary to diagnose psychological disorders accurately and to treat them effectively. Although researchers have developed statistical methods for diagnosing psychological disorders, many clinical psychologists still prefer to rely on their clinical experiences to make such diagnoses.

## Anxiety, Somatoform, and Dissociative Psychological Disorders

Anxiety Disorders • Somatoform Disorders • Dissociative Disorders

Several psychological disorders involve unrealistic and excessive anxiety, fear, or guilt. These disorders may involve anxiety that has no apparent cause, intense fear of specific objects, intrusive thoughts, compelling urges to engage in ritual-like behaviour, physical problems with no organic basis, and sudden disruptions in consciousness that affect one's sense of identity. Culture-bound syndromes are psychological disorders that are present in only one or a few cultures.

## Personality Disorders

Anti-social Personality Disorder • Borderline Personality Disorder

Personality disorders are marked by rigid traits that impair normal functioning. The most serious of these disorders is the anti-social personality disorder. Persons with this disorder are dishonest, irresponsible, incapable of feeling empathy or sympathy for others, mean-spirited, and feel no remorse for their misdeeds.

## Substance-Related Disorders

Description • Possible Causes

Psychoactive substance use disorders include both drug abuse and drug addiction. Both heredity and brain chemistry play prominent roles in these disorders.

## Schizophrenic Disorders

Description • Types of Schizophrenia • Early Signs of Schizophrenia • Possible Causes

Schizophrenic symptoms include disorganized thought, disturbances of affect, distorted perception, and disturbances of motor activity. Each of the four types of schizophrenia is diagnosed according to specific criteria based on these symptoms. Signs or characteristics of schizophrenia may appear during childhood. Researchers have found that heredity, environmental stressors, brain damage, and biochemical factors play crucial roles in the different forms of schizophrenia.

## Mood Disorders

Description • Possible Causes

Mood disorders involve extreme depression or swings between depression and extreme happiness and high energy levels. Mood disorders appear to involve one or more of the following causes: faulty cognition, heredity, brain biochemistry, and sleep/wake cycles.

PROLOGUE

## A Father's Illness, a College Son's Ambivalence

In this anonymous first-person account, a son recalls the toll of his father's psychological disorder:

"It happened when I was about seven years old. It was a Sunday afternoon, and I was watching television. I heard a lot of yelling and screaming in the kitchen. I ran to see what the matter was. They were in the midst of a fight. When they saw me, I turned and ran into the bedroom.

"That was the last time I really remember seeing my father until I was about 21. I'm told that my sister and I visited him after the divorce, but it's all pretty fuzzy to me. I know that shortly after my parents' big fight, my dad was institutionalized for the first time. His diagnosis: paranoid schizophrenia. My father has been in and out of mental institutions over the past 30 years. He is currently treated on an outpatient basis with chlorpromazine, a drug that reduces the symptoms of his disorder. He manages pretty well as long as he takes his medication.

"I didn't go looking to re-establish a relationship with my father; it was all his doing. I was going to college out west at the time. Somehow, he got my address and wrote to me. He told me very little about the past 14 years. He simply wanted to start with me anew. When I returned home for the Christmas holidays, I went to see him. He was in the intensive care unit of the local hospital. He had attempted suicide. His first words to me, after not seeing me for nearly a decade and a half, were, 'I can't do anything right—not even kill myself.'

"Despite the situation, we managed to get reacquainted. He wanted to take the relationship a little faster than I did, which brings me to the point I wish to make. About a year after I saw him at the hospital, I received a phone call from him (I was then back at school, 3000 miles away). He said he had saved some money and wanted to come to visit me. I was stunned: I thought to myself, 'What would my friends think of me having a crazy father? I can't let him come out here.' So I told him that this was a really bad time for me, that I was overloaded with schoolwork, and that I had several exams coming up—all lies. I was simply embarrassed about having a father with a psychological disorder. Disappointed, he said he understood about my heavy workload at school and that he would make other plans.

"About two weeks later, I received another call from him. He told me that he had just returned home from visiting the city in which I was living, where he had spent the previous week. He said that he knew how busy I was, but that he just wanted to learn a little more about me and my life. He told me that after spending time in the town where I lived—walking the same streets that I walked and seeing the same mountains I saw every day—he felt closer to me and could identify with me much more. And I had told him not to come. I now look back at the situation with a deep sense of humiliation and regret.

"My sharing of such a personal experience with you might have made you feel at least a bit uncomfortable. That was part of my intention. If I had told you about my father's experience with surgery for, say, a back problem, would you have felt uncomfortable? Probably not. Yet, when I tell you about my father's psychological disorder, you do. Why? That's a question I will leave for you to answer."

Life is complex, and things do not always go smoothly. We are all beset by major and minor difficulties at one time or another, and our responses to them are rarely perfect. Sometimes we find ourselves behaving irrationally, having trouble concentrating on the matter at hand, or experiencing feelings that do not seem appropriate for the circumstances. Occasionally, we may brood about imaginary disasters or harbour hurtful thoughts about people we love. For most of us, however, these problems remain occasional, and we usually manage to cope with them.

But the lives of some people, like that of the father described in the prologue, are dominated for long years by disordered thoughts, disturbed feelings, inappropriate behaviours, or some mix thereof. The problems become so severe that these individuals cannot cope with life. They may withdraw from familiar routines and those closest to them, they may turn to professionals for assistance, or they may be obliged to live in institutions.

What causes such problems? Recent studies (e.g., Caspi et al., 2002; Reif et al., 2007) have identified complex interactions between an individual's genotype, brain chemistry, and childhood environment in the **etiology** (that is, the causation) of psychological orders. Some psychological disorders—especially the less severe ones—appear to be more heavily influenced by environmental factors, such as stressors or unhealthy family interactions, or by a person's perception of these factors. For example, a child who is constantly criticized by an overbearing, demanding parent may learn to be passive and non-responding. This strategy may be adaptive in interactions with the parent but will be maladaptive in other social situations. In contrast, many of the more severe psychological disorders appear to be more heavily influenced by hereditary and other biological factors that disrupt normal cognitive processes or produce inappropriate emotional reactions.

This chapter begins with a section on the classification and diagnosis of psychological disorders; it then describes the nature of some of the better-known disorders and discusses research on their causes. (Chapter 18 will discuss the treatment of psychological disorders and the efforts of psychiatrists, clinical psychologists, and other mental health professionals to help people with problems of daily living.) The essential features of the more prominent disorders and treatment approaches are simplified here for the sake of clarity. In addition, many of the cases that clinicians encounter are less clear-cut than the conditions described here and are thus not so easily classified (Carson, Butcher, & Mineka, 2000). It is important to realize that, as more and more people now understand, the line dividing normal and abnormal behaviour is not sharp.

▲ *The dividing line between normal behaviour and abnormal behaviour is not always clear.*

# Classification and Diagnosis of Psychological Disorders

To understand, diagnose, and treat psychological disorders, psychologists need some sort of classification system. The need for a comprehensive classification system of psychological disorders was first recognized by Emil Kraepelin (1856– 1926), who provided his version in a textbook of psychiatry published in 1883. The Association of Medical Superintendents of American Institutions for the Insane, a forerunner of the American Psychiatric Association, later incorporated Kraepelin's ideas into a classification system of its own. A number of Kraepelin's original categories are retained in the classification system most widely used today.

## What Is "Abnormal"?

Psychological disorders are characterized by abnormal behaviour, thoughts, and feelings. The term *abnormal* literally refers to any departure from the norm. Thus, a short or tall person is "abnormal" and so is someone who is especially intelligent or talented. Albert Einstein was "abnormal," and so were composer George Gershwin and baseball player Babe Ruth. But, as you know, the term *abnormal* has taken on a pejorative connotation: We use it to refer to characteristics we dislike or fear.

If you have friends who insist that their pets understand them or ones who have to check several times to be sure that everything is turned off before they leave their homes, are they suffering from a psychological disorder? Are they exhibiting abnormal behaviour? The distinction between normal and abnormal behaviour can be very subjective. Psychologists stress that the most important feature of a psychological disorder is not whether a person's behaviour is "abnormal"—different from that of most other people—but whether it is *maladaptive*. Psychological disorders cause distress or discomfort and interfere with people's ability to lead satisfying, productive lives. They often make it impossible for people to hold jobs, raise families, or relate to others socially. You might rightly point out that a person who holds an unpopular

**etiology** The causes or origins of a disorder.

religious or political belief that violates a social norm may be ostracized by the community and find it impossible to obtain employment or to make friends. So the person's behaviour is maladaptive. But should we say that the person has a psychological disorder? Of course not. Depending on our own point of view, we might be tempted to label the behaviour as courageous and wise or as misguided and foolish. But simply disagreeing with the government, with established religious practices, or with popular beliefs is not sufficient evidence for a diagnosis of mental illness.

Although the diagnosis of psychological disorders should be as objective as possible, it may never be completely free from social and political judgments. In many societies, receiving direct messages from God and being transported on mystical voyages to heaven would probably be labelled as hallucinatory or delusional, whereas in other times and places they might be taken as signs of holiness and devotion. If historical records are accurate, the behaviour of many people who are now venerated as prophets or saints would be regarded quite differently if they were alive today. Understanding cultural differences in beliefs is important, especially in a multicultural society such as Canada, but the fact that diagnoses are affected by social or cultural contexts does not mean that they are invalid (Aklin & Turner, 2006; Arrindell, 2003; Lopez & Guarnaccia, 2000; Widiger & Sankis, 2000). People do have psychological disorders: They do have delusions and hallucinations, they do have thought disorders, they do experience inappropriate emotions. Psychological disorders bring pain and discomfort to these people and to their friends and families.

## Perspectives on the Causes of Psychological Disorders

There is not a single cause of psychological disorders. In general, they are caused by the interaction of hereditary, cognitive, and environmental factors. In some cases, the genetic component is strong and the person is likely to develop a psychological disorder even in a very supportive environment. In other cases, the cognitive and environmental components are strong. A complete understanding of psychological disorders requires that scientists investigate genetic, cognitive, and environmental factors. Once genetic factors are identified, the scientist faces the task of determining the physiological effects of the relevant genes and the consequences of these effects on a person's susceptibility to a psychological disorder. Understanding the cognitive factors involved in psychological disorders requires identification of the origins of distorted perceptions and maladaptive thought patterns. Environmental factors include a wide range of factors, from a person's family history and present social interactions, to their diet, exposure to drugs or alcohol, and childhood diseases.

Different psychologists and other mental health professionals approach the study of psychological disorders from different perspectives, each of which places more or less emphasis on these factors. The perspectives differ primarily in their explanation of the etiology, or origin, of psychological disorders. Because several of these perspectives were discussed in Chapters 1 and 14, I will discuss them only briefly here as they pertain to psychological disorders.

**The Psychodynamic Perspective** According to the psychodynamic perspective, which is based on Freud's early work, psychological disorders originate in intrapsychic conflict produced by the three components of the mind: the id, ego, and superego. These conflicts may centre on attempts to control potentially harmful expressions of sexual or aggressive impulses, or they may also arise from attempts to cope with external dangers and traumatic experiences. For some people, the conflict becomes so severe that the mind's defence mechanisms cannot produce a resolution that is adequate for mental health. The result is that the defence mechanisms themselves distort reality or the individual begins to function in some areas of life in a manner characteristic of an earlier developmental stage. The consequent psychological disorders may involve, among other symptoms, extreme anxiety, obsessive thoughts and compulsive behaviour, depression, distorted perceptions and patterns of thinking, and paralysis or blindness for which there is no physical cause. As we will see in Chapter 18, psychodynamic therapists attempt to make their clients aware of their intrapsychic conflicts and defence mechanism failures as part of the process of regaining mental health.

**The Medical Perspective** The origins of the medical perspective lie in the work of the ancient Greek physician Hippocrates. Recall from Chapter 14 that Hippocrates formulated the idea that excesses of the four humours (black bile, yellow bile, blood, and phlegm) led to emotional problems. Other physicians, Greek and Roman alike, extended Hippocrates' ideas and developed the concept of mental illness—illnesses of the mind. Eventually, specialized institutions or asylums were established where persons with psychological disorders were confined. Most early asylums were poorly run and the patients' problems were poorly understood and often mistreated. The conditions of asylums were so poor they may have further contributed to patients' disorders, rather than treating them. During the eighteenth and nineteenth centuries, massive reforms in the institutional care of people with psychological disorders took place. The quality of the facilities and the amount of compassion for patients improved, and physicians, including neurosurgeons and psychiatrists who were specifically trained in the medical treatment of psychological disorders, were hired to care for these patients.

Today, this perspective is a major influence in the treatment of psychological disorders. As we will see in Chapter 18, many persons with severe psychological disorders are no longer confined to mental institutions. Instead, they are treated on an outpatient basis with drugs that help decrease, and in some cases eliminate, the symptoms of psychological disorders. Usually, only those people with very severe and intractable psychological problems are institutionalized for long periods of time.

The medical model is based on the ideas that psychological disorders are caused by specific abnormalities of the brain and nervous system and that, in principle, they should be approached for treatment in the same way as physical illnesses. As we shall see, biological factors are known at least to contribute to the development of some psychological disorders, including schizophrenia and bipolar disorder, and drugs are usually used for treatment. We shall also see that genetics plays a pivotal role in the development of some of these disorders.

However, not all psychological disorders can be traced so directly and strongly to physical causes. For that reason, other perspectives, which focus on the cognitive and environmental factors involved in psychological disorders, have emerged.

**The Cognitive-Behavioural Perspective** The cognitive-behavioural perspective holds that psychological disorders are *learned* maladaptive behaviour patterns that can best be understood by focusing on environmental factors and a person's perception of those factors. In this view, a psychological disorder is not something that arises spontaneously within a person. Instead, it is caused by the person's interaction with his or her environment. For example, a person's excessive use of alcohol or other drugs may be reinforced by the relief from tension or anxiety that often accompanies intoxication.

Recall from earlier chapters that the behaviour-analytic and cognitive approaches have different historical roots and behaviour analysts and cognitive psychologists have different, often opposing, views on the causes of behaviour. Still, these approaches have become intertwined in the treatment of psychological disorders. According to the cognitive-behavioural perspective, it is not merely the environment that matters—what also counts is a person's ongoing subjective interpretation of the events taking place in his or her environment. Therapists operating from the cognitive-behavioural perspective therefore encourage their clients to replace or substitute maladaptive thoughts and behaviours with more adaptive ones.

**The Humanistic Perspective** As we saw in Chapter 14, proponents of the humanistic perspective argue that proper and natural personality development occurs when people experience unconditional positive regard. According to this view, psychological disorders arise when people perceive that they must earn the positive regard of others. Thus, they become overly sensitive to the demands and criticisms of others and come to define their personal value primarily in terms of others' reactions to them. They lack confidence in their abilities and feel as though they have no stable, internal value as persons. They may come to feel that they have no control over the outcomes of the important (and even not-so-important) events in their lives. Such feelings often accompany depression. As we will see in Chapter 18, the goal of humanistic therapy is to persuade people that they do have intrinsic value and to help them achieve their own unique, positive potential as human beings.

▲ *Cultural norms dictate what is appropriate in any given culture. For example, in the Sudan, the scars on this boy's forehead are considered normal. However, in North America such markings are apt to draw stares.*

**The Sociocultural Perspective** Psychologists and others in the field of mental health are finding that the cultures in which people live play a significant role in the development of psychological disorders (e.g., Calliess, Sieberer, Machledit, & Ziegenbein, 2008; Lopez & Guarnaccia, 2000; Manson & Kleinman, 1998; Rosenfarb et al., 2004). As you have seen time and again throughout this book, psychologists are paying more attention to the role of sociocultural factors in their attempts to understand how people think and behave, and the development of psychological disorders is no exception. Proper treatment requires an understanding of cultural issues (Dana, 2000). Cultural variables influence the nature and extent to which people interpret their own behaviours as normal or abnormal. What is considered normal in one culture may be considered abnormal in another. Moreover, psychological disorders exist that appear to occur only in certain cultures—a phenomenon called *culture-bound syndromes*.

**The Biopsychosocial Perspective** How should we make sense of these different perspectives on the causes of psychological disorders? Are disorders caused by conflict within the individual? Are they caused by genetic factors or by

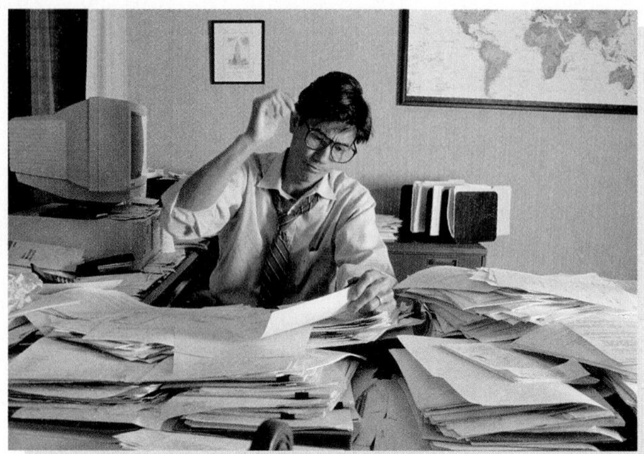

▲ *According to the diathesis–stress model, stress beyond their coping abilities may trigger the development of a psychological disorder in people predisposed toward that disorder by genetics and early leaning experiences.*

abnormalities of the brain and nervous system, or both? Are they caused by learning, by faulty subjective interpretations of environmental events, or by the way our particular culture says we should think and behave?

No single perspective is completely adequate in accounting for the origins of psychological disorders. This is not to say that any of the perspectives is unimportant, however. Different approaches can be combined to form larger, more comprehensive, perspectives. For example, the widely cited **diathesis–stress model** (die-ATH-uh-suss) asserts that the combination of a person's genes and early learning experiences may produce predispositions (*diatheses*) for a variety of psychological disorders (see Yeo, Gangestad, and Thomas, 2007, for a discussion of this concept relative to neurodevelopmental disorders such as attention-deficit/hyperactivity disorder, dyslexia, and schizophrenia). Moreover, the genes that are involved are not necessarily specific to particular disorders but may constitute a more general predisposition (Yeo, Gangestad, & Thomas, 2007). However, the symptoms of a specific disorder will emerge only if that person is confronted with stressors that exceed his or her coping abilities. In other words, a person may be predisposed toward a psychological disorder yet not develop it, either because he or she has not encountered sufficient stressors to trigger its development or because he or she possesses cognitive-behavioural coping skills adequate to counter the stressors that are present.

The diathesis–stress model represents the **biopsychosocial perspective**, which deliberately combines multiple perspectives. For example, a biopsychosocial model may use information about the way in which the genotypes of individuals diagnosed with a specific psychological disorder differ from those of individuals who do not have the disorder. A related interest may be information about the chemistry of neural pathways in individuals with the disorder and correlations between those pathways and the individuals' genotypes. From there, the model might identify the unique behavioural and cognitive symptoms of the disorder and look for evidence that certain types of family environments and other social environments are more closely related to the development of those symptoms than are other environments. Though admittedly complex, this perspective may nevertheless have greater potential for the eventual identification of successful treatments. Stravynski (2007) provides an example of the biopsychosocial approach to a specific category of anxiety disorders—social phobia.

**diathesis–stress model** A causal account of psychological disorders based on the idea that psychological disorders develop when a person possesses a predisposition for a disorder and faces stressors that exceed his or her abilities to cope with them.

**biopsychosocial perspective** A view that the causes of psychological disorders can best be understood in terms of the interaction of biological, psychological, and social factors.

***Diagnostic and Statistical Manual of Mental Disorders*** **(DSM-IV-TR)** A widely used manual for classifying psychological disorders.

## The DSM-IV-TR Classification Scheme

The classification of psychological disorders can be difficult, as the disorders can be classified in many ways. The system most commonly used is found in the American Psychiatric Association's ***Diagnostic and Statistical Manual of Mental Disorders***, Fourth Edition, Text Revision (DSM-IV-TR, 2000). (Psychiatry is a medical specialty devoted to the treatment of psychological disorders. The corresponding specialty within psychology is called clinical psychology.) **Table 17•1** lists these classifications, with several sub-classifications omitted for the sake of simplicity.

The DSM-IV-TR is the latest version of a classification scheme that was devised to provide a reliable, universal set of diagnostic categories having criteria specified as explicitly as possible. The DSM-IV-TR provides descriptions of an individual's psychological condition using five different criteria, called *axes*. Individuals undergoing evaluation are assessed on each of the axes. Axis I contains information on major psychological disorders that require clinical attention, including disorders that may develop during childhood. Personality disorders are found on Axis II. Diagnoses can be made that include both Axis I and Axis II disorders, and multiple diagnoses can occur on either axis alone. For example, major depression and alcohol dependence are both Axis I disorders, and both disorders may characterize an individual at any one period of time. A person's psychological condition may be due to several different psychological disorders described in the DSM-IV-TR, just as one person may suffer simultaneously from several different physical disorders.

Axes III through V provide information about the life of the individual in addition to the basic classification provided by Axes I and II. Axis III is used to describe any physical disorders, such as skin rashes or heightened blood pressure,

**TABLE 17•1 Summary of the DSM-IV-TR Classification Scheme for Axes I and II**

**Axis I—Major Clinical Syndromes**

- ***Disorders usually first appearing in infancy, childhood, or adolescence.*** Any deviation from normal development, including mental retardation, autism, attention deficit disorder with hyperactivity, excessive fears, speech problems, and highly aggressive behaviour.
- ***Delirium, dementia, amnestic, and other cognitive disorders.*** Disorders due to deterioration of the brain because of aging, disease (such as Alzheimer's disease, which was discussed in Chapter 12), or ingestion or exposure to drugs or toxic substances (such as lead).
- ***Psychoactive substance abuse disorders.*** Psychological, social, or physical problems related to abuse of alcohol or other drugs, not including symptomless recreational use. (Psychoactive substance use and abuse was discussed in Chapters 1, 3, 4, and 16 and is also discussed in this chapter.)
- ***Schizophrenia and other psychotic disorders.*** A group of disorders marked by loss of contact with reality, illogical thought, inappropriate displays of emotion, bizarre perceptions, and usually some form of hallucinations or delusions.
- ***Mood disorders.*** Disorders involving extreme deviations from normal mood, including severe depression (major depression), excessive elation (mania), or alternation between severe depression and excessive elation (bipolar disorder).
- ***Anxiety disorders.*** Excessive fear of specific objects (phobia); repetitive, persistent thoughts accompanied by ritualistic behaviour that reduces anxiety (obsessive-compulsive behaviour); panic attacks; generalized and intense feelings of anxiety; and feelings of dread caused by experiencing traumatic events such as natural disasters or combat.
- ***Somatoform disorders.*** Disorders involving pain, paralysis, or blindness for which no physical cause can be found. Excessive concern for one's health, as is typical in persons with hypochondriasis.
- ***Factitious disorders.*** False reports of physical symptoms, as with Munchausen's syndrome, in which the individual is frequently hospitalized because of his or her claims of illness.
- ***Dissociative disorders.*** Loss of personal identity and changes in normal consciousness, including amnesia and multiple personality disorder, in which there exists two or more independently functioning personality systems.
- ***Sexual and gender identity disorders.*** Disorders involving fetishes, sexual dysfunction (such as erectile or orgasmic dysfunctions), and problems of sexual identity (such as transsexualism).
- ***Eating disorders.*** Disorders related to excessive concern about one's body weight, such as anorexia nervosa (self-starvation) and bulimia (alternating periods of eating large amounts of food and vomiting). (Eating disorders were discussed in Chapter 13.)
- ***Sleep disorders.*** Disorders including severe insomnia, chronic sleepiness, sleepwalking, narcolepsy (suddenly falling to sleep), and sleep apnea. (Sleep disorders were discussed in Chapter 9.)
- ***Impulse control disorders.*** Disorders involving compulsive behaviours such as stealing, fire setting, or gambling.
- ***Adjustment disorders.*** Disorders stemming from difficulties adjusting to significant life stressors, such as death of a loved one, loss of a job or financial difficulties, and family problems, including divorce. (Some adjustment disorders, as they pertain to difficulty in coping with life stressors, were discussed in Chapter 16.)

**Axis II—Personality Disorders**

- ***Personality disorders*** are long-term, maladaptive, and rigid personality traits that impair normal functioning and involve psychological stress. Two examples are antisocial personality disorder (lack of empathy or care for others, lack of guilt for misdeeds, anti-social behaviour, and persistent lying, cheating, and stealing) and narcissistic personality disorder (inflated sense of self-worth and importance and persistent seeking of attention).

accompanying the psychological disorder. Axis IV specifies the severity of stress that the person has experienced (usually within the last year). This axis details the source of stress (for example, family or work) and indicates its severity and approximate duration. Axis V describes the person's overall level of psychological, social, or occupational functioning. The purpose of Axis V is to estimate the extent to which a person's quality of life has been diminished by the disorder. Ratings are made on a 100-point "Global Assessment of Functioning" (GAF) scale with 100 representing the absence or near absence of impaired functioning, 50 representing serious problems in functioning, and 10 representing impairment that may result in injury to the individual or to others.

It is also possible for the same person to suffer different disorders at different points in time. Disorders that occur together are referred to as **comorbid**. The DSM-IV-TR offers clinical psychologists, psychiatrists, and other clinical professionals a systematic means of compiling and evaluating a variety of personal and psychological information about any one specific individual. Let's consider an example to demonstrate the interrelationship among the five axes. Alcohol dependence (Axis I) can be comorbid with major depressive disorder (Axis I). A national health study in Finland

**comorbid** The appearance of two or more disorders in a single person.

(Pirkkola, Poikolainen, & Lonnqvist, 2006) found that 7.9 percent of the population reported current alcohol dependence and, of these, 8 percent were comorbid for major depression. A national survey of Canadians (Wang & El-Guebaly, 2004) showed a similar comorbidity of 8.6 percent between the two disorders.

Alcohol dependence often leads to marital problems, which may also be partly associated with an anti-social personality disorder (Axis II). Echeburúa, DeMedina, and Aizpiri (2007) reported a comorbidity of 7 percent in a Spanish sample of persons with alcohol dependence. Marital problems may lead to divorce, and these problems and the divorce are themselves stressors (Axis IV) that subsequently may contribute to an episode of major depression (Axis I). Alcohol dependence also may eventually lead to physical problems, such as cirrhosis ("seer-OH-siss"; Axis III). These problems, now acting in concert, are likely to lead to an increased impairment of overall life functioning (Axis V); eventually, the individual may have only a few friends, none of them close, and may be unable to keep a job. The evaluation of this person might be summarized as follows:

Axis I: Alcohol Dependence and Major Depressive Disorder
Axis II: Anti-social Personality Disorder
Axis III: Alcoholic cirrhosis
Axis IV: Severe stress—divorce, loss of job
Axis V: GAF evaluation = 30, which represents a very serious impairment of functioning

## Some Problems with DSM-IV-TR Classification

In North America, the DSM-IV-TR is the most widely used classification system for psychological disorders. This does not mean that it is a flawless system. Reflecting the fact that the DSM-IV-TR has been strongly influenced by psychiatrists, it tends to be more consistent with the medical perspective on psychological disorders than with other perspectives. This means that diagnosis and treatment based on the DSM-IV-TR emphasizes biological factors, which, in turn, means that potential cognitive and environmental determinants may be overlooked.

Another potential problem with the DSM-IV-TR (and perhaps with any classification scheme) is its reliability. Reliability in this context means what it did in the context of psychological testing—consistency across applications. If the DSM-IV-TR were perfectly reliable, users would be able to diagnose each case in the same way. However, evaluating psychological disorders is not so easy. Using the DSM-IV-TR is not like using a recipe; it is more like navigating your way through an unfamiliar city using a somewhat crude map. Using this map, you may or may not reach your ultimate destination. Psychological disorders do not have distinct borders that allow a mental health professional to diagnose a disorder in a person with 100 percent accuracy all of the time. For example, the diagnosis of post-traumatic stress disorder requires the persistence of symptoms for more than 30 days. If symptoms similar to those found in post-traumatic stress disorder end prior to the 30-day cut-off, the diagnosis would be acute stress disorder. The value of having two separate disorders for the same symptoms has been questioned by some psychologists (Marshall, Spitzwer, & Liebowitz, 1999).

Other critics have questioned the *validity* of the DSM-IV-TR's reliance on categories. The concern is well illustrated by a classic experiment in the social psychology of institutions performed by Rosenhan (1973). By prior assignment, Rosenhan and a small group of his professional associates who had agreed to collaborate with him in the research presented themselves at different mental hospitals in the California state system. Each used a standard introduction, offering a fictitious name and a fictitious set of symptoms (hearing voices when no one was present). Otherwise, they told the truth. Rosenhan's interest was whether such individuals (whom he styled "pseudopatients") would be admitted to the hospitals. The expert opinion of the mental health professionals to whom he had previously described the study was resoundingly that the pseudopatients would not be admitted. Hence the surprise when all were—and when their mean length of stay in the institutions was nearly three weeks! Moreover, they reported that their efforts to express their normalcy while in the hospitals only solidified the diagnosis they received—acute paranoid schizophrenia. Oddly, only the long-term residents of the hospitals detected the ruse captured in the title of Rosenhan's article, "On being sane in insane places."

Horwitz and Wakefield (2007) have focused on the DSM-IV-TR's categorization of depressive disorders, as well as the related categorizations found in previous editions of the manual. They question if inter-clinician agreement about whether a client presents the necessary and sufficient symptoms of a disorder is an adequate ground for diagnosis. Is it possible, they ask, that the symptoms are those of the natural sadness that would accompany a devastating loss and not psychological disorder at all? The issue is like that of the *false-positive* outcome of a medical test, where the test results falsely indicate the presence of a disorder. Wakefield, Schmitz, First, and Horwitz (2007) have estimated that, in as many as one in four cases, natural bereavement may be mistaken for major depressive disorder.

In active anticipation of the DSM-V, which may appear as soon as 2012, O'Donohue, Fowler, and Lilienfeld (2007) and Widiger and Trull (2007) have recommended a new perspective on psychological disorders, and personality disorders in particular. Specifically, they recommend that categorization move away from the medical model of disorder to embrace the dimensional approach to personality, as found, for example, in the five-factor model of personality. Doing so would eliminate the current practice, with its attendant confusion, of multi-axial diagnoses in which a single client is labelled as having multiple comorbid disorders.

There will probably always be dangers in classifying psychological disorders. No classification scheme is likely to be perfect, and no two people with the same diagnosis will behave in exactly the same way. Yet once people are labelled, they are likely to be perceived as having all characteristics assumed to accompany that label; their behaviour will probably be perceived selectively and interpreted in terms of the diagnosis (Rosenhan, 1973). Mental health professionals, like other humans, tend to simplify things by pigeonholing people.

An experiment by Langer and Abelson (1974) illustrated how labelling someone can affect clinical judgments. A group of psychoanalysts were shown videotape of a young man who was being interviewed. Half of the psychoanalysts were told that the man was a job applicant, while the other half were told that he was a patient. Although both groups of clinicians watched the same man exhibiting the same behaviour, those who were told that he was a patient rated him as more disturbed—that is, less well-adjusted. (See **Figure 17•1**.)

As you may have recognized, there are potential problems inherent in any system that labels human beings. It is easy to lapse into the mistaken belief that labelling disorders explains why people are the way they are. Diagnosing a psychological disorder only describes the symptoms of the disorder; it does not explain the underlying causes and psychological processes. To say, for example, that Joe spoke incoherently "because he's schizophrenic" does not explain his behaviour at all. Rather, the way Joe spoke is part of the behavioural symptom class that makes up the disorder we call schizophrenia. Consequently, we need to be on guard against associating the names of disorders with people rather than with their *symptoms*. Thus, it is more appropriate to talk about Joe as "having a schizophrenic disorder" than to call him "a schizophrenic." Labelling Joe a "schizophrenic" ignores every other aspect of Joe, except the disorder he is suffering from. If Joe were suffering from a strictly physical problem, such as a broken bone, would he still be labelled only by his injury? Most likely not.

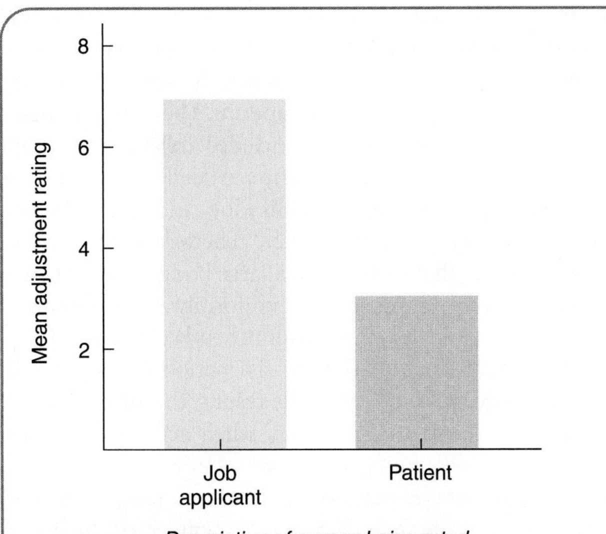


**FIGURE 17•1** The dangers of diagnosis. Adjustment ratings of the same person by psychoanalysts who were told that he was either a "job applicant" or a "patient."

*(Based on data from Langer, E. J., & Abelson, R. P. (1974). A patient by any other name . . . : Clinician group difference in labeling bias.* Journal of Consulting and Clinical Psychology, 42, *4–9.)*

## The Need for Classification

Because labelling can have negative effects, some people, such as Thomas Szasz (1960, 2002), have suggested that we should abandon all attempts to classify and diagnose psychological disorders. In fact, Szasz (pronounced "zaws") has argued that the concept of mental illness has done more harm than good because of the negative effects it has on those people who are said to be mentally ill. For example, Szasz notes that labelling people as mentally ill places the responsibility for their care with the medical establishment, thereby relieving such people of responsibility for their mental states and for taking personal steps toward improvement.

However, proper classification has advantages for a patient. One advantage is that, with few exceptions, the recognition of a specific diagnostic category precedes the development of successful treatment for that disorder. Treatments for physical diseases such as diabetes, syphilis, tetanus, and malaria were found only *after* the disorders could be reliably diagnosed. A patient may have a multitude of symptoms, but before the cause of the physical disorder (and hence its treatment) can be discovered, the primary symptoms must be identified. For example, Graves' disease is characterized by irritability, restlessness, confused and rapid thought processes, and, occasionally, delusions and hallucinations. Little was known about the endocrine system during the nineteenth century when Robert Graves identified the disease, but we now know that this syndrome results from oversecretion of thyroxine, a hormone produced by the thyroid gland. Treatment involves prescription of anti-thyroid drugs or surgical removal of the thyroid gland, followed by administration of appropriate replacement doses of thyroxine. Graves' classification scheme for the symptoms was devised many years before the physiological basis of the disease could be understood. But once enough was known about the effects of thyroxine, physicians were able to treat Graves' disease and strike it off the roll of psychological disorders.

On a less dramatic scale, different kinds of psychological disorders have different causes, and they respond to different types of psychological treatments or drugs. If future research is to reveal more about causes and treatments of these disorders, we must be able to classify specific psychological disorders reliably and accurately.

## Prevalence of Psychological Disorders

Roughly 11 percent of Canadians suffer from a psychological disorder or substance abuse problem (Health Canada, 2002). Research is conducted periodically in regions and cities of Canada to ascertain the prevalence of psychological disorders.

**TABLE 17•2 Lifetime Prevalence Rates of Several Psychological Disorders in Edmonton**

| Type of Disorder | Prevalence Rate* |
|---|---|
| Alcohol abuse/dependence | 19.1 |
| Major depression | 11.9 |
| Drug abuse/dependence | 6.7 |
| Phobias | 4.2 |
| Panic disorders | 1.8 |
| Obsessive-compulsive disorder | 1.7 |

*Source: Reprinted from* Journal of Psychiatric Research, *32(5), Newman, S. C., & Bland, R. C., Incidence of mental disorders in Edmonton: Estimates of rates and methodological issues, 273–282, (1998) with permission from Elsevier. http://www.sciencedirect.com/science/journal/00223956*

* Numbers represent the percentage of people who reported having experienced one of these psychological disorders at some time during their lives.

For example, Newman and Bland (1998) conducted a survey on the incidence of psychological disorders in Edmonton. Nearly 4000 residents were interviewed, of which almost half were re-interviewed nearly three years later. Data were also collected on the lifetime prevalence rate of psychological disorder in Edmonton. (See **Table 17•2.**) Substance use disorders, mood disorders, and anxiety disorders were found to be the most common types of psychological disorders. The findings of Newman and Bland are generally consistent with other prevalence surveys from different locations and suggest that psychological disorders occur at a fairly high frequency. For instance, the overall short-term prevalence rates for psychological disorders are quite similar for Edmontonians as they are for residents of Ontario (Offord et al., 1996). An interesting related statistic is that almost 8 percent of a large sample of adults from Ontario reported seeking some kind of mental health assistance during the past 12 months (Lin et al., 1996).

## Clinical versus Actuarial Diagnosis

Clinical psychologists and other mental health professionals are often asked to make diagnoses and to predict people's future behaviour. These decisions are important; for example, they can determine whether someone receives a treatment that may have significant side effects, whether someone receives parole, whether someone stands trial for a crime, or whether someone is placed in a psychiatric hospital. Two activities contribute to diagnoses and predictions: collection of data and interpretation of data. Accuracy is essential in both activities; unreliable or irrelevant data make interpretation questionable, and even good data can be misinterpreted.

**clinical judgments** Diagnoses of psychological disorders or predictions of future behaviour based largely on experts' experience and knowledge.
**actuarial judgments** Diagnoses of psychological disorders or predictions of future behaviour based on numerical formulas derived from analyses of prior outcomes.

Mental health professionals have many ways to collect data. They can observe people and note the presence or absence of particular behaviours. They can request medical tests such as EEG, CT, or MRI scans. They can interview people and take note of their facial expressions and their responses to questions. They can administer objective and projective personality tests. They can examine documents that already exist, such as medical records, criminal records, or reports of behaviour from mental or penal institutions.

Once data are gathered, clinicians can interpret them in two ways: using the *clinical method* or using the *actuarial (or statistical) method.* **Clinical judgments** are diagnoses based on an expert's experience. The information that is collected may come from many sources, but it is not the source of information that distinguishes the clinical method from the actuarial method—it is the processing of that information. Clinical judgments are based on experts' recollection of similar cases and on their knowledge of the symptoms that predict particular types of outcomes. The decision process may be considered less formal than that used in actuarial judgments.

**Actuarial judgments** use statistical rules that relate particular indicators (symptoms, test scores, or personal characteristics such as age, sex, and medical history) to particular outcomes. The actuarial method was first devised to set the rates for life insurance policies. For example, an insurer can estimate a person's longevity by knowing his or her age, height, weight, sex, and health-related habits such as smoking. Although the estimate may be wrong about a particular person (for example, a person may be killed in a traffic accident or may stop smoking), actuarial judgments work very well when applied to large groups of people and to the prediction of average outcomes.

Although many mental health professionals still prefer to use the clinical method, the hundreds of studies comparing actuarial and clinical judgments—not just in mental health but in the social sciences more generally—overwhelmingly show actuarial judgments to be superior. The criterion measures predicted in these studies included college grade point average, parole violation, response to particular forms of therapy, length of psychiatric hospitalization, and violent behaviour. As Meehl (1986) noted earlier, "There is no controversy in social science that shows such a large body of qualitatively diverse studies coming out so uniformly . . . as this one" (p. 373). A meta-analysis by Ægisdóttir and colleagues (2006) included 67 studies published over a period of 56 years. In their most rigorous analysis of the results, the authors found a 13 percent increase in accuracy when actuarial methods were used.

There are several reasons why actuarial judgments tend to be more accurate than clinical judgments. First, their reliability is always higher. Because a decision is based on a precise rule, the actuarial method always produces the same judgment for a particular set of data. On the other hand, an expert making a clinical judgment may make different decisions about the same set of data on different occasions, or may allow personal bias to influence his or her analysis of the data

(Rohling, Langhinrichsen-Rohling, & Miller, 2003). Experts may become tired, their judgment may be influenced by recent cases in which they were involved, or the order in which the information is presented to them may affect which factors they consider in making their decisions.

Even though the research consistently touts the actuarial method as superior, most mental health professionals still use clinical methods more often than actuarial methods of prediction. Indeed some clinicians avoid the actuarial method (Guilmette, Faust, Hart, & Arkes, 1990). Why? According to Dawes, Faust, and Meehl (2002), some clinicians may be unaware of the research showing the inferiority of the clinical method. Others find the actuarial method dehumanizing; they believe that it ignores the fact that each person is unique. As well, perhaps experts prefer to use their own judgment for a perfectly understandable reason: They find it difficult to accept that their diagnostic skills, developed over a long period of training and practice, can be bested by a rule embodied in a computer program.

## Disorders Usually Diagnosed in Childhood

The remainder of the chapter takes up several of the major categories of psychological disorders found in the DSM-IV-TR. It begins with a pair of disorders usually first diagnosed in childhood: Attention-deficit/hyperactivity disorder and autistic disorder.

**Attention-Deficit/Hyperactivity Disorder** The primary presenting symptoms of **attention-deficit/hyperactivity disorder** include inattention, hyperactivity, or impulsivity as well as combinations thereof. The symptoms associated with impairment must be presented prior to age seven; often, they have been presented for several years. The impairment must be displayed in two different settings (e.g., home and school), and must demonstrably interfere with age-appropriate functioning socially, academically, or otherwise. These symptoms are comparative—they are assessed relative to other individuals at a comparable level of development. The incidence of the disorder is estimated to be 3 to 7 percent of school-aged children. However, it may persist into adolescence and adulthood, when it presents chronic challenges to successful functioning (Young, 2007).

The inattention characteristic of the disorder is marked by the failure to attend closely to details and the tendency to make careless errors. Schoolwork, for example, is typically messy. In addition to finding it difficult to sustain attention in projects or play, children with the disorder find it difficult to complete tasks. They often appear as if their thoughts are elsewhere and fail to hear what has been said to them. They may switch frequently between unfinished tasks and fail to follow through on tasks they are instructed to complete. They may also exhibit difficulty organizing tasks and report trying to sustain attention as aversive. Not surprisingly, they tend to avoid such tasks and may lose or damage the materials required for their completion. They are readily distracted by stimuli that go unnoticed by others, are forgetful, and appear disconnected when others attempt to converse with them.

Hyperactivity is displayed by fidgeting or squirming while seated as well as by excessive running or jumping and excessive talking in situations where it is inappropriate. Activities that require being quiet or relaxing are aversive. At home, the presenting symptoms include frequently getting up from the table during meals or while watching television or doing homework. The symptoms of impulsivity include impatience, difficulty in delaying responses (such as waiting one's turn to be called on), interrupting or intruding on others inappropriately, blurting out answers before the question is asked, failing to listen to instructions, grabbing items that others have, and touching or knocking over objects that are not supposed to be touched. Individuals with the disorder may take undue risks that lead to accidents and injuries.

Despite findings of high heritability of attention-deficit/hyperactivity disorder in studies involving identical twins (Nigg, 2006), there is no clear indication of how genes and environment might produce the symptoms. Shaw and colleagues (2006, 2007) reported MRI data from 220 children diagnosed with the disorder over a 15-year period. Among their findings was an unusual trend in the developmental course of cerebral cortical thickness. On average, thickness reaches its peak at age seven or eight and then grows thinner thereafter. In the case of children with the diagnosis, maximum thickness doesn't occur until age 10. This was contrasted with the earlier-than-usual maturation of the motor cortex of children with the diagnosis. The combination of a developmental delay in areas of the brain that exert inhibitory control over movements and the premature development of the areas that produce voluntary movements is consistent with the best-known symptoms of the disorder.

A team of psychologists working in Norway has proposed a comprehensive theory of the development of the disorder (Sagvolden, Johnasen, Aase, & Russell, 2005). Specifically, they point to the insufficiency of dopamine as a modulator in neural pathways involving the neurotransmitters glutamate and GABA (see Chapter 4). In their view, the culprit is reduced activity in a dopaminergic branch of the limbic system. This interferes with the normal processes of reinforcement and extinction (see Chapter 7), which, over time, leads to the familiar symptoms of delay aversion, the development of hyperactivity in novel settings, impulsiveness, impairment of sustained attention, greater behavioural variability, and the failure to inhibit responses. However, the theory is dynamic in that it predicts when these symptoms will have their onset as a function of individual genetic predispositions and surroundings. The theory also considers the therapeutic role of parenting styles, medication, and social policy.

**attention-deficit/hyperactivity disorder** A psychological disorder found in childhood characterized by impulsivity, a lack of attention, and hyperactivity.

**Autistic Disorder** According to the DSM-IV-TR, the primary symptoms of autistic disorder are the abnormal development of social interaction and communication, accompanied by pronounced limitations of activity and interests—symptoms that must appear prior to age three. The persistent abnormality of social interaction includes the failure to use non-verbal behaviours such as eye contact and facial expressions. Children diagnosed with the disorder display little inclination to form friendships and do not spontaneously share enjoyments, interests, or achievements with other people. They prefer activities where they can be alone and are often oblivious to the presence of others and unresponsive to signs of others' distress.

## Then and Now

### Autistic Disorder

Autistic disorder was first identified in the psychiatric literature by Leo Kanner (1943). The concept of this complex disorder has changed over the years, and there are still controversial aspects of autism that are under study. As mentioned earlier, autism involves deficiencies of verbal and non-verbal communication. In addition, individuals with autistic disorder develop highly stereotyped patterns of behaviour, interests, and activities. Stereotyped movements may include clapping, finger flicking, rocking, dipping, and swaying. Postural abnormalities, such as walking on tiptoe, may also occur, as well as fascination with an object's movements and strong attachment to a specific inanimate object.

Although autism was identified in the literature in the 1940s, there are earlier accounts of cases that describe people who may fit the diagnosis. One of the more unusual cases occurred in the late eighteenth century involving an 11-year-old boy who was found in the woods near Aveyron (see Chapter 1; Malson, 1972). When he was discovered, it appeared that the boy had raised himself alone. He did not understand spoken language and exhibited a wide range of unusual behaviour. A French physician, Jean Itard, attempted to educate the boy and gave him the name Victor. Victor could not speak, would focus only on objects that were of immediate importance to him (e.g., he would grab at food if he was hungry) and he was unresponsive to many external stimuli. It was originally believed that Victor's condition was due to his unusual upbringing. Further review of his case, though, indicates that Victor may have suffered from autism. Consistent with someone suffering from autistic disorder, Victor would rock in place, and he had unusual emotional responses. For example, he would seem sullen and then burst into fits of laughter.

Before 1943, cases like Victor's were often misdiagnosed as mental retardation. After Kanner introduced autism to the psychological literature, there were still misconceptions about people with autism. For many years, autism was incorrectly labelled "childhood schizophrenia" (Bender, 1947). As you have seen throughout the text, autism and schizophrenia are vastly different disorders. Autism was also originally thought to be caused by poor parenting (Rutter, 2001), and was once believed to be a secondary symptom of a language disorder (Wolff, 2004). As research has continued on the disorder, these notions have been abandoned.

Although we now have a much better understanding of autism, there is still controversy surrounding the disorder. The DSM-IV-TR put its incidence at 5 in 10 000, but the Centers for Disease Control has more recently placed it at 1 in 166 children (Pettus, 2008)—an approximately tenfold increase! It is four times more likely to occur in males than females and is often accompanied by mental retardation. Such dramatic growth in the incidence of the disorder has created controversy: Are the increases attributable to better reporting and thus not so much a function of increased incidence per se? Or has diagnosis become liberalized so that autistic disorder itself and disorders that resemble it are now bundled together as *autistic spectrum disorders*, with a correspondingly greater incidence?

Among modern theoretical accounts of autistic disorder is the *theory of mind* (Baron-Cohen, Leslie, & Frith, 1985). It states that a child with autistic disorder fails to understand that actions may be attributed to her or his own thoughts and feelings, and that the actions of others may be attributed similarly. For example, children with autistic disorder fail the "Sally-Anne false-belief task" (see Chapter 12; Tager-Flusberg, 2007). In the task, the child is told a story that is accompanied by a picture or toys: Sally has a basket and Anne a box. Sally places a ball in her basket, then goes to play elsewhere. Anne takes the ball from Sally's basket and hides it in her box. The child is asked whether Sally will search for the ball when she returns and, if so, where she is likely to look. The failure of children diagnosed with autistic disorder to solve the problem suggested to Baron-Cohen and his colleagues that they lack the ability to invoke internal states in order to make sense of behaviour, whether it be theirs or someone else's.

Tager-Flusberg (2007) has pointed out that the theory-of-mind approach to autism fails to address a sufficiently wide range of the presenting symptoms. An adequate theory must range more widely to include social and emotional information processing. The author raises the possibility that such a theory may well include reference to the role of *mirror neurons* in developmental delays and deficits that characterize autistic disorder (see Oberman & Ramachandran, 2007).

Autistic disorder's devastating toll on children and their families has prompted a broad front of research into its possible causes: genetic, immunological, neurochemical, neurocognitive, behavioural, and beyond (Thompson, 2007). The variety of presenting symptoms of the disorder suggests a complex etiology that, according to one researcher, makes autistic disorder "a problem that no one person or discipline can figure out alone" (Pettus, 2008, p. 39).

## Interim Summary

### Classification and Diagnosis of Psychological Disorders

Mental health professionals view the causes of psychological disorders from several different perspectives. The psychodynamic perspective holds that psychological disorders arise from intrapsychic conflict that overwhelms the mind's defence mechanisms. The medical perspective asserts that psychological disorders have an organic basis, just as physical illnesses do. The cognitive-behavioural perspective maintains that psychological disorders are learned patterns of maladaptive thinking and behaving. The humanistic perspective suggests that psychological disorders arise from the demands of others when positive regard from others is conditional on meeting those demands. The sociocultural perspective focuses on how cultural variables influence the development of psychological disorders and people's subjective reactions to them. Many elements of these perspectives are integrated into the diathesis–stress model of psychological disorders. This model is based on the idea that people's biological inheritance and early learning experiences predispose them to develop psychological disorders. However, these disorders are expressed only if these people encounter stressors that overwhelm their capacities to cope with them. Thus, even though some people may be predisposed toward a disorder, the coping skills they have acquired through experience may be sufficient to prevent the actual development of that disorder.

Although clinical diagnosis is influenced by social norms, we should not abandon the attempt. The value of classification and diagnosis lies in the potential identification of disorders with common causes. Once disorders are classified, research can be carried out with the goal of finding useful therapies. The principal classification scheme in North America for psychological disorders is the DSM-IV-TR, which provides explicit criteria along five dimensions called axes. Axis I describes the major psychological disorders of clinical significance and Axis II contains personality disorders. The three remaining axes provide information about the individual, such as the presence of physical disorders, the level of stress, and the overall level of functioning. While widely used, the DSM-IV-TR is not without problems. There are issues of reliability and validity, as well as an emphasis on the biological factors involved in the diagnosis of psychological disorders. Some critics of the DSM-IV-TR claim that more attention needs to be paid to sociocultural factors.

Clinical judgments, such as diagnoses and predictions about a person's behaviour, require the collection and interpretation of information. The interpretation can use the clinical method or the actuarial method. In the clinical method, an expert uses his or her experience and judgment to make a diagnosis. The actuarial method is based on a statistical analysis of the relation between different items of information and clinical outcomes. Although research has consistently found the actuarial method to be superior, many clinicians do not use it. Some psychologists believe that clinicians should concentrate on developing new measures and making observations of behaviour that only humans can make and then employ actuarial methods to find the best ways to use the data they collect.

Disorders diagnosed in childhood include attention-deficit/hyperactivity disorder and autistic disorder. Symptoms of attention-deficit/hyperactivity disorder include inattention, hyperactivity, and impulsivity. Some researchers believe that attention-deficit/hyperactivity disorder may be due to an insufficiency of dopamine, although social factors also play a role.

The symptoms of autistic disorder include a severe lack of interest in normal childhood activities and abnormal development of social interaction and communication. One theory put forward to help explain autistic disorder is the theory of mind. This theory states that children with autistic disorder fail to make the connection between their thoughts and their actions. Other theories focus on the role of mirror neurons in the developmental delays associated with autistic disorder.

#### QUESTION TO CONSIDER

1. This section discussed diagnoses of psychological disorders and the pros and cons of basing such diagnoses on clinical versus actuarial methods. Suppose that you were the client whose mental health was in question. Which method would you prefer your therapist to use in rendering a judgment about you? Why?

# Anxiety, Somatoform, and Dissociative Psychological Disorders

Often referred to as *neuroses* (particularly from the psychoanalytic perspective), anxiety, somatoform, and dissociative psychological disorders are strategies of perception and behaviour that have gotten out of hand. They are characterized by pathological increases in anxiety. According to the psychoanalytic perspective, pathological anxiety may result from an inadequate number of defence mechanisms, from immature defences that cannot cope with the anxiety, or from defence mechanisms applied so rigidly that they have become maladaptive. People who have neuroses experience anxiety, fear, and depression, and generally are unhappy. However, unlike people who have *psychoses*, they do not suffer from delusions or severely disordered thought processes. Furthermore, they almost universally realize that they have a problem. They may not know that the source of their problems is psychological, but they know that they are unhappy and that their strategies for coping with the world are not working very well. Neurotic behaviour is usually characterized by avoidance rather than confrontation of problems. To avoid potential stressors, people with neuroses often turn, unconsciously, to imagined illnesses, oversleeping, or forgetfulness.

## Anxiety Disorders

Several important types of psychological disorders are classified as anxiety disorders, which have fear and anxiety as their most prominent symptoms. **Anxiety** is a sense of apprehension or doom that is accompanied by certain physiological reactions, such as accelerated heart rate, sweaty palms, and tightness in the stomach. Anxiety disorders are the most common psychological disorders. Anxiety disorders affect approximately 12 percent of Canadians (Health Canada, 2002). This section examines three important anxiety disorders: panic disorder, phobic disorders, and obsessive-compulsive disorder.

**Panic Disorder: Description** **Panic** is a feeling of extreme fear mixed with hopelessness or helplessness. We sometimes feel this way when we are trapped suddenly in an elevator or are in a car accident. Many people feel a tinge of panic when in a jet flying through turbulent air space. For most people, panic can be linked to specific environmental events, such as those just described.

People with **panic disorder** suffer from episodic attacks of acute anxiety—periods of acute and unremitting terror that grip them for lengths of time lasting from a few seconds to a few hours. The lifetime prevalence rate for panic disorder is estimated to be about 1.6 percent in Canada (Statistics Canada, 2002). Women are approximately twice as likely as men to suffer from panic disorder. The disorder usually has its onset between the late teen years and the mid-twenties; it rarely begins after a person reaches his or her forties.

Shortness of breath, clammy sweat, irregularities in heartbeat, dizziness, faintness, and feelings of unreality are often symptoms of panic attacks. The victim of a panic attack often feels that he or she is going to die. The symptoms are sometimes mistaken for a heart attack rather than components of psychological distress. Leon (1977) described a 38-year-old man who suffered from frequent panic attacks.

> During the times when he was experiencing intense anxiety, it often seemed as if he were having a heart seizure. He experienced chest pains and heart palpitations, numbness, shortness of breath, and he felt a strong need to breathe. He reported that in the midst of the anxiety attack, he developed a feeling of tightness over his eyes and he could only see objects directly in front of him (tunnel vision). He further stated that he feared that he would not be able to swallow.
>
> . . . The intensity of the anxiety symptoms was very frightening to him and on two occasions his wife had rushed him to a local hospital because he was in a state of panic, sure that his heart was going to stop beating and he would die. His symptoms were relieved after he was given an injection of tranquilizer medication. . . . He began to note the location of doctor's offices and hospitals in whatever vicinity he happened to be . . . and he became extremely anxious if medical help was not close by. (Leon, 1977, pp. 112, 117)

Between panic attacks, people with panic disorder tend to suffer from **anticipatory anxiety**—a fear of having a panic attack. Because attacks can occur without apparent cause, these people anxiously worry about when the next one might strike them. Sometimes, a panic attack that occurs in a particular situation can cause the person to fear that situation; that is, a panic attack can cause a phobia, presumably through classical conditioning. Anxiety is a normal reaction to many stresses of life, and none of us is completely free from it. In fact, anxiety is undoubtedly useful in causing us to be more alert and to take important things seriously. The anxiety we all feel from time to time, though, is significantly different from the intense fear and terror experienced by a person gripped by a panic attack.

▲ *For most people, anxiety is a typical reaction to circumstances that are perceived to be dangerous—for example, walking along a narrow ledge hundreds of metres above the ground—and is not considered abnormal. However, when anxiety interferes with carrying out day-to-day activities, it is considered a type of psychological disorder.*

**anxiety** A sense of apprehension or doom that is accompanied by many physiological reactions, such as accelerated heart rate, sweaty palms, and tightness in the stomach.

**panic** A feeling of extreme fear mixed with hopelessness or helplessness.

**panic disorder** Unpredictable attacks of acute anxiety that are accompanied by high levels of physiological arousal and that last from a few seconds to a few hours.

**anticipatory anxiety** A fear of having a panic attack; may lead to the development of phobias.

**Panic Disorder: Possible Causes** Panic disorders are difficult to explain, as they are extremely maladaptive. Researchers believe that such disorders are caused either by physical or cognitive factors or by interactions between the two.

**Genetic and Physiological Causes** Because the physical symptoms of panic attacks are so overwhelming, many patients reject the suggestion that they have a psychological disorder, insisting that their problem is medical. They may be correct: A considerable amount of evidence implicates biological influences in the development of panic disorder (Gratacos et al., 2007). The disorder appears to have a substantial hereditary component; there is a higher concordance rate for the disorder between identical twins than between fraternal twins (Knowles, Kaufmann, & Rieder, 1999; Torgerson, 1983), and a significant number of the first-degree relatives of a person with panic disorder also have panic disorder (Hettema, Neale, & Kendler, 2001). (*First-degree relatives* are a person's parents, children, and siblings.) According to Crowe, Noyes, Pauls, and Slymen (1983), the pattern of panic disorder within a family tree suggests that the disorder may be caused by a single, dominant gene.

People with panic disorder show physiological response patterns that seem to be biologically controlled. People with panic disorder periodically breathe irregularly both when awake (e.g., Ley, 2003) and when asleep (e.g., Stein, Millar, Larsen, & Kryger, 1995). An Internet survey found that 95 percent of respondents reported breathing changes during a panic attack, and nearly 70 percent suffered from dyspnea, a disorder with symptoms including breathing discomfort or significant breathlessness (Anderson & Ley, 2001). Although irregular breathing itself does not appear to cause panic attacks, its presence is consistent with underlying biological processes. We also know that panic attacks can be triggered in people with histories of panic disorder by giving them injections of lactic acid (a by-product of muscular activity) or by having them breathe air containing an elevated amount of carbon dioxide (Biber & Alkin, 1999; Nardi, Lopes, & Valenca, 2004; Nardi et al., 2002). People with family histories of panic attacks are more likely to react to lactic acid, even if they have never had a panic attack previously (Cowley, Dager, & Dunner, 1995; Peskind et al., 1998). Some researchers believe that what is inherited is a tendency to react with alarm to bodily sensations of many different sources that would not disturb most other people.

As usual, it is important to note that biological factors alone are unlikely to provide a full account of this disorder. There is considerable room left for environmental influence after taking into account the likely heritable component of the disorder. Thus, the amounts of stress experienced by people and how they have learned to cope with stress probably influence the expression of any biological cause.

**Cognitive Causes** The cognitive approach focuses on *expectancies*. People who suffer from panic attacks appear to be extremely sensitive to any element of risk or danger in their environments. For example, researchers brought people into a lab and asked them to look at pictures of faces that displayed negative or angry emotions. They found that people who were highly anxious were more likely to direct their gaze at the faces that exhibited an intense negative emotional expression (Mogg, Holmes, Garner, & Bradley, 2007). People with panic disorder focus on the negative aspects of the environment and expect to be threatened by situational stressors and downplay or underestimate their abilities to cope with them (Mogg & Bradley, 2003; Mogg, Bradley, Williams, & Matthews, 1993). The expectation of having to face stressors that they fear may overwhelm their coping abilities leads these people to develop a sense of dread. Soon, a full-blown panic attack results. Thus, merely anticipating that something bad is about to happen can precipitate a panic attack.

**TABLE 17•3 Names and Descriptions of Some Common Phobias**

| Name | Object or Situation Feared |
|---|---|
| Acrophobia | Heights |
| Agoraphobia | Open spaces |
| Algophobia | Pain |
| Astraphobia | Storms, thunder, lightning |
| Claustrophobia | Enclosed spaces |
| Hematophobia | Blood |
| Monophobia | Being alone |
| Mysophobia | Dirt or germs |
| Nyctophobia | Darkness |
| Ochlophobia | Crowds |
| Pathophobia | Disease |
| Pyrophobia | Fire |
| Taphophobia | Being buried alive |
| Triskaidekaphobia | Thirteen |
| Zoophobia | Animals, or a specific animal |

**Phobic Disorder: Description** Phobias—named after the Greek god Phobos, who frightened one's enemies—are persistent, irrational fears of specific objects or situations. Because phobias can be so specific, clinicians have coined a variety of inventive names. (See **Table 17•3**.)

Almost all of us have one or more irrational fears of specific objects or situations, and it is difficult to draw a line between these fears and phobic disorders. If someone is afraid of spiders but manages to lead a normal life by avoiding them, it would seem inappropriate to say that the person has a psychological disorder. Similarly, many otherwise normal people are afraid of speaking in public. The term **phobic disorder** should be reserved for people whose fear makes their lives difficult.

**phobic disorder** An unrealistic, excessive fear of a specific class of stimuli that interferes with normal activities. The object of the anxiety is readily identifiable: It may be a snake, an insect, the outdoors, or closed spaces.

The DSM-IV-TR recognizes three types of phobic disorder: agoraphobia, social phobia, and specific phobia. Agoraphobia (*agora* means "open space") is the most serious of these disorders. Most cases of agoraphobia are considered to be caused by panic attacks and are classified with them. **Agoraphobia** associated with panic attacks is defined as a fear of "being in places or situations from which escape might be difficult (or embarrassing) or in which help might not be available in the event of a panic attack. . . . As a result of this fear, the person either restricts travel or needs a companion when away from home." Agoraphobia can be severely disabling. Merely thinking about leaving the home can produce profound fear, dread, and physical symptoms such as nausea and profuse sweating. Imagine yourself unable to go to the corner store, let alone school or work, without battling what feels like a case of food poisoning combined with the most extreme fear you have ever felt. Some people with this disorder have stayed inside their houses or apartments for years, afraid to venture outside.

**Social phobia** is an exaggerated "fear of one or more situations . . . in which the person is exposed to possible scrutiny by others and fears that he or she may do something or act in a way that will be humiliating or embarrassing." Most people with social phobia are only mildly impaired. Thinking about social encounters and engaging in them still produce significant anxiety, but most people with the disorder might simply appear to the outsider to be reclusive or shy. There appears to be a self-perpetuating aspect to this disorder. Even after successful, positive interactions with others, people with social phobia feel less positive and more negative affect than people without the phobia (Wallace & Alden, 1997). People with a social phobia also tend to focus on threats in social situations (Mogg, Philippot, & Bradley, 2004). Social phobia can be rather general, with people being fearful of most social encounters, or it can be relatively circumscribed to specific situations, such as public speaking.

**Specific phobia** includes all other phobias, such as fear of snakes, darkness, or heights. These phobias are often caused by a specific traumatic experience. The lifetime prevalence rate for specific phobia is estimated to be about 15 percent for women and about 7 percent for men (Magee et al., 1996), but approximately a third of the population *sometimes* exhibits phobic symptoms (Goodwin & Guze, 1996). Both males and females are equally likely to exhibit social phobia, but females are more likely to develop agoraphobia. Phobias that begin to develop in childhood or early adolescence (primarily specific phobias) are likely to disappear, whereas those that begin to develop after adolescence are likely to endure. Social phobia tends to begin during the teenage years, whereas agoraphobia tends to begin during a person's middle or late twenties. These disorders rarely make their first appearance after age 30.

Let's try to understand what a specific phobia is really like from both an insider and an outsider point of view. A friend of mine used to have acrophobia (fear of heights), and a fairly severe case at that. Even so, I did not learn that she had this phobia until after knowing her for some five years. We were attending a meeting in Quebec City, and I wanted to take the *funiculaire* (cable car elevator) up from the old city to the new city. My friend hemmed and hawed, and eventually countered that she would rather take the land route back so that she could buy some souvenirs in a shop she had seen. I really wanted to take the gondola and persisted, suggesting that we go to the souvenir shop and then return to the *funiculaire*. It finally dawned on me that she was becoming quite upset. I had never seen her so testy. She soon told me the real reason for her resistance and emotionality—the thought of taking the *funiculaire* made her ill with apprehension. It turned out that her phobia was quite specific to circumstances in which she had a view of the ground dropping away from her feet. She was fine in aisle seats of airplanes and in most elevators—but she would not take that cable car. How could I have known my friend for so long without learning about her phobia? Like many people with phobias, she had become very proficient at avoiding those experiences that frightened her.

### Phobic Disorder: Possible Causes

What was the cause of my friend's fear? Psychoanalytical theory attributes phobias to distress caused by intolerable unconscious impulses or to the displacement of objective sources of fear to symbolic sources (e.g., from a child's realistic fear of an abusive parent to an object in the physical environment). The majority of clinical psychologists and behaviour analysts believe that phobias are learned by means of classical conditioning—whether direct or vicarious. *Direct classical conditioning* occurs when a particular animal or object is present in an especially unpleasant situation. *Vicarious classical conditioning* occurs when a person observes another person (especially a parent or someone else to whom the person is closely attached) show fright in the presence of a particular animal or object.

#### Environmental Causes—Learning

To say that phobias are learned through classical conditioning does not explain this disorder completely. Many people have traumatic, frightening experiences, but not all of them develop phobic disorders; thus, it appears that not all people are likely to develop phobias. Also, many people with phobias do not remember having had specific, early life experiences with the objects they fear (e.g., Kheriaty, Kleinknecht, & Hyman, 1999). (Of course, they may have simply forgotten the experiences.)

In addition, some objects are more likely to be feared than are others. People tend to fear animals (especially snakes,

**agoraphobia** A psychological disorder characterized by fear of and avoidance of being alone in public places; this disorder is often accompanied by panic attacks.
**social phobia** A psychological disorder characterized by an excessive and irrational fear of situations in which the person is observed by others.
**specific phobia** An excessive and irrational fear of specific things, such as snakes, darkness, or heights.

spiders, dogs, or rodents), blood, heights, and closed spaces. They are less likely to fear automobiles or electrical outlets, which are potentially more dangerous than some of the common objects of phobias, such as snakes and spiders.

You will see in Chapter 18 that the same classes of drugs useful in treating panic attacks also reduce the symptoms of agoraphobia. However, the results that last longest are obtained from behaviour therapy.

**Genetic Causes** Some investigators suggest that a tendency to develop a fear of certain kinds of stimuli may have a biological basis that reflects the evolution of our species (Seligman, 1971). The general idea is that because of our ancestors' history in relatively hostile natural environments, a capacity evolved for especially efficient fear conditioning to certain classes of dangerous stimuli (e.g., snakes). Öhman and his colleagues have reported a well-integrated series of experiments that support this analysis. Participants in these experiments are typically assigned to a condition in which they are shown pictures of either fear-irrelevant stimuli (e.g., plants) or to a condition in which they are exposed to pictures of fear-relevant stimuli (e.g., snakes). An important measure in this line of research is skin conductance, an index of emotional reactivity. A central finding of this research program is that pairing the pictures with a mild electric shock resulted in conditioned emotional responses to the fear-relevant but not to the fear-irrelevant stimuli, even though the pictures had been presented in such a way that participants could not consciously identify the content (Öhman & Soares, 1998; Soares & Öhman, 1993). Importantly, conditioning to the fear-relevant stimuli appeared more resistant to extinction than did conditioning to the fear-irrelevant stimuli. Thus, participants not only showed a special proclivity for conditioned fear to fear-relevant stimuli, but they did so without awareness. Another study in the series showed that participants who were already afraid of snakes and spiders reacted with higher skin conductance to pictures of these feared animals, again even when they were presented outside conscious awareness, than did non-fearful people (Öhman & Soares, 1994). Even five-month-old infants have exhibited predator recognition (Rakison & Derringer, 2008). Researchers have found that infants at this age appear to have a "perceptual template" for threatening objects such as spiders.

**Obsessive-Compulsive Disorder: Description** People with an **obsessive-compulsive disorder** suffer from **obsessions**—thoughts that will not leave them—and **compulsions**—behaviours that they cannot keep from performing. In one study, impaired control of mental activities, checking, urges involving loss of motor control, and feeling contaminated were found to be the major classes of obsessions and compulsions among a large sample of American university students (Sternberger & Burns, 1990). The prevalence is estimated to be about 2 percent in Canada (Health Canada, 2002).

Unlike people with panic disorder, people with obsessive-compulsive disorder have a defence against anxiety: their compulsive behaviour. Unfortunately, the need to perform this compulsive behaviour often demands more and more of their time until it interferes with their careers and daily lives. Obsessions are seen in many psychological disorders, including schizophrenia. However, unlike persons with schizophrenia, people with obsessive-compulsive disorder generally recognize that their thoughts and behaviours are senseless and wish that they would go away.

Consider the case of Beth, a young woman who had become obsessed with cleanliness.

> Beth's concern for cleanliness gradually evolved into a thorough cleansing ritual, which was usually set off by her touching her genital or anal area. In this ritual, Beth would first remove all of her clothing in a pre-established sequence. She would lay out each article of clothing at specific spots on her bed and examine each for any evidence of "contamination." She would thoroughly scrub her body, starting at her feet and working meticulously up to the top of her head, using certain washcloths for certain areas of her body. Any articles of clothing that appeared to have been "contaminated" were thrown into the laundry. Clean clothing then was put on the bed locations that were vacant. She would then dress herself in the opposite order from which she took the clothes off. If there were any deviations from this order, or if Beth began to wonder if she might have missed some contamination, she would go through the entire sequence again. It was not rare for her to do this four or five times in a row on some evenings. (Meyer & Osborne, 1982, p. 158)

Females are slightly more likely than males to have this diagnosis. Like panic disorder, obsessive-compulsive disorder most commonly begins in young adulthood (Sturgis, 1993). People with this disorder are unlikely to marry, perhaps because of the common obsessional fear of dirt and contamination or because the shame associated with the rituals they are compelled to perform causes them to avoid social contact (Turner, Beidel, Stanley, & Heiser, 2001).

There are two principal kinds of obsessions: obsessive *doubt* or *uncertainty*, and obsessive *fear of doing something prohibited*. We all experience doubts about future activities (such as whether to look for a new job, eat at one restaurant or another, wear a raincoat or take an umbrella) and about past activities (such as whether one has turned off a burner on the range and whether one remembered to lock the door upon leaving home). But these uncertainties, both trivial and important, preoccupy some people with obsessive-compulsive disorder almost completely. Others are plagued with the fear that they will do something terrible—swear aloud in church, urinate in someone's living room, kill themselves or a loved

**obsessive-compulsive disorder** Recurrent, unwanted thoughts or ideas and compelling urges to engage in repetitive ritual-like behaviour.
**obsession** An involuntary recurring thought, idea, or image.
**compulsion** An irresistible impulse to repeat some action over and over even though it serves no useful purpose.

one, or jump off a bridge—although they seldom actually do anything anti-social. And even though they are often obsessed with thoughts of killing themselves, fewer than 1 percent of them actually attempt suicide.

Most compulsions fall into one of four categories: *counting, checking, cleaning,* and *avoidance*. For example, some people feel they must count every step between their cars and the buildings they plan to enter. Others might repeatedly check burners on the stove to see that they are off or doors to be sure they are locked. Some people wash their hands hundreds of times a day, even when they become covered with painful sores. Some become afraid to leave home because they fear contamination and refuse to touch other members of their families. If they do accidentally become "contaminated," they usually perform lengthy purification rituals. The type of compulsion affects certain personality traits. For example, Radomsky, Ashbaugh, and Gelfand (2007) found a correlation between checking compulsions and increased levels of trait anger. That is, people with a checking compulsion reported feeling more anger, although this anger did not manifest itself in increased angry behaviour.

## Obsessive-Compulsive Disorder: Possible Causes

Several possible causes have been suggested for obsessive-compulsive disorder. Unlike simple anxiety states, this disorder can be understood in terms of defence mechanisms. Some cognitive investigators have suggested that obsessions serve as devices to occupy the mind and displace painful thoughts. This strategy is seen in normal behaviour: A person who "psyches himself up" before a competitive event by telling himself about his skill and stamina is also keeping out self-defeating doubts and fears. Like Scarlett O'Hara in *Gone with the Wind*, who repeatedly told herself, "I'll think about it tomorrow," we all say, at one time or another, "Oh, I'll think about something else," when our thoughts become painful.

**Cognitive Causes** Cognitive researchers also point out that persons with obsessive-compulsive disorder believe that they should be competent at all times, avoid any kinds of criticism at all costs, and worry about being punished by others for behaviour that is less than perfect (Sarason & Sarason, 1999). Thus, one reason people who have obsessive-compulsive disorder may engage in checking behaviour is to reduce the anxiety caused by fear of being perceived by others as incompetent or to avoid others' criticism that they have done something less than perfectly.

If painful, anxiety-producing thoughts become frequent, and if turning to alternative patterns of thought reduces anxiety, then the principle of reinforcement predicts that the person will turn to these patterns more frequently. Just as an animal learns to jump a hurdle to escape a painful foot shock, a person can learn to think about a "safe topic" in order to avoid painful thoughts. If the habit becomes firmly established, the obsessive thoughts may persist even after the original reason for turning to them—the situation that produced the anxiety-arousing thoughts—no longer exists. A habit can thus outlast its original causes. As we will see in Chapter 18, one effective approach to treating people with this disorder is to change their patterns of thinking.

**Tourette's syndrome** A neurological disorder characterized by tics and involuntary utterances, some of which may involve obscenities and the repetition of others' utterances.

**Genetic Causes** Evidence is beginning to accumulate suggesting that obsessive-compulsive disorder may have a genetic origin (Pato, Pato, & Pauls, 2002; Pauls & Alsobrook, 1999). Whatever the degree of heritability may turn out to be, the disorder has a strong family transmission rate. Nestadt and colleagues (2000) report that obsessive-compulsive disorder is found almost five times more frequently among first-degree relatives of those with the disorder than among first-degree relatives of people who do not have the disorder. Family studies also have found that this disorder is associated symptomatically with a neurological disorder called Tourette's syndrome, which appears during childhood (Alsobrook & Pauls, 1997; Cath et al., 2000; Leckman et al., 2003; Pauls & Leckman, 1986). In fact, approximately 30 to 50 percent of people who are diagnosed with Tourette's syndrome also meet the diagnostic criteria for obsessive-compulsive disorder (Thibault et al., 2008). **Tourette's syndrome** is characterized by muscular and vocal tics, including making facial grimaces, squatting, pacing, twirling, barking, sniffing, coughing, grunting, or repeating specific words (especially vulgarities). Pauls and his colleagues believe that the two disorders are produced by the same single, dominant gene. It is not clear why some people with the gene would develop Tourette's syndrome in childhood and others would develop obsessive-compulsive disorder later in life. There is also evidence that elevated glucose metabolic rates in certain areas of the brain are found in people suffering from obsessive-compulsive disorder (Saxena & Rauch, 2000). As well, disorders that involve basal ganglia dysfunction, such as Tourette's, are often associated with obsessive-compulsive disorder symptoms. This pattern supports the idea that the disorder may have a biological basis (Swedo, Rapaort, & Cheslow, 1989).

We do know that not all cases of obsessive-compulsive disorder have a genetic origin. The disorder sometimes occurs after brain damage caused by various means, such as birth trauma, encephalitis, and head trauma (Hollander et al., 1990). As we shall see in Chapter 18, obsessive-compulsive disorder has been treated by psychosurgery, drugs, and behaviour therapy. These treatments are sometimes effective, but the disorder often persists despite the efforts of experienced therapists. One of the problems in treating obsessive-compulsive disorder is that people are hesitant to seek treatment. In a study of more than 7000 residents of Edmonton, 172 people were diagnosed with obsessive-compulsive disorder. Only 37 percent of them had consulted a doctor about their symptoms (Mayerovitch et al., 2003).

## Somatoform Disorders

The primary symptoms of a **somatoform disorder** are a bodily or physical (*soma* means "body") problem for which there is no physiological basis. The two most important somatoform disorders are somatization disorder and conversion disorder.

**Somatization Disorder: Description** **Somatization disorder** involves complaints of wide-ranging physical ailments for which there is no apparent biological basis (Hurwitz, 2004). Regier and colleagues (1988) found that the incidence of somatization disorder in a sample of more than 18 000 people was less than 1 percent in women and non-existent in men. Somatization disorder is often chronic, lasting for decades.

Somatization disorder is characterized by persistent complaints of serious symptoms for which no physiological cause can be found. Obviously, a proper diagnosis can be made only after medical examination and laboratory tests indicate the lack of disease. The DSM-IV-TR requires that the person have a history of complaining of physical symptoms for several years. The complaints must include at least 13 symptoms from a list of 35, which fall into the following categories: gastrointestinal symptoms, pain symptoms, cardiopulmonary symptoms, pseudoneurological symptoms, and sexual symptoms. These symptoms must also have led the person to take medication, see a physician, or substantially alter her life. Almost every woman who receives the diagnosis of somatization disorder reports that she does not experience pleasure from sexual intercourse. Obviously, everyone has one or more physical symptoms from time to time that cannot be explained through a medical examination, but few people chronically complain of at least 13 of them. The person with somatization disorder will consult with many physicians and will do so frequently, often throughout her entire lifetime after onset of the disorder. Although people with somatization disorder often make suicide attempts, they rarely actually kill themselves.

Somatization disorder resembles another somatoform disorder, called **hypochondriasis.** People who suffer from hypochondriasis, more frequently women than men, interpret minor physical sensations as signs that they have a serious underlying disease. For example, a person who experiences very minor stomach discomfort might interpret the sensations as a certain sign of a malignant tumour. Normal fatigue on another occasion would then be interpreted as being consistent with the self-diagnosis that he or she is beginning to weaken from the cancerous growth. The person worries a great deal about the presumed illness and often believes that he or she is facing death. You can see that this is more than the typical anxiety that people have when they experience a symptom of illness and see their doctors. Reassurances by physicians will have only short-term ameliorative effects on the person's anxiety. You can also see that there is significant overlap in the descriptions of somatization disorder and hypochondriasis. One important distinction is that the former is characterized by many symptoms of many possible underlying disorders, whereas the latter involves a small number of symptoms. As well, the anxiety accompanying somatization disorder tends to focus on the symptoms themselves (e.g., "I'm nauseous almost every day, and want it to stop"), whereas with hypochondriasis the person usually focuses on the dangerous disease that the overinterpreted symptoms seem to implicate (e.g., "I'm going to die of stomach cancer"). Like the person with somatization disorder, the person with hypochondriasis will seek medical attention frequently.

**Somatization Disorder: Possible Causes** Somatization disorder tends to run in families. Coryell (1980) found that approximately 20 percent of first-degree female relatives of people with somatization disorder also had the disorder. In addition, many studies have shown that somatization disorder is closely associated with anti-social personality disorder (which I will describe in a later section). First-degree male relatives of women with somatization disorder have an increased incidence of alcoholism or anti-social behaviour, and first-degree female relatives of convicted male criminals have an increased incidence of somatization disorder (Guze, Wolfgram, McKinney, & Cantwell, 1967; Woerner & Guze, 1968). These findings suggest that a particular environmental or genetic history leads to different pathological manifestations in men and women.

**Conversion Disorder: Description** **Conversion disorder** is characterized by physical complaints that resemble neurological disorders but have no underlying organic pathological basis. The symptoms include blindness, deafness, loss of feeling, and paralysis. According to the DSM-IV-TR, a conversion disorder must be associated with an apparent psychological reason for the symptoms; they must occur in response to an environmental stimulus that produces a psychological conflict, or they must permit the person to avoid an unpleasant activity or to receive support and sympathy. Unlike somatization disorder, conversion disorder can afflict both men and women equally.

The term *conversion*, when applied to a psychological disorder, derives from psychoanalytical theory, which states that the energy of an unresolved intrapsychic conflict is converted into a physical symptom. The symptoms themselves

**somatoform disorder** A psychological disorder involving a bodily or physical problem for which there is no physiological basis.
**somatization disorder** A class of somatoform disorder, occurring mostly among women, that involves complaints of wide-ranging physical ailments for which there is no apparent biological cause.
**hypochondriasis** A somatoform disorder involving persistent and excessive worry about developing a serious illness. People with this disorder often misinterpret the appearance of normal physical aches and pains.
**conversion disorder** A somatoform disorder involving the actual loss of bodily function, such as blindness, paralysis, and numbness, due to excessive anxiety.

are often related to the individual's personal and work lives. For example, a telephone operator may become unable to speak, a surgeon may find her hands paralyzed, or a person with a history of doing volunteer work for music festivals may find that he cannot hear. Hofling (1963) described one such case:

> The patient had taken the day off from work to be at home with his wife and [newborn] baby. During the afternoon, he had felt somewhat nervous and tense, but had passed off these feelings as normal for a new father. . . .
>
> . . . The baby awoke and cried. Mrs. L. said that she would nurse him. . . . As she put the baby to her breast, the patient became aware of a smarting sensation in his eyes. He had been smoking heavily and attributed the irritation to the room's being filled with smoke. He got up and opened a window. When the smarting sensation became worse he went to the washstand and applied a cold cloth to his eyes. On removing the cloth, he found that he was completely blind.
>
> . . . Psychotherapy was instituted. . . . The visual symptoms disappeared rather promptly, with only very mild and fleeting exacerbations during the next several months. . . .
>
> . . . He had been jealous of the baby—this was a difficult admission to make—and jealous on two distinct counts. One feeling was, in essence, a sexual jealousy, accentuated by his own sexual deprivation during the last weeks of the pregnancy. The other was . . . a jealousy of the maternal solicitude shown the infant by its mother. (Hofling, 1963, pp. 315–316)

Although the sensory deficits or paralyses of people with conversion disorders are not caused by damage to the nervous system, these people are not faking their illnesses. People who deliberately pretend they are sick in order to gain some advantage (such as avoiding work) are said to be *malingering*. Malingering is not defined as a psychological disorder by the DSM-IV-TR. Although it is not always easy to distinguish malingering from a conversion disorder, two criteria are useful. First, people with conversion disorders are usually delighted to talk about their symptoms in great detail, whereas malingerers are reluctant to do so for fear of having their deception discovered. Second, people with conversion disorders usually describe the symptoms with great drama and flair but do not appear to be upset about them.

As we just saw, somatization disorder consists of complaints of medical problems, but the examining physician is unable to see any signs that would indicate physical illness. In contrast, a patient with conversion disorder gives the appearance of having a neurological disorder such as blindness or paralysis.

The particular physical symptoms of people with conversion disorders change with the times and with people's general sophistication. For example, around the turn of the nineteenth century, patients commonly developed "glove" or "stocking" anaesthesias, in which the skin over their hands or feet would become perfectly numb. It is physiologically impossible for these anaesthesias to occur as a result of nerve damage; the patterns of anaesthesia produced by organic means would be very different. Today people seldom suffer such a naive disorder.

**Conversion Disorder: Possible Causes** Psychoanalytical theory suggests that the psychic energy of unresolved conflicts (especially those involving sexual desires the patient is unwilling or unable to admit to having) becomes displaced into physical symptoms. In other words, psychoanalysts regard conversion disorders as primarily sexual in origin.

Behaviour analysts, on the other hand, have suggested that conversion disorders can be learned for many reasons. This assertion gains support from the finding that people with these disorders usually suffer from physical symptoms of diseases with which they are already familiar (Ullman & Krasner, 1969). A patient often mimics the symptoms of a friend. Furthermore, the patient must receive some kind of reinforcement for having the disability; he or she must derive some benefit from it.

Ullman and Krasner cited a case that was originally reported by Brady and Lind (1961). A soldier developed an eye problem that led to his discharge and his receipt of a small disability pension. He worked at a series of menial jobs, returning periodically to the hospital for treatment of his eye condition. He applied for a larger disability pension several times but was turned down because his vision had not become worse. After 12 years, the man, who was currently being forced by his wife and mother-in-law to spend his spare evenings and weekends doing chores around the house, suddenly became "blind." Because of his total disability, he was given special training for the blind and received a larger pension. He also received a family allowance from the community and no longer had to work around the house. In this case, both criteria described by Ullman and Krasner were fulfilled: The patient was familiar with the disorder (indeed, he had a real eye disorder) and his symptoms were reinforced.

## Dissociative Disorders

In somatoform disorders, anxiety is avoided by the appearance of the symptoms of serious physical disorders. In **dissociative disorders**, anxiety is reduced by a sudden disruption in consciousness, which, in turn, may produce changes in a person's memory or even in his or her identity.

**Description** A relatively simple form of dissociative disorder is called **dissociative amnesia**. Amnesia (loss of memory) can,

**dissociative disorders** A class of disorders in which anxiety is reduced by a sudden disruption in consciousness, which in turn produces changes in one's sense of identity.

**dissociative amnesia** A dissociative disorder characterized by the inability to remember important events or personal information.

of course, be produced by physical means such as brain damage, epilepsy, or intoxication. Dissociative amnesia is related instead to diverse traumatic events. For example, shortly before onset of the disorder the person may be the victim of violence, suffer a non-neurologic injury, commit an act that he or she finds repulsive, or experience a significant loss. The amnesia is typically confined to the traumatic event. The person will not be able to remember, for example, being attacked and disfigured or even who the attacker was. If the person's own actions are the source of stress, he may be unable to remember committing the act, where he was, or with whom he was at the time of the event.

A more extreme form of dissociative amnesia is called **dissociative fugue** (pronounced "fyoog"). This disorder produces considerable confusion, consternation, and worry for family, friends, and co-workers of the afflicted person. The setting conditions are the same as for dissociative amnesia, but the symptoms are much more flamboyant. Following the stressful incident, the person cannot identify himself or herself, cannot remember his or her past, will relocate to a new area, will adopt a new identity, and may establish a new family and career. Imagine your reaction if someone in your life, an apparently stable and well-functioning person, simply disappeared one night. Your thoughts would turn to the possibilities of accidents and death or perhaps kidnapping. And then imagine your reaction when you learn through coincidence that your friend has a new career and family thousands of kilometres away from his home. Just such events happen. When the fugue state ends, as often happens, the person resumes his or her normal personality and memory, except that he or she has no memory for events during the fugue. The person having the fugue state, then, will be just as confused and worried as family and friends have been about what happened.

**Dissociative identity disorder** (previously, *multiple personality disorder*) is a very rare, but very striking, dissociative disorder that is marked by the presence of two or more separate personalities within the individual, either of which may be dominant at any given time. An interesting instance of dissociative identity disorder is the case of Billy Milligan as told in the book *The Minds of Billy Milligan* (Keyes, 1981). Milligan was accused of rape and kidnapping but was deemed not guilty by reason of insanity. His psychiatric examination showed him to have 24 different personalities. Two were women and one was a young girl. There was a Briton, an Australian, and a Yugoslavian. One woman, a lesbian, was a poet, while the Yugoslav was an expert on weapons and munitions and the Briton and Australian were minor criminals.

Dissociative identity disorder has received much attention; people find it fascinating to contemplate several different personalities, most of whom are unaware of each other, existing within the same individual. Bliss (1986) suggests that dissociative identity disorder is a form of self-hypnosis, established early in life, that permits escape from painful experiences. Indeed, Ross, Miller, Bjornson, and Reagor (1991) reported that of 102 people diagnosed with dissociative identity disorder in Canada and the United States, 95 percent reported childhood sexual and/or physical abuse.

Note that such figures do not mean that childhood abuse *causes* dissociative identity disorder. Rather, they identify a very strong commonality among those who report symptoms of the disorder. Because the disorder is very rare, the rate of childhood abuse is many times higher than the incidence of dissociative identity disorder; most people who were abused as children do not develop multiple personalities. It is useful to ponder this point for a moment, because this method of statistical reporting is fairly common. To say that 95 percent of those with a particular disorder share a childhood experience is not at all to say that any other person who has the same experience has a 95 percent chance of developing the disorder. Nothing could be further from the truth. Understanding the link between childhood trauma and dissociative identity disorder remains an active and important theoretical and empirical concern (Ross, 1997).

As we saw in Chapter 9, some psychologists believe that hypnosis is not a state but, rather, a form of social role playing. In a similar vein, Nicholas Spanos (1996) advanced the theory that North Americans have learned the concept of dissociative identity disorder, and that cultural knowledge of the disorder provides a framework in which people can organize a variety of problems. Spanos argued that in attempts to understand their emotions and behaviours, people sometimes create multiple identities when doing so will help explain themselves in a congruent fashion to others. Thus, the person confused by his or her own instability in emotion and behaviour may be especially prone to develop and enact the role of a person with dissociative identity disorder. The person's confusing actions and emotions thereby become understandable both to himself or herself and to others.

But do people have the knowledge to enact the symptoms of dissociative identity disorder? In one study, Spanos and his colleagues asked people to do just that; they found that, when given appropriate instructions, people could effectively simulate two different personalities (Spanos, Weekes, & Bertrand, 1985). They adopted a new name for the new personality, and they gave different patterns of answers on a personality test when the second personality was "in control." Although people are often impressed by the remarkable differences between the various personalities of someone with dissociative identity disorder, the acting required for this task is within the ability of most people. That is not to say that everyone with multiple personality disorder is faking. The results of such research do suggest that clinicians should approach patients who appear to have multiple personalities with an open mind (Lindsay, 1999).

**dissociative fugue** Amnesia with no apparent organic cause, accompanied by adoption of a new identity and relocation.

**dissociative identity disorder** A rarely seen dissociative disorder in which two or more distinct personalities exist within the same person; each personality dominates in turn.

**Possible Causes** Dissociative disorders are usually explained as responses to severe conflicts resulting from intolerable impulses or as responses to guilt stemming from an actual misdeed. Partly because they are rare, dissociative disorders are among the least understood of the psychological disorders. In general, the dissociation is advantageous to the person. Amnesia enables the person to forget about a painful or unpleasant life. A person with fugue not only forgets but also leaves the area to start a new existence. And multiple personalities allow a person to do things that he or she would really like to do but cannot because of the strong guilt feelings that would ensue. The alternative personality can be one with a very weak conscience.

▲ *This man and his son show no signs of* nangiarpok, *a culture-bound syndrome that is today observed only rarely.*

**Culture-Bound Syndromes** People in all societies have specific rules for categorizing behaviour, and these rules can differ, often considerably, from culture to culture (Simons, 1996; Simons & Hughes, 1993). How behaviour is categorized and whether any instance of behaviour is considered appropriate is strongly influenced by social norms and values that exist at any moment in time (Bohannan, 1995). Many kinds of aberrant behaviour—behaviour that deviates from cultural norms—are not "officially" included in diagnostic manuals, such as the DSM-IV-TR, yet are considered pathological within a given culture. That is, there seem to exist highly idiosyncratic psychological disorders called **culture-bound syndromes**, which are found only within one or a few cultures. They do not exist across cultures, as schizophrenia and several other psychological disorders appear to (Al-Issa, 1995). For example, consider the following two individual cases:

> I. A. is a young Nigerian man. He recently met a stranger, whom he greeted with a handshake. He now claims that his genitals have fallen off. After a medical examination, the physician tells I. A. that his genitals are, in fact, still where they are supposed to be. But I. A. is unconvinced. He reports that his genitals are not the same since shaking hands with the stranger.
>
> I. L. was an Inuit hunter living in western Greenland. He hunted in the open sea from his kayak. He stopped because of *nangiarpok*, or an intense fear of capsizing and drowning in a kayak. He withdrew socially from his people and eventually committed suicide. Although once common among western Greenlanders, this disorder is now rare because of changes in Greenlandic culture, especially with respect to hunting and fishing, introduced through exposure to Western culture.

Many other such culture-bound syndromes appear to exist. Some Polynesian Islanders suffer from *cafard* ("ka-fawr"), a sudden display of homicidal behaviour followed by exhaustion; some male Southeast Asians develop *koro*, an intense fear that the penis will retract into the body, resulting in death (they will often hold their penises firmly to prevent this from happening); some Japanese develop an intense fear that their appearance, body odours, or behaviours are offensive to others, a condition called *Taijin kyofusho* ("ta-ee-jeen ki-yo-foo-sho") (Suzuki et al., 2004).

**culture-bound syndromes** Highly unusual psychological disorders, similar in nature to non-psychotic psychological disorders, that appear to be specific to only one or a few cultures.

What causes culture-bound syndromes? That is a very difficult question to answer for several reasons. First, a worldwide classification scheme of psychological disorders does not exist, which means that an exhaustive taxonomy of psychological disorders also does not yet exist. Second, many culture-bound syndromes have only recently been discovered, and only a few have received much empirical scrutiny. Third, we do not yet have a complete explanation for major psychological disorders that affect millions of people, such as schizophrenia and depression, so it is not unreasonable to expect that the study of psychological disorders that afflict fewer people, such as culture-bound syndromes, will be neglected. Fourth, and perhaps most important, many culture-bound syndromes are often described—and treated—using "alternative" (non–Western traditional medical) treatments. For example, in Japan, *Taijin kyofusho* is treated in a ritual that involves, among other things, massage and sweating. Because practices based on folklore are widely accepted by members of the culture, alternative explanations, based on scientific methods, are neither sought nor readily accepted when offered.

Nonetheless, we may speculate about the origins of culture-bound syndromes. Most of those we have described are *specific* to certain environmental events or situations and appear similar in nature to specific and social phobias. Thus, it appears unlikely that these problems have either a strong heritability component or an organic (physiological) basis. Syndromes such as *nangiarpok*, *koro*, and *Taijin kyofusho* seem similar to what is described by the DSM-IV-TR as a specific phobia, suggesting that they are learned responses to fear-eliciting stimuli.

Certainly, culture-bound syndromes are interesting phenomena worthy of investigation. Understanding the development of these disorders may represent an important means of learning more about how cultures influence the course of an individual's life (Kleinknecht et al., 1997).

## Interim Summary

### Anxiety, Somatoform, and Dissociative Psychological Disorders

People with anxiety, somatoform, and dissociative psychological disorders have adopted strategies that have a certain amount of immediate payoff but in the long run are maladaptive. We can understand most of their problems as exaggerations of our own. Although their fears and doubts may be unrealistic, they are not outrageously bizarre.

Anxiety disorders include panic disorder, phobias, and obsessive-compulsive disorder. All of them (except specific phobia and social phobia) appear to have a genetic component. Panic disorder is the least adaptive of all these disorders; the person has no defence against his or her discomfort. In contrast, obsessive-compulsive disorder involves thoughts or behaviours that prevent the person from thinking about painful subjects or that ward off feelings of guilt and anxiety.

Simple phobias can probably be explained by classical conditioning; some experience (usually early in life) causes a particular object or situation to become a conditioned aversive stimulus. The fear associated with this stimulus leads to escape behaviours, which are reinforced because they reduce the person's fear. Agoraphobia is a much more serious disorder, and it is apparently not caused by a specific traumatic experience. Social phobia is a fear of being observed or judged by others; in its mildest form it involves a fear of speaking in public.

Somatoform disorders include somatization disorder and conversion disorder. Somatization disorder involves persistent complaints of symptoms of a large variety of illnesses without underlying physiological causes. Almost all people with this disorder are women. Conversion disorder involves specific neurological symptoms, such as paralysis or sensory disturbance, that are not produced by a physiological disorder. In most cases, the patient derives some gain from his or her disability.

Dissociative disorders are rare but interesting. Dissociative amnesia (with or without fugue) appears to be a withdrawal from a painful situation or from intolerable guilt. Because amnesia is a common symptom of brain injury or neurological disease, physical factors must be ruled out before accepting a diagnosis of dissociative amnesia. Multiple personalities are even more rare and presumably occur because they permit a person to engage in behaviours contrary to his or her code of conduct.

Culture-bound syndromes are psychological disorders that appear to be idiosyncratic to only one or a few cultures. These disorders frequently involve fear of specific objects or situations, such as *nangiarpok*—being unable to extricate oneself from a kayak if it capsizes—or *Taijin kyofusho*—social embarrassment. The precise origins of culture-bound syndromes are unknown, but it seems likely that they involve learned responses that reduce or eliminate anxiety or stress.

#### QUESTIONS TO CONSIDER

1. When was the last time you felt especially anxious about something? Did the anxiety disrupt your behaviour, even momentarily? In what ways was your anxiety similar to or different from that that might be experienced by a person with an anxiety disorder, such as panic disorder or phobic disorder?
2. Do you have a fear of anything—heights, dark places, insects, snakes, or other things or situations? If you do, is it severe enough to be considered a phobia? How do you know?
3. Reflect for a minute on Beth, the woman who had an obsessive-compulsive cleaning ritual. How would you explain her behaviour, given what you now know about the causes of obsessive-compulsive behaviour?

# Personality Disorders

The DSM-IV-TR also classifies abnormalities in behaviour that impair social or occupational functioning—personality disorders. Although there are several types of personality disorders, the only personality disorder I will specifically discuss here is the one that has the most impact on society: *anti-social personality disorder*. **Table 17•4** provides a description of several other personality disorders.

## Anti-social Personality Disorder

There have been many different labels for what we now call **anti-social personality disorder**, which is characterized by a failure to conform to common standards of decency, repeated lying and stealing, a failure to sustain long-lasting and loving relationships, low tolerance of boredom, and a complete lack of guilt (Cleckley, 1976; De Oliveira-Souza, Moll, Azevedo Ignico, & Hare, 2008; Hare, 1998; Harpur, Hart, & Hare, 2002). Prichard (1835) used the term *moral insanity* to describe people whose intellect was normal but in whom the "moral and active principles of the mind are strongly perverted and depraved . . . and the individual is found to be incapable . . . of

**anti-social personality disorder** A disorder characterized by a failure to conform to standards of decency; repeated lying and stealing; a failure to sustain lasting, loving relationships; low tolerance of boredom; and a complete lack of guilt.

**TABLE 17•4 Descriptions of Various Personality Disorders***

| Personality Disorder | Description |
|---|---|
| Paranoid | Suspiciousness and extreme mistrust of others; enhanced perception of being under attack by others. |
| Schizoid | Difficulty in social functioning—social withdrawal and lack of caring for others. |
| Schizotypal | Unusual thought patterns and perceptions; poor communication and social skills. |
| Histrionic | Attention-seeking; preoccupation with personal attractiveness; prone to anger when attempts at attracting attention fail. |
| Narcissistic | Self-promoting; lack of empathy for others; attention seeking; grandiosity. |
| Borderline | Lack of impulse control; drastic mood swings; inappropriate anger; becomes bored easily and for prolonged periods; suicidal. |
| Avoidant | Oversensitivity to rejection; little confidence in initiating or maintaining social relationships. |
| Dependent | Uncomfortable being alone or in terminating relationships; places others' needs above one's own in order to preserve the relationship; indecisive. |
| Obsessive-compulsive | Preoccupation with rules and order; tendency toward perfectionism; difficulty relaxing or enjoying life. |

*Source: Carson and Mineka,* Abnormal Psychology & Modern Life, *pg 317, © 2000. Reproduced by permission of Pearson Education, Inc.*

* The anti-social personality disorder, not listed here, is described in detail in the text.

conducting himself with decency and propriety." Koch (1889) introduced the term *psychopathic inferiority*, which soon became simply *psychopathy* (pronounced sy-kop-a-thee); a person who displayed the disorder was called a *psychopath*. The first version of the DSM (the DSM-I) used the term *sociopathic personality disturbance*, which was subsequently replaced by the present term, *anti-social personality disorder*. Most clinicians still refer to such people as *psychopaths* or *sociopaths*, and we will, too.

**Description** Anti-social personality disorder contributes to a considerable amount of social distress. Many criminals can be diagnosed as psychopaths, and most psychopaths have a record of criminal behaviour. Anti-social personality disorder can be found in as much as 50 percent of the prison population (Health Canada, 2002). The diagnostic criteria of the DSM-IV-TR include evidence of at least three types of anti-social behaviour before age 15 and at least four types after age 18. The adult forms of anti-social behaviour include inability to sustain consistent work behaviour; lack of ability to function as a responsible parent; repeated criminal activity, such as theft, pimping, or prostitution; inability to maintain enduring attachment to a sexual partner; volatility and violence, including fights or assault; failure to honour financial obligations; impulsiveness and failure to plan ahead; habitual lying or use of aliases; and consistently reckless or drunken driving. In addition to meeting at least four of these criteria, the person must have displayed a "pattern of continuous antisocial behaviour in which the rights of others are violated, with no intervening period of at least five years without antisocial behaviour." Clearly, these are people most of us do not want to be around.

▲ *Paul Bernardo, convicted of the brutal rapes and murders of two teenage girls, is considered by many psychologists to be a classic example of the anti-social personality disorder.*

The lifetime prevalence rate for anti-social personality disorder is estimated to be about 5 percent for men and 1 percent for women (Golomb, Fava, Abraham, & Rosenbaum, 1995). However, we cannot be sure that any such estimates are accurate because psychopaths do not voluntarily visit mental health professionals for help with their "problem." Indeed, most of them feel no need to change their ways.

Cleckley (1976), one of the most prominent experts on psychopathy, has listed 16 characteristics of anti-social personality disorder. (See **Table 17•5**.) Cleckley's list of features provides a good picture of what most psychopaths are like. Psychopaths habitually tell lies, even when there is no apparent reason for doing so and even when the lie is likely to be discovered. They steal things they do not need or even appear

**TABLE 17•5 Cleckley's Primary Characteristics of Anti-social Personality Disorder**

1. Superficial charm and good "intelligence"
2. Absence of delusions and other signs of irrational thinking
3. Absence of "nervousness"
4. Unreliability
5. Untruthfulness and insincerity
6. Lack of remorse or shame
7. Inadequately motivated anti-social behaviour
8. Poor judgment and failure to learn by experience
9. Pathologic egocentricity and incapacity for love
10. General poverty in major affective reactions
11. Specific loss of insight
12. Unresponsiveness in general interpersonal relations
13. Fantastic and uninviting behaviour . . .
14. Suicide rarely carried out
15. Sex life impersonal, trivial, and poorly integrated
16. Failure to follow any life plan

*Source: From Cleckley, H. (1976).* The mask of sanity *(5th ed.). St. Louis: C. V. Mosby, pp. 337–338. Reprinted with permission.*

to want. When confronted with evidence of having lied or cheated, psychopaths do not act ashamed or embarrassed and usually shrug the incident off as a joke, or simply deny it, however obvious their guilt may be. They are unconcerned for other people's feelings and suffer no remorse or guilt if their actions hurt others. Although they may be superficially charming, they do not form real friendships; thus, they often become swindlers or confidence artists.

Psychopaths do not easily learn adaptive behaviour from experience; they tend to continue getting into trouble throughout their lives (Hare, 2006), although there is something of a decline in criminal activities around age 40 (Hare, McPherson, & Forth, 1988). They also do not appear to be *driven* to perform their anti-social behaviours; instead, they often give the impression that they are acting on whims. When someone commits a heinous crime such as a brutal murder, normal people expect that the criminal had a compelling reason, however repellant it might be, for doing so. Criminal psychopaths, though, are typically unable to supply a reason more gripping than "He had money, and I needed money," "He disrespected me," or "I just felt like it." They do not show much excitement or enthusiasm about what they are doing and do not appear to derive much pleasure from life.

**Possible Causes** Cleckley (1976) suggested that the psychopath's defect "consists of an unawareness and a persistent lack of ability to become aware of what the most important experiences of life mean to others. . . . The major emotional accompaniments are absent or so attenuated as to count for little" (p. 371). Some investigators have hypothesized that this lack of involvement is caused by an unresponsive autonomic nervous system. If a person feels no anticipatory fear of punishment, he or she is perhaps more likely to commit acts that normal people would be afraid to commit. Similarly, if a person feels little or no emotional response to other people and to their joys and sorrows, he or she is unlikely to establish close relationships with them.

**Physiological Causes and Learning** Many experiments have found that psychopaths do show less reactivity in emotional situations. For example, psychopaths were found to be relatively unresponsive, behaviourally and physiologically, to emotional words (Williamson, Harpur, & Hare, 1991). Psychopaths' speech also tends to be less emotional. Psychopaths generally speak more quietly, and do not change their voice emphasis between neutral and emotional words (Louth et al., 1998). In other work, Hare (1965) demonstrated that psychopaths show fewer signs of anticipatory fear. All participants in Hare's study watched the numerals 1 through 12 appear in sequential order in the window of a device used to present visual stimuli. They were told that they would receive a very painful shock when the numeral 8 appeared. Psychopathic participants showed much less anticipatory responsiveness than did normal controls or non-psychopathic criminals.

An important early study by Schmauk (1970) showed that although psychopaths are poor at learning to avoid aversive stimuli, they readily learn to avoid a loss of an appetitive stimulus. Schmauk trained people on an avoidance task, using three types of aversive stimuli: a physical stimulus (a painful electrical shock), a social stimulus (the researcher saying, "Wrong"), and loss of money (the researcher taking a quarter from a pile of quarters that he had given to the participant). Control participants, who were neither psychopaths nor criminals, readily learned the task in response to all three types of aversive stimuli. Non-psychopathic criminals also learned the task well, except when the motive was avoiding the aversive social stimulus; apparently, they were not very disturbed when the researcher said, "Wrong." The psychopathic prisoners learned the task only when the motive was avoiding loss of money; they did not learn to avoid a painful electrical shock and were not affected by the researcher saying, "Wrong." Thus, we can conclude that psychopaths are perfectly capable of learning an avoidance task but that social stimuli or the fear of physical pain has little effect on their behaviour. Follow-up research on non-incarcerated people who scored high on psychopathic personality traits reveals that this pattern extends beyond a prison population (Long & Titone, 2007).

**Genetic Causes** We do not yet know what causes the deficits in emotion and empathy displayed by psychopaths. These people often (but not always) come from grossly disturbed families that contain alcoholics and other psychopaths.

**FIGURE 17•2** Heritability of psychopathy. Percentage of male adoptees convicted of violent crimes or crimes against property as a function of the number of convictions of their biological fathers.

*(From Mednick, S. A., Gabrielli, W. F., & Hutchings, B. (1983). Genetic influences in criminal behavior: Some evidence from an adoptive cohort. In K. T. Van Dusen and S. A. Mednick (Eds.),* Prospective studies of crime and delinquency. *Hingham, MA: Martinus Nijhoff. Reprinted with permission.)*

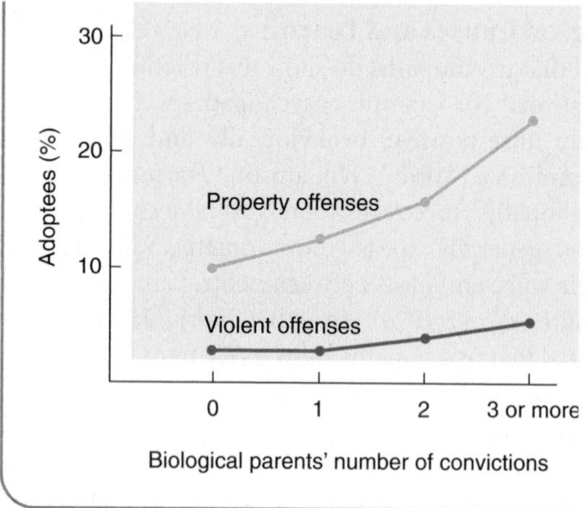


Mednick, Gabrielli, and Hutchings (1983) examined the criminal records of men who had been adopted early in life and found that the likelihood of their being convicted of a crime was directly related to the number of convictions of their biological fathers. (See **Figure 17•2.**)

**Environmental Causes—Parenting** Parenting and childhood experiences also appear to play a role in anti-social personality disorder. The quality of parenting, especially as it relates to providing supervision for children, is strongly related to the development of anti-social personality disorder. In particular, children whose parents ignore them or who leave them unsupervised for prolonged periods often develop patterns of misconduct and delinquency. When the parents do pay attention to their children, it tends to be in the form of harsh punishment or verbal abuse in response to their misdeeds. In a survey of more than 7000 people in Ontario, those reporting a history of childhood physical abuse had significantly higher lifetime rates of anti-social behaviour (MacMillan et al., 2001). Thus, the children of these parents live in an environment that ranges from no attention at all to attention in the form of physical punishment and tongue-lashings. In response, the children develop a pattern of behaviour that is characterized by increased aggression, distrust of others, concern only for themselves, and virtually no sense of right and wrong.

**Cognitive Causes** Children who have conduct problems tend to view their environments differently from well-adjusted children. They perceive the world as hostile and interpret others' actions, even those of other children, as aggressive and threatening. They may then strike out at someone else (whoever may be the object of their misperception) to avoid being attacked first. Their attack leads to retaliation, either in the form of punishment by a parent or a teacher or in the form of a counterattack by their peers. These children soon develop reputations for being aggressive and unlikeable, which further strengthens their anti-social attitudes and behaviours.

Thus, a child may be biologically predisposed to behave aggressively and to have conduct problems. The key people in the child's environment may attempt to punish these actions with a commensurate level of physical or verbal punishment. The child, in turn, perceives his or her environment as hostile and reacts even more aggressively, perhaps due to a maladaptive perception of what is necessary for his or her personal survival. Eventually, a cycle may be established that is marked by behaviours and thoughts characteristic of anti-social personality disorder. Further evidence for the biological approach has been found by Muller and colleagues (2008). It appears that people who exhibit symptoms of psychopathology have disturbed brain activation in the temporal cortex, specifically the right superior temporal gyrus.

## Borderline Personality Disorder

The historical major diagnostic categories of neuroses and psychoses allowed for the possibility of disorders that fell between their borders. Thus there was a designation of *borderline schizophrenia* and, more generally, *borderline personality*. However, reliable diagnosis was difficult (Paris, 1999).

**Description** The DSM-IV-TR diagnostic criteria for **borderline personality disorder (BPD)**, which has a lifetime prevalence rate of 2 percent, begin with the individual's strenuous efforts to resist what he or she perceives as abandonment, as might occur in a sudden change in another person's plans—cancelling an appointment, for example. The second criterion involves intense but typically short-lived relationships with others, marked by inappropriately extensive disclosure early in the relationship and rapid devaluing or disillusionment thereafter. Sudden shifts in self-image, including goals, values, and aspirations, constitute the third criterion. Impulsivity is at the heart of the fourth criterion and is marked by irresponsible spending, bingeing, and substance abuse. Finally, recurrent suicidal behaviour or self-mutilating behaviour is diagnostic, as in the following case study (Spitzer et al., 2002):

> A 26-year-old unemployed woman was referred for admission to a hospital by her therapist because of intense suicidal preoccupation and urges to mutilate

**borderline personality disorder (BPD)** An enduring pattern of instability in mood, self-image, and interpersonal relationships; includes frantic efforts to avoid real or imagined abandonment.

herself with a razor. The patient was apparently well until her junior year in high school, when she became preoccupied with religion and philosophy, avoided friends, and was filled with doubt about who she was. Academically she did well, but later, during college, her performance declined. In college she began to use a variety of drugs, abandoned the religion of her family, and seemed to be searching for a charismatic religious figure with whom to identify. At times, massive anxiety swept over her and she found it would suddenly vanish if she cut her forearm with a razor blade.

Three years ago she began psychotherapy, and initially rapidly idealized her therapist as being incredibly intuitive and empathic. Later she became hostile and demanding of him, requiring more and more sessions, sometimes two in one day. Her life centered on her therapist, by this time to the exclusion of everyone else. Although her hostility toward her therapist was obvious, she could neither see it nor control it. Her difficulties with her therapist culminated in many episodes of her forearm cutting and suicidal threats, which led to the referral for admission. (p. 233)

**Possible Causes** Skodol and colleagues (2002) and Bradley, Conklin, and Westen (2007) have identified specific features of BPD related to psychological traits that exhibit at least modest heritability—specifically, neuroticism, impulsivity, anxiousness, affect change, and insecure attachment. These genetic factors, in turn, are related to specific neural systems—for example, serotonergic systems in the case of impulsive aggression and cholinergic systems associated with affective instability. In addition, specific environmental factors that contribute to the emergence of symptoms include childhood sexual and physical abuse (Lieb et al., 2004).

## Interim Summary

### Personality Disorders

Anti-social personality disorder, also called psychopathy or sociopathy, is a serious problem for society. Many criminals are psychopaths, and many psychopaths become criminals. The hallmarks of psychopathy are an apparent indifference to the effects of one's behaviour on other people, impulsiveness, failure to learn from experience, sexual promiscuity and lack of commitment to a partner, and habitual lying. Some psychopaths are superficially charming, and many make a living cheating others out of their money.

Psychopathy tends to run in families, and it seems likely that both heredity and a poor home environment may contribute to its development. The disorder is difficult to treat because psychopaths do not see any reason for changing.

**QUESTION TO CONSIDER**

1. Suppose that you have been hired as a screenwriter for a movie about a psychopath. Before you start work in earnest, the head of the film company wants to see a sample of what you have in mind for this character and asks you to write a few paragraphs describing the opening scene of the movie. What would you write? What would your character be doing in this scene?

# Substance-Related Disorders

According to Axis I of DSM-IV-TR, **substance-related disorders** include *substance use disorders*, or what is usually called "addiction," and *substance-induced disorders*, which are less severe but still cause social, occupational, or medical problems.

Substance-related disorders have grave social consequences. Consider some of the disastrous effects caused by the abuse of humankind's oldest drug, alcohol: automobile accidents, fetal alcohol syndrome, cirrhosis, increased rate of heart disease, and increased rate of cerebral hemorrhage. Smoking (which is associated with the nicotine-related disorders) greatly increases smokers' chances of dying of lung cancer, heart attack, and stroke; and women who smoke give birth to smaller, less healthy babies. Together, tobacco and alcohol account for more than 20 percent of deaths in the United States. Cocaine addiction often causes psychosis, brain damage, and death from overdose; it produces babies born with brain damage and consequent psychological problems. Competition for lucrative drug markets terrorizes neighbourhoods, subverts political and judicial systems, and causes many deaths. People who take drugs intravenously run a serious risk of contracting AIDS.

## Description

The lifetime prevalence rate for substance-related disorder is estimated to be about 26.6 percent (Kessler et al., 1994). This means that 27 percent of individuals have reported the symptoms of substance-related disorders at least once in their lives. The 12-month prevalence rates average about 3.8 percent (Kessler, Chiu, Demler, & Walter, 2005), meaning that almost 4 percent of individuals have reported the same symptoms within the past year. The DSM-IV-TR estimates the lifetime prevalence rate for alcoholism to be about 15 percent. And although their alcohol use may not be severe enough to warrant a diagnosis of substance use disorder, as many as 25 percent of adults in North America experience

**substance-related disorders** Psychological disorders that are characterized by addiction to drugs or alcohol or by abuse of drugs or alcohol.

problems due to alcohol consumption (Cunningham, Wild, Bondy, & Lin, 2001).

There is a strong association between substance abuse and depressive disorders. In Canada, the 12-month prevalence rates for depression among people with a substance use disorder were nearly 9 percent for alcohol dependence and 16 percent for drug dependence (Currie et al., 2005). This means that people who suffer from a substance use disorder also have a greater likelihood of suffering from depression.

## Possible Causes

People abuse certain drugs because the drugs activate the reinforcement system of the brain, which is normally activated only by natural reinforcers such as food, warmth, and sexual contact. Dopamine-secreting neurons are an important component of this system. Some drugs, such as crack cocaine, activate the reinforcement system rapidly and intensely, providing immediate and potent reinforcement. For many people, the immediate effects of drug use outweigh the prospect of dangers that lie in the future. As we saw in Chapter 4, although withdrawal symptoms make it more difficult for an addict to break his or her habit, these unpleasant symptoms are not responsible for the addiction itself.

**Genetic and Physiological Causes** Not everyone is equally likely to become addicted to a drug. Many people manage to drink alcohol moderately, and even many users of potent drugs such as cocaine and heroin use them "recreationally," without becoming dependent on them. There are only two possible sources of individual differences in any characteristic: heredity and environment. Obviously, environmental effects are important; people raised in a squalid environment without any real hope for a better life are more likely than other people to turn to drugs to escape from the unpleasant world that surrounds them. But even in a given environment, poor or privileged, some people become addicts and some do not. Some of these behavioural differences are a result of genetic differences.

Most of the research on the effects of heredity on addiction has been devoted to alcoholism. As we learned in Chapter 3, most people drink alcohol sometime in their lives and thus receive first-hand experience of its reinforcing effects. The same is not true for cocaine, heroin, and other drugs that have even more potent effects. In most countries, alcohol is freely and legally available, whereas cocaine and heroin must be purchased illegally. From what we now know about the effects of addictive drugs on the nervous system, it seems likely that the results of studies on the genetics of alcoholism will apply to other types of drug addiction as well.

Although alcohol consumption is declining, about 9 percent of Canadians report problems associated with drinking, according to Health Canada. As we learned in Chapter 3, both

**TABLE 17•6 Characteristic Features of Two Types of Alcoholism**

| | Types of Alcoholism | |
|---|---|---|
| **Feature** | **Steady** | **Binge** |
| Usual age of onset (years) | Before 25 | After 25 |
| Spontaneous alcohol seeking (inability to abstain) | Frequent | Infrequent |
| Fighting and arrests when drinking | Frequent | Infrequent |
| Psychological dependence (loss of control) | Infrequent | Frequent |
| Guilt and fear about alcohol dependence | Infrequent | Frequent |
| Novelty seeking | High | Low |
| Harm avoidance | Low | High |
| Reward dependence | Low | High |

*Source: From Cloninger, C. R. (1987).* Science, 236, *410–416. Copyright 1987 by the American Association for the Advancement of Science.*

twin studies and adoption studies have shown that susceptibility to alcoholism is heritable (e.g., Kendler, Prescott, Neale, & Pedersen, 1997; Prescott & Kendler, 1999; Rhee et al., 2003). In a review of the literature, Cloninger (1987) notes that there appear to be two principal types of alcoholics: those who have anti-social and pleasure-seeking tendencies—people who cannot abstain but drink consistently—and those who are anxiety-ridden—people who are able to go without drinking for long periods of time but are unable to control themselves once they start. (For convenience, I will refer to these two groups as *steady drinkers* and *bingers*.) Binge drinking is also associated with emotional dependence, behavioural rigidity, perfectionism, introversion, and guilt feelings about one's drinking behaviour. Steady drinkers usually begin their alcohol consumption early in life, whereas binge drinkers begin much later. (See **Table 17•6**.) More generally, the age at which a person has his or her first drink correlates strongly with future alcohol abuse. Researchers found a quick progression to alcohol-related harm among those who reported their first drink between the ages of 11 and 14 (DeWit, Adlaf, Offord, & Ogborne, 2000). Thirteen and a half percent of children who consumed alcohol at the age of 11 or 12 met the criteria for alcohol abuse in adulthood, and nearly 16 percent were diagnosed as alcohol dependent.

An adoption study carried out in Sweden (Cloninger, Bohman, Sigvardsson, & von Knorring, 1985) found that men with biological fathers who were steady drinkers were almost seven times more likely to become steady drinkers themselves than were men whose fathers did not abuse alcohol. Family environment had no measurable effect; the boys began drinking whether or not the members of their adoptive families drank heavily. Very few women become steady drinkers; the daughters of steady-drinking fathers instead tend to develop somatization disorder. Thus, genes that may predispose a man to become a steady-drinking alcoholic (anti-social type) may predispose a woman to develop somatization disorder. The reason for this interaction with gender is not known.

Binge drinking is influenced both by heredity and by environment. The Swedish adoption study found that having a biological parent who was a binge drinker had little effect on the development of binge drinking unless the child was exposed to a family environment in which there was heavy drinking. The effect was seen in both males and females.

When we find an effect of heredity on behaviour, we have good reason to suspect some biological difference. That is, genes affect behaviour only by affecting the body. A susceptibility to alcoholism could conceivably be caused by differences in the ability to digest or metabolize alcohol or by differences in the structure or biochemistry of the brain.

Most investigators believe that differences in brain physiology most likely play a role. Cloninger, Sigvardsson, and Svrakic (1995) note that people with anti-social tendencies, including steady drinkers, show a strong tendency to seek novelty and excitement. These people are disorderly and distractible (many have a history of hyperactivity as children) and lack restraint in their behaviour. They do not fear dangerous situations or social disapproval and are easily bored. On the other hand, binge drinkers tend to be anxious, emotionally dependent, sentimental, sensitive to social cues, cautious and apprehensive, fearful of novelty or change, rigid, and attentive to details. Their EEGs show little slow alpha activity, which suggests that they are aroused and anxious (Propping, Kruger, & Mark, 1981). When they take alcohol, they report a pleasant relief of tension (Propping, Kruger, & Janah, 1980).

The brains of steady drinkers may be unresponsive to danger and to social disapproval, due to an undersensitive punishment mechanism. They may also have an undersensitive reinforcement system, which leads them to seek more intense thrills (including those provided by alcohol) in order to experience pleasurable sensations. Thus, they seek the euphoric effects of alcohol. On the other hand, binge drinkers may have an oversensitive punishment system. Normally, they avoid drinking because of the guilt they experience afterwards; but once they start, and once the sedative effect begins, the alcohol-induced suppression of the punishment system makes it impossible for them to stop.

Animal models have been another effective approach in the study of the physiology of addiction. Through selective breeding, two different strains of rats have been developed that differ in their response to alcohol. Alcohol-preferring rats do just what their name implies: If given a drinking tube containing a solution of alcohol along with their water and food, they become heavy drinkers. The rats that do not prefer alcohol abstain. Fadda, Mosca, Colombo, and Gessa (1990) found that alcohol appeared to produce a larger release of dopamine in the brains of alcohol-preferring rats than in the brains of rats that do not prefer alcohol. This result suggests that the reinforcing effect of alcohol is stronger in alcohol-preferring rats.

**Cognitive Causes** Cooper, Russell, and George (1988) have argued that people develop patterns of heavy drug use because of what they believe about the personal benefits of using drugs. For example, people who believe that alcohol will help them cope with negative emotions, and who also expect that alcohol will make them more likeable, sociable, or attractive, may use alcohol to obtain these *perceived positive effects*. In fact, alcohol may be abused to moderate both positive and negative emotions (Cooper, Frone, Russell, & Mudar, 1995). In this view, drug abuse or dependence is a way of coping with perceived personal shortcomings: having negative emotions, not being outgoing enough, feeling uncomfortable around others, and so on. The influence of alcohol or other drugs provides an escape from such feelings. The relief negatively reinforces the use of drugs. But the effect is temporary. The negative feelings return with sobriety, leading to further drug use. Soon, the person is intoxicated or high most or all of the time.

## Interim Summary

### Substance-Related Disorders

Drug addiction is one of the most serious problems society faces today. Apparently, all substances that produce addiction do so by activating the reinforcement system of the brain, which involves the release of dopamine. Most people who are exposed to addictive drugs—even those with high abuse potentials—do not become addicts. Evidence suggests that the likelihood of addiction, especially to alcohol, is strongly affected by heredity. There may be two types of alcoholism: one related to an anti-social, pleasure-seeking personality (steady drinkers) and another related to a repressed, anxiety-ridden personality (binge drinkers). Some investigators believe that a better understanding of the physiological basis of reinforcement and punishment will help us understand the effects of heredity on susceptibility to addiction.

**QUESTION TO CONSIDER**

1. Steady and binge drinkers appear to have different kinds of personality characteristics. Do you think these characteristics might predict which kind of alcoholic a presently non-alcoholic person might become should he or she develop a tendency to drink?

# Schizophrenic Disorders

Schizophrenia, the most common of the psychotic disorders, described in Axis I of the DSM-IV-TR, includes several subtypes, each having a distinctive set of symptoms. For many years, controversy has existed over whether schizophrenia is one disorder with various subtypes or whether each subtype constitutes a distinct disorder. Because the prognosis (the likelihood of recovery) differs for the various subtypes of schizophrenia, they appear to differ at least in severity. However, a particular individual may, at different times, meet the criteria for different subtypes. Some experts have referred to schizophrenia as the "quintessential" psychological disorder. By this they refer not only to its universal incidence but also to the characteristically tragic ways in which it transforms the lives of schizophrenic individuals and their families.

## Description

**Schizophrenia**—a group of psychological disorders involving distortions of thought, perception, and emotion; bizarre behaviour; and social withdrawal—is a problem of enormous proportions. According to the DSM-IV-TR, schizophrenia has a prevalence of 0.5 to 1.5 percent worldwide and affects approximately 1 percent of the Canadian population (Health Canada, 2002). It typically makes its appearance in the period from the late teens to the early thirties. Earlier onset, especially in children, is rare. In terms of the seriousness and prevalence of the disorder, schizophrenia is considered the "cancer" of psychological disorders. It is serious, indeed.

Descriptions of symptoms in historical writings indicate that the disorder may have existed as early as medieval times (Heinrichs, 2003). *Schizophrenia* is probably the most misused psychological term in existence. The word literally means "split mind," but it does *not* imply a split or multiple personality. People often say that they "feel schizophrenic" about an issue when they really mean that they have mixed feelings about it. A person who sometimes wants to build a cabin in the bush and live off the land and at other times wants to take over the family insurance business may be undecided, but he or she does not have schizophrenia. The man who invented the term, Eugen Bleuler, intended it to refer to a break with reality caused by such disorganization of the various functions of the mind that thoughts and feelings no longer worked together normally.

Schizophrenia is characterized by two categories of symptoms, positive and negative. **Positive symptoms** are those that make themselves known by their *presence*. These symptoms include thought disorders, hallucinations, and delusions. A **thought disorder**—a pattern of disorganized, irrational thinking—is probably the most important symptom of schizophrenia. People with schizophrenia have great difficulty arranging their thoughts logically and sorting out plausible conclusions from absurd ones. In conversation, they may jump from one topic to another as new associations come up. Sometimes, they utter meaningless words or apparently choose words for their rhyme rather than for their meaning.

*Delusions* are beliefs that are contrary to fact. Although there are debates about the exact nature of delusions (e.g., Leeser & O'Donohue, 1999; Mullen, 2003), these beliefs are readily identifiable in the context of mental illness and tend to appear in three forms. **Delusions of persecution** are false beliefs that others are plotting and conspiring against one. **Delusions of grandeur** are false beliefs in one's power and importance, such as a conviction that one has godlike powers or has special knowledge that no one else possesses. **Delusions of control** are related to delusions of persecution; the person believes, for example, that he or she is being controlled by others through such means as radar or tiny radio receivers implanted in the brain.

The third positive symptom of schizophrenia is **hallucinations**, which are perceptions of stimuli that are not actually present. When filmmakers depict hallucinations, they typically use a device to let viewers know that the sound or sight is not real. Visual hallucinations are often shown as ghostlike, and sounds have an eerie quality. For the person with schizophrenia, cues like these would likely be a relief. Unfortunately, the hallucinated perceptions and sensations seem perfectly real, as real and as substantial as this textbook.

Hallucinations can involve any of the senses. The common feature of hallucinations, in the final analysis, is that they are negative experiences. Visual hallucinations are usually threatening, frightening, or at least confusing. Gustatory (taste) and olfactory (smell) hallucinations usually are disgusting (e.g., of feces). The most common hallucinations in schizophrenia are auditory. The typical schizophrenic hallucination consists of voices talking to the person. Sometimes they order the person to do something; sometimes they criticize and humiliate him or her for being unworthy, unclean, or immoral; sometimes they just utter meaningless phrases. People with schizophrenia may hear a voice that keeps a running commentary on their behaviour.

In contrast to the positive symptoms, the **negative symptoms** of schizophrenia are known by the absence of normal behaviours: flattened emotional response, poverty of speech,

**schizophrenia** A serious psychological disorder characterized by thought disturbances, hallucinations, anxiety, emotional withdrawal, and delusions.

**positive symptoms** Symptoms of schizophrenia that may include thought disorder, hallucinations, or delusions.

**thought disorder** A pattern of disorganized, illogical, and irrational thought that often accompanies schizophrenia.

**delusions of persecution** The false belief that other people are plotting against one.

**delusions of grandeur** The false belief that one is famous, powerful, or important.

**delusions of control** The false belief that one's thoughts and actions are being controlled by other people or forces.

**hallucinations** Perceptual experiences that occur in the absence of external stimulation of the corresponding sensory organ.

**negative symptoms** Symptoms of schizophrenia that may include the absence of normal behaviours: flattened emotion, poverty of speech, lack of initiative and persistence, and social withdrawal.

lack of initiative and persistence, inability to feel pleasure, and social withdrawal. Negative symptoms are not specific to schizophrenia; they are seen in many neurological disorders that involve brain damage, especially to the frontal lobes.

As we will see later in this chapter, evidence suggests that positive and negative symptoms result from different physiological disorders. Positive symptoms appear to involve excessive activity in some neural circuits that include dopamine as a transmitter substance. Negative symptoms appear to be caused by brain damage. Many researchers suspect that these two sets of symptoms involve a common set of underlying causes, but these causes have yet to be identified with certainty.

## Types of Schizophrenia

According to the DSM-IV-TR, there are five types of schizophrenia: paranoid, disorganized, catatonic, undifferentiated, and residual.

The pre-eminent symptoms of **paranoid schizophrenia** are delusions of persecution, grandeur, or control—positive symptoms. The word *paranoid* is so widely used in ordinary language that it has come to mean "suspicious." However, not all paranoid schizophrenics believe that they are being persecuted. Some believe that they hold special powers that can save the world—that they are Superman, Napoleon, or Joan of Arc. And some hold complementary delusions of grandeur and persecution.

**Disorganized schizophrenia** is a serious progressive and irreversible disorder characterized primarily by disturbances of thought. People with disorganized schizophrenia often display signs of emotion, especially silly laughter, that are inappropriate to the circumstances. Also, their speech tends to be a jumble of words: "I came to the hospital to play, gay, way, lay, day, bray, donkey, monkey" (Snyder, 1974, p. 132). This sort of speech is often referred to as a *word salad*. Hallucinations and delusions are common.

**Catatonic schizophrenia** (from the Greek *katateinein*, meaning "to stretch or draw tight") is characterized by various motor disturbances, including both extreme excitement and stupor. People with this form of schizophrenia will display negative symptoms: catatonic postures—bizarre stationary poses that may be maintained for many hours—and waxy flexibility, in which the person's limbs can be moulded into new positions, which are then maintained for long periods.

Many patients are diagnosed as having **undifferentiated schizophrenia**; that is, they have delusions, hallucinations, and disorganized behaviour but do not meet the criteria for paranoid, disorganized, or catatonic schizophrenia. In addition, some patients' symptoms change after an initial diagnosis, and their classification changes accordingly.

**Residual schizophrenia** is the diagnosis when at least one episode of one of the four other types of schizophrenia has occurred but no single, prominent positive symptom is currently observable. However, negative symptoms are observable, as are muted forms of positive symptoms. Residual schizophrenia may mark a transition from a full-blown schizophrenic episode to remission (the absence of any symptoms). But it also may continue to linger year after year.

## Early Signs of Schizophrenia

Eugen Bleuler (1950), a pioneer in the diagnosis and study of schizophrenia, divided the disorder into *reactive* and *process* forms. Patients with a general history of good mental health were designated as having **reactive schizophrenia**, on the assumption that their disorder was a reaction to stressful life situations. Typically, these patients soon recovered, and few experienced another episode. Patients with indications of mental illness early in life were designated as having **process schizophrenia**, which was considered a chronic disorder.

If process schizophrenia does have its roots in early life, an important task is to determine what the early predictors are. The ability to identify people with a high risk of schizophrenia while they are still young will allow clinicians to institute some form of therapy before the disorder becomes advanced. The early signs may also indicate whether the causes of schizophrenia are biological, environmental, or both.

In fact, many studies of people who develop schizophrenia in adulthood have found that they were different from others even in childhood. However, these studies do not tell us whether these differences resulted from physiological disorders or from the behaviour of other family members when those who were later diagnosed with schizophrenia were in infancy and childhood. One remarkable study obtained home movies of people with adult-onset schizophrenia that showed them when they were children (Walker & Lewine, 1990). Although the schizophrenia did not manifest itself until adulthood, viewers of the films (six graduate students and one professional clinical psychologist) did an excellent job of identifying the children who would develop schizophrenia. The viewers commented on the children's poor eye contact, relative lack of responsiveness and positive affect, and generally

**paranoid schizophrenia** A form of schizophrenia in which the person suffers from delusions of persecution, grandeur, or control.

**disorganized schizophrenia** A type of schizophrenia characterized primarily by disturbances of thought and a flattened or silly affect.

**catatonic schizophrenia** A form of schizophrenia characterized primarily by various motor disturbances, including catatonic postures and waxy flexibility.

**undifferentiated schizophrenia** A type of schizophrenia characterized by fragments of the symptoms of different types of schizophrenia.

**residual schizophrenia** A type of schizophrenia that may follow an episode of one of the other types and is marked by negative symptoms but not by any prominent positive symptom.

**reactive schizophrenia** According to Bleuler, a form of schizophrenia characterized by rapid onset and brief duration; he assumed that the cause was stressful life situations.

**process schizophrenia** According to Bleuler, a form of schizophrenia characterized by a gradual onset and a poor prognosis.

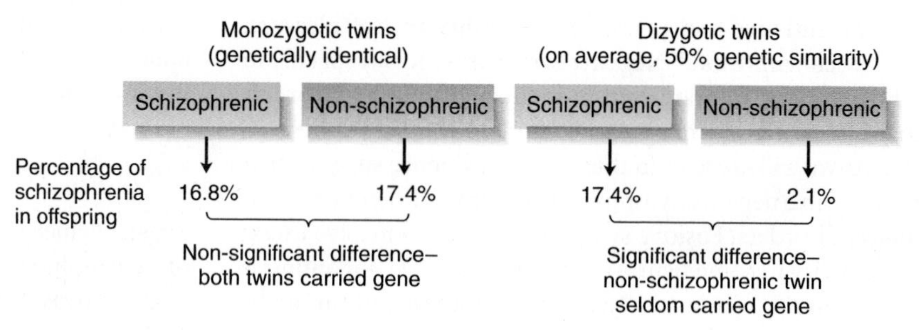


FIGURE 17•3 Heritability of schizophrenia. An explanation for evidence that people can have an unexpressed "schizophrenia gene."

poor motor coordination. Clearly, something was different about the behaviour of the people who later developed schizophrenia even early in life.

## Possible Causes

Research into the causes of all kinds and forms of schizophrenia throughout the last century reflects the challenge that psychologists face in attempting to understand how psychological and biological factors interact to influence behaviour. The diathesis–stress model of psychological disorders, discussed earlier in this chapter, is a very popular account of the causes of schizophrenia: Schizophrenia appears to result from one or more inherited biological predispositions that are activated by environmental stress.

**Genetic Causes** Schizophrenia is a disorder with a substantial genetic component (Polimeni & Reiss, 2003). Advances in genetics, and a variety of research involving twin and adoption studies, have established the heritability of schizophrenia—or more precisely, the high heritability of a *tendency* toward schizophrenia (Al-Jeshi, Epstein, & Zipursky, 2006; Gottesman & Reilly, 2003). Identical twins are much more likely to be concordant for schizophrenia than are fraternal twins, and the children of parents with schizophrenia are more likely themselves to become schizophrenic, even if they were adopted and raised by non-schizophrenic parents (Gottesman & Moldin, 1998). Twin studies of schizophrenia compare the concordance rates of identical twins with the concordance rates of siblings of different genetic relatedness who were reared either together or apart. (Recall from Chapter 3 that twins are concordant for a trait if neither or both express it and discordant if only one expresses it.) According to Gottesman and Shields (1982) and Gottesman (1991), concordance rates for identical twins are about 50 percent, but they are less than about 20 percent for fraternal twins. These results provide strong evidence that schizophrenia is heritable, and also support the conclusion that carrying a "schizophrenia gene" does not mean that a person will necessarily develop schizophrenia. (See **Figure 17•3**.) As suggested by the diathesis–stress model, environmental factors are also likely to be involved.

If a person has been diagnosed with schizophrenia, there exists the possibility that other family members also have the disorder. (See **Table 17•7**.) It is important to note that although the likelihood of developing schizophrenia increases if a person has relatives with schizophrenia, this disorder is not a simple trait, like eye colour, that is inherited. In fact, 63 percent of people suffering from schizophrenia do not have a first- or second-degree relative who also has the disorder (Gottesman & Erlenmeyer-Kimling, 2001). Even if both parents have schizophrenia, the probability that their child will develop it is 30 percent or less.

Most investigators believe that a person inherits a *predisposition* to develop schizophrenia. In their view, most environments will foster normal development, whereas certain environments will trigger various disorders, including schizophrenia. If the diathesis–stress model is valid as it applies to schizophrenia, we would expect that some people carry a "schizophrenia gene" but do not express it. Their environments do not trigger schizophrenia or they have acquired the coping skills to deal successfully with environmental stressors. Such a person might be the non-schizophrenic member of a pair of monozygotic twins discordant for schizophrenia.

Using scanning techniques that permit rapid analysis of an individual's genome, Walsh and colleagues (2008) identified rare genetic mutations that either were inherited or occurred spontaneously during or soon after conception. They found that these mutations were three times more likely

**TABLE 17•7 Summary of Major European Family and Twin Studies of the Genetics of Schizophrenia**

| Relation to Person Identified as Schizophrenic | Percentage with Schizophrenia |
|---|---|
| Spouse | 1.0 |
| Grandchild | 2.8 |
| Niece/nephew | 2.6 |
| Child | 9.3 |
| Sibling | 7.3 |
| Fraternal twin | 12.1 |
| Identical twin | 44.3 |

*Source:* Davison, G. C., & Neale, J. M. (1990). Abnormal psychology. *New York: John Wiley & Sons, after Gottesman, McGuffin, and Farmer (1987).*

to occur in individuals with schizophrenia than in matched control participants. The incidence was even higher in participants with childhood-onset schizophrenia. Of particular interest were those mutations that disrupted neurodevelopmental pathways and glutaminergic pathways.

Researchers have formulated the **dopamine hypothesis**—the proposal that abnormal activity of dopamine-containing neurons is a causal factor in schizophrenia. That is, the positive symptoms of schizophrenia are produced by the overactivity of dopamine-transmitting synapses. Amphetamines, cocaine, and the antipsychotic drugs act on synapses—the junctions between nerve cells—in the brain and can produce the symptoms of schizophrenia, both in people who have schizophrenia and in people who do not. As you may recall from Chapter 4, one neuron passes on excitatory or inhibitory messages to another by releasing a small amount of neurotransmitter from its terminal button into the synaptic cleft. The chemical activates receptors on the surface of the receiving neuron, and the activated receptors either excite or inhibit the receiving neuron. Drugs such as amphetamine and cocaine *stimulate* receptors for dopamine. In contrast, antipsychotic drugs *block* dopamine receptors and prevent them from becoming stimulated.

González-Maeso and his colleagues (2008) focused on the effects of newer antipsychotic drugs and hallucinogenic drugs, such as psilocybin and LSD (see Chapter 4), in their efforts to identify neuroreceptor complexes in schizophrenia beyond those associated with dopamine. Specifically, they found strong evidence that glutamate and serotonin receptors bind each other and that this binding may account for the effects of atypical antipsychotic drugs (see Chapter 18) in the treatment of schizophrenia. In other words, the dopamine hypothesis should be amended to become a dopamine-serotonin-glutamate hypothesis (see Berenson, 2008; Snyder, 2008).

**Physiological Causes—Neurological Disorders** Although the dopamine hypothesis has for several years been the dominant biological explanation for schizophrenia, other evidence suggests that it can offer only a partial explanation. Because antipsychotic drugs alleviate positive, but not negative, symptoms of schizophrenia (Angrist, Rotrosen, & Gershon, 1980), perhaps those patients who do not get better with medication have primarily negative symptoms.

Once investigators began paying more attention to negative symptoms, they discovered evidence for brain damage in patients exhibiting these symptoms. Several investigators have examined CT or MRI scans of patients with schizophrenia. Researchers have reported, for example, larger than normal ventricles among schizophrenic patients (Sullivan et al., 1998; Zipursky, Lambe, Kapur, & Mikulis, 1998). There is also evidence that people with schizophrenia display abnormal neural processing while trying to suppress inappropriate responses (Kiehl, Smith, Hare, & Liddle, 2000). Similarly, Pfefferbaum and colleagues (1988) found evidence that the sulci (the wrinkles in the brain) were wider in the brains of

**FIGURE 17•4** MRI scans of the brains of twins discordant for schizophrenia. (a) Normal twin. (b) Twin with schizophrenia.

*(Courtesy of D. R. Weinberger, National Institute of Mental Health, Saint Elizabeth's Hospital, Washington, DC.)*

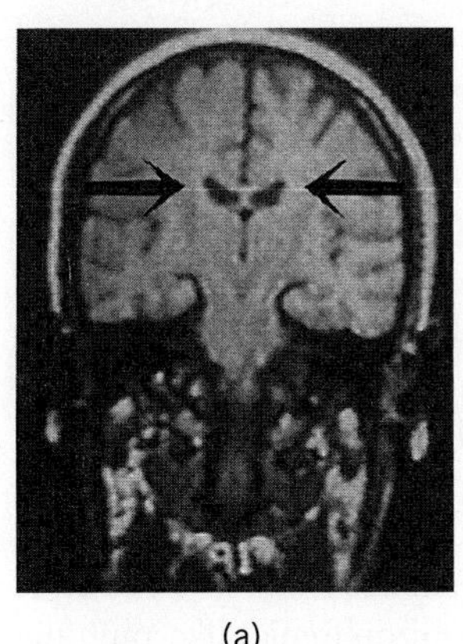

(a)

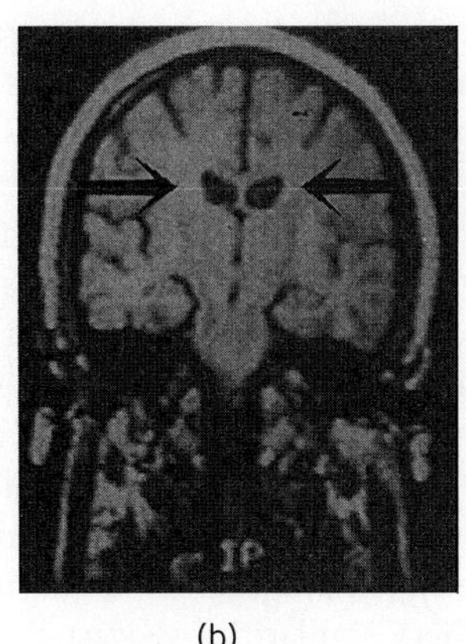

(b)

schizophrenic patients. Enlargement of the hollow ventricles of the brain and widening of the sulci indicate the absence of brain tissue. Indeed, other research shows that schizophrenic patients have less cortical grey matter than healthy control persons (Lim et al., 1998; Mitelman et al., 2003; Suddath et al., 1990). The study by Suddath and colleagues (1990) is particularly interesting because their participants were twin pairs. The investigators examined MRI scans of identical twins discordant for schizophrenia and found that in almost every case, the twin with schizophrenia had larger lateral and third ventricles. In addition, the hippocampus was smaller in the schizophrenic twin, and the total volume of the grey matter in the left temporal lobe was reduced. **Figure 17•4** shows a set of MRI scans from a pair of twins. As you can see, the lateral ventricles are larger in the brain of the twin with schizophrenia. Still other research has shown a progressive loss of grey matter during adolescence among people who develop schizophrenia during childhood (Rapoport et al., 1999). Interestingly, some brain abnormalities that had previously only been associated with chronic alcoholism have also been noted in patients with schizophrenia (Deshmukh, Rosenbloom, Pfefferbaum, & Sullivan, 2002). It appears that the abnormalities exist in people with schizophrenia, even if they do not abuse alcohol. Thus, the evidence is coming together to suggest the existence of some kind of neurological disease process.

Several studies have indicated that the cause of brain damage in schizophrenia may be a viral infection. No direct evidence for virally induced schizophrenia exists, but there are gross similarities between schizophrenia and known viral

**dopamine hypothesis** The hypothesis that the positive symptoms of schizophrenia are caused by overactivity of synapses in the brain that use dopamine.

disorders. Stevens (1988), for example, notes some interesting similarities between schizophrenia and *multiple sclerosis*, a neurological disorder. Multiple sclerosis appears to be an autoimmune disease—triggered by a virus—in which the patient's own immune system attacks the myelin sheaths that cover most axons in the central nervous system. The natural histories of multiple sclerosis and schizophrenia are similar in several ways. Both diseases are more prevalent and more severe in people who spent their childhood in latitudes far from the equator. Both diseases are more common in people with low socio-economic status who live in crowded, deprived conditions. Both diseases are characterized by one of three general courses: (1) attacks followed by remissions, many of which produce no residual deficits; (2) recurrent attacks with only partial remissions, causing an increasingly major deficit; or (3) an insidious onset with a steady and relentless progression, leading to permanent and severe deficits. These similarities suggest that schizophrenia, like multiple sclerosis, could be a virally induced autoimmune disease.

A second possible neurological cause of schizophrenia is interference with normal prenatal brain development. Several studies show that people born during the winter months are more likely to develop schizophrenia later in life (Davies et al., 2003; Torrey et al., 1997). Carrion-Baralt and his colleagues (2006) found evidence for seasonality effects in their study conducted in Puerto Rico. Individuals with schizophrenia were more likely (36.8 percent) to be born during the winter months than same-family members without schizophrenia (21.3 percent). The authors concluded that the difference in season of birth constitutes a "second hit" in a "two-hit" model of schizophrenia (Maynard, Sikich, Lieberman, & LaMantia, 2001), where the first hit is the disruption of early neural development—a model reminiscent of the diathesis–stress model discussed earlier in this chapter. Torrey, Torrey, and Peterson (1977) suggested that the causal factor could be seasonal variations in nutritional factors, or, more likely, variations in toxins or infectious agents in air, water, or food. Several diseases known to be caused by viruses, such as measles, influenza, and chicken pox, show a similar *seasonality effect*. The seasonality effect is seen most strongly in poor, urban locations, where people are at greater risk for viral infections (Machon, Mednick, & Schulsinger, 1983).

A seasonally related virus could affect either a pregnant woman or a newborn. Two pieces of evidence suggest that the damage is done prenatally. First, brain development is more susceptible to disruption prenatally. Second, a study of the offspring of women who were pregnant during an epidemic of type A2 influenza in Finland occurring in 1957 showed an elevated incidence of schizophrenia (Mednick, Machon, & Huttunen, 1990), but only among women who were in the second trimester of their pregnancies during the epidemic. Presumably, the viral infection produced toxins that interfered with the brain development of some of the fetuses, resulting in the later development of schizophrenia. Keep in mind, however, that this is just one of many potential causes of schizophrenia—a large-scale study conducted in Denmark revealed that prenatal exposure to influenza could account for only 1.4 percent of the 9462 cases of schizophrenia that were examined (Takei et al., 1996).

Birth trauma is another possible neurological cause of schizophrenia. Schwarzkopf and colleagues (1989) found that if a person with schizophrenia does not have relatives with a schizophrenic disorder—that is, if there is no evidence that the disease is a result of heredity—he or she is more likely to have had a history of complications at or around the time of childbirth. Thus, brain damage not related to heredity may also be a cause of schizophrenia.

Much more research will be needed to determine whether overactivity of dopamine synapses produces positive symptoms of schizophrenia and whether a viral infection produces brain damage that results in negative symptoms. But such biological explanations will not lessen the usefulness of psychotherapy (discussed in the next chapter) in the treatment of schizophrenia. Experience has shown that drug treatment (e.g., chlorpromazine) for people who have schizophrenic disorders is not enough. It is also important to teach the person how to structure a new life and how to cope with the many problems he or she will encounter in everyday life. Psychotherapy is at present the best hope for patients who have mainly negative symptoms, and who are not helped by antipsychotic drugs.

**Cognitive and Environmental Causes—The Family and Expressed Emotion** The personality and communicative abilities of either or both parents appear to play an influential role in the development of schizophrenic symptoms in children. Several studies have shown that children raised by parents who are dominating, overprotective, rigid, and insensitive to the needs of others are more likely to develop schizophrenia (Roff & Knight, 1995). In many cases, a parent may be verbally accepting of the child yet in other ways reject him or her, which establishes a conflict for the child called a **double-bind**. For example, a mother may encourage her son to become emotionally dependent on her yet continually reject him when he tries to hug her or sit on her lap or play with her.

Children who were reared in families wracked with discord seem to be at greater risk of developing schizophrenia. For example, in a study of 14 schizophrenic individuals, Lidz, Fleck, and Cornelison (1965) found that each of these individuals had a family that underwent either chronic discord in which the integrity of the parents' marriage was perpetually threatened or marital problems in which the bizarre behaviour of one family member was tolerated by the other members. Children in families in which parents treat them with hostility or in which parents present confusing communication to them are at risk for developing schizophrenia (Goldstein & Strachan, 1987). Further research has shown

**double-bind** The conflict caused for a child when he or she is given inconsistent messages or cues from a parent.

that excitableness in children has a strong relationship with positive symptoms of adulthood schizophrenia (Roff & Knight, 1995). However, researchers are still not sure whether marital discord, family hostility, and confusing communications are a cause or an effect of children's schizophrenia.

Researchers also have identified a social variable that affects the likelihood that a person with schizophrenia will recover. Brown and his colleagues (Brown, 1985; Brown, Bone, Dalison, & Wing, 1966) identified a category of behaviours of families of individuals recovering from schizophrenia that seemed to be related to the patients' rates of recovery. They labelled this variable **expressed emotion**, which consists of expressions of criticism, hostility, and emotional overinvolvement by the family members toward the patient. Patients living in family environments in which the level of expressed emotion was low were more likely to recover, whereas those in families in which it was high were likely to continue to exhibit schizophrenic symptoms.

Hundreds of studies investigating expressed emotion in families have been conducted, across many different cultures (Jenkins & Karno, 1992). Studies from North America, England, Denmark, Italy, France, Spain, Germany, Taiwan, India, Egypt, and Australia indicate that despite differences in the ways that people of different cultures perceive mental illness and express themselves, expressed emotion does not seem to be a culture-bound phenomenon. Two elements appear to be common to all cultures: critical comments and emotional overinvolvement. If these elements are present in families of schizophrenics at low levels, patients are likely to recover quickly; if they are present at high levels, patients are less likely to recover quickly.

Jenkins and Karno also found that expressed emotion tends to be higher in many industrialized cultures than in non-industrialized cultures. In other words, people in non-industrialized countries are more supportive of family members with schizophrenia than are people in industrialized countries. The reasons for this difference appear to centre on the role that individuals play in the two environments. For example, people in industrialized countries are generally raised with the idea that they will find a meaningful job that pays well. But people with schizophrenia who live in industrialized nations often find it hard to gain employment simply because so many jobs require specialized skills. As a result, they may be criticized for not contributing to the family income. In contrast, people with schizophrenia who live in non-industrialized nations may find less specialized jobs in agriculture or in the family business—they can still find a way to contribute to the families' economic well-being. In addition, people living in non-industrialized countries often live with an extended family where many people are contributing to the family economy. The loss or reduction in wages by a family member with schizophrenia may be partly compensated by other family members. Another advantage of living with an extended family is that there are more people who can share in the care of the family member with schizophrenia.

## Interim Summary

### Schizophrenic Disorders

The main positive symptoms of schizophrenia include thought disorders; delusions of persecution, grandeur, and control; and hallucinations. The main negative symptoms include withdrawal, apathy, and poverty of speech. The DSM-IV-TR classifies schizophrenia into several subtypes, including undifferentiated, catatonic, paranoid, and disorganized. But the distinctions between process and reactive schizophrenia and between positive and negative symptoms also seem to be important.

People who develop chronic process schizophrenia appear to be different from other people even as children, which suggests that the disorder takes root early in life. The diathesis–stress model accurately describes the course of schizophrenia: Some people seem to inherit a predisposition for the disorder, which is expressed when environmental stressors outweigh their attempts to cope with them. Recent research suggests that a low level of expressed emotion (including critical comments and emotional overinvolvement) on the part of family members facilitates the recovery of a patient with schizophrenia.

Positive symptoms of schizophrenia can be produced in normal people or made worse in schizophrenics by drugs that stimulate dopamine synapses (cocaine and amphetamine) and can be reduced or eliminated by drugs that block dopamine receptors (antipsychotic drugs). These findings have led to the dopamine hypothesis, which states that schizophrenia can be caused by an inherited biochemical defect that causes dopamine neurons to be overactive.

More recent studies indicate that schizophrenia can best be conceived of as two different disorders. The positive symptoms are produced by overactivity of dopamine neurons and can be treated with antipsychotic drugs. The negative symptoms may be caused by brain damage. Investigators have found direct evidence of brain damage by inspecting scans of living patients' brains.

Researchers have suggested three possible causes of the brain damage—and the corresponding negative symptoms—that accompany schizophrenia: a virus that triggers an autoimmune disease, which causes brain damage later in life; a virus that damages the brain early in life; and birth trauma. Heredity presumably interacts with the first two factors—many people may be exposed to the virus, but the virus will cause brain damage only in people with a genetic sensitivity.

People born during the winter months are more likely to develop schizophrenia later in life than are people born at

**expressed emotion** Expressions of criticism, hostility, and emotional overinvolvement by family members toward a person with schizophrenia.

other times of the year. The causal factor seems likely to be seasonal variations in nutritional factors, toxins, and infectious agents. This effect is especially prevalent among the urban poor, who are at the greatest risk for viral infections.

**QUESTIONS TO CONSIDER**

1. Imagine that you are a clinical psychologist. A client of yours complains of hearing voices. You suspect that this individual may be schizophrenic, but you wish to gather more information before you make your diagnosis. What sorts of information about this person do you need before you can make your diagnosis? How would you gather it?
2. Suppose that a friend of yours, who acts a little strange at times, is diagnosed as schizophrenic. Suppose further that this diagnosis is actually wrong—he truly is not schizophrenic. Your friend knows that the diagnosis is incorrect, but nobody believes him because his strange behaviour makes the diagnosis seem believable. What would your friend have to say or do to convince you that he is normal?

# Mood Disorders

Everyone experiences moods varying from sadness to happiness to elation. We're excited when our team wins a big game, saddened to learn that a friend's father has had a heart attack, thrilled at a higher-than-expected raise at work, and devastated by the death of a loved one. Such are the emotions from which the fabric of our lives is woven. Some people, though, experience more dramatic mood changes than these. Significant shifts or disturbances in mood that affect normal perception, thought, and behaviour are called **mood disorders**. They may be characterized by a deep, foreboding depression or by a combination of depression and euphoria.

**mood disorder** A disorder characterized by significant shifts or disturbances in mood that affect normal perception, thought, and behaviour. Mood disorders may be characterized by deep, foreboding depression, or a combination of depression and euphoria.

**bipolar I disorder** A mood disorder in which alternating states of depression and mania are separated by periods of relatively normal affect.

**bipolar II disorder** A mood disorder; marked by major depressive episodes that are accompanied by less severe mania (hypomanic episodes).

**major depressive disorder** Persistent and severe feelings of sadness and worthlessness accompanied by changes in appetite, sleeping, and other behaviour.

**mania** Excessive emotional arousal and wild, exuberant, unrealistic activity.

## Description

In contrast to schizophrenia, in which the principal symptom is disordered thought, the mood disorders are primarily disorders of emotion. The most severe mood disorders are the bipolar disorders and major depressive disorder. **Bipolar I disorder** is characterized by episodes of mania by itself or in a mix with anxiety, usually accompanied by episodes of major depression. **Bipolar II disorder** is marked by major depressive episodes that are accompanied by periods of less severe mania, known as *hypomanic* episodes. **Major depressive disorder** involves persistent, severe feelings of sadness and worthlessness accompanied by changes in appetite, sleeping, and other behaviour. The lifetime prevalence for major depressive disorder is about 16 percent (Nestler et al., 2002).

A less severe form of depression is called *dysthymic disorder*. The term comes from the Greek words *dus*, "bad," and *thymos*, "spirit." The primary difference between this disorder and major depressive disorder is its relatively lower severity. Similarly, *cyclothymic disorder* resembles bipolar II disorder but is less severe.

**Mania** **Mania** (the Greek word for "madness") is characterized by wild, exuberant, unrealistic activity not justified by environmental events. During manic episodes, people are usually elated and self-confident; however, contradiction or interference tends to make them very angry. Their speech (and, presumably, their thought processes) becomes very rapid. They tend to flit from topic to topic and are full of grandiose plans, but their thoughts are not as disorganized as those of people with schizophrenia. People with mania also tend to be restless and hyperactive, often pacing around ceaselessly. They often have delusions and hallucinations—typically of a nature that fits their exuberant mood. Davison and Neale (1990) recorded a typical interaction:

> *Therapist*: Well, you seem pretty happy today.
>
> *Client*: Happy! Happy! You certainly are a master of understatement, you rogue! (Shouting, literally jumping out of seat.) Why I'm ecstatic. I'm leaving for the West Coast today, on my daughter's bicycle. Only 3100 miles. That's nothing, you know. I could probably walk, but I want to get there by next week. And along the way I plan to contact a lot of people about investing in my fish equipment. I'll get to know more people that way—you know, Doc, "know" in the biblical sense (leering at the therapist seductively). Oh, God, how good it feels. It's almost like a nonstop orgasm. (Davison & Neale, 1990, p. 222)

The usual response that manic speech and behaviour evokes in another person is one of sympathetic amusement. In fact, when an experienced clinician finds that he or she is amused by a patient, the clinician begins to suspect mania. Because very few patients exhibit only mania, the DSM-IV-TR classifies all cases in which mania occurs as bipolar disorder. Patients with bipolar disorder usually experience alternate periods of mania and depression. Each period lasts from a few days to a few weeks, usually with several days of relatively normal behaviour in between. Many therapists have observed that there is often something brittle and unnatural about the happiness during the manic phase, as though the patient is making himself or herself be happy to ward off an attack of depression. Indeed, some manic patients are simply hyperactive and irritable rather than euphoric.

**Depression** People with depression have feelings of extreme sadness and are usually full of self-directed guilt, but not because of any particular environmental event. Depressed people cannot always state why they are depressed. Beck (1967) identified five cardinal symptoms of depression: (1) a sad and apathetic mood, (2) feelings of worthlessness and hopelessness, (3) a desire to withdraw from other people, (4) sleeplessness and loss of appetite and sexual desire, and (5) change in activity level, to either lethargy or agitation. Most people who are labelled "depressed" have a dysthymic disorder; a minority has a severe mood disorder. Major depression must be distinguished from grief, such as that caused by the death of a loved one. People who are grieving feel sad and depressed but do not fear losing their minds or have thoughts of self-harm. Because many people who do suffer from major depression or the depressed phase of bipolar disorder commit suicide, these disorders are potentially fatal. In fact, the mortality rate (including suicide) among people with bipolar disorder is two to three times greater than that of the general population (Fogarty, Russell, Newman, & Bland, 1994).

People with severe depression often have delusions, especially that their brains or internal organs are rotting away. Sometimes, they believe that they are being punished for unspeakable and unforgivable sins, as in the following statement, reported by Coleman (1976):

> My brain is being eaten away. . . . If I had any willpower I would kill myself. . . . I don't deserve to live. . . . I have ruined everything . . . and it's all my fault. . . . I have been unfaithful to my wife and now I am being punished . . . my health is ruined... there's no use going on . . . (sigh). . . . I have ruined everything... my family . . . and now myself. . . . I bring misfortune to everyone. . . . I am a moral leper . . . a serpent in the Garden of Eden. (Coleman, 1976, p. 346)

## Possible Causes

The possible causes of mood disorders centre on four variables: faulty cognition, heredity, brain biochemistry, and sleep/wake cycles.

**Cognitive Causes** Depressed people are generally negative about themselves and, as such, can be challenging to be around. People with mood disorders don't have the same outlook on life as others. Specifically, they are likely to make negative assertions about themselves and their abilities: "Nobody likes me"; "I'm not good at anything"; "What's the point in even trying, I'll just screw up anyway." The problem is that the depressed individual is caught in a vicious circle: Negative statements strain interpersonal relationships, which results in others withdrawing or failing to initiate social support, which in turn reinforces the depressed individual's negative statements (Klerman & Weissman, 1986; Weissman, Markowitz, & Klerman, 2000).

The changes in affect seen in depression may not be primary but are secondary to changes in cognition (Beck, 1967, 1991). That is, the primary disturbance is a distortion in the person's view of reality. For example, a depressed person may see a scratch on the surface of his or her car and conclude that the car is ruined. A person whose recipe fails may see the unappetizing dish as proof of his or her unworthiness. A nasty letter from a creditor is seen as a serious and personal condemnation. According to Beck, depressed people's thinking is characterized by self-blame (things that go wrong are always their fault), overemphasis on the negative aspects of life (even small problems are blown out of proportion), and failure to appreciate positive experiences (pessimism). This kind of thinking involves negative thoughts about the self, about the present, and about the future, which Beck collectively referred to as the *cognitive triad*. In short, depressed people see no hope for future improvement. They blame their present miserable situation on their inadequacies. Since they see these inadequacies as permanent characteristics of themselves, they have no reason to believe things will be different in the future.

Whereas psychoanalytical theory emphasizes the role of the unconscious in the emergence of psychological disorder, Beck's theory emphasizes the role of a person's judgment in contributing to his or her own emotional state. This theory has been useful in alerting therapists to the importance of considering the thought processes, as well as the feelings, of a patient with a severe mood disorder. Of course, if we observe an association between faulty cognition and depression, we cannot necessarily conclude that the faulty cognition causes the depression; in fact, the reverse could be true. In any event, Beck's method of treatment, based on his theory, has proven to be effective (as we shall see in Chapter 18).

*Attributional style* (Abramson, Metalsky, & Alloy, 1989; Abramson, Seligman, & Teasdale, 1978) appears to be another causal factor in depression. According to this idea, it is not merely experiencing negative events that causes people to become depressed. More important are the attributions people make about why those events occur. People are most likely to become depressed if they attribute negative events and experiences to their own shortcomings and believe that their lives are never going to get any better. A person's attributional style, then, serves as a predisposition or diathesis for depression. In other words, people prone to depression tend to have hopeless outlooks—"I am not good at anything I try to do and it will never get any better. I am always going to be a lousy person." According to this view, depression is most likely when people with pessimistic attributional styles encounter significant or frequent life stressors (Abramson, Alloy, & Metalsky, 1995). The pessimistic attributions are then generalized to other, perhaps smaller, stressors, and eventually a deep sense of hopelessness and despair sets in. This diathesis–stress model has been supported by research on both adults (e.g., Johnson et al., 2001; Metalsky, Joiner, Hardin, & Abramson, 1993) and young people (e.g., Abela & Sullivan, 2003; Joiner, 2000). The evidence indicates that the combination of a hopeless outlook *plus* negative life events is predictive of depression.

Such people also appear to suffer a double dose of hopelessness. Not only do they perceive negative outcomes as being their own fault, but they also perceive positive outcomes as due to circumstance or to luck. In addition, they apply pessimistic attributions to a wide range of events and experiences and apply positive attributions only to a very narrow range of events and experiences, if any.

**Genetic Causes** Like schizophrenia, the mood disorders appear to have a genetic component. People who have first-degree relatives with a serious mood disorder are 10 times more likely to develop these disorders than are people without afflicted relatives (Rosenthal, 1970). Furthermore, the concordance rate for bipolar disorder is 60 percent for monozygotic twins, compared with 15 percent for dizygotic twins (Kendler et al., 1993). First-degree relatives of people suffering from bipolar disorder are 7 percent more likely than the rest of the population to suffer from the disorder (Sadovnick et al., 1994). For major depression, the figures are 40 percent and 11 percent, respectively (Allen, 1976). Thus, a case can be made that heritable factors predispose people to develop these disorders. At the same time, it is obvious that heredity does not by itself determine whether a person will develop a serious mood disorder. Considerable variability remains that must be accounted for by environmental events.

▲ *The symptoms of major depression include apathy, feelings of worthlessness, social withdrawal, changes in sleeping and eating patterns, and lethargy or agitation.*

**Physiological Causes—Biochemical Factors** The effectiveness of certain drug therapies for mood disorders suggests to some researchers that biochemical factors might play a role in the development and course of mood disorders. Although there is logic to this argument, we will see that the issue is unsettled.

The evidence does clearly show that at least two neurotransmitters, norepinephrine and serotonin, are related to depression. People with major depression have lower levels of these neurotransmitters than do people without the disorder. It is also the case that drug therapies that increase the amount of these substances in the synapses, or make them available for a longer period of time, have beneficial effects on depression.

Other drugs, including *reserpine*, which is used to treat high blood pressure, can *cause* episodes of depression. Reserpine lowers blood pressure by blocking the release of norepinephrine in muscles in the walls of blood vessels, thus causing the muscles to relax. However, because the drug also blocks the release of norepinephrine and serotonin in the brain, a common side effect is depression. This side effect strengthens the argument that biochemical factors in the brain play an important role in depression.

Several studies have found evidence for biochemical abnormalities in the brains of people with mood disorders. Taking samples of transmitter substances directly from the living brain is not possible. But when transmitter substances are released, a small amount is broken down by enzymes in the brain, and some of the breakdown products accumulate in the cerebrospinal fluid or pass into the bloodstream and collect in the urine. Investigators have analyzed cerebrospinal fluid and urine for these substances.

For example, the level of a compound called 5HIAA in the cerebrospinal fluid of depressed people who had attempted suicide was significantly lower than in control participants (Träskmann, Asberg, Bertilsson, & Sjöstrand, 1981). The lower level of this compound, which is produced when serotonin is broken down, implies that there was less activity of serotonin-secreting neurons in the brains of the depressed people. In fact, 20 percent of the people with levels below the median subsequently killed themselves, whereas none with levels above the median committed suicide. Taube and colleagues (1978) obtained evidence for decreased activity of neurons that secrete norepinephrine; they found low levels of a compound (MHPG) produced when this transmitter substance is broken down in the urine of patients with mood disorders. Thus, decreased activity of serotonin- and norepinephrine-secreting neurons appears to be related to depression. Recently, researchers have found evidence of a genetic association between major depression and suicide (Lemonde et al., 2003). Certain genotypes (e.g., homozygous G[-1019] allele) were found twice as often in depressed patients in comparison to a control group, and four times more often in suicide victims.

Although the brain biochemistry of patients with mood disorders appears to be abnormal, we cannot be certain that a biochemical imbalance is the first event in a sequence that leads to depression. Environmental stimuli may cause the depression, which may then lead to biochemical changes in the brain. For example, the brain levels of norepinephrine are lower in dogs that have been presented with an inescapable electrical shock and have developed *learned helplessness* (Miller, Rosellini, & Seligman, 1977). The dogs certainly did not inherit the low norepinephrine levels; they acquired them as a result of their experience. The findings so far suggest that a tendency to develop serious mood disorders is heritable and that low levels of norepinephrine and serotonin are associated with these disorders. However, the cause-and-effect relations have yet to be worked out.

## Physiological Causes—Relation to Sleep Cycles

A characteristic symptom of mood disorders is sleep disturbance. Usually, people with a severe mood disorder have little difficulty falling asleep, but they awaken early and are unable to get back to sleep again. (In contrast, people with dysthymic disorder are more likely to have trouble falling asleep and getting out of bed the next day.) Kupfer (1976) reported that depressed patients tend to enter REM sleep sooner than normal people do and spend more time in this state during the last half of sleep. Noting this fact, Vogel, Vogel, McAbee, and Thurmond (1980) deprived depressed patients of REM sleep by awakening them whenever the EEG showed signs that they were entering this stage. Remarkably, the deprivation decreased their depression. These findings are supported by the observation that treatments that alleviate depression, such as electroconvulsive therapy and antidepressant drugs, profoundly reduce REM sleep in cats (Moreau, Scherschlicht, Jenck, & Martin, 1995; Scherschlicht et al., 1982).

Ehlers, Frank, and Kupfer (1988) have proposed an intriguing hypothesis that integrates behavioural and biological evidence. They suggest that depression is triggered environmentally, through loss of *social zeitgebers*. A **zeitgeber** (from the German word for "time giver") is a stimulus that synchronizes daily biological rhythms, which are controlled by an internal biological clock located in the hypothalamus. The most important zeitgeber is light; each morning, our biological clocks are synchronized ("reset to the time zero") by daylight. These clocks control sleep and waking cycles, cycles of hormone secretion and body temperature, and many other physiological systems that fluctuate each day.

Ehlers and her colleagues note that in humans, social interactions, as well as light, may serve as zeitgebers. For example, people tend to synchronize their daily rhythms to those of their spouses. After the loss of a spouse, people's daily schedules are usually disrupted and, of course, many widows and widowers become depressed. Flaherty and colleagues (1987) studied recently widowed people and found that the most depressed individuals were those with the greatest reduction in social contacts and regular daily activities. Ehlers, Frank, and Kupfer (1988) suggest that some people may be more susceptible to the disruptive effects of such changes. This susceptibility represents the genetic contribution toward developing mood disorders. Almost everyone becomes depressed, at least for a period of time, after the loss of a loved one. Other events that change a person's daily routine, such as the birth of an infant or the loss of a job, can also precipitate a period of depression. Perhaps people who "spontaneously" become depressed are reacting to minor changes in their daily routine that disrupt their biological rhythms. Clearly, this interesting hypothesis deserves further research.

Yet another phenomenon relates depression to sleep and waking—or, more specifically, to the phenomena responsible for daily rhythms. Some people become depressed during the winter season, when days are short and nights are long. The symptoms of this form of depression, called **seasonal affective disorder**, are slightly different from those of major depression. Both forms include lethargy and sleep disturbances, but seasonal depression includes a craving for carbohydrates and an accompanying weight gain. (As you will recall, people with major depression tend to lose their appetites.) Seasonal affective disorder affects between 0.4 and 2.9 percent of the population (Westrin & Lam, 2007).

Seasonal affective disorder can be treated by exposing people to natural or artificial light (Dalgleish, Rosen, & Marks, 1996; Lamberg, 1998; Lee & Chan, 1999; McColl & Veitch, 2001). Possibly, people with seasonal affective disorder require a stronger-than-normal zeitgeber to synchronize their biological clocks with the day–night cycle. Interestingly, it appears that there may be a genetic link between alcoholism and seasonal affective disorder (McGrath & Yahia, 1993). Some people who abuse alcohol tend to drink more in the fall and winter months. Family and molecular genetics studies suggest the link between alcoholism and seasonal affective disorder may be genetic (Sher, 2004). Several investigators have noticed that the symptoms of seasonal affective disorder resemble the behavioural characteristics of hibernation: carbohydrate craving, overeating and weight gain, oversleeping, and lethargy (Neuhaus & Rosenthal, 1997; Rosenthal, 2000; Rosenthal et al., 1986). Animals that hibernate do so during the winter, and the behaviour is triggered by a combination of short day length and cooler

**zeitgeber** Any stimulus, such as light, that synchronizes daily biological rhythms.

**seasonal affective disorder** A mood disorder characterized by depression, lethargy, sleep disturbances, and craving for carbohydrates. This disorder generally occurs during the winter, when the amount of daylight, relative to the other seasons, is low. This disorder can be treated with exposure to bright lights.

**FIGURE 17•5** Sleep deprivation and depression. Changes in the depression rating of a depressed patient produced by a single night's total sleep deprivation.

*(From Wu, J. C., & Bunney, W. E. (1990). The biological basis of an antidepressant response to sleep deprivation and relapse: Review and hypothesis.* American Journal of Psychiatry, 147, *14–21. Copyright 1990, the American Psychiatric Association. Reprinted by permission.)*

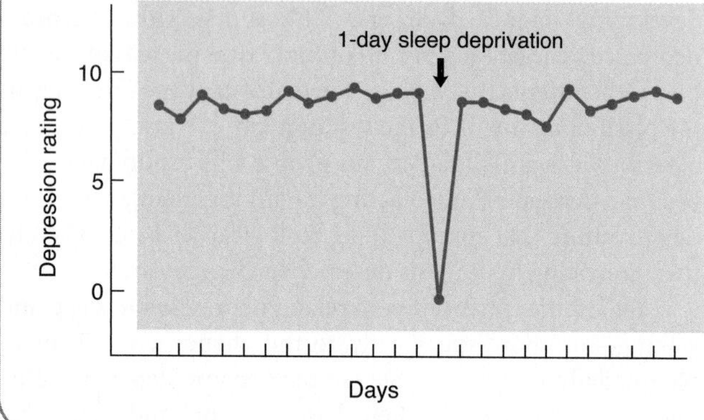


temperatures. Thus, some of the brain mechanisms involved in hibernation may also be responsible for the mood changes associated with the time of year. This hypothesis has some support. Zvolsky, Jansky, Vyskocilova, and Grof (1981) found that imipramine, an antidepressant drug, suppressed hibernation in hamsters.

As we saw, specific deprivation of REM sleep has an antidepressant effect. *Total* sleep deprivation also has an antidepressant effect. However, the effects are quite different. REM sleep deprivation takes several weeks to reduce depression and produces relatively long-lasting effects. Total sleep deprivation produces immediate effects—but the effects are short-lived (Wu & Bunney, 1990). **Figure 17•5** shows the mood rating of a patient who stayed awake one night. As you can see, the depression was lifted by the sleep deprivation but returned the next day, after a normal night's sleep.

We still do not know why some depressed people profit from total sleep deprivation while others do not. An interesting study by Reinink, Bouhuys, Wirz-Justice, and van den Hoofdakker (1990) found that we can predict a person's responsiveness from his or her circadian pattern of mood. Most people feel better at a particular time of day—generally, either the morning or the evening. Depressed people, too, show these fluctuations in mood. Reinink and his colleagues found that the depressed people who were most likely to show an improvement in mood after a night of total sleep deprivation were those who felt worst in the morning and best in the evening. Perhaps these people are most sensitive to the hypothetical depressogenic substance produced during sleep. This substance makes them feel worst in the morning. As the day progresses, the chemical is metabolized and they start feeling better. A night without sleep simply prolongs this improvement in mood.

At the present time, total sleep deprivation does not provide a practical way of reducing people's depression (people cannot stay awake indefinitely). Fortunately, partial sleep deprivation, even if only for a few hours, seems to help.

## Interim Summary

### Mood Disorders

The serious mood disorders are primarily disorders of emotion, although delusions are also characteristically present. Bipolar disorder consists of alternating periods of mania and depression, whereas major depression consists of depression alone. Beck has noted that although mood disorders involve emotional reactions, they may be, at least in part, based on faulty cognition.

Heritability studies strongly suggest a biological component to mood disorders. This possibility receives support from the finding that biological treatments reduce symptoms, while reserpine, a drug used to treat hypertension, can cause depression. Biological treatments include lithium carbonate for bipolar disorder (see Chapter 18) and electroconvulsive therapy, antidepressant drugs, and REM sleep deprivation for depression. These findings, along with evidence from biochemical analysis of the breakdown products of norepinephrine and serotonin in depressed patients, suggest that depression results from deficiencies in availability of these neurotransmitters. However, the discovery that environmental stress can affect the availability of neurotransmitters warns us to be careful in inferring cause and effect.

Evidence also suggests that the primary physiological disorder in depression may manifest itself in abnormalities in sleep/waking rhythms. Studies have shown that REM sleep deprivation alleviates the symptoms of depression, and all known biological treatments for depression themselves reduce REM sleep. Possibly, an important environmental trigger of depression may be events that disrupt a person's daily routine and social contacts. A specific form of depression, seasonal affective disorder, can be treated by exposure to bright light, which synchronizes the biological clock with the day–night cycle. In addition, total sleep deprivation temporarily reduces the symptoms of depression, particularly in people who tend to feel less depressed at the end of the day.

We close with a final thought. Besides having to simplify disorders that are typically complex, we have had to exaggerate the distinction between normalcy and psychological disorder. We must emphasize that no sharp line divides normal from abnormal. At the extremes, there is no mistaking a person with, say, a phobic disorder, schizophrenia, or a mood disorder for a person without those disorders. But most people do not fall at the extremes, and all of us recognize aspects of our own behaviour in many descriptions of people with psychological disorders.

**QUESTIONS TO CONSIDER**

1. Suppose that you have a friend whose mother has been diagnosed with major depression. Your friend is concerned about her mother, and also worries that she may become depressed because she has heard that this disorder is genetic. Knowing that you are taking a course in psychology, she asks you to tell her more about the disorder and the likelihood that she, too, will develop it. What do you tell her?
2. Medical students often diagnose themselves as having the diseases and disorders they are studying. In fact, though, their studies have simply made them more sensitive to the slightest deviations from their normal level of physical health. While reading the section on mood disorders, did something similar happen to you—did you become more sensitive to your mood and to deviations from your normal mood? Can you trace these deviations to specific events, or does there seem to be no reason for these perturbations in mood?

EPILOGUE

## Elyn Sak's Life with Schizophrenia

During her first semester at Yale, Elyn Saks (2007) experienced the onset of schizophrenia. Fears seized her, including the fear that her brain was about to explode. She was taken to a local hospital, where she was placed in restraints and given an antipsychotic drug.

Subsequently transferred to a psychiatric institute, she continued to be restrained (after confiding to her psychiatrist that she had murdered vast numbers of people with her thoughts). Once in the Psychiatric Evaluation Unit, she received a diagnosis of "chronic paranoid schizophrenia with acute exacerbation." The prognosis was "grave," and she later learned that the unit administrators, without her knowledge, had informed the law school that she likely would never return. Against these steep odds, and following a prolonged period of hospitalization, she was able to return to law school the following fall and graduate after serving as an editor of the *Yale Law Journal.*

In the nearly 30 years since the diagnosis, Saks has sustained a regimen of antipsychotic medications and psychoanalysis while achieving a very successful academic career that blends law, psychiatry, and the behavioural sciences—and a loving marriage. The medications brought tardive dyskinesia (see Chapter 18), and she has suffered other serious medical problems, but she considers herself remarkably fortunate to have carved out a quality of life that most people with schizophrenia do not experience.

Saks attributes her success to the tandem of medication and psychoanalysis. She readily acknowledges that medication is invaluable for managing the symptoms of schizophrenia. However, she is particularly indebted to psychoanalysis for bringing meaning to her experiences. It has provided her with a way to resolve what is often the most dire dilemma that individuals with schizophrenia face: "If I share my delusions with you, you will put me away; if I keep them to myself, they will only get worse." Saks cites as important the sense of "being known" by her psychoanalyst, a sense that helped her overcome the profound isolation that is too frequently the patient's lot. She tellingly remarks that though people with cancer receive flowers from others, those with schizophrenia do not. Her memoir is a testimony to extraordinary triumph over a traditionally dispiriting diagnosis.

## Canadian Connections to Research in This Chapter

Al-Issa, I. (1995). Culture and mental illness in an international perspective. In I. Al-Issa (Ed.), *Handbook of culture and mental illness: An international perspective.* Madison, CT: International Universities Press. (University of Calgary: www.ucalgary.ca)

Bland, R. C., Orn, H., & Newman, S. C. (1988). Lifetime prevalence of psychiatric disorders in Edmonton. *Acta Psychiatrica Scandinavica, 77,* 24–32. (University of Alberta: www.ualberta.ca)

Cunningham, C. E., & Boyle, M. H. (2002). Preschoolers at risk for attention-deficit hyperactivity disorder and oppositional defiant disorder: Family, parenting, and behavioral correlates. *Journal of Abnormal Child Psychology, 30*(6), 555–569. (McMaster University: www.mcmaster.ca)

Cunningham, J. A., Wild, T. C., Bondy, S. J., & Lin, E. (2001). Impact of normative feedback on problem drinkers: A small-area population study. *Journal of Studies on Alcohol, 62*(2), 228–233. (Centre for Addiction and Mental Health: www.camh.net)

DeWit, D. J., Adlaf, E. M., Offord, D. R., & Ogborne, A. C. (2000). Age at first alcohol use: A risk factor for the development of alcohol disorders. *American Journal of Psychiatry, 157*(5), 745–750. (Centre for Addiction and Mental Health: www.camh.net)

Fogarty, F., Russell, J. M., Newman, S. C., & Bland, R. C. (1994). Mania. *Acta Psychiatrica Scandinavica, 89*(376, Suppl), 16–23. (University of Alberta: www.ualberta.ca)

Hare, R. D. (1965). Temporal gradient of fear arousal in psychopaths. *Journal of Abnormal Psychology, 70*, 442–445. (University of British Columbia: www.ubc.ca)

Hare, R. D. (1998). *Without conscience: The disturbing world of the psychopaths among us.* New York: Guilford Press. (University of British Columbia: www.ubc.ca)

Hare, R. D. (1999). Psychopathy as a risk factor for violence. *Psychiatric Quarterly, 70*, 181–197. (University of British Columbia: www.ubc.ca)

Hare, R. D., McPherson, L. M., & Forth, A. E. (1988). Male psychopaths and their criminal careers. *Journal of Consulting and Clinical Psychology, 56*, 710–714. (University of British Columbia: www.ubc.ca)

Professor Hare received the Canadian Psychological Association Award for Distinguished Contributions in the Application of Psychology in 2000.

Harpur, T. J., Hart, S. D., & Hare, R. D. (2002). Personality of the psychopath. In P. T. Costa, Jr. & T. A. Widiger (Eds.), *Personality disorders and the five-factor model of personality* (2nd ed.). Washington, DC: American Psychological Association. (University of British Columbia: www.ubc.ca)

Health Canada. (2002). *A report on mental illnesses in Canada.* Retrieved April 7, 2004, from http://www.hc-sc.gc.ca/pphb-dgspsp/publicat/miic-mmac

Kiehl, K. A., Smith, A. M., Hare, R. D., & Liddle, P. F. (2000). An event-related potential investigation of response inhibition in schizophrenia and psychopathy. *Biological Psychiatry, 48*(3), 210–221. (University of British Columbia: www.ubc.ca)

Lemonde, S., Turecki, G., Bakish, D., Lisheng, D., Hrdina, P. D., Brown, C. D., Sequeira, A., et al. (2003). Impaired repression at a 5-hydroxytryptamine 1A receptor gene polymorphism associated with major depression and suicide. *The Journal of Neuroscience, 23*(25), 8788–8799. (University of Ottawa: www.uottawa.ca)

Lin, E., Goering, P., Offord, D. R., Campbell, D., & Boyle, M. H. (1996). The use of mental health services in Ontario: Epidemiologic findings. *Canadian Journal of Psychiatry, 41*, 572–577. (Centre for Addiction and Mental Health: www.camh.net)

Lindsay, D. S. (1996). Contextualizing and clarifying criticisms of memory work in psychotherapy. In K. Pezdek & W. P. Banks (Eds.), *The recovered memory/false memory debate.* San Diego, CA: Academic Press. (University of Victoria: www.uvic.ca)

MacMillan, H. L., Fleming, J. E., Streiner, D. L., Lin, E., Boyle, M. H., Jamieson, E., Duku, E. K., et al. (2001). Childhood abuse and lifetime psychopathology in a community sample. *American Journal of Psychiatry, 158*(11), 1878–1883. (McMaster University: www.mcmaster.ca)

Mayerovitch, J. I., du Fort, G. G., Kakuma, R., Bland, R. C., Newman, S. C., & Pinard, G. (2003). Treatment seeking for obsessive-compulsive disorder: Role of obsessive-compulsive disorder symptoms and comorbid psychiatric diagnoses. *Comprehensive Psychiatry, 44*(2), 162–168. (McGill University: www.mcgill.ca)

Offord, D. R., Boyle, M. H., Campbell, D., Goering, P., Lin, E., Wong, M., & Racine, Y. A. (1996). One-year prevalence of psychiatric disorder in Ontarians 15 to 64 years of age. *Canadian Journal of Psychiatry, 41*, 559–563. (McMaster University: www.mcmaster.ca)

Ross, C. A. (1997). *Dissociative identity disorder: Diagnosis, clinical features, and treatment of multiple personality* (2nd ed.). New York: John Wiley & Sons, Inc. (University of Toronto: www.utoronto.ca)

Ross, C., Miller, S. D., Bjornson, L., & Reagor, P. (1991). Abuse histories in 102 cases of multiple personality disorder. *Canadian Journal of Psychiatry, 36*, 97–101. (St. Boniface General Hospital Research Centre, Winnipeg: www.sbrc.umanitoba.ca)

Spanos, N. P. (1996). *Multiple identities & false memories: A sociocognitive perspective.* Washington, DC: American Psychological Association. (Carleton University: www.carleton.ca)

Spanos, N. P., Weekes, J. R., & Bertrand, L. D. (1985). Multiple personality: A social psychological perspective. *Journal of Abnormal Psychology, 94*, 362–376. (Carleton University: www.carleton.ca)

Stein, M. B., Millar, T. W., Larsen, D. K., & Kryger, M. H. (1995). Irregular breathing during sleep in patients with panic disorder. *American Journal of Psychiatry, 152*, 1168–1173. (University of Manitoba: www.umanitoba.ca)

Wallace, S. T., & Alden, L. E. (1997). Social phobia and positive social events: The price of success. *Journal of Abnormal Psychology, 106*, 416–424. (University of British Columbia: www.ubc.ca)

Williamson, S., Harpur, T. J., & Hare, R. D. (1991). Abnormal processing of affective words by psychopaths. *Psychophysiology, 28*, 260–273. (University of British Columbia: www.ubc.ca)

## Suggestions for Further Reading

Carson, R. C., Butcher, J. N., & Mineka, S. (2000). *Abnormal psychology and modern life* (11th ed.). New York: HarperCollins.

A highly readable, upper-division undergraduate text about psychological disorders, including their causes and treatment.

North, C. N. (1987). *Welcome, silence.* New York: Simon and Schuster.

Vonnegut, M. (1975). *The Eden express: A personal account of schizophrenia.* New York: Praeger.

Both of these books are excellent, first-hand accounts of what it is like to suffer from schizophrenia.

Goodwin, D. W., & Guze, S. B. (1996). *Psychiatric diagnosis* (5th ed.). New York: Oxford University Press.

This short book describes the characteristics of the most important psychological disorders and what is known about their causes.

Cleckley, H. (1988). *The mask of sanity* (5th ed.). Augusta, GA: Emily S. Cleckley.

The definitive volume on anti-social personality disorder (psychopathy). Along with a thorough discussion of the disorder, it contains several detailed case studies.

# 18

# The Treatment of Psychological Disorders

# CHAPTER OUTLINE

## Psychological Disorders and Psychotherapy

Early Treatment of Psychological Disorders • The Development of Psychotherapy

People with psychological disorders were once greatly misunderstood and treated inhumanely. Today, many forms of treatment are available for many different types of psychological problems. Therapists often use different methods or combine two or more methods to treat different problems.

## Insight Therapies

Psychoanalysis and Modern Psychodynamic Approaches • Humanistic Therapy • Evaluation of Insight Therapies

Insight therapies are based on the idea that a person's psychological problems can best be solved by talking about them with a specially trained therapist. Psychoanalytic and psychodynamic therapy attempt to get people to discover the unconscious and conscious forces that may be at the root of their problems. Humanistic therapy focuses more on the contribution of current thinking and emotions to maladaptive behaviour. Gestalt therapy focuses on teaching people to confront their feelings as they are presently experienced—little emphasis is placed on past experiences. An important limitation to all insight therapies is that they are mainly relevant to mild psychological disorders and not to more serious disorders, such as schizophrenia.

## Behaviour and Cognitive-Behaviour Therapies

Therapies Based on Classical Conditioning • Therapies Based on Operant Conditioning • Maintaining Behavioural Change • Cognitive-Behaviour Therapies • Evaluation of Behaviour and Cognitive-Behaviour Therapies

Therapies derived from the basic principles of classical and operant conditioning are effective in reducing anxiety and fear in people with anxiety disorders and phobias. Cognitive-behaviour therapy is also effective in changing behaviour, but in this case the emphasis is placed on changing faulty cognitions as well as environmental conditions. Despite their effectiveness, applications of these therapies are limited by ethical considerations.

## Group Therapy and Community Psychology

Family Therapy and Couples Therapy • Community Psychology • Evaluation of Group Therapy and Community Psychology

Group therapies, including family and couples therapies, provide the opportunity for the therapist to observe people's interactions with each other and to suggest ways that those people may learn more adaptive responses. Community psychology stresses public education, social change, and prevention of psychological problems as strategies for teaching more effective behaviour; it also provides important support services to those people who might otherwise be institutionalized for their problems.

## Biological Treatments

Drug Therapy • Electroconvulsive Therapy • *Then and Now: The Controversy of ECT* • Psychosurgery • Evaluation of Biological Treatments

Certain classes of drugs have been found to be highly effective in treating the symptoms of schizophrenia, depression, bipolar disorder, and anxiety-related disorders. Severe depression is often effectively treated—as a last resort—by passing electrical current through the brain and inducing a seizure. Brain surgery is no longer a common treatment of psychological disorders, although one form of it is sometimes used to treat people with severe obsessive-compulsive disorder.

## Ethical Issues in Psychotherapy

Because the therapeutic relationship can be exploited and abused, a detailed set of ethical standards has evolved to guide therapists in their practices.

## Selecting a Therapist

When selecting a therapist, one should look for someone who is licensed to practise therapy, knowledgeable about psychological disorders, ethical, and supportive.

PROLOGUE

## Life with Bipolar Disorder

Geoff was on the fast track. He had dropped out of college to start a company, then watched its sales grow non-stop in the first few years. His personal fortune zoomed up, too—at least on paper. To start a new venture, he borrowed against the company's stock. Missed deadlines and failed projections followed, and his company was forced to fold. Although his professional life was now a shambles, Geoff still believed he could do no wrong. He was bursting with ideas and energy and felt nearly indestructible. He slept only about three or four hours a night, and once told a business partner he could have jumped off the CN Tower and landed on his feet. His business reversals led Geoff to see a psychologist, who told him he might be suffering from bipolar I disorder, a serious psychological condition. Geoff brushed it off. He felt tired sometimes, but he never felt really down. The psychologist couldn't possibly be right.

Geoff decided he needed a fresh start and moved to a new city. Once there, he was sleepless for five days. Friends whom he phoned during that time recommended he seek professional help. He checked into a hospital, where he was diagnosed with bipolar I disorder and received a prescription for lithium. One of the psychiatrists who had treated him recommended that he also see a psychotherapist. Geoff's previous experience had made him skeptical, however, and he opted to depend on lithium alone to solve his problems.

Over time, additional drugs were prescribed for different aspects of the disorder. Geoff was confident that the drugs were helping him, but he hated their side effects. He developed tremors and an erratic heart rate and had to start taking other drugs to control them. He needed a different medication in order to sleep. Altogether, he was taking a dozen different medications each day, and sometimes more. He began to worry about being so dependent on them. In his more reflective moments, he wondered whether he had become less aware of himself, of others, and of life in general. He thought of himself as more and more like a ghost. Even while taking medication, he was always trying to do a hundred things at once. It was difficult to think of himself as having any stability, any substance. Sometimes he thought about going back to school, but the idea of sitting through a lecture or studying for an exam seemed impossible.

In his search for a way out, Geoff decided to give psychotherapy a second try. Following up on a friend's recommendation, he met a psychologist who seemed just right for him. Today, with his therapist's help, Geoff better understands his decision making while in a manic state. Even with medication, the manic states recur, though not as intensely, and Geoff can feel them coming on. Psychotherapy has helped him learn to recognize the early warning signs and to defer potentially important decisions until the state has subsided. As Geoff now sees it, there is no way he could have gained from psychotherapy without medication, but medication alone would not have allowed him to get his life back on track.

Geoff's story is typical of the types of treatments used in modern psychology. Psychologists often work in teams to treat disorders. Some psychiatrists might prescribe drugs and offer therapy, while other psychologists might offer group or family therapy. In Geoff's case, drug therapy allowed him to focus his attention on psychotherapy. He is happy now, is ready to enrol in another course, and eventually plans to start another business.

This chapter describes four basic approaches to the treatment of psychological disorders: insight therapies, behaviour therapy and cognitive-behaviour therapies, treatment of groups (including treatment of couples and the development of outreach programs that serve the community), and biological treatments. Therapy is a complex process, and its outcome depends to a large extent on the relationship that the client and therapist are able to form. The final section of the chapter examines some ethical issues involved in practising therapy and some practical considerations to take into account when selecting a therapist. But before we discuss the different forms of therapy, let us first briefly consider the development of psychotherapy.

# Psychological Disorders and Psychotherapy

Today, most societies view psychological disorders as illnesses, much the same as physical diseases like diabetes or cancer. Psychologists agree that maladaptive behaviour should be treated humanely. The person whose behaviour is maladaptive needs help, and the emergence of techniques to provide such help has become a hallmark of psychology. This enlightened view has not always characterized humankind's treatment of people with psychological disorders and psychological problems.

## Early Treatment of Psychological Disorders

Sometimes psychological disorders are thought of as products of relatively modern times. In truth, psychological disorders have been with us since human existence began. For most of that time, people suffering from these disorders have been regarded with awe or fear. People whom we would now probably classify as having paranoid schizophrenia may have been regarded as prophets; they were seen as instruments through which gods or spirits were speaking. More often, they were considered to be possessed by devils or evil spirits and were made to suffer accordingly. The earliest known attempts to treat psychological disorders involved drilling holes in a person's skull, a process known as **trephining**. Presumably, the opening was made to permit evil spirits to leave the victim's head. In prehistoric times, this procedure was performed with a sharp-edged stone; later civilizations, such as the Egyptians, refined the practice with more sophisticated instruments. Signs of healing at the edges of the holes in prehistoric skulls indicate that some people survived trephining. (See **Figure 18•1**.)

Many other painful and degrading practices were directed at people's presumed possession by evil spirits. People thought to be unwilling hosts for evil spirits were subjected to curses or insults designed to persuade the demons to leave. If this approach had no effect, exorcism was attempted, to make the person's body an unpleasant place for devils to reside. Other rituals included beatings, starving, near drowning, and the drinking of foul-tasting concoctions. The delusional schemes of people with psychotic disorders often include beliefs of personal guilt and unworthiness. In a society that accepted the notion that there were witches and devils, these people often were ready to imagine themselves as evil. Some confessed to unspeakable acts of "sorcery" and accepted their persecution and punishment as deserved.

As late as the eighteenth century, the idea that devils and spirits were responsible for peculiar behaviours in some people remained popular among many Europeans. Fortunately, a few people believed that these disorders reflected diseases and that they should be treated medically and with compassion. Johann Wier, a sixteenth-century physician, was among the first to challenge practices intended to combat witchcraft. He argued that most people who were being tortured and burned for practising witchcraft in fact suffered from mental illness. The Church condemned his writings as heretical and banned them. They did not re-emerge until the twentieth century.

Eventually, the belief in witchcraft and demonology waned. The clergy, medical authorities, and the general public began to regard people with psychological disorders as ill. Torture and the extremes of persecution came to an end. However, the lives of mentally ill people did not necessarily become better. Undoubtedly, many people with psychological disorders were regarded as strange but harmless and managed to maintain a marginal existence in society. Others were sheltered by their families. More often, people with psychological disorders were consigned to various "asylums" established for the care of the mentally ill. Most of these mental institutions were extraordinarily inhumane. Patients were often kept in chains and sometimes wallowed in their own excrement.

**trephining** A surgical procedure in which a hole is made in the skull of a living person.

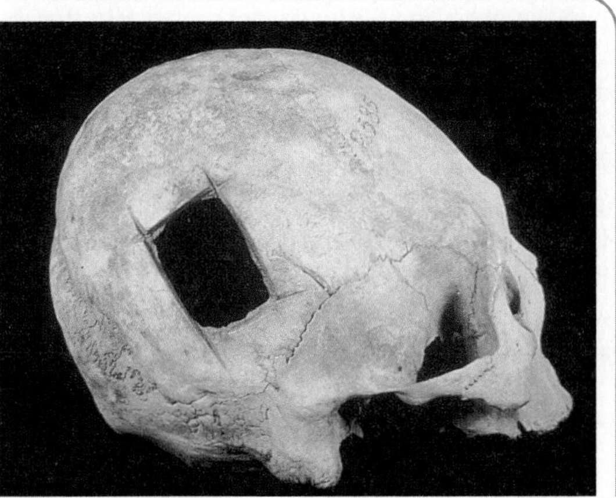

**FIGURE 18•1** Among the earliest biological approaches to the treatment of psychological disorders was the ancient practice of trephining, in which a hole was made in the skull to allow evil spirits to escape the person's head.

**FIGURE 18•2** The "tranquilizing chair" devised by Benjamin Rush.

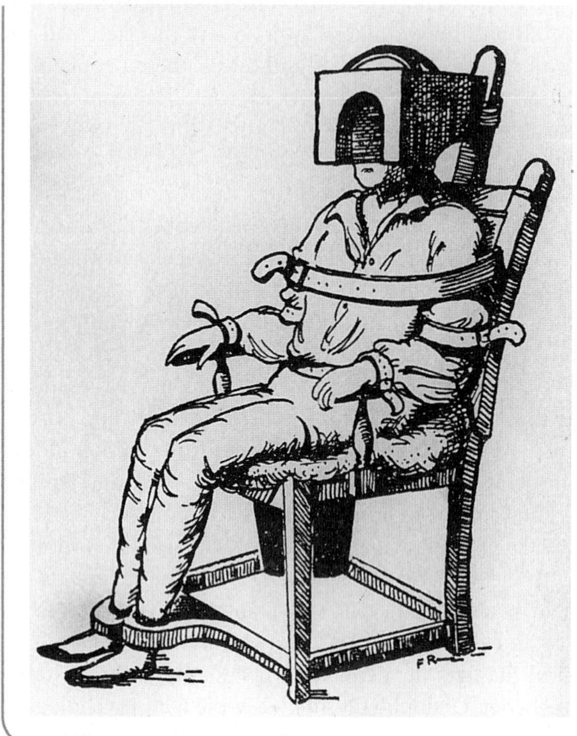

Those who displayed bizarre catatonic postures or who had fanciful delusions were sometimes exhibited to the public for a fee. Many of the treatments designed to cure mental patients were only a little better than the tortures that had previously been used to drive out evil spirits. Patients were tied up, doused in cold water, bled, made to vomit, strapped into a "tranquilizing chair" with a box placed over their head, and subjected to other terrible treatments. (See **Figure 18•2**.)

Reform began as mistreatment of the mentally ill became a cause of humanitarians. Philippe Pinel (1745–1826) was a French physician who in 1793 was appointed director of La Bicêtre, a mental hospital in Paris. Pinel believed that most mental patients would respond favourably to kind treatment. As an experiment, he removed the chains from some of the patients, took them out of the dungeons, and allowed them to walk about the hospital grounds. The experiment was a remarkable success. Orderliness and general calm replaced the previous noise, stench, and pervasive aura of despair. Many patients were eventually discharged. Pinel's success at La Bicêtre was repeated when he was given charge of Salpêtrière Hospital. Some mentally ill people eventually recover—or at least get much better—without any treatment at all. But if a person was put in a mental institution that existed prior to Pinel's time, he or she had little chance to show improvement.

Pinel's success encouraged similar reforms elsewhere. In the United States, Dorothea Dix (1802–1887) led the campaign for humane treatment of mental patients. She raised millions of dollars for the construction of mental hospitals and spurred the reform of many mental health facilities. In Canada, Dix was responsible for laying the groundwork for the first psychiatric hospital in Nova Scotia (Goldman, 1990). The process of reform in North America took a long time. Until very recently, some large mental hospitals were little more than warehouses for the mentally ill, who received little or no treatment but were merely provided with the necessities of life. Today, there is much greater emphasis on treatment. The discovery of antipsychotic drugs and improvements in psychotherapy have freed many people who otherwise would have spent their lives in institutions.

## The Development of Psychotherapy

The modern approach to therapy can be traced to Franz Anton Mesmer (1734–1815), an Austrian physician who practised in Paris in the late eighteenth and early nineteenth centuries. He devised a theory of "magnetic fluxes," according to which he attempted to effect cures by manipulating iron rods and bottles of chemicals. In reality, he hypnotized his patients and thereby alleviated some of their symptoms. As a result, hypnosis was first known as *mesmerism* (see Wegner, 2002).

Jean Martin Charcot (1825–1893), a French neurologist, began to study the therapeutic uses of hypnosis when one of his students hypnotized a woman and induced her to display the symptoms of a conversion reaction (then called *hysteria*). Charcot examined her and concluded that she was a hysterical patient. The student then woke the woman, and her symptoms vanished. Charcot had previously believed that hysteria had an organic basis, but this experience changed his opinion. He began to investigate the psychological causes of hysteria and to use hypnosis in his treatment.

Before Freud began private practice, he studied with Charcot in Paris. There, he observed the effects of hypnosis on hysteria. Freud's association with Charcot, and later with Breuer, started him on his life's study of the determinants of personality and the origins of mental illness. (These topics were discussed in Chapters 14 and 17.) He created the practice of psychoanalysis. The therapeutic methods he developed still influence how many psychologists and psychiatrists treat their clients.

Other psychologists have devised therapies based on their own theoretical views of maladaptive behaviour and its causes. Regardless of theoretical orientation, all therapists have in common a strong commitment to helping people solve their problems—whether by learning to cope with everyday stressors or with more severe psychological disorders, such as schizophrenia or depression. Some psychotherapists adopt approaches to treatment that fit their own views of why people behave the way they do. For example, therapists who believe that behaviour is strongly influenced by environmental contingencies, and people's perceptions of them, are likely to use cognitive-behavioural approaches in treating their clients' problems. Therapists who believe that behaviour is strongly influenced by biological factors are likely to use a combination of drug therapy and psychotherapy in treating their clients' problems, as was the case with Geoff in the chapter's prologue.

Most therapists adopt a more general, eclectic approach. The **eclectic approach** involves the therapist's using whatever methods he or she feels will work best for a particular client at a particular time. Such therapists are not strongly wedded to particular theoretical orientations. Instead, they seek the particular form of therapy that will best solve a particular client's problems. This often means *combining* aspects of several different treatment approaches according to a particular client's problem and personal circumstances. For example, Acierno, Hersen, and Van Hasselt (1993) have shown that combinations of behaviour and cognitive-behaviour therapies are more effective in treating panic disorder than is either one alone.

There are a large number of reasons people may seek therapy. Some need help in adjusting to everyday problems at home, work, or school. Others face more serious problems such as the death of a loved one, their own approaching death, or difficulties in getting along with other people. Still others enter therapy or are placed in therapy by mental health agencies for very serious psychological problems such as schizophrenia, major depression, or drug abuse. People who hit a low point in their lives may feel that their own efforts are insufficient and that family and friends cannot provide the help they need to solve their problems. Therapy is not just for people suffering from major psychological disorders. In fact, almost anyone can benefit from seeing a therapist if he or she is having a difficult time.

## Interim Summary

### Psychological Disorders and Psychotherapy

At different times, people suffering from emotional or behavioural problems were believed to be possessed by demons or were accused of being witches. They were often subjected to unspeakable torture, including trephining, in which a small hole was punctured in the skull of the afflicted person to allow demonic spirits to escape. Even when not being physically harmed, mental patients in sixteenth- and seventeenth-century asylums encountered abject humiliation. Philippe Pinel, a French physician, is often credited with changing the asylum environment in the late eighteenth century.

Modern therapy involves a wide array of treatment options—from psychoanalysis to drug treatment. In many cases, a person seeking therapy may find that his or her therapist uses an eclectic approach—borrowing methods from different treatments and blending them in a way that will work best in treating the patient's problem. Certainly, such options would not be available were it not for the modern view that people should have the chance to improve their level of functioning. People seeking therapy are perhaps even more diverse than those providing therapy. Although people seek therapy for many reasons, the one element they share is that they are at a low point in life and that alternative solutions, such as trying to solve the problem alone or with the help of friends and family, have not been satisfactory.

### QUESTIONS TO CONSIDER

1. What is your reaction to people with psychological disorders? Have you known anyone who has been diagnosed with a psychological disorder? If so, what was your feeling about that person when you learned that fact?
2. Do you think you would seek the help of a psychotherapist if you had a psychological problem you could not solve yourself? If so, describe what you might imagine psychotherapy to be like and how it might help you. If not, describe the reasons why you would not seek help.

# Insight Therapies

In the opening vignette, Geoff combined drug therapy and a form of insight therapy. Practitioners of *insight therapy* assume that people are essentially normal but learn maladaptive thought patterns and emotions, which are revealed in maladaptive behaviours. In other words, insight therapies view behaviour as a symptom of deeper underlying psychological problems. Once a patient understands the causes of his or her problems, the problems—and the maladaptive behaviours—will cease. Insight will lead to a cure. In this section, we will take a close look at the insight therapies: psychoanalysis, client-centred therapy, and Gestalt therapy.

The insight therapies include a variety of treatments that emphasize talk between the therapist and the client as a means of discovering the reasons for the client's problems. Insight into these reasons presumably helps the client solve the problems. Some insight therapies, such as psychoanalysis, emphasize causes in the client's past. Others, such as client-centred and Gestalt therapies, emphasize the present; they attempt to get the client to see the effects of his or her maladaptive thoughts and emotions and to find more adaptive ways of living.

## Psychoanalysis and Modern Psychodynamic Approaches

Sigmund Freud is given credit for developing **psychoanalysis**, a form of therapy aimed at providing the client with insight into his or her unconscious motivations and impulses. Recall from Chapter 14 that Freud's theory of personality suggests that unconscious conflicts based on the competing demands of the

**eclectic approach** A form of therapy in which the therapist uses whatever method he or she feels will work best for a particular client at a particular time.
**psychoanalysis** A form of therapy aimed at providing the client with insight into his or her unconscious motivations and impulses.

id (representing biological urges), the superego (representing the moral dictates of society), and the ego (representing reality) often lead to anxiety. The source of these conflicts, according to Freud, can usually be traced to inadequately defended sexual and aggressive urges or incomplete progression through the psychosexual stages.

In the early stages of therapy, the nature of the client's problems are difficult to identify because the analyst and the client are unaware of the underlying, unconscious, conflicts. The repression of these conflicts is seldom complete, though, and they frequently intrude into consciousness in subtle ways. By encouraging the client to talk, the analyst tries to bring these conflicts into view. The obscurity of the conflicts requires that the analyst interpret them in order to uncover their true meaning and gradually weave together a complete picture of the unconscious.

The purpose of therapy is to create a setting in which clues about the origins of intrapsychic conflicts are most likely to be revealed by the client. These clues are revealed in clients' dreams, physical problems, memory (or failure to remember certain things), manner of speech, and cognitive and emotional reactions to therapy. Then, by exposing the client to these clues, he or she will gain insight into the problem.

One of the main goals of the psychoanalyst is to *interpret* the clues about the origins of intrapsychic conflict given by the client. Although clients may provide their own interpretations of these phenomena, Freud argued that people are biased observers of their own problems and thus that their interpretations cannot be accurate. Instead, accurate interpretation is best accomplished by undergoing therapy with a specially trained therapist. Therapists who currently practise psychoanalysis (or one of its modern forms) still emphasize interpretation as the basic means of uncovering the root causes of their clients' problems (e.g., Busch, 2003b; LaFarge, 2000).

While the psychoanalyst's primary role is interpretation, the client's main job is to provide the psychoanalyst with something to interpret: descriptions of his or her fears, anxieties, thoughts, or repressed memories. This is not an easy task for the client to accomplish because the client unconsciously invokes one or more defence mechanisms, which, as you recall from Chapter 14, prevent anxiety-provoking memories and ideas from reaching conscious awareness. Together, the psychoanalyst and client work for insight into the client's problems.

Freud (1933) felt that the "veil of amnesia" lifts the moment that insight is achieved. It is then that the client begins to understand the true nature of his or her problems. For some clients, insight is a sudden rush of profound understanding—sort of an "Ah-ha, so that's what was causing the problem!" experience. For other clients, perhaps the majority who undergo long-term therapy, the feeling may be more one of quiet accomplishment, such as that which comes after a long struggle that finally ends with success. Successful treatment depends not only on the psychoanalyst's interpretations, but also on ensuring that the patient has the capacity to understand and integrate what is learned in therapy (Busch, 2003a). In the case of Geoff in the prologue, psychodynamic therapy would have been less effective if he had not first been prescribed medication.

**free association** A psychoanalytic procedure in which the client is encouraged to speak freely, without censoring possibly embarrassing or socially unacceptable thoughts or ideas.

**resistance** A development during therapy in which the client becomes defensive, unconsciously attempting to halt further insight by censoring his or her true feelings.

**Psychoanalytic Techniques** Freud used **free association** to encourage the client to speak freely, without censoring possibly embarrassing or socially unacceptable thoughts. Freud achieved this goal in two ways. First, the client was encouraged to report any thoughts or images that came to mind, without worrying about their meaning. Second, Freud attempted to minimize any authoritative influence over the client's disclosures by eliminating eye contact. He usually sat in a chair at the head of a couch on which the client reclined.

Freud believed that dreams were a crucial component of psychoanalysis, and these were among the topics clients were encouraged to discuss. *Dream interpretation*, the evaluation of the underlying meaning of dream content, is a hallmark of psychoanalysis (Freud, 1900). But even dream content is subject to some censoring, according to Freud, so that the analyst must be able to distinguish between the dream's *manifest* and *latent* contents. Recall that the manifest content of a dream is the actual images and events that occur within the dream; latent content is the hidden meaning or significance of the dream. The manifest content masks the latent content because the latent content is anxiety provoking and causes the person psychological discomfort. Thus, the analyst must be especially skilled in recognizing the symbolic nature of dreams, for things are not always as they appear. For example, the client may relate the image of a growling, vicious dog chasing him or her down the street. The dog may actually symbolize an angry parent or spouse. The idea of a parent or spouse being angry and upset may be so painful to the client that it has been disguised within the dream. An important step toward insight, and thus solving the client's psychological problems, is helping the client appreciate the latent content of his or her dreams.

Insight is not achieved quickly, nor do clients always find it easy to disclose private aspects of their personal lives. In fact, there is something of a paradox involved in achieving insight, for the often painful or threatening knowledge resulting from insight is precisely what led to its repression in the first place. For example, a client may have to confront the reality of being abused as a child, or of being unloved, or of feeling peculiar, inferior, or out of place. Although the client wishes to be cured, he or she does not look forward to the anxiety and apprehension that may result from recalling painful memories. The client often becomes defensive at some point during therapy, unconsciously attempting to halt further insight by censoring his or her true feelings, a process Freud called **resistance**.

A psychoanalyst may conclude that resistance is operating when the client tries to change the topic, begins to miss

▲ *Freud refined his practice of psychoanalysis in this office, where he asked his patients to recline on the couch (far right) and to tell him about their childhood experiences, their dreams, and their anxieties. Freud's goal was to discover his patients' unconscious motivations for the problems they were experiencing.*

appointments for therapy, or suddenly forgets what he or she was about to say. The skilled therapist, who is not burdened by the client's resistance, recognizes such diversions and redirects the discussion to the sensitive topics while minimizing the pain of rediscovery.

Over a period of months or even years of therapy sessions taking place as often as several times a week, the client gradually becomes less inhibited, and the discussion begins to drift away from recent events to the more distant shores of early childhood. As the client re-lives aspects of childhood, he or she may begin to project powerful attitudes and emotions onto the therapist, a process called **transference**. The client may come to love or hate the therapist with the same intensity of the powerful emotions experienced in childhood toward parents or siblings.

Originally, Freud thought of transference as a distraction from the real issues, and as an impediment to therapy. He soon realized that the experience of transference was essential to the success of therapy (Connolly, Crits-Christoph, Barber, & Luborsky, 2000). Whereas free association uncovers many of the relevant events and facts of the client's life, transference provides the means for re-living significant early experiences. By becoming a substitute for the actual people in the client's life, the therapist acts as a tool for illuminating the conflicts of the unconscious.

Freud reasoned that the analyst, being human too, could just as easily project his or her emotions onto the client, a process he called **countertransference.** Unlike transference, Freud believed countertransference to be unhealthy and undesirable. To be effective, the analyst must remain emotionally detached and objective in his or her appraisal of the client's disclosures. For this reason, he argued that the analyst, in order to understand his or her own unconscious conflicts, should undergo complete analysis with another therapist.

Although Freud was not the first to talk about the unconscious mind, he was the first to develop a significant theory of abnormal behaviour (described in Chapter 14). He also developed an equally influential therapy designed to provide the client with insight into the unconscious motives that underlie behaviour. Psychoanalysis remains a force among contemporary therapeutic practices even a century after its founding, although its practice has undergone substantial modification.

**Modern Psychodynamic Therapy** **Psychodynamic therapy** differs from Freud's original psychoanalysis and refers to a collection of therapies that, though traceable to Freud's, nevertheless depart from its tenets in substantive ways. For example, although psychodynamic therapies still focus on achieving insight into the unconscious, they tend to place less emphasis on psychosexual development and more emphasis on social and interpersonal experiences, including the complex structure and dynamics of self.

Psychodynamic therapists view the ego as playing a more active role in influencing a person's thoughts and actions. Rather than functioning merely to mediate between the demands of the id and superego, they believe that the ego is a proactive component in a person's overall psychological functioning. In other words, compared to Freud, psychodynamic therapists see the ego as having more control over the unconscious. Thus, people receiving psychodynamic therapy today are seen as being less constrained by the mind's unconscious forces than Freud had asserted (Kennedy, 2007).

Although Freud considered analysis extremely involved and demanding, often requiring years to complete, today's therapists feel that much can be gained by shortening the process and by lessening the client's dependence on the therapist (Binder, 1998; Travis, Bliwise, Binder, & Horne-Moyer, 2001). In some cases, intermittent therapy may be appropriate (Paris, 2007). With intermittent psychodynamic therapy, clients do not continuously see a therapist. Rather, they often take lengthy breaks from therapy, or stop altogether and return only when a need arises. Psychodynamic therapy, as presently practised, does not always take years to complete (e.g., Abbass, Sheldon, Gyra, Kalpin, 2008).

Another form of psychodynamic therapy is *brief psychodynamic therapy*, which takes about 10 to 25 sessions to complete (Messer, 2001). The goal of the therapist is to understand and improve the client's interpersonal skills through the interpretation of transference processes. This therapy is based on Freud's belief that our early experiences with others influence the dynamics of our current relationships. Brief psychodynamic therapy focuses on a client's schemata for interpersonal relationships and attempts to modify those that

**transference** The process by which a client begins to project powerful attitudes and emotions onto the therapist.

**countertransference** The process by which the therapist projects his or her emotions onto the client.

**psychodynamic therapy** A variation on the Freudian approach to therapy in which therapists search for unconscious conflicts and motivations but do not adhere strictly to Freud's conception of psychoanalysis.

are errant or that otherwise prevent the client from developing fulfilling relationships with others. Consider, for example, the following case (Prochaska & Norcross, 2003).

> Karen was about to be terminated from her nursing program if her problems were not resolved. She had always been a competent student who seemed to get along well with peers and patients. Now, since the beginning of her rotation on 3 South, a surgical ward, she was plagued by headaches and dizzy spells. Of more serious consequence were the two medical errors she made when dispensing medications to patients. She realized that these errors could have proved fatal, and she was as concerned as her nursing faculty about why such problems had begun in the final year of her education. Karen knew she had many negative feelings toward the head nurse on 3 South, but she did not believe these feelings could account for her current dilemma. She entered psychotherapy.
>
> After a few weeks of psychotherapy, the therapist realized that one of Karen's important conflicts revolved around the death of her father when she was 12 years old. She remembered how upset she was when her father had a heart attack and had to be rushed the hospital. For a while it looked as though her father was going to pull through, and Karen began enjoying her daily visits to see him. During one of these visits, her father clutched his chest in obvious pain and told Karen to get a nurse. She remembered how helpless she felt when she could not find a nurse, although she did not recall why this was so difficult. Her search seemed endless, and by the time she finally found a nurse, her father was dead.
>
> The therapist asked Karen the name of the ward on which her father had died. She paused and thought, and then she blurted out, "3 South." She cried at length as she told how confused she was and how angry she felt toward the nurses on the ward for not being more readily available, although she thought they might have been involved with another emergency. After weeping and shaking and expressing her resentment, Karen felt calm and relaxed for the first time in months. Her symptoms disappeared, and her problems in the nursing program were relieved. (Taken from Butcher, Mineka, & Hooley, 2007, pp. 630–631)

All forms of psychodynamic therapy share in common an interest in unconscious processes. An important corollary attaches itself to this emphasis: Behaviour or overt action is seldom important by itself. Rather, behaviour is only important to the extent that it serves as a manifestation of the real, underlying motive or conflict. But, as we will see in the next section, not all therapists agree with this idea.

**humanistic therapy** A form of therapy focusing on the person's unique potential for personal growth and self-actualization.
**client-centred therapy** A form of therapy in which the client is allowed to decide what to talk about without strong direction and judgment from the therapist.
**incongruence** A discrepancy between a client's real and ideal selves.

## Humanistic Therapy

In strong contrast to psychoanalysis, which may be considered to offer a darker view of humankind, the aim of another insight therapy, **humanistic therapy**, is to provide the client with a greater understanding of his or her unique potential for personal growth and self-actualization. Humanistic therapies proceed from the assumption that people are inherently good and have innate worth. Psychological problems represent an impediment hampering a person's potential for personal growth. The aim of therapy is to overcome this impediment and thereby retrieve the potential anew. The two major forms of humanistic therapy are client-centred therapy and Gestalt therapy.

**Client-Centred Therapy** Carl Rogers (1902–1987) developed the first humanistic therapy in the 1940s, creating a major alternative to psychoanalysis. His approach has had a major impact on therapy generally (Watson, 2007; see Freeth, 2007, for a view of its impact in the United Kingdom specifically). Rogers found the formalism of psychoanalysis too confining and its emphasis on intrapsychic conflict too pessimistic (Tobin, 1991). His discontent led him to develop his own theory of personality, abnormal behaviour, and therapy. His **client-centred therapy** is so named because of the respect given the client during therapy: The client decides what to talk about without direction or judgment from the therapist. The client takes ultimate responsibility for resolving his or her problems. The focus of the therapy is on the client, not on a method or rigid theory.

Rogers believed that the cause of many psychological problems can be traced to people's perceptions of themselves as they actually are (their *real selves*) as differing from the people they would like to be (their *ideal selves*). Rogers called this discrepancy between the real and the ideal perceptions of the self **incongruence**. The goal of client-centred therapy is to reduce incongruence by fostering experiences that will make attainment of the ideal self possible.

Because the client's and not the therapist's thoughts direct the course of therapy, the therapist strives to make those thoughts, perceptions, and feelings more noticeable to the client. This is frequently done through *reflection*, sensitive rephrasing or mirroring of the client's statements. For example:

> *Client*: I get so frustrated at my parents. They just don't understand how I feel. They don't know what it's like to be me.
>
> *Therapist*: You seem to be saying that the things that are important to you aren't very important to your parents. You'd like them now and then to see things from your perspective.

By reflecting the concerns of the client, the therapist demonstrates *empathy*, or the ability to perceive the world from another's viewpoint. The establishment of empathy is key in encouraging the client to deal with the incongruence between the real and the ideal selves.

For Rogers (1951, p. 20), the "worth and significance of the individual" is a basic ground rule of therapy. This theme

▲ *Carl Rogers (top right) taught his clients that personal growth is best achieved through the experience of unconditional positive regard.*

is represented in therapy through **unconditional positive regard**, in which the therapist tries to convey to the client that his or her worth as a human being is not dependent on anything he or she does, says, feels, or thinks.

In client-centred therapy, the therapist unconditionally accepts the client and approves of him or her as a person so that the client can come to understand that his or her feelings are worthwhile and important. We should be clear on an important point. Acceptance and approval of the person does not necessarily mean approval and acceptance of his or her behaviour. A client-centred therapist may hate the behaviour of a client if, for instance, another person has been harmed by the client. The key is that the therapist has an abiding belief in the core value and humanity of the client. The behaviour may be bad and unacceptable, but the true nature of the client is good. Once the client begins to feel valued in the therapeutic context, a self-healing process begins. For example, at first, a client usually has difficulty expressing feelings verbally. The therapist tries to understand the feelings underlying the client's confused state and to help the client put them into words. Through this process, the client learns to understand and heed his or her own drive toward self-actualization. Consider the following example:

> *Alice*: I was thinking about this business of standards. I somehow developed a sort of knack, I guess, of—well—habit—of trying to make people feel at ease around me, or to make things go along smoothly. . . .
>
> *Counsellor*: In other words, what you did was always in the direction of trying to keep things smooth and to make other people feel better and to smooth the situation.
>
> *A:* Yes. I think that's what it was. Now the reason why I did it probably was—I mean, not that I was a good little Samaritan going around making other people happy, but that was probably the role that felt easiest for me to play. I'd been doing it around the home so much. I just didn't stand up for my own convictions, until I don't know whether I have any convictions to stand up for.
>
> *C:* You feel that for a long time you've been playing the role of kind of smoothing out the frictions or differences or what not. . . .
>
> *A:* M-hum.
>
> *C:* Rather than having any opinion or reaction of your own in the situation. Is that it?
>
> *A:* That's it. Or that I haven't been really honestly being myself, or actually knowing what my real self is, and that I've been just playing a sort of false role. Whatever role no one else was playing, and that needed to be played at the time, I'd try to fill it in. (Rogers, 1951, pp. 152–153)

As this example illustrates, in Rogers' view the therapist should not manipulate the course of therapy but should create conditions under which the client can achieve his or her own insights and make his or her own decisions. Thus, the therapist in the conversation sought to confirm the client's perception of the role she had played at home and elsewhere—that of facilitator or peacemaker. The therapist then asked the client to confirm her view that having played the role for so long had left her unsure of whether she had anything of her own to offer. Doing so allowed the client to acknowledge that perhaps she had not been honest, that she had been playing a false role—a role no one else was playing at the time but that seemed called for. In doing so, she disclosed that she really didn't know what her real self was. For Rogers' purposes, this was an important achievement on the client's part.

**Gestalt Therapy** The development of client-centred therapy owes much to its founder's disenchantment with classical psychoanalysis. For much the same reason, Fritz Perls (1893–1970), though trained in Freudian techniques, disengaged himself from orthodox psychoanalysis and founded **Gestalt therapy** (Perls, 1969). Gestalt therapy emphasizes the unity of mind and body by teaching the client to "get in touch" with bodily sensations and emotional feelings long hidden from awareness. Gestalt therapy places exclusive emphasis on present experience—not on the past—and the Gestalt therapist will often be quite confrontational, challenging the client to deal honestly with his or her emotions.

Similar to Freud, Perls believed that dreams are a rich source of information and that one must be able to understand their symbolism. In Gestalt therapy, the therapist will often have the client adopt the perspective of some person or even some object in the dream in an empathic manner.

Another tool of Gestalt therapists is the *empty chair technique*, in which the client imagines that he or she is talking

**unconditional positive regard** According to Rogers, the therapeutic expression that a client's worth as a human being is not dependent on anything that he or she does, says, feels, or thinks.

**Gestalt therapy** A form of therapy emphasizing the unity of mind and body by teaching the client to "get in touch" with unconscious bodily sensations and emotional feelings.

to someone sitting in the chair beside him or her. This technique derives from Perls' belief that, for all of us, our memories, fears, and feelings of guilt affect our ongoing relationships with others. For example, a woman may be asked to say the things she always wanted to say to her deceased father but didn't while he was alive. The empty chair technique allows her to experience in the here and now the feelings and perceptions she might have suppressed while her father was alive. It also allows her to express these feelings and to gain insight into how these feelings currently influence her perception of herself and her world. The Gestalt therapist also encourages the client to gain a better understanding of his or her feelings by talking to himself or herself (to different parts of his or her personality) and to inanimate objects. Any attempt by the client to avoid the reality of his or her situation is challenged by the therapist, who constantly attempts to keep the client's attention focused on present problems and tries to guide the client toward an honest confrontation with these problems. Perls (1967, p. 331) argued, "In the safe emergency of the therapeutic situation, the neurotic discovers that the world does not fall to pieces if he or she gets angry, sexy, joyous, mournful."

## Evaluation of Insight Therapies

As we have previously learned, the processes proposed by psychoanalytic theory have not been subjected to a great deal of empirical scrutiny until relatively recently (e.g., Baumeister, Dale, & Sommer, 1998; Charman, 2004). Nevertheless, we should be able to assess the effectiveness of the psychoanalytic method—after all, it is results that count. However, evaluating the effectiveness of classical psychoanalysis is difficult because only a small proportion of people with psychological disorders qualify for this method of treatment. To participate in this kind of therapy, a client must be intelligent, articulate, and motivated enough to spend three or more hours a week working hard to uncover unconscious conflicts. These qualifications rule out many people with active psychoses, as well as people who lack the time and money to devote to such a long-term project.

Fonagy and his British colleagues (Fonagy, Roth, & Higgitt, 2005) spelled out the enormous practical and technical challenges to validly and reliably demonstrating the effectiveness of psychoanalytic and psychodynamic therapies, especially when the gold standard for such demonstration is the use of randomized controlled trials (RCT; that is, assigning clients to particular therapies on a randomized basis). Their findings are comparable to those of Leichsenring (2005), a German researcher who reviewed 22 studies of clinical outcomes involving RCT published between 1960 and 2004. The studies involved several disorders, including depressive, post-traumatic stress, somatoform, eating, personality, and substance-related disorders. Leichsenring concluded that psychoanalytic therapy is more effective than no treatment and also more effective than shorter forms of psychodynamic therapy. The latter conclusion was qualified by Finnish researchers (Knekt et al., 2008), who reported a longitudinal study in which they measured symptoms of depression and anxiety for a three-year period after treatment began. They found that short-term psychodynamic therapy produced a greater reduction of symptoms (approximately 20 percent lower) during the first year than did long-term psychodynamic therapy. However, the two therapies were approximately equivalent in effectiveness during the second year. By the third year, long-term therapy had become more effective (approximately 25 percent greater reduction of symptoms).

Rogers stimulated a considerable amount of research on the effectiveness of client-centred therapy. He recorded therapeutic sessions so that various techniques could be evaluated. One researcher, Charles Truax (1966), obtained permission from Rogers (and his clients) to record some therapy sessions, and he classified the statements made by the clients into several categories. One of the categories included statements of improving mental health, such as "I'm feeling better lately" or "I don't feel as depressed as I used to." After each of the patients' statements, Truax noted Rogers' reaction to see whether he gave a positive response. Typical positive responses were "Oh, really? Tell me more" or "Uh-huh. That's nice" or just a friendly "Mm." Truax found that of the eight categories of client statements, only those that indicated progress were regularly followed by a positive response from Rogers. Not surprisingly, during their therapy, the clients made more and more statements indicating progress.

This study attests to the power of social reinforcement and its occurrence in unexpected places. Rogers was an effective and conscientious psychotherapist, but he had not intended to single out and reinforce his clients' realistic expressions of progress in therapy. (Of course, he did not uncritically reinforce exaggerated or unrealistic positive statements.) This finding does not discredit client-centred therapy. Rogers simply adopted a very effective strategy for altering a person's behaviour. He used to refer to his therapy as *non-directive*; however, when he realized that he was reinforcing positive statements, he stopped referring to it as non-directive because it obviously was not.

As with most insight therapies, neither client-centred therapy nor Gestalt therapy is generally appropriate for serious problems such as psychoses. They are most effective for people who are motivated enough to want to change and who are intelligent enough to be able to gain some insight concerning their problems. Some of these problems include coping with everyday stressors as well as experiencing excessive anxiety and fear.

Humanistic therapies are much more affordable and less time consuming than traditional psychoanalysis. Many people would probably enjoy and profit from talking about their problems with a person as sympathetic as Carl Rogers or as direct and honest as Fritz Perls. Rogers' insights into the dynamics of the client–therapist relationship have had a major impact on the field of psychotherapy (Hill & Nakayama, 2000).

A meta-analysis of nearly 100 published studies of humanistic psychotherapy, including non-directive, client-centred therapy and Gestalt therapy, was reported by Elliott (2002). The studies were conducted in North America and Europe and largely involved clients with depressive, anxiety, and personality disorders. Few of the studies involved RCT. Humanistic therapies were more effective than no treatment and maintained their relative effectiveness beyond 12 months. Overall, there was a tendency for more directive therapies (specifically, cognitive-behaviour therapies) to be more effective.

## Interim Summary

### Insight Therapies

Insight therapies are based primarily on conversation between therapist and client. The oldest form of insight therapy, psychoanalysis, was devised by Freud. Psychoanalysis attempts to discover the forces that are warring in the client's psyche and to resolve these inner conflicts by bringing to consciousness his or her unconscious drives and the defences that have been established against them. Insight is believed to be the primary source of healing.

Humanistic therapy emphasizes conscious, deliberate mental processes, whereas the classic psychoanalytic approach regards human behaviour as motivated by intrapsychic conflict and biological urges. Client-centred therapy is based on the premise that people are basically healthy and good and that their problems result from faulty thinking. Instead of evaluating themselves in terms of their own self-concepts, they judge themselves by other people's standards. This tendency is rectified by providing an environment of unconditional positive regard in which clients can find their own way to good mental health. Gestalt therapy focuses on convincing clients that they must deal honestly with their present feelings in order to become more mentally healthy. According to Gestalt therapists, the key to becoming happier is to confront one's fears and guilt and to keep one's emotions in proper perspective.

Among the drawbacks of insight therapies is the relatively narrow range of people that may benefit by undergoing such therapy. In general, the people who seem most likely to benefit from insight psychotherapy are those who are intelligent and able to articulate their problems. Insight therapies generally are not effective with persons with serious psychological disorders, such as schizophrenia.

#### QUESTIONS TO CONSIDER

1. If you had some personal psychological problems, which kind of therapy—psychodynamic or humanistic—would you choose to use to resolve them? What factors would influence your choice?
2. Suppose that you were able to interview Freud, Rogers, and Perls. What sorts of questions would you ask each of them, and why would their answers to those questions be of interest to you?

# Behaviour and Cognitive-Behaviour Therapies

Insight therapies are based on the assumption that understanding leads to behavioural change. Once a person gains insight into the causes of his or her maladaptive behaviour, that behaviour will cease and will be replaced by adaptive behaviour. In reality, however, insight is *not* always followed by behavioural change.

In contrast, the fundamental assumption made by behaviour therapists is that people learn maladaptive or self-defeating behaviour in the same way that they learn adaptive behaviour. Undesirable behaviour, such as nail biting or alcohol abuse, is the problem, not just a reflection of the problem. The methods that behaviour therapists use to induce behaviour change are extensions of classical and operant conditioning principles. Quite literally, Pavlov's study of the conditional salivary reflex in dogs and Skinner's research on operant behaviour in pigeons and rats have yielded techniques for improving the quality of life for many people.

## Therapies Based on Classical Conditioning

Remember that in classical conditioning, a previously neutral stimulus (ultimately the CS) comes to elicit the same response as a stimulus (UCS) that naturally elicits that response because the CS reliably predicts the UCS. According to Joseph Wolpe (1958), one of the founders of behaviour therapy, many of our everyday fears and anxieties become associated with neutral stimuli through coincidence. Consider an example: Suppose that you are involved in a car accident, and although you are not seriously hurt you are upset for some time afterwards. When you get into a car for the first time after the accident, a sudden feeling of terror comes over you. You begin to perspire and breathe heavily, you feel that you are about to pass out, and it's all you can do to get out of the car without screaming. Your anxiety in response to getting into a car may be due to classical conditioning in which the pain and fear associated with the accident (the UCSs) are now associated with cars (CS).

**Systematic Desensitization** One behaviour therapy technique, developed by Wolpe, has been especially successful in eliminating some kinds of fears and phobias. This technique, called **systematic desensitization**, is designed to remove the unpleasant emotional response produced by the feared object or situation and replace it with an incompatible one—relaxation.

The first step of this technique is for the client and therapist to construct a *hierarchy* of anxiety-related stimuli.

**systematic desensitization** A method of treatment in which the client is trained to relax in the presence of increasingly fearful stimuli.

▲ *People who are treated with systematic desensitization for their phobias often show remarkable positive changes in their behaviour; for example, this person has overcome an intense fear of snakes.*

**TABLE 18•1 Sample Fear Hierarchy for Phobia of Spiders**

1. Abbie [neighbor] tells you she saw one in her garage.
2. Abbie sees you, crosses the street, says there's a tiny one across the street.
3. Betty [at work] says there's one downstairs.
4. Friends downstairs say they saw one outside their apartment and disposed of it.
5. Carrie [daughter] returns from camp; says the restrooms were inhabited by spiders.
6. You see a small, dark spot out of the corner of your eye; you have a closer look; it isn't a spider.
7. You are with your husband. You see a tiny spider on a thread outside, but you can't see it very clearly.
8. You are alone. You see a tiny spider on a thread outside, but you can't see it very clearly.
9. You are reading the paper, and you see a cartoonist's caricature of a spider (with a human-like face and smile).
10. You are reading an article about the Brown Recluse.
11. You see a clear photograph of a spider's web in the newspaper.
12. You see a spider's web on the stairs at work.
13. You suddenly see a loose tomato-top in your salad.
14. You open a kitchen cabinet and suddenly see a large spider.

*Source: Thorpe, G. L., & Olson, S. L. (1990).* Behavior therapy: Concepts, procedures, and applications. *Boston: Allyn and Bacon. Reprinted by permission.*

**Table 18•1** presents a hierarchy constructed with a person who suffered from arachnophobia, an intense fear of spiders (Thorpe & Olson, 1990). The situations provoking the least amount of fear are at the top. Next, the client is trained to achieve complete relaxation. The essential task is to learn to respond quickly to suggestions to feel relaxed and peaceful so that these suggestions can elicit an immediate relaxation response.

Finally, the conditional stimuli (fear-eliciting situations) are paired with stimuli that elicit the learned relaxation response. For example, a person with a fear of spiders is instructed to relax and then to imagine hearing from a neighbour that she saw a spider in her garage (the least fearsome event in the hierarchy). If the client reports no anxiety, he or she is instructed to move to the next, slightly more threatening, item in the hierarchy and to imagine hearing a neighbour say that there is a tiny spider across the street; and so on. Whenever the client begins feeling anxious, he or she signals to the therapist with some predetermined gesture—say, by raising a finger. The therapist instructs the client to relax and, if necessary, describes a less threatening scene. The client is not permitted to feel severe anxiety at any time. Gradually, over a series of sessions (the average is 11), the client is able to get through the entire list, vicariously experiencing even the most feared encounters while remaining in a relaxed state.

Scientific evaluations of systematic desensitization have been positive, and several experiments have found that all elements of the procedure are necessary for its success. For example, a person will not get rid of a phobia merely by participating in relaxation training or by constructing hierarchies of fear-producing situations. Only *pairings* of the anxiety-producing stimuli with instructions to relax will reduce the fear. One testimonial comes from a study by Johnson and Sechrest (1968), which attempted to reduce the fear of taking examinations in a group of university students. Students who underwent systematic desensitization received significantly higher grades on their final examination in a psychology course than did students who were also taking the course but who received either no treatment or relaxation training alone.

Whereas practitioners of systematic desensitization are careful not to permit their clients to become too anxious, practitioners of another form of exposure therapy arrange for the client to confront the feared stimulus directly. Using **in vivo exposure**, therapists attempt to rid their clients of fears by arousing those very fears at an intense level until the clients' responses diminish through extinction; that is, the clients learn that nothing bad happens when they are directly exposed to the fear-eliciting stimuli. Of course, the client is protected from any adverse physical effects of the encounter, so there are no dangerous consequences. This does not mean that every client is equally amenable to in vivo exposure. Sudden, intense fear may produce unhealthy jumps in blood pressure, fainting, or vigorous efforts to escape the situation—all of which are counterproductive for the desired outcome. Thus, it is important for therapists to consult with clients in advance about possible effects and to determine whether

**in vivo exposure** A form of therapy in which clients are exposed to intense levels of a feared stimuli in an attempt to diminish the fear through extinction.

more gradual exposure is warranted or whether an imaginal form of therapy might be more effective.

In **imaginal exposure**, the therapist describes, as graphically as possible, the most frightening possible encounters with the object of a client's phobia rather than arranging for actual encounters. The client tries to imagine the encounter and to experience intense fear. Eventually the fear response begins to subside, and the client learns that even the worst imaginable encounter can become tolerable. In other words, the client's long-entrenched avoidance responses have become extinguished. Exposure via virtual reality has become an effective form of exposure therapy (Rothbaum et al., 2002). Overall, exposure therapies have proven to be a very successful form of treatment for anxiety disorders (Emmelkamp, 2004).

**Aversion Therapy** Sometimes people are attracted by inappropriate stimuli that most of us would ignore, and they engage in maladaptive behaviour as a result of this attraction. Sexual attraction to children is one striking example. A behaviour technique called **aversion therapy** is sometimes effective in changing these behaviours. In aversion therapy, a negative reaction to a neutral stimulus is caused by pairing it with an aversive stimulus (UCS). Aversion therapy attempts to establish an unpleasant response (such as a feeling of fear or disgust) to the object that produces the undesired behaviour. For example, a man who is sexually attracted to children might be given painful electric shocks when a special apparatus detects an erectile response while he is being shown pictures of children. Aversive therapy has also been used to treat fetishes (such as sexual attraction to women's shoes), drinking, smoking, transvestism, exhibitionism, and overeating. Sometimes drugs that cause nausea (called *emetics*) are paired with the ingestion of alcohol in the treatment of problem drinking. Aversion therapy has been shown to be moderately effective for some problems, such as reducing craving among cocaine abusers (Bordnick et al., 2004). Nevertheless, the treatment is disturbing to many people because it can be characterized as punishment for having a psychological disorder (Howard, Elkins, Rimmele, & Smith, 1991). It is worth knowing that the venerable Skinner (1988) himself was opposed to aversion therapy. Because the method raises serious ethical questions and can involve significant pain, the client's participation must be voluntary. Overall, the use of aversion therapy is waning (Emmelkamp, 2004).

## Therapies Based on Operant Conditioning

**Behaviour modification**, a general term describing therapy based on operant conditioning principles, involves altering maladaptive behaviour by rearranging the contingencies between behaviour and its consequences. Increases in desirable behaviour can be brought about through either positive or negative reinforcement and undesirable behaviour can be reduced through either extinction or punishment. Practitioners have extended the use of operant principles to a wide array of behaviours and circumstances—for example, to weight management; compliance with medical regimens; and treatment of anorexia nervosa, bedwetting, and smoking (Kazdin, 1994; Martin & Pear, 2006). Behaviour modification techniques can be found in a number of settings, such as hospitals, schools, daycare centres, businesses, and even around the home (Kazdin, 2001).

**Reinforcement of Adaptive Behaviours** Behavioural techniques are often used to alter the behaviour of emotionally disturbed people, and those with mental retardation, for whom communication is difficult. Reinforcement, which was described in Chapter 7, can be a powerful method of behavioural change. If the therapist has established a warm relationship with the client, he or she can use ordinary social reinforcers, such as signs of approval (friendly smiles and nods of the head), to encourage positive behavioural change. As we saw in the section on client-centred therapy, even nonbehavioural psychologists use reinforcement—deliberately or inadvertently—to produce behavioural change.

**Token Economies** The behaviour-analytic approach sometimes has been used on a large scale in mental institutions with success. Residents are often asked to do chores to engage them in active participation in their environment. In some instances, other specific behaviours are also targeted as desirable and therapeutic, such as helping residents who have more severe problems. To promote these social behaviours, therapists have designed **token economies:** A list of tasks is compiled, and residents receive tokens as rewards for performing the tasks; later, they can exchange these tokens for snacks, other desired articles, or various privileges. The tokens become conditioned reinforcers for desirable and appropriate behaviours. **Figure 18•3** shows the strong effects of the contingencies of a pay scale used in a token economy established by Ayllon and Azrin (1968). The amount of time spent performing the desirable behaviours was high when reinforcement contingencies were imposed and low when they were not.

Implementation with token economies can be difficult. Although token economies are based on a simple principle, they require the co-operation of everyone involved. A mental institution includes patients, caretakers, housekeeping staff, and professional staff. If a token economy is to be effective, all staff members who deal with residents must learn how the system works; ideally, they should also understand

**imaginal exposure** A form of therapy in which the therapist provides a client with graphic descriptions of a feared object; its goal is to diminish fear by extinguishing avoidance responses.
**aversion therapy** A form of treatment in which the client is trained to respond negatively to a neutral stimulus that has been paired with an aversive stimulus.
**behaviour modification** Behaviour therapy based on the principles of operant conditioning.
**token economy** A program often used in institutions in which a person's adaptive behaviour is reinforced with tokens that can be exchanged for desirable goods or special privileges.

FIGURE 18•3 The effectiveness of a token economy. The effects of a token economy system of reinforcement on patients' performance of specified chores.

*(From Teodoro Ayllon and Nathan Azrin,* The Token Economy: A Motivational System for Therapy and Rehabilitation, *© 1968, pp. 249–250, 252. Reprinted by permission of Prentice-Hall, Inc., Englewood Cliffs, N.J.)*

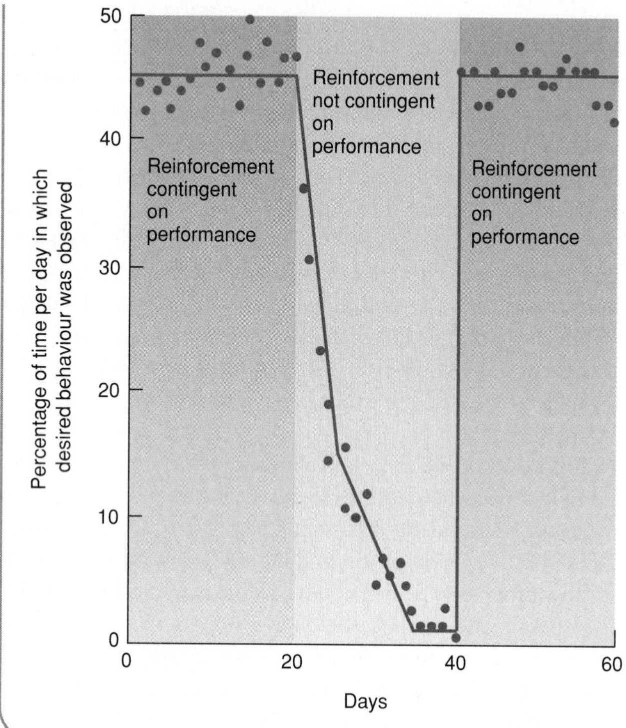


and agree with its underlying principles. A token economy can easily be sabotaged by a few people who believe that the system is foolish, wrong, or in some way threatening to themselves. If these obstacles can be overcome, token economies may work very well (Corrigan, 1995), especially in combination with other treatments (Dickerson, Tenhula, & Green-Paden, 2005). But we must also bear in mind the *overjustification effect* described in Chapter 13. Token economies use the promise of rewards to instigate activities in which people would otherwise not engage. Sometimes, for purposes of efficiency, the reward contingencies are applied to everyone in a specific area or ward of the institution, regardless of whether every individual needs to be motivated by extrinsic rewards. In such cases, there is a risk that people for whom the extrinsic rewards are superfluous may lose their intrinsic motivation.

**Modelling** Humans (and many other animals) are able to learn without directly experiencing an event. People can imitate the behaviour of other people, watching what they do and, if the conditions are appropriate, performing the same behaviour (Bandura, 1986). This capability provides the basis for the technique of modelling. Behaviour therapists have found that clients can make much better progress when they have access to a model who provides samples of successful behaviours to imitate. Bandura (1971) described a modelling session with people who had a phobic fear of snakes:

> The therapist himself performed the fearless behavior at each step and gradually led subjects into touching, stroking, and then holding the snake's body with gloved and bare hands while the experimenter held the snake securely by head and tail. If a subject was unable to touch the snake following ample demonstration, she was asked to place her hand on the experimenter's and to move her hand down gradually until it touched the snake's body. After subjects no longer felt any apprehension about touching the snake under these secure conditions, anxieties about contact with the snake's head area and entwining tail were extinguished. The therapist again performed the tasks fearlessly, and then he and the subject performed the responses jointly; as subjects became less fearful, the experimenter gradually reduced his participation and control over the snake, until eventually subjects were able to hold the snake in their laps without assistance, to let the snake loose in the room and retrieve it, and to let it crawl freely over their bodies. Progress through the graded approach tasks was paced according to the subjects' apprehensiveness. When they reported being able to perform one activity with little or no fear, they were eased into a more difficult interaction. (p. 680)

This treatment eliminated fear of snakes in 92 percent of the people who participated. Modelling is successful for several reasons. People learn to make new responses by imitating those of the therapist and, in doing so, their behaviour is reinforced. When they observe a confident person approaching and touching a feared object without showing any signs of emotional distress, they probably experience a vicarious extinction of their own emotional responses. In fact, Bandura (1971) reports that "having successfully overcome a phobia that had plagued them for most of their lives, people reported increased confidence that they could cope effectively with other fear-provoking events" (p. 684), including encounters with other people.

Modelling has been used to establish new behaviours as well as to eliminate fears. Sex therapists have used specially prepared films or videotapes showing explicit sexual activity to help clients overcome inhibitions that are interfering with their sexual relations with their partners. Other therapists have acted out examples of useful, appropriate social exchanges for clients whose maladaptive behaviours usually prevent such interactions. As we shall see in a later section, modelling is an important aspect of almost all forms of group therapy.

**Assertiveness Therapy** Assertiveness therapy is a procedure for developing coping skills in interpersonal situations in which a client might feel anxiety or be unable to function as effectively as he or she would like. Assertiveness therapy is often used to help clients who feel frustrated at not being able to speak up to defend their rights, especially in those situations in which others are trying to take advantage of them or to otherwise compromise their values or moral standards.

The first step in assertiveness therapy is to identify the variables that are causing the client to feel distressed. For instance, suppose that the client's boss is taking advantage of her and she is afraid to speak up for fear of losing her job. Once the variables controlling the situation are identified, the client practises assertive behaviours in the confines of therapy. For example, the client may practise confronting her boss with her feelings and requesting that he treat her more respectfully. Once the assertive behaviours are well practised, the therapist encourages the client to apply her new skills to real-life situations. At the same time, the client is also encouraged to develop more effective interpersonal skills. Thus, rather than merely taking more abuse from her boss, the client would learn to approach her boss tactfully to let him know her feelings. For example, if her boss makes a rude remark toward her, she may say, "Are you feeling okay today? Has something made you upset?" With this response, the client has carefully centred the situation on the boss in a non-threatening way.

Assertive behaviour is believed to be incompatible with anxious behaviour. That is, behaving assertively appears to inhibit anxious behaviours, leading to the development of more effective interpersonal skills. In those situations when people experience frustration, failure, and anxiety due to their inability to speak up for themselves or otherwise get their points across, assertiveness therapy is particularly effective.

**Extinction of Maladaptive Behaviours** Recall that *extinction* is the process through which behaviour is eliminated by removing previously available reinforcers. While it is seldom used by itself to combat undesirable behaviour, extinction is often combined with other methods in behaviour modification programs. For example, extinction might be used to eliminate a child's tantrum behaviours. If the tantrum behaviours have been reinforced—parents or caretakers have given in to the child's wishes—extinction might include ignoring the child's undesirable behaviour.

▲ *A treatment strategy that is often effective in reducing tantrum behaviours in children is extinction—simply ignoring the behaviours.*

There are two potential problems with using extinction. One is *extinction burst*. When a reinforcer that has previously followed a behaviour is no longer forthcoming, that behaviour will often intensify. You can imagine, for example, how a child whose tantrum behaviour usually meets with social attention will likely increase his or her efforts to obtain these reinforcers during the early stages of extinction. Fortunately, extinction burst is temporary, and if the extinction procedure is carried out, behaviour generally diminishes.

The other problem with using extinction is that it is not always possible to eliminate the reinforcer that maintains undesirable behaviour. For example, aggressive behaviour in the classroom may be reinforced by the peer group, so attempts by a teacher to extinguish aggression may be only minimally effective. Extinction is also not the technique of choice when the client has direct control of the reinforcer, such as in thumb sucking.

**Punishment of Maladaptive Behaviours** In general, punishment is not nearly as good a treatment method as positive reinforcement (Mazur, 2005). For one thing, the person who is being punished may learn to fear or dislike the person who administers the punishment. If this person is the therapist, such an occurrence will probably interfere with other aspects of therapy. Second, there is a tendency to *overgeneralize*—to avoid performing a whole class of responses related to the response that is specifically being punished. For example, a child might not tell her father any more lies after being punished for doing so, but she might also stop sharing her secrets with him. Unfortunately, it is usually easier to punish a response than it is to figure out how to reinforce other responses that will replace the undesirable one. And when we are angry, we often find that it is satisfying to punish someone.

However, in some therapeutic situations, especially those in which the undesirable response is clearly harmful to the client, punishment is the most effective technique for eliminating an undesirable behaviour. Cowart and Whaley (1971) reported the case of an emotionally disturbed child who persisted in self-mutilation. He banged his head against the floor until it was a swollen mass of cuts and bruises. As a result, he had to be restrained in his crib in a hospital. The consequences of such confinement are serious for a child's development. After conventional techniques had failed, the therapist attached a pair of wires to the child's leg and placed him in a room with a padded floor. The child immediately began to batter his head against the floor, and the therapist administered an electrical shock through the wires. The shock, which was certainly less damaging than the blows to the head, stopped the child short. He seemed more startled than anything else. He started banging his head against the floor again and received another shock. After a few repetitions of this sequence, the boy stopped his self-mutilation and could safely be let out of his crib.

The use of aversive methods raises ethical issues, particularly when the individual is so severely impaired that he or she is unable to give informed consent to a particular therapeutic procedure. Carr and Lovaas (1983) state that aversive methods involving stimuli such as electric shock should be used as the last resort. They should be used only when the patient's behaviour poses a serious threat to his or her own well-being and after the following methods have been employed unsuccessfully: reinforcing other behaviours, attempting to extinguish the maladaptive behaviours, temporarily removing the patient from the environment that reinforces the maladaptive behaviours (a method called *time out*), and trying to arrange for the patient to perform behaviours that are incompatible with the maladaptive ones.

Sometimes, the appropriate response need not actually be performed in the presence of the therapist but can be practised vicariously. In a method called **covert sensitization**, instead of experiencing an actual punishing stimulus after performing an actual behaviour, the client imagines that he or she is performing an undesirable behaviour and then imagines receiving an aversive stimulus. For example, Thorpe and Olson (1990) describe the case of Frank, a man in his late twenties with a variety of social problems, including exhibitionism. He would drive far from his home town and expose his genitals to unsuspecting strangers. Although he derived sexual pleasure from this practice, he was disturbed by it and wanted desperately to be able to stop.

The therapist used a variety of methods to help the client improve his social skills and reduce his anxiety. In addition, the therapist used covert sensitization to eliminate the exhibitionism. The client was encouraged to imagine vivid scenes such as the following:

> He was driving around in his car, looking for a suitable victim. A woman, walking alone, appeared. Frank stopped the car and got out. He began to loosen his clothing. He was feeling strongly aroused sexually. Suddenly a police car pulled up, its lights flashing and its siren wailing. The officers looked on Frank with contempt as they handcuffed him. At the same time one of Frank's workmates arrived on the scene. This workmate was the biggest gossip at the factory. News of Frank's arrest would soon be all over town. He would obviously lose his job. His crime would be reported in the local newspaper. Frank felt physically sick with shame. He thought ahead to the prospect of a long jail sentence in protective custody as a sex offender. (Thorpe & Olson, 1990, p. 17)

The most successful treatment for autistic disorder is a form of behaviour therapy developed by Ivar Lovaas (1987, 2003). It has a wide range of applications in mental hospitals, school, homes, and other settings and is noteworthy for its intensiveness (Hillman & Snyder, 2007). It may require one-on-one interaction with a trainer for most of the child's waking hours over several years. Training involves establishing operations and discriminative cues, as well as reinforcement and punishment contingencies. The key features of the therapy include breaking down skills to be learned in small steps, giving clear instructions, and recording client and therapist behaviour to determine progress. Although behaviour therapy for autistic disorder is being continually refined (Lord, 2007), there are limitations to its effectiveness (Butcher, Mineka, & Hooley, 2007). It is less effective for children who begin to display symptoms prior to age two, and many children who undergo therapy over many years fail to show sustained improvement in the long term. Perhaps the greatest challenge to therapists is the difficulty that children with autistic disorder have in generalizing from the training environments to other environments.

**covert sensitization** A method used by behaviour therapists in which a client imagines the aversive consequences of his or her inappropriate behaviour.

**cognitive-behaviour therapy (CBT)** A treatment method that focuses on altering the client's thoughts, beliefs, and perceptions.

## Maintaining Behavioural Change

As just noted, one of the problems with behaviour therapy is that behaviour learned under one set of conditions may fail to occur in different environments; that is, behavioural change may not generalize to other situations. Behaviour therapists have designed specific methods to ensure that positive behavioural change generalizes to situations outside the clinic or the therapist's office. As we saw in Chapter 7, intermittent reinforcement increases resistance to extinction. Thus, it is more effective to reinforce desirable responses intermittently than it is to reinforce every desirable response the client makes.

Another useful technique that helps maintain behavioural change is the practice of *self-observation*, in which the client is taught to recognize when his or her behaviour is appropriate. Therapists also frequently ask family members and friends of the client to become participants in the process of behaviour therapy. These "adjunct therapists" are taught to encourage and reward desirable behaviours and to discourage or ignore undesirable ones. By these means, a client does not shuttle back and forth between two different types of environments—one in which the therapist selectively reinforces desirable behaviours and another in which reinforcement is haphazard or even inappropriate. For example, a person with behavioural problems may receive attention from the family only when he or she acts up. Clearly, for optimal results, family members need to make an effort to ignore such outbursts and to reinforce instances of desirable behaviour instead.

## Cognitive-Behaviour Therapies

The first attempts at developing psychotherapies based on altering or manipulating cognitive processes emerged during the 1970s. These attempts were undertaken by behaviour therapists who suspected that maladaptive behaviour, or, for that matter, adaptive behaviour, might not be due to environmental variables alone. They began to explore how their clients' thoughts, perceptions, expectations, and self-statements might interact with environmental factors in the development and maintenance of maladaptive behaviour (Beck, 1991).

The focus of **cognitive-behaviour therapy (CBT)** is on changing the client's maladaptive thoughts, beliefs, and perceptions.

This form of therapy is widely practised today and has been shown to be effective in treating many kinds of psychological problems and psychological disorders (Hollon, Thase, & Markowitz, 2002; McClanahan & Antonuccio, 2002; Turkington, Dudley, Warman, & Beck, 2004). Like behaviour therapists—and unlike most insight psychotherapists—cognitive-behaviour therapists are not particularly interested in events that occurred in the client's childhood. They are interested in the here and now and in altering the client's behaviour so that it becomes more functional. Although they employ many methods used by behaviour therapists, they believe that when behaviours change, they do so because of changes in cognitive processes.

Most of the practitioners of cognitive-behaviour therapy use the methods of behaviour therapy I have just described. But in addition, they have developed some special methods designed to change the maladaptive patterns of cognition that they believe underlie maladaptive patterns of behaviour. Attempts to change these patterns of cognition is referred to as **cognitive restructuring**.

**Rational-Emotive Therapy** The first form of cognitive restructuring, called rational-emotive therapy, was developed in the 1950s by Albert Ellis, a clinical psychologist. **Rational-emotive therapy** is based on the belief that psychological problems are caused by how people think about upsetting events and situations (Ellis, 2003). In contrast to the other forms of cognitive-behaviour therapy, rational-emotive therapy did not grow out of the tradition of behaviour therapy. For many years, Ellis was regarded as outside the mainstream of psychotherapy, but now his methods are being practised by a substantial number of therapists. Ellis asserts that psychological problems are the result of faulty cognitions; therapy is therefore aimed at changing people's beliefs. Rational-emotive therapy is highly directive and confrontational. The therapist tells his or her clients what they are doing wrong and how they should change.

According to Ellis and his followers, emotions are the products of cognition. A *significant activating event* (A) is followed by a *highly charged emotional consequence* (C), but it is not correct to say that A has caused C. Rather, C is a result of the *person's belief system* (B). Therefore, inappropriate emotions (such as depression, guilt, and anxiety) can be abolished only if a change occurs in the person's belief system. It is the task of the rational-emotive therapist to dispute the person's beliefs and to convince him or her that they are inappropriate. Ellis tries to show his clients that irrational beliefs are impossible to satisfy, that they make little logical sense, and that adhering to them creates needless anxiety, self-blame, and self-doubt. The following are examples of the kinds of ideas that Ellis (1973) believes to be irrational:

> The idea that it is a necessity for an adult to be loved or approved by virtually every significant person in the community.
>
> The idea that one should be thoroughly competent, adequate, and goal-oriented in all possible respects if one is to consider oneself as having worth.
>
> The idea that human unhappiness is externally caused and that people have little or no ability to control their lives. The idea that one's past is an all-important determinant of one's present behaviour.
>
> The idea that there is invariably a right, precise, and perfect solution to human problems and that it is catastrophic if this perfect solution is not found. (pp. 152–153)

The excerpt below, taken from a therapy session with one of Ellis's own clients—a 23-year-old woman who felt guilty about her relationship with her parents—shows how Ellis challenges clients to examine their irrational beliefs (Ellis, 1989).

> *Client:* The basic problem is that I am worried about my family. I'm worried about money. And I never seem to be able to relax.
>
> *Ellis:* Why are you so worried about your family? Let's go into that, first of all. What's to be concerned about? They have certain demands that you don't want to adhere to.
>
> *C:* I was brought up to think that I mustn't be selfish.
>
> *E:* Oh, we'll have to knock that out of your head!
>
> *C:* I think that that is one of my basic problems.
>
> *E:* That's right, you were brought up to be Florence Nightingale.
>
> *C:* Yes, I was brought up in a family of would-be Florence Nightingales, now that I realize the whole pattern of my family history.... My father became really alcoholic sometime when I was away in college. My mother developed breast cancer, and she had a breast removed. Nobody is healthy.
>
> *E:* How is your father now?
>
> *C:* Well, he's doing much better.... He spends quite a bit of money every week on pills. And if he misses a day of pills, he is absolutely unlivable. My mother feels that I shouldn't have left home—that my place is with them. There are nagging doubts about what I should—
>
> *E:* That's a *belief*. Why do you have to keep believing that—at your age?... Your parents indoctrinated you with this nonsense, because it is *their* belief. But why do you still have to believe that one should not be self-interested, that one should be self-sacrificial? Who needs that philosophy? All it's gotten you, so far, is guilt. And that's all it ever *will* get you. (pp. 234–235)

Although rational-emotive therapy is much more directive than client-centred therapy, there are some similarities. Just as Rogers emphasized unconditional positive regard, so Ellis and his followers attempt to engender a feeling of full self-acceptance in their clients. They teach that self-blame is the core of emotional disturbance and that people can learn

**cognitive restructuring** The process of replacing the client's maladaptive thoughts with more constructive ways of thinking.

**rational-emotive therapy** Therapy based on the belief that psychological problems are caused not by upsetting events but by how people think about them.

to stop continuously rating their own personal worth and measuring themselves against impossible standards. They emphasize that people will be happier if they can learn to see failures as unfortunate events, not as disastrous ones that confirm the lack of their own worth. Unlike a Rogerian therapist, a rational-emotive therapist will vigorously argue with his or her client, attacking beliefs that the therapist regards as foolish and illogical. This approach also differs from the client-centred approach in that the therapist does not need to be especially empathetic to be an effective teacher and guide.

In a review of research evaluating the effectiveness of rational-emotive therapy, Solomon and Haaga (1995) concluded that the method has been shown to reduce general anxiety, test anxiety, and unassertiveness. Rational-emotive therapy has appeal and potential usefulness for those who can enjoy and profit from intellectual teaching and argumentation. The people who are likely to benefit most from this form of therapy are those who are self-demanding and who feel guilty for not living up to their own standards of perfection. People with serious anxiety disorders or with severe thought disorders, such as schizophrenia and other psychoses, are unlikely to respond to an intellectual analysis of their problems.

Many therapists who adopt an eclectic approach use some of the techniques of rational-emotive therapy with some of their clients. In its advocacy of rationality and its eschewal of superstition, the therapy proposes a common sense approach to living. However, many psychotherapists disagree with Ellis's denial of the importance of empathy in the relationship between therapist and client.

**Cognitive Therapy for Depression** Aaron Beck (1967, 1997) has developed a therapy for depression that shares with Ellis's therapy an emphasis on the client's beliefs, interpretations, and perceptions (Beck, 1967, 1997; Clark, Beck, & Alford, 1999). Beck's cognitive therapy, however, focuses more on faulty logic than on the beliefs themselves. The negative beliefs are seen as conclusions based on faulty logic. A depressed person concludes that he or she is "deprived, frustrated, humiliated, rejected or punished ('a loser,' in the vernacular)" (Beck, Rush, Shaw, & Emery, 1979, p. 120). Beck views the cognitions of the depressed individual in terms of a *cognitive triad*: a negative view of the self ("I am worthless"), of the outside world ("The world makes impossible demands on me"), and of the future ("Things are never going to get better").

Even when confronted with evidence that contradicts their negative beliefs, depressed individuals often find an illogical means of interpreting good news as bad news (Lewinsohn, Mischel, Chaplin, & Barton, 1980). For example, children who exhibit symptoms of depression tend to underestimate their abilities (McGrath & Repetti, 2002). A student who receives an A on an exam might attribute the high grade to an easy, unchallenging exam rather than to his or her own mastery of the material. The fact that few others in the class received As does little to convince the depressed student that he or she deserves congratulations for having done well. The depressed student goes on believing, against contrary evidence, that the good grade was not really deserved.

Once the faulty logic is recognized for what it is, therapy entails exploring means for correcting the distortions. Consider the following example from an actual therapy session.

> A woman who complained of severe headaches and other somatic disturbances was found to be very depressed. When asked about the cognitions that seemed to make her unhappy, she said, "My family doesn't appreciate me"; "Nobody appreciates me, they take me for granted"; "I am worthless." As an example, she stated that her adolescent children no longer wanted to do things with her. Although this particular statement could very well have been accurate, the therapist decided to determine whether it was true. He pursued the "evidence" for the statement in the following interchange:
>
> *Patient:* My son doesn't like to go to the theater or to the movies with me anymore.
>
> *Therapist:* How do you know he doesn't want to go with you?
>
> *P:* Teenagers don't actually like to do things with their parents.
>
> *T:* Have you actually asked him to go with you?
>
> *P:* No, as a matter of fact, he did ask me a few times if I wanted him to take me... but I didn't think he really wanted to go.
>
> *T:* How about testing it out by asking him to give you a straight answer?
>
> *P:* I guess so.
>
> *T:* The important thing is not whether or not he goes with you but whether you are deciding for him what he thinks instead of letting him tell you.
>
> *P:* I guess you are right but he does seem to be inconsiderate. For example, he is always late for dinner.
>
> *T:* How often has that happened?
>
> *P:* Oh, once or twice... I guess that's really not all that often.
>
> *T:* Is he coming late for dinner due to his being inconsiderate?
>
> *P:* Well, come to think of it, he did say that he had been working late those two nights. Also, he has been considerate in a lot of other ways. (Beck, Rush, Shaw, & Emery, 1979, pp. 155–156)

Actually, as the patient later found, her son was willing to go to the movies with her.

This example shows that the therapist does not accept the client's conclusions and inferences at their face value. Instead, those conclusions resulting from faulty logic are discussed so that the client may understand them from another perspective, changing his or her behaviour as a result.

*Exposure therapy*, another form of CBT, is specifically directed to the anxiety disorders, including post-traumatic stress disorder (PTSD) (Follette, Linnerooth, & Ruckstuhl, 2001). It has some of the features of in vivo exposure, which we encountered previously as an example of behaviour therapy. As in that therapy, the cognitive-behaviour therapist encourages the client to confront the anxiety-eliciting situations that she or he would ordinarily avoid and to remain there. Though the settings in which the original trauma occurred may not be reproducible, the person with PTSD may generalize from those settings to current settings and could be encouraged to prolong her or his exposure to them. Alternatively, he or she may be encouraged to imagine the original settings. Rather than merely extinguishing anxiety, however, exposure therapy encourages the client to think and feel differently while exposed to real or imagined circumstances and thus to behave in different ways that reduce the anxiety and make it more manageable. For various reasons, including lack of training and the prospect of enhanced arousal and suicidal tendency, therapists have been slow to adopt exposure therapy for the use of PTSD (Becker, Zayfert, & Anderson, 2004).

**Stress Inoculation Training** Meichenbaum (1977, 1993) developed a cognitive therapy for the treatment of stress problems that range from the familiar test anxiety that you yourself might experience to more debilitating disorders (e.g., generalized stress disorder). The therapy is well described as collaborative. The therapist helps the client learn that anxiety is affected by thoughts. The way the client represents events and his or her behaviour will influence his or her emotions.

An important initial goal of therapy is to help the client develop personalized methods of gaining insight into how his or her emotions are affected by thought. In a sense, the therapist and client develop a theory that the client can work with in order to begin coping with his or her anxiety. The client then begins to observe his or her own thinking and emotional reactions in anxiety-producing contexts. A man who is anxious about interacting with women, for example, might begin to self-monitor his reactions in such encounters in order to identify thoughts that are associated with anxiety.

Once the client and therapist have an understanding of these patterns of thinking, the therapist will help the client develop plans for stopping inappropriate and damaging thoughts. Let's say that the client in my example comes to understand that he expects to be humiliated and rejected when he meets women. During therapy, he might be armed with counter, or inoculating, thoughts about his valuable qualities to call up when he finds himself starting to fear rejection. Stress inoculation training also includes instruction in relaxation exercises that can be used to lessen physiological symptoms of anxiety.

Other techniques include having the client practise his or her new cognitive and relaxation skills during imagined anxiety-reducing encounters (Meichenbaum, 2007). Often a good strategy is to start small and then build. The client in our example might focus on brief encounters with women before trying a long conversation. If the initial attempts are not satisfactory, client and therapist go back to the drawing board until a beneficial coping program is identified and put into practice.

## Evaluation of Behaviour and Cognitive-Behaviour Therapies

Psychotherapists of traditional orientations have criticized behaviour therapy for its focus on the symptoms of a psychological problem to the exclusion of its root causes. Some psychoanalysts even argue that treatment of just the symptoms is dangerous. In their view, the removal of one symptom of an intrapsychic conflict will simply produce another, perhaps more serious, symptom through a process called *symptom substitution*.

There is little evidence that symptom substitution occurs. It is true that many people's behavioural problems are caused by conditions that existed in the past, and often these problems become self-perpetuating. Yet behaviour therapy can, in many cases, eliminate the problem behaviour without delving into the past. For example, a child may, for one reason or another, begin wetting the bed. The nightly awakening irritates the parents, who must change the bedsheets and the child's pyjamas. The disturbance often disrupts family relationships. The child develops feelings of guilt and insecurity and wets the bed more often. Instead of analyzing the sources of family conflict, a therapist who uses behaviour therapy would install a device in the child's bed that rings a bell when he or she begins to urinate. The child awakens and goes to the bathroom to urinate and soon ceases to wet the bed. The elimination of bedwetting causes rapid improvement in the child's self-esteem and in the entire family relationship. Symptom substitution does not appear to occur (Blacher & Baker, 1987).

On the other hand, there are some situations in which behaviour therapy should not be used. For example, a person who is involuntarily confined to an institution should not be subjected to aversive techniques unless he or she clearly wants to participate or unless the benefits far outweigh the discomfort. The decision to use aversive techniques must not rest only with people who are directly in charge of the patients, lest the procedures eventually be used merely for the sake of convenience. The decision must involve a committee that includes people who serve as advocates for patients.

Cognitive-behaviour therapists place a great deal of importance on unobservable constructs such as feelings, thoughts, and perceptions, but do not believe that good therapeutic results can be achieved by focusing on cognitions alone. They, like their behaviour-analytic colleagues, insist that it is not enough to have their clients introspect and analyze their thought patterns. Instead, therapists must help clients change their behaviour. Behavioural changes can cause cognitive changes. For example, when a client observes that he or she is now engaging in fewer maladaptive behaviours and more adaptive behaviours, the client's self-perceptions and self-esteem are bound to change as a result. Cognitive-behaviour therapists maintain, though, that therapy can be even more effective when specific attention is paid to cognitions as well as to behaviours.

Although cognitive-behaviour therapists also talk about unobservable cognitive processes, there are some significant differences between them and insight therapists, who also deal with unobservable processes. Unlike insight therapists, cognitive-behaviour therapists concern themselves with conscious thought processes, not with unconscious motives. They are also more interested in the present determinants of the client's thoughts and behaviours than in his or her past history. And because they come from the tradition of experimental psychology, they use rigorous empirical methods to evaluate the effectiveness of their techniques and to infer the nature and existence of cognitive processes.

Cognitive and cognitive-behaviour therapies are very popular today. Dobson and Khatri (2000) note several social influences that work in favour of these approaches. Prominent among these influences are modern society's demand for evidence of efficacy. Other factors that make the cognitive and cognitive-behaviour therapies attractive are their relative briefness and affordability (Dobson & Khatri, 2000). These observations seem to reflect accurately contemporary concerns with value for money and accountability.

The effectiveness of cognitive approaches has been strongly supported by research. Researchers have found that cognitive-behaviour therapy may produce as much change in metabolic brain activity as some drug therapies (Goldapple et al., 2004). Interestingly, not everyone's metabolic activity responds the same way to cognitive therapy. Mayberg (2003) analyzed PET scans of people suffering from depression who had undergone a variety of therapies. She identified bio-markers that showed a strong correlation between unique metabolic activity and the effectiveness of cognitive therapy. Future research incorporating the use of neuroimaging techniques may allow physicians to predict which patients will respond best to cognitive therapy or other types of treatment.

## Interim Summary

### Behaviour and Cognitive-Behaviour Therapies

Behaviour therapists attempt to use the principles of classical and operant conditioning to modify behaviour; they try to eliminate fears or replace maladaptive behaviours with adaptive ones. Systematic desensitization uses classical conditioning procedures to condition relaxation to stimuli that previously produced fear. In contrast, aversion therapy attempts to condition an unpleasant response to a stimulus with which the client is preoccupied, such as a fetish.

Whereas classical conditioning involves automatic approach and avoidance responses to particular stimuli, operant conditioning involves reinforcement, extinction, or punishment of particular behaviours in particular situations. The most formal system involves token economies, which arrange contingencies in the environment of people who reside in institutions; in this case, the system of payment and reward is obvious to the participants. Care must be taken not to produce a loss of intrinsic motivation through the use of extrinsic rewards. Not all instances of reinforcement and punishment are overt; they can also be vicarious. With the guidance of therapists, people can imagine their own behaviour with its consequent reinforcement or punishment. Modelling has been used as an important adjunct to operant conditioning; therapists who use this effective technique provide specific examples of desirable behaviours.

Although some people view behaviour therapy as a simple and rigid application of the principles of conditioning, therapists must be well-trained, sensitive people if the techniques are to be effective. The major problem with behaviour therapy is people's tendency to discriminate the therapeutic situation from similar ones in the outside world, thus failing to generalize their behaviour to situations outside the therapeutic setting. Techniques to promote generalization include the use of intermittent reinforcement and recruitment of family and friends as adjunct therapists.

With the exception of rational-emotive therapy, cognitive-behaviour therapies grew out of the tradition of behaviour therapy. These therapies attempt to change overt behaviour, but they also pay attention to unobservable cognitive processes. Rational-emotive therapy is based on the assumption that people's psychological problems stem from faulty cognitions. Its practitioners use many forms of persuasion, including confrontation, to encourage people to abandon faulty cognitions in favour of logical and healthy ones.

Other forms of cognitive-behaviour therapy involve systematic behavioural approaches to clients' problems, but their practitioners pay close attention to thinking and private verbal behaviour. For example, Beck has developed ways to help depressed people correct errors of cognition that perpetuate self-defeating thoughts.

Some critics have accused behaviour and cognitive-behaviour therapists of doing nothing more than treating the symptoms of a disorder and ignoring its basic causes. However, there is no evidence to support the idea that symptom substitution occurs in people who undergo behaviour or cognitive-behaviour therapy.

Application of behaviour and cognitive-behaviour therapy can raise ethical concerns, particularly when aversive stimuli are used. If aversive techniques are the best solution, the client's participation must be voluntary or patient advocates must participate in the decision to use this form of therapy.

#### QUESTIONS TO CONSIDER

1. Think of the stimulus—either a thing or a situation—that you fear most. Based on what you learned about systematic desensitization, create a hierarchy of fear. Consider how you might find ways to relax as you imagine the least fearful stimuli. How well can you relax as you progress through the hierarchy?
2. Think again of your hierarchy of fear. Now, instead of trying to relax, try to reconfigure your cognitions. Are there cognitive aspects of your fear that are irrational? If so, how might you change these faulty cognitions to reduce your anxiety concerning the feared stimulus?

# Group Therapy and Community Psychology

So far, we have been discussing individual forms of psychotherapy, in which a single client meets with a therapist. But in many cases, clients meet as a group, either because therapy is more effective that way or because it is more convenient or economical. In this section, we will discuss group and community therapies.

**Group psychotherapy**, in which two or more clients meet simultaneously with a therapist to discuss problems, became common during the Second World War. The stresses of combat produced psychological problems in many members of the armed forces, and the demand for psychotherapists greatly exceeded the supply. What began as an economic necessity became an institution once the effectiveness of group treatment was recognized.

Because most psychological problems involve interactions with other people, treating these problems in a group setting may be worthwhile. Group therapy provides four advantages that are not found in individual therapy:

1. The group setting permits the therapist to observe and interpret actual interactions without having to rely on clients' descriptions, which may be selective or faulty.
2. A group can bring social pressure to bear on the behaviours of its members. If a person receives similar comments about his or her behaviour from all the members of a group, the message is often more convincing than if a psychotherapist delivers the same comments in a private session.
3. The process of seeing the causes of maladaptive behaviour in other people often helps a person gain insight into his or her own problems. People can often learn from the mistakes of others.
4. Knowing that other people have problems similar to one's own can bring comfort and relief. People discover that they are not alone.

The structure of group therapy sessions can vary widely. Some sessions are little more than lectures, in which the therapist presents information about a problem common to all members of the group, followed by discussion. For example, in a case involving a person with severe mental or physical illness, the therapist explains to family members the nature, treatment, and possible outcomes of the disorder. Then the therapist answers questions and allows people to share their feelings about what the illness has done to their family. Other groups are simply efficient ways to treat several clients at the same time. But most types of group therapy involve interactions among the participants.

## Family Therapy and Couples Therapy

Very often, dealing with the problems of an individual is not enough. Family therapy and couples therapy have become important techniques for clinical psychologists. People are products of their environments, and the structure of a person's family is a crucial part of that environment. Consequently, helping an unhappy person frequently means also restructuring his or her relationship with other family members (Cox & Paley, 2003; Lefley, 2002). In addition, problems in the relations between members of a couple—with or without children—can often lead to stress and unhappiness.

▲ *Family therapy approaches psychological disorders from the perspective that the structure of relationships within the family is part of the problem and that by restructuring those relationships people will become happier.*

In many cases, a family therapist meets with all members of a client's family and analyzes the way in which individuals interact. The therapist attempts to get family members to talk to each other instead of addressing all comments and questions to him or her. As much as possible, the family therapist tries to collect data about the interactions—how individuals sit in relation to each other, who interrupts whom, who looks at whom before speaking—in order to infer the nature of interrelationships within the family. For example, there may be barriers between certain family members; perhaps a father is unable to communicate with one of his children. Or two or more family members may be so dependent on each other that they cannot function independently; they constantly seek each other's approval and, through overdependence, make each other miserable.

For example, consider the approach developed by Salvador Minuchin (1974; Minuchin & Nichols, 1998), **structural family therapy**. The therapist first observes a family's interactions and draws simple diagrams of the relationships he or she infers from their behaviours. He or she then identifies the counterproductive relationships and attempts to help the family

**group psychotherapy** Therapy in which two or more clients meet simultaneously with a therapist, discussing problems within a supportive and understanding environment.

**structural family therapy** A form of family therapy in which the maladaptive relationships among family members are inferred from their behaviour and attempts are made to restructure these behaviours into more adaptive ones.

restructure their dynamics in more adaptive ways. For example, the therapist might diagram a family structure with father (F) on one side and mother (M) on the other side, allied with son (S) but estranged from daughter (D):

$$\frac{F}{MS|D}$$

The therapist would then attempt to restructure the family as follows:

$$\frac{HW}{SD}$$

Husband (H) and wife (W) would replace mother and father, emphasizing that their primary relationship should be the one between spouses. The healthiest family interactions stem from an effectively functioning *marital subsystem*, consisting of a husband and wife. A marriage that is completely child-oriented is always dysfunctional (Foley, 1979). And alliances between one parent and one or more children are almost always detrimental to the family.

After inferring the family structure, the therapist attempts to restructure it by replacing maladaptive interactions with more effective, functional ones. He or she suggests that perhaps all members of the family must change if the client is to make real improvement. The therapist gets family members to "actualize" their transactional patterns—to act out their everyday relationships—so that the maladaptive interactions will show themselves. Restructuring techniques include forming temporary alliances between the therapist and one or more of the family members, increasing tension in order to trigger changes in unstable structures, assigning explicit tasks and homework to family members (for example, making them interact with other members), and providing general support, education, and guidance. Sometimes, the therapist visits the family at home. For example, if a child in a family refuses to eat, the therapist will visit during mealtime in order to see the problem acted out as explicitly as possible.

Behaviour therapists have also applied their methods of analysis and treatment to families. This approach focuses on the social environment provided by the family and on the ways that family members reinforce or punish each other's behaviour. The strategy is to identify the maladaptive behaviours of the individuals and the way in which these behaviours are inadvertently reinforced by the rest of the family. Then the therapist helps the family members find ways to increase positive exchanges and reinforce each other's adaptive behaviours. A careful analysis of the social dynamics of a family often reveals that changes need to be made not in the individual showing the most maladaptive behaviours but in the other members of the family.

All couples will find that they disagree on some important issues. These disagreements necessarily lead to conflicts. For example, they may have to decide whether to move to accommodate the career of one of the partners, they will have to decide how to spend their money, and they will have to decide how to allocate household chores. Their ability to resolve conflict is one of the most important factors that affects the quality and durability of their relationship.

When dealing with families and couples, which consist of people with long-established, ongoing personal relations, therapists have learned that changes in the nature of the relations can have unforeseen consequences—and that they must be alert for these consequences. For example, LoPiccolo and Friedman (1985) describe treatment of a couple with a sexual problem. At first, the problem appeared to belong to the man.

> A couple with a marriage of twenty years duration sought treatment for the male's problem of total inability to have an erection. This had been a problem for over nineteen of their twenty years of marriage. Successful intercourse had only taken place in the first few months of the marriage. . . . [The wife] reported that she greatly enjoyed sex and was extremely frustrated by her husband's inability to have an erection.

The therapists used techniques developed by Masters and Johnson (1970) to treat the man's impotence, which succeeded splendidly. Within 10 weeks the couple was able to have sexual intercourse regularly, and both had orgasms. However, even though the problem appeared to have been cured, and despite the physical gratification they received from their sexual relations, they soon stopped having them. In investigating this puzzling occurrence, the therapists discovered

> . . . that the husband had a great need to remain distant and aloof from his wife. He had great fears of being overwhelmed and controlled by her, and found closeness to be very uncomfortable.... For him, the inability to have an erection served to keep his wife distant from him, and to maintain his need for privacy, separateness, and autonomy in the relationship. (LoPiccolo & Friedman, 1985, p. 465)

The therapists also found that the wife had reasons to avoid sexual contact. For one thing, she apparently had never resolved the antisexual teachings imparted to her as a child by her family. In addition,

> . . . over the nineteen years of her husband being unable to attain an erection, she had come to have a very powerful position in the relationship. She very often reminded her husband that he owed her a lot because of her sexual frustration. Thus, she was essentially able to win all arguments with him, and to get him to do anything that she wanted. (LoPiccolo & Friedman, 1985, p. 465)

The therapists were able to address these issues and to help the couple resolve them. Eventually, they were able to alter the structure of their marriage and resumed their sexual relations.

This case illustrates the fact that a couple is not simply a collection of two individuals. Long-standing problems bring adjustments and adaptations (some of which may not be healthy). Even if the original problems are successfully resolved, the adjustments to these problems may persist and cause problems of their own.

You can appreciate how difficult the family therapist's job is. The task is formidable, as was recognized by Freud (1912) himself, who stated, "When it comes to the treatment of relationships I must confess myself utterly at a loss and I have altogether little faith in any individual therapy of them." Of course, the modern therapist enjoys the benefit of several decades of research, theory, and practice not available to Freud. There is some optimism today concerning the effectiveness of family and couples therapy.

## Community Psychology

A quite different approach to therapy involves actively seeking out people with problems or even attempting to prevent problems before they begin. Therapists who participate in prevention are practising **community psychology**, a form of education and treatment whose goal is to address psychological problems through assessment and intervention in the sociocultural contexts in which problems develop. Practitioners of community psychology deal with individuals and groups, establish educational programs, and design programs whose goal is to promote mental health by changing the environment (Butterfoss, 2007; Kirsh & Cockburn, 2007).

Several different kinds of community treatment programs have been developed. One example is the *community mental health centre*, a form of treatment designed to supplement the care provided by mental hospitals. Instead of confining patients to an institution, community mental health centres provide outpatient care within the community. A popular form of this program in Canada and the United States is called *assertive community treatment*, or ACT. ACT was developed in the 1970s by Leonard Stein and Mary Ann Test (Stein & Santos, 1998; Test & Stein, 2000). In ACT programs, a multidisciplinary team provides broad support of the needs of severely mentally ill patients. Typically, a psychiatric nurse, psychiatrist, and social worker develop a comprehensive care plan for the patient. Care under this system includes not only therapy, but also assistance in the everyday demands of living (e.g., finding a suitable place to live, finding employment when the patient is able, arranging for transportation, and ensuring that basic physical needs are met). Important goals of this type of program are maximization of the patients' ability to live independently or with minimal supervision and the reduction of their admissions to mental hospitals. A review of the research literature shows that ACT is effective in meeting these goals (Phillips et al., 2001).

A related type of community treatment program is the halfway house, a transitional setting in which patients discharged from mental hospitals may receive outpatient care as they gradually are reintegrated into the community. Using the halfway house as their base, clients may take on part-time jobs, return to school, or simply spend more time with their families and friends. Allowing previously hospitalized patients to return to their communities for treatment is called **deinstitutionalization.** For the most part, this movement has been viewed as an important advance by community psychologists. Deinstitutionalization has dramatically reduced the number of persons confined to mental institutions in North America and Europe (Lesage et al., 2000).

**Preventive Psychology** Increasingly, community psychologists have been stressing treatment strategies aimed at forestalling the development of psychological problems (Rappaport & Seidman, 2000). This emphasis on treating the sociocultural variables predictive of psychological distress is called **preventive psychology.** A useful metaphor for describing preventive psychology is that individual therapy for psychological problems can be seen as similar to rescuing people from a river (Rappaport, 1977). Each person rescued is a life saved. But a more effective solution would be to go upstream and correct the problem that is causing people to fall into the river in the first place.

Community psychologists distinguish between two kinds of prevention: primary and secondary. *Primary prevention* is any effort to eliminate the conditions responsible for psychological problems and simultaneously to bring about conditions that contribute to adaptive behaviour. For example, providing children with educational materials concerning the dangers of taking drugs while encouraging healthy recreation and exercise represents an attempt to prevent experimentation with drugs. *Secondary prevention*, on the other hand, refers to prompt identification of problems and immediate intervention to minimize development of these problems. Suicide hotlines, staffed 24 hours a day by trained volunteers, are examples of secondary prevention measures.

Community mental health centres provide individual and group therapy and counselling to members of the communities in which they are located. The goal of such centres is to provide immediate, accessible outpatient care for people who might otherwise find it difficult to get help. Such centres are generally staffed by psychologists, psychiatrists, social workers, and nurses. However, they often also employ the services of paraprofessionals who have roots in the community. The use of paraprofessionals has many advantages. People from culturally deprived backgrounds frequently have difficulty relating to—and communicating with—middle-class therapists. However, if paraprofessionals having the same social and ethnic backgrounds are available, they may be able to gain the trust and confidence of clients and enable them to profit from the help that is available. Also, having faced similar problems, the paraprofessionals may be able to provide useful advice and to

**community psychology** A form of treatment and education whose goal is to address psychological problems through an assessment of the sociocultural context in which they develop.
**deinstitutionalization** The process of returning previously hospitalized patients to their communities for treatment of psychological problems and psychological disorders.
**preventive psychology** Any attempt to forestall the development of psychological problems by altering the sociocultural variables predictive of psychological distress.

serve as role models for clients. Modelling is more effective when the model resembles the client.

## Evaluation of Group Therapy and Community Psychology

Group and community therapies and family and couples therapy have filled important gaps in the treatment of psychological disorders. Because group therapy is less expensive than private therapy, people who could not otherwise afford psychotherapy have a reasonable alternative to not getting any help.

**Assessing the Effectiveness of Psychotherapy** Evaluation of therapies and therapists is a very important issue. It has received much attention, but almost everyone who is involved agrees that too little is known about the efficacy of psychotherapeutic methods, in part because psychotherapeutic effectiveness is difficult to study.

Several factors make it extremely difficult to evaluate the effectiveness of a particular form of therapy or an individual therapist. One factor is the problem of *measurement*. Measuring a person's dysfunction is difficult; there are no easily applied, commonly agreed-upon criteria for mental health. Therefore, making valid before-and-after measurements is extremely difficult. Most studies rely on ratings by the clients or the therapists to determine whether a therapy has succeeded. These two measures are obviously correlated, because therapists primarily base their ratings on what their clients say to them. Few studies interview friends or family members to obtain independent evaluations of the clients' condition—and those that do generally find a poor correlation between these ratings and those of clients and therapists (Sloane et al., 1975).

*Ethics* also sometimes prevent clinicians from using a purely scientific method of evaluation, which requires that experimental and control groups be constituted in equivalent ways. Leaving a person who appears to be suicidal untreated so that comparisons can be made with similar people who receive therapy presents risks that therapists consider unacceptable.

*Self-selection*—the fact that clients choose whether to enter therapy, what type of therapy to engage in, and how long to stay in therapy—makes it nearly impossible to establish either a stable sample population or a control group. That is, certain kinds of people are more likely than others to enter a particular therapy and stick with it, which produces a biased sample. Lack of a stable sample and lack of a control group makes it difficult to compare the effectiveness of various kinds of therapies. Many patients change therapists or leave therapy altogether. What conclusions can we draw about the effectiveness of a therapy by looking only at the progress made by the clients who remain with it?

Yet another problem with scientific evaluation of psychotherapy is the question of an appropriate *control group*. You may recall from Chapter 2 that the effects of therapeutic drugs must be determined through comparison with the effects of *placebos* (innocuous pills that have no effects on people's thoughts and behaviour) to be sure that the improvement has not occurred merely because the patient *thinks* that a pill has done some good. Placebo effects can also occur in psychotherapy: People know that they are being treated and may get better because they *believe* that the treatment should lead to improvement. Most studies that evaluate psychotherapeutic techniques do not include control groups for these placebo effects. To do so, the investigator would have to design "mock therapy" sessions, during which the therapist does nothing therapeutic but convinces the patient that therapy is taking place; obviously, this goal is not easily achieved.

In a pioneering paper on psychotherapeutic evaluation, Eysenck (1952) examined 19 studies assessing the effectiveness of psychotherapy. He reported that of the people who remained in psychoanalysis as long as their therapists thought they should, 66 percent showed improvement. Similarly, 64 percent of patients treated eclectically showed an improvement. However, 72 percent of patients who were treated only custodially (receiving no psychotherapy) in institutions showed improvement. In other words, people got better just as fast by themselves as they did in therapy.

Subsequent studies were not much more optimistic. Some investigators, including Eysenck, concluded that it is unethical to charge a person for psychotherapy because there is little scientific evidence that it is effective. Others said that the problems involved in performing scientific research are so great that we must abandon the attempt to evaluate therapies: Validation of the effectiveness of therapy must rely on the therapist's clinical judgment. Many forms of therapy have never been evaluated objectively because their practitioners are convinced that the method works and deem objective confirmation unnecessary.

**Figure 18•4** summarizes Smith, Glass, and Miller's (1980) well-known meta-analysis of 475 studies comparing the outcome effectiveness of psychodynamic, Gestalt, client-centred, systematic desensitization, behaviour modification, and cognitive-behaviour therapies. A **meta-analysis** is a statistical procedure for estimating the magnitude of experimental effects reported by published studies. Relative to no therapy, each of these therapies was shown to be superior in helping people with their problems. As you can see, behavioural and cognitive therapies tended to exceed others in effectiveness, although these differences were often small. More recent research has confirmed these results, indicating that most people tend to improve with respect to the reason that brought them to therapy (e.g., Okiishi, Lambert, Nielsen, & Ogles, 2003). Likewise, a recent meta-analysis confirms that different forms of therapy seem to be about equally effective (Wampold, Minami, Baskin, & Callen, 2002; Wampold et al., 1997). Keep in mind that these data reflect hundreds of studies and thousands of clients. No conclusions can be drawn from studies like this as to the effectiveness of a particular therapy for any *one* client.

Each year, the editors of the popular magazine *Consumer Reports* send a large-scale survey—concerning consumer

**meta-analysis** A statistical procedure by which the results of many studies are combined to estimate the magnitude of a particular effect.

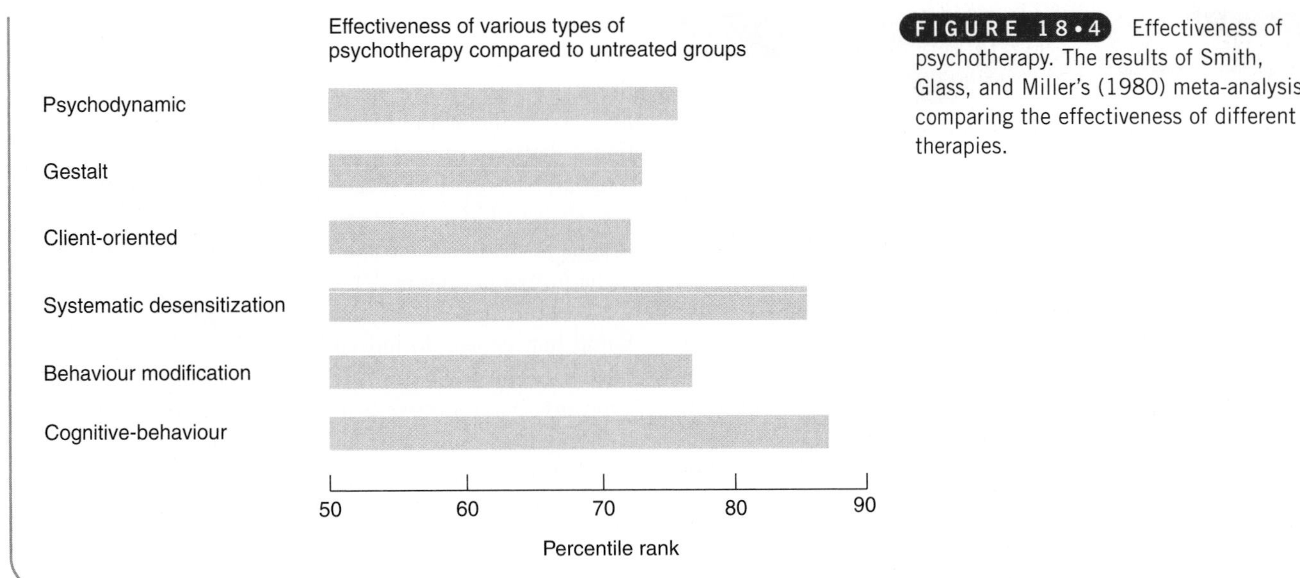


FIGURE 18•4 Effectiveness of psychotherapy. The results of Smith, Glass, and Miller's (1980) meta-analysis comparing the effectiveness of different therapies.

satisfaction with a tremendous range of goods and services—to its subscribers. The 1994 survey included 26 questions about treatment for psychological disorders. About 7000 readers responded to this portion of the survey, 2900 of whom had seen mental health professionals for help in coping with stress or emotional problems during the previous 3 years. The majority (59 percent) of these people had consulted either a psychologist or a psychiatrist; the remaining people had consulted a social worker, marriage counsellor, or some other mental health professional.

In general, the results from this survey showed that people benefited greatly from psychotherapy (*Consumer Reports*, 1995). People who had undergone long-term treatment improved more than those who had undergone short-term treatment. In addition, all forms of psychotherapy were found to be effective at making people feel better, regardless of the disorders from which they were suffering. Psychotherapy was found to be as effective as psychotherapy plus drug therapy in treating psychological disorders.

An interesting study by Luborsky and colleagues (1971) investigated the factors that influence the outcome of psychotherapy, independent of the particular method used. They examined both patient variables and therapist variables. The important *patient variables* were psychological health at the beginning of the therapy, adequacy of personality, the patient's motivation for change, level of intelligence, level of anxiety (more anxious patients tended to do better), level of education, and socio-economic status. Some of the variables seem to be self-confirming: If you are in fairly good psychological shape to begin with, you have a better chance of improving. In addition, if you are well educated and have adequate social and financial resources, your condition will probably improve. The finding that anxiety is a good sign probably indicates a motivation to improve.

Several *therapist variables* were significant. These variables were the number of years the therapist had been practising, similarity in the personality of therapist and client, and the ability of the therapist to communicate empathy to the client. The finding that the more experienced therapists had more success with their clients is very encouraging; it suggests that therapists learn something from their years of experience, which in turn implies that *there is something to learn*. Thus, we have reason to believe that the process of psychotherapy is worthwhile.

The *therapeutic alliance*, the relationship between therapist and client, is also important. Although the exact factors that contribute to a positive relationship between therapist and client differ across psychotherapies, it seems clear that a positive alliance contributes to good outcomes (Kopta, Lueger, Saunders, & Howard, 1999). According to Bordin (1994) two key underlying factors are shared goals for the therapy between client and therapist and a firm bond between the two parties. Beyond these factors, we suspect that the diverse variables that contribute to good interpersonal relationships in everyday life also promote positive alliances in therapy. Consistent with this possibility, several studies have suggested that a therapist's ability to form understanding, warm, and empathetic relationships is one of the most important traits that distinguish effective therapy. For example, Strupp and Hadley (1979) enlisted a group of college professors on the basis of their reputations as warm, trustworthy, empathetic individuals. The professors (from the departments of English, history, mathematics, and philosophy) were asked to hold weekly sessions to counsel students with psychological difficulties. Another group of students was assigned to professional psychotherapists, both psychologists and psychiatrists, and a third group received no treatment at all. Most of the students showed moderate depression or anxiety. Both groups did significantly better than the control students who received no treatment. These results suggest that sympathy and understanding are important ingredients in the therapeutic alliance, at least for treatment of mild anxiety or depression.

## Interim Summary

### Group Therapy and Community Psychology

Many types of group therapy have been developed in response to the belief that certain problems can be treated more efficiently and more effectively in group settings. Practitioners of family therapy, couples therapy, and some forms of group behaviour therapy observe people's interactions with others and attempt to help them learn how to establish more effective patterns of behaviour. Treatment of groups, including families and couples, permits the therapist to observe clients' social behaviours, and it uses social pressures to help convince clients of the necessity for behavioural change. It permits clients to learn from the mistakes of others and observe that other people have similar problems, which often provides reassurance.

Community psychology involves psychologists' attempts to reach out to a community to try to establish readily available treatment facilities or provide crisis intervention to keep problems from becoming worse. It also tries to educate the public and promote social changes in order to prevent problems from occurring in the first place.

The effectiveness of psychotherapeutic methods is difficult to assess, but given the immense expense of problems associated with psychological disorders, we must do our best to evaluate these methods. Outcomes are difficult to measure objectively, ethical considerations make it hard to establish control groups for some types of disorders, and self-selection and dropouts make it impossible to compare randomly selected groups of patients. However, what research there is suggests that many forms of psychotherapy are effective. Several experiments assessing both drug treatment and psychotherapy have found that a combined approach is the most beneficial. The most ambitious study suggested that antidepressant medication, delivered in a warm, caring atmosphere, was more effective than cognitive-behaviour therapy or interpersonal therapy alone in treating severe depression; no significant differences were seen in less severe cases. The *Consumer Reports* study found that people do indeed benefit from therapy and that, contrary to the findings of earlier studies, psychotherapy alone appears to be as effective as the combination of psychotherapy and drug therapy in treating psychological disorders.

The most important characteristic of a good psychotherapist appears to be the ability to form a warm, understanding alliance with a client. Perhaps when the therapist is empathetic, the client grows to care about the therapist's opinions, which allows the therapist to become a potent source of social reinforcement. In addition, the client may be more willing to model his or her behaviour on the behaviour of a caring therapist.

**Table 18•2** summarizes the assumptions, primary goals, and methods involved in each of the traditional forms of psychotherapy we have looked at in this section.

**QUESTIONS TO CONSIDER**

1. How effective might group therapy be in helping you cope with your problems, anxieties, or fears? Would you feel comfortable telling others about these sorts of

**TABLE 18•2 Summary of the Basic Assumptions, Goals, and Methods Involved in Traditional Forms of Psychotherapy**

| Type of Therapy | Basic Assumptions | Primary Goals | Typical Method of Analysis or Intervention |
|---|---|---|---|
| Psychoanalysis | Behaviour is motivated by intrapsychic conflict and biological urges. | Discover the sources of conflict and resolve them through insight. | Free association, dream interpretation, interpretation of transference, resistance, memory, and manner of speech. |
| Psychodynamic | Behaviour is motivated by both unconscious forces and interpersonal experiences. | Understand and improve interpersonal skills. | Interpretation of transference and modification of client's inappropriate schemata about interpersonal relationships. |
| Humanistic and Gestalt | People are good and have innate worth. | To promote personal growth and self-actualization and to enhance clients' awareness of bodily sensations and feelings. | Reduce incongruence through reflection, empathy, unconditional positive regard, and techniques to enhance personal awareness and feelings of self-worth. |
| Behaviour and cognitive-behaviour | Behaviour is largely controlled by environmental contingencies, people's perception of them, or a combination. | To change maladaptive behaviour and thinking patterns. | Manipulate environmental variables, restructure thinking patterns, and correct faulty thinking or irrational beliefs. |
| Family/couples | Problems in relationships entail everybody involved in them. | To discover how interactions influence problems in individual functioning. | Analysis of patterns of family/couples' interaction and how others reinforce maladaptive and adaptive thinking and behaving. |

things? In what ways might you benefit from hearing others discuss their problems and worries?

2. It is common practice for people to visit their physicians once a year for a checkup. It is also routine for people to visit their dentists twice a year to have their teeth cleaned and examined for cavities and other problems. Why don't people take the same preventive approach to their mental health? Suppose that you were a clinical psychologist. How might you establish or set up such a preventive exam (what would the exam consist of; what kinds of problems would you look for; how would you consider treating a problem if you found one)?

# Biological Treatments

Therapies provided by psychologists target maladaptive thoughts and behaviours, but **biomedical therapies** target abnormal neural and other physiological functions. For that reason, biomedical therapies for psychological disorders are traditionally carried out by psychiatrists or other physicians (who have medical degrees) rather than by psychologists. Besides drug therapy, there are two other forms of medical therapy: electroconvulsive therapy and psychosurgery.

## Drug Therapy

Drug therapy, often called **pharmacotherapy**, is the treatment of psychological problems with chemical agents and is the most widely used form of biomedical therapy. Although abuses have occurred, drug therapy created a revolution in the treatment of psychological disorders and is a highly active area of medical and psychological research today. **Table 18•3** lists some of the more common drugs used to improve psychological functioning, their generic names, and their more recognizable trade names. There are four classes of drugs used to treat psychological disorders: antipsychotic drugs, antidepressant drugs, antimanic drugs, and antianxiety drugs (Buschmann et al., 2007).

**Antipsychotic Drugs** In the early 1950s, physicians working at two hospitals in France found that a new drug called *chlorpromazine* (belonging to the phenothiazine class of drugs) dramatically reduced the positive symptoms of schizophrenic disorders (Lehmann & Ban, 1997; Shen & Giesler, 1998). Heinz Lehmann is generally credited with introducing chlorpromazine to North America. According to Collins (1988), Lehmann, who was clinical director at the Verdun

**biomedical therapies** A form of therapy that focuses on abnormal neural and physiological functioning.
**pharmacotherapy** The treatment of psychological problems with chemical agents.

**TABLE 18•3 Drugs Commonly Used to Treat Psychological Disorders**

| Therapeutic Function | Class of Drugs | Generic Name | Trade Name |
|---|---|---|---|
| Antipsychotic | Phenothiazines | Chlorpromazine | Largactil |
| | | Thioridazine | Mellaril |
| | | Fluphenazine | Modecate |
| | | Trifluoperazine | Stelazine |
| | | Perphenazine | Trilafon |
| | Butyrophenones | Haloperidol | Haldol |
| | Atypical | Clozapine | Clozaril |
| | | Risperidone | Risperdal |
| Antidepressant | Tricyclics | Imipramine | Tofranil |
| | Monoamine oxidase inhibitors | Phenelzine | Nardil |
| | Serotonin reuptake inhibitors | Paroxetine | Paxil |
| | | Fluoxetine | Prozac |
| | | Nefazodone | Serzone |
| | | Sertraline | Zoloft |
| Antianxiety | Benzodiazepines | Chlordiazepoxide | Librium |
| | | Diazepam | Valium |
| | | Lorazepam | Ativan |
| | | Alprazolam | Xanax |
| Antimanic | Lithium salts | Lithium carbonate | Durolith |

Protestant Hospital in Montreal, claims that his recognition of the promise of this drug was simple—he could read the French-language pharmaceutical brochures whereas most others in the psychiatric community could not.

The introduction of chlorpromazine (with the trade name *Largactil* in Canada and *Thorazine* in the U.S.) and other **antipsychotic drugs** has had a profound effect on the treatment of schizophrenia. Many people who are treated with antipsychotic drugs are able to lead happy and productive lives. My father is able to live on his own, work, and enjoy life—just like people who do not suffer from a serious mental illness.

There is still no cure for schizophrenia. The majority of antipsychotic drugs simply reduce the severity of its most prominent positive symptoms—delusions and hallucinations—apparently by blocking dopamine receptors in the brain. Presumably, overactivity of dopamine synapses is responsible for the positive symptoms of schizophrenia. Although dopamine-secreting neurons are located in several parts of the brain, most researchers believe that the ones involved in the symptoms of schizophrenia are located in the cerebral cortex and parts of the limbic system near the front of the brain.

A different system of dopamine-secreting neurons in the brain is involved in the control of movement. Occasionally, this system of neurons degenerates in older people, producing Parkinson's disease. Symptoms of this disorder include tremors, muscular rigidity, loss of balance, difficulty in initiating movement, and impaired breathing that makes speech indistinct. In severe cases, the person is bedridden.

The major problem with most antipsychotic drugs, the phenothiazines, is that they do not discriminate between these two systems of dopamine-secreting neurons. The drugs interfere with the activity of both the circuits involved in the symptoms of schizophrenia and the circuits involved in the control of movements. Consequently, when a person with schizophrenia begins to take an antipsychotic drug, he or she sometimes exhibits a movement disorder. Fortunately, the symptoms are usually temporary and soon disappear. However, after taking the antipsychotic drug for several years, some people develop a different—more serious—movement disorder known as **tardive dyskinesia** (*tardive* means "late developing"; *dyskinesia* refers to a disturbance in movement), an often irreversible and untreatable syndrome characterized by continual involuntary lip smacking, grimacing, and drooling (Cummings & Wirshing, 1989). Severely affected people have difficulty talking, and occasionally the movements interfere with breathing. The risk of developing this syndrome increases with age, dose, and duration of use (Hughes & Pierattini, 1992; Tarsy, Baldessarini, & Tarazi, 2002). For example, approximately 20 percent of older people who take these antipsychotic drugs develop tardive dyskinesia. The symptoms can temporarily be alleviated by *increasing* the dose of the antipsychotic drug, but doing so only serves to increase and perpetuate the person's dependence on the medication (Baldessarini & Tarsy, 1980). There is no cure for this disorder.

There is evidence that some of the more recent antipsychotic drugs have fewer drawbacks than previous drug treatments (Awad & Voruganti, 2004). In Chapter 17, I mentioned that most antipsychotics reduce the severity of positive symptoms of schizophrenia, such as thought disorders and hallucinations. A relatively new drug for schizophrenia called clozapine (Clozaril) is also effective for negative symptoms, such as social withdrawal and flattened emotionality. This development represents a major advance for the welfare and quality of life of people who have schizophrenia. Like all drugs, conventional antipsychotics don't work for everyone. For reasons that are not well understood, clozapine helps many people who receive no substantial benefit from the other antipsychotics (Bondolfi et al., 1998; Carpenter et al., 1995). Finally, clozapine appears to carry dramatically lower risks of tardive dyskinesia (e.g., Kane, 2001); there is even some indication that switching to clozapine may reduce the symptoms of tardive dyskinesia resulting from other drug treatments (e.g., Chakos et al., 2001). Surely this must sound like a wonder drug to you, and in many respects clozapine deserves the honour. But there is a downside. Clozapine is associated with serious adverse effects and high costs (Conley & Kelly, 2001). About 2 percent of people taking clozapine suffer an inhibition of white blood cell production, which can be fatal. For this reason, only patients with normal white cell counts can take clozapine, and they must have blood tests weekly for the first six months of therapy and then every two weeks afterwards.

**Antidepressant and Antimanic Drugs** **Antidepressant drugs** are a class of drugs used to treat the symptoms of major depression. **Antimanic drugs** are used to treat the symptoms of bipolar disorder and mania. The earliest used antidepressant drugs were derived from the family of chemicals known as tricyclics, which refers to their "three-ring" chemical structure (Lickey & Gordon, 1991). Because their chemical structure is similar to that of antipsychotic drugs, tricyclics were used in the belief that they might provide an effective treatment for schizophrenia. Although their use as an antipsychotic was quickly dismissed, researchers observed that these drugs did tend to elevate mood, suggesting their potential as an antidepressant.

Although the biology of depression is still not well understood, the most widely accepted theory is that depression may result from a deficiency of the catecholamine neurotransmitters, norepinephrine and serotonin. Each of these neurotransmitters may be involved in different types of depression, although researchers are not sure how. Antidepressant drugs seem to slow down the reuptake of these

**antipsychotic drugs** Drugs used to treat psychotic schizophrenic disorders.
**tardive dyskinesia** A serious movement disorder that can occur when a person has been treated with antipsychotic drugs for an extended period.
**antidepressant drugs** Drugs used to treat depression.
**antimanic drugs** Drugs used to treat bipolar disorder and mania.

neurotransmitters by presynaptic axons. Although tricyclics do not work for all people, about 60 to 80 percent of those whose depression has brought despair to their lives gradually return to normal after having been placed on tricyclics for two to six weeks (Hughes & Pierattini, 1992; Potter, Manji, & Rudorfer, 2001). Unfortunately, tricyclics have many side effects, including dizziness, sweating, weight gain, constipation, increased pulse, poor concentration, and dry mouth.

Another class of antidepressants is the monoamine oxidase inhibitors (MAOIs), which take one to three weeks to begin alleviating depression. MAOIs prevent enzymes in the synaptic gap from destroying dopamine, norepinephrine, and serotonin that have been released by presynaptic neurons. Although these drugs also can have many side effects—including high blood pressure (which can be fatal after the ingestion of certain foods: some wines, milk products, coffee, and chocolate), hyperthermia, blurred vision, erectile dysfunction, insomnia, and nausea—MAOIs also have been shown to be more effective in treating atypical depressions such as those involving hypersomnia (too much sleep) or mood swings (Hughes & Pierattini, 1992).

A relatively new family of drugs (with trade names such as *Prozac, Paxil,* and *Serzone*) is having a tremendous impact on pharmacotherapy for depression. Prozac, the original entry in this field, and its successors inhibit the reuptake of serotonin, leaving more of that neurotransmitter in the synaptic cleft to stimulate postsynaptic receptors. These drugs, collectively called *selective serotonin reuptake inhibitors* (or SSRIs), produce fewer negative side effects than do tricyclics and the MAOIs. Moreover, because they have fewer side effects, SSRIs can be taken in larger dosages, which generally results in more substantial reduction in depression.

Lithium carbonate is most effective in the treatment of bipolar disorders or simple mania (Schou, 2001). People's manic symptoms usually decrease as soon as their blood level of lithium reaches a sufficiently high level. In bipolar disorder, once the manic phase is eliminated, the depressed phase does not return. People with bipolar disorder have remained free of their symptoms for years as long as they have continued taking lithium carbonate. Some people with bipolar disorder require lithium in combination with other drugs for maximum effectiveness (Grof, 2003). The use of lithium greatly decreased the likelihood of suicide among people with bipolar disorder (Young & Hammond, 2007). In fact, people who have untreated bipolar disorder or mania have mortality rates two to three times that of the normal population (see Ahrens et al., 1995). Ahrens and colleagues (1995) report that continued treatment with lithium after symptoms have subsided reduces the mortality rate to that of the general population.

This drug can have some side effects, such as a fine tremor or excessive urine production; but, in general, the benefits far outweigh the adverse symptoms. However, an overdose of lithium is toxic, which means that the person's blood level of lithium must be monitored regularly.

The major difficulty with treating bipolar disorder is that people with this disorder often miss their "high." When medication is effective, the mania subsides along with the depression. But most people enjoy at least the initial phase of their manic periods, and some believe that they are more creative at that time. In addition, many of these people say that they resent having to depend on a chemical "crutch." As a consequence, many people suffering from bipolar disorder stop taking their medication. Doing so endangers the lives of these people, because the risk of death by suicide is particularly high during the depressive phase of bipolar disorder.

### Antianxiety Drugs

**Antianxiety drugs** are used in the treatment of everyday anxiety, phobias, obsessions, compulsions, panic attacks, and other anxiety-related problems. The extreme popularity of antianxiety drugs, or minor tranquilizers as they are sometimes called, is indicated by the large numbers of prescriptions filled for these drugs in Canada, the United States, and Europe. The most popular, most effective, and most abused of these drugs are the *benzodiazepines*, often known by their trade names, including Librium, Valium, and Xanax (Julien, 2000). Benzodiazepines appear to work by activating what is called the *benzodiazepine receptor*, which, in turn, produces activity in receptors sensitive to *gamma-aminobutyric acid* (GABA), an inhibitory neurotransmitter. More specifically, benzodiazepines appear to enhance the attachment of GABA molecules to the postsynaptic neuron by reconfiguring the shape of GABA receptors, thereby producing more neural activity.

Before the benzodiazepines were synthesized in the early 1960s, the major effective antianxiety drugs had been the barbiturates. The immediate success of Valium and Librium was due in part to the false belief that these newer drugs have a lower risk of abuse and are safer in cases of overdose (Lickey & Gordon, 1983). Although they are the safest of the antianxiety drugs, researchers now know that the benzodiazepines can also produce physical tolerance and withdrawal when removed. Some individuals find it very difficult to stop using benzodiazepines because of the withdrawal syndrome and, thus, show an addiction to the drug. Taken in low dosages and for short periods, though, these drugs can be effective means of reducing anxiety without incurring a high risk of physical dependence.

Besides being effective in treating depression, antidepressant drugs have also been used successfully to treat several anxiety disorders, including panic disorder and agoraphobia (Klein, 1996). These drugs appear to reduce the incidence of panic attacks, including those that accompany severe agoraphobia. However, antidepressant drugs do not reduce the anticipatory anxiety that a person feels between panic attacks.

Although the antidepressants and other drugs are useful in alleviating the symptoms of certain anxiety disorders, they do not cure any of these conditions. Because the disorders are at least partly heritable, as we saw in Chapter 17, they may have some biological causes at their root. While drug therapy

**antianxiety drugs** Drugs used to treat anxiety-related disorders.

is helpful, the most permanent and long-lasting treatment is cognitive-behaviour therapy. The drugs may be very useful in reducing symptoms so that patients can participate effectively in therapy, but they do not provide a long-term solution.

**Drug Therapy for Attention-Deficit/Hyperactivity Disorder** As mentioned earlier in the text, the symptoms of attention-deficit/hyperactivity disorder include inattentiveness, overactivity, and impulsivity. Children diagnosed with the disorder experience considerable difficulty persisting in tasks, remaining in place, and organizing their activities. Consequently they often perform poorly in school environments and are at academic risk.

Drug therapy is the most widely used treatment for attention-deficit/hyperactivity disorder and is the most commonly administered medication by school nurses (O'Connor, 2001). Among the drugs prescribed, *methylphenidate* (Ritalin) is the most common. It is an amphetamine—a stimulant—and thus might seem ill-suited to address the symptoms of the disorder. Nevertheless, it has proven effective in reducing overactivity and distractability, while at the same time increasing focus and alertness (Konrad, Gunther, Hanisch, & Herpertz-Dahlmann, 2004). It is not without multiple side effects, which include decreased cerebral blood flow, decreased production of growth hormone, insomnia, and psychotic symptoms. Nor are its long-term effects well known. *Pemoline* (Cylert), a stimulant with a very different chemical structure than methylphenidate, and *atomoxetin* (Strattera), a non-prescription drug that blocks norepinephine reuptake, are also prescribed for the disorder. Each has its own side effects.

## Electroconvulsive Therapy

**Electroconvulsive therapy (ECT)** involves applying a pair of electrodes to a person's head and then passing a brief surge of electrical current through them. The jolt produces a seizure—a storm of electrical activity in the brain that renders the person unconscious. The wild firing of neurons that control movement produces convulsions—muscular rigidity and trembling, followed by rhythmic movements of the head, trunk, and limbs. After a few minutes, the person falls into a deep sleep. Today, people are anaesthetized and temporarily paralyzed before the current is turned on. This procedure eliminates the convulsions but not the seizure, which is what causes the therapeutic effect. The seizure is believed to cause the brain to release higher than normal amounts of GABA, which decreases brain activity.

Electroconvulsive therapy has a bad reputation among many clinicians because it has been used to treat disorders such as schizophrenia, on which it has no useful effects, and because people have received excessive numbers of ECT treatments—as many as hundreds. Nevertheless, it appears to be a helpful treatment for some patients with major depression and extreme manic disorders, and is accepted as appropriate practice by the Canadian Psychiatric Association (e.g., Flint & Gagnon, 2002). No one knows for certain why ECT is effective for some patients.

A case report by Fink (1976) illustrates the response of a depressed patient to a course of ECT. A 44-year-old widow had been hospitalized for three months for severe depression. A course of three ECT treatments per week was prescribed for her by her therapist's supervisor. Unknown to her therapist (a trainee), the first 12 treatments were subthreshold; that is, the intensity of the electrical current was too low to produce seizures. (The treatments could be regarded as placebo treatments.) Although both the woman and her therapist expected her to show some improvement, none was seen. In the next 14 treatments, the current was raised to a sufficient level to produce seizures. After five actual seizures, both the woman and the therapist noticed an improvement. The woman began to complain less about various physical symptoms, to participate in hospital activities, and to make more positive statements about her mood. She became easier to talk with, and the therapist's notes of their conversations immediately proliferated. The fact that these responses occurred only after several actual seizures suggests that improvement stemmed from the biological treatment and not simply from the therapist's or the woman's expectations.

Some people with depression do not respond to antidepressant drugs, but a substantial percentage of these people improve after a few sessions of ECT. Because antidepressant medications are generally slow acting, taking 10 days to 2 weeks for their therapeutic effects to begin, severe cases of depression are sometimes treated with a brief course of ECT to reduce the symptoms right away. These people are then maintained on an antidepressant drug. Because a person with major depressive disorder runs a 15 percent chance of dying by suicide, the use of ECT may be justified in such cases (Prudic & Sackeim, 1999).

ECT treatments are not without problems. They clearly cause at least short-term memory loss (e.g., Lisanby et al., 2000). Although the evidence is inconclusive, there are concerns about the potential for permanent memory loss. Nowadays, ECT is usually administered only to the right hemisphere, in order to minimize negative effects on memory. For many years, there were concerns that ECT might cause permanent brain damage. There is no convincing evidence thus far that this is the case (e.g., Obergriesser, Ende, Braus, & Henn, 2003; Zachrisson et al., 2000). In fact, some researchers argue that the refinement of the procedure over the past several decades has led to techniques that can be effective with minimal adverse effects (Persad, 2001). For some people, there are intrapersonal consequences—they may feel ashamed and humiliated that they need what is perceived as a radical treatment (Johnstone, 1999).

**electroconvulsive therapy (ECT)** Treatment for severe depression that involves passing small amounts of electric current through the brain to produce seizure activity.

## Then and Now

### The Controversy of ECT

Electroconvulsive therapy (ECT) has been a source of controversy for many years. Treatment in the 1930s involved drug-induced seizures, resulting in unpleasant side effects. Throughout the 1940s, 1950s, and 1960s, ECT was widely practised, and criticized for being overused. The introduction of more effective drug treatments and social pressure lead to the decline of ECT in the late 1960s. However, since the 1980s, use of ECT has been steadily increasing, and it is still used today.

Around the time that the use of convulsion therapy was initiated, three key psychological disorders were most prevalent in the psychiatric community: neurosyphilis, dementia praecox (which we now call schizophrenia), and manic-depressive insanity (which is now known as major depression and bipolar disorder) (Fink, 1999a, 1999b). No effective treatments had yet been established for any of these disorders, although a number of unusual treatments had been attempted. Fink (1999a, 1999b) highlighted some of the treatments, such as removal of the sexual organs, doses of arsenic and mercury (specifically to treat syphilis), and prolonged sleep. Early theories of psychological disorder focused on bacterial infection. In an attempt to control infection, patients with psychological disorders had teeth, tonsils, gallbladder, or sections of their colon removed. These early treatments were ineffective and inhumane, and many patients died.

Although convulsive therapy has often been depicted negatively in the media, at the time of its introduction it was considered a humane response to many of the other dangerous and horrific treatments then available. This is not to say that early convulsive therapy was a pleasant experience. Its earliest form, in 1934, was induction of seizure by the drug Metrazol (Meduna, 1985). The effect of the seizure did seem to relieve some of the symptoms associated with psychological disorders, but patients found the experience extremely unpleasant. After a dose of the drug was injected to induce convulsions, patients would feel their heart race and have feelings of panic. When they awoke from the seizure, their mouths were often bleeding as a result of their jaws clamping shut on their tongues and cheeks. Patients complained of intense headaches and muscular pain after the procedure (Weigert, 1940).

ECT was introduced in 1938 (Abrams, 1997). Similar to previous methods involving drugs, the goal of administering electric shock was to induce seizure. As with the drug treatments, the therapy was effective in some cases, but had unpleasant side effects. In the preliminary form of the treatment, the patient received a bilateral electric current. This meant that the current was administered to both sides of the brain. As the therapy advanced, so did methods to make the procedure less harmful to patients. ECT now involves general anaesthetic and muscle relaxants, and it is overseen by physicians who carefully monitor the patient's vital signs (AETMIS, 2002). Before muscle relaxants became a standard component of ECT, the violent jerking of the body caused by the seizure was so strong that some patients actually broke bones! Unilateral electric currents are now used, which means that the current is applied to only one side of the brain, leading to a less severe shock.

Somewhat ironically, as the safety and efficacy of ECT increased, public perception of the treatment became more negative. Films such as *One Flew over the Cuckoo's Nest* portray ECT in a negative light. In the film, Jack Nicholson's character receives ECT, but he is not treated using a unilateral current, nor is he administered anaesthesia or muscle relaxants, which were standard procedure at the time. The film also inaccurately portrays ECT as a method of behavioural control (Beyer, Weiner, & Glenn, 1998). Although initial methods of ECT were inhumane, by the time the film was released, psychiatrists understood that ECT was primarily effective for people who suffered from depression. ECT would certainly never be used now as a means of punishing or controlling an institutionalized person.

Beyond ECT's being portrayed in a negative light in the media, there has also been a strong stigma attached to ECT and the people who have received it. One of the best-known examples of this is American Senator Thomas Eagleton, who was asked to step down as a vice-presidential running mate in 1972 after he announced that he had been in a psychiatric institution and had received ECT (Hirshbein & Sarvananda, 2008). In regards to the treatment itself, many people still incorrectly believe that ECT causes permanent memory loss and is painful, and that patients are never told what is happening during the treatment (Kerr et al., 1982).

Although many people in the general public still have a negative perception of ECT, decades of research indicate that the treatment is effective for depression (although it was used for many years to treat schizophrenia, with little success). There is evidence that ECT acts more rapidly than antidepressant drugs and can be more effective (AETMIS, 2003). Psychiatrists generally agree that ECT is a safe and effectual treatment option, but the public misunderstanding and the stigma attached to ECT are significant obstacles that contribute to the ongoing controversy.

## Psychosurgery

One other biological treatment for psychological disorders is even more controversial than electroconvulsive therapy: **psychosurgery**, which is the treatment of a psychological disorder, in the absence of obvious organic damage, through brain surgery (see Jasper, 1995, for a historical account). In contrast, brain surgery to remove a tumour or diseased neural tissue or to repair a damaged blood vessel is not psychosurgery, and there is no controversy about these procedures.

You may recall from Chapter 13 that prefrontal lobotomies were found to have serious side effects, such as apathy and severe blunting of emotions, intellectual impairments, and deficits in judgment and planning ability. Nevertheless, the procedure was once used for a variety of conditions, most of which were not improved by the surgery. Tens of thousands of prefrontal lobotomies were performed worldwide from the 1930s through the 1950s. A simple procedure, called "ice pick" prefrontal lobotomy by its critics and *leukotomy* by its proponents, was even performed on an outpatient basis. The development of antipsychotic drugs and the increasing attention paid to the serious side effects of prefrontal lobotomy led to a sharp decline in the use of this procedure during the 1950s. Today, it is no longer performed (Valenstein, 1986).

A few surgeons have continued to refine the technique of psychosurgery and now perform a procedure called a **cingulotomy**, which involves cutting the cingulum bundle, a small band of nerve fibres that connects the prefrontal cortex with parts of the limbic system (Ballantine, Bouckoms, Thomas, & Giriunas, 1987). Cingulotomies have been shown to be effective in helping some people who have severe obsessive-compulsive disorder (Jenike, 2000). In a recent study, Baer and his colleagues (1995) conducted a long-term follow-up study of 18 people who underwent cingulotomy for severe obsessive-compulsive disorder. For each of these people, other forms of therapy—drug therapy and behaviour therapy—had been unsuccessful in treating the symptoms of this disorder. However, after their surgeries, the people in Baer's study showed marked improvements in their functioning, decreased symptoms of depression and anxiety, and few negative side effects.

I must stress that psychosurgery should be used only as a last resort and never on a patient who cannot consent to treatment. The effects of psychosurgery are permanent; there is no way to reverse a brain lesion. All mental health professionals hope that more effective behavioural techniques and new drug treatments will make psychosurgical procedures obsolete.

**psychosurgery** Unalterable brain surgery used to relieve the symptoms of psychological disorders.

**cingulotomy** The surgical destruction of the cingulum bundle, which connects the prefrontal cortex with the limbic system; helps to reduce intense anxiety and the symptoms of obsessive-compulsive disorder.

## Evaluation of Biological Treatments

There can be no doubt that drug therapy is the preferred biological treatment for psychological disorders. Drug therapy, though, represents only a treatment option; it is not a cure. Usually, the drugs are effective only to the extent that the people for whom they are prescribed actually use them. In some cases, people forget to take their drugs, only to have their symptoms return. In other cases, people take their drugs, get better, and stop taking the drugs because they feel that they are no longer "sick." In these cases, too, the symptoms soon return. For some people, this cycle repeats itself over and over.

Thus, while drug therapy is an effective treatment option, it is not a panacea. But no cures for mental illness are on the horizon. And until one appears, research will continue on the development of new and more effective drugs and on finding ways to encourage people to follow their prescription regimens more closely.

## Interim Summary

### Biological Treatments

Biological treatments for psychological disorders include drugs, electroconvulsive therapy, and psychosurgery. Research has shown that treatment of the positive symptoms of schizophrenia with antipsychotic drugs, of major depression with antidepressant drugs, and of bipolar disorder with lithium carbonate are the most effective ways to alleviate the symptoms of these disorders. A new class of antipsychotic drugs shows promise for treating the negative symptoms of schizophrenia. Tricyclic antidepressant drugs can also alleviate severe anxiety that occurs during panic attacks and agoraphobia and can reduce the severity of obsessive-compulsive disorder. The antianxiety drugs help reduce anticipatory anxiety that occurs between panic attacks. Although electroconvulsive therapy is an effective treatment for depression, there are important risks; thus, this treatment is reserved for cases in which rapid relief is critical. The most controversial treatment, psychosurgery, is rarely performed today. Its only presently accepted use, in the form of cingulotomy, is for treatment of crippling compulsions that cannot be reduced by more conventional means.

#### QUESTIONS TO CONSIDER

1. Suppose that you had a friend who was about to begin drug therapy for a psychological disorder. Suppose further that you were able to accompany your friend to one of his or her pretreatment sessions with a psychiatrist (at present, only physicians, not clinical psychologists, can prescribe drugs). What kind of questions would you ask the psychiatrist about the particular kind of drug therapy he or she was recommending for your friend? Would the questions you ask differ depending on the kind of problem your friend was experiencing?

2. Suppose that your friend was treated for depression with tricyclics and the treatment failed—your friend is still extremely depressed. The psychiatrist now recommends ECT. What is your response? What sort of advice can you offer his or her family about following or not following the psychiatrist's recommendation?

# Ethical Issues in Psychotherapy

The special relationship that exists between the therapist and the client is duplicated in few other places in society. With the possible exception of the traditional role of religious leaders, few people earn their living by listening to others describe the deeply intimate details of their lives. Unfortunately, the same characteristics that give the therapeutic relationship its potential for healing may also lead to abuses. For this reason, psychologists have developed a set of ethical standards to guide their professional activities, and legislatures and courts have provided additional regulations concerning the practice of therapy.

The ethical standards for psychologists were formally defined by the publication of the *Canadian Code of Ethics for Psychologists, Third Edition* (Canadian Psychological Association, 2000). One important principle is the sexuality standard, which specifies that sexual intimacies with clients are unethical. A therapist who suggests such intimacy to a client or who allows himself or herself to be approached sexually by the client is unquestionably violating this standard. Nonetheless, the problem of sexual relations between therapist and client, although rare, remains an issue in psychotherapy (Pope, 2000).

Another ethical principle is the *confidentiality standard*, which states that any information obtained about the client during therapy is confidential. This confidentiality extends to members of the client's family.

What should the therapist do if he or she learns that the client is harming, or intends to harm, someone? Reporting the client to the police, a social service agency, or the intended victim clearly would violate the confidentiality standard. The Canadian Psychological Association ethical code recognizes that psychologists will experience conflict when they encounter this type of situation. Nevertheless, psychologists are expected to take timely action to protect others who may be at risk. If possible, the therapist should convince the client to co-operate with, or at least consent to, the disclosure. If not, the responsible therapist must take action on his or her own. The solution is that simple. Some psychologists believe that their sole responsibility should be to the client, and that a fundamental breach in the client–therapist relationship would occur if the therapist were to report a client's harmful activities or intentions. Our opinion, shared by many others, is that a therapist does a client no favour by concealing his or her harmful acts or intentions. The longer the patient goes undeterred, the greater the legal and social consequences that he or she will experience.

## Interim Summary

### Ethical Issues in Psychotherapy

To enhance and protect the therapist–client relationship, the Canadian Psychological Association has developed a set of ethical standards to guide the practice of therapy. Two especially important standards involve restraint of sexual relations between therapist and client and confidentiality.

**QUESTION TO CONSIDER**

1. Suppose that you have been asked by your psychology teacher to give a class presentation on the topic of ethical issues in psychotherapy. During the presentation, one of your fellow students asks you to provide some examples of the different ways in which a therapist could breach the confidentiality restraint. What is your response?

# Selecting a Therapist

Chances are good that at some time you or a close friend will become worried, anxious, or depressed. In most cases, people get through these times in their lives by talking with sympathetic friends, relatives, teachers, or members of the clergy. But sometimes problems persist despite this help, and the person in distress thinks about seeking professional help. How can you tell that you need to consult a therapist, and how do you go about finding a good one?

In general, if you have a problem that makes you unhappy and that persists for several months, you should seriously consider getting professional advice. If the problem is very severe, you should not wait but should look for help immediately. For example, if you experience acute panic attacks, find yourself contemplating suicide, or hear voices that you know are not there, do not wait to see whether the problems go away. You should also think about consulting a professional for specific problems, such as unhealthy habits like smoking, or specific fears, such as fear of flying. You do not have to be "mentally ill" to seek psychological help.

If you are a student at a university, the best place to turn to is the counselling service. If you are not sure what mental health support is available on campus, someone in the

**TABLE 18•4 Types of Therapists, Their Degree Credentials, and Their Training and Professional Responsibilities**

| Title | Degree | Training Background and Professional Duties |
|---|---|---|
| Clinical psychologist | Ph.D. or Psy.D. | Graduate training in research, diagnosis, and therapy plus one year clinical internship. Conducts assessment and therapy; may teach in a university setting and conduct clinical research. |
| Counselling psychologist | Ph.D., Psy.D. or Ed.D. | Graduate training in counselling. Conducts educational, vocational, and personal counselling. |
| Psychoanalyst | M.D. | Medical training plus specialized training in psychoanalysis. Conducts psychoanalytic therapy. |
| Psychiatrist | M.D. | Medical training plus psychiatry residency. Conducts diagnosis and biomedical therapy and psychotherapy. |
| Social worker | M.S.W. | Graduate work in counselling and community psychology. Conducts psychotherapy; helps patients return to community. |
| Psychiatric nurse | Diploma | Completion of approved psychiatric nursing program. Provides a variety of mental health services, usually as a member of a multidisciplinary team. |

psychology department will certainly be able to tell you where to go. In larger universities, the psychology department often operates its own clinic. If you are not a student, you should ask your physician or call your provincial or municipal mental health department and ask for advice. Or call the psychology department at a local university; you will surely reach someone who will help you find professional help.

**Table 18•4** describes some of the more common types of therapists, training and degree credentials, and the general types of responsibilities each type of therapist assumes. As you can see, the training and the types of professional duties assumed by therapists vary considerably. In addition, therapists often conduct therapy from particular theoretical orientations, as you saw earlier in this chapter. However, research suggests that the orientation of the therapist may not be a very important factor to consider when choosing a therapist, as each orientation has both advantages and limitations (Smith & Glass, 1977).

But be careful. Not mentioned in Table 18.4, because he or she is not a legitimate practitioner, is the *charlatan*, or quack, who pretends to have knowledge of something—in this case, treatment of psychological disorders—but does not. Some charlatans may attempt to treat their clients' problems through psychic healing, astrology, palm reading, or other unscientific or false approaches. Other charlatans may use respectable-sounding titles such as "psychotherapist" but lack knowledge of psychological disorders and therapeutic skills.

Charlatans can be found in almost every community, swindling unsuspecting clients out of thousands of dollars each year. They are generally very good liars, leading people to believe that they have the requisite therapeutic skills. In addition, many people seeking therapy are not very wise consumers. They don't know what to look for in a genuine therapist.

Here are three reasonable questions you should ask when you feel that you need to seek help from a therapist:

1. Is the therapist licensed to practise therapy in the province in which he or she is practising?
2. What kind of formal training does the therapist have? From what academic institution does the therapist hold advanced degrees? Did the therapist fulfill an internship during which he or she learned therapeutic techniques under the supervision of licensed practitioners?
3. What kind of reputation does the therapist have? Is he or she known for practising therapy using one or more of the unscientific approaches mentioned?

If a therapist is not licensed to practise, has little or no formal training in therapy, and is known to practise therapy using unscientific approaches, then he or she is very likely a charlatan and you should avoid consulting with this person for therapy of any sort.

You should also talk with the therapist before committing yourself to a course of therapy. Do you like the person? Do you find the person sympathetic? If not, look elsewhere. Do not be impressed by an authoritative manner or glib assurances that he or she knows best what you need. Look for someone who asks good questions about your problems and needs and who helps you formulate a specific and realistic set of goals. Find out whether the therapist specializes in your type of problem. For example, if you want to overcome a specific fear or break a specific habit, you may not want to embark on a series of sessions in which you are expected to talk about the history of your relations with other family members. On the other hand, if your problem is with family relations, then a family therapist may be the best person to consult.

What about fees? Research on this topic indicates that the amount of money a person pays has no relation to the benefits he or she receives. Ask the therapist about how much the services will cost. Find out whether your health plan will cover the fees. Do some comparison shopping. And be aware of the fact that therapists will often adjust their fees according to the ability of the client to pay.

How long should therapy continue? In some cases, the therapist will suggest a fixed number of sessions. In other cases, the arrangement will be open-ended. But how do you decide when to quit in those cases when the duration is indefinite? Here are some guidelines: If you do not make progress within a reasonable amount of time, find someone else. If the therapist seems to be trying to exploit you—for example, by suggesting that sexual relations with him or her would benefit you—run, do not walk, away. The person is violating ethical guidelines and is undoubtedly not someone who should be entrusted with your problems. If you find that therapy becomes the most important part of your life, or if you have become so dependent on your therapist that you feel unable to decide for yourself, think about quitting. If your therapist seems to want you to stay on even though your original problems have been solved, it is time to cut the cord.

Always remember that the therapist is someone *you* consult for professional advice and help. You do not owe the therapist anything other than frankness and a good-faith attempt to follow his or her advice. If you do not like the person or the advice, do not worry about hurting the therapist's feelings—look for someone else. Most people who consult therapists are glad that they did so; they usually find experienced, sympathetic people they can trust who really do help them with their problems. According to Friedman (2007), "In the end, psychotherapy is a very personal business. If you need brain surgery, it doesn't really matter if you like your surgeon as long as he's skilled and competent. But in therapy, skill and competence are necessary but not enough; personal fit, more than almost anything, can make the therapy—or break it."

## Interim Summary

### Selecting a Therapist

Most of us experience a time in life when we are plagued by a persistent personal problem that makes us unhappy. In this situation, seeking professional help is usually a good idea. Counselling services, mental health centres, and psychologists and psychiatrists can generally be found in almost any city or town.

Finding a therapist who is right for you requires that you do some homework. As a rule, a good therapist will be licensed to practise therapy, have specific training in the treatment of psychological problems and psychological disorders, and have a good reputation for being an empathetic and supportive therapist. If the therapist you choose turns out to be unsuitable for your needs, do not hesitate to look for a different therapist. The majority of people who seek therapy benefit from it and are happy that they sought help for their problems.

**QUESTIONS TO CONSIDER**

1. Sometimes people shy away from seeking therapy because of the stigma that they think will be attached to them if they do. After reading this chapter, what suggestions might you have for these people to encourage them to seek therapy?
2. Other than the fee paid to a therapist, what is the difference between a therapist and a friend? After all, doesn't a friend serve some of the same functions as a therapist: confidant, problem solver, and source of empathy, warmth, and support?

# EPILOGUE

## Losing Symptoms, Losing Self?

The prologue introduced Geoff, who, after reversals of both fortune and quality of life, found respite in a combination of drug therapy and psychotherapy following his diagnosis of bipolar I disorder. While he was still relying on lithium and other drugs to the exclusion of psychotherapy, he wondered about the authenticity of his life, questioning whether his sense of who he was had grown so thin that he was becoming a ghost. Though we weren't told this, we are probably justified in assuming that Geoff continued his treatment in subsequent years.

What about people for whom drug therapy begins at an early age and continues thereafter? What do they risk becoming? Friedman (2008) recounts the case of one of his patients, Julie, who had begun the use of antidepressant drugs when she was 14 and was now 31. She had frequently been suicidal and credited the fact that she was still alive to the medications. According to Friedman, she could remember what her depression had felt like when it was first diagnosed. In the meantime, she had moved from adolescence into adulthood and was thus different from most of Friedman's patients, who he first began to consult with when they were already adults.

The question he poses is this: To what extent had Julie's long use of drugs altered the course of her psychological development—her core identify, as he put it? To what extent was she a different Julie than she might have been had her reliance on drugs not been so long-term? Or, how might she have been different had she relied on psychotherapy instead of on a combination of drugs and psychotherapy, as in Geoff's case? In the absence of data on the long-term psychological effects of antidepressants, there is little empirical basis for an answer to such questions.

It is not unusual for clients who take drugs for psychological disorders to ask similar questions. Peter Kramer was relatively new to his psychiatric practice when he wrote a best-selling book, *Listening to Prozac* (1993). In it, he recounted case studies of his own patients following their introduction to Prozac, which many of them characterized as a wonder drug in view of its positive effects. In the final chapter of the book, Kramer picked up themes from the American novelist and essayist Walker Percy. They related to Kramer's observations of his patients and his realization that Prozac may have been doing more than simply remitting the symptoms of severe depression. The drug also may have altered who they were in some fundamental, definitive way, or at least it may have altered what they might have become.

Without in any way denying the serious threat that major depressive disorder and other mood disorders pose—the risk that, untreated, a person may well end his or her life—Kramer, like Percy, questions whether the suffering that such disorders entail might have some larger purpose. It may somehow be refining or authenticating, or may somehow deepen the contours of personhood. Quick remission of that suffering may constitute another adverse side effect of the medication.

## Canadian Connections to Research in This Chapter


Ahrens, B., Grof, P., Moller, H.-J., Muller-Oerlinghaussen, B., & Wolf, T. (1995). Extended survival of patients on long-term lithium treatment. *Canadian Journal of Psychiatry, 40,* 241–246. (University of Ottawa: www.uottawa.ca)

Dobson, K. S., & Khatri, N. (2000). Cognitive therapy: Looking backward, looking forward. *Journal of Clinical Psychology, 56,* 907–923. (University of Calgary: www.ucalgary.ca)

Enns, N., & Reiss, J. P. (1992). Electroconvulsive therapy. *Canadian Journal of Psychiatry, 37,* 671–678. (University of Manitoba: www.umanitoba.ca)

Goldapple, K., Segal, Z., Garson, C., Lau, M., Bieling, P., Kennedy, S., & Mayberg, H. (2004). Modulation of cortical-limbic pathways in major depression. *Archives of General Psychiatry, 61,* 34–41. (University of Toronto: www.utoronto.ca)

Goldman, D. L. (1990). Dorothea Dix and her two missions of mercy in Nova Scotia. *Canadian Journal of Psychiatry, 35*(2), 139–143. (Canadian Journal of Psychiatry: www.cpa-apc.org/Publications/cjpHome.asp)

Grof, P. (2003). Selecting effective long-term treatment for biopolar patients: Monotherapy and combinations. *Journal of Clinical Psychiatry, 64* (Suppl 5), 53–61. (University of Ottawa: www.uottawa.ca)

Jasper, H. H. (1995). A historical perspective: The rise and fall of prefrontal lobotomy. In H. H. Jasper & S. Riggio (Eds.), *Epilepsy and the functional anatomy of the frontal lobe.* New York: Raven Press. (Université de Montréal: www.umontreal.ca)

Lehmann, H. E., & Ban, T. A. (1997). The history of the psychopharmacology of schizophrenia. *Canadian Journal of Psychiatry, 42,* 152–162. (McGill University: www.mcgill.ca)

Lesage, A. D., Morissette, R., Fortier, L., Reinharz, D., & Contandriopoulos, A. (2000). 1. Downsizing psychiatric hospitals: Needs for care and services of current and discharged long-stay inpatients. *Canadian Journal of Psychiatry, 45,* 526–531. (Université de Montréal: www.umontreal.ca)

Mayberg, H. (2003). Modulating dysfunctional limbic-cortical circuits in depression: Towards development of brain-based algorithms for diagnosis and optimized treatment. *British Medical Bulletin, 65,* 193–207. (University of Toronto: www.utoronto.ca)

Meichenbaum, D. (1977). *Cognitive behavior modification: An integrative approach.* New York: Plenum Press. (University of Waterloo: www.uwaterloo.ca)

Meichenbaum, D. (1993). Changing conceptions of cognitive behavior modification: Retrospect and prospect. *Journal of Consulting and Clinical Psychology, 61,* 202–204. (University of Waterloo: www.uwaterloo.ca)

Persad, E. (2001). Electroconvulsive therapy: The controversy and the evidence. *Canadian Journal of Psychiatry, 46*(8), 702–703. (University of Toronto: www.utoronto.ca)

Yassa, R., Nair, N., Iskandar, H., & Schwartz, G. (1990). Factors in the development of severe forms of tardive dyskinesia. *American Journal of Psychiatry, 147,* 1156–1163. (Douglas Hospital, Verdun, QC: www.mcgill.ca/douglas)

# Suggestions for Further Reading

Aponte, J. F., & Wohl, J. (2000). *Psychological interventions and cultural diversity* (2nd ed.). Boston, MA: Allyn and Bacon.

This book addresses general issues faced by practitioners who deal with diverse ethnic, minority, and racial populations as well as specific types of interventions used for specific minority groups and problems.

Carson, R. C., Butcher, J. N., & Mineka, S. (2000). *Abnormal psychology and modern life* (11th ed.). New York: Allyn and Bacon.

A highly readable, upper-division undergraduate text about psychological disorders, including their causes and treatments.

Freud, S. (1950). *The interpretation of dreams* (A. A. Brill, Trans.). New York: Modern Library. (Original work published 1900.)

This classic book is recommended to those who wish to understand better Freud's emphasis on dreams as the "royal road" to understanding the unconscious mind.

Kazdin, A. E. (2001). *Behaviour modification in applied settings.* Pacific Grove, CA: Brooks/Cole.

Thorpe, G. L., & Olson, S. L. (1997). *Behaviour therapy: Concepts, procedures, and applications* (2nd ed.). Boston, MA: Allyn and Bacon.

These two texts provide excellent summaries of the development and uses of behaviour modification.

Rogers, C. R. (1951). *Client-centered therapy.* New York: Houghton Mifflin.

Written by the founder of the humanistic movement in psychology, this book outlines the major features of client-centred therapy.

Wedding, D., & Corsini, R. (2000). *Case studies in psychotherapy* (3rd ed.). Itasca, IL: Peacock.

A collection of case studies involving different varieties of cognitive-behaviour, humanistic, and psychoanalytic therapies. In each case study, a client's problem and the means by which it was addressed are discussed. Very interesting reading.

# References


Abbass, A., Sheldon, A., Gyra, J., & Kalpin, A. (2008). Intensive short-term dynamic psychotherapy for DSM-IV personality disorders: A randomized controlled trial. *Journal of Nervous and Mental Disease, 196*(3), 211–216.

Abela, J., & Sullivan, C. (2003). A test of Beck's cognitive diathesis-stress theory of depression in early adolescents. *Journal of Early Adolescence, 23*(4), 384–404.

Abrams, R. (1997). *Electroconvulsive therapy*. New York: Oxford University Press.

Abramson, L. Y., Alloy, L. B., & Metalsky, G. I. (1995). In G. M. Buchanan, & M. E. P. Seligman (Eds.), *Explanatory style.* Hillsdale, NJ: Lawrence Erlbaum Associates, Inc.

Abramson, L. Y., Metalsky, G. I., & Alloy, L. B. (1989). Hopelessness depression: A theory-based subtype. *Psychological Review, 96,* 358–372.

Abramson, L. Y., Seligman, M. E. P., & Teasdale, J. D. (1978). Learned helplessness in humans: Critique and reformulation. *Journal of Abnormal Psychology, 87,* 49–74.

Acierno, R. E., Hersen, M., & Van Hasselt, V. B. (1993). Interventions for panic disorder: A critical review of the literature. *Clinical Psychology Review, 18,* 561–578.

Adair, J. G. (1984). The Hawthorne effect: A reconsideration of the methodological artifact. *Journal of Applied Psychology, 69,* 334–345.

Adair, J. G. (2001). Ethics of psychological research: New policies; continuing issues; new concerns. *Canadian Psychology, 42,* 25–37.

Adair, J. G., Paivio, A., & Ritchie, P. (1996). Psychology in Canada. *Annual Review of Psychology, 47,* 341–370.

Adair-Bischoff, C. E., & Sauve, R. S. (1998). Environmental tobacco smoke and middle ear disease in preschool-age children. *Archives of Pediatrics and Adolescent Medicine, 152,* 127–133.

Addiction Research Foundation (1999). http://www.arf.org/isd/stats/alcohol.htm.

Adey, W. R., Bors, E., & Porter, R. W. (1968). EEG sleep patterns after high cervical lesions in man. *Archives of Neurology, 19,* 377–383.

Adler, A. (1939). *Social interest: A challenge to mankind*. New York: Putnam.

Ægisdóttir, S., White, M. J., SPenger, P. M., Maugherman, A. S., Anderson, L. A., Cook, R. S., Nichols, C. N., Lampropoulos, G. K., Walker, B. S., Cohen, G., & Rush, J. R. (2006). The Meta-analysis of Clinical Judgment Project: Fifty-six years of accumulated research on clinical versus statistical prediction. *The Counseling Psychologist, 34*(3), 341–382.

Agence d'évaluation des technologies et des modes d'intervention en santé (AETMIS). (2002). *L'utilisation des électrochocs au Québec.* Montreal: AETMIS.

Agranoff, B. W., Davis, R. E., & Brink, J. J. (1965). Memory fixation in the goldfish. *Proceedings of the National Academy of Sciences, 54,* 788–793.

Aharon, L., Etcoff, N., Ariely, D., Chabris, C. F., O'Connor, E., & Breiter, H. C. (2001). Beautiful faces have variable reward value: fMRI and behavioral evidence. *Neuron, 32,* 537–551.

Ahrens, B., Grof, P., Moller, H.-J., Muller-Oerlinghaussen, B., & Wolf, T. (1995). Extended survival of patients on long-term lithium treatment. *Canadian Journal of Psychiatry, 40,* 241–246.

Aiello, L. & Wheeler, P. (1995). The expensive-tissue hypothesis. *Current Anthropology, 36,* 199–221.

Aiken, L. R. (2001). *Dying, death, and bereavement* (4th ed.). Mahway, NJ: Lawrence Erlbaum Associates, Inc.

Ainslie, G. (1975). Species reward: A behavioral theory of impulsiveness and impulse control. *Psychological Bulletin, 82,* 463–496.

Ainsworth, M. D. S., Blehar, M. C., Waters, E., & Wall, S. (1978). *Patterns of attachment.* Hillsdale, NJ: Lawrence Erlbaum Associates.

Ainsworth, M. D. S., & Bowlby, J. (1991). An ethological approach to personality development. *American Psychologist, 46,* 333–341.

Ajzen, I. (2001). Nature and operation of attitudes. *Annual Review of Psychology, 52,* 27–58.

Aklin, W., & Turner, S. (2006). Toward understanding ethnic and cultural factors in the interviewing process. *Psychotherapy: Theory, Research, Practice, Training, 43*(1), 50–64.

Alais, D., Blake, R., & Lee, S.-H. (1998). Visual features that vary together over time group together over space. *Nature Neuroscience, 1,* 160–164.

Albright, L., Kenny, D. A., & Malloy, T. E. (1988). Consensus in personality judgments at zero acquaintance. *Journal of Personality and Social Psychology, 55,* 387–395.

Al-Issa, I. (1995). Culture and mental illness in an international perspective. In I. Al-Issa (Ed.), *Handbook of culture and mental illness: An international perspective.* Madison, CT: International Universities Press.

Al-Jeshi, A. A., Epstein, I., & Zipursky, R. B. (2006). An overview of the genetic risk of developing schizophrenia in relatives of schizophrenic patients. *Neurosciences, 11*(1), 7–10.

Allan, L. G., Siegel, S., Kulatunga-Moruzi, C., Eissenberg, T., & Chapman, A. (1997). Isoluminance and contingent color after-effects. *Perception & Psychophysics, 59,* 1327–1334.

Allen, L. S., & Gorski, R. A. (1992). Sexual orientation and the size of the anterior commissure in the human brain. *Proceedings of the National Academy of Sciences, USA, 89,* 7199–7202.

Allen, M. G. (1976). Twin studies of affective illness. *Archives of General Psychiatry, 33,* 1476–1478.

Allen, R. C. (1998). *The employability of university graduates in the humanities, social sciences, and education: Recent statistical evidence.* Ottawa: Social Sciences and Humanities Research Council.

Allik, J., & McCrae, R. R. (2002). A five-factor theory perspective. In R. R. McCrae & J. Allik (Eds.), *The five-factor model of personality across cultures. International and cultural psychology series.* New York: Kluwer Academic/Plenum Publishers.

Allik, J., & McCrae, R. R. (2004). Toward a geography of personality traits: Patterns of profiles across 36 cultures. *Journal of Cross-Cultural Psychology, 35*(1), 13–28.

Allis, C. D., Jenuwein, T., & Reinberg, D. (2007). Overview and concepts. In C. D. Allis, T. Jenuwein, & D. Reinberg (Eds.), *Epigenetics* (pp. 23–61). Cold Spring Harbor, NY: Cold Spring Harbor Laboratory Press.

Allport, G. W. (1968). The historical background of modern social psychology. In G. Lindzey & E. Aronson (Eds.), *The handbook of social psychology, Vol. 1.* Reading, MA: Addison-Wesley.

Allport, G. W., & Odbert, H. S. (1936). Trait-names: A psycholexical study. *Psychological Monographs, 47*(1, Whole No. 211).

Aloise-Young, P. A., Graham, J. W., & Hansen, W. B. (1994). Peer influence on adolescent smoking initiation: A comparison of group members and group outsiders. *Journal of Applied Psychology, 79,* 281–287.

Alsobrook, J. P., & Pauls, D. L. (1997). The genetics of Tourette syndrome. *Neurologic Clinics, 15,* 381–393.

Amaral, D. G., Price, J. L., Pitkänen, A., & Carmichael, S. T. (1992). Anatomical organization of the primate amygdaloid complex. In J. P. Aggleton (Ed.), *The amygdala: Neurobiological aspects of emotion, memory, and mental dysfunction.* New York: Wiley-Liss.

American Psychological Association. (2002). Ethical principles of psychologists and code of conduct. *American Psychologist, 57,* 1060–1073.

Amsel, A. (1962). Frustrative nonreward in partial reinforcement and discrimination learning: Some recent history and a theoretical extension. *Psychological Review, 69,* 306–328.

Anderson, B., & Ley, R. (2001). Dyspnea during panic attacks: An Internet survey of incidences of changes in breathing. *Behavior Modification, 25(4),* 546–554.

Anderson, C. S., Feigin, V., Bennett, D., Lin, R., Hankey, G., & Jamrozik, K. (2004). Active and passive smoking and the risk of subarachnoid hemorrhage: An international population-based case-control study. *Stroke, 35(3)*, 633–637.

Anderson, J. R., Budiu, R., & Reder, L. M. (2001). A theory of sentence memory as part of a general theory of memory. *Journal of Memory and Language, 45*, 337–367.

Andrews, B., Brewin, C. R., Philpott, R., & Stewart, L. (2007). Delayed-onset posttraumatic stress disorder: A systematic review of the evidence. *American Journal of Psychiatry, 164*(9), 1319–1326.

Angrist, B. J., Rotrosen, J., & Gershon, S. (1980). Positive and negative symptoms in schizophrenia—Differential response to amphetamine and neuroleptics. *Psychopharmacology, 72*, 17–19.

Archer, S. L., & Waterman, A. S. (1990). Varieties of identity diffusions and foreclosures: An exploration of subcategories of the identity status. *Journal of Adolescent Research, 5*, 96–111.

Ariyasu, H., Takaya, K., Tagami, T., Ogawa, Y., Hosoda, K., Akamizu, T., Suda, M., Koh, T., Natsui, K., Toyooka, S., Shirakami, G., Usui, T., Shimatsu, A., Doi, K., Hosoda, H., Kojima, M., Kangawa, K., & Nakao, K. (2001). Stomach is a major source of circulating ghrelin, and feeding state determines plasma ghrelin-like immunoreactivity levels in humans. *Journal of Clinical Endocrinology and Metabolism, 86*, 4753–4758.

Armfield, F. (1994). Preventing post-traumatic stress disorder resulting from military operations. *Military Medicine, 159*, 739–746.

Arrindell, W. A. (2003). Cultural abnormal psychology. *Behaviour Research Therapy, 41*, 749–753.

Asch, S. E. (1946). Forming impressions of personality. *Journal of Abnormal and Social Psychology, 41*, 258–290.

Asch, S. E. (1951). Effects of group pressure upon the modification and distortion of judgment. In H. Guetzkow (Ed.), *Groups, leadership, and men*. Pittsburgh: Carnegie.

Asch, S. E. (1952). *Social psychology*. New York: Prentice-Hall.

Asch, S. E. (1955). Opinions and social pressure. *Scientific American, 193*, 31–35.

Ashford, J. W., Schmitt, F. A., & Kumar, V. (1996). Diagnosis of Alzheimer's disease. *Psychiatric Annals, 26*, 262–268.

Assanand, S., Pinel, J. P. J., & Lehman, D. R. (1998). Personal theories of hunger and eating. *Journal of Applied Social Psychology, 28*, 998–1015.

Astafiev, S. V., Shulman, G. L., Stanley, C. M., Snyder, A. Z., Van Essen, D. C., Corbetta, M. (2003). Functional organization of human intraparietal and frontal cortex for attending, looking, and pointing. *Journal of Neuroscience, 23*, 4689–4699.

Astley, S. J., Clarren, S. K., Little, R. E., Sampson, P. D., & Daling, J. R. (1992). Analysis of facial shape in children gestationally exposed to marijuana, alcohol, or cocaine. *Pediatrics, 89*, 67–77.

Atkinson, R. C., & Shiffrin, R. M. (1968). Human memory: A proposed system and its control processes. In K. W. Spence & J. T. Spence (Eds.), *The psychology of learning and motivation: Advances in research and theory, Vol. 2*. New York: Academic Press.

Avey, M. T., Kanyo, R. A., Irwin, E. L., & Sturdy, C. B. (2008). Differential effects of vocalization type, singer and listener on ZENK immediate early gene response in black-capped chickadees (*Poecile atricapillus*). *Behavioural Brain Research, 188*, 201–208.

Avison, W. R., & Cairney, J. (2003). Social structure, stress, and personal control. In S. H. Zarit, L. I. Pearlin, et al. (Eds.), *Personal control in social and life course contexts: Societal impact on aging*. New York: Springer Publishing Co.

Awad, A. G., & Voruganti, L. N. P. (2004). Impact of atypical antipsychotics on quality of life in patients with schizophrenia. *CNS Drugs, 18*(13), 877–893.

Ayllon, T., & Azrin, N. H. (1968). *The token economy: A motivational system for therapy and rehabilitation*. New York: Appleton-Century-Crofts.

Azar, B. (2002, January). Social cognitive neuroscience merges three distinct disciplines in hopes of deciphering the process behind social behavior. *Monitor on Psychology, 33*(1).

Badcock, C. (1991). *Evolution and individual behavior: An introduction to human sociobiology*. Cambridge, MA: Blackwell.

Baddeley, A. (2000). The episodic buffer: A new component of working memory? *Trends in Cognitive Sciences, 4*, 417–423.

Baddeley, A. D. (1982). Domains of recollection. *Psychological Review, 89*, 708–729.

Baddeley, A. D. (1993). Working memory and conscious awareness. In A. F. Collins, S. E. Cathercole, M. A. Conway, & P. E. Morris (Eds.), *Theories of memory*. Hillsdale, NJ: Erlbaum.

Baer, L., Rauch, S. L., Ballantine, H. T., Jr., Martuza, R., Cosgrove, R., Cassem, E., Giriunas, I., Manzo, P. A., Dimino, C., & Jenike, M. A. (1995). Cingulotomy for intractable obsessive-compulsive disorder: Prospective long-term follow-up of 18 patients. *Archives of General Psychiatry, 52*, 384–392.

Bahrick, H. P. (1984). Semantic memory content in permastore: Fifty years of memory for Spanish learned in school. *Journal of Experimental Psychology: General, 113*, 12–29.

Bailey, B. A., & Sokol, R. J. (2008). Pregnancy and alcohol use: Evidence and recommendations for prenatal care. *Clinical Obstetrics and Gynecology, 51*, 436–444.

Bailey, C. H., Kandel, E. R., & Si, K. (2004). The persistence of long-term memory: A molecular approach to self-sustaining changes in learning-induced synaptic growth. *Neuron, 44*, 49–57.

Bailey, J. M., Pillard, R. C., Neale, M. C., & Agyei, Y. (1993). Heritable factors influence sexual orientation in women. *Archives of General Psychiatry, 50*, 217–223.

Bailey, J. M., & Pillard, R. C. (1991). A genetic study of male sexual orientation. *Archives of General Psychiatry, 48*, 1089–1096.

Baillargeon, R., Spelke, E. S., & Wasserman, S. (1985). Object permanence in five-month-old infants. *Cognition, 20*, 191–208.

Baker, C. (2004, February 22). Groupthink at the core of AdScam. *Winnipeg Free Press*.

Baker, R. R. (1980). Goal orientation by blindfolded humans after long-distance displacement: Possible involvment of a magnetic sense. *Science, 210*, 555–557.

Baldessarini, R. J., & Tarsy, D. (1980). Dopamine and the pathophysiology of dyskinesias induced by antipsychotic drugs. *Annual Review of Neuroscience, 3*, 23–41.

Baldwin, J. M. (1892). The psychological laboratory in the University of Toronto. *Science, 19*, 143–144.

Ball, K., & Sekuler, R. (1982). A specific and enduring improvement in visual motion discrimination. *Science, 218*, 697–698.

Ballantine, H. T., Bouckoms, A. J., Thomas, E. K., & Giriunas, I. E. (1987). Treatment of psychiatric illness by stereotactic cingulotomy. *Biological Psychiatry, 22*, 807–819.

Baltes, M. M., & Carstensen, L. L. (2003). The process of successful aging: Selection, optimization and compensation. In U. M. Staudinger & U. Lindenberger (Eds.), *Understanding human development: Dialogues with lifespan psychology*. Dordrecht, Netherlands: Kluwer Academic Publishers.

Baltes, P., & Schaie, K. (1974, October). Aging and IQ: The myth of the twilight years. *Psychology Today*, 35–38.

Bandura, A. (1963). The role of imitation in personality development. *Journal of Nursery Education, 18*, 207–215.

Bandura, A. (1971). Psychotherapy based upon modeling principles. In A. E. Bergin & S. L. Garfield (Eds.), *Handbook of psychotherapy and behavior change*. New York: John Wiley & Sons.

Bandura, A. (1978). The self system in reciprocal determinism. *American Psychologist, 33*, 344–358.

Bandura, A. (1982). Self-efficacy mechanism in human agency. *American Psychologist, 37*, 122–147.

Bandura, A. (1986). *Social foundations of thought and action: A social-cognitive theory*. Englewood Cliffs, NJ: Prentice-Hall.

Bandura, A. (1995). Exercise of personal and collective efficacy in changing societies. In A. Bandura (Ed.), *Self-efficacy in changing societies*. New York: Cambridge University Press.

Bandura, A. (1997). *Self-efficacy: The exercise of control*. New York: W. H. Freeman & Co., Publishers.

Bandura, A. (2002). Social cognitive theory in cultural context. *Applied Psychology, 51*(2), 269–290.

Bandura, A., & Locke, E. A. (2003). Negative self-efficacy and goal effects revisited. *Journal of Applied Psychology, 88*(1), 87–99.

Bandura, A., & Menlove, F. L. (1968). Factors determining vicarious extinction of avoidance behavior through symbolic modeling. *Journal of Personality and Social Psychology, 8*, 99–108.

Bandura, A., Ross, D., & Ross, S. A. (1961). Transmission of aggression through imitation of aggressive models. *Journal of Abnormal and Social Psychology, 63,* 575–582.

Barab, S. A., & Plucker, J. A. (2002). Smart people or smart contexts? Cognition, ability and talent development in an age of situated approaches to knowing and learning. *Educational Psychologist, 37,* 165–182.

Barash, D. (1982). *Sociobiology and behavior.* London: Hodder and Stoughton.

Barber, T. X. (1975). Responding to "hypnotic" suggestions: An introspective report. *American Journal of Clinical Hypnosis, 18,* 6–22.

Bard, K. A., Coles, C. D., Plaatzman, K. A., & Lynch, M. E. (2000). The effects of prenatal drug exposure, term status, and caregiving on arousal and arousal modulation in 8-week-old infants. *Developmental Psychobiology, 36,* 194–212.

Barnas, M. V., Pollina, J., & Cummings, E. M. (1991). Life-span attachment: Relations between attachment and socioemotional functioning in women. *Genetic, Social, and General Psychology Monographs, 89,* 177–202.

Barnes, M. L., & Sternberg, R. J. (1997). A hierarchical model of love and its prediction of satisfaction in close relationships. In R. J. Sternberg & M. Hojjat (Eds.), *Satisfaction in close relationships* (pp. 79–101). New York: The Guilford Press.

Bar-On, R. (1997). *BarOn Emotional Quotient Inventory: Technical manual.* Toronto: Multi-Health Systems.

Baron, R. S., Vandello, J. A., & Brunsman, B. (1996). The forgotten variable in conformity research: Impact of task importance on social influence. *Journal of Personality and Social Psychology, 71,* 915–927.

Baron-Cohen, S., Leslie, A. M., & Frith, U. (1985). Does the autistic child have a "theory of mind?" *Cognition, 21,* 37–46.

Barrick, M. R., Mount, M. K., & Judge, T. A. (2001). Personality and performance at the beginning of the new millennium: What do we know and where do we go next? *International Journal of Selection & Assessment, 9*(1–2), 9–30.

Bartholomew, R. E. (1984). Disease, disorder, or deception? Latah as habit in a Malay extended family. *Journal of Nervous and Mental Disease, 182,* 331–338.

Bartlett, F. C. (1932). *Remembering: An experimental and social study.* Cambridge, UK: Cambridge University Press.

Bartoshuk, L. M., & Beauchamp, G. K. (1994). Chemical senses. *Annual Review of Psychology, 45,* 419–449.

Basoglu, M., Salclogle, E., & Livanou, M. (2002). Traumatic stress responses in earthquake survivors in Turkey. *Journal of Traumatic Stress, 15*(4), 269–276.

Bassili, J. N. (1993). Response latency versus certainty as indexes of the strength of voting intentions in a CATI survey. *Public Opinion Quarterly, 57,* 54–61.

Bassili, J. N. (1995). Response latency and the accessibility of voting intentions: What contributes to accessibility and how it affects vote choice. *Personality and Social Psychology Bulletin, 21,* 686–695.

Basso, A. (2003). *Aphasia and its therapy.* Oxford, UK: Oxford University Press.

Bauer, P. J. (2002). Long-term recall memory: Behavioral and neuro-developmental changes in the first 2 years of life. *Current Directions in Psychological Science, 11,* 137–141.

Baumeister, R. F., Dale, K., & Sommer, K. L. (1998). Freudian defense mechanisms and empirical findings in modern social psychology: Reaction formation, projection, displacement, undoing, isolation, sublimation, and denial. *Journal of Personality, 66,* 1081–1124.

Baumrind, D. (1983). Rejoinder to Lewis' reinterpretation of parental firm control effects: Are authoritative families really harmonious? *Psychological Bulletin, 94,* 132–142.

Baumrind, D. (1991). The influence of parenting style on adolescent competence and substance use. *Journal of Early Adolescence, 11,* 56–95.

Beaupré, M. G., & Hess, U. (2005). Cross-cultural emotion recognition among Canadian ethnic groups. *Journal of Cross-cultural Psychology, 36,* 355–370.

Beauvois, M.-F., & Dérouesné, J. (1979). Phonological alexia: Three dissociations. *Journal of Neurology, Neurosurgery and Psychiatry, 42,* 1115–1124.

Bechara, A., Tranel, D., Damasio, H., Adolphs, R., Rockland, C., & Damasio, A. R. (1995). Double dissociation of conditioning and declarative knowledge relative to the amygdala and hippocampus in humans. *Science, 269,* 1115–1118.

Beck, A. T. (1967). *Depression: Clinical, experimental and theoretical aspects.* New York: Harper and Row.

Beck, A. T. (1991). Cognitive therapy: A thirty-year retrospective. *American Psychologist, 46,* 368–375.

Beck, A. T. (1997). The past and future of cognitive therapy. *Journal of Psychotherapy Practice and Research, 6,* 276–284.

Beck, A. T., Rush, A. J., Shaw, B. F., & Emery, G. (1979). *Cognitive therapy of depression.* New York: Guilford Press.

Becker, C. B., Zayfert, C., & Anderson, E. (2004). A survey of psychologists' attitudes toward and utilization of exposure therapy for PTSD. *Behaviour Research and Therapy, 42,* 277–292.

Behrend, D. A., Rosengren, K. S., & Perlmutter, M. (1992). The relation between private speech and parental interactive style. In R. M. Diaz & L. E. Berk (Eds.), *Private speech: From social interaction to self-regulation* (pp. 85–100). Hillsdale, NJ: Lawrence Erlbaum Associates, Inc.

Belin, P., Zatorre, R. J., & Ahad, P. (2002). Human temporal-lobe response to vocal sounds. *Cognitive Brain Research, 13,* 17–26.

Bell, A. P., Weinberg, M. S., & Hammersmith, S. K. (1981). *Sexual preference: Its development in men and women.* Bloomington: Indiana University Press.

Bell, S. T., Kuriloff, P. J., & Lottes, I. (1994). Understanding attributions of blame in stranger rape and date rape situations: An examination of gender, race, identification, and students' social perceptions of rape victims. *Journal of Applied Social Psychology, 24,* 1719–1734.

Bellugi, U., & Klima, E. S. (1972, June). The roots of language in the sign talk of the deaf. *Psychology Today,* 61–76.

Belmore, S. M. (1987). Determinants of attention during impression formation. *Journal of Experimental Psychology: Learning, Memory, and Cognition, 13,* 480–489.

Bem, D. J. (1972). Self-perception theory. In L. Berkowitz (Ed.), *Advances in experimental social psychology, Vol. 6.* New York: Academic Press.

Bender, L. (1947). Childhood schizophrenia, clinical study of one hundred schizophrenic children. *American Journal of Orthopsychiatry, 17,* 40–56.

Benjamin, J., Li, L., Patterson, C., Greenberg, B. D., Murphy, D. L., & Hamer, D. H. (1996). Population and familial association between the D4 dopamine receptor gene and measures of novelty seeking. *Nature Genetics, 12,* 81–84.

Benninger, M. S. (1999). The impact of cigarette smoking and environmental tobacco smoke on nasal and sinus disease: A review of the literature. *American Journal of Rhinology, 13,* 435–438.

Benzaquén, A.S. (2006). *Encounters with wild children: Temptation and disappointment in the study of human nature.* Montreal & Kingston, ON: McGill-Queen's University Press.

Berenbaum, S. A., & Snyder, E. (1995). Early hormonal influences on childhood sex-typed activity and playmate preferences: Implications for the development of sexual orientation. *Developmental Psychology, 31,* 31–42.

Berenson, A. (2008, February 24). Daring to think differently about schizophrenia. *The New York Times.*

Berk, L. E. (2005). *Infants, children, and adolescents* (5th ed.). Boston, MA: Allyn & Bacon.

Berlin, B., & Kay, P. (1969). *Basic color terms: Their universality and evolution.* Berkeley: University of California Press.

Berlyne, D. E. (1966). Motivational problems raised by exploratory and epistemic behavior. In S. Koch (Ed.), *Psychology: A study of a science, Vol. 5.* New York: McGraw-Hill.

Bernstein, I. L. (1978). Learned taste aversion in children receiving chemotherapy. *Science, 200,* 1302–1303.

Bernstein, W. M., Stephenson, B. O., Snyder, M. L., & Wicklund, R. A. (1983). Causal ambiguity and heterosexual affiliation. *Journal of Experimental Social Psychology, 19,* 78–92.

Berry, J. W. (1984). Towards a universal psychology of cognitive competence. In P. S. Fry (Ed.), *Changing conceptions of intelligence and intellectual functioning.* Amsterdam: North-Holland.

Berry, J. W. (2001). A psychology of immigration. *Journal of Social Issues, 57,* 615–631.

Berry, J. W. (2003). Origins of cross-cultural similarities and differences in human behavior: An ecocultural perspective. In A. Toomela (Ed.), *Cultural guidance in the development of the human mind: Advances in child development within culturally structured environments.* Westport, CT: Ablex Publishing.

Berry, J. W., Poortinga, Y. H., Segall, M. H., & Dasen, P. R. (2002). *Cross-cultural psychology: Research and applications* (2nd ed.). New York: Cambridge University Press.

Bertone, E. R., Snyder, L. A., & Moore, A. S. (2003). Environmental and lifestyle risk factors for oral squamous cell carcinoma in domestic cats. *Journal of Veterinary Internal Medicine, 17(4),* 557–562.

Berwick, D. M. (2003). Disseminating innovations in health care. *Journal of the American Medical Association, 289,* 1969–1975.

Berwin, C. R., Andrews, B., & Valentine, J. D. (2000). *Journal of Consulting and Clinical Psychology, 68,* 748–766.

Beyer, J. L., Weiner, R. D., & Glenn, M. D. (1998). *Electroconvulsive therapy: A programmed text* (2nd ed.). Washington, DC: American Psychiatric Press.

Biber, B., & Alkin, T. (1999). Panic disorder subtypes: Differential responses to $CO_2$ challenge. *American Journal of Psychiatry, 156,* 739–744.

Binder, J. (1998). The therapeutic alliance in the relational models of time-limited dynamic psychotherapy. In J. D. Safran & J. C. Muran (Eds.), *The therapeutic alliance in brief psychotherapy.* Washington, DC: American Psychological Association.

Binder, J. R., Frost, J. A., Hammeke, T. A., Cox, R. W., Rao, S. M., & Prieto, T. (1997). Human brain language areas identified by functional magnetic resonance imaging. *Journal of Neuroscience, 17,* 353–362.

Binder, J. R., Liebenthal, E., Possing, E. T., Medler, D. A., & Ward, B. D. (2004). Neural correlates of sensory and decision processes in auditory object identification. *Nature Neuroscience, 7,* 295–301.

Binet, A., & Henri, V. (1896). La psychologie individuelle. *Année Psychologique, 2,* 411–465.

Binkofski, F., Amunts, K., & Stephan, K. M. (2000). Broca's region subserves imagery of motion: A combined cytoarchitectonic and fMRI study. *Human Brain Mapping, 11,* 273–285.

Birbaumer, N., Veit, R., Lotze, M., Erb, M., Hermann, C., Grodd, W., & Flor, H. (2005). Deficient fear conditioning in psychopathy. *Archives of General Psychiatry, 62,* 799–805.

Birren, J. E., & Morrison, D. F. (1961). Analysis of the WISC subtests in relation to age and education. *Journal of Gerontology, 16,* 363–369.

Bishop, G. D. (1991a). Lay disease representations and responses to victims of disease. *Basic and Applied Social Psychology, 12,* 115–132.

Bishop, G. D. (1991b). Understanding the understanding of illness. In J. A. Skelton & R. T. Croyle, *Mental representation in health and illness.* New York: Springer-Verlag.

Bishop, G. D. (1994). *Health psychology: Integrating mind and body.* Boston: Allyn and Bacon.

Blacher, J., & Baker, B. L. (1987). Dry-bed training for nocturnal enuresis in three children with multiple problems. *Journal of Clinical Child Psychology, 16(3),* 240–244.

Blackburn, R. G. L. (1995). Effect of degree of weight loss on health benefits. *Obesity Research,* 3, 211–216.

Blanchard, R., & Bogaert, A. F. (1996) Homosexuality in men and number of older brothers. *American Journal of Psychiatry, 153,* 27–31.

Blanchard, R., & Ellis, L. (2001) Birth weight, sexual orientation and the sex of preceding siblings. *Journal of Biosocial Science, 33,* 451–467.

Blaxton, T. A. (1989). Investigating dissociations among memory measures: Support for a transfer appropriate processing framework. *Journal of Experimental Psychology: Learning, Memory, and Cognition, 15,* 657–668.

Bleuler, E. (1950). *Dementia praecox: or, the group of schizophrenias. Monograph series on schizophrenia.* New York: International Universities Press.

Bliss, E. L. (1986). *Multiple personality, allied disorders, and hypnosis.* New York: Oxford University Press.

Bliss, T. V., & Lomø, T. (1973). Long-lasting potentiation of synaptic transmission in the dentate area of the anaesthetized rabbit following stimulation of the perforant path. *Journal of Physiology, 232,* 331–356.

Bloom, L. (1970). *Language development: Form and function in emerging grammars.* Cambridge, MA: MIT Press.

Bloomfield, L. L., Farrell, T. M., & Sturdy, C. B. (2008). Categorization and discrimination of "chick-a-dee" calls by wild-caught and hand-reared chickadees. *Behavioural Processes, 77,* 166–176.

Bodenhausen, G. V., Macrae, C. N., & Hugenberg, K. (2003). Social cognition. In T. Millon & M. Lerner (Eds.), *Handbook of psychology: Personality and social psychology, Vol. 5.* New York: John Wiley & Sons, Inc.

Boehnke, S. E., & Phillips, D. P. (1999). Azimuthal tuning of human perceptual channels for sound location. *Journal of the Acoustical Society of America, 106,* 1948–1955.

Bogaert, A. F. (2003). The interaction of fraternal birth order and body size in male sexual orientation. *Behavioral Neuroscience, 117,* 381–384.

Bogaert, A. F. (2006) Biological versus nonbiological older brothers and men's sexual orientation. *Proceedings of the National Academy of Science (USA), 103,* 10771–10774.

Bohannan, P. (1995). *How culture works.* New York: The Free Press.

Bohannon, J. N. (1993). Theoretical approaches to language acquisition. J. B. Gleason (Ed.), *The development of language.* New York: Macmillan.

Bohbot, V. D., Lerch, J., Thorndycraft, B., Iaria, G., & Zijdenbos, A. P. (2007). Gray matter differences correlate with spontaneous strategies in a human virtual navigation task. *Journal of Neuroscience, 27,* 10078–10083.

Bolhuis, J. J., & Gahr, M. (2006). Neural mechanisms of birdsong memory. *Nature Reviews Neuroscience, 7,* 347–357.

Bolles, R. C. (1970). Species-specific defense reactions and avoidance learning. *Psychological Review, 77,* 32–48.

Bondolfi, G., Dufour, H., Patris, M., May, J. P., Billeter, U., Eap, C. B., & Baumann, P. (1998). *American Journal of Psychiatry, 155,* 499–504.

Bordin, E. S. (1994). Theory and research on the therapeutic working alliance: New directions. In A. O. Horvath & L. S. Greenberg (Eds.), *The working alliance: Theory, research, and practice.* New York: John Wiley & Sons.

Bordnick, P. S., Elkins, R. L., Orr, T. E., Walters, P., & Thyer, B. A. (2004). Evaluating the relative effectiveness of three aversion therapies designed to reduce craving among cocaine abusers. *Behavioral Interventions, 19,* 1–24.

Borgida, E., & Nisbett, R. E. (1977). The differential viewpoint of abstract vs. concrete information on decisions. *Journal of Applied Social Psychology, 7,* 258–271.

Bornstein, B., Sroka, H., & Munitz, H. (1969). Prosopagnosia with animal face agnosia. *Cortex,* 5, 164–169.

Bornstein, M. H., & Arterberry, M. E. (2003). Recognition, discrimination and categorization of smiling by 5-month-old infants. *Developmental Science, 6,* 585–599.

Bosarge, L. (1989). Educating college students about sexually transmitted diseases, AIDS, and safe-sex practices. Unpublished master's thesis, Auburn University.

Bostwick, J. M., & Martin, K. A. (2007). A man's brain in an ambiguous body: A case of mistaken gender identity. *The American Journal of Psychiatry, 164,* 1499–1505.

Bouchard, T. J., & McGue, M. (1981). Familial studies of intelligence: A review. *Science, 212,* 1055–1059.

Bouchard, T. J., & Propping, P. (Eds.). (1993). *Twins as a tool of behavior genetics.* Chichester, UK: Wiley.

Bouchard, T. J., Jr. (1997). The genetics of personality. In K. Blum & E. P. Noble (Eds.), *The handbook of psychiatric genetics.* Boca Raton, FL: CRC Press Inc.

Bouchard, T. J., Jr., & Hur, Y.-M. (1998). Genetic and environmental influences on the continuous scales of the Myers-Briggs Type Indicator: An analysis based on twins reared apart. *Journal of Personality, 66,* 135–149.

Bower, G. H., & Clark, M. C. (1969). Narrative stories as mediators for serial learning. *Psychonomic Science, 14,* 181–182.

Bowers, K. S., & Davidson, T. M. (1991). A neodissociative critique of Spanos's social-psychological model of hypnosis. In S. J. Lynn & J. W. Rhue (Eds.), *Theories of hypnosis: Current models and perspectives* (pp. 105–143). New York: Guilford Press.

Bowlby, J. (1969). *Attachment and loss. Vol. 1: Attachment.* New York: Basic Books.

Bowlby, J. (1982). Attachment and loss: Retrospect and prospect. *American Journal of Orthopsychiatry, 52,* 664–678.

Bowlby, J. (1988). *A secure base: Parent-child attachment and healthy human development.* New York: Basic Books, Inc.

Boyer, P., & Nissenbaum, S. (1972). *Salem-Village witchcraft: A documentary record of local conflict in colonial New England.* Belmont, CA: Wadsworth.

Boynton, R. M. (1979). *Human color vision.* New York: Holt, Rinehart and Winston.

Boysen, S. T., & Himes, G. T. (1999). Current issues and emerging theories in animal cognition. *Annual Review of Psychology, 50,* 683–705.

Bradley, C. L., & Marcia, J. E. (1998). Generativity-stagnation: A five-category model. *Journal of Personality, 66,* 39–64.

Bradley, R., Conklin, C. Z., & Westen, D. (2007). Borderline personality disorder. In W. O'Donohue, K A. Fowler, & S. O. Lilienfeld (Eds.), *Personality disorders: Toward the DSM-V* (pp. 167–201). Thousand Oaks, CA: Sage.

Brady, J. P., & Lind, D. L. (1961). Experimental analysis of hysterical blindness. *Archives of General Psychiatry, 4,* 331–359.

Brainerd, C. J. (2003). Jean Piaget, learning research, and American education. In B. J. Zimmerman (Ed.), *Educational psychology: A century of contributions.* Mahwah, NJ: Lawrence Erlbaum Associates.

Bransford, J. D., & Johnson, M. K. (1972). Contextual prerequisites for understanding: Some investigations of comprehension and recall. *Journal of Verbal Learning and Verbal Behavior, 11,* 717–726.

Brauer, M., Judd, C. M., & Gliner, M. D. (1995). The effects of repeated expressions on attitude polarization during group discussion. *Journal of Personality and Social Psychology, 68,* 1014–1029.

Bray, S., & Kwan, M. (2006). Physical activity is associated with better health and psychological well-being during transition to university life. *Journal of American College Health, 55,* 77–82.

Bray, S. R., & Born, H. A. (2004). Transition to university and vigorous physical activity: Implications for health and psychological well-being. *Journal of American College Health, 52*(4), 181–188.

Brehm, S. S. (1992). *Intimate relationships* (2nd ed.). New York: McGraw-Hill.

Bremner, J. D. (2006). Traumatic stress: Effects on the brain. *Dialogues in Clinical Neuroscience, 8*(4), 445–461.

Brennan, P., Buffler, P. A., Reynolds, P., Wu, W. H., Wichmann, H. E., Agudo, A., Pershagen, G., et al. (2004). Secondhand smoke exposure in adulthood and risk of lung cancer among never smokers: A pooled analysis of two large studies. *International Journal of Cancer, 109*(1), 125–131.

Brett, M. A., Roberts, L. F., Johnson, T. W., & Wassersug, R. J. (2007). Eunuchs in contemporary society: Expectations, consequences, and adjustments to castration (Part II). *Journal of Sexual Medicine, 4,* 946–955.

Briggs, S. R. (1988). Shyness: Introversion or neuroticism? *Journal of Research in Personality, 22,* 290–307.

Briskie, J. V., Montgomerie, R., Pöldmaa, T., & Boag, P. T. (1998). Paternity and paternal care in the polygynandrous Smith's longspur. *Behavioral Ecology and Sociobiology, 43,* 181–190.

Broadbent, D. E. (1958). *Perception and communication.* London, UK: Pergamon Press.

Broberg, A. G., Wessels, H., Lamb, M. E., & Hwang, C. P. (1997). Effects of day care on the development of cognitive abilities in 8-year-olds: A longitudinal study. *Developmental Psychology, 33,* 62–69.

Broberg, D. J., & Bernstein, I. L. (1987). Candy as a scapegoat in the prevention of food aversions in children receiving chemotherapy. *Cancer, 60,* 2344–2347.

Brockdorff, N., & Turner, B. M. (2007). Dosage compensation in mammals. In C. D. Allis, T. Jenuwein, D. Reinberg (Eds.) & M.-L. Caparros (Assoc. Ed.), *Epigenetics* (pp. 321–340). Cold Spring Harbor, NY: Cold Spring Harbor Laboratory Press.

Brooks-Gunn, J. (1988). Antecedents and consequences of variations in girls' maturational timing. *Journal of Adolescent Health Care, 9,* 365–373.

Brooks-Gunn, J. (1989). Pubertal processes and the early adolescent transition. In W. Damon (Ed.), *Child development today and tomorrow.* San Francisco: Jossey-Bass.

Brown, A. S. (1991). A review of the tip-of-the-tongue experience. *Psychological Bulletin, 109,* 204–223.

Brown, A. S. (2002). Consolidation theory and retrograde amnesia in humans. *Psychonomic Bulletin & Review, 9,* 403–425.

Brown, B. (2007). The utility of standardized tests [reply]. *Science, 316*(5832), 1694–1695.

Brown, G. W. (1985). The discovery of expressed emotion: Induction or deduction? In J. Leff & C. Vaughn (Eds.), *Expressed emotion in families.* New York: Guilford Press.

Brown, G. W., Bone, M., Dalison, B., & Wing, J. K. (1966). *Schizophrenia and social care.* London: Oxford University Press.

Brown, J. (1958). Some tests of the decay theory of immediate memory. *Quarterly Journal of Experimental Psychology, 10,* 12–21.

Brown, J. D., & Rogers, R. (1991). Self-serving attributions: The role of physiological arousal. *Personality and Social Psychology Bulletin, 17,* 501–506.

Brown, J. L., & Vanable, P. A. (2007). Alcohol use, partner type, and risky sexual behaviour among college students: Findings from an event-level study. *Addictive Behaviors, 32*(12), 2940–2952.

Brown, R., & Bellugi, U. (1964). Three processes in the child's acquisition of syntax. *Harvard Education Review, 34,* 133–151.

Brown, R., & Fraser, C. (1964). The acquisition of syntax. In U. Bellugi & R. Brown (Eds.), *The acquisition of language. Monographs of the Society for Research in Child Development, 29,* 43–79.

Brown, R., & McNeill, D. (1966). The "tip-of-the-tongue" phenomenon. *Journal of Verbal Learning and Verbal Behavior, 5,* 325–337.

Brown, R. D., & Bassili, J. N. (2002). Spontaneous trait associations and the case of the superstitious banana. *Journal of Experimental Social Psychology, 38,* 87–92.

Brown, R. W., & Kulik, J. (1977). Flashbulb memories. *Cognition, 5,* 73–99.

Buck, L., & Axel, R. A. (1991). Novel multigene family may encode odorant receptors: A molecular basis for odor recognition. *Cell, 65,* 175–187.

Buonomano, D. V., & Merzenich, M. M. (1998). Cortical plasticity: From synapses to maps. *Annual Review of Neuroscience, 21,* 149–186.

Burger, J. M., & Hemans, L. T. (1988). Desire for control and the use of attribution processes. *Journal of Personality, 56,* 531–546.

Burian, S. E., Liguori, A., & Robinson, J. H. (2002). Effects of alcohol on risk-taking during simulated driving. *Human Psychopharmacology, 17*(3), 141–150.

Burnstock, G., & Wood, J. N. (1996). Purinergic receptors: Their role in nociception and primary afferent neurotransmission. *Current Opinion in Neurobiology, 6,* 526–532.

Burt, C. D. B., Kemp, S., & Conway, M. (2001). What happens if you retest autobiographical memory 10 years on? *Memory & Cognition, 29,* 127–136.

Busch, F. (2003a). Back to the future. *Psychoanalytic Quarterly, 72(1),* 201–215.

Busch, F. (2003b). Telling stories. *Journal of the American Psychoanalytic Association, 51*(1), 25–42.

Buschmann, H., Diaz, J. L., Holenz, J., Párraga, A., Torrens, A., & Vela, J. M. (Eds.). (2007). *Antidepressants, antipsychotics, anxiolytics: From chemistry and pharmacology to clinical application.* Weinhelm, Germany: Wiley VCH.

Bushara, K. O., Hanakawa, T., Immisch, I., Toma, K., Kansaku, K., & Hallett, M. (2003). Neural correlates of cross-modal binding. *Nature Neuroscience, 6,* 190–195.

Bushman, B. J., & Huesmann, L. R. (2001). Effects of televised violence on aggression. In D. G. Singer & J. L. Singer (Eds.), *Handbook of children and the media.* Thousand Oaks, CA: Sage Publications.

Buskist, W., & Miller, H. L. (1986). Interaction between rules and contingencies in the control of human fixed-interval performance. *Psychological Record, 36,* 109–116.

Buss, A. H. (1995). *Personality: Temperament, social behavior, and the self.* Boston: Allyn and Bacon.

Butcher, J., Mineka, S., & Hooley, J. (2007). *Abnormal psychology.* Boston: Allyn & Bacon/Pearson Education.

Butcher, J. N., Ben-Porath, Y. S., Shondrick, D. D., Stafford, K. P., McNulty, J. L., Graham, J. R., Stein, L. A. R., et al. (2000). Cultural and subcultural factors in MMPI-2 interpretation. In J. N. Butcher (Ed.), *Basic sources on the MMPI-2.* Minneapolis: University of Minnesota Press.

Butterfoss, F. D. (2007). *The challenge of implementation: Coalitions in community intervention.* San Francisco: Jossey-Bass.

Byrne, D. (1997). An overview (and underview) of research and theory on the attraction paradigm. *Journal of Social & Personal Relationships, 14,* 417–431.

Cacioppo, J. T. (2002). Social neuroscience: Understanding the pieces fosters understanding the whole and vice versa. *American Psychologist, 57,* 819–831.

Cacioppo, J. T., Petty, R. E., & Crites, S. L. (1993). Attitude change. In V. S. Ramachandran (Ed.), *Encyclopedia of human behavior.* San Diego: Academic Press.

Calkins, M. W. (1892). Experimental psychology at Wellesley College. *American Journal of Psychology, 5*, 464–471.

Calliess, I. T., Sieberer, M., Machledit, W., & Ziegenbein, M. (2008). Personality disorders in a cross-cultural perspective: Impact of culture and migration on diagnosis and etiological aspects. *Current Psychiatry Reviews, 4*(1), 39–47.

Cambronne, D., Shih, J., & Harri, K. (1999). Innovative stress management for financial service organizations. In J. Oher (Ed.), *The employee assistance handbook.* New York: John Wiley & Sons, Inc.

Cameron, J., & Pierce, W. D. (2005). Rewards and motivation in the classroom. *Academics Exchange Quarterly, 9*(2), 67–70.

Campbell, J. D., Trapness, P. D., Heine, S. J., Katz, I. M., Lavalee, L. F., & Lehman, D. R. (1996). Self-concept clarity: Measurement, personality correlates and cultural boundaries. *Journal of Personality and Social Psychology, 70*, 141–156.

Campfield, L. A., Smith, F. J., Guisez, Y., Devos, R., & Burn, P. (1995). Recombinant mouse OB protein: Evidence for a peripheral signal linking adiposity and central neural networks. *Science, 269*, 546–549.

Canadian Institutes of Health Research, Natural Sciences and Engineering Council of Canada, & Social Sciences and Humanities Research Council of Canada (1998). *Tri-council policy statement: Ethical conduct for research involving humans.* Ottawa: Authors.

Canadian Psychological Association. (2000). *Canadian code of ethics for psychologists* (3rd ed). Ottawa: Canadian Psychological Association.

Cannon, W. B. (1927). The James-Lange theory of emotions: a critical examination and an alternative theory. Reprinted in *American Journal of Psychology, 100*, 567–586.

Cannon, W. B., & Washburn, A. L. (1912). An explanation of hunger. *American Journal of Physiology, 29*, 444–454.

Capaldi, E. J., Haas, A. I., Miller, R. M., & Martins, A. (2005). How transitions from nonrewarded to rewarded trials regulate responding in Pavlovian and instrumental learning following extensive acquisition training. *Learning and Motivation, 36*, 279–296.

Caplan, D., Alpert, N., & Waters, G. (1999). PET studies of syntactic processing with auditory sentence presentation. *NeuroImage, 9*, 343–351.

Caprara, G. V., & Perugini, M. (1994). Personality described by adjectives: Generalizability of the Big Five to the Italian lexical context. *European Journal of Personality, 8*, 357–369.

Carlson, E. A. (1998). A prospective longitudinal study of attachment disorganization/disorientation. *Child Development, 69*, 1107–1128.

Carlson, N. (2005). *Foundations of physiological psychology* (6th ed.). Boston: Pearson.

Carlston, D. E., & Skowronski, J. J. (1994). Savings in the relearning of trait information as evidence for spontaneous inference generation. *Journal of Personality & Social Psychology, 66*, 840–856.

Caroff, X. (2002). What conservation anticipation reveals about cognitive change. *Cognitive Development, 17*, 1015–1035.

Carpendale, J. I. M. (2000). Kohlberg and Piaget on stages and moral reasoning. *Developmental Review, 20*, 181–205.

Carpenter, P. A., & Just, M. A. (1983). What your eyes do while your mind is reading. In K. Rayner (Ed.), *Eye movements in reading: Perceptual and language processes.* New York: Academic Press.

Carpenter, P. A., Miyake, A., & Just, M. A. (1995). Language comprehension: Sentence and discourse processing. *Annual Review of Psychology, 46*, 91–120.

Carpenter, W. T., Conley, R. R., Buchanan, R. W., Breier, C. A., & Tamminga, C. A. (1995). Patient response and resource management: Another view of clozapine treatment of schizophrenia. *American Journal of Psychiatry, 152*, 827–832.

Carr, E. G., & Lovaas, O. J. (1983). Contingent electric shock as a treatment for severe behavior problems. In S. Axelrod & J. Apsche (Eds.), *The effect of punishment on human behavior.* New York: Academic Press.

Carrion-Baralt, J. R., Smith, C. J., Rossy-Fullana, E., Lewis-Fernandez, R., Davis, K. L., & Silverman, J. M. (2006). Seasonality effects in schizophrenic births in multiplex families in a tropical island. *Psychiatry Research, 142*, 93–97.

Carroll, J. B. (1993). *Human cognitive abilities: A survey of factor-analytic studies.* New York: Cambridge University Press.

Carroll, S. B. (2003). Genetics and the making of *Homo sapiens. Nature, 422*, 849–857.

Carson, R. C., Butcher, J. N., & Mineka, S. (2000). *Abnormal psychology and modern life* (11th ed.). Boston: Allyn & Bacon.

Caruso, D. R., Mayer, J. D., & Salovey, P. (2002). Relation of an ability measure of emotional intelligence to personality. *Journal of Personality Assessment, 79*, 306–320.

Case, R. (1998). The development of conceptual structures. In W. Damon (Ed.), *Handbook of child psychology: Vol. 2. Cognition, perception, and language.* New York: Wiley.

Caserta, M. T., O'Connor, T. G., Wyman, P. A., Wang, H., Moynihan, J., Cross, W., Tu, X., & Jin, X. (2008). The associations between psychosocial stress and the frequency of illness, and innate and adaptive immune function in children. *Brain, Behavior, and Immunity, 22*, 933–940.

Casey, J., Garrett, J., Brackett, M., & Rivers S. (2008). Emotional intelligence, relationship quality, and partner selection. In G. Geher & G. Miller (Eds.), *Mating intelligence: Sex, relationships, and the mind's reproductive system* (pp. 263–282). Mahwah, NJ: Lawrence Eribaum Associate Publishers.

Caspi, A., McClay, J., Moffitt, T. E., Mill, J., Martin, J., Craig, I. W., Taylor, A., & Poulton, R. (2002). Role of genotype in the cycle of violence in maltreated children. *Science, 297*, 851–854.

Caterina, M. J., Leffler, A., Malmberg, A. B., Martin, W. J., Trafton, J., Petersen-Zeitz, K. R., Koltzenburg, M., Basbaum, A. I., & Julius, D. (2000). Impaired nociception and pain sensation in mice lacking the capsaicin receptor. *Science, 288*, 306–313.

Cath, D. C., Spinhoven, P., van de Wetering, B. J. M., Hoogduin, C. A. H., Landman, A. D., van Woerkom, T. C. A. M., Roos, R. A. C., & Rooijmans, H. G. M. (2000). The relationship between types and severity of repetitive behaviors in Gilles de la Tourette's disorder and obsessive-compulsive disorder. *Journal of Clinical Psychology, 61*, 505–513.

Cavaco, S., Anderson, S. W., Allen, J. S., Castro-Caldas, A., & Damasio, H. (2004). The scope of preserved procedural memory in amnesia. *Brain, 127*, 1863–1867.

Cavanaugh, J. C. (1990). *Adult development and aging.* Belmont, CA: Wadsworth.

Chaiken, S. (1979). Communicator's physical attractiveness and persuasion. *Journal of Personality and Social Psychology, 37*, 1387–1397.

Chakos, M., Lieberman, J., Hoffman, E., Bradford, D., & Sheitman, B. (2001). Effectiveness of second-generation antipsychotics in patients with treatment-resistant schizophrenia: A review and meta-analysis of randomized trials. *American Journal of Psychiatry, 158*(4), 518–526.

Chandler, V. L. (2007). Paramutation: From maize to mouse. *Cell, 128*, 641–645.

Chandra, A., Martinez, G. M., Mosher, W. D., Abma, J. C., & Jones, J. (2005). Fertility, family planning, and reproductive health of U.S. women: Data from the 2002 National Survey of Family Growth. National Center for Health Statistics. *Vital Health Statistics, 23*(25), 1–160.

Chapman, K. L., Leonard, L. B., & Mervis, C. B. (1986). The effect of feedback on young children's inappropriate word usage. *Journal of Child Language, 13*, 101–117.

Chapouton, P., Jagasia, R., & Bally-Cuif, L. (2007). Adult neurogenesis in non-mammalian vertebrates. *BioEssays, 29*, 745–757.

Charman, D. P. (2004). Effective psychotherapy and effective psychotherapists. In D. P. Charman (Ed.), *Core processes in brief psychodynamic psychotherapy: Advancing effective practice.* Mahwah, NJ: Lawrence Erlbaum Associates.

Chasdi, E. H. (1994). *Culture and human development: The selected papers of John Whiting.* New York: Cambridge University Press.

Chassin, L., Presson, C. C., Rose, J. S., & Sherman, S. J. (1998). Maternal socialization of adolescent smoking: Intergenerational transmission of smoking-related beliefs. *Psychology of Addictive Behaviors, 12*, 206–216.

Chassin, L., Presson, C. C., Sherman, S. J., & Edwards, D. A. (1990). The natural history of cigarette smoking: Predicting young-adult smoking outcomes from adolescent patterns. *Health Psychology, 9*, 710–716.

Chassin, L., Presson, C. C., Sherman, S. J., & Kim, K. (2003). Historical changes in cigarette smoking and smoking-related beliefs after 2 decades in a midwestern community. *Health Psychology, 22*(4), 647–653.

Chaudhari, N., Landin, A. M., & Roper, S. D. (2000). A metabotropic glutamate receptor variant functions as a taste receptor. *Nature Neuroscience, 3*, 113–119.

Cheesman, J., & Merikle, P. M. (1986). Distinguishing conscious from unconscious perceptual processes. *Canadian Journal of Psychology, 40*, 343–367.

Cheesman, M. F. (1997). Speech perception by elderly listeners: Basic knowledge and implications for audiology. *Journal of Speech-Language Pathology and Audiology, 21,* 104–110.

Chemelli, R. M., Willie, J. T., Sinton, C. M., Elmquist, J. K., Scammell, T. E., Lee, C., Richardson, J. A., Williams, S. C., Xiong, Y., Kisanuki, Y., Fitch, T. E., Nakazato, M., Hammer, R. E., Saper, C. B., & Yanagisawa, M. (1999). Narcolepsy in orexin knockout mice: molecular genetics of sleep regulation. *Cell, 98,* 437–451.

Cheng, K., & Wehner, R. (2002). Navigating desert ants (Cataglyphis fortis) learn to alter their search patterns on their homebound journey. *Physiological Entomology, 27,* 285–290.

Cheng, P. N., & Holyoak, K. J. (1985). Pragmatic reasoning schemas. *Cognitive Psychology, 17,* 391–416.

Cheour, M., Ceponiene, R., Lehtokoski, A., Luuk, A., Allik, J., Alho, K., & Näätänen, R. (1998). Development of language-specific phoneme representations in the infant brain. *Nature Neuroscience, 1,* 351–353.

Cheour, M., Martynova, O., Näätänen, R., Erkkola, R., Sillanpää, M., Kero, P., Raz, A., Kaipio, M.-L., Hiltunen, J., Aaltonen, O., Savela, J., & Hämäläinen, H. (2002). Speech sounds learned by sleeping newborns. *Nature, 415,* 599–600.

Cherry, E. C. (1953). Some experiments on the recognition of speech, with one and with two ears. *Journal of the Acoustical Society of America, 25,* 975–979.

Chertkow, H. (2008). Diagnosis and treatment of dementia: Introduction—Introducing a series based on the Third Canadian Consensus Conference on the Diagnosis and Treatment of Dementia. *Canadian Medical Association Journal, 178,* 316–321.

Cheyne, J. A., Carriere, J. S. A., & Smilek, D. (2006). Absent-mindedness: lapses of conscious awareness and everyday cognitive failures. *Consciousness and Cognition, 15,* 578–592.

Chomsky, N. (1957). *Syntactic structure.* The Hague: Mouton Publishers.

Chomsky, N. (1965). *Aspects of the theory of syntax.* Cambridge, MA: MIT Press.

Chu, S., & Downes, J. J. (2000). Odour-evoked autobiographical memories: Psychological investigations of Proustian phenomena. *Chemical Senses, 25,* 111–116.

Chung, K. C., Kowalski, C. P., Kim, H. M., & Buchman, S. R. (2000). Maternal cigarette smoking during pregnancy and the risk of having a child with cleft lip/palate. *Plastic and Reconstructive Surgery, 105,* 485–491.

Chung, W. C. J., De Vries, G. J., & Swaab, D. R. (2002). Sexual differentiation of the bed nucleus of the stria terminalis in humans may extend into adulthood. *Journal of Neuroscience, 22,* 1027–1033.

Church, A. T., Katigbak, M. S., Ortiz, F. A., del Prado, A. M., Vargas-Flores, J., Ibanez-Reyes, J., Reyes, J. A. S., Pe-Pua, R., & Cabrera, H. F. (2005). Investigating implicit trait theories across cultures. *Journal of Cross-Cultural Psychology, 36,* 476–496.

Cialdini, R. B. (1993). *Influence: Science and practice* (3rd ed.). New York: HarperCollins.

Cialdini, R. B., & Goldstein, N. J. (2004). Social influence: Compliance and conformity. *Annual Review of Psychology, 55,* 591–621.

Clark, D. A., Beck, A. T., & Alford, B. A. (1999). *Scientific foundations of cognitive theory and therapy of depression.* New York: John Wiley & Sons, Inc.

Clark, M. M., DeSousa, D., Vonk, J., & Galef, B. G., Jr. (1997). Parenting and potency: Alternative routes to reproductive success in male Mongolian gerbils. *Animal Behaviour, 54,* 635–642.

Clark, M. M., & Galef, B. G., Jr. (1998). Where the males are. *Natural History, 107*(9), 22–24.

Clayton, D. F. (2000). The genomic action potential. *Neurobiology of Learning and Memory, 74,* 185–216.

Cleckley, H. (1976). *The mask of sanity.* St. Louis: C. V. Mosby.

Cloninger, C., Sigvardsson, S., & Svrakic, D. (1995). Personality antecedents of alcoholism in a national area probability sample. *European Archives of Psychiatry and Clinical Neuroscience, 245,* 239–244.

Cloninger, C. R. (1987). Neurogenetic adaptive mechanisms in alcoholism. *Science, 236,* 410–416.

Cloninger, C. R., Bohman, M., Sigvardsson, S., & von Knorring, A. L. (1985). Psychopathology in adopted-out children of alcoholics. The Stockholm Adoption Study. *Recent Developments in Alcoholism, 7,* 235.

Cobb, S., & Rose, R. M. (1973). Hypertension, peptic ulcer, and diabetes in air traffic controllers. *Journal of the American Medical Association, 224,* 489–492.

Cobos, P., Sanchez, M., Garcia, C., Nieves, V. M., & Vila, J. (2002). Revisiting the James versus Cannon debate on emotion: startle and autonomic modulation in patients with spinal injuries. *Biological Psychology, 61,* 251–269.

Coccaro, E. F., & Kavoussi, R. J. (1997). Fluoxetine and impulsive aggressive behavior in personality-disordered subjects. *Archives of General Psychiatry, 54,* 1081–1088.

Coccaro, E. F., Silverman, J. M., Klar, H. M., Horvath, T. B., & Siever, L. J. (1994). Familial correlates of reduced central serotonergic system function in patients with personality disorders. *Archives of General Psychiatry, 51,* 318–324.

Cohen, L. A. (1987). Diet and cancer. *Scientific American, 102,* 42–48.

Cohen, M., Brom, D., & Dasberg, H. (2001). Child survivors of the Holocaust: Symptoms and coping after fifty years. *Israel Journal of Psychiatry & Related Sciences, 38*(1), 3–12.

Cohen, M. E., Robins, E., Purtell, J. J., Altmann, M. W., & Reid, D. E. (1953). *Journal of the American Medical Association, 151,* 977–986.

Cohen, S., Doyle, W. J., & Skoner, D. P. (1999). Psychological stress, cytokine production, and severity of upper respiratory illness. *Psychosomatic Medicine, 61,* 175–180.

Cohen, S., & Hamrick, N. (2003). Stable individual differences in physiological response to stressors: Implications for stress-elicited changes in immune related health. *Brain, Behavior, & Immunity, 17*(6), 407–414.

Cohen-Bendehan, C. C., van de Beek, C., & Berenbaum, S. A. (2005). Prenatal sex hormone effects on child and adult sex-typed behavior: Methods and findings. *Neuroscience and Biobehavioral Reviews, 47,* 230–237.

Colapinto, J. (2000). *As nature made him: The boy who was raised as a girl.* Toronto: HarperCollins.

Cole, R. P., & Miller, R. R. (1999). Conditioned excitation and conditioned inhibition acquired through backward conditioning. *Learning and Motivation, 30,* 129–156.

Cole, T. J., & Mollard, R. (2007). Selective glucocorticoid receptor ligands. *Medicinal Chemistry, 3*(5), 494–506.

Coleman, J. C. (1976). *Abnormal psychology and modern life* (5th ed.). Glenview, IL: Scott, Foresman.

Collins, A. (1988). *The sleep room.* Toronto: Lester & Orpen Dennys Limited.

Collins, A. M., & Quillian, M. R. (1969). Retrieval time from semantic memory. *Journal of Verbal Learning and Verbal Behavior, 8,* 240–248.

Colucci-D'Amato, L., & di Porzio, U. (2008). Neurogenesis in adult CNS: From denial to opportunities and challenges for therapy. *BioEssays, 30,* 135–145.

Conley, R. R., & Kelly, D. L. (2001). Management of treatment resistance in schizophrenia. *Society of Biological Psychiatry, 50,* 898–911.

Conner, R. L., & Levine, S. (1969). Hormonal influences on aggressive behaviour. In S. Garattine & E. B. Sigg (Eds.), *Aggressive behaviour.* New York: John Wiley & Sons.

Connolly, M. B., Crits-Christoph, P., Barber, J. P., & Luborsky, L. (2000). Transference patterns in the therapeutic relationship in supportive-expressive psychotherapy for depression. *Psychotherapy Research, 10*(3), 356–372.

Conrad, R. (1964). Acoustic confusions in immediate memory. *British Journal of Psychology, 55,* 75–83.

Conrad, R. (1970). Short-term memory processes in the deaf. *British Journal of Psychology, 61,* 179–195.

*Consumer Reports.* (1995, November). Mental health: Does therapy help? 734–739.

Constantino, J. N., Yang, D., Gray, T. L., Gross, M. M., Abbacchi, A. M., Smith, S. C., Kohn, C. E., & Kuhl, P. K. (2007). Clarifying the associations between language and social development in autism: A study of non-native phoneme recognition. *Journal of Autism and Developmental Disorders, 37*(7), 1256–1263.

Cooper, J. (2007). *Cognitive dissonance: Fifty years of a classic theory.* Thousand Oaks, CA: Sage.

Cooper, K. (1985). Running without risk. *Runner's World, 20,* 61–64.

Cooper, K. H. (1968). *Aerobics.* New York: Evans and Company.

Cooper, M. L., Frone, M. R., Russell, M., & Mudar, P. (1995). Drinking to regulate positive and negative emotions: A motivational model of alcohol use. *Journal of Personality & Social Psychology, 69*(5), 990–1005.

Cooper, M. L., Russell, M., & George, W. H. (1988). Coping, expectancies, and alcohol abuse: A test of social learning foundations. *Journal of Abnormal Psychology, 97,* 218–230.

Cooper, R. M., & Zubek, J. P. (1958). Effects of enriched and restricted early environments on the learning ability of bright and dull rats. *Canadian Journal of Psychology, 12,* 159–164.

Coover, G. D., Murison, R., & Jellestad, F. K. (1992). Subtotal lesions of the amygdala: The rostral central nucleus in passive avoidance and ulceration. *Physiology and Behavior, 51,* 795–803.

Corbetta, M., Miezin, F. M., Doobmeyer, S., Shulman, G. L., & Petersen, S. E. (1991). Selective and divided attention during visual discriminations of shape, color, and speed: Functional anatomy by positron emission tomography. *Journal of Neuroscience, 11,* 2383–2402.

Coren, S., & Hakstian, A. R. (1988). Color vision screening without the use of technical equipment: Scale development and cross-validation. *Perception and Psychophysics, 43,* 115–120.

Corkin, S. (2002). What's new with the amnesic patient H. M.? *Nature Reviews Neuroscience, 3,* 153–160.

Corkin, S., Sullivan, E. V., Twitchell, T. E., & Grove, E. (1981). The amnesic patient H. M.: Clinical observations and test performance 28 years after operation. *Society for Neuroscience Abstracts, 7,* 235.

Cornell, E. H., & Heth, C. D. (2004). Memories of travel: Dead reckoning within the cognitive map. In G. Allen (Ed.), *Remembering where: Advances in understanding spatial memory.* Mahway, NJ: Lawrence Erlbaum Associates.

Coryell, W. (1980). A blind family history study of Briquet's syndrome: Further validation of the diagnosis. *Archives of General Psychiatry, 37,* 1266–1269.

Costa, P. T., Jr., & McCrae, R. R. (1998a). Trait theories of personality. In D. F. Barone & M. Hersen (Eds.), *Advanced personality.* New York: Plenum Press.

Costa, P. T., Jr., & McCrae, R. R. (1998b). The Revised NEO Personality Inventory (NEO-P-R). In S. R. Briggs, J. M. Cheek, & E. M. Donahue (Eds.), *Handbook of adult personality inventories.* New York: Plenum.

Covington, C. Y., Nordstrom-Klee, B., Ager, J., Sokol, R., & Delaney-Black, V. (2002). Birth to age 7 growth of children prenatally exposed to drugs: A prospective cohort study. *Neurotoxicology and Teratology, 24,* 489–496.

Cowart, J., & Whaley, D. (1971). Punishment of self-mutilation behavior. Unpublished manuscript cited by D. L. Whaley & R. W. Malott, *Elementary principles of behavior.* New York: Appleton-Century-Crofts.

Cowley, D. S., Dager, S. R., & Dunner, D. L. (1995). The lactate infusion challenge. In G. M. Asnis & H. M. van Praag (Eds.), *Panic disorder: Clinical, biological, and treatment aspects.* New York: John Wiley & Sons.

Cox, M. J., & Paley, B. (2003). Understanding families as systems. *Current Directions in Psychological Science, 12*(5), 193–196.

Craik, F. I. M., & Lockhart, R. S. (1972). Levels of processing: A framework for memory research. *Journal of Verbal Learning and Verbal Behavior, 11,* 671–684.

Craik, F. I. M., & Tulving, E. (1975). Depth of processing and the retention of words in episodic memory. *Journal of Experimental Psychology: General, 104,* 268–294.

Cramer, P. (2003). Personality change in later adulthood is predicted by defense mechanism use in early adulthood. *Journal of Research in Personality, 37,* 76–104.

Crick, F. (1970). Central dogma of molecular biology. *Nature, 227,* 561–562.

Crombag, H. F. M., Wagenaar, W.A., & van Koppen, P. J. (1996). Crashing memories and the problem of "source monitoring." *Applied Cognitive Psychology, 10,* 95–104.

Cromwell, P. F., Marks, A., Olson, J. N., & Avery, D. W. (1991). Group effects on decision-making by burglars. *Psychological Reports, 69,* 579–588.

Crowder, R.G. (1993). Short-term memory: Where do we stand? *Memory & Cognition, 21,* 142–145.

Crowe, R. R., Noyes, R., Pauls, D. L., & Slymen, D. (1983). A family study of panic disorder. *Archives of General Psychiatry, 40,* 1065–1069.

Croyle, R. T., & Cooper, J. (1983). Dissonance arousal: Physical evidence. *Journal of Personality and Social Psychology, 45,* 782–791.

Cruts, M., & Van Broeckhoven, C. (1996). Molecular genetic analysis of Alzheimer's disease. In C. N. Stefanis & H. Hippius (Eds.), *Neuro psychiatry in old age: An update.* Ashland, OH: Hogrefe & Huber Publishers.

Culham, J. C., & Kanwisher, N. G. (2001). Neuroimaging of cognitive functions in human parietal cortex. *Neuron, 32,* 737–745.

Cummings, J. L., & Wirshing, W. C. (1989). Recognition and differential diagnosis of tardive dyskinesia. *International Journal of Psychiatry in Medicine, 19,* 133–144.

Cunningham, J. A., Wild, T. C., Bondy, S. J., & Lin, E. (2001). Impact of normative feedback on problem drinkers: A small-area population study. *Journal of Studies on Alcohol, 62*(2), 228–233.

Currie, S. R., Patten, S. B., Williams, J. V. A., Wang, J., Beck, C. A., El-Guebaly, N., Maxwell, C. (2005). Comorbidity of major depression with substance use disorders. *Canadian Journal of Psychiatry, 50*(10), 660–666.

Dale, E. (1935). *The context of motion pictures.* New York: The Macmillan Company.

Dale, P. S. (1976). *Language development: Structure and function* (2nd ed.). New York: Holt, Rinehart, and Winston.

Dalgleish, T. (2004). The emotional brain. *Nature Reviews Neuroscience, 5,* 583–589.

Dalgleish, T., Rosen, K., & Marks, M. (1996). Rhythm and blues: The theory and treatment of seasonal affective disorder. *British Journal of Clinical Psychology, 35,* 163–182.

Dalton, P., Doolittle, N., Nagata, H., & Breslin, P. A. S. (2000). The merging of the senses: Integration of subthreshold taste and smell. *Nature Neuroscience, 3,* 431–432.

Daly, M., & Wilson, M. (2001). Risk-taking, intrasexual competition, and homicide. *Nebraska Symposium on Motivation, 47,* 1–36.

Daly, M., & Wilson, M. I. (1999). Human evolutionary psychology and animal behaviour. *Animal Behaviour, 57,* 509–519.

Damasio, A. R., Damasio, H., & Van Hoesen, G. W. (1982). Prosopagnosia: Anatomic basis and behavioral mechanisms. *Neurology, 32,* 331–341.

Damasio, A. R., Yamada, T., Damasio, H., Corbett, J., & McKee, J. (1980). Central achromatopsia: Behavioral, anatomic, and physiologic aspects. *Neurology, 30,* 1064–1071.

Damasio, H. (1989). Neuroimaging contributions to the understanding of aphasia. In F. Boller & J. Grafman (Eds.), *Handbook of neuropsychology, Vol. 2.* Amsterdam: Elsevier.

Damasio, H., Grabowski, T., Frank, R., Galaburda, A. M., & Damasio, A. R. (1994). The return of Phineas Gage: Clues about the brain from the skull of a famous patient. *Science, 264,* 1102–1105.

Damon, W., & Hart, D. (1992). Self-understanding and its role in social and moral development. In M. H. Bornstein & M. E. Lamb (Eds.), *Developmental psychology: An advanced textbook.* Hillsdale, NJ: Erlbaum.

Dana, R. H. (Ed.). (2000). *Handbook of cross-cultural and multicultural personality assessment.* Mahwah, NJ: Lawrence Erlbaum Associates.

Daniel, M. H. (1997). Intelligence testing: Status and trends. *American Psychologist, 52,* 1038–1045.

Darley, J. M., & Latané, B. (1968). Bystander intervention in emergencies: Diffusion of responsibility. *Journal of Personality and Social Psychology, 8,* 377–383.

Darou, W. G. (1992). Native Canadians and intelligence testing. *Canadian Journal of Counselling, 26,* 96–99.

Darwin, C. J., Turvey, M. T., & Crowder, R. G. (1972). An auditory analogue of the Sperling partial report procedure: Evidence for brief auditory storage. *Cognitive Psychology, 3,* 255–267.

Darwin, F. (1888/1950). *Charles Darwin's autobiography.* New York: Henry Schuman.

Dashiell, J. F. (1935). Experimental studies of the influence of social situations on the behavior of individual human adults. In C. Murcheson (Ed.), *A handbook of social psychology.* Worcester, MA: Clark University Press.

Davidson, T. L., & Swithers, S. E. (2004). A Pavlovian approach to the problem of obesity. *International Journal of Obesity and Related Metabolic Disorders, 28,* 933–935.

Davies, G., Welham, J., Chant, D., Torrey, E. F., & McGrath, J. (2003). A systematic review and meta-analysis of northern hemisphere season of birth studies in schizophrenia. *Schizophrenia Bulletin, 29*(3), 587–593.

Davis, J. D., & Campbell, C. S. (1973). Peripheral control of meal size in the rat: Effect of sham feeding on meal size and drinking rats. *Journal of Comparative and Physiological Psychology, 83,* 379–387.

Davis, M. (1992). The role of the amygdala in fear-potentiated startle: Implications for animal models of anxiety. *Trends in Pharmacological Sciences, 13,* 35–41.

Davis, M., & Johnsrude, I. (2007). Hearing speech sounds: Top-down influences on the interface between audition and speech perception. *Hearing Research, 229*, 132–147.

Davison, G. C., & Neale, J. M. (1990). *Abnormal psychology* (5th ed.). New York: John Wiley & Sons.

Dawda, D., & Hart, S. D. (2000). Assessing emotional intelligence: Reliability and validity of the Bar-On Emotional Quotient Inventory (EQ-i) in university students. *Personality and Individual Differences, 28*, 797–812.

Dawes, R. M., Faust, D., & Meehl, P. E. (2002). Clinical versus actuarial judgment. In T. Gilovich (Ed.), *Heuristics and biases: The psychology of intuitive judgment.* New York: Cambridge University Press.

Dawkins, R. (1986). *The blind watchmaker.* New York: Norton.

Dawkins, T. (1996). *Climbing Mount Improbable.* New York: W. W. Norton.

Deaux, K. (1985). Sex and gender. *Annual Review of Psychology, 36*, 49–81.

Deaux, K. (1999). An overview of research on gender: Four themes from 3 decades. In W. B. Swann, Jr., & J. H. Langlois (Eds.), *Sexism and stereotypes in modern society: The gender science of Janet Taylor Spence.* Washington, DC: American Psychological Association.

DeCasper, A. J., & Fifer, W. P. (1980). Of human bonding: Newborns prefer their mothers' voices. *Science, 208*, 1175–1176.

DeCasper, A. J., & Spence, M. (1986). Prenatal maternal speech influences newborns' perception of speech sounds. *Infant Behavior and Development, 9*, 133–150.

de Castro, J. M. (2002). Independence of heritable influences on the food intake of free-living humans. *Nutrition, 18*, 11–16.

Decety, J., & Keenan, J. P. (2006). Social neuroscience: A new journal. *Social Neuroscience, 1*, 1–4.

deGroot, A. D. (1965). *Thought and choice in chess.* The Hague: Mouton Publishers.

Dellas, M., & Jernigan, L. P. (1990). Affective personality characteristics associated with undergraduate ego identity formation. *Journal of Adolescent Research, 5*, 306–324.

DeLongis, A., Folkman, S., & Lazarus, R. S. (1988). The impact of daily stress on health and mood: Psychological and social resources as mediators. *Journal of Personality and Social Psychology, 54*, 486–495.

de Luis, D. A., Sagrado, M. G., Conde, R., Aller, R., & Izaola, M. D. (2008). Changes of ghrelin and leptin in response to hypocaloric diet in obese patients. *Nutrition, 24*, 162–166.

Dement, W. C. (1974). *Some must watch while some must sleep.* San Francisco: W. H. Freeman.

DeNeve, K. M., & Cooper, H. (1998). The happy personality: A meta-analysis of 137 personality traits and subjective well-being. *Psychological Bulletin, 124*, 197–229.

De Oliveira-Souza, R., Moll, J., Azevedo Ignico, F., & Hare, R. D. (2008). Psychopathy in a civil psychiatric outpatient sample. *Criminal Justice and Behaviour, 35*(4), 427–437.

DePue, R. A., Luciane, M., Arbisi, P., Collins, P., & Leon, A. (1994). Dopamine and the structure of personality: Relation of agonist-induced dopamine activity and positive emotionality. *Journal of Personality and Social Psychology, 67*, 485–498.

DePue, R. A., & Monroe, S. M. (1986). Conceptualization and measurement of human disorder in life-stress research: The problem of chronic disturbance. *Psychological Bulletin, 99*, 36–51.

De Raad, B. (1998). Five big, Big-Five issues: Rationale, content, structure, status and crosscultural assessment. *European Psychologist, 3*, 113–124.

Dérousné, J., & Beauvois, M.-F. (1979). Phonological processing in reading: Data from alexia. *Journal of Neurology, Neurosurgery, and Psychiatry, 42*, 1125–1132.

Deshmukh, A., Rosenbloom, M. J., Pfefferbaum, A., & Sullivan, E. V. (2002). Clinical signs of cerebellar dysfunction in schizophrenia, alcoholism, and their comorbidity. *Schizophrenia Research, 57*(2–3), 281–291.

Desimone, R., & Duncan, J. (1995). Neural mechanisms of selective visual attention. *Annual Review of Neuroscience, 18*, 193–222.

Deutsch, J. A., & Gonzalez, M. F. (1980). Gastric nutrient content signals satiety. *Behavioral Neural Biology, 30*, 113–116.

Deutsch, J. A., Young, W. G., & Kalogeris, T. J. (1978). The stomach signals satiety. *Science, 201*, 165–167.

Deutscher, I. (1968). The quality of postparental life. In B. L. Neugarten (Ed.), *Middle age and aging.* Chicago: University of Chicago Press.

Devane, W. A., Hanus, L., Breuer, A., Pertwee, R. G., Stevenson, L. A., Griffin, G., Gibson, D., Mandelbaum, A., Etinger, A., & Mechoulam, R. (1992). Isolation and structure of a brain constituent that binds to the cannabinoid receptor. *Science, 258*, 1946–1949.

Deverell, W. (1991). *Fatal cruise: The trial of Robert Frisbee.* Toronto: McClelland & Stewart.

deVilliers, J. G., & deVilliers, P. A. (1978). *Language acquisition.* Cambridge, MA: Harvard University Press.

DeWit, D. J., Adlaf, E. M., Offord, D. R., & Ogborne, A. C. (2000). Age at first alcohol use: A risk factor for the development of alcohol disorders. *American Journal of Psychiatry, 157*(5), 745–750.

*Diagnostic and Statistical Manual of Mental Disorders* (4th edition, Text Revision). (2000). American Psychiatric Association.

Dickerson, F., Tenhula, L., & Green-Paden, L. D. (2005). The token economy for schizophrenia: Review of the literature and recommendations for future research. *Schizophrenia Research, 75*, 405–416.

Diener, E., Suh, E. M., Smith, H., & Shao, L. (1995). National differences in reported subjective well-being: Why do they occur? *Social Indicators Research, 34*, 7–32.

Dion, K. E., Berscheid, E., & Walster, E. (1972). What is beautiful is good. *Journal of Personality and Social Psychology, 24*, 285–290.

Dion, K. K. (1986). Stereotyping based on physical attractiveness: Issues and conceptual perspectives. In C. P. Herman, M. P. Zanna, & E. T. Higgins (Eds.), *Physical appearance, stigma, and social behavior: The Ontario symposium.* Hillsdale, NJ: Lawrence Erlbaum Press.

Dion, K. L. (2003). Prejudice, racism, and discrimination. In T. Millon & M. J. Lerner (Eds.), *Handbook of psychology: Personality and social psychology, Vol. 5.* New York: John Wiley & Sons, Inc.

di Pellegrino, G., Fadiga, L., Fogassi, L., Gallese, V., & Rizzolatti, G. (1992). Understanding motor events: A neurophysiological study. *Experimental Brain Research, 91*, 176–180.

Dixon, J., Durrheim, K., & Tredoux, C. (2007). Intergroup contact and attitudes toward the principle and practice of racial equality. *Psychological Science, 18*, 867–872.

Dixon, P., Gordon, R. D., Leung, A., & Di Lollo, V. (1997). Attentional components of partial report. *Journal of Experimental Psychology, 23*, 1253–1271.

Dobson, K. S., & Khatri, N. (2000). Cognitive therapy: Looking backward, looking forward. *Journal of Clinical Psychology, 56*, 907–923.

Dodwell, P. C., & Humphrey, G. K. (1990). A function theory of the McCollough effect. *Psychological Review, 97*, 78–89.

Doetsch, F., & Hen, R. (2005). Young and excitable: The function of new neurons in the adult mammalian brain. *Current Opinion in Neuroscience, 15*, 121–128.

Donald, M. (1993). Origins of the modern mind: Three stages in the evolution of culture and cognition. Cambridge, MA: Harvard University Press.

Dong, C.-J., Swindale, N. V., & Cynader, M. S. (1999). A contingent aftereffect in the auditory system. *Nature Neuroscience, 2*, 863–865.

Donnan, G. A., Darbey, D. G., & Saling, M. M. (1997). Identification of brain region for coordinating speech articulation. *Nature, 349*, 221–222.

Dooling, D. J., & Lachman, R. (1971). Effects of comprehension on retention of prose. *Journal of Experimental Psychology, 88*, 216–222.

Doty, R. L. (2001). Olfaction. *Annual Review of Psychology, 52*, 423–452.

Downing, P. E., Jiang, Y., Shuman, M., & Kanwisher, N. G. (2001). A cortical area selective for visual processing of the human body. *Science, 293*, 2470–2473.

Doyon, J., LaForce, R., Jr., Bouchard, G., Gaudreau, D., Roy, J., Poirier, M., Bedard, P. J., Bedard, F., & Bouchard, J.-P. (1998). Role of the striatum, cerebellum and frontal lobes in the automatization of a repeated visuomotor sequence of movements. *Neuropsychologia, 36*, 625–641.

Driessen, M., Schulte, S., Luedecke, C., Scaefer, I., Sutmann, F., Olhmeier, M., et al. (2008). Trauma and PTSD in patients with alcohol, drug, or dual dependence: A multi-center study. *Alcoholism: Clinical and Experimental Research, 32*(3), 481–488.

Dronkers, N. F. (1996). A new brain region for coordinating speech articulation. *Lancet, 384*, 159–161.

Dronkers, N. F., Wilkins, D. P., Van Valin, R. D., Jr., Redfern, B. B., & Jaeger, J. J. (2004). Lesion analysis of the brain areas involved in language comprehension. *Cognition, 92,* 145–177.

Dunbar, R. (2004). From spears to speech: Could throwing spears have laid the foundations for language acquisition? *Nature, 427,* 783.

Dunbar, R. I. M. (1993). Coevolution of neocortical size, group size and language in humans. *Behavioral and Brain Sciences, 16,* 681–735.

Dutton, D. G., & Aron, A. P. (1974). Some evidence for heightened sexual attraction under conditions of high anxiety. *Journal of Personality and Social Psychology, 30,* 510–517.

Duva, C. A., Floresco, S. B., Wunderlich, G. R., Lao, T. L., Pinel, J. P. J., & Phillips, A. G. (1997). Disruption of spatial but not object-recognition memory by neurotoxic lesions of the dorsal hippocampus in rats. *Behavioral Neuroscience, 111,* 1184–1196.

Dyer, J. (2001, June 10). Ethics and orphans: The monster study. *San Jose Mercury News.*

Dzinas, K. (2000). Founding the Canadian Psychological Association: The perils of historiography. *Canadian Psychology, 41,* 205–212.

Eagly, A. H., Ashmore, R., Makhijani, M., & Longo, L. (1991). What is beautiful is good, but . . . : A meta-analytic review of research on the physical attractiveness stereotype. *Psychological Bulletin, 110,* 109–128.

Eagly, A. H., & Chaiken, S. (1998). Attitude structure and function. In D. T. Gilbert & S. T. Fiske (Eds.), *The handbook of social psychology, Vol. 1* (4th ed.). New York: McGraw-Hill.

Eagly, A. H., & Wood, W. (1999). The origins of sex differences in human behavior: Evolved dispositions versus social roles. *American Psychologist, 54,* 408–423.

Ebstein, R. P., Novick, O., Umansky, R., Priel, B., Osher, B., Blaine, D., Bennett, E. R., Nemanov, L., Katz, M., & Belmaker, R. H. (1996). Dopamine D4 receptor (D4DR) exon III polymorphism associated with the human personality trait of novelty seeking. *Nature Genetics, 12,* 78–80.

Echeburúa, E., DeMedina, R. B., & Aizpiri, J. (2007). Comorbidity of alcohol dependence and personality disorders: A comparative study. *Alcohol and Alcoholism, 42,* 618–622.

Editorial. (1999). Neuroscience for babies. *Nature Neuroscience, 2,* 849.

Egan, L. C., Santos, L. R., & Bloom, P. (2007). The origins of cognitive dissonance: Evidence from children and monkeys. *Psychological Science, 18,* 978–983.

Egan, W., & McCorkindale, C. (2007). Narcissism, vanity, personality and mating effort. *Personality and Individual Differences, 43,* 2105–2115.

Ehlers, C. L., Frank, E., & Kupfer, D. J. (1988). Social zeitgebers and biological rhythms. *Archives of General Psychiatry, 45,* 948–952.

Eichenbaum, H., Stewart, C., & Morris, R. G. M. (1990). Hippocampal representation in spatial learning. *Journal of Neuroscience, 10,* 331–339.

Eimas, P. D., Siqueland, E. R., Jusczyk, P., & Vigorito, J. (1971). Speech perception in infants. *Science, 171,* 303–306.

Ekman, P., Friesen, W. V., & Ellsworth, P. (1972). *Emotion in the human face: Guidelines for research and a review of findings.* New York: Pergamon Press.

Eldredge, N. (1998). *Life in the balance: Humanity and the biodiversity crisis.* Princeton, NH: Princeton University Press.

Ellenberger, H. F. (1972). The story of "Anna O": A critical review with new data. *Journal of the History of the Behavioral Sciences, 8,* 267–279.

Elliott, R. (2002). Research on the effectiveness of humanistic therapies: A meta-analysis. In D. Cain & J. Seeman (Eds.), *Handbook of research and practice in humanistic psychotherapies* (pp. 301–325). Washington, DC: American Psychological Association.

Ellis, A. (1973). Rational-emotive therapy. In R. Corsini (Ed.), *Current psychotherapies.* Itasca, IL: Peacock.

Ellis, A. (1989). A twenty-three-year-old woman guilty about not following her parents' rules. In D. Wedding & R. J. Corsini (Eds.), *Case studies in psychotherapy.* Itasca, IL: Peacock.

Ellis, A. (2003). Early theories and practices in rational emotive behavior therapy and how they have been augmented and revised during the last three decades. *Journal of Rational-Emotive & Cognitive Behavior Therapy, 21*(3–4), 219–243.

Elms, A. C. (1995). Obedience in retrospect. *Journal of Social Issues, 51,* 21–32.

Emmelkamp, P. M. G. (2004). Behavior therapy with adults. In M. J. Lambert (Ed.), *Bergin & Garfield's handbook of psychotherapy and behavior change* (4th ed.) (pp. 379–427). New York: Wiley.

Enard, W., Przeworski, M., Fisher, S. E., Lai, C. S., Wiebe, V., Kitano, T., Monaco, A. P., & Pääbo, S. (2002). Molecular evolution of FOXP2, a gene involved in speech and language. *Nature, 418,* 869–872.

Engberg, L. A., Hansen, G., Welker, R. L., & Thomas, D. R. (1972). Acquisition of key-pecking via autoshaping as a function of prior experience: "Learned laziness?" *Science, 178,* 1002–1004.

Enns, J. T., & Rensink, R. A. (1991). Preattentive recovery of three-dimensional orientation from line drawings. *Psychological Review, 98,* 335–352.

Ensel, W., & Lin, N. (2004). Physical fitness and the stress procedure. *Journal of Community Psychology, 32,* 81–101.

Entwisle, D. (1972). To dispel fantasies about fantasy-based measures of achievement motivation. *Psychological Bulletin, 77,* 377–391.

Enzle, M. E., & Schopflocher, D. (1978). Instigation of attribution processes by attribution questions. *Personality and Social Psychology Bulletin, 4,* 595–599.

Epstein, R. (1985). The spontaneous interconnection of three repertoires. *The Psychological Record, 35,* 131–141.

Epstein, R. (1987). The spontaneous interconnection of four repertoires of behavior in a pigeon *(Columba livia). Journal of Comparative Psychology, 101,* 197–201.

Epstein, R., Kirshnit, C., Lanza, R. P., & Rubin, L. (1984). Insight in the pigeon: Antecedents and determinants of an intelligent performance. *Nature, 308,* 61–62.

Epstein, W. (1961). The influence of syntactical structure on learning. *American Journal of Psychology, 74,* 80–85.

Erard, M. (2007a). Read my slips: Speech errors show how language is processed. *Science, 317,* 1674–1676.

Erard, M. (2007b). *UM . . . slips, stumbles, and verbal blunders, and what they mean.* New York: Pantheon Books.

Ernulf, K. E., Innala, S. M., & Whitam, F. L. (1989). Biological explanation, psychological explanation, and tolerance of homosexuals: A cross-national analysis of beliefs and attitudes. *Psychological Reports, 248,* 183–188.

Eron, L. D. (1950). A normative study of the thematic apperception test. *Psychological Monographs, 64*(Whole No. 315).

Esterling, B. A., Kiecolt-Glaser, J. K., Bodnar, J. D., & Glaser, R. (1994). Chronic stress, social support, and persistent alterations in the natural killer cell response to cytokines in older adults. *Health Psychology, 13,* 291–298.

Eysenck, H. (1998). *Dimensions of personality.* New Brunswick, NJ: Transaction Publishers.

Eysenck, H. J. (1952). The effects of psychotherapy: An evaluation. *Journal of Consulting Psychology, 16,* 319–324.

Eysenck, H. J. (1970). *The structure of human personality* (3rd ed.). London: Methuen.

Eysenck, H. J., & Eysenck, M. W. (1985). *Personality and individual differences: A natural science approach.* New York: Plenum Press, 1985.

Fadda, F., Mosca, E., Colombo, G., & Gessa, G. L. (1990). Alcohol-preferring rats: Genetic sensitivity to alcohol-induced stimulation of dopamine metabolism. *Physiology and Behavior, 47,* 727–729.

Fagan, J. R., III, & Singer, L. T. (1979). The role of simple feature differences in infants' recognition of faces. *Infant Behavior and Development, 2,* 39–45.

Faulder, L. (2006, July 2). For the love of Jennica: A family, at last. *Edmonton Journal,* E3.

Fawcett, S. L., Wang, Y.-Z., & Birch, E. E. (2005). The critical period for susceptibility of human stereopsis. *Investigative Ophthalmology & Visual Science, 46,* 521–525.

Fazio, R. H., & Roskos-Ewoldsen, D. R. (1994). Acting as we feel: When and how attitudes guide behavior. In S. Shavitt & T. C. Brock (Eds.), *Persuasion: Psychological insights and perspectives.* Boston: Allyn & Bacon, Inc.

Feather, N. T., & McKee, I. R. (1993). Global self-esteem and attitudes toward the high achiever for Australian and Japanese students. *Social Psychology Quarterly, 56,* 65–76.

Feeney, J. A., & Noller, P. (1991). Attachment style and verbal descriptions of romantic partners. *Journal of Social and Personal Relationships, 8,* 187–215.

Fegley, D., Kathuria, S., Mercier, R., Li, C., Goutopoulos, A., Makriyannis, A., & Piomelli, D. (2004). Anandamide transport is independent of fatty-acid amide hydrolase activity and is blocked by the hydrolysis-resistant inhibitor. *Proceedings of the National Academy of Science, USA, 101,* 8756–8761.

Feigenbaum, S. L., Masi, A. T., & Kaplan, S. B. (1979). Prognosis in rheumatoid arthritis: A longitudinal study of newly diagnosed younger adult patients. *American Journal of Medicine, 66,* 377–384.

Feingold, A. (1992). Good-looking people are not what we think. *Psychological Bulletin, 111,* 304–341.

Feingold, A. (1993). Cognitive gender differences: A developmental perspective. *Sex Roles, 29,* 91–112.

Feist, G. J., & Barron, F. X. (2003). Predicting creativity from early to late adulthood: Intellect, potential, and personality. *Journal of Research in Personality, 37,* 62–88.

Feldman, R. D. (1982). *Whatever happened to the quiz kids?* Chicago: Chicago Review Press.

Ferguson, C. F. (2007). The good, the bad, and the ugly: A meta-analytic review of positive and negative effects of violent video games. *Psychiatric Quarterly, 78*(4), 309–316.

Ferguson, G. A. (1982). Psychology at McGill. In M. J. Wright & C. R. Myers (Eds.), *History of academic psychology in Canada* (pp. 33–67). Toronto: Hogrefe.

Ferguson, G. O. (1916). *The psychology of the negro: An experimental study.* New York: The Science Press.

Festinger, L. (1957). *A theory of cognitive dissonance.* Stanford: Stanford University Press.

Festinger, L., & Carlsmith, J. M. (1959). Cognitive consequences of forced compliance. *Journal of Abnormal and Social Psychology, 58,* 203–210.

Festinger, L., Riecken, H. W., & Schachter, S. (1956). *When prophecy fails.* Minneapolis: University of Minnesota Press.

Festinger, L., Schachter, S., & Back, K. (1959). *Social pressures in informal groups: A study of a housing community.* New York: Harper & Row.

Feynman, R. P. (1985). *Surely you're joking, Mr. Feynman!* New York: Bantam Books.

Field, T. M. (1994). Infant day care facilitates later social behavior and school performance. In H. Goelman & E. V. Jacobs (Eds.), *Children's play in child care settings. SUNY series, children's play in society*. Albany, NY: State University of New York Press.

Fiez, J. A., Balota, D. A., Raichle, M. E., & Petersen, S. E. (1999). Effects of lexicality, frequency, and spelling-to-sound consistency on the functional anatomy of reading. *Neuron, 24,* 205–218.

Fincham, F., & Beach, S. R. H. (2007). Forgiveness and marital quality: Precursor or consequence in well-established relationships? *Journal of Positive Psychology, 2,* 260–268.

Fink, M. (1976). Presidential address: Brain function, verbal behavior, and psychotherapy. In R. L. Spitzer & D. F. Klein, *Evaluation of psychological therapies: Psycho-therapies, behavior therapies, drug therapies, and their interactions.* Baltimore: Johns Hopkins University Press.

Fink, M. (1999a). *Electroshock: Healing mental illness.* New York: Oxford University Press.

Fink, M. (1999b). *Electroshock: Restoring the mind.* New York: Oxford University Press.

Finlayson, C., Pacheco, F. G., Rodríguez-Vidal, J., Fa, D. A., Gutierrez López, J. M., Santiago Pérez, A., Finlayson, G., Allue, E., Baena-Preysler, J., Cáceres, I., Carrión, J. S., Fernández-Jalvo, Y., Gleed-Owen, C. P., Jimenez-Espejo, F. J., López, P., López-Sáez, J. A., Riquelme-Cantal, J. A., Sánchez-Marco, A., Guzman, F. G., Brown, K., Fuentes, N., Valarino, C. A., Villalpando, A., Stringer, C. B., Martinez Ruiz, F., & Sakamoto, T. (2006). Late survival of Neanderthals at the southernmost extreme of Europe. *Nature, 443,* 850–853.

Fisher, J. D., & Fisher, W. A. (1992). Changing AIDS-risk behavior. *Psychological Bulletin, 111,* 455–474.

Fisher, J. D., & Fisher, W. A. (2000). Theoretical approaches to individual-level change in HIV risk behavior. In J. L. Peterson & R. J. DiClemente (Eds.), *Handbook of HIV prevention: AIDS prevention and mental health.* New York: Kluwer Academic Publishers.

Fisher, L., Ames, E., Chisholm, K., & Savoie, L. (1997). Problems reported by parents of Romanian orphans adoped to British Columbia. *International Journal of Behavioral Development, 20,* 67–82.

Fisher, N. J., Rourke, B. P., & Bieliauskas, L. A. (1999). Neuropsychological subgroups of patients with Alzheimer's disease: An examination of the first ten years of CERAD data. *Journal of Clinical and Experimental Neuropsychology, 21,* 488–518.

Fiske, A. P., Kitayama, S., Markus, H., & Nisbett, R. E. (1998). The cultural matrix of social psychology. In D. T. Gilbert, S. T. Fiske, & G. Lindzey (Eds.), *Handbook of social psychology* (4th ed.) (pp. 915–981). Boston: McGraw-Hill.

Fiske, S. T. (1993). Social cognition and social perception. *Annual Review of Psychology, 44,* 155–194.

Fiske, S. T., & Taylor, S. E. (1991). *Social cognition* (2nd ed.). New York: McGraw-Hill.

Flaherty, J., Frank, E., Hoskinson, K., Richman, J., & Kupfer, D. (1987). *Social zeitgebers and bereavement.* Paper presented at the 140th Annual Meeting of the American Psychiatric Association, Chicago.

Flanagan, O. (1992). *Consciousness reconsidered.* Cambridge, MA: Bradford Books.

Flannery, R. B., Jr. (1999). Psychological trauma and posttraumatic stress disorder: A review. *International Journal of Emergency Mental Health, 1,* 135–140.

Flavell, J. H. (1992). Perspectives on perspective taking. In H. Beilin & P. B. Pufall (Eds.), *Piaget's theory: Prospects and possibilities.* Hillsdale, NJ: Lawrence Erlbaum Associates, Inc.

Flay, B. R., Koepke, D., Thomson, S. J., Santi, S., Best, J. A., & Brown, K. S. (1989). Six-year follow-up of the first Waterloo school smoking prevention trial. *American Journal of Public Health, 79,* 1371–1376.

Flay, B. R., Ryan, K. B., Best, J. A., Brown, K. S., Kersell, M. W., d'Avernas, J. R., & Zanna, M. P. (1985). Are social-psychological smoking prevention programs effective? The Waterloo Study. *Journal of Behavioral Medicine, 8,* 37–59.

Flexser, A. J., & Tulving, E. (1978). Retrieval independence in recognition and recall. *Psychological Review, 85,* 153–171.

Flint, A. F., & Gagnon, N. (2002). Effective use of electroconvulsive therapy in late-life depression. *Canadian Journal of Psychiatry, 47,* 734–741.

Floyd, R. L., Rimer, B. K., Giovino, G. A., Mullen, P. D., & Sullivan, S. E. (1993). A review of smoking in pregnancy: Effects on pregnancy outcomes and cessation efforts. *Annual Review of Public Health, 14,* 379–411.

Fogarty, F., Russell, J. M., Newman, S. C., & Bland, R. C. (1994). Mania. *Acta Psychiatrica Scandinavica, 89*(376, Suppl), 16–23.

Foley, V. D. (1979). Family therapy. In R. J. Corsini (Ed.), *Current psychotherapies* (2nd ed.). Itasca, IL: R. E. Peacock.

Folkman, S., & Lazarus, R. S. (1991). Coping and emotion. In A. Monat & R. S. Lazarus (Eds.), *Stress and coping: An anthology.* New York: Columbia University Press.

Follette, W., Linnerooth, P., & Ruckstuhl, L. (2001). Positive psychology: A clinical behavior analytic perspective. *Journal of Humanistic Psychology, 41,* 102–134.

Fonagy, P., Roth, A., & Higgitt, A. (2005). Psychodynamic psychotherapies: Evidence-based practice and clinical wisdom. *Bulletin of the Menninger Clinic, 69,* 1–58.

Fox, A., Bukatko, D., Hallahan, M., & Crawford, M. (2007). The medium makes a difference: Gender similarities and differences in instant messaging. *Journal of Language and Social Psychology, 26,* 389–397.

Franco, P., Groswasser, J., Hassid, S., Lanquart, J. P., Scaillet, S., & Kahn, A. (2000). Prenatal exposure to cigarette smoking is associated with a decrease in arousal in infants. *Journal of Pediatrics, 135,* 34–38.

Frank, S. L., Pirsch, L. A., & Wright, V. C. (1990). Late adolescents' perceptions of their relationships with their parents: Relationships among deidealization, autonomy, relatedness, and insecurity and implications for adolescent adjustment and ego identity status. *Journal of Youth and Adolescence, 19,* 571–588.

Frankle, W. G., Lombardo, I., New, A. S., Goodman, M., Talbot, P. S., Huang, Y., Hwang, D.-R., Slifstein, M., Curry, S., Abi-Dargham, A., Laruelle, M., & Siever, L. J. (2005). Brain serotonin transporter distribution in subjects with impulsive aggressivity: A positron emission study with [$^{11}$C]McN 5652. *American Journal of Psychiatry, 162,* 915–923.

Freedman, J. L. (2002). *Media violence and its effect on aggression: Assessing the scientific evidence.* Toronto: University of Toronto Press.

Freedman, J. L., & Fraser, S. C. (1966). Compliance without pressure: The foot-in-the-door technique. *Journal of Personality and Social Psychology, 4,* 195–203.

Freeth, R. (2007). *Humanising psychiatry and mental health care: The challenge of the person-centered approach.* Oxford, UK: Radcliffe Publishing.

Freud, S. (1900). *The interpretation of dreams.* London: George Allen and Unwin Ltd.

Freud, S. (1912). *Recommendations for physicians on the psychoanalytic method of treatment.* (J. Riviere, Trans.), Zentralblatt, Bd. II. Reprinted in Sammlung, Vierte Folge.

Freud, S. (1933). *New introductory lectures on psychoanalysis* (J. Strachey, Trans.). New York: Norton.

Frey, S. H., Vinton, D., Norlund, R., & Grafton, S. T. (2005). Cortical topography of human anterior intraparietal cortex active during visually guided grasping. *Cognitive Brain Research, 23,* 397–405.

Frey, U., & Morris, R. G. (1998). Weak before strong: Disassociating synaptic tagging and plasticity-factor accounts of late-LTP. *Neuropharmacology, 37,* 545–552.

Fridlund, A. J. (1992). The behavioural ecology and sociality of human faces. In M. S. Clark (Ed.), *Emotion: Review of personality and social psychology, Vol. 13.* Newbury Park, CA: Sage.

Fridlund, A. J. (1994). *Human facial expression: An evolutionary view.* San Diego: Academic Press.

Friedman, H. S., & Rosenman, R. F. (1974). *Type A behavior and your heart.* New York: Knopf.

Friedman, M., & Rosenman, R. H. (1959). Association of specific overt behavior patterns with blood and cardiovascular findings—Blood cholesterol level, blood clotting time, incidence of arcus senilis, and clinical coronary artery disease. *JAMA, 162,* 1286–1296.

Friedman, R. A. (2007, August 21). To reap psychotherapy's benefits, get a good fit. *The New York Times.*

Friedman, R. A. (2008, April 15). Who are we? Coming of age on antidepressants. *The New York Times.*

Fritsch, T., McClendon, M. J., Smyth, K. A., Lerner, A. J., Friedland, R. P., & Larsen, J. D. (2007). Cognitive functioning in healthy aging: The role of reserve and lifestyle factors early in life. *The Gerontologist, 47,* 307–322.

Fromkin, V. (1973). *Speech errors as linguistic evidence.* The Hague: Mouton Publishers.

Furnham, A. (1992). Just world beliefs in twelve societies. *The Journal of Social Psychology, 133,* 317–329.

Gabrieli, J. D. E., Cohen, N. J., & Corkin, S. (1988). The impaired learning of semantic knowledge following bilateral medial temporal-lobe resection. *Brain and Cognition, 7,* 157–177.

Gaillard, W. D., Pugliese, M., Grandin, C. R., Braniecki, M. A., Kondapaneni, B. A., Hunter, K., Xu, B., Petrella, J. R., Balsamo, L., & Basso, G. (2001). Cortical localization of reading in normal children. *Neurology, 57,* 47–54.

Galaburda, A., & Kemper, T. L. (1979). Observations cited by Geschwind, N. Specializations of the human brain. *Scientific American, 241,* 180–199.

Galaburda, A. M. (1993). Neurology of developmental dyslexia. *Current Opinion in Neurobiology, 3,* 237–242.

Galaburda, A. M., Menard, M. T., & Rosen, G. D. (1994). Evidence for aberrant auditory anatomy in developmental dyslexia. *Proceedings of the National Academy of Sciences, 91,* 8010–8013.

Galaburda, A. M., Sherman, G. F., Rosen, G. D., Aboitiz, F., & Geschwind, N. (1985). Developmental dyslexia: Four consecutive patients with cortical anomalies. *Annals of Neurology, 18,* 222–233.

Galambos, N. L., & Tilton-Weaver, L. C. (1998). Multiple-risk behaviour in adolescents and young adults. *Health Reports, 10,* 9–20.

Gale, C. R., O'Callaghan, F. J., Godfrey, K. M., Law, C. M., & Martyn, C. N. (2004). Critical periods of brain growth and cognitive function in children. *Brain, 127,* 321–329.

Gallistel, C. R. (1990). The organization of learning. Cambridge, MA: Bradford Books/MIT Press.

Galton, F. (1869). *Hereditary genius: An inquiry into its laws and consequences.* Cleveland, OH: World Publishing.

Ganel, T., & Goodale, M. A. (2003). Visual control of action but not perception requires analytical processing of object shape. *Nature, 426,* 664–667.

Ganong, W. F. (1980). Phonetic categorization in auditory word perception. *Journal of Experimental Psychology: Human Perception and Performance, 6,* 110–125.

Garcia, J., & Koelling, R. (1966). Relation of cue to consequence in avoidance learning. *Psychonomic Science, 4,* 123–124.

García, L. F., Antón, A., García, Ó., & Colom, R. (2007). Do parents and children know each other? A study about agreement on personality within families. *Psicothema, 19,* 120–123.

Gardner, H. (1983). *Frames of mind.* New York: Basic Books.

Gardner, H. (1993). *Multiple intelligences: The theory in practice.* New York, NY: Basic Books.

Gardner, H. (1999). *Intelligence reframed: Multiple intelligences for the 21st century.* New York: Basic Books.

Gardner, H. (2003, April 21). *Multiple intelligences after twenty years.* Paper presented at the American Educational Research Association, Chicago.

Gardner, R. A., & Gardner, B. T. (1969). Teaching sign language to a chimpanzee. *Science, 165,* 664–672.

Gardner, R. A., & Gardner, B. T. (1978). Comparative psychology and language acquisition. *Annals of the New York Academy of Sciences, 309,* 37–76.

Garnets, L., & Kimmel, D. (1991). Lesbian and gay male dimensions in the psychological study of human diversity. In J. D. Goodchilds (Ed.), *Psychological perspectives on human diversity in America.* Washington, DC: American Psychological Association.

Garrett, V., Brantley, P., Jones, G., & McKnight, G. (1991). The relation between daily stress and Crohn's disease. *Journal of Behavioral Medicine, 34,* 187–196.

Gartstein, M. A., Crawford, J., & Robertson, C. D. (2008). Early markers of language and attention: Mutual contributions and the impact of parent-infant interactions. *Child Psychiatry and Human Development, 39,* 9–26.

Gauthier, I., Skudlarski, P., Gore, J. C., & Anderson, A. W. (2000). Expertise for cars and birds recruits brain areas involved in face recognition. *Nature Neuroscience, 3,* 191–197.

Gazzaniga, M. S. (1970). *The bisected brain.* New York: Appleton-Century-Crofts.

Gazzaniga, M. S., & LeDoux, J. E. (1978). *The integrated mind.* New York: Plenum Press.

Gelman, R. (1972). Logical capacity of very young children: Number invariance rules. *Child Development, 43,* 75–90.

The Genome Sequencing Consortium. (2001). Initial sequencing and analysis of the human genome. *Nature, 409,* 860–921.

Geschwind, N., Quadfasel, F. A., & Segarra, J. M. (1968). Isolation of the speech area. *Neuropsychologia, 6,* 327–340.

Ghilardi, J. R., Röhrich, H., Lindsay, T. H., Sevcik, M. A., Schwei, M. J., Kubota, K., Halvorson, K. G., Poblete, J., Chaplan, S. R., Dubin, A. E., Carruthers, N. J., Swanson, D., Kuskowski, M., Flores, C. M., & Mantyh, P. W. (2005). Selective blockade of the capsaicin receptor TRPV1 attenuates bone cancer pain. *Journal of Neuroscience, 25,* 3126–3131.

Giaschi, D., & Regan, D. (1997). Development of motion-defined figure-ground segregation in preschool and older children, using a letter-identification task. *Optometry and Vision Science, 74,* 761–767.

Gibson, E. J., & Walk, R. R. (1960). The "visual cliff." *Scientific American, 202,* 2–9.

Gilbert, P. (1921). *The key to culture.* Girard, KS: The Geographical Publishing Company Co. Haldeman-Julius Company.

Giles, A. C., Rose, J. K., & Rankin, C. H. (2005). Investigations of learning and memory in *Caenorhabditis elegans. International Review of Neurobiology, 69,* 37–71.

Gilovich, T. (1990). Differential construal and the false consensus effect. *Journal of Personality and Social Psychology, 59,* 623–634.

Gironell, A., de la Calzada, M. D., Sagales, T., & Barraquer-Bordas, L. (1995). Absence of REM sleep and altered non-REM sleep caused by a haematoma in the pontine tegmentum. *Journal of Neurology, Neurosurgery and Psychiatry, 59,* 195–196.

Gladwin, T. (1970). *East is a big bird.* Cambridge, MA: Harvard University Press.

Glaser, R., Rice, J., Sheridan, J., Post, A., Fertel, R., Stout, J., Speicher, C. E., Kotur, M., & Kiecolt-Glaser, J. K. (1987). Stress-related immune suppression: Health implications. *Brain, Behavior, and Immunity, 1,* 7–20.

Gleicher, G., & Petty, R. E. (1992). Expectations of reassurance influence the nature of fear-stimulated attitude change. *Journal of Experimental Social Psychology, 28,* 86–100.

Glenberg, A. M., Meyer, M., & Lindem, K. (1987). Mental models contribute to foregrounding during text comprehension. *Journal of Memory and Language, 26,* 69–83.

Glowatzki, E., & Fuchs, P. A. (2002). Transmitter release at the hair cell ribbon synapse. *Nature Neuroscience, 5,* 147–154.

Gluck, M. A., & Myers, C. E. (1997). Psychobiological models of hippocampal function in learning and memory. *Annual Review of Psychology, 48,* 481–514.

Godden, D. R., & Baddeley, A. D. (1975). Context-dependent memory in two natural environments: On land and under water. *British Journal of Psychology, 66,* 325–331.

Godfrey, P. A., Malnic, B., & Buck, L. (2004). The mouse olfactory receptor gene family. *Proceedings of the National Academy of Sciences, USA, 101,* 2156–2161.

Goldapple, K., Segal, Z., Garson, C., Lau, M., Bieling, P., Kennedy, S., & Mayberg, H. (2004). Modulation of cortical-limbic pathways in major depression. *Archives of General Psychiatry, 61,* 34–41.

Goldberg, L. R. (1993). The structure of phenotypic personality traits. *American Psychologist, 48,* 26–34.

Goldberg, L. R., Johnson, J. A., Eber, H. W., Hogan, R., Ashton, M. C., Cloninger, C. R., & Gough, H. G. (2006). The international personality item pool and the future of public-domain personality measures. *Journal of Research in Personality, 40,* 84–96.

Goldin-Meadow, S., & Feldman, H. (1977). The development of language-like communication without a language model. *Science, 197,* 401–403.

Goldman, D. L. (1990). Dorothea Dix and her two missions of mercy in Nova Scotia. *Canadian Journal of Psychiatry, 35*(2), 139–143.

Goldstein, M. J., & Strachan, A. M. (1987). The family and schizophrenia. In T. Jacob (Ed.), *Family interaction and psychopathology: Theories, methods, and findings.* New York: Plenum.

Goldstone, R. L., Medink, D. L., & Gentner, D. (1991). Relational similarity and the nonindependence of features in similarity judgments. *Cognitive Psychology, 23,* 222–262.

Golomb, M., Fava, M., Abraham, M., & Rosenbaum, J. F. (1995). Gender differences in personality disorders. *American Journal of Psychiatry, 152,* 579–582.

Gomez, L. (1997). *An introduction to object relations.* New York: New York University Press.

Gonzaga, G., Haselton, M., Smurda, J., Davies, M., & Poore, J. (2008). Love, desire, and the suppression of thoughts of romantic alternatives. *Evolution and Human Behavior, 29*(2), 119–126.

González-Maeso, J., Ang, R. L., Yuen, T., Chan, P., Weisstaub, N. V., López-Giménez, J. F., Mingming, Z., Okawa, Y., Callado, L. F., Milligan, G., Gingrich, J. A., Filizola, M., Meana, J. J., & Sealfon, S. C. (2008). Identification of a serotonin/glutamate receptor complex implicated in psychosis. *Nature, 452,* 93–97.

Goodale, M. A., Meenan, J. P., Bulthoff, H. H., Nicolle, D. A., Murphy, K. J., & Racicot, C. I. (1994). Separate neural pathways for the visual analysis of object shape in perception and prehension. *Current Biology, 4,* 604–610.

Goodale, M. A., & Milner, A. D. (1992). Separate visual pathways for perception and action. *Trends in Neurosciences, 15,* 20–25.

Goodale, M. A., & Milner, A. D. (2004). *Sight unseen.* Oxford, UK: Oxford University Press.

Goodale, M. A., & Westwood, D. A. (2004). An evolving view of duplex vision: Separate but interacting cortical pathways for perception and action. *Current Opinion in Neurobiology, 14,* 203–211.

Goodglass, H. (1976). Agrammatism. In H. Whitaker & H. A. Whitaker (Eds.), *Studies in neurolinguistics.* New York: Academic Press.

Goodwin, D. W., & Guze, S. B. (1996). *Psychiatric diagnosis* (5th ed.). New York: Oxford University Press.

Goodwin, K. A., Meissner, C. A., & Ericsson, K. A. (2001). Toward a model of false recall: Experimental manipulation of encoding context and the collection of verbal reports. *Memory & Cognition, 29,* 806–819.

Gottesman, I. I. (1991). *Schizophrenia genesis: The origins of madness.* New York: Freeman.

Gottesman, I. I., & Erlenmeyer-Kimling, L. (2001). Family and twin strategies as a head start in defining prodromes and endophenotypes for hypothetical early-interventions in schizophrenia. *Schizophrenia Research, 51*(1), 93–102.

Gottesman, I. I., & Moldin, S. O. (1998). Genotypes, genes, genesis, and pathogenesis in schizophrenia. In M. F. Lenzenweger & R. H. Dworkin (Eds.), *Origins and development of schizophrenia: Advances in experimental psychopathology.* Washington, DC: American Psychological Association.

Gottesman, I. I., & Reilly, J. L. (2003). Strengthening the evidence for genetic factors in schizophrenia (without abetting genetic discrimination). In M. F. Lenzenweger & J. M. Hooley (Eds.), *Principles of experimental psychopathology: Essays in honor of Brendan A. Maher.* Washington, DC: American Psychological Association.

Gottesman, I. I., & Shields, J. (1982). *Schizophrenia: The epigenetic puzzle.* Cambridge: Cambridge University Press.

Gottfries, C. G. (1985). Alzheimer's disease and senile dementia: Biochemical characteristics and aspects of treatment. *Psychopharmacology, 86,* 27–41.

Gould, E. (2007). How widespread is adult neurogenesis in mammals? *Nature Reviews Neuroscience, 8,* 481–488.

Gould, J. L., & Able, K. P. (1981). Human homing: An elusive phenomenon. *Science, 212,* 1061–1063.

Graham, J. R. (1990). *MMPI-2: Assessing personality and psychopathology.* New York: Oxford University Press.

Graham, S. A., Baker, R. K., & Poulin-Dubois, D. (1998). Infants' expectations about object label reference. *Canadian Journal of Experimental Psychology, 52,* 103–112.

Grant, P. R., & Grant, B. R. (2002). Unpredictable evolution in a 30-year study of Darwin's finches. *Science, 296,* 707–711.

Gratacos, M., Sahun, I., Galleo, X., Amador-Arjona, A., Estivill, X., & Dierssen, M. (2007). Candidate genes for panic disorder: Insight from human and mouse genetic studies. *Genes, Brain and Behaviour, 6,* 2–23.

Gray, J. A. (1991). The neuropsychology of temperament. In J. Strelau & A. Angleitner (Eds.), *Explorations of temperament: International perspectives on theory and measurement.* London, UK: Plenum Press.

Greally, J. M. (2007). Genomics: Encyclopaedia of humble DNA. *Nature, 447,* 782–783.

Green, D. M., & Swets, J. A. (1974). *Signal detection theory and psychophysics.* New York: Krieger.

Green, J. P., Barabasz, A. F., Barrett, D., & Montgomery, G. H. (2005). Forging ahead: The 2003 APA Division 30 definition of hypnosis. *International Journal of Clinical and Experimental Hypnosis, 53,* 259–264.

Greene, J. D., Sommerville, R. B., Nystrom, L. E., Darley, J. M., & Cohen, J. D. (2001). An fMRI investigation of emotional engagement in moral judgment. *Science, 293,* 2105–2108.

Greenwald, D. F. (1990). An external construct validity study of Rorschach personality variables. *Journal of Personality Assessment, 55,* 768–780.

Greenwald, D. F. (1999). Relationships between the Rorschach and the NEO-Five Factor Inventory. *Psychological Reports, 85*(2), 519–527.

Grelotti, D. J., Gauthier, I., & Schultz, R. T. (2002). Social interest and the development of cortical face specialization: What autism teaches us about face processing. *Developmental Psychobiology, 40,* 213–225.

Griffiths, R. R., Bigelow, G. E., & Henningfield, J. E. (1980). Similarities in animal and human drug-taking behavior. In N. K. Mello (Ed.), *Advances in substance abuse, Vol. 1.* Greenwich, CT: JAI Press.

Griggs, R. A., & Cox, J. R. (1982). The elusive thematic-materials effect in Wason's selection task. *British Journal of Psychology, 73,* 407–420.

Grigorenko, E. (2001). Developmental dyslexia: An update on genes, brains, and environments. *Journal of Child Psychology and Psychiatry, 42,* 91–125.

Grill-Spector, K., & Malach, R. (2004). The human visual cortex. *Annual Review of Neuroscience, 27,* 649–677.

Grine, F. E., Bailey, R. M., Harvati, K., Nathan, R. P., Morris, A. G., Henderson, G. M., Ribot, I., & Pike, A. W. G. (2007). Late Pleistocene human skull from Hofmeyr, South Africa, and modern human origins. *Science, 315,* 226–229.

Grof, P. (2003). Selecting effective long-term treatment for biopolar patients: Monotherapy and combinations. *Journal of Clinical Psychiatry, 64* (Suppl 5), 53–61.

Grön, G., Wunderlich, A. P., Spitzer, M., Tomczak, R., & Riepe, M. W. (2000). Brain activation during human navigation: Gender-different neural networks as substrate of performance. *Nature Neuroscience, 3,* 404–408.

Grossman, D. (2000). Teaching kids to kill. In R. Moser & C. Frantz (Eds.). *Shocking violence: Youth perpetrators and victims—A multidisciplinary perspective* (pp. 17–32). Springfield, IL: Charles C. Thomas.

Grossman, E. D., & Blake, R. (2001). Brain activity evoked by inverted and imagined biological motion. *Vision Research, 41,* 1475–1482.

Grossman, E. D., Donnelly, M., Price, R., Pickens, D., Morgan, V., Neighbor, G., & Blake, R. (2000). Brain areas involved in perception of biological motion. *Journal of Cognitive Neuroscience, 12,* 711–720.

Guiller, J., & Durndell, A. (2006). "I totally agree with you": Gender interactions in educational online discussion groups. *Journal of Computer-Assisted Learning, 22,* 368–381.

Guilmette, T. J., Faust, D., Hart, K., & Arkes, H. R. (1990). A national survey of psychologists who offer neuropsychological services. *Archives of Clinical Neuropsychology, 5,* 373–392.

Guimond, S., & Dube, L. (1989). La representation des causes de l'inferiorité économique des québécois francophones. *Canadian Journal of Behavioural Science, 21,* 28–39.

Güler, A. D., Lee, J., Iida, T., Shimizu, I., Tominaga, M., & Caterina, M. (2002). Heat-activation of the ion channel, TRPV4. *Journal of Neuroscience, 22,* 6408–6414.

Guna Sherlin, D. M., & Verma, R. J. (2001). Vitamin D ameliorates fluoride-induced embryotoxicity in pregnant rats. *Neurotoxicology and Teratology, 23,* 197–201.

Gunter, B. (2008). Media violence: Is there a case for causality? *American Behavioral Scientist, 51*(8), 1061–1122.

Guthrie, R. (1998) *Even the rat was white: A historical view of psychology* (2nd ed.). Boston, MA: Allyn & Bacon.

Guze, S. B., Wolfgram, E. D., McKinney, J. K., & Cantwell, D. P. (1967). Psychiatric illness in the families of convicted criminals: A study of 519 first-degree relatives. *Disorders of the Nervous System, 28,* 651–659.

Haarmeier, T., Thier, P., Repnow, M., & Petersen, D. (1997). False perception of motion in a patient who cannot compensate for eye movements. *Nature, 389,* 849–852.

Habbick, B. F., Nanson, J. L., Snyder, R. E., Cassey, R. E., & Schulman, A. L. (1996). Foetal alcohol syndrome in Saskatchewan: Unchanged incidence in a 20-year period. *Canadian Journal of Public Health, 87,* 204–207.

Haberlandt, K. (1994). *Cognitive psychology.* Boston: Allyn & Bacon.

Hackshaw, A. K., Law, M. R., & Wald, N. J. (1997). The accumulated evidence on lung cancer and environmental tobacco smoke. *British Medical Journal, 315,* 980–988.

Haddock, G., & Zanna, M. P. (1997). Impact of negative advertising on evaluations of political candidates: The 1993 Canadian federal election. *Basic and Applied Social Psychology,* 19, 205–223.

Haddock, G., Zanna, M. P., & Esses, V. M. (1994). The (limited) role of trait-laden stereotypes in predicting attitudes toward native peoples. *British Journal of Social Psychology, 33,* 83–106.

Hadjikhani, N., Liu, A. K., Dale, A. M., Cavanagh, P., & Tootell, R. B. H. (1998). Retinotopy and color sensitivity in human visual cortical area V8. *Molecular Cell, 1,* 235–241.

Hadjistavropoulos, T., & Genest, M. (1994). The underestimation of the role of physical attractiveness in dating preferences: Ignorance or taboo? *Canadian Journal of Behavioural Science, 26,* 298–318.

Hadjistavropoulos, T., Malloy, D. C., Sharpe, D., Green, S. M., & Fuchs-Lacelle, S. (2002). The relative importance of the ethical principles adopted by the American Psychological Association. *Canadian Psychology, 43,* 254–259.

Hafer, C. L. (2000a). Do innocent victims threaten the belief in a just world? Evidence from a modified Stroop Task. *Journal of Personality and Social Psychology, 79,* 165–173.

Hafer, C. L. (2000b). Investment in long-term goals and commitment to just means drive the need to believe in a just world. *Personality and Social Psychology Bulletin, 26,* 1059–1073.

Hafer, C. L. (2002). Why we reject innocent victims. In M. Ross & D. T. Miller (Eds.), *The justice motive in everyday life.* New York: Cambridge University Press.

Haffenden, A. M., Schiff, K. C., & Goodale, M. A. (2001). The dissociation between perception and action in the Ebbinghaus illusion: Non illusory effects of pictorial cues on grasp. *Current Biology, 11,* 177–181.

Hagan, F. E. (1982). *Research methods in criminal justice and criminology.* New York: Macmillan.

Haggard, P., Clark, S., & Kalogeras, J. (2002). Voluntary action and conscious awareness. *Nature Neuroscience, 5,* 382–385.

Haggard, P., & Eimer, M. (1999). On the relation between brain potentials and the awareness of voluntary movements. *Experimental Brain Research, 126,* 128–133.

Haith, M. M. (1998). Who put the cog in infant cognition? Is rich interpretation too costly? *Infant Behavior & Development, 21,* 167–179.

Halaas, J. L., Gajiwala, K. S., Maffei, M., & Cohen, S. L. (1995). Weight-reducing effects of the plasma protein encoded by the obese gene. *Science, 269,* 543–546.

Hall, C. S., & Nordby, V. J. (1973). *A primer of Jungian psychology.* New York: New American Library.

Hall, J., & Valente, T. W. (2007). Adolescent smoking networks: The effects of influence and selection on future smoking. *Addictive Behaviours, 32,* 3054–3059.

Halliday, M. A. K. (1975). *Learning how to mean: Explorations in the development of language.* London: Edward Arnold.

Halmi, K. (1996). Eating disorders: Anorexia nervosa, bulimia nervosa, and obesity. In R. E. Hales & S. C. Yudofsky (Eds.), *The American psychiatric press synopsis of psychiatry.* Washington, DC: American Psychiatric Association.

Hamilton, W. D. (1964).The genetical evolution of social behaviour: I and II. *Journal of Theoretical Biology, 7,* 1–52.

Hamilton, W. D. (1970). Selfish and spiteful behavior in an evolutionary model. *Nature, 228,* 1218–1220.

Harakeh, Z., Engles, R. C. M. E., Vermulst, A. A., De Vries, H., & Scholte, R. H. J. (2007). The influence of best friends and siblings on adolescent smoking: A longitudinal study. *Psychology and Health, 22*(3), 269–289.

Hare, R. D. (1965). Temporal gradient of fear arousal in psychopaths. *Journal of Abnormal Psychology, 70,* 442–445.

Hare, R. D. (1998). *Without conscience: The disturbing world of the psychopaths among us.* New York: Guilford Press.

Hare, R. D. (2006). Psychopathy: A clinical and forensic overview. *Psychiatric Clinics of North America, 29*(3), 709–724.

Hare, R. D., McPherson, L. M., & Forth, A. E. (1988). Male psychopaths and their criminal careers. *Journal of Consulting and Clinical Psychology, 56,* 710–714.

Harkins, S. G., & Petty, R. E. (1982). Effects of task difficulty and task uniqueness on social loafing. *Journal of Personality and Social Psychology, 43,* 1214–1229.

Harlow, H. (1974). *Learning to love.* New York: J. Aronson.

Harmon-Jones, E., & Winkielman, P. (2007) *Social neuroscience: Integrating biological and psychological explanations of social behavior.* New York: Guilford Press.

Harper, P. S. (1995). DNA markers associated with high versus low IQ: Ethical considerations. *Behavior Genetics, 25,* 197–198.

Harpur, T. J., Hart, S. D., & Hare, R. D. (2002). Personality of the psychopath. In P. T. Costa, Jr., & T. A. Widiger (Eds.), *Personality disorders and the five-factor model of personality* (2nd ed.). Washington, DC: American Psychological Association.

Harris, M. (1991). *Cultural anthropology* (3rd ed.). New York: HarperCollins.

Hartley, T., Maguire, E. A., Spiers, H. J., and Burgess, N. (2003). The well-worn route and the path less traveled: Distinct neural bases of route following and wayfinding in humans. *Neuron, 37,* 877–888.

Harwood, R. L., Miller, J. G., & Irizarry, N. L. (1995). *Culture and attachment: Perceptions of the child in context.* New York: Guilford.

Hatfield, E. (1988). Passionate and compassionate love. In R. J. Sternberg & M. L. Barnes (Eds.), *The psychology of love.* New Haven, CT: Yale University Press.

Hatfield, E., & Rapson, R. L. (1993). *Love, sex, and intimacy: Their psychology, biology, and history.* New York: HarperCollins.

Hauser, J. D., Chomsky, N., & Fitch, W. T. (2002). The faculty of language: What is it, who has it, and how did it evolve? *Science, 298,* 1569–1579.

Hayes, E., & Plowfield, A. (2007). Smoking too young: Students' decisions about tobacco use. *The American Journal of Maternal/Child Nursing, 32,* 112–116.

Hazelwood, J. D., & Olson, J. M. (1986). Covariation information, causal questioning, and interpersonal behavior. *Journal of Experimental Social Psychology, 22,* 276–291.

He, J., Vupputuri, S., Allen, K., Prerost, M. R., Hughes, J., & Whelton, P. K. (1999). Passive smoking and the risk of coronary heart disease—a meta-analysis of epidemiologic studies. *New England Journal of Medicine, 340,* 920–926.

Health Canada. (2000). *Cardiovascular disease surveillance online.* Retrieved April 22, 2004, http://dsol-smed.hc-sc.gc.ca/dsol-smed/cvd/index_e.html.

Health Canada. (2002). *A report on mental illnesses in Canada.* Retrieved April 7, 2004, http:// www.hc-sc.gc.ca/pphb-dgspsp/publicat/miic-mmac/.

Health Canada. (2007). *Canadian Tobacco Use Monitoring Survey, 2007.* Retrieved May 2, 2008, http://www.hc-sc.gc.ca/hl-vs/tobac-tabac/research-recherche/stat/ctums-esutc_2007_e.html.

Healy, A. F., & McNamara, D. S. (1996). Verbal learning and memory: Does the Modal Model still work? *Annual Review of Psychology, 47,* 143–172.

Hebb, D. O. (1949). *The organization of behavior.* New York: Wiley-Interscience.

Hebb, D. O. (1955). Drives and the C. N. S. (conceptual nervous system). *Psychological Review, 62,* 243–254.

Hebb, D. O. (1966). *A textbook of psychology.* Philadelphia, PA: W.B. Saunders Company.

Hebb, D. O. (1980) *Essay on mind.* Hillsdale, NJ: Erlbaum.

Heeger, D. J., Juk, A. C., Geisler, W. S., & Albrecht, D. G. (2000). Spikes versus BOLD: What does neuroimaging tell us about neuronal activity? *Nature Neuroscience, 3,* 631–633.

Heider, E. R. (1971). "Focal" color areas and the development of color names. *Developmental Psychology, 4,* 447–455.

Heider, E. R. (1972). Universals in color naming and memory. *Journal of Experimental Psychology, 93,* 10–20.

Heider, F. (1958). *The psychology of interpersonal relations.* New York: John Wiley & Sons.

Heine, S. J. (2001). Self as cultural product: An examination of East Asian and North American selves. *Journal of Personality, 69,* 881–906.

Heine, S. J., Kitayama, S., Lehman, D. R., Takata, T., Ide, E., Leung, C., & Matsumoto, H. (2001). Divergent consequences of success and failure in Japan and North America: An investigation of self-improving motivations and malleable selves. *Journal of Personality and Social Psychology, 81,* 599–615.

Heinrichs, R. W. (2003). Historical origins of schizophrenia: Two early madmen and their illness. *Journal of the History of the Behavioral Sciences, 39*(4), 349–363.

Helenius, P., Salmelin, R., Service, E., & Connolly, J. F. (1999). Semantic cortical activation in dyslexic readers. *Journal of Cognitive Neuroscience, 11,* 535–550.

Helms, J. E. (1992). Why is there no study of cultural equivalence in standardized cognitive ability testing? *American Psychologist, 47,* 1083–1101.

Helms, J. E. (1997). The triple quandary of race, culture, and social classes in standardized cognitive ability testing. In D. P. Fanagan, J. L. Genshaft, et al. (Eds.), *Contemporary intellectual assessment: Theories, tests, and issues* (pp. 517–532). New York: Guilford Press.

Henderson, J., Kesmodel, U., & Gray, R. (2007). Systematic review of the fetal effects of prenatal binge-drinking. *Journal of Epidemiology and Community Health, 61,* 1069–1073.

Henderson, N. D. (1982). Human behavior genetics. *Annual Review of Psychology, 33,* 403–440.

Herdt, G. (2001). Stigma and the ethnographic study of HIV: Problems and prospects. *AIDS & Behavior, 5*(2), 141–149.

Herdt, G., & Lindenbaum, S. (Eds.). (1992). *Social analyses in the time of AIDS.* Newbury Park, CA: Sage.

Herring, S. C. (2003). Gender and power in online communication. In J. Holmes & M. Meyerhoff (Eds.), *The handbook of language and gender* (pp. 202–228). Oxford, UK: Blackwell.

Herrnstein, R. J., & Loveland, D. H. (1964). Complex visual concept in the pigeon. *Science, 146,* 549–551.

Herrnstein, R. J., & Murray, C. (1994). *The bell curve.* New York: Free Press.

Heth, C. D. (1976). Simultaneous and backward fear conditioning as a function of number of CS-US pairings. *Journal of Experimental Psychology: Animal Behavior Processes, 2,* 117–129.

Hettema, J. M., Neale, M. C., & Kendler, K. S. (2001). A review and meta-analysis of the genetic epidemiology of anxiety disorders. *American Journal of Psychiatry, 158,* 1568–1578.

Heyman, G. D., & Giles, J. W. (2004). Valence effects in reasoning about evaluative traits. *Merrill-Palmer Quarterly, 50,* 86–109.

Heywood, C. A., Gaffan, D., & Cowey, A. (1995). Cerebral achromatopsia in monkeys. *European Journal of Neuroscience, 7,* 1064–1073.

Heywood, C. A., & Kentridge, R. W. (2003). Achromatopsia, color vision, and cortex. *Neurologic Clinics, 21,* 483–500.

Higgins, S. T., Budney, A. J., & Bickel, W. K. (1994). Applying behavioral concepts and principles to the treatment of cocaine dependence. *Drug and Alcohol Dependence, 7,* 19–38.

Hilbrecht, M., Zuzanek, J., & Mannell, R. C. (2008). Time use, time pressure, and gendered behavior in early and late adolescence. *Sex Roles, 58,* 342–357.

Hilgard, E. R. (1991). A neodissociation interpretation of hypnosis. In S. J. Lynn & J. W. Rhue (Eds.), *Theories of hypnosis: Current models and perspectives* (pp. 324–361). New York: Guilford Press.

Hill, C. E., & Nakayama, E. Y. (2000). Client-centered therapy: Where has it been and where is it going? A comment on Hathaway (1948). *Journal of Clinical Psychology, 56,* 861–875.

Hilliard, S., & Domjan, M. (1995). Effects of sexual conditioning on devaluing the US through satiation. *Quarterly Journal of Experimental Psychology, 48B,* 84–92.

Hillman, J., & Snyder, S. (2007). *Childhood autism: A clinician's guide to early diagnosis and integrated treatment.* New York: Routledge.

Hilton, D. J., & Slugoski, B. R. (1986). Knowledge-based causal attributions: The abnormal conditions focus model. *Psychological Review, 93,* 75–88.

Hirschman, R. S., Leventhal, H., & Glynn, K. (1984). The development of smoking behavior: Conceptualization and supportive cross-sectional survey data. *Journal of Applied Social Psychology, 14,* 184–206.

Hirshbein, L., & Sarvananda, S. (2008). History power and electricity: American popular magazine accounts of electroconvulsive therapy, 1940–2005. *Journal of the History of Behavioural Sciences, 44*(1), 1–18.

Hobson, J. A., & Pace-Schott, E. F. (2002). The cognitive neuroscience of sleep: Neuronal systems, consciousness and learning. *Nature Reviews: Neuroscience, 3,* 679–693.

Hoff, T. L. (1992). Psychology in Canada one hundred years ago: James Mark Baldwin at the University of Toronto. *Canadian Psychology, 33,* 683–694.

Hoffman, P. (1997). The endorphin hypothesis. In W. P. Morgan (Ed.), *Physical activity and mental health* (pp. 163–177). Washington, DC: Taylor & Francis.

Hofling, C. K. (1963). *Textbook of psychiatry for medical practice.* Philadelphia: J. B. Lippincott.

Hohmann, G. W. (1966). Some effects of spinal cord lesions on experienced emotional feelings. *Psychophysiology, 3,* 143–156.

Hollander, E., Schiffman, E., Cohen, B., Rivera-Stein, M. A., Rosen, W., Gorman, J. M., Fyer, A. J., Papp, L., & Liebowitz, M. R. (1990). Signs of central nervous system dysfunction in obsessive-compulsive disorder. *Archives of General Psychiatry, 47,* 27–32.

Hollis, K. L. (1982). Pavlovian conditioning of signal-centered action patterns and autonomic behavior: A biological analysis of function. *Advances in the Study of Behavior, 12,* 1–64.

Hollis, K. L., Langworthy-Lam, K. S., Blouin, L. A., & Romano, M. C. (2004). Novel strategies of subordinate fish competing for food: Learning when to fold. *Animal Behaviour, 68,* 1155–1164.

Hollis, K. L., Pharr, V. L., Dumas, M. J., Britton, G. B., & Field, J. (1997). Classical conditioning provides paternity advantage for territorial male blue gouramis *(Trichogaster trichopterus). Journal of Comparative Psychology, 111,* 219–225.

Hollon, S. D., Thase, M. E., & Markowitz, J. C. (2002). Treatment and prevention of depression. *Psychological Science in the Public Interest, 3*(2), 39–77.

Holmes, T. H., & Rahe, R. H. (1967). The social readjustment rating scale. *Journal of Psychosomatic Research, 11,* 213, 218.

Holyoak, K. J. (1990). Problem solving. In D. N. Osherson & E. E. Smith (Eds.), *An invitation to cognitive science. Vol. 3: Thinking.* Cambridge, MA: MIT Press.

Holyoak, K. J., & Spellman, B. A. (1993). Thinking. *Annual Review of Psychology, 44,* 265–315.

Horn, J. L. (1982). The theory of fluid and crystallized intelligence in relation to concepts of cognitive psychology and aging in adulthood. In F. I. M. Craik & S. Trehub (Eds.), *Aging and cognitive processes.* New York: Plenum Press.

Horn, J. L. (1994). Theory of fluid and crystallized intelligence. In R. J. Sternberg (Ed.), *Encyclopedia of human intelligence.* New York: Macmillan.

Horn, J. L. (2002). Selections of evidence, misleading assumptions, and oversimplifications: The political message of *The Bell Curve.* In J. M. Fish (Ed.), *Race and intelligence: Separating science from myth.* Mahwah, NJ: Lawrence Erlbaum Associates.

Horn, J. L., & Cattell, R. B. (1966). Refinement and test of the theory of fluid and crystallized ability intelligences. *Journal of Educational Psychology, 57,* 253–270.

Horne, J. A. (1978). A review of the biological effects of total sleep deprivation in man. *Biological Psychology, 7,* 55–102.

Horne, J. A., & Minard, A. (1985). Sleep and sleepiness following a behaviourally "active" day. *Ergonomics, 28,* 567–575.

Horne, J. A., & Petit, A. N. (1985). High incentive effects on vigilance performance during 72 hours of total sleep deprivation. *Acta Psychologica, 58,* 123–139.

Horney, K. (1950). *Neurosis and human growth.* New York: Norton.

Horwitz, A. V., & Wakefield, J. C. (2007). *The loss of sadness: How psychiatry transformed normal sorrow into depressive disorder.* New York: Oxford University Press.

Hothersall, D. (2004). *History of psychology* (4th ed.). New York: McGraw-Hill.

Hough, L. M., & Oswald, F. L. (2000). Personnel selection: Looking toward the future—Remembering the past. *Annual Review of Psychology, 51,* 631–664.

Hovland, C. I., & Weiss, W. (1951). The influence of source credibility on communication effectiveness. *Public Opinion Quarterly, 15,* 635–650.

Howard, J. H., Cunningham, D. A., & Rechnitzer, P. A. (1976). Health patterns associated with type A behavior: A managerial population. *Journal of Human Stress, 2,* 24–31.

Howard, M. O., Elkins, R. L., Rimmele, C., & Smith, J. W. (1991). Chemical aversion treatment of alcohol dependence. *Drug and Alcohol Dependence, 29,* 107–143.

Hoyenga, K. B., & Hoyenga, K. T. (1993). *Gender-related differences: Origins and outcomes.* Boston: Allyn & Bacon.

Hubel, D. H., & Wiesel, T. (2004). *Brain and visual perception: The story of a 25-year collaboration.* New York: Oxford University Press.

Hubel, D. H., & Wiesel, T. N. (1977). Functional architecture of macaque monkey visual cortex. *Proceedings of the Royal Society of London, Series B, 198,* 1–59.

Hubel, D. H., & Wiesel, T. N. (1979). Brain mechanisms of vision. *Scientific American, 241,* 150–162.

Huesmann, L. R., Moise-Titus, J., Podolski, C.-L., & Eron, L. D. (2003). Longitudinal relations between children's exposure to TV violence and their aggressive and violent behavior in young adulthood: 1977–1992. *Developmental Psychology, 39,* 201–221.

Hughes, I. A., Houk, C., Ahmed, S. F., & Lee, P. A. (2006). Consensus statement on management of intersex disorders. *Archives of Disease in Childhood, 91,* 554–563.

Hughes, J. R., & Pierattini, R. (1992). An introduction to pharmacotherapy. In J. Grabowski & G. R. Vandenbos (Eds.), *Psychopharmacology: Basic mechanisms and applied interventions: Master lectures in psychology.* Washington, DC: American Psychological Association.

Hulit, L., & Howard, M. R. (2006). *Born to talk: An introduction to speech and language development* (4th ed.). Boston: Allyn and Bacon.

Humphrey, G. (1933). *The nature of learning: In its relation to the living system.* London, UK: Kegan, Paul, Trench, Trubner.

Humphrey, G. K., Herbert, A. M., Hazlewood, S., & Stewart, J. A. D. (1998). The indirect McCollough effect: An examination of an associative account. *Perception & Psychophysics, 60,* 1188–1196.

Humphrey, N. K. (1974). Species and individuals in the perceptual world of monkeys. *Perception, 3,* 105–114.

Hunt, E. (1985). Verbal ability. In R. J. Sternberg (Ed.), *Human abilities: An information-processing approach.* New York: W. H. Freeman.

Hunter, P. (2008). Ancient rules of memory. *EMBO Reports, 9,* 124–126.

Hur, Y.-M. (2005). Genetic and environmental influences on self-concept in female preadolescent twins: Comparison of Minnesota and Seoul data. *Twin Research and Human Genetics, 8,* 291–299.

Hurd, P. (1997). Cooperative signalling between opponents in fish fights. *Animal Behaviour, 54,* 1309–1315.

Hurwitz, T. A. (2004). Somatization and conversion disorder. *Canadian Journal of Psychiatry–Revue Canadienne de Psychiatrie, 49*(3), 172–178.

Hyman, S. E., & Malenka, R. C. (2001). Addiction and the brain: The neurobiology of compulsion and its persistence. *Nature Reviews: Neuroscience, 2,* 695–703.

Iaria, G., Petrides, M., Dagher, A., Pike, B., & Bohbot, V. D. (2003). Cognitive strategies dependent on the hippocampus and caudate nucleus in human navigation: Variability and change with practice. *Journal of Neuroscience, 23,* 5945–5952.

Inglefinger, F. J. (1944). The late effects of total and subtotal gastrectomy. *New England Journal of Medicine, 231,* 321–327.

International Human Genome Sequencing Consortium. (2004). Finishing the euchromatic sequence of the human genome. *Nature, 431,* 931–945.

Ioannidis, J. P. A. (2005). Why most published research findings are false. *PloS Medicine, 2,* 124.

Irvine, J., Garner, D. M., Craig, H. M., & Logan, A. G. (1991). Prevalence of type A behavior in untreated hypertensive individuals. *Hypertension, 18,* 72–78.

Isenberg, D. J. (1986). Group polarization: A critical review and meta-analysis. *Psychological Bulletin, 50,* 1141–1151.

Iverson, G. L. (2005). Outcome from mild traumatic brain injury. *Current Opinion in Psychiatry, 18,* 301–317.

Iversen, L. (2003). Cannabis and the brain. *Brain, 126,* 1252–1270.

Jacklin, C. N., & Maccoby, E. E. (1983). Issues of gender differentiation in normal development. In M. D. Levine, W. B. Carey, A. C. Crocker, & R. T. Gross (Eds.), *Developmental-behavioral pediatrics.* Philadelphia: Saunders.

Jackson, D. N., & Tremblay, P. F. (2002). The six-factor personality questionnaire. In B. de Raad (Ed.), *Big five assessment.* Ashland, OH: Hogrefe & Huber Publishers.

Jacobson, J. W., & Mulick, J. A. (1996). *Manual on diagnosis and professional practice in mental retardation.* Washington, DC: American Psychological Association.

Jakobson, L. S., Archibald, Y. M., Carey, D. P., & Goodale, M. A. (1991). A kinematic analysis of reaching and grasping movements in a patient recovering from optic ataxia. *Neuropsychologia, 29,* 803–809.

Jakobwitz, S., & Egan, V. (2006). The dark triad and normal personality traits. *Personality and Individual Differences, 40,* 331–339.

James, T. W., Culham, J., Humphrey, G. K., Milner, A. D., & Goodale, M. A. (2003). Ventral occipital lesions impair object recognition but not object-directed grasping: An fMRI study. *Brain, 126,* 2463–2475.

James, W. (1884). What is an emotion? *Mind, 9,* 188–205.

James, W. (1890). *Principles of psychology.* New York: Henry Holt.

James, W. (1893). *The principles of psychology: Vol. 1.* New York: Holt.

James, W. P. T., & Trayhurn, P. (1981). Thermogenesis and obesity. *British Medical Bulletin, 37,* 43–48.

Jang, K. L., Livesley, W. J., Angleitner, A., Riemann, R., & Vernon, P. (2002). Genetic and environmental influences on the covariance of facets defining the domains of the five-factor model of personality. *Personality & Individual Differences, 33*(1), 83–101.

Jang, K. L., Livesley, W. J., & Vernon, P. A. (1996). Heritability of the Big Five personality dimensions and their facets: A twin study. *Journal of Personality, 64,* 577–591.

Janis, I. L. (1972). *Victims of groupthink.* Boston: Houghton Mifflin.

Janis, I. L. (1982). *Groupthink: Psychological studies of policy decisions and fiascoes.* Boston: Houghton Mifflin.

Jasper, H. H. (1995). A historical perspective: The rise and fall of prefrontal lobotomy. In H. H. Jasper & S. Riggio (Eds.), *Epilepsy and the functional anatomy of the frontal lobe.* New York: Raven Press.

Javal, E. (1879). Essai sur la physiologie de la lecture. *Annales D'Oculistique, 82,* 242–253.

Jaynes, J. (1970). The problem of animate motion in the seventeenth century. *Journal of the History of Ideas, 6,* 219–234.

Jeffcoate, W. J., Lincoln, N. B., Selby, C., & Herbert, M. (1986). Correlations between anxiety and serum prolactin in humans. *Journal of Psychosomatic Research, 30,* 217–222.

Jelicic, M., Smeets, T., Peters, M. J. V., Candel, I., Horselenberg, R., & Merckelbach, H. (2006). Assassination of a controversial politician: Remembering details from another non-existent film. *Applied Cognitive Psychology, 20,* 591–596.

Jenike, M. S. (2000). Neurological treatment of obsessive-compulsive disorder. In W. K. Goodman, M. V. Rudorfer, & J. D. Maser (Eds.), *Obsessive-compulsive disorder: Contemporary issues in treatment.* Personality and clinical psychology series. Mahwah, NJ: Lawrence Erlbaum Associates.

Jenkins, J. G., & Dallenbach, K. M. (1924). Oblivescence during sleep and waking. *American Journal of Psychology, 35,* 605–612.

Jenkins, J. H., & Karno, M. (1992). The meaning of expressed emotion: Theoretical issues raised by cross-cultural research. *American Journal of Psychiatry, 149,* 9–21.

Jensen, A. R. (1985). The nature of the black-white difference on various psychometric tests: Spearman's hypothesis. *Behavioral and Brain Sciences, 8,* 193–263.

Jensen, T., Genefke, I., & Hyldebrandt, N. (1982). Cerebral atrophy in young torture victims. *New England Journal of Medicine, 307,* 1341.

Jitsumori, M., & Yoshihara, M. (1997). Categorical discrimination of human facial expressions by pigeons: A test of the linear feature model. *Quarterly Journal of Experimental Psychology, 50B,* 253–268.

Job, R. F. S. (2002). The effects of uncontrollable, unpredictable aversive and appetitive events: Similar effects warrant similar, but not identical, explanations. *Integrative Physiological & Behavioral Science, 37,* 59–81.

Johansson, G. (1973). Visual perception of biological motion and a model for its analysis. *Perception and Psychophysics, 14,* 201–211.

Johnsen, S., & Lohmann, K. J. (2005). The physics and neurobiology of magnetoreception. *Nature Reviews Neuroscience, 6,* 703–712.

Johnson, J. G., Alloy, L. B., Panzarella, C., Metalsky, G. I., Rabkin, J. G., Williams, J. B. W., & Abramson, L. Y. (2001). Hopelessness as a mediator of the association between social support and depressive symptoms: Findings of a study of men with HIV. *Journal of Consulting & Clinical Psychology, 69*(6), 1056–1060.

Johnson, J. G., Cohen, P., Smailes, E. M., Kasen, S., & Brook, J. S. (2002). Television viewing and aggressive behavior during adolescence and adulthood. *Science, 295,* 2468–2471.

Johnson, M. K. (2006). Memory and reality. *American Psychologist, 61,* 760–771.

Johnson, S. B., & Sechrest, L. (1968). Comparison of desensitization and progressive relaxation in treating test anxiety. *Journal of Consulting and Clinical Psychology, 32,* 280–286.

Johnson-Laird, P. N. (1985). Deductive reasoning ability. In R. J. Sternberg (Ed.), *Human abilities: An information-processing approach.* New York: W. H. Freeman.

Johnson-Laird, P. N. (1995). Deductive reasoning and the brain. In G. M. S. Gazzaniga et al. (Eds.), *The cognitive neurosciences* (pp. 999–1008). Cambridge, MA: MIT Press.

Johnson-Laird, P. N. (1999). Deductive reasoning. *Annual Review of Psychology, 50,* 109–135.

Johnson-Laird, P. N. (2001). Mental models and deduction. *Trends in Cognitive Sciences, 5,* 434–442.

Johnson-Laird, P. N., Byrne, R. M. J., & Schaeken, W. (1992). Propositional reasoning by model. *Psychological Review, 99,* 418–439.

Johnston, W. A., & Dark, V. J. (1986). Selective attention. *Annual Review of Psychology, 37,* 43–76.

Johnstone, L. (1999). Adverse psychological effects of ECT. *Journal of Mental Health, 8,* 69–85.

Joiner, T. E., Jr. (2000). A test of the hopelessness theory of depression in youth psychiatric inpatients. *Journal of Clinical Child Psychology, 29,* 167–176.

Jones, E. E. (1990). *Interpersonal perception.* New York: W. H. Freeman.

Jones, E. E., & Harris, V. A. (1967). The attribution of attitudes. *Journal of Experimental Social Psychology, 3,* 1–24.

Jones, E. E., & Nisbett, R. E. (1971). The actor and observer: Divergent perceptions of the causes of behavior. In E. E. Jones, D. E. Kamouse, H. H. Kelley, R. E. Nisbett, S. Valins, & B. Weiner (Eds.), *Attribution: Perceiving the causes of behavior.* Morristown, NJ: General Learning Press.

Jones, M. C., & Bayley, N. (1950). Physical maturing among boys as related to behavior. *Journal of Educational Psychology, 41,* 129–184.

Julesz, B. (1965). Texture and visual perception. *Scientific American, 212,* 38–48.

Julesz, B. (2006). *Fundamentals of cyclopean perception.* Cambridge, MA: MIT Press.

Julien, R. M. (2000). *A primer of drug action* (9th ed.). New York: Worth.

Jusczyk, P. W., & Hohne, E. A. (1997). Infants' memory for spoken words. *Science, 277,* 1984–1986.

Just, M. A., & Carpenter, P. A. (1987). *The psychology of reading and language comprehension.* Boston: Allyn and Bacon.

Just, M. A., Carpenter, P. A., & Wu, R. (1983). *Eye fixations in the reading of Chinese technical text* (Technical Report). Pittsburgh: Carnegie-Mellon University.

Kaernbach, C. (2004). The memory of noise. *Experimental Psychology, 51,* 240–248.

Kaewboonchoo, O., Saleekul, S., & Jaipukdee, S. (2007). Age related changes in hearing among Thai people. *Journal of the Medical Association of Thailand, 90,* 798–804.

Kagan, J., Kearsley, R. B., & Zelazo, P. R. (1978). *Infancy: Its place in human development.* Cambridge, MA: Harvard University Press.

Kagan, J., Reznick, J. S., & Snidman, N. (1988). Biological bases of childhood shyness. *Science, 240,* 167–171.

Kail, R., & Hall, L. K. (2001). Distinguishing short-term memory from working memory. *Memory & Cognition, 29,* 1–9.

Kail, R. V. (2001). *Children and their development.* Upper Saddle River, NJ: Prentice Hall.

Kalish, R. A. (1976). Death and dying in a social context. In R. H. Binstock & E. Shanas (Eds.), *Handbook of aging and the social sciences.* New York: Van Nostrand Reinhold.

Kaminsky, Z., Petronis, A., Wang, S.-C., Levine, B., Ghaffar, O., Floden, D., & Feinstein, A. (2008). Epigenetics of personality traits: An illustrative study of identical twins discordant for risk-taking behavior. *Twin Research and Human Genetics, 11,* 1–11.

Kandel, E. R., & Spencer, W. A. (1968) Cellular neurophysiological approaches in the study of learning. *Physiological Review, 48,* 65–134.

Kane, J. M. (2001). Long-term therapeutic management in schizophrenia. In A. Breier, P. V. Tran, & J. M. Herrera (Eds.), *Current issues in the psychopharmacology of schizophrenia.* Philadelphia, PA: Lippincott Williams & Wilkins Publishers.

Kanner, L. (1943). Austistic disturbances of affective contact. *Nervous Child, 2,* 217–250.

Kaplan, E. L., & Kaplan, G. A. (1970). The prelinguistic child. In J. Eliot (Ed.), *Human development and cognitive processes.* New York: Holt, Rinehart and Winston.

Kaplan, R. M. (2000). Two pathways to prevention. *American Psychologist, 55,* 382–396.

Karau, S. J., & Hart, J. W. (1998). Group cohesiveness and social loafing: Effects of a social interaction manipulation on individual motivation within groups. *Group Dynamics, 2,* 185–191.

Karau, S. J., & Williams, K. D. (1995). Social loafing: Research findings, implications, and future directions. *Current Directions in Psychological Science, 4,* 134–139.

Karbe, H., Herholz, K., Szelies, B., Pawlik, G., Wienhard, K., et al. (1989). Regional metabolic correlates of token test results in cortical and subcortical left hemispheric infarction. *Neurology, 39,* 1083–1088.

Karbe, H., Szelies, B., Herholz, K., & Heiss, W. D. (1990). Impairment of language is related to left parieto-temporal glucose metabolism in aphasic stroke patients. *Journal of Neurology, 237,* 19–23.

Kausler, D. H. (1994). *Learning and memory in normal aging.* New York: Academic Press.

Kay, P. (1975). Synchronic variability and diachronic changes in basic color terms. *Language in Society, 4,* 257–270.

Kay, P., & Regier, T. (2006). Color naming universals: The case of Berinmo. *Cognition, 102,* 289–298.

Kazdin, A. E. (1994). *Behavior modification in applied settings.* Pacific Grove, CA: Brooks/Cole.

Kazdin, A. E. (2001). *Behavior modification in applied settings* (6th ed.). Belmont, CA: Wadsworth/Thomson Learning.

Keating, D. (2004). Cognitive and brain development. In R. M. Lerner & L. Steinberg (Eds.), *Handbook of adolescent psychology* (2nd ed.) (pp. 45–84). Hoboken, NJ: John Wiley and Sons.

Keller, S. E., Weiss, J. M., Schleifer, S. J., Miller, N. E., & Stein, M. (1983). Stress-induced suppression of immunity in adrenalectomized rats. *Science, 221,* 1301–1304.

Kelley, H. H. (1950). The warm-cold variable in first impressions of persons. *Journal of Personality, 18,* 431–439.

Kelley, H. H. (1967). Attribution theory in social psychology. In D. Levine (Ed.), *Nebraska symposium on motivation, Vol. 15.* Lincoln: University of Nebraska Press.

Kelly, J. F., & Hake, D. F. (1970). An extinction-induced increase in an aggressive response with humans. *Journal of the Experimental Analysis of Behavior, 14,* 153–164.

Kelly, S. J., Day, N., & Streissguth, A. P. (2000). Effects of prenatal alcohol exposure on social behavior in humans and other species. *Neurotoxicology and Teratology, 22,* 143–149.

Kelner, F. (1997). Alcohol. In P. MacNeil & W. Ikuko (Eds.), *Canada's alcohol and other drugs survey 1994: A discussion of the findings.* Ottawa: Health Canada.

Keltikangas-Järvinen, L., & Heinonen, K. (2003). Roots of adult hostility: Family factors as predictors of cognitive and affective hostility. *Child Development, 74*, 1751–1768.

Kendler, K. S., Pedersen, N., Johnson, L., Neale, M. C., & Mathe, A. A. (1993). A pilot Swedish twin study of affective illness, including hospital- and population-ascertained subsamples. *Archives of General Psychiatry, 50*(9), 699–700.

Kendler, K. S., Prescott, C. A., Neale, M. C., & Pedersen, N. L. (1997). Temperance board registration for alcohol abuse in a national sample of Swedish male twins, born 1902 to 1949. *Archives of General Psychiatry, 54*, 178–184.

Kennedy, H. J., Evans, M. G., Crawford, A. C., & Fettiplace, R. (2003). Fast adaptation of mechanoelectrical transducer channels in mammalian cochlear hair cells. *Nature Neuroscience, 6*, 832–836.

Kennedy, R. (2007). *The many voices of psychoanalysis.* New York: Routledge.

Kerr, R. A., McGrath, J. J., & O'Kearney, T. O., et al. (1982). ECT: Misconceptions and attitudes. *Australian Journal of Psychiatry, 16*, 43–49.

Kertesz, A. (1981). Anatomy of jargon. In J. Brown (Ed.), *Jargonaphasia.* New York: Academic Press.

Kessler, R. C., Chiu, W. T., Demler, O., & Walter, E. E. (2005). Prevalence, severity, and comorbidity of 12-month DSM-IV disorders in the National Comorbidity Survey. *Archives of General Psychiatry, 62*, 617–627.

Kessler, R. C., McGonagle, K. A., Zhao, S., Nelson, C., Hughes, M., Eshleman, S., Wittchen, H., & Kendler, K. (1994). Lifetime and 12-month prevalence of DSM-III-R psychiatric disorders in the United States. *Archives of General Psychiatry, 51*, 8–19.

Key, A. P. F., Ferguson, M., Molfese, D. L, Peach, K., Lehman, C., & Molfese,V. J. (2007). Smoking during pregnancy affects speech-processing ability. *Environmental Health Perspectives, 115*, 623–629.

Keyes, D. (1981). *The minds of Billy Milligan.* New York: Bantam.

Keyes, J. B. (1995). Stress inoculation training for staff working with persons with mental retardation: A model program. In L. R. Murphy, J. J. Hurrell, Jr., S. L. Sauter, & G. P. Keita (Eds.), *Job stress interventions.* Washington, DC: American Psychological Association.

Khachaturian, Z. S., & Blass, J. P. (1992). *Alzheimer's disease: New treatment strategies.* New York: Dekker.

Kheriaty, E., Kleinknecht, R. A., & Hyman, I. E. (1999). Recall and validation of phobia origins as a function of a structured interview versus the Phobia Origins Questionnaire. *Behavior Modification, 23*, 61–78.

Kiang, N. Y.-S. (1965). *Discharge patterns of single nerve fibers in the cat's auditory nerve.* Cambridge, MA: MIT Press.

Kiehl, K. A., Smith, A. M., Hare, R. D., & Liddle, P. F. (2000). An event-related potential investigation of response inhibition in schizophrenia and psychopathy. *Biological Psychiatry, 48*(3), 210–221.

Kihlstrom, J. F. (1998) Dissociations and dissociation theory in hypnosis: Comment on Kirsch and Lynn (1998). *Psychological Bulletin, 123*, 186–191.

Kilgour, A. R., Jakobson, L. S., & Cuddy, L. L. (2000). Music training and rate of presentation as mediators of text and song recall. *Memory & Cognition, 28*, 700–710.

Kimura, D. (1999). *Sex and cognition.* Cambridge, MA: The MIT Press.

Kirasic, K. C. (1991). Spatial cognition and behavior in young and elderly adults: Implications for learning new environments. *Psychology and Aging, 6*, 10–18.

Kirasic, K. C., & Bernicki, M. R. (1990). Acquisition of spatial knowledge under conditions of temporospatial discontinuity in young and elderly adults. *Psychological Research, 52*, 76–79.

Kirchengast, S., & Hartmann, B. (2003). Nicotine consumption before and during pregnancy affects not only newborn size but also birth modus. *Journal of Biosocial Science, 35*, 175–188.

Kirsh, B., & Cockburn, L. (2007). Employment outcomes associated with ACT: A review of ACT literature. *American Journal of Psychiatric Rehabilitation, 10*(1), 31–51.

Kirsch, I., & Lynn, S. J. (1998). Dissociation theories of hypnosis. *Psychological Bulletin, 123*, 100–115.

Kisilevsky, B. S., Hains, S. M. J., Lee, K., Xie, X., Huang, H., Ye, H. H., Zhang, K., & Wang, Z. (2003). Effects of experience on fetal voice recognition. *Psychological Science, 14*, 220–224.

Kitagawa, N., & Ichihara, S. (2002). Hearing visual motion in depth. *Nature, 416*, 172–174.

Kitayama, S., Markus, H. R., & Kurakawa, M. (2000). Culture, emotion, and well-being: Good feelings in Japan and the United States. *Cognition and Emotion, 14*, 93–124.

Klaczynski, P. A. (2004). A dual-process model of adolescent development: Implications for decision making, reasoning, and identity. In R. V. Kail (Ed.), *Advances in Child Development and Behavior, Volume 32.* Amsterdam: Elsevier.

Kleim, J. A., Swain, R. A., Armstrong, K. A., Napper, R. M. A., Jones, T. A., & Greenough, W. T. (1998). Selective synaptic plasticity within the cerebellar cortex following complex motor skill learning. *Neurobiology of Learning and Memory, 69*, 274–289.

Klein, D. A., & Walsh, B. T. (2004). Eating disorders: clinical features and pathophysiology: Special issue—Reviews on ingestive science. *Physiology & Behavior, 81*, 359–374.

Klein, D. F. (1996). Panic disorder and agoraphobia: Hypothesis hothouse. *Journal of Clinical Psychiatry, 57*, 21–27.

Klein, P. (1997). Multiplying the problems of intelligence by eight: A critique of Gardner's theory. *Canadian Journal of Education, 22*(4), 377–394.

Klein, R. M. (1999). The Hebb legacy. *Canadian Journal of Psychology, 53*, 1–3.

Kleinknecht, R. A., Dinnel, D. L., Kleinknecht, E. E., Hiruma, N., & Harada, N. (1997). Cultural factors in social anxiety: A comparison of social phobia symptoms and Taijin Kyofusho. *Journal of Anxiety Disorders, 11*, 157–177.

Kleitman, N. (1961). The nature of dreaming. In G. E. W. Wolstenholme & M. O'Connor (Eds.), *The nature of sleep.* London, UK: J. & A. Churchill.

Kleitman, N. (1982). Basic rest-activity cycle—22 years later. *Sleep, 5*, 311–317.

Klerman, G. L., & Weissman, M. M. (1986). The interpersonal approach to understanding depression. In T. Millon & G. L. Klerman (Eds.), *Contemporary directions in psychopathology: Toward the DMS-IV.* New York: Guilford Press.

Kluger, A. N., Siegfried, Z., & Ebstein, R. P. (2002). A meta-analysis of the association between DRD4 polymorphism and novelty seeking. *Molecular Psychiatry, 7*, 712–717.

Knekt, P., Lindfors, O., Härkänen, T., Välikoski, M., Virtala, E., Laaksonen, M. A., Marttunen, M., Kaipainen, M., Renlund, C., & the Helsinki Psychotherapy Study Group. (2008). Randomized trial on the effectiveness of long- and short-term psychodynamic psychotherapy and solution-focused therapy on psychiatric symptoms using a 3-year follow-up. *Psychological Medicine, 38*, 689–703.

Knowles, J. A., Kaufmann, C. A., & Rieder, R. O. (1999). Genetics. In R. E. Hales, S. C. Yudofsky, & J. A. Talbot (Eds.), *Textbook of psychiatry.* Washington, DC: American Psychiatric Press.

Knowlton, B. J., Ramus, S., & Squire, L. R. (1991). Normal acquisition of an artificial grammar by amnesic patients. *Society for Neuroscience Abstracts, 17*, 4.

Knox, R. E., & Inkster, J. A. (1968). Postdecision dissonance at post time. *Journal of Personality and Social Psychology, 8*, 310–323.

Kobasa, S. C. (1979). Stress life events, personality, and health: An inquiry into hardiness. *Journal of Personality and Social Psychology, 42*, 168–177.

Kobasa, S. C. O., Maddi, S. R., Puccetti, M. C., & Zola, M. A. (1994). Effectiveness of hardiness, exercise and social support as resources against illness. In A. Steptoe & J. Wardle (Eds.), *Psychosocial processes and health: A reader.* New York: Cambridge University Press.

Koch, C., & Crick, F. (2001). The zombie within. *Nature, 411*, 893.

Koch, J. L. A. (1889). *Leitfaden der psychiatrie* (2nd ed.). Ravensburg, Austria: Dorn.

Köhler, W. (1927/1973). *The mentality of apes* (2nd ed.). New York: Liveright.

Köhnke, M. D. (2008) Approach to the genetics of alcoholism: A review based on pathophysiology. *Biochemical Pharmacology, 75*, 160–177.

Koivisto, M., & Revonsuo, A. (2008). The role of unattended distractors in sustained inattentional blindness. *Psychological Research, 72*, 39–48.

Kojima, M., Hosoda, H., Date, Y., Nakazato, M., Matsuo, H., & Kangawa, K. (1999). Ghrelin is a growth-hormone-releasing acylated peptide from stomach. *Nature, 402*, 656–660.

Kolb, B., Gibb, R., & Robinson, T. E. (2003). Brain plasticity and behavior. *Current Directions in Psychological Science, 12*, 1–5.

Kolb, B., & Stewart, J. (1995). Changes in the neonatal gonadal hormonal environment prevent behavioral sparing and alter cortical morphogenesis after early female frontal cortex lesions in male and female rats. *Behavioral Neuroscience, 109,* 285–294.

Kolb, B., & Wishaw, I. Q. (1998). Brain plasticity and behavior. *Annual Review of Psychology, 49,* 43–64.

Konrad, K., Gunther, T., Hanisch, C., & Herpertz-Dahlmann, B. (2004). Differential effects of methylphenidate on attentional functions in children with attention-deficit/hyperactivity disorder. *Journal of the American Academy of Child & Adolescent Psychiatry, 43,* 191–198.

Kopta, S. M., Lueger, R. J., Saunders, S. M., & Howard, K. I. (1999). Individual psychotherapy outcome and process research: Challenges leading to greater turmoil or a positive transition. *Annual Review of Psychology, 50,* 441–469.

Korol, M., Kramer, T. L., Grace, M. C., & Green, B. L. (2002). Dam break: Long-term follow-up of children exposed to the Buffalo Creek disaster. In A. M. La Greca, W. K. Silverman, et al. (Eds.), *Helping children cope with disasters and terrorism.* Washington, DC: American Psychological Association.

Kosslyn, S. M. (1973). Scanning visual images: Some structural implications. *Perception and Psychophysics, 14,* 90–94.

Kosslyn, S. M. (1975, July). *Evidence for analogue representation.* Paper presented at the Conference on Theoretical Issues in Natural Language Processing, Massachusetts Institute of Technology, Cambridge, MA.

Kozlowski, L. T., & Cutting, J. E. (1977). Recognizing the sex of a walker from a dynamic point-light display. *Perception and Psychophysics, 21,* 575–580.

Kozulin, A., & Falik, L. (1995). Dynamic cognitive assessment of the child. *Current Directions in Psychological Science, 4,* 192–196.

Kramer, R. (1976). *Maria Montessori.* New York: G. P. Putnam's Sons.

Kramer, U., Lemmen, C. H., Behrendt, H., Link, E., Schafer, T., Gostomzyk, J., Scherer, G., & Ring, J. (2004). The effect of environmental tobacco smoke on eczema and allergic sensitization in children. *British Journal of Dermatology, 150*(1), 111–118.

Krank, M. D., O'Neill, S., Squarey, K., & Jacob, J. (2008). Goal- and signal-directed incentive: Conditioned approach, seeing, and consumption established with unsweetened alcohol in rats. *Psychopharmacology, 196,* 397–405.

Krebs, D. L., & Denton, K. (1997). Social illusions and self-deception: The evolution of biases in person perception. In J. A. Simpson & D. T. Kenrick (Eds.), *Evolutionary social psychology.* Mahway, NJ: Lawrence Erlbaum Associates, Publishers.

Kress, M., & Zeilhofer, H. U. (1999). Capsaicin, protons and heat: New excitement about nociceptors. *Trends in Pharmacological Science, 20,* 112–118.

Krueger, R. F., Markon, D. E., & Bouchard, T. J., Jr. (2003). The extended genotype: The heritability of personality accounts for the heritability of recalled family environments in twins reared apart. *Journal of Personality, 71*(5), 809–833.

Krueger, T. H. (1976). *Visual imagery in problem solving and scientific creativity.* Derby, CT: Seal Press.

Krull, D. L., Loy, M. H.-M., Lin, J., Wang, C.-F., Chen, S., & Zhao, X. (1999). The fundamental fundamental attribution error: Correspondence bias in individualist and collectivist cultures. *Personality and Social Psychology Bulletin, 25,* 1208–1219.

Krull, D. S., & Erickson, D. J. (1995). Inferential hopscotch: How people draw social inferences from behavior. *Current Directions in Psychological Science, 4,* 35–38.

Kubitz, K. A., & Landers, D. M. (1993). The effects of aerobic exercise on cardiovascular responses to mental stress: An examination of underlying mechanisms. *Journal of Sport and Exercise Physiology, 15,* 326–337.

Kübler-Ross, E. (1969). *On death and dying.* New York: Macmillan.

Kübler-Ross, E. (1981). *Living with death and dying.* New York: Macmillan.

Kuhl, P. K., Williams, K. A., Lacerda, F., Stevens, K. N., & Lindblom, B. (1992). Linguistic experience alters phonetic perception in infants by 6 months of age. *Science, 255,* 606–608.

Kulka, R. A., & Kessler, J. R. (1978). Is justice really blind? The effect of litigant physical attractiveness on judicial judgment. *Journal of Applied Social Psychology, 4,* 336–381.

Kunda, Z. (1990). The case for motivated reasoning. *Psychological Bulletin, 108,* 480–498.

Kunda, Z. (1999). *Social cognition: Making sense of people.* Cambridge, MA: The MIT Press.

Kunda, Z., & Oleson, K. (1997). When exceptions prove the rule: How extremity of deviance determines deviants' impact on stereotypes. *Journal of Personality and Social Psychology, 72,* 965–979.

Kunda, Z., & Sinclair, L. (1999). Motivated reasoning with stereotypes: Activation, application, and inhibition. *Psychological Inquiry, 10,* 12–22.

Kuo, Z. Y. (1932). Ontogeny of embryonic behavior in Aves: VI. Relation between heart beat and the behavior of the avian embryo. *Journal of Comparative Psychology, 16,* 379–384.

Kupfer, D. J. (1976). REM latency: A psychobiologic marker for primary depressive disease. *Biological Psychiatry, 11,* 159–174.

Laeng, B., & Falkenberg, L. (2007). Women's pupillary responses to sexually significant others during the hormonal cycle. *Hormones and Behavior, 52,* 520–530.

LaFarge, L. (2000). Interpretation and containment. *International Journal of Psycho-Analysis, 81,* 67–84.

Lai, C. S. L., Fisher, S. E., Hurst, J. A., Vargha-Khadem, F., & Monaco, A. P. (2001). A forkhead-domain gene is mutated in a severe speech and language disorder. *Nature, 413,* 519–523.

Lakoff, G., & Turner, M. (1989). *More than cool reason: The power of poetic metaphor.* Chicago: University of Chicago Press.

Lakoff, R. T. (1975). *Language and woman's place.* New York: Harper & Row.

Lamberg, L. (1998). Dawn's early light to twilight's last gleaming... *Journal of the American Medical Association, 280,* 1556–1558.

Lamerson, C. D., & Kelloway, E. K. (1996). Towards a model of peacekeeping stress: Traumatic and contextual influences. *Canadian Psychology, 37,* 195–204.

Landreville, P., & Vezina, J. (1992). A comparison between daily hassles and major life events as correlates of well-being in older adults. *Canadian Journal on Aging, 11*(2), 137–149.

Lane, S. M., Mather, M., Villa, D., & Morita, S. K. (2001). How events are reviewed matters: Effects of varied focus on eyewitness suggestibility. *Memory & Cognition, 29,* 940–947.

Lange, C. G. (1887). *Über Gemüthsbewegungen.* Leipzig, East Germany: T. Thomas.

Langer, E. J., & Abelson, R. P. (1974). A patient by any other name... : Clinician group difference in labeling bias. *Journal of Consulting and Clinical Psychology, 42,* 4–9.

Langer, E. J., Bashner, R. S., & Chanowitz, B. (1985). Decreasing prejudice by increasing discrimination. *Journal of Personality and Social Psychology, 49,* 113–120.

Langhans, W. (1996). Role of the liver in the metabolic control of eating: What we know and what we do not know. *Neuroscience and Biobehavioral Reviews, 20,* 145–153.

Langhans, W., Grossman, F., & Geary, N. (2001). Intrameal hepatic-portal infusion of glucose reduces spontaneous meal size in rats. *Physiology & Behavior, 73,* 499–507.

Langlois, J. H., & Downs, A. C. (1980). Mothers, fathers, and peers as socialization agents of sex-typed play behaviors in young children. *Child Development, 51,* 1237–1247.

LaPiere, R. T. (1934). Attitudes and actions. *Social Forces, 13,* 230–237.

Latané, B., & Darley, J. M. (1970). *The unresponsive bystander: Why doesn't he help?* New York: Appleton-Century-Crofts.

Laurence, J. R., & Perry, C. (1988). *Hypnosis, will, and memory: A psycho-legal history.* New York: Guilford Press.

Lavie, P., Pratt, H., Scharf, B., Peled, R., & Brown, J. (1984). Localized pontine lesion: Nearly total absence of REM sleep. *Neurology, 34,* 1118– 1120.

Lazarus, A. A. (1971). *Behavior therapy and beyond.* New York: McGraw-Hill.

Lazarus, R. S. (2000). Toward better research on stress and coping. *American Psychologist, 55*(6), 665–673.

Lazarus, R. S., & Folkman, S. (1984). *Stress, appraisal, and coping.* New York: Springer.

Leckman, J. F., Pauls, D. L., Zhang, H., Rosario-Campos, M. C., Katsovich, L., Kidd, K. K., Pakstis, A. J., Alsobrook, J. P., et al. (2003). Obsessive-compulsive symptom dimensions in affected sibling pairs diagnosed with Gilles de la Tourette syndrome. *American Journal of Medical Genetics, 116B,* 60–68.

LeDoux, J. E. (1992). Brain mechanisms of emotion and emotional learning. *Current Opinion in Neurobiology, 2,* 191–197.

Lee, T. M. C., & Chan, C. C. H. (1999). Dose-response relationship of phototherapy for seasonal affective disorder: A meta-analysis. *Acta Psychiatrica Scandinavica, 99,* 315–323.

Lee, V., & Wagner, H. (2002). The effect of social presence on the facial and verbal expression of emotion and the interrelationships among emotion components. *Journal of Nonverbal Behavior, 26,* 3–25.

Leeser, J., & O'Donohue, W. (1999). What is a delusion? Epistemological dimensions. *Journal of Abnormal Psychology, 108,* 687–694.

Lefcourt, H. M. (1966). Internal versus external control of reinforcement: A review. *Psychological Bulletin, 65,* 206–220.

Lefcourt, H. M. (1992). Durability and impact of the locus of control construct. *Psychological Bulletin, 112,* 411–414.

Lefcourt, H. M., & Davidson-Katz, K. (1991). Locus of control and health. In C. R. Snyder & D. R. Forsyth (Eds.), *Handbook of social and clinical psychology: The health perspective.* Elmsford, NY: Pergamon Press, Inc.

Lefley, H. P. (2002). Helping families cope with mental illness: Future international directions. In H. P. Lefley & D. L. Johnson (Eds.), *Family interventions in mental illness: International perspectives.* Westport, CT: Praeger.

Leger, D. W. (1991). *Biological foundations of behavior.* New York: HarperCollins.

Lehman, D. R., Chiu, C.-Y., & Schaller, M. (2004). Psychology and culture. *Annual Review of Psychology, 55,* 689–714.

Lehmann, H. E., & Ban, T. A. (1997). The history of the psychopharmacology of schizophrenia. *Canadian Journal of Psychiatry, 42,* 152–162.

Lehne, G., & Money, J. (2000). Paraphilia treated with Depo-Provera: 40-year outcome. *Journal of Sex Education and Therapy, 25,* 213–220.

Leichsenring, F. (2005). Are psychodynamic and psychoanalytic therapies effective? A review of empirical data. *International Journal of Psychoanalysis, 86,* 841–868.

Le Mare, L., Audet, K., & Kurytnik, K. (2007). A longitudinal study of service use in families of children adopted from Romanian orphanages. *International Journal of Behavioral Development, 31,* 242–251.

Lemonde, S., Turecki, G., Bakish, D., Lisheng, D., Hrdina, P. D., Brown, C. D., Sequeira, A., et al. (2003). Impaired repression at a 5-hydroxytryptamine 1A receptor gene polymorphism associated with major depression and suicide. *The Journal of Neuroscience, 23*(25), 8788–8799.

Lennenberg, E. (1967). *Biological foundations of language.* New York: Wiley.

Leon, G. R. (1977). *Case histories of deviant behavior* (2nd ed.). Boston: Allyn and Bacon.

Leone, M., Franzini, A., Broggi, G., May, A., & Bussone, G. (2004). Long-term follow-up of bilateral hypothalamic stimulation for intractable cluster headache. *Brain, 127,* 2259–2264.

Lepage, J.-F., & Théoret, J. (2007). The mirror neuron system: Grasping others' actions from birth? *Developmental Science, 10,* 513–523.

Lepper, M. R., Greene, D., & Nisbett, R. E. (1973). Undermining children's intrinsic interest with extrinsic reward: A test of the "overjustification" hypothesis. *Journal of Personality and Social Psychology, 28,* 129–137.

Lerman, D. C., Iwata, B. A., & Wallace, M. D. (1999). Side effects of extinction: Prevalence of bursting and aggression during the treatment of self-injurious behavior. *Journal of Applied Behavior Analysis, 32,* 1–8.

Lerner, M. J. (1980). *The belief in a just world.* New York: Plenum Press.

Lesage, A. D., Morissette, R., Fortier, L., Reinharz, D., & Contandriopoulos, A. (2000). 1. Downsizing psychiatric hospitals: Needs for care and services of current and discharged long-stay inpatients. *Canadian Journal of Psychiatry, 45,* 526–531.

LeVay, S. (1991). A difference in hypothalamic structure between heterosexual and homosexual men. *Science, 253,* 1034–1037.

Lewicki, M. S. (2002). Efficient coding of natural sounds. *Nature Neuroscience, 5,* 356–363.

Lewinsohn, P. M., Mischel, W., Chaplin, W., & Barton, R. (1980). Social competence and depression: The role of illusory self-perceptions. *Journal of Abnormal Psychology, 89,* 194–202.

Lewis, J. W., Wightman, F. I., Brefczynski, J. A., Phinney, R. E., Binder, J. R., & DeYoe, E. A. (2004). Human brain regions involved in recognizing environmental sounds. *Cerebral Cortex, 14,* 1008–1021.

Lewis, M., Alessandri, S. M., & Sullivan, M. W. (1990). Violation of expectancy, loss of control, and anger expressions in young infants. *Developmental Psychology, 26,* 745–751.

Ley, R. (2003). Respiratory psychophysiology and the modification of breathing behavior. *Behavior Modification, 27*(5), 603–606.

Li, J. S., Peat, J. K., Xuan, W., & Berry, G. (1999). Meta-analysis on the association between environmental tobacco smoke (ETS) exposure and the prevalence of lower respiratory tract infection in early childhood. *Pediatric Pulmonology, 27,* 5–13.

Liaw, Y. P., Chen, H. L., Cheng, C. W., & Huang, H. L. (2005). An international epidemiological study of breast cancer mortality and total fat intake in postmenopausal women. *Nutrition Research, 26*(1), 68–73.

Liberman, A. M. (1996). *Speech: A special code.* Cambridge, MA: MIT Press.

Libet, B. (2002). The timing of mental events: Libet's experimental findings and their implications. *Consciousness and Cognition, 11,* 291–299.

Lickey, M. E., & Gordon, B. (1983). *Drugs for mental illness.* New York: Freeman.

Lickey, M. E., & Gordon, B. (1991). *Medicine and mental illness: The use of drugs in psychiatry.* New York: Freeman & Co.

Lidberg, L., Asberg, M., & Sundqvist-Stensman, U. B. (1984). 5-Hydroxyindoleacetic acid levels in attempted suicides who have killed their children. *Lancet, 2,* 928.

Lidberg, L., Tuck, J. R., Asberg, M., Scalia-Tomba, G. P., & Bertilsson, L. (1985). Homicide, suicide and CSF 5-HIAA. *Acta Psychiatrica Scandanavica, 71,* 230–236.

Lidz, T., Fleck, S., & Cornelison, A. R. (1965). *Schizophrenia and the family.* New York: International Universities Press.

Lieb, K., Zanarini, C., Schmahl, C., Linehan, M., & Bohus, M. (2004). Borderline personality disorder. *The Lancet, 364,* 453–461.

Lieberman, M. D., Ochsner, K. N., Gilbert, D. T., & Schacter, D. L. (2001). Do amnesics exhibit cognitive dissonance? The role of explicit memory and attention in attitude change. *Psychological Science, 12,* 135–140.

Liebert, R., & Baron, R. (1972). Some immediate effects of televised violence on children's behaviour. *Developmental Psychology, 6,* 469–475.

Lillard, A. S. (2005). *Montessori: The science behind the genius.* New York: Oxford.

Lim, K. O., Adalsteinsson, E., Spielman, D., Sullivan, E. V., Rosenbloom, M. J., & Pfefferbaum, A. (1998). *Archives of General Psychiatry, 55,* 346–352.

Lin, E., Goering, P., Offord, D. R., Campbell, D., & Boyle, M. H. (1996). The use of mental health services in Ontario: Epidemiologic findings. *Canadian Journal of Psychiatry, 41,* 572–577.

Lindemann, B. (2000). A taste for umami. *Nature Neuroscience, 3,* 99–100.

Lindemann, B. (2001). Receptors and transduction in taste. *Nature, 413,* 219–225.

Lindsay, D. S. (1999). Recovered-memory experiences. In S. Taub (Ed.), *Recovered memories of child sexual abuse: Psychological, social, and legal perspectives on a contemporary mental health controversy.* American series in behavioral science and law. Springfield, IL: Charles C. Thomas Publishers.

Lindsey, D. T., & Brown, A. M. (2002). Color naming and the phototoxic effects of sunlight on the eye. *Psychological Science, 13,* 506–512.

Linley, P. A., Joseph, S., Harrington, S., & Wood, A. M. (2006). Positive psychology: Past, present, and (possible) future. *Journal of Positive Psychology, 1,* 3–16.

Linsky, A. S., Bachman, R., & Straus, M. A. (1995). *Stress, culture, and aggression.* New Haven, CT: Yale University Press.

Linville, P. W., Fischer, G. W., & Salovey, P. (1989). Perceived distributions of the characteristics of in-group and out-group members: Empirical evidence and a computer simulation. *Journal of Personality and Social Psychology, 157,* 165–188.

Lisanby, S. H., Maddox, J. H., Prudic, J., Devanand, D. P., & Sackeim, H. A. (2000). The effects of electroconvulsive therapy on memory of autobiographical and public events. *Archives of General Psychiatry, 57,* 581–590.

Livesley, W. J., Jang, K. L., & Vernon, P. A. (2003). Genetic basis of personality structure. In T. Millon & M. J. Lerner (Eds.), *Handbook of psychology: Personality and social psychology, Vol. 5.* New York: John Wiley & Sons, Inc.

Locke, J. L. (1993). *The child's path to spoken language.* Cambridge, MA: Harvard University Press.

Loehlin, J. C. (1992). *Genes and environment in personality development.* London: Sage Publications.

Loehlin, J. C., McCrae, R. R., Costa, P. T., & John, O. P. (1998). Heritabilities of common and measure-specific components of the Big Five personality factors. *Journal of Research in Personality, 32,* 431–453.

Loehlin, J. C., & Nichols, R. C. (1976). *Heredity, environment, and personality.* Austin: University of Texas Press.

Loftus, E. F. (1979). *Eyewitness testimony.* Cambridge, MA: Harvard University Press.

Loftus, E. F., & Palmer, J. C. (1974). Reconstruction of automobile destruction: An example of the interaction between language and memory. *Journal of Verbal Learning and Verbal Behavior, 13,* 585–589.

Lohmann, K. J., & Lohmann, C. M. F. (1996). Detection of magnetic field intensity by sea turtles. *Nature, 380,* 59–61.

Lohmann, K. J., Luschi, P., & Hays, G. C. (2008). Goal navigation and island-finding in sea turtles. *Journal of Experimental Marine Biology and Ecology, 356,* 83–95.

LoLordo, V. M., & Drougas, A. (1989). Selective associations and adaptive specializations: Taste aversions and phobias. In S. B. Klein & R. R. Mowrer (Eds.), *Contemporary learning theories: Instrumental conditioning theory and the impact of biological constraints on learning* (pp. 145–179). Hillsdale, NJ: Lawrence Erlbaum Associates.

Lombardo, R., & Carreno, L. (1987). Relationship of type A behavior pattern in smokers to carbon monoxide exposure and smoking topography. *Health Psychology, 6,* 445–452.

Long, L. S., & Titone, D. A. (2007). Psychopathy and verbal emotion processing in non-incarcerated males. *Cognition and Emotion, 21*(1), 119–145.

Lonner, W. J., & Adamopoulos, J. (1997). Culture as antecedent to behavior. In J. W. Berry, Y. H. Poortinga, & J. Pandey (Eds.), *Handbook of cross-cultural psychology: Vol. 1. Theory and method* (pp. 43–83). Boston: Allyn and Bacon.

Loomis, W. F. (1967). Skin pigment regulation of vitamin-D biosynthesis in man. *Science, 157,* 501–506.

Lopez, S. R., & Guarnaccia, P. J. J. (2000). Cultural psychopathology: Uncovering the social world of mental illness. *Annual Review of Psychology, 51,* 571–598.

LoPiccolo, J., & Friedman, J. M. (1985). Sex therapy: An integrated model. In S. J. Lynn and J. P. Garskee (Eds.), *Contemporary psychotherapies: Models and methods.* New York: Merrill.

Lord, C. (2007). Autism in the 21st century. *Association for Behavior Analysis International Newsletter, 30,* 13–14.

Louth, S. M., Williamson, S., Alpert, M., Pouget, E. R., & Hare, R. D. (1998). Acoustic distinctions in the speech of male psychopaths. *Journal of Psycholinguistic Research, 27*(3), 375–384.

Lovaas, I. (1987). Behavioral treatment of normal educational and intellectual functioning in young autistic children. *Journal of Counseling and Clinical Psychology, 44,* 3–9.

Lovaas, I. (2003). *Teaching individuals with developmental delays: Basic intervention techniques.* Austin, TX: PRO-ED.

Luborsky, L., Chandler, M., Auerbach, A. H., Cohen, J., & Bachrach, H. M. (1971). Factors influencing the outcome of psychotherapy: A review of quantitative research. *Psychological Bulletin, 75,* 145–185.

Luck, S., Chelazzi, L., Hillyard, S., & Desimone, R. (1993). Effects of spatial attention on responses of V4 neurons in the macaque. *Society for Neuroscience Abstracts, 69,* 27.

Lumeng, J. C., & Hillman, K. H. (2007). Eating in larger groups increases food consumption. *Archives of Disease in Childhood, 92,* 384–387.

Lumia, A. R. (1972). The relationships among testosterone, conditioned aggression, and dominance in male pigeons. *Hormones and Behavior, 13,* 277–286.

Luna, K. (2007, August 18). Human "guinea pig" wins settlement in stuttering suit. *Quad-City Times.*

Lundy, A. C. (1985). The reliability of the Thematic Apperception Test. *Journal of Personality Assessment, 49,* 141–145.

Lundy, A. C. (1988). Instructional set and thematic apperception test validity. *Journal of Personality Assessment, 52,* 309–320.

Luo, Y., & Baillargeon, R. (2005). When the ordinary seems unexpected: Evidence for incremental physical knowledge in young infants. *Cognition, 95,* 297–328.

Lupfer, M. B., Clark, L. F., & Hutcherson, H. W. (1990). Impact of context on spontaneous trait and situational attributions. *Journal of Personality and Social Psychology, 58,* 239–249.

Luria, A. R. (1973). Towards the mechanisms of naming disturbance. *Neuropsychologia, 11,* 417–421.

Luzzi, S., Pucci, E., Di Bella, P., & Piccirilli, M. (2000). Topographical disorientation consequent to amnesia of spatial location in a patient with right parahippocampal damage. *Cortex, 36,* 427–434.

Lyn, H. (2007). Mental representation of symbols as revealed by vocabulary errors in two bonobos (*Panpaniscus*). *Animal Cognition, 10,* 461–475.

Lynn, R. (1978). Ethnic and racial differences in intelligence: International comparisons. In *Human variation: The biopsychology of age, race and sex.* New York: Academic Press.

Lynn, R., & Mikk, J. (2007). National differences in intelligence and educational attainment. *Intelligence, 35,* 115–121.

Lytton, H., & Romney, D. M. (1991). Parents' sex-related differential socialization of boys and girls: A meta-analysis. *Psychological Bulletin, 109,* 267–296.

Lytton, W. W., & Brust, J. C. M. (1989). Direct dyslexia: Preserved oral reading of real words in Wernicke's aphasia. *Brain, 112,* 583–594.

Maccoby, E. E. (1980). *Social development: Psychological growth and the parent-child relationship.* New York: Harcourt Brace Jovanovich.

MacDonald, G., Zanna, M. P., & Holmes, J. G. (2000). An experimental test of the role of alcohol in relationship conflict. *Journal of Experimental Social Psychology, 36,* 182–193.

MacDonald, T., Zanna, M., & Fong, G. T. (1998). Alcohol and intentions to engage in risky health-related behaviors: Experimental evidence for a causal relationship. In J. G. Adair & D. Belanger (Eds.), *Advances in psychological science (Vol. 1).* Hove, UK: Psychology Press/Erlbaum (UK) Taylor and Francis.

MacDonald, T. K., MacDonald, G., Zanna, M. P., & Fong, G. T. (2000). Alcohol, sexual arousal, and intentions to use condoms in young men: Applying alcohol myopia theory to risky sexual behavior. *Health Psychology, 19*(3), 290–298.

MacDonald, T. K., Zanna, M. P., & Fong, G. T. (1995). Decision making in altered states: Effects of alcohol on attitudes toward drinking and driving. *Journal of Personality and Social Psychology, 68,* 973–985.

Mace, F. C., Lalli, J. S., Shea, M. C., Lalli, E. P., West, B. J., Roberts, M., & Nevin, J. A. (1990). The momentum of behavior in a natural setting. *Journal of the Experimental Analysis of Behavior, 54,* 163–172.

Machon, R. A., Mednick, S. A., & Schulsinger, F. (1983). The interaction of seasonality, place of birth, genetic risk and subsequent schizophrenia in a high risk sample. *British Journal of Psychiatry, 143,* 383–388.

Macintosh, N. J., & Honig, V. R. (1969). *Fundamental issues of associative learning.* Halifax, NS: Dalhousie University Press.

MacLean, H. E., Warne, G. L., & Zajac, J. D. (1995) Defects of androgen receptor function: From sex reversal to motor-neuron disease. *Molecular and Cellular Endocrinology, 112,* 133–141.

MacLeod, M. (1991). Half a century of research on the Stroop effect: An integrative review. *Psychological Bulletin, 109,* 163–203.

MacMillan, H. L., Fleming, J. E., Streiner, D. L., Lin, E., Boyle, M. H., Jamieson, E., Duku, E. K., et al. (2001). Childhood abuse and lifetime psychopathology in a community sample. *American Journal of Psychiatry, 158*(11), 1878–1883.

MacNevin, C., & Besner, D. (2002). When are morphemic and semantic priming observed in visual word recognition? *Canadian Journal of Experimental Psychology, 56,* 112–119.

Macrae, C. N., Milne, A. B., & Bodenhausen, G. V. (1994). Stereotypes as energy-saving devices: A peek inside the cognitive toolbox. *Journal of Personality and Social Psychology, 66,* 37–47.

Maddi, S. R. (2002). The story of hardiness: Twenty years of theorizing, research, and practice. *Consulting Psychology Journal: Practice & Research, 54*(3), 175–185.

Maddi, S. R., & Kobasa, S. C. (1991). The development of hardiness. In A. Monat & R. S. Lazarus (Eds.), *Stress and coping.* New York: Columbia University Press.

Madigan, S., Moran, G., & Pederson, D. R. (2006). Unresolved states of mind, disorganized attachment relationships, and disrupted interactions of adolescent mothers and their infants. *Developmental Psychology, 42,* 293–304.

Madon, S., Smith, A., Jussim, L., Russell, D. W., Eccles, J., Palumbo, P., & Walkiewicz, M. (2001). Am I as you see me or do you see me as I am?

Self-fulfilling prophecies and self-verification. *Personality & Social Psychology Bulletin, 27,* 1214–1224.

Maess, B., Koelsch, S., Gunter, T. C., & Friederici, A. D. (2001). Musical syntax is processed in Broca's area: An MEG study. *Nature Neuroscience, 4,* 540–545.

Maffei, M., Halaas, J., Ravussin, E., Pratley, R. E., Lee, G. H., Zhang, Y., Fei, H., Kim, S., Lallone, R., & Ranganathan, S. (1995). Leptin levels in human and rodent: Measurement of plasma leptin and ob RNA in obese and weight-reduced subjects. *Nature Medicine, 11,* 1155–1161.

Magee, W. J., Eaton, W. W., Wittchen, H.-U., McGonagle, K. A., & Kessler, R. C. (1996). Agoraphobia, simple phobia, and social phobia in the National Comorbidity Survey. *Archives of General Psychiatry, 53,* 159–168.

Maguire, E. A., Gadian, D. G., Johnsrude, I. S., Good, C. D., Ashburner, J., Frackowiak, R. S. J., & Frith, C. D. (2000). Navigation-related structural change in the hippocampi of taxi drivers. *Proceedings of the National Academy of Science, USA, 97,* 4398–4403.

Maier, S. F., & Seligman, M. E. (1976). Learned helplessness: Theory and evidence. *Journal of Experimental Psychology: General, 105,* 3–46.

Main, M., & Solomon, J. (1990). Procedures for identifying infants as disorganized/disoriented during the Ainsworth Strange Situation. In M.T. Greenberg, D. Cicchetti, & M. Cummings (Eds.), *Attachment in the pre-school years: Theory, research, and intervention.* Chicago: University of Chicago Press.

Malnic, B., Godfrey, P. A., & Buck, L. B. (2004). The human olfactory receptor gene family. *Proceedings of the National Academy of Sciences, USA, 101,* 2584–2589.

Malnic, B., Hirono, J, Sato, T., & Buck, L. B. (1999). Combinatorial receptor codes for odors. *Cell, 96,* 713–723.

Malson, L. (1972). *Wolf children and the problem of human nature.* New York: Monthly Review Press.

Maltz, D. J., & Borker, R. A. (1982). A cultural approach to male-female miscommunication. In J. J. Gumpertz (Ed.), *Language and social identity* (pp. 196–216). Cambridge, UK: Cambridge University Press.

Manson, J. E., Willett, W. C., Stampfer, M. J. J., Colditz, G. A., Hunter, D. J., & Hankinson, S. E. (1995). Body weight and mortality among women. *New England Journal of Medicine, 333,* 677–685.

Manson, S. M., & Kleinman, A. (1998). DSM-IV, culture and mood disorders: A critical reflection on recent progress. *Transcultural Psychiatry, 35,* 377–386.

Manuck, S. B., Kaplan, J. R., & Clarkson, T. B. (1983). Behaviorally-induced heart rate reactivity and atherosclerosis in cynomolgous monkeys. *Psychosomatic Medicine, 45,* 95–108.

Manuck, S. B., Kaplan, J. R., & Matthews, K. A. (1986). Behavioral antecedents of coronary heart disease and atherosclerosis. *Arteriosclerosis, 6,* 1–14.

Marcia, J. E. (1980). Identity in adolescence. In J. Adelson (Ed.), *Handbook of adolescent psychology.* New York: Wiley.

Marcia, J. E. (1994). The empirical study of ego identity. In H. A. Bosma & T. L. G. Graafsma (Eds.), *Identity and development: An interdisciplinary approach (Vol. 172).* Thousand Oaks, CA: Sage Publications, Inc.

Margolin, D. I., Friedrich, F. J., & Carlson, N. R. (1985). Visual agnosia–optic aphasia: Continuum or dichotomy? Paper presented at the meeting of the International Neuropsychology Society.

Markus, H. (1977). Self-schemata and processing information about the self. *Journal of Personality and Social Psychology, 35,* 63–78.

Markus, H. R., & Kitayama, S. (1991). Culture and the self: Implications for cognition, emotion, and motivation. *Psychological Review, 98,* 224–253.

Markus, H. R., & Kitayama, S. (2003). Culture, self, and the reality of the social. *Psychological Inquiry, 14,* 277–283.

Markus, H. R., & Nurius, P. (1986). Possible selves. *American Psychologist, 41,* 954–969.

Marler, P. (1961). The filtering of external stimuli during instinctive behaviour. In W. H. Thorpe & O. L. Zangwil (Eds.), *Current problems in animal behaviour.* Cambridge, UK: Cambridge University Press.

Marois, R., & Ivanoff, J. (2005). Capacity limits of information processing in the brain. *Trends in Cognitive Science, 9,* 296–305.

Marshall, J. C., & Newcombe, F. (1973). Patterns of paralexia: A psycholinguistic approach. *Journal of Psycholinguistic Research, 2,* 175–199.

Marshall, K. (2006, July). Converging gender roles. *Perspectives,* 5–17.

Marshall, R. D., Spitzwer, R., & Liebowitz, M. R. (1999). Review and critique of the new DSM-IV diagnosis of acute stress disorder. *American Journal of Psychiatry, 156*(11), 1677–1685.

Marshark, M., Richman, C. L., Yuille, J. C., & Hunt, R. R. (1987). The role of imagery in memory: On shared and distinctive information. *Psychological Bulletin, 102,* 28–41.

Martens, R. (1969). Palmar sweating and the presence of an audience. *Journal of Experimental Social Psychology, 5,* 371–374.

Martin, G. L., & Pear, J. (2006). *Behavior modification: What it is and how to do it* (8th ed.). Englewood Cliffs, NJ: Prentice Hall.

Martin, L. (1986). "Eskimo words for snow": A case study in the genesis and decay of an anthropological example. *American Anthropologist, 88,* 418–423.

Martinez, G. M., Chandra, A., Abma, J. C., Jones, J., & Moser, W. D. (2006). Fertility, contraception, and fatherhood: Data on men and women from Cycle 6 (2002) of the National Survey of Family Growth. National Center for Health Statistics. *Vital Health Statistics, 23*(26), 1–142.

Masling, J. (1960). The influence of situational and interpersonal variables in projective testing. *Psychological Bulletin, 57,* 65–85.

Masling, J. (1998). Interpersonal and actuarial dimensions of projective testing. In L. Handler & M. J. Hilsenroth (Eds.), *Teaching and learning personality assessment. The LEA series in personality and clinical psychology.* Mahwah, NJ: Lawrence Erlbaum Associates.

Maslow, A. H. (1964). *Religions, values, and peak-experiences.* New York: Viking Press.

Maslow, A. H. (1970). *Motivation and personality* (2nd ed.). New York: Harper & Row.

Mason, R., Just, M., Keller, T., & Carpenter, P. (2003). Ambiguity in the brain: What brain imaging reveals about the processing of syntactically ambiguous sentences. *Journal of Experimental Psychology, 29,* 1319–1338.

Masuda, T., & Nisbett, R. E. (2006). Culture and change blindness. *Cognitive Science, 30,* 381–399.

Masters, W. H., & Johnson, V. E. (1970). *Human sexual inadequacy.* Boston: Little, Brown.

Matser, E. J. T., Kessels, A. G. H., Lezak, M. D., Troost, J., & Jordan, B. D. (2000). Acute traumatic brain injury in amateur boxing. *The Physician and Sportsmedicine, 28*(1), 87–92.

Matsumoto, D. (2003). Cross-cultural research. In S. F. Davis (Ed.), *Handbook of research methods in experimental psychology.* Malden, MA: Blackwell Publishers.

Maurer, D., & Maurer, C. (1988). *The world of the newborn.* New York: Basic Books.

Mayberg, H. (2003). Modulating dysfunctional limbic-cortical circuits in depression: Towards development of brain-based algorithms for diagnosis and optimized treatment. *British Medical Bulletin, 65,* 193–207.

Mayer, J. (1955). Regulation of energy intake and the body weight: The glucostatic theory and the lipostatic hypothesis. *Annals of the New York Academy of Science, 63,* 15–43.

Mayer, J. D., & Salovey, P. (1993). The intelligence of emotional intelligence. *Intelligence, 17,* 433–442.

Mayerovitch, J. I., du Fort, G. G., Kakuma, R., Bland, R. C., Newman, S. C., & Pinard, G. (2003). Treatment seeking for obsessive-compulsive disorder: Role of obsessive-compulsive disorder symptoms and comorbid psychiatric diagnoses. *Comprehensive Psychiatry, 44*(2), 162–168.

Mayes, L. C., Cicchetti, D., Acharyya, S., & Zhang, H. (2003). Developmental trajectories of cocaine-and-other-drug-exposed and non-cocaine-exposed children. *Journal of Developmental and Behavioral Pediatrics, 24,* 323–335.

Maynard, T., Sikich, L., Lieberman, J., & LaMantia, A. (2001). Neural development, cell-cell signaling, and the "two-hit" hypothesis of schizophrenia. *Schizophrenia Bulletin, 27,* 457–476.

Mayr, E. (2000). Darwin's influence on modern thought. *Scientific American, 283*(1), 79–83.

Mayr, E. (2001). *What evolution is.* New York: Basic Books.

Mazur, J. (2005). Effects of reinforcer probability, delay, and response requirements on the choices of rats and pigeons: Possible species differences. *Journal of Experimental Analysis of Behaviour, 83,* 263–279.

Mazur, J. E. (1998). *Learning and behavior* (4th ed.). Upper Saddle River, NJ: Prentice Hall.

McAlister, A., Perry, C., Killen, L. A., Slinkard, L. A., & Maccoby, N. (1980). Pilot study of smoking, alcohol, and drug abuse prevention. *American Journal of Public Health, 70,* 719–721.

McAllister, T. W., Flashman, L. A., Sparling, M. B., & Saykin, A. J. (2004). Working memory deficits after traumatic brain injury: Catecholaminergic mechanisms and prospects for treatment—A review. *Brain Injury, 18,* 331–350.

McArthur, L. (1972). The how and what of why: Some determinants and consequences of causal attribution. *Journal of Personality and Social Psychology, 22,* 171–193.

McCann, I. L., & Holmes, D. S. (1984). Influence of aerobic exercise on depression. *Journal of Personality and Social Psychology, 46,* 1142–1147.

McCarthy, R. A., & Warrington, E. K. (1990). *Cognitive neuropsychology: A clinical introduction.* San Diego: Academic Press.

McClanahan, T. M., & Antonuccio, D. O. (2002). Cognitive-behavioral treatment of panic attacks. *Clinical Case Studies, 1*(3), 211–223.

McClearn, G. E., Johansson, B., Berg, S., Pedersen, N. L., Ahern, F., Petrill, S. A., & Plomin, R. (1997). Substantial genetic influence on cognitive abilities in twins 80 or more years old. *Science, 276,* 1560–1563.

McClelland, J. L., & Rumelhart, D. E. (1981). An interactive activation model of context effects in letter perception: Part 1. An account of basic findings. *Psychological Review, 88,* 375–407.

McColl, S. L., & Veitch, J. A. (2001). Full-spectrum fluorescent lighting: A review of its effects on physiology and health. *Psychological Medicine, 31*(6), 949–964.

McCormick, P. A., Klein, R. M., & Johnston, S. (1998). Splitting versus sharing focal attention: Comment on Castiello and Umiltà (1992). *Journal of Experimental Psychology: Human Perception and Performance, 24,* 350–357.

McCrae, R. R., & Costa, P. T. (1997). Personality trait structure as a human universal. *American Psychologist, 52,* 509–516.

McCrae, R. R., & Costa, P. T., Jr. (1999). A five-factor theory of personality. In L. A. Pervin & O. P. John (Eds.), *Handbook of personality: Theory and research* (2nd ed.). New York: The Guilford Press.

McCrae, R. R., & Costa, P. T., Jr. (2004). A contemplated revision of the NEO Five-Factor Inventory. *Personality & Individual Differences, 36*(3), 587–596.

McCrae, R. R., Costa, P. T., Jr., Del Pilar, G. H., Rolland, J. P., & Parker, W. D. (1998). Cross-cultural assessment of the five-factor model: The revised NEO personality inventory. *Journal of Cross-Cultural Psychology, 29,* 171–188.

McCrae, R. R., Costa, P. T., Jr., Ostendorf, F., Angleitner, A., Hrebickova, M., Avia, M. D., Sanz, J., Sanchez-Bernardos, M. L., Kusdil, M. E., Woodfield, R., Saunders, P. R., & Smith, P. B. (2000). Nature over nurture: Temperament, personality, and life span development. *Journal of Personality and Social Psychology, 78,* 173–186.

McCrae, R. R., & Terracciano, A. (2005) Universal features of personality traits from the observer's perspective: Data from 50 cultures. *Journal of Personality and Social Psychology, 88,* 547–561.

McCrory, E., Mechelli, A., Frith, U., & Price, C. (2005). More than words: A common neural basis for reading and naming deficits in developmental dyslexia? *Brain: A Journal of Neurology, 128,* 261–267.

McDonald, R. V., & Siegel, S. (1998). Environmental control of morphine withdrawal: Context specificity or stimulus novelty? *Psychobiology, 26,* 53–56.

McEwen, B. S. (2008). Central effects of stress hormones in health and disease: Understanding the protective and damaging effects of stress and stress mediators. *European Journal of Pharmacology, 583,* 174–185.

McFarland, C., & Miller, D. T. (1990). Judgments of self-other similarity: Just like others only more so. *Personality and Social Psychology Bulletin, 16,* 475–484.

McGaugh, J. L. (1999). The perseveration-consolidation hypothesis: Mueller and Pilzecker, 1900. *Brain Research Bulletin, 50,* 445–446.

McGinty, D. J., & Sterman, M. B. (1968). Sleep suppression after basal forebrain lesions in the cat. *Science, 160,* 1253–1255.

McGovern, K. (2007). Social cognition: Perceiving the mental states of others. In B. J. Baars & N. M. Gage (Eds.), *Cognition, brain, and consciousness* (pp. 391–410). New York: Academic Press.

McGrath, E. P., & Repetti, R. L. (2002). A longitudinal study of children's depressive symptoms, self-perceptions, and cognitive distortions about the self. *Journal of Abnormal Psychology, 111*(1), 77–87.

McGrath, Y. E., & Yahia, M. (1993). Preliminary data on seasonally related alcohol dependence. *Journal of Clinical Psychiatry, 54*(7), 260–262.

McGregor, I., Newby-Clark, I. R., & Zanna, M. P. (1999). "Remembering" dissonance: Simultaneous accessibility of inconsistent cognitive elements moderates epistemic discomfort. In E. Harmon-Jones & J. Mills (Eds.), *Cognitive dissonance: Progress on a pivotal theory in social psychology.* Washington, DC: American Psychological Association.

McGuiness, D. (2004). *Early reading instruction: What science really tells us about how to teach reading.* Cambridge, MA: Harvard University Press.

McGurk, F. (1959). Negro vs. white intelligence—An answer. *Harvard Educational Review, 29,* 54–62.

McKay, A. (2004). Adolescent sexual and reproductive health in Canada: A report card in 2004. *Canadian Journal of Human Sexuality, 13,* 67–81.

McKay, D. C. (1973). Aspects of the theory of comprehension, memory and attention. *Quarterly Journal of Experimental Psychology, 25,* 22–40.

McKim, W. A. (1991). *Drugs and behavior: An introduction to behavior pharmacology* (2nd ed.). Englewood Cliffs, NJ: Prentice-Hall.

McNamara, D. S., & Scott, J. L. (2001). Working memory capacity and strategy use. *Memory & Cognition, 29,* 10–17.

McNeill, D. (1970). *The acquisition of language: The study of developmental psycholinguistics.* New York: Harper & Row.

Meadows, S. (1996). *Parenting behaviour and children's cognitive development.* East Sussex, UK: Psychology Press.

Mednick, S. A., Gabrielli, W. F., & Hutchings, B. (1983). Genetic influences in criminal behavior: Some evidence from an adoption cohort. In K. T. VanDusen & S. A. Mednick (Eds.), *Prospective studies of crime and delinquency.* Hingham, MA: Martinus Nyhoff.

Mednick, S. A., Machon, R. A., & Huttunen, M. O. (1990). An update on the Helsinki influenza project. *Archives of General Psychiatry, 47,* 292.

Meduna, L. (1985). Autobiography. *Convulsive Therapy, 1,* 43–57.

Meehl, P. E. (1986). Causes and effects of my disturbing little book. *Journal of Personality Assessment, 50,* 370–375.

Meelissen, M. R. M., & Drent, M. (2008). Gender differences in computer attitudes: Does the school matter? *Computers and Human Behavior, 24,* 969–985.

Meichenbaum, D. (1985). *Stress inoculation training.* New York: Pergamon Press.

Meichenbaum, D. (1993). Changing conceptions of cognitive behavior modification: Retrospect and prospect. *Journal of Consulting and Clinical Psychology, 61,* 202–204.

Meichenbaum, D. (1995). Disasters, stress, and cognition. In S. E. Hobfoll & M. W. deVries (Eds.), *Extreme stress and communities: Impact and intervention.* Dordrecht, Netherlands: Kluwer Academic Publishers.

Meichenbaum, D. (2007). Stress inoculation training: A preventative and treatment approach. In P. M. Lehrer, R. L. Woolfolk, & W. E. Sime (Eds.), *Principles and practice of stress management* (3rd ed.) (pp. 497–516). New York: Guilford Press.

Meichenbaum, D. H. (1977). *Cognitive-behavior modification: An integrative approach.* New York: Plenum Press.

Meindl, J. R., & Lerner, M. J. (1985). Exacerbation of extreme responses to an out-group. *Journal of Personality and Social Psychology, 47,* 71–84.

Mejia-Arauz, R., Rogoff, B, Dexter, A. & Najafi, B. (2007). Cultural variation in children's social organization. *Child Development, 78*(3), 1001–1014.

Mello, C. V., Vicario, D. S., & Clayton, D. F. (1992). Song presentation induces gene expression in the songbird forebrain. *Proceedings of the National Academy of Sciences, USA, 89,* 6818–6822.

Melzack, R. Phantom limbs. (1992). *Scientific American, 266*(4), 120–126.

Menn, L., & Stoel-Gammon, C. (1993). Phonological development: Learning sounds and sound patterns. In J. B. Gleason (Ed.), *The development of language.* New York: Macmillan.

Merikle, P. M., Smilek, D., & Eastwood, J. D. (2001). Perception without awareness: Perspectives from cognitive psychology. *Cognition, 79,* 115–134.

Merton, R. (1948). The self-fulfilling prophecy. *Antioch Review, 8,* 193–210.

Mervis, C. B., & Rosch, E. (1981). Categorization of natural objects. *Annual Review of Psychology, 32,* 89–116.

Messer, S. B. (2001). What makes brief psychodynamic therapy time efficient. *Clinical Psychology: Science and Practice, 8*(1), 5–22.

Metalsky, G. I., Joiner, T. E., Jr., Hardin, T. S., & Abramson, L. Y. (1993). Depressive reactions to failure in a naturalistic setting: A test of the hopelessness and self-esteem theories of depression. *Journal of Abnormal Psychology, 102,* 101–109.

Metter, E. J. (1991). Brain-behavior relationships in aphasia studied by positron emission tomography. *Annals of the New York Academy of Sciences, 620,* 153–164.

Meyer, R. G., & Osborne, Y. V. (1982). *Case studies in abnormal behavior*. Boston: Allyn and Bacon.

Milgram, S. (1963). Behavioral study of obedience. *Journal of Abnormal and Social Psychology, 67,* 371–378.

Milgram, S. (1974). *Obedience to authority.* New York: Harper & Row.

Miller, A. M., & Harwood, R. L. (2002). The cultural organization of parenting: Change and stability of behavior patterns during feeding and social play across the first year of life. *Parenting: Science and Practice, 2,* 241–272.

Miller, D. T., & Ross, M. (1975). Self-serving biases in the attribution of causality: Fact or fiction? *Psychological Bulletin, 82,* 213–225.

Miller, G. A. (1956). The magical number seven plus or minus two: Some limits on our capacity for processing information. *Psychological Review, 63,* 81–97.

Miller, G. A., Galanter, E., & Pribram, K. (1960). *Plans and the structure of behavior.* New York: Holt, Rinehart, and Winston.

Miller, J. L., & Eimas, P. D. (1995). Speech perception: From signal to word. *Annual Review of Psychology, 46,* 467–492.

Miller, N. E. (1983). Behavioral medicine: Symbiosis between laboratory and clinic. *Annual Review of Psychology, 34,* 1–31.

Miller, R. J., Hennessy, R. T., & Leibowitz, H. W. (1973). The effect of hypnotic ablation of the background on the magnitude of the Ponzo perspective illusion. *International Journal of Clinical and Experimental Hypnosis, 21,* 180–191.

Miller, W. R., Rosellini, R. A., & Seligman, M. E. P. (1977). Learned helplessness and depression. In J. D. Maser & M. E. P. Seligman (Eds.), *Psychopathology: Experimental models.* San Francisco: W. H. Freeman.

Miller-Jones, D. (1989). Culture and testing. *American Psychologist, 44,* 360–366.

Milner, A. D., & Goodale, M. A. (1996). *The visual brain in action.* Oxford, UK: Oxford University Press.

Milner, A. D., Perrett, D. I., Johnston, R. S., Benson, P. J., Jordan, T. R., Heeley, D. W., Bettucci, D., Mortara, F., Mutani, R., Terazzi, E., & Davidson, D. L. W. (1991). Perception and action in "visual form agnosia." *Brain, 114*(B), 405–428.

Milner, B. (1970) Memory and the temporal regions of the brain. In K. H. Pribram and D. E. Broadbent (Eds.), *Biology of memory.* New York: Academic Press.

Milner, B., Corkin, S., & Teuber, H.-L. (1968). Further analysis of the hippocampal amnesic syndrome: 14-year follow-up study of H. M. *Neuropsychologia, 6,* 317–338.

Milner, B., Squire, L. R., & Kandel, E. R. (1998). Cognitive neuroscience and the study of memory. *Neuron, 20,* 445–468.

Milner, C. E., & Cote, K. A. (2008). A dose-response investigation of the benefits of napping in healthy young, middle-aged and older adults. *Sleep and Biological Rhythms, 6,* 2–15.

Minuchin, S. (1974). *Families and family therapy.* Cambridge, MA: Harvard University Press.

Minuchin, S., & Nichols, M. P. (1998). Structural family therapy. In F. M. Dattilio & M. R. Goldfried (Eds.), *Case studies in couple and family therapy: Systemic and cognitive perspectives* (pp. 108–131). New York: Guilford Press.

Mischel, W. (1977). The interaction of person and situation. In D. Magnusson & N. S. Endler (Eds.), *Personality at the crossroads: Current issues in interactional psychology*. Hillsdale, NJ: Lawrence Erlbaum Associates.

Mischel, W. (1979). On the interface of cognition and personality: Beyond the person-situation debate. *American Psychologist, 34,* 740–754.

Mischel, W. (1990). Personality dispositions revisited and revised: A view after three decades. In L. Pervin (Ed.), *Handbook of personality: Theory and research.* New York: Guilford Press.

Mischel, W. (2003). Challenging the traditional personality psychology paradigm. In R. J. Sternberg (Ed.), *Psychologists defying the crowd: Stories of those who battled the establishment and won.* Washington, DC: American Psychological Association.

Mischel, W., Cantor, N., & Feldman, S. (1996). Principles of self-regulation: The nature of willpower and self-control. In E. T. Higgins & A. W. Kruglanski (Eds.), *Social psychology: Handbook of basic principles.* New York: Guilford Press.

Mischel, W., & Shoda, Y. (1995). A cognitive-affective system theory of personality: Reconceptualizing situations, dispositions, dynamics, and invariance in personality. *Psychological Review, 102,* 246–268.

Mischel, W., & Shoda, Y. (1998). Reconciling processing dynamics and personality dispositions. *Annual Review of Psychology, 49,* 229–258.

Misovich, S. J., Fisher, J. D., & Fisher, W. A. (1996). The perceived AIDS-preventative utility of knowing one's partner well: A public health dictum and individuals' risky sexual behavior. *The Canadian Journal of Human Sexuality, 5,* 83–90.

Mitchell, J. T. (1999). Essential factors for effective psychological response to disasters and other crises. *International Journal of Emergency Mental Health, 1,* 51–58.

Mitelman, S. A., Shihabuddin, L., Brickman, A. M., Hazlett, A. E., & Buchsbaum, M. S. (2003). MRI assessment of gray and white matter distribution in Brodmann's areas of the cortex in patients with schizophrenia with good and poor outcomes. *American Journal of Psychiatry, 160*(12), 2154–2168.

Mithen, S. (1996). *The prehistory of the mind: The cognitive origins of art and science.* London, UK: Thames and Hudson.

Miyamoto, Y., & Kitayama, S. (2002). Cultural variation in correspondence bias: The critical role of attitude diagnosticity of socially constrained behavior. *Journal of Personality & Social Psychology, 83,* 1239–1248.

Miyashita, Y. (2004). Cognitive memory: Cellular and network machineries and their top-down control. *Science, 306,* 435–440.

Mogg, K., & Bradley, B. P. (2003). Selective processing of nonverbal information in anxiety: Attentional biases for threat. In P. Philippot (Ed.), *Nonverbal behavior in clinical settings.* Series in affective science. London, UK: Oxford University Press.

Mogg, K., Bradley, B. P., Williams, R., & Matthews, A. (1993). Subliminal processing of emotional information in anxiety and depression. *Journal of Abnormal Psychology, 102,* 304–311.

Mogg, K., Holmes, A., Garner, M., & Bradley, B. P. (2008). Effects of threat cues on attentional shifting, disengagement and response slowing in anxious individuals. *Behaviour Research and Therapy, 46*(5), 656–667.

Mogg, K., Philippot, P., & Bradley, B. P. (2004). Selective attention to angry faces in clinical social phobia. *Journal of Abnormal Psychology, 113*(1), 160–165.

Mollon, J. D. (1989). "Tho' she kneel'd in that place where they grew...": The uses and origins of primate colour vision. *Journal of Experimental Biology, 146,* 21–38.

Monahan, J. L., Murphy, S. T., & Zajonc, R. B. (2000). Subliminal mere exposure: Specific, general, and diffuse effects. *Psychological Science, 11,* 462–466.

Money, J., & Ehrhardt, A. (1972). *Man & Woman, Boy & Girl.* Baltimore: Johns Hopkins University Press.

Monroe, S. M., & Hadjiyannakis, K. (2002). The social environment and depression: Focusing on severe life stress. In I. H. Gotlib & C. L. Hammen (Eds.), *Handbook of depression.* New York: Guilford Press.

Moran, G., Forbes, L., Evans, E., Tarabulsy, G. M., & Madigan, S. (2008). Both maternal sensitivity and atypical maternal behavior independently predict attachment security and disorganization in adolescent mother-infant relationships. *Infant Behavior and Development, 31,* 321–325.

Moray, N. (1959). Attention in dichotic listening: Affective cues and the influence of instructions. *Quarterly Journal of Experimental Psychology, 11,* 56–60.

Moreau, J. L., Scherschlicht, R., Jenck, F., & Martin, J. R. (1995). Chronic mild stress-induced anhedonia model of depression: sleep abnormalities and curative effects of electroshock treatment. *Behavioural Pharmacology, 6*(7), 682–687.

Morgan, A. E., Brodie, J. D., & Dewey, S. L. (1998). What are we measuring with PET? *Quarterly Journal of Nuclear Medicine, 42,* 151–157.

Morin, A. (2003, April). Inner speech and conscious experience. *Science & Consciousness Review.*

Morris, B. J., & Sloutsky, V. (2002). Children's solutions of logical versus empirical problems:

What's missing and what develops? *Cognitive Development, 16,* 907–928.

Morris, R. G. M., Garrud, P., Rawlins, J. N. P., & O'Keefe, J. (1982). Place navigation impaired in rats with hippocampal lesions. *Nature, 297,* 681–683.

Morton, J. (1979). Word recognition. In *Psycholinguistics 2: Structures and processes.* Cambridge, MA: MIT Press.

Moscovitch, M. (1995). Recovered consciousness: A hypothesis concerning modularity and episodic memory. *Journal of Clinical and Experimental Neuropsychology, 17,* 276–290.

Moynihan, J. A. (2003). Mechanisms of stress-induced modulation of immunity. *Brain, Behavior, & Immunity, 17,* S11–S16.

Muheim, R., Edgar, N. M., Sloan, K. A., & Phillips, J. B. (2006). Magnetic compass orientation in C57BL/6J mice. *Learning & Behavior, 34,* 366–373.

Mulac, A., Bradac, J., & Gibbons, P. (2001). Empirical support for the gender-as-culture hypothesis: An intercultural analysis of male/female language differences. *Human Communications Research, 27,* 121–152.

Mullen, R. (2003). Delusions: The continuum versus category debate. *Australian & New Zealand Journal of Psychiatry, 37*(5), 505–511.

Muller, J. L., Sommer, M., Sohnel, K., Weber, T., Schmidt-Wilcke, T., & Hajak, G. (2008). Disturbed prefrontal and temporal brain function during emotion and cognition interaction in criminal psychopathy. *Behavioral Sciences and the Law, 26*(1), 131–150.

Muller, U., & Carpendale, J. I. M. (2000). The role of social interaction in Piaget's theory: Language for social cooperation and social cooperation for language. *New Ideas in Psychology, 18,* 139–156.

Mundy, P., & Newell, L. (2007). Attention, joint attention, and social cognition. *Current Directions in Psychological Science, 16*(5), 269–274.

Murphy, C. M., Winters, J., O'Farrell, T. J., Fals-Stewart, W., & Murphy, M. (2005). Alcohol consumption and intimate partner violence by alcoholic men: Comparing violent and nonviolent consumption. *Journal of Family Violence, 10,* 1–21.

Murphy, S. T., Monahan, J. L., & Zajonc, R. B. (1995). Additivity of nonconscious affect: Affective priming with optimal and suboptimal exposure. *Journal of Personality and Social Psychology, 64,* 589–602.

Murray, D. M., Pirie, P., Luepker, R. V., & Pallonen, U. (1989). Five- and six-year follow-up results from four seventh-grade smoking prevention strategies. *Journal of Behavioral Medicine, 12,* 207–218.

Musseler, J., Niblein, M., & Koriat, A. (2005). German capitalization of nouns and the detection of letters in continuous text. *Canadian Journal of Experimental Psychology, 59,* 143–158.

Musso, M., Moro, A., Glauche, V., Rijntjes, M., Reichenbach, J., Büchel, C., & Weiller, C. (2003). Broca's area and the language instinct. *Nature Neuroscience, 6,* 774–781.

Muter, P. (1980). Very rapid forgetting. *Memory & Cognition, 8,* 174–179.

Myers, D. G., & Bishop, G. D. (1970). Discussion effects on racial attitudes. *Science, 169,* 778–789.

Myers, E. B., & Blumstein, S. E. (2008). The neural bases of the lexical effect: An fMRI investigation. *Cerebral Cortex, 28,* 278–288.

Myerson, J., Rank, M. R., Raines, F. Q., & Schnitzler, M. A. (1998). Race and general cognitive ability: The myth of diminishing returns to education. *Psychological Sciences, 9,* 139–142.

Nabkasorn, C., Miyai, N., Sootmongkol, A., Junprasert, S., Yamamoto, H., Arita, M., & Miyashita, K. (2007). Effects of physical exercise on depression, neuroendocrine stress hormones and physiological fitness in adolescent females with depressive symptoms. *European Journal of Public Health, 11*(1), 61–68.

Naeser, M. A., Palumbo, C. L., Helm-Estabrooks, N., Stiassny-Eder, D., & Albert, M. L. (1989). Severe nonfluency in aphasia: Role of the medial subcallosal fasciculus and other white matter pathways in recovery of spontaneous speech. *Brain, 112,* 1–38.

Nafe, J. P., & Wagoner, K. S. (1941). The nature of pressure adaptation. *Journal of General Psychology, 25,* 323–351.

Nairne, J. S. (2002). Remembering over the short-term: The case against the standard model. *Annual Review of Psychology, 53,* 53–81.

Nardi, A. E., Lopes, F. L., Valenca, A. M., et al. (2004). Psychopathological description of hyperventilation-induced panic attacks: A comparison with spontaneous panic attacks. *Psychopathology, 37*(1), 29–35.

Nardi, A. E., Valenca, A. M., Nascimento, I., Zin, W. A., & Versani, M. (2002). Carbon dioxide test as an additional clinical measure of treatment response in panic disorder. *Arquivos de Neuro-Psiquiatria, 60*(2), 358–361.

National Institute of Child Health and Human Development. (1997). The effects of infant child care on infant–mother attachment security: Results of the NICHD study of early child care. *Child Development, 68,* 860–879.

Neisser, U. (1964). Visual search. *Scientific American, 210,* 94–102.

Neisser, U., & Becklen, R. (1975). Selective looking: Attending to visually significant events. *Cognitive Psychology, 7,* 480–494.

Neisser, U., Boodoo, G., Bouchard, T. J., Jr., Boykin, A. W., Brody, N., Ceci, S. J., Halpern, D. R., Loehlin, J. C., Perloff, R., Sternberg, R. J., Urbina, S. (1996). Intelligence: Knowns and unknowns. *American Psychologist, 51,* 77–101.

Neitz, J., He, J. C., & Shevell, S. K. (1999). Trichromatic color vision with only two spectrally distinct photopigments. *Nature Neuroscience, 2,* 884–888.

Nelson, C.A. (2007). A neurobiological perspective on early human deprivation. *Child Development Perspectives, 1,* 13–18.

Nelson, G., Chandrashekar, J., Hoon, M. A., Feng, L., Zhao, G., Ryba, N. J. P., & Zuker, C. S. (2002). An amino-acid taste receptor. *Nature, 416,* 199–202.

Nestadt, G., Samuels, J., Riddle, M., Bienvenu, J., Liang, K., LaBuda, M., Walkup, J., Grados, M., & Hoen-Saric, R. (2000). A family study of obsessive-compulsive disorder. *Archives of General Psychiatry, 57,* 358–363.

Nestler, E. J., Barrot, M., DiLeone, R. J., Eisch, A. I., Gold, S. J., & Monteggia, L. M. (2002). Neurobiology of depression. *Neuron, 34,* 13–25.

Neugarten, B. L. (1974). The roles we play. In American Medical Association, *Quality of life: The middle years.* Acton, MA: Publishing Sciences Group.

Neuhaus, I. M., & Rosenthal, N. E. (1997). Light therapy as a treatment modality for affective disorders. In A. Honig & H. M. van Praag (Eds.), *Depression: Neurobiological, psychopathological and therapeutic advances.* Wiley series on clinical and neurobiological advances in psychiatry. New York: John Wiley & Sons, Inc.

Neumarker, K. J. (1997). Mortality and sudden death in anorexia nervosa. *International Journal of Eating Disorders, 21,* 205–212.

Nevin, J. A. (1988). Behavioral momentum and the partial reinforcement effect. *Psychological Bulletin, 103,* 44–56.

Nevin, J. A., & Grace, R. C. (2000). Behavioral momentum and the Law of Effect. *Behavioral and Brain Sciences, 23,* 73–130.

New, A. S., Buchsbaum, M. S., Hazlett, E. A., Goodman, M., Koenigsberg, H. W., Lo, J., Iskander, L., Newmark, R., Brand, J., O'Flynn, K., & Siever, L. J. (2004). Fluoxetine increases relative metabolic rate in prefrontal cortex in impulsive aggression. *Psychopharmacology, 176,* 451–458.

Newcomer, R. R., & Perna, F. M. (2003). Features of posttraumatic distress among adolescent athletes. *Journal of Athletic Training, 38*(2), 163–166.

Newell, A., & Simon, H. A. (1972). *Human problem solving.* Englewood Cliffs, NJ: Prentice-Hall.

Newman, S. C., & Bland, R. C. (1998). Incidence of mental disorders in Edmonton: Estimates of rates and methodological issues. *Journal of Psychiatric Research, 32,* 273–282.

Newport, E. L. (1975). *Motherese: The speech of mothers to young children.* San Diego: University of California, Center for Human Information Processing.

Nguyen-Michel, S., Unger, J., Hamilton, J., & Spruijt-Metz, D. (2006). Associations between physical activity and perceived stress/hassles in college students. *Stress and Health: Journal of the International Society for the Investigation of Stress, 22,* 179–188.

Niccols, A. (2007). Fetal alcohol syndrome and the developing socio-emotional brain. *Brain and Cognition, 65,* 135–142.

NICHD Early Child Care Research Network. (2003). Does quality of child care affect child outcomes at age 4-1/2? *Developmental Psychology, 39,* 451–469.

Nichols, T. R., Graber, J. A., Brooks-Gunn, J., & Botvin, J. I. (2004). Maternal influences on smoking initiation among urban adolescent girls. *Journal of Research on Adolescence, 14*(1), 73–97.

Nicoladis, E. (2003). What compound nouns mean to preschool children. *Brain and Language, 84,* 38–49.

Nicolas, A., Petit, D., Rompre, S., & Montplaisir, J. (2001). Sleep spindle characteristics in healthy subjects of different age groups. *Clinical Neurophysiology, 112,* 521–527.

Nicotra, A., Critchley, H. D., Mathias, C. J., & Dolan, R. J. (2006). Emotional and autonomic consequences of spinal cord injury explored using functional brain imaging. *Brain, 129,* 718–728.

Nielsen, L. L., & Sarason, I. G. (1981). Emotion, personality, and selective attention. *Journal of Personality and Social Psychology, 41,* 945–960.

Nigg, J. T. (2006). *What causes ADHD?* New York: Guilford Press.

Njegovan, M., & Weisman, R. (1997). Pitch discrimination in field- and isolation-reared black-capped chickadees *(Parus atricapillus). Journal of Comparative Psychology, 111,* 294–301.

Noonan, J. P., Coop, G., Kudaravalli, S., Smith, D., Krause, J., Alessi, J., Chen. F., Platt, D., Pääbo, S., Pritchard, J. K., & Rubin, E. M. (2006). Sequencing and analysis of Neanderthal genomic DNA. *Science, 314,* 1113–1118.

Norman, P., Bennett, P., Smith, C., & Murphy, S. (1998). Health locus of control and health behaviour. *Journal of Health Psychology, 3,* 171–180.

Norman, W. T. (1963). Toward an adequate taxonomy of personality attributes: Replicated factor structure in peer nomination personality ratings. *Journal of Abnormal and Social Psychology, 66,* 574–583.

Norton, M. B. (2003). *In the devil's snare: The Salem witchcraft crisis of 1692.* New York: Vintage Books.

Norwich, K. H., & Wong, W. (1997). Unification of psychophysical phenomena: The complete form of Fechner's Law. *Perception and Psychophysics, 59,* 929–940.

Novin, D., VanderWeele, D. A., & Rezek, M. (1973) Infusion of 2-deoxy-D-glucose into the hepatic-portal system causes eating: Evidence for peripheral glucoreceptors. *Science, 181,* 858–860.

Obergriesser, T., Ende, G., Braus, D. F., & Henn, F. A. (2003). Long-term follow-up of magnetic resonance-detectable choline signal changes in the hippocampus of patients treated with electroconvulsive therapy. *Journal of Clinical Psychiatry, 64*(7), 775–780.

Oberman, L., & Ramachandran, V. (2007). The simulating social mind: The role of the mirror neuron system and simulation in the social and communicative deficits of autism spectrum disorders. *Psychological Bulletin, 133,* 310–327.

Obhi, S. S. (2007). Evidence for feedback dependent conscious awareness of action. *Brain Research, 1161,* 88–94.

O'Brien, M., Peyton, V., Mistry, R., Hruda, L., Jacobs, A., Caldera, Y., Huston, A., & Roy, C. (2000). Gender-role cognition in three-year-old boys and girls. *Sex Roles, 42,* 1007–1025.

O'Connor, E. M. (2001, December). Medicating ADHD: Too much? Too soon? *Monitor on Psychology,* 50–51.

O'Donohue, W., Fowler, K. A., & Lilienfeld, S. O. (Eds.). (2007). *Personality disorders: Toward the DSM-V.* Thousand Oaks, CA: Sage.

Offord, D. R., Boyle, M. H., Campbell, D., Goering, P., Lin, E., Wong, M., & Racine, Y. A. (1996). One-year prevalence of psychiatric disorder in Ontarians 15 to 64 years of age. *Canadian Journal of Psychiatry, 41,* 559–563.

Öhman, A., & Soares, J. J. (1994). "Unconscious anxiety": Phobic responses to masked stimuli. *Journal of Abnormal Psychology, 103,* 231–240.

Öhman, A., & Soares, J. J. (1998). Emotional conditioning to masked stimuli: Expectancies for aversive outcomes following nonrecognized fear-relevant stimuli. *Journal of Experimental Psychology: General, 127,* 69–82.

Okagaki, L., & Sternberg, R. J. (1993). Putting the distance into students' hands: Practical intelligence for school. In R. R. Cocking & K. A. Renninger (Eds.), *The development and meaning of psychological distance.* Hillsdale, NJ: Erlbaum Associates.

Okazaki, S. (2000). Asian American and white American differences on affective distress symptoms: Do symptom reports differ across reporting methods? *Journal of Cross-Cultural Psychology, 31,* 603–625.

O'Keefe, J., & Dostrovsky, T. (1971). The hippocampus as a spatial map: Preliminary evidence from unit activity in the freely moving rat. *Brain Research, 34,* 171–175.

Okiishi, J., Lambert, M. J., Nielsen, S. L., & Ogles, B. M. (2003). Waiting for supershrink: An empirical analysis of therapist effects. *Clinical Psychology & Psychotherapy, 10*(6), 361–373.

Olds, J., & Milner, P. (1954). Positive reinforcement produced by electrical stimulation of septal areas and other regions of rat brains. *Journal of Comparative and Physiological Psychology, 47,* 419–427.

Olfert, E. D., Cross, B. M., & McWilliam, A. A. (Eds.) (1993). *Guide to the care and use of experimental animals, Vol. 1* (2nd ed.). Ottawa: Canadian Council on Animal Care.

Oliver, D. L., Beckius, G. E., Bishop, D. C., Loftus, W. C., & Batra, R. (2003). Topography of interaural temporal disparity coding in projections of medial superior olive to inferior colliculus. *Journal of Neuroscience, 23,* 7438–7449.

Oliver, R., & Williams, R. L. (2006). Performance patterns of high, medium, and low performers during and following a reward versus non-reward contingency phase. *School Psychology Quarterly, 21,* 119–147.

Olson, C. K., Kutner, L. A., & Warner, D. E. (2008). The role of violent video game content in adolescent development: Boys' perspectives. *Journal of Adolescent Research, 23,* 55–75.

Olson, J. M., Roese, N. J., & Zanna, M. P. (1996). Expectancies. In E. T. Higgins & A. W. Kruglanski (Eds.), *Social psychology: Handbook of basic principles.* New York: Guilford Press.

O'Neil, P. M., Smith, C. F., Foster, G. D., & Anderson, D. A. (2000). The perceived relative worth of reaching goal weight. *International Journal of Obesity, 24,* 1069–1076.

O'Neill, D. K. (1996). Two-year-old children's sensitivity to a parent's knowledge state when making requests. *Child Development, 67,* 659–677.

O'Regan, J. K., Rensink, R. A., & Clark, J. J. (1999). Change-blindness as a result of "mudsplashes." *Nature, 398,* 34.

Orne, M. T. (1959). The nature of hypnosis: Artifact and essence. *Journal of Abnormal and Social Psychology, 58,* 277–299.

Orvis, B. R., Kelley, H. H., & Butler, D. (1976). Attributional conflict in young couples. In J. H. Harvey, W. J. Ickes, & R. F. Kidd (Eds.), *New directions in attribution research, Vol. 1.* Hillsdale, NJ: Erlbaum.

Osborne, K. A., Robichon, A., Burgess, E., Butland, S., Shaw, R. A., Coulthard, A., Pereira, H. S., Greenspan, R. H., & Sokolowski, M. B. (1997). Natural behavior polymorphism due to a cGMP-dependent protein kinase of *Drosophila. Science, 277,* 834–836.

Ostrom, T. M., & Sedikides, C. (1992). Out-group homogeneity effects in natural and minimal groups. *Psychological Bulletin, 112,* 536–552.

Overmier, J. B. (1998). Learned helplessness: State or stasis of the art? In M. Sabourin, F. Craik, & M. Robert (Eds.), *Advances in psychological science: Biological and cognitive aspects, Vol. 2* (pp. 301–315). Hove, UK: Psychology Press/ Erlbaum.

Overmier, J. B., & Seligman, M. E. P. (1967). Effects of inescapable shock upon subsequent escape and avoidance responding. *Journal of Comparative and Physiological Psychology, 63,* 28–33.

Owen, A. M., James, M., Leigh, P. N., Summers, B. A., Marsden, C. D., Quinn, N. P., Lange, K. W., & Robbins, T. W. (1992). Fronto-striatal cognitive deficits at different stages of Parkinson's disease. *Brain, 115,* 1727–1751.

Owens, R. E. (1992). *Language development: An introduction.* New York: Merrill/Macmillan.

Paffenbarger, R. S., Hyde, J. T., Wing, A. L., & Hsieh, C. C. (1986). Physical activity, all-cause mortality, and longevity of college alumni. *New England Journal of Medicine, 314,* 605–612.

Paikoff, R. L., & Brooks-Gunn, J. (1991). Do parent-child relationships change during puberty? *Psychological Bulletin, 110,* 47–66.

Paizanis, E., Hamon, M., & Lanfumey, L. (2007). Hippocampal neurogenesis, depressive disorders, and antidepressant therapy. *Neural Plasticity,* 1–7.

Palmer, S. E. (1975). The effects of contextual scenes on the identification of objects. *Memory and Cognition, 3,* 519–526.

Papini, M. R. (2003). Comparative psychology of surprising nonreward. *Brain, Behavior, and Evolution, 62,* 83–95.

Paris, J. (1999). Borderline personality disorder. In T. Millen, P. H. Blaney, & R. D. Davis (Eds.), *Oxford textbook of psychopathology* (pp. 628–652). New York: Oxford University Press.

Paris, J. (2007). Intermittent psychotherapy: An alternative to continuous long-term treatment for patients with personality disorders. *Journal of Psychiatric Practice, 13*(3), 153–158.

Park, B. (1986). A method for studying the development of impressions in real people. *Journal of Personality and Social Psychology, 51,* 907–917.

Park, B., & Rothbart, M. (1982). Perception of out-group homogeneity and levels of social categorization: Memory for the subordinate attributes of in-group and out-group members. *Journal of Personality and Social Psychology, 42,* 1051–1068.

Parke, R. D. (2000). Father involvement: A developmental psychological perspective. *Marriage and Family Review, 29,* 43–58.

Parker-Pope, T. (2002). *Cigarettes: From seed to smoke.* New York: New Press.

Parkin, A. J., Blunden, J., Rees, J. E., & Hunkin, N. M. (1991). Wernicke-Korsakoff syndrome of nonalcoholic origin. *Brain and Cognition, 15,* 69–82.

Pato, M. T., Pato, C. N., & Pauls, D. L. (2002). Recent findings in the genetics of OCD. *Journal of Clinical Psychiatry, 63*(6), 30–33.

Patterson, D. R., & Jensen, M. P. (2003). Hypnosis and clinical pain. *Psychological Bulletin, 129,* 495–521.

Paulesu, E., Frith, U., Snowling, M., Gallagher, A., Morton, J., Frackowiak, R. S. J., & Frith, C. D. (1996). Is developmental dyslexia a disconnection syndrome? *Brain, 119,* 143–157.

Paulesu, E., McCrory, E., Fazio, F., Menoncello, L., Brunswick, N., Cappa, S. F., Cotelli, M., Cossu, G., Corte, F., Lorusso, M., Pesenti, S., Gallagher, A., Perani, D., Price, C., Frith, C. D., & Frith, U. (2000). A cultural effect on brain function. *Nature Neuroscience, 3,* 91–96.

Paulhus, D. L., Lysy, D. C., & Yik, M. S. M. (1998). Self-report measures of intelligence: Are they useful as proxy IQ tests? *Journal of Personality, 66,* 525–554.

Paulhus, D. L., & Williams, K. M. (2002). The Dark Triad of personality: Narcissism, machiavellianism, and psychopathy. *Journal of Research in Personality, 36,* 556–563.

Pauls, D. L., & Alsobrook, J. P. (1999). The inheritance of obsessive-compulsive disorder. *Child and Adolescent Psychiatric Clinics of North America, 8,* 481–496.

Pauls, D. L., & Leckman, J. F. (1986). The inheritance of Gilles de la Tourette's syndrome and associated behaviors. *New England Journal of Medicine, 315,* 993–997.

Paunonen, S. V. (2003). Big Five factors of personality and replicated predictions of behavior. *Journal of Personality & Social Psychology, 84*(2), 411–422.

Paus, T., Zijdenbos, A., Worsley, K., Collins, D. L, Blumenthal, J., Giedd, J. N., Rapoport, J. L., & Evans, A. C. (1999). Structural maturation of neural pathways in children and adolescents: In vivo study. *Science, 283,* 1908–1911.

Pavlov, I. P. (1927). Conditioned reflexes. Oxford, UK: Oxford University Press.

Pearce, J. M., & Bouton, M. E. (2001). Theories of associative learning in animals. *Annual Review of Psychology, 52,* 111–139.

Pearson, P. M., & Schaefer, E. G. (2005). Toupee or not toupee? The role of instructional set, centrality, and relevance in change blindness. *Visual Cognition, 12,* 1528–1543.

Pease, D. M., Gleason, J. B., & Pan, B. A. (1993). Learning the meaning of words: Semantic development and beyond. In J. B. Gleason (Ed.), *The development of language.* New York: Macmillan.

Peavy, G. M., Lange, K. L., Salmon, D. P., Patterson, T. L., Goldman, S., Gamst, A. C., Mills, P. J., Khandrika, S., & Galasko, D. (2007). The effects of prolonged stress and APOE genotype on memory and cortisol in older adults. *Biological Psychiatry, 62*(5), 472–478.

Pederson, D. R., Gleason, K. E., Moran, G., & Bento, S. (1998). Maternal attachment representations, maternal sensitivity, and the infant-mother attachment relationship. *Developmental Psychology, 34,* 925–933.

Pederson, D. R., & Moran, G. (1996). Expressions of the attachment relationship outside the strange situation. *Child Development, 67,* 915–927.

Pelcovitz, D., & Kaplan, S. (1996). Posttraumatic stress disorder in children and adolescents. *Child and Adolescent Psychiatric Clinics of North America, 5,* 449–469.

Pelleymounter, M. A., Cullen, M. J., Baker, M. B., Hecht, R., Winters, D., Boone, T., & Collins, E. (1997). Effects of the obese gene product on body weight regulation in ob/ob mice. *Science, 269,* 540–543.

Pembrey, M. E., Bygren, L. O., Kaati, G., Edvinsson, S., Northstone, K., Sjöström, M., Golding, J., & the ALSPAC Study Team. (2006). Sex-specific, male-line transgenerational responses in humans. *European Journal of Human Genetics, 14,* 159–166.

Pennisi, E. (2007). No sex please, we're Neandertals. *Science, 316,* 967.

Pereira, A. C., Huddleston, D. E., Brickman, A. M, Sosunov, A. A., Hen, R., McKhann, G. M., Sloan, R., Gage, F. H., Brown, T. R., & Small, S. A. (2007). An in vivo correlate of exercise-induced neurogenesis in the adult dentate gyrus. *Proceedings of the National Academy of Science, USA, 104,* 5638–5643.

Perlman, D., & Oskamp, S. (1971). The effects of picture content and exposure frequency on evaluations of Negroes and whites. *Journal of Experimental Social Psychology, 7,* 503–514.

Perlmutter, M., & Hall, E. (1992). *Adult development and aging* (2nd ed.). New York: John Wiley & Sons.

Perls, F. S. (1967). Group vs. individual therapy. *ETC: A Review of General Semantics, 34,* 306–312.

Perls, F. S. (1969). *Gestalt therapy verbatim.* Lafayette, CA: Real People Press.

Persad, E. (2001). Electroconvulsive therapy: The controversy and the evidence. *Canadian Journal of Psychiatry, 46*(8), 702–703.

Pervin, L. A. (1975). *Personality: Theory, assessment, and research.* New York: John Wiley & Sons.

Peskind, E. R., Jensen, C. F., Pascualy, M., Tsuang, D., Cowley, D., Martin, D. C., Wilkinson, C. W., & Raskind, M. A. (1998). Sodium lactate and hypertonic sodium chloride induce equivalent panic incidence, panic symptoms, and hypernatremia in panic disorder. *Biological Psychiatry, 44*(10), 1007–1016.

Pessoa, L., Japee, S., Sturman, D., & Ungerleider, L. G. (2006). Target visibility and visual awareness modulate amygdala responses to fearful faces. *Cerebral Cortex, 16,* 366–375.

Peters, E., Romer, D., Slovic, P., Jamieson, K. H., Wharfield, L., Mertz, C. K., Carpenter, S. (2007). The impact of Canadian-style cigarette warning labels among U.S. smokers and nonsmokers. *Nicotine and Tobacco Research, 9*(4), 473–481.

Peters, R. K., Cady, L. D., Bischoff, D. P., Bernstein, L., & Pile, M. C. (1983). Physical fitness and subsequent myocardial infarction in healthy workers. *JAMA, 249,* 3052–3056.

Petersen, S. E., Fox, P. T., Posner, M. I., Mintin, M., & Raichle, M. E. (1988). Positron emission tomographic studies of the cortical anatomy of single-word processing. *Nature, 331,* 585–589.

Petersen, S. E., Fox, P. T., Snyder, A. Z., & Raichle, M. E. (1990). Activation of extrastriate and frontal cortical areas by visual words and word-like stimuli. *Science, 249,* 1041–1044.

Peterson, L. R., & Peterson, M. J. (1959). Short-term retention of individual verbal items. *Journal of Experimental Psychology, 58,* 193–198.

Peterson, M. A. (2005). Object perception. In E. B. Goldstein (Ed.), *Blackwell handbook of sensation and perception* (pp. 168–203). Malden, MA: Blackwell Publishing.

Peterson, R. (1985). Pubertal development as a cause of disturbance: Myths, realities, and unanswered questions. *Genetic, Social, and General Psychology Monographs, 111,* 205–232.

Petitto, L. A., Zatorre, R. J., Gauna, K., Nikelski, E. J., Dostie, D., & Evans, A. C. (2000). Speech-like cerebral activity in profoundly deaf people processing signed languages: Implications for the neural basis of human language. *Proceedings of the National Academy of Sciences, USA, 97,* 13 961–13 966.

Pettus, A. (2008, January–February). A spectrum of disorders. *Harvard Magazine,* 27–31, 80.

Petty, R. E., & Wegener, D. T. (1999). The elaboration likelihood model: Current status and controversies. In S. Chaiken & Y. Trope (Eds.), *Dual-process theories in social psychology.* New York: Guilford Press.

Petty, R. E., Wegener, D. T., & Fabrigar, L. R. (1997). Attitude change: Multiple roles for persuasion variables. In D. Gilbert, S. Fiske, & G. Lindzey (Eds.), *Handbook of social psychology* (4th ed.). New York: McGraw-Hill.

Petty, R. E., Wheeler, S. C., & Tormala, Z. L. (2003). Persuasion and attitude change. In T. Millon & M. J. Lerner (Eds.), *Handbook of psychology: Personality and social psychology, Vol. 5.* New York: John Wiley & Sons, Inc.

Pfefferbaum, A., Zipursky, R. B., Lim, K. O., Zatz, L. M., Stahl, S. M., & Jernigan, T. L. (1988). Computed tomographic evidence for generalized sulcal and ventricular enlargement in schizophrenia. *Archives of General Psychiatry, 45,* 633–640.

Phares, E. J. (1979). *Clinical psychology: Concepts, methods, and profession.* Homewood, IL: Dorsey Press.

Phillips, S. D., Burns, B. J., Edgar, E. R., Mueser, K. T., Linkins, K. W., Rosenheck, R. A., Drake, R. E., & McDonel Herr, E. C. (2001). Moving assertive community treatment into standard practice. *Psychiatric Services, 52*(6), 771–779.

Piaget, J. (1952). *The origins of intelligence in children.* (M. Cook, Trans.). New York: International Universities Press.

Piaget, J. (1972). Intellectual evolution from adolescence to adulthood. *Human Development, 15,* 1–12.

Pichora-Fuller, M. K., & Schneider, B. A. (1998). Masking-level differences in older adults: The effect of the level of the masking noise. *Perception & Psychophysics, 60,* 1197–1205.

Pierce, J. P., Choi, W. S., Gilpin, E. A., Farkas, A. J., & Berry, C. C. (1998). Tobacco industry promotion of cigarettes and adolescent smoking. *Journal of the American Medical Association, 279,* 511–515.

Pierce, J. P., & Gilpin, E. A. (1995). A historical analysis of tobacco marketing and the uptake of smoking by youth in the United States: 1890–1977. *Health Psychology, 14,* 500–508.

Pierce, W. D., & Epling, W. F. (1997). Activity anorexia: The interplay of culture, behavior, and biology. In P. Lamal (Ed.), *Cultural contingencies: Behavior analytic perspectives on cultural practices.* Westport, CT: Prager Publishers/Greenwood Publishing Group, Inc.

Pierce, W. D., Heth, C. D., Owczarczyk, J. C., Russell, J. C., & Proctor, S. D. (2007). Overeating by young obesity-prone and lean rats caused by tastes associated with low energy foods. *Obesity, 15,* 1969–1979.

Pilleri, G. (1979). The blind Indus dolphin, *Platanista indi. Endeavours, 3,* 48–56.

Pilon, D. J., & Friedman, A. (1998). Grouping and detecting vertices in 2-D, 3-D, and quasi-3-D objects. *Canadian Journal of Experimental Psychology, 52,* 114–126.

Pinel, J. P. J., Assanand, S., & Lehman, D. R. (2000). Hunger, eating, and ill health. *American Psychologist, 55,* 1105–1116.

Pinhas, L., Toner, B. B., Ali, A., Garfinkel, P. E., & Stuckless, N. (1999). The effects of the ideal of female beauty on mood and body satisfaction. *Eating Disorders, 25,* 223–226.

Pinker, S. (1990). Language acquisition. In D. N. Osherson & H. Lasnik (Eds.), *An invitation to cognitive science. Vol. 1: Language.* Cambridge, MA: MIT Press.

Pinker, S. (1994). *The language instinct.* New York: William Morrow.

Pinker, S. (1997). *How the mind works.* New York: Norton.

Pinker, S. (1999). *Words and rules: The ingredients of language.* New York: Basic Books.

Pinker, S. (2001). Talk of genetics and vice versa. *Nature, 413,* 465–466.

Pinker, S. (2007). *The stuff of thought: Language as a window into human nature.* New York: Viking.

Pinker, S., & Jackendoff, R. (2005). The faculty of language: What's special about it? *Cognition, 96,* 201–236.

Pirkkola, S. P., Poikolainen, K., & Lonnqvist, J. K. (2006). Currently active and remitted alcohol dependence in a nationwide adult general population—Results from the Finnish health 2000 study. *Alcohol and Alcoholism, 41,* 315–320.

Pitkänen, A., Savander, V., & LeDoux, J. E. (1997). Organization of intra-amygdaloid circuits: An emerging framework for understanding functions of the amygdala. *Trends in Neuroscience, 20,* 517–523.

Pittenger, C., & Kandel, E. R. (2003). In search of general mechanisms of long-lasting plasticity: *Aplysia* and the hippocampus. Philosophical Transaction of the Royal Society of London: B. *Biological Sciences, 358,* 757–763.

Pitts, M., & Phillips, K. (1998). *The psychology of health: An introduction* (2nd ed.). London, UK, and New York: Routledge.

Plassman, B. L., Langa, K. M., Fisher, G. G., Heeringa, S. G., Weir, D. R., Ofstedal, M. B., Burke, J. R., Hurd, M. D., Potter, G. G., Rodgers, W. L., Steffens, D. C., Willis, R. J., & Wallace, R. B. (2007). Prevalence of dementia in the United States: The aging, demographics and memory study. *Neuroepidemiology, 29,* 125–132.

Plomin, R. (1990). *Nature and nurture: An introduction to behavioral genetics.* Pacific Grove, CA: Brooks/Cole.

Plomin, R., & Asbury, K. (2001). Nature and nurture in the family. *Marriage & Family Review, 33*(2–3), 273–281.

Plomin, R., & Bergeman, C. S. (1991). The nature of nurture: Genetic influence on "environmental" measures. *Behavioral and Brain Sciences, 14,* 373–427.

Plomin, R., McClearn, G. E., Smith, D. L., Vignetti, S., Chorney, M. J., Chorney, K., Venditti, C. P., Kasarda, S., Thompson, L. A., Detterman, D. K., Daniels, J., Owen, M., & McGuffin, P. (1994). DNA markers associated with high versus low IQ: The IQ quantitative trait loci (QTL) project. *Behavior Genetics, 24,* 107–118.

Plomin, R., & Rende, R. (1991). Human behavioral genetics. *Annual Review of Psychology, 43,* 161–190.

Poduslo, S. E., & Yin, X. (2001). A new locus on chromosome 19 linked with late-onset Alzheimer's disease. *Neuroreport, 12,* 3759–3761.

Polimeni, J., & Reiss, J.P. (2003). Evolutionary perspectives on schizophrenia. *Canadian Journal of Psychiatry, 48*(1), 34–39.

Polka, L., & Werker, J. (1994). Developmental changes in perception of nonnative vowel contrasts. *Journal of Experimental Psychology: Human Perception and Performance, 20,* 421–435.

Pomerleau, O. F. (1992). Smoking treatment comes of age. *Psychopharmacology and Substance Abuse Newsletter, 24,* 3.

Pope, K. S. (2000). Therapists' sexual feelings and behaviors: Research, trends, and quandaries. In L. T. Szuchman & F. Muscarella (Eds.), *Psychological perspectives on human sexuality.* New York: John Wiley & Sons, Inc.

Porter, J., Craven, B., Khan, R. M., Chang, S.-J., Kang, I., Judkewitz, B., Volpe, J., Settles, G., & Sobel, N. (2007). Mechanisms of scent-tracking in humans. *Nature Neuroscience, 10,* 27–29.

Porter, R. H., Makin, J. W., Davis, L. B., & Christensen, K. M. (1992). Breast-fed infants respond to olfactory cues from their own mother and unfamiliar lactating females. *Infant Behavior and Development, 15,* 85–93.

Posner, M. I., Snyder, C. R. R., & Davidson, B. J. (1980). Attention and the detection of signals. *Journal of Experimental Psychology: General, 109,* 160–174.

Potter, S. M., Zelazo, P. R., Stack, D. M., & Papageorgiou, A. N. (2000). Adverse effects of fetal cocaine exposure on neonatal auditory information processing. *Pediatrics, 105,* E40.

Potter, W. Z., Manji, H. K., & Rudorfer, M. V. (2001). Tricyclics and tetracyclics. In A. F. Schatzberg & C. B. Nemeroff (Eds.), *Essentials of clinical psychopharmacology.* Washington, DC: American Psychiatric Association.

Poulin-Dubois, D., Graham, S., & Sippola, L. (1995). Early lexical development: The contribution of parental labelling and infants' categorization abilities. *Journal of Child Language, 22,* 325–343.

Powell, K. E., Thompson, P. D., Caspersen, C. J., & Kendrick, J. S. (1987). Physical activity and the incidence of coronary heart disease. *Annual Review of Public Health, 8,* 253–287.

Prescott, C. A., & Kendler, K. S. (1999). Age at first drink and risk for alcoholism: A noncausal association. *Alcoholism: Clinical & Experimental Research, 23*(1), 101–107.

Prichard, J. C. (1835). *A treatise on insanity and other disorders affecting the mind.* London: Sherwood, Gilbert, and Piper.

Prochaska, J. O., & Norcross, J. C. (2003). *Systems of psychotherapy* (5th ed.). Pacific Grove, CA: Brooks/Cole.

Proeve, M., & Reilly, E. (2007). Personal and offending characteristics of child sexual offenders who have been sexually abused. *Psychiatry, Psychology, and Law, 14,* 251–259.

Propping, P., Kruger, J., & Janah, A. (1980). Effect of alcohol on genetically determined variants of the normal electroencephalogram. *Psychiatry Research, 2,* 85–98.

Propping, P., Kruger, J., & Mark, N. (1981). Genetic disposition to alcoholism: An EEG study in alcoholics and their relatives. *Human Genetics, 59,* 51–59.

Prudic, J., & Sackeim, H. A. (1999). Electroconvulsive therapy and suicide risk. *Journal of Clinical Psychiatry, 60,* 104–110.

Pulcino, T., Galea, S., Ahern, J., Resnick, H., Foley, M., Vlahov, D. (2003). Posttraumatic stress in women after the September 11 terrorist attacks in New York City. *Journal of Women's Health, 12*(8), 809–820.

Purhonen, M., Kilpeläinen-Lees, R., Valkonen-Korhonen, M., Karhu, J., & Lehtonen, J. (2005). Four-month-old infants process own mother's voice faster than unfamiliar voices—Electrical signs of sensitization in infant brain. *Cognitive Brain Research, 24,* 627–633.

Quickfall, J., & el-Guebaly, N. (2006). Genetics and alcoholism: How close are we to potential clinical applications? *Canadian Journal of Psychiatry, 51,* 461–467.

Rachlin, H. (1970). *Modern behaviorism.* New York: Freeman.

Radomsky, A., Ashbaugh, A., & Gelfand, L. (2007). Relationships between anger, symptoms, and cognitive factors in OCD checkers. *Behaviour Research & Therapy, 45*(11), 2712–2725.

Rahe, R. H., & Arthur, R. J. (1978). Life changes and illness reports. In K. E. Gunderson & R. H. Rahe (Eds.), *Life stress and illness*. Springfield, IL: Thomas.

Raine, A., Lencz, T., Bihrle, S., LaCasse, L., & Colletti, P. (2002). Reduced prefrontal gray matter volume and reduced autonomic activity in antisocial personality disorder. *Archives of General Psychiatry, 57,* 119–127.

Raine, A., Meloy, J. R., Bihrle, S., Stoddard, J., LaCasse, L., & Buchsbaum, M. S. (1998). Reduced prefrontal and increased subcortical brain functioning assessed using positron emission tomography in predatory and affective murderers. *Behavioral Science and the Law, 16,* 319–332.

Rainville, P., Duncan, G. H., Price, D. D., Carrier, B., & Bushnell, M. C. (1997). Pain affect encoded in human anterior cingulate but not somatosensory cortex. *Science, 277,* 968–971.

Rajecki, D. J. (1990). *Attitudes* (2nd ed.). Sunderland, MA: Sinauer Associates.

Rakic, P. (1985). Limits of neurogenesis in primates. *Science, 227,* 1054–1056.

Rakison, D. H., & Derringer, J. (2008). Do infants possess an evolved spider-detection mechanism? *Cognition, 107*(1), 381–393.

Ramey, C. (1994). Abecedarian project. In R. J. Sternberg (Ed.), *Encyclopedia of human intelligence.* New York: Macmillan.

Ramirez-Amaya, V., Marrone, D. F., Gage, F. H., Worley, P. F., & Barnes, C. A. (2006). Integration of new neurons into functional neural networks. *Journal of Neuroscience, 26,* 12 237–12 241.

Rapoport, J. L., Giedd, J. N., Blumenthal, J., Hamburger, S., Jeffries, N., Fernandez, T., Nicolson, R., Bedwell, J., Lenane, M., Zijdenbos, A., Paus, T., & Evans, A. (1999). Progressive cortical change during adolescence in childhood-onset schizophrenia: A longitudinal magnetic resonance imaging study. *Archives of General Psychiatry, 56,* 649–654.

Rappaport, J. (1977). *Community psychology: Values, research and action.* New York: Holt, Rinehart and Winston.

Rappaport, J., & Seidman, E. (2000). *Handbook of community psychology.* New York: Kluwer Academic/Plenum Publishers.

Rassoulzadegan, M., Grandjean, V., Gounon, P., Vincent, S., Gillot, I., & Cuzin, F. (2006). RNA-mediated non-mendelian inheritance of an epigenetic change in the mouse. *Nature, 441,* 469–474.

Rayner, K., Foorman, B. R., Perfetti, C., Petetsky, D., & Seidenberg, M. S. (2002, March). How should reading be taught? *Scientific American,* 85–91.

Rayner, K., & Pollatsek, A. (1989). *The psychology of reading.* Englewood Cliffs, NJ: Prentice-Hall.

Rayner, K., Sereno, S. C., & Raney, G. E. (1996). Eye movement control in reading: A comparison of two types of models. *Journal of Experimental Psychology: Human Perception and Performance, 22,* 1188–1200.

Réale, D., McAdam, A. G., Boutin, S., & Berteaux, D. (2003). Genetic and plastic responses of a northern mammal to climate change. *Proceedings of the Royal Society of London, 270,* 591–596.

Reber, A. S. (1992). The cognitive unconscious: An evolutionary perspective. *Consciousness and Cognition, 1,* 93–133.

Recanzone, G. H., Makhamra, S. D. D. R., & Guard, D. C. (1998). Comparison of relative and absolute sound localization ability in humans. *Journal of the Acoustical Society of America, 103,* 1085–1097.

Rees, G. (2001). Seeing is not perceiving. *Nature Neuroscience, 4,* 678–680.

Rees, G., Friston, K., & Koch, C. (2000). A direct quantitative relationship between the functional properties of human and macaque V5. *Nature Neuroscience, 3,* 716–723.

Rees, G., Kreiman, G., & Koch, C. (2002). Neural correlates of consciousness in humans. *Nature Reviews: Neuroscience, 3,* 261–270.

Regier, D. A., Boyd, J. H., Burke, J. D., Rae, D. S., Myers, J. K., Kramer, M., Ropins, L. N., George, L. K., Karno, M., & Locke, B. Z. (1988). One-month prevalence of mental disorders in the United States. *Archives of General Psychiatry, 45,* 977–986.

Regier, T., & Kay, P. (2004). Color naming and sunlight: Commentary on Lindsey and Brown (2002). *Psychological Science, 15,* 289–290.

Regier, T., Kay, P., & Cook, R. S. (2005). Focal colors are universal after all. *Proceedings of the National Academy of Sciences of the USA, 102,* 8386–8391.

Reich, W. A., & Ray, S. (2006). Domain specific effects of central traits in impression formation. *Psychological Reports, 98*(3), 885–891.

Reichle, E. D., Pollatsek, A., Fisher, D. L., & Rayner, K. (1998). Toward a model of eye movement control in reading. *Psychological Review, 105,* 125–157.

Reif, A., Rösler, M., Freitag, C. M., Schneider, M., Eujen, A., Kissing, C., Wenzler, D., Jacob, C. P. Retz-Juninger, P., Thome, J., Lesch, K.-P., & Retz, W. (2007). Nature and nurture predispose to violent behavior: Serotonergic genes and adverse childhood environment. *Neuropharmacology, 34,* 2375–2383.

Reingold, E. M., Charness, N., Pomplun, M., & Stampe, D. M. (2001). Visual span in expert chess players: Evidence from eye movements. *Psychological Science, 12,* 48–55.

Reinink, E., Bouhuys, N., Wirz-Justice, A., & van den Hoofdakker, R. (1990). Prediction of the antidepressant response to total sleep deprivation by diurnal variation of mood. *Psychiatry Research, 32,* 113–124.

Rensink, R. A. (2002). Change detection. *Annual Review of Psychology, 53,* 245–277.

Rescorla, R. A. (1966). Predictability and number of pairings in Pavlovian fear conditioning. *Psychonomic Science, 4,* 383–384.

Rescorla, R. A. (1973). Effect of US habituation following conditioning. *Journal of Comparative and Physiological Psychology, 43,* 151–160.

Rescorla, R. A. (1999). Learning about qualitatively different outcomes during a blocking procedure. *Animal Learning & Behavior, 27,* 140–151.

Rest, J. R. (1979). *Development in judging moral issues.* Minneapolis: University of Minnesota Press.

Review Panel. (1981). Coronary-prone behavior and coronary heart disease: A critical review. *Circulation, 673,* 1199–1215.

Revusky, S. H., & Garcia, J. (1970). Learned associations over long delays. In G. H. Bower & J. T. Spence (Eds.), *The psychology of learning and motivation: IV*. New York: Academic Press.

Reynolds, A. G., & Flagg, P. W. (1983). *Cognitive psychology* (2nd ed.). Boston: Little, Brown.

Reynolds, G. (2003, March 16). The stuttering doctor's "Monster Study." *New York Times Magazine,* 36–39.

Rhee, S. H., Hewitt, J. K., Young, S. E., Corely, R. P., Crowley, T. J., & Stallings, M. C. (2003). Genetic and environmental influences on substance initiation, use, and problem use in adolescents. *Archives of General Psychology, 60*(12), 1256–1264.

Rheingold, A. A., Acierno, R., & Resnick, H. S. (2004). Trauma, posttraumatic stress disorder, and health risk behaviors. In P. P. Schnurr & B. L. Green (Eds.), *Trauma and health: Physical health consequences of exposure to extreme stress.* Washington, DC: American Psychological Association.

Richards, R. J. (1987). *Darwin and the emergence of evolutionary theories of mind and behavior.* Chicago: University of Chicago Press.

Rief, J. S., Bruns, C., & Lower, K. S. (1998). Cancer of the nasal cavity and paranasal sinuses and exposure to environmental tobacco smoke in pet dogs. *American Journal of Epidemiology, 147*(5), 488–492.

Riggs, L. A., Ratliff, F., Cornsweet, J. C., & Cornsweet, T. N. (1953). The disappearance of steadily fixated visual test objects. *Journal of the Optical Society of America, 43,* 495–501.

Rips, L. J., Shoben, E. J., & Smith, E. E. (1973). Semantic distance and the verification of semantic relations. *Journal of Verbal Learning and Verbal Behavior, 12,* 1–20.

Rischer, C. E., & Easton, T. A. (1992). *Focus on human biology*. New York: HarperCollins.

Ritter, S., Dinh, T. T., & Zhang, Y. (2000). Localization of hindbrain glucoreceptive sites controlling food intake and blood glucose. *Brain Research, 856,* 37–47.

Roberson, D., Davies, I., & Davidoff, J. (2000). Color categories are not universal: Replications and new evidence from a Stone-Age culture. *Journal of Experimental Psychology: General, 129,* 369–398.

Robins, R. W., & Beer, J. S. (2001). Positive illusions about the self: Short-term benefits and long-term costs. *Journal of Personality and Social Psychology, 80,* 340–352.

Rodin, J., Schank, D., & Striegel-Moore, R. (1989). Psychological features of obesity. *Medical Clinics of North America, 73,* 47–66.

Rodrigues, A., Assmar, E., & Jablonski, B. (2005). Social-psychology and the invasion of Iraq. *Revista de Psicologia Social, 20*(3), 387–398.

Roediger, H. L. (1990). Implicit memory: Retention without remembering. *American Psychologist, 45,* 1043–1056.

Roediger, H. L., III, & McDermott, K. B. (1995). Creating false memories: Remembering words not presented in lists. *Journal of Experimental Psychology: Learning, Memory, and Cognition, 21*, 803–814.

Roelofs, K., Bakvis, P., Hermans, E. J., van Pelt, J., & van Honk, J. (2007). The effects of social stress and cortisol responses on the preconscious selective attention to social threat. *Biological Psychology, 75*(1), 1–7.

Roff, J. D., & Knight, R. A. (1995). Childhood antecedents of stable positive symptoms in schizophrenia. *Psychological Reports, 77*(1), 319–323.

Rogers, C. R. (1961). *On becoming a person*. Boston: Houghton Mifflin.

Rogers, C. T. (1951). *Client-centered therapy.* Boston: Houghton Mifflin.

Rogers, M. P., Trentham, D. E., McCune, W. J., Ginsberg, B. I., Rennke, H. G., Reike, P., & David, J. R. (1980). Effect of psychological stress on the induction of arthritis in rats. *Arthritis and Rheumatology, 23,* 1337–1342.

Rogoff, B. (1990). *Apprenticeship in thinking: Cognitive development in social context.* New York: Oxford University Press.

Rogoff, B., & Chavajay, P. (1995). What's become of research on the cultural basis of cognitive development? *American Psychologist, 50,* 859–877.

Rohling, M. L., Langhinrichsen-Rohling, J., & Miller, L. S. (2003). Actuarial assessment of malingering: Rohling's interpretive method. In R. D. Franklin (Ed.), *Prediction in forensic and neuropsychology: Sound statistical practices.* Mahwah, NJ: Lawrence Erlbaum Associates.

Roisman, G. I., Clausell, E., Holland, A., Fortuna, K., & Elieff, C. (2008). Adult romantic relationships as contexts of human development: A multimethod comparison of same-sex couples with opposite-sex dating, engaged, and married dyads. *Developmental Psychology, 44*, 91–101.

Roodenrys, S., Hulme, C., Lethbridge, A., Hinton, M., & Nimmo, L. M. (2002). Word-frequency and phonological-neighborhood effects on verbal short-term memory. *Journal of Experimental Psychology: Learning, Memory, and Cognition, 28*, 1019–1034.

Rosch, E. (1973). On the internal structure of perceptual and semantic categories. In R. E. Moore (Ed.), *Cognitive development and the acquisition of language.* New York: Academic Press.

Rosch, E. (1999). Reclaiming concepts. *Journal of Consciousness Studies, 6,* 61–77.

Rosch, E. (2002). Principles of categorization. In D. J. Levitin (Ed), *Foundations of cognitive psychology: Core readings.* Cambridge, MA: MIT Press.

Rosch, E. H. (1975). Cognitive representations of semantic categories. *Journal of Experimental Psychology: General, 104,* 192–233.

Rosch, E. H., Mervis, C. B., Gray, W. D., Johnson, D. M., & Boyes-Braem, P. (1976). Basic objects in natural categories. *Cognitive Psychology, 8,* 382–439.

Rose, G. A., & Williams, R. T. (1961). Metabolic studies of large and small eaters. *British Journal of Nutrition, 15,* 1–9.

Rose, J. K., & Rankin, C. H. (2001). Analyses of habituation in *Caenorhabditis elegans. Learning & Memory, 8,* 63–69.

Rose, R. J. (1995). Genes and human behavior. *Annual Review of Psychology, 46,* 625–654.

Rosenfarb, I. S., Bellack, A. S., Aziz, N., Kratz, M., & Sayers, S. (2004). Race, family interactions, and patient stabilization in schizophrenia. *Journal of Abnormal Psychology, 113*(1), 109–115.

Rosenhan, D. L. (1973). On being sane in insane places. *Science, 179,* 250–258.

Rosenman, R. H., Brand, R. J., Jenkins, C. D., Friedman, M., Straus, R., & Wurm, M. (1975). Coronary heart disease in the Western Collaborative Group Study: Final follow-up experience of 8½ years. *JAMA, 233,* 872–877.

Rosenman, R. H., Brand, R. J., Jenkins, C. D., Friedman, M., Straus, R., & Wurm, M. (1994). Coronary heart disease in the Western Collaborative Group Study: Final follow-up experience of 8½ years. In A. Steptoe & J. Wardle (Eds.), *Psychosocial processes and health: A reader.* New York: Cambridge University Press.

Rosenthal, D. (1970). *Genetic theory and abnormal behavior.* New York: McGraw-Hill.

Rosenthal, N. E. (2000). A patient who changed my practice: Herb Kern, the first light therapy patient. *International Journal of Psychiatry in Clinical Practice, 4,* 339–341.

Rosenthal, N. E., Genhart, M., Jacobson, F. M., Skwerer, R. G., & Wehr, T. A. (1986). Disturbances of appetite and weight regulation in seasonal affective disorder. *Annals of the New York Academy of Sciences, 499,* 216–230.

Rosenthal, R. (1985). From unconscious experimenter bias to teacher expectancy effects. In J. B. Dusek, V. C. Hall, & W. J. Meyer (Eds.), *Teacher expectancies.* Hillsdale, NJ: Lawrence Erlbaum Press.

Roskos-Ewoldsen, D. R., & Fazio, R. H. (1992). The accessibility of source likability as a determinant of persuasion. *Personality and Social Psychology Bulletin, 18,* 19–25.

Ross, C., Miller, S. D., Bjornson, L., & Reagor, P. (1991). Abuse histories in 102 cases of multiple personality disorder. *Canadian Journal of Psychiatry, 36,* 97–101.

Ross, C. A. (1997). *Dissociative identity disorder: Diagnosis, clinical features, and treatment of multiple personality* (2nd ed.). New York: John Wiley & Sons, Inc.

Ross, G., Nelson, K., Wetstone, H., & Tanouye, E. (1986). Acquisition and generalization of novel object concepts by young language learners. *Journal of Child Language, 13,* 67–83.

Ross, J., & Ma-Wyatt, A. (2004). Saccades actively maintain perceptual continuity. *Nature Neuroscience, 7,* 65–69.

Ross, L. (1977). The intuitive psychologist and his shortcomings: Distortions in the attribution process. In L. Berkowitz (Ed.), *Advances in experimental social psychology, Vol. 10.* New York: Academic Press.

Rosser, R. (1994). *Cognitive development: Psychological and biological perspectives.* Boston: Allyn & Bacon.

Roth, E. M., & Mervis, C. B. (1983). Fuzzy set theory and class inclusion relations in semantic categories. *Journal of Verbal Learning and Verbal Behavior, 22,* 509–525.

Rothbaum, B., Hodges, L., Anderson, P., Price, L., & Smith, S. (2002). Twelve-month follow-up of virtual reality and standard exposure therapies for the fear of flying. *Journal of Consulting and Clinical Psychology, 70,* 428–432.

Rothkopf, E. Z. (1971). Incidental memory for location of information in text. *Journal of Verbal Learning and Verbal Behavior, 10,* 608–613.

Rotter, J. B. (1966). Generalized expectancies for internal versus external control of reinforcement. *Psychological Monographs, 80*(1, Whole No. 609).

Rotter, J. B. (1990). Internal versus external control of reinforcement: A case history of a variable. *American Psychologist, 45,* 489–493.

Rovee-Collier, C. (1999). The development of infant memory. *Current Directions in Psychological Science, 8,* 80–85.

Rozin, P., & Royzman, E. B. (2001). Negativity bias, negativity dominance, and contagion. *Personality and Social Psychology Review, 5,* 296–320.

Rupp, H. A., & Wallen, K. (2007). Relationship between testosterone and interest in sexual stimuli: The effect of experience. *Hormones and Behavior, 52,* 581–589.

Rupp, H. A., & Wallen, K. (2008). Sex differences in response to visual sexual stimuli: A review. *Archives of Sexual Behavior, 37,* 206–218.

Ruscher, J. B. (1998). Prejudice and stereotyping in everyday communication. *Advances in Experimental Social Psychology, 30,* 241–307.

Rushing, W. A. (1995). *The AIDS epidemic: Social dimensions of an infectious disease.* Boulder, CO: Westview Press.

Russell, J. A. (1991). Culture and categorization of emotion. *Psychological Bulletin, 110,* 426–450.

Russell, J. A. (1994). Is there universal recognition of emotion from facial expression? A review of the cross-cultural studies. *Psychological Bulletin, 115,* 102–141.

Rutherford, A., & Endler, N. S. (1999). Predicting approach-avoidance: The roles of coping styles, state anxiety, and situational appraisal. *Anxiety, Stress & Coping: An International Journal, 12,* 63–84.

Rutter, M. (2001). Child psychiatry in the era following sequencing the genome. In F. Levy & D. Hay (Eds.), *Attention, genes, and ADHD* (pp. 225–248). New York: Brunner-Routledge.

Ruvolo, A., & Markus, H. (1992). Possible selves and performance: The power of self-relevant imagery. *Social Cognition, 9,* 95–124.

Ruzgis, P., & Grigorenko, E. L. (1994). Cultural meaning systems, intelligence, and personality. In R. J. Sternberg & P. Ruzgis (Eds.), *Personality and intelligence* (pp. 248–270). New York: Cambridge University Press.

Ryan, R. M., & Deci, E. L. (2000). Self-determination theory and the facilitation of intrinsic motivation, social development, and well-being. *American Psychologist, 55,* 68–78.

Ryan, R. M., & Deci, E. L. (2002). Overview of self-determination theory: An organismic-dialectical perspective. In E. L. Deci & R. M. Ryan (Eds.), *Handbook of self-determination research.* Rochester, NY: University of Rochester Press.

Ryback, R. S., & Lewis, O. F. (1971). Effects of prolonged bed rest on EEG sleep patterns in young, healthy volunteers. *Electroencephalography and Clinical Neurophysiology, 31,* 395–399.

Sacchi, D. L. M., Agnoli, F., & Loftus, E. F. (2007). Changing history: Doctored photographs affect memory for past public events. *Applied Cognitive Psychology, 21,* 1005–1022.

Sadovnick, A. D., Remick, R. A., Lam, R. W., Zis, A. P., Yee, I. M. L., & Baird, P. A. (1994). Morbidity risks for mood disorders in 3,942 first degree relatives of 671 index cases with single depression, recurrent depression, bipolar I or bipolar II. *American Journal of Medical Genetics, 54,* 132–140.

Saegert, S. C., Swap, W., & Zajonc, R. B. (1973). Exposure, context, and interpersonal attraction. *Journal of Personality and Social Psychology, 25,* 234–242.

Saffran, E. M., Marin, O. S. M., & Yeni-Komshian, G. H. (1976). An analysis of speech perception in word deafness. *Brain and Language, 3,* 209–228.

Saffran, E. M., Schwartz, M. F., & Marin, O. S. M. (1980). Evidence from aphasia: Isolating the components of a production model. In B. Butterworth (Ed.), *Language production.* London: Academic Press.

Sagvolden, T., Johansen, E. B., Aase, H., & Russell, V. A. (2005). A dynamic developmental theory of attention-deficit/hyperactivity disorder (ADHD) predominantly hyperactive/impulsive and combined subtypes. *Behavioral and Brain Sciences, 28,* 347–468.

Sakai, F., Meyer, J. S., Karacan, I., Derman, S., & Yamamoto, M. (1979). Normal human sleep: Regional cerebral haemodynamics. *Annals of Neurology, 7,* 471–478.

Saklofske, D. H., Austin, E. J., & Minski, P. S. (2003). Factor structure and validity of a trait emotional intelligence measure. *Personality and Individual Differences, 34,* 707–721.

Saks, E. (2007). *The center cannot hold: My journey through madness.* New York: Hyperion.

Salapatek, P. (1975). Pattern perception in early infancy. In L. B. Cohen & P. Salapatek (Eds.), *Infant perception: From sensation to cognition, Vol. 1.* New York: Academic Press.

Salovey, P., & Mayer, J. D. (1989–1990). Emotional intelligence. *Imagination, Cognition and Personality, 9,* 185–211.

Salter, D., McMillan, D., Richards, M., Talbot, T., Hodges, J., Bentovim, A., Hastings, R., Stevenson, J., & Skuse, D. (2003). Development of sexually abusive behaviour in sexually victimised males: A longitudinal study. *Lancet, 361,* 471–476.

Salthouse, T. A. (1984). Effects of age and skill in typing. *Journal of Gerontology, 113,* 345–371.

Salthouse, T. A. (1988). Cognitive aspects of motor functioning. In J. A. Joseph (Ed.), *Central determinants of age-related declines in motor function.* New York: New York Academy of Sciences.

Salvy, S.-J., Pierce, W. D., Heth, D. C., & Russell, J. C. (2003). Wheel running produces conditioned food aversion. *Physiology & Behavior, 80,* 89–94.

Samuels, C. (2008). Sleep, recovery, and performance: The new frontier in high-performance athletics. *Neurologic Clinics, 26,* 169–180.

Sánchez-Peña, L. C., Reyes, B.E., López-Carrillo, L., Recio, R., Morán-Martínez, J., Cebrián, M. E., & Quintanilla-Vega, B. (2004). Organophosphorous pesticide exposure alters sperm chromatin structure in Mexican agricultural workers. *Toxicology and Applied Pharmacology, 196,* 108–113.

Sande, G. N., Goethals, G. R., & Radloff, C. E. (1988). Perceiving one's own traits and others': The multifaceted self. *Journal of Personality and Social Psychology, 54,* 13–20.

Sanders, L. D., Newport, E. L., & Neville, H. J. (2002). Segmenting nonsense: An event-related potential index of perceived onsets in continuous speech. *Nature Neuroscience, 5,* 700–703.

Sandrini, G., Milanov, I., Malaguti, S., Nigrelli, M. P., Moglia, A., & Nappi, G. (2000). Effects of hypnosis on diffuse noxious inhibitory controls. *Physiology & Behavior, 69,* 295–300.

Santed, M. A., Sandin, B., Chorot, P., Olmedo, M., & García-Campayo, J. (2003). The role of negative and positive affectivity on perceived stress-subjective health relationships. *Acta Neuropsychiatrica, 15*(4), 199–216.

Santos, M. D., Leve, C., & Pratkanis, A. R. (1994). Hey buddy, can you spare seventeen cents? Mindful persuasion and the pique technique. *Journal of Applied Social Psychology, 24,* 755–764.

Sapolsky, R. M. (1996). Why stress is bad for your brain. *Science, 273,* 749–775.

Sarason, B. R., & Sarason, I. G. (1999). *Abnormal psychology: The problem of maladaptive behavior* (10th ed.). Upper Saddle River, NJ: Prentice-Hall Inc.

Sargent, J., Beach, M., Dalton, M., Mott, L., Tickle, J., Ahrens, M., & Heatherton, T. (2001). Effects of seeing tobacco use in films on trying smoking among adolescents: Cross sectional study. *BMJ: British Medical Journal, 323,* 1394.

Saudino, K. J. (2005). Behavioral genetics and child temperament. *Developmental and Behavioral Pediatrics, 26,* 214–223.

Saurer, T. B., Ijames, S. G., Carrigan, K. A., & Lysle, D. T. (2008). Neuroimmune mechanisms of opioid-mediated conditioned immunomodulation. *Brain, Behaviour, and Immunity, 22*(1), 89–97.

Savastano, H. I., & Miller, R. R. (2003). Biological significance and posttraining changes in conditioned responding. *Learning and Motivation, 34,* 303–324.

Saxena, S., & Rauch, S. L. (2000). Functional neuroimaging and the neuroanatomy of obsessive-compulsive disorder. *Pediatric Clinics of North America, 23,* 563–586.

Scarr, S., & Weinberg, R. A. (1976). IQ performance of black children adopted by white families. *American Psychologist, 31,* 726–739.

Scarr, S., & Weinberg, R. A. (1978). The influence of "family background" on intellectual attainment. *American Sociological Review, 43,* 674–692.

Schacter, D. L. (2001). *The seven sins of memory.* Boston: Houghton Mifflin.

Schacter, D. L., & Dodson, C. S. (2002). Misattribution, false recognition and the sins of memory. In A. Baddeley, M. Conway, & J. Aggleton (Eds.), *Episodic memory: New directions in research* (pp. 71–85). New York: Oxford University Press.

Schachter, S. (1982). Recidivism and self-cure of smoking and obesity. *American Psychologist, 37,* 436–444.

Schaie, K. W. (1990). Intellectual development in adulthood. In J. E. Birren & K. W. Schaie (Eds.), *Handbook of the psychology of aging* (3rd ed.). San Diego: Academic Press.

Schaie, K. W. (1996). *Intellectual development in adulthood: The Seattle Longitudinal Study.* Cambridge, UK: Cambridge University Press.

Schaie, K. W., & Strother, C. R. (1968). A cross-sequential study of age changes in cognitive behavior. *Psychological Bulletin, 70,* 661–684.

Schank, R., & Abelson, R. P. (1977). *Scripts, plans, goals, and understanding.* Hillsdale, NJ: Lawrence Erlbaum Associates.

Scherschlicht, R., Polc, P., Schneeberger, J., Steiner, M., & Haefely, W. (1982). Selective suppression of rapid eye movement sleep (REMS) in cats by typical and atypical antidepressants. In E. Costa & G. Racagni (Eds.), *Typical and atypical antidepressants: Molecular mechanisms.* New York: Raven Press.

Schiffman, H. R. (1996). *Sensation and perception: An integrated approach.* New York: Wiley.

Schleifer, S. J., Keller, S. E., Camerino, M., Thornton, J. C., & Stein, M. (1983). Suppression of lymphocyte stimulation following bereavement. *Journal of the American Medical Association, 15,* 374–377.

Schleifer, S. J., Keller, S. E., & Stein, M. (1985). Stress effects on immunity. *Psychiatric Journal of the University of Ottawa, 10*(3), 125–131.

Schmauk, F. J. (1970). Punishment, arousal, and avoidance learning in sociopaths. *Journal of Abnormal Psychology, 122,* 509–522.

Schmidt, H. G., Peeck, V. H., Paas, F., & van Breukelen, G. J. P. (2000). Remembering the street names of one's childhood neighborhood: A study of very long-term retention. *Memory, 8,* 37–49.

Schmolck, H., Buffalo, E. A., & Squire, L. R. (2000). Memory distortions develop over time: Recollections of the O. J. Simpson trial verdict after 15 and 32 months. *Psychological Science, 11,* 39–45.

Schneider, B. (1997). Psychoacoustics and aging: Implications for everyday listening. *Journal of Speech-Language Pathology and Audiology, 21,* 111–124.

Schou, M. (2001). Lithium treatment at 52. *Journal of Affective Disorders, 67*(1–3), 21–32.

Schultz, W. (2001). Reward signaling by dopamine neurons. *The Neuroscientist, 7,* 293–302.

Schwartz, C. E., Wright, C. I., Shin, L. M., Kagan, J., & Rauch, S. L. (2003). Inhibited and uninhibited infants "grown up": Adult amygdalar response to novelty. *Science, 300,* 1952–1953.

Schwartz, M. F., Marin, O. S. M., & Saffran, E. M. (1979). Dissociations of language function in dementia: A case study. *Brain and Language, 7,* 277–306.

Schwartz, M. F., Saffran, E. M., & Marin, O. S. M. (1980). The word order problem in agrammatism. I. Comprehension. *Brain and Language, 10,* 249–262.

Schwartz, R. G. (2006). Would today's IRB approve the Tudor study? Ethical considerations in conducting research involving children with communication disorders. In Goldfarb, R. (Ed.), *Ethics: A case study from fluency* (pp. 83–96). San Diego, CA: Plural.

Schwarzkopf, S. B., Nasrallah, H. A., Olson, S. C., Coffman, J. A., & McLaughlin, J. A. (1989). Perinatal complications and genetic loading in schizophrenia: Preliminary findings. *Psychiatry Research, 27,* 233–239.

Scialfa, C. T., & Joffe, K. M. (1998). Response times and eye movements in feature and conjunctive search as a function of target eccentricity. *Perception & Psychophysics, 60,* 1067–1082.

Scollon, C. N., Diener, E., Oishi, S., & Biswas-Diener, R. (2004). Emotions across cultures and methods. *Journal of Cross-Cultural Psychology, 35,* 304–326.

Scott, S. K., Blank, C. C., Rosen, S., & Wise, R. J. S. (2000). Identification of a pathway for intelligible speech in the left temporal lobe. *Brain, 123,* 2400–2406.

Scribner, S. (1977). Modes of thinking and ways of speaking: Culture and logic reconsidered. In P. N. Johnson-Laird & P. C. Wason (Eds.), *Thinking: Readings in cognitive science.* Cambridge, UK: Cambridge University Press.

Sears, D. (1983). The person-positivity bias. *Journal of Personality and Social Psychology, 44*(2), 233–250.

Seftel, A. D., Mack, R. J., Secrest, A. R., & Smith, T. M. (2004). Restorative increases in serum testosterone levels are significantly correlated to improvements in sexual functioning. *Journal of Andrology, 25,* 963–972.

Segall, M. H., Dasen, P. R., Berry, J. W., & Poortinga, Y. H. (1999). *Human behavior in global perspective: An introduction to cross-cultural psychology* (2nd ed.). Boston: Allyn and Bacon.

Seligman, M. E. P. (1971). Phobias and preparedness. *Behavior Therapy, 2,* 307–320.

Seligman, M. E. P. (1975). *Helplessness.* San Francisco: W. H. Freeman.

Seligman, M. E. P., & Csikszentmihalyi, M. (2000). Positive psychology. *American Psychologist, 55,* 5–14.

Seligman, M. E. P., & Nolen-Hoeksema, S. (1987). Explanatory style and depression. In D. Magnusson & A. Oehman (Eds.), *Psychopathology: An interactional perspective. Personality, psychopathology, and psychotherapy.* Orlando, FL: Academic Press.

Selkoe, D. J. (1989). Biochemistry of altered brain proteins in Alzheimer's disease. *Annual Review of Neuroscience, 12,* 463–490.

Selnes, O. A., & Hillis, A. (2000). Patient Tan revisited: A case of atypical global aphasia? *Journal of the History of the Neurosciences, 9,* 233–237.

Selye, H. (1956/1976). *The stress of life.* New York: McGraw-Hill.

Selye, H. (1991). History and present status of the stress concept. In A. Monat & R. S. Lazarus (Eds.), *Stress and coping.* New York: Columbia University Press.

Selye, H. (1993). History of the stress concept. In L. Goldberger & S. Breznitz (Eds.), *Handbook of stress: Theoretical and clinical aspects* (2nd ed.). New York: Free Press.

Seung, H. S. (2000). Half a century of Hebb. *Nature Neuroscience, 3,* 1116.

Shackelford, T. K., & Weekes-Shackelford, V. A. (2004). Why don't men pay child support? Insights from evolutionary psychology. In C. Crawford, A. Viviana, & C. Salmon (Eds.), *Evolutionary psychology, public policy and personal decisions* (pp. 231–247). Mahwah, NJ: Lawrence Erlbaum.

Shalom, D., & Poeppel, D. (2008). Functional anatomic models of language: Assembling the pieces. *The Neuroscientist, 14,* 119–127.

Sharpe, D., Adair, J. G., & Roese, N. J. (1992). Twenty years of deception research: A decline in subjects' trust? *Personality and Social Psychology Bulletin, 18,* 585–590.

Shattuck, R. (1980). *The forbidden experiment: The story of the Wild Boy of Aveyron.* New York: Farrar Straus Giroux.

Shavit, Y., Depaulis, A., Martin, F. C., Terman, G. W., Pechnick, R. N., Zane, C. J., Gale, R. P., & Liebeskind, J. C. (1986). Involvement of brain opiate receptors in the immune-suppressive effect of morphine. *Proceedings of the National Academy of Sciences, USA, 83,* 7114–7117.

Shavit, Y., Lewis, J. W., Terman, G. W., Gale, R. P., & Liebeskind, J. C. (1984). Opioid peptides mediate the suppressive effect of stress on natural killer cell cytotoxicity. *Science, 223,* 188–190.

Shaw, P., Gornick, M., Lerch, J., Addington, A., Seal, J., Greensten, D. Sharp, W., Evans, A, Giedd, J. N., Castellanos, F. X., & Rapaport, J. L. (2007). Polymorphisms of the dopamine $D_4$ receptor, clinical outcome, and cortical structure in attentional-deficit/hyperactivity disorder. *Archives of General Psychiatry, 64,* 921–931.

Shaw, P., Lerch, J., Greenstein, D., Sharp, W., Clasen, L., Evans, A., Giedd, J., Castellanos, F. X., & Rapaport, J. (2006). Longitudinal mapping of cortical thickness and clinical outcome in children and adolescents with attention-deficit/hyperactivity disorder. *Archives of General Psychiatry, 63,* 540–559.

Sheehy, R., & Horan, J. J. (2004). Effects of stress inoculation training for 1st-year law students. *International Journal of Stress Management, 11*(1), 41–55.

Shellenberg, G. D. (1997). Molecular genetics of Alzheimer's disease. In K. Blum & E. P. Nobel (Eds.), *Handbook of psychiatric genetics.* Boca Raton, FL: CRC Press.

Shen, W. W., & Giesler, M. C. (1998). The discoverers of the therapeutic effect of chlorpromazine in psychiatry: Qui etaient les vrais premiers practiciens? (letter). *Canadian Journal of Psychiatry, 43,* 423–424.

Shepard, R. N., & Metzler, J. (1971). Mental rotation of three-dimensional objects. *Science, 171,* 701–703.

Shepherd, G. M. (1994). Discrimination of molecular signals by the olfactory receptor neuron. *Neuron, 13,* 771–790.

Sher, L. (2004). Etiology, pathogenesis, and treatment of seasonal and non-seasonal mood disorders: Possible role of circadian rhythm abnormalities related to developmental alcohol exposure. *Medical Hypotheses, 62*(5), 797–801.

Sherif, M. (1936). *The psychology of social norms.* New York: Harper.

Sherif, M., Harvey, O. J., White, B. J., Hood, W. E., & Sherif, C. W. (1961). *Intergroup conflict and cooperation: The robbers cave experiment.* Norman, OK: Institute of Group Relations.

Sherry, D. F., & Schacter, D. L. (1987). The evolution of multiple memory systems. *Psychological Review, 94,* 439–454.

Shibley Hyde, J., & Plant, E. A. (1995). Magnitude of psychological gender differences: Another side to the story. *American Psychologist, 50,* 159–161.

Shiffman, S., Brockwell, S., Pillitteri, J., & Gitchell, J. (2008). Use of smoking-cessation treatments in the United States. *American Journal of Preventive Medicine, 34,* 102–111.

Shorter, E. (1997). *A history of psychiatry.* New York: John Wiley & Sons.

Shotland, R. L., & Heinold, W. D. (1985). Bystander response to arterial bleeding: Helping skills, the decision-making process, and differentiating the helping response. *Journal of Personality and Social Psychology, 49,* 347–356.

Si, K., Lindquist, S., & Kandel, E. (2004). A possible epigenetic mechanism for the persistence of memory. *Cold Spring Harbor Symposia on Quantitative Biology, 69,* 497–498.

Siegel, R. M., & Andersen, R. A. (1986). Motion perceptual deficits following ibotenic acid lesions of the middle temporal area in the behaving monkey. *Society of Neuroscience Abstracts, 12,* 1183.

Signorielli, N., Gerbner, G, & Morgan, M. (1995). Violence on television: The Cultural Indicators Project. *Journal of Broadcasting & Electronic Media, 39*(2), 278–283.

Simons, D. J. (2000). Current approaches to change blindness. *Visual Cognition, 7,* 1–15.

Simons, D. J., & Chabris, C. F. (1999). Gorillas in our midst: Sustained inattentional blindness for dynamic events. *Perception, 28,* 1059–1074.

Simons, D. J., & Levin, D. T. (1998). Failure to detect changes to people in a real-world interaction. *Psychonomic Bulletin and Review, 5,* 644–649.

Simons, R. C. (1996). *Boo! Culture, experience, and the startle reflex.* New York: Oxford University Press.

Simons, R. C., & Hughes, C. C. (1993). Culture-bound syndromes. In A. C. Gaw (Ed.), *Culture, ethnicity, and mental illness.* Washington, DC: American Psychiatric Press.

Simonton, D. K. (2004). Psychology's status as a scientific discipline: Its empirical placement within an implicit hierarchy of the sciences. *Review of General Psychology, 8*(1), 59–67.

Simpson, J. A., Winterheld, H. A., Rholes, W. S., & Oriña, M. M. (2007). Working models of attachment and reactions to different forms of caregiving from romantic partners. *Journal of Personality and Social Psychology, 93*, 466–477.

Singer, L. T., Arendt, R., Minnes, S., Farkas, K., Salvator, A., Kirchner, H. L., & Kliegman, R. (2002). Cognitive and motor outcomes of cocaine-exposed infants. *Journal of the American Medical Association, 287*, 1952–1960.

Singer, M., & Ritchot, K. F. M. (1996). The role of working memory capacity and knowledge access in text inference processing. *Memory & Cognition, 24*, 733–743.

Singh, R., Onglatco, M. L. U., Sriram, N., & Tay, A. B. G. (1997). The warm-cold variable in impression formation: Evidence for a positive-negative asymmetry. *British Journal of Social Psychology, 36*, 457–477.

Singh, R., & Teoh, J. B. P. (2000). Attitudes and attraction: A test of two hypotheses for the similarity-dissimilarity asymmetry. *British Journal of Social Psychology, 38*, 427–443.

Sinha, P. (2002). Recognizing complex patterns. *Nature Neuroscience, 5*, 1093–1097.

Sivacek, J., & Crano, W. D. (1982). Vested interest as a moderator of attitude-behavior consistency. *Journal of Personality and Social Psychology, 43*, 210–221.

Skaggs, W. E., & McNaughton, B. L. (1998). Spatial firing properties of hippocampal CA1 populations in an environment containing two visually identical regions. *Journal of Neuroscience, 18*, 8455–8466.

Skinner, B. F. (1948). *Walden two*. New York: Macmillan Co.

Skinner, B. F. (1953). *Science and human behavior*. New York: Macmillan.

Skinner, B. F. (1971). *Beyond freedom and dignity*. New York: Vantage.

Skinner, B. F. (1981). Selection by consequences. *Science, 213*, 501–504.

Skinner, B. F. (1986). The evolution of verbal behavior. *Journal of the Experimental Analysis of Behavior, 45*, 115–122.

Skinner, B. F. (1988, June). Skinner joins aversives debate. *American Psychological Association APA Monitor*, 22.

Skinner, B. F. (1990). Can psychology be a science of mind? *American Psychologist, 45*, 1206–1210.

Skodol, A. E., Siever, L. J., Livesley, W. J., Gunderson, J. G., Pfohl, B., & Widiger, T. A. (2002). The borderline diagnosis II: Biology, genetics, and clinical course. *Biological Psychiatry, 51*, 951–963.

Skolin, I., Wahlin, Y. B., Broman, D. A., Hursti, U.-K. K., Larsson, M. V., & Hernell, O. (2006). Altered food intake and taste perception in children with cancer after start of chemotherapy: Perspectives of children, parents and nurses. *Supportive Care in Cancer, 14*, 369–378.

Skowronski, J. J., & Carlston, D. E. (1989). Negativity and extremity biases in impression formation. *Psychological Bulletin, 105*, 131–142.

Slaughter, V., & Repacholi, B. (2003). Individual differences in Theory of Mind: What are we investigating? In B. Repacholi & V. Slaughter (Eds.), *Individual differences in Theory of Mind: Implications for typical and atypical development*. New York: Psychology Press.

Slaughter, V., & Suddendorf, T. (2007). Participant loss due to "fussiness" in infant visual paradigms: A review of the last 20 years. *Infant Behavior & Development, 30*, 505–514.

Sloane, R. B., Staples, F. R., Cristol, A. H., Yorkston, N. J., & Whipple, K. (1975). *Psychoanalysis versus behavior therapy*. Cambridge, MA: Harvard University Press.

Smeets, T., Jelicic, M., Peters, M. J. V., Candel, I., Horselenberg, R., & Merckelbach, H. (2006). "Of course I remember seeing that film"—How ambiguous questions generate crashing memories. *Applied Cognitive Psychology, 20*, 779–789.

Smith, G. P., & Gibbs, J. (1992). Role of CCK in satiety and appetite control. *Clinical Neuropharmacology, 15*(Suppl 1, Pt A), 476.

Smith, M. L., & Glass, G. V. (1977). Meta-analysis of psychotherapy outcome studies. *American Psychologist, 32*, 752–760.

Smith, M. L., Glass, G. V., & Miller, T. I. (1980). *Benefits of psychotherapy*. Baltimore: Johns Hopkins University Press.

Smylie, L., Medaglia, S., & Maticka-Tyndale, E. (2006). The effect of social capital and socio-demographics on adolescent risk and sexual health behaviours. *Canadian Journal of Human Sexuality, 15*, 95–112.

Sneed, C. D., McCrae, R. R., & Funder, D. C. (1998). Lay conceptions of the five-factor model and its indicators. *Personality and Social Psychology Bulletin, 24*, 115–126.

Snow, C. E. (1977). Mothers' speech research: From input to interaction. In C. E. Snow & C. Ferguson (Eds.), *Talking to children: Language input and acquisition*. Cambridge: Cambridge University Press.

Snow, C. E. (1986). Conversations with children. In P. Fletcher & M. Garman (Eds.), *Language acquisition* (2nd ed.). Cambridge: Cambridge University Press.

Snow, C. E., Arlman-Rupp, A., Hassing, Y., Jobse, J., Joosten, J., & Vorster, J. (1976). Mothers' speech in three social classes. *Journal of Psycholinguistic Research, 5*, 1–20.

Snow, M. E., Jacklin, C. N., & Maccoby, E. E. (1983). Sex-of-child differences in father-child interaction at one year of age. *Child Development, 54*, 227–232.

Snowling, M. J., & Hulme, C. (Eds.). (2005). *The science of reading: A handbook*. New York: Wiley.

Snyder, L. (1999). This way up: Illusions and internal models in the vestibular system. *Nature Neuroscience, 2*, 396–398.

Snyder, L. H., Batista, A. P., & Andersen, R. A. (2000). Saccade-related activity in the parietal reach region. *Journal of Neurophysiology, 83*, 1099–1102.

Snyder, M., Tanke, E. D., & Berscheid, E. (1977). Social perception and interpersonal behavior: On the self-fulfilling nature of social stereotypes. *Journal of Personality and Social Psychology, 35*, 656–666.

Snyder, S. H. (1974). *Madness and the brain*. New York: McGraw-Hill.

Snyder, S. H. (2008). A complex in psychosis. *Nature, 452*, 38–39.

Soares, J. J., & Öhman, A. (1993). Backward masking and skin conductance responses after conditioning to nonfeared but fear-relevant stimuli in fearful subjects. *Psychophysiology, 30*, 460–466.

Sokolowski, M. B., Pereira, H., S., & Hughes, K. (1997). Evolution of foraging behavior in *Drosophila* by density-dependent selection. *Proceedings of the National Academy of Sciences of the United States, 94*, 7373–7377.

Solomon, A., & Haaga, D. A. F. (1995). Rational emotive behavior therapy research: What we know and what we need to know. *Journal of Rational-Emotive & Cognitive Behavior Therapy, 13*(3), 179–191.

Solomon, G. F. (1987). Psychoneuroimmunology: Interactions between central nervous system and immune system. *Journal of Neuroscience Research, 18*, 1–9.

Sowell, E. R., Thompson, P. M., Holmes, C. J., Jernigan, T. L., & Toga, A. W. (1999). In vivo evidence for post-adolescent brain maturation in frontal and striatal regions. *Nature Neuroscience, 2*, 859–861.

Spanos, N. P. (1991). A sociocognitive approach to hypnosis. In S. J. Lynn & J. W. Rhue (Eds.), *Theories of hypnosis: Current models and perspectives* (pp. 324–361). New York: Guilford Press.

Spanos, N. P. (1996). *Multiple identities & false memories: A sociocognitive perspective*. Washington, DC: American Psychological Association.

Spanos, N. P., & Chaves, J. F. (1991). History and historiography of hypnosis. In S. J. Lynn & J. W. Rhue (Eds.), *Theories of hypnosis: Current models and perspectives*. (pp. 43–78). New York: Guilford Press.

Spanos, N. P., Weekes, J. R., & Bertrand, L. D. (1985). Multiple personality: A social psychological perspective. *Journal of Abnormal Psychology, 94*, 362–376.

Spearman, C. (1927). *The abilities of man*. London: Macmillan.

Spears, R., & Haslam, S. A. (1997). Stereotyping and the burden of cognitive load. In R. Spears (Ed.), *The social psychology of stereotyping and group life*. Oxford, UK: Blackwell Publishers, Inc.

Sperling, G. A. (1960). The information available in brief visual presentation. *Psychological Monographs, 74*(498).

Sperry, R. W. (1966). Brain bisection and consciousness. In J. Eccles (Ed.), *Brain and conscious experience*. New York: Springer-Verlag.

Spetch, M., Wilkie, D. M., & Pinel, J. P. J. (1981). Backward conditioning: A reevaluation of the empirical evidence. *Psychological Bulletin, 89*, 163–175.

Spetch, M. L., Cheng, K., MacDonald, S. E., Linkenhoker, B. A., Kelly, D. M., & Doerkson, S. R. (1997). Use of landmark configuration in pigeons and humans: II. Generality across search tasks. *Journal of Comparative Psychology, 111*, 14–24.

Spirduso, W. W., & MacRae, P. G. (1990). Motor performance and aging. In J. E. Birren & K. W.

Schaie (Eds.), *Handbook of the psychology of aging* (3rd ed.). San Diego: Academic Press.

Spitzer, R. L., Gibbon, M., Skodol, A. E., Williams, J. B. W., & First, M. B. (2002). *DSM-IV-TR case book: A learning companion to the Diagnostic and Statistical Manual of Mental Disorders, Fourth Edition, Text Revision.* Washington, DC: American Psychiatric Publishing.

Squire, L. R. (1992). Memory and the hippocampus: A synthesis from findings with rats, monkeys, and humans. *Psychological Review, 99,* 195–231.

Squire, L. R., & Bayley, P. J. (2007). The neuroscience of remote memory. *Current Opinion in Neurobiology, 17,* 185–196.

Stager, C. L., & Werker, J. F. (1997). Infants listen for more phonetic detail in speech perception than in word-learning tasks. *Nature, 388,* 381–382.

Standing, L. (1973). Learning 10,000 pictures. *Quarterly Journal of Experimental Psychology, 25,* 207–222.

Starkweather, A. (2007). The effects of exercise on perceived stress and IL-6 levels among older adults. *Biological Research for Nursing, 8,* 186–194.

Starzyk, K. B., & Quinsey, V. L. (2001). The relationship between testosterone and aggression: A meta-analysis. *Aggression and Violent Behavior, 16,* 579–599.

Stasser, G. (1991). Pooling of unshared information during group discussion. In S. Worchel, W. Wood, & J. Simpson (Eds.), *Group process and productivity.* Beverly Hills, CA: Sage.

Statistics Canada. (2002). *Canadian community health survey: Mental health and well-being.* Retrieved April 21, 2004, http://www.statcan.ca/Daily/English/030903/d030903a.htm.

Statistics Canada. (2004, June 15). *The Daily.* Retrieved http://www.statcan.ca/Daily/English/040615/d040615b.htm.

Steele, C. M., & Josephs, R. A. (1990). Alcohol myopia: Its prized and dangerous effects. *American Psychologist, 45,* 921–933.

Steenland, K. (1999). Risk assessment for heart disease and workplace ETS exposure among nonsmokers. *Environmental Health Perspectives, 107*(6), 859–863.

Steenland, K., Thun, M., Lally, C., & Heath, C., Jr. (1997). Environmental tobacco smoke and coronary heart disease in the American Cancer Society CPS-II cohort. *Circulation, 94,* 622–628.

Steeves, J. K. E., Humphrey, G. K., Culham, J. C., Menon, R. S., Milner, A. D., & Goodale, M. A. (2004). Behavioral and neuroimaging evidence for a contribution of colr and texture information to scene classification in a patient with visual form agnosia. *Journal of Cognitive Neuroscience, 16,* 955–965.

Stefanacci, L., & Amaral, D. G. (2000). Topographic organization of cortical inputs to the lateral nucleus of the macaque monkey amygdala: A retrograde tracing study. *Journal of Comparative Neurology, 22,* 52–79.

Steiger, H., Lehoux, P. M., & Gauvin, L. (1999). Impulsivity, dietary control and the urge to binge in bulimic syndromes. *Eating Disorders, 26,* 261–274.

Stein, L. I., & Santos, A. B. (1998). *Assertive community treatment of persons with severe mental illness.* New York: W. W. Norton & Co., Inc.

Stein, M. B., Millar, T. W., Larsen, D. K., & Kryger, M. H. (1995). Irregular breathing during sleep in patients with panic disorder. *American Journal of Psychiatry, 152,* 1168–1173.

Steinhauer, K., Alter, K., & Friederici, A. D. (1999). Brain potentials indicate immediate use of prosidic cues in natural speech processing. *Nature Neuroscience, 2,* 191–196.

Steinhausen, H., & Spohr, H. (1998). Long-term outcome of children with fetal alcohol syndrome: Psychopathology, behavior, and intelligence. *Alcoholism, Clinical and Experimental Research, 22,* 334–338.

Sterman, M. B., & Clemente, C. D. (1962a). Forebrain inhibitory mechanisms: Cortical synchronization induced by basal forebrain stimulation. *Experimental Neurology, 6,* 91–102.

Sterman, M. B., & Clemente, C. D. (1962b). Forebrain inhibitory mechanisms: Sleep patterns induced by basal forebrain stimulation in the behaving cat. *Experimental Neurology, 6,* 103–117.

Stern, K., & McClintock, M. K. (1998). Regulation of ovulation by human pheromones. *Nature, 392,* 177–179.

Stern, M., & Karraker, K. H. (1989). Sex stereotyping of infants: A review of gender labeling studies. *Sex Roles, 20,* 501–522.

Stern, W. (1914). *The psychological methods of testing intelligence.* Baltimore: Warwick and York.

Sternberg, R. J. (1988a). *The triarchic mind: A new theory of human intelligence.* New York, NY: Viking.

Sternberg, R. J. (1988b). Triangulating love. In R. J. Sternberg & M. L. Barnes (Eds.), *The psychology of love.* New Haven, CT: Yale University Press.

Sternberg, R. J. (1995). For whom the bell curve tolls: A review of *The bell curve. Psychological Science, 6,* 257–261.

Sternberg, R. J. (1996). *Successful intelligence.* New York, NY: Simon Schuster.

Sternberg, R. J. (1997). The triarchic theory of intelligence. In D. P. Fanagan, J. L. Genshaft, P. L. Harrison, et al. (Eds.), *Contemporary intellectual assessment: Theories, tests, and issues* (pp. 92–104). New York: Guilford Press.

Sternberg, R. J. (1999). A theory of successful intelligence. *Review of General Psychology, 3,* 292–316.

Sternberg, R. J. (2002). Beyond g: The theory of successful intelligence. In R. J. Sternberg & E. L. Grigorenko (Eds.), The *general factor of intelligence: How general is it?* Mahwah, NJ: Lawrence Erlbaum Associates.

Sternberg, R. J. (2003a). Construct validity of the theory of special intelligence. In R. J. Sternberg & J. Lautrey (Eds.), *Models of intelligence: International perspectives.* Washington, DC: American Psychological Association.

Sternberg, R. J. (2003b). *Wisdom, intelligence, and creativity synthesized.* New York: Cambridge University Press.

Sternberg, R. J., Conway, B. E., Ketron, J. L., & Bernstein, M. (1981). People's conceptions of intelligence. *Journal of Personality and Social Psychology, 41,* 37–55.

Sternberg, R. J., & Grigorenko, E. L. (1999). Myths in psychology and education regarding the gene-environment debate. *Teachers College Record, 100,* 536–553.

Sternberg, R. J., & Grigorenko, E. L. (2001). Ability testing across cultures. In L. A. Suzuki & J. G. Ponterotto (Eds.), *Handbook of multicultural assessment: Clinical, psychological, and educational applications* (2nd ed.). San Francisco: Jossey-Bass.

Sternberg, R. J., & Kaufman, J. C. (1998). Human abilities. *Annual Review of Psychology, 49,* 479–502.

Sternberg, R. J., & Lubart, T. I. (1996). Investing in creativity. *American Psychologist, 51,* 677–688.

Sternberger, L. G., & Burns, G. L. (1990). Obsessions and compulsions: Psychometric properties of the Padua inventory with an American college population. *Behavior Research and Therapy, 28,* 341–345.

Stetson, G. R. (1897). Some memory tests of whites and blacks. *Mind, 6*(24), 577–584.

Stevens, J. R. (1988). Schizophrenia and multiple sclerosis. *Schizophrenia Bulletin, 14,* 231–241.

Stewart, S. H., Mitchell, T. L., Wright, K. D., & Loba, P. (2004). The relations of PTSD symptoms to alcohol use and coping drinking in volunteers who responded to the Swissair Flight 111 airline disaster. *Journal of Anxiety Disorders, 18*(1), 51–68.

Stich, S. P. (1990). Rationality. In D. N. Osherson & E. E. Smith (Eds.), *An invitation to cognitive science, Vol. 3: Thinking.* Cambridge, MA: MIT Press.

Stine, E. L., & Bohannon, J. N. (1983). Imitations, interactions, and language acquisition. *Journal of Child Language, 10,* 589–603.

Stone, A. A., Marco, C. A., Cruise, C. E., Cox, D. S., & Neale, J. M. (1996). Are stress-induced immunological changes mediated by mood? A closer look at how both desirable and undesirable daily events influence sIgA antibody. *International Journal of Behavioral Medicine, 3,* 1–13.

Stone, A. A., Reed, B. R., & Neale, J. M. (1987). Changes in daily event frequency precede episodes of physical symptoms. *Journal of Human Stress, 13,* 70–74.

Stopfer, M., Chen, X., Tai, Y.-T., Huang, G. S., & Carew, T. J. (1996). Site specificity of short-term and long-term habituation in the tail-elicited siphon withdrawal reflex of *Aplysia. Journal of Neuroscience, 16,* 4923–4932.

Strachan, T., & Read, A. P. (1999). *Human molecular genetics.* New York: Wiley.

Strait, D. S., Grine, F. E., & Moniz, M. A. (1997). A reappraisal of early hominid phylogeny. *Journal of Human Evolution, 32,* 17–82.

Stravynski, A. (2007). *Fearing others: The nature and treatment of social phobia.* New York: Cambridge University Press.

Streissguth, A. P. (2001). Recent advances in fetal alcohol syndrome and alcohol use in pregnancy. In D. P. Agarwal & H. K. Seitz (Eds.), *Alcohol in health and disease.* New York: Marcel Dekker, Inc.

Stroop, J. R. (1935). Studies of interference in serial verbal reactions. *Journal of Experimental Psychology, 18,* 743–762.

Strupp, H. H., & Hadley, S. W. (1979). Specific vs. nonspecific factors in psychotherapy. *Archives of General Psychiatry, 36,* 1125–1136.

Stuart, T. D., & Garrison, M. E. B. (2002). The influence of daily hassles and role balance on health status: A study of mothers of grade school children. *Women & Health, 36*(3), 1–10.

Sturgis, E. T. (1993). Obsessive-compulsive disorders. In P. B. Sutker & H. E. Adams (Eds.), *Comprehensive handbook of psychopathology* (2nd ed.). New York: Plenum Press.

Suddath, R. L., Christison, G. W., Torrey, E. F., Casanova, M. F., & Weinberger, D. R. (1990). Anatomical abnormalities in the brains of monozygotic twins discordant for schizophrenia. *New England Journal of Medicine, 322,* 789–794.

Sullivan, E. V., Lim, K. O., Mathalon, D., Marsh, L., Beal, D. M., Harris, D., Hoff, A. L., Faustman, W. O., & Pfefferbaum, A. (1998). A profile of cortical gray matter volume deficits characteristic of schizophrenia. *Cerebral Cortex, 8,* 117–124.

Sullivan, M. W., & Lewis, M. (2003). Contextual determinants of anger and other negative expressions in young infants. *Developmental Psychology, 39,* 693–705.

Sun, H., & Frost, B. J. (1998). Computation of different optical variables of looming objects in pigeon nucleus rotundus neurons. *Nature Neuroscience, 1,* 296–303.

Sun, J., & Perona, P. (1998). Where is the sun? *Nature Neuroscience, 1,* 183–184.

Sundquist, K., Qvist, J., Johansson, S., & Sundquist, J. (2005). The long-term effect of physical activity on incidence of coronary heart disease: A 12-year follow-up study. *Preventive Medicine, 41,* 219–225.

Suzuki, D. T., Griffiths, A. J. F., Miller, J. H., & Lewontin, R. C. (1989). *An introduction to genetic analysis* (4th ed.). New York: Freeman.

Suzuki, K., Takei, N., Iwata, Y., Sekine, Y., Toyoda, T., Nakamura, K., Minabe, Y., et al. (2004). Do olfactory reference syndrome and Jiko-shu-kyofu (a subtype of Taijin-kyofu) share a common entity? *Acta Psychiatrica Scandinavica, 109*(2), 150–155.

Swaab, D. (2007). Sexual differentiation of the brain and behavior. *Best Practice & Research Clinical Endocrinology & Metabolism, 21,* 431–444.

Swaab, D. F., & Hofman, M. A. (1990). An enlarged suprachiasmatic nucleus in homosexual men. *Brain Research, 537,* 141–148.

Swami, V., Furnham, A., Maakip, I., Ismail, A., Nawi, N., Hudani, M., Peter, C., Andrew, N., & Garwood, J. (2008). Beliefs about the meaning and measurement of intelligence: A cross-cultural comparison of American, British and Malaysian undergraduates. *Applied Cognitive Psychology, 22*(2), 235–246.

Swedo, S. S., Rapaport, J. L., & Cheslow, D. L. (1989). High prevalence of obsessive-compulsive symptoms in patients with Sydenham's chorea. *American Journal of Psychiatry, 146,* 246–249.

Swithers, S. E., & Davidson, T. L. (2008). A role for sweet taste: Calorie predictive relations in energy regulation by rats. *Behavioral Neuroscience, 122,* 161–173.

Szasz, T. (2002). Parity for mental illness, disparity for mental patients. *Ideas on Liberty, 52,* 33–34.

Szasz, T. S. (1960). The myth of mental illness. *American Psychologist, 15,* 113–118.

Szymusiak, R., & McGinty, D. (1986). Sleep-related neuronal discharge in the basal forebrain of cats. *Brain Research, 370,* 82–92.

Tager-Flusberg, H. (2007). Evaluating the theory-of-mind hypothesis of autism. *Current Directions in Psychological Science, 16,* 311–315.

Takeda, S., Morioka, I., Miyashita, K., Okumura, A., Yoshida, Y., & Matsumoto, K. (1992). Age variation in the upper limit of hearing. *European Journal of Applied Physiology, 65,* 403–408.

Takei, N., Mortensen, P. B., Klaening, U., Murray, R. M., Sham, P. C., O'Callaghan, E., Munk, J. P. (1996). Relationship between in utero exposure to influenza epidemics and risk of schizophrenia in Denmark. *Biological Psychiatry, 40,* 817–824.

Tanenhaus, M. K. (1988). *Psycholinguistics: An overview.* Cambridge: Cambridge University Press.

Tang, Y.-P., Shimizu, E., Dube, G. R., Rampon, C., Kerchner, G. A., Zhuo, M., Lium G., & Tsien, J. Z. (1999). Genetic enhancement of learning and memory in mice. *Nature, 401,* 63–69.

Tanner, C. M., & Chamberland, J. (2001). Latah in Jakarta, Indonesia. *Movement Disorder, 16,* 526–529.

Tanser, H. A. (1939). *The settlement of negroes in Kent County, Ontario, and a study of the mental capacity of their descendents.* Catham, ON: Shephard.

Tarr, M. J., & Gauthier, I., (2000). FFA: A flexible fusiform area for subordinate-level visual processing automatized by expertise. *Nature Neuroscience, 3,* 764–769.

Tarsy, D., Baldessarini, R. J., & Tarazi, F. I. (2002). Effects of newer antipsychotics on extrapyramidal function. *CNS Drugs, 16*(1), 23–45.

Tattersall, I. (1997, April). Out of Africa again . . . and again? *Scientific American, 276,* 60–67.

Tattersall, I. (2000, January). Once we were not alone. *Scientific American, 282,* 56–62.

Taube, S. L., Kirstein, L. S., Sweeney, D. R., Heninger, G. R., & Maas, J. W. (1978). Urinary 3-methoxy-4-hydroxyphenyleneglycol and psychiatric diagnosis. *American Journal of Psychiatry, 135,* 78–82.

Tehan, G., Hendry, L., & Kocinski, D. (2001). Word length and phonological similarity effects in simple, complex, and delayed serial recall tasks: Implications for working memory. *Memory, 9,* 333–348.

Tenover, J. L. (1998). Male hormone replacement therapy including "andropause." *Endocrinology & Metabolism Clinics of North America, 27,* 969–987.

Terry, R. D., & Davies, P. (1980). Dementia of the Alzheimer type. *Annual Review of Neuroscience, 3,* 77–96.

Test, M. A., & Stein, L. I. (2000). Practical guidelines for the community treatment of markedly impaired patients. *Community Mental Health Journal, 36,* 47–60.

Thelen, E., & Corbetta, D. (2002). Microdevelopment and dynamic systems: Applications to infant motor development. In N. Granott & J. Parziale (Eds.), *Microdevelopment: Transition processes in development and learning.* Cambridge studies in cognitive perceptual development. New York: Cambridge University Press.

Thibadeau, R., Just, M. A., & Carpenter, P. A. (1982). A model of the time course and content of reading. *Cognitive Science, 6,* 157–203.

Thibault, G., Felezeu, M., O'Connor, K. P., Todorov, C., Stip, E., & Lavoie, M. E. (2008). Influence of comorbid obsessive-compulsive symptoms on brain event-related potentials in Gilles de la Tourette syndrome. *Progress in Neuro-Psychopharmacology and Biological Psychiatry, 32*(3), 803–815.

Thompson, T. (2007). *Making sense of autism.* Baltimore: Brookes.

Thomas, R. M. (1996). *Comparing theories of child development* (4th ed.). Pacific Grove, CA: Brooks/Cole.

Thompson, M. S., Judd, C. M., & Park, B. (2000). The consequences of communicating social stereotypes. *Journal of Experimental Social Psychology, 36,* 567–599.

Thompson, R., Emmorey, K., & Gollan, T. (2005). "Tip of the fingers" experiences by deaf signers. *Psychological Science, 16,* 856–860.

Thompson, S. C., Kent, D. R., Thomas, C., & Vrungos, S. (1999). Real and illusory control over exposure to HIV in college students and gay men. *Journal of Applied Social Psychology, 29,* 1128–1150.

Thompson, T., & Schuster, C. R. (1968). *Behavioral pharmacology.* Englewood Cliffs, NJ: Prentice-Hall.

Thorndike, E. L. (1905). *The elements of psychology.* New York: Seiler.

Thorpe, G. L., & Olson, S. L. (1990). *Behavior therapy: Concepts, procedures, and applications.* Boston: Allyn and Bacon.

Thurstone, L. L. (1938). *Primary mental abilities.* Chicago: University of Chicago Press.

Tobin, S. A. (1991). A comparison of psychoanalytic self-psychology and Carl Rogers's person-centered therapy. *Journal of Humanistic Psychology, 31,* 9–33.

Todrank, J., Byrnes, D., Wrzesniewski, A., & Rozin, P. (1995). Odors can change preferences for people in photographs: A cross-modal evaluative conditioning study with olfactory USs and visual CSs. *Learning and Motivation, 26,* 116–140.

Tomasello, M., & Farrar, J. (1986). Joint attention and early language. *Child Development, 57,* 1454–1463.

Toni, N., Teng, E. M., Bushong, E. A., Aimone, J. B., Zhao, C., Consiglio, A., van Praag, H., Martone, M. E., Ellisman, M. H., & Gage, F. H. (2007). Synapse formation on neurons in the adult hippocampus. *Nature Neuroscience, 10,* 727–734.

Tooby, J., & Cosmides, L. (1989). Evolutionary psychology and the generation of culture, Part I: Theoretical considerations. *Ethology and Sociobiology, 10,* 39–49.

Tootell, R. B., Reppas, J. B., Dale, A. M., & Look, R. B. (1995). Visual motion aftereffect in human cortical area MT revealed by functional magnetic resonance imaging. *Nature, 375,* 139–141.

Tordoff, M. G., & Friedman, M. I. (1988). Hepatic control of feeding: Effect of glucose, fructose, and mannitol infusion. *American Journal of Physiology, 254,* 969–976.

Torgerson, S. (1983). Genetic factors in anxiety disorders. *Archives of General Psychiatry, 40,* 1085–1089.

Torrey, E., Fuller, E., Miller, J., Rawlings, R., & Yolken, R. H. (1997). Seasonality of births in schizophrenia and bipolar disorder: A review of the literature. *Schizophrenia Research, 28,* 1–38.

Torrey, E. F., Torrey, B. B., & Peterson, M. R. (1977). Seasonality of schizophrenic births in the United States. *Archives of General Psychiatry, 34,* 1065–1070.

Tosteson, A. N., Weinstein, M. C., Hunink, M. G., Mittleman, M. A., Williams, L. W., Goldman, P. A., & Goldman, L. (1997). Cost-effectiveness of population-wide educational approaches to reduce serum cholesterol levels. *Circulation, 95,* 24–30.

Transport Canada. (2002). *The alcohol-crash problem in Canada: 2000.* Retrieved April 23, 2004, http://www.tc.gc.ca/roadsafety/tp/tp11759/2000/pdf/tp11759e_2000.pdf.

Träskmann, L., Åsberg, M., Bertilsson, L., & Sjöstrand, L. (1981). Monoamine metabolites on CSF and suicidal behavior. *Archives of General Psychiatry, 38,* 631–636.

Travis, L. A., Bliwise, N. G., Binder, J. L., & Horne-Moyer, H. L. (2001). Changes in clients' attachment styles over the course of time-limited dynamic psychotherapy. *Psychotherapy: Theory, Research, Practice, Training, 38*(2), 149–159.

Trehub, S. E., & Thorpe, L. A. (1989). Infants' perception of rhythm: Categorization of auditory sequences by temporal structure. *Canadian Journal of Psychology, 43,* 217–229.

Treisman, A. M. (1960). Contextual cues in selective listening. *Quarterly Journal of Experimental Psychology, 12,* 242–248.

Treit, D., & Menard, J. (1997). Dissociations among the anxiolytic effects of septal, hippocampal, and amygdaloid lesions. *Behavioral Neuroscience, 111,* 653–658.

Tremblay, S., Shiller, D. M., & Ostry, D. J. (2003). Somatosensory basis of speech production. *Nature, 423,* 866–869.

Triplett, N. (1898). The dynamogenic factors in pacemaking and competition. *American Journal of Psychology, 9,* 507–533.

Trivers, R. L. (1971). The biology of reciprocal altruism. *Quarterly Review of Biology, 46,* 35–57.

Trivers, R. L. (1972). Parental investment and sexual selection. In B. Campbell (Ed.), *Sexual selection and the descent of man.* Chicago: Aldine.

Tronick, E., Als, H., Adamson, L., Wise, S., & Brazelton, T. B. (1978). The infant's response to entrapment between contradictory messages in face-to-face interaction. *Journal of the American Academy of Child Psychiatry, 17,* 1–13.

Truax, C. B. (1966). Reinforcement and nonreinforcement in Rogerian psychotherapy. *Journal of Abnormal Psychology, 71,* 1–9.

Trussell, L. O. (2002). Transmission at the hair cell synapse. *Nature Neuroscience, 5,* 85–86.

Tryon, R. C. (1940). Genetic differences in maze-learning ability in rats. *Yearbook of the National Society for the Study of Education, 39,* 111–119.

Tsao, D. Y., Vanduffel, W., Sasaki, Y., Fize, D., Knutsen, T. A., Mandeville, J. B., Wald, L. L., Dale, A. M., Rosen, B. R., Van Essen, D. C., Livingstone, M. S., Orban, G. A., & Tootell, R. B. H. (2003). Stereopsis activates V3A and caudal intraparietal areas in macaques and humans. *Neuron, 39,* 555–568.

Tsuchiya, N., & Adolphs, R. (2007). Emotion and consciousness. *Trends in Cognitive Sciences, 11,* 158–167.

Tulving, E. (1972). Episodic and semantic memory. In E. Tulving & W. Donaldson (Eds.), *Organization of memory.* New York: Academic Press.

Tulving, E. (2002). Episodic memory: From mind to brain. *Annual Review of Psychology, 53,* 1–25.

Tulving, E., & Schacter, D. L. (1990). Priming and human memory systems. *Science, 247,* 301–306.

Tupes, E. C., & Christal, R. E. (1961). Recurrent personality factors based on trait ratings. *USAF ASD Technical Report,* 61–97.

Turkington, D., Dudley, R., Warman, D. M., & Beck, A. T. (2004). Cognitive-behavioral therapy for schizophrenia: A review. *Journal of Psychiatric Practice, 10*(1), 5–16.

Turner, S. M., Beidel, D. C., Stanley, M. A., & Heiser, N. (2001). Obsessive-compulsive disorder. In P. B. Sutker & H. E. Adams (Eds.), *Comprehensive handbook of psychopathology* (3rd ed.). New York: Kluwer Academic/Plenum Publishers.

Tversky, A., & Kahneman, D. (1974). Judgment under uncertainty: Heuristics and biases. *Science, 185,* 1124–1131.

Tversky, A., & Kahneman, D. (1982). Judgment under uncertainty: Heuristics and biases. In D. Kahneman, P. Slovic, & A. Tversky (Eds.), *Judgment under uncertainty.* New York: Cambridge University Press.

Tyrell, J. B., & Baxter, J. D. (1981). Glucocorticoid therapy. In P. Felig, J. D. Baxter, A. E. Broadus, & L. A. Frohman (Eds.), *Endocrinology and metabolism.* New York: McGraw-Hill.

Ullman, L. P., & Krasner, L. (1969). *Psychological approach to abnormal behavior.* Englewood Cliffs, NJ: Prentice-Hall.

Ungerleider, L. G., & Mishkin, M. (1982). Two cortical visual systems. In D. J. Ingle, M. A. Goodale, & R. J. W. Mansfield (Eds.), *Analysis of visual behavior.* Cambridge, MA: MIT Press.

Uno, H., Tarara, R., Else, J. G., Suleman, M. A., & Sapolsky, R. M. (1989). Hippocampal damage associated with prolonged and fatal stress in primates. *The Journal of Neuroscience, 9,* 1705–1711.

Urgesi, C., Berlucchi, G., & Aglioti, S. M. (2004). Magnetic stimulation of extrastreate body area impairs visual processing of nonfacial body parts. *Current Biology, 14,* 2130–2134.

Uyeda, L., Tyler, I., Pinzon, J., & Birmingham, C. L. (2002). Identification of patients with eating disorders: The signs and symptoms of anorexia nervosa and bulimia nervosa. *Eating & Weight Disorders, 7,* 116–123.

Vahtera, J., Kivimaki, M., Vaananen, A., Linna, A., Pentti, J., Helenius, H., & Elovainio, M. (2006). Sex differences in health effects of family death or illness: Are women more vulnerable than men? *Psychosomatic Medicine, 68*(2), 283–291.

Vaillant, G. E. (2002). The study of adult development. In E. Phelps, F. F. Furstenberg, Jr., et al. (Eds.), *Looking at lives: American longitudinal studies of the twentieth century.* New York: Russell Sage Foundation.

Vaillant, G. E., & Milofsky, E. S. (1982). The etiology of alcoholism. *American Psychologist, 37,* 494–503.

Valenstein, E. S. (1986). *Great and desperate cures: The rise and decline of psychosurgery and other radical treatments for mental illness.* New York: Basic Books.

Valentine, D., Hedrick, M. S., & Swanson, L. A. (2006). Effect of an auditory training program on reading, phoneme awareness, and language. *Perceptual and Motor Skills, 103*(1), 183–196.

Vallerand, R. J., & Ratelle, C. F. (2002). Intrinsic and extrinsic motivation: A hierarchical model. In E. L. Deci & R. M. Ryan (Eds.), *Handbook of self-determination research.* Rochester, NY: University of Rochester Press.

Vanderwolf, C. H., & Cain, D. P. (1994). The behavioral neurobiology of learning and memory: A conceptual reorientation. *Brain Research Reviews, 19,* 264–297.

Van der Hal-van Raalte, E., Van Ijzendoorn, M. H., & Bakermans-Kranenburg, M. J. (2007). Quality of care after early childhood trauma and well-being in later life: Child holocaust survivors reaching old age. *American Journal of Orthopsychiatry, 77*(4), 514–522.

Van Goozen, S., Wiegant, V., Endert, E., Helmond, F., & Van de Poll, N. (1997). Psychoendocrinological assessments of the menstrual cycle: The relationship between hormones, sexuality, and mood. *Archives of Sexual Behavior, 26,* 359–382.

van Kesteren, P. J., Gooren, L. J., & Megens, J. A. (1996). An epidemiological and demographic study of transsexuals in the Netherlands. *Archives of Sexual Behavior, 25,* 589–600.

Vartanian, L. R. (2000). Revisiting the imaginary audience and personal fable constructs of adolescent egocentrism: A conceptual review. *Adolescence, 35,* 639–661.

Vecera, S. P., & Farah, M. J. (1994). Does visual attention select objects or locations? *Journal of Experimental Psychology, 123,* 146–160.

Vellutino, F. R., & Fletcher, J. M. (2005). Developmental dyslexia. In M. J. Snowling & C. Hulme (Eds.), *The science of reading: A handbook* (pp. 362–378). New York: Wiley.

Vernon, P. A., Villani, V. C., Vickers, L. C., & Harris, J. A. (2008). A behavioral genetic investigation of the Dark Triad and the Big 5. *Personality and Individual Differences, 44,* 445–452.

Vernon, P. A., Jang, K. L., Harris, J. A., & McCarthy, J. M. (1997). Environmental predictors of personality differences: A twin and sibling study. *Journal of Personality and Social Psychology, 72,* 177–183.

Vernon, P. E. (1979). *Intelligence: Heredity and environment.* San Francisco: W. H. Freeman.

Virkkunen, M., De Jong, J., Bartko, J., & Linnoila, M. (1989). Psychobiological concomitants of history of suicide attempts among violent offenders and impulsive fire setters. *Archives of General Psychiatry, 46,* 604–606.

Vitaliano, P. P., Zhang, J. P., & Scanlan, J. M. (2003). Is caregiving hazardous to one's physical health? A meta-analysis. *Psychological Bulletin, 129*(6), 946–972.

Voets, T., Droogmans, G., Wissenbach, U., Janssens, A., Flockarzi, V., & Nilius, B. (2004). The principle of temperature-dependent gating in cold- and heat-sensitive TRP channels. *Nature, 430,* 748–754.

Vogel, G. W., Vogel, F., McAbee, R. S., & Thurmond, A. G. (1980). Improvement of depression by REM sleep deprivation. *Archives of General Psychiatry, 37,* 247–253.

Vogt, J., Hagemann, T., & Kastner, M. (2006). The impact of workload on heart rate and blood pressure in en-route and tower air traffic control. *Journal of Psychophysiology, 20*(4), 297–314.

Vollrath, M. (2000). Personality and hassles among university students: A three-year longitudinal study. *European Journal of Personality, 14,* 199–215.

Volpe, B. T., LeDoux, J. E., & Gazzaniga, M. S. (1979). Information processing of visual stimuli in an "extinguished" field. *Nature, 282,* 722–724.

von Békésy, G. (1960). *Experiments in hearing.* New York: McGraw-Hill.

Voyat, G. (1998). In tribute to Piaget: A look at his scientific impact in the United States. In R. W. Reiber & K. Salzinger (Eds.), *Psychology: Theoretical-historical perspectives* (2nd ed.). Washington, DC: American Psychological Association.

Vroomen, J., Bertelson, P., & de Gelder, B. (2001). The ventriloquist effect does not depend on the direction of automatic visual attention. *Perception & Psychophysics, 63,* 651–659.

Vygotsky, L. S. (1934/1987). Thinking and speech. In R. W. Rieber & A. S. Carton (Eds.), *The collected works of L. S. Vygotsky: Vol. 1. Problems of general psychology* (N. Minick, Trans.). New York: Plenum.

Wadden, T. A., Brownell, K. D., & Foster, G. D. (2002). Obesity: Responding to the global epidemic. *Journal of Consulting and Clinical Psychology, 70,* 510–525.

Wagner, R. K., & Sternberg, R. J. (1983). Executive control of reading. Cited by Sternberg, R. J. (1985). *Beyond IQ: A triarchic theory of human intelligence.* Cambridge: Cambridge University Press.

Wagstaff, G. F., Cole, J. C., & Brynas-Wagstaff, J. (2007). Effects of hypnotic induction and hypnotic depth on phonemic fluency: A test of the frontal inhibition account of hypnosis. *International Journal of Psychology and Psychological Theory, 7,* 27–40.

Wahlsten, D. (1997a). Leilani Muir versus the philosopher king: Eugenics goes on trial in Alberta. *Genetica, 99,* 185–198.

Wahlsten, D. (1997b). The malleability of intelligence is not constrained by heritability. In B. Devlin, S. E. Fienberg, D. P. Resnick, & K. Roeder (Eds.), *Intelligence, genes, and success.* New York: Copernicus.

Wahlsten, D. (1999). Single gene influences on brain and behavior. *Annual Review of Psychology, 50,* 599–624.

Wakefield, J. C., Schmitz, M. F., First, M. B., & Horwitz, A. V. (2007). Extending the bereavement exclusion for major depression to other losses: Evidence from the National Comorbidity Survey. *Archives of General Psychiatry, 64,* 433–440.

Wakelin, A., & Long, K. M. (2003). Effects of victim gender and sexuality on attributions of blame to rape victims. *Sex Roles, 49,* 477–487.

Walker, E., & Lewine, R. J. (1990). Prediction of adult-onset schizophrenia from childhood home movies of the patients. *American Journal of Psychiatry, 147,* 1052–1056.

Wallace, S. T., & Alden, L. E. (1997). Social phobia and positive social events: The price of success. *Journal of Abnormal Psychology, 106,* 416–424.

Wallace, W. T. (1994). Memory for music: Effect of melody on recall of text. *Journal of Experimental Psychology: Learning, Memory, and Cognition, 20,* 1471–1485.

Wallston, K. A., Wallston, B. S., & DeVellis, R. (1978). Development of multidimensional health locus of control (MHLC) scales. *Health Education Monographs, 6,* 160–170.

Walsh, T., McClellan, J. M., McCarthy, S. E., Addington, A. M., Pierce, S. B., Cooper, G. M., et al. (2008, March 27). Rare structural variants disrupt multiple genes in neurodevelopmental pathways in schizophrenia. *Science Online.*

Walsh, V., Ellison, A., Battelli, L., & Cowey, A. (1998). Task-specific impairments and enhancements induced by magnetic stimulation of human visual area V5. *Proceedings of the Royal Society B: Biological Sciences, 265,* 537–543.

Walster, E., Aronson, V., Abrahams, D., & Rottman, L. (1966). Importance of physical attractiveness in dating behavior. *Journal of Personality and Social Psychology, 4,* 508–516.

Walster, E., & Berscheid, E. (1971). Adrenaline makes the heart grow fonder. *Psychology Today,* June, pp. 47–62.

Wampold, B. E., Minami, T., Baskin, T. W., and Callen, S. (2002). A meta-(re)analysis of the effects of cognitive therapy versus "other therapies" for depression. *Journal of Affective Disorders, 69*(2–3), 159–165.

Wampold, B. E., Mondin, G. W., Moody, M., Stich, F., Benson, K., & Ahn, H. (1997). A meta-analysis of outcome studies comparing *bona fide* psychotherapies: Empirically "all must have prizes." *Psychological Bulletin, 122,* 203–215.

Wang, J., & El-Guebaly, N. (2004). Sociodemographic factors associated with comorbid major depressive episodes and alcohol dependence in the general population. *Canadian Journal of Psychiatry, 49,* 37–44.

Ward-Robinson, J. (2004). An analysis of second-order autoshaping. *Learning and Motivation, 35,* 1–21.

Washburn, M. F. (1922). Introspection as an objective method. *Psychological Review, 29,* 89–112.

Wason, P. (1968). Reasoning about a rule. *Quarterly Journal of Experimental Psychology, 20,* 273–281.

Wason, P. C., & Johnson-Laird, P. N. (1972). *Psychology of reasoning: Structure and content.* Cambridge, MA: Harvard University Press.

Watkins, C. E., Campbell, V. L., Nieberding, R., & Hallmark, R. (1995). Contemporary practice of psychological assessment by clinical psychologists. *Professional Psychological Research and Practice, 26,* 54–60.

Watkins, C. E., Jr. (2000). Some final thoughts about using tests and assessment procedures in counseling. In C. E. Watkins, Jr., & V. L. Campbell (Eds.), *Testing and assessment in counseling practice* (2nd ed.). Contemporary topics in vocational psychology. Mahwah, NJ: Lawrence Erlbaum Associates.

Watson, J. B. (1930). *Behaviorism* (rev. ed.). New York: W. W. Norton.

Watson, J. B., & Rayner, R. (1920). Conditioned emotional reactions. *Journal of Experimental Psychology, 3,* 1–14.

Watson, J. C. (2007). Reassessing Rogers' necessary and sufficient conditions of change. *Psychotherapy, 44*(3), 268–273.

Watson, J. S., & Ramey, C. T. (1972). Reactions to responsive contingent stimulation in early infancy. *Merrill-Palmer Quarterly, 18,* 219–227.

Watt, A., & Honey, R. C. (1997). Combining CSs associated with the same or different USs. *Quarterly Journal of Experimental Psychology, 50B,* 350–367.

Weaver, I. C. G., Champagne, F. A., Brown, S. E., Dymov, S., Sharma, S., Meaney, M. J., & Szyf, M. (2005). Reversal of maternal programming of stress responses in adult offspring through methyl supplementation: Altering epigenetic marking later in life. *Journal of Neuroscience, 25,* 11 045–11 054.

Webster, D. M., Richter, L., & Kruglanski, A. W. (1996). On leaping to conclusions when feeling tired: Mental fatigue effects on impressional primacy. *Journal of Experimental Social Psychology, 32,* 181–195.

Wegner, D. M. (2003). The mind's best trick: How we experience conscious will. *Trends in Cognitive Sciences, 7,* 65–69.

Weidner, G., Sexton, G., McLellarn, R., Connor, S. L., & Matarazzo, J. D. (1987). The role of type A behavior and hostility in an elevation of plasma lipids in adult women and men. *Psychosomatic Medicine, 49,* 136–145.

Weigel, R. H., Vernon, D. T. A., & Tognacci, L. N. (1974). Specificity of the attitude as a determinant of attitude-behavior congruence. *Journal of Personality and Social Psychology, 30,* 724–728.

Weigert, E. (1940). Psychoanalytic notes on sleep and convulsion treatment in functional psychoses. *Psychiatry, 3,* 189–209.

Weinstein, C. S., Fucetola, R., & Mollica, R. (2001). Neuropsychological issues in the assessment of refugees and victims of mass violence. *Neuropsychology Review, 11*(3), 131–141.

Weissman, M. M., Markowitz, J. C., & Klerman, G. L. (2000). *Comprehensive guide to interpersonal psychotherapy*. New York: Basic Books.

Weissman, M. M., Warner, V., Wickramaratne, P. J., & Kandel, D. B. (1999). Maternal smoking during pregnancy and psychopathology in offspring followed to adulthood. *Journal of the American Academy of Child and Adolescent Psychiatry, 38*, 892–899.

Weltzin, T. E., Hsu, L. K. G., Pollice, C., & Kaye, W. H. (1991). Feeding patterns in bulimia nervosa. *Biological Psychiatry, 30*, 1093–1110.

Wen, J. Y. M., Kumar, N., Morrison, G., Rambaldini, G., Runciman, S., Rousseau, J., & van der Kooy, D. (1997). Mutations that prevent associative learning in *C. elegans*. *Behavioral Neuroscience, 111*, 354–368.

Werker, J. F., Pegg, J. E., & McLeod, P. J. (1994). A cross-language investigation of infant preference for infant-directed communication. *Infant Behavior and Development, 17*, 323–333.

Werker, J. F., & Tees, R. C. (1999). Influences on infant speech processing: Toward a new synthesis. *Annual Review of Psychology, 50*, 509–535.

Wernicke, K. (1874). *Der Aphasische Symptomenkomplex.* Breslau, Poland: Cohn & Weigert.

West-Eberhard, M. J. (2005). The maintenance of sex as a developmental trap due to sexual selection. *Quarterly Review of Biology, 80*, 47–53.

Westen, D. (1998). The scientific legacy of Sigmund Freud: Toward a psychodynamically informed psychological science. *Psychological Bulletin, 124*, 333–371.

Westrin, A., & Lam, R. W. (2007). Long-term and preventative treatment for seasonal affective disorder. *CNS Drugs, 21*(11), 901–909.

Wheeler, L., & Kim, Y. (1997). What is beautiful is culturally good: The physical attractiveness stereotype has different content in collectivist cultures. *Personality and Social Psychology Bulletin, 23*, 795–800.

Whishaw, I. Q. (2000). Loss of the innate cortical engram for action patterns used in skilled reaching and the development of behavioral compensation following motor cortex lesions in the rat. *Neuropharmacology, 39*, 788–805.

White, G. L. (1980). Physical attractiveness and courtship progress. *Journal of Personality and Social Psychology, 39*, 660–668.

Whitlock, J. R., Heynan, A. J., Shuler, M. G., & Bear, M. F. (2006). Learning induces long-term potentiation in the hippocampus. *Science, 313*, 1093–1097.

Whorf, B. L. (1956). Science and linguistics. In J. B. Carroll (Ed.), *Language, thought and reality: Selected writings of Benjamin Lee Whorf.* Cambridge, MA: MIT Press.

Wicks, S. R., & Rankin, C. H. (1997). Effects of tap withdrawal response habituation on other withdrawal behaviors: The localization of habituation in the Nematode. *Behavioral Neuroscience, 111*, 342–353.

Widiger, T. A., & Sankis, L. M. (2000). Adult psychopathology: Issues and controversies. *Annual Review of Psychology, 51*, 377–404.

Widiger, T. A., & Trull, T. J. (2007). Plate tectonics in the classification of personality disorder: Shifting to dimensional model. *American Psychologist, 62*, 71–83.

Widom, C. S. (1989). Does violence beget violence? A critical examination of the literature. *Psychological Bulletin, 106*, 3–28.

Wiggins, J. S., & Pincus, A. L. (2002). Personality structure and the structure of personality disorders. In P. T. Costa, Jr., & T. A. Widiger (Eds.), *Personality disorders and the five-factor model of personality* (2nd ed.). Washington, DC: American Psychological Association.

Wiggins, J. S., & Trapnell, P. D. (1997). Personality structure: The return of the Big Five. In R. Hogan, J. A. Johnson, & S. Briggs (Eds.), *Handbook of personality psychology*. San Diego: Academic Press.

Williams, K., Harkins, S., & Latané, B. (1981). Identifiability as a deterrent to social loafing: Two cheering experiments. *Journal of Personality and Social Psychology, 40*, 303–311.

Williamson, S., Harpur, T. J., & Hare, R. D. (1991). Abnormal processing of affective words by psychopaths. *Psychophysiology, 28*, 260–273.

Willingham, D. G., & Koroshetz, W. J. (1993). Evidence for dissociable motor skills in Huntington's disease patients. *Psychobiology, 21*, 173–182.

Winkler, I., & Cowan, N. (2005). From sensory to long-term memory evidence from auditory memory reactivation studies. *Experimental Psychology, 52*, 3–20.

Winzeler, R. L. (1999). Is *latah* always fakery and deception? *Transcultural Psychiatry, 36*, 385–390.

Wiseman, R., & Smith, M. D. (2002). Assessing the role of cognitive and motivational biases in belief in the paranormal. *Journal of the Society for Psychical Research, 66*, 157–166.

Wiseman, R., Watt, C., Stevens, P., Greening, E., & O'Keeffe, C. (2003). An investigation in alleged "hauntings." *British Journal of Psychology, 94*, 195–211.

Woerner, P. L., & Guze, S. B. (1968). A family and marital study of hysteria. *British Journal of Psychiatry, 114*, 161–168.

Wolfe, J. M., Butcher, S. J., Lee, C., & Hyle, M. (2003). Changing your mind: On the contributions of top-down and bottom-up guidance in visual search for feature singletons. *Journal of Experimental Psychology: Human Perception and Performance, 29*, 483–502.

Wolff, S. (2004). The history of autism. *European Child & Adolescent Psychiatry, 12*, 201–208.

Wolpe, J. (1958). *Psychotherapy by reciprocal inhibition*. Stanford, CA: Stanford University Press.

Wood, D. L., Sheps, S. G., Elveback, L. R., & Schirder, A. (1984). Cold pressor test as a predictor of hypertension. *Hypertension, 6*, 301–306.

Wood, R. M., & Gustafson, G. E. (2001). Infant crying and adults' anticipated caregiving responses: Acoustic and contextual influences. *Child Development, 72*, 1287–1300.

Wood, W. (2000). Attitude change: Persuasion and social influence. *Annual Review of Psychology, 51*, 539–570.

Wood, W., & Eagly, A. H. (2002). A cross-cultural analysis of the behavior of women and men: Implications for the origins of sex differences. *Psychological Bulletin, 128*, 699–727.

Woods, S. C., Seeley, R. J., Porte, D., Jr., & Schwartz, M. W. (1998). Signals that regulate food intake and energy homeostasis. *Sciences, 280*, 1378–1383.

Woody, E., & Sadler, P. (1998). On reintegrating dissociated theories: Comment on Kirsch and Lynn (1998). *Psychological Bulletin, 123*, 192–197.

Worchel, F. F., Aaron, L. L., & Yates, D. F. (1990). Gender bias on the Thematic Apperception Test. *Journal of Personality Assessment, 55*, 593–602.

World Health Organization. (2003). *The World Health Report 2003—Shaping the future.* Retrieved April 23, 2004, http://www.who.int/en/.

World Health Organization (2007). AIDS epidemic update. Retrieved May 3, 2008, http://www.unaids.org/en/KnowledgeCentre/HIVData/EpiUpdate/EpiUpdArchive/2007/.

Wright, M. J., & C. R. Myers (Eds.). (1982). *History of academic psychology in Canada* Toronto: Hogrefe.

Wu, H., Wang, J., Cacioppo, J. T., Glaser, R., Kiecold-Glaser, J. K., & Malarkey, W. B. (1999). Chronic stress associated with spousal caregiving of patients with Alzheimer's dementia is associated with down regulation of B-lymphocyte CH mRNA. *Journals of Gerontology Series A–Biological Sciences & Medical Sciences, 54A*(4), M212–M215.

Wu, J. C., & Bunney, W. E. (1990). The biological basis of an antidepressant response to sleep deprivation and relapse: Review and hypothesis. *American Journal of Psychiatry, 147*, 14–21.

Wunsch, A., Philippot, P., & Plaghki, L. (2003). Affective associative learning modifies the sensory perception of nociceptive stimuli without participant's awareness. *Pain, 102*, 27–38.

Wyer, R. R., Jr., & Srull, T. K. (Eds.). (1994). *Handbook of social cognition* (2nd ed.). Hillsdale, NJ: Erlbaum.

Xu, Y. (2005). Revisiting the role of the fusiform face area in visual expertise. *Cerebral Cortex, 15*, 1234–1242.

Yairi, E. (2006). The Tudor study and Wendell Johnson. In R. Goldfarb (Ed.), *Ethics: A case study from fluency* (pp. 35–62). San Diego, CA: Plural.

Yalch, R. F. (1991). Memory in a jingle jungle: Music as a mnemonic device in communicating advertising slogans. *Journal of Applied Psychology, 76*, 268–275.

Yang, X., Sheng, B., & Bao, L. (2003). The relationship of Type A behaviour to cerebrovascular diseases. *Chinese Journal of Clinical Rehabilitation, 7*(7), 1105–1106.

Yarmey, A. D. (2003). Eyewitness identification: Guidelines and recommendations for identification procedures in the United States and in Canada. *Canadian Psychology, 44,* 181–189.

Yates, W. R., Perry, P., & Murray, S. (1992). Aggression and hostility in anabolic steroid users. *Biological Psychiatry, 31,* 1232–1234.

Yeo, R., Gangestad, S., & Thoma, R. (2007). Developmental instability and individual variation in brain development: Implications for the origin of neurodevelopmental disorders. *Current Directions in Psychological Science, 16,* 245–249.

Yeo, R. A., Gangestad, S. W., & Thomas, R. J. (2007). Developmental instability and individual variation in brain development: Implications for the origin of neurodevelopmental disorders. *Current Directions in Psychological Science, 16,* 245–249.

Young, A., Stokes, M., & Crowe, M. (1984). Size and strength of the quadriceps muscles of old and young women. *European Journal of Clinical Investigation, 14,* 282–287.

Young, A. H., & Hammond, J. M. (2007). Lithium in mood disorders: Increasing evidence base, declining use? *British Journal of Psychiatry, 191,* 474–476.

Young, J. L. (2007). *ADHD grown up: A guide to adolescent and adult ADHD.* New York: Norton.

Young, M. C. (1998). *The Guinness book of world records.* New York: Bantam Books.

Zachrisson, O. C. G., Balldin, J., Ekman, R., Naesh, O., Rosengren, L., Agren, H., & Blennow, K. (2000). No evident neuronal damage after electroconvulsive therapy. *Psychiatry Research, 96,* 157–165.

Zajonc, R. B. (1965). Social facilitation. *Science, 149,* 269–274.

Zajonc, R. B. (1968). Attitudinal effects of mere exposure. *Journal of Personality and Social Psychology, Monograph Supplement, 9,* 1–27.

Zandian, M., Ioakimidis, I., Bergh, C., & Södersten, P. (2007). Cause and treatment of anorexia nervosa. *Physiology & Behavior, 92,* 283–290.

Zanna, M. P., & Rempel, J. K. (1988). Attitudes: A new look at an old concept. In D. Bar-Tal & A. W. Kruglanski (Eds.), *The social psychology of knowledge.* Cambridge, UK: Cambridge University Press.

Zaslow, M. J. (1991). Variation in child care quality and its implications for children. *Journal of Social Issues, 47,* 125–138.

Zatorre, R. J., Bouffard, M., Ahad, P., & Belin, P. (2002). Where is "where" in the human auditory cortex? *Nature Neuroscience, 5,* 905–909.

Zentner, M., & Renaud, O. (2007). Origins of adolescents' ideal self: An intergenerational perspective. *Journal of Personality and Social Psychology, 92,* 557–574.

Zhao, C., Deng, W., & Gage, F. H. (2008). Mechanisms and functional implications of adult neurogenesis. *Cell, 132*(4), 645–660.

Zhong, L. J., Goldberg, M. S., Parent, M. E., & Hanley, J. A. (2000). Exposure to environmental tobacco smoke and the risk of lung cancer: A meta-analysis. *Lung Cancer, 27,* 3–18.

Zhou, J.-N., Hofman, M. A., Gooren, L. J. G., & Swaab, D. F. (1995). A sex difference in the human brain and its relation to transsexuality. *Nature, 378,* 68–70.

Zhu, S., Melcer, T., Sun, J., Rosbrook, B., & Pierce, J. P. (2000). Smoking cessation with and without assistance: A population-based analysis. *American Journal of Preventive Medicine, 18*(4), 305–311.

Zhuo, M. (2005). Targeting central plasticity: A new direction of finding painkillers. *Current Pharmaceutical Design, 11,* 2797–2807.

Zipursky, R. B., Lambe, E. K., Kapur, S., & Mikulis, D. J. (1998). Cerebral gray matter volume deficits in first episode psychosis. *Archives of General Psychiatry, 55,* 540–546.

Zola, D. (1984). Redundancy and word perception during reading. *Perception and Psychophysics, 36,* 277–284.

Zuckerman, B., & Brown, E. R. (1993). Maternal substance abuse and infant development. In C. H. Zeanah, Jr. (Ed.), *Handbook of infant mental health.* New York: Guilford Press.

Zuckerman, M. (1991). *Psychobiology of personality.* Cambridge, UK: Cambridge University Press.

Zurif, E. G. (1990). Language and the brain. In D. N. Osherson & H. Lasnik (Eds.), *Language: An invitation to cognitive science, Vol. 1.* Cambridge, MA: MIT Press.

Zvolsky, P., Jansky, L., Vyskocilova, J., & Grof, P. (1981). Effects of psychotropic drugs on hamster hibernation: Pilot study. *Progress in Neuropsychopharmacology, 5,* 599–602.

# Photo Credits

## Chapter 1

Page 2, Diana Ong/SuperStock; p. 5, Dennis Hallinan/(re)view/Jupiter Images; p. 10, Kurt Scholz/SuperStock; p. 11, (left) Mary Evans Picture Library/The Image Works, (right) Stock Montage; p. 13, National Library of Medicine; p. 14, National Library of Medicine; p. 16, photograph courtesy of the Archives of the Association Montessori Internationale; p. 18, National Library of Medicine; p. 19, The Ferdinand Hamburger Archives of The John Hopkins University; p. 21, (bottom) Corbis-Bettmann, (top) Archives of the History of American Psychology—The University of Akron; p. 22, Archives of the History of American Psychology—The University of Akron; p. 24, McGill University, PR000387/McGill University Archives.

## Chapter 2

Page 28, © Diana Ong/SuperStock; p. 31, © Gary W. Priester; p. 33, (left) Tony Stone Worldwide, (right) Harcourt/Anthro-Photo File; p. 42, Clifford Skarstedt/CP Photo Archive; p. 46, Quad-City (Ia) Times; p. 47, Jonathan Selig/Stone/Getty Images; p. 53, Don Spiro/Tony Stone Images.

## Chapter 3

Page 56, © Dian Ong/SuperStock; p. 60, North Wind Picture Archives; p. 65, (top) CNRI/SPL/Photo Researchers, Inc, (bottom) David Phillips/Photo Researchers, Inc; p. 70, Will & Deni McIntyre/Photo Researchers, Inc; p. 73, Peter Cade/Getty Images; p. 79, (left) Jmmohn Reader/Science Photo Library/Photo Researchers, Inc, (middle) Topham/The Image Works, (right) Robert E. Demmrich/Tony Stone Images; p. 80, David Madison/Tony Stone Images; p. 81, Barag Schuler/Anthro-Photo File.

## Chapter 4

Page 86, © Purestock/SuperStock; p. 101, Alan Morgan/Peter Arnold, Inc; p. 102, Jack Fields/Photo Researchers, Inc; p. 103, Science Photo Library/Photo Researchers; p. 107, (top) Hitoshi Sakano, PhD, The University of Tokyo, (bottom) Larry Mulvehill/Rainbow.

## Chapter 5

Page 126, © Diana Ong/SuperStock; p. 129, Digital Vision/Getty Images; p. 133, SuperStock; p. 136, (both) National Eye Institute, National Institutes of Health; p. 141, Gary Yeowell/Tony Stone Images; p. 147, Joe Sohm/The Image Works; p. 155, Omikron/Photo Researchers, Inc; p. 160, Photo Researchers, Inc/Gerard Vandystadt/Agence Vandystadt.

## Chapter 6

Page 166, © Diana Ong/SuperStock; p. 173, Photo courtesy of Neil Carlson; p. 177, Patricia Thomson/Tony Stone Images; p. 178, Scott Tysick/Masterfile; p. 187, (top left) Bohdan Hrynewch/Stock Boston, (top right) SuperStock; p. 189, Andre Forget/CP Photo Archive.

## Chapter 7

Page 194, © Diana Ong/SuperStock; p. 197, © Culver Pictures/SuperStock; p. 207, David young Wolff/Tony Stone Images; p. 209, (left) L. Kolvoord/The Image Works, (right) Bob Daemmrich/Stock Boston; p. 211, Bob Daemmrich/The Image Works; p. 213, Randy Lincks/Image Network; p. 214, Bob Daemmrich/Stock Boston; p. 218, Chris Gardner/CP Photo Archive; p. 233, (all) © SuperStock.

## Chapter 8

Page 228, Diana Ong/SuperStock; p. 233, Chad Ehlers/Getty Images; p. 236, Ron Sherman/Stock Boston; p. 239, AP/World Wide Photos; p. 240, Steve Prezant/Corbis; p. 242, Greg Atkinson/Shutterstock; p. 244, (both) Ogust/The Image Works; p. 247, Courtesy of the Canadian Broadcasting Corporation; p. 249, (left) Syracuse Newspapers/Jennifer Grimes/The Image Works, (right) Ryan McVay/Getty Images; p. 256, © Photos 12/Alamy; p. 258, AP/World Wide Photos.

## Chapter 9

Page 264, © Diana Ong/SuperStock; p. 267, S. Lousada/Petit Format/Photo Researchers, Inc.; p. 272, Cary Wolinsky/Stock Boston; p. 274, Royalty-Free/Corbis; p. 283, Philippe Platilly/Science Photo Library/Photo Researchers, Inc; p. 286, Michael Heron/Woodfin Camp & Associates; p. 290, Tom Grille/A.G.E. FotoStock/First Light.

## Chapter 10

Page 294, © Purestock/SuperStock; p. 296, Courtesy of CNN; p. 297, Jack Brink/Royal Alberta Museum, Edmonton; p. 304, Peter Poulides/Tony Stone World Wide; p. 308, Michael Ventura/Tony Stone Images; p. 310, Lawrence Migdale.Tony Stone World Wide; p. 313, Frank Pedrick/The Image Works; p. 316, James Wilson/Woodfin Camp & Associates, Inc.

## Chapter 11

Page 324, © Purestock/SuperStock; p. 328, Nicolas DeVore/Getty Images; p. 331, Nigel Dickinson/Tony Stone Images; p. 337, Bob Daemmrich/The Image Works; p. 340, James Shaffer/PhotoEdit; p. 344, (top) © EyeWire, Inc, (bottom) Marc Pokempner/Tony Stone Images; p. 352, AP World Wide Photos; p. 354, Roger Tully/Stone/Getty Images.

## Chapter 12

Page 356, © Diana Ong/SuperStock; p. 361, Mike Abrahams/Alamy; p. 363, Neil Harding/Getty Images; p. 369, The Copyright Group/SuperStock; p. 370, Steve Gordon/Dorling Kindersley; p. 373, Will Hart; p. 379, Owen Franken/Stock, Boston; p. 382, Robert Harbison; p. 385, (left) Peter Cade/Tony Stone Images, (right) Kindra Clineff/Tony Stone Images; p. 394, Alfred Pasieka/Photo Researchers; p. 395, Richard Hutchings/PhotoEdit; p. 398, Brian J. Gavriloff/Edmonton Journal.

## Chapter 13

Page 402, © Purestock/SuperStock; p. 408, Eastcott/The Image Works; p. 412, Wayne Eastep/Getty Images; p. 415, AP Photo/Diane Bondareff; p. 422, © Alex Segre/Alamy.

## Chapter 14

Page 434, © Diana Ong/SuperStock; p. 437, AP Photo/The Canadian Press/Paul Pritchard, HO; p. 438, (all) Bettmann/Corbis; p. 439, Jon Riley/Tony Stone Images; p. 443, (left) Robert Harding World Imagery/Getty Images, (right) Alistair Berg/Digital Vision/Getty Images; p. 444, Myrleen Ferguson Cate/PhotoEdit; p. 448, Sue Ann Miller/Tony Stone Images; p. 451, Paula Lerner/Saga Agency; p. 456, Andy Sacks/Tony Stone Images; p. 457, Phil Degginger/Tony Stone Images; p. 461, Topham; p. 462, SuperStock.

## Chapter 15

Page 470, © Diana Ong/SuperStock; p. 475, (bottom) Anders Ryman/Corbis, (top) Statistics Canada Population Density 2001 by Dissemination Area from the Statistics Canada website http://geodepot.statcan.ca/Diss/Maps/ThematicMaps/population/National/pop_dens_colour_e.pdf; p. 476, Keren Su/Getty Images; p. 484, Robert E Daemmrich/Tony Stone Images; p. 490, Scott Houston/Corbis; p. 493, Peter M. Fisher/Corbis; p. 495, John Doman/AP Wide World Photos; p. 500, Shaney Komulainen/CP Photo Archive; p. 506, Ken Chernus/Getty Images.

## Chapter 16

Page 510, © Diana Ong/SuperStock; p. 513, Robert Frerck/Woodfin Camp & Associates; p. 525, Michael Abramson/Woodfin Camp & Associates; p. 526, Rich Iwasaki/Stone/Getty Images; p. 531, CP Photo Archive; p. 533, Andrejs Liepins/Science Photo Library/Photo Researchers, Inc; p. 537, © EyeWire.

## Chapter 17

Page 544, © Diana Ong/SuperStock; p. 547, Jonathan Hayward/CP Photo Archive; p. 549, Betty Press/Woodfin Camp & Associates; p. 550, Larry Dale Gordon/Getty Images; p. 558, Bill Horsman/Stock Boston; p. 566, John Eastcott/Yva Momatiuk/Woodfin & Camp Associates; p. 568, Phil Snell/CP Photo Archive; p. 582, Zave Smith/Corbis.

## Chapter 18

Page 588, © Diana Ong/SuperStock; p. 591, Loren McIntyre/Woodfin Camp & Associates; p. 592, Corbis/Bettmann; p. 595, Photo Researchers, Inc; p. 597, Michael Rougier/Life Magazine; p. 600, Jerry Howard/Stock, Boston; p. 603, Paula Lerner/Woodfin Camp & Associates; p. 609, Frank Pedrick/The Image Works.

# Name Index

# Subject Index

**Note:** Page numbers followed by an *f* indicate figures; page numbers followed by a *t* indicate tables.